Fromm...

Australia 2004

POSTCARDS FROM

On beautiful Fitzroy Island in Queensland, you can find deserted beaches surrounded by clear water. Don't forget sunscreen! See "The Best Beaches" in chapter 1. Fitzroy Island is easily accessible from Cairns (see chapter 6). © *Queensland Tourist & Travel Corporation.*

Sydney's Opera House is both a symbol of the city and the home of world-class musical performances. For information on touring the building or obtaining event tickets, see chapter 3, "Sydney." © Paul Chesley/Getty Images.

Sydney grew up around its harbor, and traveling by ferry is an easy and scenic way to get to many destinations. See chapter 3 for information on ferries and a map of their routes. © George Hall/Getty Images.

The Outback is known for amazing, eerie natural formations like The Walls of China on the shores of dry Lake Mungo. See "The Best Places to Experience the Outback" in chapter 1. © Dave G. Houser/Houserstock, Inc.

Divers come from all over the world to experience the beauty of the Great Barrier Reef. There's nothing else like it, except for the barrier reef on the other side of Australia! See chapter 6 for Great Barrier Reef information and chapter 9 for Western Australia's reef. © Carl Roessler Photography.

The variety of flora and fauna that makes the Great Barrier Reef its home is unparalleled. See "The Best Diving & Snorkeling Sites" in chapter 1. © Kelvin Aitken/Peter Arnold, Inc.

Uluru (Ayers Rock), a mysterious icon of Outback Australia, rises serenely out of the desert. For information about getting here, see chapter 7, "The Red Centre."
© Doug Armand/Getty Images.

The haunting sounds of the didgeridoo form the soundtrack of a trip to the Outback. See "The Best Places to Learn About Aboriginal Culture" in chapter 1. © Paul Souders/Getty Images.

Many cattle stations, such as those in the Kimberley, offer visitors the opportunity to experience ranch life as guests. For information on the Kimberley, see chapter 9.
© Dave G. Houser/Houserstock, Inc.

A pod of wild dolphins has visited the remote outpost of Monkey Mia in Western Australia almost every day for decades. Other marine mammals, like dugongs (manatees), are also resident in these waters. See chapter 9, "Perth & Western Australia."
© Thomas Schmitt/Getty Images.

Port Arthur, on the island-state of Tasmania, was once Australia's most notorious penal colony. Convict labor created many local roads and buildings, some of which you can still see today. See chapter 14, "Tasmania." © Greg Probst Photography.

Kakadu National Park in the Northern Territory is rich in wildlife and also contains some 5,000 ancient Aboriginal art sites. See chapter 8, "The Top End." © *Tom Till Photography.*

Frommer's

Australia

2004

by Marc Llewellyn & Lee Mylne

Here's what the critics say about Frommer's:

"After examining a slew of guidebooks to Australia, this was my clear favorite, the one that's torn and underlined; pages folded back; in other words the one I really used. Unlike so many guides that are just full of facts, this, in the style of other Frommer books, is written in a chatty manner, as if an expert acquaintance is helping you make your plans."
—*Times-Picayune, New Orleans, LA*

"Amazingly easy to use. Very portable, very complete."
—*Booklist*

"Detailed, accurate, and easy-to-read information for all price ranges."
—*Glamour Magazine*

"Hotel information is close to encyclopedic."
—*Des Moines Sunday Register*

"Frommer's Guides have a way of giving you a real feel for a place."
—*Knight Ridder Newspapers*

WILEY

Wiley Publishing, Inc.

Published by:

Wiley Publishing, Inc.

111 River St.
Hoboken, NJ 07030

ISBN 0-7645-3872-1
ISSN 1040-9408

Editor: Lisa Torrance Duffy
Production Editor: Tammy Ahrens
Cartographer: Nicholas Trotter
Photo Editor: Richard Fox
Production by Wiley Indianapolis Composition Services

For information on our other products and services or to obtain technical support, please contact our Customer Care Department within the U.S. at 800-762-2974, outside the U.S. at 317-572-3993 or fax 317-572-4002.

Wiley also publishes its books in a variety of electronic formats. Some content that appears in print may not be available in electronic formats.

Manufactured in the United States of America

5   4   3   2   1

Contents

3 Sydney   89

by Marc Llewellyn

4 New South Wales   180

by Marc Llewellyn

5 Brisbane   231

by Lee Mylne

6 Queensland & the Great Barrier Reef   260

by Lee Mylne

7 The Red Centre   363

by Marc Llewellyn

8 The Top End   393

by Lee Mylne

9 Perth & Western Australia   420

by Lee Mylne

⑩ Adelaide & South Australia   483

by Marc Llewellyn

⑪ Melbourne   528

by Marc Llewellyn

⑫ Victoria   575

by Marc Llewellyn

⑬ Canberra   594

by Marc Llewellyn

14 Tasmania   609

by Marc Llewellyn

Appendix: Australia in Depth   638

by Marc Llewellyn

Index   647

List of Maps

An Invitation to the Reader

In researching this book, we discovered many wonderful places—hotels, restaurants, shops, and more. We're sure you'll find others. Please tell us about them, so we can share the information with your fellow travelers in upcoming editions. If you were disappointed with a recommendation, we'd love to know that, too. Please write to:

Frommer's Australia 2004
Wiley Publishing, Inc. • 111 River St. • Hoboken, NJ 07030

An Additional Note

Please be advised that travel information is subject to change at any time—and this is especially true of prices. We therefore suggest that you write or call ahead for confirmation when making your travel plans. The authors, editors, and publisher cannot be held responsible for the experiences of readers while traveling. Your safety is important to us, however, so we encourage you to stay alert and be aware of your surroundings. Keep a close eye on cameras, purses, and wallets, all favorite targets of thieves and pickpockets.

About the Authors

Marc Llewellyn is the winner of several travel writing awards, including the Australian Society of Travel Writer's Travel Writer of the Year award 2001/2002. His latest travelogue, *Riders to the Midnight Sun,* tells of his cycle journey from the Ukrainian Black Sea to Arctic Russia—in a bid to escape the Australian heat.

Lee Mylne writes for a broad range of consumer and travel trade publications. Born and raised in New Zealand, she traveled widely before finally figuring out she could make a living out of it. She has lived in Australia for the past 17 years and is a Full Member of the Australia Society of Travel Writers. Her books include *Frommer's Portable Australia's Great Barrier Reef.*

Frommer's Star Ratings, Icons & Abbreviations

Every hotel, restaurant, and attraction listing in this guide has been ranked for quality, value, service, amenities, and special features using a **star-rating system.** In country, state, and regional guides, we also rate towns and regions to help you narrow down your choices and budget your time accordingly. Hotels and restaurants are rated on a scale of zero (recommended) to three stars (exceptional). Attractions, shopping, nightlife, towns, and regions are rated according to the following scale: zero stars (recommended), one star (highly recommended), two stars (very highly recommended), and three stars (must-see).

In addition to the star-rating system, we also use **seven feature icons** that point you to the great deals, in-the-know advice and unique experiences that separate travelers from tourists. Throughout the book, look for:

Finds	Special finds—those places only insiders know about
Fun Fact	Fun facts—details that make travelers more informed and their trips more fun
Kids	Best bets for kids and advice for the whole family
Moments	Special moments—those experiences that memories are made of
Overrated	Places or experiences not worth your time or money
Tips	Insider tips—great ways to save time and money
Value	Great values—where to get the best deals

The following **abbreviations** are used for credit cards:

AE	American Express	DISC	Discover	V	Visa
DC	Diners Club	MC	MasterCard		

Frommers.com

Now that you have the guidebook to a great trip, visit our website at **www.frommers.com** for travel information on more than 3,000 destinations. With features updated regularly, we give you instant access to the most current trip-planning information available. At Frommers.com, you'll also find the best prices on airfares, accommodations, and car rentals—and you can even book travel online through our travel booking partners. At Frommers.com, you'll also find the following:

- Online updates to our most popular guidebooks
- Vacation sweepstakes and contest giveaways
- Newsletter highlighting the hottest travel trends
- Online travel message boards with featured travel discussions

What's New in Australia

The land Down Under continues to change in exciting ways. Travelers have new possibilities for getting to and around the country. Hotel renovations and openings provide travelers with more options. Here's a brief summary of the latest happenings. You'll find more detail in each of the regional chapters.

PLANNING YOUR TRIP The Australian skies have seen many changes in recent years, the most notable being the growth of no-frills carrier **Virgin Blue** (© 07/3295 2296; www.virginblue.com.au). Rapidly expanding routes now see Virgin Blue servicing all capital cities as well as an ever-growing list of smaller centers such as Cairns, Townsville, Mackay, the Whitsunday Coast, Rockhampton, and Gold Coast in Queensland; Coffs Harbour in New South Wales; Hobart and Launceston in Tasmania; Alice Springs in the Red Centre; and Broome in Western Australia.

Another newcomer is **Regional Express** (© 13 17 13 in Australia; www.regionalexpress.com.au), which picked up the pieces from the old Kendell Airlines. Its many routes include Sydney to Broken Hill, Ballina, and Merimbula, all in New South Wales; Melbourne to northern Tasmania; and Adelaide to Kangaroo Island and Broken Hill. You can often find good Internet deals on Regional Express and Virgin Blue.

GETTING AROUND AUSTRALIA Train travel has also undergone some changes. Australia's Orient Express, the luxury **Great South Pacific Express,** which traveled from Sydney to Cairns, "suspended" operations indefinitely in June 2003, citing a downturn in international business.

On the positive side, beginning in early 2004, the opening of the long-awaited Alice Springs–Darwin railway line will give the Top End its first rail link. Great Southern Railway's **The Ghan** (© 13 21 47 in Australia; www. trainways.com.au) will run one weekly return journey between the two cities, leaving Alice Springs on Mondays and arriving in Darwin about 24 hours later.

In Queensland, the new high-speed Brisbane-Cairns **Tilt Train** has knocked about 7 hours off the journey between those cities. The 160kmph (about 100 mph) "business class" trip takes 25 hours. For more details, contact **Queensland Rail** (© 07/3235 1122; www.traveltrain.qr.com.au).

As for road travel, an extension of the M5 motorway south of Sydney has cut 45 minutes off the road trip to Canberra and the Snowy Mountains. You can now make Canberra in less than 3½ hours.

SYDNEY The latest newcomer to the Sydney hotel scene is the **Sydney Harbour Marriott,** on Pitt Street (© 800/228-9290 in the U.S.; www. marriott.com). The hotel, which occupies the shell of the former Renaissance Hotel, was opened in mid-2003 after a A$35 million (about US$23 million) refurbishment. Many of the rooms have good Sydney Harbour and Opera House views.

New entrants to the bar scene in Sydney include the groovy **Cargo Bar & Lounge,** 52–60 The Promenade, King Street Wharf (✆ **02/9262 1777**), which has outdoor areas that are great on a sultry evening, and **The Establishment,** 252 George St. (✆ **02/9240 3000**), in the city center.

MELBOURNE The new place to hang out is **Federation Square,** a collection of attractions around a large square, which planners estimate will attract six million visitors a year. The architecture is weird: a kind of postindustrial cubic look with a large piazza paved with very irregular stones. There are plenty of cafes, restaurants, and art spaces nearby. One eatery to look out for is **Chocolate Buddha** (✆ **03/9654 5688**), a Japanese-inspired noodle place.

The latest hotel of note is the **Ramada Melbourne** (270 Flinders St.; ✆ **1300/726 232** in Australia, or 03/9654 6888), a new four-star hotel opposite Flinders Street Railway Station. It's cozy, friendly and offers special deals—especially on weekends.

BRISBANE Brisbane's pub scene has taken on new life, with the renovation of several of its historic hotels. The heritage-listed **Breakfast Creek Hotel,** 2 Kingsford Smith Dr. (✆ **07/ 3262 5988**), has undergone a A$4 million (US$2.6 million) renovation and restoration, and the **Regatta Hotel,** 543 Coronation Dr. (✆ **07/ 3870 7063**), now one of the trendiest places in town, has also undergone a facelift. Access to the Regatta has been improved by the opening of a new CityCat terminal practically on its doorstep.

The **Queensland Museum,** adjacent to South Bank Parklands (✆ **07/ 3840 7555**), underwent a major revamp in 2003, adding a smart new entrance and interactive Sciencentre, a kid magnet.

Brisbane's new **Cultural Industries Precinct** at Kelvin Grove, still under construction at press time, is the new home to the established and innovative **La Boite Theatre** (www.laboite. com.au), which was due to move into its new 400-seat theater-in-the-round in late 2003.

QUEENSLAND A major redevelopment of Cairns's **Esplanade,** including a massive new saltwater swimming lagoon, has transformed that city. Another new addition is the **Reef Fleet Terminal,** the departure point for Great Barrier Reef boats.

Many island resorts are undergoing major refurbishment programs. **Hayman Resort** (✆ **800/223-6800** in the U.S. or 1800/075 175 in Australia) has completed a staggering A$50 million (US$33 million) refurbishment of its rooms and introduced new accommodations levels.

P&O Australian Resorts opened new "super premium" pavilion-style accommodations, called **The Point** (✆ **800/225-9849** in the U.S. or 1800/737 678 in Australia), at its fabulous Lizard Island and Bedarra resorts in mid-2003.

THE RED CENTRE Ayers Rock Resort has undergone a revamp and now includes two new places to stay. At the top of the price scale is **Longitude 131,** Yulara Dr., Yulara (✆ **08/ 8957 7888**), a A$9 million (about US$6 million) development consisting of 15 luxury tents. They're smack-dab in the middle of the sand dunes, with fabulous views of the Rock. It's like being in Africa, only with kangaroos. Staying here is terrifically expensive, though. The other newcomer is

The Lost Camel, Yulara Dr., Yulara (© 08/8957 7888), a trendy hotel aimed at urbanites who want similar surroundings to back home.

PERTH & WESTERN AUSTRALIA
The **Mining Hall of Fame** (© 08/9026 2700;** www.mininghall.com) in the Outback gold town of Kalgoorlie continues to expand, with new attractions, including a Chinese garden and more galleries, opening in late 2003.

1

The Best of Australia

by Marc Llewellyn & Lee Mylne

Maybe we're biased because we live here, but Australia has a lot of bests—world bests, that is. It's got some of the best natural scenery, the weirdest wildlife, the most brilliant scuba diving and snorkeling, the best beaches (shut up, California), the oldest rainforest (110 million years and counting), the oldest human civilization (some archaeologists say 40,000 years, some say 120,000; whatever—it's old), the best wines (come see what we mean), the best weather (give or take the odd wet season in the north), the most innovative East-meets-West-meets-someplace-else cuisine—all bathed in sunlight that brings everything up in Technicolor.

"Best" means different things to different people, but scarcely a visitor lands on these shores without having the Great Barrier Reef at the top of his "Things to See" list. So they should, because it really is a glorious natural masterpiece. Also high on most folks' lists is Ayers Rock. This monolith must have some kind of magnet inside it designed to attract planeloads of tourists. We're not saying the Rock isn't special, but we think the vast Australian desert all around it is even more so. The third attraction on most visitors' lists is Sydney, the Emerald City that glitters in the Antipodean sunshine on—here we go with the "bests" again—the best harbor, spanned by the best bridge in the world (yes it is, San Francisco).

But as planes zoom overhead delivering visitors to these "big three" attractions, Aussies in charming country towns, on far-flung beaches, on rustic sheep stations, in rainforest villages, and in mountain lodges shake their heads and say sadly, "They don't know what they're missin'." Well, that's the aim of this chapter—to show you what you're missin'. Read on, and consider the road less traveled.

1 The Top Travel Experiences

- **Hitting the Rails on the *Indian Pacific* Train:** This 3-day train journey across the Outback regularly makes it onto the "Top Rail Journeys in the World" lists compiled by travel magazines. The desert scenery ain't all that magnificent—it's the unspoiled, empty vastness that passengers appreciate. It includes the longest straight stretch of track in the world, 478km (296 miles) across the treeless Nullarbor Plain. Start in Sydney and end in Perth, or vice versa, or just do a section. See "Getting Around Australia" in chapter 2.

- **Experiencing Sydney** (NSW): Sydney is more than just the magnificent Harbour Bridge and Opera House. No other city has beaches in abundance like Sydney, and few have such a magnificently scenic harbor. Our advice is to get aboard a ferry, walk from one side of the bridge to the other, and try to spend a week here, because

---

Tips **A Note on Abbreviations**

In the listings below, NSW stands for New South Wales, QLD for Queensland, NT for the Northern Territory, WA for Western Australia, SA for South Australia, VIC for Victoria, TAS for Tasmania, and ACT for the Australian Capital Territory.

---

you're going to need it. See chapter 3, "Sydney."

- **Seeing the Great Barrier Reef** (QLD): It's a glorious 2,000km (1,240-mile) long underwater coral fairyland with electric colors and bizarre fish life—and it comes complete with warm water and year-round sunshine. This is what you came to Australia to see. When you're not snorkeling over coral and giant clams almost as big as you, scuba diving, calling in at tropical towns, or lazing on deserted island beaches, you're trying out the sun lounges or enjoying the first-rate food. See chapter 6, "Queensland & the Great Barrier Reef."

- **Exploring the Wet Tropics Rainforest** (QLD): Folks who come from skyscraper cities like Manhattan or Los Angeles can't get over the moisture-dripping ferns, the neon-blue butterflies, and the primeval peace of this World Heritage rainforest stretching north, south, and west from Cairns. Hike it, four-wheel-drive it, or glide over the treetops in the Skyrail gondola. See "Cairns" in chapter 6.

- **Bareboat Sailing in the Whitsundays** (QLD): Bareboat means unskippered—that's right, even if you think port is an after-dinner drink, you can charter a yacht, pay for a day's instruction from a skipper, and then take over the helm yourself and explore these 74 island gems. It's easy. Anchor in deserted bays, snorkel over dazzling reefs, fish for coral trout, and feel the wind in your sails. See "The Whitsunday Coast & Islands" in chapter 6.

- **Exploring the Olgas (Kata Tjuta) & Ayers Rock (Uluru)** (NT): Just why everyone comes thousands of miles to see the big red stone of Ayers Rock is a mystery—that's probably why they come, because the Rock is a mystery. Just 50km (31 miles) from Ayers Rock are the round red heads of the Olgas, a second rock formation more significant to Aborigines and more intriguing to many visitors. See "Uluru-Kata Tjuta National Park (Ayers Rock/The Olgas)" in chapter 7.

- **Taking an Aboriginal Culture Tour** (Alice Springs, NT): Eating female wasps, contemplating a hill as a giant resting caterpillar, and imagining that the stars are your grandmother smiling down at you will give you a new perspective on Aboriginal culture. See what we mean on a half-day tour from the Aboriginal Art & Culture Centre. See p. 370.

- **Discovering the Kimberley** (WA): Australia's last frontier, the Kimberley is a romantic cocktail of South Sea pearls, red mountain ranges, aqua seas, deadly crocodiles, Aboriginal rock art, and million-acre farms in a never-ending wilderness. Cross it by four-wheel-drive, stay in safari tents on a cattle ranch, swim under ferny waterfalls, ride a camel along the beach in Broome, and more. See chapter 8, "The Top End."

Australia

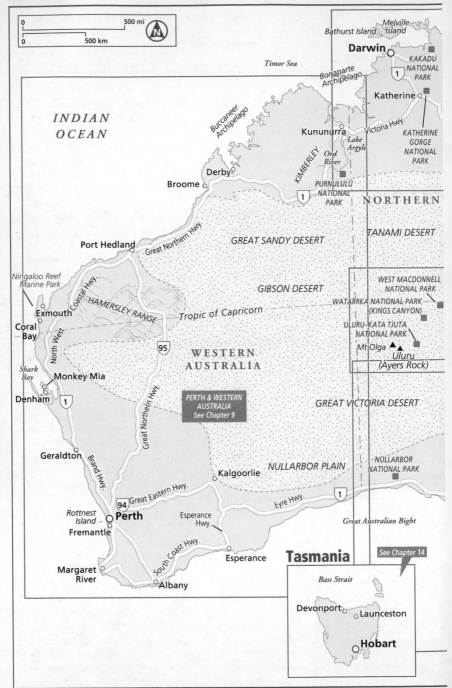

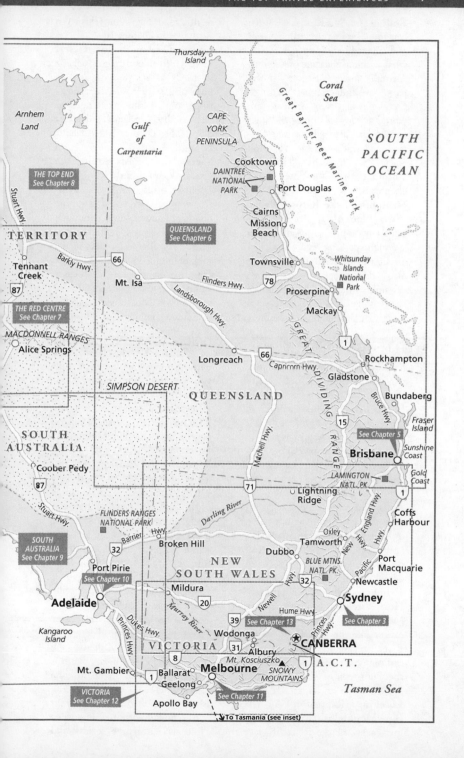

Coral Sea

SOUTH PACIFIC OCEAN

Thursday Island

Arnhem Land

Gulf of Carpentaria

CAPE YORK PENINSULA

Great Barrier Reef Marine Park

Cooktown

DAINTREE NATIONAL PARK

Port Douglas

THE TOP END
See Chapter 8

Cairns
Mission Beach

TERRITORY

Barkly Hwy.

66

Mt. Isa

Tennant Creek

87

THE RED CENTRE
See Chapter 7

MACDONNELL RANGES

Alice Springs

Stuart Hwy.

Flinders Hwy.

Landsborough Hwy.

78

Townsville

Whitsunday Islands National Park

Proserpine

Mackay

1

SIMPSON DESERT

QUEENSLAND
See Chapter 6

Longreach

66

Capricorn Hwy.

GREAT

Rockhampton

Gladstone

QUEENSLAND

Mitchell Hwy.

DIVIDING

15

Bundaberg

Fraser Island

SOUTH AUSTRALIA

Coober Pedy

87

FLINDERS RANGES NATIONAL PARK

Barrier Hwy.

Broken Hill

RANGE

See Chapter 5

Bruce Hwy.

Brisbane

LAMINGTON NATL. PK.

Sunshine Coast

Gold Coast

1

Stuart Hwy.

Darling River

71

Lightning Ridge

Coffs Harbour

SOUTH AUSTRALIA
See Chapter 9

32

Port Pirie
See Chapter 10

Adelaide

Kangaroo Island

Dukes Hwy.

Princes Hwy.

Mildura

Murray River

20

NEW SOUTH WALES

Dubbo

Oxley Hwy.

Tamworth

New England Hwy.

Pacific Hwy.

Port Macquarie

Newcastle

32

BLUE MTNS. NATL. PK.

Sydney

See Chapter 3

Newell Hwy.

Hume Hwy.

39

See Chapter 13

Wodonga

31

Albury

Mt. Kosciuszko

SNOWY MOUNTAINS

CANBERRA

A.C.T.

Princes Hwy.

1

VICTORIA

8

Ballarat

Melbourne

Mt. Gambier

1

Geelong

Apollo Bay

VICTORIA
See Chapter 12

See Chapter 11

Tasman Sea

To Tasmania (see inset)

- **Rolling in Wildflowers** (WA): Imagine Texas three times over and covered in wildflowers. That's what much of the state of Western Australia looks like every spring from around August through October when pink, mauve, red, white, yellow, and blue wildflowers bloom. Aussies flock here big-time for this spectacle, so book ahead. See the box "Tiptoeing Through the Wildflowers" in chapter 9.

- **Drinking in the Barossa Valley** (SA): One of Australia's four largest wine-producing areas, this German-speaking region less than an hour's drive from Adelaide is also the prettiest. Adelaide's restaurants happen to be some of the country's best, too, so test out your wine purchases with the city's terrific food. See "Side Trips from Adelaide" in chapter 10.

- **Getting Dusty in the Desert** (SA): Head inland from Adelaide to the Outback to visit remote pubs and settlements, the craggy ridges of the Flinders Ranges, as well as dry salt lakes and stony deserts. See chapter 10, "Adelaide & South Australia."

- **Seeing the Sights Along the Great Ocean Road** (VIC): This 106km (66-mile) coastal road carries you past wild and stunning beaches, forests, and dramatic cliff-top scenery—including the Twelve Apostles, 12 pillars of red rock standing in isolation in the foaming Southern Ocean. See "The Great Ocean Road: One of the World's Most Scenic Drives" in chapter 12.

2 The Best Outdoor Adventures

- **Sea Kayaking:** Kayaking is a great way to explore Queensland's Whitsunday Islands as well as Dunk Island off Mission Beach in Queensland. **Rivergods** (© 08/ 9259 0749; www.rivergods.com. au) in Perth even takes you on a sea-kayaking day trip to snorkel with wild sea lions and watch penguins feeding. This Western Australian company also runs multiday expeditions past whales, dolphins, and sharks in Shark Bay, and over coral at Ningaloo Reef on the Northwest Cape. For details on the Whitsunday Islands and Dunk Island, see chapter 6.

- **Horse Trekking in the Snowy Mountains** (NSW): Ride the ranges like the man from Snowy River, staying in bush lodges or camping beneath the stars. See "In the Footsteps of the Man from Snowy River" in chapter 4.

- **Abseiling (Rappelling) in the Blue Mountains** (NSW): Careering backward down a cliff face with the smell of eucalyptus in your nostrils is not everyone's idea of fun, but you sure know you're alive. Several operators welcome both novices and the more experienced. See "The Blue Mountains" in chapter 4.

- **White-Water Rafting on the Tully River** (Mission Beach, QLD): The Class III to IV rapids of the Tully River swoosh between lush, rainforested banks. The guides are professional, and the rapids are just hairy enough to be fun. It's a good choice for first-time rafters. See "The North Coast: Mission Beach, Townsville & the Islands" in chapter 6.

- **Four-Wheel-Driving on Fraser Island** (QLD): Burning down 75-Mile Beach in a 4×4 on the biggest sand island in the world is liberating, if not great for the environment. Paradoxically, the island is ecologically important and popular with nature lovers. Hike its eucalyptus forests and rainforests, swim its clear lakes, and fish off the beach. See "Fraser Island: Ecoadventures & Four-Wheel-Drive Fun" in chapter 6.

- **Game Fishing:** Battle a black marlin off Cairns and you might snare the world record; that's how big they get down there. Marlin and other game catches run around much of the Australian coastline—Exmouth on the Northwest Cape in Western Australia (see chapter 9), and Broome and Darwin in the Top End (see chapter 8) are two other hot spots.
- **Canoeing the Top End** (NT): Paddling between the sun-drenched ocher walls of Katherine Gorge sharpens the senses, especially when a (harmless) freshwater crocodile pops up! **Gecko Canoeing** (© **1800/634 319** in Australia, or 08/8972 2224; www.geckocanoeing.com.au) will take

you downriver to the rarely explored Flora and Daly River systems to meet Aboriginal communities, shower under waterfalls, hike virgin bushland, and camp in swags on the banks. See "Katherine" in chapter 8.

- **Surfing in Margaret River** (WA): A 90-minute surf lesson with four-time Western Australia surf champ Josh Palmateer is a great introduction to the sport—if only to hear Josh's Aussie accent! In July and August, Josh shifts his classes to Cable Beach in Broome. See chapter 9.
- **Skiing in the Victorian Alps** (VIC): Skiing in Australia? Sure. When you've had enough coral and sand, you can hit the slopes in Victoria. Where else can you swish down the mountain between gum trees? See "The High Country" in chapter 12.

3 The Best Places to View Wildlife

- **Pebbly Beach** (NSW): The eastern gray kangaroos, which inhabit Murramarang National Park, 20 minutes south of Ulladulla on the south coast of New South Wales, tend to congregate along this ocean beach and the adjoining dunes. See "South of Sydney Along the Princes Highway" in chapter 4.
- **Montague Island** (Narooma, NSW): This little island just offshore from the seaside town of Narooma, on the south coast, is a haven for nesting seabirds, but it's the water around it that's home to the main attractions. Dolphins are common, fairy penguins, too; in whale-watching season, you're sure to spot southern right and humpback whales. See "South of Sydney Along the Princes Highway" in chapter 4.
- **Jervis Bay** (NSW): This is probably the closest place to Sydney

where you're certain to see kangaroos in the wild and where you can pet them, too. The national park here is home to hundreds of bird species, including black cockatoos, as well as plenty of possums. See "South of Sydney Along the Princes Highway" in chapter 4.
- **Lone Pine Koala Sanctuary** (Brisbane, QLD): Cuddle a koala (and have your photo taken doing it) at this park, the world's first and largest koala sanctuary. Apart from some 130 koalas, lots of other Aussie wildlife—including wombats, Tasmanian devils, 'roos (which you can hand-feed), and colorful parakeets—are on show. See p. 246.
- **Hervey Bay** (QLD): The warm waters off Hervey Bay, and in particular the lovely Platypus Bay, on the Queensland coast, are where the humpback whales come each year between June and October in

increasing numbers to give birth. The long journey from Antarctica brings them up the coast to frolic with their young for several months before making the return trip. Hervey Bay's many cruises can bring you closer to these gentle giants than you'll ever come elsewhere. See "Fraser Island: Ecoadventures & Four-Wheel-Drive Fun" in chapter 6.

• **Australian Butterfly Sanctuary** (Kuranda, near Cairns, QLD): Walk through the biggest butterfly "aviary" in Australia and see some of Australia's most gorgeous butterflies, including the electric-blue Ulysses. See many species of butterfly feed, lay eggs, and mate, and inspect caterpillars and pupae. Wearing pink, red, or white encourages the butterflies to land on you. See p. 281.

• **Wait-a-While Rainforest Tours** (QLD): Head into the World Heritage–listed Wet Tropics rainforest behind Cairns or Port Douglas with this ecotour operator to spotlight possums, lizards, pythons, even a platypus, so shy that most Aussies have never seen one in the wild. About once a month one group will spot the rare, bizarre Lumholtz's tree kangaroo. See "Cairns" in chapter 6.

• **Heron Island** (off Gladstone, QLD): There's wonderful wildlife on this "jewel in the reef" any time of year, but the best time to visit is November to March, when the life cycle of giant green loggerhead and hawksbill turtles is in full swing. From November to January, the turtles come ashore to lay their eggs. From late January to March, the hatchlings emerge and head for the water. You can see it all by just strolling down to the beach, or join a university researcher to get the full story. See "The Capricorn Coast & the

Southern Reef Islands" in chapter 6. Mon Repos Turtle Rookery, near Bundaberg in Queensland (see "Up Close & Personal with a Turtle" in chapter 6) and the Northwest Cape in Western Australia (see "The Midwest & the Northwest: Where the Outback Meets the Sea" in chapter 9) are two other good turtle-watching sites.

• **Currumbin Wildlife Sanctuary** (The Gold Coast, QLD): Tens of thousands of unbelievably pretty red, blue, green, and yellow rainbow lorikeets have been screeching into this park for generations to be hand-fed by delighted visitors every morning and afternoon. There are 'roos and other Australian animals at the sanctuary, too, but the birds steal the show. See p. 355.

• **Kakadu National Park** (NT): One-third of Australia's bird species live in Kakadu; so do lots of saltwater crocs. A cruise on the Yellow Waters Billabong or aboard the Original Jumping Crocodiles cruise en route to the park, are some of the best places to see them in the wild. See "Kakadu National Park" in chapter 8.

• **The Northwest Cape** (WA): For the thrill of a lifetime, go snorkeling with a whale shark. No one knows where they come from, but these mysterious monsters (up to 18m/60 ft. long) surface in the Outback waters off Western Australia every year from March to early June. A mini-industry takes snorkelers out to swim alongside the sharks as they feed (on plankton, not snorkelers). See "The Midwest & the Northwest: Where the Outback Meets the Sea" in chapter 9.

• **Tangalooma** (QLD), **Bunbury & Monkey Mia** (WA): There are several places you can see, hand-feed, or swim with wild dolphins Down Under. At Bunbury, south of Perth, you can swim with them or join cruises to see them (they come right up to the boat). If you want an almost guaranteed dolphin sighting, head to Tangalooma Wild Dolphin Resort on Moreton Island, off Brisbane, where you can hand-feed them, or to Monkey Mia on the lonely Outback coast, where they cruise past your legs. Even better is a cruise on the *Shotover* catamaran to see some of the area's 10,000 dugongs (manatees), plus turtles, sea snakes, sharks—and more. See chapters 5 and 9.

- **Kangaroo Island** (SA): You're sure to see more native animals here—including koalas, wallabies, birds, echidnas, reptiles, seals, and sea lions—than anywhere else in the country, apart from a wildlife park. Another plus: The distances between major points of interest are not great, so you won't spend half the day just getting from place to place. See "Kangaroo Island" in chapter 10.

4 The Best Places to Experience the Outback

- **Broken Hill** (NSW): There's no better place to experience real Outback life than in Broken Hill. There's the city itself, with its thriving art scene and the Royal Flying Doctor service; a historic ghost town on its outskirts; a national park with Aboriginal wall paintings; an opal mining town nearby; and plenty of kangaroos, emus, and giant wedge-tailed eagles. See "Outback New South Wales" in chapter 4.
- **Lightning Ridge** (NSW): This opal-mining town is as rough and ready as the stones they pull out of the ground. Meet amazing characters, share in the eccentricity of the place, and visit opal-rush areas with molehill scenery made by the old sun-bleached mine tailings. See "Outback New South Wales" in chapter 4.
- **Uluru-Kata Tjuta National Park** (Ayers Rock, NT): Sure, Ayers Rock will enthrall you with its eerie beauty; but the nearby Olgas are more soothing, more interesting, and taller than the Rock, so make the time to wander through them, too. Hike the Rock's base, burn around it on a Harley-Davidson, saunter up to it on a camel, climb it if you must. Don't go home until you've felt the powerful heartbeat of the desert. See "Uluru-Kata Tjuta National Park (Ayers Rock/The Olgas)" in chapter 7.
- **The MacDonnell Ranges** (NT): The Aborigines say these red rocky hills were formed by the Aboriginal "Caterpillar Dreaming" that wriggled from the earth here. To the west of Alice Springs are dramatic gorges, idyllic (and bloody cold) waterholes, and cute wallabies. To the east are Aboriginal rock carvings, and the Ross River Homestead, where you can crack a cattle whip, throw a boomerang, feast on damper and billy tea, and ride a horse or camel in the bush. See "Road Trips from Alice Springs" in chapter 7.
- **Kings Canyon** (NT): Anyone who saw the cult flick *The Adventures of Priscilla, Queen of the Desert* will remember the scene where the transvestites climb a soaring orange cliff and survey the desert floor. That was Kings Canyon, about 320km (198 miles) from Alice Springs in one direction and Ayers Rock in the other. Trek the dramatic rim or

take the easier shady route along the bottom. Don't forget your lipstick, guys. See "Kings Canyon" in chapter 7.

• **The Northwest Cape** (WA): This treeless moonscape of red anthills, spiky spinifex, and blazing heat seems to go on forever, so it's all the more amazing to find a beautiful coral reef offshore. Drive the rugged hills in a four-wheel-drive, dodging kangaroos on the way; swim with giant manta rays; snorkel right off the beach; scuba dive coral outcroppings; and laze on blindingly white beaches. This is where the Outback meets the sea. See "The Midwest & the Northwest: Where the Outback Meets the Sea" in chapter 9.

• **Coober Pedy** (SA): It may be hot and dusty, but you'll get a true taste of the Outback as you tag along with the local mail carrier as he makes his rounds to the area's remote cattle stations (ranches). It's a 12-hour, 600km (372-mile) journey along sun-baked dirt roads. See "Outback South Australia" in chapter 10.

5 The Best Beaches

• **Palm Beach** (Sydney): At the end of a string of beaches stretching north from Sydney, Palm Beach is long and white, with good surfing and a golf course. See chapter 3, "Sydney."

• **Hyams Beach** (Jervis Bay, NSW): This beach in off-the-beaten-path Jervis Bay is said to be the whitest in the world. You need to wear sunblock if you decide to stroll along it, because the reflection from the sun, even on a cloudy day, can give you a nasty sunburn. The beach also squeaks as you walk. See "South of Sydney Along the Princes Highway" in chapter 4.

• **Four Mile Beach** (Port Douglas, QLD): The sea is turquoise, the sun is warm, the palms sway, and the low-rise hotels starting to line this country beach can't spoil the feeling that it is a million miles from anywhere. But isn't there always a serpent in paradise? In this case the "serpents" are north Queensland's seasonal, potentially deadly marine stingers. Come June through September to avoid them, or confine your swimming to the area in the stinger net the rest of the year. See "Port Douglas, Daintree & the Cape Tribulation Area" in chapter 6.

• **Mission Beach** (QLD): Azure blue water, islands dotting the horizon, and white sand edged by vine forests make this beach a real winner. The bonus is that hardly anyone comes here. Cassowaries (giant emulike birds) hide out in the rainforest, and the tiny town of Mission Beach makes itself invisible behind the leaves. Visit June through September to avoid marine stingers. See "The North Coast: Mission Beach, Townsville & the Islands" in chapter 6.

• **Whitehaven Beach** (Whitsunday Island, QLD): It's not a surf beach, but this 6km (3¾-mile) stretch of white silica sand on uninhabited Whitsunday Island is pristine and peaceful. Bring a book, curl up under the rainforest lining its edge, and fantasize that the cruise boat is going to leave without you. See "The Whitsunday Coast & Islands" in chapter 6.

• **Surfers Paradise Beach** (Gold Coast, QLD): Actually, all 35 of the beaches on the 30km (19-mile) Gold Coast strip in south Queensland are worthy of inclusion here. Every one has sand so clean it squeaks, great surf, and fresh breezes—ignore the tacky high-rises. Surfers will like

Burleigh Heads. See "The Gold Coast" in chapter 6.

- **Cable Beach** (Broome, WA): Is it the South Sea pearls they pull out of the Indian Ocean, the camels loping along the sand, the sunsets, the surf, or the red earth meeting the green sea that gives this beach an exotic appeal? Maybe it's the 26km (16 miles) of glorious white sand. The only time to swim here is June through September, when deadly marine stingers aren't around. See "The Kimberley: A Far-Flung Wilderness" in chapter 9.

- **Cottesloe Beach** (Perth, WA): Perth has 19 great beaches, but this petite crescent is the prettiest. After you've checked out the scene, join the fashionable set for brunch in the Indiana Tea House, a mock-Edwardian bathhouse fronting the sea. Surfers head to Scarborough and Trigg. See chapter 9, "Perth & Western Australia."

6 The Best Diving & Snorkeling Sites

- **Port Douglas** (QLD): Among the fabulous dive sites found off Port Douglas, north of Cairns, are Split-Bommie, with its delicate fan corals and schools of fusiliers; Barracuda Pass, with its coral gardens and giant clams; and the swim-through coral spires of the Cathedrals. Snorkelers can glide over coral and reef fish life of Agincourt Reef. See "Port Douglas, Daintree & the Cape Tribulation Area" in chapter 6.

- **Lizard Island** (QLD): Snorkel over 150-year-old giant clams—as well as gorgeous underwater coral—in the Clam Garden, off this exclusive resort island northeast of Cairns. Nearby is the famous Cod Hole, where divers can hand-feed giant potato cod. See p. 287.

- **Cairns** (QLD): Moore, Norman, Hardy, Saxon, and Arlington reefs and Michaelmas and Upolu cays—all about 90 minutes off Cairns—offer great snorkeling and endless dive sites. Explore on a day trip from Cairns or join a live-aboard adventure. See "Cairns," chapter 6.

- **Coral Sea** (QLD): In this sea east of the Great Barrier Reef off north Queensland, you'll see sharks feeding at Predator's Playground; 1,000m (3,280 ft.) drop-offs in the Abyss; reefs covering hundreds of square miles; and tropical species not found on the Great Barrier Reef. This is not a day-trip destination; many dive operators run multiday trips on live-aboard vessels. Visibility is excellent—up to 100m (328 ft.). See "The North Coast: Mission Beach, Townsville & the Islands" in chapter 6.

- ***Yongala* wreck** (QLD): Sunk by a cyclone in 1911, the 120m (394 ft.) SS *Yongala* lies in the Coral Sea off Townsville. Schools of trevally, kingfish, barracuda, and batfish surround the wreckage; giant Queensland grouper live under the bow, lionfish hide under the stern, turtles graze on the hull, and hard and soft corals make their home on it. It's too far for a day trip; live-aboard trips run from Townsville and Cairns. See "The North Coast: Mission Beach, Townsville & the Islands" in chapter 6.

- **The Whitsunday Islands** (QLD): As well as Blue Pearl Bay, these 74 breathtaking islands offer countless dive sites both among the islands themselves and on the Outer Great Barrier Reef 90 minutes away. Bait Reef on the Outer

Reef is popular for its cascading drop-offs. Snorkelers can explore not just the Outer Reef, but also patch reefs among the islands and rarely visited fringing reefs around many island shores. See "The Whitsunday Coast & Islands" in chapter 6.

- **Heron Island** (QLD): Easily the number-one snorkel and dive site in Australia. If you stayed in the water for a week, you couldn't snorkel all the acres of coral stretching from shore. Take your pick of 22 dive sites: the Coral Cascades, with football trout and anemones; the Blue Pools, favored by octopus, turtles, and sharks; and Heron Bommie, with its rays, eels, and Spanish dancers; and more. Absolute magic. See "The Capricorn Coast & the Southern Reef Islands" in chapter 6.

- **Lady Elliot Island** (QLD): Gorgeous coral lagoons, perfect for snorkeling, line this coral cay island off the town of Bundaberg. Boats take you farther out to snorkel above manta rays, plate coral, and big fish. Divers can swim through the blow hole, 16m (52 ft.) down, and see Gorgonian fans, soft and hard corals, sharks, barracudas, and loads of reef fish. See "The Capricorn Coast & the

Southern Reef Islands" in chapter 6.

- **Rottnest Island** (WA): Just 19km (12 miles) off Perth, this former prison island has excellent snorkeling and more than 100 dive sites. Wrecks, limestone overhangs, and myriad fish will keep divers entertained. There are no cars, so snorkelers should rent a bike and snorkel gear, buy a visitor center map of suggested snorkel trails, and head off to find their own private coral garden. The sunken grotto of Fishhook Bay is great for fish life. See "Side Trips from Perth" in chapter 9.

- **Ningaloo Reef** (WA): A well-kept secret is how we'd describe Australia's second great barrier reef, stretching 260km (161 miles) along the Northwest Cape halfway up Western Australia. Coral starts right on shore, not 90 minutes out to sea as at the Great Barrier Reef. You can snorkel or dive with manta rays, and dive to see sharks, angelfish, turtles, eels, grouper, potato cod, and much more. Snorkel with whale sharks up to 18m (59 ft.) long from March to early June. See "The Midwest & Northwest: Where the Outback Meets the Sea" in chapter 9.

7 The Best Places to Bushwalk (Hike)

- **Blue Mountains** (NSW): Many bushwalks in the Blue Mountains National Park offer awesome views of valleys, waterfalls, cliffs, and forest. All are easily reached from Sydney. See "The Blue Mountains" in chapter 4.

- **Whitsunday Islands** (QLD): Most people think of snorkeling and watersports when they come to these subtropical national-park islands clad in dense rainforest and bush, but every resort island

we recommend has hiking trails. Some are flat, some are hilly. Wallabies and butterflies are common sights. South Molle has the best network of trails and 360-degree island views from its peak. See "The Whitsunday Coast & Islands" in chapter 6.

- **Lamington National Park** (QLD): Few other national parks in Australia have such a well-marked network of trails (160km/99 miles in all) as this one, just 90 minutes from the Gold Coast. Revel in dense subtropical rainforest, marvel at mossy 2,000-year-old Antarctic beech trees, delight in the prolific wallabies and birds, and soak up the cool mountain air. See "The Gold Coast Hinterland: Back to Nature" in chapter 6.

- **Larapinta Trail** (The Red Centre, NT): You can now start off from Alice Springs and walk the entire 250km (155-mile) semidesert trail that winds through the stark crimson McDonnell Ranges. You don't have to walk the entire length, as plenty of day-length and multiday sections are possible. This one's for the cooler months only (Apr–Oct). See "Alice Springs" in chapter 7.
- **Kakadu National Park** (NT): Whether a pleasant wetlands stroll or a tough overnight hike in virgin bushland, you can find it in this World Heritage–listed park. You'll see red cliffs, cycads, waterfalls, lily-filled lagoons hiding man-eating crocodiles, what sometimes looks like Australia's entire bird population, and Aboriginal rock art. See "Kakadu National Park" in chapter 8.

- **Cape-to-Cape** (WA): Rugged sea cliffs, a china-blue sea, eucalyptus forest, white beaches, and coastal heath are what you will find hiking between Cape Naturaliste and Cape Leeuwin, in the southwest corner of Western Australia. In season, you'll see whales and wildflowers. See "Margaret River & the Southwest: Wine Tasting in the Forests" in chapter 9.
- **Freycinet National Park** (TAS): The trek to Wine Glass Bay passes pink granite outcrops, with views over an ocean sliced by a crescent of icy sand. It's prehistorically beautiful. See "Freycinet National Park" in chapter 14.
- **Cradle Mountain & Lake St. Clair National Park** (TAS): The 80km (50-mile) Overland Track is the best hike in Australia. The trek, from Lake St. Clair to Cradle Mountain, takes anywhere from 5 to 10 days, depending on your fitness level. Shorter walks, some lasting just half an hour, are also accessible. See "Cradle Mountain & Lake St. Clair National Park" in chapter 14.

8 The Best Places to Learn About Aboriginal Culture

- **The Umbarra Aboriginal Cultural Centre** (Wallaga Lake, near Narooma, NSW): This center offers boomerang- and spear-throwing instruction, painting with natural ochers, discussions on Aboriginal culture, and guided walking tours of Aboriginal sacred sites. See chapter 4.
- **Tjapukai Aboriginal Cultural Park** (Cairns, QLD): This multi-million-dollar center showcases the history of the Tjapukai people—their Dreamtime creation history and their often-harrowing experiences since the white man arrived—using a film, superb

theatrical work, and a dance performance. Its Aboriginal art and crafts gift shop is one of the country's best. See p. 275.
- **Aboriginal Art & Culture Centre** (Alice Springs, NT): You'll taste bush food, see a dance, throw boomerangs and spears, and learn about Aboriginal family values in one half-day tour of this Aborigine-owned center in Alice Springs. Be sure to hang around for the 1-hour didgeridoo lesson at the end. See p. 370.
- **Anangu Tours** (Ayers Rock, NT): The Anangu are the owners of Ayers Rock, or Uluru, as it is

called in their native tongue. Join them for walks around the Rock as you learn about the poisonous "snake men" who fought battles here, pick bush food off the trees, throw spears, visit rock paintings, and watch the sun set over the monolith. Their Cultural Centre near the base of the Rock has good displays about the Aboriginal Dreamtime. See "Uluru-Kata Tjuta National Park (Ayers Rock/ The Olgas)" in chapter 7.

- **Manyallaluk: The Dreaming Place** (Katherine, NT): This Aboriginal community welcomes visitors to their bush home and teaches them to paint, weave, throw boomerangs, and other tasks of daily life. A low-key day and the chance to chat one-on-one with Aboriginal people. See "Katherine" in chapter 8.

- **Mangarrayi People** (Katherine, NT): Mike Keighley of **Far Out Adventures** (© **08/8972 2552** or 0427 152288; www.farout.com.au) takes tours to beautiful Elsey Station (a ranch) near Katherine, where you visit with the children of the local Mangarrayi people. Sample bush tucker, learn a little bush medicine, and swim in a natural "spa-pool" in the Roper River. See "Katherine" in chapter 8.

- **Yamatji Bitja Aboriginal Bush Tours** (Kalgoorlie, WA): Geoffrey Stokes (© **08/9093 3745** or 0407/378 602), brought up the traditional Aboriginal way in the bush, takes you out to track emus, forage for bush food, and maybe even hunt a 'roo for dinner (with a gun, not a boomerang!). Explore the bush, learn about Aboriginal Dreamtime creation myths, and find out more about his childhood. See "The Goldfields" in chapter 9.

- **Tandanya Aboriginal Cultural Institute** (Adelaide, SA): This is a great place to experience life through Aboriginal eyes. You might catch one of the dances or other performances, although there are plenty of other opportunities to find out more about Aboriginal culture. See p. 499.

9 The Best of Small-Town Australia

- **Central Tilba** (NSW): Just inland from Narooma on the south coast, this historic hamlet is one of the cutest you'll see, complete with its own blacksmiths and leatherwork outlets. The ABC cheese factory offers free tastings, and you can spend hours browsing antiques stalls or admiring the period buildings. See "South of Sydney Along the Princes Highway" in chapter 4.

- **Broken Hill** (NSW): Known for its silver mines, the quirky town of Broken Hill has more pubs per capita than just about anywhere else. It's the home of the School of the Air—a "classroom" that transmits lessons by radio to communities spread over thousands of miles of Outback. Here you'll also find the Palace Hotel, made famous in *The Adventures of Priscilla, Queen of the Desert*, as well as plenty of colonial mansions and heritage homes. See "Outback New South Wales" in chapter 4.

- **Port Douglas** (QLD): What happens when Sydneysiders and Melbournites discover a one-street fishing village in tropical north Queensland? Come to Port Douglas and find out. A strip of groovy restaurants and a championship golf course have not diminished "Port's" old-fashioned air. Four Mile Beach is at the end of the street, and boats depart daily for the Great Barrier Reef. See "Port Douglas, Daintree &

the Cape Tribulation Area" in chapter 6.

- **Mission Beach** (QLD): You'd never know this tidy village existed (it's hidden in lush rainforest off the highway) if you weren't well informed. Aussies know it's here, but few bother to patronize its dazzling beach, offshore islands, and rainforest trails, so you'll have the place all to yourself. There's great white-water rafting on the nearby Tully River, too. See "The North Coast: Mission Beach, Townsville & the Islands" in chapter 6.

- **Broome** (WA): This romantic pearling port on the far-flung Kimberley coast on the Indian Ocean blends Aussie corrugated-iron architecture with red pagoda roofs left by the Chinese pearl divers. The town fuses a sophisticated international ambience with Outback attitude. Play on Cable Beach (see "The Best Beaches," earlier in this chapter) and stay at glamorous Cable Beach Club Resort. This is the place to add to your South Sea pearl collection. See "The Kimberley: A Far-Flung Wilderness" in chapter 9.

- **Kalgoorlie** (WA): This is it, the iconic Australian country town. Vibrant Kalgoorlie sits on what used to be the richest square mile of gold-bearing earth ever. It still pumps around 2,000 ounces *a day* out of the ground. Have a beer in one of the gracious 19th-century pubs, peer into the world's biggest open-cut gold mine, and wander the ghost-town streets of its sister town, Coolgardie. See "The Goldfields" in chapter 9.

- **Hahndorf** (SA): A group of Lutheran settlers founded this German-style town in the Adelaide Hills, in the 1830s. You'll love the churches, the wool factory and crafts shops, and the delicious German food served up in the local cafes, restaurants, and bakeries. See "Side Trips from Adelaide" in chapter 10.

- **Coober Pedy** (SA): For an Outback experience that's *fair dinkum* (genuine), few places are as weird and wonderful as this opal-mining town in the middle of nowhere. Visit mines, see wacky museums, and stay in a hotel underground—not all that unusual, considering that the locals live like moles anyway. See "Outback South Australia" in chapter 10.

- **Launceston** (TAS): Tasmania's second city is not much larger than your average European or American small town, but it's packed with Victorian and Georgian architecture and remnants of Australia's convict past. Spend a few days and discover the scenery; splurge a little on a stay in a historic hotel. See "Launceston" in chapter 14.

10 The Best Museums

- **Australian National Maritime Museum** (Sydney, NSW): The best things about this museum are the ships and submarines often docked in the harbor out front. You can climb aboard and explore what it's like to be a sailor. Inside are some fascinating displays relating to Australia's dependence on the oceans. See p. 149.

- **Alice Springs Telegraph Station Historical Reserve** (NT): It's not called a museum, but that's what this restored telegraph-repeater station out in the picturesque hills by a spring—Alice Springs—really is. From the hot biscuits turned out of the wood-fired oven to the old telegraph equipment, this 1870s settlement is as real as history can get. See p. 371.

- **Australian Aviation Heritage Centre** (Darwin, NT): The pride of this hangar is a B-52 bomber on permanent loan from the United States. But there's loads more, and not just planes, engines, and other aviation paraphernalia—there are stories, jokes, and anecdotes associated with the exhibits that will appeal even if you don't have avgas (aviation fuel) running in your veins. See "Darwin" in chapter 8.

- **Warradjan Aboriginal Cultural Centre** (NT): Reader Mari Fagin of Oklahoma City wrote that this small, stylish museum in Kakadu National Park makes for a "very memorable and moving experience! This museum is one of the best of its type we've ever seen." Learn about Dreamtime myths and daily life of Aboriginal people in Kakadu. See "Kakadu National Park" in chapter 8.

- **Western Australian Maritime Museum** & the Adjacent **Shipwrecks Museum** (Perth, WA): Housed in a brand-new building in the historic port precinct of Fremantle, Perth, this museum tells tales of the harsh Western Australian coastline since the Dutch first bumped into it and abandoned it as useless in the 1600s. Anyone who ever dreamed of finding a shipwreck laden with pieces of eight will relish the displays of treasure recovered from the deep. See p. 442.

- **New Norcia Museum & Art Gallery** (New Norcia, WA): The collection of European Renaissance art in this tiny museum in the Spanish Benedictine monastery town of New Norcia is mind-boggling. The museum has all kinds of memorabilia from the monks' past manuscripts, clothing, instruments, and gifts from Queen Isabella of Spain. See "Side Trips from Perth" in chapter 9.

- **The Migration Museum** (Adelaide, SA): This museum gives visitors insight into the people who came to Australia, how and where they settled, and how many suffered getting here. Don't expect a lot of musty displays because this museum is full of hands-on activities. See p. 498.

- **Australian War Memorial** (Canberra, ACT): Given its name, you might think this museum is a bleak sort of place, but you'd be wrong. The museum gives important insight into the Anzac (Australian and New Zealand Army Corps) spirit, including an exhibit on the tragic battle of Gallipoli. There's also a pretty good art collection. See p. 604.

- **National Museum of Australia** (ACT): Using state-of-the-art technology and hands-on exhibits, Australia's newest and most impressive museum concentrates on Australian society and its history since 1788, the interaction of people with the Australian environment, and Aboriginal and Torres Strait Islander cultures and histories. See p. 605.

11 The Best Luxury Accommodations

- **Sir Stamford at Circular Quay,** Sydney (© **1300/301 391** in Australia, or 02/9252 4600): This AAA-rated five-star hotel combines old-world luxury with a wonderful bar and nice views. I

like the top-hatted doorman who valet-parked my rusting 1976 Toyota without a comment. See p. 112.

- **Park Hyatt Sydney** (© **800/633-7313** in the U.S. and Canada or

02/9241 1234 in Australia): You'll have to book well in advance to snag a room at Sydney's best-positioned property, at the edge of the city's historic Rocks district. Many rooms have fabulous views across the harbor to the Sydney Opera House. See p. 109.

- **Sebel Reef House** (Cairns, QLD; ℂ 1800/079 052 in Australia): Everyone who stays here says the same thing: "It feels like home." Airy rooms look into tropical gardens, waterfalls cascade into the pools, mosquito nets drape over the beds, and you could swear pith-helmeted colonial officers will be back any minute to finish their gin-and-tonics in the Brigadier Bar. Idyllic Palm Cove Beach is just across the road. See p. 285.
- **Lizard Island** (off Cairns, QLD; ℂ 1800/737 678 in Australia, 800/225-9849 in the U.S. and Canada, or 020/7805 3875 in the U.K.): Lizard Island has long been popular with Americans for its game fishing, wonderful coral and diving, smart food, and simple upscale lodge accommodations. See p. 287.
- **Bedarra Island** (off Mission Beach, QLD; ℂ 1800/737 678 in Australia, 800/225-9849 in the U.S. and Canada, or 020/7805 3875 in the U.K.): Presidents and princesses in need of a little time out come to this small rainforest island ringed by beaches. The timber villas are cozy, and the discreet staff assures privacy. Best of all, though, is the extravagant 24-hour open bar. See p. 306.
- **Orpheus Island Resort** (off Townsville or Cairns, QLD; ℂ 1800/077 167 in Australia): Beloved of film stars and others who relish privacy, this resort has simple, attractive rooms; good food; a marvelous sense of seclu-

sion; and a beautiful location in the curve of a palm-lined bay. The only way in is by seaplane. See p. 314.
- **Hayman** (Whitsunday Islands, QLD; ℂ 1800/075 175 in Australia, or call Leading Hotels of the World at ℂ 800/223-6800 in the U.S. and Canada, 0800/181 123 in the U.K., 1800/409 063 in Ireland, or 0800/44 1016 in New Zealand): Located on Hayman Island in the Whitsundays, this is Australia's most glamorous resort. It's got classy rooms, excellent restaurants, staff keen to please, a superb hexagonal swimming pool, and a fleet of charter boats waiting to spirit you off to the Reef or your own deserted isle. See p. 324.
- **Longitude 131** (Uluru/Ayres Rock, Red Centre, NT; ℂ 08/8957 7888): A newcomer to the Ayres Rock resort scene, Longitude 131 is an African-style luxury safari camp set in the sand dunes and with great views of Uluru/Ayres Rock. It's very exclusive and very expensive, but you experience the Outback in style. See p. 390.
- **El Questro Homestead** (The Kimberley, WA; ℂ 1300/65 65 65 in Australia, 800/221 4542 in the U.S. and Canada, 020/8283 4500 in the U.K., 0800/44 4422 in New Zealand, or 08/9169 1777): Charming country decor spiced up with Indonesian antiques, good cooking, and a dramatic gorge location make this glamorous homestead on a million-acre cattle station popular with jet-setters. Cruise wild gorges, heli-fish for barramundi, and hike to Aboriginal rock art while you're here. See p. 475.
- **Cable Beach Club Resort Broome** (Broome, WA; ℂ 1800/099 199 in Australia, or 08/9192 0400): Chinatown meets the Outback at this elegant corrugated-iron-and-pagoda-studded

resort lying low along glorious Cable Beach in the romantic pearling port of Broome. Three to-die-for suites, decorated with superb Asian antiques and paintings by luminaries of the Australian art world. See p. 480.

- **The Hotel Como** (Melbourne, VIC; ℂ **1800/033 400** in Australia, or 03/9825 2222): Great service, nice rooms, and free plastic ducks make this one of our

favorite top-flight Australian hotels. See p. 543.

- **Hyatt Hotel Canberra** (Canberra, ACT; ℂ **800/233-1234** in the U.S. and Canada, or 02/6270 1234): Visiting heads of state and pop stars make this their residence when staying in Canberra. It's a 2-minute drive from the central shopping district, and a stone's throw from Lake Burley Griffin and the Parliamentary Triangle. See p. 599.

12 The Best Moderately Priced Accommodations

- **Explorers Inn Hotel** (ℂ **1800/ 623 288** in Australia) and **Hotel George Williams** (ℂ **1800/064 858** in Australia), both in Brisbane, QLD: These two hotels around the corner from each other are shining examples of what affordable hotels should be— trendy, clean, and bright with useful facilities like 24-hour front desk, hair dryers, helpful staff, and a pleasant, inexpensive restaurant attached. See p. 242.

- **The Reef Retreat** (Cairns, QLD; ℂ **07/4059 1744**): It's not often you find so much decorating taste—wooden blinds, teak furniture, and colorful upholstery—at a price you want to pay, but that's what you get at the apartments in trendy Palm Cove, one of Cairns's most desirable beachfront suburbs. There's a swimming pool in the lovely landscaped grounds, but the beach is just a block away. See p. 286.

- **Archipelago Studio Apartments** (Port Douglas, QLD; ℂ **07/4099 5387**): They may be tiny, but these pretty apartments have a homey atmosphere and are seconds from Four Mile Beach. Some units have sea views. The solicitous proprietor is a font of advice on things to see and do. See p. 297.

- **Miss Maud Swedish Hotel** (Perth, WA; ℂ **1800/998 022** in Australia): Staying here is like staying at Grandma's—just as she's finished a major redecoration job. You're right in the heart of Perth, and the friendly staff and huge buffet breakfasts (included in the rate) complete the picture. See p. 432.

- **North Adelaide Heritage Group** (Adelaide, SA; ℂ **08/8272 1355**): These accommodations consist of 18 fabulous properties in North Adelaide and Eastwood. The former Friendly Meeting Chapel Hall resembles a small church stocked with Victorian antiques. Another memorable place is the George Lowe Esq. Apartment, done up in the style of a 19th-century gentleman's bachelor pad. See p. 493.

- **York Mansions** (Launceston, TAS; ℂ **03/6334 2933**): If you feel that where you stay is as important to your visit as what you see, then don't miss out on a night or two here. This National Trust–classified building has five spacious apartments, each with a distinct character. It's like living the high life in the Victorian age. See p. 631.

13 The Best Alternative Accommodations

- **Underground Motel** (White Cliffs, NSW; ℂ **1800/021 154** in Australia, or 08/8091 6677): All but two of this motel's rooms are underground in this opal-mining town. Rooms are reached by a maze of spacious tunnels dug out of the rock. See p. 228.

- **Whitsunday Wilderness Lodge** (The Whitsunday Islands, QLD; ℂ **07/3357 3843**): The 10 comfy beachfront cabins are basic, but your vacation at this island ecoretreat will be anything but. Sea kayak, sail, snorkel, hike rainforest trails, dine with other guests outside under the Milky Way, and maybe even swim with Myrtle, the pet kangaroo. Considering you'll only shell out for wine and maybe a seaplane trip to the Reef, this is a great value. See p. 326.

- **Kingfisher Bay Resort** (Fraser Island, QLD; ℂ **1800/072 555** in Australia): If it weren't for the ranger station and natural-history videos in the lobby, the wildlife walks, the guided four-wheel-drive safaris, and other ecoactivities taking place, you'd hardly know that this hotel is an ecoresort as comfortable and modern as it is. See p. 340.

- **Binna Burra Mountain Lodge** (ℂ **1800/074 260** in Australia) & **O'Reilly's Rainforest Guesthouse** (ℂ **1800/688 722** in Australia), both in the Gold Coast Hinterland, QLD: Tucked almost 1,000m (3,280 ft.) up on rainforested ridges, these cozy retreats offer fresh mountain air, activities, and instant access to the hiking trails of Lamington National Park. At O'Reilly's you can hand-feed brilliantly colored rainforest birds every morning. See p. 361.

- **Emma Gorge Resort** (The Kimberley, WA; ℂ **800/221-4542** in the U.S. and Canada, or 08/9169 1777): At this spick-and-span little safari camp on the 400,000-hectare (1-million-acre) El Questro cattle station, guests stay in cute tents with wooden floors and electric lights, eat at a rustic gourmet restaurant, and join in the many hikes, bird-watching tours, river cruises, and more. See p. 475.

- **Prairie Hotel** (Flinders Ranges, SA; ℂ **08/8648 4844**): This remarkable tin-roofed, stone-walled Outback pub in the Flinders Ranges has quaint rooms, a great bar out front where you can meet the locals, and some of the best food in Australia. See p. 523.

- **Freycinet Lodge** (Freycinet National Park, Coles Bay, TAS; ℂ **03/6257 0101**): These eco-friendly bush cabins are right next to one of the nation's best walking trails. The ocean views from the magnificent restaurant and the surrounding balconies are spectacular. See p. 627.

- **Cradle Mountain Lodge** (Cradle Mountain, TAS; ℂ **03/6492 1303**): Just minutes from your comfortable cabin are 1,500-year-old trees, moss forests, craggy mountain ridges, limpid pools and lakes, and hordes of scampering marsupials. See p. 635.

14 The Best B&Bs & Guesthouses

- **The Russell** (The Rocks, Sydney; ℂ **02/9241 3543**): This B&B, wonderfully positioned in the city's old quarter, is the coziest place to stay in Sydney. It's got creaky floorboards, a ramshackle feel, brightly painted corridors, and rooms with immense character. See p. 113.

• **Echoes Hotel & Restaurant** (Katoomba, Blue Mountains, NSW; ℂ 02/4782 1966): Echoes is right on the edge of a dramatic drop into the Jamison Valley. The views from the balconies are breathtaking. See p. 186.

• **Barrington Guest House** (Barrington Tops National Park, The Hunter, NSW; ℂ 02/4995 3212): Nestled in a valley just outside the Barrington Tops National Park, this charming guesthouse and luxury cabin property offers magnificent rainforest walks, plenty of native animals, and excellent activities, such as horseback riding through the bush. See p. 199.

• **Ulladulla Guest House** (Ulladulla, NSW; ℂ 02/4455 1796): Works of art on the walls, fabulous food, and a lagoonlike pool among the palm trees—all this and lovely rooms with hosts that can't do enough for you. See p. 218.

• **Waverley** (Brisbane, QLD; ℂ 07/3369 8973): This gorgeous old timber Queenslander house has pretty rooms and a cool deck within earshot of rainbow lorikeets chirping in the mango trees. And the cute shops and galleries of fashionable Paddington are right outside your door. See p. 243.

• **Lilybank Bed & Breakfast** (Cairns, QLD; ℂ 07/4055 1123): This rambling 1890s homestead used to be the Cairns mayor's residence. Today, owners Pat and Mike Woolford welcome guests to its comfy rooms, wide verandas, and blooming gardens. You can also stay in the renovated gardener's cottage. See p. 284.

• **Marae** (near Port Douglas, QLD; ℂ 07/4098 4900): Lush bushland full of butterflies and birds is the setting for this gorgeous contemporary Queenslander house with hip rooms and an outdoor plunge pool. Hostess Andy Crowe serves a wonderful breakfast, and Cactus, the crazy pet cockatoo, gives you a warm welcome, too. See p. 299.

• **The Rocks** (Townsville, QLD; ℂ 07/4771 5700): Victorian charm has been poured into this old Queenslander with stylish, not frilly, results. Eat off antique china in the old dining room, bathe in a claw-foot tub in the main bathroom, and meet other guests for sherry on the wide old veranda at dusk. See p. 311.

• **The Summer House** (Darwin, NT; ℂ 08/8981 9992): Groovy guest rooms with hip furniture, funky bathrooms, louvered windows, and tropical gardens make this converted apartment block an oasis of cool—in both senses of the word. See p. 403.

• **Hansons Swan Valley** (near Perth, WA; ℂ 08/9296 3366): Good-bye faded lace, hello Art Deco—here is a B&B with cutting-edge style for young sophisticates. Jon and Selina Hanson have created a stylish retreat nestled among the Swan Valley vineyards, an easy drive from Perth. See p. 450.

• **Heritage Trail Lodge** (Margaret River, WA; ℂ 08/9757 9595): How many B&Bs do you know that provide a double Jacuzzi in every room? These salmon-pink cabins abut tall karri forest where parrots flit. 'Roos hop into the parking lot on occasion, and the fabulous Margaret River wineries surround you. See p. 458.

• **Collingrove Homestead** (Angaston, the Barossa Valley, SA; ℂ 08/8564 2061): This country house, built in 1856, has a real air of colonial manor farm living, with hallways festooned with hunting trophies, rifles, and oil paintings, and plenty of oak paneling and antiques scattered about. See p. 506.

- **Robinson's by the Sea** (St. Kilda, Melbourne; ✆ **03/9534 2683**): This 1870s heritage B&B just across the road from St. Kilda

beach has a comfortable living room and dining room stocked with antiques and five individually decorated bedrooms. It's a very friendly place and a good value. See p. 542.

15 The Best Restaurants

- **MG Garage** (Sydney, NSW; ✆ **02/9383 9383**): Causing a stir in Sydney with the fashionable crowd, MG Garage is set in a car showroom and serves up great Modern Australian cuisine. See p. 136.
- **Mezzaluna** (Sydney, NSW; ✆ **02/9357 1988**): Come here for exquisite food, flawless service, and a great view across the city's western skyline. The main dining room opens onto an all-weather terrace kept warm in winter by giant, overhead fan heaters. Don't miss it. See p. 137.
- **Quay** (Sydney, NSW; ✆ **02/9251 5600**): Sydney's best seafood restaurant offers perhaps the loveliest view in Sydney. Gaze through the large windows towards the Opera House, the city skyline, the North Shore suburbs, and the Harbour Bridge. See p. 130.
- **Tetsuya's** (Sydney, NSW; ✆ **02/ 9267 2900**): Chef Tetsuya Wakuda is arguably Sydney's most famous chef, and his nouveau Japanese creations are imaginative enough to guarantee that this hip eatery is a constant number one in Australia. See p. 134.
- **Salt** (Sydney, NSW; ✆ **02/9332 2566**): You'll need to dress up in your coolest outfit to fit into the scene happening at this modernist restaurant in the Kirketon Hotel in Darlinghurst. Inside it's all sleek and chrome, and the menu is innovative Modern Australian all the way. See p. 137.

- **e'cco bistro** (Brisbane, QLD; ✆ **07/3831 8344**): Simple food, elegantly done, has won this small but elegant bistro a stack of awards, and you'll soon see why. Not least among its titles is Australia's top restaurant award, the Remy Martin Cognac/Gourmet Traveller Restaurant of the Year. Booking ahead is essential. See p. 243.
- **Fishlips Bar & Bistro** (Cairns, QLD; ✆ **07/4041 1700**): Clever ways with fresh seafood and other Aussie ingredients—think crocodile—make this cheerful blue beach house on a Cairns highway a real winner, the pick of the bunch in Cairns. See p. 288.
- **Fraser's** (Perth, WA; ✆ **08/9481 7100**): The city center and Swan River sparkling in the sunshine seem so close that you can almost reach out and touch them from the terrace of this parkland restaurant. Sensationally good Modern Australian food turned out with flare and flavor is what you come here for; seafood is a specialty. See p. 434.
- **Lamont's Winery, Restaurant & Gallery** (in the Swan Valley near Perth, WA; ✆ **08/9296 4485**): Hearty, tasty, yet sophisticated fare is what this rustic restaurant in the vineyards is all about. It's worth the 20-minute drive from Perth, but if you can't make the trip, there's a second Lamont's in East Perth. See p. 451.

- **Newtown House** (Vasse, near Margaret River, WA; © **08/9755 4485**): Chef Stephen Reagan makes intelligent, flavorsome food that beautifully partners with premium Margaret River wines. Stay in his homestead B&B overnight and explore the wineries the next day. See p. 459.

- **Prairie Hotel** (Flinders Ranges, SA; © **08/8648 4844**): Chef Darren ("Bart") Brooks serves up some very high-class cuisine in the middle of nowhere. His "feral" foods, such as kangaroo tail soup and a mixed grill of emu sausages, camel steak, and kangaroo, is remarkable. See p. 523.

- **Flower Drum** (Melbourne, VIC; © **03/9662 3655**): Praise pours in for this upscale eatery serving Cantonese food. The food is exquisite and the service impeccable. See p. 544.

- **The Tryst** (Canberra, ACT; © **02/ 6239 4422**): Canberra has far grander and more expensive restaurants, but this place has found a spot in our hearts for its constantly delicious food. It's also relaxed, feeling almost communal on busy nights. See p. 603.

> ⌒ *Tips* **Size Does Matter**
>
> When planning your trip, keep in mind that Australia is as big as western Europe and about the same size as the 48 contiguous U.S. states. Melbourne and Brisbane are a long day's drive from Sydney, and driving from Sydney to Perth takes the better part of a week.

wildlife, art galleries, and Aboriginal influences), and Outback opal-mining towns White Cliffs and Lightning Ridge, which exist in a wacky underground world of their own.

QUEENSLAND   Without a doubt, the biggest draw for visitors to Queensland is the Great Barrier Reef. Ogling the tropical fish, sea creatures, and rainbow-hued corals is a holiday highlight for most people. The Reef stretches more than 2,000km (1,240 miles) along Queensland's coast, as far south as Bundaberg, 384km (238 miles) north of Brisbane. Alluring island resorts dot the coast; while most are expensive, we've found a few that won't break the bank.

Queensland is also known for its white-sand beaches. Many of the best are on the Gold Coast in the state's south (about an hour's drive from Brisbane), and the Sunshine Coast, a 2-hour drive north of Brisbane. Cairns and Port Douglas in the north have their fair share of beaches, too, but be warned: Swimming in their waters can be *very* hazardous to your health. Deadly box jellyfish, or "stingers," call a halt to all ocean swimming at beaches in the northern third of the country October through May. In Queensland, stingers may be found in all coastal waters north of Gladstone. Most patrolled beaches in these areas have "stinger nets," which aim to keep the little blighters out, but the thimble-sized Irakandji jellyfish is small enough to sneak through the mesh and its sting can be fatal. All patrolled beaches have warning signs and the lifeguards do regular net drags to see if there are any in the water. If they find any, the beach is promptly closed. But to be absolutely sure, you should stick to the waterfront lagoons at Airlie Beach and Cairns, or your hotel pool this time of year. The jellyfish are mainly found in coastal waters and do not interfere with Great Barrier Reef activities like snorkeling or diving, as these are out of the habitat of marine stingers.

Island swimming is mostly stinger-free, but be careful and take advice from the lifeguards before plunging into that inviting water.

One of the most appealing of Queensland's destinations is the aquatic playground made up of the 74 Whitsunday Islands in the Great Barrier Reef Marine Park. These mostly uninhabited islands are a paradise for kayaking, snorkeling, diving, fishing, hiking, watersports, bird-watching, and bareboat sailing.

Another big attraction is the lush 110-million-year-old Daintree rainforest, just north of Port Douglas.

The capital, Brisbane, has Australia's largest koala sanctuary, (you can cuddle one if you like) and you can hand-feed wild dolphins on a day trip across Brisbane's Moreton Bay. In the Gold Coast hinterland is Lamington National Park, a rainforested mountain region great for hiking and spotting wildlife.

THE RED CENTRE   The eerie silence of Uluru, also known as Ayers Rock, is what draws everyone to the sprawling ocher sands of the Red Centre, the heart of the Northern Territory. For many, there is the delightful

2

Planning Your Trip to Australia

by Lee Mylne

This chapter aims to answer all the practical questions that may pop up as you're planning your trip: How will you get there; how much will it cost; the ins and outs of traveling Down Under; and myriad other details. We've done the legwork—ferreting out deals on airfares, listing package companies, locating outdoor adventure operators, and more—so you won't have to.

1 The Regions in Brief

About 84% of Australia's 19 million people huddle in cities around the coast covering a mere 1% of this vast continent. The reason is simple: Much of Australia is harsh Outback country, characterized by savanna land, spectacular rocky outcrops, shifting deserts, and dry salt lakes. In these parts of the country, the soil is poor, the rainfall scarce, and some rivers don't even make it to the ocean. The roads that traverse the interior are sometimes barely distinguishable as roads, and most people choose air travel or stick to the coastal fringe.

In spectacular contrast, on the coast—particularly the east, where most people live—Nature's bounty has almost overdone it. Here, Australia is blessed with one of the greatest natural attractions in the world—the Great Barrier Reef. There are also rainforests in Queensland, alpine scenery in Tasmania, wildflowers in Western Australia, rolling wine country in South Australia, a great coastal drive in Victoria, bird-filled wetlands in the Northern Territory, and countless sand beaches more or less everywhere.

Australia is made up of six states—New South Wales, Queensland, Victoria, South Australia, Western Australia, and Tasmania—and two internal territories—the Australian Capital Territory (ACT) and the Northern Territory. The national capital is Canberra, in the ACT.

See the map on p. 6 or the map on the inside back cover to visualize the regions described here.

NEW SOUTH WALES Australia's most populated state is also the most-visited by tourists. They come to see Sydney—and who can blame them? It's one of the most glamorous and beautiful cities in the world, with dozens of harbor and ocean beaches within and around the city, and a mixture of bushland and city development around Sydney Harbour itself. Sydney is also a good base for day trips or overnight excursions inland, especially to the scenic Blue Mountains and the wineries of the Hunter Valley.

Farther afield, a string of quaint beachside towns stretches all the way down the southern coast to Victoria. Along the north coast are remnant areas of rainforest and a more tropical air in the laid-back hangout of Byron Bay, where "Croc Dundee" himself, movie star Paul Hogan, has a home.

The inland is dry and sparsely forested. Highlights include the mining town of Broken Hill (known for discovery that the lesser-known nearby domes of Kata Tjuta, or "the Olgas" are even more spectacular (if that's possible). A half-day's drive from the Rock brings you to Kings Canyon, an awesomely lovely desert gorge popular with hikers. If you visit the Red Centre, try to spend at least a few days in Alice Springs. This laid-back Outback town has the best Aboriginal arts-and-crafts shopping in Australia, Aboriginal tours, a world-class desert wildlife park, stunning scenery, hikes through the stark MacDonnell Ranges, an Outback ranch to stay at, and even camel rides along a dry riverbed.

THE TOP END The northwest reaches of the country (from the rocky red ranges of the Kimberley in Western Australia to the northern third of the Northern Territory) encompass what Aussies eloquently dub "the Top End." This is Crocodile Dundee territory, a remote, vast, semidesert region where the cattle probably outnumber the people. In this book, we have concentrated on the Northern Territory section of the "Top End," with the Kimberley included in the Western Australia chapter.

Near the tropical city of Darwin, the territory's capital, is Kakadu National Park, where you can cruise past crocodiles on inland billabongs (ponds), bird-watch, and visit ancient Aboriginal rock-art sites. Closer to Darwin is Litchfield National Park, where you can take a dip in fern-fringed swimming holes surrounded by red cliffs—stuff straight from Eden. You can cruise the waterways of Katherine Gorge, a few hours' drive south of Darwin, or explore them by canoe. Near Katherine you can canoe rarely explored, croc-infested inland rivers and learn to make your own didgeridoo (a large wooden, traditional Aboriginal musical instrument).

WESTERN AUSTRALIA Distance and high airfares work against Western Australia's tourism industry, which is a shame because this is one of Australia's most wild and beautiful regions. The seas teem with whales in season, and thrill seekers can swim alongside gigantic but gentle whale sharks on the Northwest Cape every fall (Mar–June). This cape is home to one of Australia's best-kept secrets, a second barrier reef called Ningaloo Marine Park, which runs for 260km (161 miles), one of the few reefs in the world to grow on a western coast. You can snorkel with manta rays here or try the fantastic diving. Just 19km (12 miles) off Perth, snorkelers can gaze at corals and fish on Rottnest Island, and in Shark Bay at Monkey Mia, tourists can greet wild dolphins (or is it the other way around?).

In the southwest "hook" of the continent lies the Margaret River wine region. Wild forests, thundering surf, dramatic cliffs, rich bird life, and wild 'roos make it one of the country's most attractive wine regions. The state's capital, Perth, has surf beaches and a restored 19th-century port with a fun atmosphere and some great museums. One or 2 hours' drive from the city brings you to some cute towns, like the Spanish Benedictine monastery town of New Norcia. Inland, the state is mostly wheat fields and desert, but if you have the inclination, head west 600km (372 miles) from Perth to the gold-mining town of Kalgoorlie, where you'll find the world's largest open-cast gold mine. With its gracious old pubs lining the wide bustling streets, it's what an Aussie country town should look like.

In the Kimberley, you can visit the ancient Geikie and Windjana gorges, pearl farms where the world's best South Sea pearls grow, and the charming (in a corrugated-iron sort of way) beachside frontier town of Broome. This tract of the country is so little populated and so underexplored that most Aussies never contemplate coming here. Getting around is expensive, because it's so vast. Near Kununurra, on the eastern edge of the Kimberley, is a million-acre cattle station, El Questro, where you can camp in safari tents (or stay in an upmarket—read "expensive"—homestead), fish for barramundi, hike through the bush to Aboriginal rock art, take all kinds of active tours from horseback riding to four-wheel-drive jaunts, and dine every night on terrific Modern Australian cuisine. From Kununurra you can fly over or hike into the beehive-shaped rock formation of the Bungle Bungles, cruise on the bird-rich, croc-infested Ord River, and tour the Argyle Diamond Mine—the world's biggest.

SOUTH AUSTRALIA Stretched between Western Australia and Victoria is the nation's breadbasket, South Australia. The capital, Adelaide, is a stately place known for its conservatism, parks, and churches, and is an ideal base for exploring Australia's illustrious wine region, the Barossa Valley. Big labels like Penfolds, Seppelts, and Wolf Blass are here, but take time to sniff out the many smaller but no less outstanding vineyards. And it's less than an hour from the city!

Bring your binoculars for the massive waterbird sanctuary, the Coorong. Stay in an underground hotel in the offbeat opal-mining town of Coober Pedy (it's too hot above ground), or order a 'roo-burger at the historic Prairie Hotel in the craggy, ancient lands of the Flinders Ranges in the South Australian Outback.

The greatest of South Australia's attractions (apart from wine, of course) is Kangaroo Island, the best place in Australia to see native animals. In a day you can spot wallabies, kangaroos, koalas, oodles of birds from black swans to kookaburras, echidnas, and penguins. The beach teems with sea lions.

VICTORIA Australia's second-largest city, Melbourne, is the capital of Victoria. Melbourne is more stately and "Old World" than Sydney, and offers an exciting mix of ethnicity and the country's best fashion shopping. Nearby Phillip Island is famous for its Penguin Parade, where hundreds of tiny penguins dash up the beach to their burrows at dusk; and, the historic gold-mining city of Ballarat is not far away. Victoria is also the site of one of Australia's great road trips, the Great Ocean Road, which stretches for 106km (66 miles) along the southern coast, where the eroded rock towers named the Twelve Apostles stand tall in the sea. Then there's the inland "high country," the stomping ground of the title character in Banjo Patterson's 1890 poem "The Man from Snowy River."

AUSTRALIAN CAPITAL TERRITORY (ACT) Surrounded entirely by New South Wales is the Australian Capital Territory. The ACT is made up of bushland and the nation's capital, Canberra, a planned city similar in architectural concept to Washington, D.C. Many Australians consider the capital boring, but Canberra will surprise you. It has some of the country's best museums and great restaurants, so don't automatically exclude it from your itinerary.

TASMANIA Last stop before Antarctica is the island state of Tasmania. Visit the Apple Isle for its beautiful national parks, stretches of alpine wilderness and gloomy forests, fruit and lavender farms, the world's best trout fishing, and an exquisitely slow pace of life rarely experienced anywhere else. If you're up to it, you could tackle the Overland Track, an 85km (53-mile) hiking trail between Cradle Mountain and Lake St. Clair that passes through highland moors, dense rainforests, and several mountains. A more leisurely option is a visit to the picturesque stone ruins of Port Arthur, Australia's version of Devil's

Island, where thousands of convicts brought in to settle the new British colony were imprisoned and died. All of Tasmania is spectacular, but you haven't seen anything until you've experienced Freycinet National Park, with its pink granite outcrops set against an emerald-green sea.

2 Visitor Information

The **Australian Tourist Commission** (ATC) is the best source of information on traveling Down Under. Its website, www.australia.com, has more than 10,000 pages of listings of tour operators, hotels, car-rental companies, specialist travel outfitters, holidays, maps, distance charts, suggested itineraries, and much more. The site provides you with information tailored to travelers from your country of origin, including packages and deals. By signing up for the free online Travel Club, you will be e-mailed news of hot deals, events, and the like on a regular basis, and you can also order brochures online. The ATC operates a website only, no telephone lines. Other good sources are the websites of Australia's state tourism marketing offices. They are as follows:

- **Canberra Tourism:** www.canberra tourism.com.au.

- **Northern Territory Tourist Commission:** www.Ntholidays.com or www.australiasoutback.com, the latter written for international visitors.
- **South Australian Tourism Commission:** www.southaustralia.com.
- **Tourism New South Wales:** www.visitnsw.com.au or www.sydney australia.com.
- **Tourism Queensland:** www.queenslandholidays.com.au or www.destinationqueensland.com, the latter geared for North Americans.
- **Tourism Tasmania:** www.discover tasmania.com.au.
- **Tourism Victoria:** www.visit victoria.com.
- **Western Australian Tourism Commission:** www.western australia.net.

3 Entry Requirements & Customs

ENTRY REQUIREMENTS
Along with a current passport valid for the duration of your stay, the Australian government requires a visa from visitors of every nation, except New Zealand, to be issued before you arrive. If you are short-term visitor or business traveler, the process is easy and can be done in a few minutes on the Internet, using the Australian government's Electronic Travel Authority (ETA). This is an electronic visa that takes the place of a stamp in your passport.

You can apply for an ETA yourself, or have your travel agent or airline do it for you when you book your plane ticket. (They may charge you extra to

---

Tips Get Help from the ATC

The ATC maintains a network of "Aussie Specialist" travel agents in hundreds of cities across the United States, Canada, the United Kingdom, New Zealand, and other countries. The agents are trained on the best destinations, hotels, deals, and tours Down Under. Get a referral to the nearest two Aussie Specialists by clicking the "Certified Aussie Specialist" button on the home page on the ATC's website, www.australia.com.

Australia: Red Alert Checklist

- Don't forget that you will need a visa to enter Australia (unless you are a New Zealand citizen).
- Do any theater, restaurant, or travel reservations need to be booked in advance?
- Did you make sure your favorite attraction is open? Call ahead for opening and closing times.
- If you purchased traveler's checks, have you recorded the check numbers, and stored the documentation separately from the checks?
- Did you stop the newspaper and mail delivery, and leave a set of keys with someone reliable?
- Did you pack your camera and an extra set of camera batteries, and purchase enough film? If you packed film in your checked baggage, did you invest in protective pouches to shield film from airport X-rays?
- Do you have a safe, accessible place to store money?
- Did you bring your ID cards that could entitle you to discounts such as AAA and AARP cards, student IDs, etc.?
- Did you bring emergency drug prescriptions and extra glasses and/or contact lenses?
- Did you find out your daily ATM withdrawal limit?
- Do you have your credit card PIN? Is there a daily withdrawal limit on credit card cash advances?
- If you have an E-ticket, do you have documentation?
- Did you leave a copy of your itinerary with someone at home?
- Do you have the address and phone number of your country's embassy with you?

do this.) Apply online at www.eta.immi.gov.au. There is a A$20 (US$13) charge, payable by credit card (Amex, Diners Club, Master-Card, or Visa). Assuming you do not have a criminal conviction and are in good health, your ETA should be approved quickly. You can also apply for the visa at Australian embassies, high commissions, and consulates (see below). Children traveling on their parent's passport must have their own ETA.

Fees mentioned in this section are in Australian dollars; the exact amount charged by the Australian embassy, consulate, or high commission in your country will depend on the foreign currency exchange rate.

Tourists should apply for a Visitor ETA. It's free and valid for as many visits to Australia as you like of up to 3 months each within a 1-year period. Tourists may not work in Australia, so if you are visiting for business, you have two choices: Apply for a free Short Validity Business ETA, which is valid for a single visit of 3 months within a 1-year period, or pay A$65 (US$42) to apply for a Long Validity Business visa, which entitles you to as many 3-month stays in Australia as you like for the life of your passport but cannot be done online.

If your travel agent or airline is not connected to the ETA system, you will need to apply for a visa the old-fashioned way—by taking or mailing your passport, a completed visa application form, and the appropriate payment to your nearest Australian embassy or consulate. In the United States, Canada, the United Kingdom, Ireland, and many other countries, most agents and airlines are ETA-compatible. You will also need to go the old-fashioned route if you are someone other than a tourist or a business traveler—for example, a student studying in Australia; a businessperson staying longer than 3 months; a long-term resident; a sportsperson; a member of the media; a performer; or a member of a social group or cultural exchange. If you fall into one of these categories, you will need to apply for a Temporary Residence visa. There is a A$65 (US$42) fee for non-ETA tourist and business visas for stays of up to 3 months, and A$160 (US$104) for business visas for stays between 3 months and 4 years. Non-ETA visa application fees for other kinds of travelers vary, from nil to thousands of dollars. Contact the nearest Australian embassy, consulate, or high commission to check what forms of payment they accept.

Apply for non-ETA visas at Australian embassies, consulates, and high commissions. In the United States, apply to the Australian Embassy, 1601 Massachusetts Ave. NW, Washington, DC 20036 (© **202/797 3000;** dima-washington@dfat.gov.au). The website of the Australian Embassy in North America is www.austemb.org. In Canada, contact the Australian High Commission, 50 O'Connor St., No. 710, Ottawa, ON K1P 6L2 (© **613/783 7665;** www.ahc-ottawa. org). For business-visa inquiries in the United States and Canada, call © **800/ 579 7664.** In the United Kingdom and Ireland, contact the Australian High Commission, Australia House, The Strand, London WC2B 4LA (© **020/09065 508900** for 24-hr.

recorded information, or 020/7379 4334; www.australia.org.uk). You can obtain an application form for a non-ETA visa via the Internet at the Australian Department of Immigration and Multicultural Affairs website (www.immi.gov.au). This site also has a good explanation of the ETA system.

Allow at least a month for processing of non-ETA visas.

For information on how to get a passport, go to the "Fast Facts" section of this chapter—the websites listed provide downloadable passport applications as well as the current fees for processing passport applications. For an up-to-date country-by-country listing of passport requirements around the world, go the "Foreign Entry Requirement" Web page of the U.S. State Department at http://travel. state.gov/foreignentryreqs.html.

CUSTOMS
WHAT YOU CAN BRING INTO AUSTRALIA

The duty-free allowance in Australia is A$400 (US$260) or, for those under 18, A$200 (US$130). Anyone over 18 can bring in up to 250 cigarettes or 250 grams of cigars or other tobacco products, 1.125 liters (41 fl. oz.) of alcohol, and "dutiable goods" to the value of A$400 (US$260), or A$200 (US$130) if you are under 18. "Dutiable goods" are luxury items such as perfume, watches, jewelry, furs, plus gifts of any kind. Keep this in mind if you intend to bring presents for family and friends in Australia; gifts given to you also count toward the dutiable limit. Personal goods that you're taking with you are usually exempt from duty but if you are returning with valuable goods that you already own, file form B263. Customs officers do not collect duty of less than A$50 (US$33) as long as you declared the goods in the first place. A helpful brochure, available from Australian consulates or Customs offices,

---

Tips Passport Savvy

Allow plenty of time before your trip to apply for a passport; processing normally takes 3 weeks but can take longer during busy periods (especially spring). And keep in mind that if you need a passport in a hurry, you'll pay a higher processing fee. When traveling, safeguard your passport in an inconspicuous, inaccessible place like a money belt and keep a copy of the critical pages with your passport number in a separate place. If you lose your passport, visit the nearest consulate of your native country as soon as possible for a replacement.

---

is *Know Before You Go.* For more information, contact Australian Customs Services, GPO Box 8, Sydney NSW 2001 (© **02/6275 6666**), or check out www.customs.gov.au.

Cash in any currency, and other currency instruments such as traveler's checks, under a value of A$10,000 (US$6,500) need not be declared. Firearms in Australia are strictly controlled; contact the nearest Australian diplomatic post for advice on importing a handgun.

Australia is a signatory to the Convention on International Trade in Endangered Species (CITES), which restricts or bans the import of products made from protected wildlife. Examples of the restricted items are coral, giant clam, wild cats, monkey, zebra, crocodile or alligator, bear, some types of caviar, American ginseng, and orchid products. Banned items include ivory, tortoise (marine turtle) shell, products from rhinoceros or tiger, and sturgeon caviar. Bear this in mind if you stop in other countries en route to Australia where souvenirs made from items like these may be sold. Australian authorities may seize and not return the items to you.

Because Australia is an island, it is free of many agricultural and livestock diseases. To keep it that way, strict quarantine applies to importing plants, animals, and their products, including food. "Sniffer" dogs are used at Australian airports to detect these

products (as well as drugs). Some items may be held for treatment and returned to you; others may be confiscated; and others may be held over for you to take with you when you leave the country. Amnesty trash bins are available before you reach the immigration counters in airport arrivals halls for items such as fruit. Don't be alarmed if, just before landing, the flight attendants spray the aircraft cabin (with products approved by the World Health Organization) to kill potentially disease-bearing insects. For more information on what is and is not allowed, contact the nearest Australian embassy or consulate, or Australia's Department of Agriculture, Fisheries, and Forestry, which runs the Australian Quarantine and Inspection Service (© **02/6272 4143;** www.affa. gov.au). Its website contains a list of many restricted or banned foodstuffs, animal and plant products, and other items.

WHAT YOU CAN TAKE HOME FROM AUSTRALIA

Returning **U.S. citizens** who have been away for at least 48 hours are allowed to bring back, once every 30 days, $800 worth of merchandise duty-free. You'll be charged a flat rate of 4% duty on the next $1,000 worth of purchases. Be sure to have your receipts handy. On mailed gifts, the duty-free limit is $200. With some exceptions, you cannot bring fresh fruits and vegetables into the United

States. For specifics on what you can bring back, download the invaluable free pamphlet *Know Before You Go* online at **www.customs.gov**. (Click on "Travel," then "Know Before You Go Online Brochure.") Or contact the **U.S. Customs Service,** 1300 Pennsylvania Ave., NW, Washington, DC 20229 (© **877/287-8867**) and request the pamphlet.

For a clear summary of **Canadian** rules, write for the booklet *I Declare,* issued by the **Canada Customs and Revenue Agency** (© **800/461-9999** in Canada, or 204/983-3500; www.ccra-adrc.gc.ca). Canada allows its citizens a C$750 exemption, and you're allowed to bring back duty-free one carton of cigarettes, one can of tobacco, 40 imperial ounces of liquor, and 50 cigars. In addition, you're allowed to mail gifts to Canada valued at less than C$60 a day, provided they're unsolicited and don't contain alcohol or tobacco (write on the package "Unsolicited gift, under $60 value"). All valuables should be declared on the Y-38 form before departure from Canada, including serial numbers of valuables you already own, such as expensive foreign cameras. *Note:* The $750 exemption can only be used once a year and only after an absence of 7 days.

U.K. citizens returning from **a non-EU country** have a customs allowance of: 200 cigarettes; 50 cigars; 250 grams of smoking tobacco; 2 liters of still table wine; 1 liter of spirits or strong liqueurs (over 22% volume); 2 liters of fortified wine, sparkling wine or other liqueurs; 60cc (ml) perfume; 250cc (ml) of toilet water; and £145 worth of all other goods, including gifts and souvenirs. People under 17 cannot have the tobacco or alcohol allowance. For more information, contact HM Customs & Excise at © **0845/010 9000** (from outside the U.K., 020/8929 0152), or consult their website at www.hmce.gov.uk.

The duty-free allowance for **New Zealand** is NZ$700. Citizens over 17 can bring in 200 cigarettes, 50 cigars, or 250 grams of tobacco (or a mixture of all three if their combined weight doesn't exceed 250g); plus 4.5 liters of wine and beer, or 1.125 liters of liquor. New Zealand currency does not carry import or export restrictions. Fill out a certificate of export, listing the valuables you are taking out of the country; that way, you can bring them back without paying duty. Most questions are answered in a free pamphlet available at New Zealand consulates and Customs offices: *New Zealand Customs Guide for Travellers, Notice no. 4.* For more information, contact **New Zealand Customs,** The Customhouse, 17–21 Whitmore St., Box 2218, Wellington (© **04/473 6099** or 0800/428 786; www.customs.govt.nz).

4 Money

For American and European travelers, Australia is very affordable because of the perilous state of the Australian dollar the past few years. Most travelers will find money matters are relatively easy in Australia, but beware the small town where traveler's checks may not be readily accepted.

CURRENCY

The Australian dollar is divided into 100¢. Coins are 5¢, 10¢, 20¢, and 50¢ pieces (silver) and $1 and $2 pieces (gold). Prices often end in a variant of 1¢ and 2¢ (for example, 78¢ or $2.71), a relic from the days before 1-cent and 2-cent pieces were phased out. Prices are rounded to the nearest 5¢—so 77¢ rounds down to 75¢, and 78¢ rounds up to 80¢). Bank notes come in denominations of A$5, A$10, A$20, A$50, and A$100.

The Australian Dollar, the U.S. Dollar & the British Pound

For U.S. Readers   The rate of exchange used to calculate the dollar values given in this book was US$1 = approximately A$1.54 (or A$1 = US65¢).

For British Readers   The rate of exchange used to calculate the pound values in the accompanying table was £1 = A$2.60 (or A$1 = 38p).

Note: International exchange rates for the Australian dollar can fluctuate markedly. Check the latest rate when you plan your trip. The table below, and all the prices in this book, should be used only as a guide.

A$	US$	UK£	A$	US$	UK£
0.25	0.16	0.09	30.00	19.50	11.40
0.50	0.33	0.19	35.00	22.75	13.30
1.00	0.65	0.38	40.00	26.00	15.20
2.00	1.30	0.76	45.00	29.25	17.10
3.00	1.95	1.14	50.00	32.50	19.00
4.00	2.60	1.52	55.00	35.75	20.90
5.00	3.25	1.90	60.00	39.00	22.80
6.00	3.90	2.28	65.00	42.25	24.70
7.00	4.55	2.66	70.00	45.50	26.60
8.00	5.20	3.04	75.00	48.75	28.50
9.00	5.85	3.42	80.00	52.00	30.40
10.00	6.50	3.80	85.00	55.25	32.30
15.00	9.75	5.70	90.00	58.50	34.20
20.00	13.00	7.60	95.00	61.75	36.10
25.00	16.25	9.50	100.00	65.00	38.00

The Universal Currency Converter at the website www.xe.com/ucc will give you up-to-the-minute conversions for your dollar or pound in dozens of countries.

It's a good idea to exchange at least some money—just enough to cover airport incidentals and transportation to your hotel—before you leave home, so you can avoid lines at airport ATMs (automated teller machines). You can exchange money at your local American Express or Thomas Cook office or your bank. If you're far away from a bank with currency-exchange services, **American Express** offers traveler's checks and foreign currency, though with a $15 order fee and additional shipping costs, at www.american express.com or © 800/807-6233.

ATMS

The easiest and best way to get cash away from home is from an ATM (automated teller machine). The **Cirrus** (© 800/424-7787; www. mastercard.com) and **PLUS** (© 800/ 843-7587; www.visa.com) networks span the globe; look at the back of your bank card to see which network you're on, then call or check online for ATM locations at your destination. Be sure you know your personal identification number (PIN) before you leave home and be sure to find out your daily withdrawal limit before you depart. Also keep in mind that many banks impose a fee every time a card is used at a different bank's ATM, and that fee can be higher for international transactions (up to $5 or more) than for domestic ones (where they're rarely more than $1.50). On top of this, the bank from which you withdraw cash may charge its own fee. For international withdrawal fees, ask your bank. You can also get cash advances on your credit card at an ATM. Keep in mind that credit card companies try to protect themselves from theft by limiting the funds someone can withdraw outside their home country, so call your credit card company before you leave home.

Most ATMs in Australia will be linked to a network that likely includes your bank at home, but in Outback areas, carry cash and a credit card because ATMs can be hard to find in small country towns, and shopkeepers in remote parts may not cash traveler's checks.

TRAVELER'S CHECKS

Traveler's checks are something of an anachronism from the days before the ATM made cash accessible at any time. Traveler's checks used to be the only sound alternative to traveling with dangerously large amounts of cash. They were as reliable as currency, but, unlike cash, could be replaced if lost or stolen.

These days, traveler's checks are less necessary because most cities have 24-hour ATMs that allow you to withdraw small amounts of cash as needed. However, keep in mind that you will likely be charged an ATM withdrawal fee if the bank is not your own, so if you're withdrawing money every day, you might be better off with traveler's checks—provided that you don't mind showing identification every time you want to cash one.

However, be warned that traveler's checks are not as widely accepted in Australia, and if you do opt for them, get them in Australian dollars. Checks in U.S. dollars are accepted at banks, big hotels, currency exchanges, and some shops in major tourist regions, but smaller shops, restaurants, and other businesses will have no idea what the exchange rate is when you present a U.S. check. Another advantage of Australian-dollar checks is that the two largest Aussie banks, ANZ and Westpac, cash them for free; it will cost you around A$5 (US$3.25) to A$11 (US$7) to cash checks in foreign currency at most Australian banks.

You can get traveler's checks at almost any bank. **American Express** offers denominations of $20, $50, $100, $500, and (for cardholders only) $1,000. You'll pay a service charge ranging from 1% to 4%. You can also get American Express traveler's checks over the phone by calling ℂ **800/221-7282;** Amex gold and platinum cardholders who use this number are exempt from the 1% fee.

Visa offers traveler's checks at Citibank locations nationwide, as well as at several other banks. The service charge ranges between 1.5% and 2%; checks come in denominations of $20, $50, $100, $500, and $1,000. Call ℂ **800/732-1322** for information. AAA members can obtain Visa checks without a fee at most AAA offices or by calling ℂ **866/339-3378. MasterCard** also offers traveler's checks. Call ℂ **800/223-9920** for a location near you.

ℂ *Tips* **Small Change**

When you change money, ask for some small bills or loose change. Petty cash will come in handy for tipping and public transportation. Consider keeping the change separate from your larger bills, so that it's readily accessible and you'll be less of a target for theft.

Tips **Dear Visa: I'm Off to Kununurra!**

Some credit card companies recommend that you notify them of any impending trip abroad so that they don't become suspicious when the card is used numerous times in a foreign destination and your charges are blocked. Even if you don't call your credit card company in advance, you can always call the card's toll-free emergency number (see "Fast Facts," later in this chapter) if a charge is refused—a good reason to carry the phone number with you. But perhaps the important lesson here is to carry more than one card with you on your trip; a card might not work for any number of reasons, so having a backup is the smart way to go.

American Express, Visa, and MasterCard offer checks in Australian dollars.

If you choose to carry traveler's checks, be sure to keep a record of their serial numbers separate from your checks in the event that they are stolen or lost. You'll get a refund faster if you know the numbers.

CREDIT CARDS

Credit cards are a safe way to carry "money"; they provide a convenient record of all your expenses and they generally offer good exchange rates. You can also withdraw cash advances from your credit cards at banks or ATMs, provided you know your PIN. If you've forgotten yours, or didn't even know you had one, call the number on the back of your credit card and ask the bank to send it to you. It usually takes 5 to 7 business days,

though some banks will provide the number over the phone if you tell them your mother's maiden name or some other personal information. Your credit card company will likely charge a commission (1% or 2%) on every foreign purchase you make, but don't sweat this small stuff; for most purchases, you'll still get the best deal with credit cards when you factor in things like ATM fees and higher traveler's check exchange rates.

Visa and MasterCard are universally accepted in Australia, but American Express and Diners Club are considerably less popular. Always carry a little cash because many merchants will not take cards for purchases under A$15 (US$9.75) or so.

For tips and telephone numbers to call if your wallet is stolen or lost, go to "Lost & Found" in the "Fast Facts" section of this chapter.

5 When to Go

When it is winter in the Northern Hemisphere, Australia is basking in the Southern Hemisphere's summer, and vice versa. Midwinter in Australia is July and August, and the hottest months are November through March. Remember, unlike in the Northern Hemisphere, the farther south you go in Australia, the colder it gets.

THE TRAVEL SEASONS

Airfares to Australia offered by U.S. airlines are lowest from mid-April to

late August—the best time to visit the Red Centre, the Top End, and the Great Barrier Reef!

HIGH SEASON   The peak travel season in the most popular parts of Australia is the Aussie winter. In much of the country—Queensland from around Townsville and northward, all of the Top End and the Red Centre, and most of Western Australia—the most pleasant time to travel is April through September, when daytime temperatures are 66°F to 88°F (19°C–31°C) and it rarely rains. June, July, and August are the busiest months in these parts; you'll need to book accommodations and tours well in advance, and you will pay higher rates then, too.

On the other hand, Australia's summer is a nice time to visit the southern states—New South Wales, Victoria, South Australia, Western Australia from Perth to the south, and Tasmania. Even in winter, temperatures rarely dip below freezing, and snow falls only in parts of Tasmania, in the ski-fields of Victoria, and in the Snowy Mountains of southern New South Wales.

The best months to visit Australia, I think, are September and October, when it's often still warm enough to hit the beach in the southern states, cool enough to tour Ayers Rock and the humidity and rains have not come to Cairns and the Top End (although it will be very hot by Oct). And the wildflowers are in full bloom in Western Australia.

LOW SEASON October through March (summer) it is just too hot, too humid, too wet, or all three, to tour the Red Centre, the Top End, and anywhere in Western Australia except Perth and the southwest. The Top End, the Kimberley, and North Queensland, including Cairns, suffer an intensely hot, humid Wet Season November or December through March or April. In the Top End and Kimberley, this is preceded by an even stickier "build-up" in October and November. Some attractions and tour companies close, floodwaters render others off-limits, and hotels drop their rates, often dramatically. So if you decide to travel in these areas at this time—and lots of people do—be prepared to take the heat, the inconvenience of floods, and in tropical coastal areas, the slight chance of encountering cyclones.

HOLIDAYS

In addition to the period from December 26 to the end of January, when Aussies take their summer vacations, the 4 days at Easter (from Good Friday to Easter Monday) and all school holidays are very busy, so book ahead. The school year in Australia is broken into four semesters, with 2-week holidays around Easter-time, the last week of June and the first week of July, and the last week of September and the first week of October. Some states break at slightly different dates. There's a 6-week summer/Christmas vacation from mid-December to the end of January.

Almost everything shuts down on Christmas Day, Boxing Day (Dec 26), and Good Friday, and much is closed New Year's Day, Easter Sunday, and Easter Monday. Most things are closed until 1pm, if not all day, on Anzac Day, a World War I commemorative day on April 25.

Among the major public holidays are: New Year's Day (Jan 1); Australia Day (Jan 26); Labor Day (2nd Mon in Mar, WA); Eight Hours Day (1st Mon in Mar, TAS); Labor Day (2nd Mon in Mar, VIC); Canberra Day, (3rd Mon in Mar, ACT); Good Friday; Easter Sunday; Easter Monday; Anzac Day (Apr 25); May Day (1st Mon in

---

Tips **Steer Clear of the Vacation Rush**

Try to avoid Australia from Boxing Day (Dec 26) to the end of January, when Aussies take their summer vacations. In popular seaside holiday spots, hotel rooms and airline seats get scarce as hen's teeth, and it's a rare airline or hotel that will discount even a dollar off their full tariffs.

May, NT); Labour Day (1st Mon in May, QLD); Adelaide Cup (3rd Mon in May, SA); Foundation Day (1st Mon in June, WA); Queen's Birthday (2nd Mon in June, except WA); Royal National Show Day (2nd or 3rd Wed in Aug, QLD); Queen's Birthday (Mon in late Sept/early Oct, WA); Labour Day (1st Mon in Oct, NSW/SA); Melbourne Cup Day (1st Tues in Nov, Melbourne only); Christmas (Dec 25); and Boxing Day (Dec 26, or on the next Mon if 26th falls on a weekend; if Christmas Day is a Sat and Boxing Day a Sun, then both the following Mon and Tues are holidays).

AUSTRALIA CALENDAR OF EVENTS

January

Sydney Festival. Highlights of Sydney's visual and performing arts festival are free jazz or classical music concerts held outdoors on 2 Saturday nights near the Royal Botanic Gardens. (Take a picnic and arrive by 4pm to get a place.) Contact ℂ **02/8248 6500** or go to www.sydneyfestival.org.au. Three weeks in January.

Hyundai Hopman Cup, Perth. Tennis greats from the world's nine top tennis nations are invited to battle it out in a 7-day mixed-doubles competition. Contact the booking agent, BOCS Ticketing (ℂ **08/ 9484 1133**), or check www.hopman cup.com.au. Late December/early January.

Tamworth Country Music Festival, Tamworth (459km/285 miles northwest of Sydney), New South Wales. It may look like an Akubra Hat Convention, but this gathering of rural folk and city folk who would like to be rural folk is Australia's biggest country music festival. The Tamworth Information Centre (ℂ **02/6755 4300;** www.tamworth. nsw.gov.au) takes bookings.

Australia Day. Australia's answer to the Fourth of July marks the landing of the First Fleet of convicts at Sydney Cove in 1788. Every town puts on some kind of celebration; in Sydney, there are ferry races and tall ships on the harbor, food and wine stalls in Hyde Park, open days at museums and other attractions, and fireworks in the evening. January 26.

February

Johnnie Walker Classic, Perth. The country's richest golf tourney with A$2.8 million (US$1.8 million) up for grabs draws top players to Perth. South African golfer Ernie Els was the 2003 winner, with past winners including Tiger Woods and Greg Norman. Contact IMG (ℂ **03/9639 2333**) or check the Western Australian Tourism Commission's events site at www.events corp.com.au for ticketing details.

March

Sydney Gay & Lesbian Mardi Gras. A spectacular parade of costumed dancers and decorated floats, watched by several hundred thousand onlookers, followed by a giant warehouse party (by invitation only). Contact Sydney Gay & Lesbian Mardi Gras (ℂ **02/9557 4332;** www.mardigras.com.au). Usually the last Saturday night in February or first Saturday in March.

Australian Formula One Grand Prix, Melbourne. The first Grand Prix of the year on the international FIA Formula One World Championship circuit is battled out on one of its fastest circuits, in Melbourne. For tickets, contact Ticketmaster (ℂ **13 16 41** (in Australia) or order online at www.grandprix.com.au. Four days in the first or second week of March.

Australian Surf Life Saving Championships, Kurrawa Beach,

Gold Coast, Queensland. Up to 6,000 bronzed Aussie and international men and women swim, ski paddle, sprint relay, pilot rescue boats, parade past admiring crowds, and resuscitate "drowning" swimmers in front of 10,000 spectators. Contact Surf Life Saving Australia (© 02/9130 7370; www.slsa.asn. au). March 18 to 21, 2004.

June

Sydney Film Festival. World and Australian premieres of Aussie and international movies are shown in the State Theatre and other venues. Contact the Sydney Film Festival (© 02/9660 3844; www.sydney filmfestival.org). Two weeks from first or second Friday in June.

August

Sun-Herald City to Surf, Sydney. Fifty thousand Sydneysiders pound the pavement (or walk or wheelchair it) in this 14km (8.75-mile) "fun run" from the city to Bondi Beach. Entry details are posted on the website www.smh.com.au/marketing/citytosurf from June onward. If there are still slots available, you can enter the day of the race. The fee is around A$25 (US$16). Second Sunday in August.

September

Floriade, Canberra. A million tulips, daffodils, hyacinths, and other blooms carpet the banks of Canberra's Lake Burley Griffin in stunning themed flower bed designs at this celebration, which features performing arts and other entertainment. Contact Canberra Visitors Centre (© 1300/554 114 in Australia; www.canberratourism. com.au or www.floriadeaustralia. com. September 18 to October 17, 2004.

Henley-on-Todd Regatta, Alice Springs. Sounds sophisticated, doesn't it? It's actually a harumscarum race down the dry bed of the Todd River in homemade "boats" made from anything you care to name—an old four-wheeldrive chassis, say, or beer cans lashed together. The only rule is the vessel has to look *vaguely* like a boat. Contact the organizers at © 08/8952 3040; www.henleyon todd.com.au. One Saturday in late September.

October

Lexmark Indy 300 Carnival, Surfers Paradise, Queensland. The world's best Indy-car drivers race a street circuit around Surfers Paradise on the glitzy Gold Coast, as part of the international FedEx Championship champ car motorsport series. Contact Ticketek (© 1300/303 103 in Australia or 07/3404 6700 in Brisbane; www. ticketek.com), or check the event's website at www.indy.com.au. Four days in mid- or late October.

November

Melbourne Cup. They say the whole nation stops to watch this horse race. That's about right. If you're not actually there, you're glued to the TV for this A$3½-million (US$2½-million) race, or well, you're probably not an Australian. Women wear hats to the office, files on desks all over the country make way for a late chicken and champagne lunch, and don't even think about flagging a cab at the 3:20pm race time. First Tuesday in November.

December

Sydney-to-Hobart Yacht Race. Find a cliff-top spot near the Heads to watch the glorious show of spinnakers as 100 or so yachts leave Sydney Harbour for this grueling world-class event. The organizer is the Sydney-based Cruising Yacht Club of Australia (© 02/9363 9731; www.cyca.com.au). The event's website is www.s2h.tas.gov.au. Starts December 26.

New Year's Eve. Watching the Sydney Harbour Bridge light up with fireworks is a treat. The main show is at 9pm, not midnight, so young kids don't miss out. Pack a picnic and snag a Harbour-side spot by 4pm, or even earlier at the best vantage point—Mrs. Macquarie's Chair in the Royal Botanic Gardens.

6 Travel Insurance

Check your existing insurance policies and credit-card coverage before you buy travel insurance. You may already be covered for lost luggage, canceled tickets or medical expenses. The cost of travel insurance varies widely, depending on the cost and length of your trip, your age, health, and the type of trip you're taking.

TRIP-CANCELLATION INSURANCE Trip-cancellation insurance helps you get your money back if you have to back out of a trip, if you have to go home early, or if your travel supplier goes bankrupt. Allowed reasons for cancellation can range from sickness to natural disasters to the State Department declaring your destination unsafe for travel. (Insurers usually won't cover vague fears, though, as many travelers discovered who tried to cancel their trips in October 2001 because they were wary of flying.) In this unstable world, trip-cancellation insurance is a good buy if you're getting tickets well in advance—who knows what the state of the world, or of your airline, will be in 9 months? Insurance policy details vary, so read the fine print—and especially make sure that your airline or cruise line is on the list of carriers covered in case of bankruptcy. For information, contact one of the following insurers: **Access America** (© 866/807-3982; www.accessamerica.com); **Travel Guard International** (© 800/826-4919; www.travelguard.com); **Travel Insured International** (© 800/243-3174; www.travelinsured.com); and **Travelex Insurance Services** (© 888/457-4602; www.travelex-insurance.com).

MEDICAL INSURANCE Most health insurance policies cover you if you get sick away from home—but check, particularly if you're insured by an HMO. With the exception of certain HMOs and Medicare/Medicaid, your medical insurance should cover medical treatment—even hospital care—overseas. However, most out-of-country hospitals make you pay your bills up front, and send you a refund after you've returned home and filed the necessary paperwork. And in a worst-case scenario, there's the high cost of emergency evacuation. In Australia, hygiene standards are high, hospitals are modern, and doctors and dentists are well qualified, but the continent's immense distances mean you can sometimes be a long way from a hospital or a doctor. Make sure your policy covers medical evacuation by helicopter or Australia's Royal Flying Doctor Service airlift. (You might well need this if you become sick or injured in the Outback.)

One of the most potentially financially ruinous situations arising from getting sick in Australia is evacuation to your home country. Your policy should cover the cost to fly you back home in a stretcher, along with a nurse, should that be necessary. A stretcher takes up three coach-class seats, plus you may need extra seats for a nurse and medical equipment.

Australia has a reciprocal medical-care agreement with Great Britain and a limited agreement with Ireland and New Zealand in which travelers are covered for medical expenses for immediately necessary treatment in a public hospital (but not evacuation to

---

Tips **Quick ID**

Tie a colorful ribbon or piece of yarn around your luggage handle, or slap a distinctive sticker on the side of your bag. This makes it less likely that someone will mistakenly appropriate it. And if your luggage gets lost, it will be easier to find.

---

your home country, ambulances, funerals, and dental care) by Australia's national health system, called Medicare, which is similar to the program by the same name in the United States. It's crucial to buy insurance, though, because medical care in Australia is expensive and the national health-care system typically covers only 85%, sometimes less, of treatment; you will not be covered for treatment in a private hospital; and evacuation insurance is a must. Most foreign students must take out the Australian government's Overseas Student Health Cover as a condition of entry.

If you require additional medical insurance, try **MEDEX International** (© 800/527-0218 or 410/453-6300; www.medexassist.com) or **Travel Assistance International** (© 800/821-2828; www.travelassistance.com; for general information on services, call the company's Worldwide Assistance Services, Inc., at © 800/777-8710.

LOST-LUGGAGE INSURANCE
On domestic flights, checked baggage is covered up to $2,500 per ticketed passenger. On international flights (including U.S. portions of international trips), baggage is limited to approximately $9.05 per pound, up to approximately $635 per checked bag. If you plan to check items more valuable than the standard liability, see if your valuables are covered by your homeowner's policy, get baggage insurance as part of your comprehensive travel-insurance package, or buy Travel Guard's "BagTrak" product. Don't buy insurance at the airport, as it's usually overpriced. Be sure to take any valuables or irreplaceable items with you in your carry-on luggage, as many valuables (including books, money, and electronics) aren't covered by airline policies.

If your luggage is lost, immediately file a lost-luggage claim at the airport, detailing the luggage contents. For most airlines, you must report delayed, damaged, or lost baggage within 4 hours of arrival. The airlines are required to deliver luggage, once found, directly to your house or destination free of charge.

7 Health & Safety

STAYING HEALTHY
You don't have to worry much about health issues on a trip to Australia. Hygiene standards are high, hospitals are modern, and doctors and dentists are well qualified. Australia's immense distances mean that you can sometimes be a long way from a hospital or a doctor, but help is never far away thanks to the Royal Flying Doctor Service. However, standard medical travel insurance may be advisable (see previous section on insurance).

GENERAL AVAILABILITY OF HEALTH CARE
No vaccinations are needed to enter Australia unless you have been in a yellow-fever danger zone—that is, South America or Africa—in the past 6 days.

Australian pharmacists may only fill prescriptions written by Australian doctors, so carry enough medication with you for your trip. Doctors are listed under "M" for Medical Practitioners in the Yellow Pages, and most large towns and cities have 24-hour clinics. Failing that, go to the local hospital's emergency room.

BUGS, BITES & OTHER WILD-LIFE CONCERNS   Snake and spider bites may not be as common as the hair-raising stories you will hear would suggest, but it pays to be wary. Australia's two deadly spiders are the large hairy funnel web and the tiny red-back, which has a distinctive red slash on its back. Snakes are common throughout Australia and you are most likely to see one if you are in the bush or hiking. If you are bitten, keep calm; moving as little as possible may save your life. Demobilize the limb and wrap that whole section of the limb tightly (but not tight enough to restrict the blood flow) with a wide cloth or bandage (not a narrow tourniquet). Then send someone to the nearest hospital, where antivenin should be available.

If you go bushwalking, check your whole body for ticks, which are common. If you find one, dab it with methylated spirits or some other noxious chemical. Wait for a while, and then gently pull the tick out with tweezers, carefully ensuring that you don't leave its head buried inside the wound.

Many Aussie marine creatures are deadly. Avoid stingrays, stonefish (which look like stones, so don't walk on underwater "rocks"), lionfish, and puffer fish. Never touch a blue-ringed octopus (it has blue circles all over its body) or a cone shell (a large shellfish shaped like a blunt cone). Marine stingers, or box jellyfish, inhabit the coastal waters of the northern third of the country in summer. Their sting is very painful and can cause heart failure and death. If you are stung, pour vinegar over the affected site immediately—local authorities leave bottles of vinegar on the beach specifically for this purpose. On beaches in Sydney and other areas, you might come across "blue bottles." These long-tentacled blue jellyfish inflict a generally harmless but painful sting that can last for hours. Sometimes you'll see warning signs on patrolled beaches. The best remedy if you are stung is to rinse the area liberally in seawater or fresh water to remove any tentacles stuck to the skin. For intense pain, apply heat or cold, whichever feels better. If you experience breathing difficulties or disorientation following a box jellyfish or blue bottle sting, seek medical attention immediately.

There are two types of crocodiles in Australia: the freshwater crocodile, which grows to almost 3m (10 ft.), and the highly dangerous estuarine (or saltwater) crocodile, which reaches 5m to 7m (17 ft.–23 ft.). Freshwater crocs are considered harmless; unfortunately, estuarine crocs aren't. They are called "saltwater" crocs but live mostly in freshwater rivers, wetlands, gorges, and billabongs (ponds). They are very dangerous, move at lightning speed, and are invisible even an inch beneath the water; few people survive an attack. *Never* swim in, or stand near the bank of, any river, swamp, or pool in the northern third of Australia, unless you know for certain it's croc-free, and don't swim at beaches near stream or river mouths.

SUN/ELEMENTS/EXTREME WEATHER EXPOSURE   Australians have the world's highest death rate from skin cancer because of the country's intense sunlight. Limit your exposure to the sun, especially during the first few days of your trip, and from 11am to 3pm in summer and 10am to 2pm in winter. Remember that UV rays reflected off walls, water, and the ground, can burn you even when you're not in direct sunlight. Use a broad-spectrum sunscreen with a high protection factor (SPF 30+). Wear a broad-brimmed hat that covers the back of your neck, ears, and face (a baseball cap won't do it), and a long-sleeved shirt. Remember that children need more protection than adults do. Don't even think about traveling without sunglasses, or you'll spend your entire vacation squinting against Australia's "diamond light."

Cyclones are occasionally experienced in tropical areas such as Darwin and Queensland's coastal regions from about Gladstone north, during January and February, but serious damage is relatively rare.

WHAT TO DO IF YOU GET SICK AWAY FROM HOME

In most cases, your existing health plan will provide the coverage you need. But double-check; you may want to buy **travel medical insurance** instead. (See the section on insurance, above.) Bring your insurance ID card with you when you travel.

If you suffer from a chronic illness, consult your doctor before your departure. For conditions like epilepsy, diabetes, or heart problems, wear a **Medic Alert Identification Tag** (© 800/825-3785; www.medicalert.org), which will immediately alert doctors to your condition and give them access to your records through Medic Alert's 24-hour hot line.

Pack **prescription medications** in your carry-on luggage, and carry prescription medications in their original containers, with pharmacy labels—otherwise they won't make it through airport security. Also bring along

copies of your prescriptions in case you lose your pills or run out. Don't forget an extra pair of contact lenses or prescription glasses. Carry the generic name of prescription medicines, in case a local pharmacist is unfamiliar with the brand name.

Contact the **International Association for Medical Assistance to Travelers (IAMAT)** (© 716/754-4883 or 416/652-0137; www.iamat.org) for tips on travel and health concerns in Australia, and lists of local doctors. The United States **Centers for Disease Control and Prevention** (© 800/311-3435; www.cdc.gov) provides up-to-date information on necessary vaccines and health hazards by region or country.

If you get sick, consider asking your hotel concierge to recommend a local doctor—even his or her own.

STAYING SAFE

Driving probably poses one of the greatest risks to visitors to Australia. Australians drive on the left, something that North American and European visitors still often have difficulty remembering. Drivers and passengers, including taxi passengers, must wear a seat belt at all times, by law. Avoid driving between dusk and dawn in country areas, because this is when kangaroos are most active, and a collision with a 'roo is something to be avoided at all costs. Road trains—as many as three big truck carriages linked together can be up to 54m (177 ft.) long—are another danger, particularly in the Outback. *Warning:* If you break down or get lost, never leave your vehicle. Most people who get lost do so in Outback spots, and those who wander off to look for help or water usually die in the attempt. If it happens to you, stay with your car. See "Getting Around by Car," later in this chapter.

8 Specialized Travel Resources

TRAVELERS WITH DISABILITIES

Most disabilities shouldn't stop anyone from traveling. There are more options and resources out there than ever before. Most hotels, major stores, attractions, and public restrooms in Australia have wheelchair access. Many smaller lodges and even B&Bs are starting to cater to guests with disabilities, and some diving companies cater to scuba divers with disabilities. National parks make an effort to include wheelchair-friendly pathways, too. Taxi companies in bigger cities can usually supply a cab equipped for wheelchairs. TTY facilities are still limited largely to government services. For information on all kinds of facilities and services in Australia for people with disabilities (not just travel-related organizations), contact **National Information Communication Awareness Network (NICAN)**, P.O. Box 407, Curtin, ACT 2605 (© **1800/806 769** voice and TTY in Australia, or 02/6285 3713; www.nican.com.au). This free service can put you in touch with accessible accommodations and attractions throughout Australia, as well as with travel agents and tour operators who understand your needs.

Many travel agencies offer customized tours and itineraries for travelers with disabilities. **Flying Wheels Travel** (© **507/451-5005;** www.flying wheelstravel.com) offers escorted tours and cruises that emphasize sports and private tours in minivans with lifts. **Accessible Journeys** (© **800/846-4537** or 610/521-0339; www.disability travel.com) caters specifically to slow walkers and wheelchair travelers and their families and friends.

Organizations that offer assistance to travelers with disabilities include the **Moss Rehab Hospital** (www.moss resourcenet.org), which provides a library of accessible-travel resources online; the **Society for Accessible Travel and Hospitality** (© 212/447-7284; www.sath.org; annual membership fees: $45 adults, $30 seniors and students), which offers a wealth of travel resources for all types of disabilities and informed recommendations on destinations, access guides, travel agents, tour operators, vehicle rentals, and companion services; and the **American Foundation for the Blind** (© 800/232-5463; www.afb.org), which provides information on traveling with Seeing Eye dogs.

For more information specifically targeted to travelers with disabilities, the community website **iCan** (www. icanonline.net/channels/travel/index. cfm) has destination guides and several regular columns on accessible travel. Also check out the quarterly magazine *Emerging Horizons* ($15 per year, $20 outside the U.S.; www. emerginghorizons.com); **Twin Peaks Press** (© 360/694-2462; http:// disabilitybookshop.virtualave.net/blist 84.htm), offering travel-related books for travelers with special needs; and *Open World Magazine,* published by the Society for Accessible Travel and Hospitality (see above; subscription: $18 per year, $35 outside the U.S.).

GAY & LESBIAN TRAVELERS

Sydney is one of the most gay-friendly cities in the world, and across most of Australia, the gay community has a high profile and lots of support services. There are plenty of gay and lesbian bars, and most Saturday nights see a privately operated gay dance party taking place in an inner-city warehouse somewhere. The cafes and pubs of Oxford Street in Darlinghurst, a short cab ride or long stroll from Sydney's downtown area, are the liveliest gay spots. The annual Sydney Gay & Lesbian Mardi Gras, culminating in a huge street parade and party in late

February/early March, is a high point on the city's calendar.

In rural areas of Australia, you may still encounter a little conservative resistance to gays and lesbians, but Australians everywhere are generally tolerant. Noosa, on Queensland's Sunshine Coast, was a favored destination for revelers after the 2002 Mardi Gras, and there are a couple of resorts in north Queensland catering to gay and lesbian travelers.

Liberty Resort at Kuranda near Cairns (ℂ **1300/650 464** in Australia, or 07/4093 7556; www.liberty resort.com.au), opened in late 2002, billing itself as the world's most luxurious gay and lesbian resort. It has 56 villas, 8 apartments, and an 80-bed backpacker hostel set on 3.2 hectares (8 acres) of tropical rainforest. By the time you get to Australia, there may be more resorts in the Liberty chain, including possibly one in the Blue Mountains, west of Sydney.

Turtle Cove Resort (ℂ **1300/727 979** in Australia, or 07/4059 1800; www.turtlecove.com.au), located on a private beach between Cairns and Port Douglas, is another well-known resort for lesbians and gay men.

Some services you may find useful are the **Gay & Lesbian Counselling Service** of NSW (ℂ **02/9207 2888** for the administration office), which runs a hot line from 4pm to midnight daily (ℂ **1800/805 379** in Australia, or 02/9207 2800). In Sydney, the **Albion Street Centre** (ℂ **02/9332 9600** for administration, or 1800/451 600 in Australia outside Sydney and 02/9332 9700 in Sydney for the information line) is an AIDS clinic and information service.

The International Gay & Lesbian Travel Association (IGLTA) (ℂ **800/ 448-8550** or 954/776-2626; www. iglta.org) is the trade association for the gay and lesbian travel industry, and offers an online directory of gay and lesbian-friendly travel businesses;

go to their website and click on "Members."

Many agencies offer tours and travel itineraries specifically for gay and lesbian travelers. **JMS Global Travel,** 263 Liverpool St., Darlinghurst, NSW 2010 (ℂ **1800/672 120** in Australia, or 02/9360 9611), is one of the biggest travel agencies specializing in gay travel in Australia. **Above and Beyond Tours** (ℂ **800/ 397-2681;** www.abovebeyondtours. com) is the exclusive gay and lesbian tour operator for United Airlines. **Now, Voyager** (ℂ **800/255-6951;** www.nowvoyager.com) is a well-known San Francisco–based gay-owned and -operated travel service.

Fellow Traveller (ℂ **03/9429 6110**), Australia's only free gay and lesbian accommodations guide, is produced annually by Melbourne's weekly gay and lesbian newspaper *MCV.* It is distributed nationally. The following travel guides are available at most travel bookstores and gay and lesbian bookstores, or you can order them from **Giovanni's Room** bookstore, 1145 Pine St., Philadelphia, PA 19107 (ℂ **215/923-2960;** www. giovannisroom.com): *Out and About* (ℂ **800/929-2268** or 415/644-8044; www.outandabout.com), which offers guidebooks and a newsletter 10 times a year packed with solid information on the global gay and lesbian scene; *Spartacus International Gay Guide* and *Odysseus,* both good, annual English-language guidebooks focused on gay men; and *Gay Travel A to Z: The World of Gay & Lesbian Travel Options at Your Fingertips,* by Marianne Ferrari (Ferrari Publications; Box 35575, Phoenix, AZ 85069), a very good gay and lesbian guidebook series.

SENIOR TRAVEL

Mention the fact that you're a senior when you make your travel reservations. Although all of the major U.S.

airlines except America West have canceled their senior discount and coupon book programs, many hotels still offer discounts for seniors.

Seniors—often called "pensioners" in Australia—from other countries don't always qualify for the discounted entry prices to tours, attractions, and events that Australian seniors enjoy, but mostly they do. Always inquire about discounts when booking hotels, flights, and train or bus tickets. The best ID to bring is something that shows your date of birth or something that marks you as an "official" senior, like a membership card from AARP.

Members of **AARP** (formerly known as the American Association of Retired Persons), 601 E St. NW, Washington, DC 20049 (© **800/ 424-3410** or 202/434-2277; www. aarp.org), get discounts on hotels, airfares, and car rentals. AARP offers members a wide range of benefits, including *AARP: The Magazine* and a monthly newsletter. Anyone over 50 can join.

Many reliable agencies and organizations target the 50-plus market. **Elderhostel** (© **877/426-8056;** www. elderhostel.org) arranges study programs for those 55 and over (and a spouse or companion of any age) in the U.S. and in more than 80 countries around the world. Most international courses last 2 to 4 weeks, and many include airfare, accommodations in university dormitories or modest inns, meals, and tuition. **ElderTreks** (© **800/741-7956;** www. eldertreks.com) offers small-group tours to off-the-beaten-path or adventure-travel locations, restricted to travelers 50 and older.

Recommended publications offering travel resources and discounts for seniors include: the quarterly magazine *Travel 50 & Beyond* (www.travel 50andbeyond.com); *Travel Unlimited: Uncommon Adventures for the Mature Traveler* (Avalon); *101 Tips for Mature Travelers,* available from Grand Circle Travel (© **800/221- 2610** or 617/350-7500; www.gct. com); *The 50+ Traveler's Guidebook* (St. Martin's Press); and *Unbelievably Good Deals and Great Adventures That You Absolutely Can't Get Unless You're Over 50* (McGraw Hill).

FAMILY TRAVEL

If you have enough trouble getting your kids out of the house in the morning, dragging them thousands of miles away may seem like an insurmountable challenge. But family travel can be immensely rewarding, giving you new ways of seeing the world through smaller pairs of eyes.

Australians travel widely with their own kids, so facilities for families, including family passes to attractions, are common.

A great accommodations option for families is Australia's huge stock of serviced or unserviced apartments. Often less expensive than a hotel room, they offer a living room, a kitchen, a bathroom or two, and the privacy of a separate bedroom for adults. "Tips on Accommodations," later in this chapter, has details on the major apartment chains. Most Australian hotels will arrange babysitting given a day's notice.

International airlines and domestic airlines in Australia charge 67% of the adult fare for kids under 12. Most charge 10% for infants under 2 not occupying a seat. Australian transport companies, attractions, and tour operators typically charge half price for kids under 12 or 14 years.

Many Australian resorts have "kids clubs" with extensive programs designed for under 12s and in some cases teenagers. The French-owned Accor chain of hotels and resorts, which is Australia's largest chain, has kids' clubs, kids' menus designed by a nutritionist (and not just the same boring fodder you get everywhere else), and other family-friendly facilities including family rooms, while other resorts such as Hamilton Island have "kids stay, eat, and play free" offers, particularly during holiday periods. Many hotels will offer interconnecting rooms or "family rooms." Ask when booking, and look out for our "kid friendly" icon in this book.

Don't forget that children entering Australia on their parent's passport still need their own visa. See "Entry Requirements," earlier in this chapter. **Rascals in Paradise** (© 415/921-7000; www.rascalsinparadise.com) sells family vacation packages to Australia.

Familyhostel (© 800/733-9753; www.learn.unh.edu/familyhostel) takes the whole family, including kids 8 to 15, on moderately priced domestic and international learning vacations. Lectures, fields trips, and sightseeing are guided by a team of academics.

You can find good family-oriented vacation advice on the Internet from sites like the **Family Travel Network** (www.familytravelnetwork.com); **Traveling Internationally with Your Kids** (www.travelwithyourkids.com), a comprehensive site offering sound advice for long-distance and international travel with children; and **Family Travel Files** (www.thefamilytravel files.com), which offers an online magazine and a directory of off-the-beaten-path tours and tour operators for families.

How to Take Great Trips with Your Kids (The Harvard Common Press) is full of good general advice that can apply to travel anywhere.

WOMEN TRAVELERS
Women Welcome Women World Wide (5W) (© 203/259-7832 in the U.S.; www.womenwelcomewomen. org.uk) works to foster international friendships by enabling women of

different countries to visit one another (men can come along on the trips; they just can't join the club). It's a big, active organization, with more than 3,500 members from all walks of life in some 70 countries.

Check out the website **Journeywoman** (www.journeywoman.com), a lively travel resource, with "GirlTalk Guides" to destinations like New York, Hong Kong, and Toronto and a free e-mail newsletter; or the travel guide *Safety and Security for Women Who Travel,* by Sheila Swan Laufer and Peter Laufer (Travelers' Tales, Inc.), offering commonsense advice and tips on safe travel.

STUDENT TRAVEL
If you're planning to travel to Australia, you'd be wise to arm yourself with an **International Student Identity Card (ISIC),** which offers substantial savings on rail passes, plane tickets, and entrance fees. It also provides you with basic health and life insurance and a 24-hour help line. The card is available for $22 from **STA Travel** (© 800/781-4040, and if you're not in North America there's probably a local number in your country; www.statravel.com), the biggest student travel agency in the world. If you're no longer a student but are still under 26, you can get a **International Youth Travel Card (IYTC)** for the same price from the same people, which entitles you to some discounts (but not on museum admissions). (*Note:* In 2002, STA Travel bought competitors **Council Travel** and **USIT Campus** after they went bankrupt. It's still operating some offices under the Council name, but it's owned by STA.)

Travel CUTS (© 800/667-2887 or 416/614-2887; www.travelcuts.com) offers similar services for both Canadians and U.S. residents. Irish students should turn to **USIT** (© 01/602 1600; www.usitnow.ie).

SINGLE TRAVELERS

Many people prefer traveling alone, and for independent travelers, solo journeys offer infinite opportunities to make friends and meet locals. Unfortunately, if you like resorts, tours, or cruises, you're likely to get hit with a "single supplement" to the base price. Single travelers can avoid these supplements, of course, by agreeing to room with other single travelers on the trip. One Australian resort that will fix you up with a same-sex roommate if you're traveling alone is Contiki Great Keppel Island Resort (© **1800/245 658** in Australia, or 07/4939 5044; www. contikiresorts.com), off the Queensland coast (p. 331).

An even better idea is to find a compatible roommate before you go from one of the many roommate locator agencies. **Travel Buddies Singles Travel Club** (© **800/998-9099;** www.travelbuddiesworldwide.com), based in Canada, runs small, intimate, single-friendly group trips to a range of destinations including Australia

and will match you with a roommate free of charge and save you the cost of single supplements. **TravelChums** (© **212/787-2621;** www.travelchums. com) is an Internet-only travel-companion matching service with elements of an online personals-type site, hosted by the respected New York–based Shaw Guides travel service. Many reputable tour companies offer singles-only trips. **Backroads** (© **800/462-2848;** www.backroads. com) offers more than 160 active trips to 30 destinations worldwide, including Australia.

For more information, check out Eleanor Berman's *Traveling Solo: Advice and Ideas for More Than 250 Great Vacations* (Globe Pequot), a guide with advice on traveling alone, whether on your own or on a group tour. Or turn to the **Travel Alone and Love It** website (www.travelaloneand loveit.com), designed by former flight attendant Sharon Wingler, the author of the book of the same name. Her site is full of tips for single travelers.

9 Planning Your Trip Online

SURFING FOR AIRFARES

The "big three" online travel agencies—**Expedia.com, Travelocity.com,** and **Orbitz.com**—sell most of the air tickets bought on the Internet. (Canadian travelers should try expedia.ca and Travelocity.ca; U.K. residents can go for expedia.co.uk and opodo.co. uk.) Each has different business deals with the airlines and may offer different fares on the same flights, so it's wise to shop around. Expedia and Travelocity will also send you **e-mail notification** when a cheap fare becomes available to your favorite destination. Of the smaller travel agency websites, **SideStep** (www.sidestep.com) has gotten the best reviews from Frommer's authors. It's a browser add-on that purports to "search 140 sites at once," but in reality only beats competitors' fares as often as other sites do.

Also remember to check **airline websites.** Even with major airlines, you can often shave a few bucks from a fare by booking directly through the airline and avoiding a travel agency's transaction fee. But you'll get these discounts only by **booking online:** Most airlines now offer online-only fares that even their phone agents know nothing about. For the websites of airlines that fly to and from Australia, go to "Getting There," later in this chapter.

Great **last-minute deals** are available through free weekly e-mail services provided directly by the airlines. Most of these are announced on Tuesday or Wednesday and must be purchased online. Most are only valid for travel that weekend, but some can be booked weeks or months in advance.

Frommers.com: The Complete Travel Resource

For an excellent travel-planning resource, we highly recommend Frommers.com (www.frommers.com). We're a little biased, of course, but we guarantee that you'll find the travel tips, reviews, monthly vacation giveaways, and online-booking capabilities thoroughly indispensable. Among the special features are our popular **Message Boards,** where Frommer's readers post queries and share advice (sometimes even our authors show up to answer questions); **Frommers.com Newsletter,** for the latest travel bargains and insider travel secrets; and **Frommer's Destinations Section,** where you'll get expert travel tips, hotel and dining recommendations, and advice on the sights to see for more than 3,000 destinations around the globe. When your research is done, the **Online Reservations System** (www.frommers.com/book_a_trip) takes you to Frommer's preferred online partners for booking your vacation at affordable prices.

Sign up for weekly e-mail alerts at airline websites or check megasites that compile comprehensive lists of last-minute specials, such as **Smarter Living** (smarterliving.com). For last-minute trips, **site59.com** in the U.S. and **lastminute.com** in Europe often have better deals than the major-label sites.

If you're willing to give up some control over your flight details, use an **opaque fare service** like **Priceline** (www.priceline.com; www.priceline.co.uk for Europeans) or **Hotwire** (www.hotwire.com). Both offer rock-bottom prices in exchange for travel on a "mystery airline" at a mysterious time of day, often with a mysterious change of planes en route. The mystery airlines are all major, well-known carriers—but your chances of getting a 6am or 11pm flight are pretty high. Hotwire tells you flight prices before you buy; Priceline usually has better deals than Hotwire, but you have to play their "name our price" game. If you're new at this, the helpful folks at **BiddingForTravel** (www.biddingfortravel.com) do a good job of demystifying Priceline's prices. Priceline and Hotwire are great for flights within

North America and between the U.S. and Europe. But for flights to other parts of the world, consolidators will almost always beat their fares.

For much more about airfares and savvy air-travel tips and advice, pick up a copy of *Frommer's Fly Safe, Fly Smart* (Wiley Publishing, Inc.).

SURFING FOR HOTELS

Shopping online for hotels is much easier in the U.S., Canada, and certain parts of Europe than it is in the rest of the world, but Australian hotels—even the small ones—are pretty Internet savvy, as are B&Bs. Of the "big three" sites, **Expedia** may be the best choice, thanks to its long list of special deals. **Travelocity** runs a close second. Hotel specialist sites **hotels.com** and **hoteldiscounts.com** are also reliable. An excellent free program, **TravelAxe** (www.travelaxe.net), can help you search multiple hotel sites at once.

SURFING FOR RENTAL CARS

For booking rental cars online, the best deals are usually found at rental-car company websites, although all the major online travel agencies also offer rental-car reservations services. Priceline and Hotwire work well for rental cars, too; the only "mystery" is which major rental company you get, and for most travelers the difference between Hertz, Avis, and Budget is negligible.

10 The 21st-Century Traveler

INTERNET ACCESS AWAY FROM HOME

Travelers have any number of ways to check their e-mail and access the Internet on the road. Of course, using your own laptop—or even a PDA (personal digital assistant) or electronic organizer with a modem—gives you the most flexibility. But even if you don't have a computer, you can still access your e-mail and even your office computer from cybercafes.

WITHOUT YOUR OWN COMPUTER

It's hard nowadays to find a city that *doesn't* have a few cybercafes, and that certainly applies in Australia. Although there's no definitive directory for cybercafes—these are independent businesses, after all—three places to start looking are at **www.cybercaptive. com**, **www.netcafeguide.com**, and **www.cybercafe.com**. In major tourist cities like Cairns and Darwin, there are whole streets full of cybercafes. Aside from formal cybercafes, most **youth hostels** nowadays have at least one computer that accesses the Internet. And most **public libraries** offer Internet access free or for a small charge. Avoid **hotel business centers,** which often charge exorbitant rates.

Most major airports now have **Internet kiosks** scattered throughout their gates. These kiosks, which you'll also see in shopping malls, hotel lobbies, and tourist information offices around the world, give you basic Web access for a per-minute fee that's usually higher than cybercafe prices. The kiosks' clunkiness and high price means they should be avoided whenever possible.

To retrieve your e-mail, ask your **Internet service provider (ISP)** if it has a Web-based interface tied to your existing e-mail account. If your ISP doesn't have such an interface, you can use the free **mail2web** service (www. mail2web.com) to access your home e-mail. For more flexibility, you may want to open a free, Web-based e-mail account with **Yahoo! Mail** (mail. yahoo.com). (Microsoft's Hotmail is another popular option, but Hotmail has severe spam problems.) Your home ISP may be able to forward your e-mail to the Web-based account automatically.

If you need to access files on your office computer, look into a service called **GoToMyPC** (www.gotomypc. com). The service provides a Web-based interface for you to access and manipulate a distant PC from anywhere—even a cybercafe—provided your "target" PC is on and has an always-on connection to the Internet (such as with Road Runner cable). The service offers top-quality security, but if you're worried about hackers, use your own laptop rather than a cybercafe to access the GoToMyPC system.

WITH YOUR OWN COMPUTER

Major Internet service providers (ISPs) have **local access numbers** around the world, allowing you to go online by simply placing a local call. Check your ISP's website or call its toll-free number and ask how you can use your current account away from home, and how much it will cost.

If you're traveling outside the reach of your ISP, the **iPass** network has dial-up numbers in most of the world's countries. You'll have to sign up with an iPass provider, which will then tell you how to set up your computer for your destination(s). For a list of iPass providers, go to www.ipass.com and click on "Reseller Locator." Under "Select a Country," pick the country that you're coming from, and under "Who is this service for?" pick "Individual." One solid provider is **i2roam** (www.i2roam.com; © **866/811-6209** or 920/235-0475).

Wherever you go, bring a **connection kit** of the right power and phone adapters, a spare phone cord, and a spare Ethernet network cable. Australia's electricity supply is 240 volts, 50 Hz. North Americans and Europeans will need to buy a converter before they leave home, as Australian stores usually only stock converters for Aussie appliances to fit American and European outlets. Most business-class hotels throughout the world offer dataports for laptop modems, and a few thousand hotels in the U.S. and Europe now offer high-speed Internet access using an Ethernet network cable. You'll have to bring your own cables either way, so **call your hotel in advance** to find out what the options are.

Community-minded individuals have also set up **free wireless networks** in major cities around the U.S., Europe, and Australia. These networks are spotty, but you get what you (don't) pay for. Each network has a home page explaining how to set up your computer for its particular system; start your explorations at www.personaltelco.net/index.cgi/Wireless Communities.

USING A CELLPHONE IN AUSTRALIA

The three letters that define much of the world's **wireless capabilities** are GSM (Global System for Mobiles), a big, seamless network that makes for easy cross-border cellphone use throughout Europe and dozens of other countries worldwide. In the U.S., T-Mobile, AT&T Wireless, and Cingular use this quasi-universal system; in Canada, Microcell and some Rogers customers are GSM, and all Europeans and most Australians use GSM.

If your cellphone is on a GSM system, and you have a world-capable phone such as many (but not all) Sony Ericsson, Motorola, or Samsung models, you can make and receive calls across civilized areas on much of the globe. Just call your wireless operator and ask for "international roaming" to be activated on your account.

World-phone owners can bring down their per-minute charges with a bit of trickery. Call up your cellular operator and say you'll be going abroad for several months and want to "unlock" your phone to use it with a local provider. Usually, they'll oblige. Then, in your destination country, pick up a cheap, prepaid phone chip at a mobile phone store and slip it into your phone. (Show your phone to the salesperson, as not all phones work on all networks.) You'll get a local phone number in your destination country— and much, much lower calling rates.

Otherwise, **renting** a phone is a good idea. In Australia—reputed to have one of the world's largest per-capita ownership of cellular or "mobile" telephones, as they are known here—they are available for daily rental at major airports and in big cities, and increasingly from car- and motor-home-rental companies. The cell network is digital, not analog. Calls to, or from, a mobile telephone are generally more expensive than a call to, or from, a fixed telephone— A60¢ (US40¢) a minute is a ballpark guide, although the price varies depending on the telephone company, the time of day, the distance between caller and recipient, and the telephone's pricing plan.

An advantage of renting the phone before you leave home is that way you can give loved ones your new number, make sure the phone works, and take the phone wherever you go—especially helpful when you rent overseas, where

Online Traveler's Toolbox

Veteran travelers usually carry some essential items to make their trips easier. Following is a selection of online tools to bookmark and use.

- **Visa ATM Locator** (www.visa.com), for locations of Plus ATMs worldwide, or **MasterCard ATM Locator** (www.mastercard.com), for locations of Cirrus ATMs worldwide.
- **Intellicast** (www.intellicast.com) and **Weather.com** (www.weather.com). Gives weather forecasts for all 50 states and for cities around the world.
- **Mapquest** (www.mapquest.com). This best of the mapping sites lets you choose a specific address or destination, and in seconds, it will return a map and detailed directions.
- **Universal Currency Converter** (www.xe.com/ucc). See what your dollar or pound is worth in more than 100 other countries.
- **Travel Warnings** (http://travel.state.gov/travel_warnings.html, www.fco.gov.uk/travel, www.voyage.gc.ca, www.dfat.gov.au/consular/advice). These sites report on places where health concerns or unrest might threaten American, British, Canadian, and Australian travelers. Generally, U.S. warnings are the most paranoid; Australian warnings are the most relaxed.

phone-rental agencies bill in local currency and may not let you take the phone to another country.

In Australia, mobile phone company **Vodafone** (www.vodarent.com.au) has outlets at Brisbane, Cairns, Sydney, Perth, and Melbourne international airports as well as stores in Surfers Paradise on the Gold Coast and at 50 Park St. in Sydney. They cost between A$8 and A$10 (US$5–US$6.50) a day, plus call charges and insurance, depending on the kind of phone and coverage you want.

Two good wireless rental companies are **InTouch USA** (© **800/872-7626;** www.intouchglobal.com) and **Road-Post** (© **888/290-1606** or 905/272-5665; www.roadpost.com). Give them your itinerary, and they'll tell you what wireless products you need. InTouch will also, for free, advise you on whether your existing phone will work overseas; simply call © **703/222-7161** between 9am and 4pm

Eastern Standard Time, or go to http://intouchglobal.com/travel.htm.

For trips of more than a few weeks spent in one country, **buying a phone** becomes economically attractive, as many nations have cheap, no-questions-asked prepaid phone systems. Stop by a local cellphone shop and get the cheapest package; you'll probably pay less than US$100 for a phone and a starter calling card. Local calls may be as low as US10¢ per minute, and in many countries incoming calls are free.

True wilderness adventurers, or those heading to less-developed countries, should consider renting a **satellite phone** (see above). Per-minute call charges can be even cheaper than roaming charges with a regular cellphone, but the phone itself is more expensive (up to US$150 a week), and depending on the service you choose, people calling you may incur high long-distance charges.

11 Getting There

BY PLANE

Australia is a long, long haul from any-where except New Zealand. Sydney is a nearly 15-hour nonstop flight from Los Angeles, longer if you come via Hon-olulu. From the east coast, add 5½ hours. If you're coming from the States via Auckland, add transit time in New Zealand plus another 3 hours for the Auckland-Sydney leg. If you are com-ing from the United Kingdom, brace yourself for a flight of more or less 12 hours from London to Asia; then pos-sibly a long day in transit, because flights to Australia have a habit of arriv-ing in Asia early in the morning and departing around midnight; and finally the 8- to 9-hour flight to Australia.

Sydney, Cairns, Melbourne, Bris-bane, Adelaide, Darwin, and Perth are all international gateways, but most airlines fly only into Sydney, and a few fly to Melbourne and Brisbane.

THE MAJOR CARRIERS

Here are toll-free reservations numbers and websites for the major interna-tional airlines serving Australia. The "13" prefix in Australia means that the number is charged at the cost of a local call from anywhere in the country.

CARRIERS FLYING FROM NORTH AMERICA

- **Air Canada** (*✆* **888/247-2262** in the U.S. and Canada, 02/9286 8900 in Sydney, or 1300/655 757 from elsewhere in Australia; www.aircanada.ca)
- **Air New Zealand** (*✆* **800/262-1234** in the U.S., 310/615-1111 in the Los Angeles area, or 13 24 76 in Australia; in Canada: 800/663-5494 for English, 800/799-5494 for French, or 604/606-0150 in Vancouver; www.airnewzealand.com)
- **Qantas** (*✆* **800/227-4500** in the U.S. and Canada or 13 13 13 in Australia; www.qantas.com.au)

- **United Airlines** (*✆* **800/538-2929** in the U.S. and Canada or 13 17 77 in Australia; www.ual.com or www.united.ca)

CARRIERS FLYING FROM THE UNITED KINGDOM

- **British Airways** (*✆* **0845/773 3377** in the U.K., 1800/626 747 in Ireland, or 1300/767 177 in Australia; www.britishairways.com.
- **Cathay Pacific** (*✆* **020/8834 8888** in the U.K. or 13 17 47 in Australia; www.cathaypacific.com/uk)
- **Malaysia Airlines** (*✆* **0870/607 9090** in the U.K. and Ireland or 13 26 27 in Australia; www.malaysiaairlines.com.my or www.malaysiaairlineseurope.com)
- **Qantas** (*✆* **0845/774 7767** in the U.K. or 13 13 13 in Australia; www.qantas.com.au)
- **Singapore Airlines** (*✆* **0870/608 8886** in the U.K. or 13 10 11 in Australia; www.singaporeair.com/uk)
- **Thai Airways International** (*✆* **0870/6060 911** in the U.K. or 1300/651 960 in Australia; www.thaiair.com)

GETTING THROUGH THE AIRPORT

With the federalization of airport security, security procedures at U.S. airports are more stable and consistent than ever. Generally, you'll be fine if you arrive at the airport **1 hour** before a domestic flight and **2 hours** before an international flight; if you show up late, tell an airline employee and you'll probably be whisked to the front of the line.

Bring a **current, government-issued photo ID** such as a driver's license or passport, and if you've got an E-ticket, print out the **official con-firmation page;** you'll need to show your confirmation at the security

---

ⓘ Tips   Don't Stow It—Ship It

If ease of travel is your main concern and money is no object, you can ship your luggage with one of the growing number of luggage-service companies that pick up, track, and deliver your luggage (often through couriers such as Federal Express) with minimum hassle for you. Traveling luggage-free may be ultraconvenient, but it's not cheap: One-way overnight shipping can cost from $100 to $200, depending on what you're sending. Still, for some people, especially the elderly or the infirm, it's a sensible solution to lugging heavy baggage. Specialists in door-to-door luggage delivery are Virtual Bellhop (www.virtualbellhop.com), SkyCap International (wwww.skycapinternational.com), and Luggage Express (www.usxpluggageexpress.com).

---

checkpoint, and your ID at the ticket counter or the gate. (Children under 18 do not need photo IDs for domestic flights, but the adults checking in with them need them.)

Security lines are getting shorter than they were during 2001 and 2002, but some doozies remain. If you have trouble standing for long periods of time, tell an airline employee; the airline will provide a wheelchair. Speed up security by **not wearing metal objects** such as big belt buckles or clanky earrings. If you've got metallic body parts, a note from your doctor can prevent a long chat with the security screeners. Keep in mind that only **ticketed passengers** are allowed past security, except for folks escorting passengers with disabilities or children.

Federalization has stabilized **what you can carry on** and **what you can't.** The general rule is that sharp things are out, nail clippers are okay, and food and beverages must be passed through the X-ray machine—but that security screeners can't make you drink from your coffee cup. Bring food in your carry-on rather than checking it, as explosive-detection machines used on checked luggage have been known to mistake food (especially chocolate, for some reason) for bombs. Travelers in the U.S. are allowed one carry-on bag,

plus a "personal item" such as a purse, briefcase, or laptop bag. Carry-on hoarders can stuff all sorts of things into a laptop bag; as long as it has a laptop in it, it's still considered a personal item. The Transportation Security Administration (TSA) has issued a list of restricted items; check its website (http://www.tsa.gov/public/index. jsp) for details.

In 2003, the TSA started phasing out **gate check-in** at all U.S. airports. Passengers with E-tickets and without checked bags can still beat the ticket-counter lines by using **electronic kiosks** or even **online check-in.** Ask your airline which alternatives are available, and if you're using a kiosk, bring the credit card you used to book the ticket. If you're checking bags, you will still be able to use most airlines' kiosks; again call your airline for up-to-date information. **Curbside check-in** is also a good way to avoid lines, although a few airlines still ban curbside check-in entirely; call before you go.

At press time, the TSA is also recommending that you **not lock your checked luggage** so screeners can search it by hand if necessary. The agency says to use plastic "zip ties" instead, which can be bought at hardware stores and can be easily cut off.

FLYING FOR LESS: TIPS FOR GETTING THE BEST AIRFARE

If you're flying from the U.S., keep in mind that the airlines' low season is from mid-April to the end of August—and this happens to be the best time to travel most parts of Australia. High season is December through February, and shoulder season is September through November, and again from March to mid-April.

Keep an eye out for special deals throughout the year. Unexpected lows in airline passenger loads often lead airlines to put cheap offers on the market. The catch is these usually have a short lead-time, requiring you to travel in the next 6 weeks or so. Some deals involve taking a circuitous route, via Fiji or Japan, for instance.

Some travel agents specializing in cheap fares include **Austravel** (© **800/633-3404** in the U.S. and Canada or 0870/055 0239 in the U.K.; www.austravel.net); **Downunder Direct,** a division of Swain Australia (© **800/642-6224** in the U.S. and Canada; www.downunderdirect. com); and **Goway** (© **800/387-8850** in the U.S. and Canada; www.goway. com).

Here are some other ways to keep your airfare costs down.

- Passengers who can book their ticket **long in advance,** who can stay over **Saturday night,** or who fly **midweek** or at **less-trafficked hours** will pay a fraction of the full fare. If your schedule is flexible, say so, and ask if you can secure a cheaper fare by changing your flight plans.
- You can also save on airfares by keeping an eye out in local newspapers for **promotional specials** or **fare wars,** when airlines lower prices on their most popular routes. You rarely see fare wars offered for peak travel times, but if you can travel in the off-months, you may snag a bargain.
- Search **the Internet** for cheap fares (see "Planning Your Trip Online," earlier in this chapter).
- Try to book a ticket **in its country of origin.** For instance, if you're planning a one-way flight from Sydney to Auckland, an Australia-based travel agent such as Flight Centres will probably have the lowest fares. For multileg trips, book in the country of the first leg; for example, book Melbourne–Auckland–Los Angeles in Australia.
- **Consolidators,** also known as bucket shops, are great sources for international tickets. Start by looking in Sunday newspaper travel sections; U.S. travelers should focus on the *New York*

Tips Travel in the Age of Bankruptcy

At press time, two major U.S. airlines were struggling in bankruptcy court and most of the rest weren't doing very well either. To protect yourself, **buy your tickets with a credit card,** as the Fair Credit Billing Act guarantees that you can get your money back from the credit card company if a travel supplier goes under (and if you request the refund within 60 days of the bankruptcy). **Travel insurance** can also help, but make sure it covers against "carrier default" for your specific travel provider. And be aware that if a U.S. airline goes bust midtrip, a 2001 federal law requires other carriers to take you to your destination (albeit on a space-available basis) for a fee of no more than $25, provided you rebook within 60 days of the cancellation.

Times, Los Angeles Times, and *Miami Herald.* **Beware:** Bucket shop tickets are usually nonrefundable or rigged with stiff cancellation penalties, often as high as 50% to 75% of the ticket price, and some put you on charter airlines with questionable safety records. Several reliable consolidators are worldwide and available on the Net. **STA Travel** (© **800/781-4040;** www.statravel.com) is now the world's leader in student travel, thanks to their purchase of Council Travel. It also offers good fares for travelers of all ages.

- Join **frequent-flier clubs.** Accrue enough miles, and you'll be rewarded with free flights and elite status. It's free, and you'll get the best choice of seats, faster response to phone inquiries, and prompter service if your luggage is stolen, your flight is canceled or delayed, or if you want to change your seat. You don't need to fly to build frequent-flier miles—**frequent-flier credit cards** can provide thousands of miles for doing your everyday shopping.

- For many more tips about air travel, including a rundown of the major frequent-flier credit cards, pick up a copy of *Frommer's Fly Safe, Fly Smart* (Wiley Publishing, Inc.).

LONG-HAUL FLIGHTS: HOW TO STAY COMFORTABLE

Long flights can be trying; stuffy air and cramped seats can make you feel as if you're being sent parcel post in a small box. But with a little advance planning, you can make an otherwise unpleasant experience almost bearable.

- Your choice of airline and airplane will definitely affect your legroom. Research firm Skytrax has posted a list of average seat pitches for international airlines at www.airlinequality.com.

- Emergency exit seats and bulkhead seats typically have the most

---

(Tips Coping with Jet Lag

Jet lag is a pitfall of traveling across time zones. If you're flying north-south, say from Canada to Australia, and you feel sluggish when you touch down, your symptoms will be caused by dehydration and the general stress of air travel. When you travel east to west or vice-versa, however, your body becomes thoroughly confused about what time it is, and everything from your digestion to your brain gets knocked for a loop. Traveling east is more difficult on your internal clock than traveling west, as most people's bodies find it more acceptable to stay up late than to fall asleep early.

Here are some tips for combating jet lag:

- Reset your watch to your destination time before you board the plane.
- Drink lots of water before, during, and after your flight. Avoid alcohol.
- Exercise and sleep well for a few days before your trip.
- If you have trouble sleeping on planes, fly eastward on morning flights.
- Daylight is the key to resetting your body clock. At the website for Outside In (www.bodyclock.com), you can get a customized plan of when to seek and avoid light.
- If you need help getting to sleep earlier than you usually would, doctors recommend taking either the hormone melatonin or the sleeping pill Ambien—but not together. Take 2 to 5 milligrams of melatonin about 2 hours before your planned bedtime.

Flying with Film & Video

Never pack film—developed or undeveloped—in checked bags, as the new, more powerful scanners in U.S. airports can fog film. The film you carry with you can be damaged by scanners as well. X-ray damage is cumulative; the faster the film and the more times you put it through a scanner, the more likely the damage. Film under 800 ASA is usually safe for up to five scans. If you're taking your film through additional scans, U.S. regulations permit you to demand hand inspections. In international airports, you're at the mercy of airport officials. On international flights, store your film in transparent bags, so you can remove it easily before you go through scanners. Keep in mind that airports are not the only places where your camera may be scanned: Highly trafficked attractions are X-raying visitors' bags with increasing frequency.

Most photo supply stores sell protective pouches designed to block damaging X-rays. The pouches fit both film and loaded cameras. They should protect your film in checked baggage, but they also may raise alarms and result in a hand inspection.

An organization called **Film Safety for Traveling on Planes, FSTOP** (© **888/301-2665**; www.f-stop.org), can provide additional tips for traveling with film and equipment.

Carry-on scanners will not damage **videotape** in video cameras, but the magnetic fields emitted by the walk-through security gateways and handheld inspection wands will. Always place your loaded camcorder on the screening conveyor belt or have it hand-inspected. Be sure your batteries are charged, as you will probably be required to turn the device on to ensure that it's what it appears to be.

legroom. Emergency exit seats are usually held back to be assigned the day of a flight (to ensure that the seat is filled by someone able bodied); it's worth getting to the ticket counter early to snag one of these spots for a long flight. Keep in mind that bulkheads are where airlines often put baby bassinets, so you may be sitting next to an infant.

• To have two seats for yourself, try for an aisle seat in a center section toward the back of coach. If you're traveling with a companion, book an aisle and a window seat. Middle seats are usually booked last, so chances are good you'll end up with three seats to yourselves. And in the event that a third passenger is assigned the middle seat, he or she will probably be more than happy to trade for a window or an aisle.

• Ask about entertainment options. Many airlines offer seat-back video systems where you get to choose your movies or play video games—but only on some of their planes. (Boeing 777s are your best bet.)

• To sleep, avoid the last row of any section or a row in front of an emergency exit, as these seats are the least likely to recline. Avoid seats near highly trafficked toilet areas. You also may want to reserve a window seat so that you can rest your head and avoid being bumped in the aisle.

- Get up, walk around, and stretch every 60 to 90 minutes to keep your blood flowing. This helps avoid deep vein thrombosis, or "economy-class syndrome," a rare and deadly condition that can be caused by sitting in cramped conditions for too long.
- Drink water before, during, and after your flight to combat the lack of humidity in airplane cabins—which can be drier than the Sahara. Bring a bottle of water on board. Avoid alcohol, which will dehydrate you.
- If you're flying with kids, don't forget to carry on toys, books, pacifiers, and chewing gum to help them relieve ear pressure buildup during ascent and descent. Let each child pack his or her own backpack with favorite toys.

12 Packages for the Independent Traveler

Before you start your search for the lowest airfare, you may want to consider booking your flight as part of a travel package. Package tours are not the same thing as escorted tours. Package tours are simply a way to buy the airfare, accommodations, and other elements of your trip (such as car rentals, airport transfers, and sometimes even activities) at the same time and often at discounted prices—kind of like one-stop shopping. Packages are sold in bulk to tour operators—who resell them to the public at a cost that usually undercuts standard rates.

Several big **online travel agencies**—Expedia, Travelocity, Orbitz, Site59, and Lastminute.com—also do a brisk business in packages. If you're unsure about the pedigree of a smaller packager, check with the Better Business Bureau in the city where the company is based, or go online at www.bbb.org. If a packager won't tell you where it's based, don't fly with them.

Austravel (© 800/633-3404 in the U.S. and Canada or 0870/055 0239 in the U.K.; www.austravel.net) is an American company offering independent packages Down Under. The following companies offer both independent and escorted tours: **ATS Tours** (© 800/423-2880 in the U.S. and Canada; www.atstours.com); **Collette Vacations** (© 800/340-5158 in the U.S., 416/626-1661 in Canada, or 0189/581 2333 in the U.K. through Adventures Unlimited, Inc.; www.collettevacations.com); **Goway** (© 800/387-8850 in the U.S. and Canada; www.goway.com); **Inta-Aussie South Pacific Tours** (© 800/633-3404, or 212/693-0677 in the U.S.; www.inta-oz.com); **Maupintour** (© 800/255-4266 in the U.S. and Canada; www.maupintour.com); **Qantas Vacations** (© 800/348-8139 in the U.S. or 800/268-7525 in Canada; www.qantasvacations.com); **Sunbeam Tours** (© 800/955-1818 in the U.S. and Canada; www.sunbeamtours.com); **Swain Australia Tours** (© 800/22-SWAIN in the U.S. and Canada; www.swainaustralia.com); Swain Australia's budget-travel division, **Downunder Direct** (© 800/642-6224 in the U.S. and Canada; www.downunderdirect.com); and **United Vacations** (© 800/917-9246 in the U.S. and Canada; www.unitedvacations.com). Swain Australia is operated and largely staffed by Aussies. Collette Vacations, Inta-Aussie South Pacific, Sunbeam Tours, Swain Australia, and Goway have offices in Australia.

Travel packages are also listed in the travel section of your local Sunday newspaper. Or check ads in the national travel magazines such as *Arthur Frommer's Budget Travel Magazine, Travel & Leisure, National Geographic Traveler,* and *Condé Nast Traveler.*

Package tours can vary by leaps and bounds. Some offer a better class of hotels than others. Some offer the same hotels for lower prices. Some offer flights on scheduled airlines, while others book charters. Some limit your choice of accommodations and travel days. You are often required to make a large payment up front. On the plus side, packages can save you money, offering group prices but allowing for independent travel. Some even let you to add on a few guided excursions or escorted day trips (also at prices lower than if you booked them yourself) without booking an entirely escorted tour.

Before you invest in a package tour, get some answers. Ask about the accommodations choices and prices for each. Then look up the hotels' reviews in your Frommer's guide and check their rates for your specific dates of travel online. You'll also want to find out what **type of room** you get. If you need a certain type of room, ask for it; don't take whatever is thrown your way. Request a nonsmoking room, a quiet room, a room with a view, or whatever you fancy.

Finally, look for **hidden expenses.** Ask whether airport departure fees and taxes, for example, are included in the total cost.

13 Escorted General-Interest Tours

Escorted tours are structured group tours, with a group leader. The price usually includes everything from airfare to hotels, meals, tours, admission costs, and local transportation. **Connections for 18 to 35's** (call Australian Pacific Touring ℗ **800/ 290-8687** in the U.S.; Goway ℗ **800/387-8850** in Canada; or the main office ℗ **1800/077 251** or 07/3839 7877 in Australia; www. connections1835.com.au), and **Contiki** (℗ **888/CONTIKI** in the U.S.; 800/268-1835 in Canada; 020/8290 6777 in the U.K.; 09/309 8824 in New Zealand; or 02/9511 2200 in Australia; www.contiki.com) specialize in escorted tours for 18- to 35-year-olds. These trips attract a lot of Australians, too, so they are a good way to meet locals. Australian company **Connections for 18 to 35's** also does a Connections Plus range of active holidays for people of any age. **Premier Vacations** (℗ **800/321-6720** in the U.S. and Canada; www.premierdown under.com) is another reliable escorted tour operator.

Many people derive a certain ease and security from escorted trips. Escorted tours—whether by bus, motor coach, train, or boat—let travelers sit back and enjoy their trip without having to spend lots of time behind the wheel. All the little details are taken care of; you know your costs up front; and there are few surprises. Escorted tours can take you to the maximum number of sights in the minimum amount of time with the least amount of hassle—you don't have to sweat over the plotting and planning of a vacation schedule. Escorted tours are particularly convenient for people with limited mobility.

On the downside, an escorted tour often requires a big deposit up front, and lodging and dining choices are predetermined. As part of a cloud of tourists, you'll get little opportunity for serendipitous interactions with locals. The tours can be jam-packed with activities, leaving little room for individual sightseeing, whim, or adventure—plus they also often focus only on the heavily touristed sites, so you miss out on the lesser-known gems.

Before you invest in an escorted tour, ask about the **cancellation policy:** Is a deposit required? Can they cancel the trip if they don't get enough people? Do you get a refund if they cancel? If *you* cancel? How late can you cancel if you are unable to go? When do you pay in full? *Note:* If you choose an escorted tour, think strongly about purchasing trip-cancellation insurance, especially if the tour operator asks you to pay up front. See the section on "Travel Insurance," earlier in this chapter.

You'll also want to get a complete **schedule** of the trip to find out how much sightseeing is planned each day and whether enough time has been allotted for relaxing or wandering solo.

The **size** of the group is also important to know up front. Generally, the smaller the group, the more flexible the itinerary, and the less time you'll spend waiting for people to get on and off the bus. Find out the **demographics** of the group as well. What is the age range? What is the gender breakdown? Is this mostly a trip for couples or singles?

Discuss what is included in the **price.** You may have to pay for transportation to and from the airport. A box lunch may be included in an excursion, but drinks might cost extra. Tips may not be included. Find out if you will be charged if you decide to opt out of certain activities or meals.

Finally, if you plan to travel alone, you'll need to know if a **single supplement** will be charged and if the company can match you up with a roommate.

14 The Active Traveler

Australia's wide-open spaces and great weather cry out to even the most dedicated lazybones. Most operators and outfitters listed below specialize in adventure vacations for small groups. Meals, accommodations, equipment rental, and guides are usually included in their packages, though international airfares are not. Where you end up spending the night varies depending on the package you select—on a sea-kayaking trip you almost always camp on the beach; on a hiking expedition you may stay at a wilderness lodge, and on a biking trip you often stop over at B&B-style lodgings. More information on the outdoor activities discussed below is contained in the relevant regional chapters. *Tip:* Before you hit the outdoors, review the safety tips in the "Insurance, Health & Safety" section earlier in this chapter.

SCUBA DIVING

Diving Down Under is one of the best travel experiences in the world. There are good dive sites all around the coastline, not just on the Great Barrier Reef. A second barrier reef in Ningaloo Reef Marine Park stretches 260km (161 miles) off the coast of Western Australia. (See chapter 9 or Exmouth Diving Centre's website at www.exmouthdiving.com.au for a good description of dive sites there.) Not all the good sites are on coral. In Tasmania, for instance, you can dive kelp beds popular with seals, and in South Australia you can cage-dive with great white sharks. For a rundown on the country's outstanding dive areas, see "The Best Diving & Snorkeling Sites," in chapter 1.

Wherever you find coral in Australia, you'll find dive companies offering learn-to-dive courses, day trips, and, in some cases, extended journeys on live-aboard vessels. Most international dive certificates, including PADI, NAUI, SSI, and BSAC, are recognized. It's easy to rent gear and wet suits wherever you go, or you can bring your own.

Beginners' courses are known as "open-water certification" and usually require 2 days of theory in a pool at the dive company's premises, followed by 2 or 3 days on a live-aboard boat where you make between four and nine dives, including a night dive if you opt for the 5-day course. Open-water certification courses range from an intensive 3 to 5 days, for which you can expect to pay between about A$350 and A$600 (US$228–US$390). A 5-day course is seen as the best. When comparing the value offered by dive schools, keep in mind that if the practical section of your course does not take place on a live-aboard boat, you will have to budget for accommodations and meals. Most operators offer courses right up to instructor level. If you're pressed for time, a PADI Referral course might suit you. It allows you to do your theory work at home, do a few hours of pool work at a PADI dive center in your home country, and then spend 2 or 3 days in the Australian ocean doing your qualifying dives. Remember to allow time in your itinerary for a medical exam in Australia (see the next paragraph), and expect the dive instructor to grill you on your theory again before you hit the water.

If you're already a certified diver, remember to bring your "C" card and log book. If you're going to do a dive course, you'll need a medical certificate from an Australian doctor that meets Australian standard AS4005.1, stating that you are fit for scuba diving. (An all-purpose physical is not enough.) Virtually all dive schools will arrange the medical exam for you; expect to pay around A$50 (US$33) for it. Remember, you must complete your last dive 24 hours before you fly in an aircraft. This catches a lot of people off guard when they are preparing to fly on to their next destination the day after a visit to the Reef. You won't be able to helicopter off the Reef

back to the mainland, either. Check to see if your travel insurance covers diving. **The Divers Alert Network** (© 800/446-2671; www.diversalert network.org) sells diving insurance and has diving and nondiving medical emergency hot lines, and an information line for dive-related medical questions.

If you've never been diving and don't plan to become qualified, you can see what all the fuss is about on an "introductory" dive that lets you dive in the company of an instructor on a one-time basis, with a briefing before-hand. Most dive operators on the Great Barrier Reef and other dive locations offer introductory dives.

See "Exploring the Great Barrier Reef" in chapter 6 for more information.

For information on dive regions and operators, try the state tourism marketing boards' websites (see "Visitor Information," earlier this chapter). Tourism Queensland's website (www. queensland-holidays.com.au; click the "Special Interests" tab) links to most dive operators working the Great Barrier Reef. If you know where you want to dive, you may obtain an even more detailed list of operators by bypassing the big tourism boards and contacting the local tourist office for a list of local dive operators. **Dive Queensland** (the Queensland Dive Tourism Association; © 07/4051 1510; fax 07/4051 1519; www.dive-queensland.com.au) requires its member operators to abide by a code of ethics. Its website has a list of members and the services they offer. It includes a few in other states, too. Another good source is **Diversion Dive Travel & Training** (© 07/ 4039 0200; www.diversionoz.com), a

---

⌒Tips Peak Time on the Reef

August through January is peak visibility time on the Great Barrier Reef, but the marine life will amaze you any time of year.

Cairns-based travel agent that specializes in dive holidays on the Great Barrier Reef, as well as in other good dive spots in Australia. It books day trips and extended diving excursions on a choice of live-aboard vessels, as well as dive courses, island resorts with diving, accommodations, and non-diving tours. It also sells diving insurance. Its proprietors are both dive instructors, and one of them is trained as a Handicapped Diving Instructor for divers with disabilities.

Peter Stone's Dive Australia is a 608-page guidebook to more than 2,000 dive sites all over Australia. It by no means lists every site, but it does contain many sites off the dive-tourist trail (many not on the Great Barrier Reef), so divers in search of new territory may find it handy. It also contains a lot of background such as dive operators and associations, a chapter on Australian diving law, the nearest hyperbaric chambers, and travel tips. Order from the publisher, Oceans Enterprises (© 03/5182 5108; www. oceans.com.au). The book costs A$36 (US$23) plus postage.

BUSHWALKING (HIKING)

With so much unique scenery and many rare animals and plants, it's not surprising Australia is full of national parks crisscrossed with hiking trails. You're never far from a park with a bushwalk, whether it's an easy stroll, or a 6-day odyssey on the Cape-to-Cape trail in Western Australia.

A good Australian bushwalking Web page is at www.bushwalking.org. au. However, the best place to get information about bushwalking is the National Parks & Wildlife Service, or its equivalent in each state; sources include:

- **Environmental Protection Agency** (QLD Parks & Wildlife Service; © 07/3227 7111; www. epa.qld.gov.au).

- **NSW National Parks & Wildlife Service** (© 02/9585 6444 administration; www.npws.nsw. gov.au). It has a visitor information center at 110 George St., The Rocks, Sydney (© 02/9247 5033).
- **Parks & Wildlife Commission of the Northern Territory** (© 08/8999 5511; www.nt.gov. au/ipe/pwcnt). The Northern Territory Tourist Commission (see "Exploring the Red Centre," in chapter 7) is the official dispenser of information on parks and wildlife matters.
- **Parks Victoria** (© 13 19 63; www.parkweb.vic.gov.au).
- **South Australian Department for Environment and Heritage** (© 08/8204 1910; www.denr.sa. gov.au).
- **Tasmania Parks and Wildlife Service** (© 1300/135 513; www. dpiwe.tas.gov.au).
- **Western Australian Department of Conservation and Land Management** (CALM; © 08/9334 0333; www.calm.wa.gov.au).

Some parks charge an entry fee, often ranging from A$6 to A$18 (US$3.90–US$12).

MORE ACTIVE VACATIONS FROM A TO Z

ABSEILING Rappelling is another name for this sport that involves backing down vertical cliff faces on a rope and harness. The rugged, beautiful Blue Mountains near Sydney are Australia's abseiling capital. In the Margaret River region in Western Australia, you can do it as mighty breakers crash on the cliffs below. You can even do it in the heart of Brisbane on riverside cliffs.

BIKING Much of Australia's countryside is flat and ideal for cycling, as Aussies call biking, but consider the heat and vast distances before setting

---

(Fun Fact **Something Different: Camel Trekking**

Camels Down Under? You bet. Australia has one of the world's largest camel populations, and even exports racing camels to the Middle East. Camels were imported to negotiate waterless deserts in the 1900s but were later set free. They are now a popular way to trek the country. Short rambles of an hour or two in Alice Springs and at Ayers Rock are a novel way to see the Outback, or you can join extended camel treks through Outback deserts offered by a number of operators. Several companies in Broome lead guided rides along beautiful Cable Beach.

---

out. There are plenty of biking trails. The rainforest hills behind Cairns hosted the world mountain-biking championships in 1996, and Sydney's Blue Mountains have good mountain-biking trails. On Rottnest Island off Perth, it's the only mode of transport from one coral-filled bay to the next. All major towns and most resort centers rent regular bikes and mountain bikes.

If you're interested in taking an extended trip, you may find a copy of *Cycling Australia: Bicycle Touring Throughout the Sunny Continent,* by Australian Ian Duckworth (Motorbooks, 1996) useful. This 224-page guide outlines short trips and eight long trips with maps and route descriptions. Any bookstore can order it, or it is available for US$2.55 from the Adventurous Traveler Bookstore (✆ 800/282-3963 in the U.S. and Canada; www.adventuroustraveler. com), or for £9.95 from the Quayside Bookshop in the United Kingdom (✆ 01626/77 5436; quaybooks@aol. com).

Remote Outback Cycle Tours (✆ 08/9279 6969; www.cycletours. com.au) takes novice and expert riders, young and old, on extended tours across the country. The distances are vast, but the trip is combined with four-wheel-drive travel. Itineraries include the Red Centre, the historic Oodnadatta Track cattle-driving route from Alice Springs to Adelaide via the underground opal-mining town of Coober Pedy in South Australia, and from Adelaide to Perth across the Nullarbor Plain desert and through the pretty Margaret River wine region in southern Western Australia.

BIRD-WATCHING Australia's unique geography as an island continent ensures it has species you won't see anywhere else. It is probably best known for its brilliant parrots, but you will see species from the wetlands, savanna, mulga scrub, desert, oceans, dense bushland, rainforest, mangroves, rivers, and other habitats. More than half of the country's species have been spotted in the Daintree Rain Forest area in north Queensland, and one third live in wetlands-rich Kakadu National Park in the Top End. The Coorong in South Australia and Broome in the Top End are home to marvelous waterfowl populations.

To get in touch with bird-watching clubs all over Australia, contact **Birds Australia** (✆ 03/9882 2622; www. birdsaustralia.com.au).

Kirrama Wildlife Tours (✆ 07/ 4065 5181; www.gspeak.com.au/ kirrama) operates birding expeditions to remote regions in northern Australia from a base in north Queensland. Broome-based ornithologist George Swann of **Kimberley Birdwatching, Wildlife & Natural History Tours** (✆ 08/9192 1246; www. kimberleybirdwatching.com.au) leads extended birding trips throughout the

Kimberley and the Northern Territory. Fine Feather Tours (© **07/4094 1199;** www.finefeathertours.com.au) based near Port Douglas near the Daintree Rain Forest, operates bird-watching day trips and afternoon river cruises.

CANOEING & SEA KAYAKING Katherine Gorge in the Northern Territory offers some spectacular flat canoeing. You'll find delightful canoeing on the bird-rich Ord River in the Top End. Katherine Gorge and the Ord are full of generally harmless freshwater crocodiles, but *never* canoe in saltwater-crocodile territory. White-water canoeing can be found in Barrington Tops National Park north of Sydney.

A growing number of operators all around the coastline rent kayaks and lead guided expeditions. Popular spots are the Whitsunday Islands in north Queensland, the cold southern seas around Tasmania, and Byron Bay, where you can take a 3-hour "dolphin kayaking" trip to see wild dolphins (and whales June–Oct) and "kayak-surf" the waves.

Rivergods (© **08/9259 0749;** www.rivergods.com.au) conducts multiday sea kayaking, canoeing, and white-water-rafting adventures throughout Western Australia's pristine ocean and rivers, in which whales, sharks, dugongs (manatees), sea snakes, turtles, and dolphins abound. They also run a "sea kayak with wild seals" day outing from Perth. **Gecko Canoeing** (© **08/8972 2224;** www.geckocanoeing.com.au) leads canoeing trips of 1 to 21 days from Katherine along remote Top End rivers between April and September.

CAVING Australia doesn't have a lot of caves, but the ones it has are spectacular. The best spots are the Blue Mountains west of Sydney, and the Margaret River region in southwest Western Australia. For tourists who want to see caves and stay clean and safe (as opposed to spelunkers), the best caves are the spectacular Jenolan Caves in the Blue Mountains, a honeycomb of caverns bursting with intricate stalactites and stalagmites; and the 350 limestone caves in Margaret River, of which five are open to the public. Two are "adventure caves," which any novice caver (as opposed to an experienced spelunker) can explore on a 2- or 3-hour tour. You can also go caving at Olssen's Capricorn Caverns, near Rockhampton, in Central Queensland.

FISHING   Reef, game, deep sea, beach, estuary, and river fishing—Australia's massive coastline lets you do it all. Drop a line for coral trout on the Great Barrier Reef; go for the world record black marlin off Cairns; hook a fighting "barra" (barramundi) in the Northern Territory or the Kimberley; or cast for trout in Tasmania's highland lakes. Charter boats will take you out for the day from most towns all around the coast.

GOLF   Australians are almost as passionate about golf as they are about football and cricket—after all, Greg Norman started life as an Aussie! Queensland has the lion's share of the most stunning resort courses, such as the Sheraton Mirage in Port Douglas, Laguna Quays Resort near the Whitsundays, and the Hyatt Regency Sanctuary Cove Resort on the Gold Coast. The Gold Coast has more than 40 courses. Joondaloop Country Club in Western Australia was voted Number One Resort Course in Australia by *Golf Australia* magazine for 2003. One of the world's best desert courses is at Alice Springs.

Most courses rent clubs for around A$30 (US$20). Greens fees start at around A$20 (US$13) for 18 holes but average A$65 (US$42) or more on a championship course. **Koala Golf** (© **02/9980 9073;** www.koalagolf.com) offers escorted day trips and package tours to excellent golf courses in major cities and holiday areas around Australia. It has offices in Sydney, Melbourne, Brisbane, Perth, Cairns, and Queensland's Gold and Sunshine coasts.

HORSEBACK RIDING Horseback-riding operators are everywhere in Australia. A particularly pleasant vacation is a multiday riding and camping trek in "The Man from Snowy River" country in the Snowy Mountains in New South Wales.

SAILING The 74 islands of the Whitsundays in Queensland are an out-of-this-world backdrop for sailing. And you don't have be an expert sailor—the Whitsunday region is Australia's "bareboating" capital. Bareboating means you can charter an unskippered yacht and sail yourself. Even those without a scrap of experience can do it, although it's best to have someone on board who knows aft from fore. Perth and Sydney are mad about sailing; experienced sailors can head to the nearest yacht club to offer themselves as crew, especially during summer twilight races. The clubs are often short of sailors and most will welcome out-of-towners.

SURFING You'll have no trouble finding a good surf beach along the Australian coast. Perth and Sydney are blessed with loads right in the city. Other popular spots include the Gold and Sunshine Coasts in Queensland, the legendary Southern Ocean swells along Victoria's southern coast, and magnificent sets off Margaret River in Western Australia. Don't take your board much north of the Sunshine Coast—the Great Barrier Reef puts a stop to the swell from there all the way to the northern tip of Queensland. Loads of companies rent surf gear. Beginner's lessons are offered at many surf beaches. Remember, surf only at patrolled beaches and never surf alone.

WHITE-WATER RAFTING The best rapids are the Class V torrents on the Nymboida and Gwydir rivers behind Coffs Harbour in New South Wales. More Class V rapids await you on the Johnstone River in north Queensland, although they must be accessed by helicopter. Loads of tourists who have never held a paddle hurtle down the Class III to IV Tully River or the gentler Class II to III Barron River on a day trip from Cairns. The Snowy River National Park in Victoria and the Franklin River in the wilds of Tasmania are other popular spots. See also "Canoeing & Sea Kayaking," above.

AUSTRALIA-BASED OUTFITTERS & OPERATORS

The Adventure Company (© 888/ **SNORKEL** or 720/494-1530 in the U.S., or 07/4051 4777; www. adventures.com.au) runs day and extended trips that incorporate all kinds of activities—hiking, biking, canoeing, rafting, snorkeling, kayaking, scuba diving, sailing, balloon flights, and four-wheel-driving— mostly on the Great Barrier Reef and in the Daintree Rain Forest and other wilderness areas in North Queensland. The company is based in Cairns.

Auswalk (© 02/6457 2220; www. auswalk.com.au) offers self drive or escorted accommodated walking tours through picturesque parts of Australia such as the Great Ocean Road in Victoria, tropical Magnetic Island in Queensland, and the Fraser Island wilderness.

Tasmanian Expeditions (© 03/ 6334 3477; www.tas-ex.com) conducts day trips and extended expeditions featuring hiking, cycling, rafting, abseiling, canoeing, sea kayaking, and rock-climbing throughout Tasmania's national parks and unspoiled rural areas.

World Expeditions (© 415/989- 2212 in the U.S., 020/8870 2600 in the U.K., 09/368 4161 in New Zealand, or 02/9279 0188 or 1300/720 000 in Australia; www.worldexpeditions.com.au) runs expeditions in many parts of Australia, including to places less traveled such as Hinchinbrook Island in the Great Barrier Reef Marine Park, and the long-distance Bibbulmun Track in Western Australia's Southwest. Some trips incorporate other pursuits like rafting, sailing, or biking.

U.S.-BASED OUTFITTERS & OPERATORS

The **Great Outdoor Recreation Pages (GORP)** site at www.gorp.com not only has links to adventure-tour operators to Australia, but also contains articles, sells books and maps, and has links to heaps of sites on Australia with an action slant.

Adventure Express (② 800/443-0799 or 206/441-3482) sells diving packages and custom-built itineraries on the Great Barrier Reef.

Outer Edge Expeditions (② 800/322-5235 or 517/552-5300; www.outer-edge.com) and **The World Outdoors** (② 800/488-8483 or 303/413-0938; www.theworldoutdoors.com) both offer ecologically minded multisport diving, hiking, mountain-biking, canoeing, and kayaking packages to the Great Barrier Reef and North Queensland rainforest.

15 Getting Around Australia

Lesson number one: You won't be able to see Uluru (Ayers Rock) from your Sydney hotel room window. It's 2,841km (1,761 miles) away. Possibly the biggest mistake tourists make Down Under (apart from getting horribly sunburned) is failing to comprehend the distances between popular locations. Another of the urban legends that grew up around the 2000 Olympics was the tale of the tourist who asked where in Sydney Harbour he could catch the boat to the Great Barrier Reef. That's a mere 2,800km (1,736 miles) north. Don't try to cram too much into your trip.

Traveling overland may make sense in Europe or North America, but in Australia flying is the best way between most points. People who go by train, bus, or car are often disappointed at Australia's flat vistas of desert, wheat fields, and gum trees—the same landscape can go on for days. A good compromise is to take to the air for long trips and save the land travel for short hops of a few hours. Try not to backtrack, which eats up valuable time and money.

BY PLANE

Australia is a big country with a small population to support its air routes. Airfares are high. This section contains some tips to help you save.

Most domestic air travel is operated by **Qantas** (② 800/227-4500 in the U.S. and Canada, 0845/7747 767 in the U.K., 09/357 8900 in Auckland, 0800/808 767 in New Zealand, and 13 13 13 in Australia; www.qantas.om.au). You may get a cheaper fare with the no-frills airline **Virgin Blue** (② 13 67 89 in Australia, or 07/3295 2296; www.virginblue.com.au). Virgin flies to every capital, as well as Cairns, Townsville, Mackay, Rockhampton, Gold Coast and Sunshine Coast, all in Queensland, Coffs Harbour in New South Wales, and Launceston in Tasmania. Because its network is growing, Virgin may have added more cities by the time you read this.

Australia's air network is not as well developed as that of North America or Europe, so don't assume there is a direct flight to your chosen destination, or that there is a flight every hour or even every day. *Note:* All flights in Australia are nonsmoking.

FARES FOR INTERNATIONAL TRAVELERS Qantas typically offers international travelers a discount of around 30% off the full fares that Australians pay for domestic flights bought within Australia. To qualify, quote your passport number and international ticket number when reserving. Don't assume the fare for international travelers is the best deal, though—the latest deal in the market that day (or even better, perhaps, a package deal with accommodations thrown in) may be cheaper still.

AIR PASSES If you are planning on whipping around to more than one city, purchasing a Qantas **Boomerang Pass** is much cheaper than buying regular fares. You must buy the minimum-size pass before you arrive in Australia and it can be extended to other cities once you get there; residents of Australia and New Zealand cannot purchase them.

With Qantas's Boomerang Pass, for example, you must purchase a minimum of two coupons (with a maximum of 10) priced at different fares depending on where you travel, and whether the flights are in high demand. Fares are A$260 (US$169) or A$300 (US$195) per coupon for travel within one zone, or A$330 (US$215) or A$390 (US$254) per coupon for travel between zones. The difference between the higher and lower fares depends on the availability of seats, so your coupons may cost the lower or higher amount depending on the day you buy them and how many seats are available on the flight you book.

Passes are a great value when you consider that a fully-flexible one-way fare from Melbourne to Cairns—a (2,254km) 1,400-mile, 2-hour journey—is around A$530 (US$345), compared with the Boomerang pass fare of A$260 (US$169).

Coupons are also good for travel to and from New Zealand and to the most popular South Pacific nations, and can also be used with Air Pacific. Zone 1 covers Western Australia; Zone 2 covers the Red Centre and Darwin; Zone 3 covers major towns in South Australia, Tasmania, Victoria, New South Wales, and Queensland; and Zone 4 covers many small towns in the east coast states, including island gateways like Hayman Island, Hamilton Island, and Gladstone. You must book your first two coupon destinations before you arrive, but you can book the rest as you go by phoning or calling in to any Qantas office. Another great thing about these fares is that they are changeable and the unused portion is refundable; you will incur an A$50 (US$33) fee to change destinations after the coupons have been issued. Many small towns and short flight sectors, some island resorts, and some airports served by subsidiaries of Qantas are not covered by the passes, but most times you can find local fares to these places which are just as good a value as the Boomerang pass, and passes will still get you to loads of places.

AERIAL TOURS The great thing about aerial touring is that it allows you to whiz around the vast Australian continent to see many highlights, and you get to skip all the featureless countryside that typically separates Australia's most fascinating bits. Much of the landscape is best seen from the air, anyhow (such as the weird Bungle Bungles formations in the Kimberley). **Aircruising Australia** *✈* (*©* **02/9693 2233;** www.aircruising.com.au) operates upscale aerial tours of 8 to 13 days in a private aircraft, usually a 40-passenger Fokker Friendship, which is nimble enough to "flight-see" at a low 150m (500 ft.). One factor you may regard as a plus is that the company mainly markets within Australia, so your fellow passengers are likely to be Aussies. Perhaps because the tours are expensive for Australians, most passengers are over 55. Those who have taken these tours recommend them, saying they are extremely well organized, with lots of time for the land-based sightseeing, some free time, and a maximum 2 hours in the air most days. Accommodations are usually the best available, and the itineraries include "fun extras." Fares in 2003 for a 12-day Great Australian Aircruise around the Outback, departing from Sydney, were A$9,994 to A$10,450 (US$6,496–US$6,792) per person, twin-share, **depending on the season.** The **Captain's Choice** Tour (© **1800/650 738;** www.captains choice.com.au) offers a program of air tours through some of Australia's best-known outback towns, traveling aboard a beautifully restored 24-seat historic Douglas DC-3 airliner. In 2003, two "Back of Beyond" tours operated between Sydney and North Queensland in alternate directions.

A typical tour includes stops at Broken Hill, Australia's biggest inland city, where visits include a local gallery featuring "The Brushmen of the Bush," Australian painters including Pro Hart and Jack Absalom; 2 nights in South Australia's Flinders Ranges, including a Mountain Tops four-wheel-drive tour; a scenic flight over Lake Eyre, sometimes a massive salt pan, and sometimes an inland sea after heavy rains; the Queensland Outback towns of Birdsville, Longreach, and Winton, where "Waltzing Matilda" was written; Undara, home of the longest lava tube system in the world; Cape York, 400m (1,312 ft.) from the northernmost tip of Australia; and a short cruise across the Torres Strait to Thursday Island. Two Top End tours, from North Queensland to Darwin, with a 3-day East Timor extension, are also available. The 10-night tours are priced from A$8,985 (US$5,840) per person, twin-share.

You may not think of Antarctica as part of your Australian vacation, but **Antarctica Sightseeing Flights** (© **1800/633 449** in Australia, or 03/ 9725 8555; www.antarcticaflights. com.au) offers once-in-a-lifetime visits to the icy continent. The 12-hour journey offers spectacular viewing over the frozen beauty of Antarctica— a truly memorable experience that comes at a high price for a day trip. Flights are seasonal (Nov–Feb, including a New Year's Eve flight), with most leaving from Sydney or Melbourne, with connections from Brisbane and Adelaide. The tours have been running for 9 years, operated by Croydon Travel with chartered Qantas jumbo jets carrying 350 passengers. You reach the Antarctic coastline after about 4 hours flying and spend the next 4 hours above some of the world's most pristine and spectacular territory. Below are magnificent glaciers, mountain ranges, soaring coastal cliffs, and ice floes. There's no problem viewing all this, despite the fact that you might not have a window seat—everyone moves around and takes turns, and a rotating seating system works well. In 2003 and 2004, fares ranged from A$899 (US$584) in economy to A$4,499 (US$2,924) in first class— but this is unlike any other flight you've been on.

BY TRAIN

Australia's trains are clean, comfortable, and safe, and for the most part service standards and facilities are perfectly adequate. The rail network in Australia links Perth to Adelaide, and continues on to Melbourne and north to Canberra, Sydney, Brisbane, and right up the coast to Cairns. There's also a line from Adelaide to Alice Springs and Darwin, and some rural towns, such as Broken Hill, also have rail services. Trains generally cost more than buses, but are still reasonably priced. The exceptions are two trains promoted as "experiences" rather than a mere mode of transport—the *Indian Pacific* and *The Ghan* (described below)—that can be frightfully expensive.

Most long-distance trains have sleepers with big windows, air-conditioning, electric outlets, wardrobes, hand basins, and fresh sheets and blankets. First-class sleepers have en-suite bathrooms, and meals are often included. Second-class sleepers use shared shower facilities, and meals are not included. Some second-class sleepers are private cabins; on other trains you share with strangers. Single cabins are usually of broom-closet dimensions but surprisingly comfy and have their own toilet and basin. The food ranges from mediocre to pretty good. Smoking is usually banned, or allowed only in the club cars or special "smoking rooms."

Australia's rail routes are managed either by the private enterprise **Great Southern Railway** (© **13 21 47** in Australia, or 08/8213 4592; www.gsr.com.au), which runs the *Indian Pacific,* the *Overland,* and *The Ghan,* or by one of the following government bodies: **Traveltrain,** the long distance train division of Queensland Rail (© **13 22 32** in Australia; www.traveltrain.qr.com.au), which handles rail within that state; **Countrylink** (© **13 22 32** in Australia; www.countrylink.nsw.gov.au), which manages travel within New South Wales and from Sydney to Canberra, Melbourne, and Brisbane; and **WAGR** (Western Australian Government Railways; © **13 10 53** in Western Australia, or 08/9229 2065; www.wagr.wa.gov.au), which operates trains in Western Australia.

Outside Australia, the umbrella organization Rail Australia (www.rail australia.com.au) handles inquiries and makes reservations for all long-distance trains, with the exception of WAGR, through its overseas agents: **ATS Tours** (© **310/643 0044**) in the U.S.; **Goway** (© **416/322 1034**) in Canada; **International Rail** (© **0871/ 201 606**) in the U.K.; and **Tranz Scenic** (© **03/339 3809**) in New Zealand.

Great Southern Railway's *Indian Pacific* ☞ is a glamorous train linking Sydney, Broken Hill, Adelaide, and Perth in a 3-day Outback run twice a week. Slightly less posh but still comfortable, *The Ghan* (named after Afghani camel trainers who traveled the Outback in the 19th century) travels between Sydney, Melbourne, Adelaide, and Alice Springs twice a week, with connections from Sydney and Perth on the Indian Pacific and from Melbourne on the Overland. With the opening of a new rail line linking Alice Springs and Darwin, expected in early 2004, the iconic train will operate one weekly return service between Adelaide and Darwin and twice weekly return services between Adelaide and Alice Springs. Both *The Ghan* and the *Indian Pacific* offer a choice of economy seats and second- or first-class sleepers.

Great Southern Railway's third train, the *Overland,* provides a more prosaic journey between Adelaide and Melbourne twice a week. Countrylink runs daily trains from Sydney to Melbourne, Canberra, and Brisbane, and to a number of New South Wales country towns.

Queensland Rail's Traveltrain operates two trains on the Brisbane–Cairns route: *The Sunlander* runs twice a week from Brisbane to Cairns offering a choice of the premium, all-inclusive Queenslander Class; single, double or triple berth sleepers; or economy seats. Two services also run as far as Townsville on this route without Queenslander Class. The high-speed *Tilt Train* operates three weekly trips on the same route in less time—by about 8 hours—with business-class–style seating. Tilt Trains also service Rockhampton daily from Brisbane. Traveltrain also operates trains to Outback towns. All Traveltrain and most Countrylink long-distance trains stop at most towns en route, so they're useful for exploring the eastern states.

PACKAGES Great Southern Railway, Countrylink, and Queensland Rail Traveltrain (see above) offer rail packages that include accommodations and sightseeing.

RAIL PASSES National, East Coast, New South Wales, Queensland and Great Southern Railway rail passes are available from Rail Australia (see above) at its overseas agents. National passes must be bought before you arrive and are available only to holders of non-Australian passports. East Coast (Melbourne-Sydney-Brisbane-Cairns) and Queensland passes can be purchased before or after you arrive in Australia. Passes are not valid for first-class travel but upgrades are available.

The national **Austrail Flexipass** is good for economy seats and second-class sleepers on all long-distance trains (except WAGR services in Western Australia) and is even good for suburban city train networks. It allows you to travel for any 8, 15, 22, or 29 days, consecutive or not, within a 6-month period. An 8-day Flexipass is A$560 (US$364), with the price going up to A$1,570 (US$1,021) for a 29-day Flexipass. *Note:* You cannot use the 8-day pass on the *Indian Pacific* or *The Ghan,* meaning not on the Adelaide-Perth or on the Sydney–, Melbourne–, or Adelaide–Alice Springs routes.

BY BUS

Bus travel in Australia is a big step up from the low-rent affair it can be in the United States. Terminals are centrally located and well lit, the coaches are clean and air-conditioned, you sit in adjustable seats, videos are shown on board, and the drivers are polite and sometimes even point out places of interest along the way. Some buses even have restrooms. Unlike Australia's train service, there are few places the extensive bus network won't take you. Buses are all nonsmoking.

Australia has two national coach operators: **Greyhound Pioneer Australia** (© 13 20 30 in Australia, or 07/4690 9888; www.greyhound.com. au; no relation to Greyhound in the U.S.) and **McCafferty's** (© 13 14 99 in Australia, or 07/4690 9888; www. mccaffertys.com.au). McCafferty's owns Greyhound Pioneer, hence the same telephone number, above. While the coach lines operate as separate brands with their own networks, passes are combined and can be used interchangeably on either network. The coaches and service standards of both companies are virtually identical. The only real difference between them is that McCafferty's does not travel in Western Australia, while Greyhound Pioneer does (although McCafferty's reservations offices can book your travel in Western Australia aboard Greyhound Pioneer buses, anyhow).

Neither bus company operates within Tasmania; however, McCafferty's provides a booking and transfer service from Melbourne across the Bass Strait aboard the *Spirit of Tasmania* ferry to connect with one of Tasmania's Redline Coaches. As well as point-to-point services, both coach companies offer a limited range of tours at popular locations on their networks. McCafferty's/Greyhound Pioneer has many international agents, including **Inta-Aussie South Pacific** (© 310/568-2060) in the U.S., **Goway** (© 800/387-8850) in Canada, and **Bridge the World** (© 020/7911 0900) in the United Kingdom.

BUS PASSES Bus passes are a great value. There are several kinds—Day passes, Pre-set Itinerary passes, and Kilometre passes. Look into the one that suits you best. Note that even with a pass, you may still need to book the next leg of your trip 12 or 24 hours ahead as a condition of the pass, and in school vacation periods, which are always busy, booking as much as 7 days ahead may be smart.

The **Aussie Day Pass** is good for 7, 10, 15, 21, or 30 days of travel, consecutive or not, within a 1- to 2-month period depending on how many days you buy. The pass is valid for unlimited travel, and backtracking is allowed. Fares range from A$781 (US$508) for a 7-day pass to A$1,879 (US$1,221) for a 30-day pass.

Greyhound Adventures (© 1800/ 800 260 in Australia; www.greyhound adventures.com.au) has packages that can be tailor-made to combine bus travel with accommodations, some meals, and an "adventure" component.

SAMPLE TRAVEL TIMES & BUS FARES

Here are some sample bus fares and travel times, to give you an idea of what you're getting yourself into as you step aboard. All fares and travel times are one-way.

Route	Travel Time (Approx.)	Fare
Broome-Darwin	27 hr.	A$255 (US$166)
Sydney-Brisbane	17 hr.	A$93 (US$60)
Cairns-Brisbane	29 hr.	A$192 (US$125)

Note: Fares and some passes will be considerably cheaper if you're a student, a senior, a backpacker cardholder, or a Hostelling International/YHA member.

If you know where you are going and are willing to obey a "no back-tracking" rule, consider an **Aussie Explorer** predetermined itinerary pass. These passes allow unlimited stops in a generous time frame on a preset one-way route (you are permitted to travel the route in either direction). There is a huge range of itineraries to choose from. As an example, the **Aussie Reef and Rock** pass takes in Alice Springs, Katherine, Darwin, Mt. Isa, Cairns, and the whole east coast down to Sydney. The pass is valid for 6 months and costs A$1,106 (US$719) from Sydney including tours to Ayers Rock, Kakadu National Park, and Kings Canyon. You don't have to start in Sydney; you can start at any point along any of the pass routes, in which case the pass may be cheaper. In the case of the Reef and Rock pass that means you could start further up the track at Brisbane (in which case the pass costs A$1,022/US$664), or Cairns (from where the pass costs A$682/US$443). McCafferty's does

not serve Western Australia, so if you want a pass that covers the whole country, go for Greyhound Pioneer's All Australian Pass for A$2,403 (US$1,561); it's valid for a year.

The **Aussie Kilometre Pass** allows unlimited stops in any direction within the mileage you buy. Passes are available in increments of 1,000km (620 miles). Prices range from A$321 (US$209) for 2,000km (1,240 miles)—enough to get you from Cairns to Brisbane—to A$2,258 (US$1,467) for a whopping 20,000km (12,400 miles).

BY CAR

Australia's roads sometimes leave a bit to be desired. The taxes of 19 million people get spread pretty thin when it comes to maintaining roads across a continent. Most highways are two-lane affairs with the occasional rut and pothole, often no outside line markings, and sometimes no shoulders to speak of.

When you are poring over the map of Australia, remember that what looks like a road may be an unsealed (unpaved) track suitable for four-wheel-drive vehicles only. Many roads in the Top End are passable only in the Dry Season (about Apr–Nov). If you plan long-distance driving, get a road map (see below for sources) that marks paved and unpaved roads.

You cannot drive across the middle of the country (except along the north-south Stuart Highway linking Adelaide and Darwin) because most of it is desert. In most places you must travel around the edge on Highway 1. The map inside the back cover of this book marks the major highways.

You can use your current driver's license or an international driver's permit in every state of Australia. By law you must carry your license with you when driving. The minimum driving age is 16 or 17, depending on which state you visit, but some car-rental companies require you to be 21, or sometimes 26, if you want to rent a four-wheel-drive vehicle.

CAR RENTALS

Think twice about renting a car in tourist hot spots such as Cairns. In these areas most tour operators pick you up and drop you back at your hotel door, so having a car may not be worth the expense.

The "big four" car-rental companies all have networks across Australia:

- **Avis** (© **13 63 33** in Australia, www.avis.com.au; 800/230-4898 in the U.S., www.avis.com; 800/72-5871 in Canada; 08700/100 287 in the U.K. and Ireland, www.avis.co.uk; 0800/655-111 in New Zealand, www.avis.co.nz)
- **Budget** (© **1300/362 848** in Australia, www.budget.com.au; 800/527-0700 in the U.S., www.budget.com; 800/268-8900 in Canada, www.budget.ca; 0035/9032 7711 in the U.K., www.budget-uk.com; 903/ 27711 in

Ireland, www.budget-ireland.com; 0800/652 227 in New Zealand, www.budget.co.nz)
- **Hertz** (© **13 30 39** in Australia, www.hertz.com.au; 800/654-3131 in the U.S., www.hertz.com; 800/263-0600 in English or 800/263-0678 in French in Canada, or 416/620-9620 in Toronto, www.hertz.ca; 020/7026 0077 in the U.K., www.hertz.co.uk; 1/676 7476 in Ireland; 0800/654 321 in New Zealand)
- **Thrifty** (© **1300/367 227** in Australia, www.thrifty.com.au; 800/THRIFTY [847-4389] in the U.S. and Canada, www.thrifty.com; 01494/751 600 in the U.K., www.thrifty.co.uk; 1800/51 5800 in Ireland, www.thrifty.ie; 0800/73 7070 in New Zealand, www.thrifty.co.nz)

Two other large companies with offices around Australia are:

- **Europcar** (© **1300/13 13 90** in Australia or 03/9330 6160, www.deltaeuropcar.com.au; 877/940 6900 in the U.S. and Canada; 1132/422 233 in the U.K., www.europcar.co.uk; 1/614 2800 in Ireland, www.europcar.ie; 1800/556 680 in New Zealand). Europcar has the third largest fleet in Australia.
- **Red Spot Car Rentals** (© **1300/668 810** in Australia, or 02/9317 5771; www.redspotrentals.com.au). It has depots in Sydney, Melbourne, Brisbane, and Cairns, and about 25 other outlets, mainly in New South Wales and Victoria.

SAMPLE DRIVING DISTANCES & TIMES

Here are a few sample road distances between popular points and the minimum time it takes to drive between them.

Route	Distance	Approx. Driving Time
Cairns-Sydney	2,495km (1,547 miles)	29 hr. (allow 4–5 days)
Sydney-Melbourne	873km (541 miles)	15 hr. (allow 1–2 days)
Sydney-Perth	4,131km (2,561 miles)	51 hr. (allow 6–7 days)
Adelaide-Darwin	3,024km (1,875 miles)	31 hr. (allow 4–6 days)
Perth-Darwin	4,163km (2,581 miles)	49 hr. (allow 6–8 days)

A small sedan for zipping around a city or touring a wine region will cost from about A$45 to A$80 (US$29–US$52) a day. A feistier vehicle with enough grunt to get you from state to state will cost around A$70 to A$100 (US$46–US$65) a day. Rentals of a week or longer usually reduce by A$5 (US$3.25) a day or so.

A regular car will get you to most places in this book, but because the country has a high number of unpaved roads, it can make sense to rent a four-wheel-drive vehicle. All of the major car-rental companies rent them. They are more expensive than a regular car but you can get them for as little as A$75 (US$49) per day if you shop around, cheaper for rentals of a week or longer.

The rates quoted here are only a guide. Many smaller local companies, and the big guys, too, do competitive specials, especially in tourist areas with distinct off-seasons. Advance purchase rates, usually 7 to 21 days, can offer significant savings.

INSURANCE Insurance for loss of, or damage to, the car, and third-party property insurance are usually included, but read the agreement carefully, because the fine print contains information the front-desk staff may not tell you. For example, damage to the car body may be covered, but not damage to the windshield or tires, or damage caused by water or driving too close to a bushfire.

The deductible, known as "excess" in Australia, on insurance may be as high as A$2,000 (US$1,300) for regular cars and up to A$5,500 (US$3,575) on four-wheel-drives and

motor homes. You can reduce it, or avoid it altogether, by paying a premium of between about A$17 to A$47 (US$11–US$31) per day on a car or four-wheel-drive, and around A$25 to A$47 (US$16–US$31) per day on a motor home. The amount of the excess reduction premium depends on the vehicle type and the extent of reduction you choose. Your rental company may bundle personal accident insurance and baggage insurance into this premium. And again, check the conditions; some excess reduction payments do not reduce excesses on single-vehicle accidents, for example.

ONE-WAY RENTALS Australia's distances often make one-way rentals a necessity, for which car-rental companies can charge a hefty penalty amounting to hundreds of dollars. A one-way fee usually applies to motor-home renters, too—usually around A$200 to A$220 (US$130–US$143), more for remote outback areas such as Broome and Alice Springs. And there's a 7-day rental minimum.

MOTOR HOMES Motor homes (Aussies also call them camper vans) are popular in Australia. Generally smaller than the RVs in the United States, they come in two-, three-, four-, or six-berth versions, and usually have everything you need, such as a minifridge/freezer (icebox in the smaller versions), microwave, gas stove, cooking and cleaning utensils, linens, and touring information including maps and campground guides. All have showers and toilets, except some two-berthers. Most have

---

⎛Tips⎞ Insurance Alert

Damage to a rental car caused by an animal (hitting a kangaroo, for instance) is not covered by car-rental companies' insurance policies, nor is driving on an unpaved road—and Australia has a lot of those.

---

air-conditioned driver's cabins, but not all have air-conditioned living quarters, a necessity in most parts of the country November through March. Four-wheel-drive campers are available, but tend to be small and some lack hot water, toilet, shower, and air-conditioning. Minimum driver age for motor homes is usually 21.

Australia's biggest national motor-home-rental companies are **Apollo Motorhome Holidays** (© 1800/777 779 in Australia, or 07/3260 5466; www.apollocamper.com), **Britz Campervan Rentals** (© 1800/331 454 in Australia, or 03/8379 8890; www.britz. com), **Hertz Campervans** (© 1800/ 33 5888 in Australia, or 08/8271 8281; www.hertzcampervans.com.au), and **Maui** (© 1300/363 800 in Australia, or 03/8379 8891; www.maui-rentals.com).

Frustratingly, most local councils take a dim view of "free camping," the practice of pulling over by the roadside to camp for the night. Instead, you will likely have to stay in a campground.

For a two-berth motor home with shower and toilet, Britz's 2003/2004 rates range from A$114 and A$230 (US$74–US$150) per day, over a 5- to 20-day rental period. For a four-berth with shower and toilet over the same period, you are looking at between A$211 and A$297 (US$137–US$193) per day. Rates vary with the seasons. May and June are the slowest months; December and January are the busiest. It's sometimes possible to get better rates by booking in your home country before departure. Renting for longer than 3 weeks knocks around A$15 (US$9.75) off the daily rate. Most

companies will demand a minimum 4- or 5-day rental. Give the company your itinerary before booking because some routes, such as the ferry across to Tasmania, or in a four-wheel-drive motorhome's case, the Gibb River Road in the Kimberley, may need the company's permission. Companies may not permit you to drive their two-wheel-drive motor home on unpaved roads; Apollo, Britz and Hertz do not, while Maui does allow two-wheel-drive campers to travel on unsealed access roads to recognized campgrounds.

ON THE ROAD

GAS   The price of petrol (gasoline) will elicit a cry of dismay from Americans and a whoop of delight from Brits. Prices go up and down, but roughly, you're looking at around A90¢ a liter (or US$2.20 per U.S. gallon) for unleaded petrol in Sydney, and A$1.20 a liter (or US$2.45 per U.S. gallon), or more, in the Outback. One U.S. gallon equals 3.78 liters. Most rental cars take unleaded gas, and motor homes run on diesel, which costs around A90¢ to A$1.20 a liter (US$2.20–US$2.45 per U.S. gallon), depending on your location.

DRIVING   RULES   Australians drive on the left, which means you give way to the right. Left turns on a red light are not permitted unless a sign says so.

Roundabouts (traffic circles) are common at intersections; approach these slowly enough to stop if you have to, and give way to all traffic on the roundabout. Flash your indicator as you leave the roundabout (even if you're going straight, as technically that's a left turn).

The only strange driving rule is Melbourne's requirement that drivers turn right from the left lane at certain intersections in the city center. This allows the city's trams to carry on uninterrupted in the right lane. Pull into the left lane opposite the street you are turning into, and make the turn when the traffic light in the street you are turning into becomes green. These intersections are signposted. The maximum permitted blood alcohol level when driving is 0.05%, which equals approximately two 200-milliliter (6.6 fl. oz.) drinks in the first hour for men, one for women, and one drink per hour for both sexes after that. The police set up random breath-testing units (RBTs) in cunningly disguised and unlikely places all the time, so getting caught is easy. You will face a court appearance if you do.

The speed limit is 50kmph (31 mph) or 60kmph (37 mph) in urban areas and 100kmph (62 mph) or 110kmph (68 mph) in most country areas. Speed-limit signs are black numbers circled in red on a white background.

Drivers and passengers, including taxi passengers, must wear a seat belt at all times when the vehicle is moving forward, if a belt is fitted in the car. Young children are required to sit in the rear seat in a child-safety seat or harness; car-rental companies will rent these to you, but be sure to book them. Tell the taxi company you have a child when you book a cab so that they can send a car with the right restraints.

MAPS The maps published by the state automobile clubs listed below in "Auto Clubs" will likely be free if you are a member of an affiliated auto club in your home country. None will mail them to you overseas; pick them up on your arrival. Remember to bring your auto-club membership card to qualify for discounts or free maps.

Two of the biggest map publishers in Australia are **HEMA Maps** (© 07/3340 0000; www.hemamaps.com.au) and **Universal Press** (© 1800/021 987 in Australia, or 02/9857 3700; www.universalpress-online.com). Both publish an extensive range of national, state, regional, and city maps. HEMA has a strong list of regional maps ("Gold Coast and Region" and "The Red Centre" are just a few), while Universal produces a complete range of street directories by city, region, or state under the "UBD" and "Gregory's" labels. HEMA produces four-wheel-drive and motorbike road atlases and many regional four-wheel-drive maps—good if you plan to go off the trails—an atlas of Australia's national parks, and maps to Kakadu and Lamington national parks.

Both companies produce a range of national road atlases. Universal's UBD *Motoring Atlas of Australia* helpfully publishes street maps of small regional towns in each state. HEMA publishes a national road atlas on CD. As Australia is such as big country, a national atlas is good for overall trip planning and long-distance or interstate journeys, but sometimes of limited use on day trips or short journeys because it is not detailed enough. Then, you may find it worthwhile to purchase a map to the local area—say, a "Cairns to Cooktown" map if you wanted to explore Cairns, Kuranda, Port Douglas, and other towns within an hour or two's drive of Cairns.

HEMA and Universal Press maps are distributed in the United States by **Map Link** (© 800/962-1394; www.maplink.com). HEMA Maps are also distributed in Canada, by **ITMB** (International Travel Maps and Books: © 604/879-3621; www.itmb.com) and in the U.K. by Estate Publications (© 01580/76 4225; www.estatepublications.co.uk).

In Australia, auto clubs (see below), bigger newsdealers, and bookstores are your best source of maps. Gas stations stock a limited range relating to their location, and visitor information centers sometimes stock a range of maps to the area and the whole state.

ROAD SIGNS   Australians navigate by road name, not road number. The easiest way to get where you're going is to familiarize yourself with the major towns along your route and follow the signs toward them.

AUTO CLUBS   Every state and territory in Australia has its own auto club. Your auto association back home probably has a reciprocal agreement with Australian clubs, which may entitle you to free maps, accommodations guides, and emergency roadside assistance. Don't forget to bring your membership card.

Even if you're not a member, the clubs are a good source of advice on local traffic regulations, touring advice, road conditions, traveling in remote areas, and any other motoring questions you may have. They sell maps, accommodations guides, and camping guides to non-members at reasonable prices. You can drop into numerous regional offices as well as the head office locations listed here.

- **New South Wales & ACT: National Roads and Motorists' Association (NRMA),** 74–76 King St. (at George St.), Sydney, NSW 2000 (ℭ **13 21 32** in New South Wales, or 02/9848 5201).
- **Victoria: Royal Automobile Club of Victoria (RACV),** 550 Princes Hwy., Noble Park, VIC 3174 (ℭ **13 19 55** in Australia, or 03/9790 2211). A more convenient city office is located at 422 Little Collins St., Melbourne.
- **Queensland: Royal Automobile Club of Queensland (RACQ),** 300 St. Pauls Terrace, Fortitude Valley, QLD 4006 (ℭ **13 19 05**

in Australia, or 07/3872 8456). A more convenient city office is in the General Post Office building at 261 Queen St., Brisbane (ℭ **07/3872 8465**).
- **Western Australia: Royal Automobile Club of WA (RAC),** 228 Adelaide Terrace, Perth, WA 6000 (ℭ **13 17 03**).
- **South Australia: Royal Automobile Association of South Australia (RAA),** 41 Hindmarsh Sq., Adelaide, SA 5000 (ℭ **08/8202 4600**).
- **Northern Territory: Automobile Association of the Northern Territory (AANT),** 79–81 Smith St., Darwin, NT 0800 (ℭ **08/8981 3837**).
- **Tasmania: Royal Automobile Club of Tasmania (RACT),** corner of Murray and Patrick streets, Hobart, TAS 7000 (ℭ **13 27 22** in Tasmania, or 03/6232 6300).

All these clubs can be accessed on www.aaa.asn.au.

ROAD CONDITIONS & SAFETY

Here are some common motoring dangers and ways to avoid them:

FATIGUE   Fatigue is a killer on Australia's roads. The rule is to take a 20-minute break every 2 hours, even if you don't feel tired. In some states, "driver reviver" stations on major roads are set up during holiday periods. They serve free tea, coffee, and cookies, and are often at roadside picnic areas that have restrooms.

KANGAROOS & OTHER WILDLIFE   It's a sad fact, but kangaroos are a road hazard. Avoid driving between dusk and dawn in country areas, because this is when 'roos are most active. If you hit one, always stop and check its pouch for live joeys (baby kangaroos), because females usually have one in the pouch. Wrap the joey tightly in a towel or old sweater, don't feed or overhandle it, and take it to a vet in the nearest town or call one of the following wildlife care groups: **Wildlife Information & Rescue Service (WIRES)** in New South Wales (© 02/8977 3333); **Wildlife Victoria** (© 0500/540 000 or 03/9663 9211); **Wildlife Rescue** in Queensland (© 0418 792 598); **RSPCA Wildlife** in the ACT (© 02/ 6287 8100 or 0413/495 031); **FAWNA Inc.** in Western Australia (© 08/9753 2118); **Wildlife Rescue** in the Northern Territory (© 08/8999 4536); **Fauna Rescue of S.A.** (© 08/ 8289 0896) in South Australia; or **Wildcare** in Tasmania (© 03/6233 6556). Most vets will treat native wildlife for free.

Some highways run through unfenced stations (ranches), where sheep and cattle pose a threat. Cattle like to rest on the warm bitumen road at night, so put your lights on high to spot them. If an animal does loom up, slow down but never swerve or you may roll, and, if you have to, hit it. Tell ranchers within 24 hours if you have hit their livestock.

Car-rental companies will not insure for animal damage to the car, which should give you an inkling of how common an occurrence this is.

ROAD TRAINS Road trains consist of as many as three big truck carriages linked together to make a "train" up to 54m (177 ft.) long. If you're in front of one, give them plenty of warning when you brake, because they need a lot of distance to slow down. Allow at least 1 clear kilometer (over ½ mile) before you pass one, but don't expect the driver to make it easy—"truckies" are notorious for their lack of concern for motorists.

UNPAVED ROADS Many country roads are unsealed (unpaved). They are usually bone-dry, which makes them more slippery than they look, so travel at a moderate speed—35kmph (22 mph) is not too cautious and anything

over 60kmph (37 mph) is dangerous. Don't overcorrect if you veer to one side. Keep well behind any vehicles because the dust they throw up can block your vision.

FLOODS Floods are common in the Top End and north of Cairns November or December through March or April (the wet season). Never cross a flooded road unless you are sure of its depth. Crocodiles may be in the water, so do not wade in to test it! Fast-flowing water is dangerous, even if very shallow. When in doubt, stay where you are and wait for the water to drop, because most flash floods subside in 24 hours. Check the road conditions ahead at least once a day in the wet season.

RUNNING OUT OF GAS Gas stations (also called "roadhouses" in rural areas) can be few and far between in the Outback, so fill up at every opportunity.

WHAT IF YOUR VEHICLE BREAKS DOWN?

Warning: If you break down or get lost, never leave your vehicle. Many a motorist, often an Aussie who should know better, has died wandering off on a crazy quest for help or water, knowing full well that neither is to be found for maybe hundreds of miles. Most people who get lost do so in Outback spots; if that happens to you, conserve your body moisture by doing as little as possible and staying in the shade of your car. Put out distress signals in patterns of three—three yells, three columns of smoke, and so on. The traditional Outback call for help is "Coo-*ee*," with the accent on the "ee" and yodeled in a high pitch; the sound travels a surprisingly long way.

The state auto clubs listed above provide free breakdown emergency assistance to members of many affiliated automobile associations around the world.

EMERGENCY ASSISTANCE

The emergency breakdown assistance telephone number for every Australian auto club is ℭ **13 11 11** from anywhere in Australia. It is billed as a local call. If you are not a member of an auto club at home that has a reciprocal agreement with the Australian clubs, you'll have to join the Australian club on the spot before they will tow/repair your car. This usually costs only around A$80 (US$52), not a big price to pay when you're stranded (although in the Outback, the charge may be considerably higher). Most car-rental companies also have emergency assistance numbers.

TIPS FOR FOUR-WHEEL DRIVERS

Always keep to the four-wheel-drive track, as going off-road causes soil erosion, a significant environmental problem in Australia. Leave gates as you found them. Obtain permission from the owners before venturing onto private station (ranch) roads. On an extended trip or in remote areas, carry 5 liters (1.3 gal.) of drinking water per person per day (dehydration occurs fast in the Australian heat); enough food to last 3 or 4 days more than you think you will need; a first-aid kit; spare fuel; a jack and two spare tires; spare fan belts, radiator hoses, and air-conditioner hoses; a tow rope; and a good map that marks all gas stations. In seriously remote areas outside the scope of this book, carry a high-frequency and CB radio. (A cellphone may not work in the Outback.) Advise a friend, your hotel manager, the local tourist bureau, or a police station of your route and your expected time of return or arrival at your destination.

16 Tips on Accommodations

Accommodations properties in Australia are given a star rating by AAA Tourism, which has been awarding ratings since the 1950s. This independent assessment is based on facilities, amenities, maintenance, and cleanliness, and awards between one and five stars. Stars are featured in AAA Tourism guides, and recent research shows 70% of travelers use the star ratings when choosing their accommodations (these star ratings are noted below using asterisks). The rating scheme covers over 18,000 accommodations throughout every state and territory.

* Offers a basic standard of accommodations, simply furnished, with a resident manager.

** Similar standard to one star but offers more comfort and value with additional features. These are well-maintained properties offering an average standard of accommodations with average furnishings, bedding, and floor coverings.

*** Well appointed, with a comfortable standard of accommodations, above average furnishings and floor coverings.

**** Exceptionally well-appointed establishments with high quality furnishings, a high degree of comfort, high standard of presentation, and guest services.

***** International standard establishments offering superior appointments, furnishings, and decor, with an extensive range of first class guest services. Reception, room service, and housekeeping available 18 hours a day with restaurant/bistro facilities available 7 nights a week. A number and variety of room styles and/or suites are available. Choice of dining facilities, 24-hour room service, housekeeping, and valet parking. Porter and concierge service available as well as a dedicated business center and conference facilities.

Note: All accommodations listed in this book have private bathrooms unless otherwise noted.

HOTELS   It's a rare hotel room that does not have reverse-cycle air-conditioning for heating and cooling, a telephone, a color TV, a clock radio, a minifridge if not a minibar, an iron and ironing board, and self-serve tea and coffee. Private bathrooms are standard, although they often have only a shower, not a tub. The largest hotel group in Australia is the French chain Accor, which has more than 100 properties (that's about 15,000 rooms) under its Sofitel, Novotel, Mercure and All Seasons, Ibis, and Formule 1 brands.

Many other international chains, such as Marriott, Sheraton, and Hilton, have properties in Australia.

SERVICED APARTMENTS   Serviced apartments are favored by many Aussie families and business travelers. You get a fully furnished apartment with one, two, or three bedrooms, a living room, a kitchen or kitchenette, a laundry, and often two bathrooms—in other words, all the facilities of a hotel suite and more, often for less than the cost of a four-star hotel room. A nice two-bedroom apartment will usually cost anywhere from around A$165 to A$255 (US$130–US$455) a night, depending on your location and the season. (Not every apartment kitchen has a dishwasher, so check if that's important to you.) Australia's apartment inventory is enormous and ranges from clean and comfortable, if a little dated, to luxurious. Most apartments can be rented for 1 night, especially in cities, but in popular vacation spots, some proprietors will insist on a minimum 3-night stay, or even a week in high season.

Medina Serviced Apartments (*©* **1300/300 232** in Australia, or 02/ 9356 1000; www.medinaapartments. com.au) has a chain of midrange to upscale properties in Sydney, Melbourne, Brisbane, Canberra, Adelaide and—beginning in mid-2004—Perth. Australia's biggest apartment chain is the **Quest Serviced Apartments** (*©* **1800/334 033** in Australia, or 03/9645 2566, 0800/944 400 in New Zealand; www.questapartments.com. au). It has four brands: the upscale Quest Establishments, the midrange Quest Inns, Quest Lodgings for longer stays, and Quest Resorts, in every state and territory except the Northern Territory.

MOTELS & MOTOR INNS   Australia's plentiful motels are neat and clean, if often a little dated. You can count on them to provide air-conditioning, a telephone, a color TV, a clock radio, a minifridge or minibar, and self-serve tea and coffee. Most have only showers, not bathtubs. Some have restaurants attached, and many have swimming pools. Motor inns offer a greater range of facilities and a generally higher standard of rooms than motels. Rates average A$70 to A$110 (US$46–US$72) double.

BED & BREAKFAST INNS   B&Bs are cheap and plentiful in Australia. It is easy to find charming rooms for around A$80 (US$52) for a double. Bathroom facilities are often shared, although more properties now offer private, if not always en-suite, bathrooms.

Travel agents rarely list B&Bs because the establishments are not big enough to pay commission, so they can be hard to find. A good source is *The Australian Bed & Breakfast Book* (published by Moonshine Press; *©* **02/9985 8500**), which lists more than 600 B&Bs across Australia. Although the B&Bs pay to be in the book, they have to meet standards required by the editors. The entire book is posted on the Web at www.bbbook.com.au. In Australia, it's widely available in bookshops and newsdealers; you can also order it on www.amazon.com or contact Moonshine Press, which retails it for A$17 (US$11) plus A$10 (US$6.50) for overseas postage.

Orangewood, a Northern Territory B&B, provides an index of Australian B&B directories at this address: http://members.ozemail.com.au/~ora ngewo/owdirdir.htm. **What Next? Productions Pty. Ltd.** (© **03/9537 0833;** www.beautiful accommodation.com) publishes a color guide titled *Beautiful B&Bs & Small Hotels,* 190 exquisite properties in Victoria and Tasmania, many in charming country areas. The properties listed are more upscale than most, roughly in the A$100 to A$200 (US$65–US$130) range. The guide sells for A$30 (US$20) in Australian bookstores and can be ordered online.

PUBS Aussie pubs are really made for drinking, not spending the night, but many offer rooms upstairs, usually with shared bathroom facilities. Because most pubs are decades old, the rooms may be either old-fashioned or just plain old. Pub accommodations are dying out in the cities but still common in the country. Australians are rowdy drinkers, so sleeping over the bar can be hellishly noisy, but the pub's saving grace is incredibly low rates. Most charge per person, not per room, and you will rarely pay more than A$50 (US$33) per person a night.

HOUSE SWAPS Many international visitors to Australia have happily swapped homes with locals using the Internet to find their "perfect match." There is a plethora of sites that you can use to make your search. Two that list up to 100 Australian homes each are www.holi-swaps.com/ swapsau.htm and www.homebase-hols. com. You can browse the listings for free, but it costs around US$37 to view the contact details, or to list your own home.

FARM STAYS The Aussie answer to the dude ranch is a farm stay. Australian farm stays are rarely as well set up for tourists as the dude ranch visited by Billy Crystal's character in *City Slickers.* Most are farms first, tourist operations second, so you may have to find your own fun and know how to take care of yourself, at least to a degree. Accommodations on farms can be anything from a basic bunkhouse (ask if it's air-conditioned, because most farms are in very hot areas) to rustically luxurious digs. Do some research on your farm—a lot of activities are seasonal, some farmers will not allow you to get involved in dangerous work, not all will offer horseback riding, and *farm* means different things in different parts of Australia. If you like green fields and dairy cows, Victoria may be the place for you. If checking fences on a dusty 500,000-hectare (200,000-acre) Outback station (ranch) sounds wildly romantic, head to Western Australia or the Northern Territory.

Australian Farm & Country Tourism (www.farmstaysaustralia.com) is a cooperative marketing organization for farm-stay properties. It has no office, so

---

Tips Meet the People Down Under

If you want to see an Australian Rules football game in the company of a knowledgeable local in Melbourne or swim at Bondi Beach with a Sydneysider, contact **Friends Overseas—Australia** (© **718/261-0534;** www. friendsoverseas.org). This program is designed to match visitors with friendly Aussies of like age and interests, so you can spend time with them. The membership fee is US$25.

your best contact is Farm & Country Tourism Victoria (℃ **1300/132 358** or 03/9614 0892; www.factv.com), which dispenses free brochures, one each for Victoria, New South Wales, Queensland, South Australia, and Western Australia, which detail the accommodations, activities, and rates at a range of farm-stay properties. Rates vary, but you will find many properties charging between A$100 and A$140 (US$65–US$91) for a double, which sometimes includes breakfast. Meals are often available as an optional extra.

SAVING ON YOUR HOTEL ROOM

The **rack rate** is the maximum rate that a hotel charges for a room. Hardly anybody pays this price, however. To lower the cost of your room:

- **Ask about special rates or other discounts.** Always ask whether a room less expensive than the first one quoted is available, or whether any special rates apply to you. You may qualify for corporate, student, military, senior, or other discounts. Mention membership in AAA, AARP, frequent-flier programs, or trade unions, which may entitle you to special deals as well. Find out the hotel policy on children—do kids stay free in the room or is there a special rate?
- **Dial direct.** When booking a room in a chain hotel, you'll often get a better deal by calling the individual hotel's reservation desk than at the chain's main number.
- **Book online.** Many hotels offer Internet-only discounts, or supply rooms to Priceline, Hotwire, or Expedia at rates much lower than the ones you can get through the hotel itself.
- **Remember the law of supply and demand.** Resort hotels are most crowded and therefore most expensive on weekends, so discounts are usually available for midweek stays. Business hotels in downtown locations are busiest during the week, so you can expect big discounts over the weekend. Many hotels have high-season and low-season prices, and booking the day after high season ends can mean big discounts.
- **Look into group or long-stay discounts.** If you come as part of a large group, you should be able to negotiate a bargain rate, since the hotel can then guarantee occupancy in a number of rooms. Likewise, if you're planning a long stay (at least 5 days), you might qualify for a discount. As a general rule, expect one night free after a 7-night stay.
- **Avoid excess charges and hidden costs.** When you book a room, ask whether the hotel charges for parking. Use your own cellphone, pay phones, or prepaid phone cards instead of dialing direct from hotel phones, which usually have exorbitant rates. And don't be tempted by the room's minibar offerings: Most hotels charge through the nose for water, soda, and snacks. Finally, ask about local taxes and service charges, which can increase the cost of a room by 15% or more. If a hotel insists upon tacking on a surprise "energy surcharge" that wasn't mentioned at check-in or a "resort fee" for amenities you didn't use, you can often make a case for getting it removed.
- **Consider the pros and cons of all-inclusive resorts and hotels.** The term "all-inclusive" means different things at different hotels. Many all-inclusive hotels will include three meals daily, sports equipment, spa entry, and other amenities; others may include all or most drinks. In general, you'll save money going the "all-inclusive"

Tips **Dial E for Easy**

For quick directions on how to call Australia, see the "Telephone" listing in the "Fast Facts" section at the end of this chapter or check out the "Telephone Tips" on the inside front cover of the book.

---

way—as long as you use the facilities provided. The down side is that your choices are limited and you're stuck eating and playing in one place for the duration of your vacation.

- **Book an efficiency.** A room with a kitchenette allows you to shop for groceries and cook your own meals. This is a big money saver, especially for families on long stays.

LANDING THE BEST ROOM

Somebody has to get the best room in the house. It might as well be you. You can start by joining the hotel's frequent-guest program, which may make you eligible for upgrades. Always ask about a corner room. They're often larger and quieter, with more windows and light, and they often cost the same as standard rooms. When you make your reservation, ask if the hotel is renovating; if it is, request a room away from the construction. Ask about non-smoking rooms, rooms with views, rooms with twin, queen- or king-size beds. If you're a light sleeper, request a quiet room away from vending machines, elevators, restaurants, bars, and discos. Ask for one of the rooms that have been most recently renovated or redecorated.

If you aren't happy with your room when you arrive, say so. If another room is available, most lodgings will be willing to accommodate you.

In resort areas, particularly in warm climates, ask the following questions before you book a room:

- What's the view like? Cost-conscious travelers may be willing to pay less for a back room facing the parking lot, especially if they don't plan to spend much time in their room.
- Does the room have air-conditioning or ceiling fans? Do the windows open? If they do, and the nighttime entertainment takes place alfresco, you may want to find out when show time is over.
- What's included in the price? Your room may be moderately priced, but if you're charged for beach chairs, towels, sports equipment, and other amenities, you could end up spending more than you bargained for.
- How far is the room from the beach and other amenities? If it's far, is there transportation to and from the beach?

17 Recommended Books & Films

Australian literature has come a long way since the days when the bush poets A. B. "Banjo" Paterson and Henry Lawson penned their odes to a way of life now largely lost. The best known of these is Patterson's epic *The Man from Snowy River* (Buccaneer Books, 1996), which hit the bestseller list in 1895 and was made into a film.

But the literary scene has always been lively, and Australia has a wealth of classics, many of them with the Outback at their heart.

Miles Franklin wrote *My Brilliant Career* (HarperCollins, 2001) in 1901, the story of a young woman faced with the dilemma of choosing between marriage and a career;

Colleen McCullough's *Thorn Birds* (Avon, 1996) is a romantic epic about forbidden love between a Catholic priest and a young woman; *We of the Never Never* (Avon, 1984) by Mrs. Aeneas Gunn, tells the story of a young woman who leaves the comfort of her Melbourne home to live on a cattle station in the Northern Territory; and *Walkabout* (Sundance, 1984) by James V. Marshall explores the relationship between an Aboriginal and two lost children in the bush. It was later made into a powerful film.

If you can find it, *The Long Farewell* (Penguin Books, 1983) by Don Charlwood tells firsthand diary accounts of long journeys from Europe to Australia in the last century. A good historical account of the early days is Geoffrey Blainey's *The Tyranny of Distance* (Pan Macmillan, 1977), first published in 1966. Robert Hughes's *The Fatal Shore: The Epic of Australia's Founding* (Vintage Books, 1988), is a bestselling nonfiction study of the country's early days. For a contemporary, if somewhat dark, take on the settlement and development of Sydney, delve into John Birmingham's

Leviathan (Random House, 1999). From an Aboriginal perspective, *Follow the Rabbit-Proof Fence* (University of Queensland Press, 1997) by Doris Pilkington tells the true story of three young girls from the "Stolen Generation" who ran away from a mission school to return to their families (a movie of the book was released in 2002).

Modern novelists include David Malouf, Elizabeth Jolley, Helen Garner, Sue Woolfe, and Peter Carey, whose *True History of the Kelly Gang* (Vintage Books, 2001), a fictionalized autobiography of the outlaw Ned Kelly, won the Booker Prize in 2001. West Australian Tim Winton evokes his part of the continent in stunning prose, with his latest novel *Dirt Music* (Scribner, 2002) being no exception.

Two outsiders who have tackled Australia include Jan Morris and Bill Bryson. Morris's *Sydney* (Viking) was published in 1992, and Bryson's *In a Sunburned Country* (Broadway Books, 2001), while not always a favorite with Australians, may appeal to American readers.

 FAST FACTS: Australia

American Express For all travel-related customer inquiries regarding any American Express service, including reporting a lost card, call ✆ **1800/230 100**. To report lost or stolen traveler's checks there is a separate line (✆ **1800/251 902**).

Area Codes See "Telephones," later in this section.

ATM Networks See "Money," earlier in this chapter.

Business Hours Banks open Monday through Thursday from 9:30am to 4pm, until 5pm on Friday. General business hours are Monday through Friday from 8:30am to 5:30pm. Shopping hours are usually from 8:30am to 5:30pm weekdays and 9am to 4 or 5pm on Saturday. Many shops close on Sundays, although major department stores and shops in tourist precincts are open 7 days.

Car Rentals See "Getting Around," earlier in this chapter.

Currency See "Money," earlier in this chapter.

Dates Australians write their dates day/month/year; so March 6, 1958, is 06/03/58.

Driving Rules See "Getting Around," earlier in this chapter.

Drugstores These are called "chemists" or "pharmacies." Australian pharmacists are permitted to fill only prescriptions written by Australian doctors.

Electricity The current is 240 volts AC, 50 hertz. Sockets take two or three flat, not rounded, prongs. North Americans and Europeans will need to buy a converter before they leave home (don't wait until you get to Australia, because Australian stores are only likely to stock converters for Aussie appliances to fit American and European outlets). Some large hotels have 110V outlets for electric shavers or dual voltage, and some will lend converters; but don't count on it in smaller, less expensive hotels, motels, or B&Bs. Power does not start automatically when you plug in an appliance; you need to flick the switch located beside the socket to the "on" position.

Embassies & Consulates Most diplomatic posts are in Canberra: **British High Commission,** Commonwealth Avenue, Canberra, ACT 2600 (© 02/6270 6666); **Embassy of Ireland,** 20 Arkana St., Yarralumla, ACT 2600 (© 02/6273 3022); **High Commission of Canada,** Commonwealth Avenue, Yarralumla, ACT 2600 (© 02/6270 4000); **New Zealand High Commission,** Commonwealth Avenue, Canberra, ACT 2600 (© 02/6270 4211); and the **United States Embassy,** 21 Moonah Place, Yarralumla, ACT 2600 (© 02/6214 5600). Embassies or consulates with posts in state capitals are listed in "Fast Facts" in the relevant state chapters of this book.

Emergencies Dial © **000** anywhere in Australia for police, ambulance, or the fire department. This is a free call from public and private telephones and needs no coins. The TTY emergency number is © **106.**

Holidays See "Calendar of Events," earlier in this chapter.

Information See "Visitor Information," earlier in this chapter.

Internet Access Internet access is available just about everywhere, including some of the smallest outback towns, which generally have at least one cybercafe and/or coin-operated machines, which are also available at larger airports. Major tourist towns such as Darwin and Cairns sometimes have whole streets full of cybercafes.

Liquor Laws Hours vary from pub to pub, but most are open daily from around 10am or noon, to 10pm or midnight. The minimum drinking age is 18. Random breath tests to catch drunk drivers are common, and drunk-driving laws are strictly enforced. Getting caught drunk behind the wheel will mean a court appearance, not just a fine. The maximum permitted blood alcohol level is 0.05%. Alcohol is sold only in liquor stores, or in the "bottle shops" attached to every pub, and in some states in supermarkets.

Lost & Found Be sure to contact your credit card companies the minute you discover that your wallet has been lost or stolen and file a report at the nearest police precinct. Your credit card company or insurer may require a police report number or record of the loss. Most credit card companies have an emergency toll-free number to call if your card is lost or stolen; they may be able to wire you a cash advance immediately or deliver an emergency credit card in a day or two. Visa's U.S. emergency number is © 800/847-2911 or 410/581-9994. American Express cardholders and traveler's check holders should call © 800/221-7282. MasterCard holders should call © 800/307-7309 or 636/722-7111. In Australia, call toll-free: **American Express** (© **1800/230 100**), **MasterCard** (© **1800/120 113**), and **Visa** (© **1800/125 440**).

If you need emergency cash over the weekend when all banks and American Express offices are closed, you can have money wired to you via **Western Union** (© 800/325-6000; www.westernunion.com). Identity theft or fraud are potential complications of losing your wallet, especially if you've lost your driver's license along with your cash and credit cards. Notify the major credit-reporting bureaus immediately; placing a fraud alert on your records may protect you against liability for criminal activity. The three major U.S. credit-reporting agencies are **Equifax** (© **800/766-0008**; www.equifax.com), **Experian** (© **888/397-3742**; www.experian.com), and **TransUnion** (© **800/680-7289**; www.transunion.com). Finally, if you've lost all forms of photo ID, call your airline and explain the situation; they might allow you to board the plane if you have a copy of your passport or birth certificate and a copy of the police report you've filed.

Mail A postcard costs A$1 (US65¢) to the United States, Canada, the United Kingdom, or New Zealand.

Maps Newsdealers, auto clubs, and bookstores are your best sources for maps (see "Getting Around," earlier in this chapter).

Newspapers & Magazines The national daily newspaper is *The Australian,* which publishes an expanded edition with a color magazine on Saturdays. Most capital cities have their own daily papers, usually a tabloid and a broadsheet. The Australian current affairs magazine, *The Bulletin with Newsweek,* is published weekly, and there is an Australian edition of *Time.*

Passports **For Residents of the United States:** Whether you're applying in person or by mail, you can download passport applications from the U.S. State Department website at **http://travel.state.gov.** For general information, call the **National Passport Agency** (© **202/647-0518**). To find your regional passport office, either check the U.S. State Department website or call the **National Passport Information Center** (© **900/225-5674**); the fee is US55¢ per minute for automated information and US$1.50 per minute for operator-assisted calls.

For residents of Canada: Passport applications are available at travel agencies throughout Canada or from the central **Passport Office,** Department of Foreign Affairs and International Trade, Ottawa, ON K1A 0G3 (© **800/567-6868**; www.dfait-maeci.gc.ca/passport).

For residents of the United Kingdom: To pick up an application for a standard 10-year passport (5-yr. passport for children under 16), visit your nearest passport office, major post office, or travel agency or contact the **United Kingdom Passport Service** at © **0870/521 0410** or search its website at www.ukpa.gov.uk.

For residents of Ireland: You can apply for a 10-year passport at the **Passport Office,** Setanta Centre, Molesworth Street, Dublin 2 (© **01/671**

1633; www.irlgov.ie/iveagh). Those under age 18 and over 65 must apply for a €12 3-year passport. You can also apply at 1A South Mall, Cork (© 021/272 525) or at most main post offices.

For residents of New Zealand: You can pick up a passport application at any New Zealand Passports Office or download it from their website. Contact the **Passports Office** at © **0800/225 050** in New Zealand or 04/ 474-8100, or log on to www.passports.govt.nz.

Pets Leave 'em at home. You will be back home planning your next vacation before Fluffy clears quarantine Down Under.

Police Dial © **000** anywhere in Australia. This is a free call from public and private telephones and requires no coins.

Safety Violent crime is uncommon, and the political situation is stable. Guns are strictly controlled. Purse snatchers are the same threat they are all over the world. See "Insurance, Health & Safety," earlier in this chapter.

Smoking Smoking in most public areas, such as museums, cinemas, and theaters, is restricted or banned. Increasingly Aussie restaurants are banning smoking (those in Western Australia and New South Wales already ban it), though in many states, restaurants have smoking and nonsmoking sections. Pubs are a territorial victory for smokers; after a night in one, nonsmokers smell as if they smoked a whole pack (which they probably did, secondhand). Most hotels have smoking and nonsmoking rooms. Australian aircraft on all routes are completely nonsmoking, as are all airport buildings.

Taxes Australia applies a 10% tax called Goods and Services Tax (GST) on most products and services. Your international airline tickets to Australia are not taxed, nor are domestic airline tickets for travel within Australia *if you bought them outside Australia*. If you buy more Australian airline tickets once you arrive in Australia, you will pay GST on them.

Through the Tourist Refund Scheme (TRS), Australians and international visitors can claim a refund of the GST (and of a 14.5% wine tax called Wine Equalisation Tax, or WET) paid on a purchase of more than A$300 (US$195) from a single outlet, within the last 30 days before you leave. More than one item may be included in that A$300. For example, you can claim back the GST you paid on 10 T-shirts each worth A$30 (US$20), as long as they were bought from a single store. Do this as you leave by presenting your receipt or "tax invoice," to the Australian Customs Service's TRS booths, located beyond passport control in the International Terminal departure areas at most airports. If you buy several things on different days from one store, which together add up to A$300 or more, you must ask the store to total all purchases on one tax invoice (or receipt)—now there's a nice piece of bureaucracy to remember Australia by! Carry the items in your carry-on baggage, as you must show them to Customs. You can use the goods before you leave Australia and still claim the refund, but you cannot claim a refund on things you have consumed (film you shoot off in the camera, say, or food). You cannot claim a refund on alcohol other than wine. Allow an extra 15 minutes to stand in line at the airport and get your refund.

You can also claim a refund if you leave Australia as a cruise passenger from Circular Quay or Darling Harbour in Sydney, Cairns, Darwin, or

Fremantle (Perth). If your cruise departs from elsewhere in Australia, or if you are flying out from an airport other than Sydney, Melbourne, Brisbane, Adelaide, Cairns, Perth, Darwin, Gold Coast, or Broome, telephone the Australian Customs Service (📞 **1300/363 263** in Australia, or 02/6275 6666) to see if you can still claim the refund.

Items bought in duty-free stores will not be charged GST. Nor will items you export—such as an Aboriginal painting, say, that you buy in a gallery in Alice Springs and have shipped straight to your home outside Australia.

Basic groceries are not GST-taxed, but restaurant meals are.

Other taxes include departure tax of A$38 (US$25) for every passenger 12 years and over, included in the price of your airline ticket when you buy it in your home country; landing and departure taxes at some airports, also included in the price of your ticket; and "reef tax," officially dubbed the Environmental Management Charge, of A$5.50 (US$3.60) for every person over the age of 4 every time he or she enters the Great Barrier Reef Marine Park. (This charge goes toward park upkeep.)

Telephones The primary telecommunications network in Australia is Telstra (www.telstra.com).

To call Australia: If you're calling Australia from the United States:
1. Dial the international access code 011
2. Dial the country code 61
3. Dial the city code (drop the 0 from any area code given in this book) and then the number. So, if you're calling Sydney, the whole number you'd dial would be 011-61-2-0000-0000.

To make international calls: To make international calls from Australia, first dial 0011 and then the country code (U.S. or Canada 1, U.K. 44, Ireland 353, New Zealand 64). Next dial the area code and number. For example, if you wanted to call the British Embassy in Washington, D.C., you would dial 0011-1-202-588-7800. For other country codes, call 📞 **1222** or look in the back of the Australian White Pages.

For directory assistance: Dial 12455 if you're looking for a number inside Australia, and dial 1225 for numbers to all other countries.

For operator assistance: If you need operator assistance in making a call, dial 📞 **1234**. To make a collect call, dial 📞 **12550**. To find a number, call Directory Assistance at 📞 **1223** for numbers in Australia and 📞 **1225** for international numbers.

Toll-free numbers: Numbers beginning with 1800 in Australia are toll-free, but calling a U.S. 1-800 number from Australia is not toll-free; it costs the same as an overseas call.

Other numbers: Numbers starting with 13 or 1300 in Australia are charged at the local fee of A25¢ anywhere in Australia. Numbers beginning with 1900 (or 1901 or 1902 and so on) are pay-for-service lines and you will be charged as much as A$5 (US$3.25) a minute.

Time Zone Eastern Standard Time (EST, also written as AEST sometimes) covers Queensland, New South Wales, the Australian Capital Territory, Victoria, and Tasmania. Central Standard Time (CST) is used in the Northern Territory and South Australia, and Western Standard Time (WST) is the standard in Western Australia. When it's noon in New South Wales, the ACT, Victoria, Queensland, and Tasmania, it's 11:30am in South Australia and the Northern Territory and 10am in Western Australia. All states except Queensland, the Northern Territory, and Western Australia observe daylight saving time, usually from the last Sunday in October (the 1st Sun in Oct in Tasmania) to the last Sunday in March. However, not all states switch over to daylight saving on the same day or in the same week.

The east coast of Australia is GMT (Greenwich Mean Time) plus 10 hours. When it is noon on the east coast, it is 2am in London that morning, and 6pm in Los Angeles and 9pm in New York the previous night. These times are based on standard time, so allow for daylight saving in the Australian summer, or in the country you are calling. New Zealand is 2 hours ahead of the east coast of Australia, except during daylight saving, when it is 3 hours ahead of Queensland.

Tipping Tipping is not expected in Australia. It is usual to tip around 5% or round up to the nearest A$10 (US$6.50) for a substantial meal in a restaurant. Some passengers round up to the nearest dollar in a cab, but it's okay to insist on every bit of change back. Tipping bellboys and porters is sometimes done but no one tips bar staff, barbers, or hairdressers.

Water Water is fine to drink everywhere. In the Outback, the taps may carry warm brackish water from underground called "bore water" for showers and laundry, while drinking water is collected in rainwater tanks.

Sydney

by Marc Llewellyn

Sunny, sexy, and sophisticated, Sydney (pop. 4.1 million) basks in its worldwide recognition as the shining star of the Southern Hemisphere. The "emerald city" is one of the most attractive on earth. Some people compare it to San Francisco—it certainly has that relaxed feel—but the gateway to Australia is far from a clone of an American city.

First, of course, there's the Sydney Opera House, one of the most recognized buildings in the world. This white-sailed construction on Sydney Cove, designed by Danish architect Jørn Utzon, is the pride of the city—but there's far, far more on offer.

For example, you can walk across that other great icon, the Sydney Harbour Bridge, on the pathway beside the trains and traffic and catch the CityRail train back into town. Those with a daredevil spirit can join a Bridge Climb tour venture across catwalks and ladders to the top of the main arch for 360-degree views across the Opera House and the ferries and boats below.

Sydney is one of the biggest cities in the world—but fortunately most of the interesting things are concentrated in a relatively compact area around one of the finest urban harbors in the world.

As it is, there's so much to do in Sydney that you could easily spend a week here and still find yourself crashing into bed at night exhausted by trying to see all the main attractions.

Sydney's greatest summer experience is on the beaches—and with over 20 strung along the city's oceanfront and dozens more around the harbor, you'll be spoiled for choice. The most famous of them all is Bondi, a strip of golden sand legendary for its Speedo-clad lifesavers and surfboard riders. From here a "must do" is the 3.2km (2-mile) coastal path that leads off across the cliff tops, via cozy Tamarama Beach (dubbed "Glamourama" for its chic sun worshippers), to glorious Bronte Beach, where you can cool down again in the crashing waves of the Pacific.

Another beach favorite is Manly, a 30-minute ferry trip from Circular Quay. Pick up some fish and chips and head for the main beach, flanked by a row of giant pines that chatter with hundreds of colorful lorikeets at dusk.

The best time to return is in the early evening, when the lights of the skyscrapers around Circular Quay are streaked like rainbows across the water of the harbor, and the sails of the Opera House and the girders of the Harbour Bridge are lit up—it's magical.

History is enshrined in its many museums and art galleries, while modern Sydney comes alive in the more recent developments around Darling Harbour and the restaurant and entertainment area nearby at Cockle Bay and Kings Wharf. At Darling Harbour you'll find the world-class Sydney Aquarium. You can also start your gourmet tour of Sydney's "Modern Australian" cooking style, which encompasses the best of freshness with spices from the Orient and flavors from the Mediterranean.

Add to all this the side trips to the gorges and cliffs of the Blue Mountains, the wineries of the Hunter Valley, and the dolphin- and whale-watching around Port Stephens (see "Port Stephens: Dolphin- & Whale-Watching" in chapter 4), and you'll see why Sydney gets so much praise.

The frugal traveler will find that, compared to other major international cities, Sydney offers good value for your money. Food and public transport are cheap, and attractions are generally not prohibitively expensive. (Senior and student prices are almost always available if you have identification.) The price of a hotel room is far cheaper than in other major population centers such as New York and London.

1 Orientation

ARRIVING

BY PLANE   Sydney International Airport is 8km (5 miles) from the city center. The international and domestic terminals are separate but linked by free shuttle buses. In both terminals, you'll find luggage carts, wheelchairs, a post office (open Mon–Fri 9am–5pm), mailboxes, currency exchange, duty-free shops (including one before you go through customs on arrival, selling alcohol and perfumes), restaurants, bars, stores, showers, luggage lockers and a Baggage Held Service for larger items, ATMs, and tourist information desks. You can hire mobile phones from the international terminal. There is also a Sydney Visitors Centre Bookings desk (© 02/9667 6050) offering cheap deals on hotels (see "Where to Stay," later in this chapter), as well as offering car rental, phone cards, and maps and brochures. Here you can also buy the SydneyPass (see section 2, "Getting Around") and Airport Express tickets (see below). The airport is efficient, has extremely strict quarantine procedures—you must declare all food— and is completely nonsmoking. On arrival, pick up a copy of *Sydney The Official Guide,* from the rack just before passport control, which contains tear-out discount tickets for some of Sydney's major attractions. Luggage trolleys are free in the arrival terminals, but cost A$2 (US$1.30) outside the departure terminal where you'll need a A$2 coin.

GETTING INTO TOWN   The **Sydney Airport Train Link** connects the international and domestic airports to the city stations of Central, Museum, St. James, Circular Quay, Wynyard, and Town Hall. You'll need to change trains for other Sydney stations. Unfortunately, the line has no dedicated luggage areas and, as it's on a scheduled route into the city from the suburbs, it gets very crowded during rush hours (approximately 7–9am and 4–6:30pm). If you have lots of luggage and you're traveling into the city at these times, it's probably best to take an airport bus (below) or a taxi. Otherwise walk to the end of the platform where there should be more room onboard. There are elevators at the Airport Train Link

---

Tips **Tourist Refund Scheme**

Visitors to Australia are entitled to claim any Goods and Services Tax (GST) on purchases over A$300 (US$195) per store. The GST component is 10% of the sale price. Do this at the refund booth located past Customs. After doing the paperwork—you need to have the goods and receipt with you, not in your checked luggage—you will be refunded by check on the spot. You can convert this to cash at any foreign exchange booth at Sydney Airport.

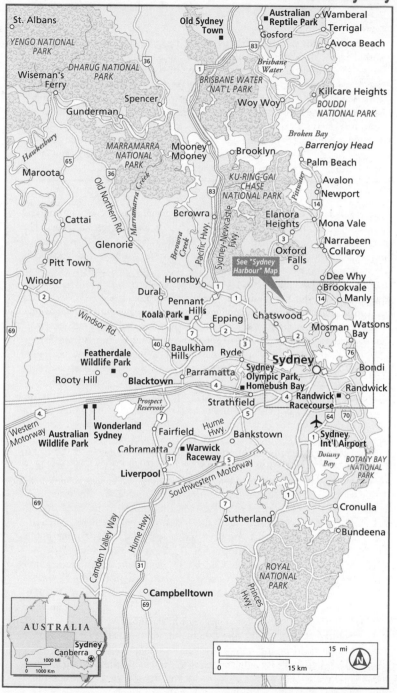

Greater Sydney

St. Albans
YENGO NATIONAL PARK
Wiseman's Ferry
Gunderman
Spencer
DHARUG NATIONAL PARK
36
Old Sydney Town
Australian Reptile Park
Gosford
Wamberal
Terrigal
Avoca Beach
83
Brisbane Water
BRISBANE WATER NAT'L PARK
Woy Woy
Killcare Heights
BOUDDI NATIONAL PARK
Broken Bay
Barrenjoy Head
MARRAMARRA NATIONAL PARK
Mooney Mooney
Brooklyn
Palm Beach
Maroota
65
36
Hawkesbury
Old Northern Rd.
Marramarra Creek
KU-RING-GAI CHASE NATIONAL PARK
83
Avalon
Newport
14
Cattai
Glenorie
Berowra
Elanora Heights
Mona Vale
Berowra Creek
Pacific Hwy.
Sydney-Newcastle Fwy.
3
Narrabeen
Collaroy
Pitt Town
Oxford Falls
Windsor
2
Hornsby
See "Sydney Harbour" Map
Dee Why
Dural
1
Brookvale
Manly
69
Pennant Hills
Koala Park
Epping
1
Chatswood
14
Mosman
Watsons Bay
Windsor Rd.
7
2
2
76
40
Baulkham Hills
Ryde
3
Featherdale Wildlife Park
Sydney
Bondi
Rooty Hill
Blacktown
Parramatta
Sydney Olympic Park, Homebush Bay
Randwick
Prospect Reservoir
4
4
Randwick Racecourse
4.
7
Strathfield
5
Western Motorway
Australian Wildlife Park
Wonderland Sydney
Fairfield
Hume Hwy.
Bankstown
64
70
Cabramatta
Warwick Raceway
Sydney Int'l Airport
1
Liverpool
31
5
Southwestern Motorway
Botany Bay
BOTANY BAY NATIONAL PARK
69
7
1
Cronulla
Sutherland
Bundeena
Camden Valley Way
Hume Hwy.
31
ROYAL NATIONAL PARK
Princes Hwy.
69
Campbelltown

AUSTRALIA
Sydney
Canberra
0   1000 Mi
0   1000 Km

0   15 mi
0   15 km
N

Tips **Taxi Savvy**

Especially in busy periods, taxi queues can be long, and drivers may try to cash in by insisting you share a cab with other passengers in line at the airport. Here's the scam: After dropping off the other passengers, the cab driver will attempt to charge you the full price of the journey, despite the fact that the other passengers paid for their sections. You certainly won't save any money sharing a cab if this happens, and your journey will be a long one. I find it's often better to wait until you can get your own cab, or catch an airport bus to the city center (and then take a taxi from there to your hotel, if necessary). If you are first in line in the taxi rank, the law states that you can refuse to share the cab with anyone else.

---

stations and some at the city train stations (but the crowds and lack of staff and signs mean you'll probably end up lugging it all up loads of steps anyway). The train takes 10 minutes to reach the Central Railway Station and then continues on to Circular Quay. Trains leave every 15 minutes or so and cost A$11 (US$6.90) one-way for adults and A$7.30 (US$4.50) for children, and A$16 (US$11) return for adults (A$14/US$9 off-peak—for travel before 9am weekdays, and all day on weekends and public holidays), and A$11 (US$6.90) for children. Ask about special "Group Fares" for 3 or 4 people traveling together.

Fast and comfortable green-and-yellow **Airport Express buses** travel between the city center and both the international and domestic terminals from 5am to 9:30pm. The buses stop at Central Railway Station, Town Hall, Queen Victoria Building, Wynyard Station, Circular Quay, The Rocks, Kings Cross, and Potts Point before returning to the airport. The **Airport Express** operates every day of the year from approximately 6:30am to 7:50pm, leaving every 20 minutes on Monday to Friday and every 30 minutes on weekends and public holidays. The trip to Circular Quay takes about 45 minutes. One-way tickets cost A$7 (US$4.55) for adults, A$3.50 (US$2.30) for kids under 16, and A$18 (US$11) for families (any number of children). A round-trip ticket costs A$12 (US$7.80) for adults, A$6 (US$3.90) for kids, and A$30 (US$20) for families. You must use the return portion within 2 months.

Buy your tickets from the Airport Express booth outside the airport terminal, or on the bus. Purchase the SydneyPass and the Airport Express transfers are included. The Airport Express buses also travel between the international and domestic terminals every 15 minutes and cost A$3 (US$1.95) for adults, A$1.50 (US95¢) for children, and A$7.50 (US$4.90) for a family.

The **Kingsford Smith Airport Coach** also operates to the city center from bus stops outside the terminals. This service will drop you off (and pick you up) at your hotel (pickups require at least 1 hr. advance notice; call © **02/9667 3221**). Tickets cost A$7 (US$4.55) one-way and A$11 (US$7.15) round-trip. (The return portion can be used at any time in the future.)

The **Bondi Jetbus** (© **0500/886 008** mobile phone; fax 02/9487 3554) will deliver you anywhere on the eastern beaches, including Bondi and Bronte. Tickets are A$10 (US$6.50) for single adult, A$8 (US$5.20) each for two or more, and A$4 (US$2.60) for children. Call when you arrive at the airport, and they'll come pick you up within 15 minutes or less.

A **taxi** from the airport to the city center costs about A$25 (US$16). An expressway, the Eastern Distributor, opened in 2000, is the fastest way to reach the city from the airport. There's a $3.50 (US$2.30) toll from the airport to the city (the taxi driver pays the toll and then adds the cost to your fare), but there is no toll to the airport. A 10% credit card charge applies. *Note:* A dispute with Visa means this credit card isn't accepted by Australian taxis, so make sure you have an alternative card, or get money from the ATM or currency exchange booths at the airport.

BY TRAIN   Central Station (© **13 15 00** for CityRail and 13 22 32 for Countrylink interstate trains) is the main city and interstate train station. It's at the top of George Street in downtown Sydney. All interstate trains depart from here, and it's a major CityRail hub. Many city buses leave from neighboring Railway Square for places like Town Hall and Circular Quay.

BY BUS   The **Greyhound Pioneer Australia terminal** is on the corner of Oxford and Riley streets in Darlinghurst (© **13 20 30** in Australia, or 02/9283 5977). **McCafferty's** (© **13 14 99** in Australia) operates from the **Sydney Coach Terminal** (© **02/9281 9366**) on the corner of Eddy Avenue and Pitt Street, bordering Central Station.

BY CRUISE SHIP   Cruise ships dock at the **Overseas Passenger Terminal** in The Rocks, just opposite the Sydney Opera House, or in Darling Harbour if The Rocks facility is already occupied by another vessel.

BY CAR   Drivers coming into Sydney from the north enter the city on the Pacific Highway, drivers from the south enter the city via the M5 and Princes highways, and those coming from the west enter via the Great Western Highway.

VISITOR INFORMATION

The **Sydney Visitor Centre, 106 George St., The Rocks** (© **02/9255 1788**), is a good place for maps, brochures, and general tourist information, including for towns in New South Wales; it also has two floors of displays on The Rocks. The office is open daily from 9am to 6pm. Also in The Rocks is the **National Parks & Wildlife Centre** (© **02/9247 8861**), in Cadmans Cottage, 110 George St. Elsewhere City Host information kiosks, located near the Town Hall (George St.), at Circular Quay (corner of Pitt and Alfred sts.) and at Martin Place (between Elizabeth and Castlereagh sts.) provide comprehensive information on Sydney. Two more Visitor Centres are located at the International Terminal at the airport and at Darling Harbour. If you want to inquire about destinations and holidays within Sydney or the rest of New South Wales, call **Tourism New South Wales's** help line at © **13 20 77** in Australia.

Electronic information on cinema, theater, exhibitions, and other events can be accessed through **Talking Guides** (© **13 16 20** in Australia). You'll need a code number for each topic, which you can find on page 3 of the A-K section of the *Sydney Yellow Pages.* The service costs the same as a local call.

A good website is **CitySearch Sydney** (www.sydney.citysearch.com.au), for events, entertainment, dining, and shopping.

CITY LAYOUT

Sydney is one of the largest cities in the world by area, covering more than 1,730 sq. km (675 sq. miles) from the sea to the foothills of the Blue Mountains. Thankfully the city center is compact. The jewel in Sydney's crown is its harbor, which empties into the South Pacific Ocean through headlands known simply as North Head and South Head. On the southern side of the harbor are the high rises of the city center; the Sydney Opera House; a string of beaches, including Bondi; and the inner-city suburbs. The Sydney Harbour Bridge and a tunnel connect the city center to the high rises of the North Sydney business district and the affluent northern suburbs and beautiful ocean beaches beyond.

MAIN ARTERIES & STREETS   The city's main thoroughfare, **George Street,** runs up from **Circular Quay** (pronounced key), past Wynyard CityRail station, Town Hall, and to Central Station. A whole host of streets bisect the city parallel to George, including Pitt, Elizabeth, and Macquarie streets. **Macquarie Street** runs up from the Sydney Opera House, past the Royal Botanic Gardens and Hyde Park. **Martin Place** is a pedestrian thoroughfare that stretches from Macquarie to George streets. It's about halfway between Circular Quay and Town Hall—in the heart of the city center. The easy-to-spot **A.M.P. Centerpoint Tower,** facing onto the pedestrian-only **Pitt Street Mall** on Pitt Street, is the main city-center landmark. Next to Circular Quay and across from the Opera House is **The Rocks,** a cluster of small streets that was once city slums but is now a tourist attraction. Roads meet at Town Hall from Kings Cross in one direction and Darling Harbour in the other. From Circular Quay to The Rocks it's a 5- to 10-minute stroll, to Wynyard about 10 minutes, and to Town Hall about 20 minutes.

NEIGHBORHOODS IN BRIEF
South of the Harbour

Circular Quay This transport hub for ferries, buses, and CityRail trains is tucked between the Harbour Bridge and the Sydney Opera House. The Quay, as it's called, is a good spot for a stroll, and its outdoor restaurants and street performers are popular. The Rocks, the Royal Botanic Gardens, the Contemporary Art Museum, and the start of the main shopping area (centered on Pitt and George sts.) are a short walk away. To reach the area via public transport, take a CityRail train, ferry, or city-bound bus to Circular Quay.

The Rocks This small historic area, a short stroll west of Circular Quay, is packed with colonial stone buildings, intriguing back streets, boutiques, pubs, tourist stores, and top-notch restaurants and hotels. It's the most exclusive place to stay in the city because of its beauty and its proximity to the Opera House and harbor. Shops are geared toward Sydney's yuppies and wealthy Asian tourists—don't expect bargains. On weekends a portion of George Street is blocked

off for The Rocks Market, with street stalls selling souvenirs and crafts. To reach the area via public transport, take any bus for Circular Quay or The Rocks (via George St.) or a CityRail train or ferry to Circular Quay.

Town Hall In the heart of the city, this area is home to the main department stores and two Sydney landmarks, the Town Hall and the Queen Victoria Building (QVB). In this area are the A.M.P. Centerpoint Tower (A.M.P. is the name of a local insurance company) and the boutique-style chain stores of Pitt Street Mall. Farther up George Street are major movie houses, the entrance to Sydney's Spanish district (around Liverpool St.), and the city's Chinatown. To reach the area via public transportation, take any bus from Circular Quay via George Street, or take a CityRail train to the Town Hall stop.

Darling Harbour Designed as a tourist precinct, Darling Harbour features Sydney's main convention, exhibition, and entertainment centers; a waterfront promenade; the Sydney Aquarium; the Panasonic

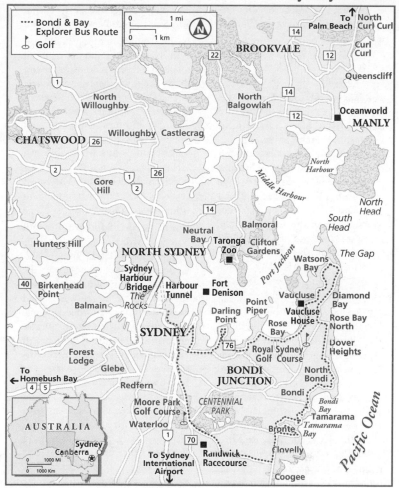

To North
Palm Beach   Curl Curl

BROOKVALE

14

12   Curl
Curl

22

Queenscliff

1

North
Willoughby

North
Balgowlah

14

12   Oceanworld
MANLY

CHATSWOOD   26

Willoughby   Castlecrag

North
Harbour

2

26

1

Gore
Hill

2

14

North
Head

Middle Harbour

South
Head

Neutral
Bay

Balmoral

Taronga
Zoo

Clifton
Gardens

The Gap

Hunters Hill

NORTH SYDNEY

Watsons
Bay

Port Jackson

40   Birkenhead
Point

Sydney
Harbour
Bridge

Harbour
Tunnel

Fort
Denison

Vaucluse

Diamond
Bay

The
Rocks

Point
Piper

Vaucluse
House

Balmain

Darling
Point

Rose
Bay

Rose Bay
North

SYDNEY

76

Dover
Heights

Forest
Lodge

Royal Sydney
Golf Course

North
Bondi

To
← Homebush Bay

4   5

Glebe

BONDI
JUNCTION

Redfern

Bondi

Bondi
Bay

Moore Park
Golf Course

CENTENNIAL
PARK

Tamarama

AUSTRALIA

Waterloo

1

Tamarama
Bay

Sydney
Canberra ⊛

0   1000 Mi
0   1000 Km

70

Bronte

Bronte
Bay

Pacific Ocean

To Sydney
International
Airport
↓

Randwick
Racecourse

Clovelly

Coogee

IMAX Theatre; the Australian Maritime Museum; the Powerhouse Museum; Star City, Sydney's casino; a major food court; and plenty of shops. Nearby are the funky restaurants of Cockle Bay and Kings Wharf. To reach Darling Harbour via public transport, take a ferry from Circular Quay (Wharf 5), the monorail from Town Hall, or the light rail (tram) from Central Station.

Kings Cross & the Suburbs Beyond "The Cross," as it's known, is the city's red-light district—

though it's also home to some of the city's best-known nightclubs and restaurants. The area houses plenty of backpacker hostels, a few bars, and some upscale hotels. The main drag, Darlinghurst Road, is short but crammed with strip joints, prostitutes, addicts, drunks, and such. Also here are cheap e-mail centers that offer discount overseas phone rates. Fortunately, there's a heavy police presence, but do take care. Beyond the strip clubs and glitter, the suburbs of Elizabeth Bay, Double Bay, and Rose Bay hug the waterfront. To reach the area via public transport, take a CityRail train to Kings Cross. From the next train stop, Edgecliff, it's a short walk to Double Bay and a longer one to Rose Bay along the coast.

Paddington/Oxford Street This inner-city suburb, centered on trendy Oxford Street, is known for its expensive terrace houses, off-the-wall boutiques and bookshops, and restaurants, pubs, and nightclubs. It's also the heart of Sydney's large gay community and has a liberal scattering of gay bars and dance spots. To reach the area via public transport, take bus no. 380 or 382 from Circular Quay (via Elizabeth St.); no. 378 from Railway Square, Central Station; or nos. 380 and 382 from Bondi Junction. The lower end of Oxford Street is a short walk from Museum CityRail Station (take the Liverpool St. exit).

Darlinghurst Between grungy Kings Cross and upscale Oxford Street, this extroverted, grimy terraced suburb is home to some of Sydney's best cafes. It's probably not wise to wander around at night. Take the CityRail train to Kings Cross and head right from the exit.

Central The congested and polluted crossroads around Central Station, the city's main train station, has little to recommend it. Buses run from here to Circular Quay, and it's a 20-minute walk to Town Hall. The Sydney Central YHA (youth hostel) is here.

Newtown This popular student area is centered around car-clogged King Street, which is lined with alternative shops, bookstores, and ethnic restaurants. People-watching is the thing to do—see how many belly-button rings, violently colored hairdos, and Celtic arm tattoos you can spot. To reach the area via public transport, take a CityRail train to Newtown Station.

Glebe Young professionals and students come to this inner-city suburb for the cafes, restaurants, pubs, and shops along the main thoroughfare, Glebe Point Road. All this, plus a location 15 minutes from the city and 30 minutes from Circular Quay, makes it a good place for budget-conscious travelers. To reach Glebe, take bus no. 431, 433, or 434 from Millers Point, The Rocks (via George St.), or bus no. 459 from behind Town Hall.

Bondi & the Southern Beaches Some of Sydney's most glamorous surf beaches—Bondi, Bronte, and Coogee—can be found along the South Pacific coastline southeast of the city center. Bondi has a wide sweep of beach (crowded in summer), some interesting restaurants and bars, and plenty of attitude and beautiful bodies—and no CityRail station. To reach Bondi via public transport, take bus no. 380 or 382 to Bondi Beach from Circular Quay—it takes up to an hour—or a quicker alternative is a CityRail train to Bondi Junction to connect with the same buses. Bus no. 378 from Railway Square, Central Station goes to Bronte, and bus no. 373 or 374 travels to Coogee from Circular Quay.

Watsons Bay Watsons Bay is known for The Gap—a section of dramatic sea cliffs—as well as several good restaurants, such as Doyles on the Beach, and the Watsons Bay Hotel beer garden—also run by Doyles. It's a terrific spot to spend a sunny afternoon. To reach it via public transportation, take bus no. 324 or 325 from Circular Quay. There's a limited ferry service daily from Circular Quay (Wharf 2), starting at 10:15am on weekdays, 9:15am on weekends and holidays.

North of the Harbour

North Sydney Across the Harbour Bridge, the high rises of North Sydney attest to its prominence as a major business area. There's little for tourists here, except the possibility of being knocked over on a busy thoroughfare. Chatswood (take a CityRail train from Central or Wynyard stations) has some good suburban-type shopping, and Milsons Point has a decent pub, the Kirribilli Hotel, as well as Luna Park, an ill-fated amusement park that's basically out of action due to wealthy locals who complained the roller coaster was too noisy—you can see the giant smiling clown face from Circular Quay.

The North Shore Ferries and buses provide access to these wealthy neighborhoods across the Harbour Bridge. Gorgeous Balmoral Beach, Taronga Zoo, and upscale boutiques are the attractions in Mosman. Take a ferry from Circular Quay (Wharf 2) to Taronga Zoo—10 minutes—and a bus from there to Balmoral Beach (another 10 min.).

Manly & the Northern Beaches Half an hour away by ferry, or 15 minutes by the faster JetCat, Manly is famous for its ocean beach—it gives Bondi a run for its money—and scores of cheap food outlets. Farther north are more beaches popular with surfers. CityRail train lines do not go to the northern beaches. The farthest beach from the city, Palm Beach, has magnificent surf and lagoon beaches, walking paths, and a golf course. To reach the area via public transport, take the ferry or JetCat from Circular Quay (Wharves 2 and 3) to Manly. Change at Manly interchange for various buses to the northern beaches, nos. 148 and 154 through 159. You can also take bus no. L90 from Wynyard station.

West of the City Center

Balmain West of the city center, a short ferry ride from Circular Quay, Balmain was once Sydney's main ship-building area. In the last few decades the area has become trendy and expensive. The suburb has a village feel to it, is filled with restaurants and pubs, and hosts a popular Saturday market at the local church. Take bus no. 441, 442, or 432 from Town Hall or George Street, or a ferry from Circular Quay (Wharf 5), and then a short bus ride up the hill to the main shopping area.

Homebush Bay Sydney Olympic Park was the main site of the 2000 Olympic Games. You'll find Stadium Australia, the Aquatic Center, and Homebush Bay Information Centre, parklands, and a waterbird reserve. To reach the area via public transport, take a CityRail train from Circular Quay to the Olympic Park station.

2 Getting Around

BY PUBLIC TRANSPORTATION

State Transit operates the city's buses and the ferry network, CityRail runs the urban and suburban trains, and Sydney ferries runs the public passenger ferries. Some private bus lines operate buses in the outer suburbs. In addition, a monorail connects the city center to Darling Harbour and a light rail line (tram) runs between Central Station and Wentworth Park in Pyrmont.

MONEY-SAVING TRANSIT PASSES   Several passes are available for visitors who will be using public transportation frequently—all work out to be much cheaper than buying individual tickets.

Sydney Transportation Systems

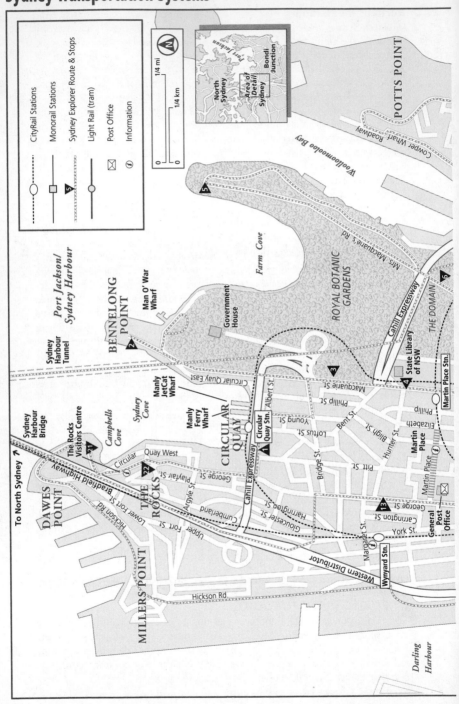

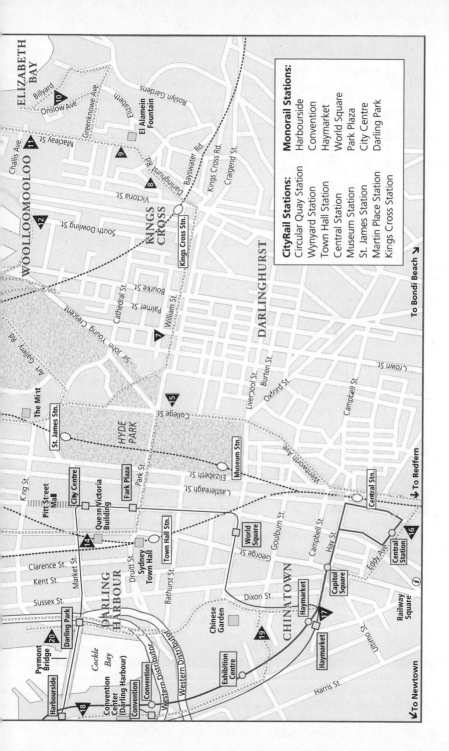

CityRail Stations:
Circular Quay Station
Wynyard Station
Town Hall Station
Central Station
Museum Station
St. James Station
Martin Place Station
Kings Cross Station

Monorail Stations:
Harbourside
Convention
Haymarket
World Square
Park Plaza
City Centre
Darling Park

ELIZABETH BAY

WOOLLOOMOOLOO

KINGS CROSS

DARLINGHURST

HYDE PARK

CHINATOWN

DARLING HARBOUR

Cockle Bay

Billyard
Onslow Ave.
Greenknowe Ave.
Macleay St.
Challis Ave.
Elizabeth
Roslyn Gardens
El Alamein Fountain
Darlinghurst Rd.
Bayswater Rd.
Kings Cross Rd.
Craigend St.
Victoria St.
South Dowling St.
Bourke St.
Palmer St.
Cathedral St.
William St.
Sir John Young Crescent
Art Gallery Rd.
College St.
Liverpool St.
Burton St.
Oxford St.
Crown St.
Campbell St.
Wentworth Ave.
The Mint
St. James Stn.
Park St.
Elizabeth St.
Castlereagh St.
Museum Stn.
King St.
Pitt Street Mall
City Centre
Queen Victoria Building
Park Plaza
Clarence St.
Kent St.
Sussex St.
Market St.
Druitt St.
Bathurst St.
Sydney Town Hall
Town Hall Stn.
George St.
World Square
Goulburn St.
Campbell St.
Hay St.
Central Stn.
Eddy Ave.
Central Station
Railway Square
Dixon St.
Chinese Garden
Haymarket
Capitol Square
Haymarket
Exhibition Centre
Harris St.
Ultimo St.
Western Distributor
Convention Center (Darling Harbour)
Convention
Convention
Darling Park
Pyrmont Bridge
Harbourside
Kings Cross Stn.

To Bondi Beach ➜
➜ To Redfern
↙ To Newtown

99

⟨Tips⟩ Transit Information

For timetable information on buses, ferries, and trains, call **Infoline** at ⓒ **13 15 00** (in Australia) daily from 6am to 10pm. Otherwise check the website for Sydney buses and ferries (www.sydneybuses.nsw.gov.au) or CityRail (www.staterail.nsw.gov.au). Pick up a **Sydney Transport Map** (a guide to train, bus, and ferry services) at any rail, bus, or ferry office.

The **SydneyPass** includes return Airport Express transfers, unlimited travel on Sydney Explorer coaches and Bondi & Bay Explorer coaches, unlimited travel on any or each of four Sydney Harbour cruises (see "What to See & Do in Sydney," later in this chapter), unlimited travel on the JetCat to Manly and the high-speed RiverCat to Parramatta (linking the city center to this important heritage and business center along a historic waterway), and unlimited travel on all Sydney buses, Sydney ferries, and CityRail trains (within the "Red Travel-Pass" travel zone, which includes the entire city center, as well as to Bondi Junction). The SydneyPass costs A$90 (US$59) for adults and A$45 (US$29) for children for 3 days travel over a 7-day period; A$120 (US$78) for adults and A$60 (US$39) for children for 5 days over a 7-day period; and A$140 (US$91) for adults and A$70 (US$45) for children for 7-days' consecutive travel. Family fares are also available. Buy tickets at the Airport Express offices at the airport, the TransitShop at Circular Quay (outside McDonald's), from the Sydney Ferries ticket office (Wharf 4, Circular Quay), and from Explorer bus drivers.

A **Weekly Travel Pass** allows unlimited travel on buses, trains, and ferries. There are six different passes (denoted by color) depending on the distance you need to travel. The passes most commonly used by visitors are the Red Pass and the Green Pass. The Red Pass costs A$30 (US$20) for adults and A$15 (US$9.75) for kids and covers all transportation within the city center and near surroundings. This pass will get you aboard inner harbor ferries, for example, but not the ferry to Manly. The Green Pass, which costs A$38 (US$25) for adults and A$19 (US$12) for kids, will take you to more far-flung destinations, including Manly (aboard the ferry but not the JetCat before 7pm). You can buy either pass at newsdealers or bus, train, and ferry ticket outlets.

The **Day Tripper** ticket gives you unlimited bus, train, and ferry travel for 1 day. Tickets cost A$13 (US$8.70) for adults and A$6.70 (US$4.30) for children. The pass is available at all bus, train, and ferry ticket outlets.

A CityHopper ticket allows unlimited all-day travel on CityRail trains bounded by Kings Cross, North Sydney, and Redfern. Peak time tickets cost A$6.40 (US$4.15) for adults and A$3.20 (US$2) for children, and off-peak tickets cost A$4.60 (US$3) for adults and A$2.30 (US$1.50) for children.

A **Travelten ticket** offers 10 bus or ferry rides for a discounted price. A blue Travelten covers two sections on the bus route and costs A$10 (US$6.50) for adults and A$5.20 (US$3.40) for children; a BrownTravelten covers up to nine sections and costs A$18 (US$12) for adults and A$8.80 (US$6.15) for children. The Travelten ferry ticket costs A$26 (US$17) for adults and A$13 (US$8.50) for kids for 10 trips within the inner harbor (this excludes Manly). The Manly ferry Travelten costs A$39 (US$25) for adults and A$19 (US$12) for children, while the JetCat Travelten to Manly (before 7pm) costs A$55 (US$36) for adults (no kids' price). Buy Travelten tickets at newsdealers, bus depots, or at the Circular

Quay ferry terminal. Tickets are transferable, so if two or more people travel together, you can use the same ticket.

A 7-day **Rail Pass** costs A$16 (US$11) for adults and A$8.20 (US$5.30) for children, traveling within the city center. For a full day's unlimited travel by bus, you can't go wrong with the One-Day Bus Tripper. It costs A$9 (US$5.85) for adults and A$4.50 (US$2.90) for children 4 to 15, and can be bought from newsdealers and at bus depots. An unlimited One-Day Bus/Ferry Tripper costs A$13 (US$8.45) for adults and A$6.50 (US$4.20) for children.

BY PUBLIC BUS   Buses are frequent and reliable and cover a wide area of metropolitan Sydney—though you might find the system a little difficult to navigate if you're visiting some of the outer suburbs. The minimum fare (which covers most short hops in the city) is A$1.50 (US$1) for adults and A70¢ (US45¢) for children for a 4km (2½-mile) "section." The farther you go, the cheaper each section is. For example, the 44km (27-mile) trip to Palm Beach, way past Manly, costs A$4.60 (US$3) for adults and $2.30 (US$1.50) for kids. Sections are marked on bus-stand signs (though most Sydneysiders are as confused about the system as you will be—when in doubt, ask the bus driver).

Most buses bound for the northern suburbs, including night buses to Manly and the bus to Taronga Zoo, leave from Wynyard Park on Carrington Street, behind the Wynyard CityRail station on George Street. Buses to the southern beaches, such as Bondi and Bronte, and the western and eastern suburbs leave from Circular Quay. Buses to Balmain leave from behind the QV.

Call the **Transport Info Line** (© 13 15 00) for information, or ask the staff at the bus information kiosk on the corner of Alfred and Loftus streets, behind Circular Quay CityRail station (© 02/9219 1680). The kiosk is open Monday through Saturday from 8am to 8pm and Sunday from 8am to 6pm. Buses run from 4am to around midnight during the week, less frequently on weekends and holidays. Some night buses to outer suburbs run after midnight and throughout the night. You can purchase single tickets onboard; exact change is not required.

BY SYDNEY EXPLORER BUS   These bright red buses operate every day, traveling a 28km (18-mile) circuit and stopping at 26 places of interest. These include Sydney Opera House, the Royal Botanic Gardens, the State Library, Mrs. Macquarie's Chair, the Art Gallery of New South Wales, Kings Cross, Elizabeth Bay House, Wynyard CityRail station, the QVB, A.M.P. Centerpoint Tower, the Australian Museum, Central Station, Chinatown, and Darling Harbour and The Rocks. Buses depart from Circular Quay at 18-minute intervals from 8:40am with the last "round-trip" service departing Circular Quay at 5:20pm. This service returns to Circular Quay at 7pm. Board anywhere along the route where you see the distinctive red Sydney Explorer stop sign, and leave at any attraction along the way. If you want to stay on the bus from start to finish, the full circuit takes 1½ hours to complete. Your Sydney Explorer ticket entitles you to free travel on regular "blue and white" Sydney Buses within the same zone covered by your Sydney Explorer Ticket until midnight. When planning your itinerary for the day, remember that some attractions, such as museums, close at 5pm. Tickets cost A$30 (US$20) for adults, A$15 (US$9.75) for children 4 to 16, and A$75 (US$49) for a family. Buy tickets onboard the bus. You can also buy a 2-day Twin Ticket for both the Sydney Explorer Bus and the Bondi Explorer Bus (see below). The tickets cost A$50 (US$33) for adults, A$25 (US$16) for children, and A$125 (US$81) for a family.

BY BONDI EXPLORER BUS   The Bondi Explorer operates every day, traveling a 30km (19-mile) circuit around the eastern harborside bays and coastal beaches and back. Stops along the way include Kings Cross, Double Bay, Watsons Bay, Bondi Beach, Bronte Beach, Coogee Beach, Paddington, Oxford Street, and Martin Place. The bus departs from Circular Quay at 25-minute intervals from 9:15am, with the last "round-trip" service departing Circular Quay at 4:20pm. This service returns to Circular Quay at 5:55pm. Board anywhere along the route where you see the Bondi & Bay Explorer sign, and get off at any attraction along the way. If you wish to stay on board from start to finish without making any stops, the entire circuit takes 1½ hours to complete. Your ticket entitles you to free travel on regular "blue and white" Sydney Buses within the same zone covered by your Bondi & Bay Explorer ticket until midnight. The 1-day fare is A$30 (US$20) for adults, A$15 (US$9.75) for children 4 to 16, and A$75 (US$49) for families. Buy the ticket onboard.

BY FERRY & JETCAT   The best way to get a taste of a city that revolves around its harbor is to jump aboard a ferry. The main ferry terminal is at Circular Quay. Tickets can be bought at machines at each wharf. (There are also change machines.) For ferry information call ℂ **13 15 00,** or visit the ferry information office opposite Wharf 4. Timetables are available for all routes.

One-way journeys within the inner harbor (virtually everywhere except Manly and Parramatta) cost A$4.20 (US$2.75) for adults and A$2.10 (US$1.40) for children. The ferry to Manly takes 30 minutes and costs A$5.30 (US$3.50) for adults and A$2.60 (US$1.70) for children. It leaves from Wharf 3. The rapid JetCat service to Manly takes 15 minutes and costs A$6.60 (US$4.30) for both adults and children. After 7pm all trips to and from Manly are by JetCat at ferry prices. Ferries run from 6am to midnight.

BY CITYRAIL   Sydney's publicly owned train system is a cheap and efficient way to see the city. The system is limited, though, with many tourist areas—including Manly, Bondi Beach, and Darling Harbour—not connected to the network. CityRail trains have a reputation of running late and out of timetable order. All train stations have ticket machines, and most have ticket offices.

The single fare within the city center at any time of day is A$2.20 (US$1.40) for adults and A$1.10 (US70¢) for kids. An off-peak (after 9am) return ticket costs A$2.60 (US$1.70) for adults and A$2.20 (US$1.40) for kids, while a peak return will cost A$4.40 (US$2.85) for adults and A$2.20 (US$1.45) for kids. Information is available from **Infoline** (ℂ **13 15 00** in Australia).

Comfortable and efficient **Countrylink** trains out of Central Station link the city with the far suburbs and beyond. For reservations call ℂ **13 22 32** in Australia between 6:30am and 10pm, or visit the **Countrylink Travel Center** (ℂ **02/9224 2742**), Station Concourse, Wynyard CityRail station for brochures and bookings.

BY METRO MONORAIL   The metro monorail, with its single overhead line, is seen by many as a blight and by others as a futuristic addition. The monorail connects the central business district to Darling Harbour—though it's only a 15-minute walk from Town Hall. The system operates Monday through Wednesday from 7am to 10pm, Thursday and Friday from 7am to midnight, Saturday from 7am to midnight, and Sunday from 8am to 10pm. Tickets are A$4 (US$2.60), free for children under 5. An all-day monorail pass costs A$8 (US$5.20) for adults and A$24 (US$16) for a family. The trip from the city center to Darling Harbour takes around 12 minutes. Look for the gray overhead line and the plastic tubelike structures that are the stations. Call **Metro Monorail** at © **02/8584 5288** (www.metrolightrail.com.au) for more information.

BY METRO LIGHT RAIL   A system of "trams" opened in late 1997 with a route that traverses a 3.6km (2¼-mile) track between Central Station and Wentworth Park in Pyrmont. It provides good access to Chinatown, Paddy's Markets, Darling Harbour, the Star City casino, and the Sydney Fish Markets. The trams run every 10 minutes. The one-way fare is A$2.50 (US$1.60) or $4.80 (US$3.15), depending on distance. There are no child fares. A day pass costs A$8 (US$5.20), and a family-of-five day pass is A$24 (US$16). Call **Metro Light Rail** at © **02/8584 5288** (www.metrolightrail.com.au) for details.

BY TAXI

Taxis are a relatively economical way to get around. Several companies service the city center and suburbs. All journeys are metered. If you cross either way on the Harbour Bridge or through the Harbour Tunnel, it will cost you an extra A$3 (US$1.95)—a rip-off considering there's only an official toll on the way into the city, and if you take the Eastern Distributor from the airport, it's A$3.50 (US$2.30). An extra 10% will be added to your fare if you pay by credit card. *Note:* Visa cards are not accepted in Australian taxis.

Taxis line up at stands in the city, such as those found opposite Circular Quay and Central Station. They are also frequently found in front of hotels. A yellow light on top of the cab means it's vacant. Cabs can be hard to get on Friday and Saturday nights and between 2 and 3pm every day, when cabbies are changing shifts after 12 hours on the road. Tipping is not necessary, but appreciated—a dollar or so is plenty. Some people prefer to sit up front, but it's certainly not considered rude if you don't. Passengers must wear seat belts in the front and back seats. The **Taxi Complaints Hotline** (© **1800/648 478** in Australia) deals with problem taxi drivers. Taxis are licensed to carry four people.

The main cab companies are **A** (© **132 522**); **Taxis Combined Services** (© **02/9332 8888**); **RSL Taxis** (© **02/9581 1111**); **Legion Cabs** (© **13 14 51**); and **Premier** (© **13 10 17**).

BY WATER TAXI

Harbour Taxis, as they are called, operate 24 hours a day and are a quick, convenient way to get to waterfront restaurants, harbor attractions, and some suburbs. They can also be hired for private cruises. A journey from Circular Quay to Watsons Bay, for example, costs about A$60 (US$39) for two. An extra passenger costs around A$8 (US$5.20); some taxis can hold up to 28 people. An hour's sightseeing excursion around the harbor costs A$181 (US$118) for two. The main operator is **Water Taxis Combined** (© **02/9555 8888**).

BY CAR

Traffic restrictions, parking, and congestion can make getting around by car frustrating, but if you plan to visit some of the outer suburbs or take excursions elsewhere in New South Wales, then renting a car will give you more flexibility. The **NRMA's** (National Roads and Motorists' Association—the New South Wales auto club) emergency breakdown service can be contacted at © **13 11 11.**

Car-rental agencies in Sydney include **Avis,** 214 William St., Kings Cross (© 1800/225 553); **Budget,** 93 William St., Kings Cross (© 13 27 27 in Australia, or 02/9339 8888); **Dollar,** Domain Car Park, Sir John Young Car Park (© 02/9223 1444); **Hertz,** corner of William and Riley streets, Kings Cross

Sydney Ferries

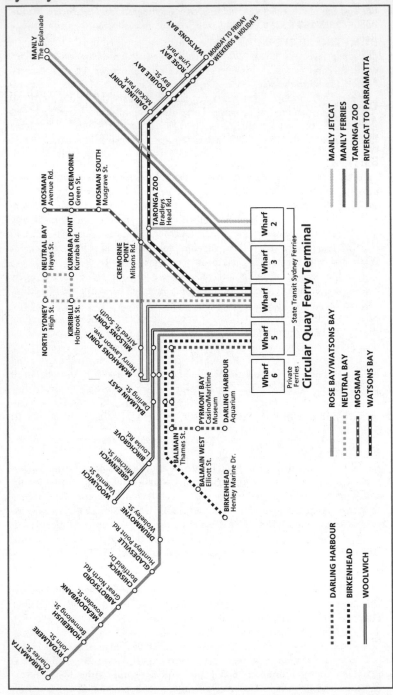

(② 13 30 39 in Australia); and **Thrifty,** 75 William St., Kings Cross (② 02/ 9380 5399). Avis, Budget, Hertz, and Thrifty also have desks at the airport. Rates average about A$60 (US$39) per day for a small car. One of the best value operations is **Bayswater Car Rentals,** 180 William St., Kings Cross (② 02/ 9360 3622), which has small cars for A$48 (US$31) a day and A$25 (US$16) a day for 6 days or more.

You can rent a motor home (called a camper van by some Aussies) from **Britz Campervans,** 653 Gardeners Rd., Mascot, NSW 2020 (② **1800/331 454** in Australia, or 02/9667 0402; www.britz.com). Plan on about A$105 (US$68) a day for a two-person van in winter and around $145 (US$94) in summer. You can drop off your van at most state capitals and in Cairns, a convenience that costs an extra A$200 (US$130).

 FAST FACTS: Sydney

American Express The main Amex office is at Level 3, 130 Pitt St., near Martin Place (② **02/9236 4200**). You can cash traveler's checks here, and it also acts as a travel booking service. It's open Monday through Friday from 8:30am to 5pm and Saturday from 9am to noon. Another foreign exchange office is located on the walkway leading up to the Sydney Opera House (② **02/9251 1970**). If you've lost your traveler's checks, then you need to go to the head office at 175 Liverpool St. (② **02/9271 1111**). It's a locked security building so you'll need to call ahead first.

Babysitters Dial an Angel (② **02/9416 7511** or 02/9362 4225) offers a well-regarded babysitting service.

Business Hours General office and banking hours are Monday through Friday from 9am to 5pm. Many banks, especially in the city center, are open from around 9.30am to 12:30pm on Saturday. Shopping hours are usually from 8:30am to 5:30pm daily (9am–5pm Sat), and most stores stay open until 9pm on Thursday. Most city-center stores are open from around 10am to 4pm on Sunday.

Currency Exchange Most major bank branches offer currency exchange services. Small foreign-currency exchange offices are clustered at the airport and around Circular Quay and Kings Cross. **Thomas Cook** can be found at the airport; at 175 Pitt St. (② **02/9231 2877**), open Monday through Friday from 6:45am to 5:15pm and Saturday from 10am to 2pm; and on the lower ground floor of the QVB (② **02/9264 1133**), open Monday through Friday from 9am to 6pm (until 9pm Fri), Saturday from 9am to 6pm, and Sunday from 11am to 5pm.

Dentist A well-respected dentist office in the city is **City Dental Practice,** Level 2, 229 Macquaire St., near Martin Place (② **02/9221 3300**). For dental problems after hours, call **Dental Emergency Information** (② 02/9369 7050).

Doctor The **Park Medical Centre,** Shop 4, 27 Park St. (② 02/ **9264 4488**), in the city center near Town Hall, is open Monday through Friday from 8am to 6pm; consultations cost A$40 (US$26) for 15 minutes. (*Note:* If you plan to take a dive course in Australia, get your medical exam done here. It costs A$70/US$46, about the cheapest in Australia.) The **Kings Cross Travelers'**

Clinic, Suite 1, 13 Springfield Ave., Kings Cross, just off Darlinghurst Road (*C* **1300/369 359** in Australia, or 02/9358 3066), is great for travel medicines and emergency contraception pills among other things. Hotel visits in the Kings Cross area cost A$80 (US$52); consultations cost A$40 (US$26). The **Travelers' Medical & Vaccination Centre,** Level 7, 428 George St., in the city center (*C* **02/9221 7133**), stocks and administers travel-related vaccinations and medications.

Embassies/Consulates　All foreign embassies are based in Canberra. You'll find the following consulates in Sydney: **United Kingdom,** Level 16, Gateway Building, 1 Macquarie Place, Circular Quay (*C* **02/9247 7521**); **New Zealand,** 55 Hunter St. (*C* **02/9223 0144**); **United States,** Level 59, MLC Centre, 19–29 Martin Place (*C* **02/9373 9200**); and **Canada,** Level 5, 111 Harrington St., The Rocks (*C* **02/9364 3000**).

Emergencies　Dial *C* **000** to call police, the fire service, or an ambulance. Call the **Emergency Prescription Service** (*C* **02/9235 0333**) for emergency drug prescriptions, and the NRMA for car breakdowns (*C* **13 11 11**).

Eyeglass Repair　**Perfect Vision,** Shop C22A, in the Centerpoint Tower, 100 Market St. (*C* **02/9221 1010**), is open Monday through Friday from 9am to 6pm (until 9pm Thurs) and Saturday from 9am to 5pm. It's the best place to replace lost contact lenses, but bring your prescription.

Holidays　See "When to Go" in chapter 2. New South Wales also observes Labor Day on the first Monday in October.

Hospitals　Make your way to **Sydney Hospital,** on Macquarie Street, at the top end of Martin Place (*C* **02/9382 7111** for emergencies). **St. Vincents Hospital** is on Victoria and Burton streets in Darlinghurst, near Kings Cross (*C* **02/9339 1111**).

Hot Lines　Contact the **Poisons Information Center** at *C* **13 11 26**; the **Gay and Lesbian Counseling Line** (4pm–midnight) at *C* **02/9207 2800**; the **Rape Crisis Center** at *C* **02/9819 6565**; and the **Crisis Center** at *C* **02/9358 6577**.

Internet Access　Several Internet/e-mail centers are scattered around the Kings Cross, Bondi, and Manly.

Lost Property　There is no general lost property bureau in Sydney. Contact the nearest police station if you think you've lost something. For items lost on trains, contact the **Lost Property Office,** 494 Pitt St., near Central Railway Station (*C* **02/9379 3000**). The office is open Monday through Friday from 8:30am to 4:30pm. For items left behind on planes or at the airport, go to the Federal Airport Corporation's administration office on the top floor of the International Terminal at Sydney International Airport (*C* **02/9667 9583**). For stuff left behind on buses or ferries, call *C* **02/9245 5777**. Each taxi company has its own lost property office.

Luggage Storage　You can leave your bags at the International Terminal at the airport. A locker here costs A$5 (US$3.25) per day, or you can put them in the storage room for A$7 (US$4.55) per day per piece. The room is open from 4:30am to the last flight of the day. Call *C* **02/9667 9848** for information. Otherwise, leave luggage at the cloakroom at Central Station, near the front of the main building (*C* **02/9219 4395**). Storage at the rail station costs A$4.50 (US$2.90) per article per day. The **Travelers Contact**

Point, 7th floor, 428 George St. (above the Dymocks bookstore) (© **02/9221 8744**), stores luggage for A$15 (US$9.75) per piece per month. It also operates a *poste restante* service, has Internet access, a travel agency, a jobs board, and ships items to the U.K. and Ireland.

Newspapers The *Sydney Morning Herald* is considered one of the world's best newspapers—by its management at least—and is available throughout metropolitan Sydney. The equally prestigious *Australian* is available nationwide. The metropolitan *Daily Telegraph* is a more casual read and has a couple of editions a day. The *International Herald Tribune, USA Today,* the British *Guardian Weekly,* and other U.K. newspapers can be found at Circular Quay newspaper stands and most newsdealers.

Pharmacies Most suburbs have pharmacies that are open late. For after-hours referral, contact the **Emergency Prescription Service** (© **02/9235 0333**).

Police In an emergency dial © **000.** Make nonemergency police inquiries through the Sydney Police Centre (© **02/9281 0000**).

Post Office The General Post Office (G.P.O.) is at 130 Pitt St., not far from Martin Place (© **13 13 18** in Australia). It's open Monday through Friday from 8:30am to 5:30pm and Saturday from 10am to 2pm. Letters can be sent c/o Poste Restante, G.P.O., Sydney, NSW 2000, Australia (© **02/9244 3733**), and collected at 310 George St., on the third floor of the Hunter Connection shopping center. It's open Monday through Friday from 8:15am to 5:30pm. For directions to the nearest post office, call © **1800/043 300.**

Restrooms These can be found in the QVB (second floor), most department stores, at Central Station and Circular Quay, near the escalators by the Sydney Aquarium, and in the Harbourside Festival Marketplace in Darling Harbour.

Safety Sydney is an extremely safe city, but as anywhere else, it's good to keep your wits about you and your wallet hidden. If you wear a money belt, keep it under your shirt. Be wary in Kings Cross and Redfern at all hours and around Central Station and the cinema strip on George Street near Town Hall station in the evening—the latter is a hangout for local gangs, though they're usually busy holding each other up for their sneakers. Other places of concern are the back lanes of Darlinghurst, around the naval base at Woolloomooloo, and along the Bondi restaurant strip when the drunks spill out after midnight. Several people have reported thieves at the airport on occasions. If traveling by train at night, travel in the carriages next to the guard's van, marked with a blue light on the outside.

Taxes Beginning July 1, 2000, Australia adopted a 10% Goods and Services Tax (GST) on most goods sold in Australia and most services. The GST applies to most travel-related goods and services, including transport, hotels, tours, and restaurants. By law, the tax has to be included in the advertised price of the product, though it doesn't have to be displayed independently of the pretax price.

Taxis See "Getting Around," earlier in this chapter.

Telephones Sydney's public phone boxes take coins, while many also take credit cards and A$10 (US$6.50) phone cards available from newsdealers. Local calls cost A40¢ (US25¢).

Transit Information Call the **Infoline** at 🕾 **13 15 00** in Australia (daily 6am–10pm).

Useful Telephone Numbers For news, dial 🕾 **1199**; for the time, 🕾 **1194**; for Sydney entertainment, 🕾 **11 688**; for directory assistance, 🕾 **12 455**; for Travelers Aid Society, 🕾 **02/9211 2469**.

Weather For the local forecast, call 🕾 **1196**.

3 Where to Stay

The 2000 Sydney Olympics, and the increased exposure the city received as a result, led to more visitors to the city and more hotels to cater to them. Unfortunately, the worldwide threat of terrorism has had an adverse affect too. Although it's unlikely you'll find the city's hotels completely booked if you turn up looking for a bed for the night, it's probably wise to reserve rooms in advance.

DECIDING WHERE TO STAY   The best location for lodging in Sydney is in The Rocks and around Circular Quay—a short stroll from the Sydney Opera House, the Harbour Bridge, the Royal Botanic Gardens, and the ferry terminals.

Hotels around Darling Harbour offer good access to the local facilities, including museums, the Sydney Aquarium, and the Star City casino. Most Darling Harbour hotels are a 10- to 15-minute walk, or a short monorail or light rail trip, from Town Hall and the central shopping district in and around Centerpoint Tower and Pitt Street Mall.

LAST-MINUTE ROOM DEALS

If you turn up in town without a reservation, you should definitely make use of the Sydney Visitors Centre Booking desk (🕾 **02/9667 6050**) in the arrivals hall of the airport's International Terminal. It negotiates deals with many of Sydney's hotels (but not hostels) and offers exceptional value discounts on rooms that haven't been filled that day—you can save up to 50% on a room. The desk is open from 6am to the last flight of the day and also offers discounts on tours (to the Blue Mountains, for example), and cheap tickets for flights within Australia.

More hotels are grouped around Kings Cross, Sydney's red-light district. While some of the hotels here are among the city's best, you'll also find a range of cheaper lodgings, including several backpacker hostels. Kings Cross can be unnerving at any time, but especially on Friday and Saturday nights when the area's strip joints and nightclubs are jumping. Staying here does have its advantages: You get a real inner-city feel, and it's close to excellent restaurants and cafes around the Kings Cross/Darlinghurst and Oxford Street areas.

Glebe, with its ethnic restaurants, is another inner-city suburb popular with tourists. It's well served by local buses, as well as Airport Express Bus route 352.

If you want to stay near the beach, check out the options in Manly and Bondi, though you should consider their distance from the city center and the lack of CityRail trains to these areas. A taxi to Manly from the city will cost around A$35 (US$23) and to Bondi around A$26 (US$17).

The prices given below for very expensive and expensive hotels are the **"rack rates,"** the official published rates, which almost nobody pays. Always ask about discounts rates, package deals, and any other special offerings when booking a hotel, especially if you are traveling in winter when hotels are less likely to be full. Ask about weekend discounts, corporate rates, and family plans. **Serviced**

apartments are also well worth considering because you can save a bundle by cooking your own meals; many also have free laundry facilities.

Almost all hotels offer nonsmoking rooms; inquire when you make a reservation if it's important to you. Most moderately priced to very expensive rooms will have tea- and coffeemaking facilities, and an iron. Like elsewhere, there's an increasing trend to rip off guests with pay-per-view movie channels (around A$14/US$9.10 per movie), rather than to provide full access to a range of free cable TV channels. In Australia, by the way, a "double" room means you get one double, queen-size, or king-size bed in a room.

The websites www.wotif.com.au and www.lastminute.com.au offer substantial discounts year-round.

The price categories used below are defined as follows (for a double room): Very Expensive, A$250 (US$162) and up; Expensive, A$150 to $250 (US$97–US$162); Moderate, A$80 to A$150 (US$52–US$97); Inexpensive, below A$80 (US$52).

THE ROCKS/CIRCULAR QUAY
VERY EXPENSIVE
Observatory Hotel ✿✿✿   This exclusive hotel, a 10-minute walk uphill from The Rocks and George Street, is a turn-of-the-20th-century beauty competing for top-hotel-in-Sydney honors. (In 2001, Zagats named it hotel of the year in Australia, and the 11th-best hotel in the world.) Up there with the Ritz-Carlton Sydney for unadulterated style, it's fitted out with antiques, objets d'art, and the finest carpets, wallpapers, and draperies. Plus, it's renowned for its personalized service. Rooms are plush and quiet, and the huge bathroom is a great place for a glass of champagne and some takeout sushi. Some rooms have city views while others look out over the harbor. The pool here is one of the best in Sydney: Note the Southern Hemisphere constellations on the roof. The health club offers a free float in the flotation tank for early arrivals coming in from overseas.

89–113 Kent St., Sydney, NSW 2000. ✆ **1800/806 245** in Australia, or 02/9256 2222. Fax 02/9256 2233. www.observatoryhotel.com.au. 100 units. A$415–A$450 (US$270–US$292) double; from A$510 (US$331) suite. Extra person A$66 (US$43). Children under 14 stay free in parent's room. AE, DC, MC, V. Parking A$30 (US$20). Bus: 339, 431, or 433 to Millers Point. **Amenities:** Restaurant; bar; chemical-free heated indoor pool; floodlit tennis court; sauna; health club with flotation tank; concierge; business center; 24-hr. room service; laundry service; dry cleaning. *In room:* TV w/pay movies, VCR, CD player, dataport, minibar, hair dryer, safe.

Park Hyatt Sydney ✿✿   This artistically curving property on The Rocks foreshore is the best-positioned hotel in Sydney. It's right on the water, with some rooms having fantastic views across the harbor to the Sydney Opera House. Its location and general appeal mean it's usually full and frequently has to turn guests away. The room rates have skyrocketed in recent years, and unless you have money to burn, there are plenty of places that are far cheaper and just as nice.

The building itself is a pleasure to look at, and from a ferry on the harbor it looks like a wonderful addition to the toy town feel of The Rocks. Every possible luxury has been incorporated into the good-size rooms. Room rates here depend on views; the least expensive units have only glimpses of the harbor. (The most expensive rooms look over the Opera House.) Each of the 33 executive suites has two balconies with a telescope.

The **Verandah on the Park** restaurant offers good buffet food indoors or outside on the edge of the harbor, and is worth a visit even if you don't stay here.

7 Hickson Rd., The Rocks, Sydney, NSW 2000. ✆ **02/9241 1234** or 02/9241 1234. Fax 02/9256 1555. www. sydney.hyatt.com. 158 units. A$650–A$700 (US$422–US$455) double depending on view; A$820–A$920 (US$533–US$598) executive studio; from A$1,000 (US$650) suite. Extra person A$55 (US$36). Children under

Central Sydney Accommodations

ANA Harbour Grand Sydney **8**
Bernly Private Hotel **24**
DeVere Hotel **26**
The Grace Hotel Sydney **11**
Hotel 59 **22**
The Hughenden **21**
The Kirketon **23**
The Lord Nelson Brewery Hotel **3**
Medina Grand, Harbourside **12**
Observatory Hotel **4**
Park Hyatt Sydney **1**
Park Regis Sydney **15**
Quay Grand Suites Sydney **7**
The Russell **6**
Saville Park Suites, Sydney **18**
The Sebel Pier One Sydney **2**
Sir Stamford at Circular Quay **9**
The Stafford **5**
Star City Hotel **13**
Sullivans Hotel **20**
Sydney Central YHA **16**
Travelodge, Wentworth Avenue **17**
Victoria Court Sydney **25**
Wattle Private Hotel **19**
Westin Sydney **10**
Wool Brokers Arms **14**

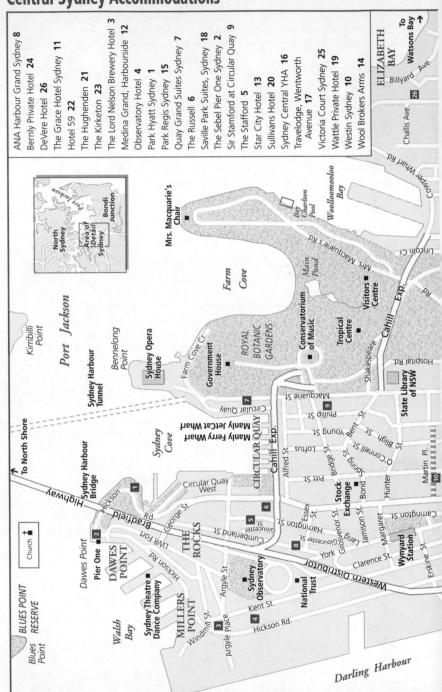

110

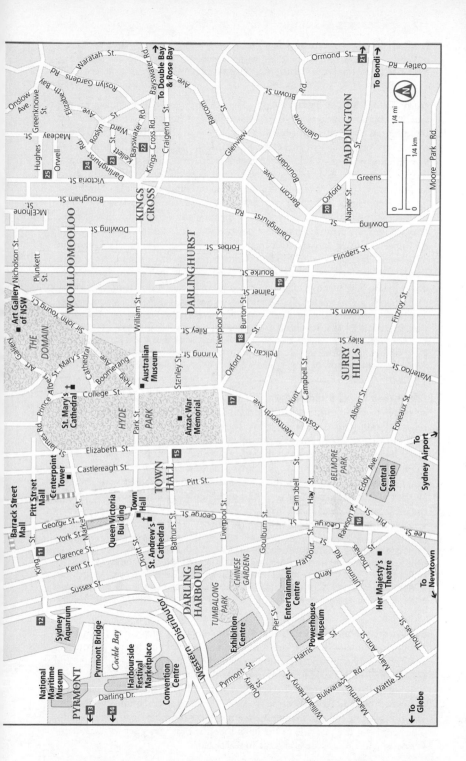

18 stay free in parent's room. Ask about lower weekend rates and packages. AE, DC, MC, V. Parking A$22 (US$14). CityRail, bus, or ferry: Circular Quay. **Amenities:** 2 restaurants; bar/lounge; heated outdoor pool; health club/spa; concierge; business center; 24-hr. room service; babysitting; laundry service. *In room:* A/C, TV, dataport, minibar, coffeemaker, hair dryer, iron, safe.

Quay Grand Suites Sydney ★★   The best serviced-apartment complexes, like this one, can outdo superior AAA-rated five-star hotels—even in price. This building, on the pedestrian concourse leading up to the Sydney Opera House, also houses private apartments costing upward of A$750,000 (US$487,500)— so you know you are in exclusive territory. The apartments here are spacious and ultramodern, and either face onto the Botanic Gardens or have fantastic views looking across the ferry terminals and the Sydney Harbour Bridge. Rooms are fully self-contained and come with a balcony to admire the views. The noises from the CityRail train station, including the train announcements as well as the ferry hooters, are captivating but can easily be shut out. Bathrooms are large and feature a good-size Jacuzzi. You might want to eat at the hotel's **Quadrant** restaurant, which serves up Modern Australian food; otherwise, there are two separate and excellent eateries—**Aqua Luna** and **Aria**—on the promenade down below. The Dendy cinema, in the same strip, has good art-house movies.

61 Macquarie St., E. Circular Quay, Sydney, NSW 2000. ℭ **1800/091 954** in Australia, or 02/9256 4000. Fax 02/9256 4040. www.mirvachotels.com.au. A$335–A$507 (US$218–US$330) 1-bedroom apt, depending on view. Extra person A$35 (US$23). Ask about weekend packages and rates for long-term stays. AE, DC, MC, V. Valet Parking A$20 (US$13). CityRail, bus, or ferry: Circular Quay. **Amenities:** Restaurant; bar (the trendy ECQ); small health club; concierge; 24-hr. room service; massage; babysitting; laundry service; dry cleaning; nonsmoking rooms. *In room:* A/C, TV w/pay movies, dataport, kitchen, minibar, coffeemaker, hair dryer, iron, washing machine, dryer.

Shangri-la Hotel Sydney ★★   For a room with a view, you're not going to do better than this ultramodern landmark hotel a 5-minute walk from Circular Quay. All rooms look out onto Darling Harbour or across the Opera House and Harbour Bridge. Try to book a room on the 20th floor or above: From here Sydney is laid out at your feet, with the ferries buzzing around below you like bathtub toys. If you really want to splurge, book a corner room for an extraordinary vista. Rooms are comfortably furnished and decorated to blend with sky, city, and sea. The hotel is popular with tour groups, particularly from Japan, hence the great Japanese restaurants here.

176 Cumberland St., The Rocks, Sydney, NSW 2000. ℭ **1800/801 088** in Australia, or 02/9250 6000. Fax 02/9250 6250. www.shangri-la.com. 563 units. A$450–A$500 (US$292–US$325) double depending on view; A$750 (US$487) corner rooms with views; A$550–A$4,900 (US$357–US$3,185) suites. Extra person A$60 (US$39). Children stay free in parent's room. Ask about packages. AE, DC, MC, V. Parking A$21 (US$14). CityRail or ferry: Circular Quay. **Amenities:** 2 restaurants; lounge; 2 bars; heated indoor pool; Jacuzzi; sauna; exercise room; concierge; business center; salon; 24-hr. room service; babysitting; laundry service; currency exchange; early-arrivals/late-departures lounge. *In room:* A/C, TV w/pay movies, dataport, minibar, hair dryer, iron, safe.

Sir Stamford at Circular Quay ★★★   Talk about plush! This is Sydney's most deluxe hotel—from the moment the doorman doffs his top hat to you, you enter the world of aristocracy, complete with the slight scent of cigar smoke and aged brandy in the air. This hotel, formally the Ritz Carlton, has a prime location, just a short walk from Circular Quay and the Opera House, and just across the road from the Royal Botanic Gardens. Rooms are exceptionally large and luxurious with good-size marble bathrooms. Most rooms have a small balcony. The rooms on the east side of the hotel have the best views across the Botanic Gardens. Most rooms are accessible to wheelchairs.

93 Macquarie St., Sydney, NSW 2000. ℂ **1300/301 391** in Australia, or 02/9252 4600. Fax 02/9252 4286. www.stamford.com.au. 105 units. A$540 (US$351) double; A$580 (US$377) deluxe harbor-view double; A$705–A$3,000 (US$487–US$1,950) Sir Stamford presidential suite. AE, DC, MC, V. Parking A$40 per day (US$26). CityRail, bus, or ferry: Circular Quay. **Amenities:** Restaurant; bar; solar heated outdoor pool; exercise room; sauna; concierge; business center with secretarial services; 24-hr. room service; babysitting; laundry service; currency exchange. *In room:* A/C, TV w/pay movies, fax, dataport, minibar, hair dryer, iron, safe.

EXPENSIVE

The Russell 🕸🕸 *(Finds* This is the coziest place to stay in The Rocks, and perhaps in all of Sydney. It's more than 100 years old, and it shows its age wonderfully in the creak of the floorboards and the ramshackle feel of its brightly painted corridors. Every room is different in style, size, and shape; all come with a queen-size bed and most have cable TV. (Others can have a TV moved in if requested.) All rooms have immense character, including a series of rooms added on in 1990 above the Fortune of War Hotel next door. There are no harbor views, but from some rooms you can see the tops of the ferry terminals at Circular Quay. Guests have the use of a comfortable sitting room, a living room with magazines and books, and a rooftop garden. The apartment is large, open plan with a king-size bed and small kitchen suitable for three people. (There's a double sofa bed.) It overlooks Circular Quay. The place was refurbished in 2000 and 2001.

143A George St., The Rocks, Sydney, NSW 2000. ℂ **02/9241 3543**. Fax 02/9252 1652. www.therussell.com. au. 29 units, 19 with bathroom. A$140–A$195 (US$91–$127) double without bathroom; A$235–A$290 (US$153–$188) double with bathroom (the most expensive overlook Circular Quay); A$320 (US$208) suite and apt. Extra person A$15 (US$9.75). Rates include continental breakfast. AE, DC, MC, V. Parking not available. CityRail or ferry: Circular Quay. **Amenities:** Restaurant; lounge. *In room:* TV, coffeemaker, iron.

The Sebel Pier One Sydney 🕸 *(Finds* A premier waterfront hotel, the Sebel is located within the historic Woolloomooloo Wharf complex and has been painstakingly renovated so as to leave as much of the original structure intact as possible. It's a wonderfully intoxicating blend of old wooden beams and tasteful modern art. The only drawback to staying in one of their tastefully appointed waterfront rooms is that the harbor views through windows that run all the way to the floor could make you want to stay in for the rest of the day. But then again, perhaps the cocktail bar is more your scene, touted as one of the trendiest in town.

11 Hickson Rd., Walsh Bay, Sydney NSW 2000. ℂ **1800/780 485** in Australia. Fax 02/8298 9777. www. mirvachotel.com.au. 161 units. A$235 (US$153) double; A$290 (US$189) waterfront room. Rates include breakfast. AE, DC, MC, V. CityRail, ferry: Circular Quay; Bus: George St. **Amenities:** Restaurant; bar; outdoor terrace; Jacuzzi; gym. *In room:* A/C, TV, dataport, minibar, hair dryer, iron, safe.

The Stafford The Stafford offers some of the best-positioned serviced apartments in Sydney, right in the heart of The Rocks, very close to the harbor and Circular Quay, and a short stroll from the central business district. The property consists of modern apartments in a six-story building (the best units, for their harbor and Opera House views, are on the top three floors) and seven two-story terrace houses dating from 1870 to 1895. The Stafford is highly recommended for its location, spacious rooms, and fully equipped kitchen.

75 Harrington St., The Rocks, Sydney, NSW 2000. ℂ **02/9251 6711**. Fax 02/9251 3458. www.stafford apartments.com.au. 61 units. A$235–A$275 (US$153–US$179) studio double; A$280 (US$182) 1-bedroom apt; A$320 (US$208) executive 1-bedroom apt; A$295 (US$192) terrace house; A$370 (US$240) 1-bedroom penthouse. Extra person A$15 (US$9.75). Children under 12 stay free in parent's room. Ask about lower weekly rates. AE, DC, MC, V. Parking A$15 (US$9.75). CityRail or ferry: Circular Quay. **Amenities:** Small outdoor pool; exercise room; Jacuzzi; sauna; tour/car-rental desk; business center; limited room service; babysitting; free self-service laundry; dry cleaning. *In room:* A/C, TV, dataport, kitchen, minibar, coffeemaker, hair dryer, iron.

MODERATE

The Lord Nelson Brewery Hotel   Sydney's oldest pub was established in 1841 after serving as a private residence since its construction in 1836. It's an attractive, three-story sandstone building with a busy pub on the ground floor, a good brasserie on the second, and hotel accommodations on the third. The rooms were totally renovated in 1999 and while compact, are spacious enough to swing your bags around without hitting the walls. From its creaky floorboards and bedroom walls made from convict-hewn sandstone blocks, to the narrow corridors, the wood fire, and homemade beer down in the bar, the Lord Nelson positively wallows in colonial atmosphere.

At the corner of Kent and Argyle sts., The Rocks, Sydney, NSW 2000. ℂ **02/9251 4044.** Fax 02/9251 1532. www.thelordnelson.com.au. 9 units, 8 with bathroom. A$120 (US$78) double without bathroom; A$180 (US$117) double with bathroom. Extra person A$30 (US$20). Rates include continental breakfast. AE, DC, MC, V. No parking. CityRail or ferry: Circular Quay. **Amenities:** 2 restaurants; bar. *In room:* TV, fax, coffee-maker, hair dryer, iron.

CITY CENTRE

VERY EXPENSIVE

The Grace Hotel Sydney 🎯🎯   Situated within the historic Grace Building, a replica of the *Chicago Tribune* Building in the United States and one of Australia's finest examples of commercial Gothic architecture, the Grace is one of the city's newest centrally located hotels. The 11-story building's L-shaped lobby has marble flagstones, stained-glass windows, a lace ironwork balcony, Art Deco furniture and light fittings, and high ceilings supported by marble columns. Guest rooms vary in size (the more expensive doubles labeled "deluxe," the cheaper "executive"), with king-size beds or a pair of doubles, and are fronted by almost surreally wide corridors. Three rooms are suitable for travelers with disabilities.

77 York St., Sydney, NSW 2000. ℂ **1800/682 692** in Australia, or 02/9299 8777. Fax 02/9299 8189. www. gracehotel.com.au. 382 units. A$374–A$396 (US$243–US$257) double; A$572 (US$372) suite. Extra person A$50 (US$32). Children under 17 stay free in parent's room. AE, DC, MC, V. Parking A$28 (US$18). CityRail: Wynyard. **Amenities:** 2 restaurants; bar; heated outdoor pool; sauna; gym; concierge; business services; 24-hr. room service; massage; babysitting; laundry service; currency exchange. *In room:* A/C, TV, dataport, mini-bar, coffeemaker, hair dryer, iron, safe.

Westin Sydney 🎯   One of Sydney's newest and most celebrated AAA-rated five-star hotels, the Westin is in the center of the city in the Martin Place pedestrian mall. Integrated into a former post office from the 19th century, the Westin has a charm that is modern and classic all at once. The large rooms have comfortable beds and floor-to-ceiling windows. The hotel is home to several bars, restaurants, and clothing shops. Just steps from the central shopping streets, the QVB, and a 10- to 15-minute walk to both Sydney Opera House and Darling Harbour, the hotel features an impressive seven-story atrium, a wonderful two-level health club, and an exclusive day spa.

1 Martin Place, Sydney, NSW 2000. ℂ **800/WESTIN-1** in the U.S., or 02/8223 1111. Fax 02/8223-1222. www. westin.com.au. 416 units. A$286 (US$186) double. AE, DC, MC, C. Parking A$25 (US$16). **Amenities:** Cafe; bar; day spa; massage; babysitting; same-day laundry service; currency exchange. *In room:* A/C, TV, dataport, minibar, coffeemaker, hair dryer, iron, safe.

EXPENSIVE

Park Regis Sydney   This hotel occupies the top 15 floors of a 45-story building and is well placed in the central business district, just 2 blocks from Hyde Park and Town Hall. There's nothing spectacular about the place, but the rooms are light, modern, and equally practical. The bathrooms have a shower and no tub. Many of the guests are business travelers, which gives the hotel a corporate

---

(Tips Where to Stay During Gay & Lesbian Mardi Gras

The **Saville Park Suites, Sydney** (see below) is a fabulous place from which to watch Sydney's annual Gay and Lesbian Mardi Gras, held every February. (The parade is usually the last Sat in Feb or first Sat in Mar.) Make your plans early, as most rooms are booked a year in advance. Four-night Mardi Gras packages range from around A$1,600 to A$2,000 (US$1,040–US$1,300). **Sullivans Hotel** (p. 119) on Oxford Street is another popular place to stay during Mardi Gras.

---

feel. Nevertheless, it's a relatively good value considering the location. Rooms at the front have views over the city and park.

27 Park St. (at Castlereagh St.), Sydney, NSW 2000. (C) **02/9267 6511,** or 1800/221 138 in Australia. Fax 02/9264 2252. www.parkregissydney.com.au. 120 units. A$165 (US$107) double; A$198 (US$129) suite. Extra person A$22 (US$14). Children under 14 stay free in parent's room. Ask about lower rates available through Aussie auto clubs. AE, DC, MC, V. Free parking. CityRail: Town Hall. Monorail: Park Plaza. **Amenities:** Small heated outdoor pool; concierge; tour desk; 24-hr. room service; babysitting; laundry service; dry cleaning; nonsmoking rooms. *In room:* A/C, TV, fridge, coffeemaker, hair dryer.

Saville Park Suites, Sydney (*)   Although the serviced apartments here are pleasant and nicely furnished and the complex is well situated right at the start of Oxford Street and just a short walk across Hyde Park from the Pitt Street Mall shopping area, I feel it's overpriced. You may be able to negotiate a cheaper rate with the management, though; it never hurts to ask. Each room has a sofa and a couple of armchairs, a separate kitchen, a balcony, and a bathroom with a smallish tub and separate shower. Guests get free membership at a gym just down the road.

16–32 Oxford St., Sydney, NSW 2010. (C) **02/8268 2599,** or 1800/221 2599 in Australia. Fax 02/8268 2599. www.savillesuites.com.au. 135 units. A$250 (US$162) 1-bedroom apt; A$270 (US$176) 2-bedroom apt. Extra person A$25 (US$16). Children under 15 stay free in parent's room. Ask about special rates. AE, DC, MC, V. Parking A$5 (US$3.25). CityRail: Museum. **Amenities:** Restaurant; small heated outdoor pool; sauna; Jacuzzi. *In room:* A/C, TV, minibar, iron, washing machine, dryer.

MODERATE

Travelodge, Wentworth Avenue (*)   This business-oriented hotel is cheap for Sydney, and comfortable and well located—making it a good option for some travelers. The clean, brown-colored rooms are motel-like in appearance, with a queen-size bed. Many come with a sofa. From here it's a short walk to Oxford Street, Town Hall, Hyde Park, and the monorail to Darling Harbour.

27–33 Wentworth Ave., Sydney, NSW 2000. (C) **02/8267 1700.** Fax 02/8267 1800. www.travelodge.com.au. 406 units. A$119 (US$77) double and twin rooms. Extra person A$16 (US$10). AE, DC, MC, V. Parking around corner A$17 (US$11). CityRail: Museum. **Amenities:** Restaurant; massage; babysitting; nonsmoking rooms. *In room:* A/C, TV, dataport, kitchenette, fridge, coffeemaker, hair dryer, iron.

INEXPENSIVE

Sydney Central YHA (**) (*Value*)   This multi-award-winning hostel is one of the biggest and busiest in the world. And it's just one of 140 YHA hostels in Australia (for the full list check the website below). With a 98% year-round occupancy rate, you'll have to book early. It's in a historic nine-story building, which offers far more than standard basic accommodations. In the basement is the **Scu Bar,** a popular drinking hole with pool tables and occasional entertainment. There's also an entertainment room with more pool tables and e-mail facilities, TV rooms on every floor, and an audiovisual room showing movies. Try the heated swimming pool and the sauna. Rooms are clean and basic. The YHA is accessible to travelers with disabilities. Check the website for other hostels in Sydney—including the Glebe Point YHA, the Sydney Beachhouse YHA in the beachside suburb of Collaroy, and Pittwater YHA in Ku-ring-gai Chase National Park (only accessible by boat and a fabulous way to experience the "bush" around Sydney).

11 Rawson Place, Sydney, NSW 2000. ⓒ **02/9281 9111.** Fax 02/9281 9199. www.yha.com.au. 151 rooms or 532 beds (54 twin rooms). A$25–A$31 (US$16–US$20) dorm bed; A$78 (US$51) twin without bathroom, A$88 (US$57) twin with bathroom. Non-YHA members A$3 (US$1.95) extra. MC, V. Parking A$10 (US$6.50). On the corner of Pitt St., outside Central Station. CityRail: Central. **Amenities:** Restaurant; bar; small heated outdoor pool; sauna; 2 kitchens; TV room. *In room:* No phone.

AT DARLING HARBOUR
VERY EXPENSIVE

Star City Hotel 🌟🌟 Opened at the end of 1997, this A$900 million (US$585 million) gambling and entertainment complex includes a AAA-rated five-star hotel, with rooms overlooking Darling Harbour and the architecturally interesting Pyrmont Bridge. Although the four split-level Royal Suites are spectacular, each with three TVs, a giant Jacuzzi, a full kitchen, two bathrooms, its own sauna, and the services of the former butler to the governor of Queensland, the standard rooms are somewhat small and sterile. Executive suites are very nice. If you stay here, pay the extra money for a room with spectacular views over Darling Harbour.

80 Pyrmont St., Pyrmont, Sydney, NSW 2009. ⓒ **1800/700 700** in Australia, or 02/9777 9000. Fax 02/9657 8344. www.starcity.com.au. 491 units. A$350–A$370 (US$228–US$241) double, depending on view; from A$510 (US$332) and way up for apts. Extra person A$40 (US$26). Ask about special packages. AE, DC, MC, V. Parking A$15 (US$9.75). Ferry: Pyrmont Bay. Monorail: Harbourside. Light Rail: Star City. Free shuttle buses run from the central business district. **Amenities:** 4 restaurants; large heated outdoor pool; sauna; Jacuzzi; gaming rooms; concierge; business center; shopping arcade; salon; 24-hr. room service; massage; laundry service; 2 theaters; currency exchange. *In room:* A/C, TV, dataport, minibar, coffeemaker, hair dryer.

MODERATE

Wool Brokers Arms You'll find this friendly 1886 heritage building on the far side of Darling Harbour, next to the prominent AAA-rated four-star Novotel hotel and hidden behind a monstrous aboveground parking garage. It's set on a noisy road, so unless you're used to traffic avoid the rooms at the front. Rooms are simply furnished with a double bed and a sink. Room no. 3 is one of the nicer ones. Family rooms have a king-size bed, a set of bunks, and two singles through an open doorway. There are 19 shared bathrooms. It's adequate for a few nights.

22 Allen St., Pyrmont, Sydney, NSW 2009. ⓒ **02/9552 4773.** Fax 02/9552 4771. www.ozemail.com. au/~woolbrokers. 26 units, none with bathroom. A$89 (US$58) double; A$110 (US$72) triple; A$130 (US$85) family room for 4. Rates include continental breakfast. Extra person A$20 (US$13). AE, MC, V. Parking A$11 (US$7) nearby. Bus: 501 from central business district or Central Station. Light Rail: Convention Centre. **Amenities:** Tour desk; coin-op laundry; nonsmoking rooms. *In room:* TV.

SERVICED APARTMENTS

Medina Grand, Harbourside 🌟🌟 This impressive serviced hotel offers modern and very comfortable rooms at competitive prices. It's a little oddly placed—reached by an offshoot road and a short, unattractive walk from the Sydney Aquarium in Darling Harbour—but it makes up for it by being close to all the Darling Harbour, Cockle Bay, and Town Hall attractions and shops. You can choose between studio and one-bedroom apartments, which all come with Italian designer furniture, large windows, and balconies (some with good harbor views). Studio units come with a kitchenette, and one-bedroom units come with a fully equipped kitchen and a second TV. All have dataports. Medina offers very good package and weekend rates, which means this place can work out to be a real bargain.

Medina has a series of other serviced-apartment complexes in Sydney, including the **Medina Executive,** Sydney Central (© **02/8396 9800**), in a historic building near Central station; the pleasant **Medina Classic** in Martin Place (© **02/9224 6400**); coastal **Medina Executive,** near Coogee Beach (© **02/ 9578 6000**); the gorgeous **Medina Executive** in Paddington (© **02/9361 9000**); and the AAA-rated five-star **Medina Grand,** Sydney (© **02/9274 0000**), between Town Hall and Darling Harbour. Check the website below for more details on these highly recommended properties. Rates range from A$165 (US$109) for a studio for two guests at the Medina Grand to A$488 (US$322) for a "Premier Plus" two-bedroom apartment, with many prices and combinations in between (check the website).

Corner of Shelley and King sts., King St. Wharf, Sydney, NSW 2000. © 1300/300 232 in Australia, or 02/9249 7000. Fax 02/9249 6900. www.medinaapartments.com.au. 114 units. AE, DC, MC, V. CityRail: Town Hall. **Amenities:** Small heated indoor pool; exercise room; concierge; tour desk; business center; laundry service; nonsmoking rooms. *In room:* A/C, TV, dataport, kitchenette, minibar, coffeemaker, hair dryer, iron.

IN KINGS CROSS & THE SUBURBS BEYOND
EXPENSIVE
The Kirketon ⟨⁀⟩   If you want to stay somewhere a bit offbeat and class yourself as a "hip, fashionable type," then this boutique hotel in Darlinghurst is a fascinating option. Rooms come with either a king, queen, double, or twin beds, and are lightly stocked with modernist furniture and custom-made fittings, including mirrored headboards, sleek bathrooms hidden away behind mirrored doors, and interestingly textured bedspreads and areas of wallpaper. All in all the decor is fun if you like this sort of thing, although personally I found it jarred with my more conventional taste. Junior rooms are quite compact, some of the Premium rooms come with a tub as well as shower, and the quite large executive rooms have a VCR, with some having a small balcony overlooking the main road. (The road can be noisy at night.) The inside scoop is that the best Junior room is no. 330, the best Premium room no. 340, and the best executive room no. 323. I would definitely ask for a room away from the main road. The same company also operates another stylish boutique hotel, **Medusa,** at 267 Darlinghurst Rd. (© **02/9331 1000**).

229 Darlinghurst Rd., Darlinghurst. © **02/9332 2011.** Fax 02/9332 2499. www.kirketon.com.au. 40 rooms. Junior rooms (single) A$220 (US$143); premium rooms (double) A$275 (US$179); executive rooms (double) A$365 (US$238). 1 or 2 people only per room. AE, DC, MC, V. Free parking in garage around corner. **Amenities:** Restaurant; bar. *In room:* A/C, TV, dataport, minibar, hair dryer.

MODERATE
DeVere Hotel   The DeVere has been recommended by several readers who comment on the friendly staff and the bargain-basement prices when booked at the Tourism New South Wales Travel Centre at the Sydney airport. Although the rooms are very modern, they are a little too standard gray for my liking (although the owner says some are now yellow). Superior rooms are a bit larger, and the executive room is larger still and comes with nicer furniture. They are certainly a bargain compared to similar, but far more expensive, rooms elsewhere in Sydney. The suites have views of Elizabeth Bay, a Jacuzzi, and a king-size bed rather than a queen. Some suites have a kitchenette with no cooking facilities.

Some standard rooms have an extra single bed. Breakfast is available from A$8 (US$5.20).

44–46 Macleay St., Potts Point, NSW 2011. ℂ 1800/818 790 in Australia, 0800/441 779 in New Zealand, or 02/9358 1211. Fax 02/9358 4685. www.devere.com.au. 100 units. A$126 (US$82) double; A$163 (US$106) superior room; A$189 (US$123) executive room or self-contained studio; A$237 (US$154) suite. Extra person A$36 (US$23). Children under 12 stay free in parent's room. AE, DC, MC, V. Parking at nearby Landmark Hotel A$12 (US$7.80) per exit. CityRail: Kings Cross. Bus: 311 from Circular Quay. **Amenities:** Tour desk; car-rental desk; business center; laundry service; dry cleaning. *In room:* A/C, TV, fridge, coffeemaker, hair dryer.

Hotel 59 *(Kids*   This popular and friendly B&B is well worth considering if you want to be near the Kings Cross action, but far enough away to get a decent night's sleep. Deluxe rooms have either a queen- or king-size bed and a combined shower and tub, while the smaller standard rooms come with a double bed and a shower (no tub). The two large superior rooms come with a separate living room, two single beds, and two more that can be locked together to form a king. One comes with a small kitchen with a microwave and hot plates. All rooms are very clean and comfortable, and have private bathrooms. A fully cooked breakfast is served up in the cafe below. A flight of stairs and no elevator might make this a bad choice for older travelers or those with disabilities.

59 Bayswater Rd., Kings Cross, NSW 2011. ℂ 02/9360 5900. Fax 02/9360 1828. www.hotel59.com.au. 8 units. A$115 (US$75) standard double; A$125 (US$81) deluxe double; A$135 (US$88) superior room. Extra person A$15 (US$9.75), extra children 2–12 A$10 (US$6.50). Rates include cooked breakfast. MC, V. No parking. CityRail: Kings Cross. **Amenities:** Cafe; TV lounge; tour/car rental desk; nonsmoking rooms. *In room:* A/C, TV, kitchen, fridge, coffeemaker, hair dryer, iron.

INEXPENSIVE

Bernly Private Hotel *(Finds*   This place, tucked just off Darlinghurst Road, is a find. It's a rabbit warren of rooms run by friendly staff, catering to everyone from short-term travelers to newly arrived immigrants. All rooms are new and clean. The more expensive rooms are superior to most others of their price in the area. Budget rooms are a bit scruffier and smaller than the standards, but are perfectly livable. Some come with a microwave oven, and all have a small TV. Backpacker rooms have two sets of bunk beds, though just two people seem to occupy most. Some of the backpacker rooms have a shower. There's a rooftop sun deck and a lounge with cable TV. Five family rooms come with double beds and two singles.

15 Springfield Ave., Potts Point, NSW 2011. ℂ 02/9358 3122. Fax 02/9356 4405. www.bernlyprivatehotel.com.au. 95 units, 12 with bathroom. $A60 (US$39) budget double without shared bathroom; A$80 (US$52) double with en-suite bathroom; A$100 (US$65) triple with en-suite bathroom; A$125 (US$81) family room with en-suite bathroom; A$25 (US$16) dorm bed. Additional person A$22 (US$14) extra. AE, DC, MC, V. On-street meter parking. CityRail: Kings Cross. **Amenities:** Rooftop sun deck; TV lounge. *In room:* A/C, TV, fridge, coffeemaker, iron.

Victoria Court Sydney 🌟 *(Value*   This cute, good-value place is made up of two 1881 terrace houses joined together; it's situated near a string of backpacker hostels and popular cafes in a leafy street running parallel to sleazy Darlinghurst Road. The glass-roofed breakfast room on the ground floor is a work of art decked out with hanging ferns, giant bamboo, wrought-iron tables and chairs, and a trickling fountain. Just off this space is a peaceful guest lounge stacked with books and newspapers. The very plush rooms come with either king- or queen-size beds, but lack a tub in the bathroom. There's a coin-op laundry just down the road.

122 Victoria St., Potts Point, NSW 2011. ℂ 1800/630 505 in Australia, or 02/9357 3200. Fax 02/9357 7606. www.victoriacourt.com.au. 22 units. A$75–A$115 (US$49–US$75) double, depending on the season; A$165

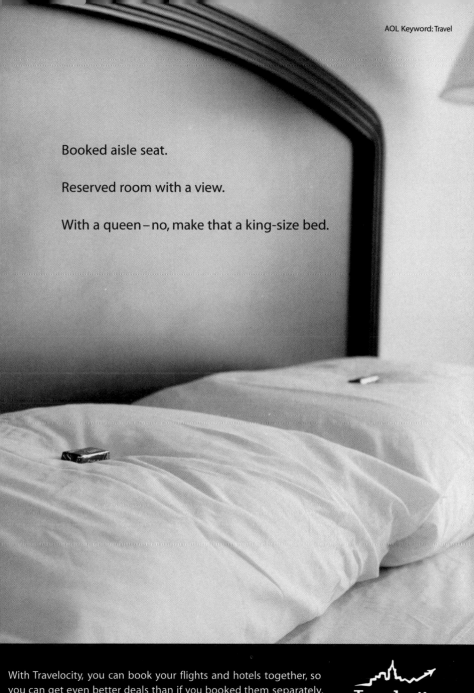

Booked aisle seat.

Reserved room with a view.

With a queen – no, make that a king-size bed.

With Travelocity, you can book your flights and hotels together, so you can get even better deals than if you booked them separately. You'll save time and money without compromising the quality of your trip. Choose your airline seat, search for alternate airports, pick your hotel room type, even choose the neighborhood you'd like to stay in

Travelocity

Visit www.travelocity.com or call 1-888-TRAVELOCITY

(US$108) deluxe double with sun deck; A$250 (US$163) honeymoon suite with balcony. Extra person A$20 (US$13). Rates include buffet breakfast. AE, DC, MC, V. Free parking in secured lot. CityRail: Kings Cross. **Amenities:** Guest lounge. *In room:* A/C, TV.

OXFORD STREET/DARLINGHURST
MODERATE

The Hughenden ⊛ *Finds*   This boutique hotel in a restored 1870 Victorian mansion is a real find and is situated in Woollahra's tree-lined antiques district (just opposite the entrance to Centennial Park). Pleasant and reassuring, it's a bit like visiting your grandparents and comes complete with warmly romantic rooms, opulent iron beds, blue-on-white linen, and antique furniture. The owners, two artist sisters, have lent their personal touch to the place. Check out their paintings, book readings, and high teas incorporating classical recitals on Sundays. Breakfasts are served in their leafy conservatory.

14 Queen St., Woollahra, NSW 2025. ℂ 02/9363 4863. Fax 02/9362 0398. hughenden@ozemail.com.au. 33 units. A$174 (US$113) double; A$204 (US$132) deluxe room. Rates include English breakfast. AE, MC, V. Free parking. Bus: 380, 382, or 387. **Amenities:** Restaurant; piano bar. *In room:* A/C, TV.

Sullivans Hotel   About half of this boutique hotel's guests come from overseas, mainly from the United Kingdom, Europe, and the United States. There's also a small corporate following. Sullivans is right in the heart of the action in one of Sydney's most popular shopping, entertainment, restaurant, and gay pub and club areas. The hotel is particularly popular with Americans during the Gay and Lesbian Mardi Gras, held during the month of February. All rooms are simple and compact, but good for a few nights. They come with an attached shower. Standard rooms have two single beds, and the garden rooms have a queen-size bed and pleasant garden views.

21 Oxford St., Paddington, NSW 2021. ℂ 02/9361 0211. Fax 02/9360 3735. www.sullivans.com.au. 64 units. A$122 (US$79) standard double; A$144 (US$94) garden room double and triple; A$195 (US$127) family room. AE, DC, MC, V. Limited free parking. Bus: 378 from Central Station or 380 from Circular Quay. **Amenities:** Breakfast cafe; small heated outdoor pool; free bike rental, coin-op laundry; garden courtyard area; free Internet. *In room:* A/C, TV w/free movies, fridge, hair dryer, iron, safe (garden rooms only).

Wattle Private Hotel   This attractive Edwardian-style house built between 1900 and 1910 offers homey accommodations in the increasingly fashionable inner-city suburb of Darlinghurst, known for its great cafes, nightlife, and restaurants. Rooms are found on four stories, but there's no elevator, so if you don't fancy too many stairs try to get a room on the lower floor. Rooms are smallish but are opened up by large windows. Twin rooms have a better bathroom, with a tub. The decor is a jumble of Chinese vases, ceiling fans, and contemporary bedspreads. The owners are very friendly.

108 Oxford St. (at corner of Palmer St.), Darlinghurst, NSW 2010. ℂ 02/9332 4118. Fax 02/9331 2074. wattlehotel@yahoo.com.au. 12 units. A$99 (US$64) double. Extra person A$11 (US$7.15). Rates include continental breakfast. MC, V. No parking. Bus: Any to Taylor Square from Circular Quay. **Amenities:** Coin-op laundry. *In room:* A/C, TV, minibar.

IN NEWTOWN

Billabong Gardens   For that real inner-city feel, you can't beat Newtown with its busy street happenings, cheap restaurants, and grunge look. It's also easily accessed by buses and the Newtown CityRail station. Billabong Gardens is just off the main drag, King Street, and is classed with a five-star backpackers rating by the National Roads and Motorists' Association. While there are dormitory accommodations here, you might also consider the double or twin rooms, which offer pretty good value. The more expensive rooms have their own bathrooms. It's a friendly place with lots of native plants scattered around and a pool set in a pleasant courtyard. Rooms are simply furnished in pine and have exposed brickwork. They are cleaned daily. On the property is a comfortable TV lounge and a large kitchen. It's very secure and offers 24-hour access. Motel-style rooms are also offered here.

5–11 Egan St., Newtown, NSW 2042. © 02/9550 3236. Fax 02/9550 4352. www.billabonggardens.com.au. 37 units. A$20–A$23 (US$13–US$15) dorm; A$66–A$88 (US$43–US$57) double/twin. Motel rooms: A$88 (US$57) double; A$105 (US$68) triple. Family rooms available. MC, V. A$5 (US$3.25) parking. CityRail: Newtown. Bus: 422, 423, 426, or 428. **Amenities:** Small heated outdoor pool; Jacuzzi; coin-op laundry; TV room; games room; barbecue; fax; free Internet; kitchen; pay phones; safe. *In room:* No phone.

IN GLEBE
EXPENSIVE
Tricketts Luxury Bed & Breakfast 𝒜𝒜   As soon as I walked into this atmospheric old place, I wanted to ditch my modern Sydney apartment and move in. Your first impression as you enter the tessellated, tiled corridor of this 1880s Victorian mansion is the jumble of plants and ornaments, the high ceilings, the Oriental rugs, and the leaded windows. Guests play billiards over a decanter of port or relax among magazines and wicker furniture on the balcony overlooking the fairly busy Glebe Point Road. The bedrooms are quiet and homey (no TVs). My favorites are no. 2, with its wooden floorboards and king-size bed, and no. 7, with its queen-size bed, extra single bed, and very large bathroom. Rooms all have showers. There's a nice courtyard out back with a barbecue.

270 Glebe Point Rd., Glebe, NSW 2037. © 02/9552 1141. Fax 02/9692 9462. www.tricketts.com.au. 7 units. A$150–A$176 (US$98–US$114) double; A$198 (US$129) honeymoon suite. Rates include continental breakfast. Free parking. Bus: 431 from George St. **Amenities:** Tour desk; massage; nonsmoking rooms. *In room:* A/C, TV, hair dryer.

MODERATE
Alishan International Guest House   The Alishan is another quiet place with a real Aussie feel. It's at the city end of Glebe Point Road, just 10 minutes by bus from the shops around Town Hall. It's a mixture between an upmarket youth hostel and a typical guesthouse. Standard dorm rooms are spotless, light and bright, and come with two sets of bunks. Doubles have a double bed, a sofa and armchair, and an en-suite shower. Grab room no. 9 if you fancy sleeping on one of two single mattresses on the tatami mat floor, Japanese style.

100 Glebe Point Rd., Glebe, NSW 2037. © 02/9566 4048. Fax 02/9525 4686. www.alishan.com.au. 19 units. A$30 (US$20) dorm bed; A$110 (US$72) double; A$154 (US$100) family room. Extra person A$16 (US$10). AE, MC, V. Secured parking available for 6 cars; otherwise, metered on-street parking. Bus: 431 or 433 from George St., or Kingsford Smith Shuttle from airport. **Amenities:** Coin-op laundry; TV room; barbeque area; Internet access. *In room:* TV, fridge.

IN BONDI
Bondi Beach is a good place to stay if you want to be close to the surf and sand, though if you're getting around by public transport you'll need to catch a bus to Bondi Junction, then a train to the city center. (You can stay on the bus all the way, but it takes forever.)

As well as the properties recommended below, there are two good backpacker hostels: **Indy's** (© **02/9365 4900**) at 35a Hall St. offers four- to eight-person dorm rooms for A$16 (US$11) in winter and A$20 (US$14) in summer, and double rooms in a separate building opposite North Bondi Surf Club for the same price per person; **Noah's**, 2 Campbell Parade (© **02/9365 7100**), has a great ambience and offers clean, modern four- to eight-person dorm rooms from

A$21 to A$24 (US$14–US$16) as well as doubles for A$50 (US$33) and beach doubles for A$55 (US$36). Weekly rates range from A$126 to A$330 (US$82–US$215).

VERY EXPENSIVE

Swiss-Grand Hotel 🐸🐸   Situated right on Bondi Beach, overlooking the Pacific, the Swiss-Grand is the best hotel in Bondi. The lobby is grand indeed, with high ceilings and stylish furniture. A renovation in 2002 made each room into a suite, with separate bedroom and living room. All suites are spacious, and each comes with a rather luxurious bathroom. All rooms have two TVs; some have Jacuzzis. All oceanfront rooms have balconies.

Corner of Campbell Parade and Beach Rd. (P.O. Box 219, Bondi Beach, NSW 2026). © **02/9365 5666**, or 1800/655 252 in Australia, 800/344-1212 in the U.S., 0800/951 000 in the U.K., or 0800/056 666 in New Zealand. Fax 02/9365 9710. www.swissgrand.com.au. 230 units. A$308 (US$200) standard double; A$352 (US$229) double with ocean view; from A$396 (US$257) suite. Extra person A$44 (US$29). AE, DC, MC, V. Free parking. Bus: 380 from Circular Quay. **Amenities:** 2 restaurants; rooftop and indoor heated pools; fitness center; Jacuzzi; tour desk. *In room:* A/C, TV, coffeemaker, hair dryer, iron.

MODERATE

Bondi Beachside Inn 🐸 *Kids*   With such a great location, right on the beachfront, you can't get much better value than this. A modern seven-story hotel, which prides itself on being family-friendly, the Beachside Inn has quite large rooms with compact bathrooms. The more expensive rooms have balconies with ocean views. It's well loved by return travelers, so it's very advisable to book well ahead, especially during the Australian summer.

152 Campbell Parade, Bondi Beach, NSW 2026. © **02/9130 5311**. Fax 02/9365 2646. www.bondiinn. com.au. 70 units. A$100–A$120 (US$63–US$76) double. AE, DC, MC, V. Free parking. Bus: 380 or 382 from Circular Quay. **Amenities:** 24-hr reception; free security parking. *In room:* A/C, TV, fridge, tea/coffeemaking facilities, toaster.

Ravesi's on Bondi Beach 🐸🐸   Right on Australia's most famous golden sands, this boutique property reopened in May 2002 after major renovations to the restaurant, bar, and many of its rooms. Now, this AAA-rated three-star hotel offers modern minimalist rooms with white marble bathrooms—all very chic with African tribal wall hangings. Standard doubles are spacious; there's a one-bedroom suite and a split-level one-bedroom option with the bedroom upstairs. Room nos. 5 and 6 and the split-level suite have the best views of the ocean. All rooms have Juliet balconies, and the split-level suite has its own terrace. If you're a light sleeper, request a room on the top floor because the popular Ravesi's Restaurant can cook up quite a bit of noise with its Modern Australian cuisine on busy nights. An attractive glass-sided ground floor bar is the "in" place on the Bondi scene, with lounge, house, and "chill" music every evening. The bar is a great place to watch the outside street scene.

Corner of Hall St. and Campbell Parade, Bondi Beach, NSW 2026. © **02/9365 4422**. Fax 02/9365 1481. www.ravesis.com.au. 16 units. A$120 (US$78) standard double; A$185–A$195 (US$120–US$127) double with side view; A$275 (US$179) beachfront room; A$245 (US$159) 1-bedroom suite; A$245–US$275 (US$159–US$179) split-level suites with terrace; $A450 (US$292) penthouse. Extra person A$25 (US$16.25). 2 children under 12 stay free in parent's room. AE, DC, MC, V. Parking at the Swiss-Grand Hotel nearby for A$8 (US$5.20) for 24 hr. CityRail: Bondi Junction; then Bus 380. Bus: 380 from Circular Quay. **Amenities:** Restaurant; bar; tour desk; 24-hour room service; laundry service; dry cleaning. *In room:* AC, TV, minibar, hair dryer, iron, safe.

SERVICED APARTMENTS

Bondi Serviced Apartments   If you plan on staying a week or more in Sydney then these pleasant, privately-owned apartments could be ideal. They're on busy Bondi Road, a 25-minute walk to the beach, and opposite from a post office (with phones—the apartment complex doesn't have any), an Internet parlor, and a 24-hour supermarket. The rooms at the front of the hotel suffer from traffic noise, but are larger than the quieter ones in the back. That said, all are good-size and have a nice feel about them. Each has a double bed (the front rooms also have an extra single) and a full kitchen. There's no air-conditioning (though the sea breeze does tend to cool Bondi down a bit in summer). You must book for a week or more, but if there are free rooms you can negotiate a 4-night stay. The owner describes it as a "no frills" complex—hence the lack of phones, Internet address, fax number, credit card payments, and once-weekly servicing.

164–166 Bondi Rd., Bondi Beach, NSW 2026. ℭ **02/9363 5529.** No fax. 12 units. A$385–A$550 (US$250–US$357) apt, per week. Ask about cheaper rates for longer stays. No credit cards. Free parking. Bus 380 or 382 from city center and Bondi Junction. **Amenities:** Coin-op laundry; weekly cleaning service. *In room:* TV, kitchen, iron and ironing board.

IN MANLY

If you decide to stay at my favorite beachside suburb, you'll need to be aware that ferries from the city stop running at midnight. If you get stranded, you'll be facing either an expensive taxi fare (around A$35/US$23), or you'll need to make your way to the bus stand behind Wynyard CityRail station to catch a night bus. Consider buying a Ferry Ten or JetCat Ten ticket, which will save you quite a bit of money in commuting expenses if you're staying in Manly for a few days.

As well as the recommendations below, Manly has several backpacker places worth checking out. The best is **Manly Backpackers Beachside,** 28 Ragland St. (ℭ **02/9977 3411;** fax 02/9977 4379), which offers dorm beds for A$24 (US$16), doubles without bathroom for A$70 (US$46), and doubles with bathroom for A$80 (US$52). The hostel charges a A$30 (US$20) key deposit.

VERY EXPENSIVE

Manly Pacific Parkroyal ⭐⭐   If you could bottle the views from this top-class hotel—across the sand and through the Norfolk Island Pines to the Pacific Ocean—you'd make a fortune. Standing on your private balcony in the evening with the sea breeze in your nostrils and the chirping of hundreds of lorikeets is nothing short of heaven. The Manly Pacific is the only hotel of its class in this wonderful beachside suburb. There's nothing claustrophobic here, from the broad expanse of glittering foyer to the wide corridors and spacious rooms. Each standard room is light and modern with two double beds, a balcony, limited cable TV, and all the necessities from bathrobes to an iron and ironing board. Views over the ocean are really worth the extra money. The hotel is a 10-minute stroll, or a A$4 (US$2.60) taxi ride, from the Manly ferry.

55 North Steyne, Manly, NSW 2095. ℭ **02/9977 7666,** or 800/835-7742 in the U.S. and Canada. Fax 02/9977 7822. www.sixcontinentshotels.com/sixcontinentshotels. 169 units. A$283–A$327 (US$184–US$212) double, depending on view; A$512 (US$333) suite. Extra person A$32 (US$21). AE, DC, MC, V. Parking A$10 (US$6.50). Ferry or JetCat: Manly. **Amenities:** 2 restaurants; 2 bars; heated rooftop pool; Jacuzzi; exercise room; sauna; concierge; tour desk; 24-hr. room service; laundry service. *In room:* A/C, TV, dataport, minibar, coffeemaker, hair dryer, iron.

MODERATE

Manly Lodge ⭐ *Kids*   At first sight this ramshackle building halfway between the main beach and the harbor doesn't look like much—especially the cramped hostel-like foyer bristling with tourist brochures. But don't let the tattiness put you off. Some of the rooms are lovely, and the whole place has a nice atmosphere and plenty of character. Double rooms are not exceptional and come with a double bed, stone or carpet floors, a TV and VCR, and either a Jacuzzi or a tub/shower combination. Some of the standard doubles, and all of the deluxe doubles have a kitchen. Family rooms have a set of bunk beds and a double in one room, and a shower. Family suites are very classy; each has a small kitchen area, one double and three singles in the bedroom, and two sofa beds in the living area. The lodge also has table tennis and even an Olympic-size trampoline.

22 Victoria Parade, Manly, NSW 2095. ℂ **02/9977 8655.** Fax 02/9976 2090. www.manlylodge.com.au. 24 units. Standard double A$132–A$154 (US$86–US$100) peak season, A$108–A$132 (US$70–US$86) off season; deluxe double A$154–A$198 (US$100–US$128) peak season, A$132–A$154 (US$86–US$100) off season; family suite with Jacuzzi A$264–A$330 (US$172–US$215) peak season, A$187–A$262 (US$122–US$170) off season. Peak season: Christmas, Easter, and school holidays. Extra person A$30 (US$20), extra child under 10 A$17 (US$11). Ask about weekly rates; management will also negotiate off-season prices. Rates include continental breakfast. AE, MC, V. Free parking. Ferry or JetCat: Manly. **Amenities:** Exercise room; Jacuzzi; sauna; coin-op laundry. *In room:* A/C, TV.

Manly Paradise Motel and Beach Plaza Apartments 🅰   I walked into this place after taking a look around the modern Manly Waterfront Apartment Hotel next door and immediately felt more at home here. The motel and the apartment complex are separate, but share the same reception area. The irregularly shaped rooms are big yet cozy, and come with a shower (no tub) and a springy double bed. Though there is no restaurant, you can get breakfast in bed. My only concern is that the traffic can make it a little noisy during the day (but, you'll probably be on the beach anyway). Some rooms have glimpses of the sea. A swimming pool (with views) on the roof is shared with the apartment complex.

The apartments are magnificent—very roomy, with thick carpets. They're stocked with everything you need, including a washing machine and dryer, a full kitchen with dishwasher, and two bathrooms (one with a tub). The sea views from the main front balcony are heart-stopping.

54 North Steyne, Manly, NSW 2095. ℂ **1800/815 789** in Australia, or 02/9977 5799. Fax 02/9977 6848. www.manlyparadise.com.au. 40 units. A$105–A$165 (US$62–US$94) double motel unit; A$295 (US$192) 2-bedroom apt. Extra person A$25 (US$16). Ask about lower rates for long-term stays. AE, DC, MC, V. Free secured parking. Ferry or JetCat: Manly. **Amenities:** Indoor heated pool; dry cleaning; nonsmoking rooms. *In room:* A/C, TV, dataport, hair dryer, iron.

Periwinkle-Manly Cove Guesthouse   Nicely positioned across the road from one of Manly's two harbor beaches, the Periwinkle is a short walk from the ferry, the shops along the Corso, and the main ocean beach. Rooms are small and come with a double bed. Some have a shower and toilet (these go for the higher prices noted below), but otherwise you'll have to make do with one of four separate bathrooms. (One has a tub.) A full kitchen next to a pleasant-enough communal lounge means you could save money by not eating out. Room nos. 5 and 10 are the nicest and have screened balconies overlooking the harbor (but no bathrooms). For atmosphere I prefer the Manly Lodge (see above). No smoking inside.

18–19 E. Esplanade, Manly, NSW 2095. ℂ **02/9977 4668.** Fax 02/9977 6308. www.periwinkle.citysearch.com.au. 18 units, 12 with bathroom. A$126 (US$82) double without bathroom; A$165 (US$107) double with bathroom. Units with harbor views A$10 (US$6.50) extra. Extra person A$25 (US$16). Rates include continental breakfast. MC, V. Free parking. Ferry or JetCat: Manly. **Amenities:** Kitchen; common lounge; coin-op laundry; nonsmoking rooms. *In room:* TV, fridge.

IN MOSMAN

Buena Vista Hotel   If you want to see how wealthy Sydneysiders live, then stay in this upmarket northern suburb a 10-minute walk from Taronga Zoo. The rooms above this popular local pub, just down the road from some of Sydney's most exclusive boutiques, are clean and comfortable, and a bargain by Sydney standards. Each comes with a springy queen-size bed or two singles, a small TV, and a sink; a few have balconies. All except room no. 13 have good city views. The best is room no. 1, which is larger and brighter than the rest, and comes with a large balcony with good views. Family rooms come with a double bed, a foldout sofa bed, and a trundle bed—all in one room. All rooms share nice bathrooms. The fabulous Balmoral Beach is a 10-minute walk away, or just 5 minutes by bus. Ask hotel staff for ferry times and bus/ferry connection details from Taronga Zoo and Mosman wharves. The taxi from the city is around A$22 (US$14). If you stay here I highly recommend the Japanese restaurant, Kyushu, at Shop 5, 9–11 Grosvenor St., Neutral Bay (✆ **02/9953 8272**), about 5 minutes away by taxi.

76 Middle Head Rd., Mosman, NSW 2095. ✆ **02/9969 7022.** Fax 02/9968 2879. 13 units (5 doubles, 6 single, 1 twin, 1 family room), none with bathroom. A$75 (US$49) single; A$85 (US$55) double/twin; A$100 (US$65) family room. Rates include continental breakfast. AE, DC, MC, V. Ferry: Taronga Zoo, then a 5-min. bus ride. Bus: Taronga Zoo from Wynyard station. **Amenities:** Restaurant; 2 bars. *In room:* TV.

AT THE AIRPORT

Stamford Sydney Airport 🏵🏵   This is the best airport hotel. Opened in 1992, it has the largest rooms, each with a king-size bed or two doubles, access to airport information, and a good-size bathroom with tub. The location is 7 minutes from the airport via a free pickup service. Day-use rates for 2 to 4 hours cost A$85 (US$55) and from 4 to 8 hours A$115 (US$75).

Corner of O'Riordan and Robey sts. (P.O. Box 353, Mascot, Sydney, NSW 2020). ✆ **1300/301 391** in Australia, or 02/9317 2200. Fax 02/9317 3855. www.stamford.com.au. 314 units. A$270 (US$176) double; from A$370 (US$240) and up for suite. Extra person A$25 (US$16). Children under 17 stay free in parent's room. Ask about discount packages and weekend rates. AE, DC, MC, V. A$5 (US$3.25) self-parking fee for up to 10 days. **Amenities:** 2 restaurants; bar; good-size outdoor pool; fitness center; Jacuzzi; sauna; concierge; business center 24-hr. room service; babysitting; laundry service; currency exchange; nonsmoking rooms; executive rooms. *In room:* A/C, TV, minibar, dataport, coffeemaker, hair dryer, iron.

4 Where to Dine

Sydney is a gourmet paradise, with an abundance of fresh seafood, a vast range of vegetables and fruit always in season, prime meats at inexpensive prices, and top-quality chefs making an international name for themselves. You'll find that Asian and Mediterranean cooking have had a major influence on Australian cuisine, with spices and herbs finding their way into most dishes. Immigration has brought with it almost every type of cuisine you could imagine, from African to Tibetan, from Russian to Vietnamese, with whole areas of the city dedicated to one type of food, while other areas are a true melting pot of styles.

Sydney is a great place to try "Modern Australian," or "Mod Oz," cuisine, which has been applauded by chefs and food critics around the world. Modern Australian cuisine emphasizes fresh ingredients and a creative blend of European styles with Asian influences. (Some foodies complain that some restaurants use the label "Modern Australian" as an excuse to serve skimpy portions—like one lamb chop atop a tiny mound of mashed potatoes sprinkled with curry sauce.) At its best, Modern Australian food is world-class, but you'll probably have to go to the best of Sydney's restaurants to really see what the scene is all about.

Australians think American-style coffee tastes like ditch water and largely favor a range of Italian-style coffee creations. Ask for a latte if you just want coffee with milk. "Bottomless" cups of coffee are very rare in Australia. By the way, in Australia, the first course is called the entree and the second course the main.

> ### *Value* What to Know About BYO
>
> Most moderate and inexpensive restaurants in Sydney are **BYO,** as in "bring your own" bottle, though some places may also have extensive wine and beer lists. More moderately priced restaurants are introducing "corkage" fees, which mean you pay anywhere from A$1 to A$4 (US65¢–US$2.60) per person for the privilege of the waiter opening your bottle of wine. Very expensive restaurants discourage BYO.
>
> Sydney's **cheap eats** are congregated in inner-city areas such as along King Street in Newtown, Crown Street in Darlinghurst, and Glebe Point Road in Glebe. There are also inexpensive joints scattered among the more upscale restaurants in Kings Cross and along trendy Oxford Street.
>
> I would avoid the takeout booths along the ferry wharves at Circular Quay, after revelations showed that some of them harbored nasty bugs. The fish-and-chip shop opposite the "bottle shop" (liquor store) is an exception—it also has some of the best french fries in Sydney.
>
> Smoking is banned in all Sydney restaurants, except if you're eating from sidewalk tables.

NEAR CIRCULAR QUAY
VERY EXPENSIVE

Forty One ✶✶ MODERN AUSTRALIAN   Powerful people, international celebrities, and average Sydneysiders out for a special celebration all come here to feel exclusive. It's won plenty of awards including the Amex Best Restaurant in NSW and Best Restaurant in Sydney City 2002. The views over the city are terrific, the service is fun, the cutlery is the world's best, and Swiss chef and owner Dietmar Sawyere has given the food a wickedly good Asian slant. In all, it's a glamorous place to experience the best of Australian cuisine. The signature dish is the crown roast wild hare, with celeriac and potato purée, Viennoise carrots, and chartreuse jus. The menu changes every 2 weeks to keep up with seasonal produce.

Level 41, Chifley Tower, 2 Chifley Sq. (℗ **02/9221 2500.** forty.one@chifleytower.com.au. Reservations required. 3-course menu A$120 (US$78); 3-course menu with matched wine A$140 (US$91); 6 courses with wine A$200 (US$130). AE, DC, MC, V. Tues–Fri noon–4pm; Mon–Sat 7–10pm. CityRail: Wynyard.

Guillaume at Bennelong ✶ FRENCH   If you go to Bondi, you have to swim in the Pacific; if you see the Harbour Bridge, you have to walk across it; if you visit the Opera House, you must eat at Guillaume at Bennelong. The restaurant is as uniquely designed as the building itself, with tall glass windows that furrow around in an arch and grab the harbor and Circular Quay by the throat. Reopened after renovations in 2002, renowned French chef Guillaume Brahini's offerings could include sealed veal sweetbreads with broad beans, asparagus, peas and shiitake mushrooms, or a confit of Atlantic salmon on braised endive with red wine sauce. It's hardly innovative but sometimes tradition wins through. Many would rather miss the first half of the opera they've paid a fortune to see rather than leave before dessert. The best bar in town is upstairs where you can see over the water to the bridge and up to the other "sails." Good bar food is

Central Sydney Dining

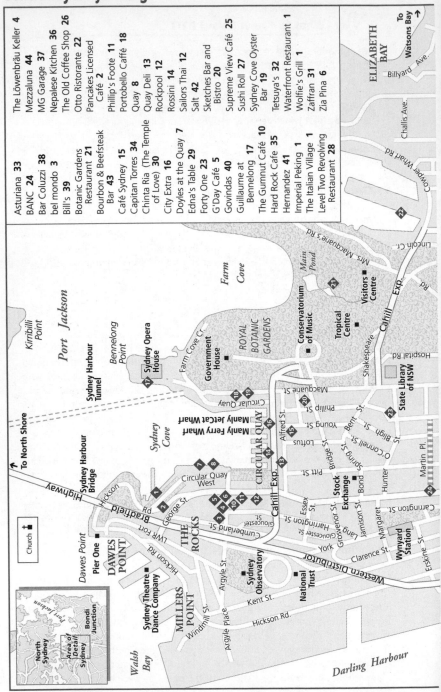

Asturiana **33**
BANC **24**
Bar Coluzzi **38**
bel mondo **3**
Bill's **39**
Botanic Gardens Restaurant **21**
Bourbon & Beefsteak Bar **43**
Café Sydney **15**
Capitan Torres **34**
Chinta Ria (The Temple of Love) **30**
City Extra **16**
Doyles at the Quay **7**
Edna's Table **29**
Forty One **23**
G'Day Café **5**
Govindas **40**
Guillaume at Bennelong **17**
The Gumnut Café **10**
Hard Rock Cafe **35**
Hernandez **41**
Imperial Peking **1**
The Italian Village **1**
Level Two Revolving Restaurant **28**

The Löwenbräu Keller **4**
Mezzaluna **44**
MG Garage **37**
Nepalese Kitchen **36**
The Old Coffee Shop **26**
Otto Ristorante **22**
Pancakes Licensed Café **2**
Phillip's Foote **11**
Portobello Caffé **18**
Quay **8**
Quay Deli **13**
Rockpool **12**
Rossini **14**
Sailors Thai **12**
Salt **42**
Sketches Bar and Bistro **20**
Supreme View Café **25**
Sushi Roll **27**
Sydney Cove Oyster Bar **19**
Tetsuya's **32**
Waterfront Restaurant **1**
Wolfie's Grill **1**
Zaffran **31**
Zia Pina **6**

126

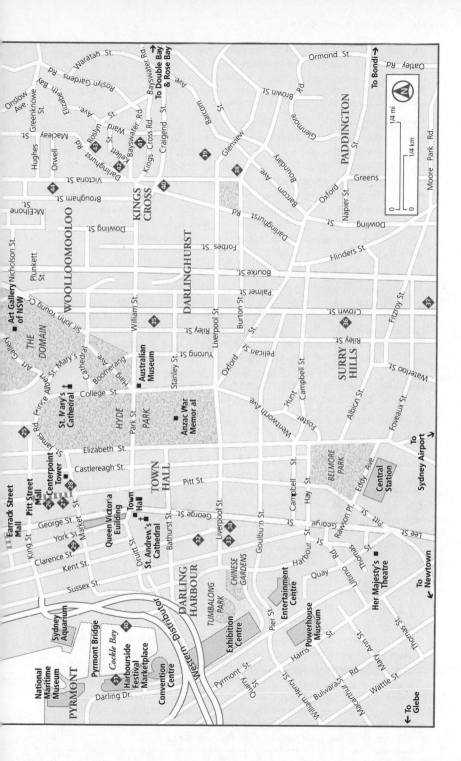

Waratah St.

Roslyn Gardens Rd

Elizabeth Bay
Onslow Ave.
Greenknowe St.

Hughes St.
Macleay St.
Orwell

Roslyn Ave.
Ward Ave.
Kellett St.
Darlinghurst Rd.

Bayswater Rd.
Kings Cross Rd.
Craigend St.

To Double Bay
& Rose Bay

Ormond St.

Brown St.

Ormond St.

Glennmore St.

Bayswater Rd

Ave.

Barcom St.

Glenview

PADDINGTON

Greens

Oxford St.

Napier St.

Dowling St.

Moore Park Rd.

Oatley Rd.

To Bondi

1/4 mi
1/4 km

Victoria St.

WOOLLOOMOOLOO

McElhone St.
Brougham St.

KINGS CROSS

Dowling St.

Nicholson St.

Plunkett St.

Forbes St.

DARLINGHURST

Darlinghurst Rd

Flinders St.

Bourke St.

Palmer St.

Burton St.

Oxford St.

Pelican St.

Crown St.

Fitzroy St.

SURRY HILLS

Riley St.

Waterloo St.

Albion St.

Foveaux St.

To Sydney Airport

Art Gallery of NSW

Art Gallery Rd.

THE DOMAIN

Sir John Young Cr.

St. Mary's Cathedral

Cathedral
Prince Albert Rd.

St. Mary's
Boomerang
Haig Ave.

College St.

William St.

Australian Museum

Riley St.
Stanley St.
Yurong St.
Liverpool St.

Wentworth Ave.

Foster St.
Hunt St.

Campbell St.

HYDE PARK

Park St.

Anzac War Memorial

Hay St.

Eddy Ave.

BELMORE PARK

Central Station

Lee St.

To Newtown

St. James Rd.

Elizabeth St.

Castlereagh St.

TOWN HALL

Pitt St.

George St.

Pitt St.
King St.

Farrack Street Mall
Pitt Street Mall
Centerpoint Tower

George St.

York St.

Clarence St.

Kent St.

Sussex St.

Market St.

Queen Victoria Building

Druitt St.

St. Andrew's Cathedral

Bathurst St.

Liverpool St.

George St.

Goulburn St.

Campbell St.

Hay St.

George St.

Rawson Pl.

Pitt St.

DARLING HARBOUR

TUMBALONG PARK

CHINESE GARDENS

Exhibition Centre

Pier St.

Entertainment Centre

Harris St.

Powerhouse Museum

Quay St.

Ultimo Rd.

Thomas St.

Her Majesty's Theatre

Mary Ann St.

Macarthur St.

Bulwara Rd.

William Henry St.

Wattle St.

Thomas St.

To Glebe

Sydney Aquarium

Pyrmont Bridge

Cockle Bay

Harbourside Festival Marketplace

National Maritime Museum

PYRMONT

Convention Centre

Darling Dr.

Western Distributor

Pyrmont St.

Quarry St.

127

available until 11:30pm. It won the 2003 "Best Restaurant" Award from the *Sydney Morning Herald's Good Food Guide.*

In the Sydney Opera House, Bennelong Point. © 02/9241 1999. Fax 02/9241 3795. enquiries@guillaume atbennelong.com.au. Reservations recommended. Main courses A$35 (US$23). AE, DC, MC, V. Mon–Sun 5:30–10:30pm; Fri noon–3pm. CityRail, bus, or ferry: Circular Quay.

EXPENSIVE

Botanic Gardens Restaurant MODERN AUSTRALIAN   You couldn't ask for a better walk to get to a restaurant than through the Royal Botanic Gardens, next to the Sydney Opera House. Enjoying lunch on the wisteria-covered balcony in the middle of Sydney's most beautiful park is a treat every visitor should enjoy. Main courses include the very popular white sausage *(boudin blanc)* with lentils and braised fennel. Try the perfect crème brûlée with underlying plum purée for dessert (A$11.50/US$7.50).

In the Royal Botanic Gardens. © 02/9241 2419. Reservations recommended. Main courses A$22–A$28 (US$14–US$18). AE, DC, MC, V. Daily noon–3pm. Bus or ferry: Circular Quay.

City Extra ITALIAN/AUSTRALIAN   Because this place stays open 24 hours, it's convenient if you get the munchies at a ridiculous hour. It's also nicely placed right next to the Manly ferry terminal. The plastic chairs and tables placed outside make it a pleasant spot to while away an inexpensive meal. A range of pastas are on offer as well as salads, pies, steaks, ribs, fish, and Asian-influenced dishes. There's also a fat selection of desserts. The food is much nicer and a better value next door at Rossini (see below).

Shop E4, Circular Quay. © 02/9241 1422. Reservations not accepted. Main courses A$13–A$26 (US$8.45–US$17). 10% surcharge midnight–6am, Sun, and public holidays. AE, DC, MC, V. Daily 24 hr. CityRail, bus, or ferry: Circular Quay.

Sketches Bar and Bistro 🍴 PASTA   Sketches is a favorite with people on their way to the Opera House and those who know a cheap meal when they taste one. Here's how it works: After getting the barman's attention, point to one of three different sized plates stuck to the bar above your head—the small size is adequate if you're an average eater, the medium plate is good for filling up after a hard day of sightseeing (and no lunch), but I've yet to meet the person who can handle the large serving with its accompanying bread, pine nuts, and Parmesan cheese. Then, with ticket in hand, head toward the chefs in white hats and place your order. There are 12 pastas to choose from and several sauces, including carbonara, marinara, pesto, vegetarian, and some unusual ones to dishearten pasta purists, such as south Indian curry. Meals are cooked in front of you while you wait.

Finds   A Great Place for Picnic Grub

If you're looking for something to take with you on a harbor cruise or on a stroll through the Royal Botanic Gardens, you can't go wrong with **Quay Deli,** E5 Alfred St. (next to the pharmacy under the Circular Quay CityRail station, facing the road; © 02/9241 3571). Everything is fresh and tasty, and there are all sorts of goodies, including gourmet sandwiches and takeout foods such as olives, Greek dishes, pasta, salads, meat pies, and the best English-style custard tarts around. Lunch items go for A$1.80 to A$4.50 (US$1.25–US$3.15). It's open Monday through Friday from 5am to 6:45pm, Saturday from 9am to 4pm. No credit cards.

What's the Restaurant Surcharge?

Some Australian restaurants charge surcharges on public holidays and Sundays. Typically this can amount to an extra A$2 to up to A$6 or more per person. Restaurants argue that it's difficult to get staff to work on these days so they need to provide them with a cash incentive not to call in with a hangover from the previous night.

In the Hotel Inter-Continental, 117 Macquarie St. (enter from Bridge St.). © 02/9240 1210. Reservations recommended. Pasta A$11–A$17 (US$7–US$11). AE, DC, MC, V. Mon–Fri 5:30–9:30pm; Sat 5:30–10:30pm. CityRail, bus, or ferry: Circular Quay.

Sydney Cove Oyster Bar SEAFOOD   Just before you reach the Sydney Opera House you'll notice a couple of small shedlike buildings with tables and chairs set up to take in the stunning views of the harbor and the Harbour Bridge. The first is a Sydney institution, serving some of the best oysters in town. Light meals such as Asian-style octopus and seared tuna steak are also on the menu.

No. 1 Eastern Esplanade, Circular Quay East. © 02/9247 2937. www.sydneycoveoysterbar.com. Main courses A$25–A$35 (US$16–US$23). 10% surcharge weekends and public holidays. AE, DC, MC, V. Mon–Sat 11am–11pm; Sun 11am–8pm. CityRail, bus, or ferry: Circular Quay.

MODERATE

Rossini *Kids* ITALIAN   This cafeteria-style Italian restaurant opposite Ferry Wharf No. 5 at Circular Quay is wonderfully positioned for people-watching. The outside tables are perfect for breakfast or a quick bite before a show at the Opera House. Breakfast croissants, Italian donuts, muffins, and gorgeous Danish pastries cost A$2 (US$1.30), and bacon and eggs A$8 (US$5.20). Wait to be seated for lunch or dinner, make your choice, pay at the counter, take a ticket, and then pick up your food. Meals, including veal parmigiana, cannelloni, ravioli, chicken crepes, and octopus salad, are often huge. You could easily get away with one meal for two people—ask for an extra plate—and while not the best Italian you'll ever eat, it is tasty. Coffee fanatics rate the Rossini brew as average.

Shop W5, Circular Quay. © 02/9247 8026. Main courses A$10–A$15 (US$6.50–US$9.75). Cash only. Daily 7am–10pm. CityRail, bus, or ferry: Circular Quay.

INEXPENSIVE

Portobello Caffé PIZZA/SANDWICH   Sharing the same address as the Sydney Cove Oyster Bar (and the same priceless views), the Portobello Caffé offers first-class gourmet sandwiches on Italian wood-fired bread, small but delicious gourmet pizzas, breakfast croissants, snacks, cakes, and hot and cold drinks. Walk off with sensational ice cream in a cone for around A$3 (US$1.95).

No.1 Eastern Esplanade, Circular Quay East. © 02/9247 8548. Main courses A$8 (US$5.20). 10% surcharge Sun and public holidays. AE, DC, MC, V. Minimum credit card purchase A$30 (US$20). Daily 8am–11:50pm. CityRail, bus, or ferry: Circular Quay.

IN THE ROCKS
VERY EXPENSIVE

bel mondo NORTHERN ITALIAN   With its uncomplicated northern Italian cuisine, bel mondo has deservedly positioned itself alongside the best of Sydney's upscale restaurants. At this family-run affair, chef Stefano Manfredi is helped out in the kitchen by his mum, Franca, a pasta diva in her own right. The restaurant is large and long with high ceilings, and the energetic pace and the banging and clashing coming from the open kitchen give the place a New York feel. Standout appetizers include grilled sea scallops with soft polenta and pesto. Favorite main courses include roast lamb with rosemary and roast potatoes, and potato gnocchi with burnt butter and Parmesan. The wine list is extensive. Bel mondo's **Antibar** is cheaper and more relaxed; it offers some of the best antipasto I've tasted, as well as light meals (from A$14–A$22/US$8.80–US$14) and features jazz on Friday evenings from 5:30 to 7:30pm.

In the Argyle Department Store, 3rd floor, 18–24 Argyle St., The Rocks. ℂ 02/9241 3700. reservations@bel mondo.com.au. Reservations recommended. Main courses A$27–A$46 (US$17–US$30). 10% surcharge Sun and public holidays. AE, DC, MC, V. Tues–Fri 12:30–2:30pm; Mon–Thurs 6:30–10:30pm; Fri–Sat 6:30–11pm; Sun 6:30–10pm. CityRail, bus, or ferry: Circular Quay.

Café Sydney MODERN AUSTRALIAN   Located in the historic Customs House—the building with the clock tower across the square and behind the ferry wharfs at Circular Quay—Café Sydney is a fabulous spot to watch the world go by on the harbor and has spectacular views of the Sydney Harbour Bridge. The interior design is fresh and modern with lots of wood and soft lighting, and the menu features plenty of European-style classics and others with a distinct Asian influence with an emphasis on seafood. A couple of options are the tandoori roast salmon with *chana masala* (curried chickpeas, Indian-style) and *coconut sambol* (a hot coconut side dish from Sri Lanka), and the wood-grilled veal with figs and Gorgonzola and *speck* (bits of bacon, German-style). The Havana Bar here offers cozy wood cubicles and great cocktails. Downstairs on the courtyard is an informal cafe, which is also nice for cocktails or a quick unassuming lunch.

Level 5, Customs House, corner Loftus and Alfred sts., Circular Quay. ℂ 02/9251 8683. Reservations recommended in restaurant. Main courses A$23–A$30 (US$15–US$20). AE, DC, MC, V. Lunch daily 12:30–2:30pm; dinner Mon–Sat 6:30–10:30pm. CityRail, bus, or ferry to Circular Quay.

Quay ✸✸✸ MODERN AUSTRALIAN   Some feel this is Sydney's best restaurant—and with its enviable location on top of the cruise-ship terminal, it offers perhaps the loveliest view. In good weather the sun sparkles off the water and through the large glass windows while the Opera House, city skyline, North Shore suburbs, and the Harbour Bridge all look magnificent. At night, when the lights from the city wash over the harbor and the bridge and the Opera House's sails are lit up, the view is even better. The new menu from chef Peter Gilmore is a revelation of French, Italian, and Australian ideas. The signature dishes include the crisped pressed duck, with garlic purée and porcini mushrooms, and the seared yellowfin tuna with tomato jelly, roasted eggplant, and basil oil. Expensive, yet select, this restaurant has tempted all the big-name visitors to Sydney. Quay was named Restaurant of the Year in 2003 by the *Sydney Morning Herald's Good Food Guide*.

On the upper level of the Overseas Passenger Terminal, Circular Quay West, The Rocks. ℂ 02/9251 5600. info@quay.com.au. Reservations recommended well in advance. Main courses A$38 (US$25). A$6 (US$3.90) per-person surcharge on public holidays. AE, DC, MC, V. Mon–Fri noon–2:30pm; Mon–Sun 6–10pm. CityRail, bus, or ferry: Circular Quay.

Rockpool ✸✸ MODERN AUSTRALIAN   The Rockpool is an institution in Sydney known for its inventive food. It's approached by a steep ramp and opens up into two stories of ocean-green carpet, designer chairs, and stainless steel. Along with the bar, the kitchen—with its busy chefs and range of copper pots and pans—is very much at the center of things. Menus change regularly, but you can expect to find anything from a dozen fresh oysters and spanner crab with

bel mondo **3**
Café Sydney **13**
Doyles at the Quay **7**
G'Day Café **5**
The Gumnut Café **9**
Imperial Peking **1**
The Italian Village **1**
The Löwenbräu Keller **4**
Pancakes Licensed Café **2**
Phillip's Foote **10**
Quay **8**
Rockpool **12**
Sailors Thai **11**
Waterfront Restaurant **1**
Wolfie's Grill **1**
Zia Pina **6**

Church
Pedestrian Walkway
Stairs

lemon ravioli to fish cooked with coconut milk and Indian garam masala and
served with snow peas and semolina noodles. On my last visit, the desserts were
a letdown after the fabulous main courses.

109 George St., The Rocks. ℂ **02/9252 1888**. Reservations required. Main courses A$38 (US$25). AE, DC,
MC, V. Mon–Sat 6–11pm. CityRail, bus, or ferry: Circular Quay.

Sailors Thai ⍟ THAI   With a reputation as hot as the chiles in its jungle curry,
Sailors Thai canteen attracts lunchtime crowds who come to eat great-tasting
noodles and the likes of pork and prawn won-ton soup, red curry with lychees,
and Thai salads at its single, stainless steel table lined with some 40 chairs. Four
other tables overlook the cruise-ship terminal and the quay. Downstairs, the a la
carte restaurant serves inventive food (which is a far cry from your average Thai
restaurant), such as stir-fried pineapple curry with chiles and cashew nuts and a
wonderfully glutenous coconut ash pudding, made from the ash of burnt
coconuts cooked with licorice root, coconut water, rice flower, and sugar.

106 George St., The Rocks. ℂ **02/9251 2466**. Reservations required well in advance in restaurant; not
accepted in canteen. Main courses A$26–A$32 (US$17–US$21) in restaurant; A$15–A$23 (US$9.75–US$15)
in canteen. AE, DC, MC, V. Restaurant Mon–Fri noon–2pm; Mon–Sat 6–10pm; canteen daily noon–9pm.
CityRail, bus, or ferry: Circular Quay.

EXPENSIVE

Doyles at the Quay *Overrated* SEAFOOD   Just below Quay (see above) is
Doyles, a name synonymous with seafood in Sydney. Most customers sit outside

to enjoy the fabulous views across the harbor, though a set of thick green railings does somewhat interrupt the view of the Opera House. Businesspeople and tourists come here if they don't want to lay out the cash for Quay or if they fancy a more relaxed style. The most popular dish is basically pricey fish and chips (choose between ocean trout, garfish, John Dory, swordfish, whiting, and salmon). You can also get a dozen oysters for A$20 (US$13) or a lobster for A$65 (US$42).

A second Doyles, **Doyles on the Beach** 🐟🐟 (𝄢 **02/9337 2007**), at Watsons Bay, is a much better option, with lovely beach and water views. Food here includes Tasmanian "Atlantic" salmon cutlets (A$33.50), and the lobster and prawn salad (A$63). Nearby is **Doyles Fisherman's Wharf** (𝄢 **02/9337 1572**), located on the ferry wharf; it used to be a takeout joint, but now also has sit-down service. Doyles also runs the food service at the wonderful Watsons Bay Hotel nearby. Ferries run to Watsons Bay from Circular Quay in time for lunch at 10:30 and 11:30am, and 12:30pm Monday through Friday, and at 11:15am and 1:15pm on Saturday, Sunday, and public holidays. On weekdays the last ferry returns at 3:50pm, and on weekends at 4:15 and 6:10pm.

Overseas Passenger Terminal, Circular Quay. 𝄢 02/9252 3400. Main courses A$20–A$33 (US$13–US$21). DC, MC, V. Daily 11:30am–3pm; Mon–Sat 5:30–10:30pm; Sun 5:30–9:30pm. CityRail, bus, or ferry: Circular Quay.

The Löwenbräu Keller 🐟 BAVARIAN

Renowned for celebrating Oktoberfest every day for the past 20 years, this is the place to come to watch Aussies let their hair down. Come for lunch and munch a club sandwich or focaccia in the glassed-off atrium while watching the daytime action of The Rocks. For a livelier scene, head here on a Friday or Saturday night, when mass beer-sculling (chugging) and yodeling are accompanied by a brass band, and costumed waitresses ferry foaming beer steins about the atmospheric, cellarlike inside. Options include hearty southern German and Austrian fare and no less than 17 varieties of German beers in bottle or on draught (tap). There's a good wine list, and, surprisingly, vegetarians have a few choices, too.

18 Argyle St. (at Playfair St.), The Rocks. 𝄢 02/9247 7785. Reservations recommended. Main courses A$15–A$22 (US $9.75–US$14). AE, DC, MC, V. Daily 9:30am–2am (kitchen closes at 11pm). CityRail, bus, or ferry: Circular Quay.

Pancakes Licensed Café AMERICAN/PANCAKES

Buttermilk and chocolate pancakes, and French crepes filled with seafood, chicken, and mushrooms; vegetables in a basil-cream sauce; or smoked ham and cheese are the most popular dishes served up in this old warehouse done up in Art Deco style. The beef ribs, pastas, and pizzas are also good sellers.

10 Hickson Rd. (enter from Hickson Rd. or George St.), The Rocks. 𝄢 02/9247 6371. Reservations not accepted. Main courses A$13–A$22 (US$8.40–US$14); breakfast (served 24 hr.) A$8.95–A$12 (US$5.80–US$7.80). AE, DC, MC, V. Daily 24 hr. CityRail, bus, or ferry: Circular Quay.

Phillip's Foote BARBECUE

Venture behind this historic pub and you'll find a courtyard strung with tables and benches and large barbecues. Choose your own steak, lemon sole, trout, chicken, or pork, and throw it on the "barbie." It's fun, it's filling, and you might even make some new friends while your meal's sizzling.

101 George St., The Rocks. 𝄢 02/9241 1485. Main courses A$23 (US$15). AE, DC, MC, V. Mon–Sat noon–midnight; Sun noon–10pm. CityRail, bus, or ferry: Circular Quay.

Waterfront Restaurant 🐟

You can't help but notice the mast, rigging, and sails that mark this restaurant set in a converted stone warehouse. It's one of four in a row right next to the water below the main spread of The Rocks. It's very popular at lunchtime when businesspeople snap up the best seats outside in the sunshine, but at night with the colors of the city washing over the harbor it can be magical. You get a choice of such things as steaks, mud crab, fish filets, prawns, or the seafood plate—including lobsters, Balmain bugs (small, odd-looking crayfish), prawns, scallops, baby squid, fish pieces, and octopus (A$53). The food is simple and fresh, with a price markup added for the glorious position and views.

In the same building you'll find sister restaurants **Wolfie's Grill** (② 02/9241 5577), which serves good chargrilled beef and seafood dishes for A$22 to A$26 (US$14–US$17), and **The Italian Village** (② 02/9247 6111), which serves regional Italian cuisine for A$22 to $A30 (US$14–US$20). The third in the line is an excellent Chinese restaurant, the **Imperial Peking** ✿ (② 02/9247 7073), which serves excellent food for similar prices. All four restaurants offer fantastic water views and indoor and outdoor dining.

In Campbell's Storehouse, 27 Circular Quay West, The Rocks. ② 02/9247 3666. Reservations recommended. Main courses A$26–A$29 (US$17–US$19). A$3.30 (US$2.15) per person surcharge weekends and public holidays. AE, DC, MC, V. Daily 12–10:30pm. CityRail, bus, or ferry: Circular Quay.

MODERATE

The Gumnut Café *(Kids)* MODERN AUSTRALIAN   A hearty lunch in a courtyard shaded from the sun by giant umbrellas—ah, heaven. With a great location in the heart of The Rocks, this 1890 sandstone cottage restaurant also has an extensive indoor seating area, so it's a perfect place to take a break from all that sightseeing. On weekends live jazz sets the mood. The breakfast specials (A$8.50/US$5.50) are popular with guests from surrounding hotels, while at lunchtime it's bustling with tourists and local office workers. Lunchtime blackboard specials cost A$11 (US$7.15). More regular fare includes the disappointing Ploughman's Lunch (why spoil a traditional English meal of bread, cheese, and pickles by limiting the bread and adding unappealing vegetables and salad?) and the better chicken and leek pies, and good pasta and noodle dishes. Filling Turkish sandwiches cost between A$7.70 and A$9 (US$5–US$5.85). The courtyard is heated in winter, making it quite cozy. It's BYO with no corkage fee.

28 Harrington St., The Rocks. ② 02/9247 9591. Main courses A$8.50–A$14 (US$5.50–US$9.10). AE, DC, MC, V. Sun–Wed 8am–5pm; Thurs–Sat 8am–10:30pm. CityRail, bus, or ferry: Circular Quay.

INEXPENSIVE

G'Day Café *(Value)* CAFE   According to the manager, about half the tourists who visit Sydney visit this little place in the heart of The Rocks. That's not surprising considering it offers simple but satisfying food at around half the price you'd expect to pay in such a tourist precinct. The interior is uninspiring, but out the back there's a pleasant leafy courtyard. Among the offerings are focaccia sandwiches, hearty soups, salads, burgers, lasagna, chili con carne, and beef curry.

83 George St., The Rocks. ② 02/9241 3644. Main courses A$3–A$7 (US$1.95–US$4.55). AE. Sun–Thurs 5am–midnight; Fri–Sat 5am–3am. CityRail, bus or ferry: Circular Quay.

Zia Pina PIZZA/PASTA   With 10 tables crammed downstairs and another 24 upstairs, there's not much room to breathe in this cramped traditional pizzeria and spaghetti house. But squeeze in between the close-fit bare-brick walls and wallow in the clashes and clangs coming from the hard-working chefs in the kitchen. Pizzas come in two sizes; the larger feeds two people. Servings of delicious gelato go for a cool A$4 (US$2.60).

93 George St., The Rocks. ℂ 02/9247 2255. Reservations recommended well in advance. Main courses A$9–A$22 (US$5.85–US$14). AE, DC, MC, V. Daily noon–3pm; Sun–Mon 5–9pm; Tues–Thurs 5–10:30pm; Fri–Sat 5–11:30pm. CityRail, bus, or ferry: Circular Quay.

NEAR MARTIN'S PLACE

BANC ⋒⋒ MODERN FRENCH   Winner of "Best Restaurant" in 2001 from the *Sydney Morning Herald's Good Food Guide,* Banc is an upmarket establishment that serves up top-class French-inspired food in a formal atmosphere of columns and white linen-clothed tables. It's popular with business executives and high flyers. Service is excellent, and the cellar has over 900 wine labels from Australia and abroad. The specialties are a mouthful: among them "Assiette of Lamb with Haricot Blanc and a Ragout of Vegetables," "Open Ravioli of Crustacea with a Vanilla and Oyster Nage," and "Pan-Fried John Dory and Roasted Scallops with a Curry Emulsion." Dress to impress. Downstairs is **Wine Banc,** great for cocktails and cigars (and live jazz on Fri nights).

53 Martin Place. ℂ 02/9233 5300. Fax 02/9233 5311. banc@pacific.net.au. Reservations essential. Main courses A$38–A$45 (US$25–US$30); 7-course meal with wines A$125 (US$81); vegetarian option A$110 (US$72). AE, DC, MC, V. Tues–Fri noon–2:30pm; Tues–Sat 6:30–10pm. CityRail: Martin Place.

NEAR TOWN HALL
VERY EXPENSIVE

Level Two Revolving Restaurant *(Overrated* GRILLS/ROASTS/SEAFOOD/ ASIAN   For those not scared of heights, Level Two offers a self-service all-you-can-eat buffet—ideal for those who don't want to pay for the a la carte goodies a floor down at its sister restaurant, **Level One.** This place is popular with tourists, who come here for the stupendous views across Sydney and, on a clear day, as far as the Blue Mountains. The dining area takes about an hour to fully rotate, but even going this slowly I find it a bit off-putting—especially when you're some 250m (820 ft.) up. You can heap your plate with a selection of five appetizers, then choose between 15 main courses, including steaks, roasts, pork knuckles, beef Stroganoff, seafood, and Asian dishes. There are also five desserts to choose from. The prices are as sky-high as the views.

A.M.P. Centerpoint Tower Market St. (between Pitt and Castlereagh sts.). ℂ 02/9233 3722. reservations@ sydney-tower-restaurant.com. Reservations recommended. Lunch Mon–Sat A$40 (US$26), Sun A$49 (US$32); early dinner A$49 (US$32), regular dinner A$49 (US$32). A$20 (US$13) for children 3–12 at lunch and early dinner. 10% surcharge (on drinks only) weekends and public holidays. AE, DC, MC, V. Daily 11:30am–3:30pm and 5–11:45pm. CityRail: St. James. Monorail: City Centre.

Tetsuya's ⋒⋒⋒ MODERN JAPANESE   Chinese chef Tetsuya Wakuda is arguably Sydney's most famous chef, and his food is certainly cutting edge. This is not Japanese food as you might know it, but a fusion of Eastern and Western styles that has made him the darling of Australian cuisine. Everybody who is anybody wants to eat here in the tranquil Japanese garden that serves as the restaurant space—getting a table is difficult. To have a chance you need to book 4 weeks in advance. (They don't take bookings before this time.) The restaurant is stylish and light, and the food mind-blowing. The menu is constantly changing, but to give you an idea, think tofu with duck foie gras and sherry vinegar; marinated roast breast of duck with coffee; tartare of tuna with olive oil and wasabi jelly; and seared filet of veal with porcini mushrooms, sautéed green beans, and asparagus.

529 Kent St., Sydney. ℂ 02/9267 2900. Reservations essential. Lunch A$100 (US$65) per person (8 courses); dinner A$155 (US$101) per person (12 courses). AE, DC, MC, V. Fri noon–3pm; Tues–Sat 6–10pm. CityRail: Town Hall.

EXPENSIVE

Capitan Torres SPANISH   Sydney's Spanish quarter, based on Liverpool Street (a 10-min. walk from Town Hall station on your right just past Sydney's main cinema strip) offers some great restaurants, of which Capitan Torres is my favorite. Downstairs is a tapas bar with traditional stools, Spanish serving staff, and lots of authentic dark oak. Upstairs on two floors is a fabulous restaurant with heavy wooden tables, chairs, and an atmosphere thick with sangria and regional food. The garlic prawns are incredible, and the whole snapper a memorable experience. The tapas are better at **Asturiana** (© **02/9264 1010**), another Spanish restaurant a couple of doors down. Make sure you insist on eating at the bar for that authentic experience. *Warning:* Spanish serving staff in Sydney can be a bit gruff, so come armed with your own sense of humor.

73 Liverpool St. (just past the cinema strip on George St., near Town Hall). © **02/9264 5574.** Fax 02/9283 2292. Main courses A$18–A$23 (US$12–US$15); tapas A$8–A$11 (US$5.20–US$7.15). AE, DC, MC, V. Daily noon–3pm; Mon–Sat 6–11pm; Sun 6–10pm. CityRail: Town Hall.

Edna's Table 🏵🏵 AUSTRALIAN   Jennice Kersch and brother Raymond have Australian native cuisine in their hearts, and it shows as they introduce diners to such exotic specialties as crocodile and assorted local seafood. Interesting combinations include barramundi (a big freshwater fish from the Northern Territory) cooked in paperbark, carpaccio of tuna with native anise, and Balmain bug (an unusually-armored, small native crayfish), and ravioli in pepper-berry sauce. One of Australia's national icons—the kangaroo—also hops onto the menu, despite calls to preserve native wildlife in the wild, rather than in the refrigerator. It's all served up in one of Sydney's most beautiful heritage buildings—refurbished in a light and elegant style—close to the Town Hall and Queen Victoria Building.

204 Clarence St. © **02/9267 3933.** Reservations recommended. Main courses A$28–A$33 (US$18–US$21). AE, DC, MC, V. Lunch Mon–Fri noon–3pm; dinner Tues–Sat 6–10pm. CityRail: Townhall. Monorail: Park St.

INEXPENSIVE

Supreme View Café 🏵 *Finds* CAFE   If you happen to be in the city center, then this fabulous, largely undiscovered restaurant/cafe is a must for the great value food and absolutely fantastic views reaching over Hyde Park and even to the harbor. It's very large inside, has panoramic windows, and serves meals from the counter. Breakfasts are hearty and include bacon and eggs, omelets, and cereals. It's particularly handy if you are staying in the lower Oxford Street area. All-day dishes include the likes of sandwiches, Caesar salad, homemade pies, pastas, and lasagna. Even if you're not hungry it's well worth popping in for a coffee.

Level 14, Law Courts Bldg., 184 Phillip St. (Queens Sq.). © **02/9230 8224.** Main courses A$8–A$13 (US$5.20–US$8.45); coffee and cake A$5 (US$3.25). No credit cards. Mon–Fri 7am–5pm. CityRail or bus: Museum.

Sushi Roll 🏵 SUSHI   The fresh, simple food at this bargain-basement take-out is a healthy alternative to the greasy edibles with which many travelers end up satisfying their hunger. A large range of sushi and nori rolls peek out from behind the counter if you turn up at lunchtime, and you can eat at the tables opposite. The gourmet sandwiches and meals served up by other establishments in the food court here make it a good stopover after a morning's shopping and sightseeing.

Sydney Central Plaza (downstairs in the food court next to Grace Brothers department store on Pitt St. Mall). © **02/9233 5561.** Sushi rolls A$1.70 (US$1.10) each. No credit cards. Mon–Wed and Sat 8am–7pm; Thurs 8am–10pm; Sun 10am–6pm. CityRail or bus: Town Hall.

DARLING HARBOUR
EXPENSIVE

Zaaffran 𝄞𝄞 INDIAN Sydney certainly hasn't seen an Indian restaurant like this one before. Forget the dark interiors and Indian murals. Here you find white surfaces, a glass-fronted wine cellar, and magnificent views of water and the Sydney skyline from the far side of Darling Harbour. (An outdoor terrace provides the best views.) The restaurant started life when two brothers from Bombay combined with chef Vikrant Kapoor (formerly the chef de cuisine at Raffles in Singapore). Together, they've revolutionized classic Indian cuisine. Expect such delights as chicken breast morsels in a yogurt-onion sauce with mustard seeds, curry leaf, and mountain chiles; or scallops, calamari, and tiger prawns in a ragout of puréed onions, tomato, and green coconut cream infused with Kashmiri chile, green cardamom, and cloves. Even fans of traditional Indian food are impressed by the creations here. It's a world away from almost anything you'd find back on the Indian subcontinent.

Level 2, 345 Harbourside Shopping Centre, Darling Harbour. ℂ **02/9211 8900**. Reservations recommended. Main courses A$20–A$25 (US$13–US$16). AE, DC, MC, V. Daily noon–2:30pm and 6–11pm. Ferry or monorail: Darling Harbour.

MODERATE

Chinta Ria (The Temple of Love) 𝄞 MALAYSIAN Cockle Bay's star attraction for those who appreciate good food and fun ambience without paying a fortune, Chinta Ria is on the roof of the three-story Cockle Bay development. In a round building dominated by a giant golden Buddha in the center, Chinta Ria serves up fairly good "hawker-style" (read: cheap and delicious) Malaysian food. While the food is good, the atmosphere is even more memorable. The service is slow, but who cares in such an interesting space, with plenty of nooks, crannies, and society folk to look at. There are seats outside (some get the noise of the highway), but the best views unfold inside. The hot-and-sour soup—a broth made with tofu, mushrooms, bamboo shoots, and preserved cabbage—makes an interesting starter, and I recommend the chile prawns and the *Hokkeien Char* (soft-cooked egg noodles with extras) as main dishes.

Cockle Bay Wharf Complex. ℂ **02/9264 3211**. Main courses A$11–A$28 (US$7.15–US$18). AE, DC, MC, V. Daily noon–2:30pm and 6–11pm. Ferry or monorail: Darling Harbour.

WOOLLOOMOOLOO WHARF

Otto Ristorante 𝄞𝄞 MODERN ITALIAN Recognized as one of Sydney's premier restaurants, Otto's lush designer appointments and dim lighting make it popular with both local celebrities and socialites alike. You must book well ahead to taste the delectable taleggio and cauliflower panna cotta or the twice-roasted duck in a rich lentil and red-wine sauce. For dessert I recommend you try the Campari and grenadine poached pear, which is simply out of this world.

8 the Wharf Woolloomooloo, 6 Cowper Wharf Rd. ℂ02/9368 7488. Reservations essential. Main courses A$30–A$36 (US$20–US$24); desserts A$15 (US$9.75). AE, DC, MC, V. Tues noon–10:30pm, Sat noon–midnight; Sun noon–9pm. Limited street parking. Bus: 311 from Circular Quay. Water taxi (drop off at Berth 53).

SURRY HILLS
VERY EXPENSIVE

MG Garage 𝄞𝄞𝄞 MODERN AUSTRALIAN This Greek influenced fine-dining restaurant has caused a stir in Sydney, and not just because it's in a car showroom. It's a glamorous, modern eatery with good service and a fashionable crowd. Tables are difficult to get, so you'll need to book at least a week in advance. The food is different to say the least, and I have never been as surprised by the combination of tastes and textures anywhere else. It really is a must-do Sydney dining experience for the adventurous. Among the offerings you might find are the roasted pigeon with roasted cauliflower, green lentils, dauphine potatoes, and a jus of Indian spices, or the twice cooked veal shanks stuffed with bread and thyme, semolina, and pumpkin gnocchi. The complicated dishes always have a taste surprise in store. It's best to get here by taxi, or it's a 20-minute walk from Central Station.

490 Crown St., Surry Hills. (C) 02/9360 7007. dpearce@trivettclassic.com.au. Reservations essential. Main courses A$34–A$43 (US$21–US$28). AE, DC, MC, V. Mon–Fri noon–2:30pm; Mon–Sat 6:30–10pm.

INEXPENSIVE

Nepalese Kitchen NEPALESE   Adventurous gourmands around here dig into this somewhat mildly spiced cuisine, which is something like a mixture of Indian and Chinese. Steamed dumplings, called *momo,* and stuffed crispy pancakes made with black-lentil flour are interesting appetizers, and the goat curry is the pick of the main courses. Also popular is the chargrilled lamb or chicken marinated in roasted spices. The curries are very tasty, and there's a large selection of vegetarian dishes, including flavorsome eggplant curry. Accompany your food with *achars* (relishes) to highlight the flavors of your dishes.

481 Crown St., Surry Hills. (C) 02/9319 4264. Main courses A$8–A$12 (US$5.60–US$8.40); 2-course meal A$18 (US$13). AE, DC, MC, V. Daily 6–11pm. CityRail: Central, then a 10-min. walk up Devonshire St.

IN KINGS CROSS/DARLINGHURST
EXPENSIVE

Mezzaluna 𝄐𝄐 MODERN ITALIAN   Exquisite food, flawless service, and an almost unbeatable view across the city's western skyline have all helped Mezzaluna position itself firmly among Sydney's top restaurants. A cozy, candlelit place with white walls and polished wooden floorboards, the main dining room opens up onto a huge, all-weather terrace kept warm in winter by giant, overhead fan heaters. The restaurant's owner, Sydney culinary icon Beppi Polesi, provides an exceptional wine list to complement a menu that changes daily. There's always a fabulous risotto on the menu, though, while other delights may include rack of lamb roasted with olives and oregano and served with baked baby eggplant, or roasted muscovy duck breast served with figs and pomegranate. Whatever you choose, you can't really go wrong. I highly recommend this place—of all Sydney's restaurants, I brought my long-term girlfriend here on her birthday, partly because she's special and partly because it doesn't break the bank.

123 Victoria St., Potts Point. (C) 02/9357 1988. Fax 02/9357 2615. www.mezzaluna.com.au. Reservations recommended. Main courses A$20–A$45 (US$13–US$29). AE, DC, MC, V. Mon–Fri noon–3pm; Mon–Sat 6–11pm. CityRail: Kings Cross.

Salt 𝄐𝄐𝄐 MODERN AUSTRALIAN   Renowned chef Luke Mangan is behind the food at this "in" place for the fashion crowd; dress up in your coolest outfit to fit into the scene. Inside it's all sleek molded plastic seats and chrome, with tables just big enough for two. The food is innovative and frankly superb, and could include anything from appetizers of quail eggs encrusted with salt and sugar or grilled salmon with tea infused zucchini, cucumber, and poached oyster to such main courses as snapper filet baked with shallots and thyme served with caramelized whitlof (endive or chicory) and snow peas. A martini is the drink of choice. Some less trendy people might find the scene a bit pretentious.

Something Fishy

If you like fresh seafood at cheap prices, then saunter down to the **Sydney Fishmarket** 𝒾, on the corner of Bank Street and Pyrmont Bridge Road, Pyrmont (𝒸 **02/9660 1611**, or call the **Fishline** at 𝒸 **02/ 9552 2180** for information on special events such as seafood cooking classes). The major fish retailers here sell sashimi at the cheapest prices in Sydney, but if you prefer your seafood cooked, then stay for lunch at one of the eateries scattered along the boardwalk and inside the main building.

To get to the Fishmarket, take the light rail (tram) from Central Station, Chinatown, or Darling Harbour to the Fishmarket stop, or you can walk from Darling Harbour. (Follow the signs.)

In the Kirketon Hotel, 229 Darlinghurst Rd., Darlinghurst. 𝒸 02/9332 2566. www.saltrestaurant.com.au. Reservations essential. Main courses A$35–A$42 (US$23–US$28). AE, DC, MC, V. Mon–Fri noon–3pm; daily 6–11pm.

MODERATE

Bourbon & Beefsteak Bar INTERNATIONAL   Extensively renovated in 2002, Bourbon & Beefsteak has been a Kings Cross institution for more than 30 years, and still attracts everyone from visiting U.S. sailors and tourists to businesspeople and ravers. The fact that it's open 24 hours means many people never seem to leave—occasionally you'll find someone taking a nap in the bathroom. The American-themed restaurant is always busy, churning out steaks, seafood, salads, Tex-Mex, ribs, and pasta, under the supervision of their new award-winning chef, Colin Holt. Breakfast is also served daily from 6 to 11am.

Every night there's live music in the Piano Bar from 5 to 9pm, followed by a mixture of jazz, Top 40, and rock 'n' roll until 5am. A disco downstairs starts at 11pm every night (finishing at 6am), and a larger one takes off in **The Penthouse at the Bourbon** bar on Friday and Saturday nights. The music is geared toward the 18-to-25 crowd of locals and tourists.

24 Darlinghurst Rd., Kings Cross. 𝒸 02/9358 1144. Reservations recommended Fri–Sun. Main courses A$13–A$28 (US$8.15–US$18). A$2 (US$1.30) surcharge weekends and public holidays. AE, DC, MC, V. Daily 24 hr. (happy hour 4–7pm). CityRail: Kings Cross.

Hard Rock Cafe AMERICAN   The obligatory half a Cadillac through the wall beckons you into this shrine to rock 'n' roll. Among the items on display are costumes worn by Elvis, John Lennon, and Elton John, as well as guitars from Sting and the Bee Gees, drums from Phil Collins and the Beatles, and one of Madonna's bras. The mainstays here are the burgers, with ribs, chicken, fish, salads, and T-bone steaks on the menu, too. Most meals come with french fries or baked potatoes and a salad. It's really busy on Friday and Saturday evenings from around 7:30 to 10:30pm, when you might have to line up to get a seat.

121–129 Crown St., Darlinghurst. 𝒸 02/9331 1116. Reservations not accepted. Main courses A$9.95–A$22 (US$6.50–US$14). 10% surcharge weekends and public holidays. AE, DC, MC, V. Daily noon–midnight. Shop daily 10am–midnight. Closed Christmas. CityRail: Museum; then walk across Hyde Park, head down the hill past the Australian Museum on William St., and turn right onto Crown St. Sydney Explorer Bus: Stop no. 7.

INEXPENSIVE

Govindas VEGETARIAN   When I think of Govindas, I can't help smiling. Perhaps it's because I'm reliving the happy vibe from the Hare Krishna center it's based in, or maybe it's because the food is so cheap! Or maybe it's because they even throw in a decent movie with the meal. (The movie theater is on a different floor.) The food is simple vegetarian, served buffet style and eaten in a basic room off black-lacquer tables. Typical dishes include pastas and salads, lentil dishes, soups, and casseroles. It's BYO and doctrine-free.

112 Darlinghurst Rd., Darlinghurst. ℂ 02/9380 5155. Dinner A$16 (US$10), including free movie. AE, MC, V. Daily 6–11pm. CityRail: Kings Cross.

IN GLEBE

The Boathouse on Blackwattle Bay ⋆⋆ (Finds) SEAFOOD   Located above Sydney University's rowing club and looking over a working area of Sydney Harbour, this converted boat shed offers water views across to the city and the Anzac Bridge. Terrific French-inspired seafood is served up in an elegant, yet informal, atmosphere of white tablecloths and good natural lighting. The service is good, and you can see the chefs at work in the open-plan kitchen. You can't go wrong with the signature dish, the fabulous snapper fish pie with roasted tomatoes and mashed potatoes. There are also usually nine varieties of oysters on the menu. A good wine list and delicious desserts cap off a truly memorable experience. I highly recommend the Boathouse, particularly as a lunchtime treat. Catch a taxi, as it's a little hard to find.

End of Ferry Rd., Glebe. ℂ 02/9518 9011. http://www.bluewaterboathouse.com.au. Main courses A$36–A$41 (US$23–US$27). AE, DC, MC, V. Tues–Sun noon–2:30pm and 6:30–10pm. Bus 431, 433, or 434 from Millers Point, The Rocks (via George St.), or 459 from behind Town Hall.

IN PADDINGTON

The top end of Oxford Street, which runs from Hyde Park in central Sydney toward Bondi, has a profusion of trendy bars and cafes and a scattering of cheaper eateries among the more glamorous ones.

Bistro Lulu ⋆ FRENCH/AUSTRALIAN   Gabrielle, my delightful French friend, raves about Bistro Lulu. "It's the worn floorboards and smell of coffee—it's like being back in Paris," she says. But Gabrielle won't find the same Australian influence in the food back home. Here chef Luke Mangan, also behind Salt (above), serves undemanding yet elegant food, which to me tastes a little ho-hum international, the sort of stuff you might find in good hotel restaurants worldwide. The duck confit and the vegetarian artichoke and fig gallette were Gabrielles' favorites, but the menu changes frequently. Such a long list of good wines by the glass is pleasing and rare to find in Sydney. The place is always busy.

257 Oxford St., Paddington ℂ 02/9380 6888. Main courses A$25–A$26 (US$16–US$17). AE, DC, MC, V. Thurs–Sat noon–3pm; daily 6-11pm (10pm Sun). Bus: Oxford St.

CAFE CULTURE

Debate rages over which cafe serves the best coffee in Sydney, which has the best atmosphere, and which has the tastiest snacks. The main cafe scenes are centered around Victoria Street in Darlinghurst, Stanley Street in East Sydney, and King Street in Newtown. Other places, including Balmoral Beach on the north shore, Bondi Beach, and Paddington, all have their favored hangouts as well.

Note: Americans will be sorry to learn that, unlike in the States, free refills of coffee are rare in Australian restaurants and cafes. Sip slowly. Expect a cup of coffee to cost between A$2.50 and A$3 (US$1.65–US$1.95); main courses between A$8 and A$15 (US$5.20–US$9.75). This section includes my favorite cafes around town.

Balmoral Boatshed Kiosk ⊛ *(Finds* A real find, this beautiful rustic cafe is right on the water beside the dinghies and sailing craft of the wooden Balmoral Boatshed (located to the far right of the central beach as you look at the water). It's a heavenly place for enjoying a breakfast muffin or a ham-and-cheese croissant while basking in the sun. This place is popular with families on weekend mornings, so if you hate kids, find somewhere else. (The nearby Sandbar has the best takeout food and coffee.)

2 The Esplanade, Balmoral Beach. ℂ **02/9968 4412.** Daily 8am–6pm in summer; 8am–5pm in winter. Ferry to Taronga Zoo, then bus to Balmoral Beach.

Bar Coluzzi Although it may no longer serve the best coffee in Sydney, this cafe's claim to fame is that long ago it served up real espresso when the rest of the city was drinking Nescafé. People-watching is a favorite hobby at this fashionably worn-around-the edges spot in the heart of Sydney's cafe district.

322 Victoria St., Darlinghurst. ℂ **02/9380 5420.** Daily 5am–8pm. CityRail: Kings Cross.

Bill's This bright and airy place, strewn with flowers and magazines, serves nouveau cafe–style food. It's so popular you might have trouble finding a seat. The signature breakfast dishes—including ricotta hotcakes with honeycomb butter and banana, and sweet corn fritters with roast tomatoes and bacon—are the stuff of legends. Last time I was here I asked for fried instead of scrambled eggs and was brusquely told I had to stick to the menu—a response that is really unforgivable.

433 Liverpool St., Darlinghurst. ℂ **02/9360 9631.** Fax 02/9360 7302. AE, MC, V. Mon–Sat 7:30am–3pm. CityRail: Kings Cross.

Hernandez ⊛ *(Finds* The walls of this tiny, cluttered cafe are crammed with eccentric fake masterpieces, and the air is permeated with the aroma of 20 types of coffee roasted and ground on the premises. It's almost a religious experience for discerning inner-city coffee addicts. The Spanish espresso is a treat.

60 Kings Cross Rd., Potts Point. ℂ **02/9331 2343.** Daily 24 hr. CityRail: Kings Cross.

The Old Coffee Shop ⊛ Sydney's oldest coffee shop opened in the Victorian Strand Arcade in 1891. The shop may or may not serve Sydney's best java, but the old-world feel of the place and the sugary snacks, cakes, and pastries make up for it. It's a good place to take a break from shopping and sightseeing.

Ground floor, The Strand Arcade. ℂ **02/9231 3002.** Mon–Fri 7:30am–5pm; Sat 8:30am–5pm; Sun 10:30am–4pm. CityRail: Town Hall.

IN NEWTOWN: GREAT ETHNIC EATS

Inner-city Newtown is three stops from Central Station on CityRail, and 10 minutes by bus from central Sydney. On Newtown's main drag, King Street, many inexpensive restaurants offer food from all over the world.

Le Kilimanjaro AFRICAN With so many excellent restaurants in Newtown—they close down or improve quickly enough if they're bad—I picked Kilimanjaro because it's the most unusual. It's a tiny place, with limited seating on two floors. Basically, you enter, choose a dish off the blackboard menu (while standing), and are escorted to your seats by one of the waiters. On a recent visit I had couscous, African bread (similar to an Indian chapati), and the *Saussou-gor* *di guan* (tuna in a rich sauce). Another favorite dish is *Yassa* (chicken in a rich African sauce). All meals are served on traditional wooden plates.

280 King St., Newtown. © 02/9557 4565. Reservations not accepted. Main courses A$8.50–A$9.50 (US$5.50–US$6.20). No credit cards. CityRail: Newtown.

Old Saigon *(Value* VIETNAMESE   Another Newtown establishment bursting with atmosphere, Old Saigon was owned until 1998 by a former American Vietnam War correspondent who loved Vietnam so much he ended up living there and marrying a local, before coming to Australia. Just to make sure you know his history, he's put up his photos on the walls and strewn the place with homemade tin helicopters. His Vietnamese brother-in-law has taken over, but the food is still glorious, with spicy squid dishes among my favorites. A popular pastime is grilling your own strips of venison, beef, wild boar, kangaroo, or crocodile over a burner at your table, then wrapping the meat in rice paper with lettuce and mint, and dipping it in a chile sauce. I highly recommend this place for a cheap night out.

107 King St., Newtown. © 02/9519 5931. Reservations recommended. Main courses A$12–A$43 (US$7.80–US$28). AE, DC, MC, V. Wed–Fri noon–3pm; Tues–Sun 6–11pm. BYO only. CityRail: Newtown.

AT BONDI BEACH

The seafront drag of Campbell Parade is packed with restaurants. A new addition in 2003 to the restaurant scene was Moorish Restaurant and Bar beneath the **North Bondi R.S.L. Club,** at the far end of Bondi Beach to your left as you look at the ocean. It's run by chef Luke Mangan, also behind Salt in Darlinghurst and Bistro Lulu, so the pedigree is excellent. It's a bit more casual than those two places and features a modern interpretation of Spanish and North African food, with a range of dishes from tapas to wood-fired grills. The views of the beach are terrific. A poolside cafe also opened in mid-2003 at the Bondi Icebergs Club at the other end of the beach.

MODERATE

Thai Terrific *☆* THAI   Thai Terrific by name, terrific Thai by nature. This superb place around the corner from the Bondi Hotel is run with flair and efficient service. The large back room can be noisy, so if you prefer less din with your dinner, sit at one of the sidewalk tables. The servings here are enormous—three people could easily fill up on just two main courses. The *tom yum* (hot and sour) soups and the prawn or seafood *laksa* noodle soups (spicy soup made with coconut milk) are the best I've tasted in Australia and are very filling. I also highly recommend the red curries.

Equally as nice (and quieter) is the Bangkok-style **Nina's Ploy Thai Restaurant** *☆,* at 132 Wairoa Ave. (© **02/9365 1118**), at the corner of Warners Avenue at the end of the main Campbell Parade strip. Main courses here cost between A$8 and A$12.50 (US$5.60 and US$8.75); cash only.

147 Curlewis St., Bondi Beach. © 02/9365 7794. Reservations recommended Fri–Sat nights. Main courses A$11–A$20 (US$7–US$13). AE, DC, MC, V. Daily noon–11pm. Bus: 380 to Bondi Beach.

INEXPENSIVE

Pompei's *☆☆* *(Finds* PIZZA/PASTA/ICECREAM   The recipe is simple: Use good ingredients and you'll get good pizzas—regulars swear they are the best in Sydney. Toppings include figs, prosciutto, fresh goat cheese, and pumpkin. They also have a selection of pizzas without cheese. And leave some room for the homemade gelati, the best in Sydney by far—the last time I had anything so good was recently in Pompeii, Italy, itself, and I swore then it was the best I'd ever eaten. Try the dense raspberry, the thick chocolate, the tiramisu, or the lemoncello. The water views and outside tables are another plus.

126–130 Roscoe St. at Gould St., Bondi Beach. © 9365 1233. Reservations recommended. Pizza A$13–A$17 (US$8.40–US$11). AE, DC, MC, V. Tues–Sun 11am–11pm.

Turenne's *☆* *(Finds* CARIBBEAN   Being greeted by the owner Turenne himself armed with his delicious complimentary punch and welcoming smile, makes you feel at home the moment you enter this beautifully understated restaurant. You will then discover the service to be both attentive and professional as you dine on such creations as prawns, cashews, and crispy coconut served on fresh betel leaf; I recommend the Court bouillon of a whole snapper with lentils and the crème brûlée with fresh fruit. The Caribbean music rounds off this relaxed experience perfectly.

49 Hall St. © 02/9363 7609. Reservations recommended. Main courses A$15–A$24 (US$9.75–US$16). Daily 6–11pm. Closed Tues in winter.

Yulla ISRAELI   Good value for money, this trendy restaurant is best enjoyed if you are able to score a spot out on the balcony overlooking Bondi. Go with the mixed plate, a generous selection of dips and chargrilled mushrooms with lots of hot pita bread. The spinach salad is another favorite, shredded green leaves roasted pumpkin, corn, Parmesan, avocado, and croutons.

1st floor, 38 Campbell Parade. © 02/9365 1788. Main courses A$7.50–A$18 (US$5–US$12); breakfast A$5.50–A$9.50 (US$3.60–US$6.20). AE, DC, MC, V. Daily 7am–11pm. Bus: Bondi Beach.

IN MANLY

Manly is 30 minutes from Circular Quay by ferry, or 15 minutes by JetCat. The takeout shops that line the Corso, as well as the pedestrian mall that runs between the ferry terminal and the main Manly Beach, offer everything from Turkish kebaps to Japanese noodles.

Ashiana *☆* INDIAN   You'll be hard-pressed to find a better cheap Indian restaurant in Sydney. Tucked away up a staircase next to the Steyne Hotel (just off the Corso and near the main beach), Ashiana has won a few prizes for its traditional spicy cooking. Portions are large and filling, and the service is very friendly. The butter chicken is magnificent, while the *Malai Kofta* (cheese and potato dumplings in a mild, creamy sauce) is the best this side of Bombay. Beer is the best drink with everything. Work off the heavy load in your stomach with a beachside stroll afterward.

Corner of Sydney Rd. and Corso Manly. © 02/9977 3466. Reservations recommended. Main courses A$8.50–A$18 (US$5.50–US$12). AE, MC, V. Daily 5:30–11pm. Ferry or JetCat: Manly.

VEGETARIAN

Green's Eatery VEGETARIAN   Of the many eateries in Manly, this nice little vegetarian place, just off the Corso on the turnoff just before the Steyne

---

(Finds Sydney's Best Fries

If you're looking for the best french fries in Sydney, head to **Manly Ocean Foods,** three shops down from the beach on the Corso. Avoid the fish and chips here (the shark is not the best in my opinion), and spend a few dollars extra on barramundi, salmon, perch, or snapper.

Hotel, does the best lunchtime business. The food is healthy and good quality. The menu includes 11 different vegetarian burgers, vegetable curries and noodle dishes, patties and salads, soups, smoothies, and wraps. They serve some exceptionally nice cakes here, too, which despite being incredibly wholesome are still surprisingly tasty. On a nice day you can sit outside.

1–3 Sydney Rd., Manly. ℂ 02/9977 1904. Menu items A$1.20–A$7.40 (US80¢–US$4.80). No credit cards. Daily 8am–7pm. Ferry or JetCat: Manly.

5 What to See & Do in Sydney

The only problem with visiting Sydney is fitting in everything you want to do and see. Of course, you won't want to miss the iconic attractions: the **Opera House** and the **Harbour Bridge.** Everyone seems to be climbing over the arch of the bridge these days on the Bridge Climb Tour, so look up for the tiny dots of people waving to the ferry passengers below.

You should also check out the native wildlife in **Taronga Zoo** and the **Sydney Aquarium,** stroll around the tourist precinct of **Darling Harbour,** and get a dose of Down Under culture at the not-too-large **Australian Museum.** Also try to take time out to visit one of the nearby national parks for a taste of the Australian bush, and if it's hot take your "cozzie" (swimming suit) and towel to **Bondi Beach** or **Manly.**

I also recommend a quick trip out of town. Go bushwalking in the **Blue Mountains,** wine tasting in the **Hunter Valley,** or dolphin spotting at **Port Stephens** (see chapter 4 for details on all three).

Whatever you decide to do, you won't have enough time. Don't be surprised if you start planning ahead for your next visit before your first is even finished.

THE OPERA HOUSE & SYDNEY HARBOUR

Officially called Port Jackson, **Sydney Harbour** is the focal point of Sydney and one of the features—along with the beaches and easy access to surrounding national parks—that makes this city so special. It's entered through **the Heads,** two bush-topped outcrops (you'll see them if you take a ferry or JetCat to Manly), beyond which the harbor laps at some 240km (149 miles) of shoreline before stretching out into the Parramatta River. Visitors are often awestruck by the harbor's beauty, especially at night when the sails of the Opera House and the girders of the Harbour Bridge are lit up, and the waters are swirling with the reflection of lights from the abutting high-rises—reds, greens, blues, yellows, and oranges. During the day, it buzzes with green-and-yellow ferries pulling in and out of busy Circular Quay, sleek tourist craft, fully-rigged tall ships, giant container vessels making their way to and from the wharves of Darling Harbour, and hundreds of white-sailed yachts.

The greenery along the harbor's edges is a surprising feature, and thanks to the **Sydney Harbour National Park,** a haven for native trees and plants, and a feeding and breeding ground for lorikeets and other nectar-eating bird life. In the center of the harbor is a series of islands, the most impressive is the tiny isle supporting **Fort Denison,** which once housed convicts and acted as part of the city's defense.

THE HARBOUR ON THE CHEAP   The best way to see Sydney Harbour, of course, is from the water. Several companies operate tourist craft for fare-paying customers (see "Harbor Cruises & Organized Tours," later in this chapter), but it's easy enough just to hop on a regular passenger ferry (see "Getting Around," earlier in this chapter). The best ferry excursions are over to the beachside suburb

Central Sydney Attractions

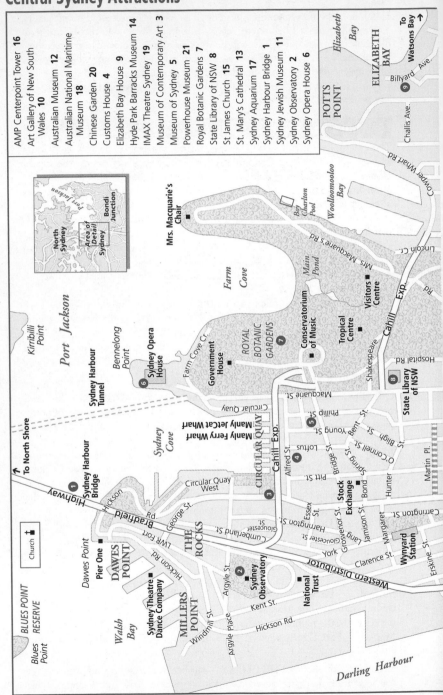

AMP Centerpoint Tower **16**
Art Gallery of New South Wales **10**
Australian Museum **12**
Australian National Maritime Museum **18**
Chinese Garden **20**
Customs House **4**
Elizabeth Bay House **9**
Hyde Park Barracks Museum **14**
IMAX Theatre Sydney **19**
Museum of Contemporary Art **3**
Museum of Sydney **5**
Powerhouse Museum **21**
Royal Botanic Gardens **7**
State Library of NSW **8**
St James Church **15**
St. Mary's Cathedral **13**
Sydney Aquarium **17**
Sydney Harbour Bridge **1**
Sydney Jewish Museum **11**
Sydney Observatory **2**
Sydney Opera House **6**

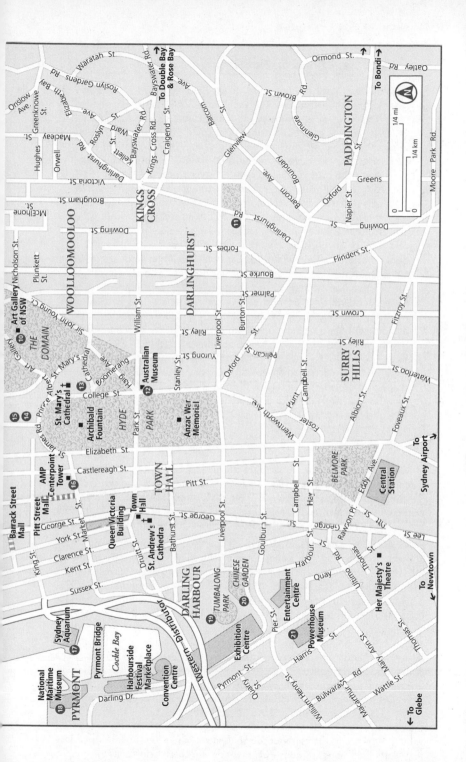

Value Great Deals on Sightseeing

The **Privileges Card** is a great way to save money if you plan to visit Sydney's biggest attractions. The card costs A$25 (US$16), is good for up to 1 month, and can be used in Sydney, Canberra, and Melbourne. In Sydney, all the major attractions offer some sort of discount if you show a Privileges Card, such as two-for-one admission or reduced-price admission if you're traveling alone, and buy-one-get-one-free reductions. With the card you'll also get discounts on harbor cruises (typically 20%), as well as discounts at certain restaurants (sometimes a free main course if two of you are dining, or a 20% rebate off the total bill for the cardholder and three others). To get a card, you'll need to fill out an application form, available on the Internet (www.privileges card.com) or at tourist information centers in Sydney; you'll receive a booklet with details on where you can save. Call Privileges at © **1800/ 675 500** (in Australia), or fax at 02/6254 8788. If you book in advance, the company can arrange to have the card sent to your hotel.

The **See Sydney & Beyond** card, a cashless smart card packaging more than 40 of the city's main attractions and tours, is valuable for avoiding lines and saving money, although you'll have to plan well to get the most out of it. The card can be purchased for a 1-, 2-, 3-, or 7-day period; the one-day pass costs A$59 (US$38) for adults and A$39 (US$25) for children. You can also purchase cards including public transporation; a one-day card with this option costs A$75 (US$49) for adults and A$47 (US$30) for children. For more information, call © **02/ 9247 6611** or see www.seesydneycard.com.

---

of **Manly** (come back after dusk to see the lights ablaze around The Rocks and Circular Quay); to **Watsons Bay,** where you can have lunch and wander along the cliffs; to **Darling Harbour,** for all the area's entertainment and the fact that you travel right under the Harbour Bridge; and to **Mosman Bay,** just for the ride and to see the grand houses that overlook exclusive harbor inlets.

FAST ACTION ON THE HARBOR   For a thrill ride, you can board a 420-horsepower jet boat, which zooms about on three high-speed waterway tours at speeds of up to 40 knots (about 80kmph/50 mph), with huge 240-degree turns with instant stops. **Harbour Jet** (© **1300 88 73 73** in Australia, or 02/9212 3555; www.harbourjet.com) offers a 35-minute Jet Blast Adventure costing A$50 (US$33) for adults, and A$35 (US$23) for kids under 15, and A$135 (US$88) for a family. A 50-minute Sydney Harbour Adventure costs A$65 (US$42) for adults, A$45 (US$29) for kids, and A$175 (US$114) for a family; a 1-hour-and-20-minute Middle Harbour Adventure cruise costs A$90 (US$59) for adults, A$60 (US$39) for kids, and A$240 (US$156) for a family. Rides are fast and furious and pump with rock music. A 1¼-hour Ultimate Scenic Adventure, which goes through Sydney Heads and out to sea, and ends up at Bondi, costs A$175 (US$114) for adults and A$160 (US$104) for kids. There's no family price for this one. The boat leaves from the Convention Jetty, between the Convention Centre and the Harbourside Shopping complex on the far side of Darling Harbour. These trips don't leave every day, so check beforehand.

Another option is **Oz Jet Boat** (© **02/9808 3700;** wwwozjetboating.com), which departs every hour from the Eastern Pontoon at Circular Quay (on the walkway to the Opera House). These large red boats are a bit more powerful than the blue Harbour Jet ones, but you might not notice the difference. This company offers a 30-minute ride for A$45 (US$29) for adults, A$30 (US$20) for kids, and A$130 (US$85) for a family; and a 1-hour trip out to Sydney Heads on weekends for A$80 (US$52) for adults, A$50 (US$33) for children, and A$240 (US$156) for a family.

SEAPLANE ESCAPE   Sydney Harbour Sea Planes (© **02/8274 7777;** www.sydneyseaplanes.com.au) take off from Sydney Harbour, fly around and over it, and go as far as Bondi (for A$110/US$72) or the Northern Beaches (for A$190/US$124). Or zoom up to Cottage Point on the Hawkesbury River and have a nice boozy lunch before swooping back down again (A$335/US$218).

Sydney Harbour Bridge (★★★ (Moments   One thing so few tourists do, but which only takes an hour or so, is to walk across the Harbour Bridge. The bridge, completed in 1932, is 1,150m (3,772 ft.) long and spans 503m (1,650 ft.) from the south shore to the north. It accommodates pedestrian walkways, two railway lines, and an eight-lane road. The 30-minute stroll from one end to the other offers some excellent harbor views. Once on the other side, you can take a CityRail train from Milsons Point train station back to the city (to Wynyard— change here for Circular Quay, Town Hall, or Central stations).

As you walk across, stop off at the **Pylon Lookout** (© **02/9247 3408**), at the southeastern pylon. Admission is A$5 (US$3.25) for adults, A$3 (US$1.95) for children, and A$12 (US$7.80) for a family. From the top of this bridge support, 89m (292 ft.) above the water, you get panoramic views of Sydney Harbour, the ferry terminals of Circular Quay, and beyond. An interesting museum charts the building of the bridge. Reach the pylon by walking to the far end of George Street in The Rocks toward the Harbour Bridge. Just past the Mercantile Pub you'll see some stone steps that take you onto Cumberland Street. From there, it's a 2-minute walk to the steps underneath the bridge on your right. Climb four flights of stairs to reach the bridge's Western Footway, and then walk along to the first pylon. **Note:** Climbing up inside the pylon involves 200 steps. The Pylon Lookout is open daily from 10am to 5pm (closed Christmas).

Sydney Opera House (★★★   Only a handful of buildings around the world are as architecturally and culturally significant as the Sydney Opera House. But what sets it apart from, say, the Taj Mahal and the Great Pyramids of Egypt is that this white-sailed construction caught midbillow over the waters of Sydney Cove is a working building. Most are surprised to learn it's not just an Opera House, but a full-scale performing-arts complex with five major performance spaces. The biggest and grandest of the lot is the 2,690-seat **Concert Hall,** which has the best acoustics of any man-made building of its type in the world. Come here to experience opera, but also chamber music, symphonies, dance, choral performances, and even rock 'n' roll. The **Opera Theatre** is smaller, seating 1,547, and is home to operas, ballets, and dance. The **Drama Theatre,** seating 544, and the **Playhouse,** seating 398, specialize in plays and smaller-scale performances. The Boardwalk, seating 300, is used for dance and experimental music.

The history of the building is as intriguing as the design. The New South Wales Government raised the construction money with a lottery. Danish Architect Jørn Utzon won an international competition to design it. From the start, the project was controversial, with many Sydneysiders believing it was a

---

(Moments **A Walk on the Wild Side: Climbing the Harbour Bridge**

At one time, only bridge workers had the opportunity to view Sydney from the top of the main bridge arch. But since October 1998, Sydneysiders and tourists have been able to experience the spectacular view and the exhilarating achievement of climbing to the top of one of Australia's icons. The experience takes 3 hours from check-in at the **Bridge-Climb** 𝄞𝄞 base at 5 Cumberland St., The Rocks (© **02/9240 1100** or 02/8274 7777; fax 02/9240 1122; www.bridgeclimb.com) to completion. The office is open daily from 8am to 6pm, and climbers leave in small groups every 10 minutes or so. Climbers wear "Bridge Suits" and are harnessed to a line. Participants are also breath-tested for alcohol and are banned from carrying anything, including cameras. Climbs cost A$145 (US$94) for adults and A$110 (US$72) for children ages 12 to 16 on weekdays during the day and for night climbs Monday to Thursday; and A$175 (US$114) for adults and $125 (US$81) for children for twilight climbs daily, night climbs on Friday and Saturday, and day climbs on Saturday and Sunday. Children under 12 are not allowed to climb.

---

monstrosity. Following a disagreement, Utzon returned home, without ever seeing his finished project, and the interior fell victim to a compromise design, which, among other things, left too little space to perform full-scale operas. And the cost? Initially the project was budgeted at a cool A$7 million (US$5.44 million), but by the time it was finished in 1973 it had cost a staggering A$102 million (US$66.3 million), most raised through a series of lotteries. Since then, continual refurbishment and the major task of replacing the asbestos-laden grouting between the hundreds of thousands of white tiles that make up its shell has cost many millions more.

Tours & Tickets: Guided tours of the Opera House last about an hour and are conducted daily from 9am to 4pm, except Good Friday and Christmas. Though guides try to take groups into the main theaters and around the foyers, if you don't get to see everything you want it's because the Opera House is not a museum but a workplace, and there's almost always some performance, practice, or setting up to be done. Reservations are essential. Tours include approximately 200 stairs. (Tours for people with disabilities can be arranged.) Specialized tours, focusing on the building's architecture and engineering, for example, can also be arranged.

The Tourism Services Department at the Sydney Opera House can book **combination packages,** including dinner and a show; a tour, dinner, and a show; or a champagne interval performance. Prices vary depending on shows and dining venues. Visitors from overseas can buy tickets by credit card and then pick them up at the box office on arrival, or contact a local tour company specializing in Australia. Advance ticket purchases are a good idea, as performances are very popular. The views from the back rows are hardly worth the effort and expense if you turn up on the day of performance. Tickets for performances vary from as little as A$12 (US$7.80) for children's shows to A$180 (US$117) for good seats at the opera. Plays cost between A$40 and A$60 (US$26–US$39) on average.

Free performances are given outside on the Opera House boardwalks on Sunday afternoons and during festival times. The shows range from musicians and performance artists to school groups.

Bennelong Point. © **02/9250 7250** for guided tours and inquiries. www.soh.nsw.gov.au. For box office bookings, call © **02/9250 7777**; fax 02/9251 3943; bookings@soh.nsw.gov.au. Box office open Mon–Sat 9am–8:30pm; Sun 2 hr. before performance. Tours A$15 (US$9.75) adults, A$11 (US$7.15) children (family prices available on application); backstage tours A$25 (US$16) (no children's price). Tours run Mon–Sun 8:30am–5pm (around every 45 min.) subject to theater availability. (Tour sizes are limited, so be prepared to wait.) CityRail, bus, or ferry: Circular Quay. Sydney Explorer bus. Parking: Daytime A$7 (US$4.50) per hr.; evening A$23 (US$15) flat rate.

ATTRACTIONS AT DARLING HARBOUR

Many tourists head to Darling Harbour for the Harbourside Festival Market-place, a huge structure beside the Pyrmont pedestrian and monorail bridge that's crammed full of cheap eateries and a few interesting shops. However, Sydney's tourist precinct has a lot more to offer.

Australian National Maritime Museum ⚡ *Kids*   Modern Australia owes almost everything to the sea, so it's not surprising there's a museum dedicated to the ships, from Aboriginal vessels to submarines. You'll find ships' logs, things to pull and tug at, and the fastest boat in the world, the *Spirit of Australia*. Docked in the harbor are a fully rigged tall ship; an Australian Naval Destroyer, the *Vampire;* (which you can clamber over); and an Oberon Class submarine. Allow 2 hours.

Darling Harbour. © **02/9298 3777**. www.anmm.gov.au. A$10 (US$6.50) adults, A$6 (US$3.90) children, A$25 (US$16) families (for entry without access to navy ships). A$14 (US$9.10) adults, A$7 (US$4.55) children, A$30 (US$20) families (for museum entry and navy ships). Daily 9:30am–5pm (until 6:30pm in Jan). Ferry: Darling Harbour. Monorail: Harbourside. Sydney Explorer bus.

Chinese Garden   The largest Chinese garden of its type outside China offers a pleasant escape from the city concrete. Expert gardeners from China's Guang-dong Province designed the garden according to principles of garden design dating back to the 5th century. Allow 30 minutes.

Darling Harbour (adjacent to the Entertainment Centre). © **02/9281 6863**. Admission A$4.50 (US$2.90) adults, A$2 (US$1.30) children, A$10 (US$6.50) families. Daily 9:30am–dusk. Ferry: Darling Harbour. Mono rail: Convention. Sydney Explorer bus.

IMAX Theatre Sydney   Four different IMAX films are usually showing on the gigantic eight-story-high screen. Each flick lasts about 50 minutes or so. If you've ever been to an IMAX theater before, you know what to expect. As you watch, your mind is tricked into feeling that it's right in the heart of the action. Also shown are 3-D movies, which cost A$1 (US65¢) extra.

Southern Promenade, Darling Harbour. © **02/9281 3300**. Admission A$15 (US$9.75) adults, A$12 (US$7.80) students, A$10 (US$6.50) children 3–15, A$35 (US$23) families. Daily 10am–10pm (until 11:30pm Fri–Sat). Ferry: Darling Harbour. Monorail: Convention. Sydney Explorer bus.

Powerhouse Museum *Kids*   Sydney's most interactive museum is also one of the largest in the Southern Hemisphere. Inside the postmodern industrial interior you'll find all sorts of displays and gadgets relating to the sciences, transportation, human achievement, decorative art, and social history. The many hands-on exhibits make this fascinating museum worthy of a couple of hours of your time.

500 Harris St., Ultimo (near Darling Harbour). © **02/9217 0111**. Admission A$10 (US$6.50) adults, A$3 (US$1.95) students and children 5–15, A$23 (US$15) families. Free admission 1st Sat of every month. Daily 10am–5pm. Ferry: Darling Harbour. Monorail: Harbourside. Sydney Explorer bus.

Sydney Aquarium 🎈🎈 *Kids*   This is one of the world's best aquariums and should be near the top of any Sydney itinerary. The main attractions are the underwater walkways through two enormous tanks—one with an impressive collection of creatures found in Sydney Harbour, the other full of giant rays and gray nurse sharks. Other excellent exhibits include a giant Plexiglas room suspended inside a pool patrolled by rescued seals, and a magnificent section on the Great Barrier Reef, where thousands of colorful fish school around coral outcrops. Also on display are two saltwater crocodiles and some fairy penguins. Try to visit during the week when it's less crowded. Allow around 2 hours.

Aquarium Pier, Darling Harbour. © **02/9262 2300.** Admission A$22 (US$14) adults, A$13 (US$8.45) students, A$10 (US$6.50) children 3–15, A$48 (US$31) families. Daily 9am–10pm. Seal Sanctuary closes at 7pm in summer. CityRail: Town Hall. Ferry: Darling Harbour. Sydney Explorer bus.

OTHER TOP ATTRACTIONS: A SPECTACULAR VIEW, SYDNEY'S CONVICT HISTORY & MORE

A.M.P. Centerpoint Tower 🎈   The tallest building in the Southern Hemisphere is not hard to miss—it resembles a giant steel pole skewering a golden marshmallow. Standing more than 300m (984 ft.) tall, the tower offers stupendous 360-degree views across Sydney and as far as the Blue Mountains. Fortunately, an elevator takes you to the indoor viewing platform. Unfortunately, prices have rocketed in recent years, too. Don't be too concerned if you feel the building tremble slightly, especially in a stiff breeze—I'm told it's perfectly natural. Below the tower are three floors of stores and restaurants. Allow 1 hour.

Pitt and Market sts. © **02/9223 0933.** Admission A$20 (US$13) adults, A$13 (US$8.45) children 5–16, A$55 (US$36) families (up to 3 kids). Daily 9am–10:30pm. CityRail: St. James or Town Hall. Sydney Explorer bus.

Hyde Park Barracks Museum 🎈   These Georgian-style barracks were designed in 1819 by the convict/architect Francis Greenway. They were built by convicts and inhabited by fellow prisoners. These days they house relics from those early days in interesting, modern displays, including log books, early settlement artifacts, and a room full of ships' hammocks in which visitors can lie and listen to fragments of prisoner conversation. If you are interested in Sydney's early beginnings, then I highly recommend a visit—the displays are also far more straightforward that those at the Museum of Sydney (see later in this chapter). The courtyard cafe is excellent. Allow for 1 hour or more.

Queens Sq., Macquarie St. © **02/9223 8922.** Admission A$7 (US$4.55) adults, A$3 (US$1.95) children, A$17 (US$11) families. Daily 9:30am–5pm. CityRail: St. James or Martin Place. Sydney Explorer bus.

Museum of Contemporary Art (MCA)   This imposing sandstone museum set back from the water on The Rocks side of Circular Quay offers wacky, entertaining, inspiring, and befuddling displays of what's new (and dated) in modern art. It houses the J. W. Power Collection of more than 4,000 pieces, including works by Andy Warhol, Christo, Marcel Duchamp, and Robert Rauschenberg, as well as temporary exhibits. As it's relatively new and still building up its collection, this museum isn't as impressive as major modern art museums in say London or New York. In mid-2001 there was talk of the museum closing because of financial concerns. Guided tours are offered Monday through Saturday at noon and 2pm, and Sunday at 2pm. Worth at least 1 hour.

140 George St., Circular Quay West. © **02/9252 4033.** www.mca.com.au. Free general admission. Daily 10am–6pm (5pm in winter). CityRail, bus, ferry: Circular Quay. Sydney Explorer bus.

Sydney Olympic Park 🎈   The site of the 2000 Sydney Olympic Games is still very much a tourist attraction, as well as a major sporting venue. Most of the Olympic venues are at this dedicated Olympic precinct at Homebush Bay, which also has plenty of bars and restaurants. First port of call should be the Homebush Bay Information Centre (✆ **02/9714 7888**), which offers displays, walking maps, and tour tips. It's open daily from 9am to 5pm.

Nearby is **Stadium Australia** (✆ **02/8765 2300;** www.stadiumaustralia. com.au), the site of the Opening and Closing ceremonies, the track and field events, and some Olympic soccer games. Today it stages Australian Rules games, rugby league, rugby union, and soccer matches. A 20-minute tour of the stadium costs A$15 (US$9.50) for adults, A$7.50 (US$4.90) for children, and A$42 (US$27) for a family. A 1-hour "behind the scenes" tour is A$26 (US$17) for adults, A$13 (US$8.45) for children, and A$60 (US$39) for a family.

Also at the Olympic Park is the **Sydney International Aquatic Centre** (✆ **02/9752 3666;** www.siac.nsw.gov.au), which comprises the Olympic pool, diving pool, and training facilities. To swim here costs a whopping A$16 (US$10) for adults and A$10 (US$6.50) for children. I hope they towel you off afterward.

There are wonderful views of the Sydney Olympic Park and the city from Level 17 of the **Novotel hotel** (✆ **02/8762 1111**), located in the park. Entry to the observation area costs A$4 (US$2.60) for adults, A$2 (US$1.30) for children (free for under 8 yr. old). You can purchase a SuperPass entitling you to entry to the Observation Center at the Novotel and a guided tour of Stadium Australia and the Sydney Aquatic Center (including swimming). Tickets are available from participating venues or the visitor center for A$40 (US$26) for adults, A$20 (US$13) for children, and A$79 (US$51) for a family.

One of the best ways to get to the Olympic Site is via the Sydney Explorer bus.

Sydney Olympic Site, Olympic Park, Homebush Bay. www.sydneyolympicpark.nsw.gov.au. CityRail: Olympic Park. Sydney Explorer bus.

Wonderland Sydney If you're used to big Disneyesque extravaganzas, then this theme park (until recently called Australia's Wonderland) might be a bit of a disappointment—though I guarantee The Demon roller coaster will more than satisfy in the terror department. Other big rides are Space Probe 7, which is basically a heart-stopping drop, and a cute and rattly wooden roller coaster called the Bush Beast. Live shows and bands round out the entertainment options. The entry ticket also includes admission to a wildlife park, with all the old favorites—koalas, wombats, kangaroos, wallabies, and more. Allow half a day.

100 Wallgrove Rd., Eastern Creek. ✆ 02/9830 9100. www.wonderland.com.au. Admission (includes rides, shows, attractions, and entrance to Australian Wildlife Park) A$46 (US$30) adults, A$30 (US$20) children, family tickets only available for wildlife park. Daily 10am–5pm. CityRail: Rooty Hill (trip takes less than 1 hr.); Wonderland buses leave from Rooty Hill station every half hr. on weekends, and at 8:55, 9:32, 10:10, and 11:35am, and 12:14pm weekdays. Wonderland express coach is a convenient way to get to Wonderland Sydney, with city return transfers available daily from major CBD locations. For bookings and information call ✆ 02/9830 9187. Free parking.

'ROOS, KOALAS & OTHER AUSSIE WILDLIFE

The Sydney Aquarium is discussed on p. 150.

Australian Reptile Park What started off as a one-man operation supplying snake antivenin in the early 1950s has ended up a nature park teeming with the slippery-looking creatures. But it's not all snakes and lizards; you'll also find saltwater crocodiles, American alligators, as well as plenty of somewhat cuddlier creatures, such as koalas, platypuses, wallabies, dingoes, and flying foxes. The park is set in beautiful bushland dissected by nature trails. A truly devastating fire burned down the entire park in mid-2000, killing all of the animals. The staff has worked valiantly to start up a new collection.

Pacific Hwy., Somersby. ℭ **02/4340 1022**. Admission A$16 (US$10) adults, A$8 (US$5.20) children, A$40 (US$26) families. Daily 9am–5pm. Closed Christmas. Somersby is near Gosford, 84km (52 miles) north of Sydney. By car: Take the Pacific Hwy. and the Sydney-Newcastle Fwy. (F3); the trip takes about 1 hr. CityRail trains leave from Central Station for Gosford every 30 min. From Gosford, take the bus marked Australian Wildlife Park (10-min. ride).

Featherdale Wildlife Park 🦘🦘 *Kids*   If you only have time to visit one wildlife park in Sydney, make it this one. The selection of Australian animals is excellent, and most importantly, the animals are very well cared for. You could easily spend a couple of hours here despite the park's compact size. You'll have the chance to hand-feed friendly kangaroos and wallabies, and get a photo taken next to a koala. (There are many here, both the New South Wales variety and the larger Victorian type.) The park's newest addition is the "Reptilian Pavilion." It houses 30 different native species of reptiles in 26 spectacularly lifelike exhibits.

217 Kildare Rd., Doonside. ℭ **02/9622 1644**. Fax 02/9671-4140. www.featherdale.com.au. Admission A$16 (US$10) adults, A$8 (US$5.20) children 4–14, A$40 (US$26) families. Daily 9am–5pm. CityRail: Blacktown station, then take bus 725 to park. (Ask driver to tell you when to get off.) By car: Take the M4 motorway to Reservoir Rd., turn off, travel 4km (2½ miles), then turn left at Kildare Rd.

Koala Park   This is probably the only place in the country (unless you travel all the way to Kangaroo Island in South Australia) where you'll be able to spot this many koalas in one place. In all, there are around 55 koalas roaming within the park's leafy boundaries. Koala cuddling sessions are free, and take place at 10:20 and 11:45am, and 2 and 3pm daily. There are also wombats, dingoes, kangaroos, wallabies, emus, and native birds here, too. You can hire a private guide to take you around for A$70 (US$46) for a 2-hour session, or hitch onto one of the free "hostess" guides who wander around the park like Pied Pipers.

84 Castle Hill Rd., West Pennant Hills. ℭ **02/9484 3141** or 02/9875 2777. www.koalapark.com. Admission A$15 (US$9.75) adults, A$8 (US$5.20) children, A$40 (US$26) families. Daily 9am–5pm. Closed Christmas. CityRail: Pennant Hills station via North Strathfield (45 min.), then take any bus nos. 651–655 to park.

Oceanworld Manly *Kids*   Though not as impressive as the Sydney Aquarium, Oceanworld can be combined with a visit to Manly Beach (see "North of Sydney Harbour," below) for a nice day's outing. There's a decent display of Barrier Reef fish, and more giant sharks. Also here are the five most venomous snakes in the world. Shark feeding is at 11am on Monday, Wednesday, and Friday. There is also a dive with the sharks program.

West Esplanade, Manly. ℭ **02/9949 2644**. Admission A$16 (US$10) adults, A$8 (US$5.20) children, A$40 (US$26) families. Daily 10am–5:30pm. Ferry or JetCat: Manly.

Taronga Zoo 🦘 *Kids*   Taronga has the best view of any zoo in the world. Set on a hill, it looks out over Sydney Harbour, the Opera House, and the Harbour Bridge. It's better on the legs to explore the zoo from the top down. The main attractions are the fabulous chimpanzee exhibit, the gorilla enclosure, and the Nocturnal Houses, where you can see some of Australia's many nighttime marsupials out and about, including the platypus and the cuter-than-cute bilby (the official Australian Easter bunny). There's an interesting reptile display, a couple of impressive Komodo dragons, a scattering of indigenous beasties— including a few koalas, echidnas, kangaroos, dingoes, and wombats—and lots more. The kangaroo and wallaby exhibit is unimaginative; you'd be better off going to Featherdale Wildlife Park (see above) for happier-looking animals. Animals are fed at various times during the day. The zoo can get crowded on weekends, so I strongly advise visiting during the week or going early in the morning on weekends. Interestingly, the three sun bears near the lower ferry entrance/exit were rescued by an Australian businessman, John Stephens, from a restaurant in Cambodia, where they were to have their paws cut off and served in a soup. Allow around 2 hours.

Bradley's Head Rd., Mosman. 🅒 **02/9969 2777.** Admission A$21 (US$14) adults, A$12 (US$7.80) children 4–15. Ask about family prices. A Zoopass (includes entry, round-trip ferry from Circular Quay, and Aerial Safari cable-car ride from ferry terminal to upper entrance of zoo) is available from CityRail stations for A$25 (US$16) for adults and A$13 (US$8.10) for children (no family pass). Daily 9am–5pm (Jan 9am–9pm). Ferry: Taronga Zoo. At Taronga Zoo wharf, a bus to the upper zoo entrance is A$1.30 (US85¢), or take a cable car to the top for A$2.50 (US$1.60). The lower zoo entrance is a 2-min. walk up the hill from the wharf.

HITTING THE BEACH

One of the big bonuses of visiting Sydney in the summer months (Dec–Feb) is that you get to experience the beaches in their full glory.

Most major city beaches, such as Manly and Bondi, have lifeguards on patrol, especially during the summer. They check the water conditions and are on the lookout for **"rips"**—strong currents that can pull a swimmer far out to sea. Safe places to swim are marked by red and yellow flags. You must always swim between these flags. If you are using a foam or plastic body board or "boogie board," it's advisable to use it between the flags. Fiberglass surfboards must be used outside the flags. (Expect a warning from the beach loudspeakers and an A$100/US$65 fine if you fail to take notice.)

WHAT ABOUT SHARKS & OTHER NASTIES? One of the first things visitors wonder when they hit the water in Australia is: *Are there sharks?* The answer is yes, but fortunately they are rarely spotted inshore—you are far more likely to spot a migrating whale. In reality, sharks have more reason to be scared of us than we of them; most of them end up as the fish in your average packet of fish and chips. (Shark filets are often sold as "flake.") Though some beaches—such as the small beach next to the Manly ferry wharf in Manly and a section of Balmoral Beach in Mosman—have permanent shark nets, most rely on portable nets that are moved from beach to beach.

Another common problem off Sydney's beaches are **"blue bottles"**—small blue jellyfish, often called "stingers" in Australia, and "Portuguese-Man-o'-War" elsewhere. You'll often find these creatures washed up along the beach; they become a hazard for swimmers when there's a strong breeze coming off the ocean and they're blown in to shore (watch out for warning signs erected on the shoreline). Minute individual stinging cells often break off the main body of the creature, and they can cause minor itching or stinging. Or you might be hit by the full force of a blue bottle, which will often stick to your skin and wrap its tentacles around you. Blue bottles deliver a hefty punch from their many stinging cells, causing a severe burning sensation almost immediately. Wearing a T-shirt in the water reduces the risk somewhat (though a pair of waterlogged jeans isn't a good idea). If you are stung, rinse the area liberally with seawater or fresh water to remove any tentacles stuck in the skin. For intense pain, apply heat or cold, whichever feels better. If you experience breathing difficulties or disorientation, seek medical attention immediately.

SOUTH OF SYDNEY HARBOUR

Sydney's most famous beach is **Bondi** 𝄠𝄠. In many ways it's a raffish version of a Californian beach, with plenty of tanned skin and in-line skaters. Though the beach is nice, it's cut off from the cafe and restaurant strip that caters to beach-goers by a road that pedestrians have to funnel across in order to reach the sand.

On summer weekend evenings it's popular with souped-up cars and groups of disaffected youths. To reach Bondi Beach, take the CityRail train to Bondi Junction, then transfer to bus no. 380 (a 15-min. bus journey). You can also catch bus no. 380 directly from Circular Quay (but it can take an hour or so in peak time).

If you follow the water along to your right at Bondi, you'll come across a very scenic cliff-top trail that takes you to **Bronte Beach** (a 20-min. walk), via gorgeous little **Tamarama,** nicknamed "Glamourama" for its trendy sun-worshippers. This boutique beach is known for its dangerous rips. Bronte has better swimming than Bondi. To get to Bronte, catch bus no. 378 from Circular Quay, or pick up the bus at the Bondi Junction CityRail station.

Clovelly Beach, farther along the coast, is blessed with a large rock pool carved into a rock platform and sheltered from the force of the Tasman Sea. This beach is accessible for visitors in wheelchairs via a series of ramps. To reach Clovelly, take bus no. 339 from Circular Quay.

The cliff walk from Bondi will eventually bring you to **Coogee,** which has a pleasant strip of sand with a couple of hostels and hotels nearby. To reach Coogee, take bus no. 373 or 374 from Circular Quay (via Pitt, George, and Castlereagh sts., and Taylor Sq. on Oxford St.) or bus no. 314 or 315 from Bondi Junction.

NORTH OF SYDNEY HARBOUR

On the north shore you'll find **Manly** ★★, a long curve of golden sand edged with Norfolk Island pines. (Don't be fooled by the two small beaches on either side of the ferry terminal as some people have been—including the famous novelist Arthur Conan Doyle, who traveled to Manly by ferry and presuming the small beach near the ferry station was the best the suburb had to offer did not bother to disembark.) Follow the crowds shuffling through the pedestrianized "Corso" to the main ocean beach. You'll find one of Sydney's nicest walks here, too. Looking at the ocean, head to your right along the beachfront and follow the coastal path to the small and sheltered **Shelly Beach** ★, a nice area for snorkeling and swimming. (There's also a small takeout outlet here selling drinks and snacks, next to the good, but pricey, Le Kiosk beachfront restaurant.) Follow the bitumen path up the hill to the car park. Here, a track cuts up into the bush and leads toward a fire wall, which marks the entrance to Sydney Harbour National Park. Around here you'll get some spectacular ocean views across to Manly and the northern beaches (the headland farther in the distance is Palm Beach). The best way to reach Manly is on a ferry or JetCat from Circular Quay.

Farther along the northern coast are a string of ocean beaches, including the surf spots of **Curl Curl, Dee Why, Narrabeen, Mona Vale, Newport, Avalon,** and finally **Palm Beach** ★, a long and beautiful strip of sand cut from the calmer waters of **Pittwater** by sand dunes and a golf course. Here you'll also find the Barrenjoey Lighthouse, which also offers fine views along the coast (see the "Greater Sydney" map earlier in this chapter for a map of this area.) Bus nos. 136 and 139 run from Manly to Curl Curl, while Bus no. 190 runs from Wynyard to Newport and then via the other northern beaches as far as Palm Beach.

The best harbor beach is at **Balmoral** ★, a wealthy North Shore hangout complete with some good cafes (The Sandbar is the best for food) and two good, upmarket beach-view restaurants—the **Bathers Pavillion** (☏ 02/9969 5050) and **The Watermark** (☏ 02/9968 3433). The beach itself is split into three parts. As you look toward the sea, the middle section is the most popular with sunbathers, while the wide expanse to your left and the sweep of surreally beautiful sand to your right have a mere scattering. There's a caged pool area for

---

Fun Fact **Grin & Bare It**

If getting an all-over tan is your scene, you have a couple of options in Sydney. Head either to the nudist beach at **Lady Jane Bay,** a short walk from Camp Cove Beach (accessed from Cliff St. in Watsons Bay, reached by walking along the strip of sand—to the right as you look at the sea—at the back of the Watsons Bay Hotel). Or, you can try **Cobblers Beach,** accessed via a short, but steep, bush track that leads from the far side of the playing field oval next to the main HMAS *Penguin* naval base at the end of Bradley's Head Road in Mosman. (Follow the procession of men in shorts.) Be prepared for a largely male-orientated scene—as well as the odd boatload of beer-swigging peeping toms.

---

swimming. Reach Balmoral via a ferry to Taronga Zoo and then a 5-minute ride on a connecting bus from the ferry wharf, or catch the bus from the stop outside the zoo's top entrance.

MUSEUMS, GALLERIES, HISTORIC HOUSES & MORE

Art Gallery of New South Wales 🏵 The numerous galleries here present some of the best of Australian art and many fine examples by international artists, including good displays of Aboriginal and Asian art. You enter from The Domain parklands on the third floor of the museum. On the fourth floor you will find an expensive restaurant and a gallery often showing free photography displays. On the second floor is a wonderful cafe overlooking the wharves and warships of Woolloomooloo. Every January and February there is a fabulous display of the best work created by school students throughout the state. Allow at least 1 hour.

Art Gallery Rd., The Domain. ℂ **02/9225 1744.** www.artgallery.nsw.gov.au. Free admission to most galleries. Special exhibitions vary; expect to pay around A$12 (US$7.80) adults, A$7 (US$4.55) children. Daily 10am–5pm. Tours of general exhibits Tues–Fri 11am, noon, 1 and 2pm; Mon 1 and 2pm; Sat–Sun 11am, 1 and 2pm. Tours of Aboriginal galleries Tues–Sun 11am. Free Aboriginal performance Tues–Sat noon. CityRail: St. James. Sydney Explorer bus.

Australian Museum Though nowhere near as impressive as, say, the Natural History Museum in London, Sydney's premier natural history museum is still worth a look. Displays are presented thematically, the best being the Aboriginal section with its traditional clothing, weapons, and everyday implements. There are some sorry examples of stuffed Australian wildlife, too. Temporary exhibits run from time to time. Allow 1 to 2 hours.

6 College St. ℂ **02/9320 6000.** www.austmus.gov.au. Admission A$8 (US$5.20) adults, A$3 (US$1.95) children, A$19 (US$12) families. Special exhibits extra. Daily 9:30am–5pm. Closed Christmas. CityRail: Museum, St. James, or Town Hall. Sydney Explorer bus.

Customs House This museum, in the sandstone building with the clock and flags across the large square opposite the Circular Quay CityRail station and the ferry wharves, opened in December 1998. It's worth a look inside if you're interested in architecture. You might be hooked by the series of modern-art objects displayed on the ground floor, and the traveling exhibits on the third floor—though often you won't be. Outside in the square is a popular cafe selling reasonably priced coffee, cakes, sandwiches, and the like. Allow 15 minutes.

Alfred St., Circular Quay. ℂ **02/9320 6429.** Free general admission. Daily 9:30am–5pm. CityRail, bus, or ferry: Circular Quay.

Elizabeth Bay House This good example of colonial architecture was built in 1835 and was described at the time as the "finest house in the colony." Visitors can tour the whole house and get a real feeling of the history of the fledgling settlement. The house is situated on a headland and has some of the best harbor views in Sydney. Allow 1 hour.

7 Onslow Ave., Elizabeth Bay. ℂ 02/9356 3022. Admission A$7 (US$4.55) adults, A$3 (US$1.95) children, A$17 (US$11) families. Tues–Sun 10am–4:30pm. Closed Good Friday and Christmas. Bus: 311 from Circular Quay. Sydney Explorer bus.

Museum of Sydney You'll need your brain in full working order to make the most of the contents of this three-story postmodern building near Circular Quay, which encompasses the remnants of Sydney's first Government House. This place is far from being a conventional showcase of history; instead, it houses a rather minimalist collection of first-settler and Aboriginal objects and multimedia displays that "invite" the museum-goer to discover Sydney's past for him- or herself. Some Frommer's readers have criticized the place, saying it's not just minimalist—it's simply unfathomable. By the way, that forest of poles filled with hair, oyster shells, and crab claws in the courtyard adjacent to the industrial-design cafe tables is called *Edge of Trees*. It's a metaphor for the first contact between Aborigines and the British. There's a reasonable cafe out the front. Allow anywhere from an hour to a lifetime to understand.

37 Phillip St. ℂ 02/9251 5988. Admission A$7 (US$4.55) adults, A$3 (US$1.95) children under 15, A$17 (US$11) families. Daily 9:30am–5pm. CityRail, bus, or ferry: Circular Quay. Sydney Explorer bus.

St. James Church Sydney's oldest surviving colonial church, begun in 1822, was designed by the government architect, and former convict, Francis Greenway. At one time the church's spire served as a landmark for ships coming up the harbor, but today it looks totally lost amid the skyscrapers. It's well worth seeking out, though, especially for the plaques on the wall, which pay testament to the hard early days of the colony when people were lost at sea, "speared by blacks," and died while serving the British Empire overseas.

Queens Sq., Macquarie St. ℂ 02/9232 3022. Daily 8am–5pm.

St. Mary's Cathedral Sydney's most impressive worship place is a giant sandstone construction between The Domain and Hyde Park. The original St Mary's was built in 1821, but the chapel was destroyed by fire. Work on the present cathedral began in 1868, but due to lack of funds remained unfinished until work began in 1999 to build the two spires. The stained-glass windows inside are impressive. St. Mary's is Roman Catholic and was built for Sydney's large population of Irish convicts. In perhaps Sydney's worst pre-Olympic planning, the beautiful brown sandstone building was marred by a wide stretch of dark gray paving outside—now the battleground of skateboarders and city council rangers. The two spires were completed in extra-quick time for the Olympics, too.

College and Cathedral sts. ℂ 02/9220 0400. Mon–Fri 6:30am–6:30pm; Sat 8am–7:30pm; Sun 6:30am–7:30pm.

State Library of NSW The state's main library is divided into two sections, the Mitchell and Dixon libraries, next door to one another. A newer reference-library complex nearby has two floors of reference materials, local newspapers, and microfiche viewers. Leave your bags in the free lockers downstairs. (You'll need an A$2 coin, which is refundable.) I highly recommend the library's leafy **Glasshouse Café,** in my opinion one of the best walk-in lunch spots in Sydney.

The older building contains many older books on the ground floor, and often hosts free art and photography displays in the upstairs galleries. A small library section in the Sydney Town Hall building has international newspapers.

Macquarie St. (℃ **02/9273 1414.** Free admission. Mon–Fri 9am–5pm; Sat–Sun and selected holidays 11am–5pm. Closed New Year's Day, Good Friday, Christmas, and Boxing Day (Dec 26). CityRail: Martin Place. Sydney Explorer bus.

Sydney Jewish Museum   Harrowing exhibits here include documents and objects relating to the Holocaust and the Jewish culture, mixed with soundscapes, audiovisual displays, and interactive media. There's also a museum shop, a resource center, a small theater, and a traditional kosher cafe. It's considered one of the best museums of its type in the world. Allow 1 to 2 hours.

148 Darlinghurst Rd., Darlinghurst. (℃ **02/9360 7999.** Fax 02/9331 4245. www.sjm.com.au. Admission A$10 (US$6.50) adults, A$6 (US$3.90) children, A$22 (US$14) families. Sun–Thurs 10am–4pm; Fri 10am–2pm. Closed Jewish holidays, Christmas, and Good Friday. CityRail: Kings Cross.

Sydney Observatory   The city's only major museum of astronomy offers visitors a chance to see the southern skies through modern and historic telescopes. The best time to visit is during the night on a guided tour, when you can take a close-up look at some of the planets. Night tours are offered at 8:15pm from the end of May to the end of August and at 6:15 and 8:15pm the rest of the year; be sure to double-check the times when you book your tour. The planetarium and hands-on exhibits are also interesting.

Observatory Hill, Watson Rd., Millers Point. (℃ **02/9217 0485.** Free admission in daytime; guided night tours (reservations essential) A$10 (US$6.50) adults, A$5 (US$3.25) children, A$25 (US$16) families. Daily 10am–5pm. CityRail, bus, or ferry: Circular Quay.

Vaucluse House   Also looking over Sydney Harbour, this house includes lavish entertainment rooms and impressive stables and outbuildings. It was built in 1803 and was the home of Charles Wentworth, the architect of the Australian Constitution. It's set in 11 hectares (27 acres) of gardens, bushland, and beach frontage—perfect for picnics. Allow 1 hour.

Wentworth Rd., Vaucluse. (℃ **02/9337 1957.** www.hht.nsw.gov.au. Admission A$7 (US$4.55) adults, A$3 (US$1.95) children. House Tues–Sun 10am–4:30pm; grounds daily 7am–5pm. Free guided tours. Closed Good Friday and Christmas. Bus: 325 from Circular Quay, or Bondi and Bay Explorer.

PARKS & GARDENS
IN SYDNEY
ROYAL BOTANIC GARDENS   If you are going to spend time in one of Sydney's green spaces, then make it the **Royal Botanic Gardens** ✿ (℃ **02/9231 8111**), next to Sydney Opera House. The gardens were laid out in 1816 on the site of a farm dedicated to supplying food for the colony. They're informal in appearance with a scattering of duck ponds and open spaces, though there are several areas dedicated to particular plant species, such as the rose garden, the cacti and succulent display, and the central palm and the rainforest groves (watch out for the thousands of large fruit bats, which chatter and argue among the rainforest trees). **Mrs. Macquarie's Chair,** along the coast path, offers superb views of the Opera House and the Harbour Bridge. (It's a favorite stop for tour buses.) The sandstone building dominating the gardens nearest to the Opera House is the **Government House,** once the official residence of the governor of New South Wales. (He moved out in 1996 in the spirit of republicanism.) The pleasant gardens are open to the public daily from 10am to 4pm, and the house is open Friday through Sunday from 10am to 3pm. Entrance to both

is free. If you plan to park around here, note that parking meters cost upwards of A$3 (US$1.95) per hour, and you need A$1 coins.

A popular walk takes you through the Royal Botanic Gardens to the **Art Gallery of New South Wales.** The gardens are open daily from 7am to dusk. Admission is free.

HYDE PARK   In the center of the city is Hyde Park, a favorite with lunching businesspeople. Of note here are the **Anzac Memorial** to Australian and New Zealand troops killed in the wars, and the **Archibald Fountain,** complete with spitting turtles and sculptures of Diana and Apollo. At night, avenues of trees are lit up with twinkling lights giving the place a magical appearance.

MORE CITY PARKS   Another Sydney favorite is giant **Centennial Park** (✆ **02/9339 6699**), usually accessed from the top of Oxford Street. It opened in 1888 to celebrate the centenary of European settlement, and today encompasses huge areas of lawn, several lakes, picnic areas with outdoor grills, cycling and running paths, and a cafe. It's open from sunrise to sunset. To get there, take bus no. 373, 374, 378, 380, or 382 from the city, or via the Bondi & Bay Explorer.

A hundred years later, **Bicentennial Park,** at Australia Avenue, in Homebush Bay, came along. Forty percent of the park's total 100 hectares (247 acres) is general parkland reclaimed from a city dump; the rest is the largest remaining remnant of wetlands on the Parramatta River and is home to many species of both local and migratory wading birds, cormorants, and pelicans. Follow park signs to the **visitor information office** (✆ **02/9763 1844**), open Monday through Friday from 10am to 4pm, and Saturday and Sunday from 9:30am to 4:30pm. To reach the park, take a CityRail train to Homebush Bay station.

BEYOND SYDNEY

SYDNEY HARBOUR NATIONAL PARK   You don't need to go far to experience Sydney's nearest national park. The Sydney Harbour National Park stretches around parts of the inner harbor and includes several small harbor islands. (Many first-time visitors are surprised at the amount of bushland still remaining in prime real-estate territory.) The best walk through the Sydney Harbour National Park is the **Manly to Spit Bridge Scenic Walkway** (✆ **02/9977 6522**). This 10km (6-mile) track winds its way from Manly (it starts near the Oceanarium), via Dobroyd Head to Spit Bridge (where you can catch a bus back to the city). The walk takes around 3 hours at a casual pace, and the views across busy Sydney Harbour are fabulous. There are a few Aboriginal stone carvings, which are signposted along the route. Maps are available from the **Manly Visitors Information Bureau** (✆ **02/9977 1088**), right opposite the main beach.

Other access points to the park include tracks around Taronga Zoo (ask the zoo staff to point you toward the rather concealed entrances) and above tiny Shelly Beach, opposite the main beach at Manly.

Also part of the national park is the recently restored **Fort Denison,** in the middle of the harbor between Circular Quay and Manly. The fort was built during the Crimean War due to fears of a Russian invasion, and was later used as a penal colony. One- to 2-hour **Heritage Tours** of the island leave from Cadmans Cottage, in The Rocks (✆ **02/9247 5033**). They cost A$22 (US$14) for adults and A$18 (US$12) for students and children. Call ahead for times and bookings. Pickup maps of Sydney Harbour National Park at Cadmans Cottage.

Another great walk in Sydney can be combined with lunch or a drink at Watsons Bay. A 15-minute bush stroll to **South Head** is accessed from the small beach outside the Watsons Bay Hotel. Walk to the end of the beach (to your right as you look at the water) then up the flight of steps into Short Street, then left along Cliff Street to the end of Camp Cove Beach. Continue along the coast past the nudist Lady Bay Beach to the lighthouse at South Head, where there are some great views (of the coastline, not the nudists). Across the road in front of the Watsons Bay Hotel is another section of the national park, known for its cliff-top views. Here you'll find The Gap, a sheer cliff popular for suicides, sadly. Watsons Bay is reached by ferries from Circular Quay, and via the Bondi & Bay Explorer.

MORE NATIONAL PARKS   Forming a semicircle around the city are Sydney's biggest parks of all. To the west is the **Blue Mountains National Park** (see chapter 4); to the northeast is **Ku-ring-gai Chase National Park;** and to the south is the magnificent **Royal National Park.** All three parks are home to marsupials such as echidnas and wallabies, numerous bird and reptile species, and a broad range of native plant life. Walking tracks, whether they stretch for half an hour or a few days, make each park accessible to the visitor.

   Ku-ring-gai Chase National Park (© 02/9457 9322 or 02/9457 9310) is a great place to take a bushwalk through gum trees and rainforest on the lookout for wildflowers, sandstone rock formations, and Aboriginal art. There are plenty of tracks through the park, but one of my favorites is a relatively easy 2.5km (1.5-mile) tramp to **The Basin** (Track 12). The well-graded dirt path takes you down to a popular estuary with a beach and passes some significant Aboriginal engravings. There are also some wonderful water views over Pittwater from the picnic areas at **West Head.** Pick up a free walking guide at the park entrance, or gather maps and information in Sydney at the National Parks & Wildlife Service's center at **Cadmans Cottage,** 110 George St., The Rocks (© **02/9247 8861**). The park is open from sunrise to sunset, and admission is A$10 (US$6.50) per car. You can either drive to the park or catch a ferry from Palm Beach to The Basin (from where you can walk up Track 12 and back). Ferries run on the hour (except at 1pm) from 9am to 5pm daily and cost A$4 (US$2.60) one-way; call © **02/ 9918 2747** for details. Shorelink bus no. 577 runs from the Turramurra CityRail station to the nearby park entrance every hour on weekdays and every 2 hours on weekends; call © **02/9457 8888** for details. There is no train service to the park. Camping is allowed only at The Basin (© **02/9457 9853**) and costs A$12 (US$7.80) for two people booked in advance.

   If you have a car you could visit the **Ku-ring-gai Wildflower Garden,** 420 Mona Vale Rd., St Ives (© **02/9440 8609**), which is essentially a huge area of natural bushland and a center for urban bushland education. There are plenty of bushwalking tracks, self-guided walks, and a number of nature-based activities. It's open daily from 8am to 4pm. Admission is A$2.50 (US$1.60) for adults, A$1 (US65¢) for children, and A$6 (US$3.90) for families.

   To the south of Sydney is the remarkable **Royal National Park,** Farrell Avenue, Sutherland (© **02/9542 0648**). It's the world's oldest national park, having been gazetted as such in 1879. (The main competitor to the title is Yellowstone in the United States, which was set aside for conservation in 1872 but not designated as a national park until 1883.) Severe bushfires almost destroyed the whole lot in early 1994, but the trees and bush plants have recovered remarkably. There's no visitor center, but you can get park information at park entrances, where you'll have to pay a A$10 (US$6.50) per car entry fee.

   There are several ways to access the park, but my favorites are the little-known access points from Bundeena and Otford. To get to Bundeena, take a CityRail train from Central Station to Cronulla. Just below the train station you'll find Cronulla Wharf. From there, hop on the delightful ferry run by **National Park**

Ferries (© **02/9523 2990**) to Bundeena; ferries run on the half-hour (except 12:30pm) and stop at around 7pm. After you get off the ferry, the first turn on your left just up the hill will take you to **Bundeena Beach.** It's another 5km (3 miles) or so to the wonderfully remote **Little Marley Beach,** via Marley Beach (which has dangerous surf). The ferry returns to Cronulla from Bundeena hourly on the hour (except 1pm). The fare is A$3 (US$1.95) each way.

An alternative way to reach the park is to take the train from Central Station to **Otford,** then climb the hill up to the sea cliffs. If you're driving, you might want to follow the scenic cliff-edge road down into Wollongong. The entrance to the national park is a little tricky to find, so you might have to ask directions—but roughly it's just to the left of a cliff top popular for hang gliding, radio-controlled airplanes, and kites. A 2-hour walk from the sea cliffs through beautiful and varying bushland and a palm forest will take you to **Burning Palms Beach.** There is no water along the route. The walk back up is steep, so only attempt this trek if you're reasonably fit. Trains to the area are irregular, and the last one departs around 4pm, so give yourself at least 2½ hours for the return trip to the train station to make sure you don't get stranded. It's possible to walk the memorable 26km (16 miles) from Otford to Bundeena, or vice versa, in 2 days. (Take all your food, water, and camping gear.) The track sticks to the coast, crosses several beaches, and is relatively easy to follow.

ESPECIALLY FOR KIDS

There are plenty of places kids can have fun in Sydney, but my choices below are particularly suitable for youngsters. (All of the places are reviewed in full above.)

Taronga Zoo (p. 152) is an all-time favorite with kids, where the barnyard animals, surprisingly, get as much attention as the koalas. If your kids want hands-on contact with the animals, though, you'd better head to **Featherdale Wildlife Park** (p. 152), where they can get their photo taken next to a koala, and hand feed and stroke kangaroos and wallabies. You can't stroke koalas in New South Wales. Even more interactive are the exhibits just crying out to be touched and bashed at the **Powerhouse Museum** (p. 149).

The sharks at **Oceanworld** (p. 152) in Manly and at the **Sydney Aquarium** (p. 150) in Darling Harbour are big lures for kids, too, and the thrill of walking through a long Plexiglas tunnel as giant manta rays perch over their heads will lead to more squeals of excitement.

Another outing for both adults and children is to crawl around inside boats and submarines at the **Australian National Maritime Museum** (p. 149).

And, of course, what kid wouldn't enjoy a day at the beach, and Sydney's got plenty to choose from, like **Bondi** or **Manly.**

Tips **A Stroll on The Rocks**

Sydney is relatively compact, so it's a wonderful city for exploring on foot. I particularly recommend a wander through The Rocks, site of the oldest settlement in Australia, a rough-and-tumble place where prostitutes, gang members, and other shady characters loitered more than a century ago. **The Rocks Walking Tour** (© **02/9247 6678**) has an organized stroll (see "Walking Tours," below). For my own take on the neighborhood, consult the self-guided walk that appears in *Frommer's Portable Sydney* (Wiley Publishing, Inc.).

---

6 Harbor Cruises & Organized Tours

For details on the Sydney Explorer bus, see "Getting Around," earlier this chapter.

HARBOR CRUISES

The best thing about Sydney is the harbor, so you shouldn't leave without taking a harbor cruise. **Sydney Ferries** (*C* **13 15 00** in Australia, or 02/9245 5600; www.sta.nsw.gov.au) offers a 1-hour morning harbor cruise with commentary departing Circular Quay, Wharf 4, daily at 10 and 11:15am. It costs A$15 (US$9.75) for adults, A$7.50 (US$4.90) for children under 16, and A$38 (US$24) for families (any number of children under 16). A 2½-hour afternoon cruise explores more of the harbor and leaves from Wharf 4 at 1pm on weekdays and 1:30pm on weekends and public holidays. This tour costs A$22 (US$14) for adults, A$11 (US$7.15) for children, and A$55 (US$36) for families. The highly recommended 1½-hour **Evening Harbour Lights tour,** which takes in the city lights as far east as Double Bay and west to Goat Island, leaves Monday through Saturday at 8pm from Wharf 5. The evening tour costs A$19 (US$12) for adults, A$9.50 (US$6.20) for children, and A$48 (US$31) for families.

Another option is a trip on the paddle-steamer the *Sydney Showboat* (*C* **02/ 9552 2722;** www.bluelinecruises.com.au). A daily lunch cruise on this oddly placed vessel starts at either 11.15am or 1:15pm and costs A$51 (US$33) for adults and A$31 (US$20) for children 4 to 12; it includes a good buffet lunch, a jazz band, and commentary. A daily 2½-hour dinner cruise and variety show runs from 7:30pm and costs from A$99 (US$65) for adults and A$69 (US$45) for children. Ask about other cruises, including afternoon excursions.

HARBOR CRUISE TICKETS & INFO

The one-stop shop for tickets and information on all harbor cruises is the **Australian Travel Specialists** (*C* **02/9247 5151;** www.atstravel.com.au). Find outlets at jetty no. 6 at Circular Quay; at the Harbourside Festival Marketplace at Darling Harbour; and on the Podium Level of the A.M.P. Centerpoint Tower. It's a good idea to check the website before you come to Australia as cruise options and prices are frequently changing. You can book on the Net, too.

If you're going to splurge on a cruise, though, the best are aboard the fully rigged replica of **Captain Bligh's** *Bounty* (*C* **02/9247 1789;** www.the bounty.com). Based at Campbell's Cove in The Rocks, it was built for the movie *The Bounty* (1984), which starred Mel Gibson and Anthony Hopkins. Standard 2-hour and lunch cruises run from 12:30pm Monday through Friday and cost A$65 (US$42). Dinner cruises lasting 2½ hours depart daily at 7pm in high season (Sept 1–Apr 30) and Friday and Saturday only from May 1 to August 31, and cost A$99 (US$64) for adults. On Saturday and Sunday (and public holidays) a 2½-hour Buffet Lunch Sail starts at 12:30pm and costs A$95 (US$62), and a 1½-hour predinner sail on Saturdays from 4pm costs A$53 (US$34). An extra 1½-hour brunch sail on Sundays and public holidays also costs A$53 (US$34). There's a 40% discount for children under 12 on all cruises.

Alternatively, you can cruise like a millionaire aboard the **MV** *Oceanos* (*C* **02/9555 4599**), a 21.5m (71-ft.) luxury motor cruiser. A 3-hour cruise, which leaves Campbells Cove at 12:30pm Tuesday, Thursday, and Sunday, costs A$75 (US$49) per person and includes a quality seafood lunch. It's essential to book 2 days in advance. **Sail Venture Cruises** (*C* **02/9262 3595**) also has a range of cruises aboard its catamarans.

Tips Top Gun

If you have time and money to spare you might want to try your hand at riding in a real-life jet fighter over trees and water on Sydney's outskirts There are several options, including a 20-minute aerobatic and patrol run, costing A$1,595 (US$1,036); a 30-minute low-level simulated attack run for A$1,995 (US$1,296); and a dogfight (bring along a rich friend) for A$2,495 (US$1,621). Contact **Jet Fighter Flights** on ✆ **1800/880 501** in Australia, or look them up at www.jetfighterflights.com.

Captain Cook Cruises, departing jetty no. 6, Circular Quay (✆ **02/9206 1111;** www.captaincook.com.au), offers several harbor excursions on its sleek vessels, with commentary along the way. The Harbour Highlights cruise operates several times daily and takes in most of the main points of interest in 1¼ hours, for A$20 (US$13) for adults and A$10 (US$6.50) for children. Another offering is the *Sydney Harbour Explorer* cruise, which departs at 9:30 and 11:30am, and 1:30 and 3:30pm and combines visits to five major Sydney attractions with a 2-hour cruise. You can get off where you want and join the boat again later. Tickets cost A$25 (US$16) for adults and A$15 (US$9.75) for children. An Aquarium and Zoo Cruise, costing A$37 (US$24) for adults and A$19 (US$12) for children, includes the *Sydney Harbour Explorer* cruise and admission to either the Sydney Aquarium or the Taronga Zoo.

The company also offers a 1½-hour Lunch Cruise, which leaves daily at 12:30pm. It costs A$49 (US$32) for adults and A$29 (US$19) for children. A Starlight Dinner Cruise leaves nightly at 7:30pm and costs A$59 (US$39) for adults and A$35 (US$23) for children.

Its nightly 1½-hour Sunset Cruise aboard the **John Cadman Cruising Restaurant boat,** departing just before sunset, costs A$69 (US$45) for adults and A$35 (US$23) for children, and includes a two-course meal and drinks. Yet another option is the Opera Afloat Dinner (including opera singers of course). This costs A$99 (US$64) for adults and A$55 (US$36) for children.

Matilda Cruises (✆ **02/9264 7377;** www.matilda.com.au) offers a 1-hour Matilda Rocket sightseeing tour leaving the pontoon at the far end of Sydney Aquarium at Darling Harbour eight times daily beginning at 9:30am (six times daily in winter, Apr 1–Sept 30, beginning at 10:30am). You can stay on for the full hour, or get off and on again at Circular Quay, the Opera House, Watsons Bay, and Taronga Zoo. The last boat leaves Taronga Zoo at 5:10pm in summer (4:10pm in winter). There's commentary and tea and coffee on board. The cruise costs A$21 (US$13) for adults, A$11 (US$7.15) for children 5 to 12, and A$50 (US$33) for a family. The company also runs morning and afternoon cruises, and lunch and dinner cruises with good food.

WALKING TOURS

The center of Sydney is compact, and you can see a lot in a day on foot. If you want to learn more about Sydney's early history, then book a guided tour with **The Rocks Walking Tour** (✆ **02/9247 6678**), based at the Shop K4, Kendall Lane (off Argyle St., The Rocks). Excellent walking tours leave Monday through Friday at 10:30am, 12:30, and 2:30pm, and Saturday and Sunday at 11:30am and 2pm (in Jan only 10:30am and 2:30pm on weekdays). The 1½-hour tour costs A$16 (US$10) for adults, A$11 (US$7.15) for children 10 to 16, and A$41 (US$27) for families. Free for accompanied children under 10.

For other historical walks contact **Sydney Guided Tours** (ⓒ **02/9660 7157**). The company's owner, Maureen Fry, has been in the business for over 12 years and employs trained guides qualified in disciplines such as history, architecture, and botany. She offers a range of tours including an introductory tour of Sydney, a tour of Macquarie Street, and many others. Walking tours cost A$17 (US$11) for 2 hours as part of a group. (Call in advance to find out what's available.)

A journey with a difference is **Weird Sydney Ghost and History Tours** (ⓒ **02/9555 2700;** www.destinytours.com.au). The tour—in a hearse—is fascinating and fun, and explores a section of historic Sydney (and more modern additions) including a former VD Clinic, the Sydney Opera House, and some buildings along Macquarie Street. It costs A$149 (US$97) for the 1½- to 2-hour trip.

MOTORCYCLE TOURS

Blue Thunder Motorcycle Tours (ⓒ **02/9977 7721** or 0414/278 983) runs Harley-Davidson tours of Sydney, the Blue Mountains, and places around New South Wales. A 1-hour ride (you sit on the back of the bike) around the city costs A$90 (US$59). A half-day trip to the northern beaches or down the south coast through the Royal National Park costs A$265 (US$172), including lunch. Full-day trips cost A$370 (US$240) including lunch and snacks, and go to the Hunter Valley, the south coast, Bathurst, or the Blue Mountains.

If you love motorbikes and want to take one out on your own for a self-guided or guided tour, contact **Bikescape** (ⓒ **02/9356 2453;** www.bikescape. com.au). They'll rent you a bike to go around Sydney, or as far afield as Byron Bay or the Great Ocean Road in Victoria.

7 Staying Active

BIKING The best place to cycle in Sydney is in Centennial Park. Rent bikes from Centennial Park Cycles, 50 Clovelly Rd., Randwick (ⓒ **02/9398 5027**), which is 200m (656 ft.) from the Musgrave Avenue entrance. (The park has five main entrances.) Mountain bikes cost A$9 (US$5.85) for the first hour, A$13 (US$8.45) for 2 hours, and A$20 (US$13) for 4 hours.

Bicycles in The City, 722 George St. (near Central Station) (ⓒ **02/9280 2229**), rents mountain bikes from A$5 (US$3.25) per hour, or $25 ($16) per day. You can rent in-line skates here, too, for the same daily rate with all protective clothing. Helmets are compulsory in Australia.

FITNESS CLUBS The **City Gym,** 107 Crown St., East Sydney (ⓒ **02/9360 6247**), is a busy gym near Kings Cross. Drop-in visits are A$10 (US$6.50), and it's open daily 24 hours.

GOLF Sydney has over 90 golf courses and plenty of fine weather. The 18-hole championship course at **Moore Park Golf Club,** at Cleveland Street and Anzac Parade, Waterloo (ⓒ **02/9663 1064**), is the nearest to the city. Visitors are welcome every day except all day Friday and Sunday mornings. Greens fees are A$24 (US$16) Monday through Friday, and A$27 (US$18) Saturday and Sunday.

One of my favorite courses is **Long Reef Golf Club,** Anzac Avenue, Colloroy (ⓒ **02/9982 2943**). This northern beaches course is surrounded by the Tasman Sea on three sides and has gorgeous views. Greens fees are A$25 (US$16) midweek, and A$35 (US$23) on weekends.

For general information on courses call the **New South Wales Golf Association** (© **02/9264 8433**).

IN-LINE SKATING The best places to go in-line skating are along the beachside promenades at Bondi and Manly beaches and in Centennial Park. **Manly Blades,** 49 North Steyne (© **02/9976 3833**), rents skates for A$12 (US$7.80) for the first hour and A$6 (US$3.90) for each subsequent hour, or A$25 (US$16) per day. Lessons are A$25 (US$16) including 1-hour skate rental and a half-hour lesson. **Bondi Boards & Blades,** 148 Curlewis St., Bondi Beach (© **02/9365 6555**), rents skates for A$11 (US$7.15) for the first hour, A$5.50 (US$3.60) for each subsequent hour, and A$20 (US$13) for 24 hours. Ask about a free lesson. **Total Skate,** 36 Oxford St., Paddington, near Centennial Park (© **02/9380 6356**), rents skates for A$10 (US$6.50) for the first hour, A$5 (US$3.25) for subsequent hours, and A$30 (US$20) for 24 hours. Ask about a free lesson.

JOGGING The **Royal Botanic Gardens, Centennial Park,** or any **beach** are the best places to kick-start your body. You can also run across the Harbour Bridge, though you'll have to put up with the car fumes. Another popular spot is along the sea cliffs from Bondi Beach to Bronte Beach.

PARASAILING If being strapped to a parachute 100m (328 ft.) above Sydney Harbour while being towed by a speedboat is your idea of fun, contact **Sydney Harbour Parasailing and Scenic Tours** (© **02/9977 6781**). A regular flight will see you in the air for 8 to 10 minutes at the end of a 100m (328-ft.) line. Flights cost A$55 (US$36) per adult. Tandem rides (for children and adults) are also available. The boat departs next to the Manly ferry wharf in Manly.

SCUBA DIVING Plenty of people learn to dive in Sydney before taking off for the Barrier Reef. Don't expect coral reefs, though. **Pro Dive,** 27 Alfreda St., Coogee (© **02/9665 6333**), offers a 4-day learn-to-dive program costing A$345 (US$224). A day of diving for registered divers costs A$105 (US$68).

SURFING **Bondi Beach** and **Tamarama** are the best surf beaches on the south side of Sydney Harbour, while **Manly, Narrabeen, Bilgola, Colloroy, Long Reef,** and **Palm** beaches are the most popular on the north side. Most beach suburbs have surf shops where you can rent a board. At Bondi Beach, the **Bondi Surf Co.,** 72 Campbell Parade (© **02/9365 0870**), rents surfboards for A$45 (US$29) for 4 hours or A$60 (US$39) all day. Body boards cost A$20 (US$13) for 2 hours and A$60 (US$39) all day. In Manly, **Aloha Surf,** 44 Pittwater Rd., Manly (© **02/9977 3777**), also rents surfboards. **Manly Surf School** (© **02/9977 6977**) offers 2-hour surf classes for A$40 (US$26), 2-day sessions for A$70 (US$46), and 3-day classes for A$90 (US$59). **Wave Action Surf School** (© **02/9970 6813,** or mobile 0413/177 242) offers a similar service with the same rates as Manly Surf School, on the breakers at Palm Beach. Also, it offers a 1-day surf tour from central Sydney to Palm Beach and other northern Sydney beaches with sightseeing and lunch for A$100 (US$65).

SWIMMING The best place to swim indoors in Sydney is the **Sydney Aquatic Centre,** at Olympic Park, Homebush Bay (© **02/9752 3666**). It's open Monday through Friday from 5am to 9:45pm, and Saturday, Sunday, and public holidays from 6am to 7:45pm (6:45pm May–Oct; A$5.80 (US$3.75) adult, A$4.60 (US$3) child 4–15).

Another good bet is the **North Sydney Olympic Pool,** Alfred South Street, Milsons Point (© **02/9955 2309**). It's just over the Harbour Bridge, near the amusement park, so why not have a swim after a walk over from the city. Swimming here costs A$3.50 (US$2.30) for adults and A$1.65 (US$1.10) for children. More world records have been broken in this pool than in any other. In 1999, the pool was renovated, and there's now a separate indoor pool, too. The Bondi Icebergs Club, on the rocks to the right of the beach as you look at the sea, also has a new Olympic-size swimming pool, and a children's pool. Entrance costs $3.30 and includes a sauna.

TENNIS　There are hundreds of places around the city to play one of Australia's most popular sports. A nice spot is the **Miller's Point Tennis Court,** Kent Street, The Rocks (✆ **02/9256 2222**). It's run by the Observatory Hotel and is open daily from 7:30am to 10pm. The court costs A$25 (US$16) per hour. The **North Sydney Tennis Centre,** 1A Little Alfred St., North Sydney (✆ **02/9371 9952**), has three courts available daily from 6am to 10pm. They cost A$16 (US$10) until 5pm on weekdays and A$20 (US$13) other times.

WINDSURFING　My favorite spot to learn to windsurf or to set out onto the harbor is at **Balmoral Beach,** in Mosman on the North Shore. Rent boards at **Balmoral Windsurfing, Sailing and Kayaking School & Hire,** 3 The Esplanade, Balmoral Beach (✆ **02/9960 5344**). Windsurfers cost A$27 (US$18) per hour for beginners and A$38 (US$28) for advanced windsurfing equipment. Lessons cost A$175 (US$114) for 5 hours teaching over a weekend, for beginners, and A$195 (US$127) for advanced lessons. This place also rents fishing boats.

YACHTING　**Balmoral Boat Shed,** Balmoral Beach (✆ **02/9969 6006**), rents catamarans, 3.5m (11-ft.) aluminum runabouts, canoes, and surf skis. The catamarans and runabouts cost A$35 (US$23) for the first hour (with an A$80/US$52 deposit); a full day costs A$120 (US$78). Other vessels, such as canoes, cost A$12 (US$7.80) per hour with an A$10 (US$6.50) deposit.

　Sydney by Sail (✆ **02/9280 1110,** or mobile 0419/367 180) offers sailing courses on Sydney Harbour. A long, 1-day introductory course costs A$450.

8 Spectator Sports

CRICKET　The **Sydney Cricket Ground,** at the corner of Moore Park and Driver Avenue, is famous for its 1-day and test matches, played October through March. Phone the **New South Wales Cricket Association** at ✆ **02/9339 0999** for match details, and **Sportspace Tours** (✆ **02/9380 0383**) for stadium tours.

FOOTBALL　In this city, "football" means rugby league. If you want to see burly chaps pound into each other while chasing an oval ball, then be here between May and September. The biggest venue is the **Sydney Football Stadium,** Moore Park Road, Paddington (✆ **02/9360 6601**). Match information is available at ✆ **1900/963 133.** Buy tickets at **Ticketek** (✆ **02/9266 4800**).

HORSE RACING　Sydney has four horse-racing tracks: Randwick, Canterbury, Rosehill, and Warwick Farm. The most central and most well known is **Randwick Racecourse,** Alison Street, Randwick (✆ **02/9663 8400**). The biggest race day of the week is Saturday. Entry costs A$9 (US$5.85) per person. Call the **Sydney Turf Club** at ✆ **02/9930 4000** with questions about Rosehill and Canterbury, and the Randwick number above for Warwick Farm.

SURFING CARNIVALS　Every summer these uniquely Australian competitions bring large crowds to Sydney's beaches, as surf clubs compete against each other in various watersports. Contact the **Surf Lifesaving Association** (✆ **02/ 9597 5588**) for times and locations. Other beach events include Iron Man and

---

Finds A Surf Adventure

If you've always fancied learning to surf, then head for **Waves Surf School** (© **1800/851 101** in Australia, or mobile 0414/682 228; www.wavessurf school.com.au). They take budding surfers on 1-day trips from Sydney to the Royal National Park with equipment and lunch provided. Trips cost A$65 (US$42). If you're young enough to sleep the night in a "double-decker party bus" then you might consider a 2-day surfing trip to Seal Rocks, north of Sydney, for A$169 (US$110). The company also takes adventurous travelers on a 4-day surfing trip for A$399 (US$259).

Iron Woman competitions, during which Australia's fittest struggle it out in combined swimming, running, and surfing events.

YACHT RACING While sailing competitions take place on the harbor most summer weekends, the start of the **Sydney to Hobart Yacht Race** on Boxing Day (Dec 26) is something not to be missed. The race starts from the harbor near the Royal Botanic Gardens.

9 Shopping

You'll find plenty of places to keep your credit cards in action in Sydney. Most shops of interest to the visitor are located in The Rocks and along George and Pitt streets (including the shops below the A.M.P. Centerpoint Tower and along the Pitt Street Mall). Other shopping precincts worth checking out are Mosman on the North Shore and Double Bay in the eastern suburbs for exclusive boutique shopping, Chatswood for its general shopping centers, the Sydney Fishmarket for the sake of it, and the various weekend markets (listed below).

Don't miss the **Queen Victoria Building (QVB),** on the corner of Market and George streets. This Victorian shopping arcade is one of the prettiest in the world and has some 200 boutiques—mostly men's and women's fashion—on four levels. The arcade is open 24 hours, but the shops do business Monday through Saturday from 9am to 6pm (Thurs to 9pm) and Sunday from 11am to 5pm.

SHOPPING HOURS Regular shopping hours are generally Monday through Wednesday and Friday from 8:30 or 9am to 6pm, Thursday from 8:30 or 9am to 9pm, Saturday from 9am to 5 or 5:30pm, and Sunday from 10 or 10:30am to 5pm. Exceptions are noted in the store listings below.

Several other arcades in the city center also offer good shopping potential, including the **Sydney Central Plaza,** beside the Grace Brothers department store on Pitt Street Mall; and the **Skygarden Arcade,** which runs from Pitt Street Mall to Castlereagh Street. The **Strand Arcade** (between Pitt St. Mall and George St.) was built in 1892 and is interesting for its architecture and small boutiques, food stores and cafes, and the Down Town Duty Free store on the basement level.

On **Pitt Street Mall** you'll find record shops, including HMV, a branch of The Body Shop, and boutiques such as Just Jeans, Jeans West, Katies, and Esprit.

Oxford Street runs from the city to Bondi Junction through Paddington and Darlinghurst and is home to countless clothing stores for the style conscious. You could quite easily spend anywhere from 2 hours to a whole day making your way from one end to the other. Detour down the small William Street once you get to Paddington to visit the headquarters of celebrated international Australian designer Collette Dinnigan. On the same street are the trendy boutiques Belinda and Corner Store for cutting edge designs, and Pelle and Di Nuovo for luxury recycled goods.

SYDNEY SHOPPING FROM A TO Z
ABORIGINAL ARTIFACTS & CRAFTS

Aboriginal & Tribal Art Centre   This center carries a wide range of desert paintings and bark paintings, mostly of very high quality. Collectibles such as didgeridoos, fabrics, books, and boomerangs are on sale, too. Open daily from 10am to 5pm. Amex, Diner Card, MasterCard, and Visa are accepted. 1st floor, 117 George St., The Rocks. ℂ 02/9247 9625. Fax 02/9247 4391.

Coo-ee Aboriginal Art Gallery and Shop   The proprietors of Coo-ee collect artifacts and fine art from more than 30 Aboriginal communities and dozens of individual artists throughout Australia. The gallery also stocks the largest collection of limited-edition prints in Australia. There are also plenty of hand-painted fabrics, T-shirts, didgeridoos, boomerangs, sculpture, bark paintings, jewelry, music, and books. Don't expect bargain prices, though; you pay for the quality here. Open Monday through Saturday from 10am to 6pm and Sunday from 11am to 5pm. 98 Oxford St., Paddington. ℂ 02/9332 1544.

Didj Beat Didjeridoo's   Here you'll find the most authentic and well-priced didgeridoos in Sydney. Open daily from 10am to 6:30pm. Shop 2, The Clock Tower Sq., corner of Argyle and Harrington sts. ℂ 02/9251 4289.

Gavala Aboriginal Art & Cultural Education Centre   I'd head here first if I were in the market for a decent boomerang or didgeridoo. Gavala is entirely owned and operated by Aborigines, and there are plenty of authentic Aboriginal crafts for sale, including carved emu eggs, grass baskets, cards, and books. A first-rate painted didgeridoo will cost anywhere from A$100 to A$450 (US$65–US$293). Gavala also sponsors cultural talks, didgeridoo-making lessons, and story-telling sessions. Open daily from 10am to 9pm. Shop 377, Harbourside Festival Marketplace, Darling Harbour. ℂ 02/9212 7232.

Original & Authentic Aboriginal Art   Quality Aboriginal art is on sale here from some of Australia's best-known painters, including Paddy Fordham Wain-burranga, whose paintings even hang in the White House in Washington, and Janet Forrester Nangala, whose work has been exhibited in the Australian National Gallery in Canberra. Expect to pay in the range of A$1,000 to

---

Value Discount Shopping

If you're looking for bargains, head to **Foveraux Street** between Elizabeth and Waterloo streets in Surry Hills for factory clearance shops selling last season's fashions and seconds at deep discounts. If you're keen on bargain shopping, consider joining up with **Shopping Spree Tours** (ℂ **1800/625 969** in Australia, or 02/9360 6220; fax 02/9332 2641), which offers tours to outlets and warehouses selling everything from clothes to cookware to electrical appliances. Full-day tours cost A$70 (US$46) for adults and A$20 (US$13) for children 3 to 12 and include pickup at your hotel, visits to 8 to 10 outlets and warehouses, and a two-course lunch at a good restaurant. Tours depart at 8:15am daily except Sunday and public holidays.

A$4,000 (US$650–US$2,600) for the larger paintings. There are some nice painted pots here, too, costing from A$30 to A$80 (US$20–US$52). Open daily from 10am to 6:30pm. 79 George St., The Rocks. ℂ **02/9251 4222.**

ART PRINTS & ORIGINALS

Done Art and Design   The art is by Ken Done, who's well known for having designed his own Australian flag, which he hopes to raise over Australia should it abandon its present one following the formation of a republic. The clothing designs—which feature printed sea- and beachscapes, the odd colorful bird, and lots of pastels—are by his wife Judy. Ken Done's gallery is in Hickson Road, just off George Street, in the Rocks. Open daily from 10am to 5:30pm. 1 Hickson Rd., The Rocks. ℂ **02/9247 2740.**

Ken Duncan Gallery   This photographer-turned-salesman is making a killing from his exquisitely produced large-scale photographs of Australian scenery. Open daily from 9am to 8pm in summer, until 9pm on Thursday and from 9am to 7pm in winter. 73 George St., The Rocks (across from The Rocks Visitor Centre). ℂ **02/9241 3460.** Fax 02/9241 3462.

BOOKS

You'll find a good selection of specialized books on Sydney and Australia for sale at the **Art Gallery of New South Wales,** the Garden Shop in the **Royal Botanic Gardens,** the **Museum of Sydney,** the **Australian Museum,** and the **State Library of New South Wales.**

Abbey's Bookshop   This interesting, centrally located bookshop specializes in literature, history, and mystery, and has a whole floor on language and education. 131 York St. (behind the QVB). ℂ **02/9264 3111.**

Angus & Robertson Bookworld   One of Australia's largest bookshops, with two stories of books—including a good guidebook and Australiana section—and games. 168 Pitt St., Pitt Street Mall. ℂ **02/9235 1188.**

Dymocks   One of the largest book department stores in the city, Dymocks has three levels of general books and stationery. There's a good travel section with plenty of guides. Open Monday through Wednesday and Friday from 9am to 6pm, Thursday from 9am to 9pm, Saturday from 9am to 5pm, and Sunday from 10am to 5pm. 424–428 George St. (just north of Market St.). ℂ **02/9235 0155.**

Gleebooks Bookshop   Specializing in art, general literature, psychology, sociology, and women's studies, Gleebooks also has a secondhand store (with a large children's department) down the road at 191 Glebe Point Rd. Open daily 8am to 9pm. 49 and 191 Glebe Point Rd., Glebe. ℂ **02/9660 2333.**

Goulds Book Arcade   Come here to search for unusual dusty volumes. Located about a 10-minute walk from the Newtown CityRail station, the place is bursting at the seams with many thousands of secondhand and new books all in a very rough order. You can browse for hours here. Open daily from 8am to midnight. 32–38 King St., Newtown. ℂ **02/9519 8947.**

Travel Bookshop   Hundreds of travel guides, maps, Australiana titles, coffee-table books, and accessories line the shelves of this excellent bookshop. There's also an Amex counter. Open Monday through Friday from 9am to 6pm and Saturday from 10am to 5pm. Shop 3, 175 Liverpool St. (across from the southern end of Hyde Park, near the Museum CityRail station). ℂ **02/9261 8200.**

CRAFTS

Australian Craftworks   This place showcases some of Australia's best arts and crafts, collected from some 300 Australian artists from around the country. It's all displayed in a former police station built in 1882, a time of economic depression when mob riots and clashes with police were common in this area. The cells and administration areas are today used as gallery spaces. Open daily from 8:30am to 7pm. 127 George St., The Rocks. ℭ 02/9247 7156.

The Puppet Shop at the Rocks *(Finds*   I can't believe I kept walking past the sign outside this place for so many years without looking in. Deep down in the bowels of a historic building, I eventually came across several cramped rooms absolutely packed with puppets, costing from a couple of dollars to a couple of hundred. The owners make their own puppets—mostly Australian in style (emus, koalas, and that sort of thing)—as well as import things from all over the world. Wooden toys abound, too. It's the best shop in Sydney! Open daily from 10am to 5:30pm. 77 George St., The Rocks. ℭ 02/9247 9137.

Telopea Gallery   This shop is run by the New South Wales Society of Arts and Crafts, which exhibits works by its members, all of whom are New South Wales residents. There are some wonderful glass, textile, ceramic, jewelry, fine-metal, and wood-turned items for sale. Open daily from 9:30am to 5:30pm. Shop 2 in the Metcalfe Arcade, 80–84 George St., The Rocks. ℭ 02/9241 1673.

DEPARTMENT STORES

The two big names in Sydney shopping are David Jones and Grace Brothers. **David Jones** (ℭ 02/9266 5544) is the city's largest department store, selling everything from fashion to designer furniture. You'll find the women's section on the corner of Elizabeth and Market streets, and the men's section on the corner of Castlereagh and Market streets.

Grace Brothers (ℭ 02/9238 9111) is similar to David Jones, but the building is newer and flashier. It's located on the corner of George and Market streets. Both stores are open Monday through Wednesday and Friday through Saturday from 9am to 6pm, Thursday from 9am to 9pm, and Sunday from 11am to 5pm.

DUTY-FREE SHOPS

Sydney has several duty-free shops selling goods at a discount. To take advantage of the bargains, you need a passport and a flight ticket, and you must export what you buy. The duty-free shop with the best buys is **Downtown Duty Free,** which has two city outlets, one on the basement level of the Strand Arcade, off Pitt Street Mall (ℭ 02/9233 3166) and one at 105 Pitt St. (ℭ 02/9221 4444). Five more stores are at Sydney International Airport and are open from the first to the last flight of the day.

FASHION

The best places to shop for fashion are the QVB and the Sydney Central Plaza (on the ground floor of the mall next to the Grace Brothers department store on Pitt Street Mall). Otherwise, the major Pitt Street Mall outlets will keep you up-to-date. For really trendy clothing head to Paddington, and for alternative clothes, go to Newtown.

Australian Outback Clothing

R.M. Williams   Moleskin trousers may not be the height of fashion at the moment, but you never know. R.M. Williams boots are famous for being both tough and fashionable. You'll find Akubra hats, Driza-bone coats, and kangaroo-skin belts here, too. 389 George St. (between Town Hall and Central CityRail stations). ℂ 02/ 9262 2228.

Thomas Cook Boot & Clothing Company   Located on George Street between Town Hall and Central CityRail stations, this place specializes in Australian boots, Driza-bone coats, and Akubra hats. There's another shop at 129 Pitt St., near Martin Place (ℂ **02/9232 3334**). 790 George St., Haymarket. ℂ 02/9212 6616. www.thomascookclothing.com.au.

Men's Fashion

Esprit Mens   Not so cheap, but certainly colorful clothes come out of this designer store where bold hues and fruity patterns are the in thing. Quality designer shirts cost around A$60 (US$39). Shop 10G, Sydney Central Plaza, 450 George St. ℂ 02/9233 7349.

Gowings   Probably the best all-round men's clothing store in Sydney, Gowings sells quality clothing on several levels. There's also an eclectic mix of gardening equipment, gourmet camping gear, odds and ends for the extrovert, a good range of Australian bush hats, and R. M. Williams boots (at around A$250/US$163 a pair). If you want to risk it, you can even get a cheap haircut here. There's a similar store at 319 George St., near Wynyard CityRail station (ℂ **02/9262 1281**). 45 Market St. ℂ 02/9264 6321.

Outdoor Heritage   Quality clothing with a yachting influence is what you'll find at this good-looking store specializing in casual, colorful gear. Shop 13G, Sydney Central Plaza, 450 George St. ℂ 02/9235 1560.

Unisex Fashion

Country Road   This chain store has outlets all across Australia as well as in the United States. The clothes, for both men and women, are good quality but tend to be quite expensive (though you might find something smart if you forgot to pack something). You'll find other branches in the QVB and the Skygarden Arcade, and in Bondi Junction, Darling Harbour, Double Bay, Mosman, and Chatswood. 142–146 Pitt St. ℂ 02/9394 1818.

Mostrada   If you're looking for good-quality leather items at very reasonable prices, then this is your place. Leather jackets for men and women go for between A$199 and A$899 (US$129–US$584), with an average price of around A$400 (US$260). There are also bags, belts, and other leather accessories on offer. Store 15G, Sydney Central Plaza, 450 George St. ℂ 02/9221 0133.

Women's Fashion

In addition to the places listed below, head to Oxford Street (particularly Paddington), for more avant-garde designers.

Carla Zampatti   There are some 30 Carla Zampatti stores around Australia offering stylish fashions at hard-to-swallow prices. Open Monday through Saturday from 10am to 5pm. 143 Elizabeth St. ℂ 02/9264 3257.

Dorian Scott   Probably the best place to go for hand-knit sweaters—called "jumpers" in Australia—Dorian Scott has a wide range of colorful garments from more than 200 leading Australian designers. While some items go for A$80 (US$52), others will set you back several hundred. You'll also find clothing accessories for men, women, and children in this two-story emporium, including Hot Tuna surfwear and Thomas Cook adventure clothing. Open Monday through Saturday from 9:30am to 7pm and Sunday from 10am to

6pm. There are also two Dorian Scott stores at Sydney International Airport (© **02/9667 3255**) and another at the Inter-Continental Hotel at 117 Macquarie St. (© **02/9247 1818**). 105 George St., The Rocks. © **02/9221 8145**. Fax 02/9251 8553.

FOOD

The goodies you'll find in the downstairs food section of **David Jones** department store on Castlereagh Street (the men's section) are enough to tempt anyone. The store sells the best local and imported products to the rich and famous.

Coles   One of the few supermarkets in the city center, this place is a good bet if you want to cater for yourself or are after ready-made food (including tasty sandwiches) and cheap soft drinks. There's another Coles beneath the giant Coca-Cola sign on Darlinghurst Road, Kings Cross. Open daily from 6am to midnight. Wynyard station, Castlereagh St., Wynyard (directly opposite the Menzies Hotel and the public bus stands). © **02/9299 4769.**

Darrell Lea Chocolates   This is the oldest location of Australia's most famous chocolate shop. Pick up some wonderful handmade chocolates as well as other unusual candies, including the best licorice this side of the Kasbah. At the corner of King and George sts. © **02/9232 2899.**

Sydney Fishmarket   Finding out about what people eat can be a good introduction to a new country and, in my opinion, nowhere is this more fascinating than a visit to the local fish market. Here you'll find seven major fish retailers selling everything from shark to Balmain bugs, with hundreds of species in between. Watch out for the local pelicans being fed the fishy leftovers. There's also a Doyles restaurant (p. 131) and a sushi bar, a couple of cheap seafood eateries, a fruit market, and a good deli. The retail sections are open daily from 7am to 4pm. Get here by light rail (get off at the Fishmarket stop), or walk from Darling Harbour. Parking costs A$2 (US$1.30) for the first 3 hours. At the corner of Bank St. and Pyrmont Bridge Rd., Pyrmont. © **02/9660 1611.**

GIFTS & SOUVENIRS

The shops at **Taronga Zoo,** the **Oceanarium** in Manly, the **Sydney Aquarium,** and the **Australian Museum** are all good sources for gifts and souvenirs. There are many shops around **The Rocks** worth browsing, too.

Australian Geographic   A spinoff from the Australian version of *National Geographic* magazine, this store sells good-quality crafts and Australiana. On hand are camping gadgets, telescopes and binoculars, garden utensils, scientific oddities, books and calendars, videos, music, toys, and lots more. Harbourside Festival Marketplace, Darling Harbour. © **02/9212 6539**. A.M.P. Centerpoint Tower, Pitt St. © **02/9231 5055.**

Ikonstore   This interesting little store located on the pedestrian pathway to the Sydney Opera House from Circular Quay has a fascinating collection of watches and gadgets for the gourmet collector. 16, Opera Quays, East Circular Quay. © **02/9252 6352.**

National Trust Gift and Bookshop   You can pick up some nice souvenirs, including books, Australiana crafts, and indigenous foodstuffs here. An art gallery on the premises presents changing exhibits of paintings and sculpture by Australians. There's also a cafe. Closed Monday. Observatory Hill, The Rocks. © **02/9258 0154.**

The Wilderness Society Shop   Australiana is crawling out of the woodwork at this cute little crafts emporium dedicated to spending all its profits on saving the few remaining untouched forests and wilderness areas of Australia. You'll find some quality crafts items, cute children's clothes, books, cards, and knickknacks. A.M.P. Centerpoint Tower, Castlereagh St. ℂ 02/9233 4674.

MARKETS

Balmain Market   Active from 8:30am to 4pm every Saturday, this market has some 140 vendors selling crafts, jewelry, and knickknacks. Take the ferry to Balmain (Darling St.); the market is a 10-minute walk up Darling Street. On the grounds of St. Andrew's Church, Darling St., Balmain ℂ 02/9555 1791.

Bondi Markets   A nice place to stroll around on Sunday after your brunch on Campbell Parade and discover the upcoming young Australian designers. This market has somewhat specialized in clothing and jewelry, new, secondhand, and retro. Bondi Beach School, Campbell Parade. ℂ 02/9398 5486.

Paddington Bazaar   At this Saturday-only market you'll find everything from essential oils and designer clothes to New Age jewelry and Mexican hammocks. Expect things to be busy from 10am to 4pm. Take bus no. 380 or 389 from Circular Quay. On the grounds of St. John's Church on Oxford St., on the corner of Newcome St. (just follow the crowds). ℂ 02/9331 2646.

Paddy's Markets   A Sydney institution, Paddy's Markets has hundreds of stalls selling everything from cheap clothes and plants to chickens. It's open Friday through Sunday from 9am to 4:30pm. Above Paddy's Markets is **Market City** (ℂ **02/9212 1388**), which has three floors of fashion stalls, food courts, and specialty shops. Of particular interest is the largest Asian-European supermarket in Australia, on level 1, and the **Kam Fook yum cha** Chinese restaurant on level 3, also the largest in Australia. At the corner of Thomas and Hay sts., in Haymarket, near Chinatown. ℂ **1300/361 589** in Australia, or 02/9325 6924.

The Rocks Market   Held every Saturday and Sunday, this very touristy market has more than 100 vendors selling everything from crafts, housewares, posters, jewelry, and curios. The main street is closed to traffic from 10am to 4pm to make it easier to stroll around. On George St., The Rocks. ℂ 02/9255 1717.

MUSIC

Birdland   This is the best store in Sydney for jazz and blues, and it stocks a sizable collection of rare items. The staff is very knowledgeable. 3 Barrack St. ℂ 02/9299 8527. www.birdland.com.au.

HMV   This is one of the best music stores in Sydney. The jazz section is impressive. CDs in Australia are not cheap, with most new releases costing around A$30 to A$35 (US$20–US$23). Pitt Street Mall. ℂ 02/9221 2311.

Red Eye Records   These two shops, tucked away downstairs in a small arcade not far from Pitt Street Mall and the Strand Arcade, are directly across from one another. The larger store sells a wide range of modern CDs, but the smaller store sells a great collection of quality secondhand and end-of-the-line CDs for around A$20 (US$13) each. Tank Stream Arcade (downstairs), at the corner of King and Pitt sts. (near Town Hall). ℂ 02/9233 8177 (new recordings), or 02/9233 8125 (secondhand CDs). www.redeye.com.au.

Sounds Australian   You can find anything you've ever heard that sounds Australian here. From rock and pop to didgeridoo and country, it's all here. And if you haven't a clue what's good and what's bad you can spend some time listening before you buy. The management is quite knowledgeable. In the Argyle Stores department store, The Rocks. ℂ 02/9247 7290. Fax 02/9241 2873.

OPALS

There are plenty of opal shops around in Sydney, but don't expect to walk away with any bargains. Best just to choose one you like and haggle.

Altman & Cherry   A good selection of opals—black, white, and boulder varieties—as well as jewelry are on sale here. Ask to see "The Aurora Australis," the world famous black opal valued at A$1 million (US$650,000). 19–31 Pitt St. (near Circular Quay). © 02/9251 4717.

Australian Opal Cutters   Learn more about opals before you buy at this shop. The staff here will give you lessons about opals to help you compare pieces. Suite 10, Level 4, National Bldg., 250 Pitt St. © 02/9261 2442.

WINE

Australian Wine Centre   This is one of the best places in the country to pick up Australian wines by the bottle or the case. The shop stocks a wide range of wines from all over Australia, including bottles from small boutique wineries you're unlikely to find anywhere else. Individual tastings are possible at any time, though there are formal tastings every Thursday and Friday from 4 to 6pm. Wine is exported all over the world from here, so if you want to send home a crate of your favorite, you can be assured it will arrive in one piece. The center owns the wine bar and bistro next door, which is open Monday through Saturday from 6am until 10pm. You can drink here without dining. 1 Alfred St., Shop 3 in Goldfields House, Circular Quay. © 02/9247 2755.

10 Sydney After Dark

Australians are party animals when they're in the mood; whether it's a few beers around the barbecue with friends or an all-night rave at a trendy dance club, they're always on the lookout for the next event. You'll find that alcohol plays a big part in the Aussie culture.

WHERE TO FIND OUT WHAT'S ON

The best way to find out what's on is to get hold of the "Metro" section of the Friday *Sydney Morning Herald* or the "Seven Days" pullout from the Thursday *Daily Telegraph*.

THE PERFORMING ARTS

If you have an opportunity to see a performance in the **Sydney Opera House,** jump at it. The "House" is actually not that impressive inside, but the walk back after the show toward the ferry terminals at Circular Quay, with the Sydney Harbour Bridge lit up to your right and the crowd all around you debating the best part of this play or who dropped a beat in that performance—well, it's like hearing Gershwin while on the streets of New York—you'll want the moment to stay with you forever. For details on Sydney's most famous performing-arts venue, see "What to See & Do in Sydney," earlier in this chapter.

THE OPERA, SYMPHONY & BALLET

Australian Ballet   Based in Melbourne, the Australian Ballet tours the country with its performances. The Sydney season, at the Opera House, is from mid-March until the end of April. A second Sydney season runs November through December. Level 15, 115 Pitt St. © 02/9223 9522. www.australianballet.com.au.

Australian Chamber Orchestra   Based in Sydney, this well-known company performs at various venues around the city, from nightclubs to specialized

---

Tips **It's a Festival!**

If you happen to be in Australia in January, plan to attend one of the many events that are part of the annual Sydney Festival. The festival kicks off just after New Year's and continues until the last week of the month, with recitals, plays, films, and performances at venues throughout the city, including Town Hall, the Royal Botanic Gardens, the Sydney Opera House, and Darling Harbour. Some events are free. "Jazz in The Domain" and "Symphony in The Domain" are two free outdoor performances held in the Royal Botanic Gardens, generally on the third and fourth weekend in Jan; each event attracts thousands of Sydneysiders. For more information, contact **Festival Ticketek** (✆ **02/9266 4111**; fax 02/9267 4460). Buy tickets and find out about performances on the Web at **www.sydneyfestival.org.au**.

---

music venues, including the Concert Hall in the Sydney Opera House. Opera Quays, 2 East Circular Quay. ✆ **02/9357 4111**; box office ✆ **02/8274 3888**. www.aco.com.au.

Opera Australia   Opera Australia performs at the Sydney Opera House's Opera Theatre. The opera season runs January through March and June through November. 480 Elizabeth St., Surry Hills. ✆ **02/9699 1099**; bookings 02/9319 1088. www.opera-australia.org.au.

Sydney Symphony Orchestra   Sydney's finest symphony orchestra is conducted by the renowned Edo de Waart. It performs throughout the year in the Opera House's Concert Hall. The main symphony season runs March through November, and there's a summer season in February. Level 5, 52 William St., East Sydney. ✆ **02/9334 4644**; box office 02/9334 4600. www.symphony.org.au.

THEATER

Sydney's blessed with plenty of theaters, many more than I have space for here—check the *Sydney Morning Herald,* especially the Friday edition, for information on what's currently in production.

Belvoir Street Theatre   The hallowed boards of the Belvoir are home to Company B, which pumps out powerful local and international plays upstairs in a wonderfully moody main theater, formerly part of a tomato-sauce factory. Downstairs, a smaller venue generally shows more experimental productions, such as Aboriginal performances and dance. 25 Belvoir St., Surry Hills. ✆ **02/9699 3444**. Tickets around A$34 (US$22).

Capital Theatre   Sydney's grandest theater plays host to major international and local productions like [cough] Australian singing superstar Kylie Minogue. It's also been the Sydney home of musicals such as *Miss Saigon* and *My Fair Lady.* 13–17 Campbell St., Haymarket, near Town Hall. ✆ **02/9320 5000**. Ticket prices vary.

Her Majesty's Theatre   A quarter of a century old, this large theater is still trawling in the big musicals. Huge productions that have run here include *Evita* and *Phantom of the Opera.* 107 Quay St., Haymarket, near Central Station. ✆ **02/9212 3411**. Ticket prices average A$55–A$75 (US$36–US$49).

Wharf Theatre   This wonderful theater is situated on a refurbished wharf on the edge of Sydney Harbour, just beyond the Harbour Bridge. The long walk from the entrance of the pier to the theater along old creaky wooden floorboards builds up excitement for the show. Based here is the Sydney Theatre Company, a group well worth seeing whatever the production. Dinner before the show at the Wharf's restaurant offers special views of the harbor. Pier 4, Hickson Rd., The Rocks. ℂ 02/9250 1777. www.sydneytheatre.com.au. Ticket prices vary.

THE CLUB & MUSIC SCENE
JAZZ, FOLK & BLUES
The Basement   Australia's hottest jazz club also manages to squeeze in plenty of blues, folk, and funk. Acts appear every night, and it's best to book ahead. Call for the schedule, pick up one at the club, or visit the website. 29 Reiby Place, Circular Quay. ℂ 02/9251 2797. www.thebasement.com.au/club_info.htm. Cover A$15–A$20 (US$9.75–US$13) for local acts, A$20–A$40 (US$13–US$26) for international performers.

side-on café   Known by locals as one of the few live venues in Sydney to showcase deliciously diverse jazz nearly every night of the week, this surprisingly decent restaurant is part of a multiarts complex and serves a two-course meal for A$27 (US$18). Patrons are a decent cross-sectional blend of artists, musicians, and various other assorted jazz lovers. The side-on endeavors to promote upcoming local talent as well as established acts and is also home to an art gallery upstairs. Located just over 5km (3 miles) from the center of town, it's not all that central but is very easily reached by public transport and well worth the detour. Daily 7pm until late. 83 Parramatta Rd., Anandale, near Anandale Hotel. www.side-on.com.au. Cover charge: A$13 (US$8.45).

ROCK
Metro   A medium-size rock venue with space for 1,000, the Metro is the best place in Sydney to see local and international acts. Tickets sell out quickly. 624 George St. ℂ 02/9264 2666. Cover varies.

DANCE CLUBS
Clubs come and go, and change names and music, so check the latest by planning ahead with a phone call. You can also check the "Metro" section in *Sydney Morning Herald* on Friday; otherwise, you might find free giveaway newspapers in some bars along Oxford Street that have info about the latest clubs.

Nightclub entrance charges change regularly, but generally cost between A$10 and A$15 (US$6.50–US$9.75). The Bourbon & Beefsteak Bar, with its A$5 (US$3.25) cover charge, is an oddity.

Bourbon & Beefsteak Bar   Right in the middle of Sydney's red-light district, this 24-hour restaurant and nightspot has a small dance floor. Bands play on the ground level Friday and Saturday nights. It's popular with a whole range of ages, from 18 to 60. 24 Darlinghurst Rd., Kings Cross. ℂ 02/9358 1144. Cover $5 (US$3.25).

Chinese Laundry   A couple of dance floors, one with rock walls to enhance the beat of the hip-hop, trance, and dance. What to wear? Dress like you want to *un*-impress. Open Friday and Saturday from 11pm to 4am. Sussex St. (turn right as you face the bridge from Cockle Bay across to Darling Harbour, and it's a 2-min. walk, below the Slip Inn bar). ℂ 02/9299 4777.

Home   Cavelike in shape and feel with a balcony to look down upon the throng, Home has a reputation for bad bouncers—like the time the *Sydney Morning Herald* newspaper had a Christmas party there and even the influential journalists were abused. Still it's managed to survive—hope you can. DJs spin funk and heavy drum-and-bass-style music, good for the serious clubber. Cockle Bay Wharf, Darling Harbour. ℂ 02/9266 0600. Cover A$25 (US$16).

Mister Goodbar   A young, trendy, local crowd inhabits Mister Goodbar's two good-size dance floors, where they can groove to a range of rap, funk, and hip-hop music Wednesday through Saturday. 11a Oxford St., Paddington. © **02/9360 6759.**

Riche Nightclub   This hot spot for dancing is popular with the local over-25 club set, as well as with hotel guests wanting to shake their booties to typical dance music. Open only Friday and Saturday. In the Sydney Hilton, 259 Pitt St. © **02/ 9266 2000.** Cover varies. Free for hotel guests.

Tantra   "Upmarket nightclubbing for the likes of models and beautiful people from the [affluent] north shore of Sydney," is how the manager describes this place. The interior is pseudo-Roman with lots of pillars. The club offers hardcore club/dance music: "'70s Boogie Wonderland" night Friday, commercial house music Saturday, and "funky" house music Sunday. Dress code is fashionable, with a shirt collar required for men and no sneakers. 169 Oxford St., Darlinghurst. © **02/9331 7729.**

GAY & LESBIAN CLUBS

Sydney has a huge gay community, so there's a very happening scene. The center of it all is Oxford Street, though Newtown has established itself as a major gay hangout, too. For information on events concerning gays and lesbians pick up a copy of the *Sydney Star Observer* or *Lesbians on the Loose* available at arthouse cinemas, cafes, and stores around Oxford Street. Nightclub entrance charges generally range from A$10 to A$15 (US$6.50–US$9.75).

Arq   This 24-hour club has an amazing light show and the best DJs in town. A very big place specializing in the latest dance tunes. Daily 24 hours. 16 Flinders St., Darlinghurst. © **02/9380 8700.**

Civic   This original Art Deco hotel has been tastefully decked up to accommodate three levels of entertainment. There's a theater on the lower first floor (basement), a saloon bar on the ground floor, and an Australian restaurant with live jazz upstairs, as well as an outdoor cocktail terrace. Great bands. Corner of Pitt and Goulburn sts., Sydney © **02/8267 3181.**

Gilligan's & Ginger's   A cocktail bar on the first floor of The Oxford Hotel, Gilligan's & Ginger's is home to a thriving social scene and great views of Oxford Street and the city skyline. DJs spin the latest handbag hits for the drag queens. 134 Oxford St., Darlinghurst, corner of Taylor Sq. © **02/9331 3467.**

The Stonewall Hotel   An institution with three levels of entertainment and many special nights. Don't miss Sydney's Diva, Ricca Paris, at the pickup night Malebox on Wednesdays. Daily noon to 5am. 175 Oxford St., Darlinghurst. © **02/9360 1963.** Free entry on most nights.

Taxi Club   "Tacky Club," as it's affectionately known, is another Sydney institution good for "handbag music"—or old pop and new pop. 40 Flinders St., Darlinghurst (near Taylor Sq., Oxford St.). © **02/9331 4256.**

THE BAR SCENE

Most of Australia's drinking holes are known as "hotels," after the tradition of providing room and board alongside a good drink in the old days. Occasionally you might hear them referred to as pubs. You tend to find the term *bar* used in upscale hotels and trendy establishments. Bars close at various times, generally from midnight to around 3am. Unless mentioned otherwise, these bars do not charge a cover.

Bondi Hotel   This huge, conglomerate across the road from Bondi Beach offers pool upstairs, a casual beer garden outside, and a resident DJ Thursday through Sunday from 8pm to 4am. There's also a free nightclub on Friday nights. Watch yourself; too much drink and sun turns some people nasty here. 178 Campbell Parade, Bondi Beach. (C) **02/9130 3271.**

Cargo Bar & Lounge Thus split-level waterfront bar on the city side of Darling Harbour (past the Sydney Aquarium) has a large ground-floor bar with access to an outdoor beer garden. The lounge upstairs features trendy leather and red footstools (apparently you sit on them). Cocktails and cigars are upstairs and more casual beers downstairs. Some nice pizzas here, too—if you like them topped with emu, crocodile, or kangaroo. 52-60 The Promenade, King Street Wharf. (C) **02/9262 1777.**

The Establishment Another trendy night out is in store if you set foot in this restored historic building with its 42m (138-ft.) bar, lots of floor-to-ceiling columns, and pressed-metal ceilings. It's fashionable, and the food downstairs— fish and chips and the like—is nice but unadventurous. There's better eating upstairs in the fine-dining restaurant. 252 George St., City. (C) **02/9240 3000.**

The Friend in Hand In the same location as the fantastically cheap Caesar's No Names spaghetti house, The Friend in Hand offers cheap drinks, poetry readings on Tuesday evenings from 8:30pm, a trivia night on Thursday evenings from 8:30pm, and the distinctly unusual Crab Racing Party every Wednesday from around 8pm. Crab fanciers buy a crustacean for around A$4 (US$2.60), give it a name, and send it off to do battle in a race against about 30 others. There are heats and finals, and victorious crustaceans win their owners prizes. 58 Cowper St., Glebe. (C) **02/9660 2326.**

Henry the Ninth Bar This mock-Tudor drinking hole gets very busy on Friday and Saturday nights. They serve up some good ales in an oaky atmosphere. An Irish band whips up the patrons on Thursday and Friday nights, and a cover band does the same on Wednesday and Saturday nights. A good-value happy hour brings beer prices tumbling Monday through Thursday from 5:30 to 7:30pm, Friday 5:30 to 8:30pm, and Saturday 8 to 10pm. In the Sydney Hilton, 259 Pitt St. (C) **02/9266 2000.**

Hero of Waterloo Hotel This sandstone landmark, built in 1845, was once allegedly the stalking ground of press gangs, who'd whack unsuspecting land-lubbers on the head, push them down a trapdoor out the back, and cart them out to sea. Today, this strangely shaped drinking hole is popular with the locals, and hosts old-time jazz bands (the musicians are often in their 70s and 80s) on Saturday and Sunday afternoons from 1:30 to 6:30pm, and Irish and cover bands Friday to Sunday evenings from 8:30pm. 81 Lower Fort St., The Rocks. (C) **02/ 9252 4553.**

Jacksons on George A popular drinking spot, this place has four floors of drinking, eating, dancing, and pool playing, and is a popular haunt with tourists and after-work office staff. Pool is expensive here at A$3 (US$1.95) a game (you'll need to ask the rules, as Australians have their own) and drinks have a nasty habit of going up in price without warning as the evening wears on. The nightclub plays commercial dance, and there's a smart/casual dress code. Happy hour is Monday through Friday from 5 to 7pm, when drinks cost around one-third less than normal. 178 George St., The Rocks. (C) **02/9247 2727.** Cover A$10 (US$6.50) for nightclub Fri–Sat after 10pm.

Lord Dudley Hotel The best way to get to this great English-style pub is via the Edgecliff CityRail station (between Kings Cross and Bondi Junction). From

there, bear right along the edge of the bus station, walk up the hill for 5 minutes and then take a right onto Jersey Road—ask the railway staff for the correct
exit if you can find anyone working. The Lord Dudley has the best atmosphere
of just about any drinking hole in Sydney, with log fires in winter, couches to
relax in, three bars, and a restaurant. 236 Jersey Rd., Woollahra. © 02/9327 5399.

Lord Nelson Hotel *(Value)*   Another Sydney sandstone landmark, the Lord Nelson rivals the Hero of Waterloo for the title of Sydney's oldest pub. The drinks
are sold English-style, in pints and half-pints, and the landlord even makes his
own prize-winning beers. Of these beers, Three Sheets is the most popular, but
if you can't handle falling over on your way home you might want to try a drop
of Quail (a pale beer), Victory (based on an English bitter), and a dark beer
called Admiral. You can get some good pub grub here, too. Upstairs there's a
more formal brasserie. At Kent and Argyle sts., The Rocks. © 02/9251 4044.

Marble Bar   Once part of a hotel demolished in the 1970s, the Marble Bar is
unique as the only grand-cafe–style drinking hole in Australia. With oil paintings, marble columns, and brass everywhere, it's the picture of 15th-century Italian Renaissance architecture, a tourist attraction in itself. Live music, generally
jazz or soul, is played here Tuesday through Saturday beginning at 8:30pm.
Dress smart on Friday and Saturday evenings. Drinks are normally very expensive, but the happy hour (daily 7–9pm) cuts prices down to what you'd pay during normal drinking hours elsewhere. In the Sydney Hilton, 259 Pitt St. © 02/9266 2000.

The Mercantile   Sydney's original Irish bar is scruffy and loud when the Irish
music's playing in the evening, but an essential stop on any pub crawl in The
Rocks. The Guinness is some of the best you'll taste in Sydney. Irish bands kick
off every night at around 8pm. 25 George St., The Rocks. © 02/9247 3570.

Slip Inn   This multifunctioning bar and bistro setup is a popular city place to
drink and meet. There's a garden bar downstairs set in a courtyard, along with a
trattoria selling pizzas. Upstairs there's a Thai bistro open for lunch and a large
square bar. It's crowded on Friday evenings, but you'll never feel like a sardine.
Sussex St., Darling Harbour. © 02/9299 4777. A 2-min. walk toward the city from the Town
Hall/Cockle Bay side of the pedestrian bridge across to Darling Harbour.

Watsons Bay Hotel   If it's a sunny afternoon, get over to Watsons Bay for the
best food you'll find in the sun anywhere. The beer garden serves good seafood
and barbecue meat dishes, while you sip your expensive wine or beer overlooking the harbor. Nearby are the fabulous Doyles Wharf Restaurant and Doyles at
the Beach takeout. 1 Military Rd., Watsons Bay. © 02/9337 4299.

MOVIES
The city's major movie houses, **Hoyts** (© **13 27 00** in Australia), **Greater
Union** (© **02/9267 8666**), and **Village** (© **02/9264 6701**), are right next to
each other on George Street just past Town Hall. They tend to show big-budget
movie releases. Other options are the **Dendy Cinemas,** located at 19 Martin
Place, City (© **02/9233 8166**); 261–263 King St., Newtown (© **02/9550
5699**); and the latest Dendy Quay movie theater located just before you reach
the Opera House, at 2 East Circular Quay (© **02/9247 3800**). All show art-
house movies; the latter allows wine and beer bought on the premises to be consumed in the cinema. In Paddington, the **Verona,** 17 Oxford St. (© **02/9360
6099**), and the **Academy Twin,** 2 Oxford St. (© **02/9361 4455**), conveniently
located next to each other, are always screening the best local and foreign films
in Sydney.

Another exceptional art-house/recent blockbuster cinema is the **Hayden Orpheum Picture Palace,** 380 Military Rd., Cremorne (© **02/9908 4344**). This eight-screen Art Deco gem is an experience in itself, especially on Saturday and Sunday evenings when a Wurlitzer pops up from the center of the Cinema 2 stage, and a musician in a tux gives a stirring rendition of times gone by. Eat "Jaffas," round candy-coated chocolates, if you want to fit in.

Movie prices hover around A$15 (US$9.40), with a half-price night generally on Tuesdays.

THE CASINO

Star City   This huge entertainment complex has 15 main bars, 12 restaurants, 2 theaters—the Showroom, which presents Las Vegas–style revues, and the Lyric, Sydney's largest theater—and a huge complex of retail shops. All the usual gambling tables are here, in four main gambling areas. In all there are 2,500 slot machines to gobble your change. Open 24 hours. 80 Pyrmont St., Pyrmont (adjacent to Darling Harbour). © **02/9777 9000.** Ferry: Pyrmont (Darling Harbour). Monorail: Casino.

4

New South Wales

by Marc Llewellyn

With so much to experience in a state as big as New South Wales, you're not going to see all the major attractions in one hit, so you must prioritize. If you have just a few days to spare, you should certainly head out to the Blue Mountains, part of the Great Dividing Range that separates the lush eastern coastal strip from the more arid interior. Although these mountains are more like hills, they are spectacular, with tall eucalyptus trees, deep river valleys, waterfalls, and craggy cliffs. Or spend a day in the vineyards of the lower Hunter (also known as the Hunter Valley). If you have a few more days, I recommend heading to Barrington Tops National Park, north of the Hunter, for the rainforest and native animals, or down to the pristine beaches of Jervis Bay for gorgeous scenery and great bushwalks.

For longer trips, you can head north toward the Queensland border on the 964km (598-mile) route to Brisbane. You'll pass pretty seaside towns, deserted beaches, and tropical hinterland. Another option is to travel along the south coast 1,032km (640 miles) to Melbourne. Along the way are some of the country's most spectacular beaches, quaint hamlets, good opportunities to spot dolphins and whales, and extensive national parks. If you want to experience the Outback, then head west across the Blue Mountains. You are sure to see plenty of kangaroos, emus, reptiles, and giant wedge-tailed eagles. The main Outback destination is the extraordinary opal-mining town of Lightning Ridge, where you can meet some of the most eccentric *fair-dinkum* (that means "authentic" or "genuine") Aussies you'll come across anywhere.

EXPLORING THE STATE

VISITOR INFORMATION The **Sydney Visitors Centre,** 106 George St., The Rocks (© **13 20 77** in Australia; www.tourism.nsw.gov.au) will give you general information on what to do and where to stay throughout the state. Otherwise, **Tourism New South Wales** (© **02/9931 1111**) will direct you to the regional tourist office in the town or area you are interested in.

GETTING AROUND   By Car   From Sydney, the **Pacific Highway** heads along the north coast into Queensland, and the **Princes Highway** hugs the south coast and runs into Victoria. The **Sydney-Newcastle Freeway** connects Sydney with its industrial neighbor and the vineyards of the Hunter. The **Great Western Highway** and the **M4 Motorway** head west to the Blue Mountains, while the **M5 Motorway** and the **Hume Highway** (via Canberra) are the quickest (and least interesting) ways to get to Melbourne.

The state's automobile association, the **National Roads and Motorists' Association (NRMA),** 151 Clarence St., Sydney (© **13 11 22** in Australia), offers free maps and touring guides to members of overseas motoring associations,

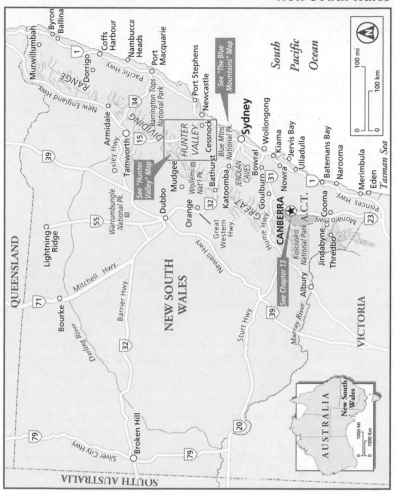

including AAA in the United States, CAA in Canada, AA and RAC in the United Kingdom, and NZAA in New Zealand.

By Train   Countrylink (© **13 22 32** in Australia) trains travel to most places of interest in the state and as far south as Melbourne in Victoria and across the border into southern Queensland. Countrylink also has special rates for car rental through Thrifty.

By Plane   Qantas (© **13 13 13** in Australia) and **Eastern Australia Airlines** (book through Qantas) fly to most major cities and towns within the state.

1 The Blue Mountains ★★

Although the **Blue Mountains** are today where Sydneysiders go to escape the humidity and crowds of the city, in the early days of the colony, the mountains kept at bay those who would explore the interior. In 1813, three explorers— Gregory Blaxland, William Charles Wentworth, and William Lawson—managed to conquer the sheer cliffs, valleys, and dense forest, and cross the mountains (which are hardly mountains at all, but rather a series of hills covered in bush and ancient fern trees) to the plains beyond. There they found land urgently needed for grazing and farming. The Great Western Highway and Bells Line of Road are the access roads through the region today—winding and steep in places, they are surrounded by the Blue Mountains and Wollemi national parks.

The area is known for its spectacular scenery, particularly the cliff-top views into the valleys of gum trees and across to craggy outcrops that tower up from the valley floor. It's colder up here than down on the plains, and the clouds can sweep in and fill the canyons with mist in minutes, while waterfalls cascade down sheer drops, spraying the dripping fern trees that cling to the gullies. You'll need at least a couple of days up here to get the best out of it—a single-day tour, with all the traveling involved, can only just scratch the surface.

The Blue Mountains is also one of Australia's best-known adventure playgrounds. Rock climbing, caving, abseiling (rappelling), bushwalking, mountain biking, horseback riding, and canoeing are practiced here year-round.

BLUE MOUNTAIN ESSENTIALS

VISITOR INFORMATION   You can pick up maps, walking guides, and other information and book accommodations at **Blue Mountains Tourism,** with locations at Echo Point Road, Katoomba, NSW 2780 (© **1300/653 408** in Australia, or 02/4739 6266), and on the Great Western Highway at Glenbrook, a small settlement 61km (38 miles) from Sydney (same telephone number). The Katoomba information center is an attraction itself, with glass windows overlooking a gum forest and cockatoos and lorikeets feeding on seed dispensers. Pick up a copy of the *Blue Mountains Pocket Guide,* a free guide to dining, accommodations, bushwalking, and entertainment. Both offices are open from 9am to 5pm daily (the office at Glenbrook closes at 4:30pm Sat–Sun).

The **National Park Shop,** Heritage Centre, the end of Govetts Leap Rd., Blackheath (© **02/4787 8877;** www.npws.nsw.gov.au), is run by the National Parks and Wildlife Service and offers detailed information about the Blue Mountains National Park. The staff can also arrange personalized guided tours of the mountains. It's open daily from 9am to 4:30pm (closed Christmas).

Check the website, www.bluemts.com.au, for more information on the area.

GUIDED TOURS FROM SYDNEY   Many private bus operators offer day trips from Sydney, but it's important to shop around because some offer a guided coach tour where you just stretch your legs occasionally, while others let you get your circulation going with a couple of longish bushwalks. One highly recommended operator is **Oz Trek Adventure Tours** (© 02/9360 3444; www.oztrek.com.au). Their trips include a tour of the Olympic site, a visit to Glenbrook National Park (where you'll see kangaroos and wallabies in the wild), tours of all the major Blue Mountain sites, and a 1½-hour bushwalk. It costs

---

(Fun Fact   **Color Me Blue**

The Blue Mountains derive their name from the ever-present blue haze that is caused by light striking the droplets of eucalyptus oil that evaporate from the leaves of the dense surrounding forest.

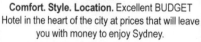

Inset map:
New South Wales
Blue Mountains National Park
Canberra — Sydney

Map labels:
WOLLEMI NATIONAL PARK
Bilpin
Panorama Point Lookout
To Hunter Valley via Putty Road
Kurrajong
Richmond
To Australian Pioneer Village
BLUE MOUNTAINS NATIONAL PARK
Mt. Tomah Botanic Gardens
Castlereagh
Lithgow
GROSE GORGE
Hawkesbury Heights
To Featherdale Wildlife Park
Western Hwy. Mount Victoria Medlow Bath
Pulpit Rock
Springwood
Elizabeth Lookout
Penrith
Hartley
Faulconbridge
Govetts Leap
Blackheath
Mt. Blackheath Lookout
Evans Lookout
Wentworth Falls
Woodford
Blaxland
Glenbrook
Marges Lookout
Hargreaves Lookout
Scenic Railway
Lawson
Katoomba Leura
The Oaks Fire Track
Echo Point
Three Sisters
BLUE MOUNTAINS NATIONAL PARK
Euroka
MEGALONG VALLEY
JAMISON VALLEY
Warragamba Dam
JENOLAN STATE FOREST
Jenolan Caves
KANANGRA BOYD NATIONAL PARK
Lake Burragorang
0   10 mi
0   10 km

A\$54 (US\$35) for adults and A\$43 (US\$28) for kids. You can also add on overnight packages, horseback riding and abseiling.

Oz Experience (© **1300/300 028** in Australia, or 02/9213 1766; www.oz experience.com) offers tours ranging from 1 day including lunch to 4 days aimed at younger people. A day trip including a visit to Featherdale Wildlife Park costs A\$70 (US\$46); and a 4-day trip including abseiling and canyoning costs A\$395 (US\$257).

Visitours (© **02/9909 0822**; www.visitours.com.au) runs a fabulous minibus trip to the mountains, stopping off at Featherdale Wildlife Park and the Olympic site. You get to see all the usual 1-day sights, learn to throw a boomerang and play the didgeridoo, and take a ferry ride down the Parramatta River back to Circular Quay in Sydney.

Cox's River Escapes, P.O. Box 81, Leura, NSW 2780 (© **02/4784 1621,** or mobile 0407/400 121; www.bluemts.com.au/CoxsRiver), offers recommended tours for those wanting to get off the beaten track. Half-day trips with morning or afternoon tea cost A\$110 (US\$72); full-day trips with morning tea, lunch, and afternoon refreshments and entry into Jenolan Caves cost A\$220 (US\$143).

AAT Kings, Shop 1, corner of Alfred Street and Ferry Wharf no. 1, Circular Quay (© **02/9518 6095;** www.aatkings.com), operates three typical big-bus tours of the mountains, taking in most of the usual sights, with a couple of short walks included. One tour includes a visit to Jenolan Caves. Tours range in cost

> **Tips Timing Is Everything: When to Visit**
>
> If you can, try to visit the Blue Mountains on **weekdays,** when most Syd-neysiders are at work and the prices are lower. Note that the colder win-ter months (June–Aug) are the busiest season. This period is known as **Yuletide**—the locals' version of the Christmas period, when most places offer traditional Christmas dinners and roaring log fires.

from A$85 to A$113 (US$55–US$73) for adults, and A$43 to A$86 (US$28–US$60) for children. Another large operator, **Australian Pacific Tours** (© **1300/655 965;** fax 02/9660 5016), offers a similar trip with a visit to the Australian Wildlife Park and a quick visit to the Sydney Olympic site at Home-bush·Bay. This tour costs A$94 (US$61) for adults and A$47 (US$31) for chil-dren. If you hate big-group travel then choose another option.

BUSHWALKING & OTHER ACTIVE ENDEAVORS

Whereas almost every other activity costs money, bushwalking (hiking) is the exception to the rule that nothing in life is free. There are some 50 walking trails in the Blue Mountains, ranging from routes you can cover in 15 minutes to the 3-day **Six Foot Track** ⚜ that starts just outside Katoomba and finishes at Jenolan Caves. If you are planning on some bushwalking, I highly recommend picking up *Sydney and Beyond—Eighty-Six Walks in NSW* by Andrew Mevissen (Macstyle Publishing). It features eight walks in the Blue Mountains, from easy 1-hour treks to 6-hour tramps. Buy it at bookshops and tourist information cen-ters. Otherwise, the staff at the tourist offices and National Park office will be happy to point you in the right direction, whether it be for an hour's stroll or a full-day's hike.

Great Australian Walks, 81 Elliot St., Balmain, NSW 2041 (© **1300/360 499** in Australia, or 02/9555 7580; www.greatwalks.com.au), is a superb operator offering walks in the Blue Mountains. I had great fun on their 3-day "Six Foot Track Walk" from Katoomba to Jenolan Caves. Though not a wilderness trek, it goes through pockets of rainforest and gum forests and traverses farming country.

One of the best adventure operators in the area, **High 'n' Wild,** Unit 3, No. 5 Katoomba St., Katoomba, NSW 2780 (© **02/4782 6224;** www.high-n-wild.com.au), offers a series of canyoneering expeditions, taking in scenic rain-forest gullies and caverns made up of dramatic rock formations and fern-lined walls. Generally there's a bit of swimming and plenty of walking, wading, and squeezing through tight spaces involved—and sometimes rappelling—but for-tunately being double-jointed is not a prerequisite.

If you really want to test your head for heights, though, then try High 'n' Wild's 150m (492-ft.) "Mega Jump"—the highest continuous rappel in the Southern Hemisphere. This heart-pumping descent down a sheer cliff is suitable for the fearless beginner, but they assure me you soon settle in by learning the ropes on the 10-story-high junior slopes beforehand.

If that's too much to handle, though, then you could always try a day's raft-ing on an inflatable raft between huge towering rock walls on the Wollangambe River. There are a few minor rapids to navigate, and the bushwalk down to the river and back up again can be a little testing, but it's certainly suitable for a fam-ily outing. Rappelling costs from A$69 (US$45) and canyoning from $85 (US$55). Raft adventures cost $169 (US$110).

Other excellent adventure operators are **The Blue Mountains Adventure Company,** P.O. Box 242, Katoomba, NSW 2780 (© **02/4782 1271;** bmac@ bmac.com.au), located in Katoomba at 84a Bathurst Rd. (above the Summit Gear Shop); and the **Australian School of Mountaineering,** 166b Katoomba St., Katoomba, NSW 2780 (© **02/4782 2014**). Both offer rock climbing, rappelling, and canyoning trips. The company also offers caving and mountain biking, and the Australian School of Mountaineering offers bushcraft and survival training. Expect to pay around A$100 (US$65) for a daylong introductory rock-climbing course including rappelling, and between A$99 and A$125 (US$64–US$81) for a day's canyoning.

If you feel like some adventure on your own, you could always rent a mountain bike from **Cycletech,** 182 Katoomba St., Katoomba (© **02/4782 2800**). Standard mountain bikes cost A$19 (US$12) for half a day and A$28 (US$18) for a full day (superior front-suspension mountain bikes cost A$28/US$18 for a half day and A$50/US$33 for a full day).

KATOOMBA: GATEWAY TO THE BLUE MOUNTAINS
114km (71 miles) W of Sydney

Katoomba (pop. 11,200) is the largest town in the Blue Mountains and the focal point of the Blue Mountains National Park. It's an easy 1½- to 2-hour trip by train, bus, or car. The town is a low-socioeconomic pocket in a very affluent region, with one of the highest unemployment rates in the State.

GETTING THERE   By car from central Sydney travel along Parramatta Road and turn off onto the M4 motorway (around 2 hr. to Katoomba). Another route is via the Harbour Bridge to North Sydney, along the Warringah Freeway (following the signs to the M2). Then, travel along the M2 to its end and follow the signs to the M4, and the Blue Mountains. This takes around 1½ hours.

Frequent rail services connect Sydney to Katoomba from Central Station; contact **CityRail** (© **13 15 00**) or **Countrylink** (© **13 22 32**) for details. The train trip takes 2 hours, leaving from platform nos. 12 and 13 of Central Station. Trains leave almost hourly, stopping at Katoomba, and then at Mt. Victoria and Lithgow. An adult day-return round-trip ticket costs A$12 (US$7.80) off-peak and A$20 (US$13) during commuter hours. A child's day-return round-trip ticket costs A$3 (US$1.95).

GETTING AROUND   The best way to get around the Blue Mountains without your own transport is with the **Blue Mountains Explorer Bus** (© **02/4782 4807;** www.explorerbus.com.au). This double-decker bus leaves from outside Katoomba train station every hour from 9:30am until 4:30pm and stops at 27 attractions, resorts, galleries, and tearooms in and around Katoomba and Leura. You can get on and off as often as you want. Tickets cost A$25 (US$16) for adults, A$13 (US$8) for children, and A$63 (US$41) for a family. You can also link this tour bus with the CityRail train from Sydney. The Blue Mountains Explorer Link Ticket, available from CityRail stations cost A$39 (US$25) for adults, A$15 (US$10) for children, and A$62 (US$40) for a family, and includes return train fare and Explorer Bus tickets.

Another option is **Trolley Tours** (© **1800/801 577** in Australia; www.trolley tours.com.au), which is a kind of tram on wheels with commentary. An all-day pass costs A$12 (US$7.80) and includes stops at various attractions around Katoomba and Leura, too. The trolley leaves Katoomba Station each hour, connecting with the trains from Sydney.

Fantastic Aussie Tours (© **02/4782 1866;** www.fantastic-aussie-tours.com.
au) runs several tours of the area, including a Blue Mountains Highlight Tour
which takes you to many of the best sites. Tours leave at 10:30am (and finish at
1:15pm), 11:30am (to 3:15pm), and 2pm (to 5:15pm). Tours cost A$38
(US$24) for adults, A$19 (US$12) for children, and A$88 (US$57) for a family.

EXPLORING THE AREA

The most visited and photographed attractions in the Blue Mountains are the
rock formations known as the **Three Sisters** ✦✦. For the best vantage point,
head to **Echo Point Road,** across from the Blue Mountains Tourism office. Or
try Evans Lookout, Govetts Leap, and Hargreaves Lookout, all at Blackheath
(see "Blackheath," below)—none of which are serviced by the Blue Mountains
Explorer Bus or Trolley Tours.

One thing you have to do in the Blue Mountains is ride the **Scenic Railway,**
the world's steepest. It consists of a carriage on rails that is lowered 415m (1,361
ft.) down into the Jamison Valley at a maximum incline of 52 degrees. Originally the rail line was used to transport coal and shale from the mines below in
the 1880s. The trip only takes a few minutes; at the bottom are some excellent
walks through forests of ancient tree ferns. Another popular attraction is the
Skyway, a cable car that travels 300m (984 ft.) above the Jamison Valley. The
trip takes 6 minutes round-trip. The Scenic Railway and the Skyway (© **02/
4782 2699**) each cost A$8 (US$5.20) round-trip for adults and A$3 (US$1.95)
for children, and operate from 9am to 5pm daily (last trip at 4:50pm). They
depart from the ticket office at 1 Violet St., Katoomba. (Follow the signs.)

Canyons, waterfalls, underground rivers—the Blue Mountains has them all,
and before you experience them in person you can catch them on the (giant)
screen in *The Edge* at the **MAXVISION Cinema,** 225–237 Great Western
Hwy., Katoomba (© **02/4782 8900**). The special effects shown on the screen,
18m (59 ft.) high and 24m (79 ft.) wide, make you feel like you're part of the
action. The 38-minute film *The Edge* is shown every 40 to 50 minutes from
10am to 5:45pm. Tickets are A$13 (US$8.45) for adults, A$11 (US$7.15) for
students, and A$7.50 (US$4.90) for children. The cinema is a 5- to 10-minute
walk from the train station. Recent release movies are shown on part of the giant
screen in the evenings. There is a restaurant and a snack bar on the premises.

To get back to Sydney, I highly recommend taking the Bell's Line of Road
through Bilpin. It's up to 3-hour's driving via this route, but you can stop off at
the wonderful **Mt. Tomah Botanic Gardens** ✦. (You can't miss the large sign
on your right about 10 min. before you get to Bilpin.) An adjunct of the Royal
Botanic Gardens in Sydney, Mt. Tomah is dedicated to cold climate plants. It's
compact and has a very good cafe serving lunch daily. Allow around 2 hours for
a stop here.

WHERE TO STAY

There are plenty of places to stay throughout the Blue Mountains, including historic guesthouses, B&Bs, resorts, motels, and homestays.

Very Expensive

Echoes Hotel & Restaurant, Blue Mountains ✦ *Finds* Lilianfels (see
below) might be more expensive, but Echoes, just across the road on a cliff overlooking the Jamison Valley, has superior views. Large windows, balconies, and a
sizeable deck allow guests to soak up the fantastic scenery. Rooms are simply furnished and smaller than those at Lilianfels; all have underfloor heating and are
recommended.

> **Tips** **Seeing the Blue Mountains from the Back of a Harley**
>
> A thrilling way to see the Blue Mountains is on the back of a chauffeur-driven Harley-Davidson. **Blue Thunder Bike Tours** (℃ **02/4571 1154**) leaves from Manly Wharf in Sydney (but they'll pick you up anywhere in the city). Rides cost A$80 (US$52) for the first hour, A$130 (US$85) for 2 hours, A$255 (US$166) for half a day, and A$360 (US$234) for a full day with lunch. The same company runs **Hot Heritage Tours**, operating out of the Blue Mountains (pickup anywhere in the Mountains), for the same prices.

---

3 Lilianfels Ave., Katoomba, NSW 2780. ℃ **02/4782 1966.** Fax 02/4782 3707. www.echoeshotel.com.au. 12 units. Weekend rate A$425 (US$276) double including breakfast; midweek rate A$325 (US$211) double including dinner and breakfast. AE, DC, MC, V. Free parking. **Amenities:** Restaurant; bar; Jacuzzi; sauna; nonsmoking rooms. *In room:* A/C, TV, minibar, coffeemaker, hair dryer, iron.

Lilianfels Blue Mountains ⭐⭐ Set just over a road from Echo Point, this Victorian country-house hotel—a member of the Small Luxury Hotels of the World—is a full-service yet still cozy establishment. Rooms are spacious and furnished with antiques. Most have king-size beds and both a tub and shower. Those with views are more expensive. The living areas are just as grand, with roaring log fires and more antiques. Views are impressive, especially from the lounge, which overlooks the Jamison Valley. On the grounds is an 1889 cottage. Meant for two, it has a sitting room, a bedroom with a four-poster bed, a Jacuzzi, an intimate fireplace, and its own gardens. Among the other offerings at Lilianfels are a billiards room, a library and reading room, and a lawn for French boules.

Lilianfels Ave., Katoomba, NSW 2780. ℃ **1800/024 452** in Australia, or 02/4780 1200. Fax 02/4780 1300. www.slh.com. 85 units, 1 cottage. A$380–A$470 (US$247–US$305) double; A$530–A$685 (US$345–US$445) suite; A$1,050 (US$682) cottage. Extra person A$55 (US$36). Ask about off-season packages. AE, DC, MC, V. Free parking. **Amenities:** 2 restaurants; small indoor swimming pool; health club with flotation tank; exercise room; Jacuzzi; sauna; bike rental; tour desk; secretarial services; 24-hr. room service; massage; laundry service; dry cleaning; nonsmoking rooms. *In room:* A/C, TV, minibar, coffeemaker, hair dryer, iron.

Moderate

The Carrington Hotel ⭐⭐ *Finds* Construction started on this grand Victorian hotel in 1880, and it reopened in 2000 after a major renovation. A ramshackle building, The Carrington is a must-stay if you're into buildings of the British-Raj style. Downstairs is a restaurant/breakfast room (once a ballroom), a couple of lounges scattered with antiques, and a gorgeous wood-paneled billiard room. Chandeliers and 1930s-style lamps reflecting off silver trophies won by the local Rifle Club give everything a warm glow. Unfortunately, heavy Plexiglas doors greet you as you enter each of the many corridors—a necessary fire precaution. All the rooms are delightful, with royal gold and blue carpets and drapes which would probably be considered gaudy if they didn't seem to fit in with the overall style. Traditional rooms share bathrooms; Colonial rooms come with a deep tub in the bathroom (with a noisy fan) and no view to speak of; Deluxe Colonial rooms have a balcony and mountain views; Premier rooms have Jacuzzis and great views; and the suites are fit for a duke and duchess. Dinner here costs A$100 (US$65) per person, and the full breakfast is one of the best I've encountered.

15–47 Katoomba St., Katoomba (P.O. Box 28, NSW 2780). ℃ **02/4782 1111.** Fax 02/4782 1421. www.the carrington.com.au. 63 units. Traditional rooms Mon–Thurs A$100 (US$65), Fri–Sat A$155 (US$101); colonial rooms Mon–Thurs A$150 (US$98), Fri–Sat A$225 (US$166); deluxe colonial rooms Mon–Thurs A$185

(US$120), Fri–Sat A$300 (US$195); premier rooms Mon–Thurs A$225 (US$146), Fri–Sat A$350 (US$228); suites Mon–Thurs A$265–A$450 (US$172–US$293), Fri–Sat A$410–A$630 (US$267–US$409). Ask about weekend packages. Rates include breakfast. AE, DC, MC, V. **Amenities:** Restaurant; bar; snooker room. *In room:* TV, coffeemaker, iron.

Echo Point Holiday Villas ⚶ These are the closest self-contained accommodations to the Three Sisters Lookout. The two front-facing villas are the best because of their beautiful mountain views. Some villas have one double and two single beds, plus a foldout double bed in the lounge room. Bathrooms contain a shower, with no tub. There are barbecue facilities in the backyard. The two cottages are also fully self-contained, sleeping up to eight, and have a tub, central heating, and access to nice gardens.

36 Echo Point Rd., Katoomba, NSW 2780. ✆ **02/4782 3275.** Fax 02/4782 7030. www.echopointvillas.com. au. 5 villas, 2 cottages (all with shower only). Fri–Sat and public holidays A$140 (US$91) villa; Sun–Thurs A$105 (US$68) villa; A$150 (US$98) cottage for 2. Minimum 2-night stay required. Extra person A$12 (US$7.80). AE, DC, MC, V. *In room:* TV, kitchen, fridge, hair dryer, iron.

Inexpensive

Katoomba Mountain Lodge This two-star property is quite cozy, with rooms looking out across the mountains. Dorm rooms are clean and come with three to six beds. Doubles are basic and lack a TV, but adequate for a couple of nights. All share bathrooms. On the premises you'll find a TV lounge with a log fire, a BYO dining room, and a game room. The staff can arrange tour packages. Breakfast costs an additional A$9 to A$10 (US$5.85–US$6.50) per person, and dinner and breakfast costs an extra A$30 to A$32 (US$20–US$21) per person.

31 Lurline St., Katoomba, NSW 2780. ✆ and fax **02/4782 3933.** 23 units, none with bathroom. Sun–Thurs A$58 (US$38) double; Fri–Sat A$78 (US$50) double; A$11–A$15 (US$7.15–US$9.75) dorm bed. Ask about packages. AE, DC, MC, V. **Amenities:** Tour desk; coin-op laundry. *In room:* No phone.

WHERE TO DINE

Katoomba Street has many ethnic dining choices, whether you're hungry for Greek, Chinese, or Thai. Restaurants in the Blue Mountains are generally more expensive than equivalent places in Sydney.

Expensive

Lindsay's ⚶⚶ INTERNATIONAL Swiss chef Beat Ettlin has been making waves in Katoomba ever since he left some of the best European restaurants behind to try his hand at dishes such as pan-fried crocodile nibbles on pumpkin scones with a ginger dipping sauce. The food in this upscale, New York–style speakeasy is as glorious as its decor—Tiffany lamps, sketches by Australian artist Norman Lindsay, and booths lining the walls. The three-level restaurant is warmed by a cozy fire surrounded by an antique lounge stage and resounds every night to piano, classical music, or a jazz band. The menu changes every few weeks, but a recent popular dish was grilled veal medallions topped with Balmain bugs (small, saltwater crayfish), with potato and béarnaise sauce.

122 Katoomba St., Katoomba. ✆ **02/4782 2753.** Reservations recommended. Main courses A$14–A$24 (US$9.10–US$16). AE, MC, V. Dinner Wed-Sun 6pm–midnight.

TrisElies GREEK Perhaps it's the belly dancers and the plate smashing, or the smell of moussaka, but as soon as you walk through the door of this lively eatery you feel like you've been transported to an authentic Athenian *taberna*. The restaurant folds out onto three tiers of tables, all with a good view of the stage where every night Greek or international performances take place. The food is solid Greek fare—souvlaki, traditional dips, fried haloumi cheese, Greek salads, casseroles like Mother could have made, whitebait (tiny fried fish), and sausages in red wine—with a few Italian and Spanish extras. If it's winter, come in to warm up beside one of two log fires.

287 Bathurst Rd, Katoomba. © **02/4782 4026.** Fax 02/4782 1128. www.triselies.com.au. Reservations recommended. Main courses A$17–A$26 (US$11–US$17). AE, DC, MC, V. Sun–Thurs 5pm–midnight; Fri–Sat 5pm–3am.

Inexpensive

Chork Dee Thai Restaurant THAI   Loved by the locals, Chork Dee offers good Thai food in a pleasant but modest eatery. Served up is the usual Thai fare, including satay, spring rolls, and fish cakes to start, and lots of curries, noodles, and sweet-and-sour dishes for mains. While vegetarians won't find anything without meat or fish to start with, there are plenty of veggie and tofu dishes available as main courses. BYO.

216 Katoomba St., Katoomba. © **02/4782 1913.** Main courses A$7.70–A$17 (US$5–US$11). AE, MC, V. Sun–Thurs 5:30–9pm; Fri–Sat 5:30–10pm.

Paragon Café *Value* CAFE   The Paragon has been a Blue Mountains' institution since it opened for business in 1916. Inside, it's decked out with dark wood paneling, bas-relief figures guarding the booths, and chandeliers. The homemade soups are delicious. The cafe also serves pies, pastas, grills, seafood, waffles, cakes, and a Devonshire tea of scones and cream.

65 Katoomba St., Katoomba. © **02/4782 2928.** Menu items A$3–A$10 (US$1.95–US$6.50). AE, MC, V. Tues–Fri 10am–3:30pm; Sat–Sun 10am–4pm.

LEURA

107km (66 miles) W of Sydney; 3km (2 miles) W of Katoomba

The fashionable capital of the Blue Mountains, Leura is known for its gardens, its pretty old buildings (many of them holiday homes for Sydneysiders), and its cafes and restaurants. The National Trust has classified Leura's main street as an urban conservation area. Just outside Leura is the **Sublime Point Lookout,** which has spectacular views of the Three Sisters in Katoomba. From the southern end of **Leura Mall,** a cliff drive takes you all the way back to Echo Point in Katoomba; along the way you'll get some spectacular views across the Jamison Valley.

WENTWORTH FALLS ☆☆

103km (64 miles) from Sydney; 7km (4½ miles) from Katoomba

This pretty little town has numerous crafts and antiques shops, but the area is principally known for its 281m (922-ft.) waterfall, situated in **Falls Reserve.** On the far side of the falls is the **National Pass Walk**—one of the best in the Blue Mountains. It's cut into a cliff face with overhanging rock faces on one side and sheer drops on the other. The views over the Jamison Valley are spectacular. The track takes you down to the base of the falls to the **Valley of the Waters.** Climbing up out of the valley is quite a bit more difficult, but just as rewarding.

A NICE SPOT FOR LUNCH

Conservation Hut Café CAFE   This pleasant cafe is in the national park itself on top of a cliff overlooking the Jamison Valley. It's a good place for a bit of lunch on the balcony if you're famished after the Valley of the Waters walk, which leaves from outside. It serves the usual cafe fare—burgers, salads, sandwiches, and pastas. There are vegetarian options, too. There's a nice log fire inside in winter.

At the end of Fletcher St., Wentworth Falls. © **02/4757 3827.** Menu items A$6–A$15 (US$3.90–US$9.75). AE, MC, V. Daily 9am–5pm.

MEDLOW BATH

150km (93 miles) W of Sydney; 6km (3¾ miles) E of Katoomba

In between Katoomba and Blackheath, Medlow Bath is a cozy place, with its own railway station, a secondhand bookstore, and a few properties hidden between the trees. Its one claim to fame is the **Hydro Majestic Hotel** (℃ 02/ **4788 1002**), a must-do stop for any visitor to the Blue Mountains. The historic Hydro Majestic has fabulous views over the Megalong Valley; the best time to appreciate the views is at sunset with a drink on the terrace. Otherwise, it sells Devonshire tea all day, and plenty of cakes, snacks, coffee, and tea.

WHERE TO STAY

Mercure Grand Hydro Majestic Hotel 🐾🐾   This, the most famous of all the hotels in the Blue Mountains, was built in 1904 by Mark Foy, a retail baron, world traveler, sportsman, and hypochondriac. Once called "A Palace in the Wilderness," this former health resort underwent a huge renovation and was reopened in late 2001 in the style Mr. Foy might have liked. The long, white-washed building, with great bushland views from the restaurant and many of its more expensive rooms, is reminiscent of those grand hotels that were all the rage in Queen Victoria's time. The standard rooms, called Heritage Rooms, are fur-nished in Art Deco style and have views of the garden. The similar Gallery Rooms have slightly better views, some with valley glimpses. Cloister Rooms, mostly in another wing, are decorated in both Art Deco and Edwardian (think country style), and have sweeping valley views. Some of these have Jacuzzis. Rooms in the Delmonte Wing are decorated in French provincial style, and also have views. The suites are truly sumptuous.

Medlow Bath, NSW 2780. ℃ 02/4788 1002. Fax 02/4788 1063. www.hydromajestic.com.au. 84 units. Her-itage rooms A$250–A$290 (US$163–US$189); Gallery Rooms A$290–A$330 (US$189–US$215); Cloister Rooms A$330–A$370 (US$215–US$241); Cloister Room with Jacuzzi A$370–A$410 (US$241–US$267); $A830–A$1070 (US$540–US$696) suite. Higher rates Fri–Sat. All rates include breakfast. Extra person A$30 (US$20). Ask about great packages. AE, MC, V. **Amenities:** Restaurant; bar; 2 outdoor lighted tennis courts; health club; tour desk; limited room service; croquet lawn; English lawn bowls. *In room:* TV, minibar, coffee-maker, hair dryer.

BLACKHEATH

114km (71 miles) W of Sydney; 14km (8¾ miles) W of Katoomba

Blackheath is the highest town in the Blue Mountains at 1,049m (3,441 ft.). The **Three Brothers** at Blackheath are not as big or as famous as the Three Sis-ters in Katoomba, but you can climb two of them for fabulous views. Or you could try the **Cliff Walk** from **Evans Lookout** to **Govetts Leap** (named after a surveyor who mapped the region in the 1830s), where there are magnificent views over the **Grose Valley** and **Bridal Veil Falls**. The 1½-hour tramp passes through banksia, gum, and wattle forests, with spectacular views of peaks and valleys. If you want a guide while you're in the area contact **Blue Mountains Magic** (℃ 02/4787 6354; www.bluemts.com.au), based in Blackheath. The guide, Phil Foster, is a trained botanist.

Blackheath itself has some interesting tearooms and antiques shops.

GETTING THERE   The Great Western Highway takes motorists west from Katoomba to Blackheath. CityRail trains also stop at Blackheath.

VISITOR INFORMATION   The **Heritage Centre** (℃ 02/4787 8877; www. npws.nsw.gov.au), operated by the National Parks and Wildlife Service, is located close to Govetts Leap Lookout on Govetts Leap Road. It has information on guided walks, camping and hiking, as well as information on local European and Aboriginal historic sites. It's open daily from 9am to 4:30pm.

EXPLORING THE AREA ON HORSEBACK

One of the nicest ways to get around is on horseback. **Werriberri Trail Rides** (© 02/4787 9171; fax 02/4787 6680), found at the base of the Blue Mountains, 10km (6 miles) from Blackheath on Megalong Road in the Megalong Valley, offers guided ½-hour to 3-hour rides through the Megalong Valley. Suitable for beginners to advanced riders. Half-hour rides cost A$17 (US$11).

WHERE TO STAY

Jemby-Rinjah Lodge ℱ   The Blue Mountains National Park is just a short walk away from this interesting alternative accommodations option. There are nine standard cabins (seven two-bedroom cabins, and two one-bedroom loft cabins), one deluxe cabin called Treetops Retreat, and three pole-frame lodges good for groups. The cabins are right in the bush, can sleep up to six people, and are well spaced. Each has a slow combustion heater, carpets, a bathroom, a fully equipped kitchen, and a lounge and dining area. There are also laundry and barbecue areas nearby. The lodges each have five bedrooms, two bathrooms, and a common lounge area with a circular fireplace. You can rent linens, but bring your own food. Free pickup can be arranged from Blackheath train station. Treetops Retreat has a Japanese hot tub, TV, VCR, stereo, and three private balconies with bush views. It sleeps two, making it a perfect romantic getaway. The nearby walking trails take you to the spectacular Grand Canyon; the Grose Valley Blue Gum forests; and Walls Cave, a resting place for local Aborigines 10,000 years ago.

336 Evans Lookout Rd., Blackheath, NSW 2785. © 02/4787 7622. Fax 02/4787 6230. www.Jembyrinjah lodge.com.au. 10 cabins, 3 lodges. Cabins (occupied by up to 2 adults and 2 children): Fri–Sun and public holidays A$195–A$250 (US$127–US$163); Mon–Thurs A$150–A$195 (US$98–US$127). Extra adult A$22 (US$14), extra child A$14 (US$9.10). Linen A$14 (US$8.80) per bed. AE, DC, MC, V. **Amenities:** Restaurant with lounge area; coin-op laundry; nonsmoking rooms. *In room:* TV, kitchenette, fridge, coffeemaker.

JENOLAN CAVES ℱ

182km (113 miles) W of Sydney; 70km (43 miles) W of Katoomba

The winding road from Katoomba eventually takes you to a spur of the Great Dividing Range and a series of underground limestone caves considered some of the world's best. Known to the local Aborigines as "Binoomea," meaning "dark place," the caves are an impressive amalgamation of stalactites, stalagmites, and underground rivers and pools. They have been open to the public since 1866.

GETTING THERE   It's a 1½-hour drive from Katoomba to the caves. CityRail trains run to Katoomba and link up with daily Jenolan Caves excursions run by **Fantastic Aussie Tours** (© 02/4782 1866, or 1300 300 915 in Sydney; www.fantastic-aussie-tours.com.au). The day tour departs Katoomba at 10:30am and returns at 5:15pm. It costs A$80 to A$99 (US$52–US$64) depending on which cave you visit. The more expensive tour also includes a short wilderness walk. The company also runs transfers to Jenolan from Katoomba departing at 10:30am and leaving Jenolan at 3:45pm daily. They cost A$47 (US$31) for adults and A$23 (US$15) for children each way.

Day trips from Sydney are operated by **AAT King's** (© 02/9252 2788) and **Australian Pacific Tours** (© 02/9252 2988; fax 02/9247 2052). Coach tours depart from the coach terminal at Circular Quay. Since you end up spending 6 hours on a coach on these day trips, I recommend staying overnight in either Jenolan Village or somewhere else in the Blue Mountains.

EXPLORING THE CAVES

Nine caves are open for exploration, with guided tours operated by **Jenolan Caves Reserves Trust** (© **02/6359 3311;** www.jenolancaves.org.au). The first cave tour starts at 10am weekdays and 9:30am weekends and holidays. The final tour departs at 4:30pm (5pm in warmer months). Tours last 1 to 2 hours, and each costs between A$15 and A$22 (US$9.75–US$14) for adults, and between A$10 and A$15 (US$6.50–US$9.75) for children under 15. Family concessions and multiple cave packages are available. The best all-around cave is **Lucas Cave; Imperial Cave** is best for seniors. **Adventure Cave Tours,** which include canyoning, last from 3 hours to a full day and cost from A$55 to A$188 (US$36–US$122) per person.

WHERE TO STAY

The Gatehouse Jenolan   The Gatehouse is a clean and cozy budget-style lodge, with a separate cottage nearby. It's opposite the caves. The Gatehouse sleeps 66 people in all, in seven six-bed rooms and six four-bed rooms in the main building. The cottage can accommodate up to four couples. There are also two common rooms, lockers, washing machines and dryers, and kitchen facilities. There are outdoor barbecues on the premises, and apparently at least one ghost.

Jenolan Caves Village, NSW 2790. © **02/6359 3322.** Fax 02/6359 3227. 13 units. Weekend rates: 4-person dorm room A$90 (US$59); 6-person dorm room A$120 (US$78). Weekday rates: 4-person dorm room A$60 (US$40), 6-person dorm room A$80 (US$52). Linen A$3.30 (US$2.15) per person. AE, MC, V. **Amenities:** Coin-op laundry.

Jenolan Caves House ⚐   This heritage-listed hotel was built between 1888 and 1906 and is one of the most outstanding structures in New South Wales. The main part of the enormous three-story building is made of sandstone and fashioned in Tudor-style black and white. Around it are several cottages and former servants quarters. Rooms vary within the main house from simple budget bunk rooms, to "traditional" rooms with shared bathrooms and "classic" rooms with private bathrooms. The traditional and classic rooms are old-world and cozy, with heavy furniture and views over red-tile rooftops or steep slopes. "Mountain lodge" rooms are in a building behind the main house and are more motel-like.

Jenolan Caves Village, NSW 2790. © **02/6359 3322.** Fax 02/6359 3227. www.jenolancaves.com. 101 units, some with bathroom. Weekend rates: Classic A$255 (US$166), grand classic A$225 (US$146), traditional A$125 (US$81), mountain lodge A$145 (US$94). Weekday rates: Classic A$185 (US$120), grand classic A$165 (US$107), traditional A$95 (US$62), mountain lodge A$105 (US$68). Additional person A$60 (US$39). Family rooms and suites also available. AE, DC, MC, V. **Amenities:** 2 restaurants; bar; tour desk; nonsmoking rooms. *In room:* TV, coffeemaker, hair dryer.

2 The Hunter Valley: Wine Tasting & More ⚐

Cessnock: 190km (118 miles) N of Sydney

The Hunter Valley (or the Hunter as it's also called) is the oldest commercial wine-producing area in Australia, as well as a major site for coal mining. Internationally acclaimed wines have poured out of here since the early 1800s. Though the region falls behind the major wine-producing areas of Victoria in terms of volume, it has the convenient advantage of being just 2 hours from Sydney.

People come here to visit the vineyards' "cellar doors" for free wine tasting, to enjoy the scenery, to sample the area's highly regarded cuisine, or to escape from the city for a romantic weekend. The whole area is dedicated to the grape and the plate, and you'll find many superb restaurants amid the vineyards and farmland.

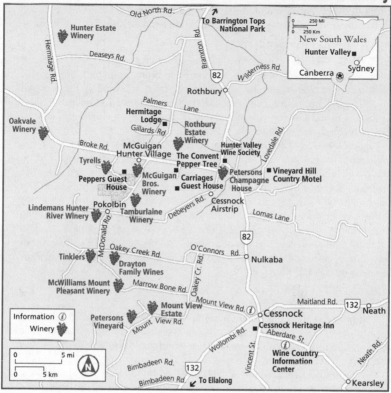

In the **Lower Hunter,** centered around the towns of Cessnock and Pokolbin, you'll find around 110 wineries and cellar doors, including well-known producers such as Tyrell, Rothbury, Lindemans, Draytons, McGuigans, and McWilliams. Many varieties of wine are produced here, including semillon, shiraz, chardonnay, cabernet sauvignon, and pinot noir.

Farther north, the **Upper Hunter** offers the very essence of Australian rural life, with its sheep and cattle farms, historic homesteads, more wineries, and rugged bushland. The vineyards here tend to be larger than those in the south, and produce more aromatic varieties, such as traminers and rieslings. February through March is when the harvest takes place.

The Upper Hunter gives way to the forested heights of the World Heritage–listed Barrington Tops National Park. The park is ruggedly beautiful and

---

Tips A Wine-Buying Tip

The best years ever for red wines in this part of Australia were 1988 and 2000, when long, hot summers produced fewer, but more intensely flavored grapes. Stock up on anything you can find from these vintages. At the other end of the scale, 1997 was a bad year, and 1996, 1999, 2001, and 2002 produced average vintages. The year 2003 is expected to be outstanding.

home to some of the highest Antarctic beech trees in the country. It abounds with animals, including several marsupial species and an abundance of birds.

HUNTER VALLEY ESSENTIALS

GETTING THERE   To get to the wine-producing regions of the Hunter, leave Sydney via the Harbour Bridge or Harbour Tunnel and follow the signs for Newcastle. Just before Hornsby, turn off the highway and head up the National 1/F3 freeway. After around an hour take the Cessnock exit and follow the signs to the vineyards. The trip will take about 2½ hours. Barrington Tops National Park is reached via the Upper Hunter town of Dungog.

Keynes Buses (© **1800/043 339** in Australia, or 02/6543 1322) run coaches to Scone in the Hunter Valley from Sydney's Central Station. Buses depart Monday through Saturday at 3pm and arrive in Scone at 6:50pm; a second service on Friday leaves at 6pm, and on Sunday the bus leaves at 6:40pm. Round-trip tickets are A$74 (US$48) for adults and A$38 (US$25) for children.

A rental car should cost you from A$45 (US$29) a day from Sydney, and you might put in around A$40 (US$26) worth of gas or so for a couple of day's of touring (gasoline in Australia hovers around A90¢ a liter, or US$2.20 a gal.). In the Hunter, contact **Hertz,** 1A Aberdare Rd., Cessnock (© **13 30 39** in Australia, or 02/4991 2500).

ORGANIZED TRIPS FROM SYDNEY   Several companies offer day trips to the Hunter Valley from Sydney.

Visitours (© **02/9909 0822;** www.visitours.com.au) takes small groups to the Hunter to visit up to six wineries as well as cheese and fudge producers. The trip costs A$89 (US$58). The company also transfers passengers to the Hunter and back for A$55 (US$36) one-way.

Oz Trek Adventure Tours (© **02/9360 3444;** www.oztrek.com.au) also offers a highly recommended tour, with a visit to the Australian Reptile and Wildlife Park. The trip includes a barbecue lunch and wine tasting, and costs A$85 (US$55).

VISITOR INFORMATION   **Wine Country Visitors Information Centre,** Main Road, Pokolbin, NSW 2325 (© **02/4990 4477;** fax 02/4991 4518; www. winecountry.com.au), is open Monday through Friday from 9am to 5pm, Saturday from 9:30am to 5pm, and Sunday from 9:30am to 3:30pm. The staff can make accommodations bookings and answer any questions. The **Dungog Visitors Information Centre,** on Dowling Street, Dungog (© **02/4992 2212**), has plenty of information on the Barrington Tops area. A good general website is www.winecountry.com.au.

VISITING THE WINERIES

Many people start their journey through the Hunter by popping into the **Hunter Valley Wine Society,** at the corner of Broke and Branxton roads in Pokolbin (© **1300/303 307** in Australia, or 02/4941 3000). The club basically acts as a

---

Tips **Remember a Designated Driver!**

Australia's drunk-driving laws are strict and rigidly enforced. If you are interested in tasting some grapes in the Hunter Valley, choose a designated driver or take a guided tour (see above). Both easily identifiable and unmarked police cars patrol the vineyard regions.

> **Tips A Wine-Tasting Tip**
>
> Some wineries routinely offer some of their inferior wines for tastings. I've made a habit of asking for a list of their premium wines available for tasting. Most wineries usually have a bottle or two of their better wines uncorked for those with a serious interest.

Hunter Valley wine clearinghouse, sending bottles and cases to members all over Australia, and some overseas. It's also a good place to talk to the experts about the area's wines, and to taste a few of them. It's open daily from 9am to 5pm.

You might also like to visit the **Small Winemakers Centre,** McDonalds Road, Pokolbin (© **02/4998 7668**). At any one time it represents around six of the region's smaller producers.

Most of the wineries in the region are open for cellar-door tastings, and it's perfectly acceptable just to turn up, taste a couple of wines or more, and then say your good-byes without buying anything. Though you will come across some unusual vintages, especially at the boutique wineries, don't expect to find any bargains—city bottle shops buy in bulk and at trade price, which means you can probably get the same bottle of wine for less in Sydney than at the cellar door in the Hunter.

Drayton Family Wines   Drayton's produces some spectacular shiraz. Oakey Creek Rd., Pokolbin. © 02/4998 7513. Mon–Fri 9am–5pm; Sat–Sun 10am–5pm.

Hunter Estate Winery   The Hunter's largest winery crushes some 6,500 tons of grapes a year. Come here for excellent semillon and shiraz. Hermitage Rd., Pokolbin. © 02/4998 7777. Daily 10am–5pm. Tours daily 11am and 2pm.

Lindemans Hunter River Winery   This famous winery offers an interesting sparkling red shiraz. McDonald Rd., Pokolbin. © 02/4998 7684. Mon–Fri 9am–4:30pm, Sat–Sun 10am–4:30pm.

McGuigan Brothers Winery   Another winery worth visiting in the area, McGuigan Brothers also has a cheese factory and bakery on the site. McDonald Rd., Pokolbin. © 02/4998 7402. Daily 9:30am–5pm. Tours daily at noon.

McWilliams Mount Pleasant Winery   Famous for both its Elizabeth Semillon, which has won 39 trophies and 214 gold medals since 1981, and its Lovedale Semillon, which has won 39 trophies and 74 gold medals since 1984. Marrowbone Rd., Pokolbin. © 02/4998 7505. Daily 10am–4:30pm. Tours daily 11am.

Mount View Estate   The pioneer of Verdelho wines in Australia—a grape attributed to Portugal, but it's also grown in small quantities in Italy and France. It's a very crisp and dry white wine, which I like with seafood. Mount View Rd., Mount View. © 02/4990 3307. Daily 10am–5pm.

Peterson's Champagne House   This is the only specialist champagne winery in the Hunter. At the corner of Broke and Branxton roads, Pokolbin. © 02/4998 7881. Daily 9am–5pm.

Peterson's Vineyard   Peterson's produces fine chardonnay, semillon, and shiraz. Mount View Rd., Mount View. © 02/4990 1704. Mon–Sat 9am–5pm, Sun 10am–5pm.

Rothbury Estate ℛ   This very friendly winery produces the magnificent Brokenback Shiraz and the nice Mudgee Shiraz. The Rothbury Café (p. 201) serves meals. Broke Rd., Pokolbin. © 02/4998 7555. Daily 9:30am–4:30pm.

Tamburlaine Winery Don't miss this boutique winery, the winner of many wine and tourism awards. McDonald Rd., Pokolbin. © 02/4998 7570. Daily 9:30am–5pm.

Tinklers If you want to taste the grapes in season, head to Tinklers. It sells some 30 different varieties of eating grapes between December and March, and nectarines, plums, peaches, and vegetables at other times of the year. It also offers wine tasting and free vineyard walks at 11am on Saturday and Sunday. Pokolbin Mountains Rd., Pokolbin. © 02/4998 7435. Daily 10am–4pm.

Tyrell's Tyrell's has produced some famous wines and exports all over the world. Broke Rd., Pokolbin. © 02/4993 7000. Tours daily 1:30pm.

DAY TOURS, HOT-AIR BALLOON RIDES & OTHER FUN STUFF

If you don't have a car, you'll have to get around as part of a tour, as there is no public transport running between the wineries.

Trekabout Tours (© 02/4990 8277) offers half-day and full-day winery tours for a maximum of six people. Half-day tours cost A$28 (US$18), with visits to five or six wineries, and full-day tours cost A$44 (US$29), and take in up to nine wineries. The company can pick you up from your hotel in either Cessnock or Pokolbin.

Also offering local pickup is **Hunter Vineyard Tours** (© 02/4991 1659), which has a full-day tour on either 12- or 21-seat buses, taking in five wineries. They charge A$38 (US$25) or A$55 (US$36) with a two-course meal.

A tranquil way to see the wineries is from above. **Balloon Aloft,** in Cessnock (© 1800/028 568 in Australia, or 02/4938 1955; fax 02/6344 1852), offers year-round dawn balloon flights that include a post-flight champagne and optional breakfast costing A$15 (US$9.75). Flights last about an hour and cost A$225 (US$146) for adults on weekdays and A$250 (US$162) on weekends. Children 7 to 12 fly for A$130 (US$85) daily.

If you like adventure, try **Grapemobile Bicycle and Walking Tours** (© 0500/ 804 039 in Australia, or 02/4991 2339 phone and fax). This company supplies you with a mountain bike, helmet, guide, and support bus, and takes you on a peaceful meander through the wineries. Tours cost A$98 (US$64), including lunch in a restaurant. They also rent bicycles—A$22 (US$14) for a half day and A$30 (US$20) for a full day.

WHERE TO STAY

The Hunter Valley is far more expensive on weekends and during public holidays, when room prices jump significantly and some properties insist on a 2-night stay. It's worthwhile checking out the information board located inside the Wine Country Visitors Information Centre (see "Visitor Information," above) for special deals, including self-contained accommodations, cottages, resorts, and guesthouses.

IN CESSNOCK

Staying in Cessnock is a good idea if you don't have a car and are relying on local tour companies to pick you up and show you around the area.

Cessnock Heritage Inn This 1920s building, built as a pub, is right in the center of Cessnock, so there's easy access to all the local pubs and restaurants. All the rooms are done in country style, with dried grasses, floral bedspreads, and the like. All are quite large with high ceilings but differ greatly—the smallest room has a double bed, others have queen beds and singles, and there are two family rooms (sleeping five). All have ceiling fans and free video movies. There's also a guest lounge where you can chat with the owners.

Bunking Down in a Caravan, Man

Two trailer (caravan) parks offer reasonably comfortable accommodations in trailers and cabins. **Cessnock Cabins and Caravan Park** (© 02/ **4990 5819**; fax 02/4991 2944), Allandale/Branxton Road, Nulkaba (2km/ 1¼ miles north of Cessnock), has four on-site vans for A$30 to A$40 (US$20–US$26); a double and 12 cabins with shower from A$48 to A$69 (US$31–US$45)—the more expensive prices for weekends. There are also camping sites here for A$14 (US$9) and powered sites for A$16 (US$10).

The **Valley Vineyard Tourist Park** (© and fax **02/4990 2573**) on Mount View Road (on the way out to the vineyards) has five trailers for A$35 (US$23) and 12 cabins with shower for A$55 (US$36). Two two-bedroom units cost A$75 (US$49). Powered sites cost A$16 to A$20 (US$10–US$13), and a camping site A$12 (US$7.80). There's a BYO restaurant, a camper's kitchen, and a swimming pool on-site.

Vincent St., Cessnock (P.O. Box 714, NSW 2325). © **02/4991 2744.** Fax 02/4991 2720. www.hunterweb. com.au/heritageinn.html. 13 units. Weekend rates A$110–A$120 (US$72–US$78) per person with full breakfast; 2-night weekend package A$180–A$200 (US$117–US$130). Midweek rates A$90–A$100 (US$59–US$65) double with full breakfast. AE, MC, V. **Amenities:** Tour desk; lounge room; nonsmoking rooms. *In room:* A/C, TV, minibar, coffeemaker.

IN POKOLBIN
Very Expensive
Peppers Convent Hunter Valley 🐨🐨 Originally a convent for Brigidine nuns in the early part of the 20th century, this building was transported some 600km (372 miles) from Coonamble in central New South Wales to its present location in 1990. A year later, it opened as a hotel. Rooms are elegant and spacious, with baroque decor, including plaster frieze ceilings, and thick, rich drapes. French doors open onto private verandas overlooking patches of bushland. King rooms are larger and have wicker lounge areas. There is an elegant sitting area where drinks are served, and a light and airy breakfast room serving the best breakfasts in the Hunter. The Pepper Tree Complex includes Pepper Tree Wines and the excellent **Robert's restaurant.**

In the Pepper Tree Complex, Halls Rd., Pokolbin, NSW 2320. © **02/4998 7764.** Fax 02/4998 7323. www. peppers.com.au. 17 units. Weekend rates A$323–A$387 (US$210–US$252) double per night (minimum stay 2 nights, either Fri–Sat or Sat–Sun). Midweek rates A$291–A$332 (US$189–US$216) double. Ask about packages and check website the week before for specials. Children under 5 stay free in parent's room; children 5–15 A$22 (US$14) extra; extra adult A$44 (US$29). AE, DC, MC, V. **Amenities:** Restaurant; medium-size heated outdoor pool; outdoor lighted tennis court; Jacuzzi; bike rental (free); concierge; tour desk; car-rental desk; business center; massage; babysitting; laundry service, cleaning service; nonsmoking rooms. *In room:* A/C, TV, minibar, coffeemaker, hair dryer, iron.

Peppers Guest House This tranquil escape is set in beautiful bush gardens. The spot is so peaceful that kangaroos hop up to the veranda in the evenings looking for treats. The "classic" rooms downstairs have French doors that you can fling open in abandonment, while upstairs rooms express just a tad more old-fashioned charm and come with air-conditioning. All rooms have king-size beds and are furnished with colonial antiques. Guests don't come here for action; they come to relax. The Pampering Place offers massages and facials, while a gentle 30-minute trail winds through the bush. There's a pleasant guest lounge with an open fireplace and a bar. The inn's restaurant, **Chez Pok,** is an upscale establishment with mismatched china and pretty good country food.

Ekerts Rd., Pokolbin, NSW 2321. ℂ **02/4998 7596.** Fax 02/4998 7739. www.peppers.com.au. 47 units, 1 cottage. Weekend rates (minimum 2-night stay): A$277 (US$180) colonial double; A$303 (US$197) classic double; A$315 (US$205) vintage double; A$347 (US$225) heritage suite. Weekday rates (including buffet breakfast): A$273 (US$177) colonial double; A$283 (US$184) classic double; A$292 (US$190) vintage double; A$327 (US$213) heritage suite. AE, DC, MC, V. **Amenities:** Restaurant; small heated indoor pool; outdoor lighted tennis court; bike rental; laundry service; nonsmoking rooms. *In room:* A/C, TV, minibar, coffeemaker, hair dryer, iron.

Expensive

Carriages Guest House 🏵🏵   Tucked away on 15 hectares (37 acres), a kilometer off the main road, Carriages is a secluded retreat in the heart of Pokolbin. A two-suite cottage called the Gatehouse is on a separate part of the grounds. In the main two-story house, a veranda circles downstairs rooms, which are furnished with antique country pine. Upstairs, the two lofty gable suites are centered around huge fireplaces. The Gatehouse suites offer five-star luxury; although relatively new, the stained-glass windows and rescued timber give them a rustic feel (these two Jacuzzi rooms share a lounge with a full kitchen and an open fire). There are open fires in six of the rooms. (The two standard doubles don't have them.) Breakfast is served in your room, and **Robert's Restaurant** is next door. The friendly owner, Ben Dawson, assures me he'll take Frommer's readers up to the top of a nearby hill where they can see plenty of wild kangaroos.

Halls Rd., Pokolbin, NSW 2321. ℂ **02/4998 7591.** Fax 02/4998 7839. www.thecarriages.com.au. 10 units. A$185 (US$120) double; A$240–A$265 (US$156–US$172) suite; A$285 (US$185) Jacuzzi suite. Rates include breakfast. Minimum 2-night stay on weekends. Ask about 10%–20% discounts midweek. AE, MC, V. **Amenities:** Large heated outdoor pool; outdoor lighted tennis court; Jacuzzi; massage; babysitting; laundry service; nonsmoking rooms. *In room:* A/C, TV, kitchenette, fridge, coffeemaker, hair dryer, iron.

Hermitage Lodge   If you want to be in the heart of vineyard country, stay at this property, which is surrounded by vineyards. Standard rooms are large, sunny, and nicely decorated, and come with a queen-size bed and a double sofa bed. The spa suites are larger with queen-size beds and double sofas, cathedral ceilings, Jacuzzis, and separate showers. The more expensive suites have a separate bedroom and bathrobes. Breakfast is served in all rooms. **Il Cacciatore** restaurant is one of the best in the region.

At Gillards and McDonalds roads, Pokolbin, NSW 2320. ℂ **02/4998 7639.** Fax 02/4998 7818. www.ozemail. com.au/~hlodge. 10 units. Weekend rates A$220 (US$143) standard double; A$240 (US$156) spa suite. Midweek rates A$145 (US$94) standard double; A$165 (US$107) spa suites. Extra person A$15 (US$9.75). Minimum 2-night stay on weekends. Rates include continental breakfast. Ask about midweek packages. AE, MC, V. **Amenities:** Restaurant; bar; medium-size outdoor pool; golf course nearby; Jacuzzi; bike hire (free for Frommer's readers); limited room service; babysitting; free self-service laundry; nonsmoking rooms. *In room:* A/C, TV, fridge, coffeemaker, hair dryer, iron.

Moderate

Vineyard Hill Country Motel 🏵   Motel is a bit of a misnomer for this place; it's more aptly described as a "fully self-contained chalet." Units are modern, with a separate bedroom, lounge and dining area, a full kitchen, and a balcony with views across a valley of vineyards to the Brokenback Ranges in the distance. It's all terrifically rural, with cows wandering about and kangaroos and possums creeping around at dusk. There's no restaurant, but there is a gourmet deli on the premises. In the garden are a large swimming pool and a Jacuzzi.

Lovedale Rd., Pokolbin, NSW 2321. ℂ **02/4990 4166.** Fax 02/4991 4431. www.vineyardhill.com.au. 8 units. Weekend rates A$155 (US$100) 1-bedroom unit; A$218 (US$142) 2-bedroom unit (for 4 people). Midweek

Something Special: A Cattle Station in the Upper Hunter

Located just off the Golden Highway, 1 hour north of Mudgee, 2½ hours west of Cessnock, and 4 hours northwest of Sydney, **Runnymede,** Golden Highway, Runnymede, Cassilis, NSW 2329 (© **02/6376 1183;** fax 02/6376 1187), is an 800-hectare (2,000-acre) sheep-and-cattle ranch (called a station in Australia) where you can get a taste of Aussie ranch life. The ranch offers farm-style lodgings in a 1930s California-style bungalow. Two rooms have an en-suite shower, while the third shares the hosts' bathroom down the hall. The homestead has an open fire in the living room (and a rarely used TV). There are plenty of native birds in the gardens, and kangaroos are common. May is the best time to see sheep shearing, and August is the best time to witness lambing and calving. Guests rave about hosts Libby and David Morrow. David offers 1-hour tours of the property for around A$30 (US$20) per "Toyota-load," and other tours throughout the district.

Doubles go for A$80 to A$90 (US$52–US$59). Rates include breakfast, but dinner is A$20 (US$13) per person extra (BYO wine or beer). No credit cards.

rates A$107 (US$70) 1-bedroom unit; A$165 (US$107) 2-bedroom unit. Extra person A$20 (US$13). Ask about midweek and long-weekend packages. AE, MC, V. **Amenities:** Large heated outdoor pool; Jacuzzi; limited room service; massage; babysitting; free laundry service; nonsmoking rooms. *In room:* A/C, TV, kitchen, minibar, fridge, coffeemaker, hair dryer, iron.

IN THE UPPER HUNTER

Barrington Guest House 🌟🌟 *Value*   Barrington Guest House is nestled in a valley just outside the Barrington Tops National Park. It retains an old-world charm and serves bacon and eggs for breakfast, scones and cream, and vegetables boiled soft enough for your dentures. The place has lace tablecloths in the dining room, a log fire beneath a higgledy-piggledy brick chimney, mahogany walls, high ceilings, and personalized service—despite the communal mealtimes and the lack of a menu. Rooms range from the original guesthouse chambers adjoining the dining room, to new and almost luxurious two-story self-contained cottages (sleeping up to five) that cling to a hillside. I highly recommend the latter—the former are basic, with no TV and can be noisy if a party's in full swing in the dining room. This place is very popular with older travelers during the week but attracts a range of ages on the weekends. The guesthouse grounds attract plenty of animals and act as a wildlife reserve for several rescued kangaroos. Activities include horseback riding, guided walks through the rainforest, "billy tea" tours, and night spotting for quolls (native cats) and possums, bush dancing, tennis, film evenings, and skeet shooting. It can be a very social scene, too.

Salisbury (via Dungog), NSW 2420. © **02/4995 3212.** Fax 02/4995 3248. www.barringtonguesthouse.com. au. 20 rainforest cottages, 21 guesthouse units, 13 with bathroom. Midweek (all rates per person) A$69 (US$5) in a guesthouse room without bathroom, including meals and activities; A$120 (US$78) in a guesthouse room with bathroom, including meals and activities; A$145 (US$94) self-catering cottage, including activities. Weekend rates (2 nights) room without bathroom A$138 (US$90) inclusive; A$210 (US$137) room with bathroom; A$290 (US$189) cottage. Ask about packages. AE, DC, MC, V. The guesthouse is about 3½ hr.

from Sydney and 1½ hr. from the main Hunter wine region. Free pickup from Dungog railway station. **Amenities:** Restaurant; bar; 2 lit tennis courts; tour desk; massage; laundry service; nonsmoking rooms. *In room:* Cottages only: TV, kitchen, fridge, coffeemaker, hair dryer, iron.

WHERE TO DINE
IN CESSNOCK

Amicos MEXICAN/ITALIAN PIZZERIA You can't mistake the Mexican influence in the decor, with bunches of chile peppers, cow skulls, ponchos, masks, and frescoes, but the Mediterranean/Italian connection is more evident in the menu. Mexican dishes include the usual nachos, enchiladas, burritos, barbecued chicken, and the like, while there are a few pastas and Mediterranean dishes, such as crumbed lamb brains, too. The pizzas are pretty good, and one could just about serve four people. They will deliver, too.

138 Wollombi Rd., Cessnock. ℂ 02/4991 1995. Fax 02/4990 9302. Reservations recommended. Main courses A$12–A$20 (US$7.80–US$13); pizzas A$14–A$18 (US$9.10–US$12). MC, V. Daily 6–10pm.

IN POKOLBIN

The three restaurants in the Hunter with the biggest reputations are **Robert's Restaurant,** which is part of the Pepper Tree Complex (see "Where to Stay," above) along with the Convent guesthouse; **Chez Pok** in Peppers Guest House (see "Where to Stay," above); and **Casuarina** (see below).

Blaxland's Restaurant ⟨ MODERN INTERNATIONAL This very atmospheric restaurant revolves around a winery theme, with pictures of vineyards on the walls, one of the most comprehensive Hunter wine lists in the area, and even the owner's homemade vintages on the menu. Parts of the building date from 1829, with wooden trusses holding up the ceiling and exposed sandstone block walls. Popular here is the roast spatchcock (baby chicken) and the steamed balcak mussels. A large open fire brings a glow to the white tablecloths in winter.

Broke Rd., Pokolbin. ℂ 02/4998 7550. Fax 02/4998 7802. www.blaxlandsrestaurant.com.au. Reservations recommended. Main courses A$20–A$26 (US$13–US$17). A$3 (US$1.40) per person surcharge weekends and public holidays. AE, DC, MC, V. Daily 11am–10pm.

Café Enzo MODERN AUSTRALIAN This charming little cafe offers a nice ambience and good cuisine. Pastas, pizzettas, antipasti, and steaks dominate the menu. The pizzetta with chargrilled baby octopus, squid, and king prawns, Kalamata olives, fresh chile and onion, and freshly shaved Parmesan is particularly nice. Cakes and cheese plates are a specialty.

At the corner of Broke and Ekerts roads (adjacent to Peppers Creek Antiques, near Peppers Guest House), Pokolbin. ℂ 02/4998 7233. Main courses A$10–A$18 (US$6.50–US$12). Devonshire tea A$7.50 (US$4.90). AE, DC, MC, V. Wed–Sun 10am–5pm (until 10pm Sat).

Casuarina Restaurant ⟨⟨ MODERN AUSTRALIAN This superb restaurant has taken a slew of awards for its cooking in recent years. The surroundings are elegant, with lots of antiques below the very high wooden ceilings. Flambés are the signature meal here, the most popular being a flambé of chile lobster and prawn (for two people). Other meals to write home about are the Thai-style chicken curry and the Caesar salad.

Hermitage Rd., Pokolbin. ℂ 02/4998 7888. Fax 02/4998 7692. www.casuarina.com. Reservations recommended. Main courses A$27–A$34 (US$18–US$22). AE, DC, MC, V. Daily 7–11pm.

Robert's Restaurant ⟨⟨ MODERN AUSTRALIAN Chef and owner Robert Molines has become a legend in Hunter Valley gourmet circles for coming up with great dishes that perfectly complement the region's wines. His restaurant is known for its eclectic mix of antiques and his country-style dishes, such as rabbit with olives and vegetables, rack of lamb from the wood-fired oven, and twice-roasted duckling. The meat-free specialty is the wild mushroom risotto.

In the Pepper Tree complex, Halls Rd., Pokolbin. © 02/4998 7330. Main courses A$29–A$34 (US$19–US$22). A$4 (US$2.60) per-person surcharge weekends and public holidays. AE, DC, MC, V. Daily noon–5pm and 7pm–midnight.

The Rothbury Café ✿ MODERN AUSTRALIAN   This second-floor cafe has some of the best views across the valley; occasionally you can even spot kangaroos grazing in the farmers' fields across the way. The cafe has a Mediterranean feel about it, with timber tables loaded with bread and olives. Signature dishes are the chickpea-battered squid with yogurt and eggplant relish for a first course, and the venison and beet pie or the braised oxtail with orange, walnuts, olives, and polenta for main courses. Desserts include the fabulously rich chocolate-chestnut torte with berries.

Upstairs at the Rothbury Estate, Broke Rd., Pokolbin. © 02/4998 6622. Main courses A$8.80–A$16 (US$10–US$12). AE, DC, MC, V. Daily 9:30–4:30pm.

3 Port Stephens: Dolphin- & Whale-Watching ✿✿

209km (136 miles) N of Sydney

Port Stephens, just 2½ hours north of Sydney, should be at the top of any New South Wales itinerary. It's a perfect add-on to a trip to the Hunter Valley (see above). Though you can come up from Sydney for the day, I recommend staying in the general area for at least 1 night. The sheltered Port Stephens bay itself is more than twice the size of Sydney Harbour, and is as clean as a newly poured bath. The sea literally jumps with fish, and the creamy islands and surrounding Tomaree National Park boast more species of birds than even Kakadu National Park in the Northern Territory. Two pods of bottle-nosed dolphins, around 70 individuals in all, call the bay home, and you are almost certain to see some on a dolphin-watching cruise. Port Stephens is also a fabulous place to watch whales during their migration to the breeding grounds farther north (roughly from June 1 to mid-Nov—though they are less frequently seen in Aug). There is also a large breeding colony of koalas in Lemon Tree Passage on the south side of the Tomaree Peninsula, which makes up the southern shoreline of the bay.

The main town, **Nelson Bay** (pop. 7,000) is on the northern side of the peninsula. The township of Shoal Bay, farther along the peninsula, has a spectacular beach edged with wildflowers. Another small resort town, **Anna Bay,** is the largest development on the southern side of the peninsula, and has excellent surf beaches. The Stockton Bight stretches some 32km (20 miles) from Anna Bay south to the large industrial town of Newcastle. The beach here is popular with ocean fishermen who have the awful habit of driving their four-wheel-drives along it. The first 500m (1,640 ft.) of the beach is swimming and surfing only. The Stockton Sand Dunes, which run behind the beach, are the longest in the Southern Hemisphere.

Opposite the Tomaree Peninsula, across the bay, are the small tourist townships of Tea Gardens and Hawks Nest, both at the mouth of the Myall River. See the Wonderbus tour of The Hunter (above) for details on a tour to Port Stephens.

ESSENTIALS

GETTING THERE   To get to Port Stephens, take the Sydney to Newcastle Freeway (F3) to its end, then follow the Pacific Highway signs to Hexham and

---

Finds **Through the Dunes on Horseback**

You can ride a horse through the dunes with **Sahara Horse Trails** (© 02/ 4981 9077). A 2-hour trip costs A$60 (US$39), and a half-day excursion is A$120 (US$78). Bookings required 1 day in advance.

Port Stephens. **Port Stephens Coaches** (© **1800/045 949** in Sydney, or 02/ 4982 2940) travel between Port Stephens and Newcastle, and to Nelson Bay from Sydney daily at 2pm. Buses from Sydney leave from Eddy Avenue, near Central Station; the journey takes 3½ hours. Return tickets cost A$44 (US$29) for adults and A$31 (US$20) for children.

VISITOR INFORMATION The **Port Stephens Visitor Information Centre,** Victoria Parade, Nelson Bay (© **1800/808 900** in Australia, or 02/4981 1579; fax 02/4984 1855; www.portstephens.org.au), is open Monday through Friday from 9am to 5pm and Saturday and Sunday from 9am to 4pm.

SEEING THE AREA

Several operators have vessels offering **dolphin- and whale-watching cruises.** Some of the best are aboard *Imagine* (© 02/4984 9000; www.portstephens. com.au/imagine), a 15m (49-ft.) catamaran operated by Frank Future and Yves Papin, two real characters. They offer a daily "Island Discovery" trip that includes dolphin-watching and a trip around the offshore islands. The 4-hour cruise departs from **D'Albora Marina** in Nelson Bay daily at 11am and costs A$49 (US$32) for adults, and A$25 (US$16) for children 4 to 14, including lunch.

Four-hour whale-watching tours cost the same and leave at 11am from June 1 to November 15. You are most likely to spot humpback whales, but there's also a chance to see minke and southern right whales.

A morning dolphin-watching cruise runs from 10:30am to 12:30pm daily during summer and costs A$20 (US$13) for adults, A$13 (US$8.45) for children, and A$53(US$34) for families. If you happen to be around on the weekend nearest a full moon, ask about overnight **"Full Moon Tours."**

The **Port Stephens Ferry Service** (© 02/4981 3798, or 0419/417 689 mobile phone) operates a 2½-hour "Early Bird Dolphin Watch" daily at 8:30am with a stop off at Tea Gardens. A similar 3½-hour cruise departs at noon (you can eat lunch at Tea Gardens), and a 2-hour dolphin-watching cruise departs at 3:30pm. All cruises cost A$17 (US$11) for adults, A$9 (US$5.85) for children, and A$40 (US$26) for families.

Wonderbus (© **1800/669 800** in Australia, or 02/9555 9800; www.wonder bus.com.au) transfers passengers from Sydney and back for A$55 (US$36) oneway. Otherwise it offers wine tasting in the Hunter Valley, a 2-hour dolphin-watch cruise, a visit to Oakdale wildlife farm, and lunch for A$168 (US$109).

WHERE TO STAY

Port Stephens is very popular with Sydneysiders, especially during the Christmas holidays, January, and Easter, so you'll need to book well in advance then.

Peppers Anchorage Port Stephens 🏨🏨 This low-rise resort, split into a main guesthouse and four separate lodges, is built onto a headland and runs almost directly into the bay—it's only stopped from sliding in by a boardwalk and a picturesque marina. Rooms are light and luxurious; the suites each have a good-size Jacuzzi, perfect for two. Rooms on the top floor have a large balcony, from which you have uninterrupted views across the bay and the islands; those below have their own private verandas. Two rooms are designed for wheelchairs. A nearby beach is the perfect spot for a sunset stroll.

Corlette Point Rd., Corlette, NSW 2315. © 1800/809 142 in Australia, or 02/4984 2555. Fax 02/4984 0300. www.peppers.com.au. 80 units. Weekend rates A$345 (US$224) double; A$396 suite. Midweek (including breakfast) rates A$291 (US$189) double; A$337 (US$219) suite. Ask about packages. AE, DC, MC, V. **Amenities:** Restaurant; bar; good-size heated outdoor pool; exercise room; Jacuzzi; sauna; children's program (public holidays only); tour desk; 24-hr. room service; massage; babysitting; laundry service; nonsmoking rooms. *In room:* A/C, TV, fax, dataport, minibar, coffeemaker, hair dryer, iron.

Port Stephens Motor Lodge   Surrounded by tall trees and gardens, this motor lodge is a peaceful place to stay and a short stroll from the main township. The standard rooms are quite plain with raw-brick walls, a comfy double (and an extra single bed in most rooms), a private balcony, and an attached shower with half-tub. Adjacent to the lodge is a self-contained family unit with two bedrooms, a laundry, and water views. There's a barbecue area on the grounds.

44 Mangus St., Nelson Bay, NSW 2315. © 02/4981 3366. Fax 02/4984 1655. psmlodge@aol.com. 17 units. A$60–A$120 (US$39–US$78) standard double (Christmas holiday period most expensive); A$88 (US$57) family unit on weekdays and A$120 (US$78) on weekends. Extra person A$10 (US$6.50), extra person under 15 A$5 (US$3.25). AE, DC, MC, V. **Amenities:** Heated outdoor pool; coin-op laundry; nonsmoking rooms. *In room:* A/C, TV, coffeemaker, hair dryer, iron.

Salamander Shores ⊛   Salamander Shores looks like a beached, ramshackle paddle steamer—it's all white-painted bricks and rails and stairs, fixed to the bay by a jetty. Set in a well-tendered, sloping garden, this five-story hotel retains a certain 1960s charm, despite undergoing selective modernization. Standard rooms are similar to most motel rooms, but you really should throw caution to the wind and get a sea-view room—you won't regret it. These rooms have Jacuzzis and large balconies with extensive views of the bay. When the sun rises over the water and the garden is full of lorikeets and corellas, it couldn't be more picture-book perfect. Down below is a pub and shop selling alcohol.

147 Soldiers Point Rd., Soldiers Point, NSW 2317. © 1800/655 029 in Australia, or 02/4982 7210. Fax 02/ 4982 7890. www.salamander-shores.com. 90 units. A$109 (US$80) standard double; A$142 (US$92) garden-view double; A$161 (US$105) sea-view double; A$229 (US$149) family suite; A$264 (US$172) penthouse. A$18 (US$12) extra person. Ask about packages. AE, DC, MC, V. **Amenities:** 2 restaurants; bar; small heated outdoor pool; sauna; tour desk; babysitting; laundry service; nonsmoking rooms. *In room:* A/C, TV, minibar, coffeemaker, hair dryer, iron.

WHERE TO DINE

Most people head down to Nelson Bay for their meals because of the great views across the bay. You'll also find a host of cheap takeout joints here, including **The Pure Pizza Café,** D'Albora Marina (© **02/4984 2800**), which offers pizzas for around A$10 to A$24 (US$6.50–US$15), depending on toppings, pastas for between A$10 and A$15 (US$6.50–US$9.75), and salads, too.

Rob's on the Boardwalk CAFE   You can pick up a hearty American break-fast at this busy cafe overlooking the bay, or a snack throughout the day. The Caesar salad is popular, as are the half-dozen oysters for A$13 (US$8.20). One of the best main courses is the mixed seafood bouillabaisse, while the prime scotch filet with sautéed forest mushrooms, Jerusalem artichokes, gratin pota-toes, and a red-wine sauce, would tempt the most red-blooded carnivore.

D'Albora Marina. © **02/4984 4444**. Main courses A$12–A$23 (US$8–US$15). AE, DC, MC, V. Daily 8am until the last customer leaves.

Rock Lobster SEAFOOD   Eat inside or out at this peaceful yet stylish restaurant. The plump Port Stephens Oysters should be enough to tempt you to start, while main courses such as smoked salmon in layers of wonton pastry with salad and wasabi sauce, or calamari flavored with chile and cilantro in bread crumbs with spicy passion-fruit dip should fill you up. There are usually a couple of meat dishes and a vegetarian option on the menu, too.

D'Albora Marina. ℂ **02/4981 1813.** Main courses A$24 (US$16). Seafood platter for 2 A$105 (US$68). AE, DC, MC, V. Daily 12–2:30pm and 5:30–9pm.

4 North of Sydney Along the Pacific Highway: Australia's Holiday Coast

The Pacific Highway leads over the Sydney Harbour Bridge and merges into the Sydney-Newcastle Freeway. It continues to the industrial coast town of Newcastle, bypassing Tuggerah Lake and Lake Macquarie (neither of real interest compared to what follows). From here, the Pacific Highway stays close to the coast until it reaches Brisbane, some 1,000km (620 miles) from Sydney.

Though the road is gradually being upgraded, the conditions vary, and the distances are long. Travelers should be aware that the route is renowned for its accidents. Though you could make it to Brisbane in a couple of days, you could also easily spend more than a week stopping off at the attractions along the way. The farther north you travel the more obviously tropical the landscape gets. By the time visitors reach the coastal resort town of Coffs Harbour, temperatures have noticeably increased, and banana palms and sugar cane plantations start to appear.

Along the coast, you'll find excellent fishing and some superb beaches, most of them virtually deserted. Inland, the Great Dividing Range, which separates the wetter eastern plains from the dry interior, throws up rainforests, extinct volcanoes, and hobby farms growing tropical fruit as you head farther north toward Queensland. Along the way, are a series of national parks, most of them requiring detours of several kilometers. Those you shouldn't miss include the **Dorrigo** and **Mount Warning** national parks, both of which offer some of the country's best and most accessible rainforests.

PORT MACQUARIE
423km (262 miles) N of Sydney

Port Macquarie (pop. 28,000), about halfway between Sydney and the Queensland border, boasts some fabulous beaches; Flynn's Beach in particular is a haven for surfers. Boating and fishing are other popular pastimes.

ESSENTIALS
GETTING THERE   From Sydney, motorists follow the Pacific Highway and then the Sydney-Newcastle Freeway (F3). **Eastern Australia Airways** (ℂ **02/ 9691 2333**) flies between Sydney and Port Macquarie. The coach trip from Sydney takes about 7 hours.

VISITOR INFORMATION   The **Port Macquarie Visitor Information Centre,** at the corner of Clarence and Hay streets, under the Civic Centre (ℂ **1800/025 935** in Australia, or 02/6581 8000; www.portmacquarieinfo. com.au), is open Monday through Friday from 8:30am to 5pm and Saturday and Sunday from 9am to 4pm.

EXPLORING THE AREA

The Billabong Koala and Wildlife Park, 61 Billabong Dr., Port Macquarie (© **02/6585 1060**), is a family-owned nature park where you can get up close to hand-raised koalas, kangaroos, emus, wombats, many types of birds, and fish. You can pat the koalas at 10:30am, and 1:30 and 3:30pm. There are also barbecue facilities, picnic grounds, and a restaurant. Allow 2 hours to fully experience this recommended wildlife park. It's open daily from 9am to 5pm; admission is A$8 (US$5.20) for adults and A$5 (US$3.25) for children.

The 257-passenger vessel ***Port Venture*** (© **02/6583 3058**) leaves from the wharf at the end of Clarence Street Tuesday and Thursday through Sunday at 10am and 2pm, for a 2-hour scenic cruise on the Hastings River. Cruises cost A$20 (US$13) for adults, A$8 (US$5.20) for children 6 to 14, and A$49 (US$32) for families. Reservations are essential. The boat also travels up the river on a 5-hour Barbecue Cruise every Wednesday morning leaving at 10am. It docks at a private bush park along the way and passengers can tuck into a traditional Aussie barbecue of steaks, fish, and salad. You can then fish, take a bushwalk, go swimming, or take a 20-minute four-wheel-drive trip. The cruise costs A$37 (US$24) for adults, A$18 (US$12) for children, and A$94 (US$61) for families. A 4-hour cruise also leaves on Monday at 10am. It costs A$35 (US$23) for adults, A$15 (US$9.75) for children, and A$88 (US$57) for families.

WHERE TO STAY

El Paso Motor Inn   Located right on the waterfront, this motel offers standard motel–type rooms; the more expensive deluxe doubles are a little larger and have newer furniture and a fresher coat of paint after being refurbished in 1998. Two rooms come with Jacuzzis, and some come with kitchenettes. The third-floor three-room suite has good ocean views and a kitchenette.

29 Clarence St., Port Macquarie, NSW 2444. © **1800/027 965** in Australia, or 02/6583 1944. Fax 02/6584 1021. 55 units. A$87 (US$57) standard double; A$97 (US$63) deluxe double; A$130 (US$85) Jacuzzi room; A$150 (US$98) suite. Extra person A$10 (US$6.50). A$30 (US$20) per-room surcharge Easter, Christmas, and some long weekends. DC, MC, V. **Amenities:** Restaurant; bar; good-size heated outdoor pool; sauna; Jacuzzi; game room; tour desk; babysitting; nonsmoking rooms. *In room:* A/C, TV, minibar, coffeemaker, hair dryer, iron.

COFFS HARBOUR: BANANA CAPITAL OF AUSTRALIA ⊛

554km (344 miles) N of Sydney; 427km (265 miles) S of Brisbane

Rainforests, beaches, and sand surround the relaxed capital of Australia's Holiday Coast. The state's "banana republic" headquarters—the area produces more bananas than anywhere else in Australia—is bordered by hillsides furrowed with rows of banana palms. Farther inland, the rolling hills plateau into Dorrigo National Park, one of the best examples of accessible rainforests anywhere. Also inland is the Nymboida River, known for its excellent white-water rafting.

Coffs Harbour is a rather disjointed place, with an old town-center retail area; the Jetty Strip (with restaurants and fishing boats) near the best swimming spot, Park Beach; and a new retail area called The Plaza. Wide sweeps of suburbia separates these three areas; it's a difficult town to negotiate if you don't have a car.

ESSENTIALS

GETTING THERE   It takes around 7 hours to drive from Sydney to Coffs Harbour without stops; from Brisbane it takes around 5 hours. The Pacific Highway in this region is notoriously dangerous; there have been many serious accidents involving drivers enduring long hours behind the wheel. Ongoing road-widening projects should improve things. **Qantas** (© **13 13 13** in Australia) flies non-stop to Coffs Harbour from Sydney. Several coach companies, including **Greyhound Pioneer** (© **13 20 30** in Australia) and **McCafferty's** (© **13 14 99** in Australia), make the trip from Sydney in about 9 hours. A **Countrylink** (© **13 22 32** in Australia) train from Sydney costs A$79 (US$52).

VISITOR INFORMATION   The **Coffs Harbour Visitors Information Centre** (© **1800/025 650** in Australia, or 02/6652 1522) is just off the Pacific Highway, at the corner of Rose Avenue and Marcia Street, 2 blocks north of the city center. It's open daily from 9am to 5pm. A good general website is www.holiday coast.com.au.

GETTING AROUND   If you don't have a car, you can get around on the **Coffs Harbour Coaches** (© **02/6652 2877**), which runs day trips around the local area on weekdays (including a town tour on Mon, and a trip to the magnificent Dorrigo National Park on Wed). **Blue Tongue Transport** ✆ (© **1800/ 258 386** in Australia, or 02/6651 8566) offers smaller group tours of Dorrigo National Park daily costing A$50 (US$33) for adults and A$40 (US$26) for children; a morning city tour for A$11 (US$7.15); and an upmarket afternoon champagne tour of town for A$22 (US$14).

VISITING THE BIG BANANA & OTHER THINGS TO DO

You can't miss the 10m (33-ft.) reinforced concrete banana alongside the highway at the **Big Banana Theme Park** (© **02/6652 4355**), 3km (2 miles) north of town. The park includes an air-conditioned, diesel-powered train that takes visitors on a 1-hour tour of the 18-hectare (44-acre) banana plantation that contains some 18,000 banana trees. Along the route it passes various off-the-wall exhibits relating to farming, Aborigines, and local history. It stops at the property's hydroponic glasshouses and at a viewing platform and cafeteria, which serves up all things banana—cakes, breads, splits, shakes, and so on. The park is open daily from 9am to 4:30pm (3pm in winter). Admission is free, but the train tour costs A$10 (US$6.50) for adults, A$6 (US$3.90) for children, and A$25 (US$16) for families. I had my doubts about this place before I visited, but I ended up charmed—even if it was simply by the wackiness of the place.

The **Coffs Harbour Zoo** (© **02/6656 1330**), 10 minutes north of town on the Pacific Highway, has plenty of koalas, as well as wombats, kangaroos, dingoes, Tasmanian devils, waterbirds, and aviaries. The award-winning native gardens are full of wild birds expecting a feed. The zoo is open daily from 8:30am to 4pm. Admission is A$12 (US$7.80) for adults, A$6 (US$3.90) for children, and A$30 (US$20) for families.

A free natural attraction is **Mutton Bird Island,** which you can get to via the Coffs Harbour jetty. A steep path leads up the side of the island, but views from the top are worth it. Between September and April the island is home to thousands of shearwaters (or mutton birds), which make their nests in burrows in the ground.

If you prefer fish, try diving with gray nurse sharks, manta rays, and moray eels with **Island Snorkle and Dive** (© **02/6654 2860**) or **Dive Quest** (© **02/ 6654 1930**). The *Pamela Star* (© **02/6658 4379**) offers good-value deep-sea-fishing trips including all tackle and bait, and lunch, for A$60 (US$39). The boat leaves Coffs Harbour jetty at 7:30am and returns at 1:30pm daily.

For a taste of gold fever, head to **George's Gold Mine,** 40km (25 miles) west of Coffs Harbour on Bushman's Range Road (© **02/6654 5355** or 02/6654 5273). You get to go into an old-time gold mine, see the "stamper battery" crushing the ore, and pan for gold yourself. The mine is open Wednesday through Sunday (daily during school and public holidays) from 10:30am to 4pm. Admission is A$9 (US$5.85) for adults, A$4.50 (US$2.90) for children, and A$26 (US$17) for families.

You might also like to visit **Kiwi Down Under Farm** (℘ **02/6653 4449**), a fascinating organic farm growing kiwi fruit and macadamia nuts, among other things. No nasty sprays are used here. Free 30- to 45-minute guided tours of the property leave at 2, 3, and 4pm on weekends and school holidays. The tea shop on the premises serves amazing scones and jam for A$4.50 (US$2.90) and excellent vegetarian lunches for A$8.50 (US$5.50). The farm is 14km (8½ miles) south of Coffs Harbour; turn off at Gleniffer Road, just south of Bonville, and follow the signs for 4km (2½ miles).

SHOPPING FOR ARTS & CRAFTS

There are several recognized "crafts drives" in the area, where tourists can go in search of quality souvenirs. Pick up a free copy of *Discover the Coffs Harbour Region* from the tourist information center for more details on the dozens of crafts shops in the area. One of the best is the **Australian Wild Flower Gallery** (℘ **02/6651 5763**), just off West High Street and Bennetts Road. Wolfgang Shultze carves intricate designs out of pewter, silver, and gold to make detailed animal- and plant-inspired jewelry, charms, and spoons. Pieces cost between A$5 and A$36 (US$3.25–US$23). The gallery is open daily from 9am to 5pm.

On the way to or from the Dorrigo rainforest, stop off at the township of **Bellingen,** 20 minutes south of Coffs Harbour on Waterfall Way. It's a pleasant place with several crafts shops. Among the best is **The Old Church** (℘ **02/6655 0438**), 8 Church St. (just off the main road), crammed full of wooden crafts items, cards, furniture, wacky mobiles, incense, hats, and knickknacks, and surrounded by gardens and fruit trees. It's open daily from 8:30am to 5:30pm.

EXPLORING THE RAINFORESTS & OTHER OUTDOOR ADVENTURES

Coffs Harbour's main tourist attraction is its position as a good base for exploring the surrounding countryside. You must see the World Heritage–listed **Dorrigo National Park** ⋆⋆, 68km (42 miles) west of Coffs Harbour, via Bellingen. Perched on the Great Dividing Range that separates the lush eastern seaboard from the arid interior, the rainforest here is one of the best I've seen in Australia. (It's a pity that so much fell to the axes of early settlers.) Entry to the rainforest is free.

The **Dorrigo Rainforest Centre** (℘ **02/6657 2309**) is the gateway to the park and has extensive information on the rainforest. Just outside is the 21m (69-ft.) high **Skywalk,** which offers a bird's-eye view of the forest canopy. There are several walks leaving either the Rainforest Centre, the Glade Picnic Area (about 1km/½ mile away), and the Never-Never Picnic Area (a 10km/6¼-mile drive along Dome Road). Most tracks are suitable for wheelchairs. Bring a raincoat or an umbrella; it is a rainforest after all! The **Dorrigo Tourist Information** office (℘ **02/6657 2486**) is in the center of Dorrigo township.

One of the best tour operators in the area is the award-winning **Mountain Trails 4WD Tours** (℘ **02/6658 3333;** fax 02/6658 3299). Full-day tours that include visits to two rainforest areas and a good lunch cost A$80 (US$52) for adults and A$60 (US$39) for children under 16. Half-day tours of one rainforest cost A$56 (US$36) for adults and A$40 (US$26) for children.

For a bit more personal action, try horseback riding through the rainforest 23km (14 miles) southwest of Coffs Harbour with **Valery Trails** (© **02/6653 4301**). Two-hour rides leave at 10am and 2pm daily and cost A$35 (US$23) per person, bookings essential.

More hectic still are **white-water rafting trips** 🎿 through the wilderness on the furious Nymboida River with **Wow Rafting**, 1448 Coramba Rd., Coramba via Coffs Harbour, NSW 2450 (© **1800/640 330** in Australia, or 02/6654 4066; www.wowrafting.com.au). Full-day trips, including morning tea, a high-energy snack, and a barbecue meal, cost A$153 (US$99). These adventurous trips operate year-around, depending on water levels. A 2-day trip costs A$325 (US$211), including all meals and overnight camping. If the water level in the Nymboida is low then you raft on the Goolang Creek, a shorter but still exciting run. Most of the rapids are Class III; some of them can be pretty hairy. The rafting guides are real characters; although they're safety-conscious, you're sure to be dunked a few times.

Rapid Rafting (© **1800/629 797** in Australia, or 02/6652 1741) also runs rafting trips on the Goolang River, costing $77 (US$50) for a half-day trip, and A$120 (US$78) for a full day.

Looking for yet another adrenaline rush? Then head to the **Raleigh International Raceway** (© **02/6655 4017**), where you can zip around the track behind the wheel of your very own go-kart. It's 23km (14 miles) south of Coffs Harbour and 3km (2 miles) along Valery Road off the Pacific Highway north of Nambucca Heads. Six high-speed laps cost A$16 (US$10), 11 cost A$23 (US$15), and 16 cost A$32 (US$21). It's open daily from 9am to 5pm (6pm in summer).

The *Pacific Explorer* catamaran (© **0418/663 815** mobile phone or 02/6652 7225 after working hours) operates **whale-watching trips** between June and October; the 2½-hour cruises cost A$44 (US$29). Between November and May, they run half-day dolphin-watching cruises for the same price.

WHERE TO STAY

Coffs Harbour is a popular beachside holiday spot with plenty of motels along the Pacific Highway offering standard roadside rooms from A$35 to A$49 (US$23–US$32) per night. Vacancy signs are common outside Australian school holiday periods and the Christmas and Easter periods (when Coffs really fills up). A few to try are the **Caribbean Motel**, 353 High St., Coffs Harbour, NSW 2450 (© **02/6652 1500**; fax 02/6651 4158), with doubles ranging from A$55 to A$120 (US$36–US$78) depending on the season and the view; and the **Coffs Harbour Motor Inn**, 22 Elizabeth St., Coffs Harbour, NSW 2450 (© **02/6652 6388**; fax 02/6652 6493), with doubles ranging from A$72 to A$108 (US$47–US$70) depending on the season.

Pelican Beach Resort Australis 🎿 *Value* This Bali-style resort complex is situated 7km (4½ miles) north of Coffs Harbour beside a long stretch of creamy sand. (The beach is dangerous for swimming.) Terraced over six levels, the resort's rooms all have balconies and many have ocean views. Standard rooms are light and modern, with either twin or queen beds. Family rooms have a kitchenette, dining area, and one queen and two single beds divided by a half wall. Suites have a separate bedroom, kitchenette, lounge area, and Jacuzzi. Two rooms are equipped for travelers with disabilities. Outside in the landscaped gardens is a minigolf course and a volleyball court.

Pacific Hwy., Coffs Harbour, NSW 2450. © 1300/650 464 in Australia, or 02/6653 7000. Fax 02/6653 7066. 112 units. www.australishotels.com. A$120–A$215 (US$78–US$140) standard room for 1 or 2 depending on season; A$184–A$330 (US$120–US$215) family room for up to 4; A$236–A$463 (US$153–US$300) suite. Extra person A$33 (US$21). Ask about packages and discounts. The highest rates apply Dec 26–Jan 18. AE, DC, MC, V. **Amenities:** Restaurant; bar; large lagoon-style swimming pool; 3 tennis courts; exercise room; 2 Jacuzzis; sauna; game room; concierge; children's center (weekends); tour desk; car-rental desk; 24-hr. room service; babysitting; massage; free self-service laundry; dry cleaning; nonsmoking rooms. *In room:* A/C, TV, dataport, kitchenette (some rooms), minibar, hair dryer, iron.

Sanctuary Motor Inn Resort   If you like animals you'll love this animal-sanctuary/guesthouse complex 2km (1¼ miles) south of town. Wandering around the grounds are wallabies, kangaroos, peacocks, and several species of native birds. The rooms are comfortable, with the more expensive rooms being larger and more recently renovated. The executive room comes with a Jacuzzi.

Pacific Hwy., Coffs Harbour, NSW 2450. © 02/6652 2111. Fax 02/6652 4725. phciscato@hotmail.com.au. 38 units. A$88 (US$57) standard double; A$94 (US$60) superior double; A$150 (US$98) executive double. Extra person A$15 (US$9.75). Holiday surcharges A$25 (US$16). Ask about lower rates through Aussie auto clubs. AE, DC, MC, V. **Amenities:** Restaurant; bar; large heated outdoor pool; lighted tennis and squash courts; minigolf; Jacuzzi; sauna; room service 7–9am and 6–8pm; coin-op laundry. *In room:* A/C, TV w/free satellite channels, kitchen (in 4 units), fridge, coffeemaker, hair dryer.

WHERE TO DINE

Seafood Mama's *ITALIAN/SEAFOOD*   This charming, informal award-winning Italian restaurant packs a mean barbecue seafood dish of octopus, prawns, fish, calamari, and mussels. Also on the menu in this rustic, bottles-hanging-from-the-ceiling Italian joint are some well-regarded veal and steak dishes, and plenty of pastas. Seafood Mama's is right on the ocean, near the Pelican Beach and the older Nautilus resorts, 7km (4½ miles) north of Coffs Harbour. The restaurant will do takeout and deliver to your hotel.

Pacific Hwy. © 02/6653 6733. Reservations recommended. Main courses A$13–A$25 (US$8.45–US$16). AE, DC, MC, V. Tues–Sat 6–10pm.

BYRON BAY: A BEACH BOHEMIA
78km (48 miles) SE of Murwillumbah

As the most easterly point on the Australian mainland, the sun's rays hit Byron before anywhere else. This geographical position is good for two things: you can spot whales as they migrate north in June and July, and it's attractive to the town's "alternative" community. Painters, craftspeople, glass blowers, and poets are so plentiful they almost fall from the macadamia nut trees. The place is loaded with float tanks, "pure body products," beauty therapists, and massage centers. Though it attracts squadrons of backpackers each summer to its party scene and discos, many of the locals simply stay at home, sipping their herbal tea and preparing for the healing light of the coming dawn. Families love Byron Bay for the beautiful beaches, and surfers flock here for some of the best surfing in the world.

ESSENTIALS
GETTING THERE   If you're driving up the north coast, leave the Pacific Highway at Ballina and take the scenic coast road via Lennox Head. It's around 10 hours by car from Sydney (790km/490 miles), and 2 hours (200km/124 miles) south of Brisbane. **Regional Express** airline (www.regionalexpress.com. au) flies from Sydney to Ballina. The round-trip costs around A$280 (US$182). **Byron Bus Transfers** (© 02/6681 3354) meets all flights and transfers to Byron Bay for A$20 (US$13) single and A$35 (US$23) return. **Coolangatta airport** is 1 hour north of Byron Bay (112km/69 miles). **Countrylink** (© 13 22 32 in Australia) runs daily trains from Sydney to Byron Bay; the one-way fare

is A$98 (US$64) for adults and A$47 (US$31) for children, and the trip takes 12¾ hours. **Greyhound Pioneer** (© **13 20 30** in Australia) buses from Sydney take 13½ hours; the one-way coach fare is A$69 (US$45).

ORGANIZED TOURS FROM SYDNEY   An unusual way to get to Byron is on a 5-day surf safari from Sydney with **Surfaris** (© **1800/634 941** in Australia; www.surfaris.com). You can learn to surf along the way as you stop off at several beaches, with camping overnight. Trips leave Sydney on Monday mornings and Byron Bay on Sunday mornings. It costs A$499 (US$324) all-inclusive—though you need to bring a sleeping bag.

Another great trip is with **Ando's Outback Tours** (© **1800/228 828** in Australia; www.outbacktours.com.au), which operates from Sydney every Sunday and heads inland deep into the Outback on a 5-day trip. Among the highlights are visits to Lightning Ridge and the wild Glengarry opal fields (see "Outback New South Wales" later in this chapter). The trip costs A$435 (US$283). A return trip to Sydney costs A$35 (US$23).

VISITOR INFORMATION   The **Byron Visitors Centre,** 80 Jonson St., Byron Bay, NSW 2481 (© **02/6680 9271**), is open daily from 9am to 5pm. A half-hour farther south is the **Ballina Tourist Information Centre,** on the corner of Las Balsas Plaza and River Street, Ballina (© **02/6686 3484**), open daily from 9am to 5pm. Two good websites on the area are **www.byronbay.net.au** and **www.byronbay-online.com**.

SPECIAL EVENTS   Byron really goes to town during 4 days over the Easter weekend with the **East Coast Blues & Roots Festival** (www.bluesfest.com.au). Up to 30,000 people camp out to listen to up to 80 acts, including the likes of Ben Harper, Midnight Oil, and Joan Armatrading. Book tickets on the Web. The first Sunday of every month is when the extraordinary local **crafts market** brings hippies and funky performers out from the hinterland. Byron Bay is very popular over the Christmas period so book well in advance.

HITTING THE SURF & SAND

Many accommodations in Byron Bay offer free surfboards for guests, or else head to the **Byron Bay Surf Shop,** on Lawson Street at the corner of Fletcher Street (© **02/6685 7536**), which rents boards for A$12 (US$7.80) for 4 hours and A$20 (US$13) for 24 hours. The shop can also arrange surf lessons for around A$25 (US$16) per hour.

Wategos Beach and an area off the tip of Cape Byron called **"The Pass"** are two particularly good surf spots, however, since each of the beaches faces a different direction, you are bound to find the surf is up on at least one. **Main Beach,** which stretches along the front of the town (it's actually some 50km/31 miles long), is good for swimming. West of Main Beach is **Belongil Beach,** the unofficial nudist beach (when authorities aren't cracking down on covering up). **Clarke's Beach** curves away to the east of Main Beach toward Cape Byron.

The **Cape Byron Lighthouse** on Cape Byron is one of Australia's most powerful. It's eerie to come up here at night to watch the stars and see the light reach some 40km (25 miles) out to sea. A nice walk just south of town goes through the rainforest of the **Broken Heads Nature Reserve.**

The best place to dive around Byron Bay is at **Julian Rocks,** about 3km (2 miles) offshore. Cold currents from the south meet warmer ones from the north here, which makes it a good spot to find a large variety of marine sea life. **Byron Bay Dive Centre,** 111 Jonson St. (© **02/6685 7149**), charges A$70 (US$46) for the first dive and A$35 (US$23) for each subsequent dive. **Sundive,** in the Byron Hostel complex on Middleton Street (© **02/6685 7755**), has cheaper initial dives at A$60 (US$39) each.

EXPLORING THE HILLS & RAINFORESTS

Behind Byron you'll find hills that could make the Irish weep, as well as rainforests, waterfalls, and small farms burgeoning with tropical fruits. A good operator taking trips inland is **Forgotten Country Ecotours** (© **02/6687 7843**). **Byron Bay to Bush Tours** (© **02/6685 6889** or 04/1866 2684; bush@mullum. com.au) operates day trips to the hippie hangout of **Nimbin** 𝒻—where during my last visit I was approached four times in 10 minutes by people selling marijuana—and up into the rainforest, visiting a macadamia-nut farm and having a barbecue on their organic farm. The trip leaves at 11am Monday through Saturday and costs A$30 (US$20). This company also operates trips to the Sunday market at Channon the second Sunday of each month and the one at Bangalow on the fourth Sunday. These trips cost A$15 (US$9.75).

WHERE TO STAY

Real-estate agents **Elders R Gordon & Sons** (© **02/6685 6222;** eldersbb@ omcs.com.au) can book rooms and cottages in Byron Bay and in the hinterland. Rates vary.

The Byron Bay Waves Motel (The Waves) 𝒻   This exceptional motel is just 60m (197 ft.) from Main Beach and just around the corner from the town center. The rooms are very nice, and each comes with a queen-size bed, a marble bathroom with shower, and a king-size tub. Four rooms on the ground floor have a courtyard, and one is suitable for travelers with disabilities. Toasters, inhouse massage, and beauty treatments are also available. The suites each have a king-size bed and a large balcony. The penthouse is a very plush and fully self-contained one-bedroom apartment. There are six family rooms sleeping three adults, or two adults and two children.

Corner of Lawson and Middleton sts. (P.O. Box 647, Byron Bay 2481). © 02/6685 5966. Fax 02/6685 5977. www.byron-bay.com/waves. 19 units. A$150–A$320 (US$98–US$208) double depending on season; A$250–A$380 (US$162–US$247) suite; A$250–A$480 (US$163–US$312) penthouse. Extra person A$20 (US$13). AE, DC, MC, V. **Amenities:** Massage; babysitting; laundry service; nonsmoking rooms. *In room:* A/C, TV, fax, minibar, coffeemaker, hair dryer, iron, safe.

Byron Central Apartments   If you don't want to eat out all the time then this is the place for you. The self-contained apartments come with a queen-size sofa bed and free in-house movies. Those on the first floor come with balconies. There are also a few loft-style apartments with separate dining, lounge, and sleeping areas. Units for people with disabilities are available. The landscaped garden has a barbecue. The apartments are a 2-minute walk from the beach and town.

Byron St., Byron Bay, NSW 2481. © 02/6685 8800. Fax 02/6685 8802. www.byronbay.com/bca. 26 units. A$120–A$260 (US$78–US$169) standard apt 1 night (depending on season). Higher rates apply Christmas/New Year period; low season is Apr–Sept. Ask about discounts for multiple-night stays. AE, DC, MC, V. **Amenities:** Medium-size saltwater pool; coin-op laundry; nonsmoking rooms. *In room:* TV, kitchen, fridge, coffeemaker, hair dryer.

Holiday Village Backpackers 𝒻   Byron Bay's original hostel is still one of the best. It's in the center of town next door to Woolworth's supermarket and only a few minutes' walk from the bus and train stops, the main beach, and the town center. The National Roads and Motorists' Association gives this place a five-star backpackers rating, which is as good as it gets. Dorm rooms are clean, and doubles in the hostel are above average and come with a double bed, a fan, and a wardrobe. For a couple of dollars more you can stay in a self-contained unit with a separate bedroom, lounge, and kitchen area. On the premises are a volleyball court, Jacuzzi and pool, TV and video lounge (with a library), barbecues, basketball hoop, Internet and e-mail, and free surfboards, body boards, and bikes.

116 Jonson St., Byron Bay, NSW 2481. ℭ **02/6685 8888.** Fax 02/6685 8777. 42 units, 13 with bathroom. A$55–A$65 (US$36–US$42) double in hostel; A$70–A$85 (US$46–US$55) self-contained double; A$21–A$29 (US$14–US$19) dorm bed. MC, V. **Amenities:** Medium-size heated outdoor pool; Jacuzzi; bike rentals; tour desk; coin-op laundry; nonsmoking rooms. *In room:* TV/VCR (some rooms); fridge.

Taylor's Guest House 🐨🐨 This truly beautiful guesthouse is set in 2 secluded hectares (5 acres) of gardens and rainforest. Rooms vary in price depending on whether you stay for 1 night or more. The guest rooms are lavishly decorated in a country style and come with either a queen- or king-size bed. The cottage is huge, has wraparound verandas and long French windows, and is done up in bright Santa Fe–style colors. The cottage also comes with a laundry and has the largest bed in Australia—a 2.4m-×-2.1m (8-ft.-×-7-ft.) antique English "Emperor" bed. The guesthouse is renowned for its cooking.

160 McGettigan's Lane, Ewingsdale, Byron Bay, NSW 2481. ℭ **02/6684 7436.** Fax 02/6684 7526. www. taylors.net.au. 5 units, 1 cottage. A$220 (US$143) double; A$330 (US$215) cottage. Rates include breakfast, cakes, and biscuits, and predinner champagne cocktails. Dinner is A$60 (US$39) per person. Surcharge of 20% for doubles and 50% for cottage at Christmas and Easter. AE, DC, MC, V. Not suitable for children. **Amenities:** Restaurant; lounge; large heated outdoor pool; nonsmoking rooms. *In room:* TV, hair dryer, iron.

WHERE TO DINE

Beach Hotel Barbecue PUB/BARBECUE The outdoor meals at this pub near the beach make it popular with visitors and locals. About the cheapest thing on the menu is the burger, and the most expensive is steak. The Beach Hotel Bistro is open from 10am to 9pm daily and serves coffee, cakes, and snacks throughout the day; a lunch menu is served from noon to 3pm and dinner from 6 to 9pm.

In the Beach Hotel, at Bay and Johnson sts. ℭ **02/6685 6402.** Main courses A$3.90–A$14 (US$2.50–US$8.80). No credit cards. Daily noon–3pm.

Earth 'n' Sea PIZZA/PASTA This popular spot has been around for years and offers a fairly extensive menu of pastas and pizzas, including some unusual combinations such as prawns, banana, and pineapple. Pizzas come in three sizes, and the small is just enough to satisfy the average appetite.

11 Lawson St. ℭ **02/6685 6029.** Reservations recommended. Main courses A$9.50–A$24 (US$6.20–US$15). AE, MC, V. Daily 5:30–11pm.

The Pass Café 🐨 MEDITERRANEAN Though not as well positioned as Rae's Restaurant and Bar (see below), the Pass Café rivals Rae's for breakfasts and lunches, and if you happen to be heading to or from the local rainforest on the Cape Byron Walking Track, you'll find this a great place to stop off. Breakfast items range from simple fresh fruit and muffins to gourmet chicken sausages. Lunch specials include Cajun chicken, octopus, and calamari salad, as well as fresh fish, meat dishes, and plenty of good vegetarian options.

At the end of Brooke Dr., on Cape Byron Walking Track, Palm Valley. ℭ **02/6685 6074.** Main courses A$10–A$25 (US$6.50–US$16). MC, V. Daily 8am–3pm; Thurs–Sat until 6pm.

Rae's Restaurant and Bar 🐨 MODERN AUSTRALIAN/SEAFOOD You can't beat Rae's for either its location or its food. It's right on the beach, about a

2-minute drive from the town center, and has a secluded, privileged air about it in the nicest of ways. Inside it's all Mediterranean blue and white, which complements perfectly the waves hitting the sand. The menu changes daily, but you may find the likes of grilled Atlantic salmon, red curry of roast beef filet, braised lamb shanks, and yellowfin tuna. If you have any special dietary requirements, tell the chef, and he will go out of his way to please you. Next door to the restaurant, but part of the same establishment, is **Rae's on Watago's,** an exclusive five-star guesthouse offering luxury accommodations. There are seven rooms and prices start from A$350 (US$228) for a double suite to A$990 (US$644) for the penthouse suite.

Watago's Beach, Byron Bay. ℂ **02/6685 5366.** Fax 02/6685 5695. www.raes.com.au. Reservations recommended. Dinner main courses A$35–A$50 (US$23–US$33), lunch A$30–A$35 (US$20–US$23). AE, DC, MC, V. Daily 7–10pm; Sat–Sun noon–3pm.

Raving Prawn ⓡ SEAFOOD Fish cover the walls at this excellent place, but there's more than that on the menu. You can tuck into veal, chicken, or vegetarian dishes if you want to, but I wouldn't miss out on the fabulous signature dish, the jewfish (a kind of grouper) with an herb-mustard crust. The forest-berry tart is the best dessert on the menu.

Feros Arcade (between Jonson and Lawson sts.). ℂ **02/6685 6737.** Reservations recommended. Main courses A$19–A$27 (US$12–US$18). AE, DC, MC, V. Tues–Sat 6–10pm (until around 9pm in winter). Open daily during school holidays.

MURWILLUMBAH

321km (199 miles) N of Coffs Harbour; 893km (554 miles) N of Sydney; 30km (19 miles) S of Queensland border

The main town of the Tweed Valley, Murwillumbah is a good base for touring the surrounding area, which includes **Mount Warning,** picturesque country towns, and countryside dominated by sugar cane and banana.

ESSENTIALS

GETTING THERE Murwillumbah is inland from the Pacific Highway. The nearest airport is at **Coolangatta,** 34km (21 miles) away, over the Queensland border. **Countrylink** trains (ℂ **13 22 42** in Australia) link Murwillumbah with Sydney, taking around 13 hours. **Greyhound Pioneer** buses (ℂ **13 20 30** in Australia) run from Sydney to Murwillumbah; the trip takes 14½ hours.

VISITOR INFORMATION The **Murwillumbah Visitors Centre,** at the corner of the Pacific Highway and Alma Street, Murwillumbah, NSW 2484 (ℂ **02/6672 1340**), is worth visiting before heading out to see more of the Tweed Valley or the beaches to the east. Another option is the **Tweed Heads Visitors Centre,** at the corner of Bay and Wharf streets, Tweed Heads, NSW 2485 (ℂ **07/5536 4244**). Both are open Monday through Friday from 9am to 5pm, and Saturday from 9am to 1pm.

SEEING THE AREA

If you're looking for a Big Avocado to go with your Coffs Harbour Big Banana, then head for **Tropical Fruit World,** on the Pacific Highway (ℂ **02/6677 7222**), 15km (9½ miles) north of Murwillumbah and 15km (9½ miles) south of Coolangatta. The Tweed Valley's top attraction grows some 400 varieties of tropical fruit, which can be discovered on an interesting 1½-hour tractor-train tour of the 81-hectare (200-acre) tropical fruit plantation, as well as on four-wheel-drive rainforest drives and riverboat rides. It's open daily from 10am to

5pm. Also on the property are a kiosk, fruit market, and gift shop. Admission to food and shopping areas is free. Guided tours cost A$22 (US$14) for adults, A$12 (US$7.80) for children 4 to 12.

The 1,154m (3,785-ft.) **Mount Warning** is part of the rim of an extinct volcano formed from volcanic action some 20 million to 23 million years ago. You can hike around the mountain and to the top on trails in the Mount Warning World Heritage Park.

WHERE TO STAY & DINE
Crystal Creek Rainforest Retreat 🐟🐟   Crystal Creek is tucked away in a little valley of rainforest just 25 minutes by car from the Pacific Highway. Self-contained cabins skirt the edge of the rainforest that borders the Border Ranges National Park, a World Heritage site. There are plenty of native birds, possums, echidnas, wallabies, and bandicoots around and about. Though the water is always cold, guests can swim in the natural pools and laze around on hammocks strung up in the bush. Cabins have two comfortable rooms, a balcony, kitchen, barbecue, and plenty of privacy. Two glass-terrace cabins overlook the rainforest and mountain. All rooms have a king-size bed and a double Jacuzzi—no curtains in the bathroom because the rainforest gives enough privacy. Several tours are offered, including four-wheel-drive rainforest tours and visits to local country markets and arts-and-crafts galleries, as well as walking tours around the property. Guests cook their own food or eat at the casual restaurant.

Brookers Rd., Upper Crystal Creek, Murwillumbah, NSW 2484. © 02/6679 1591. Fax 02/6679 1596. www. crystalcreekrainforestretreat.com.au. 7 cabins. A$240–A$260 (US$156–US$169). Ask about midweek specials. AE, DC, MC, V. Pickup service from the airport, bus, and train stations available. Not suitable for children. **Amenities:** Restaurant; Jacuzzi; 24-hr. room service; massage; nonsmoking rooms. *In room:* TV, CD player, kitchen, fridge, coffeemaker, hair dryer, iron.

AFTER DARK
The clubs up here on the border of Queensland are huge and offer cheap bistro meals as well as pricier ones in the more upscale restaurants, inexpensive drinks at the bar, entertainment, and hundreds of poker machines. The biggest in New South Wales is the **Twin Towns Services Club,** Wharf Street, Tweed Heads (© 07/5536 2277). Another worth checking out is **Seagulls Rugby League Club,** Gollan Drive, Tweed Heads (© 07/5536 3433). Major entertainers such as Tom Jones, Joe Cocker, and Bob Hope have played here over the last few years. It's open 24 hours. To gain admittance to these "private" clubs, you must sign the registration book just inside the door.

5 South of Sydney Along the Princes Highway

There are two main roads leading south out of Sydney: the Hume Highway and the Princes Highway. Both routes connect Sydney to Melbourne, but the Hume Highway is quicker. A favorite with truckers and anyone in a hurry, the Hume Highway will get you to Melbourne in about 12 hours. The Princes Highway is a scenic coastal route that can get you to Melbourne in 2 days, though the many attractions along the route make it well worth taking longer.

KIAMA
119km (74 miles) S of Sydney

Kiama (pop. 10,300) is famous for its **blowhole.** In fact, there are two, a large one and a smaller one, but both spurt seawater several meters into the air. The larger of the two can jet water up to 60m (197 ft.), but you need a large swell and strong southeasterly winds to force the sea through the rock fissure with enough force to achieve that height. The smaller of the two is more consistent, but fares better with a good northeasterly wind.

Pick up a map from the **Kiama Visitors Centre** (see below) to guide you on a Heritage Walk through the historic district of this quaint village, where you can tour a row of National Trust workers' cottages built in 1896. There's little reason to stay in Kiama the night, as plenty more scenic places await farther south.

ESSENTIALS
GETTING THERE   From Sydney, travel south on the Princes Highway via the steel-works city of Wollongong. There's also a regular train service from Sydney and a Greyhound Pioneer (© **13 20 30** in Australia) coach service. The trip by coach takes about 2 hours, the train trip a little less.

VISITOR INFORMATION   The **Kiama Visitors Centre** at Blowhole Point, Kiama (© **02/4232 3322;** fax 02/4226 3260; www.kiama.net/default.htm), is open daily from 9am to 5pm.

JERVIS BAY: AN OFF-THE-BEATEN-TRACK GEM 🐾🐾
182km (113 miles) S of Sydney

Booderee National Park (formally known as Jervis Bay National Park), at Jervis Bay, is nothing short of spectacular. You should come here even if it means missing out on some of Sydney's treasures. How does this grab you—miles of deserted beaches, the whitest sand imaginable, kangaroos you can stroke, lorikeets that mob you for food during the day time and possums that do the same at night, pods of dolphins, some great walks through gorgeous bushland, and a real Aboriginal spirituality-of-place? I could go on, but see for yourself.

ESSENTIALS
GETTING THERE   It's best to reach Jervis Bay via Huskisson, 24km (15 miles) southeast of Nowra on the Princes Highway. Approximately 16km (10 miles) south of Nowra, turn left onto the Jervis Bay Road to Huskisson. The entrance to Booderee National Park is just after Huskisson. It's about a 3-hour drive from Sydney. You'll probably need at least 2 days to get to know the area. Watch out for the black cockatoos.

Australian Pacific Tours (© **02/9247 7222;** fax 02/9247 2052; www. aptours.com.au) runs a dolphin-watching cruise to Jervis Bay from Sydney every day between early October and mid-April, and Monday and Thursday in winter. The 12-hour trip—7 hours of which are on the coach—includes a visit to the Kiama blowhole, a 3-hour luncheon cruise looking for bottlenose dolphins, and a stop off on the way back at Fitzroy Falls in the Southern Highlands. The trip costs A$117 (US$76) for adults and A$109 (US$71) for children.

East Coast Adventure Tours (© **1800/666 000** in Australia; www.beachn bush.com.au) takes backpackers and adventurous oldies on a 2-night trip to Jervis Bay every Friday evening. You walk deep into the huge Morton National Park, go on a dolphin cruise, and spend the rest of the weekend in Jervis Bay. The trip costs A$219 (US$142) per person.

VISITOR INFORMATION   For information on the area, contact the **Shoalhaven Visitors Centre,** at the corner of Princes Highway and Pleasant Way, Nowra (© **1800/024 261** in Australia, or 02/4421 0778; www.shoalhaven.nsw. gov.au). Pick up maps and book camping sites at the **Booderee National Park** office (© **02/4443 0977;** www.ea.gov.au/parks/booderee), located just beyond

Huskisson; it's open daily from 9am to 4pm. **Hyams Beach Store** (✆ **02/4443 0242**) has an accommodations guide listing 34 rental properties from A$100 (US$65) a weekend.

SEEING THE AREA

If you want to see the best spots, you'll need to pay the rather extortionate park-entrance fee of A$10 (US$6.50) a day. Some of the places you could visit include **Hyams Beach** 👍, reputed to have the whitest sand in the world. Notice how it squeaks when you walk on it. Wear sunscreen! The reflection off the beach can burn your skin in minutes on a sunny day. **Hole in the Wall Beach** has interesting rock formations and a lingering smell of natural sulfur. **Summer Cloud Bay** is secluded and offers excellent fishing.

Dolphin Watch Cruises, 74 Owen St., Huskisson (✆ **1800/246 010** in Australia, or 02/4441 6311; www.dolphinwatch.com.au), runs a hardy vessel out of Huskisson on the lookout for the resident pod of bottlenose dolphins—you have "more than a 95% chance of seeing them," the company claims. A 2-hour coffee cruise runs at 10am on Saturdays and Sundays, public holidays, and school holidays, and costs A$20 (US$13) for adults and A$10 (US$6.50) for children. A 2½-hour dolphin watch and bay cruise leaves at 1pm and costs A$25 (US$16) for adults and A$12 (US$7.80) for children. It's possible to see humpback and southern right whales June to July and mid-September to mid-November. A 3-hour whale-watch cruise costs A$40 (US$26) for adults and A$30 (US$20) for children.

WHERE TO STAY & DINE

If you have a tent and camping gear, all the better. **Caves Beach** is a quiet spot (except when the birds chorus at dawn) located just a stroll away from a good beach; it's home to resident eastern gray kangaroos. A campsite here costs A$8 (US$5.20) per tent in winter and A$10 (US$6.50) in summer and on public holidays, though at press time moves were afoot to increase prices. It's about a 250m (about ¹⁄₁₀-mile) walk from the car park to the campground. **Greenpatch** is more dirt than grass, but you get your own area and it's suitable for motor homes. It's infested with overfriendly possums around dusk. A camp spot here costs A$13 (US$8.45) in winter and A$16 (US$10) in summer.

For supplies, head to the area's main towns, **Huskisson** (pop. 930) and **Vincentia** (pop. 2,350). The **Huskisson RSL Club,** overlooking the wharf area on Owen Street (✆ **02/4441 5282**), has a good bistro and a bar. You'll have to sign in inside the main entrance. The Huskissson Hotel (also called the "Husskie Pub") is just down the road and has a nice beer garden and cheapish meals at lunchtime.

Huskisson Beach Tourist Resort   This resort is the very pinnacle of cabin accommodations on this part of the east coast. Cabins vary in price depending on size, but even the smallest has room enough for a double bed, triple bunks, and a small kitchen with microwave. Larger cabins have two separate bedrooms. There's a game room and barbecue facilities on the grounds.

Beach St., Huskisson, Jervis Bay, NSW 2540. ✆ and fax **02/4441 5142.** 38 units. Fri–Sat A$75–A$105 (US$49–US$68) cabin; Sun–Thurs A$60–A$95 (US$39–US$62) cabin. DC, MC, V. **Amenities:** Small heated outdoor pool; lighted tennis court; coin-op laundry; nonsmoking rooms. *In room:* TV, kitchen, fridge, coffeemaker, hair dryer, iron.

Jervis Bay Guest House 👍   After the Jervis Bay Hotel, take the second road to the left—Nowra Street—and follow it to the end. This relatively new guesthouse has four distinctly different rooms (different color schemes, beds, and so

---

Tips **A Safety Warning**

Jervis Bay is notorious for its car break-ins, a situation the local police force has been unable to control. If you park your car anywhere in the national park, remove all valuables, including things in the trunk.

---

on), each with a private bathroom. One room has a Jacuzzi, and two rooms face the water. Breakfast is a hearty affair and could include emu sausages and thick slabs of bacon followed by a tropical fruit platter. Children under 16 not allowed.

1 Beach St., Huskisson, NSW 2540 (℃) **02/4441 7658.** Fax 02/4441 7659. www.jervisbayguesthouse.com.au. 4 units. A$130–A$220 (US$85–US$143) double depending on season. Rates include breakfast. AE, DC, MC, V. **Amenities:** Lounge/game room; tour desk; massage; nonsmoking rooms. *In room:* A/C, coffeemaker (waterview rooms), hair dryer, iron.

ULLADULLA
220km (136 miles) south of Sydney

Very much a supply town on the south coast as well as a fishing center, especially for tuna, Ulladulla is a pleasant stopover on your journey south. This is also a good place to stock up on supplies from local supermarkets. On the outskirts of town (just to the south) are a series of saltwater lakes that make for good fishing, though you'll have competition from the pelicans. Inland is the giant Morton National Park, marked by the peak of Pigeonhouse Mountain. The 3- to 4-hour walk to the top and back starts at a car park a 30-minute drive from Ulladulla. The going is steep at first but levels out as it crosses a sandstone plateau. Another upward climb and you're rewarded with a magnificent view of peaks and ocean.

Several side roads worth exploring spur off between Ulladulla and Batemans Bay (see below). These lead to the tiny villages of Bawley Point and Kioloa, where holiday cottages nestle between isolated beaches, gum forests, and green patches studded with gray kangaroos.

There are more kangaroos at the pristine **Pebbly Beach** 🐾 in Murramarang National Park, a short hop—20 minutes south—of Ulladulla. These furry creatures actually wander around the beach and adjacent campsite, or gather on the grassy dunes to graze. It's a good area for bird-watching, too.

ESSENTIALS
GETTING THERE   Ulladulla is about a 3-hour drive from Sydney Central Business District down the Pacific Highway.

VISITOR INFORMATION   **Ulladulla Visitors Centre,** Civic Center, Princes Highway (℃ **02/4455 1269;** www.shoalhaven.nsw.gov.au), is open Monday through Friday from 10am to 5pm; Saturday and Sunday from 9am to 5pm.

WHERE TO STAY & DINE
Ulladulla is well known for its food (particularly seafood and beef) and wine. (There are a few boutique wineries in the area.) For some of the best fish in Australia, head to one of the fish-and-chip shops on Wason Street, close to the harbor. The best of these is **Tiger Fish and Chips** (no phone). On the same street is **Torys Takeaway** (℃ **02/4454 0888**), where you can buy good fish and chips on the ground floor at about a third of the price of the very nice restaurant

above—**Torys Seafood Restaurant** (open in the evenings, same number)—and take them down to the harbor to eat amongst the seagulls.

Ulladulla Guest House ★★★   This fabulous, award-winning property is one of the best places to stay in Australia. Run by the friendly Andrew and Elizabeth Nowosad—try and guess his accent—the Ulladulla Guest House is an impressive AAA-rated five-star establishment. It's surrounded by small but lovely tropical gardens—Andrew insists his coconut palms are the only ones this far south—and overlooks the harbor. Unusually, the house is also a registered art gallery, and the walls are festooned with paintings for sale. Past the cozy lounge are three types of rooms. Two self-contained units with private entrances to the garden are the lowest in price. The one-bedroom unit has a queen-size bed and a foldout sofa bed, and the two-bedroom unit has a double bed in one room, two singles in another, and a double foldout sofa bed in the lounge. Luxury rooms have a queen-size bed, custom-made furniture, and original artwork. Executive rooms come with a marble bathroom and a private Jacuzzi. There are three masseurs on standby.

39 Burrill St., Ulladulla, NSW 2539. ℂ **02/4455 1796.** Fax 02/4454 4660. www.guesthouse.com.au. 10 units. Self-contained 1-bedroom unit: A$98 (US$64) midweek standby, A$188 (US$122) weekend and peak period (see below). 2-bedroom unit: A$120 (US$78) midweek, A$238 (US$155) weekend/peak. Luxury units: A$118 (US$77) midweek, A$198 (US$129) weekend/peak. Executive units A$150 (US$98) midweek, A$238 (US$155) weekend/peak. Peak periods: weekends, public holidays, Easter, and Christmas school holidays. AE, DC, MC, V. **Amenities:** Restaurant; lagoon-style heated outdoor pool; golf course nearby; exercise room; Jacuzzi; watersports equipment rental; bike rental; room service (7am–10pm); in-room massage; babysitting; free self-service laundry; laundry service; same-day dry cleaning; nonsmoking rooms. *In room:* A/C, TV, fax, dataport, fridge, coffeemaker, hair dryer, iron.

BATEMANS BAY
275km (171 miles) S of Sydney

This laid-back holiday town offers good surfing beaches, arts-and-crafts galleries, boat trips up the Clyde River, good game fishing, and bushwalks in Morton and Deua national parks.

ESSENTIALS
GETTING THERE   Batemans Bay is a 3- to 4-hour drive from Sydney, depending on the traffic. (Avoid leaving Sydney at rush hour, and prepare for long delays on holidays.) **Premier Motor Service** (ℂ **1300/368 100** in Australia, or 02/4423 5233) runs coaches to Batemans Bay from Sydney's Central Station.

VISITOR INFORMATION   **Batemans Bay Visitor Information Centre,** at the corner of Princes Highway and Beach Road (ℂ **1800/802 528** in Australia, or 02/4472 6800), is open daily from 9am to 5pm.

GAME FISHING & A RIVER CRUISE
If you fancy some serious fishing contact **OB1 Charters,** Marina, Beach Road, Batemans Bay (ℂ **1800/641 065** in Australia, 02/4471 2738, or 0416/241 586 mobile; www.southcoast.com.au/ob1). The company runs full-day game-fishing trips and morning snapper-fishing trips (afternoon snapper trips in summer, too). Expect to encounter black marlin, blue marlin, giant kingfish, mako sharks, albacore tuna, yellow-fin tuna, and blue tuna from November through June. The trip includes all tackle, bait, and afternoon and morning teas, but you must provide your own lunch. It costs A$900 (US$585) to hire the six-person boat; if there are just a couple of you, the charter company may be able to fill the rest of the boat

if you make your reservations far enough in advance. Trips to catch snapper (a nice-tasting fish, which is not the same as red snapper) include all gear, bait, and morning or afternoon tea for A$80 (US$52) per person.

A river cruise on the **MV *Merinda,*** Innes Boatshed, Orient St., Batemans Bay (© **02/4472 4052;** fax 02/4472 4754), is a pleasant experience. The 3-hour cruise leaves at 11:30am daily and travels inland past townships, forests, and farmland. It costs A$22 (US$14) for adults, A$11 (US$7.15) for children, and A$50 (US$33) for families; a fish-and-chip lunch is A$6 (US$3.90) extra and a seafood basket for two is A$12 (US$7.80).

A NICE PLACE TO STAY

The Bay Soldiers Esplanade Motor Inn ⭐   This four-star motel right on the Batemans Bay river estuary has fabulous views and is close to the town center. Rooms are light and well furnished, and all have balconies (some with water views). Some doubles and suites have Jacuzzis; they cost the same as non-Jacuzzi rooms, so specify if you want one when booking. Eat at the hotel's restaurant or at the Batemans Bay Soldiers' Club just opposite, which has a restaurant, a bistro, cheap drinks, and a free evening kids club.

23 Beach Rd. (P.O. Box 202), Batemans Bay, NSW 2536. © **1800/659 884** in Australia, or 02/4472 0200. Fax 02/4472 0277. www.esplanade.com.au/motel. 23 units. A$107–A$179 (US$70–US$116) double, depending on season, view, and Jacuzzi; A$156–A$330 (US$101–US$215) suite. Extra person A$12 (US$7.80). Children under 18 stay free in parent's room. AE, DC, MC, V. **Amenities:** Restaurant; coin-op laundry; nonsmoking rooms. *In room:* A/C, TV, kitchenette, fridge, coffeemaker, hair dryer, iron.

NAROOMA ⭐
345km (214 miles) SW of Sydney

Narooma is a seaside town with beautiful deserted beaches, a golf course right on a headland, a natural rock formation in the shape of Australia (popular with camera-wielding tourists), and excellent fishing. However, its major attraction is **Montague Island** ⭐⭐, the breeding colony for thousands of shearwaters (or mutton birds, as they're also called) and a hangout for juvenile seals.

Just 18km (11 miles) farther south is **Central Tilba** ⭐, one of the prettiest towns in Australia and the headquarters of the boutique **ABC Cheese Factory.** You'll kick yourself if you miss this charming historical township (pop. 35; 1 million visitors annually).

ESSENTIALS
GETTING THERE   Narooma is a 7-hour drive from Sydney down the Princes Highway. **Premier Motor Service** (© **1300/368 100** in Australia, or 02/4423 5233) runs coaches to Narooma from Sydney's Central Station.

VISITOR INFORMATION   The **Narooma Visitors Centre,** Princes Highway, Narooma (© **02/4476 2881;** fax 02/4476 1690; www.naturecoast-tourism. com.au), is open daily from 9am to 5pm.

WHAT TO SEE & DO: WHALES, GOLF & MORE
A must if you're visiting the area is a boat tour with **Narooma Charters** (© 02/ 4476 2240; www.acr.net.au/~charters). It offers spectacular tours of the coast on the lookout for dolphins, seal colonies, and little penguins, and also includes a tour of Montague Island. Morning and afternoon tours take 3½ hours and cost A$69 (US$45) for adults, A$50 (US$33) for children, and A$198 (US$129) for families. A 4½-hour tour includes some of the world's best whale-watching (between mid-Sept and early Dec) and costs A$89 (US$58) for adults, A$70

(US$46) for children, and A$299 (US$194) for families. The last time I went on this trip we saw no fewer than eight humpback whales, some of them mothers with calves. An evening tour to see fairy penguins on Montague Island and a visit to the seal colony costs A$69 (US$45) for adults, A$50 (US$35) for children, and A$198 (US$128) for a family. The company also offers game fishing from February to the end of June and scuba diving in the seal colonies from August to the end of December. You could also see giant fish-eating gray nurse sharks, dolphins and even orcas. Dives cost A$66 (US$43) for a double dive, plus approximately A$33 (US$21) for gear rental.

Narooma Golf Club, Narooma (© **02/4476 2522**), has one of the most interesting and challenging coastal courses in Australia. A round of golf will cost you A$25 (US$16).

While in the area I recommend stopping off at the **Umbarra Aboriginal Cultural Centre** ✸, Wallaga Lake, off the Princes Highway on Bermagui Road (© **02/4473 7232;** umbarra@acr.net.au). The center offers activities such as boomerang and spear throwing, and painting with natural ochres for A$6.25 (US$4.05) per person, or A$20 (US$13) per family. There are also discussions, Aboriginal archival displays, and a retail store. It's open Monday through Friday from 9am to 5pm and Saturday and Sunday from 9am to 4pm (closed Sun in winter). The center's guides also offer 2- to 4-hour four-wheel-drive/walking trips of nearby **Mount Dromedary** ✸ and **Mumbulla Mountain,** taking in sacred sites. The tours cost A$45 (US$29) per person. Reservations are essential.

If you want to attempt Mt. Dromedary without a guide, ask for directions in Narooma. The hike to the top takes around 3 hours.

WHERE TO STAY
Whale Motor Inn ✸   This nice, quiet motor inn has the best panoramic ocean views on the south coast and the largest rooms in town. Standard rooms have a queen-size and a single-person sofa bed. Standard suites have a separate bedroom, two sofa beds, and a kitchenette. Executive and Jacuzzi suites are very spacious, better furnished, and have a kitchenette and a large balcony or patio.

Princes Hwy., Narooma, NSW 2546. © **02/4476 2411.** Fax 02/4476 1995. www.whalemotorinn.com.au. 17 units. A$90–A$145 (US$59–US$94). Extra person A$10 (US$6.50). AE, DC, MC, V. **Amenities:** Restaurant; small unheated outdoor pool; nonsmoking rooms. *In room:* A/C, TV, kitchenette (in all rooms except A$90/US$59 rooms), fridge, coffeemaker, hair dryer, iron.

MERIMBULA
480km (298 miles) S of Sydney; 580km (360 miles) NE of Melbourne

This seaside resort (pop. approx. 7,000) is the last place of interest before the Princes Highway crosses the border into Victoria. Merimbula is a good center from which to discover the surrounding **Ben Boyd National Park** and **Mimosa Rocks National Park;** both offer bushwalking. Another park, **Bournda National Park,** is situated around a lake and has good walking trails and a surf beach.

Golf is the game of choice in Merimbula itself, and the area's most popular venue is the **Pambula-Merimbula Golf Club** (© **02/6495 6154**), where you can spot kangaroos grazing on the fairways of the 27-hole course. It costs A$14 (US$9.10) for nine holes, or A$25 (US$16) for the day. Another favorite is **Tura Beach Country Club** (© **02/6495 9002**), which is known for its excellent coastal views. A round of 18 holes costs A$20 (US$13).

Eden, 20km (12½ miles) south of Merimbula, was once a major whaling port. The rather gruesome **Eden Killer Whale Museum,** on Imlay Street in

Eden (© **02/6496 2094**), is the only reason to stop here. It has a dubious array of relics, including boats, axes, and remnants of the last of the area's killer whales, called Old Tom. The museum is open Monday through Saturday from 9:15am to 3:45pm, Sunday from 11:15am to 3:45pm. In January it's open daily from 9:15am to 4:45pm daily. Admission is A$5.50 (US$3.60) for adults and A$1.50 (US$1) for children. You can still see a scattering of whales off the coast in October and November.

ESSENTIALS

GETTING THERE   The drive from either Sydney or Melbourne takes about 7 hours. The **Greyhound Pioneer** (© **13 20 30** in Australia) bus trip from Sydney takes more than 8 hours.

VISITOR INFORMATION   The **Merimbula Tourist Information Centre,** at Beach Street, Merimbula (© **1800/150 457** in Australia, or 02/6495 1129; fax 02/6495 1250), is open daily from 9am to 5pm (10am–4pm in winter).

SPECIAL EVENTS   Jazz fans should head for the **Merimbula Jazz Festival** held over the long Queens Birthday weekend, the second weekend in June. A country-music festival takes place the last weekend in October.

WHERE TO STAY

Ocean View Motor Inn   This pleasant motel has good water views from 12 of its rooms (the best are nos. 9, 10, and 11). The rooms are spacious and modern, with plain brick walls, patterned carpets, and one long balcony serving the top six rooms. Fourteen rooms have kitchenettes. All have showers. It's a friendly place. Breakfast is served to your room for A$7.70 (US$5) extra.

Merimbula Dr. and View St., Merimbula, NSW 2548. © **02/6495 2300.** Fax 02/6495 3443. www.oceanview motorinn.com.au. 20 units. A$66–A$120 (US$43–US$78) double (depending on season). Extra person A$11 (US$6.50). MC, V. **Amenities:** Medium-size solar-heated outdoor pool; limited room service; babysitting; coin-op laundry; nonsmoking rooms. In room: A/C, TV, kitchenette, fridge, coffeemaker.

6 The Snowy Mountains: Australia's Ski Country ⭐

Thredbo: 519km (322 miles) SW of Sydney; 208km (129 miles) SW of Canberra; 543km (337 miles) NE of Melbourne

Made famous by Banjo Paterson's 1890 poem "The Man from Snowy River," the Snowy Mountains are most commonly used for what you'd least expect to happen in Australia—skiing. It starts to snow around June and carries on until September. During this time hundreds of thousands of people flock here to ski at the major ski resorts—Thredbo and Perisher Blue, and, to a lesser extent, Charlotte Pass and Mount Selwyn. It's certainly different skiing here, with ghostly white gum trees as the obstacles instead of pine trees.

The whole region is part of the **Kosciuszko** (pronounced ko-zi-*os*-co) **National Park,** the largest alpine area in Australia. During the summer months the park is a beautiful place for walking, and in spring the profusion of wildflowers is exquisite. A series of lakes in the area, including the one in the resort town of Jindabyne, are favorites with trout fishermen.

Visitors stay at **Jindabyne,** 62km (38 miles) south of Cooma, or **Thredbo Village,** 36km (22 miles) southwest of Jindabyne. Jindabyne is a bleak-looking resort town on the banks of the man-made Lake Jindabyne, which came into existence when the Snowy River was dammed to provide hydroelectric power.

Thredbo Village is set in a valley of Mt. Crackenback and resembles European-style resorts. From here, the Crackenback Chairlift provides easy access to an easy-grade pathway which leads to the top of Mt. Kosciuszko, which at 2,228m (7,308 ft.) is Australia's highest peak. The mountain has stunning views of the alpine region and some good walks.

SNOWY MOUNTAIN ESSENTIALS

GETTING THERE   From Sydney, take the Eastern Distributor road towards Sydney Airport and turn right just before the planes, following the signs to Wollongong and then Canberra, via the M5 motorway and the Hume Highway. Follow the Hume Highway south to Goulburn, where you turn onto the Federal Highway toward Canberra. From there take the Monaro Highway to Cooma, then follow the Alpine Way through Jindabyne and on to Thredbo. Chains may have to be used on the slopes in winter and can be rented from local service stations. The trip takes around 6 hours from Sydney with short breaks.

Qantas (© 13 13 13 in Australia) has daily flights from Sydney to Cooma. A connecting bus to the ski fields takes about 1 hour and is available June through October. It's run by **Snowy Mountain Hire Cars** (© **02/6456 2957**) and costs A$48 (US$31) one-way.

In winter only (from around June 19–Oct 5), **Greyhound Pioneer** (© **13 20 30** in Australia) operates daily buses between Sydney and Cooma, via Canberra. The journey takes around 7 hours from Sydney and 3 hours from Canberra. A one-way ticket costs A$50 (US$33).

VISITOR INFORMATION   Pick up information about the ski fields and accommodations options either at the **Cooma Visitors Centre,** 119 Sharp St., Cooma, NSW 2630 (© **02/6450 1740;** fax 02/6450 1798), or at the **Snowy Region Visitor Centre,** Kosciuszko Rd., Jindabyne, NSW 2627 (© **02/6450 5600;** fax 02/6456 1249; srvc@npws.nsw.gov.au).

HITTING THE SLOPES & OTHER ADVENTURES

Obviously, skiing is the most popular activity here. More than 50 ski lifts serve the fields of Perisher Valley, Mt. Blue Cow, Smiggins Holes, and Guthega. Perisher Valley offers the best overall slopes; Mt. Blue Cow is generally very crowded; Smiggins Holes offer good slopes for beginners; and Guthega has nice light, powdery snow and is less crowded. Thredbo has some very challenging runs and the longest downhill runs, but I still prefer Perisher for atmosphere. A day's ski pass costs around A$77 (US$50) for adults, and A$42 (US$27) for children.

A ski-tube train midway between Jindabyne and Thredbo on the Alpine Way travels through the mountains to Perisher Valley and then to Blue Cow. It costs A$15 (US$9.75) a day for adult skiers and A$9 (US$5.85) for child skiers; A$30 (US$20) for non-skiing adults and A$17 (US$11) for non-skiing children. Prices are cheaper in summer. Ski gear can be rented at numerous places in Jindabyne and Thredbo.

In summer, the region is popular for hiking, canoeing, fishing, and golf. Thredbo Village has tennis courts, a nine-hole golf course, and mountain-bike trails.

Tips **Ski Condition Updates**

For up-to-date ski field information call the **Snowy Region Visitor Centre** (© **02/6450 5600**).

Moments **In the Footsteps of the Man from Snowy River**

Horseback riding is a popular activity for all those wanting to ride like the "Man from Snowy River." **Reynella Kosciusko Rides,** located in Adamanaby, 44km (27 miles) northwest of Cooma (✆ **1800/029 909** in Australia, or 02/6454 2386; fax 02/6454 2530; reynellarides.com.au), offers multinight rides through the Kosciuszko National Park from October to the end of April. Three-day/4-night rides costs A$799 (US$519), and the 5-day/6-night ride A$1,207 (US$784). Transfers from Cooma cost A$33 (US$21) each way. The trips are all-inclusive and include camping and homestead accommodations. Shorter rides are offered by **Jindabyne Trail Rides** (✆ **02/6456 2421;** fax 02/6456 1254). Gentle, 1½-hour rides on the slopes above Jindabyne cost A$25 (US$16) per person.

WHERE TO STAY

You'll have to book months ahead to find a place during the ski season (especially on weekends). And don't expect to find a lot of bargains. The **Kosciuszko Accommodation Centre,** Nuggets Crossing, Jindabyne, NSW 2627 (✆ **1800/ 026 354** in Australia, or 02/6456 2022; fax 02/6456 2945), can help find and book accommodations in the area. Other private agents who can help find you a spot for the night include **The Snowy Mountains Reservation Centre** (✆ **02/ 6456 2633**) and the **Thredbo Resort Centre** (✆ **1800/020 622** in Australia).

IN THREDBO

Riverside Cabins   These self-contained studio and one-bedroom cabins are above the Thredbo River and overlook the Crackenback Range. They're also a short walk from the Thredbo Alpine Hotel and local shops. Most rooms have balconies. Rates vary wildly from weekday to weekend and season, so check before you come here.

Thredbo, NSW 2625. ✆ **02/6459 4196** in Australia, or 02/6459 4299. Fax 02/6459 4195. www.thredbo.com. 36 units. Winter A$160–A$516 (US$104–US$335) double. Summer A$117–$164 (US$76–US$107) double. Ask about weekly rates. AE, DC, MC, V. *In room:* TV, kitchen, coin op laundry, fridge, coffeemaker, hair dryer, iron.

Thredbo Alpine Apartments   These apartments are very similar to the Riverside Cabins (see above) and are managed by the same people. All have balconies with mountain views. Some have queen-size beds. There's a limited daily maid service and in-room movies.

Thredbo, NSW 2628. ✆ **1800/026 333** in Australia, or 02/6459 4299. Fax 02/6459 4195. 35 units. Winter weekends A$210–A$441 (US$137–US$287) 1-bedroom apt; A$289–A$628 (US$188–US$408) 2-bedroom apt; A$394–A$770 (US$256–US$500) 3-bedroom apt; midweek rates approx. 20% cheaper. Summer A$127–A$164 (US$83–US$107) 1-bedroom apt; A$159–A$190 (US$103–US$124) 2-bedroom apt; A$180–A$210 (US$117–US$137) 3-bedroom apt. Summer rates apply July 30–Sept 2. Ask about weekly rates. AE, DC, MC, V. Covered parking. *In room:* TV, kitchen, coin-op laundry, fridge, coffeemaker, hair dryer, iron.

Thredbo Alpine Hotel   After the skiing is finished for the day, the center of activity in Thredbo is this large resort-style lodge. Rooms vary; those on the top floor of the three-story hotel have a king-size bed instead of a standard queen. The rooms are all wood-paneled. Thredbo's only nightclub is here.

Thredbo (P.O. Box 80, Thredbo NSW 2625). ✆ **02/6459 4200.** Fax 02/6459 4201. www.thredbo.com.au. 65 units. Winter A$198–A$498 (US$129–US$324) double. Summer A$129–A$189 (US$84–US$123) double. Ask about weekly rates and packages. Rates include breakfast. AE, DC, MC, V. **Amenities:** 2 restaurants; bistro;

4 bars; heated outdoor pool; 3 lit tennis courts; golf course nearby; Jacuzzi; sauna; tour desk; massage; room service (winter only); coin-op laundry; nonsmoking rooms. *In room:* TV/VCR w/in-house movies, minibar, coffeemaker, hair dryer.

7 Outback New South Wales

The Outback is a powerful Australian image. Hot, dusty, and prone to flies, it can also be a romantic place where wedge-tailed eagles float in the shimmering heat as you spin in a circle, tracing the unbroken horizon. If you drive out here, you have to be constantly on the lookout for emus, large flightless birds that dart across roads open-beaked and wide-eyed. When you turn off the car engine, it's so quiet you can hear the scales of a sleepy lizard, as long as your forearm, scraping the rumpled track as it turns to taste the air with its long, blue tongue.

The scenery is a huge canvas with a restricted palette: blood red for the dirt, straw yellow for the blotches of Mitchell grass, a searing blue for the surreally large sky. There is room to be yourself in the Outback, and you'll soon find that personalities often tilt toward the eccentric. It's a hardworking place, too, where miners, and sheep and cattle farmers try to eke out a living in Australia's hard center.

BROKEN HILL 😊😊
1,157km (717 miles) W of Sydney; 508km (315 miles) NE of Adelaide

At heart, Broken Hill—or "Silver City" as it's been nicknamed—is still very much a hardworking, hard-drinking mining town. Its beginnings date back to 1883 when the trained eye of a boundary rider named Charles Rasp noticed something odd about the craggy rock outcrops at a place called the Broken Hill. Today, the city's main drag, Argent Street, bristles with finely crafted colonial mansions, heritage homes, hotels, and public buildings. Look deeper and you see the town's quirkiness. Around one corner you'll find the radio station built to resemble a giant wireless set with round knobs for windows, and around another the headquarters of the Housewives Association, which ruled the town with an iron apron for generations. Then there's the Palace Hotel—made famous in the movie *The Adventures of Priscilla, Queen of the Desert*—with its high painted walls and a mural of Botticelli's *Birth of Venus* on the ceiling two flights up.

Traditionally a hard-drinking but religious town, Broken Hill has 23 pubs (down from 73 in its heyday) and plenty of churches, as well as a Catholic cathedral, a synagogue, and a mosque to serve its 21,000 inhabitants.

ESSENTIALS
GETTING THERE   By Car   Take the Great Western Highway from Sydney to Dubbo, then the Mitchell Highway to the Barrier Highway, which will take you to Broken Hill. **Southern Australian Airlines** (book through Qantas, © 13 13 13 in Australia) also connects Broken Hill to Adelaide, Melbourne, and Mildura.

The *Indian Pacific* train stops here on its way to Perth twice a week. The fare from Sydney is A$415 (US$270) for adults and A$283 (US$184) for children in a first-class sleeper, A$329 (US$214) for adults and A$198 (US$129) for children in an economy sleeper, and A$117 (US$76) for adults and A$53 (US$34) for children in an economy seat. Call **Great Southern Railways** (© 08/8213 4530) for more information and bookings, or check out the timetables and fares on their website (www.gsr.com.au).

Greyhound Pioneer (© 13 20 30 in Australia; www.greyhound.com.au) runs buses from Adelaide for A$58 (US$38); the trip takes 7 hours. The 16-hour trip from Sydney costs from A$93 (US$60).

VISITOR INFORMATION   The **Broken Hill Visitors Information Centre,** at Blende and Bromide streets, Broken Hill, NSW 2880 (© **08/8087 6077;** fax 08/8088 5209; www.murrayoutback.org.au), is open daily from 8:30am to 5pm. The **National Parks & Wildlife Service (NPWS)** office is at 183 Argent St. (© **08/8088 5933),** and the **Royal Automobile Association of South Australia,** which offers reciprocal services to other national and international autoclub members, is at 261 Argent St. (© **08/8088 4999).**

Note: The area code in Broken Hill is **08,** the same as the South Australia code, not 02, the New South Wales code.

GETTING AROUND   **Silver City Tours,** 380 Argent St. (© **08/8087 3144),** conducts tours of the city and surrounding Outback. City tours take around 4 hours and cost A$45 (US$26) for adults and A$20 (US$13) for children. They also offer a range of other tours of the area.

Broken Hill Corner Country Adventure Tours (© **08/8087 5142;** www.cornercountryadventure.com.au), operates several small group tours into the desert from Broken Hill, staying in rural properties and bush pubs. The regular 4-day/3-night Corner Country Tour takes in a sheep station, White Cliffs, Mootwingee, and the red-sand Sturt National Park. It costs A$850 (US$552) all-inclusive. Other offerings include a 5-day trip to the Flinders Ranges and Lake Eyre—usually a vast dry bowl of clay, which sometimes floods—for A$1,235 (US$803); and an 8-day Birdsville and Outback tour, May through October, stopping off at the very impressive red sand dunes on the edge of the Simpson Desert, as well as the one-camel bush towns of Birdsville, Marree, and Innamincka in South Australia. This costs A$1,790 (US$1,163).

Another recommended small group tour operator, **Goanna Safari** (© **08/8087 6057;** www.goanna-safari.com.au), offers personalized tours of the Outback from Broken Hill, and a range of regular camping (with good camp beds and cooking fires) or accommodated tours. Among them is a 3-day/2-night trip to Mootwingee, White Cliffs, and Menidee Lakes, where giant dams on the Darling River bristle with the half-drowned skeletons of gum trees and flutter with numerous species of wading birds, pelicans, and ducks. This trip costs A$656 (US$426) camping and A$694 (US$450) accommodated. Also on the agenda is a 3-day trip to Minindee, Kinchega National Park, and Lake Mungo, a dry lake famous for the 45,000-year-old skeletons and artifacts discovered in it and for huge sand dunes and shimmering white cliffs known as the Walls of China. This costs A$582 (US$378) camping and A$694 (US$452) accommodated.

Hertz (© **08/8087 2719;** fax 08/8087 4838) rents four-wheel-drive vehicles suitable for exploring the area.

EXPLORING THE TOWN: GALLERIES, A MINE TOUR & THE WORLD'S LARGEST SCHOOLROOM

With the largest regional public gallery in New South Wales and 27 private **galleries,** Broken Hill has more places per capita to see art than anywhere else in Australia. The **Broken Hill Regional Art Gallery,** Chloride Street, between Blende and Beryl streets (© **08/8088 5491),** houses an extensive collection of Australian colonial and Impressionist works. Look for the *Silver Tree,* a sculpture created out of the pure silver mined from beneath Broken Hill. This is also a good place to see works by the "Brushmen of the Bush," a well-known group of artists, including Pro Hart, Jack Absalom, Eric Minchin, and Hugh Schultz, who spend many days sitting around campfires in the bush trying to capture its essence in paint. The gallery is open Monday through Friday from 10am to

---

Fun Fact **What Time Is It, Anyway?**

Broken Hill runs its clocks to Central Standard Time, to correspond with South Australia. The surrounding country, however, runs half an hour faster at Eastern Standard Time.

5pm, and Saturday and Sunday from 1 to 5pm. Admission is A$3 (US$1.95) for adults, A$2 (US$1.30) for children, and A$6 (US$3.90) for families.

Other galleries worth visiting around town include **Absalom's Gallery,** 638 Chapple St. (© **08/8087 5881**), and the **Pro Hart Gallery,** 108 Wyman St. (© **08/8087 2441**). All are open daily. Pro Hart's gallery is really worth a look. Apart from his own works—including works based on incidents and scenes relating to Broken Hill—his gallery is crammed with everything from a bas-relief of Salvador Dalí to a landscape by Claude Monet.

To get a real taste of mining in Broken Hill, take an underground tour at **Delprat's Mine** (© **08/8088 1604**). Visitors go 120m (394 ft.) below the surface. Children under 6 are not allowed. Tours run Monday through Friday at 10:30am and Saturday at 2pm. The 2-hour tour costs A$23 (US$15) for adults and A$18 (US$12) for children.

Be sure not to miss the School of the Air and the Royal Flying Doctor Service base, both of which help show the enormity of the Australian interior. The **School of the Air**—the largest schoolroom in the world, with students scattered over 800,000 sq. km (312,000 sq. miles)—conducts lessons via two-way radios. Visitors can listen in on part of the day's first teaching session Monday through Friday at 8:30am (except public holidays). Bookings are essential and must be made through the **Broken Hill Visitors Information Centre** (see "Visitor Information," above). Tours costs A$2 (US$1.30) per person. The **Royal Flying Doctor Service base** is at the Broken Hill Airport (© **08/8080 1777**). The service maintains communication with more than 400 outback stations, ready to fly at once in case of an emergency. The base at Broken Hill covers 25% of New South Wales, as well as parts of Queensland and South Australia. Explanations of the role of the flying doctor service are given continuously at the base Monday through Friday from 9am to 5pm. Admission is A$3 (US$1.95) for adults, free for children.

OTHER THINGS TO SEE & DO NEARBY

VISITING A GHOST TOWN   At least 44 movies have been filmed in the Wild West town of **Silverton** ᙭ (pop. 50), 23km (14 miles) northwest of Broken Hill. It's the Wild West Australian-style, though, with camels instead of horses sometimes placed in front of the **Silverton Pub,** which is well worth a visit for its kitschy Australian appeal. Silverton once had a population of 3,000 following the discovery of silver here in 1882, but within 7 years almost everyone had left. There are some good art galleries here, as well as a restored jail and hotel.

DISCOVERING ABORIGINAL HANDPRINTS   **Mutawintji National Park** ᙭ (also known and pronounced by its old name, Mootwingee), 130km (81 miles) northeast of Broken Hill, was one of the most important spiritual meeting places for Aborigines on the continent. Groups came from all over to peck out abstract engravings on the rocks with sharpened quartz tools and to sign their handprints to show they belonged to the place. The ancient, weathered fireplaces are still here, laid out like a giant map to show where each visiting group came from. Hundreds of ocher outlines of hands and animal paws, some up to 30,000 years old, are stenciled on rock overhangs. The fabulous 2-hour Outback trip from Broken Hill to Mootwingee is along red-dirt tracks not really suitable for two-wheel-drives and should not be attempted after a heavy rain.

Mootwingee Heritage Tours (© **08/8088 7000**) organizes inspections of the historical sites every Wednesday and Saturday morning at 10:30am Broken Hill time (11am Mootwingee, or Eastern Standard, time). The tours may be canceled in very hot weather. The **NPWS office** in Broken Hill (© **08/8088 5933**) also has details. You can camp at the **Homestead Creek** campground for A$11 (US$7.15) a night. It has its own water supply.

EXPLORING WHITE CLIFFS 🐨🐨 White Cliffs, 290km (180 miles) east of Broken Hill, is an opal-mining town bigger than it looks. Unlike Lightning Ridge (below), which produces mainly black opals, White Cliffs is known for its less valuable white opals (as is Coober Pedy in South Australia). To escape the summer heat, most houses are built underground in mine shafts, where the temperature is a constant 73°F (23°C). Prospecting started in 1889, when kangaroo shooters found the colorful stones on the ground. A year later the rush was on and by the turn of the 20th century about 4,000 people were digging and sifting in a lawless, waterless hell of a place. White Cliffs is smaller than Coober Pedy and less touristy—which is its great charm. You also have a lot more freedom to wander around the old opal tailings here, whereas in Coober Pedy they discourage it. However, given the choice between White Cliffs and Lightning Ridge (below), I'd opt for the latter (though if you have time you should see both).

If you fancy an after-hours round of golf in the dirt (and who doesn't?), contact the secretary of the **White Cliffs Golf Club,** John Painter (© **08/8091 6715** after hours). He'll be happy to supply you with a golf club or two and a couple of balls for A$2 (US$1.30). Otherwise, put A$2 (US$1.30) in the black box at the first tee if you have your own clubs—but be warned, bush playing can damage your clubs, and crows often make off with the balls. Visitors can play day or night, but if you want some company, come on Sunday when club members shoot it out.

Today, the countryside looks like an inverted moonscape, pimpled with bone-white heaps of gritty clay dug from the 50,000 mine shafts that surround the town. These days, White Cliffs is renowned for its eccentricity. Take **Jock's Place,** for instance, an underground museum full to the beams with junk pulled from old mine shafts. Then there's a house made of beer flagons and a nine-hole **dirt golf course** where locals play at night with fluorescent green golf balls.

WHERE TO STAY: ABOVEGROUND & BELOW

One option is to rent a local cottage from **Broken Hill Historic Cottages** (© **08/8087 9966**) for A$80 (US$52) a night.

Finds **A Fabulous Place to Enjoy the Sunset**

Just outside Broken Hill in the **Living Desert Nature Park** is the best collection of sculptures this side of Stonehenge. Twelve sandstone obelisks, up to 3m (10 ft.) high and carved totemlike by artists from as far away as Georgia, Syria, Mexico, and the Tiwi Islands, make up the Sculpture Symposium. Surrounding them on all sides is brooding mulga scrub. It's fantastic at sunset.

Broken Hill Overlander Motor Inn   This is my favorite place to stay in Broken Hill, although admittedly that's not really saying much in this Outback town. It's set way back from the road, has nice green areas and barbecue facilities, and is very quiet. The more expensive AAA-rated four-star rooms are much nicer than the cheaper variants, and considerably larger. Two family rooms sleep up to six in a combination of single and queen-size beds. You can order off several menus supplied by local restaurants, and with the hotel supplying plates and cutlery.

142 Iodide St., Broken Hill, NSW 2880. (℃ 08/8088 2566. Fax 08/8088 4377. www.bestwestern.com.au/overlander. Reservations can be made through Best Western (℃ 800/780-7234 in the U.S. and Canada, 0800/39 3130 in the U.K., 0800/237 893 in New Zealand, or 13 17 79 in Australia). 15 units. A$85–A$135 (US$55–US$88) double; A$135 (US$88) 2-bed unit. Extra person A$10 (US$6.50). AE, DC, MC, V. **Amenities:** Small heated outdoor pool; sauna; tour desk; laundry service; dry cleaning; nonsmoking rooms. *In room:* A/C, TV, dataport, coffeemaker, fridge, hair dryer, iron.

Mario the Palace Hotel (Value   With its high painted walls, a mural of Botticelli's *Birth of Venus* on the ceiling two flights up, and an office crammed with stuffed animal heads and crabs, the Palace Hotel is an intriguing sanctuary for the night. The owners have put a lot of work into restoring the place. The more expensive doubles are larger and come with a small lounge area, but all are comfortable and cool. Ten double rooms come with an attached shower. The Priscilla Suite is famous because that's where the transvestites stayed in *The Adventures of Priscilla, Queen of the Desert.* Mario owned the place for "donkey's years," as he says, but he's now retired. It's still run by his family.

227 Argent St., Broken Hill, NSW 2880. (℃ 08/8088 1699. Fax 08/8087 6240. mariospalace@bigpond.com. 51 units, 10 with bathroom. A$44 (US$29) double without bathroom; A$53–A$70 (US$35–US$46) double with bathroom. Priscilla suite $90 (US$59) for 2. AE, MC, V. **Amenities:** Bar; dining room. *In room:* A/C, TV, fridge, coffeemaker, iron.

Underground Motel ★★   I love this place; it's worth making the scenic trip out to White Cliffs just to stay here for the night. All but two of the rooms are underground; they're reached by a maze of spacious tunnels dug out of the rock and sealed with epoxy-resin to keep out the damp and the dust. The temperature below ground is a constant 72°F (22°C), which is decidedly cooler than a summer day outside. Rooms are comfortable though basic, and toilets and showers are shared. Turn the light off, and it's dark as a cave. Every night guests sit around large tables and dig into the roast of the day. (Vegetarians are catered to, also.)

Smiths Hill, White Cliffs (P.O. Box 427), NSW 2836. (℃ 1800/021 154 in Australia, or 08/8091 6677. Fax 08/8091 6654. 30 units, none with bathroom. A$83 (US$54) double. A$25 (US$16) 3-course meal. Extra person A$24 (US$16). MC, V. **Amenities:** Restaurant; bar; small heated outdoor pool; coin-op laundry; nonsmoking rooms.

WHERE TO DINE

The best place for a meal Aussie-style is at one of the local clubs. You'll find one of the best bistros at the **Barrier Social & Democratic Club,** at 218 Argent St. (℃ **08/8088 4477**). It serves breakfast, lunch, and dinner. There's also a host of Chinese restaurants around town, including the **Oceania Chinese Restaurant** on Argent Street (℃ **08/8087 3695**), which has a A$7 (US$4.55) lunch special.

LIGHTNING RIDGE: OPALS GALORE ★★

793 (492 miles) NW of Sydney; 737km (457 miles) SW of Brisbane

Lightning Ridge, or "The Ridge" as the locals call it, is perhaps the most fascinating place to visit in all of New South Wales. Essentially, it's a hard-working opal-mining town stuck out in the arid far northern reaches of New South Wales—where summer temperatures hover around the 113°F (45°C) mark. Lightning Ridge thrives off the largest deposit of black opal in the world. Good quality opals can fetch a miner around A$8,000 (US$5,200) per carat, and stones worth upward of A$500,000 (US$325,000) each are not unheard of. Tourists come here to get a taste of life in Australia's "Wild West." A popular tourist activity in the opal fields is to pick over the old heaps of mine tailings. Stories (perhaps tall tales) abound of tourists finding overlooked opals worth thousands.

I strongly recommend you visit the **Grawin** and **Glengarry opal fields** ⋆⋆, both about an hour or so from Lightning Ridge on a dirt track suitable for two-wheel-drive cars in dry weather only. (Check with the Tourist Information Centre before you go.) These full-on frontier townships are bristling with drills and hoists pulling out bucket-loads of dirt and buzzing with news of the latest opal rush. If you can convince a local to take you there, all the better, as the tracks can be misleading. **Ando's Outback Tours** (see "Byron Bay: A Beach Bohemia," earlier in this chapter) takes in Glengarry and Lightning Ridge on its 5-day trip.

ESSENTIALS
GETTING THERE   From Sydney it takes about 9 hours to drive to Lightning Ridge, via Bathurst, Dubbo, and the fascinating town of Walgett. **Airlink** (© **02/6884 2435**) flies to Lightning Ridge from Sydney via Dubbo.

VISITOR INFORMATION   The **Lightning Ridge Tourist Information Centre** on Morilla Street, P.O. Box 1779, Lightning Ridge, NSW 2834 (© **02/ 6829 0565;** fax 02/6829 0565), is open Monday through Friday from 8:30am to 4pm. On weekends call © **02/6829 0429,** or e-mail lridge@walgettshire.com.

SPECIAL EVENTS   If you're in Australia around Easter, make sure you come to Lightning Ridge for the **Great Goat Race** and the rodeo. A decent website for information is www.lightningridge.net.au.

SEEING THE TOWN
Any visit to Lightning Ridge should start with an orientation trip with **Black Opal Tours** (© **02/6829 0368;** fax 02/6829 1206). The company offers a 5-hour tour of the opal fields for A$70 (US$46) per person. Three-hour morning tours cost A$35 (US$23), and slightly shorter afternoon tours A$30 (US$20).

Among the many points of interest is the 15m (49-ft.) tall homemade **Amigo's Castle,** which dominates the worked-out opal fields surrounding the modern township of Lightning Ridge. Complete with turrets, battlements, dungeons, and a wishing well, the castle has been rising out of these arid lands for the past 17 years, with every rock scavenged from the surrounding area and lugged in a wheelbarrow or in a rucksack on Amigo's back. The wonderful Amigo hasn't taken out insurance on the property, so there are no official tours, though if he feels like a bit of company he'll show you around.

The **Artesian Bore Baths,** 2km (1¼ mile) from the post office on Pandora Street, are free, open 24 hours a day, and said to have therapeutic value. The water temperature hovers between 104°F and 122°F (40°C–50°C). A visit at night when the stars are out is amazing.

The **Bevan's Black Opal & Cactus Nursery** (© **02/6829 0429**) contains more than 2,000 species of cactus and succulent plants, including rare specimens. Betty Bevan cuts opals from the family's mine, and many are on display. Admission is A$4 (US$2.60) to the cactus nursery, but free to see her opals.

There are plenty of opal shops, galleries, walk-in opal mines, and other distinctly unique things to see in Lightning Ridge. You might want to take a look at **Gemopal Pottery** (② **02/6829 0375**), on the road to the Bore Baths. The resident potter makes some nice pots out of clay mine tailings and lives in one of his five old Sydney railway carriages.

WHERE TO STAY & DINE

An interesting addition to the Lightning Ridge hotel scene is the **Lightning Ridge Hotel/Motel** (② **02/6829 0304;** www.lightning-ridge-hotel-motel.com), set in 4 hectares (10 acres) of Australian bush, complete with birdbath to attract the native parrots. There are 40 log cabins here as well as a trailer park (for your own trailer or motor home) and camping sites. Cabins cost A$46 (US$30) without bathroom, and A$52 (US$34) with a bathroom, and motel rooms A$60 (US$39) for a double, A$80 (US$52) for a triple, and A$122 (US$79) for a quad. If you want to stay at the Glengarry opal fields then your only option is at the **Glengarry Hilton,** a rustic outback pub (not associated with the major hotel chain). Here you stay in mobile units sleeping 24. A night costs A$12 (US$7.80).

The Wallangulla Motel   My choice of the four motels in town, the Wallangulla offers two standards of rooms, the cheaper ones being in an older section of the property. Newer rooms are better furnished and generally nicer; they're worth the extra money. Two large family rooms each have two bedrooms and a living room; one has a Jacuzzi. Guests can use the barbecue facilities, and there is an arrangement with the bowling club across the road for meals there to be charged back to your room. The Bowling Club has a restaurant with pretty good food and a very cheap bistro.

Morilla St. (at Agate St.), Lightning Ridge, NSW 2834. ② **02/6829 0542.** Fax 02/6829 0070. www.wj.com. au/wallangulla. 43 units. A$55–A$85 (US$36–US$55) double; A$75–A$95 (US$49–US$62) triple; A$95–A$110 (US$62–US$72) family room with Jacuzzi. AE, DC, MC, V. **Amenities:** Coin-op laundry; non-smoking rooms. *In room:* A/C, TV, coffeemaker.

Brisbane

by Lee Mylne

Queensland's capital is relaxed, laid-back, and subtropical. Set along the banks of the wide, brown Brisbane River, this is a city that has grown up in recent years, confident in its appeal. It's one of those places that people don't always appreciate until they spend time there but where the welcome is as warm as the weather. The city is green and leafy; Moreton Bay fig trees give shade, and in summer the purple haze of jacarandas competes with the scarlet blaze of poinciana trees. A mango tree in the backyard is practically de rigueur.

The theme parks are south of the city, on the Brisbane–Gold Coast corridor. Brisbane folk don't consider that a drawback. They'll urge you to discover the city, rich in history and character, and get to know the locals. That's easy; friendly folk of Queensland will start chatting with just about anyone.

Brisbane (pronounced *Briz*-bun) is known for its timber "Queenslanders," cottages and houses set high on stumps to catch the breeze, with wide verandas to keep out the midday sun. In some inner city suburbs, Queenslanders have been converted to trendy cafes and restaurants, or into shops selling antiques, clothes, and housewares.

In the city center, gracious colonial sandstone buildings stand next to modern glass towers. Wander in the city botanic gardens, in-line skate or bike along the riverfront pathways, have a drink in a pub beer garden, or get out on the river on a CityCat. There are several bridges across the river, the most famous and attractive being the Story Bridge, on the Town Reach of the river. Getting around is cheap and easy, good food—including fantastic seafood—is abundant, and accommodations are affordable, especially in some of the city's comfortable, elegant B&Bs.

Brisbane is on the southern coast of the state, flanked by the Sunshine Coast, about 2 hours to the north, and the Gold Coast, 1 hour to the south. The Brisbane River flows into Moreton Bay, dotted with beautiful islands you can explore.

1 Orientation

ARRIVING

BY PLANE About 20 international airlines fly into **Brisbane International Airport** from Europe, Asia, and New Zealand, including Qantas, Air New Zealand, Singapore Airlines, Thai International, Malaysia Airlines, and Cathay Pacific. From North America you will likely fly to Sydney and connect on one of several direct flights on Qantas, or fly direct from Auckland, in New Zealand.

Qantas (© **13 13 13** in Australia; www.qantas.com.au) operates daily flights from state capitals, Cairns, and several other regional towns. No-frills **Virgin Blue** (© **13 67 89** in Australia; www.virginblue.com.au) offers cheaper fares and services from all capital cities as well as Cairns, Townsville, Mackay and the

Gold Coast in Queensland; Coffs Harbour in New South Wales; and Launceston in Tasmania. **Brisbane International Airport** is 16km (10 miles) from the city, and the domestic terminal is 2km (1¼ miles) farther away. The Arrivals Floor, on Level 2, has an information desk open to meet all flights, help you with flight inquiries, dispense tourist information, and make your hotel bookings, and a check-in counter for passengers transferring to domestic flights.

Travelex currency-exchange bureaus are located on both the departures and arrivals floors. **Avis** (© 07/3860 4200), **Budget** (© 07/ 3860 4466), **Hertz** (© 07/3860 4522), and **Thrifty** (© 1300/367 227) have desks on Level 2; in the airport there is also a free-call board connecting you to smaller local car-rental companies that sometimes offer better rates. Free showers and baby change rooms are located on Levels 2, 3, and 4; Level 4 has an ATM.

The domestic terminal has a Travelex currency-exchange bureau, showers, and the big four car-rental desks. (Call the telephone numbers above.) An interterminal shuttle runs every 15 to 20 minutes and is free if you have an airline ticket or costs A$2.70 (US$1.70) otherwise, or you can catch Airtrain, which costs A$3 (US$1.95).

Due to current security measures, lockers at both airport terminals are only available by contacting airport staff. Details are posted on the lockers, which cost A$6 to A$11 (US$3.90–US$7.15) for 24 hours.

Coachtrans (© 07/3860 6999; www.coachtrans.com.au) runs a shuttle between the airport and Roma Street Transit Centre every 15 minutes from 5am to 7:30pm and every 30 minutes from 7:30 to 10pm. The cost is A$9 (US$5.85) per person one-way or A$11 (US$7.15) for hotel drop-off. Return fare is A$15 (US$9.75) or A$17 (US$11). Family tickets are A$24 (US$16) or A$29 (US$19) one-way. The trip takes about 40 minutes, reservations not needed. No public buses serve the airport. A taxi to the city costs around A$20 (US$13) from the international terminal and A$25 (US$16) from the domestic terminal, plus A$2 (US$1.30) for departing taxis.

Airtrain (© 07/3211 2855; www.airtrain.com.au), a rail link between the city and Brisbane's domestic and international airport terminals, runs every 15 minutes from 5:30am to 9pm daily, with a fare from Central Station to the airport costing A$9 (US$5.85) adults, A$4.50 (US$2.90) children, or A$22 (US$14) for a group of four (only from airport stations) and taking about 20 minutes. Airtrain also links the airport with the Gold Coast.

BY TRAIN   **Queensland Rail** (© 13 22 32 in Queensland; www.qr.com.au) operates several long-distance trains to Brisbane from Cairns. The fast new Tilt Train takes about 25 hours and costs A$280 (US$182) for a business class fare. The slower Sunlander takes 32 hours and costs A$187 (US$122) for a sitting berth, A$235 (US$153) for an economy-class sleeper, A$352 (US$229) for a first-class sleeper, or A$646 (US$420) for the all-inclusive Queenslander class. **Countrylink** (© 13 22 32 in Australia; www.countrylink.nsw.gov.au) runs daily train service to Brisbane from Sydney. The 14-hour trip from Sydney costs A$110 to A$154 (US$72–US$100) in a sitting berth, and A$231 (US$150) for a sleeper. Be sure to book the through-service; some services transfer to coach in Murwillumbah, south of the border, tacking an extra 2 hours to the trip. This train/coach service has no sleepers.

All intercity and interstate trains pull into **Brisbane Transit Centre at Roma Street** (in the city center), often called the Roma Street Transit Centre. From here,

Greater Brisbane

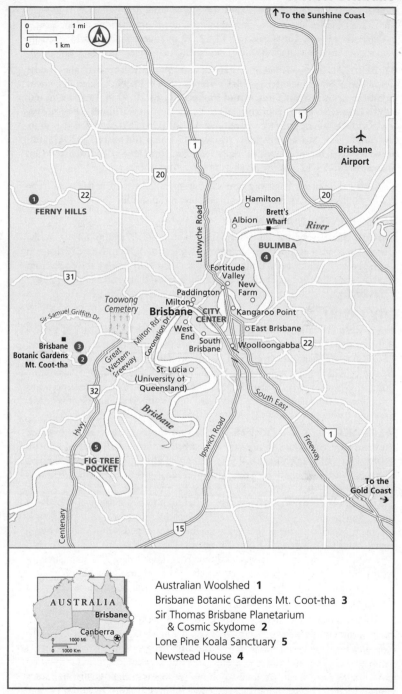

0 | 1 mi
0 | 1 km

↑ To the Sunshine Coast

1
FERNY HILLS

22

20

Lutwyche Road

1

20

✈
Brisbane
Airport

Hamilton

Albion
Brett's
Wharf

River

BULIMBA
4

31

Toowong Cemetery

Sir Samuel Griffith Dr.

Brisbane
Botanic Gardens
Mt. Coot-tha
3
2

Fortitude Valley

Paddington
Milton

New Farm

Brisbane
CITY CENTER

Kangaroo Point

Great Western Freeway

Milton Rd.

Coronation Dr.

West End

South Brisbane

East Brisbane

Woolloongabba

22

32

St. Lucia
(University of Queensland)

Brisbane

Ipswich Road

South East

Freeway

1

5
FIG TREE POCKET

Centenary Hwy.

15

To the
Gold Coast
→

AUSTRALIA

Brisbane

Canberra ★

0 | 1000 Mi
0 | 1000 Km

Australian Woolshed **1**
Brisbane Botanic Gardens Mt. Coot-tha **3**
Sir Thomas Brisbane Planetarium
 & Cosmic Skydome **2**
Lone Pine Koala Sanctuary **5**
Newstead House **4**

most city and Spring Hill hotels are a few blocks' walk or a quick cab ride away. The Transit Centre has food outlets, showers, tourist information, and lockers.

Queensland Rail CityTrain (© **13 12 30** in Queensland) provides a daily train service from the Sunshine Coast, and plentiful services from the Gold Coast.

BY BUS   All intercity and interstate coaches pull into the Brisbane Transit Centre (see "By Train," above). **McCafferty's** (© **13 14 99** in Australia; www.mccaffertys.com.au) and **Greyhound Pioneer** (© **13 20 30** in Australia, or 07/3258 1670; www.greyhound.com.au) serve the city several times daily. A one-way Cairns-Brisbane ticket costs around A$192 (US$125), and the trip takes 28½ hours. The Sydney-Brisbane trip takes 18 hours and costs A$93 (US$60) one-way. Coachtrans provides daily services from the Gold Coast. Call **Transinfo** (© **13 12 30**) for details.

BY CAR   The Bruce Highway from Cairns enters the city from the north. The Pacific Highway enters Brisbane from Sydney in the south.

VISITOR INFORMATION

Brisbane Marketing has an information booth (© **07/3006 6290**) in the Queen Street Mall at Albert Street, open from 9am to 5:30pm Monday through Thursday, to 7pm or later Friday, and 4pm Saturday; Sunday it's open from 10am to 4pm. The Roma Street Transit Centre is another source of info (© **07/3236 2020**).

CITY LAYOUT

The city center's office towers shimmer in the sun on the north bank of a curve of the Brisbane River. In the tip of the curve are the lush Brisbane City Gardens. The 30m (98 ft.) sandstone cliffs of Kangaroo Point rise on the eastern side of the south bank; to the west are the South Bank Parklands and the Queensland Cultural Centre, known as South Bank. The Goodwill Bridge (for pedestrians only) links South Bank with the City Gardens. To the west 5km (3 miles), Mt. Coot-tha (pronounced *Coo*-tha) looms out of the flat plain.

MAIN ARTERIES & STREETS   It's easy to find your way around central Brisbane once you know all the east-west streets are named after female British royalty, and all the north-south streets are named after their male counterparts. The most northerly is Ann, followed by Adelaide, Queen, Elizabeth, Charlotte, Mary, Margaret, and Alice. From east to west, the streets are Edward, Albert, George, and William, which becomes North Quay, flanking the river's northeast bank.

Queen Street, the main thoroughfare, becomes a pedestrian mall between Edward and George streets. Roma Street exits the city diagonally to the northwest. Ann Street leads all the way east into Fortitude Valley. The main street in Fortitude Valley is Brunswick Street, which runs right into New Farm.

A new pedestrian bridge links the Brisbane City Gardens (off Alice St.) to the eastern end of South Bank Parklands.

STREET MAPS   The **Brisbane Map,** free from Brisbane Marketing (see "Visitor Information," above) or your concierge, is a lightweight map that shows the river and outlying suburbs, as well as the city. It's great for drivers because it shows parking lots and one-way traffic directions on the confusing city-center grid. Rental cars usually come with street directories. Newsagents and some bookstores sell this map, and the state auto club, the **R.A.C.Q.,** in the General Post Office, 261 Queen St. (© **13 19 05**), is also a good source.

NEIGHBORHOODS IN BRIEF

City Center The vibrant city center is where residents eat, shop, and socialize. Queen Street Mall, in the heart of town, is popular with shoppers and moviegoers, especially on weekends and Friday nights (when stores stay open until 9pm). The Eagle Street financial/legal office precinct houses some great restaurants with river views, and on Sundays there are markets by the Riverside Centre office tower and the Pier. Much of Brisbane's colonial architecture is in the city center, too. Strollers, bike riders, and in-line skaters shake the summer heat in the green haven of the Brisbane City Gardens at the business district's southern end.

Fortitude Valley Ten years ago, this suburb of derelict warehouses just east of the city center was one of the sleazier parts of town. Today, "the Valley" is a stamping ground for street-smart young folk who meet in restored pubs and eat in cool cafes. The lanterns, food stores, and shopping mall of Chinatown are here, too. Take Turbot Street to the Valley's Brunswick Street.

New Farm Always an appealing suburb, New Farm is becoming the city's "in" spot for cafe-hopping, shopping, and cinema-going. Merthyr Street is where the action is, especially on Friday and Saturday nights. From the intersection of Wickham and Brunswick streets, follow Brunswick southeast for 13 blocks to Merthyr.

Paddington This hilltop suburb, a couple of miles northwest of the city, is one of the most attractive in Brisbane. Brightly painted Queenslander cottages line the main street, Latrobe Terrace, as it winds west along a ridge top. Many of the houses have been turned into shops and cafes, where you can browse, enjoy coffee and cake, or just admire the charming architecture.

Milton & Rosalie Park Road in Milton might not quite be a little bit of Europe, but it tries hard—even right down to a replica Eiffel Tower above the cafes and shops. Italian restaurants line the street, buzzing with white-collar office workers who down cappuccinos at alfresco restaurants, scout interior design stores for a new objet d'art to grace the living room, and stock up on European designer rags. A few minutes' drive away, Baroona Road and Nash Street (in Rosalie) are doing their best to catch up.

West End This small inner-city enclave is alive with ethnic restaurants, cafes, and the odd, interesting housewares or fashion store. Most action is centered at the intersection of Vulture and Boundary streets, where Asian grocers and delis abound.

Bulimba One of the emerging fashionable suburbs, Bulimba has a long connection with the river through the boat-building industry. One of the nicest ways to get there is by CityCat. Oxford Street is the main drag, around which trendy cafes and shops are springing up.

2 Getting Around

BY PUBLIC TRANSPORTATION

Bus, train, and ferry services are all run by **Brisbane Transport**. For timetable and route inquiries, call **Transinfo** (© **13 12 30;** www.transinfo.qld.gov.au; 6am–9pm Mon–Fri; 7am–9pm weekends). The most convenient places to buy

Brisbane Accommodations, Dining & Attractions

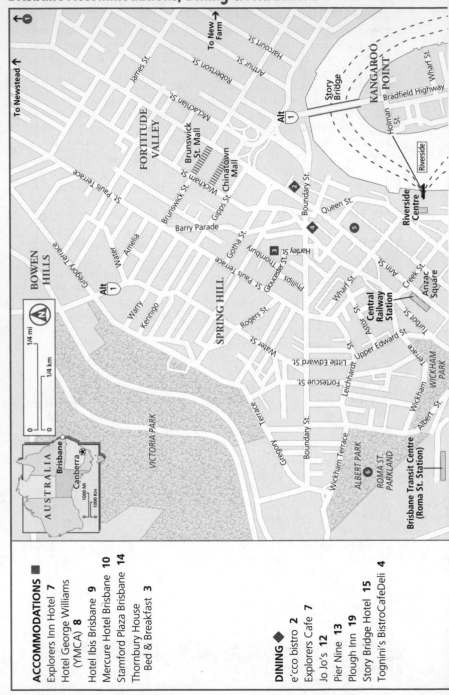

ACCOMMODATIONS ■

Explorers Inn Hotel **7**

Hotel George Williams (YMCA) **8**

Hotel Ibis Brisbane **9**

Mercure Hotel Brisbane **10**

Stamford Plaza Brisbane **14**

Thornbury House Bed & Breakfast **3**

DINING ◆

e'cco bistro **2**

Explorers Cafe **7**

Jo Jo's **12**

Pier Nine **13**

Plough Inn **19**

Story Bridge Hotel **15**

Tognini's BistroCafeDeli **4**

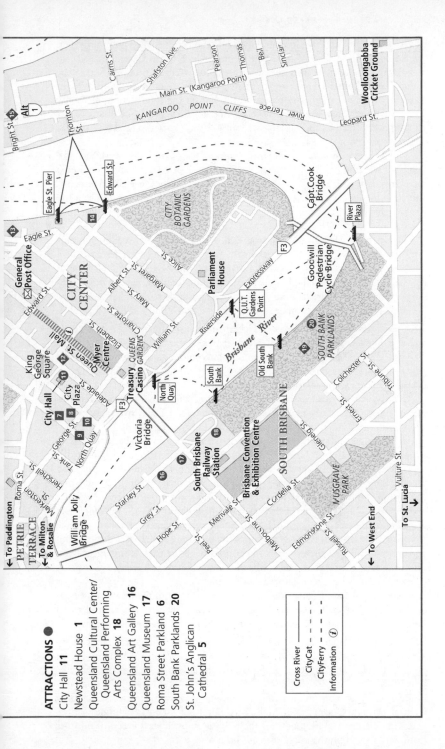

ATTRACTIONS ●

City Hall **11**
Newstead House **1**
Queensland Cultural Center/
Queensland Performing
Arts Complex **18**
Queensland Art Gallery **16**
Queensland Museum **17**
Roma Street Parkland **6**
South Bank Parklands **20**
St. John's Anglican
Cathedral **5**

Cross River	——
CityCat	– – –
CityFerry	– – –
Information	ⓘ

passes and to pick up timetables and maps are the Brisbane Transport outlets on the Elizabeth Street level of the Myer Centre, which fronts Queen Street Mall; at Brisbane Transport's Brisbane Administration Centre, 69 Ann St.; at the Roma Street Transit Centre; or at Brisbane Marketing's kiosk in the Queen Street Mall. You can also buy passes on the bus, at the train station, or on the CityCat or ferry. Any news agency displaying a yellow-and-white BUS & FERRY TICKETS SOLD HERE banner sells passes, but not train passes, special tour tickets, or family passes.

A single sector or zone on the bus, train, or ferry costs A$1.80 (US$1.15). Whether traveling with a parent on a single ticket or a pass, kids under age 5 travel free, kids ages 5 to 15 pay half fare; all seniors except Queensland residents and all students pay full fare. If you plan on using the buses and ferries a lot, weekly passes and Ten Trip Saver tickets are available from the outlets described above.

The **Brisbane Mobility Map,** produced by the Brisbane City Council, outlines wheelchair access to buildings in the city center, and includes a detailed guide to the Queen Street Mall and a map of the Brisbane Botanic Gardens at Mt. Coot-tha. The council's disability services unit also has a range of other publications including a Braille Trail and an access guide to parks. These can all be obtained from council customer service centers (© **07/3403 8888**).

TRANSPORT PASSES   A 1-2-3 Ticket can be used for up to 2 hours on a one-way journey with any combination of bus, train, or ferry, and only costs A$3.80 (US$2.45). There are limits to how far you can go on the trains, but the pass will get you as far as the Australian Woolshed at Ferny Grove, which is probably as far as you will be traveling anyhow.

It's possible you won't use trains to get around Brisbane, as most attractions are on the bus and ferry networks. In that case, get a Day Rover pass, which allows unlimited travel on buses, CityCats, and ferries for A$8.40 (US$5.50).

On weekends and public holidays, it's cheaper to buy an Off-Peak Saver pass, which lets you travel on buses all day for A$4.60 (US$3) for adults. The Off-Peak Saver is also available on weekdays, but remember to plan your sightseeing around the fact that it cannot be used before 9am or between 3:30 and 7pm. And it can't be used on CityCats or ferries.

Note that Day Rover and Off-Peak Saver passes can't be used on tour buses like City Sights (see "Organized Tours," later in this chapter).

If you see peak-hour buses displaying a full-fare-only sign, that does not mean you cannot travel on them with a discounted ticket or pass. It just means you cannot purchase a ticket or pass on the bus; you will have to purchase your ticket or pass from a ticket agent before boarding the bus.

The excellent **City Sights** bus tour entitles you to unlimited travel on buses, ferries, and CityCats for the day, and at the same time gets you around to 19 points of interest—see "Organized Tours," later in this chapter, for details.

BY BUS   Buses operate from around 5am to 11pm weekdays, with fewer services on weekends. On Sunday, many routes stop around 5pm. Most buses depart from City Hall at King George Square, from Adelaide or Ann streets. The Downtown Loop is a free bus service that circles the city center. The Loop's distinctive red buses run on two routes stopping at convenient places including Central Station, Queen Street Mall, City Botanic Gardens, Riverside Centre, and King George Square. Look for the red bus stops. It runs every 10 minutes from 7am to 5:50pm Monday through Friday.

BY FERRY   The fast **CityCat** ferries run to many places of interest, including South Bank and the Queensland Cultural Centre; the restaurants and Sunday markets at the Riverside Centre; and New Farm Park, not far from the cafes of Merthyr Street. They run every half-hour between Queensland University, approximately 9km (5½ miles) along the river to the south, and Brett's Wharf, about 9km (5½ miles) to the north. Slower but more frequent Inner City and Cross-River ferries stop at a few more points, including the south end of South Bank Parklands, Kangaroo Point, and Edward Street right outside the City Botanic Gardens. Ferries run from around 6am to 10:30pm daily.

To stop people from riding the CityCats all day—a real temptation—you cannot travel on them for more than 2 hours at a time, even with a transit pass; you are free to do another 2 hours later in the day if you wish. Two hours on the CityCat takes you the entire length of the run.

BY TRAIN   Brisbane's suburban rail network is fast, quiet, safe, and clean. Trains run from around 5am to midnight, stopping at about 11pm on Sundays. All trains leave Central Station, between Turbot and Ann streets at Edward Street.

BY CAR OR TAXI

Brisbane's grid of one-way streets can be confusing, so plan your route before you set off. Brisbane's biggest car park is at the Myer Centre (enter from Elizabeth St.) and is open 24 hours (© **07/3229 1699**). Most hotels and motels have free parking for guests.

Avis (© **13 63 33** or 07/3221 2900), **Budget** (© **1300/362 848** in Australia, or 07/3220 0699), and **Hertz** (© **13 30 39** or 07/3221 6166) all have outlets in the city center. **Thrifty** (© **1300/367 227**) is on the edge of the city center at 49 Barry Parade, Fortitude Valley.

For a taxi, call **Yellow Cabs** (© **13 19 24** in Australia) or **Black and White Taxis** (© **13 10 08** in Australia). There are taxi stands at each end of Queen Street Mall, on Edward Street and George Street (outside the Treasury Casino).

 FAST FACTS: Brisbane

American Express   The office at 131 Elizabeth St. (© **1300/139 060**) cashes traveler's checks, exchanges foreign currency, and refunds lost traveler's checks.

Business Hours   Banks are open Monday through Thursday from 9:30am to 4pm, until 5pm on Friday. See "The Shopping Scene," later in this chapter, for store hours. Some restaurants close Monday and/or Tuesday nights, and bars are generally open from 10 or 11am until midnight.

Currency Exchange   **Travelex**, Lennons Plaza, Queen Street Mall between Albert and George streets (© **07/3229 8610;** www.travelex.com.au), is open Monday through Friday from 9am to 6pm, Saturday from 9:30am to 5pm, and Sunday from 10:30am to 4:30pm.

Dentist   The **Adelaide and Albert Dental Centre** (© **07/3229 4121**), located next to the Travellers Medical Service (see "Doctor," below), is open Monday through Friday from 8am to 6pm.

Doctor   **Travellers Medical Service** is at 245 Albert St. (at Adelaide St.), opposite City Hall (© **07/3211 3611;** www.travmed.com.au). It's open

Monday through Friday from 7:30am to 7pm, Saturday from 9am to 5pm, and Sunday from 10am to 4pm; for after-hours emergencies call © 0412/ 452 400.

Drugstores (Chemist Shops) **Queen Street Mall Day & Night Pharmacy,** 141 Queen Street Mall (© 07/3221 4585), is open Monday through Thursday from 7am to 9pm, Friday from 7am to 9:30pm, Saturday from 8am to 9pm, Sunday from 8:30am to 5:30pm, and public holidays from 9am to 7:30pm. There is also a pharmacy under the Travellers Medical Service (see "Doctor," above).

Embassies/Consulates The United States, Canada, and New Zealand have no representation in Brisbane; see chapter 3, "Sydney," for those countries' nearest offices. The British Consul General is at Level 26, Waterfront Place, 1 Eagle St. (© 07/3223 3200).

Emergencies Dial © 000 for fire, ambulance, or police help in an emergency. This is a free call from a private or public telephone.

Hospitals The nearest one is **Royal Brisbane Hospital,** about a 15-minute drive from the city at Herston Road, Herston (© 07/3636 8111).

Hot Lines **Lifeline** (© 13 11 14) is a 24-hour emotional crisis counseling service.

Internet Access **Dial Up Cyber Lounge,** in the Mayfair Arcade, 126 Adelaide St. (© 07/3211 9095), is open from 10am to 7pm Monday through Thursday and Saturday, and to 8pm Friday. In Paddington, **The Computer Café,** 107 Latrobe Terrace (© 07/3368 3190), above Woolworths, is open Monday, Tuesday, and Thursday from 10am to 9pm, and Wednesday, Friday, and Saturday from 10am to 6pm. There's also Internet access at the **South Bank Information Centre,** open from 9am to 5:30pm Saturday to Thursday and until 8:30pm Fridays, for A$2 (US$1.30) per 15 minutes.

Luggage Storage/Lockers **The Brisbane Transit Centre** on Roma Street (© 1800/632 640) has baggage lockers.

Newspapers/Magazines The *Courier-Mail* (Mon–Sat) and the *Sunday Mail* are Brisbane's daily newspapers. The free weekly *Brisbane News* is a good guide to dining, entertainment, and shopping.

Police Dial © 000 in an emergency, or © 07/3364 6464 for police headquarters. Police are stationed 24 hours a day in the Pavilion Arcade, at 130 Queen Street (in the Queen St. Mall), near Albert Street (© 07/3224 4444).

Safety Brisbane is relatively crime free, but as in any large city, personal safety should be considered especially when out at night. Stick to well-lit streets and busy precincts.

Time Zone Brisbane is Greenwich Mean Time plus 10 hours. It does not observe daylight saving time, which means it's on the same time as Sydney and Melbourne in winter, and 1 hour behind those cities October through March, when they go to daylight saving. For the exact local time, call © 1194.

Weather Call © 1196 for the southeast Queensland weather forecast.

3 Where to Stay

IN THE CITY CENTER
VERY EXPENSIVE

Stamford Plaza Brisbane ⭐⭐⭐   The Stamford is one of Brisbane's most beautiful hotels; its marble lobby is dotted with brocade chairs and sofas, enormous still-life oils, gilt mirrors, and palms. It's also one of the few city hotels to have river views from every room—especially stunning at night from the southern rooms when the Story Bridge lights up. The plush rooms are not enormous, but all fit a king-size bed or two twins. What must be the biggest bathrooms in Brisbane sport small TVs. A riverside boardwalk leads from the hotel to the Eagle Street Pier restaurants, and the Brisbane City Gardens abut the hotel. In an historic sandstone building adjacent to the hotel is one of Brisbane's grandest fine-dining restaurants, **Siggi's,** which also boasts a wine bar where you can puff on cigars with your cognac.

Edward and Margaret sts. (adjacent to the Brisbane City Gardens), Brisbane, QLD 4000. ⓒ **1800/773 700** in Australia, or 07/3221 1999. Fax 07/3221 6895. www.stamford.com.au. 252 units. A$415 (US$270) double; A$630–A$3,080 (US$410–US$2,002) suite. Extra person A$38 (US$25). Children under 12 stay free in parent's room with existing bedding. Ask about packages. AE, DC, MC, V. Free valet parking. Train: Central, then taxi or walk 6 blocks. Bus: Downtown Loop. Ferry: Edward St. **Amenities:** 3 restaurants; 3 bars; smallish outdoor heated lap pool and sun deck; health club; Jacuzzi; sauna; bike rental; concierge; tour desk; car-rental desk; business center; salon; 24-hr. room service; in-room massage; babysitting; same-day dry cleaning; 24-hr. butler service; nonsmoking rooms. *In room:* A/C, TV/VCR w/pay movies, dataport, minibar, coffeemaker, hair dryer, iron.

EXPENSIVE

Mercure Hotel Brisbane ⭐   Sweeping views of the Brisbane River come with many rooms at this bright 14-story hotel (given four stars by AAA) across the water from South Bank. A A$3 million (US$1.9 million) refurbishment of all rooms in late 2002 has given them a fresh, contemporary look in red and cream. The four suites have river views, and the standard rooms are comfortable and unassuming. Rooms without water views have nice city views. Roma Street Transit Centre, Queen Street Mall, South Bank Parklands, and the Queensland Cultural Centre are a short walk away.

85–87 North Quay (between Ann and Turbot sts.), Brisbane, QLD 4000. ⓒ **1300/65 6565** in Australia, or 800/221-4542 In the U.S. and Canada, 020/8283 4500 in the U.K., 0800/44 4422 in New Zealand, or 07/3236 3300. Fax 07/3236 1035. www.mercurebrisbane.com.au. 194 units. A$137–A$226 (US$89–US$147) double; A$207–A$266 (US$135–US$173) studio suite; A$237–A$296 (US$154–US$192) executive suite. Extra person A$36 (US$23). Children under 16 stay free in parent's room with existing bedding. Ask about packages. AE, DC, MC, V. Parking A$10 (US$6.50) per day. Airport shuttle. Train: Roma St. Bus: Downtown Loop. Ferry: North Quay (CityCat and CityFerry). **Amenities:** Restaurant; bar; outdoor heated pool; access to nearby health club; car-rental desk; concierge; 24-hr. room service; babysitting; dry cleaning; nonsmoking rooms. *In room:* A/C, TV w/pay movies, minibar, coffeemaker, hair dryer, iron.

MODERATE

Hotel Ibis Brisbane   What you get is what you pay for at this three-star sister property to the Mercure, around the corner (see above). In this case, it is basically a room, with few amenities you might expect in a large hotel. But if you don't mind doing without river views, porters, pool, or other small luxuries, this could be the place for you. Rebuilt inside an office building in 1998, the hotel has rooms furnished in a contemporary decor with sizable work desks and small but smart bathrooms.

27–35 Turbot St. (between North Quay and George St.), Brisbane, QLD 4000. ⓒ **1300/65 6565** in Australia, or 800/221-4542 in the U.S. and Canada, 020/8283 4500 in the U.K., 0800/44 4422 in New Zealand, or

07/3237 2333. Fax 07/3237 2444. www.accorhotels.com.au. 218 units. A$109 (US$71) double. Extra person A$30 (US$20). Children under 16 stay free in parent's room with existing bedding. Ask about packages. AE, DC, MC, V. Parking at Mercure Hotel Brisbane (see above) at A$10 (US$6.50) per day. Airport shuttle. Train: Roma St. Bus: Downtown Loop. Ferry: North Quay (CityCat and CityFerry). **Amenities:** Restaurant (breakfast, dinner only); coin-op laundry and laundry service; nonsmoking rooms. *In room:* A/C, TV w/pay movies, fridge, coffeemaker, hair dryer, iron.

INEXPENSIVE

Explorers Inn Hotel 🍂   You'll be astonished to find such spruce decor and terrific value in one place—and in the heart of the city! Each tiny room at this former YWCA was designed by its architect owners to contain just the necessities—including a narrow desk. The front desk lends hair dryers and the friendly staff will help with booking tours and sending e-mails. All of the rooms are non-smoking, but there is a smokers' lounge. Downstairs is the good-value **Explorers Cafe** restaurant and bar (p. 244). South Bank, the casino, the Roma Street Transit Centre, and Queen Street Mall are all close by.

63 Turbot St. (near George St.), Brisbane, QLD 4000. ℂ 1800/623 288 in Australia, or 07/3211 3488. Fax 07/3211 3499. www.explorers.com.au. 58 units (all with shower only). A$75–A$97 (US$49–US$63) double; A$97 (US$63) family (sleeps 4). AE, DC, MC, V. Train: Roma St. Bus: Downtown Loop. **Amenities:** Restaurant; tour desk; car-rental desk; secretarial services; coin-op laundry and laundry service; dry-cleaning; nonsmoking rooms. *In room:* A/C, TV, fridge, coffeemaker.

Hotel George Williams 🍂   It's hard to believe this smart 4-year-old hotel is a YMCA. Rooms have vivid bedcovers, chrome chairs, and artsy bedside lamps on chrome stands. Rooms are small, but can accommodate up to four adults. Among the useful facilities are a 24-hour front desk, safe-deposit boxes, and a hip cybercafe. Hair dryers are available on request. Four rooms are designed for guests with disabilities, and there is access for those with disabilities to the gym and elevators. The City Y health club is the largest hotel gym in Australia, and offers free aerobics classes to guests, personal trainers, and massages.

317–325 George St. (between Turbot and Ann sts.), Brisbane, QLD 4000. ℂ 1800/064 858 or 07/3308 0700. Fax 07/3308 0733. www.hgw.com.au. 55 units (most with shower only). A$92–A$96 (US$60–US$62) double; additional person A$22 (US$14). Children 4 and under stay free. Ask about packages. AE, DC, MC, V. Free secure covered parking. Airport shuttle. Train: Roma St. Bus: Downtown Loop. Ferry: North Quay (CityCat and CityFerry). **Amenities:** Restaurant; bar; health club; tour desk; car-rental desk; babysitting; coin-op laundry with iron and ironing board; laundry service; same-day dry cleaning; nonsmoking rooms. *In room:* A/C, TV, fridge, coffeemaker.

Thornbury House Bed & Breakfast 🍂 *Finds*   A 15-minute walk to Spring Hill from the city center brings you to this 1886 Queenslander cottage on a quiet street. Owner Michelle Bugler has decked out every room individually with Oriental rugs, comfortable beds, bathrobes, and lovely old furniture and knickknacks. Those without en suite bathrooms have their own pretty, clean private bathrooms down the hall. Downstairs is a self-contained apartment with contemporary decor. Breakfast is served in the ferny courtyard (a cool and restful place on a humid day), where you can help yourself to tea, coffee, cookies, and the newspaper any time of day.

In early 2003, Michelle opened a second B&B, **Eton** (ℂ **07/3236 0115;** www.babs.com.au/eton), in a Heritage-listed cottage at 436 Upper Roma St., Brisbane, not far from the Brisbane Transit Centre. It's similar in style and price to Thornbury, with five rooms and an attic suite (sleeps three). Ask for room no. 1, at the front of the house, for its claw-foot bathtub and king-size bed. My pick is Eton, but Thornbury's location is quieter and more residential.

1 Thornbury St., Spring Hill, Brisbane, QLD 4000. (C) **07/3832 5985.** Fax 07/3832 7756. www.babs.com.au/ thornbury. 6 units, all with bathroom (5 with shower only). A$110–A$120 (US$72–US$78) double; A$420 (US$273) apt weekly. Rates include breakfast. AE, MC, V. Limited free off-street parking and on-street meter parking A$5 (US$3.25) per day. Airport bus stop at front door. Train: Central. **Amenities:** Dinner on request; access to nearby swimming pools, golf club, and health club; children's play area and toys; room service (8am–8pm); dry cleaning; free access to washing machine, dryer, iron, fridge and microwave; fax, computer and dataport available; pay phone; nonsmoking rooms. *In room:* A/C, TV, hair dryer.

IN PADDINGTON

Waverley (★★ *Finds*   On the main shopping and restaurant strip in Paddington, this lovely three-story 1888 residence retains most of its original features such as bay windows, tongue-and-groove walls, soaring ceilings, and polished timber floors. The two air-conditioned front rooms are freshly painted, spacious, and individually furnished with supportive mattresses, comfy sofas, and attractive bathrooms. You can also stay in two self-contained apartments (with fans) downstairs. Your hostess, Annette Henry, cooks a hearty breakfast in the homey yellow kitchen. (Her fresh muffins are popular.) A rear deck on both levels overlooks two old mango trees, busy with possums at night and visited regularly by day by a pair of native butcher-birds. There's also a lounge. No smoking indoors.

5 Latrobe Terrace at Cochrane St., Paddington, Brisbane, QLD 4064. (C) **07/3369 8973,** or 0419/741 282 mobile phone. Fax 07/3876 6655. www.babs.com.au/paddington. 4 units (all with en-suite shower only). A$110 (US$72) double; A$440 (US$286) self-contained apts per week. Additional person A$25 (US$16) extra. Rates include full breakfast for B&B guests. AE, DC, MC, V. Free off-street parking for 4 cars. Bus stop 20m (65 ft.). Pickup available on request from Roma St. Transit Centre. **Amenities:** Coin-op laundry; safe; nonsmoking rooms. *In room:* A/C, TV, kitchenette (apts only), refrigerator, coffeemaker, hair dryer, iron.

4 Where to Dine

Visitors are often surprised to find Brisbane has a sophisticated dining scene. Stylish bistros and cafes line Merthyr Street in New Farm; cute cafes are plentiful in Paddington; Asian eateries are a good choice around the intersection of Vulture Street and Boundary Street in West End; and in Fortitude Valley ("the Valley" for short), you'll find Chinatown. There's a street full of upscale but laid-back restaurants under the kitsch replica Eiffel Tower on Park Road in Milton, many with a Mediterranean flavor, and in the city center you can find slick riverfront restaurants at Eagle Street Pier and Riverside. The intersection of Albert and Charlotte streets buzzes with inexpensive, good-quality cafes.

IN THE CITY CENTER
EXPENSIVE

e'cco bistro (★★★ MODERN AUSTRALIAN   "Here it is" is one of the Italian translations for *e'cco,* and that's the philosophy behind the food at this multi-award–winning bistro. Simple food, done exceptionally well. E'cco counts the title of Australia's top restaurant award (the Remy Martin Cognac/Gourmet Traveller Restaurant of the Year) among its claims to fame and deservedly so. Set in a former tea warehouse on the city fringe, it is enormously popular, and bookings are essential. Large windows, bold colors, and modern furniture make it a pleasant setting in a small but popular restaurant enclave. There's a nice, simple price structure (each course's offerings are all the same price), and there's an extensive wine list—many by the glass. You can BYO wine for a corkage fee of A$5.50 (US$3.60) per bottle.

100 Boundary St. (at Adelaide St.). (C) **07/3831 8344.** Fax 07/3831 8460. www.eccobistro.com. Reservations required. Main courses A$30 (US$19). AE, DC, MC, V. Tues–Fri noon–2:30pm; Tues–Sat 6–10pm. Also open Mon mid-Nov to Christmas. Closed for 10 days from Christmas. On-street meter parking.

Pier Nine 🅠🅠🅠 MODERN AUSTRALIAN/SEAFOOD   Ask the locals for the best seafood in town, and this light-filled contemporary restaurant overlooking the river and Story Bridge is where they'll send you. The menu changes daily, but the specialties include fresh local Moreton Bay bugs (a kind of crustacean) and oysters shucked to order and served several ways or au naturel for the purist. Another is Tasmanian salmon, and I'm a fan of the spanner crab omelet. It's always busy, so prepare to cool your heels at the oyster bar if you turn up without a reservation.

Eagle St. Pier, 1 Eagle St. ℂ 07/3229 2194. www.piernine.com.au. Reservations recommended. Main courses A$21–A$40 (US$14–US$26). AE, DC, MC, V. Daily 11:30am–10pm, but the oyster bar is open (with a supper menu) until midnight. Ferry: Riverside (CityCat); Edward St. or Riverside (CityFerry); Eagle Street Pier (Cross River Ferry). Underground parking, but charges are steep.

MODERATE

Jo Jo's INTERNATIONAL/CAFE FARE   A spectacular timber, limestone, and glass bar dominates the center of this casual cafe-style eating spot, housing more than 1,000 bottles of wine. Four different menus—chargrill, Thai, pizza, and Mediterranean—are on offer, and the locals have been dropping in here for years to make a shopping pit stop, or to eat after the cinema. The food is well priced and good. You order at the bar, but meals are delivered to the table (try to get one on the balcony overlooking the Queen St. Mall). Among your options are steaks and seafood from the grill; curries and stir-fries from the Thai menu; pastas, antipasto and designer sandwiches from the Mediterranean; and gourmet toppings for the wood-fired oven pizzas.

1st floor, Queen St. Mall at Albert St. ℂ 07/3221 2113. www.jojos.com.au. Reservations not needed. Main courses A$8–A$27 (US$5.20–US$18). AE, DC, MC, V. Daily 9:30am–midnight; happy hour daily 4:30–6pm. Central Station.

INEXPENSIVE

Explorers Cafe *Value* CAFE FARE   After 6 years with one of the best-value a la carte menus in town, this basement restaurant under the Explorers Inn (p. 242) continues to offer great value, with all meals under A$17 (US$11). There are soups, pasta, seafood, steaks, and chicken dishes, with a choose-and-pay-at-the-counter format but with table service. There are vegetarian and gluten-free dishes on the lunch and dinner menus.

63 Turbot St. (near corner of George St.). ℂ 07/3211 3488. Fax 07/3211 3499. www.explorers.com.au. Reservations recommended at lunch. Main courses A$10–A$17 (US$6.55–US$11); breakfast A$3.50–A$10 (US$2.25–US$6.50). AE, DC, MC, V. Daily 7–9:30am and 6–8pm; noon–2pm Mon–Fri. Train: Roma St. Bus: Downtown Loop.

IN SPRING HILL
MODERATE

Tognini's BistroCafeDeli MODERN AUSTRALIAN   Owners Mark and Narelle Tognini opened this relaxed modern bistro, incorporating an extensive deli and walk-in cheese room, in April 2002. It is the third of the popular deli-cafes to bear their name around Brisbane. (The other two are at Main St., Kangaroo Point, and Baroona Rd., Milton.) Popular with inner-city dwellers and business folk, it has an extensive take-home range of gourmet delights you can also find on the menu. Or you can sit at one of the communal tables and try the roast pumpkin and goats cheese ravioli or maybe the blue swimmer crab and prawns with Pernod and Moreton Bay bugs with roasted red capsicum. Don't pass up the cinnamon poached pears and vanilla panna cotta—it's divine.

Turbot and Boundary sts., Spring Hill. ℭ **07/3831 5300.** Fax 07/3831 5311. www.togninis.com. No reservations taken. Main courses A$9–A$15 (US$5.85–US$9.75). AE, DC, MC, V. Mon–Fri 7am–7pm; Sat 7:30am–5:30pm; Sun 8am–5:30pm. Closed Christmas and Easter.

IN MT. COOT-THA
EXPENSIVE

The Summit ✿✿ MODERN AUSTRALIAN   It would be hard to find a better view of Brisbane than from this spot. A teahouse of some kind has been on this mountaintop for more than a century. Part 19th-century Queenslander house and part modern extension, the restaurant has wraparound covered decks with a view to the city and Moreton Bay. A changing menu features local produce and dishes with Asian and Mediterranean influences, teamed with Australian wines. Try grilled swordfish steak from North Queensland, or grilled kangaroo loin on rosemary skewers. And when you've finished dining, spend some time on the observation deck—at night the city lights provide a glittering panorama.

At the Mt. Coot-tha Lookout, Sir Samuel Griffith Dr., Mt. Coot-tha. ℭ **07/3369 9922.** Fax 07/3369 8937. www.mtcoot-tha.com. Reservations recommended Fri–Sat nights. Main courses A$25–A$33 (US$16–US$21); Chef's Selection 3-course menu A$46 (US$30); 2- or 3-course early-bird menu A$24–A$30 (US$16–US$20) available from 3pm if you finish by 7pm. AE, DC, MC, V. Daily 11:30am–midnight; Sun brunch 8am–10:30am; Christmas Day for lunch only; New Year's Day, Boxing Day (Dec 26), and Good Friday, dinner only. Bus: 471. From Roma St. Transit Centre, take Upper Roma St. and Milton Rd. 3.5km (2¼ miles) west to the Western Fwy. roundabout at Toowong Cemetery, veer right into Sir Samuel Griffith Dr., and go approx. 3km (2 miles). Free parking.

IN EAST BRISBANE
MODERATE

Green Papaya ✿ (Value) NORTH VIETNAMESE   Clean, fresh, and simple are the key words to describe owner/chef Lien Yeoman's approach to her native cuisine. Two cheerful rooms—painted yellow and blue—are usually crowded with a faithful clientele. If you don't know your *Bo xao cay ngot* (spicy beef) from your *Nom du du* (green papaya salad), the staff willingly gives advice. The restaurant is licensed, but you can bring your own bottled wine (no beer or spirits) for a corkage charge of A$3 (US$1.95) per person. Cooking classes are also run from time to time, so call for a schedule. They also do takeout.

898 Stanley St. East (at Potts St.), East Brisbane. ℭ **07/3217 3599.** www.greenpapaya.com.au. Reservations recommended. Main courses A$12–A$30 (US$7.80–US$20); banquet menus (for minimum of 4 people) A$35–A$40 (US$23–US$26). AE, DC, MC, V. Tues–Sun 6–10pm. Closed Good Friday, and from Christmas to early Jan. Located a 10-min. drive from town and 1 block from the Woolloongabba Cricket Ground. Train: Woolloongabba station. Parking at rear of restaurant and on-street.

IN ALBION
MODERATE

Breakfast Creek Hotel ✿ STEAK   A A$4 million (US$2.6 million) renovation and restoration has given fresh life to this Brisbane treasure. Built in 1889 and listed by the National Trust, the Breakfast Creek Hotel is fondly known as the Brekky Creek—or simply The Creek. It is quintessentially Queensland, with a new outdoor dining area overlooking Breakfast Creek, and is famed for its gigantic steaks and XXXX (Fourex) beer "off the wood" (from the keg). The beer garden is always popular and there's usually a band on Sunday afternoons.

2 Kingsford Smith Dr. (at Breakfast Creek Rd.), Albion. ℭ **07/3262 5988.** Main courses A$17–A$25 (US$11–US$16). AE, DC, MC, V. Meals daily noon–2:30pm; Mon–Fri 5:30–9:30pm; Sat 5–9:30pm; Sun 5–8:30pm. Pub Sun–Thurs 10am–10pm; Fri–Sat 10am–11pm. Bus: 300 or 322. Wickham St. becomes Breakfast Creek Rd; the hotel is just off the route to the airport.

5 Exploring Brisbane

CUDDLING A KOALA & OTHER TOP ATTRACTIONS

Australian Woolshed   If you've never seen a sheep or visited a farm, this might be a novelty for you, but don't be surprised if your Aussie friends cringe when you mention your intention to visit it. That said, this is a popular attraction with overseas visitors and school groups—you may have to contend with busloads of them. The ram show features eight trained Australian rams that "answer" to their names and walk through the audience to take their place beside their named spots on the stage. There's also sheep shearing, spinning, and sheepdog demonstrations, and you can get your hands dirty classing wool, milking cows, feeding kangaroos, and cuddling koalas (a photo will cost you A$14/US$9). The gift shop has quality Australian-made souvenirs. A rustic restaurant serves Aussie specialties, including billy tea and damper.

Some Friday and Saturday nights the Woolshed hosts a traditional bush dance and dinner, featuring country dancing, spoon-playing, singalongs, a live band, and a two-course dinner. Tickets cost A$39 (US$25) per adult and A$17 (US$11) for children 5 to 14. The fun starts at 7pm and goes until midnight. Bookings are essential.

148 Samford Rd., Ferny Hills. ℂ 07/3872 1100. www.auswoolshed.com.au. Admission to ram show A$17 (US$11) adults, A$12 (US$7.80) seniors and students, A$11 (US$7.15) children 3–14, A$46 (US$30) family (2 adults/3 children). Billy tea and damper A$6.50 (US$4.20) adults, A$4.10 (US$2.65) children 3–14. Water slide A$6.50 (US$4.20) for 1 hr.; A$10 (US$6.50) for 4 hr. Minigolf A$5.50 (US$3.60) for 9 holes. AE, MC, V. Daily 8:30am–4:30pm (ram show 9:30 and 11am and 1 and 2:30pm) except Christmas Day and Anzac Day (Apr 25) morning. Train: Ferny Grove (station is 800m/2,624 ft. from the Woolshed). Car: Kelvin Grove Rd. from the city becomes Enoggera Rd., then Samford Rd.; the trip is 14km (8½ miles). Large off-street free parking lot.

Brisbane Botanic Gardens Mt. Coot-tha   These 52-hectare (128-acre) gardens at the base of Mt. Coot-tha feature Aussie natives and exotics you probably won't see at home, including an arid zone, a Tropical Dome conservatory housing rainforest plants, a cactus house, bonsai house, fragrant plants, a Japanese garden, African and American plants, wetlands, and a bamboo grove. There are lakes and trails, usually a horticultural show or arts-and-crafts display in the auditorium on weekends, and a cafe. Free 1-hour guided tours leave the kiosk at 11am and 1pm Monday through Saturday (except public holidays).

Mt. Coot-tha Rd., Toowong, 7km (4 miles) from the city. ℂ 07/3403 8888. www.brisbane.qld.gov.au. Free admission to Botanic Gardens. Gardens open daily 8am–5pm (5:30pm Sept–Mar). Bus: 471. Free parking.

City Hall   Once the tallest building in Brisbane, City Hall is now dwarfed by the office blocks that surround it. Nevertheless, a ride in the old elevator to the top of the sandstone clock tower gives you a different perspective on the city center. Take a peek into the spacious art gallery on the ground floor, then take the elevator from outside the gallery entrance to the third floor (there's a A$2/US$1.30 charge). A cheery elevator operator will give you a history of the building on your short ride up before letting you out into the glassed-in observation floor in the bell tower. If you're there on the quarter hour you'll get a close-up experience of the chimes. Try not to be there at midday, when the clock chimes 12—it's deafening.

King George Square (Ann and Adelaide sts.). ℂ 07/3403 8888. Clock tower open Mon–Fri 10am–3pm; Sat 10am–2:30pm. Closed Sun and public holidays.

Lone Pine Koala Sanctuary 𝒌𝒌 *(Kids)*   This is the best place in Australia to cuddle a koala—and one of the few places where koala cuddling is still allowed. Banned in New South Wales and Victoria, koala cuddling is allowed in

Queensland under strict conditions which ensure each animal is handled for less than 30 minutes a day and they get every third day off! When it opened in 1927, Lone Pine had only two koalas, Jack and Jill, but is now home to more than 130 of the furry marsupials. You can cuddle them any time and have a photo taken holding one for A$10 (US$6.50); once you've purchased a photograph, your companions can take as many photos of you as they like with their own cameras. Lone Pine isn't just koalas—you can also hand-feed kangaroos and wallabies and get up close with emus, parrots, wombats, Tasmanian devils, skinks, lace monitors, frogs, bats, turtles, possums, and other native wildlife. There is currency exchange, a gift shop, and restaurant and cafe. You can also take advantage of the picnic and barbecue facilities. The nicest way to get to Lone Pine is a cruise down the Brisbane River aboard the MV *Miramar* (© 07/ 3221 0300), which leaves North Quay at the Queen Street Mall, next to Victoria Bridge, at 10am. The 19km (12-mile) trip to Lone Pine takes 90 minutes and includes a commentary. You have 2 hours to explore Lone Pine before returning, arriving in the city at 2:45pm. The fare is A$25 (US$16) for adults and A$15 (US$10) for children 3 to 13, including a map and hotel pickups. Cruises are every day except Christmas and Anzac Day.

Jesmond Rd., Fig Tree Pocket. © 07/3378 1366. Fax 07/3878 1770. www.koala.net. Admission A$15 (US$9.75) adults, A$10 (US$6.50) children 3–13, A$38 (US$25) family pass, A$13 (US$8.45) seniors, backpackers, and students with ID. AE, DC, MC, V. Daily including Christmas 7:30am–5pm; 1:30–5pm on Anzac Day (Apr 25). By car, take Milton Rd. to the roundabout at Toowong cemetery, and then the Western Fwy. towards Ipswich. Signs will direct you to Fig Tree Pocket and Lone Pine. The sanctuary is 20 min. from the city center by car. There's a free parking lot. Bus 430 goes directly to the Sanctuary from the Koala platform "N" at the Myer Centre, Queen St. Mall, and leaves hourly from 8:45am–3:45pm weekdays; 8:30am–4:30pm weekends and public holidays. Bus fare is A$2.80 (US$1.80) adults and A$1.40 (US91¢) children. A taxi will cost about A$22 (US$14) from the city center.

Newstead House 🐾   Brisbane's oldest surviving home has been restored to its late Victorian splendor in a peaceful park overlooking the Brisbane River. Wander the rooms, admire the gracious exterior dating from 1846, and on Sundays and public holidays between March and November, take Devonshire tea. The U.S. Army occupied the house during World War II, and the first American war memorial built in Australia stands on Newstead Point on the grounds.

Newstead Park, Breakfast Creek Rd., Newstead. © 1800/061 846 or 07/3216 1846. A$4.40 (US$2.85) adults, A$3.30 (US$2.15) seniors and students, A$2.20 (US$1.45) children 6–16, A$11 (US$7.15) family pass. Mon–Fri 10am–4pm; Sun and most public holidays 2–5pm. Last admittance 30 min. before closing. Closed Christmas, Boxing Day (Dec 26), Good Friday, and Anzac Day (Apr 25). Bus: 300, 306, or 322. Limited parking.

Queensland Cultural Centre _Kids_   This low-rise, modern complex stretching along the south bank of the Brisbane River houses many of the city's performing arts venues as well as the state art gallery, museum, and library. Thanks to plenty of open plazas and fountains inserted by thoughtful architects, it is a pleasing place to wander or to just sit and watch the river and the city skyline.

The **Queensland Performing Arts Complex** (© 07/3840 7444 administration Mon–Fri 9am–5pm, or 136 246 for all bookings) houses the 2,000-seat Lyric Theatre for musicals, ballet, and opera; the 1,800-seat Concert Hall for orchestral performances; the 850-seat Optus Playhouse Theatre for plays; and the 315-seat Cremorne Theatre for theater-in-the-round, cabaret, and experimental works. The complex has a restaurant and a cafe. Free 40-minute front-of-house tours leave from the box office at noon Monday through Friday; no bookings are needed. One hour backstage tours are available by arrangement for A$5.50 (US$3.60) per person (© 07/3840 7431).

The **Queensland Art Gallery**   (© 07/3840 7303) is one of Australia's most attractive galleries, with vast light-filled spaces and interesting water features both inside and out. It is a major player in the Australian art world, attracting international blockbuster exhibitions of works by the likes of Renoir, Picasso, and van Gogh, and showcasing diverse modern Australian painters, sculptors, and other artists. It also has an impressive collection of Aboriginal art. Admission is free. Free guided tours run Monday through Friday at 11am, and 1 and 2pm; Saturdays at 11am, and 2 and 3pm; Sundays at 11am, and 1 and 3pm. There is a gift shop and bistro. The gallery is open 10am to 5pm from Monday through Friday, 9am to 5pm on weekends; closed Good Friday, Christmas, and until noon on Anzac Day (Apr 25).

The **Queensland Museum** (© 07/3840 7555) on the corner of Grey and Melbourne streets is undergoing a major revamp in 2003. New additions include a smart new entrance and an interactive Sciencentre to open in 2004. The museum houses an eclectic collection ranging from natural history specimens and fossils to a World War I German tank. Children will like the blue whale model and the dinosaurs, which include Queensland's own Muttaburrasaurus. The museum has a cafe and gift shop. Admission is free, except to the Sciencentre (rates still to be set at press time) and traveling exhibitions, and it is open daily from 9:30am to 5pm; closed Christmas, Good Friday, and until noon on Anzac Day (Apr 25).

Adjacent to South Bank Parklands, across Victoria Bridge at western end of Queen St. © 07/3840 7100. Ferry: South Bank (CityCat) and Old South Bank (Inner City Ferry). Bus: Countless bus routes depart Adelaide St. near Albert St., cross the Victoria Bridge, and stop outside. Plentiful underground parking. The Centre is a 7-min. walk from town.

Roma Street Parkland   Thousands of plants, including natives and some of the world's most endangered, have been used to create lush subtropical gardens in an unused railway yard. The effect is stunning. Areas of the gardens are themed and there are guided walks twice a day (10am and 2pm Sept–May, 11am and 2pm June–Aug) Thursday through Sunday (including public holidays), self-guided walking tours for each, or you can take the "art walk" and discover the great public art on display. There are barbeques and picnic areas and a children's playground. Brisbane people have taken to this new park, so it is busy and lively, but is large enough to handle the crowds.

Walk there from Roma St. train station. From King George Sq., it's about a 500m (1,640-ft.) walk along Albert St. By car, access is from Roma St. or the Wickham Terrace/College Rd./Gregory Terrace intersection. © 07/ 3006 4545. Open 24 hr., except Spectacle Garden closed 7pm–6:30am. Information booths are located in the Spectacle Garden and at the Activity Centre.

Sir Thomas Brisbane Planetarium & Cosmic Skydome *Kids* The planetarium is part of the Botanic Gardens at Mt. Coot-tha. A fascinating 45-minute astronomical show re-creates the Brisbane night sky using the Ziess projector. Kids over 6 will like this.

Mt. Coot-tha Rd., Toowong © 07/3403 2578. A$11 (US$7.15) adults, A$9 (US$6) seniors and students, A$6.50 (US$4.20) children under 15 (not recommended for children under 6), A$30 (US$20) families. Show times Wed–Fri 3:30pm; Sat 1:30, 3:30, and 7:30pm; Sun 1:30 and 3:30pm; more often during Queensland school holiday periods. Reservations not necessary but advisable. Open Wed–Sun noon–7pm.

South Bank Parklands *Kids* Follow the locals' lead and spend some time at this delightful 16-hectare (40-acre) complex of parks, restaurants, shops, playgrounds, street theater, and weekend markets. The former World Expo '88 site has been happily transformed into a people's place that really works. There's even a man-made beach, lined with palm trees, with real waves and sand, where you can swim, stroll, and cycle the meandering pathways; sit over a caffe latte in one of the cafes and enjoy the city views. From the parklands it's an easy stroll to the museum, art gallery, and other parts of the adjacent Queensland Cultural Centre (see above).

From the Queen St. Mall, cross the Victoria Bridge to South Bank or walk across the Goodwill Bridge from Gardens Point Rd. entrance to the City Gardens. (☎ 07/3867 2051 for Visitor Information Centre, or 07/3867 2020 for recorded entertainment information. Free admission. Park daily 24 hr.; Visitor Information Centre Sat–Thurs 9am–6pm; Fri 9am–10pm. Train: South Brisbane. Ferry: CityCats and Cross River Ferries both leave from the Clem Jones Promenade at South Bank. Bus: Countless bus routes depart Adelaide St. near Albert St., cross the Victoria Bridge, and stop at the Queensland Cultural Centre; walk through the Centre to South Bank Parklands. Plentiful underground parking in Queensland Cultural Centre. The Parklands are a 7-min. walk from town.

St. John's Anglican Cathedral 𝒜𝒜 Brisbane's stunning neo-Gothic Anglican cathedral is in the final stages of its completion—a mere 100 years after it was begun. Don't be put off by the scaffolding which will likely still be swaddling it when you visit—from a glassed off area inside, you can watch the stonemasons as they work on the western transept (fronting Ann St.), due to be completed in 2006. Friendly, knowledgeable volunteer guides run tours and will point out some of the details which make this cathedral uniquely Queensland—like the carved possums on the organ screen and the hand-stitched cushions.

373 Ann St. (between Wharf and Queen sts.). (☎ 07/3835 2248. www.stjohnscathedral.com.au. Daily 9:30am–4:30pm; free tours 10am and 2pm Mon–Sat; Sun 2pm only.

TAKING A CITY STROLL

Because Brisbane is leafy, warm, and full of colonial-era Queenslander architecture, it is a great city for strolling. Pick up one of the free Heritage Trail Maps from the Brisbane Marketing information booths (see "Visitor Information," earlier in this chapter) and set off to explore on your own. The map books have a history of the area and excellent detailed information of historic buildings and other sights along the way.

For organized walking tours, see below.

6 Organized Tours

RIVER CRUISES   The best way to cruise the river, in my view, is aboard the fast **CityCat ferries** 𝒜𝒜. Board at Riverside and head downstream under the Story Bridge to New Farm Park, past Newstead House to the restaurant row at Brett's Wharves; or cruise upriver past the city and South Bank to the University of Queensland's lovely campus. (Take a look at its impressive Great Court while you're there.) This trip in either direction will set you back a whole A$3.80 (US$2.45). Or you can stay on for the full trip, which takes about 2 hours. For those who'd like a commentary and maybe a meal as they cruise, the **Kookaburra River Queen** paddle-wheeler ((☎ 07/3221 1300) is a good option. You can choose from a lunch or dinner cruise, and from a three-course menu or a seafood platter. Lunch prices are A$38 (US$25) and A$58 (US$38) for the seafood; dinner is A$52 (US$34) and A$68 (US$44). Prices are slightly higher on Friday and Saturday nights and on Sundays and public holidays. The boat departs from the Eagle Street Pier. Parking is available under the City Rowers tavern in Eagle Street. A A$24 (US$16) "coffee, tea, and cookies" fare is part of the lunch cruise, but without the full meal.

BUS TOURS   For a good introduction to Brisbane, look no further than a **City Sights** or **City Nights** bus tour, both run by Brisbane Transport (℃ **13 12 30** in Australia). City Sights buses stop at 19 points of interest in a continuous loop around the city center, South Bank, and Fortitude Valley, including Chinatown, South Bank Parklands, the Queensland Cultural Centre, Sciencentre, the Riverside Centre (where markets are held Sun), the City Botanic Gardens, the casino, and various historical buildings. The driver of the blue and yellow bus gives a commentary, and you can hop on and off at any stop you like, getting onto the next bus that comes along. The tour is good value as your ticket also gives unlimited access to buses, ferries, and CityCats for the day as well as discounts to some attractions. The bus departs every 45 minutes from 9am to 3:45pm daily except Christmas, Good Friday, and Anzac Day. The whole trip, without stopping, takes 90 minutes. Tickets cost A$20 (US$13) for adults, A$15 (US$9.75) for children 5 to 15. Buy your ticket on board. You can join anywhere along the route, but the most central stop is City Hall, Stop 2 on Adelaide Street at Albert Street. Daily except Christmas, Good Friday, and Anzac Day (Apr 25).

The City Nights tour shows you the city lights from Mt. Coot-tha, the Brisbane River at South Bank, and the illuminated cliffs at Kangaroo Point, New Farm Park, and Fortitude Valley. It departs City Hall, Stop 2 on Adelaide Street, at 6pm daily (Mar–Oct) and 6:30pm (Nov–Feb) and takes about 2½ hours. Daily except Christmas, New Year's Eve, Good Friday, and Anzac Day. Tickets are A$20 (US$13) for adults, A$15 (US$9.75) for kids 5 to 15. The trip also includes a sector by CityCat from South Bank to New Farm Park, where the bus is waiting to pick you up again.

WALKING TOURS   The Brisbane City Council has a wonderful program called **Walking for Pleasure** (℃ 07/3403 8888). Most days a free guided walk departs from somewhere in the city or suburbs, exploring all kinds of territory from bushland to heritage buildings to riverscapes to cemeteries. The walks are aimed at locals, not tourists, so you get to explore Brisbane side by side with the townsfolk. Every walk has a flexible distance option and usually lasts about 2 hours. Most are easy, but some are more demanding. Most start and finish near public transport and end near a food outlet of some kind. **Historical Walking Tours** are run by local history expert Brian Ogden (℃ 07/3217 3673), who leads visitors on a journey into Brisbane's past, regaling them with tales dating from convict settlement right to the present day. Four different routes are taken and each tour takes about 2 hours and costs A$15 (US$10). Prepare for shivers up your spine if you take one of Jack Sim's **Ghost Tours** ⚡ (℃ 07/3844 6606), to relive Brisbane's gruesome past. City walking tours (A$25/US$16) are run on Friday nights and there are also tours of the historic Toowong Cemetery and the now-disused Boggo Road Gaol. Bookings essential.

Free guided walks of the **City Botanic Gardens** (℃ 07/3403 8888) at Alice Street leave from the rotunda at the Albert Street entrance Monday through Saturday at 11am and 1pm (except public holidays and the first Mon of each month).

7 Enjoying the Great Outdoors
OUTDOOR ACTIVITIES
ABSEILING & ROCK CLIMBING   The Kangaroo Point cliffs just south of the Story Bridge are a breeze for first-time abseilers (rappellers) to scale—so they say. **Outdoor Pursuits** (℃ 07/3391 8776; www.outdoorpursuits.com.au)

stages rock climbs up the cliffs every second Sunday from 8:30am. The experience lasts 3½ hours and costs A$39 (US$25) per person. At 1pm you can abseil back during a 4-hour session for A$39 (US$25) per person. You will fit in four or five abseils in the course of the afternoon. If you want to climb in the morning and abseil in the afternoon, you can buy both experiences as a package for A$59 (US$38).

BIKING   Bike tracks stretch for 400km (248 miles) around Brisbane, often shared with pedestrians and in-line skaters. One great scenic route—about 9km (5½ miles) long—starts just west of the Story Bridge, sweeps through the City Botanic Gardens, and follows the river all the way to the University of Queensland campus at St. Lucia. **Brisbane Bicycle Sales and Hire,** 87 Albert St. (© **07/3229 2433;** www.brizbike.com), will rent you a bike and furnish you with the Brisbane City Council's free detailed bike maps. Rentals start at A$12 (US$7.80) for 1 hour and go up to A$25 (US$16) for the day; overnight (A$45/US$29), weekly (A$80/US$52), and biweekly (A$120/US$78) rentals are available. The price includes helmets, which are compulsory in Australia. **Valet Cycle Hire (© 0408 003 198** mobile phone) rents bikes, helmets, and maps for A$30 (US$20) for a half day, A$40 (US$26) for a full day, and A$70 (US$46) for 2 days. The company also operates an easy escorted tour each afternoon for about 2½ hours, departing from the Brisbane City Gardens, which costs A$38 (US$25) adults and A$30 (US$20) children 7 to 12. Bookings essential. The Brisbane City Council at City Hall (© **07/3403 8888**) and Brisbane Marketing's information booths (see "Visitor Information," earlier in this chapter) also give out bike maps.

BUSHWALKING   **Brisbane Forest Park** 🌊🌊, a 28,500-hectare (71,395-acre) expanse of bushland, waterfalls, and rainforest a 20-minute drive north of the city, has hiking trails ranging from just a few hundred meters up to 8km (5 miles). Some tracks have themes—one highlights the native mammals that live in the park, for example, and another, the 1.8km (just over 1 mile) **Mt. Coot-tha Aboriginal Art Trail,** showcases contemporary Aboriginal art with tree carvings, rock paintings, etchings, and a dance pit. Because the park is so big, most walks depart from seven regional centers that are up to a 20-minute drive from headquarters, so you will need a car. Make a day of it and pack a picnic. Park Headquarters (© **07/3300 4855;** www.brisbaneforestpark.qld.gov.au) is at 60 Mt. Nebo Rd., The Gap. Here you will find a wildlife display, a restaurant, a crafts shop, and an information center.

IN-LINE SKATING   In-line skaters can use the network of bike/pedestrian paths. See "Biking," above, for locations of where to find a map, or just head down to the City Botanic Gardens at Alice Street and find your own way out along the river. **SkateBiz,** 101 Albert St. (© **07/3220 0157**), rents blades for A$13 (US$9) for 2 hours, or A$20 (US$13) for any time up to 24 hours. Protective gear is included. Take photo ID. The store is open from 9am to 5.30pm Monday through Thursday, 9am to 9pm Friday, 9am to 4pm Saturday, and 10am to 4pm Sunday.

8 The Shopping Scene

Brisbane's best shopping is centered on **Queen Street Mall,** which has around 500 stores. Fronting the mall at 171–209 Queen St., under the Hilton, is the three-level **Wintergarden** shopping complex (© **07/3229 9755**), housing upscale jewelers and Aussie fashion designers. Farther up the mall at 91 Queen St. (at Albert St.) is the **Myer Centre** (© **07/3223 6900**), which has Brisbane's biggest department store and five levels of moderately priced stores, mostly fashion. The **Brisbane Arcade,** 160 Queen Street Mall (© **07/3221 5977**), is lined with the boutiques of local Queensland designers. Just down the mall from it you will find the **Broadway on the Mall** arcade (© **07/3229 5233**), which stocks affordable fashion, gifts, and accessories on two levels. Across from the Edward Street end of the mall is a smart new fashion and lifestyle shopping precinct, **MacArthur Central,** right next door to the GPO and taking up the block between Queen and Elizabeth streets. This is where you'll find top name designer labels, Swiss watches, galleries and accessory shops.

The trendy suburb of **Paddington,** just a couple of miles from the city by cab (or take the no. 144 bus to Bardon), is the place for antiques, books, art, crafts, one-of-a-kind clothing designs, and unusual gifts. The shops—colorfully painted Queenslander cottages—line the main street, Given Terrace, which becomes Latrobe Terrace. Don't miss the second wave of shops around the bend.

SHOPPING HOURS   Brisbane shops are open from 8:30am to 5:30pm Monday through Friday, 8:30am to 5pm on Saturday, and 10:30am to 4pm on Sunday. They stay open until 9pm Friday in the city, when the Queen Street Mall is abuzz with cinema-goers and revelers, and until 9pm Thursday in Paddington.

MARKETS   Authentic retro '50s and '60s fashion, offbeat stuff like old LPs, secondhand crafts, fashion by up-and-coming young designers, and all kinds of junk and treasure are all up for sale at Brisbane's only alternative market, **Valley Markets,** Brunswick Street and Chinatown malls, in Fortitude Valley (© **07/3006 6200**). Hang around in one of the many coffee shops and listen to live music. It's held Saturday and Sunday from 8am to 4pm.

Friday night is a fun time to visit the **South Bank Art and Craft Markets,** Stanley Street Plaza, South Bank Parklands (© **07/3846 4500** or 0414/754 082 mobile phone), when the buzzing outdoor handcrafts market is lit by fairy lights. The market is held Friday from 5 to 10pm, Saturday from 11am to 5pm, and Sunday from 9am to 5pm.

Brisbane's glamour set likes trawling the **Riverside Markets** ⚛ at the Riverside Centre, 123 Eagle St. (© **07/3870 2807**) and the adjacent Eagle Street Pier Craft and Deli Markets (**07/3846 4500,** or 0417/635822 mobile phone) to buy attractive housewares, colorful pottery, wooden blanket chests, handmade toys, painted flowerpots, and other stylish wares. It's held Sunday from 8am to 4pm.

For an authentic taste of Queensland's best produce, the **Farmers Markets** ⚛⚛ (© **0439/999 009**) operates every Saturday, from 7am to 1pm, in the grounds of

---

Finds **Fireworks for Your Wall**

If the Aboriginal art you see in the usual tourist outlets doesn't do it for you, what you'll see at Brisbane's **Fire-Works Gallery** will. Upstairs in an old printery at 11 Stratton St., Newstead (© **07/3216 1250**), this renowned gallery shows art by established and emerging artists from all over Australia. You may pale at some of the prices, but the stockroom at the back of the gallery may have something within your price range. They'll also arrange to get your new acquisition shipped home for you. Open Wednesday to Saturday, 11am to 6pm, or by appointment on Tuesdays.

the Brisbane Powerhouse, Lamington Street, New Farm. Here you'll find much to tempt your palate, brought into the city fresh that morning by farmers from around the south east of the state. There's everything from fresh fruit and vegetables to homemade chutneys, quail, fresh seafood, free-range eggs, and patés. Foodies will find themselves in heaven.

9 Brisbane After Dark

You can find out about other festivals, concerts and events, and book tickets, through **Ticketek** (© **13 19 31** in Queensland or 07/3404 6700 outside Queensland; www.ticketek.com). You can book in person at Ticketek agencies, the most convenient of which are on Level E at the Myer Centre at 91 Queen Street Mall, in the Roma Street Transit Centre, and in the Visitor Information Centre at South Bank Parklands. Or try **Ticketmaster** (© **13 16 00;** www.ticketmaster7.com).

QTIX (© **13 62 46** in Australia) is a major booking agent for performing arts and classical music, including all events at the Queensland Performing Arts Complex (QPAC). There is a A$6.60 (US$4.30) fee per booking, not per ticket. You can also inquire and book in person at the box office at QPAC between 8:30am and 9pm Monday through Saturday, and at its outlet at the South Bank Parklands Visitor Information Centre.

The free, color weekly newspaper *Brisbane News* lists performing arts; jazz and classical music performances; art exhibitions; rock concerts; and public events. The free weekly *TimeOff,* which comes out Wednesdays and can be found in bars and cafes, is a good guide to live music, as is Thursday's *Courier-Mail* newspaper.

THE PERFORMING ARTS

Many of Brisbane's performing-arts events are held at the **Queensland Performing Arts Centre (QPAC)** in the Queensland Cultural Centre (see "Exploring Brisbane," earlier in this chapter), but the city also has a lively independent theater scene, with smaller companies making an increasing impact on cultural life. To find out what's playing and to book tickets, call QTIX (see above) or visit www.qtix.com.au.

Queensland Theatre Company, the state theater company, offers eight or nine productions a year, from the classics to new Australian works, attracting some of the country's best actors and directors. Most performances are at either the Optus Playhouse or Cremorne Theatre at the Queensland Performing Arts Centre (QPAC), South Bank. Call © **07/3840 7000** for administration and information, or check out www.qldtheatreco.com.au. Tickets cost A$17 (if you are age 24 or under) to A$50 (US$11–US$33).

La Boite Theatre ℛ (**www.laboite.com.au**) is a well-established innovative company, which performs contemporary all-Australian plays in the round. In late 2003, La Boite moved to a new 400-seat theater in the new Cultural Industries Precinct that's being constructed at Kelvin Grove. Check the website for address and phone details. Tickets for the 2003 season were around A$30 (US$20), previews A$25 (US$16).

Brisbane Powerhouse–Centre for the Live Arts, 119 Lamington St., New Farm (© **07/3358 8600**), is a venue for innovative (some might say fringe) contemporary works. A former electricity powerhouse, this massive brick factory is now a dynamic new art space for exhibitions, contemporary performance, and live art. The building retains its unique character, an industrial mix of metal, glass, and stark surfaces etched with 20 years of graffiti. It's a short walk from the New Farm ferry terminal along the riverfront through New Farm Park.

The state opera company, **Opera Queensland,** performs a lively repertoire of traditional opera as well as modern works, musicals, and choral concerts. Free talks on the opera you are about to see start in the foyer 45 minutes before every performance, and free close-up tours of the set are held after every performance (except the final night). Most performances take place at the Queensland Performing Arts Centre (QPAC). Call © 07/3875 3030 for administration. Tickets average A$33 to A$118 (US$21–US$77) or A$37 (US$24) at some performances if you're age 30 or under.

The **Queensland Orchestra** (© 07/3377 5000 for administration) provides classical music lovers with a diverse mix of orchestral and chamber music, with the odd foray into fun material, such as Cole Porter hits and gospel music, performing about 30 concerts a year. Free talks are given in the foyer 1 hour before all major performances. The occasional "Tea and Symphony" concerts at City Hall include tea and coffee. The orchestra plays at the Concert Hall in the Queensland Performing Arts Centre (QPAC) or City Hall, though more intimate works are sometimes staged at its studios at 53 Ferry Rd., West End. Tickets cost A$35 to A$50 (US$23–US$33), less if you are a full-time student or under 26.

NIGHTCLUBS & BARS

Friday's   This indoor/outdoor bar, restaurant, and nightclub complex overlooking the Brisbane River is a haunt for "the Zoolander generation" of 18 to 40 year olds. Every Tuesday to Saturday night sees some kind of happy-hour deal, cocktail club, or drinks special, and the dance action starts pumping around 11pm on Fridays and Saturdays. Every third Wednesday of the month from 6 to 8:30pm the Wine Club welcomes over-30s with all the wine, champagne, spirits, beer, food, and live bands they can take for A$30 (US$20). Sounds on Sunday, from 2pm till very late, features top DJs from around Australia. Upstairs in Riverside Centre, 123 Eagle St. © 07/3832 2122. Cover A$7–A$10 (US$4.55–US$6.50). CityCat to Riverside.

Margaux's   A smart mid-30s to mid-40s crowd gathers to dance and chat over cocktails and supper at this clubby joint. It's open Friday and Saturday from 9pm to 3am; happy hour is 9:30 to 10:30pm. 5th fl., Brisbane Hilton, 190 Elizabeth St. © 07/3234 2000. Cover A$5 (US$3.25) Sat night. Train: Central.

Treasury Casino   This lovely heritage building—built in 1886 as, ironically enough, the state's Treasury offices—houses a modern casino. Three levels of 100 gaming tables offer roulette, blackjack, baccarat, craps, sic-bo, and traditional Aussie two-up. There are more than 1,000 slot machines, five restaurants and seven bars, and it's open 24 hours. Live bands appear nightly in the Livewire Bar. Ask about Ride and Dine deals, in which your bus, train, ferry, or taxi fare entitles you to buy a package of cheap gaming chips and a meal. Queen St. between George and William sts. © 07/3306 8888. Must be 18 years old to enter; neat casual attire required (no beachwear or thongs). Closed Christmas, Good Friday, and until 1pm Anzac Day (Apr 25). No cover. Train: Central or South Brisbane (then walk across the Victoria Bridge).

Zenbar   Minimalist Manhattan style interiors with an 8m-high (26-ft.) glass wall overlooking a bamboo garden make this one of the hippest joints in town. It's a restaurant as well, but the bar is packed on Friday and Saturday nights with office workers and beautiful people. There are about 40 wines by the glass, but in this kind of place you should be drinking a margarita or martini. The music ranges from '70s underground jazz and lounge to ultramodern funk house on Fridays, and on Saturdays the mood changes to easy background music. Park level, Post Office Sq., 215 Adelaide St. © 07/3211 2333. No cover. Train: Central.

Finds   Brisbane's Historic Pubs

Brisbane's attractive historic pubs, many of them recently revitalized, have wide shady verandas and beer gardens just perfect for whiling away a sunny afternoon or catching a quick meal at night.

The best known is undoubtedly the **Breakfast Creek Hotel** on Kingsford Smith Drive, Breakfast Creek (© **07/3262 5988;** see "Where to Dine," earlier in this chapter). Built in 1889, the hotel is a Brisbane institution and for many people a visit to the city isn't complete without a steak and beer "off the wood" at the Brekkie Creek.

Another landmark is the **Regatta Hotel,** 543 Coronation Dr., Toowong (© **07/3870 7063).** This heritage hotel with three stories of iron lace balconies is the perfect spot for a cool drink overlooking the Brisbane River. After a 2002 multi-million-dollar renovation, the place now bursts at the seams on weekends. The new Boat Shed restaurant is popular but not inexpensive—tables around the hotel verandas are a better choice.

Not far from the Regatta, in High Street, Toowong, is the **Royal Exchange Hotel** (© **07/3371 2555),** known simply as "the RE." The RE is popular with students, probably because of its proximity to the University of Queensland. It has a great garden bar at the back.

The **Story Bridge Hotel,** at 200 Main St. (© **07/3391 2266),** Kangaroo Point, is well known as the venue for some of Brisbane's most unusual events, such as the annual Australia Day (Jan 26) cockroach races. Built in 1886, the pub is also a great place to find live music.

COOL SPOTS FOR JAZZ & BLUES

Brisbane Jazz Club ★ *Finds*   On the riverfront under the Story Bridge, this is the only Australian jazz club still featuring big band dance music (every Sun night). Watch out for the slightly sloping dance floor—it was once a boat ramp! Traditional and mainstream jazz is featured on Saturday nights. Once a month on Sunday afternoons guest artists play on the deck. It's open Saturday 8 to 11pm and Sunday 7 to 10:30pm and sometimes on Friday nights, but the best thing is to phone and check what's on first. 1 Annie St., Kangaroo Point. © **07/3391 2006.** A$10 (US$6.50) most nights, with higher cover charges for some guest acts. CityCat to Holman St. Free parking lot.

Holiday Inn Jazz-n-Blues Bar   One of Brisbane's leading live jazz venues is in the unlikely setting of this busy hotel. A mixed crowd in their 20s to 40s turns up to hear local, Australian, and international acts. Get there early, as there are only seats for 30, the rest is standing-room only. Open Wednesday, Thursday, and Saturday 6pm to late, and Friday from 4pm. Ground floor of the hotel, next to Brisbane Transit Centre, Roma St. © **07/3238 2222.** Varying cover charges. Train: Roma Street.

10 Brisbane's Moreton Bay & Islands

The Brisbane River runs into Moreton Bay, which is studded with hundreds of small islands—and a few large ones. Some of them can only be reached by private vessel. Others are national parks, and are accessible by tour boat or public ferry.

NORTH STRADBROKE ISLAND 🐢🐢

Affectionately called "Straddie" by the locals, the island was once home to a large Aboriginal population and still retains much of their history. Dunwich was later used as a convict outstation, a Catholic mission, quarantine station, and benevolent institution. The historical museum at Dunwich has a display of historic photographs, items salvaged from shipwrecks, and information about the early settlement of the island; it's open from 10am to 2pm Wednesdays and Saturdays. A self-guided historical walk begins at the information center, where you can pick up a free map. A "must" for all visitors is the North Gorge Headlands Walk, for breathtaking views and for spotting turtles, dolphins, and whales.

GETTING THERE & GETTING AROUND   Stradbroke Ferries (℃ 07/3286 2666) operates a water-taxi service from Toondah Harbour, Middle Street, Cleveland, to Dunwich (about 30 min.) for A$11 (US$7.15) return (round-trip) adult fare. The vehicle barge takes walk-on passengers for A$8.50 (US$5.50) return (this takes about 1 hr.). A bus service meets almost every water taxi or ferry, and operates between the three main settlements, Dunwich, Amity, and Point Lookout. The trip takes about 30 minutes to either place and costs A$8.60 (US$5.60) for adults.

VISITOR INFORMATION   The **Tourist Information Centre** (℃ 07/3409 9555) is on Junner Street, Dunwich (about 200m/656 ft. from the ferry terminal), and is open weekdays from 8:30am to 5pm and weekends 9am to 3pm.

SOUTH STRADBROKE ISLAND 🐢🐢

A turn-of-the-20th-century shipwreck (with a cargo of whiskey and explosives) weakened the link between this lovely island and North Stradbroke, and nature did the rest. South Stradbroke is less well known than its sister island, but that's changing. There are four camping grounds and three resorts on the island. South Stradbroke Island is accessible from Runaway Bay near Southport, at the Gold Coast—about a 45-minute drive south of Brisbane city.

GETTING THERE & GETTING AROUND   From Brisbane, take the Pacific Highway exit after Dreamworld (exit 57), follow signs to Sanctuary Cove/Hope Island and to the marina. The resorts run boats for guests only, so the only other way to get there is by water taxi. **Gold Coast Water Taxi** (℃ 0418 759 789) takes groups to the campgrounds and resorts for about A$10 (US$6.50) per person (minimum of six people plus camping gear, if necessary). **Couran Cove Island Resort** (℃ 1800/632 211 or 07/5597 9000) runs day tours from A$55 (US$36) per person which includes return transfers from Runaway Bay, morning tea, guided rainforest tour, lunch, and use of resort facilities. Fastcat leaves Runaway Bay at 10am, and you can return on the 3 or 5pm boat.

MORETON ISLAND 🐢🐢

At more than 200 sq. km (78 sq. miles), Moreton is the second-largest sand mass in the world (after Queensland's Fraser Island) and has the world's largest sandhill, Mt. Tempest. There are three settlements and the Tangalooma Wild Dolphin Resort, where guests and visitors on an extended day cruise can take part in hand-feeding a pod of wild dolphins which come in to the jetty each evening. Moreton has other claims to fame. For instance, you can visit the 42-hectare (104-acre) "desert" and toboggan down the sand dunes. Or you can snorkel around the 12 wrecks just north of the resort, and visit historic points of interest including the sandstone lighthouse at Cape Moreton, built in 1857. A four-wheel-drive vehicle

Moreton Bay & Islands

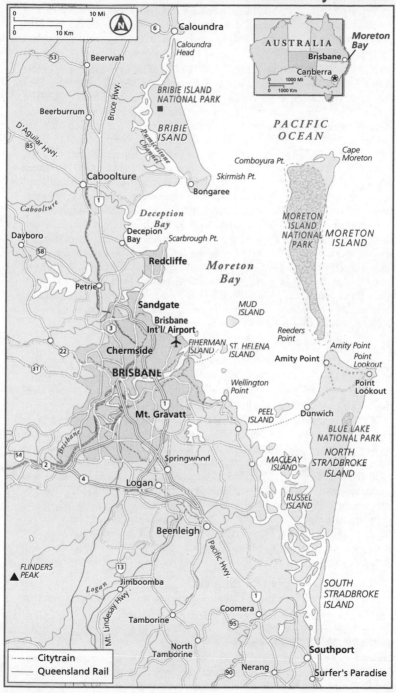

AUSTRALIA
Brisbane
Canberra

Moreton Bay

0   10 Mi
0   10 Km

N

Caloundra

Caloundra Head

Beerwah

53

BRIBIE ISLAND NATIONAL PARK

Beerburrum

D'Aguilar Hwy.

85

Bruce Hwy.

BRIBIE ISLAND

Pumicestone Channel

PACIFIC OCEAN

Comboyura Pt.

Cape Moreton

Caboolture

1

Caboolture

Skirmish Pt.

Bongaree

Deception Bay

MORETON ISLAND NATIONAL PARK

MORETON ISLAND

Dayboro

58

Decepion Bay

Scarbrough Pt.

Redcliffe

Moreton Bay

Petrie

MUD ISLAND

Reeders Point

Sandgate

Brisbane Int'l/ Airport

FIHERMAN ISLAND

ST. HELENA ISLAND

Amity Point

Amity Point

Point Lookout

Chermside

3

22

BRISBANE

Wellington Point

Point Lookout

31

Mt. Gravatt

1

PEEL ISLAND

Dunwich

BLUE LAKE NATIONAL PARK

brisbane

Springwood

MACLEAY ISLAND

NORTH STRADBROKE ISLAND

54

2

Logan

4

RUSSEL ISLAND

Beenleigh

FLINDERS PEAK

13

Logan

Jimboomba

Mt. Lindesay Hwy.

Pacific Hwy.

1

SOUTH STRADBROKE ISLAND

Tamborine

Coomera

95

North Tamborine

90

Nerang

Southport

Surfer's Paradise

- - - Citytrain
— Queensland Rail

6

is essential for getting around, but tours are run from the resort. Permits for access (A$30/US$20 per vehicle) and camping (A$4/US$2.60 per person or A$16/US$10 for a family of six per night) are available from National Park rangers and ferry operators.

GETTING THERE & GETTING AROUND   The high-speed catamarans *Tangalooma Flyer* and *Tangalooma Express* (© **1300/652 250**) leave Brisbane's Pinkenba wharf at Eagle Farm twice daily, at 10am and 5pm (10am and 2pm on Sat). The trip takes 75 minutes. Coaches pick up from Roma Street Transit Centre at 9am daily to connect with the Flyer and will pick up from city and Spring Hill hotels on request. Return transfers leave Tangalooma at 3:30pm daily except Saturday, when they leave at noon and 4:30pm. The return fare is A$56 (US$36) adults and A$28 (US$18) children 3 to 14. The *Combie Trader* vehicular and passenger ferry (© **07/3203 6399**; www.moreton-island.com) departs from Scarborough on the Redcliffe Peninsula for Bulwer daily except Tuesday. The trip takes about 2 hours and costs A$27 (US$18) adults, A$24 (US$16) students 16 and over, and A$16 (US$10) children 5 to 15, round-trip for walk-on passengers. The cost to take a four-wheel-drive and up to five passengers is A$125 (US$81). Day trips operate on Saturdays (11am–4pm) and cost A$20 (US$13) adults, A$12 (US$7.80) children, and A$72 (US$47) family of four. Combie Trader also runs four-wheel-drive trips to the island on Mondays, Fridays, and Sundays. The cost of A$85 (US$55) adults and A$60 (US$39) children under 14 includes the ferry crossing, tour, and lunch. Timetables are subject to change so check first.

ST. HELENA ISLAND 🎭🎭

For 65 years, from 1867 to 1932, St. Helena was a prison island, known as "the hell hole of the Pacific" to the nearly 4,000 souls incarcerated there. Today, the prison ruins are a tourist attraction, with a small museum in the restored and reconstructed Deputy Superintendent's Cottage.

GETTING THERE & GETTING AROUND   Entry to the island is by guided tour only. Excellent tours, most involving a re-enactment of life on the island jail, are run by **AB Sea Cruises** (© **07/3893 1240**; 7am–7pm daily) on the launch *Cat-o-Nine-Tails,* leaving from Manly Boat Harbour. The cost is A$65 (US$42) adults, A$55 (US$36) concessions, A$35 (US$23) children 4 to 14, and $139 (US$90) family of four. The tour leaves at 9:15am weekdays, returning at 2:15pm, and 11am to 4pm on weekends and public holidays, and includes a box lunch. **St. Helena By Night Ghost Tours** are run on some Friday and Saturday nights. They include dinner, a dramatized version of life in the prison, and a few spooky surprises. Night tours cost A$75 (US$49) adults, A$40 (US$26) children, and A$159 (US$103) family of four. Bookings essential.

WHERE TO STAY ON THE ISLANDS

Moreton and South Stradbroke islands have resorts, while North Stradbroke has plenty of existing low-key accommodations and is likely to have a major resort development in the next year or so. The smaller islands offer a variety of motels, cabins, motor-home parks, and camping grounds.

Couran Cove Resort 🎭🎭🎭 *Finds*   You'll be lucky to find a more peaceful resort than this one, which is an island idyll in a class of its own. On South Stradbroke Island, there are no cars, with everyone getting around on foot or bicycle or silent electric shuttle. And whether you're a beach or bush person, you'll find it here. You can hang around the pools or lagoon, head to the spectacular surf beach about 2km (1¼ miles) from the main resort, or stroll through remnants of primeval rainforest. The resort is committed to environmentally friendly practices, and is unique for its range of more than 100 recreational and sporting activities including a 9m (30-ft.) rock-climbing wall, three-lane sprint track, baseball and softball pitching cage, and a High Ropes Challenge course. There's also beach volleyball, bocce and lawn bowls, shuffleboard, surfing, fishing, and a stargazing observatory, and for gentler pursuits an extensive day spa and a resident artist who'll give you lessons. Guests can take in a wildlife show at the amphitheater. There are lots of accommodations choices. My favorite is a nature-cabin in the bush, but for water views and closer access to the restaurants and spa, choose one of the colorful waterfront units. All have kitchens, and there's a general store and "pantry service" which will deliver supplies to your room. Smoking is only allowed in designated outdoor areas and on balconies, and no tobacco products are sold at the resort.

South Stradbroke Island, Moreton Bay, QLD or P.O. Box 224, Runaway Bay, QLD 4216. © 1800/632 211 or 07/5597 9000. Fax 07/5597 9090. www.couran-cove.com.au. 357 units. Nature cabins (sleep from 3–8) from A$308 (US$200) per night with a minimum 3-night stay; waterfront rooms from A$299 (US$194) per night (no minimum stay). AE, DC, MC, V. **Amenities:** 3 restaurants; poolside cafe; 10-lane heated pool; children's swimming pool; golf driving range and putting green, free transfers to mainland golf courses; 2 tennis courts; 2 fully equipped exercise rooms; spa; extensive watersports equipment rentals; bike rental; children's programs and ½-acre adventure playground; game room; tour desk; massage; babysitting; laundry service; dry-cleaning. *In room:* A/C (waterfront units only, others have ceiling fans), TV w/pay movies, VCR, fax, dataport, kitchen, minibar (marine resort only), hair dryer, safe.

Tangalooma Wild Dolphin Resort 🏊 *Kids*   Once the Southern Hemisphere's largest whaling station, Tangalooma is the only resort on Moreton Island. The resort's big attraction is the pod of wild dolphins that comes into the jetty each evening. Guests are guaranteed one chance during their visit to hand-feed the dolphins; but you can't swim with, or touch, the dolphins. The feeding is regulated for the health of the pod, and your turn is over in a few seconds. Tangalooma is a good base for exploring the rest of the island, and a variety of tours are available, among them seasonal (late June to Oct) whale-watching cruises for A$95 (US$62) adults, A$55 (US$36) children. A dolphin research center is also based here. In the past year, 96 new hotel rooms have been added to the accommodations, which also includes 56 modern two-story family villas only a year or so older. Villas are pricier than regular rooms, and are a little farther from the resort facilities. The new hotel rooms sleep up to four guests and have such amenities as air-conditioning, minibar, and hair dryers, which the other rooms do not. However, older rooms have a kitchenette. Units in the main resort area each sleep four to five people, and each has a private balcony. A general store is on-site.

Moreton Island, off Brisbane, QLD, or P.O. Box 1102, Eagle Farm, QLD 4009. © 1300/652 250 or 07/3268 6333. Fax 07/3268 6299. www.tangalooma.com. 288 units (all with shower only). A$328–A$433 (US$213–US$281) including dolphin feeding. AE, DC, MC, V. **Amenities:** 2 restaurants; cafe; 2 outdoor pools; driving range and putting green; archery; tennis and squash courts; Jacuzzi; watersports equipment rental; children's programs and playground; tour desk; 4WD rental; babysitting; coin-op washers and dryers. *In room:* A/C in newer rooms, TV, kitchenette in older rooms, full kitchen in villas, minibar, fridge, coffeemaker, hair dryer (some rooms only).

Queensland & the Great Barrier Reef

by Lee Mylne

With a landscape three times the size of Texas and a population that clings to the coast but embraces the Outback for its icons, Queensland is a sprawling amalgam of stunning scenery, fantastic yarns, and eccentric personalities. Its most famous attraction is the Great Barrier Reef—by no means the only thing worth seeing. Great beaches and tropical weather make it hard to decide where to go first, and for how long.

White sandy beaches grace almost the entire Queensland coastline, and a string of lovely islands and coral atolls dangle just offshore. At the southern end of the state, Gold Coast beaches and theme parks keep tourists happy. In the north, from Townsville to Cape York, the rainforest teems with exotic flora and fauna.

Brisbane is the state capital, a former penal colony that today brims with style. While Brisbane boasts world-class theater, shopping, markets, art galleries, and restaurants, it still conveys the relaxed warmth of a country town. For more on this city, see chapter 5.

Less than an hour's drive south of Brisbane is the **Gold Coast** "glitter strip," with its 35km (22 miles) of rolling surf and sandy beaches. North of Brisbane lies the aptly named **Sunshine Coast**—more white sandy beaches, crystal-clear waters, and rolling mountains dotted with villages.

Don't miss the wild beauty of the largest sand island in the world, World Heritage–listed **Fraser Island.** Each year from August to October, humpback whales frolic in the sheltered waters between Fraser Island and Hervey Bay.

As you travel north, you'll be tempted by one tropical island after another until you hit the cluster of 74 that makes up the **Whitsunday** and **Cumberland** groups.

Then you enter a land where islands, rainforest, mountains, and rivers unite. Green sugar cane fields are everywhere—**Mackay** is the largest sugar-producing region in Australia. This attractive city has its own beach, but the harbor is a departure point for cruises to the Great Barrier Reef and the Whitsunday Islands. The Whitsundays are on the same latitude as Tahiti, and for my money are equally lovely. The idyllic island group is laced with coral reefs rising out of calm, blue waters teeming with colorful fish—warm enough for swimming year-round.

North of the Whitsundays is **Dunk Island** and the rainforest settlement of **Mission Beach**—a perfect illustration of the regional contrasts found in Tropical North Queensland. The port city of **Townsville** boasts 320 days of sunshine a year, and marks the start of the Great Green Way—an area of lush natural beauty on the way to Cairns.

Then you come to **Cairns,** with rainforest hills and villages to explore and a harbor full of boats waiting to take you to the Reef.

Cairns is a good base, but savvy travelers head an hour north to the trendy village of **Port Douglas.**

EXPLORING THE QUEENSLAND COAST

VISITOR INFORMATION   The **Queensland Travel Centre** is a great resource on traveling and touring the state, including the Great Barrier Reef. Visit the Destination Queensland website at www.destinationqueensland.com or call ✆ **13 88 33** in Australia. Tourism Queensland has offices in the United States and the United Kingdom—see "Visitor Information" in chapter 2.

You will also find excellent information on the **Great Barrier Reef Visitors Bureau**'s website at www.great-barrier-reef.com. This is not an official tourist office but part of a private company, **Travel Online** (✆ **07/3876 4644;** fax 07/ 876 4645), which offers itinerary planning and booking services for a wide range of accommodations and tours throughout north Queensland.

For information on B&Bs and farm stays in Cairns, Port Douglas, Mission Beach, and Townsville, contact the **Bed & Breakfast and Farmstay Association of Far North Queensland,** P.O. Box 595, Ravenshoe, QLD 4888 (✆ **07/4097 7022;** www.bnbnq.com.au).

WHEN TO GO   Australia's winter (June–Aug) is high season in Queensland; the water can be chilly, but its temperature rarely drops below 72°F (22°C). August through January is peak visibility time for divers. Summer is hot and sticky across the state. North Queensland (Mission Beach, Cairns, and Port Douglas) gets a monsoonal Wet Season November or December through March or April, which brings heavy rains, high temperatures, extreme humidity, and cyclones. It's no problem to visit then, but if the wet turns you off, consider the beautiful Whitsundays, which are generally beyond the reach of the rains and the worst humidity (but not of cyclones).

GETTING AROUND   **By Car**   The Bruce Highway travels along the coast from Brisbane to Cairns. It is mostly a narrow two-lane highway, and the scenery most of the way is eucalyptus bushland, but from Mackay north you will pass through sugar cane fields adding some variety to the trip.

Tourism Queensland publishes regional motoring guides. All you are likely to need, however, is a state map from the **Royal Automobile Club of Queensland** (RACQ), 300 St. Pauls Terrace, Fortitude Valley, Brisbane, QLD 4006 (✆ **13 19 05** in Australia). If you are already in Brisbane, you can get maps and motoring advice from the more centrally located RACQ office in the General Post Office (GPO) building at 261 Queen St. For road condition reports, call ✆ **1300/ 130 595** (recorded message), or 07/3361 2406. The state's Department of Natural Resources (✆ **07/3896 3216**) publishes an excellent range of "Sunmaps"

⟨ Tips ⟩ When to Visit the Reef

April through November is the best time to visit the Reef. December through March can be uncomfortably hot and humid, particularly as far north as the Whitsundays, Cairns, and Port Douglas. In the winter months (June–Aug), the water can be a touch chilly (Aussies think so, anyway), but it rarely drops below 72°F (22°C).

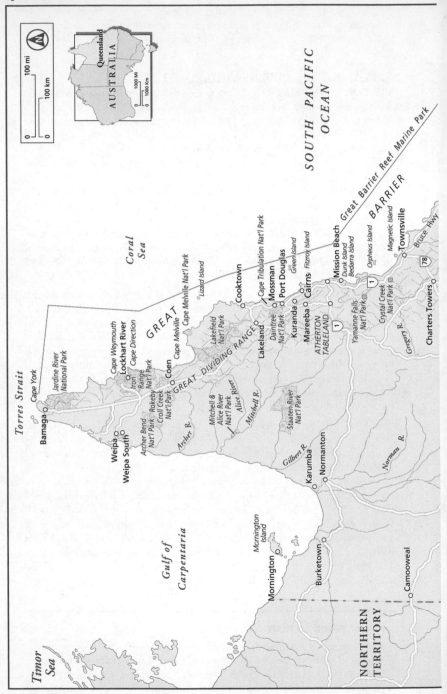

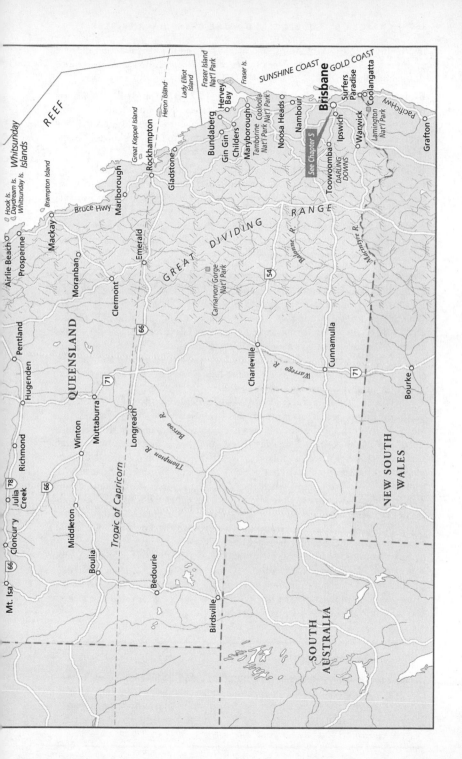

that highlight tourist attractions, national parks, and the like, although they are of limited use as road maps. You can get them at newsdealers and gas stations throughout the state.

By Train   Queensland Rail's **Traveltrain** (© **13 22 32** in Australia; www.travel train.qr.com.au) operates two long-distance trains along the Brisbane-Cairns route, a 32-hour trip aboard *The Sunlander* or about 8 hours less on the new high-speed **Tilt Train.** Traveltrain also operates trains to Outback towns. See the "Getting Around Australia" section in chapter 2 for more details.

By Plane   This is the fastest way to see a lot in such a big state. Beware the "milk run" flights that stop at every tiny town en route; these can chew up time. **Qantas** (© **13 13 13** in Australia; www.qantas.com.au) and regional airline **Sunstate Airlines** (book through Qantas) serve most coastal towns from Brisbane, and a few from Cairns. **Virgin Blue** (© **13 67 89** in Australia; www.virginblue.com. au) services Brisbane, Cairns, Townsville, Mackay, Rockhampton, Gold Coast, and Maroochydore on the Sunshine Coast.

1 Exploring the Great Barrier Reef

It's the only living structure on Earth visible from the moon; at 348,700 sq. km (135,993 sq. miles), it's bigger than the United Kingdom; it's over 2,000km (1,240 miles) long, stretching from Lady Elliot Island off Bundaberg to just south of Papua New Guinea; it's home to 1,500 kinds of fish, 400 species of corals, 4,000 kinds of clams and snails, and who knows how many sponges, starfish, and sea urchins. The Great Barrier Reef is listed as a World Heritage site and is the biggest marine park in the world.

There are three kinds of reef on the Great Barrier Reef—fringing, ribbon, and platform. **Fringe reef** is the stuff you will see just off the shore of islands and along the mainland. **Ribbon reefs** create "streamers" of long, thin reef along the outer edge of the Reef, and are only found north of Cairns. **Platform** or **patch reefs** are splotches of coral emerging up off the continental shelf all the way along the Queensland coast. Platform reefs, the most common kind, are what most people are thinking of when they refer to the Great Barrier Reef. Island resorts in the Great Barrier Reef Marine Park are either "continental," meaning part of the Australian landmass, or "cays," crushed dead coral and sand amassed over time by water action. Cays are surrounded with dazzling coral and marine life. On continental islands, the coral can be of varying quality.

Apart from the dazzling fish life around the corals, the Reef is home to large numbers of green and loggerhead turtles, one of the biggest dugong (manatee) populations in the world, sharks, giant manta rays, and sea snakes. In winter (June–Aug), humpback whales gather in the warm waters around the Hervey Bay and the Whitsunday Islands to give birth to calves.

Tips The Reef Tax

Every passenger over 4 years old must pay a A$5.50 (US$3.60) daily Environmental Management Charge (EMC), commonly called "reef tax," every time they visit the Great Barrier Reef. This money goes toward the management and conservation of the Reef. Your tour operator will collect it from you when you pay for your trip.

The Great Barrier Reef

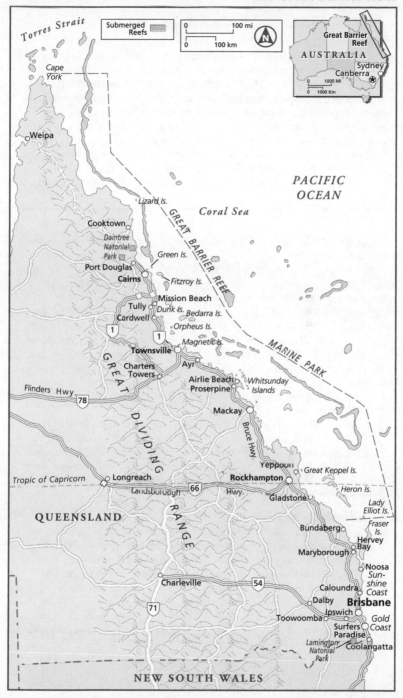

Tips Reef Health & Safety Warnings

Coral is very sharp and coral cuts get infected quickly and badly. If you cut yourself, ask your cruise boat for antiseptic cream and apply it to grazes as soon as you come out of the water.

The sun and reflected sunlight off the water can burn you fast. Remember to put sunscreen on your back and the back of your legs, especially around your knees and the back of your neck, even behind your ears—all places that rarely get exposed to the sun but will be exposed as you swim face down. Apply more when you leave the water.

Remember, the Great Barrier Reef is a marine park. Removing coral (living or dead), shells, or any other natural item is an offense. If everyone who has ever visited the Reef took a piece, it would not be worth coming to see what's left.

To see the Reef you can snorkel, dive, fish, or fly over it. For most people, the Great Barrier Reef means the "Outer Reef," the network of platform and ribbon reefs that lie an average of 65km (40 miles) off the coast (about 1 hr., 90 min. by boat from the mainland). You should get out and see that, but there is plenty of fringing reef to explore around islands closer to the mainland.

Learning about the Reef before you get there will enhance your visit. **Reef Teach** 𝄞𝄞 (© **07/4031 7794**) is an evening multimedia presentation by Paddy Colwell, an enthusiastic marine biologist and scuba diver. He tells you everything you need to know about the Reef, from how it was formed to how coral grows, from what dangerous creatures to avoid, to how to take successful underwater photos. The presentation takes place throughout the year at 14 Spence St., Cairns, Monday through Saturday from 6:15 to 8:30pm, and costs A$13 (US$8.45) per person.

Townsville is the headquarters of the Great Barrier Reef Marine Park Authority, and a visit to its showcase, Reef HQ (p. 309) is a superb introduction. The star attraction at the aquarium is a re-created living-reef ecosystem in a massive viewing tank. Find out more about the Reef from the **Great Barrier Reef Marine Park Authority** (© **07/4750 0700;** fax 07/4772 6093; www.gbrmpa. gov.au or www.reefhq.org.au).

DISCOVERING THE REEF

Snorkeling the Reef can be a wondrous experience. Green and purple clams, pink sponges, red starfish, purple sea urchins, and fish from electric blue to neon yellow to lime are a truly magical sight. The rich colors of the coral only survive with lots of light, so the nearer the surface, the brighter and richer the marine life. That means snorkelers are in a prime position to see it at its best.

If your Reef cruise offers a guided snorkel tour or "snorkel safari," take it. They are worth the extra cost of A$30 (US$20) or so. Most safaris are suitable for both beginners and advanced snorkelers, and are led by marine biologists who tell you about the fascinating sea creatures you are seeing. Snorkeling is an easy skill to master, and the crew on cruise boats are always happy to tutor you if you are unsure.

A day trip to the Reef also offers a great opportunity to go scuba diving—even if you have never dived before. Every major cruise boat listed in "Day Trips to the Reef" (below) and many dedicated dive boats listed in "Diving the Reef" (also below) offer introductory dives that allow you to dive without certification to a depth of 6m (20 ft.) in the company of an instructor. You will need to complete a medical questionnaire and undergo a 30-minute briefing on the boat. Intro dives are also called "resort dives" because many resorts offer something similar, giving you 1 or 2 hours' instruction before taking you to a nearby reef to dive.

CHOOSING A GATEWAY TO THE REEF

Cairns and **Port Douglas** are both good places from which to access the Reef—but the quality of the coral is just as good off any town along the coast between **Gladstone** and Cairns. The Reef is pretty much equidistant from any point on the coast—about 90 minutes away by high-speed catamaran. An exception is **Townsville,** where the Reef is about 2½ hours away. Think carefully about where to base yourself.

The main gateways, north to south, are **Port Douglas, Cairns, Mission Beach, Townsville, the Whitsunday Islands, Gladstone** (for Heron Island), and **Bundaberg.** The Whitsundays has the added attractions of dazzling islands to sail among; beautiful island resorts offering a wealth of watersports and other activities; and a large array of diving, fishing, and day cruises. Most important, you can snorkel every day off your island or join a sailing or cruise day trip to a number of magnificent inner reefs much nearer than the main Outer Reef. Many people stay in Cairns simply because of easy international airport access.

If you are a nonswimmer, choose a Reef cruise that visits a coral cay, because a cay slopes gradually into shallow water and the surrounding coral. The **Low Isles** at Port Douglas; **Green Island, Michaelmas Cay,** or **Upolu Cay** off Cairns; **Beaver Cay** off Mission Beach; and **Heron Island** are all good locations.

DAY TRIPS TO THE REEF

The most common way to get to the Reef is on one of the big motorized catamarans that carry up to 300 passengers each and depart from Cairns, Port

---

(Moments Overnighting on the Reef

Down Under Dive (© 1800/079 099 in Australia, or 07/4052 8300; fax 07/4031 1373; www.downunderdive.com.au) in Cairns offers a chance to "sleep on the Reef" aboard a 43m (141-ft.) 1890s-style brigantine, the SV *Atlantic Clipper.* It's a sleek, romantic sailing ship with towering masts, a roomy Jacuzzi on the foredeck, a cocktail bar, a comfortable dining room, and single, double, triple, or quad-share air-conditioned cabins. A motorized launch takes you from Cairns to the ship's reef mooring; from there you sail up to the four popular reef complexes of Norman, Hastings, and Saxon reefs, and Michaelmas Cay. The emphasis is on fun and relaxation, with lots of snorkeling and diving. Choose between a 2-day/1-night stay in a two-, three-, or four-berth cabin for A$210 (US$137) for snorkelers or A$290 (US$189) for divers, and a 3-day/2-night journey for A$340 (US$221) for snorkelers or A$400 (US$260) for divers. Add a surcharge of A$20 (US$13) per person per night for a twin cabin and A$30 (US$20) for a double cabin with shower. The all-inclusive prices include all dive and snorkel gear (including prescription masks), meals, and pickups from your Cairns city accommodations. Transfers from Port Douglas are available for an extra A$27 (US$18).

Douglas, Townsville, Mission Beach, and the Whitsunday mainland and islands. The boats are air-conditioned and have a bar, videos, and educational material on board, as well as a marine biologist who gives a brief talk on the Reef's ecology en route. The boats tie up at their own private permanent pontoons anchored to a platform reef. The pontoons have glass-bottom boats for passengers who don't want to get wet, dry underwater viewing platforms, usually a bar, sun decks, shaded seats, and often showers.

An alternative to traveling on a big tour boat is to go on one of the many smaller boats. These typically visit two or three Reef sites rather than just one. There are usually no more than 20 passengers, so you get more personal attention, and you get to know the other passengers. Another advantage is that you will have the coral pretty much all to yourself. The drawbacks of a small boat are that you have only the cramped deck to sit on when you get out of the water, and your traveling time to the Reef may be longer. If you're a nervous snorkeler, you may feel safer on a boat where you will be swimming with 300 other people.

Most day-trip fares include snorkel gear—fins, mask, and snorkel, and wet suits in winter, although you rarely need them—free use of the underwater viewing chambers and glass-bottom-boat rides, a plentiful buffet or barbecue lunch, and morning and afternoon refreshments. Diving is an optional activity for which you pay extra. The big boats post snorkeling scouts to keep a lookout for anyone in trouble and to count heads periodically. If you wear glasses, ask whether your boat offers prescription masks as this could make a big difference to the quality of your experience! Don't forget, you can travel as a snorkel-only passenger on most dive boats, too.

> ### Tips Feeling Green?
>
> If you are inclined to be seasick, come prepared with medication. Some boats sell a ginger-based anti-seasickness pill, but it doesn't always work!

The major launching points for day trips to the Reef are Port Douglas, Cairns, Mission Beach, Townsville, and the Whitsundays (see individual sections on these regions later in this chapter).

DIVING THE REEF 🤿

Divers have a big choice of dive boats that make 1-day runs to the Outer Reef and live-aboard dive boats making excursions that last up to a week. As a general rule, on a typical 5-hour day trip to the Reef, you will fit in about two dives. The companies listed in this section give you an idea of the kinds of diving trips that are available and how much they cost. This is by no means an exhaustive list, as there are far too many to include here. The section on "The Active Vacation Planner" in chapter 2 has more pointers for locating a dive operator. The prices quoted here include full gear rental; knock off about A$20 (US$13) if you have your own gear.

> ### Fun Fact The Floating P.O.
>
> Australia's only "floating post office" is on Agincourt Reef, about 72km (45 miles) offshore from Port Douglas. The facility floats on the Quicksilver Connections pontoon, and your letter or postcard will be stamped with a special postmark from the Great Barrier Reef.

Tips **Pressed for Time?**

If you don't have time for a full day on the Reef, don't forget that you can dive the coral cay of Green Island, just 27km (16 miles) off Cairns, in half a day (see "Exploring the Islands" in the Cairns section, later in this chapter).

FROM CAIRNS Tusa Dive (© 07/4040 6464; www.tusadive.com) runs two 20m (66-ft.) dive boats daily to two dive sites from a choice of 21 locations on the Outer Reef. The day costs A$175 (US$114) for divers and A$115 (US$75) for snorkelers, with wet suits, guided snorkel tours, lunch, and transfers from your Cairns or northern beaches hotel. For an extra A$66 (US$43) you can get a video done of the day's dive. If you want to be shown the best spots under the water, you can take a guided dive with the dive team for an extra A$20 (US$13). Day trips for introductory divers cost A$180 (US$117) for one dive or A$215 (US$140) for two. The groups are kept to a maximum of 25 people, so you get personal attention. The company is the Nitrox and Rebreather facility for north Queensland, and certified divers can take two introductory dives on Nitrox/Safe Air in 1 day for A$200 (US$130).

FROM PORT DOUGLAS The waters off Port Douglas are home to dramatic coral spires and swim-throughs at the Cathedrals; giant clams at Barracuda Pass; a village of parrot fish, anemone fish, unicorn fish, and two moray eels at the soaring pinnacle of Nursery Bommie; fan corals at Split-Bommie; and many other wonderful sites.

Poseidon (© 07/4099 4772; www.poseidon-cruises.com.au) is a fast 24m (79-ft.) vessel that visits three Outer Reef sites. The day-trip price of A$135 (US$88) for adults, A$100 (US$65) for kids 3 to 12, includes snorkel gear, a marine biology talk, snorkel safaris, lunch, and pickups from Port Douglas hotels. Certified divers pay A$40 (US$26) extra for two dives or A$55 (US$36) for three, plus A$20 (US$13) gear rental. Guides will accompany you, free of charge, to show you great locations. Introductory divers pay A$50 (US$33) extra for one dive, and A$40 (US$26) each for the second and third. The vessel carries no more than 48 passengers, one-third its capacity, and gets you to the Reef in just over an hour, giving you 5 hours on the coral. The boat departs Marina Mirage daily at 8:30am.

FROM TOWNSVILLE Off Townsville, you can dive not only the Reef but also a wreck, the *Yongala* ✵, which lies off the coast in 30m (98 ft.) of water with good visibility. A cyclone sent the *Yongala* with 49 passengers and 72 crew members to the bottom of the sea in 1911. Today it's surrounded by a mass of coral and rich marine life, including barracuda, grouper, rays, and turtles. **Diving Dreams** (© 07/4721 2500; fax 07/4721 2549; www.divingdreams.com) runs a day trip for around A$220 (US$143) and 2- or 3-day trips, which include dives at the *Yongala*, with prices at around A$395 to A$495 (US$257–US$322).

FROM THE WHITSUNDAYS In and around the Whitsunday Islands, you can visit the Outer Reef and explore the many excellent Reef dive sites close to shore. Two of the more established companies are **Reef Dive** (© 07/4946 6508; www.reefdive.com.au) and **Kelly Dive** (© 1800/063 454 in Australia, or 07/ 4946 6122). Expect to pay about A$550 (US$358) per person for a 3-day/3-night trip.

DIVE COURSES   Many dive companies in Queensland offer dive courses, from initial open-water certification all the way to dive master, rescue diver, and instructor level. To take a course, you will need to have a medical exam done by a Queensland doctor. (Your dive school will arrange it.) You will also need two passport photos for your certificate, and you must be able to swim! Some courses take as little as 3 days, but 5 days is generally regarded as the best. Open-water certification usually requires 2 days of theory in a pool, followed by 2 or 3 days out on the Reef, where you make between four and nine dives.

> **Tips Diving Tips**
>
> Don't forget your "C" certification card. Bringing along your dive log is also a good idea. Remember not to fly for 24 hours after diving.

Deep Sea Divers Den (© 07/4046 7333; fax 07/4031 1210; www.diversden.com) has been in operation since 1974 and claims to have certified about 55,000 divers. The 5-day open-water course involves 2 days of theory in the pool in Cairns, and 3 days and 2 nights on a live-aboard boat. The course costs A$550 (US$358) per person, including all meals on the boat, nine dives (including a guided night dive), all your gear and a wet suit, and transfers from your city hotel. The same course over 4 nights, with 1 night on the boat and four dives, costs A$440 (US$286). New courses begin every day of the week.

Virtually every Great Barrier Reef dive operator offers dive courses. Most island resorts offer them, too. You will find dive schools in Cairns, Port Douglas, Mission Beach, Townsville, and the Whitsunday Islands.

Most dive companies teach from beginner level ("open-water certification") through to Advanced, Rescue, Dive Master, and Dive Instructor level. Courses usually begin every day or every week. Prices vary considerably, but are generally around A$550 to A$600 (US$358–US$390) for a 5-day open-water certification course, or A$450 (US$293) for the same course over 4 nights.

Companies offering dive courses appear under the relevant regional sections throughout this chapter.

2 Cairns

346km (215 miles) N of Townsville; 1,807km (1,120 miles) N of Brisbane

This is the only place in the world where two World Heritage–listed sites—the Great Barrier Reef and the Wet Tropics Rainforest—lie side by side. In parts of the far north, the rainforest touches the reef, reaching right down to sandy beaches from which you can snorkel the reef. Cairns is the gateway to these natural attractions, plus to man-made tourist attractions such as the Skyrail Rainforest Cableway. It's also a stepping-stone to islands of the Great Barrier Reef and the grasslands of the Gulf Savannah.

When international tourism to the Great Barrier Reef boomed a decade or two ago, the small sugar-farming town of Cairns boomed along with it. The town now boasts outstanding hotels, island resorts off shore, big Reef-cruise catamarans in the harbor, and too many souvenir shops. The only beach right in town is a man-made 4,000-sq.-m (43,000-sq.-ft.) saltwater lagoon and artificial beach on the Esplanade, which opened in early 2003 as part of a multimillion-dollar redevelopment of the city and port.

The 110-million-year-old rainforest, the Daintree, where plants that are fossils elsewhere in the world exist in living color, is just a couple of hours north of

Cairns

Map labels: See Map of Port Douglas, Daintree & Cape Tribulation For Areas North; To Kuranda & Skyrail Rainforest Cableway; To Airport & Northern Beaches; AUSTRALIA; Cairns; Canberra; 1000 Mi; 1000 Km; 1/4 mi; 1/4 km; GREAT BARRIER REEF; Trinity Bay; Lily St.; Smith St.; Sheridan St.; Digger St.; Lake St.; McKenzie St.; THE ESPLANADE; James St.; Thomas St.; Charles St.; Martyn St.; Severin St.; Kuranda Railway Line; Captain Cook Highway; Gatton St.; Kerwin St.; Grove St.; Gatton St.; Draper St.; Water St.; McLeod St.; Upward St.; Abbott St.; Lake St.; Grafton St.; Sheridan St.; Florence St.; Minnie St.; Bruce Highway; Aplin St.; THE ESPLANADE; City Place; The Pier Marketplace; Mulgrave Road; PARRAMATTA PARK; Shields St.; Reef Fleet Terminal; Bunda St.; Spence St.; Cairns Railway Station (Cairns Central); Wharf St.; Scott St.; Information (i); Post Office; To Tully & Mission Beach; Hartley St.; Kenny St.; Trinity Inlet

Cairns. The Daintree is part of the Wet Tropics, a World Heritage–listed area that stretches from north of Townsville to south of Cooktown, beyond Cairns, and houses half of Australia's animal and plant species.

If you are spending more than a day or two in the area, consider basing yourself on the city's pretty northern beaches, in Kuranda, or in Port Douglas (see "Port Douglas, Daintree & the Cape Tribulation Area," later in this chapter). Although prices will be higher in the peak season (Australian winter and early spring, July–Oct), there are affordable accommodations year-round.

ESSENTIALS

GETTING THERE   By Plane   Qantas (© **13 13 13** in Australia) has direct flights throughout the day to Cairns from Sydney and Brisbane, and at least one flight a day from Darwin and Uluru (Ayers Rock). From Melbourne you can fly direct some days, but most flights connect through Sydney or Brisbane. **Sunstate Airlines** (book through Qantas) also flies several times a day from Townsville, and **Airlink** (book through Qantas) has flights from Alice Springs and Uluru. **Virgin Blue** (© **13 67 89** in Australia) flies to Cairns direct from Brisbane, Sydney, and Melbourne. Several international carriers fly to Cairns from various Asian cities, and from New Zealand.

Cairns Airport is 8km (5 miles) north of downtown, and a 5-minute walk or a A$2 (US$1.30) shuttle ride separates the domestic and international terminals. The **Australia Coach** (© **07/4048 8355**) shuttle, which costs A$7 (US$4.55) adults, A$3.50 (US$2.25) children 3 to 12, meets major flights at both terminals for transfers to city hotels. **Sun Palm Express Coaches** (© **07/4099 4850**) provides transfers from the airport to the city and northern beaches. The one-way fare is A$13 (US$8.45) adults and A$7.50 (US$4.85) children to the city, and A$16 (US$10) adults and A$8.75 (US$5.70) children to Palm Cove.

A taxi from the airport costs around A$15 (US$9.75) to the city, A$30 (US$20) to Trinity Beach, and A$40 (US$26) to Palm Cove. Call **Black & White Taxis** (© **13 10 08** in Australia).

Avis, Budget, Hertz, and **Thrifty** all have car-rental offices at the domestic and international terminals (see "Getting Around," below).

By Train   Long-distance trains operate from Brisbane several times a week. Queensland Rail's **Traveltrain** (© **13 22 32** in Queensland; www.qr.com.au) operates the services. The new 160kmph Tilt Train takes about 25 hours and costs A$280 (US$182) for a business class fare between Brisbane and Cairns. Northbound services leave Brisbane at 6.25pm on Mondays, Wednesdays, and Fridays; southbound services depart Cairns at 8:15am on Wednesdays, Fridays, and Sundays. The train features luxury "business class" seating, with an entertainment system for each seat including multiple movie and audio channels.

The Sunlander, which runs twice a week between Brisbane and Cairns, takes 32 hours and costs A$187 (US$122) for a sitting berth, A$235 (US$153) for an economy-class sleeper, A$352 (US$229) for a first-class sleeper, or A$646 (US$420) for the all-inclusive Queenslander class. Trains pull into the Cairns Central terminal (© **13 22 32** in Australia for reservations or inquiries 24 hr. a day, or 07/4052 6297 for the terminal from 8am–6pm, 07/4052 6203 after hours) on Bunda Street in the center of town. The station has no showers, lockers, or currency exchange booths, but you will find 24-hour ATMs outside the Cairns Central shopping mall, right above the terminal.

By Bus   McCafferty's (© **13 14 99,** or 07/4051 5899 for Cairns terminal) and **Greyhound Pioneer** (© **13 20 30,** or 07/4051 5899 for terminal) buses

---

Finds Staying Connected

You can surf the Web and check your e-mail at **The Inbox Café**, 119 Abbot St. (© 07/4041 4677; fax 07/4041 4322), for A$1.50 (US95¢) for 15 minutes, A$2.50 (US$1.60) for 30 minutes, or A$4 (US$2.60) an hour. It's open daily from 7am to midnight. The Inbox Café, which has 12 computers on line, is Cairns's only licensed Internet cafe. The cafe food is by the **Red Ochre Grill** (see "Where to Dine," later in this chapter). It's fresh, tasty, and afford-able, with breakfast available all day. There is a bar with lots of newspa-pers and magazines, and resident DJs play groovy tunes to set a relaxed mood with an extra beat on weekend nights.

---

pull into Trinity Wharf Centre on Wharf Street in the center of town. Buses travel from the south via all towns and cities on the Bruce Highway, and from the west from Alice Springs and Darwin via Tennant Creek on the Stuart High-way and the Outback mining town of Mt. Isa to Townsville, where they join the Bruce Highway and head north. The 45-hour Sydney-Cairns trip costs A$285 (US$186), the 28½-hour trip from Brisbane is A$192 (US$125), and from Dar-win, the journey takes about 41 hours and costs A$402 (US$261).

By Car   From Brisbane and all major towns in the south, you'll enter Cairns on the Bruce Highway. To reach the northern beaches or Port Douglas from Cairns, take Sheridan Street in the city center, which becomes the Captain Cook Highway.

VISITOR INFORMATION   Tourism Tropical North Queensland, 51 The Esplanade, Cairns, QLD 4870 (© **07/4051 3588;** fax 07/4051 0127; www.tropicalaustralia.com.au), has information on Cairns and its environs, and on Mission Beach, Port Douglas, the Daintree Rain Forest, Cape York, and Out-back Queensland. It's open daily from 8:30am to 5:30pm, and 8:30am to 1pm on public holidays. Closed Christmas and New Year's Day.

CITY LAYOUT   A major redevelopment of the Cairns Esplanade, completed in 2003, has transformed the face of the city. The focal point is a 4,000-sq.-m (40,000-sq.-ft.) saltwater swimming lagoon with a wide sandy beach and sur-rounding parkland with public artworks and picnic areas. Suspended over the mudflats and providing a platform for bird-watching, a timber boardwalk runs 600m (1,800 ft.) along the waterfront. The boardwalk is lit for nighttime use. A walkway now links the Esplanade to the new Reef Fleet Terminal, the departure point for Great Barrier Reef boats.

Downtown Cairns is on a grid 5 blocks deep, bounded in the east by the Esplanade on the water, and in the west by McLeod Street, where the train sta-tion and the Cairns Central shopping mall are located. In between are shops, offices, and restaurants.

Heading 15 minutes north from the city along the Captain Cook Highway, you come to the **northern beaches:** Holloway's Beach, Yorkey's Knob, Trinity Beach, Kewarra Beach, Clifton Beach, Palm Cove, and Ellis Beach.

GETTING AROUND   By Bus   Sunbus (© 07/4057 7411) buses depart City Place Mall at the intersection of Lake and Shields streets. Buy all tickets and passes on board, and try to have correct change. You can hail buses anywhere it's convenient for the driver to stop. Buses 2 and 2A travel to Trinity Beach; 1 and 1X (weekend express) travel to Palm Cove. The N route runs along the highway

---

Tips Croc Alert!

Dangerous crocodiles inhabit Cairns waterways. Do not swim in, or stand on the bank of, any river or stream.

---

from the city to Palm Cove all night until dawn on Friday and Saturday nights, stopping at all beaches in between. Most other buses run from early morning until almost midnight.

By Car Avis (© 07/4051 5911), **Budget** (© 07/4051 9222), **Hertz** (© 07/ 4051 6399), and **Thrifty** (© 07/4051 8099) all have offices in Cairns city and at the airport. One long-established local outfit, **Sugarland Car Rentals,** has reasonable rates and offices in Cairns (© 07/4052 1300) and Palm Cove (© 07/ 4059 1087). **Britz Australia** (© 1800/331 454 in Australia), **Budget Campervan Rentals** (© 07/4032 2065), and **Maui Rentals** (© 1300/363 800 in Australia, or 07/4032 2065) rent motor homes. Britz and most major rental-car companies rent four-wheel-drive vehicles.

By Taxi Call **Black & White Taxis** at © **13 10 08.**

DAY TRIPS TO THE REEF

Cairns passengers can board the most luxurious vessel visiting the Reef, the **Quicksilver Cruises** wave-piercer catamaran (© **07/4087 2100;** www. quicksilver-cruises.com), which departs from the Reef Fleet Terminal at 8am and at Palm Cove Jetty on Cairns's northern beaches at 8:35am. It arrives at Port Douglas at 9:30am and leaves for the Reef at 10am. All of these trips run daily except Christmas. For the whole day from Cairns or Palm Cove, passengers pay A$175 (US$114) for adults, A$90 (US$59) for kids 4 to 14. A free pickup from your hotel is included in the price.

If you prefer to visit the Reef straight from Cairns, large-scale operator **Great Adventures** (© **1800/079 080** in Australia, or 07/4044 9944; www.great adventures.com.au) does daily cruises in fast, air-conditioned catamarans to a three-level pontoon on the Outer Reef. The pontoon has a children's swimming area, a semisubmersible, and an underwater observatory. You get at least 3 hours on the Reef. The cost for the day is A$152 (US$99) for adults, A$79 (US$51) for children 4 to 14, and A$388 (US$252) for a family. Hotel transfers are available from Cairns and the northern beaches for an extra cost. The boat departs the Great Adventures terminal at the new Reef Fleet Terminal at 10:30am.

You have an option to depart Cairns with Great Adventures at 8:30am and spend 2 hours on Green Island en route. This gives you time to walk nature trails, rent snorkel gear and watersports equipment, or laze on the beach before continuing to the Outer Reef. This cruise costs an extra A$16 (US$10) per adult and A$8 (US$5.20) per child.

Sunlover Cruises (© **1800/810 512** in Australia, or 07/4050 1333; www. sunlover.com.au) has a choice of Outer Reef trips aboard its large, fast catamarans. One trip stops at Fitzroy Island for a guided rainforest walk before heading on to Moore Reef on the Outer Reef. Transfers from city and northern beaches hotels are included. The day costs A$159 (US$103) for adults, A$80 (US$52) for children 4 to 14, and A$398 (US$258) for a family. This trip includes a glass-bottom boat ride and semisubmersible viewing.

Another Sunlover trip departs Cairns and picks up passengers at Palm Cove before heading to Arlington Reef. In total, you spend about 4 hours on the Reef.

The price is A$141 (US$92) for adults, A$71 (US$46) for kids, and A$353 (US$229) for a family, from Cairns.

Introductory dives on either trip cost A$107 (US$70). Certified divers pay the same price, including all gear. Both cruises include lunch and transfers from Cairns and northern beaches hotels. Both boats depart from the Reef Fleet Terminal in Cairns at 9:30am daily.

Great Adventures, Quicksilver, and Sunlover all offer helicopter flights over the Reef from their pontoons—a truly spectacular experience. There are also fly/cruise trips.

An alternative to motoring to the Reef is to sail to it. **Ocean Spirit Cruises** (✆ **07/4031 2920;** www.oceanspirit.com.au) operates two sailing cats that take no more than 100 or 150 passengers to Michaelmas Cay or Upolu Cay, lovely white-sand cays on the Outer Reef surrounded by rich reefs. This trip is a good value because it includes a pleasant 2 hours sailing to either cay, a guided snorkeling safari, guided beach walk, and a free glass of bubbly and live music on the way home—in addition to the usual reef ecology talks, semisubmersible rides, lunch, and transfers from your Cairns or northern beaches hotel. Another plus is that you spend your out-of-water time on a beautiful beach, not on a pontoon or boat deck. You get about 4 hours on the Reef.

The day trip to Michaelmas Cay is A$155 (US$101) for adults, A$78 (US$51) for children 4 to 14, and A$425 (US$276) for a family. The day trip to Upolu Cay costs A$89 (US$58) for adults, A$45 (US$29) for kids, and A$240 (US$156) for a family. Transfers from Cairns and the northern beaches are free, but from Port Douglas they cost an extra A$39 (US$25) adults and A$19 (US$12) children. Introductory dives cost A$89 (US$58), and certified divers pay A$59 (US$38) for one or A$95 (US$62) for two, all gear included, at Michaelmas Cay, less at Upolu. The boats depart Reef Fleet Terminal at 8:30am daily.

WHAT TO SEE & DO IN & AROUND CAIRNS

If you're staying in Cairns, also check out what there is to see and do in and around Port Douglas (see section 3 of this chapter) and Mission Beach (see section 4 of this chapter). Many tour operators in Port Douglas, and a few in Mission Beach, offer transfers from Cairns.

LEARNING ABOUT ABORIGINAL CULTURE

Tjapukai Aboriginal Cultural Park ✸✸✸   Don't miss this. Whether you choose the day or night experience, the Tjapukai (pronounced jab-oo-guy) cultural park is one of the best chances you'll have to discover the history and culture of the Aborigines without going to Central Australia. American theater director Don Freeman and his French-Canadian dancer wife, Judy, founded the dance show in 1987, working with local Aborigines, including acclaimed dancer and songwriter David Hudson. Today it is a sophisticated, multi-award-winning cultural park with an international reputation. Don and Judy are still heavily involved, but the park is 51% owned by the Aborigines who work in it.

Housed in a striking modern building that incorporates Aboriginal themes and colors, the Tjapukai experience needs at least 2 to 3 hours. Start in the Creation Theatre, where the latest in illusion, theatrics, and technology are used to tell the story of the creation of the world according to the spiritual beliefs of Tjapukai people. Actors work with spectacular special effects and holographic images to illustrate the legends. The production is performed in the Tjapukai language, translated through headsets.

Move on through the Magic Space museum and gallery section of the complex to the History Theatre, where a 20-minute film relates the history of the Tjapukai people since the coming of white settlers 120 years ago.

Outside, a suspension bridge links the main building with a cultural village where you can try boomerang and spear throwing, fire-making and didgeridoo playing, and learn about bush foods and medicines. In the open-sided Dance Theatre, Aboriginal men and women perform dances incorporating ancient and modern steps. Shows and demonstrations are planned so visitors can move from one to another easily, without missing anything. The complex also includes a restaurant and coffee shop. An arts-and-crafts gallery and shop is stocked with the work of Aboriginal artists and crafts workers.

"Tjapukai by Night" tours operate on Tuesday, Friday, and Sunday, from 7:30 to 11pm, and include transfers to and from accommodations, interactive time in the Magic Space museum, a Creation Show performance, and an outdoor Serpent Circle—a new, interactive show featuring tap sticks for each guest, a join-in corroboree (an Aboriginal nighttime dance), and a dramatic ceremony involving fire and water. It is followed by a buffet dinner and dance show, and the chance to meet the Tjapukai dancers. The cost is A$92 (US$60) adults, A$46 (US$30) children.

Captain Cook Hwy. (beside the Skyrail terminal), Smithfield. © 07/4042 9900. Fax 07/4042 9990. www. tjapukai.com.au. Admission A$28 (US$18) adults, A$14 (US$9) children 4–14, A$70 (US$46) family. AE, DC, MC, V. Ask about packages that include transfers, lunch, and a guided Magic Space tour, or Skyrail and/or Scenic Rail travel to and from Kuranda. Daily 9am–5pm. Closed Christmas and New Year's Day. Bus: 1C or 1E. Book shuttle transfers from Cairns and northern beaches hotels (A$17/US$11 adults and A$8.50/US$5.50 children) through the park. Park is 15 min. north of Cairns and 15 min. south of Palm Cove along the Captain Cook Hwy. Free parking.

MORE ATTRACTIONS
In Cairns

Hartley's Crocodile Adventures *Kids* Hartley's is the original Australian croc show, and after a move to a new location and a multimillion-dollar redevelopment in mid-2002, quite possibly the best. What makes it different from others is the fantastic natural setting—a 2-hectare (5-acre) lagoon surrounded by melaluca (paperbark) and bloodwood trees and home to 23 estuarine crocs. The best time to visit is for the 3pm "croc attack" show, when you can witness the saltwater crocodile "death roll" during the 45-minute performance. At 11am you can see these monsters get hand-fed or hear an eye-opening talk on the less aggressive freshwater crocodiles. There are tours of the croc farm at 10am and 1:30pm; at 2pm there is a snake show; and at 4:30pm it's koala-feeding time. This attraction makes a good stop en route to Port Douglas, and also has cassowaries, which are fed at 9:30am and 4:15pm.

Capt. Cook Hwy. (40km/24 miles north of Cairns; 25km/16 miles south of Port Douglas). © 07/4055 3576. Fax 07/4059 1017. www.crocodileadventures.com. Admission A$25 (US$16) adults, A$13 (US$8.10) children

---

Tips **Wait Till You Get There . . .**

Unless you are sure which tours you want to take, it often pays to wait until you get to Cairns to book them. Local travel agents, your hotel or B&B host, and other travelers in Cairns are often valuable sources of advice. Cairns has about 600 tour operators, so even in peak season, tours are rarely booked up more than 24 hours in advance.

4–15, A$60 (US$39) families. Tickets allow return entry for 3 days. Daily 8:30am–5pm. Closed Christmas. Transfers from Cairns available through All In A Day Tours (© 07/4032 5050). Free parking.

Royal Flying Doctor Visitors Centre   The Royal Flying Doctor Service (RFDS), the free aeromedical service that provides a "mantle of safety" for all Outback Australians, has a base in Cairns. Tours of their center are run every 30 minutes from 9am to 4:30pm. You can also watch a film, attend a talk on how the service began, browse through memorabilia, and board a former RFDS plane. Allow about 45 minutes.

1 Junction St., Edge Hill. © 07/4053 5687. Admission A$5.50 (US$3.55) adults, A$2.75 (US$1.80) children, A$17 (US$11) families. Mon–Sat 8:30am–5pm. Closed Sun and public holidays. Bus: 6 or 6A.

Wild World—The Tropical Zoo *(Kids*   Get a dose of your favorite Aussie wildlife here—some kind of talk or show takes place just about every 15 or 30 minutes throughout the day, including koala cuddling (have your photo taken for an extra A$13/US$8.45), saltwater crocodile and lorikeet feedings, and cane toad racing. Lots of other animals are on show, too, like kangaroos (which you can hand-feed for A$1/US65¢ a bag), emus, cassowaries, dingoes, and native birds in a walk-through aviary. The park also runs a nocturnal tour, in which you can see many of the more elusive creatures on show. To take the park's 3-hour Cairns Night Zoo tour, book by 4pm that day, earlier if you want transfers. The evening starts at 7pm and includes a wildlife spotlighting walk, where you can pat a koala and a possum and feed kangaroos; a stargazing interlude; a barbecue dinner with beer and wine, billy tea and damper and supper; and dancing to an Aussie bush band.

Captain Cook Hwy. (22km/14 miles north of the city center), Palm Cove. © 07/4055 3669. Fax 07/4059 1160. www.wildworld.com.au. Admission A$24 (US$16) adults, A$12 (US$7.80) children 4–15. Cairns Night Zoo experience (daily except Fri and Sun) A$109 (US$71) adults, A$55 (US$36) children 4–15. AE, DC, MC, V. Daily 8:30am–5pm. Closed Christmas. Bus: 1B. Cairns Night Zoo transfers from Cairns through All In A Day Tours (© 07/4032 5050) or from Port Douglas with Night Zoo Tours (© 07/4098 4929). Free parking.

EXPLORING THE ISLANDS

You don't have to go all the way to the outer Reef to see coral. Less than an hour from the city wharf, Green Island has snorkeling equal to that on the Great Barrier Reef. Fitzroy Island has rainforest walks, coral accessible by dive and snorkel boat trips from the island, and watersports. See "Where to Stay," later in this section, for details of the resorts on both islands.

GREEN ISLAND   This 15-hectare (37-acre) coral cay, surrounded by dazzling coral and marine life, is just 27km (17 miles) east of Cairns. You can rent snorkel gear, windsurfers, and paddle-skis; take glass-bottom-boat trips; go parasailing; take an introductory or certified dive; walk vine-forest trails; or laze on the beach. The beach is coral sand, so it's a little rough underfoot. Day visitors can use one of Green Island Resort's pools, its main bar, casual or upscale restaurants, and lockers and showers. Ask beach staff for their recommendations for the best snorkeling spots. If you don't snorkel, it's worth the admission charge to see the display of clown fish, potato cod, and anemones at the little underwater observatory, despite its cloudy old viewing windows. The island has a small attraction called **Marineland Melanesia** (© 07/4051 4032), where you can see old nautical artifacts, primitive art, a turtle and reef aquarium, and live crocodiles. Admission is A$10 (US$6.50) adults, A$4.50 (US$2.90) kids; croc shows are at 10:30am and 1:45pm.

   Great Adventures (© 07/4044 9944; www.greatadventures.com.au) and **Big Cat Green Island Reef Cruises** (© 07/4051 0444; www.bigcat-cruises.com.au)

both make trips to Green Island from Cairns. Expect to pay around A$65 (US$42) for a half-day trip with snorkel gear or a glass-bottom-boat cruise. A full-day trip can be as much as A$96 (US$62), but Big Cat makes a day trip for as little as A$60 (US$39). Big Cat's boat is slower, but you still get 5½ hours on the island. Great Adventures also has transfer-only rates of A$50 (US$30), which also gives access to the island's day facilities. Both companies pick up from hotels in Cairns, the northern beaches, and Port Douglas for an extra cost; Big Cat also runs to the island direct from Palm Cove.

FITZROY ISLAND   Scenic Fitzroy Island is a rainforested national park 45 minutes from Cairns, offering good diving. You can rent windsurfers, catamarans, and canoes; hike to the mountain-top lighthouse; view coral from a glass-bottom boat or take a short boat trip from the island to snorkel it; take a beginner's or certified dive; and swim in the pool. A day trip is simply the price of the round-trip ferry fare at A$36 (US$23) for adults, A$18 (US$12) for kids 4 to 14, or A$90 (US$59) for a family. Departures from Cairns are daily at 8:30 and 10:30am, and 4pm, returning at 9:30am, and 3 and 5pm. Make reservations at © **07/4030 7907**, or through **Raging Thunder Adventures** (© **07/4030 7990**; www.ragingthunder.com.au). Raging Thunder also runs guided sea-kayak expeditions around Fitzroy Island. The trips include 3 hours of kayaking, snorkeling gear, lunch on a deserted beach, and a rainforest walk to the lighthouse. The full-day trip costs A$115 (US$75), but you must be age 13 or over. You can also stay on the island for as little as A$31 (US$20) per person per night in a multishare bunkhouse accommodations (See "Where to Stay," later in this chapter).

EXPLORING THE WET TROPICS RAINFOREST

The 110-million-year-old World Heritage–listed Daintree Rainforest, 2 hours north of Cairns, gets most of the attention (see the "Port Douglas, Daintree & the Cape Tribulation Area" section, later in this chapter), but tracts of rainforest closer to Cairns are just as pristine. These rainforests and the Daintree are part of the Wet Tropics, a World Heritage area that stretches from Cape Tribulation to Townsville. This dense, lush environment has remained unchanged by ice ages and other geological events, and the plants and animals here retain primitive characteristics. Within the tract's mangroves, eucalyptus woodlands, and tropical rainforest are 65% of Australia's bird species, 60% of its butterfly species, and many of its frogs, reptiles, bats, marsupials, and orchids.

Because so much rainforest wildlife is nocturnal and often difficult to spot, consider joining **Wait-a-While Rainforest Tours** (© **07/4098 7500**) on one of their afternoon-into-night trips into Daintree and Cape Tribulation national parks. The tours cost A$265 to A$285 (US$172–US$185) and are designed to maximize your encounters with the wild things.

A SIDE TRIP TO KURANDA, A RAINFOREST VILLAGE ☞

Few travelers visit Cairns without making at least a day trip to the mountain village of Kuranda, 34km (21 miles) west of Cairns near the Barron Gorge National Park. Although it's undeniably touristy, the cool mountain air and mist-wrapped rainforest refuse to be spoiled, no matter how many tourists clutter the streets. The shopping in Kuranda—for leather goods, Australian-wool sweaters, opals, crafts, and more—is more unusual than in Cairns, and the handful of cafes and restaurants are much more atmospheric. The town is easily negotiated on foot, so pick up a visitors' guide and map at the Skyrail gondola station or train station (see below for how to get there) when you arrive.

GETTING THERE

Getting to Kuranda is part of the fun. Some people drive up the winding 25km (16-mile) mountain road, but undoubtedly the most popular routes are to chuff up the mountainside in a scenic train, or to glide silently over the rainforest canopy in the world's longest gondola cableway, the Skyrail Rainforest Cableway.

The most popular way to get there is to go one way on the Skyrail (mornings are best for photography from the Skyrail) and the other way on the train.

BY SKYRAIL   The **Skyrail Rainforest Cableway** ☆☆☆ (© 07/4038 1555; www.skyrail.com.au) is a magnificent feat of engineering and one of Australia's top tourism attractions. About 114 six-person gondolas leave every few seconds from the terminal in the northern Cairns suburb of Smithfield for the 7.5km (4½-mile) journey. The view of the coast as you ascend is so breathtaking that even those afraid of heights will find it worthwhile overcoming their nervousness. As you rise over the foothills of the coastal range, watch the lush green of the rainforest take over beneath you. Looking back, there are spectacular views over Cairns and north towards Trinity Bay. On a clear day, you can see Green Island. There are two stops along the way—at Red Peak and Barron Falls—and about 90 minutes is needed to make the trip properly. After about 10 minutes, you reach Red Peak. You are now 545m (1,788 ft.) above sea level, and massive kauri pines dominate the view. You must change gondolas at each station, so take the time to stroll around the boardwalks for the ground view of the rainforest. Guided walks are run every 20 minutes.

On to Barron Falls station, built on the cleared site of an old construction camp for workers on the first hydroelectric power station on the Barron River in the 1930s. A rainforest information center has been established here, and there are boardwalks to the lookouts for wonderful views of the Barron Gorge and Falls. From Barron Falls station, the gondola travels over the thick rainforest of the range. It's easy to spot ferns and orchids and the brilliant blue butterflies of the region. As you reach the end of the trip, the gondola passes over the Barron River and across the Kuranda railway line into the station. A one-way ticket is A$32 (US$21) for adults and A$16 (US$10) for children 4 to 14; a round-trip ticket, including transfers from your Cairns or northern beaches hotel, is A$61 (US$40) for adults, A$31 (US$20) for children, or A$153 (US$99) for a family, and A$78 (US$51) for adults, A$39 (US$25) for children, or A$195 (US$127) for a family from Port Douglas. You must make a reservation to travel within a 15-minute time frame. Don't worry if it rains on the day you've chosen to go—one of the best trips I've made on Skyrail was in a misty rain, which added a new dimension to the rainforest. The cableway operates from 8am to 5pm, with last boarding at the Cairns end at 3:45pm. The Skyrail terminal is on the Captain Cook Highway at Kamerunga Road, Caravonica Lakes, 15km (9½ miles) north of Cairns' city center.

BY SCENIC RAILWAY   The 34km (21-mile) Kuranda Scenic Railway (© **1800/620 324** in Australia, or 07/4031 3636; www.traveltrain.qr.com.au) is one of the most scenic rail journeys in the world. The train snakes through the magnificent vistas of the Barron Gorge National Park, past gorges and waterfalls on the 90-minute trip from Cairns to Kuranda. It rises 328m (1,076 ft.) and goes through 15 tunnels before emerging at the pretty Kuranda station, which is smothered in ferns. Built by hand over 5 years in the late 1880s, the railway track is today a monument to the 1,500 men who toiled to link the two towns, and the ride on the steam train adds to the atmosphere. The train departs Cairns Central at 8:30am daily and 9:30am Sunday through Friday (except Christmas), and leaves Kuranda at 2pm Sunday through Friday and 3:30pm every day. The fare is A$31 (US$20) one-way for adults and A$15 (US$9.75) for children 4 to 14. A pass for a family is A$77 (US$50) one-way.

SKYRAIL/TRAIN COMBINATION TICKETS   In most cases, these packages represent convenience rather than savings. A package combining one-way travel on the Skyrail and a trip back on the Scenic Railway is A$63 (US$41) for adults and A$31 (US$20) for children; A$78 (US$51) for adults and A$39 (US$25) for kids with round-trip transfers from Cairns or the northern beaches. A shuttle bus operates between the Skyrail terminal and the nearest train station at Freshwater, 7km (4½ miles) away, for A$5 (US$3.25) adults, A$2.50 (US$1.60) kids one-way. A three-way package including the Skyrail, the Scenic Railway, and entry to the Tjapukai Aboriginal Cultural Park (see above) is A$91 (US$59) for adults and A$45 (US$29) for kids, or A$106 (US$69) for adults and A$53 (US$34) for kids including transfers from Cairns/northern beaches. A Skyrail/Scenic Railway/Rainforestation option is A$103 (US$67) for adults, A$51 (US$33) kids. Book packages through Skyrail, Queensland Rail, or Tjapukai.

BY BUS   Whitecar Coaches (© 07/4091 1855) operates several daily bus services to Kuranda departing from 46 Spence St., Cairns. The fare is A$1 (US65¢) per person.

EXPLORING KURANDA

Kuranda is known for its markets that sell locally made arts and crafts, fresh produce, boomerangs, T-shirts, and jewelry. There are two markets—the small "original" markets at 7 Therwine St., behind Kuranda Market Arcade (open Wed–Fri and Sun), which mainly sell cheap imports; and the 90-stall Heritage markets (open daily 9am–3pm), which offer better quality and a wider variety of goods. Try to visit Kuranda when both markets are open.

Even the Heritage markets have been invaded by commercial imported products, and in response, a group of about 50 local artisans sell their work in the **Kuranda Arts Co-Operative** ✿ (© 07/4093 9026) at Shop 6, "The Settlement," Rob Veivers Drive, next to the Butterfly Sanctuary. It's open from 10am to 4pm daily. You will find quality furniture crafted from recycled Australian hardwoods, jewelry, handicrafts, and all kinds of stuff here.

You can explore the rainforest, the river esplanade, or Barron Falls along a number of easy walking trails. If you want to learn about the rainforest, explore it with Brian Clarke of **Kuranda Riverboat & Rainforest Tours** (© 07/4093 7476 or 0412/159212), who runs informative 45-minute river cruises. The cruises depart from 10:15am to 2:30pm from the riverside landing across the railway footbridge near the train station. He also runs a daily 400m (1,312-ft.) walk through the rainforest, leaving at 11:45am and returning at 12:45pm. Brian is a former crocodile hunter and has lived in the rainforest for more than 30 years. The cruise or the walk costs A$12 (US$7.80) for adults, A$6 (US$3.90) for children 5 to 15, and A$30 (US$20) for families. Buy your tickets on board.

KURANDA'S NATURE PARKS

Of Kuranda's two walk-through aviaries, **Birdworld** (© 07/4093 9188), behind the Heritage markets off Rob Veivers Drive, is probably the most interesting, as it has eye-catching macaws and a cassowary. **The Aviary**, 8 Thongon St. (© 07/4093 7411), is good if you want to see a bigger range of Australian species. Birdworld is open daily from 9am to 4pm; admission is A$11 (US$7.15) for adults, A$4 (US$2.60) for children 4 to 14, A$28 (US$18) for families. The Aviary is open from 10am to 3:30pm; admission is A$12 (US$7.80) for adults, $6 (US$3.90) for kids 4 to 16. Both aviaries are closed Christmas.

Australian Butterfly Sanctuary 🅪 *(Kids)* A rainbow-hued array of 1,500 tropical butterflies—including the electric blue "Ulysses" and Australia's largest species, the Cairns bird wing—is housed in a lush walk-through enclosure here. Take the free, guided tour and learn about the butterfly's fascinating life cycle. The butterflies will land on you if you wear pink, red, and other bright colors.

8 Rob Veivers Dr. ℂ 07/4093 7575. Fax 07/4093 8923. www.australianbutterflies.com. Admission A$13 (US$8.45) adults, A$12 (US$7.15) seniors, A$6.50 (US$4.25) children 5–16, A$30 (US$20) family pass. AE, DC, MC, V. Daily 9:45am–4pm. Free guided tours every 15 min. from 10am; last tour departs 3:15pm. Closed Christmas. On-street parking. Bus stop 7 min. from sanctuary.

Rainforestation Nature Park At this 40-hectare (99-acre) nature and cultural complex, you can take a 45-minute ride into the rainforest in a World War II amphibious Army Duck. You'll hear commentary on orchids and other rainforest wildlife along the way. You can also see a performance by Aboriginal dancers; learn about Aboriginal legends and throw a boomerang on the Dreamtime Walk; or have your photo taken cuddling a koala in the wildlife park. You can do any of these activities separately, or do them all (except cuddle a koala) in a package that costs A$34 (US$22) for adults, A$17 (US$11) for kids 4 to 14, or A$84 (US$55) for a family. Koala photos are A$12 (US$7.80). The Army Duck runs on the hour beginning at 10am; the Aboriginal dancers perform at 10:30am, noon, and 2pm; and the 30-minute Dreamtime Walk leaves at 10, 11, and 11:30am, noon, and 12:30, 1:30, and 2:30pm.

On the Kennedy Hwy., a 5-min. drive from the center of Kuranda. ℂ 07/4093 9033. Fax 07/4093 7578. www.rainforest.com.au. Shuttle from Thongon St., Kuranda (opposite the Post Office), every 30 min. from 10:45am–2:45pm costs A$6 (US$3.90) adults, A$3 (US$1.95) children, and A$15 (US$8.95) families, round-trip. AE, DC, MC, V. Daily 9am–4pm. Closed Christmas. Ample parking.

WHITE-WATER RAFTING & OTHER THRILLS

RnR Rafting 🅪 (ℂ **1800/079 039** in Australia, or 07/4051 7777; www. rnrrafting.com) and **Raging Thunder Adventures** (ℂ **07/4030 7990;** www. ragingthunder.com.au) serve as one-stop booking shops for action pursuits in and around Cairns, including hot-air ballooning, skydiving, jet-boating, horseback riding, ATV (all-terrain vehicle) safaris, parasailing, and rafting. Ask them about multipursuit packages.

BIKING Dan's Mountain Biking (ℂ **07/4033 0128**) runs a wide range of full- and half-day guided tours in small groups from A$75 to A$135 (US$49–US$88) per person.

BUNGEE JUMPING Contact **A. J. Hackett Bungy** (ℂ **1800/622 888** in Australia, or 07/4057 7188). The cost is A$109 (US$71) per person including transport to the site, which is 20 minutes north of town on McGregor Road.

FISHING Cairns is the world's giant black marlin capital. Catches of more than 1,000 pounds hardly raise an eyebrow in this neck of the woods. The game-fishing season is September through December, with November the busiest.

(*Tips* **Staying Warm in Kuranda**

If you visit Kuranda, don't forget to bring some warm clothing in winter. It can get nippy in the mountains, especially at night.

Book early, as game boats are reserved months in advance. Game fishers can also battle Pacific sailfish, dogtooth and yellow-fin tuna, Spanish mackerel, wahoo, dolphinfish, barracuda, and tiger shark. Reef anglers can expect to land coral trout, red emperor (sea perch), and sweetlip. Mangrove jack, barramundi, and tarpon lurk in the estuaries. Check out www.fishingcairns.com.au or contact **Destination Cairns Marketing,** 36 Aplin St. (at Sheridan St.; © **1800/807 730** in Australia, or 07/4051 4066), to book a charter. Expect to pay around A$400 (US$260) per person or about A$1,900 (US$1,235) per day for a sole charter for heavy-tackle game fishing, A$295 (US$192) per person for light tackle stuff, from A$145 (US$94) for reef fishing, and A$130 (US$85) for a day or A$75 (US$49) for a half day in the Cairns Inlet estuary.

WHITE-WATER RAFTING   Several companies offer exciting white-water-rafting trips from Cairns on the Class III to IV **Tully River** *๙๙*, 90 minutes south of Cairns near Mission Beach; the Class III Barron River in the hills behind the city; and the Class IV to V rapids of the inland Johnstone River. One of the best is **RnR Rafting** (© **07/4051 7777**).

One-day trips on the Tully are the most popular (see "Mission Beach: The Cassowary Coast," later in this chapter). The trip costs A$145 (US$94) from Cairns, or A$160 (US$104) from Port Douglas, including transfers.

Closer to Cairns, the gentler **Barron River** is a good choice for the timid. The half-day trip with RnR Rafting costs about A$83 (US$54) from Cairns or A$94 (US$61) from Port Douglas, including pickup from your accommodations and 2-hours' rafting. There is also a A$6 (US$3.90) National Park fee.

WHERE TO STAY

High season in Cairns includes 2 weeks at Easter, the period from early July to early October, and the Christmas holiday through January. Book ahead in those periods, and in low season (Nov–June) many hotels offer discount rates or are willing to negotiate.

Cairns has a good supply of affordable accommodations, both in the heart of the city and along the northern beaches. Or you can choose to stay in the peaceful village of Kuranda, or get away from it all at an island resort.

Don't think you have to stay in Cairns city if you don't have a car. Most tour and cruise operators will pick you up and drop you off in Cairns, on the northern beaches, or even in Port Douglas (see section 3, later in this chapter).

IN CAIRNS

Unless noted otherwise, all accommodations below are within walking distance of shops, restaurants, cinemas, the casino, the tourist office, bus terminals, the train station, and the departure terminals for Great Barrier Reef cruises.

Very Expensive

Hotel Sofitel Reef Casino *๙*   Arguably the most stylish property in Cairns, this six-story hotel is 1 block from the water, with partial water views from some rooms, and nice city/hinterland outlooks from others. All the rooms, which have lots of light and high-quality amenities, come with Jacuzzis, bathrobes, and small balconies with smart timber furniture. The Cairns casino is attached to the hotel (see "Cairns After Dark," later in this chapter).

35–41 Wharf St., Cairns, QLD 4870. © **1800/808 883** in Australia, 800/221-4542 in the U.S. and Canada, 020/8283 4500 in the U.K., 0800/44 4422 in New Zealand, or 07/4030 8888. Fax 07/4030 8777. www.accor hotels.com. 128 units. A$325–A$600 (US$211–US$390) double; A$710–A$2,000 (US$462–US$1,300) suite. Extra person A$33 (US$21). Children under 15 stay free in parent's room with existing bedding. AE, DC, MC, V.

Free valet and self-parking. Airport shuttle. **Amenities:** 3 restaurants; bar; small rooftop pool; health club; Jacuzzi; sauna; concierge; tour desk; business center; 24-hr. room service; babysitting; laundry service; dry cleaning. *In room:* A/C, TV/VCR, dataport, minibar, hair dryer, iron, safe.

Radisson Plaza Hotel at The Pier 🐾 There's a definite "wow!" factor to this hotel on Trinity Bay. When you walk into the lobby, you're surrounded by rainforest. Tall trees (real ones) and cockatoos (papier-mâché) give the place a great atmosphere. Sporting the best views of any city-center hotel, the rooms were renovated in 1999 with smart maple entryways and a gold, burgundy, and navy decor. Each has a VCR, a balcony, and a view of the harbor, the city, tropical gardens, or the big free-form pool. The bathrooms all have marble and maple fittings, and big corner tubs. The hotel is connected to The Pier shopping mall and is not far from the Reef Fleet Terminal.

Pierpoint Rd., Cairns, QLD 4870. ℂ 1800/333 333 in Australia and New Zealand, 800/333-3333 in the U.S. and Canada, 0800/37 4411 in the U.K., 1800/55 7474 in Ireland, or 07/4031 1411. Fax 07/4031 3226. www. radisson.com. 216 units. A$396–A$437 (US$257–US$284) double; A$413–A$1,100 (US$268–US$715) suite. Children under 17 stay free in parent's room with existing bedding. AE, DC, MC, V. Free outdoor and covered self-parking. Airport shuttle. **Amenities:** 2 restaurants; bar; large outdoor swimming pool and children's pool; nearby golf course; health club; Jacuzzi; sauna; video arcade; concierge; tour desk; car-rental desk; business center; shopping arcade; salon; 24-hr. room service; in-room massage; babysitting; coin-op laundry; dry cleaning; executive level rooms. *In room:* A/C, TV/VCR w/pay movies, fax, dataport, minibar, coffeemaker, hair dryer, iron, safe.

Expensive

Matson Resort Cairns Despite its lack of obvious glitz, the 14-story Matson has been the choice of a number of movie stars—most famously Marlon Brando—while on location in Cairns. A 20-minute waterfront walk from downtown, the hotel offers a range of accommodations, from hotel rooms to four-bedroom penthouses (with private rooftop pool), which have been refurbished over the past 5 years. The one- and two-bedroom apartments look out to the sea; hotel rooms have sea or mountain views. The rooms are spacious, but the bathrooms are not, perhaps reflecting the hotel's Japanese market. Out back are cheaper studios and apartments, with newly upgraded furnishings, and out front is a pretty pool and sun deck.

The Esplanade (at Kerwin St.), Cairns, QLD 4870. ℂ 1800/079 105 in Australia, or 07/4031 2211. Fax 07/ 4031 2704. www.matsonresort.com.au. 342 units. A$220–A$260 (US$143–US$169) double; A$160 (US$104) studio; A$165–A$360 (US$107–US$234) tower apt (sleeps 5); A$205 (US$133) 1-bedroom apt (sleeps 4); A$250 (US$163) 2-bedroom apt (sleeps 6); A$950 (US$618) 3 bedroom penthouse; A$1,200 (US$780) 4-bedroom penthouse. Extra person A$28 (US$18). Ask about packages. AE, DC, MC, V. Free covered parking. Courtesy transfers to and from airport, hotel-shuttle service around the city. Bus stop about 100m (328 ft.) from the hotel. **Amenities:** 2 restaurants; 3 bars; 3 outdoor swimming pools; golf course about 20 min. away; 2 lit tennis courts; health club with facilities including aerobics classes; Jacuzzi; sauna; bike rental; concierge; tour desk; car-rental desk; salon; 24-hr. room service; massage (in-room or at the health club); babysitting; coin-op laundry and laundry service; same-day dry cleaning; nonsmoking rooms. *In room:* A/C, TV w/pay movies, dataport in some rooms, kitchenette in studios and apts only, minibar in hotel rooms and apts, fridge in studios, hair dryer, iron, safe.

Oasis Resort Cairns *Value* The large swimming pool, complete with swim-up bar and a little sandy beach, is the focus of this attractive six-story resort built in 1997. All the colorful, contemporary rooms have balconies with views over the tropical gardens, mountains, or the pool. The suites, with a TV in the bedroom and a large Jacuzzi bathtub, could well be the best-value suites in town.

122 Lake St., Cairns, QLD 4870. ℂ 07/4080 1888. Fax 07/4080 1889. www.oasis-cairns.com.au. 314 units. A$215 (US$140) double; A$385 (US$250) suite. Extra person A$44 (US$29). Children under 16 stay free in parent's room with existing bedding. Free crib. Ask about packages. AE, DC, MC, V. Free valet and self-parking.

Airport shuttle. **Amenities:** Restaurant; 2 bars; outdoor pool; health club; concierge; tour desk; limited room service; babysitting; coin-op laundry or laundry service; dry cleaning. *In room:* A/C, TV w/pay movies, dataport, coffeemaker, minibar, hair dryer, iron, safe.

Moderate

Tuna Towers   The harbor views at this multistory motel and apartment complex are better than those at most of the more luxurious hotels in Cairns. Two blocks from town, the accommodations are good size, with fresh, appealing furnishings and modern bathrooms. If your balcony does not have a water vista, you overlook a nice aspect of the city or mountains instead.

145 The Esplanade (at Minnie St.), Cairns, QLD 4870. ⓒ **1800/117 787** in Australia, or 07/4051 4688. Fax 07/4051 8129. www.tunatowers.com.au. 60 units. A$120–A$135 (US$78–US$88) double; A$131–A$146 (US$85–US$95) studio apt double; A$150–A$170 (US$98–US$111) suite. Extra person A$12 (US$7.80). AE, DC, MC, V. Limited free parking. Airport shuttle. **Amenities:** Restaurant; small outdoor pool; golf course (1km/½ mile away); 4 lit tennis courts nearby; access to nearby health club; Jacuzzi; tour desk; car-rental desk; limited room service; massage; babysitting; coin-op laundry; dry cleaning. *In room:* A/C, TV w/free movies, dataport, kitchenettes in suites and studios, coffeemaker, hair dryer, iron.

Inexpensive

Coral Tree Inn *⟨Value⟩*   The focal point of this airy, modern resort-style motel just a 5-minute walk from the city center is the clean, friendly communal kitchen that overlooks the palm-lined saltwater pool and paved sun deck. It's a great spot to cook up a steak or reef fish filet on the free barbecue and join other guests at the big communal tables. Local restaurants deliver, free fresh-roasted coffee is on the boil all day, and a vending machine sells wine and beer, so you don't even have to go down to the pub for supplies! The smallish, basic but neat motel rooms have painted brick walls, terra-cotta tile or carpeted floors, and clean new bathrooms sporting marble-look laminate countertops. In contrast, the eight suites are huge and stylish enough to do any corporate traveler proud. They are some of the best-value accommodations in town. All rooms have a private balcony or patio; some look out onto the drab commercial buildings next door, but most look out over the pool. Ask about packages that include cruises and other tours.

166–172 Grafton St., Cairns, QLD 4870. ⓒ **07/4031 3744.** Fax 07/4031 3064. www.coraltreeinn.com.au. 58 units. A$110 (US$72) double; A$136 (US$88) suite (sleeps 4). Additional person A$10 (US$6.50). AE, DC, MC, V. Limited free parking; ample on-street parking. Airport shuttle. **Amenities:** Bar; outdoor pool; access to nearby health club; bike rental; tour desk; car-rental desk; babysitting; coin-op laundry and laundry service; same-day dry cleaning; nonsmoking rooms, safe (at reception). *In room:* A/C, TV, dataport, kitchenette in suites, fridge, coffeemaker, hair dryer, iron.

Lilybank Bed & Breakfast *⟨R⟩*   This 1870s Queenslander homestead, originally a mayor's residence, is in a leafy suburb 6km (3¾ miles) from the airport and a 10-minute drive from the city. Guests sleep in large, attractive rooms, all individually decorated with such features as wrought-iron beds and patchwork quilts. Each bathroom is a good size. The largest room has French doors opening onto a "sleep-out," an enclosed veranda with two extra beds. You can also stay in the gardener's cottage, renovated with slate floors, stained-glass windows, a king-size bed, and a bar. The house is set in gardens with an attractive rock-lined saltwater pool. Breakfast is served in the garden room by the fishpond. Your gregarious hosts Mike and Pat Woolford also share their house with three poodles, an irrepressible galah, and a giant green tree frog. There's a guest TV lounge and kitchen, and phone, fax, and e-mail access. Many tours pick up at the door, and several good restaurants are a stroll away, so you don't need a car to stay here. No smoking indoors.

75 Kamerunga Rd., Stratford, Cairns, QLD 4870. ℭ **07/4055 1123.** Fax 07/4058 1990. www.lilybank.com. au. 6 units (4 with shower only). A$88–A$110 (US$57–US$72) double. Additional person A$33 (US$21). Rates include full breakfast. AE, MC, V. Free parking. Bus: 1E or 1G. Taxi from airport approximately. A$15 (US$9.75). Bus stop 120m (394 ft.). Children not permitted. **Amenities:** Outdoor pool; tour desk; massage can be arranged; coin-op laundry; nonsmoking rooms. In room: A/C, hair dryer, no phone.

ON THE NORTHERN BEACHES

A string of white sandy beaches starts 15 minutes north of the city center. Trinity Beach, 15 minutes from the airport, is secluded, elegant, and scenic. The most upscale is Palm Cove, 20 minutes from the airport. Here rainbow-hued shops and tasteful apartment blocks nestle among giant paperbarks and palms fronting a postcard-perfect beach. It has several advantages over other beach suburbs: a nine-hole resort golf course and a gym are within walking distance, the Quicksilver Wavepiercer Great Barrier Reef cruise boat picks up passengers here daily, and it has the greatest choice of places to eat. Add 5 to 10 minutes to the traveling times above to reach the city.

Very Expensive

The Sebel Reef House & Spa Palm Cove 𝕽𝕽𝕽   Picture yourself inside a Somerset Maugham novel—but substitute the Queensland tropics for Singapore—and you've almost got it right. This must be one of the most romantic hotels in Queensland, or all of Australia. The Reef House's guest list has read like an excerpt from Who's Who—the most recent addition being Bob Dylan and his band. But no matter who you are, you will never want to leave. The white walls are swathed in bougainvillea, and the beds with mosquito netting. Airy interiors are furnished with rustic handmade artifacts and white wicker furniture. The Verandah Spa rooms, which have a Jacuzzi on the balcony, overlook the pool, waterfalls, and lush gardens and there are all the extra touches such as bathrobes and CD player, as well as generous balconies within earshot of the ocean. The beachfront restaurant, set on a large covered wooden deck beneath towering paperbarks, is a favorite with locals and tourists alike for its unsurpassed ocean views, gentle breezes, and unpretentious food. In mid-2003, the hotel opened a health spa operated by Daintree Spa (see "A Spa in the Rainforest" on p. 300).

99 Williams Esplanade, Palm Cove, Cairns, QLD 4879. ℭ **1800/079 052** in Australia, or 07/4055 3633. Fax 07/4055 3305. www.reefhouse.com.au. 69 units (14 with shower only). A$275–A$480 (US$179–US$312) double; A$480–A$595 (US$312–US$387) suite. Extra person A$30 (US$20). Children under 14 stay free in parent's room with existing bedding. AE, DC, MC, V. Free undercover parking (for limited number of cars); ample on-street parking. Courtesy airport shuttle. Bus: 1, 1B, 1X, 2X, or N. **Amenities:** Restaurant; bar; cafe; honor bar; 3 small heated outdoor pools; nearby golf course; spa; access to nearby health club; concierge; tour desk; limited room service; massage; babysitting; coin-op laundry; laundry service; same-day dry cleaning. In room: A/C, TV/VCR, kitchenette, minibar, coffeemaker, hair dryer, iron, safe.

Expensive

Outrigger Beach Club & Spa 𝕽   Ask for a room overlooking the beach at this new, three-story hotel on the waterfront. Still somewhat stark and new looking, the Outrigger tries to mix the style of an elegant hotel with a Queensland colonial house. By the time you get there, some of the newness may have rubbed off. Hotel rooms are small, but have Jacuzzis on the decks. You can also choose an apartment—the two penthouses have private rooftop terraces and pools. There's no elevator. The first block of 48 rooms opened in late 2002, with another 180 due to open in August 2003. Rates for the new rooms were not available at press time.

123 Williams Esplanade, Palm Cove, Cairns, QLD 4879. ℭ **800/688-7444** in the U.S. and Canada, 1800/134 444 in Australia, or 07/4059 9200. Fax 07/4059 9222. www.outrigger.com.au. 228 units. A$280–A$400

Tips **Safe Swimming**

All of the northern beaches have small, netted enclosures for safe swimming October through May, when deadly box jellyfish (stingers) render all mainland beaches in north Queensland off-limits.

(US$182–US$260) double rooms with Jacuzzi; A$340–A$480 (US$221–US$312) double 1-bedroom suite; A$430–A$510 (US$280–US$332) double 2-bedroom suite with Jacuzzi; A$650 (US$423) 2-bedroom penthouse suite. Extra person A$30 (US$20). Minimum 3 night stay at Easter and Christmas to mid-January. AE, DC, MC, V. Bus: 1, 1B, 1X, 2X, or N. Security car parking. **Amenities:** Restaurant; coffee shop; heated outdoor pool; golf course nearby; spa; gymnasium; concierge; tour desk; nonsmoking rooms. *In room:* A/C, TV w/pay movies, dataport, kitchen (suites only), fridge, coffeemaker, hair dryer, iron, safe, Jacuzzi, washing machine and dryer (suites only).

Moderate

Ellis Beach Oceanfront Bungalows 🅐 *Finds*   Located on what is arguably the loveliest of the northern beaches, about 30 minutes from Cairns, these bungalows and cabins are set under palm trees between the Coral Sea and a backdrop of mountainous rainforest. Lifeguards patrol the beach, and there are stinger nets in season as well as a shady swimming pool and toddlers' wading pool. There's plenty of privacy, and the accommodations are basic but pleasant. You can sit on the veranda and gaze at the ocean. Keep an eye out for dolphins. Each bungalow and cabin sleeps four and has full kitchen facilities (with microwave, fridge, and freezer), but cabins have no en-suite bathroom. There are coin-operated barbecues and phone and fax facilities.

Captain Cook Hwy., Ellis Beach, QLD 4879. 🅒 **1800/637 036** in Australia, or 07/4055 3538. Fax 07/4055 3077. www.ellisbeachbungalows.com.au. 15 units (all with shower only). A$68 (US$44) double cabins; A$155 (US$101) double bungalows. Extra person A$15 (US$9.75) cabins, A$24 (US$16) bungalows. AE, MC, V. **Amenities:** Restaurant; 2 outdoor pools; golf course nearby; tour desk; car-rental desk; coin-op laundry. *In room:* A/C and ceiling fans, TV, kitchen, iron, no phone.

The Reef Retreat 🅐🅐   Tucked back one row of buildings from the beach is this little gem—a low-rise collection of contemporary studios and suites built around a swimming pool in a peaceful grove of palms and silver paperbarks. All the rooms in the newer or extensively renovated wings have cool tile floors and smart teak and cane furniture. The studios are a terrific value and much larger than the average hotel room. In the oceanview suites, you can even lie in bed and see the sea. The extra-private honeymoon suites (and some oceanview suites) have a Jacuzzi and a kitchenette outside on the balcony. There's a barbecue on the grounds and a Jacuzzi. There's no elevator. Units are cleaned twice weekly; one free cleaning for stays of 5 days or longer. Extra cleanings A$20 (US$13).

10–14 Harpa St., Palm Cove, Cairns, QLD 4879. 🅒 **07/4059 1744.** Fax 07/4059 1745. www.reefretreat.com.au. 36 units (16 with shower only, 20 with shower and Jacuzzi). A$140 (US$91) studio double; A$150 (US$98) suite with Jacuzzi; A$160 (US$104) oceanview suite; A$260 (US$169) 2-bedroom apt (sleeps 4). Additional person A$25 (US$16). Children under 3 stay free in parent's room with existing bedding; crib A$25 (US$16). AE, MC, V. Free parking. Bus: 1, 1B 1X, 2X, or N. Airport shuttle A$15 (US$9.75) per person one-way. **Amenities:** Outdoor saltwater pool; nearby golf course; nearby tennis courts; Jacuzzi; tour desk; car-rental desk; coin-op laundry; laundry service; dry cleaning. *In room:* A/C, TV, dataport, kitchenette, fridge, coffeemaker, hair dryer, iron.

ON AN ISLAND

Several island resorts are located off Cairns. They afford you safe swimming year-round, because the October-to-May infestations of deadly marine stingers don't make it to the islands.

Very Expensive

Green Island Resort ⚡️ Step off the beach at this Great Barrier Reef national-park island, and you are surrounded by acres of coral. The resort is a high-class cluster of rooms tucked away in a dense vine forest. Each room is private, roomy, and elegantly outfitted, with polished wooden floors and a balcony looking into the forest. Windsurfing, paddle skiing, canoeing, diving and snorkeling (both on the island and on day trips to the outer Reef), learn-to-dive courses, glass-bottom-boat trips, walking rainforest trails, parasailing, and beach volleyball are among the activities available, or you can simply laze on the coarse white-coral sand. Helicopter and seaplane flights and cruises are available to the Outer Reef. Many activities and equipment are free for guests, such as non-motorized sports, snorkel gear, and glass-bottom-boat trips, while there's a charge for scuba diving and other activities using fuel. Both the island and the resort are small, so you may feel a bit cramped when the day-trippers from Cairns descend; but after most of them leave at 4:30pm, the place is blissfully peaceful.

27km (17 miles) east of Cairns (P.O. Box 898, Cairns, QLD 4870). ℂ 1800/67 3366 in Australia, or 07/4031 3300. Fax 07/4052 1511. www.greenislandresort.com.au. 46 units. A$465 (US$302) double; A$565 (US$367) suite. Extra person A$86 (US$56). Ask about packages. AE, DC, MC, V. Great Adventures (ℂ 07/4044 9944) runs transfers (50 min.) from Cairns 4 times a day for A$50 (US$33) adults, A$25 (US$16) children 4–14, round-trip. Helicopter and seaplane transfers are available through resort. **Amenities:** 2 restaurants; 2 bars; 2 outdoor saltwater pools; wide array of watersports equipment available; concierge; tour desk; laundry service and free guest laundry. *In room:* A/C, TV, free cable TV, minibar, hair dryer, safe.

Lizard Island ⚡️⚡️⚡️ Luxury lodges, huge potato cod so tame divers can pet them, snorkeling off the beach, and isolation—that's what lures the well-heeled to this small, exclusive resort. Lizard is a rugged 1,000-hectare (2,470-acre) national-park island on the Great Barrier Reef, sparsely vegetated but stunningly beautiful, ringed by 24 white sandy beaches, with fringing reefs that support a multitude of marine life including giant clams. No day-trippers are allowed. Many activities are free: snorkeling and glass-bottom-boat trips, catamarans, paddle-skis, fishing tackle, tennis, and hiking trails, such as the muscle-straining 545m (½-mile) climb to Cook's Look, where Captain Cook spied his way out of the treacherous reefs in 1770. You pay for fishing and diving trips to nearby Reef sites, including Cod Hole. Introductory dive lessons and night dives are available. Lizard's waters are home to the world-record black marlin; half- and full-day game-fishing trips are available.

The resort underwent renovation in 2000. The 40 villas are freestanding lodges tucked under palms along the beach or perched on cliff tops overlooking the bay. They are of elegant timber and stone construction, in a casual tropical style, with earth and sea tone finishes. A guest lounge has Internet facilities, TV and video, bar facilities, and a book and games library. At press time, the resort was gearing up to open The Point, "super premium" pavilion-style accommodations with cascading decks and a plunge pool. Other recent additions include a gymnasium and expanded spa facilities.

240km (149 miles) north of Cairns; 27km (16¾ miles) offshore (P&O Australian Resorts, G.P.O. Box 478, Sydney, NSW 2001). ℂ 1800/737 678 in Australia, 800/225-9849 in the U.S. and Canada, 020/7805 3875 in the U.K., or 02/9277 5050 (Sydney reservations office). Fax 02/9299 2477 (Sydney reservations office). www.poresorts.com. 40 units (all with shower only). A$1,480 (US$962) double room; A$1,800 (US$1,170) double suites and villas; A$2,140 (US$1,391) double Premium Villa; A$2,900 (US$1,885) double The Point. Extra person A$440 (US$286). Rates include all meals and many activities. Ask about packages; some combine stays at Silky Oaks Lodge (Port Douglas), Sebel Reef House (Cairns), and Bedarra Island (off Mission Beach). AE, DC, MC, V. Transfers are by twice-daily 1-hr. flight from Cairns (book through Qantas); round-trip advance purchase fare is about A$480 (US$312) per person. Aircraft luggage limit 15kg (33 lb.) per person. Air-charter transfers also available. No children under 10. **Amenities:** Restaurant; freshwater pool; night/day tennis court; gymnasium; spa; laundry service. *In room:* A/C and fans, dataport, minibar, coffeemaker, hair dryer, iron.

Moderate/Inexpensive

Fitzroy Island Resort   This is probably the most affordable island resort on the Great Barrier Reef. It's targeted at a young crowd looking for action and eco-fun in a pristine, beautiful location. It's no glamour-puss palace, but was revamped in 2000 to include a Hard Rock Cafe–style restaurant and spruced-up interiors. Fitzroy is a continental island offering little in the way of fringing coral and only a few narrow strips of coral sand. What it does have are catamarans, outrigger canoes, and surf skis; glass-bottom-boat rides; and hiking trails through dense national park forest to a lighthouse. Divers can make drift dives over the reefs dotted around the island to see manta rays, reef sharks, turtles, and coral. There is good snorkeling at two points around the island that you can reach twice a day on the dive boat, at an extra fee. You can also catch the Sunlover Cruises day trip to the outer Great Barrier Reef. The dive shop runs introductory and certified dives and certification courses. Each of the modestly comfortable beach cabins has a queen-size bed and two bunks in the back, and the rooms have ceiling fans and a large balcony with views through the trees to the sea. The bunkhouse accommodations are basic fan-cooled carpeted rooms with bunks and/or beds. Bunkhouse guests can use the communal kitchen, but must bring their own supplies from the mainland.

The restaurant is moderately priced, a kiosk sells takeout food, and the poolside grill and bar offers casual meals. The **Raging Thunder Beach Bar,** billed as "the only nightclub on the Reef," gets going on Saturday nights.

35km (22 miles) southeast of Cairns (P.O. Box 1109, Cairns, QLD 4870). (C) **07/4051 9588.** Fax 07/4052 1335. www.fitzroyislandresort.com.au. 52 cabins (all with shower only); 32 bunkhouses, none with private bathroom. Cabins A$220 (US$143) double. Extra person A$35 (US$23). Bunkhouses A$31 (US$20) per person per bed (sharing with up to 3 other people); A$116 (US$76) double (sole use); A$124 (US$81) family bunkhouse (sleeps 4). AE, DC, MC, V. Round-trip transfers 3 times daily from Cairns (approx. 45 min.) cost A$36 (US$23) adults, A$18 (US$12) children 4–14. **Amenities:** Restaurant; bar; outdoor pool; watersports equipment; tour desk; dive shop. *In room* (cabins only): TV, minifridge, coffeemaker, hair dryer, iron.

WHERE TO DINE
IN CAIRNS
Expensive

Fishlips Bar & Bistro ☒☒ MODERN AUSTRALIAN/SEAFOOD   Ask locals where they go for seafood—as opposed to where they send tourists—and they direct you to this 1920s bluebird-blue shack about 2km (1¼ miles) from town. Chef Ian Candy is renowned for his flair and innovation with seafood. All dishes come in small or large servings, and the local barramundi, or "barra," shows up in several incarnations, maybe beer-battered with rough-cut chips (fries) and fresh tartar sauce, simply grilled, or served with eggplant pickle and rocket pesto on chargrilled zucchini and onion with charred polenta. There are plenty of non-seafood options as well. Be daring—try the crocodile, pan-fried with pine nuts, coriander, and cumin. For dessert, don't go past the homemade ice cream with flavors that change each week. How nice to see that almost every choice on the wine list comes by the glass. Dine inside (air-conditioned for those humid nights) or on the front deck, with its bright blue pots and palm trees. Licensed Sunday through Thursday, and BYO wine only (no BYO beer or spirits).

228 Sheridan St. (between Charles and McKenzie sts.) (C) **07/4041 1700.** www.fishlips.com.au. Reservations recommended. Main courses A$12–A$19 (US$7.80–US$12) small sizes, A$20–A$41 (US$13–US$27) large sizes. AE, DC, MC, V. Fri noon–2:30pm; daily 6pm–late.

Red Ochre Grill *&* *(Kids* GOURMET BUSH TUCKER   You could accuse this restaurant/bar of using weird and wonderful Aussie ingredients as a gimmick to pull in crowds, but the diners who flock here know good food when they taste it. Daily specials are big on fresh local seafood, and the regular menu—which changes often—lets you devour the Aussie coat of arms in several different ways. Try the emu paté with bush tomato chile sauce, or kangaroo filets done over a mallee wood-fired grill. Although the place is slick enough for a night out, it is also informal enough for a casual meal, and there's a kids' menu.

43 Shields St. © 07/4051 0100. www.redochregrill.com.au. Reservations recommended. Main courses A$5.50–A$24 (US$3.60–US$16) at lunch, A$24–A$32 (US$16–US$21) at dinner. Australian game platter A$42 (US$27) per person; seafood platter A$50 (US$33) per person. AE, DC, MC, V. Daily noon–midnight; 6pm–midnight public holidays. Closed Christmas.

Moderate

Perrotta's MODERN AUSTRALIAN   The locals flock here for brunch and lunch, particularly on the weekends, and you can team it with a visit to the Cairns Regional Art Gallery, as the cafe is just outside. Breakfast differs from the usual bacon and eggs or pancakes fare, offering delights such as smoked salmon and Klimera hash browns with roasted Roma tomatoes, sour cream, and avocado. Sweet-tooths may go for the French toast with star anise–scented pineapple and lime mascarpone. For lunch there's a choice of bruschettas, focaccia, or panini, pasta dishes, or more individual dishes such as Thai style calamari with roasted peanuts, lemon grass, and chile. At dinner, try the barramundi, local swordfish, or Tasmanian salmon. Remember to check out the specials board.

Abbott and Shields sts. © 074031 5899. www.cairnsregionalgallery.com.au. Reservations recommended. Breakfast A$4 A$10 (US$2.60–US$6.50). Main courses (at dinner) all A$25 (US$16). MC, V. Daily 8am–late.

ON THE NORTHERN BEACHES

Colonies MODERN AUSTRALIAN   It may not have the ocean frontage of the grander restaurants along Williams Esplanade, but you are still within earshot of the waves from the veranda of this cheery little aerie upstairs behind a seafront building. The atmosphere is simple and the menu includes loads of inexpensive choices such as pastas, soups, green chicken curry, and seafood. Licensed and BYO.

Upstairs in Paradise Village shopping center, Williams Esplanade, Palm Cove. © 07/4055 3058. Fax 07/4059 1559. www.palmcoveonline.com/colonies. Reservations recommended. Main courses A$16–A$29 (US$10–US$19). AE, DC, MC, V. Daily 10am–10.30pm. Closed mid-Jan to mid-Mar. Bus: 1, 1B, 1X, 2X, or N.

Far Horizons MODERN AUSTRALIAN   You can't quite sink your toes into the sand, but you are just yards from the beach at this pleasant restaurant within the Angsana Resort. The laid-back fine-dining fare includes plenty of fresh seafood—the catch of the day comes with chunky homemade fries and tartar sauce, and there are interesting choices like Vietnamese salad with chargrilled reef fish. The restaurant sometimes sets up dining on the lawn among the palm trees beside the beach. The service is relaxed and friendly and the crowd is a mix of hotel guests from this and other nearby resorts. On Friday and Saturday nights a guitarist plays in the cocktail bar.

Angsana resort, 1 Veivers Rd. (southern end of Williams Esplanade), Palm Cove. © 07/4055 3000. Reservations recommended. Main courses A$24–A$29 (US$16–US$19). AE, DC, MC, V. Daily 6:30pm–midnight (last orders at 9:30pm). Bus: 1, 1B, 1X, 2X, or N.

CAIRNS AFTER DARK

Pick up a copy of the free entertainment newspaper *Barfly,* published every Thursday, for a guide to the week's after-hours action in Cairns. Top spots recommended by the locals include **Metropolis,** upstairs at 15 Spence St. (© **07/4041 0277**), which is popular with the 25-to-45 market and features a sophisticated chocolate decor and a cigar lounge. The **Hotel Sofitel Reef Casino,** 35–41 Wharf St. (© **07/4030 8888**), has two levels of blackjack, baccarat, reef routine, roulette, sic-bo, money wheel, paradise pontoon, Keno, and slot machines. It's open from 10am to 4am Monday through Thursday, and 24 hours from 10am Friday until 4am Monday (closed Good Friday, Anzac Day, and Christmas). No entry for children under 18. The **Casino Nightclub 1936** is open Thursday through Saturday from 8pm to 3am; cover is A$5 (US$3.25).

If you're over 18, but under 35 or so, and it's Saturday night, you may want to take the boat to the DJs or live bands at the **Raging Thunder Nightclub Beach Bar** on Fitzroy Island (see "Where to Stay," above). A$25 (US$16) will get you the boat to the island, nightclub entry, overnight accommodations, and the return trip at 9:30am the next day. There's a A$5 (US$3.25) burger bar operating as well. You must book ahead, through Raging Thunder Adventures (© **07/4030 7907**).

---

3 Port Douglas ⟨★★⟩, Daintree & the Cape Tribulation Area

Port Douglas 67km (42 miles) N of Cairns; Mossman 19km (11½ miles) N of Port Douglas; Daintree 49km (30 miles) N of Port Douglas; Cape Tribulation 34km (21 miles) N of Daintree

The tiny fishing village of Port Douglas is the only place in the world where two World Heritage areas—the Daintree Rain Forest and the Great Barrier Reef—lie side by side. This is truly where "the rainforest meets the reef." Just over an hour's drive from Cairns, through rainforest and along the sea, Port Douglas may be a one-horse town, but it's main street is lined with stylish shops and seriously trendy restaurants, and beautiful Four Mile Beach is not to be missed. This is a favorite spot with celebrities big and small—you may find yourself dining at a table next to anyone from Bill Clinton to Kylie Minogue, Sean Penn to Australian rock band Midnight Oil or minor soap stars.

People often base themselves in "Port," as the locals call it, rather than in Cairns, because they like the peaceful rural surroundings, the uncrowded beach, and the charmed absence of tacky development (so far, anyway). Don't think you will be isolated—many reef and rainforest tours originate in Port Douglas and many of the tours discussed in the Cairns section earlier in this chapter pick up from Port Douglas.

Daintree National Park lies just north of Port Douglas; and just north of that is Cape Tribulation National Park, another wild tract of rainforest and hilly headlands sweeping down to the sea. Exploring these two national parks is easy on a four-wheel-drive day safari from Port Douglas.

ESSENTIALS

GETTING THERE Port Douglas is a scenic 65-minute drive from Cairns, in part along a narrow winding road that skirts the coast. Take Sheridan Street north out of the city as it becomes the Captain Cook Highway; follow the signs to Mossman and Mareeba until you reach the Port Douglas turnoff on your right.

One of the most pleasant ways to get to Port Douglas is to take one of the giant **Quicksilver Wavepiercer** ⟨★⟩ (© **07/4087 2100**) catamarans along the coast. They depart Reef Fleet Terminal in Cairns at 8am, Palm Cove jetty at 8:35am, and arrive in Port Douglas at 9:30am. You can also stay onboard and go straight to the Great Barrier Reef for the day for an extra charge (see "Discovering the

Port Douglas, Daintree & Cape Tribulation

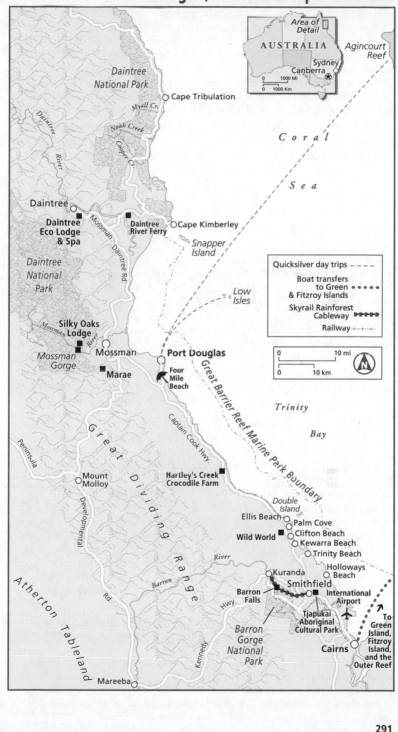

Great Barrier Reef," below). The cost of the trip from Cairns is A$24 (US $16) one-way, A$36 (US$23) round-trip, half price for kids 4 to 14.

A one-way ticket aboard **Sun Palm Express Coaches** (© 07/4031 7577) to Port Douglas hotels is A$28 (US$18) from the Cairns airport. Fares for children are half price.

There is no **train** to Port Douglas, and no scheduled air service. A small airport handles light aircraft and helicopter charters. A **taxi** from Cairns would run close to A$100 (US$65); call **Black & White Taxis** (© 13 10 08 in Cairns).

VISITOR INFORMATION Write for information to the **Port Douglas Daintree Tourism Association,** P.O. Box 511, Port Douglas, QLD 4871 (© 07/4099 4588; www.pddt.com.au). The association has no visitor information office in Port Douglas. Instead, visitors should visit one of several private tour information and booking centers in town. One of the biggest and most centrally located is the **Port Douglas Tourist Information Centre,** 23 Macrossan St. (© 07/4099 5599), open from 7:30am to 6pm daily.

GETTING AROUND Of the major rental companies, only **Avis** (© 07/ 4099 4331) has an office in Port Douglas. Check out the local companies, including **Port Douglas Car Rental** (© 07/4099 4988) and **Crocodile Car Rentals** (© 07/4099 5555). All rent regular vehicles as well as four-wheel-drives, which are needed if you plan to drive to Cape Tribulation. If you need a taxi, call **Port Douglas Taxis** (© 07/4099 5345).

A good way to get around the town's flat streets is by bike. **Bike 'n' Hike** (© 07/4099 4000; www.bikenhike.com.au), 40 Macrossan St, is open daily from 8am to 6pm or later and has a large range of good mountain bikes from A$17 (US$11) a day or A$11 (US$7.15) a half day. **Port Douglas Bike Hire** (© 07/4099 5799), corner Warner and Wharf streets, rents bikes for A$14 (US$9.10) a day or A$10 (US $6.50) for a half day. The shop is open from 9am to 5pm daily.

EXPLORING THE REEF & THE RAINFOREST

DISCOVERING THE GREAT BARRIER REEF Without a doubt the most glamorous large vessels visiting the Outer Reef are the **Quicksilver Wavepiercers** (© 07/4099 5500) based in Port Douglas. These ultrasleek, high-speed, air-conditioned 37m (121-ft.) and 46m (151-ft.) catamarans carry 300 or 440 passengers to Agincourt Reef, a ribbon reef 39 nautical miles (72km/ 45 miles) from shore on the very outer edge of the Reef. After the 90-minute trip to the Reef you tie up at a two-story pontoon, where you spend 3½ hours.

Quicksilver departs Marina Mirage at 10am daily except Christmas Day. The cost for the day is A$165 (US$107) for adults and A$85 (U.S$55) for kids 4 to 14, or A$415 (US$270) for a family. Coach transfers from your Port Douglas hotel are an extra A$5 (US$3.25) adults, A$2.50 (US$1.60) children. Guided snorkel safaris cost A$35 (US$23) per person, and introductory dives cost A$119 (US$77) per person. Qualified divers take a dive-tender boat to make two dives for A$119 (US$77) per person, all gear included. Because Quicksilver carries so many passengers, booking snorkel safaris and dives in advance is a good idea.

The dive boat **Poseidon** (see "Diving the Reef," earlier in this chapter) welcomes snorkelers. It presents a Reef ecology talk en route and takes you on a guided snorkel safari. Lunch and transfers from Port Douglas hotels are included in Poseidon's price of A$135 (US$88) for adults and A$100 (US$65) for children 3 to 12.

Snorkeling specialist boat *Wavelength* (© 07/4099 5031; www.wavelength-reef.com.au) does a full-day trip to the Outer Reef for A$134 (US$87) for adults, A$90 (US$59) for children 2 to 12, or A$410 (US$267) for a family. The trip visits three different snorkel sites each day and incorporates a guided snorkel tour and a reef presentation from a marine biologist. It caters to up to 30 passengers and includes snorkel gear, sunsuits, lunch, and transfers from your hotel. Both beginners and experienced snorkelers will like this trip. It departs daily from the Wavelength jetty in Wharf Street at 8:15am.

Another way to spend a pleasant day on the Great Barrier Reef, closer to shore, is to visit the **Low Isles,** 15km (9½ miles) northeast of Port Douglas. The isles are 1.5-hectare (3¾-acre) coral-cay specks of lush vegetation surrounded by white sand and 22 hectares (54 acres) of coral—which is what makes them so appealing. The coral is not quite as good as the outer Reef's, but the fish life is rich, and the proximity makes for a relaxing day.

The trip aboard the 30m (98-ft.) luxury sailing catamaran *Wavedancer* (© **07/4087 2100**), operated by Quicksilver, is A$115 (US$75) adults, A$60 (US$39) kids 4 to 14, and A$290 (US$189) families. You have the option of making an introductory scuba dive for an extra A$98 (US$64) per person. The Wavepiercer departs Reef Fleet Terminal in Cairns at 8am and Palm Cove Jetty on the northern beaches at 8:35am to connect with Wavedancer departures from Port Douglas at 10am. The company picks you up free of charge from your hotel.

EXPLORING DAINTREE NATIONAL PARK & CAPE TRIBULATION

The World Heritage–listed Daintree Rain Forest has remained largely unchanged over the past 110 million years. It is now home to rare plants that provide key links in the evolution story. In the 56,000-hectare (138,320-acre) **Daintree National Park** you will find cycads, dinosaur trees, fan palms, giant strangler figs, and epiphytes like the basket fern, staghorn, and elkhorn. Nighttime croc-spotting tours on the Daintree River vie for popularity with early morning cruises to see the rich bird life. Pythons, lizards, frogs, and electric blue Ulysses butterflies attract photographers, and sport fishermen come here to do battle with the big barramundi.

Just about everyone who visits Port Douglas takes a guided four-wheel-drive day trip into the beautiful Daintree and Cape Tribulation rainforests. Although they are two separate national parks, the forests merge into one.

You can rent a four-wheel-drive and explore on your own, but you won't understand much about what you are seeing unless you have a guide to explain it to you. Most companies basically cover the same territory and sights, including a 1-hour Daintree River cruise to spot crocs, a visit to the lovely Marrdja Botanical Walk, a stroll along an isolated beach, lunch at a pretty spot somewhere in the forest, and a visit to Mossman Gorge. Some tours also go to the picturesque Bloomfield Falls in Cape Tribulation National Park. Expect to pay about A$130 (US$85) per adult and about A$90 (US$59) per child. Trips that include Bloomfield Falls are more. A company that provides an excellent, gently adventurous alternative is Pete Baxendell's **Heritage & Interpretive Tours** (© **07/4098 7897**; www.nqhit.com.au). On a day-long bushwalk into a tract of privately owned rainforest with Pete, a naturalist and professional tour guide, you taste green ants (be brave, it's quite an experience) and other native "bush tucker," discover how to rustle up a toothbrush from a shrub if you forgot to pack yours, learn about bush medicine and the wildlife around you, and clamber up a stream to a waterfall. He takes a maximum six people at a time. Lunch and pickups are included in the price of A$110 (US$72). His walks run Tuesday and Saturday, leaving Port at 8:30am. You can also charter Pete and his 4WD on other days for day bushwalks for A$160 (US$104) per person (minimum of two) or for a "go anywhere" adventure for A$540 (US$351) per day. Pickups from the northern beaches cost A$30 (US$20) extra for bushwalks, but are included in the price for "go anywhere" charters. The charter prices compare favorably to a regular Daintree four-wheel-drive tour if there's three or more of you—and you get a tailored itinerary, Pete's knowledge, and the vehicle all to yourself. He often takes charter customers inland to Outback gold mining ghost towns, or north to tiny Cooktown, which boasts an excellent museum devoted to Australia's "discoverer," Captain James Cook. If you have 2 days, he can take you farther west to see Aboriginal rock art and stay at an upscale tented camp, or to the Undara Lava Tubes, which have been hollowed from rock by lava flows. Other established operators are **Trek North Safaris** (✆ 07/4051 4328) and **BTS Tours** (✆ 07/4099 5665). As is the case in most tourist hot spots, some tour operators battle fiercely to pay tour desks the highest commission to recommend their tours, even though those tours may not necessarily be the best for your needs. Take tour desks' recommendations with a grain of salt, and ask other travelers for their recommendations. You may not see too much wildlife, as rainforest animals are shy, camouflaged, nocturnal, or all three! Most four-wheel-drive tours will pick you up in Port Douglas at no charge, although there is usually a small fee from Cairns and the northern beaches. Floods and swollen creeks can quash your plans to explore the Daintree in the Wet Season (Dec–Mar or Apr), so keep your plans flexible.

If your chosen safari does not visit Mossman Gorge, 21km (13 miles) northwest of Port Douglas near the sugar town of Mossman, try to get there under your own steam. The gushing river tumbling over boulders and the network of short forest walks are magical. (Don't climb on the rocks or enter the river, as strong currents are extremely dangerous and have claimed at least one life in recent years.)

Most four-wheel-drive Daintree tours include a 1-hour cruise on the **Daintree River** ☆, but if yours does not, or you want to spend more time on the river, cruises are available on a variety of boats, ranging from open-sided "river trains" to small fishing boats. One of the best is offered by **Dan Irby's Mangrove Adventures** ☆ (✆ 07/4090 7017; www.mangroveadven.citysearch.com.au), whose small open boat can get up side creeks the bigger boats can't. Originally from Oklahoma, Dan has been in Australia for 30 years, and is extremely knowledgeable about the wildlife and habitat. He takes no more than 10 people at a time on 2-, 3-, and 4-hour cruises. Chances are you will spot lots of fascinating wildlife on his 2-hour night cruise, and even if you don't, it's worth it just to see the stars! A 2-hour trip costs A$45 (US$29). Night trips depart from the Daintree Eco Lodge, 20 Mossman Daintree Rd., 4km (2½ miles) south of Daintree village; day trips leave from the public jetty next to the Daintree River ferry crossing. Take the Captain Cook Highway north to Mossman, where it becomes

---

⟮Tips⟯ Drat Those Aussie Mozzies!

Mozzies, as Aussies call mosquitoes, love the rainforest as much as people do, so throw some insect repellent in your day pack when touring the Daintree and Cape Tribulation.

the Mossman Daintree Road, and follow it for 24km (15 miles) to the sign-posted turnoff for the ferry on your right. The ferry is 5km (3 miles) from the turnoff. You'll need a car to get there.

Bird-watchers love the Wet Tropics rainforests of which the Daintree and Cape Tribulation national parks are part. More than half of Australia's bird species have been recorded within 200km (120 miles) of this area. **Fine Feather Tours** (© 07/ 4094 1199; www.finefeathertours.com.au) has a full-day bird-watching safari through the Wet Tropics to the edge of the Outback for A$185 (US$120), an afternoon cruise on the Daintree River for A$135 (US$88), and other tours.

Rainforest Habitat wildlife sanctuary (© 07/4099 3235; www.rainforest habitat.com.au) is a great place to get to see the animals that are too shy to be spotted in the wild. Here, 180 animal species from the Wet Tropics are gathered in one place for you to see up close. You can see saltwater and freshwater croco-diles, hand-feed kangaroos, and have your photo taken beside (but not holding) a koala (from 10–11am and 3–4pm for the cost of a donation). The highlight is the walk-through aviary, which houses 70 Wet Tropics bird species including cassowaries. You'll get the most out of your visit if you take one of the excellent free guided tours that leave every hour on the hour between 9am and 3pm. Rainforest Habitat is located on Port Douglas Road at the turnoff from the Cap-tain Cook Highway. It's open daily (except Christmas) from 8am to 5:30pm (last entry at 4:30pm). Admission is A$25 (US$16) for adults, A$13 (US$8.45) for kids 4 to 14. Between 8am and 11am, the park serves a champagne buffet breakfast for A$38 (US$25) for adults and A$19 (US$12) for kids, including admission. Allow 2 hours here.

DISCOVERING ABORIGINAL CULTURE   The native KuKu-Yalanji tribe will teach you about bush medicines and foods, Dreamtime legends, and the sacred sites their families have called home for tens of thousands of years. **KuKu-Yalanji Dreamtime Tours** ⋔ (© 07/4098 2595; www.yalanji.com.au) offers a guided walk through the rainforest to see cave paintings and visit "special sites"; the tour is followed by a Dreamtime story over billy tea and damper in a bark warun (shelter). You can buy artifacts from the tribe's information center, gift shop, and art gallery. The tours depart Monday through Friday at 10am, noon, and 2pm from the Kuku-Yalanji community on the road to Mossman Gorge (1km/½ mile before you reach the Gorge parking lot). Tours cost A$17 (US$11) for adults and A$8.25 (US$5.35) for children. Allow 2 hours.

Hazel Douglas of **Native Guide Safari Tours** ⋔ (© 07/4098 2206; www. nativeguidesafaritours.com.au) runs four-wheel-drive tours of the rainforest from an Aboriginal perspective. Hazel is a full-blooded Aboriginal who grew up in a tribal lifestyle in the Daintree. She imparts her traditional knowledge of the plants, animals, Dreamtime myths, and Aboriginal history on a full-day tour departing at 9:15am from your Port Douglas hotel. Passengers from Cairns transfer up on the Quicksilver catamaran and return either by coach (northern beaches) or catamaran (Cairns city). The trip costs A$120 (US$78) for adults and A$80 (US$52) for children 3 to 14 from Port Douglas, and A$10 (US$6.50) extra from Cairns or the northern beaches. Charter and half-day tours are also available.

MORE TO SEE & DO
Some companies in Cairns that offer outdoor activities will provide pickups from Port Douglas hotels. See "White-Water Rafting & Other Thrills," in the Cairns section earlier in this chapter for details.

Tips The Secret of the Seasons

High season in Port Douglas is from roughly June 1 through October 31.

The best outdoor activity in Port Douglas, however, is to do absolutely nothing on spectacular **Four Mile Beach** 👧👧. May through September the water is stinger-free. October through April, swim in the stinger safety net. **Get High Parafly** (© 07/4099 6366, or call the boat at 0407/996 366) offers parasailing, jet-skiing, tube rides, water-skiing, and other watersports on the beach. Expect to pay from A$35 to A$70 (US$23–US$46) for each activity. A boat runs every hour on the hour between 9am and 5pm from the booking office at Berth C4 at Marina Mirage to the company's beach location at Four Mile Beach.

Visitor greens fees at the championship **Sheraton Mirage** golf course on Port Douglas Road are A$145 (US$94) for 18 holes or A$85 (US$5.25) for 9 holes, including a cart. Club rental ranges from A$38 to A$60 (US$25–US$40). Whacking a ball on the hotel's aquatic driving range costs A$6.50 (US$4.20) for a bucket of 25 balls, A$13 (US$8.45) for 50 balls, plus A$2.15 (US$1.40) for club rental. Contact the **Pro Shop** (© 07/4099 5537).

Mowbray Valley Trail Rides (© 07/4099 3268), located 13km (8 miles) inland from Port Douglas, offers 2-hour horseback rides for A$66 (US$43) or half-day rides through rainforest and sugar cane fields to Collards Falls, or to a swimming hole in the Hidden Valley, for A$88 (US$57), including morning or afternoon tea and lunch. It also runs full-day trips along the mountainous Bump Track, followed by a dip in a rainforest pool and barbecue lunch at Mowbray Falls for A$125 (US$81). Transfers from your Port Douglas accommodations are included. Transfers from Cairns are A$20 (US$13) per person. **Wonga Beach Trail Rides** (© 07/4098 7583) does 3-hour rides through the rainforest and along Wonga Beach, 35 minutes north of Port Douglas, for A$81 (US$53), including transfers from Port Douglas and insurance.

Bike 'n' Hike (© 07/4099 4000; www.bikenhike.com.au) takes small groups biking, hiking, and swimming in natural lagoons in the Mowbray Valley in the rainforest near Port Douglas. You don't need to be a strong cyclist to take part. Half-day tours cost A$84 (US$55). Full-day tours cost A$128 (US$83). Pickups from your Port Douglas hotel, a 27-speed mountain bike, a snack, and drinks (and lunch on the full-day trip) are included. Transfers from Cairns and Palm Cove are extra. Experienced mountain bikers can descend the steep 14km (8½-mile) Bump Track through dense rainforest from the top of the Great Dividing Range on a half-day trip designed for a maximum of eight riders.

Every Sunday, a colorful handicrafts and fresh food market sets up on the lawns under the mango trees beside Dickson Inlet at the end of Macrossan Street. Stalls sell everything from foot massages to fresh coconut milk. It runs from 7:30am to 1pm. While you're here, take a peek, or attend a nondenominational service, inside the pretty timber St. Mary's by the Sea church.

WHERE TO STAY

Port Douglas Accommodation Holiday Rentals (© 1800/645 566 in Australia, or 07/4099 4488; www.portdouglasaccom.com.au) has a wide range of apartments and homes for rent.

VERY EXPENSIVE

Sheraton Mirage Port Douglas 🌟🌟🌟   One of Australia's most luxurious properties, this low-rise Sheraton has 2 hectares (5 acres) of saltwater pools, and a championship Peter Thomson–designed 18-hole golf course. It is a bit too far from Port's main street by foot, but a free shuttle runs from 9am to 6pm to the golf course's country club/health center, to Marina Mirage shopping center, and into town. All the rooms are large and light-filled. You might fancy upgrading to a Mirage room with a corner Jacuzzi and king beds, but I thought the standard rooms just fine. The 101 privately owned two-, three-, and four-bedroom luxury villas with golf course, garden, or sea views are rented out by Sheraton; the decor varies, but each has a Jacuzzi and two bathrooms.

Davidson St. (off Port Douglas Rd.), Port Douglas, QLD 4871. 🕐 **1800/07 3535** in Australia; 800/325-3535 in the U.S. and Canada; 00800/325 353535 in the U.K., Ireland, and New Zealand; or 07/4099 5888. Fax 07/4099 4424, or Starwood Hotels reservation fax 07/4099 5398. www.sheraton-mirage.com.au. 394 units (including 101 villas). A$619–A$830 (US$402–US$540) double; A$2,895 (US$1,882) 1- or 2- bedroom suite; A$950–A$1,250 (US$618–US$813) 2-, 3-, or 4-bedroom villa. Extra person A$70 (US$46). Children under 17 stay free in parent's room with existing bedding. Rates include full breakfast. Discounted rates available. AE, DC, MC, V. Free valet and self-parking. Helicopter transfers available. **Amenities:** 3 restaurants; 2 bars; 25m (82-ft.) outdoor lap pool; 18-hole championship golf course with country club and pro shop, aquatic driving range (with targets in a lake), putting green, and golf clinics; 9 day/night tennis courts; health club; spa; Jacuzzi; bike rental; daily day care for kids under 5, kids' club for children 5–15 during school vacations (for additional fee); concierge; tour desk; car-rental desk; business center (with extra charge for Internet access); salon; 24-hr. room service; massage; babysitting; dry cleaning; nonsmoking rooms. *In room:* A/C, TV, kitchenette (villas only), minibar (hotel rooms only), coffeemaker, hair dryer, iron, safe.

EXPENSIVE

Port Douglas Peninsula Boutique Hotel 🌟🌟   Built in 1999 over three levels, this intimate studio apartment hotel fronting Four Mile Beach is one of the nicest places to stay in town. Every apartment features an open-plan living room/bedroom, a contemporary kitchenette (with microwave and dishwasher), and a groovy bathroom boasting a giant double tub (or Jacuzzi, in some units). Corner apartments are a little bigger. The decor is a stylish mélange of terra cotta, mosaic tiles, granite, and wicker, with classy extra touches like a CD player and boxed Twining's teas. Most have great beach views from the roomy balcony or patio, while a few look onto the green and mauve complex of petite Art Deco-ish pools, waterfalls, hot and cold Jacuzzis, and sun deck rising and falling on several levels. A 2-minute walk brings you to the main street. There's also a picnic hamper service on offer.

9–13 The Esplanade, Port Douglas, QLD 4871. 🕐 **1800/676 674** in Australia, or 07/4099 9100. Fax 07/4099 5440. www.peninsulahotel.com.au. 34 units. A$312–A$400 (US$202–US$260) double. Rates include full breakfast. Ask about packages. AE, DC, MC, V. Complimentary round-trip transfers from Cairns airport. Covered parking. **Amenities:** Restaurant; small bar; large outdoor pool; hot and cold Jacuzzis (no kids under 15 without an adult in either); bike rental; tour desk; laundry/dry cleaning. *In room:* A/C, TV/VCR, dataport, kitchenette, coffeemaker, hair dryer, iron, safe.

MODERATE

Archipelago Studio Apartments 🌟   You won't find a friendlier or more convenient place to stay in Port Douglas than these apartments, 10 seconds from the beach and less than 10 minutes' walk from town. Your hosts Wolfgang Klein and Christel Bader are eager to help with tour bookings and to give useful advice—and they also speak fluent German, conversational French, and some Spanish. The apartments are on the small side (most suit only three people, at the most), but all are well cared for and were refurbished in 2001. You can opt for a tiny Garden apartment with a patio; or upgrade to a Balcony or Seaview apartment, both a bit larger and with private balconies. Seaview apartments are quite roomy, and have side views of Four Mile Beach. Towels are changed daily and linen weekly, but general servicing will cost A$20 (US$13) extra. There's no elevator and no porter, so be prepared to carry your luggage upstairs. No children under 3 permitted.

72 Macrossan St., Port Douglas, QLD 4871. Ⓒ 07/4099 5387. Fax 07/4099 4847. www.archipelago.com.au. 21 units (all with shower only). High season (June–Oct) A$118–A$199 (US$77–A$129) double; low season A$96–A$169 (US$62–US$110) double. Additional person A$20 (US$13). 3-night minimum stay applies. MC, V. Free undercover parking. **Amenities:** Outdoor saltwater pool; nearby golf course; 6 nearby day/night tennis courts; access to nearby health club; Jacuzzi; tour desk; coin-op laundry; laundry service; same-day dry cleaning can be arranged; nonsmoking rooms. *In room:* A/C, TV, kitchenette, fridge, coffeemaker, hair dryer.

Port Douglas Retreat   This well-kept two-story studio apartment complex on a quiet street, featuring the white-battened balconies of the Queenslander architectural style, is a good value, because even some of the ritzier places in town can't boast its lagoonlike saltwater pool surrounded by dense jungle and wrapped by an ample shady sun deck that cries out to be lounged on with a good book and a cool drink. The apartments are not enormous, but are fashionably furnished with terra-cotta tile floors, wrought-iron beds, cane seating, and colorful bedcovers. All have large furnished balconies or patios looking into tropical gardens (some on the ground floor open onto the common-area boardwalk, so maybe ask for a first-floor unit). Town and the beach are a 5-minute walk away. No smoking indoors. The newer **Cayman Villas** (www.caymanvillas.com.au) next door are run by the same management but are more expensive.

31–33 Mowbray St. (at Mudlo St.), Port Douglas, QLD 4871. Ⓒ 07/4099 5053. Fax 07/4099 5033. www. portdouglasretreat.com.au. 36 units (all with shower only). High season A$143 (US$93) double; low season A$107 (US$70) double. Crib A$5.50 (US$3.60) per night. AE, MC, V. Security covered parking. **Amenities:** Outdoor saltwater pool; tour desk; car-rental desk; coin-op laundry. *In room:* A/C, TV w/free movies, kitchenette, iron.

INEXPENSIVE

Port O'Call Lodge   There's a nice communal feeling to this modest motel on a suburban street a 10-minute walk from town. Backpackers, families, and anyone on a budget seem to treat it like a second home, swapping travel stories as they cook up a meal in the communal kitchen and dining room. The rooms are light, cool, and fresh with tile floors, loads of luggage and bench space, and small patios. The compact bathrooms are efficiently laid out with old but neat fixtures (bring your own hair dryer). Only the deluxe rooms have a TV, clock radio, self-serve tea and coffee facilities, and a minifridge. The hostel rooms have private bathrooms and no more than five beds and/or bunks in each. A 26-bed bunkhouse opened in 2001, and includes facilities for travelers with disabilities. At night the lively poolside bistro, **Port O' Call Bistro** (p. 301) is the place to be. Other facilities include free board games, a pay phone, Internet access, guest safe, and a kiosk selling refreshments.

Port St. at Craven Close, Port Douglas, QLD 4871. Ⓒ 1800/892 800 in Australia, or 07/4099 5422. Fax 07/ 4099 5495. www.portocall.com.au. 28 units (all with shower only). High season (June–Sept, Christmas, and Easter) A$89–A$99 (US$58–US$64) double; shoulder season (May and Oct) A$79–A$89 (US$51–US$58) double; low season (Nov–Apr) A$69–A$79 (US$45–US$51) double. Additional person A$11 (US$7.15). Hostel rooms A$23 (US$15) or A$22 (US$14) YHA/Hostelling International members; bunkhouse A$21 (US$14) or A$20 (US$13) YHA/Hostelling International members. Children under 3 stay free. MC, V. Free minibus to and from Cairns Mon, Wed, and Sat. Free on-site parking. Bus stop at front door. **Amenities:** Restaurant; outdoor pool; 3 golf courses nearby; access to nearby health club; bike rental; tour desk; coin-op laundry; nonsmoking rooms. *In room:* A/C, TV, fridge (double motel rooms only).

A LUXURY B&B HIDEAWAY IN THE COUNTRY

Marae 𝕽𝕽   Your hostess Andy Crowe has turned her architecturally stunning timber home, on a rural hillside 15km (9½ miles) north of Port Douglas, into a glamorous and soothing retreat. The rustic-meets-sleek contemporary bedrooms have white mosquito nets and smart linens on timber beds, and elegant bathrooms. The downstairs room opens onto a plunge pool overlooking the valley. Wallabies and bandicoots (a kind of small marsupial) feed in the garden, kingfishers and honeyeaters use the pool, and butterflies are everywhere. You can enjoy the company of Andy's Jack Russell terrier and an irrepressible cockatoo called Cactus, laze on the two decks, or wander the rainforest trails of Mossman Gorge just a few miles away.

Lot 1, Chook's Ridge, Shannonvale (P.O. Box 133, Port Douglas, QLD 4871). ℭ **07/4098 4900.** Fax 07/4098 4099. www.marae.com.au. 3 bedrooms (2 with shower only). From A$140 (US$91) double. Minimum 2-night stay. Rates include full breakfast. MC, V. From Port Douglas take Captain Cook Hwy. toward Mossman for 10km (6¼ miles), turn left onto Mt. Molloy turnoff for 1km (½ mile), then right onto Ponzo Rd. for 2km (1¼ miles); Chook's Ridge is on your left. You need your own transport. Covered parking. Pets by arrangement. No children under 13 permitted. **Amenities:** Outdoor pool; nearby golf course; tour desk; use of laundry; non-smoking rooms. *In room:* A/C, TV, hair dryer.

RAINFOREST HIDEAWAYS

Silky Oaks Lodge & Healing Waters Spa 𝕽𝕽   Relax in the hammock on your veranda and listen to the waters of the Mossman River gushing through the rainforest. Stroll down for a swim—no crocs here. Despite its popularity and relatively large size, this luxury resort tucked away at the edge of cane fields still exudes a restful feeling. Treehouses are scattered through the rainforest and gardens; the 6 Riverhouses overlook the river frontage, and some have Jacuzzis. Each has timber floors, attractive furnishings, bathrobes, a CD player—but no TV—and a double hammock to string up. The resort's most recent renovation was completed in September 2001, and included the addition of the Healing Waters Day Spa, where I had the best facial of my life. Last year, the Spa was tripled in size (no doubt word has got out how good it is), and the central lodge and Treehouse Restaurant were given a fresh, contemporary new look. Guided nature walks, mountain bikes, and nature slide shows are free, and there is a daily activities program. A car is necessary to access Mossman Gorge's lovely walking trails across the river.

7km (4½ miles) west of Mossman; 27km (17 miles) from Port Douglas (c/o P&O Australian Resorts, G.P.O. Box 478, Sydney, NSW 2001). ℭ **1800/737 678** in Australia, 800/225-9849 in the U.S. and Canada, 020/7805 3875 in the U.K., 02/9277 5050 (Sydney reservations office), or 07/4098 1666 (lodge). Fax 02/9299 2477 (Sydney reservations office), or 07/4098 1983 (lodge). www.poresorts.com. 50 units. A$660–A$790 (US$429–US$514) double. Extra person A$150 (US$98). Rates include continental breakfast and 4-course dinner. Ask about packages. AE, DC, MC, V. Free morning and afternoon shuttle from Port Douglas. Sun Palm Express Coaches does transfers from Port Douglas for A$25 (US$16), the northern beaches for A$30 (US$20), or Cairns airport for A$40 (US$26) one-way. Town-car transfers A$135 (US$88) per car one-way from Cairns city or airport; stretch limousine transfers A$180 (US$117). Take Captain Cook Hwy. to Mossman, where it becomes the Mossman-Daintree Rd.; follow approx. 3.5km (2¼ miles) past Mossman and turn left onto Finlayvale Rd. at the small white-on-blue Silky Oaks sign. No children under 10. **Amenities:** Restaurant; bar; outdoor pool; day/night tennis court; spa; tour desk; coin-op laundry; laundry service. *In room:* A/C, ceiling fans, minibar, coffeemaker, hair dryer, iron.

Thala Beach Lodge 𝕽𝕽   "Where are the walls?" may be your first question on arriving at this Balinese-style luxury hideaway in the rainforest outside Port Douglas. The lodge's reception area and lobby are open, to stunning effect. And from the elevated restaurant the impact is even greater, with sweeping views from the Daintree to Cape Grafton, south of Cairns. Thala (pronounced *Ta*-la)

Beach is set on a 59-hectare (146-acre) private peninsula, bordered on three sides by private beaches and coves. Owners Rob and Oonagh Prettejohn also own the well-established Kewarra Beach Resort on Cairns' northern beaches. Thala Beach opened in 1998, taking its inspiration from the flora and fauna of the World Heritage area that surrounds it. The secluded bungalows are built on high poles in the trees, where dazzling lorikeets and small red-faced flying foxes feed on blossoms and hang contentedly from the branches. Some of the bungalows are a bit of a hike from the public areas, but I thought it was a small price to pay for the privacy and the rainforest setting.

16km (10 miles) south of Port Douglas (P.O. Box 199, Smithfield, Cairns, QLD 4878). ℂ 1800/251 958 in Australia (Small Luxury Hotels of the World), or 07/4098 5700 (lodge). Fax 07/4098 5837. www.slh.com/thala. 85 units. A$335–A$533 (US$218–US$346) double. AE, DC, MC, V. Transfers from Cairns A$26 (US$17) per person. Valet parking. **Amenities:** Restaurant; bar; 2 outdoor pools; nearby golf course; tour desk. *In room:* A/C and ceiling fans, TV, minibar, coffeemaker, hair dryer, iron, safe.

A SPA IN THE RAINFOREST

Daintree Eco Lodge & Spa ⟨ Check in to your room and head straight for the Daintree Spa. Here you can relax and soak up all kinds of pampering treatments, including the 90-minute A$195 (US$127) Mala Mayi body treatment in which you are wrapped in mud as you recline on a magnificent carved timber "wet bed," and the Jalaymba rain therapy treatment. It's bliss.

A multi-award winner for "green tourism," the lodge hosts only a small number of guests and has a position in the primeval forest. Don't think "eco" means sacrificing creature comforts: The large rooms, refurbished in 2000, boast marble floors, timber and bamboo furniture, and tiled bathrooms with robes. Five have Jacuzzis on their balconies, which are screened to keep out the mosquitoes that are an inevitable part of a rainforest visit at certain times of year.

You can also join a yoga or Ki (based on Japanese Aikido) session, laze by the small solar-heated pool and sun deck, walk rainforest trails, join members of the local Aboriginal Kuku tribe on a bush tucker and native medicine stroll, or take a four-wheel-drive day trip to modern-day Aboriginal communities. The Bilngkumu Restaurant overlooks a lily pond, and serves food with a gourmet bushtucker slant.

20 Daintree Rd., Daintree, QLD 4873 (4km/2½ miles south of Daintree village). ℂ 1800/808 010 in Australia, or 07/4098 6100. Fax 07/4098 6200. www.daintree-ecolodge.com.au. 15 units (10 with shower only). A$476–A$531 (US$309–US$345) double. Extra person A$33–A$50 (US$21–US$33). Cribs A$33 (US$21) for duration of stay. Rates include full breakfast. Ask about packages. AE, DC, MC, V. Scheduled minibus picks up and drops off once a day at Port Douglas hotels, Cairns hotels, and Cairns airport for A$50 (US$33) (Port Douglas) or A$55 (US$36) (Cairns) per person, one-way. Transfers at any time are available at higher cost. Private car transfers A$143 (US$93) from Port Douglas or A$165 (US$107) from Cairns, per car, one-way. Stretch limousine transfers (A$242/US$157 one-way), and helicopter transfers can be arranged. The lodge is 98km (61 miles) north of Cairns and 40km (25 miles) north of Port Douglas. Take Captain Cook Hwy. north to Mossman, where it becomes the Mossman-Daintree Rd.; follow this all the way to the lodge. The road is paved all the way. **Amenities:** Restaurant; pool; spa; tour desk; laundry service. *In room:* A/C, TV, minibar, coffeemaker, hair dryer.

WHERE TO DINE IN PORT DOUGLAS

Nautilus ⟨⟨ TROPICAL/SEAFOOD Bill and Hillary Clinton dined here during a visit Down Under, and by all accounts loved it. So did I. The restaurant, which has been keeping the locals happy since 1953, is set under the palm trees and stars, with a clever seating plan and unusual high-backed chairs which give a wonderfully intimate atmosphere. Local produce and seafood is the mainstay of the menu, which serves such delights as deep fried whole coral trout, served with lotus root and bean shoot salad, sweet chile sauce, and steamed rice or yellowfin tuna poached in broth with tofu, Vietnamese mint, cilantro, chile, and Nori tempura oysters. Or you may prefer to go for the fresh mud crab, barramundi, or one of the many choices for non-seafood eaters.

17 Murphy St. (entry also from Macrossan St.), Port Douglas. (C) **07/4099 5330**. www.nautilus-restaurant. com.au. Reservations recommended. Main courses A$26–A$38 (US$17–US$25). AE, DC, MC, V. Daily 6:30–10:30pm or until the last diners leave. Closed Feb.

Port O' Call Bistro *(Kids* CAFE/BISTRO   Locals patronize this poolside bistro and bar at the Port O' Call Lodge (p. 298) almost as often as guests do, because it offers good, honest food like lamb shanks and steaks in hearty portions at painless prices. The atmosphere is fun and friendly. Tuesday is curry night, and if it's Sunday, there's a roast. Every night you can try one of the "chef's blackboard surprises," including local seafood. Kids' meals are all A$6 (US$3.90), and there are burgers, nachos, and pastas to appeal to everyone.

Port St. at Craven Close. (C) **07/4099 5422**. Main courses A$7.50–A$14 (US$4.90–US$9). MC, V. Daily 6–9pm. Happy hour 5–7pm. Bar opens 4pm.

Salsa Bar & Grill *(Kids* MODERN/TROPICAL   This trendy restaurant, in its lovely timber Queenslander with wrap-around verandas, has terrific food, great value prices, and lively, fun service. Open for brunch, lunch, or dinner, here you can choose between the simplest of fare such as gnocchi, Caesar salad, or fantastic spring rolls, or such mouth-watering delights as sand crab panna cotta or panfried Atlantic salmon with pickled ginger, coriander mash, and green papaya salad. Even if you usually resist dessert, don't. The buttermilk and almond nougat panna cotta is to-die-for, and the chocolate Cointreau soufflé is a must. On Sundays there's a salsa band and the place really gets jumping.

26 Wharf St. (at Warner St.). (C) **07/4099 4922**. www.salsa-port-douglas.com.au. Reservations essential. Main courses A$20–A$25 (US$13–US$17). AE, DC, MC, V. Mon–Sat 10am–midnight; Sun 8am–midnight.

4 The North Coast: Mission Beach *(★★*, Townsville & the Islands

For years the lovely town of **Mission Beach** was a well-kept secret. Farmers retired here; then those who liked to drop out and chill out discovered it; today, it's a small, prosperous and stunningly pretty rainforest town. The beach here is one of the most beautiful in Australia, a long white strip fringed with dense tangled vine forests, the only surviving lowlands rainforest in the Australian tropics. It is also one of the least crowded and least spoiled, so clever has **Mission Beach** been at staying out of sight, out of mind, and off the tourist trail.

The nearby **Tully River** is white-water-rafting heaven for thrill-seekers. You can also bungee jump and tandem sky dive when you're not rushing down the rapids, flanked by lush rainforest.

From Mission Beach it's a short ferry ride to **Dunk Island,** a large resort island that welcomes day-trippers. You can even sea kayak there from the mainland. Mission Beach is closer to the Great Barrier Reef than any other point along the coast—just an hour—and cruise boats depart daily from the jetty, stopping en route at Dunk Island.

A few hours' drive south brings you to the city of **Townsville,** also a gateway to the Great Barrier Reef, but more important to visitors as a gateway to Magnetic Island, a picturesque, laid-back haven for hikers and watersports enthusiasts.

MISSION BEACH: THE CASSOWARY COAST

140km (87 miles) S of Cairns; 240km (149 miles) N of Townsville

Tucked away off the Bruce Highway, the township of Mission Beach has managed to duck the tourist hordes. It's actually a conglomeration of four beachfront towns: South Mission Beach, Wongaling Beach, Mission Beach proper, and Bingil Bay. Most commercial activity centers on the small nucleus of shops and businesses at Mission Beach proper. It's so isolated that signs on the way into town warn you to watch out for ultra-shy cassowaries emerging from the jungle to cross the road. Dense rainforest hides the town from view, until you round the corner to Mission Beach proper and discover appealing hotels, neat shops, and smart little restaurants. Just through the trees is the fabulous beach. A mile or so north of the main settlement of Mission Beach is Clump Point Jetty.

ESSENTIALS

GETTING THERE   From Cairns, follow the Bruce Highway south. The Mission Beach turnoff is at the tiny town of El Arish, about 15km (9½ miles) north of Tully. Mission Beach is 25km (16 miles) off the highway. It's a 90-minute trip from Cairns. If you're coming from Townsville, there is an earlier turnoff just north of Tully that leads 18km (11 miles) to South Mission Beach.

Airport Connections (© 07/4099 5950) operates door-to-door shuttles twice a day from Cairns for A$39 (US$25) adults and A$20 (US$13) children, and from the northern beaches for A$44 (US$29) adults and A$25 (US$16) children. **McCafferty's** (© 13 14 99 in Australia) and **Greyhound Pioneer** (© 13 20 30 in Australia) coaches both stop in Mission Beach proper (not South Mission Beach) several times daily on their Cairns-Brisbane-Cairns runs. The fare is A$16 (US$10) from Cairns, or A$187 (US$122) for the 26-hours-plus trip from Brisbane.

Five trains a week on the Cairns-Brisbane-Cairns route call at the nearest train station, Tully, about 20km (12½ miles) away. One-way travel from Cairns on the Tilt Train costs A$43 (US$28) for the 2-hour 50-minute journey. From Brisbane, fares range from A$183 (US$119) in an economy seat to A$345 (US$224) for a first-class sleeper on *The Sunlander*. For more information, call Queensland Rail's long-distance division, **Traveltrain** (© 13 22 32 in Australia, or 07/3235 1122). A taxi from Tully to Mission Beach with **Tully Taxis & Buses** (© 07/4068 3937) is about A$40 (US$26).

A bus transfer to Mission Beach with **Mission Beach Bus & Coach** (© 07/ 4068 7400) is A$7 (US$4.55). You must book the transfer in advance.

VISITOR INFORMATION   The **Mission Beach Visitor Centre,** Porters Promenade, Mission Beach, QLD 4852 (© 07/4068 7099; fax 07/4068 7066; www.missionbch.com), is located at the northern end of town. It's open Monday through Saturday from 9am to 5pm, and Sunday from 9am to 4pm.

GETTING AROUND   Mission Beach Bus & Coach (© 07/4068 7400) travels day and night between the beach communities, stopping outside all the accommodations houses listed below, at Clump Point Jetty, and at Wongaling

---

Tips Mission Beach Money Matters

There's no bank in Mission Beach; in fact, the only ATM is at Mission Beach Resort, Wongaling Beach, so come with enough cash, traveler's checks, and/or a credit card.

Tips **Safety Tips When Encountering Wildlife**

Endangered cassowaries (spectacular ostrichlike birds with a blue boney crown on their head) can kill with their enormous claws, so never approach one. If you disturb one, back off slowly and hide behind a tree. Dangerous crocodiles inhabit the local waterways. Do not swim in, or stand on the bank of, any river or stream.

You will spend plenty of time lazing and strolling the area's 14km (8¾ miles) of beaches, but be careful about where you swim. Deadly marine stingers inhabit the sea October through May; in these times swim only in the stinger nets erected at the north and south ends of Mission Beach.

Beach near the water taxi to Dunk Island. **Sugarland Car Rentals (℃ 07/4068 8272)** is the only rental-car company in town. For Mission Beach taxi service, call ℃ **07/4068 8155.**

WHAT TO SEE & DO

EXPLORING THE REEF Mission Beach is the closest point on the mainland to the Reef, just 1 hour by the high-speed **Quick Cat Cruises** catamaran (℃ **1800/654 242** in Australia, or 07/4068 7289). The trip starts with an hour at Dunk Island 20 minutes offshore, where you can walk rainforest trails, play on the beach, or parasail or jet ski for an extra fee. Then it's a 1-hour trip to sandy Beaver Cay on the Outer Reef, where you have 3 hours to snorkel or to check out the coral from a semi-submersible or glass-bottom boat. There's no shade on the cay, so come prepared with a hat and sunscreen. The trip departs daily from Clump Point Jetty at 9:30am. It costs A$148 (US$96) for adults, A$74 (US$48) for children 4 to 14, and A$370 (US$241) for a family. An introductory scuba dive costs A$80 (US$52) for the first dive and A$35 (US$23) for the second. You should prebook your introductory scuba dive to ensure a place. Qualified divers pay A$60 (US$39) for the first dive, A$35 (US$23) for the second, all gear included. Free pickups from Mission Beach are included. You can also join this trip from Cairns; coach connections from your Cairns or northern beaches hotel will cost extra. Ask about Sunday and Wednesday specials during high season.

WHITE-WATER RAFTING ON THE TULLY A day's rafting through the rainforest on the Class III to IV Tully River is an adventure you won't soon forget. In raft-speak, Class IV means "exciting rafting on moderate rapids with a continuous need to maneuver rafts." On the Tully, that translates to regular hair-raising but manageable rapids punctuated by calming stretches that let you just float downstream. You don't need experience, just a decent level of agility and an enthusiastic attitude. **RnR Rafting** (℃ **07/4051 7777**) runs a trip, which includes 5 hours on the river with fun, expert guides, a barbecue lunch in the rainforest, and a video screening of your adventure. With transfers, the day costs A$135 (US$88) from Mission Beach, A$145 (US$94) from Cairns, Palm Cove, or Townsville, and A$160 (US$104) from Port Douglas, plus a A$10 (US$6.50) national park fee. The trip runs daily; you must be 13 years or older.

EXPLORING THE RAINFOREST & COAST Walking, wildlife spotting, canoeing in the forest, and kayaking along the pristine coast are all worth doing. Hiking trails abound through national parks, rainforests, fan palm groves, and along the beach. The 8km (5-mile) **Licuala Fan Palm** track starts at the parking lot on the Mission Beach–Tully Road about 1.5km (1 mile) west of the turnoff to South Mission Beach. The track leads through dense forest, over creeks, and comes out on the El Arish–Mission Beach Road about 7km (4.5 miles) north of the post office. When you come out, you can cross the road and keep going on the 1km (less than a mile) Lacey Creek loop in the Tam O'Shanter State Forest. A shorter Rainforest Circuit option leads from the parking lot at the start of the Licuala Fan Palm track and makes a 1km (less than a mile) loop incorporating a fan palm boardwalk. There's also a 10-minute "follow the cassowary footprints to the nest" children's walk leading from the parking lot.

If you would rather see the sea than rainforest, take the 7km (4.5-mile) Edmund Kennedy track, which starts below the Horizon resort at the southern end of the Kennedy Esplanade in South Mission Beach. You get views of the ocean and the rainforest on this trail. The Mission Beach Visitor Centre has free trail maps.

Ingrid Marker of **Sunbird Adventures** (© 07/4068 8229; sunbird. adventures@bigpond.com) offers a range of sea-kayaking and trekking expeditions that interpret the rich environment around you. No more than eight people are allowed on each trip, so you get personal attention and time to ask questions. Her half-day sea-kayak expedition (A$55/US$36 per person) journeys around Bingil Bay. Night walks, starting at 7pm and returning around 9:30pm, are held on Bicton Hill and are great for kids because they spot glow-in-the-dark fungi, and frogs and shrimps in the streams (A$30/US$20 per person). Ingrid also runs 3-day sea kayak/camping trips, and a 3-day Misty Mountain Trails hike in the Tully River Gorge. They can be combined to make a 6-day trip, and prices for both can be worked out with Ingrid according to your needs. All trips include pickup from your accommodations, and all food is locally grown organic produce. Not all tours depart every day, so check with her first.

HITTING THE BEACH   Of course, relaxing on the uncrowded beach is why everyone comes to Mission Beach. June through September you can swim anywhere, and the water is warm; October through May stick to areas with stinger nets at Mission Beach proper (behind Castaways resort) and South Mission Beach.

A DAY TRIP TO DUNK ISLAND   If you're a beachcomber at heart, Dunk will fulfill your dreams. Just 5km (3 miles) offshore from Mission Beach, Dunk was the inspiration for writer E. J. Banfield's book *Confessions of a Beachcomber.* Banfield moved to Dunk at the turn of the 20th century to live out what he thought would be a short life. He lived on for another 23 years, which must say something about the restorative powers of a piece of paradise. Ed and Bertha Banfield's graves are alongside the track to Mt. Kootaloo.

Thick bushland and rainforest cover much of the island's 12 sq. km (4¾ sq. miles), most of which is a national park. The island is renowned for its myriad birds and electric-blue Ulysses butterflies.

You can stay at the upscale Dunk Island resort (see below in this section) or just pop over for the day to snorkel, hike in the forest, or do all sorts of watersports. **Dunk Island Ferry & Cruises** (© 07/4068 7211) runs day trips for A$69 (US$45) for adults and A$25 (US$16) for kids 4 to 14 (free for younger kids). The cruise includes lunch, boom-netting, a swing around Bedarra Island, and free snorkeling gear (with a A$20/US$13 refundable deposit). Daily departures are from Clump Point Jetty at 8:45 and 10:30am. You can also get to

Dunk by the **water taxi** (© **07/4068 8310**), which runs five times a day from Wongaling Beach. The round-trip fare is A$29 (US$19) for adults and A$15 (US$9.75) for kids 4 to 14. Ask at your accommodations about transfers between Clump Point and South Mission Beach.

Once on Dunk, you pay as you go for activities and equipment rental on the island. Everything from water-skiing to catamaran sailing is available, and Dunk has lovely beaches and half a dozen rainforest walking trails, ranging in duration from 15 minutes to 4 hours. On Monday and Thursday mornings, you can visit an artist's gallery reached via a 40-minute trail through the rainforest; admission is A$4 (US$2.60).

Ingrid Marker of Sunbird Adventures (see above) runs full-day guided **sea-kayak expeditions** ⚓ to Dunk Island. Ingrid says if you can pedal a bike for an hour, you can sea kayak for the hour it takes to get to the island. You glide over reefs, looking for sea turtles; spend the morning snorkeling in Coconut Bay; have a picnic lunch of oysters, mussels, and fresh produce (all organic) in Hidden Palm Valley; then hike the rainforest. At morning and afternoon tea you get a choice of nine organic teas and coffees. The trip costs A$95 (US$62) per person.

WHERE TO STAY IN MISSION BEACH

The Horizon ⚓   With its beguiling views across the pool to Dunk Island, its rainforest setting, and its impressive rooms, this resort perched on a steep hillside is one of the most comfortable and beautiful you will find. Even the least expensive rooms are spacious and have luxurious bathrooms. All but a handful of rooms have some kind of sea view; a half dozen retain the older-style bathrooms from a previous resort development, but the sea views from these rooms are the best. It's just a minute or two down the rainforest track to the beach.

Explorer Dr., South Mission Beach, QLD 4852. © **1800/079 090** in Australia, or 07/4068 8154. Fax 07/4068 8596. www.thehorizon.com.au. 55 units. A$220–A$420 (US$143–US$273) double. Children A$20 (US$13) extra. Ask about packages and specials. Rates are higher Dec 22–Jan 2. AE, DC, MC, V. **Amenities:** 3 restaurants; bar; large saltwater pool; day/night tennis courts; tour desk. *In room:* A/C, TV w/cable, minibar, coffeemaker, hair dryer, iron.

Mackays *(Value)*   This delightfully well-kept motel is one of the best-value places to stay in town. It's just 80m (262 ft.) from the beach and 400m (¼ mile) from the heart of Mission Beach. The friendly Mackay family repaints the rooms annually, so the place always looks brand new. All the rooms are pleasant and spacious with white-tiled floors, cane sofas, colorful bedcovers, and very clean bathrooms. Those in the newer section are air-conditioned, and some have views of the attractive granite-lined pool and gardens. Rooms in the older painted-brick wing have garden views from a communal patio and no air-conditioning. Ask about special packages; they can be extremely good deals and may include extras like rafting on the Tully River and day trips to the Reef and Dunk Island.

7 Porter Promenade, Mission Beach, QLD 4852. © **07/4068 7212.** Fax 07/4068 7095. www.mackaysmission beach.com. 22 units, 12 with bathroom (10 with shower only). A$85–A$110 (US$55–US$72) double; A$110 (US$72) 1- and 2-bedroom apt. Higher rates apply at Easter. Additional person A$17 (US$11) extra; children under 14 A$6.50 (US$4.20) extra. Crib A$6.50 (US$4.20) extra. Ask about packages. AE, DC, MC, V. Free covered off-street parking. **Amenities:** Outdoor pool; access to nearby tennis courts; access to bike rental; tour desk; car-rental desk; room service at breakfast; in-room massage; babysitting; coin-op laundry; nonsmoking rooms. *In room:* A/C (in 12 units only), TV, fax, kitchenettes (4 units only), fridge, safe.

WHERE TO STAY ON THE ISLAND

Dunk Island ⚓ *(Kids)*   Families love Dunk Island because there's so much to do, but that doesn't mean it's not just as appealing for honeymooners or retired couples. For those who are more inclined to relaxation Dunk has beautiful beaches and gentle pastimes like champagne sunset cruises. Just 5km (3 miles) offshore from Mission Beach, Dunk is a thickly rainforested 12 sq. km (7½-sq.-mile) island that attracts everyone. The island is renowned for bird life and neon-blue Ulysses butterflies, which you will see everywhere.

Among the free activities are windsurfing, catamaran sailing, paddle skiing, tennis and squash courts, fitness classes and aqua-aerobics, beach and pool volleyball, badminton, bocce, and archery, to name just a few. You pay for a range of other activities, including guided jet-ski tours, parasailing, water-skiing, tube rides, tandem skydiving, game-fishing trips, motorboats, sunset wine-and-cheese cruises, and horse riding. A yacht calls to make trips around nearby islands, and a game-fishing boat picks up here regularly. The kids will love the playground and a visit to Coonanglebah (the island farm), as well as the kids' club. A private artists' colony in the rainforest sells works Monday and Thursday, from 10am to 1pm.

There were big changes at Dunk in the past year. All four kinds of low-rise accommodations have been refurbished, with new furniture in the Garden Cabana, Banfield and Beachfront rooms, while the Bayview suites have been gutted and given a new modern style. The golf course has expanded from 6 to 18 holes, making it Australia's only island resort course. The Spa of Peace and Plenty, which offers facials, massage, body wraps, and other treatments, has been extended and is now housed in two large tropical-style buildings connected by a floating boardwalk on a man-made lake.

Off Mission Beach. C/o P&O Australian Resorts, G.P.O. Box 478, Sydney, NSW 2001. ℂ 1800/737 678 in Australia, 800/225-9849 in the U.S. and Canada, 020/7805 3875 in the U.K., or 02/9277 5050 (Sydney reservations office). Fax 02/9299 2477 (Sydney reservations office). www.poresorts.com. 146 units (72 with shower only). A$480–A$740 (US$312–US$481) double. Rates include full breakfast and dinner daily. Extra adult A$140 (US$91), extra child 3–14 A$80 (US$52). Ask about packages; some combine stays at Bedarra Island and Silky Oaks Lodge (p. 299). AE, DC, MC, V. Daily 45-min. flights operate from Cairns (book through Qantas or the resort). Aircraft luggage limit 16kg (35 lb.) per person. Dunk Island Ferry & Cruises (ℂ 07/4068 7211) makes round-trip ferry transfers from Mission Beach for A$28 (US$18) adults. Including the ferry fare, the company does daily door-to-door coach connections from Port Douglas for A$126 (US$82), Cairns for A$84 (US$55), and Cairns northern beaches for A$104 (US$68) adult. Fares for children 4–14 are half price. Disembarkation from the ferry is sometimes into shallow water—be prepared to get your feet wet! Airport pickups must be booked. Transfers also available by air charter and "Quick Cat" Great Barrier Reef cruise boat (see earlier in this chapter). **Amenities:** 3 restaurants; bar; 2 large outdoor pools; 18-hole golf course; 3 day/night tennis courts (1 indoor); exercise room; spa; extensive watersports equipment rental; bike rental; daily kids' club for ages 3–14 (an additional fee); babysitting; coin-op laundry. *In room:* A/C and ceiling fans, TV, minibar (beachfront units and suites only), fridge, coffeemaker, hair dryer, iron.

BEDARRA ISLAND: THE ULTIMATE LUXURY GETAWAY

Only a mile long, Bedarra is home to an exclusive 15-room resort favored by the rich, the famous, and anyone who treasures privacy. The staff is discreet, and day-trippers are banned. Rainforested and fringed by beaches, Bedarra is a few miles south of Dunk Island.

Bedarra Island 🐠🐠🐠   Bedarra is one of those rare and fabulous places that throws not just meals but vintage French champagnes, fine cognacs and wines, and other potable treats into the price, shocking though that price may be. If you feel like Louis Roederer Champagne at 3am, help yourself. The new-look Bedarra was injected with some contemporary style during 2001. The private villas have large verandas, and there's a sense of light and space in the public areas. The lobby, restaurant, and 24-hour bar are open, with ironbark and recycled timber beams, and feature panels of volcanic stone. Each villa is tucked into the rainforest with a balcony and sea views. All come with generous living areas, king beds, CD players, bathrobes, and the important things in life, like double hammocks on the veranda, big double bathtubs, and aromatherapy oil-burners. Bathrooms offer divine pampering treats including signature Bedarra aromatherapy oils.

Two premium villas, The Pavilions at Bedarra, are set away from the main resort, perched on cliff tops overlooking Wedgerock Bay, and offer superior facilities including separate living and sleeping areas and large decks and outdoor area with a private plunge pool. In 2003, one of the villas was converted into a similarly exclusive retreat The Point, with many of the same features as the Pavilions, and the additional luxury of a gorgeous outdoor living area.

The emphasis here is on relaxation. Walk along rainforest trails, fish off the beach, snorkel, or take a catamaran, paddle-ski, or windsurf out on the water. These activities are free; chartering a yacht or game-fishing boat costs extra. To visit the Great Barrier Reef, you will need to transfer to Dunk Island to join the Quick Cat catamaran (see earlier in this section). The Beachclub offers watersports facilities and a gym and massage therapy room as well as a lounge area with Internet access. Many guests do nothing more strenuous than have the chef pack a gourmet picnic with a bottle of bubbly and set off in search of a deserted beach. Dress at night is smart casual.

Off Mission Beach (c/o P&O Australian Resorts, G.P.O. Box 478, Sydney, NSW 2001). ⓒ 1800/737 678 in Australia, 800/225-9849 in the U.S. and Canada, 020/7805 3875 in the U.K., or 02/9277 5050 (Sydney reservations office). Fax 02/9299 2477 (Sydney reservations office). www.poresorts.com.au. 17 villas. A$1,900–A$2,900 (US$1,235–US$1,885) double. Rates include all meals, 24-hr. open bar and transfers from Dunk Island. Ask about packages; some combine stays at Dunk Island (see above), Silky Oaks Lodge, and Lizard Island (both described in this chapter). AE, DC, MC, V. Air or coach/ferry transfer to Dunk Island from Cairns (see above), then 15-min. boat transfer. Water transfers can be arranged from Mission Beach. No children under 16. **Amenities:** Restaurant; bar; secluded outdoor pool with timber decking and private Jacuzzi area; day/night tennis court; watersports (see above); gym; massage; laundry service. *In room:* A/C and ceiling fan, TV/VCR, free minibar, hair dryer, iron.

WHERE TO DINE IN MISSION BEACH

Friends HOME COOKING   The cozy interior and a hearty menu favoring local seafood make this place a long-standing favorite with locals. Appetizers include mussels Normandy, oysters done three ways, and garlic prawns; main courses feature lamb shanks; steak with mushrooms or green peppercorn sauce; and chicken hot pot. Settle in with a homemade dessert and liqueur coffee after dinner. Licensed and BYO.

Porters Promenade (opposite Campbell St.), Mission Beach. ⓒ 07/4068 7107. Reservations recommended. Main courses A$15–A$25 (US$9.75–US$16). AE, MC, V. Mon–Sat 6:30–10:30pm or until the last diners leave. Open Sun on long weekends. Closed for 1 month during Feb–Mar.

TOWNSVILLE & MAGNETIC ISLAND
346km (215 miles) S of Cairns; 1,371km (850 miles) N of Brisbane

With a population of 140,000, Townsville claims to be Australia's largest tropical city. Because of its size, and an economy based on mining, manufacturing, education, and tourism, it is sometimes overlooked as a holiday destination. Unjustly so, I think. The people are friendly, the city pleasant, and there's plenty to do. The town is nestled by the sea below the pink face of Castle Rock, which looms 300m (about 1,000 ft.) directly above, and the beachfront had a A$29 million (US$18.9 million) revamp a couple of years ago.

Townsville's major attraction is the world-class **Museum of Tropical Queensland,** where a full size replica of the HMS *Pandora* is the stunning centerpiece.

The museum is next door to one of the city's most enduring attractions, the Reef HQ aquarium.

Remnants of bygone times are still apparent in some of the surrounding towns, particularly **Charters Towers** and **Ravenswood,** where there are splendid examples of colonial architecture, historic hotels, museums, and displays of old gold mining machinery and cottages.

Cruises depart from the harbor for the Great Barrier Reef, about 2½ hours away, and just 8km (5 miles) offshore is Magnetic Island—"Maggie" to the locals—a popular place for watersports, hiking, and spotting koalas in the wild.

Although Townsville can be hot and humid in the summer—and sometimes in the path of cyclones—it is generally spared the worst of the wet season rains.

ESSENTIALS

GETTING THERE   Townsville is on the Bruce Highway, a 3-hour drive north of Airlie Beach and 4½ hours south of Cairns. The Bruce Highway breaks temporarily in the city. From the south, take Bruce Highway Alt. 1 route into the city. From the north, the highway leads into the city.

Qantas (© **13 13 13** in Australia; www.qantas.com) and subsidiary **Sunstate Airlines** (book through Qantas) have many flights a day from Cairns, and several from Brisbane. Sunstate flies from Proserpine and Hamilton Island airports in the Whitsundays. **Virgin Blue** (© **13 67 89** in Australia) flies to Townsville from Brisbane daily, and newcomer **Alliance Airlines** (© **1300/130 092;** www.allianceairlines.com.au) also flies between Brisbane and Townsville.

Airport Transfers & Tours (© **07/4775 5544**) runs a door-to-door airport shuttle. It meets only flights from Brisbane, not from Cairns or elsewhere. A trip into town is A$7 (US$4.55) one-way or A$11 (US$7.15) return. A taxi from the airport to most central hotels costs about A$12 (US$7.80).

Seven **Queensland Rail** (© **13 22 32** in Queensland, or 07/3235 1122) long-distance trains stop at Townsville each week. The 19-hour **Tilt-Train** journey from Brisbane costs A$244 (US$159). The 24-hour *Sunlander* journey costs from A$162 (US$105) for an economy seat to A$316 (US$205) for a first-class sleeper.

Greyhound Pioneer (© **13 20 30** in Australia) and McCafferty's (© **13 14 99** in Australia) coaches stop at Townsville many times a day on their Cairns-Brisbane-Cairns routes. The fare from Cairns is A$51 (US$33); trip time is 6 hours. The fare from Brisbane is A$166 (US$108); trip time is 22½ hours.

VISITOR INFORMATION   For an information packet, contact **Townsville Enterprise Limited,** P.O. Box 1043, Townsville, QLD 4810 (© **07/4726 2728;** www.townsvilleonline.com.au). It has two Information Centres. One is in the heart of town on Flinders Mall (© **1800/801 902** in Australia, or 07/4721 3660); it's open Monday through Friday from 9am to 5pm, and weekends from 9am to 1pm. The other is on the Bruce Highway 10km (6¼ miles) south of the city (© **07/4778 3555**); it's open daily from 9am to 5pm. For information on Magnetic Island, also check www.magnetic-island.com.au.

GETTING AROUND   Local **Sunbus** (© **07/4725 8482**) buses depart Flinders Street Mall. Car-rental chains include **Avis** (© **07/4721 2688**), **Budget** (© **07/4725 2344**), **Hertz** (© **07/4775 5950**), and **Thrifty** (© **07/4725 4600**).

Detours Coaches (© **07/4721 5977**) runs tours to most attractions in and around Townsville.

DAY TRIPS TO THE REEF

Most boats visiting the Reef from Townsville are live-aboard vessels that make trips of 2 or more days, designed for serious divers. **Barrier Reef Dive, Cruise & Travel** (✆ **1800/636 778** in Australia, or 07/4772 5800) has day trips to Keeper Reef and John Brewer Reef. It takes only 1½ hours to reach John Brewer Reef, where you can make introductory dives for A$60 (US$39) for the first and A$30 (US$20) for the second, while certified divers can make two dives for a very reasonable A$60 (US$39); all gear is included. The cruise costs A$104 (US$68) for adults, A$84 (US$56) for seniors, A$54 (US$35) for children 5 to 15, and A$270 (US$176) for a family. The price includes lunch and morning and afternoon tea. There are fresh water showers on board. Cruises depart Townsville at 9am, with a pickup at Magnetic Island en route, and returns by about 5:45pm. Several other operators including **The Dive Bell** (✆ **07/4721 1155**), and **Adrenalin Dive** (✆ **07/4724 0600**) have trips to the Yongala Wreck, the Coral Sea, and the Reef.

THE TOP ATTRACTIONS

Museum of Tropical Queensland ✷✷   A stunning 2002 addition to Townsville's skyline is this A$22 million (US$14.3 million) museum, with its curved roof reminiscent of a ship in full sail. In pride of place is the amazing exhibition of relics salvaged from the wreck of HMS *Pandora,* which lies 33m (108 ft.) underwater on the edge of the Great Barrier Reef, 120km (74 miles) east of Cape York. The *Pandora* exhibit includes a built-to-scale replica of a section of the ship's bow and its 17m (56-ft.) high foremast. Standing three stories high, the replica and its copper-clad keel were crafted by local shipwrights for the museum. *Pandora* sank in 1791, and the wreck was discovered in 1977. The exhibition traces the ship's voyage and the retrieval of the sunken treasure. The museum has six galleries, including a hands-on science center, and a natural history display that looks at life in tropical Queensland—above and below the water. Another is dedicated to north Queensland's indigenous heritage, with items from Torres Strait and the South Sea Islands as well as stories from people of different cultures about the settlement and labor of north Queensland. Touring exhibitions change every 3 months. Allow 2 to 3 hours.

70–102 Flinders St. (next to Reef HQ). ✆ 07/4726 0600, or 07/4726 0606 info line. www.mtq.qld.gov.au. Admission A$9 (US$5.85) adults, A$6.50 (US$4.20) seniors and students, A$5 (US$3.25) children 4–16,, A$24 (US$16) families. MC, V. Daily 9am–5pm. Closed Christmas, Good Friday, and until 1pm on Anzac Day (Apr 25).

Reef HQ ✷ *Kids*   Reef HQ is the education center for the Great Barrier Reef Marine Park Authority's headquarters and is the largest living coral reef aquarium in the world. It underwent a A$6.4 million (US$4.1 million) upgrade in 2002, but the highlight is still walking through a 20m-long (66-ft.) see-through acrylic tunnel, gazing right into a giant predator tank where sharks cruise silently. The wreck of the SS *Yongala* provides an eerie backdrop for blacktip and whitetip reef sharks, leopard sharks, and nurse sharks, sharing their 750,000-liter (195,000-gal.) home with stingrays, giant trevally, and a green turtle. Watching them feed is quite a spectacle. The tunnel also reveals the 2.5-million-liter (650,000-gal.) coral reef exhibit, with its hard and soft corals providing a home for thousands of colorful fish, giant clams, sea cucumbers, sea stars, and other creatures. There's a regular scuba dive show where the divers speak to you via intercom while they swim with the sharks and feed the fish. Other highlights include a marine creature touch-tank, a wild sea-turtle rehabilitation center, plus great interactive activities for children. Reef HQ is an easy walk from the city center.

2–68 Flinders St. ℂ 07/4750 0800. www.reefHQ.org.au. Admission A$20 (US$13) adults, A$15 (US$9.75) seniors and students, A$9.50 (US$6.20) children 4–16. AE, DC, MC, V. Daily 9am–5pm. Closed Christmas. Public parking lot opposite Reef HQ. Bus stop 3-min. walk away.

MORE THINGS TO SEE & DO

The Strand is a 2.5km (1½-mile) strip with safe-swimming beaches, a fitness circuit, a great water park for the kids, and plenty of covered picnic areas and free gas barbecues. Stroll along the promenade or relax at one of the many cafes, restaurants, and bars while you gaze across the Coral Sea to Magnetic Island. For the more active, there are areas to in-line skate, cycle, walk, or fish, and a basketball half-court. Four rocky headlands and a picturesque jetty adjacent to Strand Park provide good fishing spots, and there are two surf lifesaving clubs to service the three swimming areas along The Strand. With 300 days of sunshine each year, Townsville is a place where you'll enjoy cooling off—in either the Olympic-size Tobruk Pool, the seawater Rockpool, or at the beach itself. During summer (Nov–Mar), three swimming enclosures operate to keep swimmers safe from marine stingers, and if watersports are on your agenda try a jet ski, hire a canoe, or take to the latest in pedal skis. A state-of-the-art water-park, complete with an assortment of wet and wild fun has waterfalls, hydrants, water slides, and water cannons, plus a huge bucket of water which continually fills until it overturns and dumps water on laughing children.

Don't miss the views of Cleveland Bay and Magnetic Island from **Castle Hill;** it's a 2.5km (1½-mile) drive or a shorter, but steep, walk up from town. To drive to the top, follow Stanley Street west from Flinders Mall to Castle Hill Drive; the walking trails up are posted en route.

At the **Billabong Sanctuary** (ℂ **07/4778 8344;** www.billabongsanctuary. com.au) on the Bruce Highway 17km (11 miles) south of town, you can see Aussie wildlife in a natural setting; hold a koala, a (baby) crocodile, a python, or a wombat; and hand-feed kangaroos (all for free). Bring your own camera. There are talks and shows continuously from 8:30am; one of the most popular is the saltwater-crocodile feeding at 12:15 and 2:30pm. There are also Aboriginal cultural talks, a food kiosk, gas barbecues, and a pool. Admission is A$22 (US$14) for adults, A$18 (US$12) for students and seniors, A$11 (US$7.15) for kids 4 to 16, and A$58 (US$38) for a family. The sanctuary is open every day except Christmas from 8am to 5pm.

WHERE TO STAY

Holiday Inn Townsville The "Sugar Shaker" (you'll know why when you see it) has been Townsville's favorite hotel for years, especially with the corporate set. Right on Flinders Mall, it's a stroll from Reef HQ, Museum of Tropical Queensland, and Magnetic Island ferries. The rooms are fitted out in sleek blonde-wood decor, and because the 20-story building is circular, every one faces the city, the bay, or Castle Hill. The star attraction is the rooftop pool and sun deck with barbecues.

334 Flinders Mall, Townsville, QLD 4810. ℂ **1800/079 903** in Australia, 800/835-7742 in the U.S. and Canada, 0345/581 666 in the U.K. or 020/8335 1304 in London, 0800/801 111 in New Zealand, or 07/4729 2000. Fax 07/4721 1263. www.sixcontinentshotels.com. 197 units. A$140–A$280 (US$91–US$182) double; A$375 (US$243) suite. Extra person A$33 (US$22). Children under 20 stay free in parent's room with existing bedding. Free crib. Ask about weekend rates, advance-purchase rates, and packages. AE, DC, MC, V. Free undercover valet parking. **Amenities:** Restaurant; 2 bars; rooftop pool; free access to nearby gym; bike rental; secretarial services; 24-hr. room service; massage; babysitting; coin-op laundry; laundry service; dry cleaning. *In room:* A/C, TV w/pay movies, kitchenette (in suites only), dataport, minibar, coffeemaker, hair dryer, iron.

The Rocks ⚷ *Finds* If you have a weakness for Victoriana, you will sigh with delight when you enter this exquisitely renovated old Queenslander home. The owners have fitted it with 19th-century antiques, from the crimson velvet settee to the grandfather clock in the drawing room. Even your meals are served on collectible dinnerware. Every room is decorated with lovely linens, old trunks, and in a few, even original washbasins tastefully wrapped in muslin "gowns." One has an en-suite bathroom; the others share a historically decorated bathroom with a cast-iron claw-foot bath. Complimentary sherry is served at 6pm on the wide veranda, where you have lovely views of Magnetic Island and Cleveland Bay. Despite the old-world ambience, the house has telephone, fax, Internet, and e-mail access for guests (although not in your room). Free tea and coffee are available. There's also an outdoor Jacuzzi, a billiards table (antique, of course), a small croquet court, and a guest laundry. The Strand is a minute's stroll away, and you are a 10- to 15-minute walk from town and the Magnetic Island ferries.

20 Cleveland Terrace, Townsville, QLD 4810. © 07/4771 5700, or 0416/044 409 mobile phone. Fax 07/4771 5711. www.therocksguesthouse.com. 9 units, 3 with private bathroom (shower only). A$105–A$119 (US$68–US$77) double. Extra person A$25 (US$16). Rates include continental breakfast. AE, DC, MC, V. Airport shuttle. Limited free on-street parking. **Amenities:** Outdoor Jacuzzi; tour desk; business center; laundry service. *In room:* A/C (5 rooms only).

Seagulls Resort This popular low-key resort, a 5-minute drive from the city, is built around an inviting free-form saltwater pool in 1.2 hectares (3 acres) of dense tropical gardens. Despite its Esplanade location, the motel-style rooms do not boast waterfront views, but they are comfortable and a good size. The larger Reef Rooms have painted brick walls, a sofa, dining furniture, and a kitchen sink. Apartments have a main bedroom and a bunk bedroom, a kitchenette, dining furniture, and a roomy balcony. The rooms were last refurbished in late 1997, and the modest fittings are in good condition. The foyer was refurbished in late 2000, and the whole resort is wheelchair-friendly, with bathroom facilities for people with disabilities. The accommodations wings surround the pool and its pretty open-sided restaurant, which is popular with locals. It's a 10-minute walk to The Strand; the resort makes free transfers to the city and Magnetic Island ferry terminals, and most tour companies pick up at the door.

74 The Esplanade, Belgian Gardens, QLD 4810. © 1800/079 929 in Australia, or 07/4721 3111. Fax 07/4721 3133. www.seagulls.com.au. 70 units (all with shower only). A$103–A$114 (US$67–US$74) double; A$139 (US$90) 2-bedroom apt. Additional person A$15 (US$9.75), extra children under 14 A$9 (US$5.85); crib A$9 (US$5.85). AE, DC, MC, V. Airport shuttle A$3 (US$1.95) one-way. Bus: 7. Free parking. **Amenities:** Restaurant; bar; 2 large outdoor saltwater pools, children's wading pool; access to nearby golf course; small tennis court; access to nearby health club; children's playground; business center; tour desk; limited room service; coin-op laundry; limited laundry service; dry cleaning. *In room:* A/C, TV w/free movies, dataport, kitchenette (Reef rooms and suites), fridge, coffeemaker, hair dryer, iron.

WHERE TO DINE

Apart from the suggestions below, you will find more restaurants and cafes on Palmer Street, an easy stroll across the river from Flinders Mall, Flinders Street East, and The Strand.

Michel's Cafe and Bar MODERN AUSTRALIAN This big contemporary space is popular with Townsville's "in" crowd. Choose a table on the sidewalk, or opt for air-conditioning inside. Owner/chef Michel Flores works in the open kitchen where he can keep an eye on the excellent service. You might choose a Louisiana blackened rib filet, or kangaroo, or something more casual like the stylish pizzas, pastas, seafood, or warm salads.

7 Palmer St. ℂ **07/4724 1460.** Reservations recommended. Main courses A$11–A$23 (US$7.10–US$15). AE, DC, MC, V. Tues–Fri 11:30am–2pm; Tues–Sun 5:30–10pm.

Zouí Alto ⭐⭐ MODERN AUSTRALIAN This is not just one of the best restaurants in Townsville, it's one of the best in the country. Chef Mark Edwards, who has cooked for the king of Norway, turns out terrific food, while his effusive wife Eleni runs the front of the house, which is idiosyncratically decked out in primary splashes and Greek urns. Main courses include ravioli with choice of filling—pumpkin and blue vein cheese, sweet potato and ginger, or sun-dried tomato and goat's cheese. Arrive before sunset, to make the most of the spectacular views of Castle Hill on one side and the bay on the other.

On 14th floor at Aquarius on the Beach, 75 The Strand. ℂ **07/4721 4700.** Reservations recommended. Main courses A$18–A$22 (US$12–US$14). AE, MC, V. Tues–Sat 6:30–9:30pm. Bus: 1B.

A SIDE TRIP TO MAGNETIC ISLAND
8km (5 miles) E of Townsville

"Maggie" is a delightful 51-sq.-km (20-sq.-mile) national-park island 20 minutes from Townsville by ferry. About 2,500 people live here, but it's also popular with Aussies, who love its holiday atmosphere. It is a busy little place as visitors and locals zip about between the small settlements dotted around its coast; in fact, the island has a good range of restaurants, laid-back cafes, and takeout joints. But peace-seeking visitors will find plenty of unspoiled nature to restore their souls. Most people come for the 20 or so pristine (and amazingly uncrowded) bays and white beaches that rim the island, but hikers, botanists, and bird-watchers may want to explore the eucalyptus woods, patches of gully rainforest, and granite tors. (The island got its name when Captain Cook thought the "magnetic" rocks were interfering with his compass readings.) The place is famous for wild koalas that are easily spotted up in the gum trees by the side of the road; ask a local to point you to the nearest colony. Rock wallabies are often spotted in the early morning. Maggie, off the tourist trail by and large, is definitely a flip-flops kind of place.

GETTING THERE & GETTING AROUND Sunferries (ℂ 07/4771 **3855** for Flinders St. terminal, or 07/4721 4798 for Breakwater terminal) runs services from the 168–192 Flinders Street East terminal and the Breakwater terminal on Sir Leslie Thiess Drive throughout the day. The company has a courtesy coach that will pick you up from your hotel for the 10:30am ferry. Round-trip tickets are A$22 (US$14) for adults, A$14 (US$9.10) for children 5 to 15, and A$38 (US$25) for a family. Combination tickets combining the ferry with an all-day Magnetic Island bus pass or *minimoke* (similar to a golf cart) rental can save you a bit.

You can take your car across on the ferry, but most people get around by renting an open-sided minimoke from the many moke-rental outfits on the island. Minimokes are unlikely to send your speedometer much over 60kmph (36 mph). **Moke Magnetic** (ℂ 07/4778 5377) right near the jetty rents them for around A$47 (US$31) a day. The **Magnetic Island Bus Service** (ℂ 07/4778 **5130**) runs a 3-hour guided tour of the island for A$30 (US$20) for adults, A$15 (US$9.75) for kids, or A$75 (US$49) for a family.

OUT & ABOUT ON THE ISLAND
There is no end to the things you can do on Maggie—snorkeling, swimming in one of a dozen or more bays, catamaran sailing, water-skiing, paraflying, horseback riding on the beach, biking, tennis or golf, scuba diving, sea kayaking, sailing or

---

Tips **Magnetic Island Travel Tips**

If you're going to Magnetic Island for the day, pick up a copy of the free *Magnetic Island Guide* from any tourist information center or hotel lobby or at the ferry terminal in Townsville before you go. Because there are so many choices of activities and tours, it will help if you plan your day before you arrive. Also, there is no bank on the island, so carry cash (not every business will cash traveler's checks) and a credit card.

Be warned: Deadly marine stingers make swimming and snorkeling a bad idea October through May, except at the safe swimming enclosures at Picnic Bay and Horseshoe Bay. Alma Bay is swept and patrolled by life-savers so it is usually safe. You can still do watersports on top of the water, if your rental outlet provides a protective Lycra stinger-suit, but you won't want to wear one of those in the sticky summer heat from November through March.

---

cruising around the island, taking a Harley-Davidson tour, fishing, and more. Equipment for all these activities is for rent on the island.

Most activities are spread out around Picnic Bay (where the ferry pulls in) and the island's three settlements: Arcadia, Nelly Bay, and Horseshoe Bay.

The island is not on the Great Barrier Reef, but surrounding waters are part of the Great Barrier Reef Marine Park. There is good reef snorkeling at Florence Bay on the southern edge, Arthur Bay on the northern edge, and Geoffrey Bay, where you can even reef-walk at low tide. (Wear sturdy shoes and do not walk directly on coral to avoid damaging it.) First-time snorkelers will have an easy time of it in Maggie's weak currents and softly sloping beaches. Outside stinger season, there is good swimming at any number of secluded bays found all around the island. Alma Bay is a good choice for families as it is reef free and has shady lawns and a playground; Rocky Bay is a small, secluded cove.

One of the best, and therefore most popular, of the island's 20km (12.5 miles) of hiking trails is the Nelly Bay–Arcadia trail, a one-way journey of 5km (3 miles) that takes 2½ hours. The first 45 minutes, starting in rainforest and climbing to a saddle between Nelly Bay and Horseshoe, are the most interesting. Another excellent walk is the 2km (1.25-mile) trail to the Forts, remnants of World War II defenses, which, not surprisingly, have great 360-degree sea views. The best koala spotting is on the track up to the Forts off Horseshoe Bay Road. Carry water when walking, as some bays and hiking trails are not near shops.

If you feel like splurging, consider the jet-ski circumnavigation of the island offered by **Adrenalin Jet Ski Tours & Hire** (© **07/4778 5533**). The 3-hour tour is conducted on two-seat jet skis and costs A$115 (US$75) per person, which includes your wet suit, life jacket, and stinger suits in season. Tours depart from Horseshoe Bay morning and afternoon. Keep your eyes peeled for dolphins, dugongs (manatees), and sea turtles.

ORPHEUS ISLAND
80km (50 miles) N of Townsville; 190km (118 miles) S of Cairns

In the 1930s, actress Vivien Leigh and novelist Zane Grey were among the stars who sought seclusion at this beautiful island. More recently, rock star Elton John vacationed here. One of the Great Barrier Reef's most exclusive retreats, Orpheus Island Resort is a popular getaway for executives, politicians, and any savvy traveler eager for peace and beauty. Although it takes 74 guests, guest numbers usually sit at around 40 or so. The surrounding waters are home to 340 of the 350 or so coral species found on the Great Barrier Reef, 1,100 species of fish, green and loggerhead turtles, dolphins, manta rays, and, from June through September, humpback whales. The only other people you will see are resort staff, a handful of guests, and the occasional scientist from the James Cook University marine research station in the next bay. Day-trippers are not allowed.

Transfers are by eight-seater Cessna seaplane from Townsville three times a day. Fares are A$380 (US$247) per person round-trip, trip time 30 minutes. Book through the resort. Luggage limit is 25 kilograms (55 lb.) per person.

Orpheus Island Resort ⑄   The resort is a cluster of rooms lining one of the prettiest turquoise bays you'll find anywhere. Most guests spend their time snorkeling over coral reefs, chilling with a good book or magazine in the Polynesian-style Quiet Lounge, or lazing in a hammock. Free activities include water-skiing (and lessons), snorkeling, catamaran sailing, a "Discover Scuba" lesson, canoeing, windsurfing, paddle skiing, fishing, and taking a dinghy around the shore to explore some of the island's 1,300 national-park hectares (3,211 acres). You can pay to go game fishing, charter a boat or seaplane to the outer Reef, or do a dive course.

Apart from the hillside Osprey Villas, all the rooms and suites on Orpheus are absolute beachfront. The 17 Orpheus Retreats are set in blocks of three, and each has a personal patio and a Jacuzzi. Four Nautilus Suites are more spacious, with separate lounge and bedroom areas, large private patios and large Jacuzzi. Two have enclosed garden courtyards. The six palatial villas, furnished in terra cotta and Tuscan style, are about a 3-minute walk from the beach, and have hillside views of the sea or gardens. Don't expect marbled splendor on Orpheus; the rooms and facilities are attractive and comfortable rather than luxurious—although the complimentary champagne, fruit, and chocolates, and fresh flowers in your room when you arrive are extravagant touches. What you are paying for is seclusion and tranquillity.

Orpheus Island, Great Barrier Reef via Townsville (PMB 15, Townsville, QLD 4810). ⓒ **1800/077 167** in Australia, or 07/4777 7377. Fax 07/4777 7533. www.orpheus.com.au. 27 units. A$1,300 (US$845) double Orpheus Retreat, A$1,580 (US$1,027) double Nautilus Suite, A$1,800 (US$1,170) Osprey Villas. Rates include all meals and snacks; drinks cost extra. Ask about packages. AE, DC, MC, V. No children under 15. **Amenities:** Restaurant; 2 bars; 2 small outdoor pools, 1 with swim-up bar; day/night tennis court; exercise room; Jacuzzi; watersports rentals; concierge; business center; in-room massage. *In room:* A/C (except villas), minibar, coffeemaker, hair dryer, iron.

5 The Whitsunday Coast & Islands

A day's drive or a 1-hour flight south of Cairns brings you to the dazzling collection of 74 islands known as the Whitsundays. No more than 3 nautical miles separates most of the islands, and altogether they represent countless bays, beaches, dazzling coral reefs, and fishing spots that comprise one fabulous Great Barrier Reef playground. Sharing the same latitude as Rio de Janeiro and Hawaii, the water is at least 72°F (22°C) year-round, the sun shines most of the year, and winter requires only a light jacket at night.

All the islands are composed of densely rainforested national park land, mostly uninhabited, and the surrounding waters belong to the Great Barrier Reef Marine Park. Don't expect palm trees and coconuts—these islands are covered with dry-looking pine and eucalyptus forests full of dense undergrowth,

The Whitsunday Region

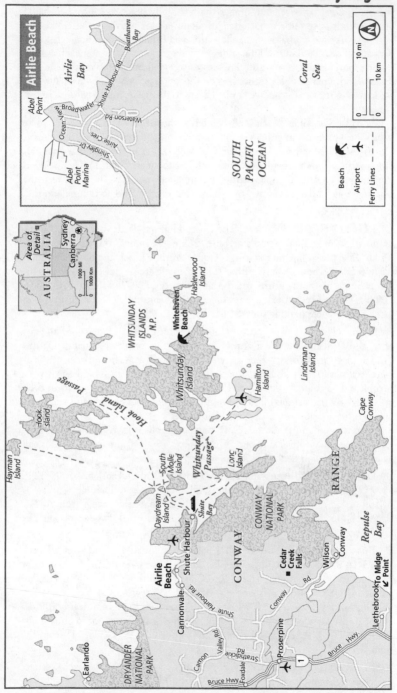

and rocky coral coves far outnumber the few sandy beaches. More than half a dozen islands have resorts that offer just about all the activities you could ever want—snorkeling, scuba diving, sailing trips, reef fishing, water-skiing, jet-skiing, parasailing, sea kayaking, hiking, rides over the coral in semisubmersibles, fish feeding, putt-putting around in dinghies to secluded beaches, playing tennis or squash, and aqua-aerobics classes. Accommodations range from small, low-key wilderness retreats to mid-range family havens to Australia's most luxurious resort, Hayman.

The village of Airlie Beach is the center of the action on the mainland. The Whitsundays are just as good a stepping-stone to the outer Great Barrier Reef as Cairns—some people think it is better because you don't have to make the 90-minute trip to the Reef before you hit coral. Just about any Whitsunday island has fringing reef around its shores, and there are good snorkeling reefs between the islands, a quick boat ride away from your island or mainland accommodations.

ESSENTIALS

GETTING THERE   By Car   The Bruce Highway leads south from Cairns or north from Brisbane to Proserpine, 26km (16 miles) inland from Airlie Beach. Take the "Whitsunday" turnoff to reach Airlie Beach and Shute Harbour. Allow a good 8 hours to drive from Cairns. There are several car-storage facilities at Shute Harbour. **Whitsunday Car Security** (© 07/4946 9955 or 0419/ 729 605) will collect your car anywhere in the Whitsunday area and store it in locked undercover parking for A$14 (US$9) per 24 hours.

By Plane   There are two air routes into the Whitsundays: Hamilton Island airport, and Whitsunday Coast Airport at Proserpine on the mainland. **Qantas** (© 13 13 13 in Australia) flies direct to Hamilton Island from Brisbane. **Sunstate Airlines** (book through Qantas) flies from Sydney, Cairns, and Townsville. Airlink and Sunstate Airlines fly to Proserpine direct from Brisbane. **Virgin Blue** (© 13 67 89 in Australia) flies to Proserpine direct from Sydney and with connections from Perth, Adelaide, and Melbourne.

If you stay on an island, the resort may book your launch transfers automatically. These may appear on your airline ticket, in which case your luggage will be checked through to the island.

By Train   Several **Queensland Rail** (© 13 22 32 in Queensland, or 07/3235 1122) long-distance trains stop at Proserpine every week. The one-way fare is A$134 (US$87) from Cairns on the Tilt Train. Brisbane fares range from A$217 (US$141) on the Tilt Train to A$288 (US$187) for a first-class sleeper on *The Sunlander.*

By Bus   **Greyhound Pioneer** (© 13 20 30 in Australia) and **McCafferty's** (© 13 14 99 in Australia) operate plentiful daily services to Airlie Beach from Brisbane (trip time: around 18 hr.) and Cairns (trip time: 9–10½ hr.). The fare is A$144 (US$94) from Brisbane and A$83 (US$54) from Cairns.

Whitsunday Transit (© 07/4946 1800) meets all flights and trains at Proserpine to provide door-to-door transfers to Airlie Beach hotels, or to Shute Harbour. The fare is A$29 (US$19) from the airport, or A$17 (US$11) from the train station.

VISITOR INFORMATION   For information before you travel, contact **Tourism Whitsundays,** P.O. Box 83, Whitsunday, QLD 4802 (© 07/4946 6673; fax 07/4946 7387; www.whitsundaytourism.com). Another useful website is www.whitsunday.net.au. **Tourism Whitsundays'** information center (© 1800/ 801 252 in Australia, or 07/4945 3711) is in Proserpine, on the Bruce Highway in the town's south. It's open Monday to Saturday from 9am to 5pm and Sundays and public holidays (except Christmas) from 8:30am to 1:30pm.

If you're staying in Airlie Beach, it's easier to pick up information from the private booking agents lining the main street, which all stock a vast range of cruise, tour, and hotel information, and which make bookings free of charge. They all have pretty much the same stuff; but because some manifest certain boats exclusively, and prices can vary a little from one to the next, shop around.

GETTING AROUND   Island ferries and Great Barrier Reef cruises leave from Shute Harbour, a 10-minute drive south of Airlie Beach on Shute Harbour Road. Most other tour-boat operators and bareboat charters anchor at Abel Point Marina, a 15-minute walk west from Airlie Beach.

Avis (© **07/4946 6318**), **Hertz** (© **07/4946 4687**), and **Thrifty** (© **07/4946 7727**) have outlets in Airlie Beach and Proserpine Airport (telephone numbers serve both locations). Budget has no Whitsundays office.

Local bus company **Whitsunday Transit** (© **07/4946 1800**) runs a half-hourly service between Airlie Beach and Shute Harbour to meet all ferries. The fare is A$7.80 (US$5.05).

Most tour-boat operators pick up guests free from Airlie Beach hotels and call at some or all island resorts.

Whitsunday All Over (© **07/4946 6900**), **Whitsunday Island Adventure Cruises** (© **07/4946 5255** for the booking agent), and **Fantasea Cruises** (© **1800/650 851** in Australia, or 07/4946 5111) make ferry transfers from Shute Harbour to the islands and between the islands. One-way transfers from the mainland cost A$18 (US$12) to South Molle Island, and A$29 (US$19) from Hamilton Island. Children 4 to 14 pay around half price. It is not necessary to book, but do book your arrival and departure ferry so that you don't miss your connections. Most islands receive a boat only every 2 to 4 hours, some only once or twice a day, so it's a long wait if you miss your boat.

CHOOSING A WHITSUNDAY BASE

The advantages of staying on the mainland are cheaper accommodations, a choice of restaurants, and freedom to visit a different island each day. There is jet-skiing, kayaking, parasailing, catamaran rental, and windsurfing on the mainland.

The main advantage of staying on an island is that swimming, snorkeling, bushwalking, and a huge range of watersports, many of them free, are right outside your door. The deadly stingers that can infest Airlie's shores do not make it to the islands, so swimming in the islands is safe year-round. You won't be isolated if you stay on an island, as most Great Barrier Reef cruise boats, "sail and snorkel" yacht excursions, Whitehaven Beach cruises, dive boats, fishing tour vessels, and so on stop at the island resorts every day or on a frequent basis. Be warned, however, that once you're "captive" on an island, you may be slugged

---

Tips **Safety Tips**

Although they have not been sighted at Airlie Beach for several years, deadly marine stingers may inhabit the shorelines October through April. The best place to swim then is in the beachfront Airlie Beach lagoon.

The rivers in these parts are home to dangerous saltwater crocodiles (which mostly live in fresh water, contrary to their name), so no swimming in streams, rivers, and water holes.

Moments Come Sail with Me

If "bareboating" is a mystery to you, take heart. You're not alone, but it simply means you are sailing the boat yourself. And if that seems daunting, rest assured that thousands of people do it safely every year. Most of the many bareboat-yacht-charter companies in the islands will want one person on the boat to have a little experience at the helm of a vessel, but don't worry if you don't know one end of a boat from another. You do not need a license, and sailing is surprisingly easy in these uncrowded waters, where the channels are deep and hazard-free and the seas are protected from big swells by the Great Barrier Reef. The 74 islands are so close to each other that one is always in sight, and safe anchorages are everywhere.

If you have absolutely no boating experience, the company may require you to take a skipper along for the first day at an extra cost of around A$200 (US$130) a day or A$230 (US$150) for overnight. And if you think you know what you're doing but just want extra reassurance, you can take a skipper along for an extra fee for the first couple of hours for A$60 (US$39) to help you get the hang of things. Most companies mail you a preparation kit before you leave home, and you have a thorough 2- to 3-hour briefing before departure and are given easy-to-read maps marking channels, anchorage points, and the very few dangerous reefs. Your charter company will radio in once or twice a day to check that you're still afloat, and you can contact them any time for advice.

Most yachts are fitted for two to eight passengers. Try to get a boat with two berths more than you need if your budget will bear it, as space is always tight. The boats usually have a galley kitchen, a barbecue mounted to the stern, hot showers, toilet, linens, a radio and/or stereo, a motorized dinghy, and snorkeling equipment. Sleeping quarters are usually not all that luxurious and include a mix of single galley berths and one or two very compact private cabins. You can buy your own provisions or have the charter company stock the boat for you at an extra cost of about A$35 (US$23) per person per day. Most operators will load a Windsurfer, fishing tackle, and scuba-diving equipment on request for an extra fee, if they are not already standard.

with high food and drink prices. Bear in mind, too, that although most island resorts offer nonmotorized watersports, such as Windsurfers and catamarans, free of charge, you will pay for activities that use fuel, such as parasailing, waterskiing, and dinghy rental.

In some places in the Whitsundays, extreme low tides may reveal rocky mud flats below the sand line. Watersports can be limited at low tide because of the low water level.

EXPLORING THE ISLANDS & THE REEF

REEF CRUISES **Fantasea Cruises** (© 07/4946 5111; www.fantasea.com. au) makes a daily trip to Hardy Reef from Shute Harbour, near Airlie Beach, in a high-speed, air-conditioned catamaran. The boat has a bar, and a biologist

In peak season you may have to charter the boat for a week. At other times, most companies stipulate a minimum of 5 days, but many will rent for 3 nights if you ask, rather than let a vessel sit idle in the marina. Five nights is a good length of time as it allows you to get familiar enough with the boat to relax and enjoy yourself.

In peak season, expect to pay around A$530 to A$730 (US$345–US$475) for a four- to six-berth yacht, per boat, per night. Rates in the off season, and even in the Whitsundays' busiest time June through August, will be anywhere from A$40 to A$90 (US$26–US$59) less. If you are prepared to book within 14 days of when you want to sail, the deals can be even better; you should be able to find a boat at such late notice in the off season. You will be asked to lodge a credit-card bond of between A$1,200 and A$1,500 (US$780–US$975). Mooring fees apply if you want to call into one of the island resorts overnight. A number of bareboat-charter companies offer "sail 'n' stay" packages that combine a few days sailing with a few days at an island resort.

Most bareboat charter companies will make complete holiday arrangements for you in the islands, including accommodations, transfers, tours, and sporting activities. Most companies operate out of Airlie Beach or Hamilton Island, or both. Two of the largest bareboat charter companies, **Australian Bareboat Charters** and **Whitsunday Rent-A-Yacht** operate under the banner of Trinity Marine and share the same contact details: © **1800/075 000** in Australia, or 07/4946 9232; www. rentayacht.com.au. Other well-known operators include **Queensland Yacht Charters** (© **1800/075 013** in Australia, or 07/4946 7400; fax 07/4946 7698; www.yachtcharters.com.au); **Sail Whitsunday** (© **1800/075 045** in Australia, or 07/4946 7070; fax 07/4946 7044); and **The Moorings** (© **888/952-8420** in the U.S., in Australia 1800/553 720 or 07/4946 8044.; www.moorings.com). Tourism Whitsundays (see "Visitor Information," above) can furnish you with a complete list of operators.

If you don't want to sail yourself, there are countless skippered sailing trips through the islands (see the "Sailing & Snorkeling Trips," below).

gives a marine ecology talk en route. You anchor at the massive Fantasea Reefworld pontoon, which holds up to 600 people, and spend up to 3½ hours on the Reef. The day trip costs A$152 (US$99) for adults, A$130 (US$85) for seniors and students, A$81 (US$53) for children 4 to 14, and A$355 (US$231) for a family of four. Guided snorkel safaris cost A$19 (US$12) extra. Cruise/dive packages are available for A$78 (US$51) extra for both introductory and certified dives. Cruises depart at 8am and pick up passengers at South Molle, Daydream, and Hamilton island resorts. Passengers from Long and Lindeman islands connect by water taxi.

A fun alternative is Fantasea's 2-day, 1-night **ReefSleep,** in which you spend the night on the pontoon. This gives you a fabulous chance to snorkel at night when the coral is luminescent in the moonlight and nocturnal sea creatures get busy. The trip includes a marine biologist's slide presentation, two scuba dives, plenty of night snorkeling, two buffet lunches, dinner under the stars with wine, and breakfast and more snorkeling on the second day. You can stay in either a clean, comfortable bunk room for four for A$325 (US$211) per person, or in the double cabin, which has a king-size bed for A$383 (US$249) per person. With so few guests per night, you have the Reef all to yourself.

SAILING & SNORKELING TRIPS ⊛   A cheaper alternative to skippering your own yacht—also called "bareboating"—around the Whitsundays (see the box "Come Sail with Me," above) is to join one of the numerous yachts offering 3-day, 2-night sailing adventures around the islands. You can get involved with sailing the boat as much or as little as you want, snorkel to your heart's content over one dazzling reef after another, beachcomb, explore national-park trails, learn to sail, call into secluded bays, swim, sunbathe, and generally have a laid-back good time. A few companies offer introductory and qualified scuba diving for an extra cost per dive. Most boats carry a maximum of 12 passengers, so the atmosphere is always friendly and fun. The food is generally good, the showers are usually hot, and you sleep in comfortable but small berths off the galley. Some have small private twin or double cabins.

In peak season, expect to pay around A$500 (US$325) per person. Prices usually include all meals, any Marine Park entrance fees, snorkel gear, and courtesy transfers to the departure point (Abel Point Marina or Shute Harbour). In the off season, the boats compete fiercely for passengers; you'll see signboards on the main street in Airlie Beach advertising standby deals. Among the better-known operators are *Ragamuffin* (© 07/4946 7777), a 17m (56-ft.) oceangoing yacht; and **Prosail** (© 1800/810 116 in Australia, or 07/4946 5433; www.prosail.com.au), which runs trips on a fleet of 19 yachts. Prosail offers day trips (around A$90/US$58) as well as multiday sailing, specializing in 3-day, 2-night guided sailing trips through the Marine and Great Barrier Reef Marine parks for around A$500 to A$550 (US$325–US$358). All trips include sailing, snorkeling, scuba diving, and bush walking and you can sail on maxi-yachts such as *Matador, Condor, Broomstick* and *Hammer*. They also offer 6-day packages. Contact **Tourism Whitsundays** (see "Visitor Information," above) for details on other charters.

ISLAND HOPPING   Day-trippers to Hamilton, Daydream, South Molle, Club Crocodile Long Island, and Hook Island resorts can rent the hotels' watersports equipment, laze by the beaches and pools, scuba dive, join the resorts' activities programs, hike their trails, and eat at some or all of their restaurants. See "The Whitsunday Island Resorts," below, for details on where to stay. Club

---

Tips The Secret of the Seasons

High season in the Whitsundays is school vacations, which occur mid-April, from late June to early July, from late September to early October, late December, and all of January. The Aussie winter, June through August, is popular, too. You have to book months ahead to secure high-season accommodations, but at any other time you can get some very good deals indeed. Specials on accommodations, sailing trips, day cruises, and diving excursions fairly leap off the blackboards outside the tour-booking agents in Airlie Beach.

Finds **Hitting the Sand at Whitehaven Beach**

The 6km (3¾-mile) stretch of pure-white silica sand on **Whitehaven Beach** 🏆🏆 will leave you in rapture. The beach, on uninhabited Whitsunday Island, does not boast a lot of coral, but the swimming is good, and the forested shore is beautiful. Take a book and chill out. Some sailboat day trips visit it, as do several motorized vessel operators, including **Lindeman Pacific** (© **07/4946 6922**, or 07/4946 5580 after hours), **Fantasea Cruises** (© **07/4946 5111**), and **Whitsunday All Over** (© **07/4946 6900**). Expect to pay around A$70 (US$46) per person for the day, with lunch.

Crocodile Long Island is a rather noisy, unpretentious resort that nonetheless has plentiful watersports, picturesque hiking trails, wild wallabies, and a large beach–cum–tidal flat where you can relax on sun lounges.

You can get to the islands on your own by ferry (see "Getting Around," above), or take an organized day trip that visits one, two, or even three islands in a day. **Fantasea Cruises** (© **1800/650 851** in Australia, or 07/4946 5111; www.fantasea.com.au), **Whitsunday All Over** (© **1300/366 494** in Australia, or 07/4946 6900), and **Whitsunday Island Adventure Cruises** (© **07/4946 5255** for the booking agent) all offer them, as do several yachts. **Whitsunday All Over** also does a day trip to Whitehaven Beach and Bali Hai, an uninhabited isle where you can snorkel, dive, view the coral from a large submersible, or laze on the sand for A$86 (US$56) adults, half price for kids.

SCENIC FLIGHTS   Expect to pay around A$200 (US$130) for a 1-hour flight over the outer Reef (a spectacular sight from the air), about A$295 (US$192) for a seaplane flight to a private Reef pontoon to snorkel for a couple of hours, way up to A$390 (US$254), even more, for a helicopter to drop you on a deserted coral-edged island with a champagne seafood picnic and snorkel gear. **Hamilton Island Aviation** (© **07/4946 8249**) and **Air Whitsunday Seaplanes** (© **07/4946 9111**) both do a range of such tours.

FISHING   Reef fishing is superb throughout the islands; red emperor, coral trout, sweetlip, and snapper are common catches. One of the most popular charter vessels is the 16m (52-ft.) timber cruiser *Moruya* (© **07/4946 7127,** or 0415/185 653 mobile phone; www.fishingwhitsunday.com.au). Day trips depart Shute Harbour daily at 9:30am and return at 5:30pm. They include lunch, bait, and fishing rods. The crew will even clean your catch for you. Adults pay A$100 (US$65), seniors A$90 (US$59), children 4 to 14 A$65 (US$42), and a family of four A$265 (US$172).

The 12m (39-ft.) *Marlin Blue* (© **07/4948 0999** for the booking office) takes reef and game anglers out from Abel Point Marina and South Molle Island Resort for A$245 (US$159) per person for a full day, based on a shared charter. That includes lunch, bait, and tackle; drinks are extra. The boat departs the mainland at 7am and returns around 5:30pm.

If you want to undertake your own fishing expedition, **Harbourside Boat Hire** (© **07/4946 9330**), in Shute Harbour, rents motorized dinghies for A$60 (US$39) for a half day or A$90 (US$59) for a full day. Half-cabin cruisers cost A$90 (US$59) for a half day or A$150 (US$98) for a full day. They also hire fishing rods and sell tackle, bait, ice, and all your fishing needs.

Moments Whale-Watching in the Whitsundays

Humpback whales migrate to the Whitsundays every July through September to give birth. These fearless giants of the deep come right up to the boat. **Fantasea Cruises** (② 07/4946 5111; www.fantasea.com.au) runs whale-watching cruises in season; trips feature an onboard talk and videos. The cost is about A$95 (US$62) per adult, and if you don't see any whales, you can go again another day for free, or choose another of Fantasea's cruises as an alternative.

ECOTOURS   Visitors to the Whitsundays can get up-close-and-personal with crocodiles in their natural habitat with **Proserpine River Eco Tours** (② 07/ 4946 5111), which combines an open-air wagon ride through the pristine Goorganga wetlands and a boat trip on the river to learn more about one of Queensland's major crocodile-breeding grounds. This is the only place to see crocs in safety in the wild south of the Daintree. Bus pickups operate from Airlie Beach, Cannonvale, and Proserpine for the morning and afternoon tours, which each run for about 4 hours, depending on tides, and cost A$59 (US$38) adults, A$40 (US$26) kids 4 to 14, and A$158 (US$103) family of four. You finish up with a talk over billy tea and the best damper I've ever tasted (and they'll even give you the recipe).

HIKING & FOUR-WHEEL-DRIVE SAFARIS   The hills behind Airlie Beach stretch into the nearby Conway State Forest and are rich in giant strangler figs, ferns, and palms. If you're lucky you'll spot a giant blue Ulysses butterfly. Several companies run half-day four-wheel-drive safaris. Hiking trails ranging in length from 1km (just over .5 mile) to 5.5km (3.5 miles) lead through open forest or down to the beach in Conway National Park, which spans Shute Harbour Road between Airlie Beach and Shute Harbour. One trail has signboards explaining the Aboriginal uses of the plants you are passing; several trails offer impressive views of the islands. The trails depart from one of three parking lots along Shute Harbour Road. The **Queensland Parks and Wildlife Service information center** (② 07/4946 7022), on Shute Harbour Road at Mandalay Road, 2.5km (1½ miles) northeast of Airlie Beach has maps and self-guiding brochures; it's open Monday through Friday from 8am to 5pm and most, but not all, Saturdays from 9am to 1pm.

GOLF   Serious golfers should not miss a round on arguably Australia's best resort course, the championship **Turtle Point golf course** ᚷ at Laguna Quays Resort, Kunapipi Springs Road, Midge Point (② 1800/812 626 in Australia, or 07/4947 7777), a 45-minute drive south of Airlie Beach. An 18-hole round dodging wallabies, goannas, and kookaburras on these difficult fairways will set you back A$55 (US$36) midweek, A$66 (US$43) weekends, plus A$30 (US$20) for clubs, A$10 (US$6.50) for shoes, and A$25 (US$16) for a round-trip shuttle transfer.

SEA KAYAKING ᚷ   If you have strong arms, sea kayaking is a wonderful way to enjoy the islands. Daydream Island and the beaches and bays of the North, Mid, and South Molle group of islands are all within paddling distance of the mainland. It's common to see dolphins, turtles, and sharks along the way. One of the area's most established operators is **Salty Dog Sea Kayaking** (© **07/4946 1388;** www.saltydog.com.au), which takes escorted trips through the islands. Half-day trips run on Tuesday, Wednesday, and Saturday and full-day trips on Monday, Thursday, and Friday, departing Shute Harbour at 8:30am. A half-day trip is A$50 (US$33) per person, and a day trip is A$90 (US$59). Three- and 6-day trips, where you camp out, are A$395 (US$257) and A$995 (US$647); rates include snorkel gear, meals, hotel pickup, and, on overnight trips, camping gear. They also deliver sea kayaks to you anywhere in the Whitsundays. A full day's rental is from A$50 (US$33) for a single kayak, A$60 (US$39) for a double, including delivery and pickup and all safety equipment. A security deposit of A$200 (US$130) is required for rentals.

AIRLIE BEACH
640km (397 miles) S of Cairns; 1,146km (711 miles) N of Brisbane

The little town of Airlie Beach is the focal point of activity on the Whitsunday mainland. The town is only a few blocks long, but you will find an adequate choice of decent accommodations, a small selection of good restaurants and bars, a nice boutique or two, and facilities such as banks and a supermarket. Cruises and yachts depart from either Shute Harbour, a 10-minute drive south on Shute Harbour Road, or Abel Point Marina, a 10-minute walk west along the foreshore or a quick drive over the hill on Shute Harbour Road.

Airlie Beach has a massive beachfront artificial lagoon, with sandy beaches and landscaped parkland, which solves the problem of where to swim in stinger season. The lagoon is the size of about six full-size Olympic swimming pools, set in 4 hectares (10 acres) of botanic gardens, with a children's pool, plenty of shade, barbecues, picnic shelters, toilets and showers, and parking.

Perched on the edge of the Coral Sea, with views across Pioneer Bay and the Whitsunday Passage, Airlie Beach has a village atmosphere where life revolves around the beach and the marina by day, and the bars and restaurants by night.

The spit of land between Airlie Bay and Boathaven Bay is home to the Airlie Beach Sailing Club. Shute Harbour, 11km (7¾ miles) from Airlie Beach, is one of Queensland's busiest ports, filled with yachts, cruisers, water taxis, ferries, and fishermen. For a bird's-eye view, head to the Lions Lookout

---

Great Whitsunday Walking
The Whitsundays will have the first of six **Great Walks of Queensland,** which are being developed over the next 4 years. The Queensland Parks and Wildlife Service (© **07/4946 7022;** www.env.qld.gov.au) is planning tracks that will highlight some of Queensland's most valuable parks and forests in World Heritage areas. The Whitsundays Great Walk is due to open in June 2004 and will cover 36km (22 miles) in Conway State Forest and Conway National Park, behind Airlie Beach. Half-day walks to extended overnight adventures will be available.

The walk will begin at the parking lot at the end of Brandy Creek Road, a short drive from Cannonvale. The trail will wind in three stages from Brandy Creek to Airlie Beach, with two campsites at 12km (7.5-mile) intervals. Walkers should take drinking water with them, as the water in natural systems is not good for drinking.

A second Great Walk will open on Fraser Island in June 2004 (p. 341).

WHERE TO STAY

Coral Sea Resort ⋒ Set in Airlie Beach's best location, on the edge of Paradise Point, with 280-degree views of the ocean, this 5-year-old resort is one of the best places to stay on the Whitsunday mainland. There's a wide range of great accommodations styles to suit everyone from honeymooners to families, and although its relatively sprawling, the design is such that you can easily feel you're alone. All the rooms have a nautical feel, and the Coral Sea suites are divine, complete with a Jacuzzi and double hammock on the balcony. There are four styles of suites, apartments, and family units, all serviced daily. Bayview suites have a Jacuzzi inside. It's a 3-minute walk along the waterfront to Airlie Beach village.

25 Oceanview Ave., Airlie Beach, QLD 4802. ⓒ 1800/075 061 in Australia, or 07/4946 6458. Fax 07/4946 6516. www.coralsearesort.com. 78 units. A$185–A$300 (US$120–US$195) double suite; A$240–A$295 (US$156–US$192) double 1-bedroom apt; A$295–A$325 (US$192–US$211) double 2-bedroom apt; A$255 (US$166) family unit (sleeps 5); A$280 (US$182) 1-bedroom penthouse; A$375 (US$244) 2-bedroom penthouse; A$520 (US$338) 3-bedroom penthouse. Cribs A$12 (US$7.80). Minimum 2-night stay at Easter, 3-night stay Dec 26–Jan 5. Ask about packages. AE, DC, MC, V. Free parking. **Amenities:** Restaurant; bar; 25m/82 ft. outdoor pool; exercise room; games room; tour desk; car-rental desk; 24-hr. room service; massage; babysitting; coin-op laundry; dry cleaning. In room: A/C and ceiling fans, TV w/satellite and free movies, kitchenette, minibar, coffeemaker, hair dryer, iron.

Martinique Whitsunday Resort ⋒ Your apartment in this French Caribbean–style complex high on the hill above Airlie Beach has views which make the short but very steep walk from the town well worthwhile. The one-, two-, and three-bedroom apartments are roomy and light, and each has a big balcony. The wet edge lap pool also overlooks the Coral Sea, and is surrounded by tropical gardens and waterfalls. There's a barbecue area, and you can also order kitchen supplies to be ready when you arrive. Apartments are serviced weekly, and each has a washing machine and dryer.

18 Golden Orchid Dr. (off Shute Harbour Rd.), Airlie Beach, QLD 4802. ⓒ 07/4948 0401. Fax 07/4948 0402. www.martiniquewhitsunday.com.au. A$175 (US$114) double 1-bedroom apt; A$190 (US$124) double 2-bedroom apt; A$330 (US$215) 3-bedroom apt (sleeps 6). Extra person A$22 (US$14). AE, DC, MC, V. Covered parking. **Amenities:** Outdoor lap pool; 2 Jacuzzis; exercise room; tour desk. In room: A/C and ceiling fans, TV, full kitchen, minibar, hair dryer, iron.

WHERE TO DINE

Mangrove Jack's Café Bar PIZZA/CAFE FARE Bareboat sailors, local sugar farmers, Sydney yuppies, and European backpackers all flock to this big open-fronted sports bar/restaurant. The mood is upbeat but pleasantly casual, the surrounds are spic-and-span, and the food passes muster. Wood-fired pizza with trendy toppings is the specialty. There is no table service; just place your order at the bar and collect your food when your number is called. The more than 50 wines come by the glass.

In the Airlie Beach Hotel, 16 The Esplanade (enter via Shute Harbour Rd.). ⓒ 07/4946 6233. Reservations recommended. Main courses A$7.90–A$20 (US$5.15–US$13). AE, DC, MC, V. Daily 10am–midnight.

THE WHITSUNDAY ISLAND RESORTS

There are about 10 resorts of varying degrees of splendor; accommodations range from positively glitzy to comfortably midrange to downright old-fashioned.

VERY EXPENSIVE

Hayman ⋒⋒⋒ This is the most luxurious, glitzy, and glamorous resort in Australia. And a recent A$50 million (US$32.5 million) redevelopment has ensured that it is even more so. Check-in is done over a glass of bubbly aboard the resort's sleek launch that meets you at Hamilton Island airport. On arrival, you won't take long to find your way through the open-air sandstone lanais, cascading ponds, and tropical foliage to the fabulous hexagonal complex of swimming pools by the sea. Despite the luxury, Hayman is relaxed. Dress is beachwear by day, smart casual at night (but pack something elegant for dinner, if you wish). An impressive lineup of activities is available, and it's probably fair to say the staff at Hayman can organize almost anything you desire.

While Hayman is renowned for the antiques, artworks, and fine objets d'art gracing its public areas, the accommodations are welcoming. Every room, suite, villa, and penthouse has a balcony or terrace, bathrobes, and valet service (and butler service in the penthouses). Pool Wing rooms with marble floors and bathrooms and tropically elegant furnishings have views over the pool, and also to the sea from the third and fourth floors. Lagoon Wing rooms overlook a lagoon and have sea views from the third floor. There are new Lagoon rooms, suites and penthouses, and 16 new Retreat Rooms (each with private veranda, open patios, and outdoor rinse showers), a Jacuzzi, and a contemporary beachfront restaurant. For even greater privacy, the Beach Villa, opened in late 2002, has a private Balinese style courtyard, walled gardens, its own private infinity plunge pool, and personalized concierge service.

Hayman, Great Barrier Reef, QLD 4801. ⓒ 1800/075 175 in Australia, or call The Leading Hotels of the World at ⓒ 800/223-6800 in the U.S. and Canada, 0800/181 123 in the U.K., 1800/409 063 in Ireland, 0800/44 1016 in New Zealand, or 02/9268 1888 (Sydney sales office), or 07/4940 1234 (the island). Fax 02/9268 1899 (Sydney sales office), or 07/4940 1567 (the island). www.hayman.com.au. 244 units. A$585–A$1,100 (US$380–US$715) double; A$1,900(US$1,235) suite; A$2,500–A$4,200 (US$1,625–US$2,730) penthouse; A$2,800 (US$1,820) Beach Villa. A surcharge of 10% and 4-night minimum stay Dec 24–Jan 5. Children under 13 stay free in parent's room; A$140 (US$91) children 13 and over sharing parent's room; 50% of room rate for children in adjoining room. Children 5–12 charged 50% for all dining costs. Ask about packages. AE, DC, MC, V. Resort launch meets all flights at Hamilton Island Airport for the 55-min. transfer. Helicopter and seaplane transfers available. Hayman Island is 33km (20 miles) from Shute Harbour. **Amenities:** 4 restaurants; 2 bars; 3 swimming pools (1 saltwater and 2 heated freshwater); beachside 9-hole golf putting green; 5 day/night tennis courts (with ball machine and coaching); extensive health club with massage and sauna; outdoor Jacuzzi; watersports (including parasailing, water-skiing, windsurfing, and catamarans; dive center offering dive day trips, courses, and gear rental); daily kids' club for children ages 5–14, and day care for younger kids; game room; concierge; tour desk; business center and secretarial services; shopping arcade; salon; 24-hr. room service; babysitting; dry cleaning; laundry service. In room: A/C, TV w/free and pay-per-view movies, fax, minibar, fridge, coffeemaker, hair dryer, iron, safe.

Peppers Palm Bay 🦀 A A$7 million (US$4.5 million) upgrade in 2001 transformed this Long Island hideaway. The Balinese-style beachfront hures (a kind of hut common in Polynesia) have a new glamour to them, with new decks and furnishings, and there are plans for a spa in the next few years. The resort's small swimming pool has been extended and surrounded by timber decking, and a small massage studio has opened in the former gym. This is a private and romantic spot, with no phone, radio, television, or air-conditioning in the rooms, but there's a hammock on your veranda. The large Club Crocodile Long Island resort is a 20-minute walk across the hill to the other side of the island and is completely hidden from Palm Bay, but guests at Palm Bay Hideaway can use Club Crocodile's watersports facilities. Nonmotorized watersports such as kayaks are available at Palm Bay.

Palm Bay, Long Island (16km/10 miles SE of Shute Harbour), Whitsunday Islands. (Postal address: P.M.B. 28, Mackay, QLD 4741). ⓒ 1800/095 025 in Australia, or 07/4946 9233. Fax 07/4946 9309. www.palmbay.com.au. 21 units. A$380 (US$247) double cabins; A$570 (US$371) double bure; A$684 (US$444) 2-bedroom bungalows. Children 3–14 A$80 (US$52); cribs A$40 (US$26). Rates include breakfast. Ask about packages. AE, DC, MC, V. Fantasea Cruises (ⓒ 1800/650 851 in Australia, or 07/4946 5111) provide launch transfers from Hamilton Island airport, and water taxi transfers are available from Shute Harbour. **Amenities:** Restaurant and bar; outdoor pool; Jacuzzi; watersports; tour desk; massage; coin-op laundry; dry cleaning/laundry service. *In room:* Ceiling fan, fridge, coffeemaker, no phone.

Whitsunday Wilderness Lodge ⋦⋩ This resort was designed to show off the Whitsundays' natural beauty. Tucked in a cove under towering hoop pines and palms, it is an environmentally sensitive lodge on a national-park island for people who want to explore the wilderness in basic comfort, but without the crowds, noisy watersports, or artificial atmosphere of a resort. It's also a great place to meet other travelers. A maximum 16 guests stay in simple but smart cabins facing the sea, each with a double and single bed, modern bathrooms, and a private deck facing the sea. Solar power rules, so there is no air-conditioning, TV, hair dryer, iron, or other appliances. There is one public phone. Social life centers on an open-sided gazebo by the beach, equipped with a natural-history library and CDs, where everyone dines together at slab tables under the Milky Way on fabulous buffet-style campfire meals. Access is only by a short but stunning helicopter flight from Hamilton Island.

Daily excursions include sailing away on the lodge's gleaming 10.2m (33-ft.) catamaran, a seaplane flight to the Outer Reef and Whitehaven Beach, sea kayaking the mangroves to spot giant green sea turtles (which are common around the lodge), snorkeling the fringing reef on uninhabited islands, or bushwalking to a magical milkwood grove no one else knows about. Or you may prefer to just laze in the hammocks, or head off with a free sea kayak and snorkel gear. The beach is more tidal flat than sand, but clean and firm enough to sunbathe on. Wildlife abounds, including Myrtle, the lodge's pet kangaroo. Those who stay on this 1,215-hectare (3,001-acre) island consider it a plus that no ferries or cruise boats call and that the lodge is inaccessible to day-trippers.

Paradise Bay, Long Island (16km/10 miles SE of Shute Harbour), Whitsunday Islands (P.O. Box 842, Airlie Beach, QLD 4802) ℭ 07/4946 9777. Fax 07/4946 9777. www.southlongisland.com. 10 units (all with shower only). A$5,980 (US$3,887) double for 5 nights (minimum stay). A$800 (US$520) double extra nights. Rates include all meals, helicopter transfers from Hamilton Island Airport, daily excursions, and equipment. Rates decrease with longer stays. On "Beachcomber Weeks," held several times a year, there's a 50% discount on 6-night rates—in exchange for helping clean up the island's shores for an hour a day. MC, V. No children under 15. *In room:* No phone.

EXPENSIVE

Daydream Island Resort ⋦⋩ *(Kids)* After a A$40 million (US$26 million) refurbishment, one of the Whitsunday's oldest resorts has emerged as one of Australia's most extensive and modern spa resorts. The 16 therapy rooms at the Rejuvenation Spa have some of the most sophisticated equipment in the country and since reopening in September 2001 the resort has found a new clientele while retaining many of the features—such as the outdoor cinema and kids' club—which have always made it popular with families. The state-of-the-art Daydream Rejuvenation Spa has an in-house naturopath and a range of computerized health analyses using equipment and tests usually only found in clinics in Europe and the United States, such as iridology and measurement of vitamin and mineral imbalances and antioxidant levels. The "village" at the southern end of the island, a short stroll along the boardwalk from the resort, has shops, cafes, a pool and bar, water activities center, and a tavern serving bistro-style meals. A rainforest walk stretches almost the entire length of the kilometer-long island, and other activities include snorkeling, sailboarding, jet-skiing, parasailing, coral viewing, reef fishing, diving and dive school, tennis, volleyball, badminton and croquet, and mini golf. The resort's makeover includes the addition of balconies—some of them very small—to upper-level rooms, providing uninterrupted ocean views.

Daydream Island (40km/25 miles NE of Shute Harbour), Whitsunday Islands. (Postal address: P.M.B. 22, Mackay, QLD 4741.) © 07/4948 8488. Fax 07/4948 8499. www.daydream.net.au. 296 units. A$224–A$584 (US$146–US$380) double. Minimum 3-night stay. Rates include breakfast. Children 4–14 stay free with existing bedding. Ask about packages. AE, MC, V. Whitsunday All Over ((© 1300/366 494 in Australia, or 07/4946 9499) provides 15-min. launch transfers from Shute Harbour as well as from Long Island, South Molle, and Hamilton Island. **Amenities:** 3 restaurants; 3 bars; 3 freshwater outdoor pools (1 heated); 3 Jacuzzis; 2 day/night tennis courts; watersports equipment; tour desk; coin-op laundry. In room: A/C, TV w/pay movies and PlayStation, dataport, minibar, coffeemaker, hair dryer, iron.

Hamilton Island 📷📷 *Kids*   More a vacation village than a single resort, Hamilton has the widest range of activities, accommodations styles, and restaurants of any Great Barrier Reef island resort. Thanks to a A$56 million (US$36 million) refurbishment over the past 5 years, the place is looking fresh. Accommodations choices are extra-large rooms and suites in the high-rise hotel, high-rise one bedroom apartments, Polynesian-style bungalows in tropical gardens (ask for one away from the road for real privacy), and glamorous rooms in the two-story, adults-only Beach Club, which sports minimalist decor and a personal "host" to cater to every whim, as well as a choice of two-, three-, and four-bedroom self-contained apartments and villas. The best sea views come from the second-floor Beach Club rooms, from floor nos. 5 to 18 of the Reef View Hotel, and from most apartments. In-room amenities vary depending on your accommodations choice, so check when booking.

On one side of the island is a marina village with cafes, restaurants, shops, and a yacht club. On the other are the accommodations, a large and inviting free-form pool and swim-up bar, and the wide curve of Cat's Eye Beach. Hamilton offers a huge range of watersports, fishing trips, and cruises, speedboat rides, Go-Karts, a "wire flyer" flying-fox hang glider, a pistol/clay target/rifle range, minigolf, an aquatic driving range, beach barbecue safaris in an army truck, hiking trails, an Aussie wildlife sanctuary where you can cuddle a koala or hold a baby crocodile, and an extensive daily activities program. Because the resort is split by a steep hill, you need to get around by the free shuttle (which runs half-hourly or hourly 10am–8pm), by golf buggy (A$35/US$23 per hr. or A$60/US$39 for 24 hr.), or on foot. Despite the price, everyone seems to go for the buggies, so the place can feel like rush hour. To get away, hit the beach or the hiking trails, because most of the 750-hectare (1,853-acre) island is virgin bushland. The biggest drawback is that just about every activity costs extra (and it's usually not cheap) so you are constantly adding to your holiday bill.

Hamilton Island (16km/10 miles SE of Shute Harbour), Whitsunday Islands, QLD 4803. © 1800/075 110 in Australia, or 02/8353 8444 (reservations office in Sydney), or 07/4946 9999 (the island). Fax 02/8353 8498 (reservations office in Sydney), or 07/4946 8888 (the island). www.hamiltonisland.com.au. 737 units (some with shower only). A$249–A$335 (US$162–US$218) bungalow or Palm Terrace; A$340–A$690 (US$221–US$449) apt (to sleep 5 or 6). Hotel A$332–A$398 (US$216–US$259) double; A$589 (US$383) suite. Beach Club A$531 (US$345) double. Children under 12 stay free in parent's room with existing bedding and eat free from kids' menu at 5 restaurants. No children in Beach Club rooms. Ask about packages. AE, DC, MC, V. Airlines fly into Hamilton Island Airport. Free airport-resort transfers for all guests. Fantasea Cruises ((© 1800/650 851 in Australia, or 07/4946 5111) provides launch transfers from Shute Harbour and most other islands. **Amenities:** 10 restaurants; 7 bars; 6 outdoor pools; minigolf and driving range; day/night tennis courts; health club and spa; extensive range of watersports and activities; bike rental; child-care center for kids from 6 weeks to 14 years (in 3 groups); concierge (hotel and Beach Club only); tour desk; business center and secretarial services; shopping arcade; salon; limited room service (18 hr. for Beach Club guests; 16 hr. for hotel guests); massage; babysitting; coin-op laundry; laundry service (hotel only). In room: A/C, TV (some rooms have VCR, some have pay movies), fax, kitchen (apts only), minibar, coffeemaker, hair dryer, iron, safe.

MODERATE

Hook Island Wilderness Resort   This humble collection of cabins and campsites on a white sandy beach is one of the few really affordable island resorts on the Great Barrier Reef. That makes it popular with backpackers and anybody who just wants to dive, rent canoes, play beach volleyball, visit the underwater observatory, hike, fish in the four-person flat-bottom boat, laze in the pool and Jacuzzi, and chill out. Good snorkeling is footsteps from shore, and the resort's dive center conducts first-time and regular dives off the beach. Hook is a national park and the second-largest Whitsunday island. The cabins are very basic, with beds or bunks sleeping six or eight. All come with fresh bed linen, but bring your own bath towels. A store sells essentials, but try to bring everything you need.

Hook Island (40km/25 miles NE of Shute Harbour), Whitsunday Islands. (Postal address: P.M.B. 23, Mackay, QLD 4741.) ℂ 07/4946 9380. Fax 07/4946 9470. www.hookislandresort.com.au. 20 tent sites; 2 10-bed dormitories; 10 cabins, 4 with bathroom (shower only). A$79 (US$51) cabin without bathroom double; extra adult A$24 (US$16), extra child 4–14 A$18 (US$12). A$119 (US$77) cabin with bathroom double; extra adult A$29 (US$19), extra child A$22 (US$14). Dorm bed A$24 (US$16) adult, A$18 (US$12) child 4–14. Tent site A$15 (US$9.75) adult, A$7.50 (US$4.90) child 4–14. Ask about packages. MC, V. Transfers from the mainland cost A$36 (US$23) per person, round-trip. Boat leaves Shute Harbour at 9am and leaves Hook Island for the return trip at 3pm (trip time: 1 hr). Book through the resort. **Amenities:** Cafe and bar; outdoor pool; Jacuzzi; watersports equipment (snorkel gear, canoes, and sea kayaks); tour desk. *In room:* A/C, minifridge, coffeemaker.

6 The Capricorn Coast & the Southern Reef Islands

South of the Whitsundays, the Bruce Highway travels through rural country until it hits the beaches of the Sunshine Coast just north of Brisbane. It may not be the tourism heartland of the state, but there's still plenty to discover. The most spectacular of the Great Barrier Reef islands, Heron Island, is off the coast from Gladstone. Heron's reefs are a source of enchantment for divers and snorkelers, its waters boasting 21 fabulous dive sites. In summer giant turtles nest on its beaches, and in winter humpback whales cruise by.

North of Gladstone is Rockhampton and the Capricorn Coast, named after the Tropic of Capricorn that runs through it. Rockhampton is also a stepping-stone to the resort island, Great Keppel. To the south, off the small town of Bundaberg, lies another tiny coral cay, Lady Elliot Island, which is a nesting site for tens of thousands of sea birds, and has a first-rate fringing reef. Two little-known attractions in Bundaberg are its good shore scuba diving and a loggerhead turtle rookery that operates in summer on the beach. Farther south lies the world's largest sand island, the World Heritage–listed Fraser Island, which can be negotiated only on foot or by four-wheel-drive (see section 7 in this chapter).

ROCKHAMPTON: THE BEEF CAPITAL

1,055km (654 miles) S of Cairns; 638km (3 miles) N of Brisbane

You may hear Queenslanders talk dryly about "Rockvegas." Don't be fooled. "Rocky" is the unofficial capital of the sprawling beef-cattle country inland, and the gateway to Great Keppel Island, which boasts some of the few inexpensive island retreats in Queensland, but bears no resemblance to Las Vegas. Heritage buildings line the Fitzroy River, where barramundi await keen fishermen. Every Friday night at the Great Western Hotel, bull-riding cowboys take to the rodeo ring to test their skills against local Brahman bulls.

ESSENTIALS

GETTING THERE   Rockhampton is on the Bruce Highway, a 3½-hour drive south of Mackay, and almost 2 hours north of Gladstone.

Qantas (© **13 13 13** in Australia) has flights from Brisbane, Mackay, Bundaberg, and Gladstone. **Virgin Blue** (© **13 67 89** in Australia) flies direct from Brisbane.

Queensland Rail (© **13 22 32** in Queensland, or 07/3235 1122) trains call into Rockhampton daily. The trip from Brisbane takes just 7 hours on the high-speed Tilt Train; the fare is A$94 (US$61) economy class and $141 (US$92) business class.

McCafferty's (© **13 14 99** in Australia) and **Greyhound Pioneer** (© **13 20 30** in Australia) call at Rockhampton on their many daily coach services between Brisbane and Cairns. The fare is A$83 (US$54) from Brisbane (trip time: just over 11 hr.) and A$128 (US$83) from Cairns (trip time: about 17 hr.).

VISITOR INFORMATION Drop by the **Capricorn Tourism** information center at the city's southern entrance on Gladstone Road at the Capricorn Spire (© **07/4927 2055**). It's open daily from 9am to 5pm.

GETTING AROUND **Avis** (© **07/4927 3344**), **Budget** (© **07/4926 4888**), **Hertz** (© **07/4922 2721** airport, or 07/4927 8700 city), and **Thrifty** (© **07/4927 8755**) have offices in Rockhampton. The local bus is **Sunbus** (© **07/4936 2133**).

EXPLORING THE AREA: CAVERNS, ABORIGINAL CULTURE & MORE

The **Capricorn Caves** ☆ (© **07/4934 2883**), 23km (14 miles) north of Rockhampton at Olsen's Caves Road, off the Bruce Highway, have been a popular attraction in this part of the world ever since Norwegian pioneer John Olsen stumbled upon them in 1882. The limestone caves have origins in an ancient coral reef (380 million yr. old) and today are a maze of small tunnels and larger chambers. The 1-hour tour, which winds through large caverns with stalactite and stalagmite formations before entering the 20m (66-ft.) high Cathedral Cave, is A$13 (US$8.45) for adults, A$12 (US$7.80) for seniors and students, and A$6.50 (US$4.20) for children 5 to 15. It departs daily (except Christmas) on the hour from 9am to 4pm (closing time is 5pm). Spelunkers (over 16) can squeeze through tunnels and chimneys and rock climb on a 3-hour adventure tour that costs A$55 (US$36); book 24 hours ahead for this. From December 1 to January 10, you can catch the Summer Solstice light cave on a tour departing every morning at 11am. On the longest day of the year the sun moves slowly over the Tropic of Capricorn and a ray of pure light pours through a hole in the limestone caves. It's known as the Summer Solstice phenomenon and is the only time of year when the sun is directly over the Tropic of Capricorn. The caves are also home to thousands of small insectivorous bats, which leave the cave at sunset to feed. Plan enough time here to walk the 30-minute dry rainforest trail, watch the video on bats in the interpretive center, and feed the wild kangaroos. If you like it so much you want to stay, there's a motor-home park and campground attached. Bus tours operate from Rockhampton; contact the Caves for details.

The **Dreamtime Cultural Centre** (© **07/4936 1655;** www.dreamtimecentre. com.au), located on the Bruce Highway opposite the Yeppoon turnoff, 6km (3¾ miles) north of town, showcases Aboriginal culture. There's a sandstone cave replica, a display on the dugong (manatee) culture of the Torres Strait Islanders, and an Aboriginal crafts shop. The center is open Monday to Friday from 10am to 3:30pm. Admission, including the tour, is A$13 (US$8.45) for adults, A$9 (US$5.85) for seniors, A$6 (US$3.90) for students and backpackers, and A$11

(US$7.15) for kids. Regular tours of burial sites and rock art, with didgeridoo demonstrations and boomerang-throwing classes, run from 10:30am.

Rockhampton has two free public botanic gardens, both nice for a stroll and a barbecue picnic. The **Kershaw Gardens,** which display Aussie rainforest, wetland, and fragrant plants from north of the 30th parallel, also have a monorail and a pioneer-style slab hut where Devonshire teas are served. Enter off Charles Street. The **Rockhampton Botanic Gardens** (© 07/4936 8000) were established in 1869, and are quite lovely. Admission is free to the small zoo inside the grounds, which features 'roos, koalas, lorikeets, cassowaries, and a range of other creatures, including—rather bizarrely—two chimpanzees. The gardens are open 6am to 6pm daily, with the zoo open from 8am to 5pm. Enter off Ann Street or Spencer Street.

WHERE TO STAY

Rydges Capricorn Resort ⭑   The 20km (12½ miles) of unbroken beach which fronts this resort—and the fact that it is the only resort of any size or style in this region—are reason enough to visit. The resort is about 9km (5½ miles) from the pretty seaside town of Yeppoon, about 45km (28 miles) north of Rockhampton Airport. Open since 1986, the resort was built and is still owned by Japanese businessman Yohachiro Iwasaki, and you will still hear the locals refer to it as "the Iwasaki Resort" despite its several changes of name over the years. Now showing its age a little, the resort is nevertheless cheerful and pleasant, and the rooms are spacious. The best of the three accommodations blocks is The Palms for its views over the beach and out to Great Keppel Island. The main resort block is dominated by one of the largest freshwater swimming pools in the southern hemisphere, popular with visiting local families, especially at weekends. Set in 8,910 hectares (22,000 acres) of bushland, the resort also has an extensive wetlands teeming with bird life. This is not the place for a quiet getaway—it is very popular with large and sometimes noisy conference groups—but there are lots of activities, and it may be just the place to break your coastal trek.

Farnborough Rd. (P.O. Box 350), Yeppoon, QLD 4703. © **1800/075 902** in Australia, or 07/4939 5111. Fax 07/4939 5666. www.capricornresort.com. 279 units. A$200 (US$130) hotel room; A$250 (US$163) junior suite; A$275 (US$179) junior suite with kitchenette; A$325 (US$211) capricorn suite; A$355 (US$230) capricorn suite with kitchenette; A$270 (US$176) 1-bedroom apt; A$345 (US$224) 2-bedroom apt; A$350–A$425 (US$228–US$277) interconnecting family rooms. Free crib. Packages, including golf packages, available year-round. AE, DC, MC, V. Free transfers from airport, bus, or train station; free covered parking. **Amenities:** 4 restaurants; 2 bars; outdoor freshwater pool, with adjoining heated beach-style pool; 2 18-hole golf courses; 4 day/night tennis courts; exercise room; outdoor Jacuzzi; sauna; extensive watersports and other activities free of charge; bike rental; free kids' club during the day (charges apply for evening sessions); game room for children over 14; children's playground; concierge; tour desk; car-rental desk; free transfers to airport, rail or coach terminal; business center; salon; limited room service; massage (in-room and poolside); babysitting; laundry service; coin-op laundry in The Palms and Araucaria buildings; dry cleaning service Mon–Thurs only; activities which cost include horseback riding, land yachting, fishing, canoeing, clay-pigeon shooting, wetlands tours, WaveRunners, and rifle shooting. In room: A/C, TV w/pay movies, kitchenette in some suites and all apts, minibar in all hotel rooms and on request in apts, tea/coffeemaking facilities, hair dryer, iron, safe (Royal Palm Building only), 2-bedroom apts and Capricorn Suites with kitchens have washing machine and dryer.

GREAT KEPPEL ISLAND
15km (9½ miles) E of Rockhampton

This 1,454-hectare (3,591-acre) island is home to one major resort, for the 18-to-35s, and a couple of smaller, family-oriented ones. You can stay at one of the resorts, or take a day trip from the mainland and pay to use many of the facilities including watersports equipment, pools, and food outlets. Seventeen beaches on the island are accessible by walking trails or dinghy (which you can rent). The shallow waters and fringing reef make the island a good choice for beginner divers; experienced divers will see corals, sea snakes, turtles, and rays. If you stay overnight, you will most likely be rewarded with one of the spectacular sunsets for which the island is famous.

GETTING THERE   Launches operated by **Keppel Tourist Services** (© 07/ **4933 6744**) and **Freedom Fast Ferries** (© 07/4933 6244) each make the 30-minute crossing from Rosslyn Bay Harbour, approximately 55km (34 miles) east of Rockhampton, three times daily. The return trip costs about A$31 (US$20) adults, A$16 (US$10) children 5 to 15, and A$78 (US$51) families of four.

From Rockhampton, take the Capricorn Coast scenic drive Route 10 to Emu Park and follow the signs to Rosslyn Bay Harbour. If you're coming to Rockhampton from the north, the scenic drive turnoff is just north of the city, and from there it's 46km (29 miles) to the harbor. You can leave your car in undercover storage at **Great Keppel Island Security Car Park** (© 07/4933 6670) at 422 Scenic Hwy., near the harbor, for A$6.50 to A$8 (US$4.20–US$5.20) per day.

Rothery's Coaches (© 07/4922 4320) runs a daily service from Kern Arcade on Bolsover Street in Rockhampton to Rosslyn Bay Harbour and back, three times a day. You can request a free pickup from the airport, train station, or your hotel. Round-trip fares from town are A$14 (US$9.10) for adults, A$11 (US$7.15) for seniors and students, A$7 (US$4.55) for children 5 to 14. The round-trip fare to/from the airport is A$28 (US$18) for adults, A$22 (US$14) for seniors and students, A$14 (US$9.10) for children, and A$69 (US$45) for families.

Guests at Contiki Resort Great Keppel Island can fly from Rockhampton on a light plane, which takes about 15 minutes and costs A$149 (US$97) round-trip. Book through the resort (see below).

VISITOR INFORMATION   The **Great Keppel Island Information Centre**, at the ferry terminal at Rosslyn Bay Harbour (© **1800/774 488** in Australia), dispenses information about activities and accommodations.

WHERE TO STAY & DINE

Contiki Resort Great Keppel Island   I can't tell you what it is like to stay at this resort, because I'm too old. But the word is out: If you're a young adult looking for a very good time, this is the resort for you. Following the old adage "If you can't beat 'em, join 'em," the new owners and managers of this popular 30-year-old resort have closed the doors to everyone outside the ages of 18 to 35. Great Keppel made its name in Australia in the '70s with an advertising campaign that it has never managed to shake. "Get wrecked!" it screamed and they came in droves for sex, sun, and good times. Firmly stuck with an image that it later didn't deserve—for my money in recent years it has been one of the best places to take a family—this resort is reverting to what made its name and was relaunched in April 2002 as Australia's first Contiki Resort. About 70 water- and land-based sports are offered, and many, including catamarans, paddle-skis, and Windsurfers, are free. Activities that cost extra include scuba diving, tandem sky diving, parasailing, guided snorkeling safaris, jet-skiing, sunset champagne sails, and reef-fishing trips, to name only a few. There are three types of accommodations: Hillside Villas with sea or bush views, garden rooms, or beachfront units—my pick because of their location. If you're traveling alone, they'll even fix you up with a same-sex roommate. The whole resort was given a A$3 million (US$1.95 million) face-lift in 2001.

Great Keppel Island, QLD 4700. ℂ 1800/245 658 in Australia, or 07/4939 5044. Fax 07/4939 1775. www.
contikiresorts.com. 181 units. A$479–A$549 (US$311–US$356) twin, for 3-night minimum stay; extra nights
A$160–A$184 (US$104–US$119) twin. Rates include brunch and dinner. Ask about packages. AE, DC, MC, V.
Amenities: 3 restaurants; 4 bars; 4 outdoor freshwater pools; 9-hole golf course; 2 day/night tennis courts;
2 Jacuzzis; gymnasium (7am–10pm); extensive watersports equipment and rental; concierge; tour desk;
salon; massage; coin-op laundry; laundry service; dry cleaning; nonsmoking rooms. *In room:* A/C, TV, minibar
(villas and beachfront units only), coffeemaker, hair dryer, iron.

Keppel Haven   Not far from the ferry drop-off point at the beach is this
campground-style enclave of humble but pretty cabins and tents, which is a
good choice for families. Renovated in 1998, the cabins have terra cotta–look
floors, bright new kitchenettes, a small double bedroom, four bunks in the living/
dining area for the kids, fans, and a little porch. The permanent tents come with
twin or double beds, four bunks separated by a canvas partition, and electricity.
Catamarans, Windsurfers, fishing tackle, snorkel gear, and dinghies are available
for hire on a pay-as-you-go basis. There's a general store selling basic groceries,
and three communal kitchens and barbecues. BYO towels or rent them (towels
in cabins).

Great Keppel Island via Rockhampton, QLD 4700. ℂ 1800/35 6744 in Australia, or 07/4933 6744. Fax 07/
4933 6429. ktsgki@networx.com.au. 40 permanent tents, none with bathroom; 6 family tents (double bed
and 3 single beds); 12 cabins (each sleeps 6), all with bathroom (shower only). 12 bunkhouses (with 1 bathroom per 2 rooms). Tent A$18 (US$12) per person triple or quad share, A$20 (US$13) per person twin/dou-
ble, A$28 (US$18) single. Cabins A$120 (US$78) twin or double; additional person A$20 (US$13) extra.
Bunkhouses A$80 (US$52) double/twin; A$25 (US$16) quad share. Family tents A$20 (US$13) per adult and
A$12 (US$7.80) children 5–14. Free for children under 5. A$5 (US$3.25) per person linen for duration of stay
for tents. Cabins and bunkhouses have linen supplied. Ask about 3-day, 2-night packages with Keppel Tourist
Services that include ferry transfers and a ½-day snorkeling or boom-netting cruise. MC, V. **Amenities:**
Restaurant; watersports rentals; hair dryers at front desk. *In room:* Kitchenettes in cabins.

GLADSTONE: GATEWAY TO HERON ISLAND
550km (341 miles) N of Brisbane; 1,162 (720 miles) S of Cairns

The industrial port town of Gladstone is the departure point for the breathtak-
ingly beautiful Heron Island. It is also home to the delectable mud-crab, best
savored over a glass of wine at the award-winning **Flinders Seafood Restaurant.**
About 25km (16 miles) south of the town (but off the Bruce Hwy.) are the twin
beach towns of Boyne Island and Tannum Sands, which are worth the detour.

ESSENTIALS
GETTING THERE & GETTING AROUND   Gladstone is on the coast
21km (13 miles) off the Bruce Highway. **QantasLink** (book through Qantas)
has many flights a day from Brisbane (trip time: 75 min.) and two direct flights
a day from Rockhampton and Bundaberg.

   Queensland Rail (ℂ 13 22 32 in Queensland, or 07/3235 1122) operates
trains most days to Gladstone from Brisbane and Cairns. The fare from Brisbane
(trip time: 6 hr. on the high-speed Tilt Train) is A$84 (US$55); fares from
Cairns (trip time: 20 hr.) range from A$151 (US$98) for a seat to A$298
(US$194) for a first-class sleeper on *The Sunlander.*

   McCafferty's and **Greyhound Pioneer** operate many daily coaches to Gladstone on their Brisbane-Cairns runs. The fare is A$78 (US$51) from Brisbane
(trip time: 10½ hr.) and A$142 (US$92) from Cairns (trip time: 17½ hr.).

   Avis (ℂ 07/4978 2633), **Budget** (ℂ 07/4972 8488), **Hertz** (ℂ 07/4978
6899), and **Thrifty** (ℂ 07/4972 5999) all have offices in Gladstone.

VISITOR INFORMATION   The **Gladstone Information Centre** is located
in the ferry terminal at Gladstone Marina, Bryan Jordan Dr., Gladstone, QLD

4680 (© **07/4972 9000;** www.gladstoneregion.org.au). It's open from 8:30am to 5pm Monday through Friday, and from 9am to 5pm Saturday and Sunday.

WHERE TO STAY IN GLADSTONE

Country Plaza International   This four-level hotel in the center of town runs a free shuttle to the wharf for guests bound for Heron Island. Gladstone's largest and best hotel, it caters primarily to business travelers, so it has ample facilities— spacious rooms with balconies, modern bathrooms, an upscale seafood restaurant, and a pool and sun deck. Most rooms have views over the port or the city. There are six three-bedroom apartments and one two-bedroom apartment.

100 Goondoon St., Gladstone, QLD 4680. © **07/4972 4499.** Fax 07/4972 4921. www.plazahotels. com.au/gladstone.htm. 80 units. A$130 (US$85) double; A$140–A$150 (US$91–US$98) apts. AE, DC, MC, V. Free covered parking. **Amenities:** Restaurant; bar; outdoor pool; business center; free transfers from airport, coach terminal, marina, and train station; 24-hr. room service; laundry service; dry cleaning. *In room:* A/C, TV w/free movies, fax, dataport, minibar, coffeemaker, hair dryer, iron.

HERON ISLAND: JEWEL OF THE REEF ✸✸✸
72km (45 miles) NE of Gladstone

The difference between Heron and other islands is that once there, you have no need to travel farther to the reef. Step off the beach, and you enter magnificent fields of coral that seem to stretch for miles. And the myriad life-forms that abound here are accessible to everyone through diving, snorkeling, reef walks at low tide, or aboard a semisubmersible vessel that allows you to view the ocean floor without getting wet. When geologist Joseph Beete Jukes named this piece of paradise in 1843, he overlooked the turtles for which it is now famous and favored the reef herons that abounded on the island. There has been a resort on Heron since 1932, and in 1943 the island was made a National Park. It is a haven for wildlife and people, and an experience of a lifetime is almost guaranteed at any time of year. Heron is a rookery for giant green and loggerhead turtles. Resort guests gather on the beach from late November to February to watch the female turtles lay eggs, and from February to mid-April to see the hatched babies scuttle down the sand to the water. Humpback whales pass through June through September.

Three days on Heron gives plenty of time to see everything. The island is so small you can walk around it at a leisurely pace in about half an hour. One of the first things to do is to take advantage of the organized activities which operate several times a day and are designed so guests can plan their own days. Snorkeling and reef walking are major occupations for visitors—if they're not diving, that is, for the island is home to 21 of the world's most stunning dive sites.

Guided island walks provide another way to explore the island. Walks include a visit to the research station based on the island. As for the reef walk, just borrow a pair of sandshoes, a balance pole, and a viewing bucket, and head off with a guide at low tide. The walk can take up to 90 minutes, but there's no compulsion to stay; if it gets too hot, you can head back for the sanctuary of your room or the shady bar area.

A fishing trip should also be put on the agenda, even for the most inexperienced. The reef fish seem to just jump onto the hook, and the resort chef is happy to cook them for you for dinner!

GETTING THERE   A courtesy coach meets flights at 10:30am to take guests to Gladstone Marina for the launch transfer to the island (trip time: 1hr., 40 min); it departs 11am daily (except Christmas). Round-trip boat transfer costs A$170

(US$111) for adults, half price for kids 3 to 14. A new 130-seater catamaran to be launched in August 2003 was designed to make the sometimes rough trip smoother; at press time, we hadn't been able to test it out, so make sure you take seasickness medication with you just in case. Helicopter transfers can be arranged for A$274 (US$178) adults and A$137 (US$89) kids, one-way.

WHERE TO STAY ON HERON ISLAND

Heron Island Resort 🏆🏆🏆 *(Kids)*   This lovely, low-key resort has been transformed over the past few years, and changes to the accommodations mix continue alongside cosmetic changes. The latest are the chic new Wistari Suites, each with a private garden and veranda. But new accommodations, a revamped central complex and a stylish, contemporary new look have not changed the focus on the outdoors. The brilliant colors of the island's surrounding water and Reef are reflected in the interiors, and everything is light-filled and breezy. Heron's central complex is equal parts grand Queenslander home and sophisticated beach house, with smart bar and lounge areas open to ocean views and sunsets. Duplex-style Turtle Rooms are designed for couples or families, both with en-suite bathrooms, casual living area, and a shady veranda, or you can go for greater luxury in the suites or the private beach house.

Heron Island, via Gladstone, QLD 4680 (P&O Resorts, G.P.O. Box 5287, Sydney, NSW 2001). ☎ **1800/737 678** in Australia, 800/225-9849 in the U.S. and Canada, 020 7805 3875 in the U.K., 02/9257 5050 or fax 02/9299 2477 (Sydney reservations office). www.poresorts.com. 109 units (some with shower only). Turtle Rooms A$460 (US$299) double; Reef Suite A$550 (US$358) double; Heron Beachside Suite A$660 (US$429) double; Point Suite, Wistari Suite, or private Beach House A$890 (US$579) double. Extra adult A$150 (US$98), extra children 3–14 A$90 (US$59). Free crib. Rates include all meals and many activities. Ask about special packages. AE, DC, MC, V. No children allowed in Point suites or Beach House. **Amenities:** Restaurant; bar; outdoor pool; 2 day/night tennis courts; Jacuzzi; massage; limited watersports equipment rental; Heron Kids Junior Rangers program (7–12 only) in Australian school vacations only; game room; activities desk; babysitting; coin-op laundry; lounge with TV; public phones; Internet access. *In room:* Ceiling fan, fridge, coffeemaker, hair dryer, iron, no phone (except in the 4 Point Suites and the Beach House).

BUNDABERG: GATEWAY TO LADY ELLIOT ISLAND

384km (238 miles) N of Brisbane; 1,439km (892 miles) S of Cairns

The small sugar town of Bundaberg is the closest to the southern-most point of the Great Barrier Reef. If you visit the area between November and March, allow an evening to visit the Mon Repos turtle rookery. Divers may want to take in some of Australia's best shore diving right off Bundaberg's beaches.

GETTING THERE & GETTING AROUND   Bundaberg is on the Isis Highway, about 50km (31 miles) off the Bruce Highway from Gin Gin in the north and 53km (33 miles) off the Bruce Highway from just north of Childers in the south.

Sunstate Airlines (book through Qantas at ☎ **13 13 13** in Australia) flies from Brisbane daily and from Gladstone three times a week.

Queensland Rail (☎ **13 22 32** in Queensland, or 07/3235 1122) trains stop in Bundaberg every day en route between Brisbane and Cairns. The fare is A$59 (US$38) from Brisbane economy class on the Tilt Train; fares range from A$163 (US$106) for a seat to A$316 (US$205) for a first-class berth on *The Sunlander* from Cairns.

McCafferty's (☎ **13 14 99** in Australia) and **Greyhound Pioneer** (☎ **13 20 30** in Australia) call here many times a day on their coach runs between Brisbane and Cairns. The 7-hour trip from Brisbane costs A$58 (US$38). From Cairns it is a 22-hour trip, for which the fare is A$155 (US$101).

Moments Up Close & Personal with a Turtle

The egg in my hand is warm, soft, and about the size of a Ping-Pong ball. At our feet, a giant green turtle sighs deeply as she lays a clutch of about 120 eggs in a pear-shaped chamber dug from the sand. A large tear rolls from her eye. In the distance the wedge-tailed shearwaters call eerily to each other, backed by the sound of the ocean.

The egg-laying ritual of the turtles is central to a trip to Heron Island in the summer months. At night and in the early morning, small groups of people gather on the beaches to witness the turtles lumber up the beach, dig a hole in the sand, and lay their eggs. (The turtles are not easily disturbed, and you can get very close.) Every night during the season, volunteer guides from the University of Queensland research station based on the island are on hand; you can watch and ask questions as the researchers tag and measure the turtles before they return to the water. The laying season runs December through February, and only one in 5,000 hatchlings will live to return in about 50 years to lay their own eggs.

Another good place to watch the turtles nesting is at Mon Repos Beach, outside Bundaberg. Mon Repos Conservation Park is one of the two largest loggerhead-turtle rookeries in the South Pacific. The visitor center by the beach has a great display on the turtle life cycle and shows films at approximately 7:30pm each night in summer. Visitors can turn up anytime after 7pm; the action goes on all night, sometimes until as late as 6am. Nesting happens around high tide; hatching usually occurs between 8pm and midnight. Try to get there early to join the first group of 70 people, the maximum allowed at one laying or hatching. Take a flashlight if you can.

The **Mon Repos Turtle Rookery** 🐾 (𝒞 **07/4159 1652** for the visitor center) is 14km (8¾ miles) east of Bundaberg's town center. Follow Bourbong Street out of town toward Burnett Heads as it becomes Bundaberg-Bargara Road. Take the Port Road to the left and look for the Mon Repos signs to the right. Admission to the visitor center is free April through November (9am–4pm), but when the turtles start nesting, you pay A$5 (US$3.25) for adults, A$2 (US$1.30) for children. November through March, the center is open daily from 7pm until midnight.

Avis (𝒞 07/4152 1877), **Budget** (𝒞 07/4153 1600), **Hertz** (𝒞 07/4155 2403), and **Thrifty** (𝒞 07/4151 6222) all have offices in Bundaberg.

VISITOR INFORMATION   The **Bundaberg Region Visitor Centre** is at 271 Bourbong St. at Mulgrave Street, Bundaberg, QLD 4670 (𝒞 **1800/308 888** in Australia, or 07/4153 8888; www.bundabergregion.info). It's open daily from 9am to 5pm.

WHAT TO SEE & DO

The best shore diving in Queensland is in **Bundaberg's Woongarra Marine Park.** It has soft and hard corals, urchins, rays, sea snakes, and 60 fish species, plus a World War II Beaufort bomber wreck. There are several scuba operators.

Salty's Dive Centre (© **1800/625 476** in Australia, or 07/4153 4747; fax 07/ 4152 6707; www.saltys.net) rents dive gear for A$45 (US$29). They also run day trips for A$100 (US$65) including all equipment. Five-day open water and 4-day shore courses are A$580 (US$377) and A$169 (US$110), respectively. A 3-day/3-night southern Great Barrier Reef dive cruise costs A$495 (US$322), plus A$65 (US$42) for all equipment rental. Night dives are free but you pay A$10 (US$6.50) for chemical sticks and light.

WHERE TO STAY
Acacia Motor Inn   This tidy motel is a short stroll from the town center. It has undergone a complete refit inside and out in the past 2 years, with new furniture, carpets and TVs, as well as a repaint and the addition of shade sails around the pool area. The rooms are clean and well-kept, extra-large family rooms at a decent price. Local restaurants provide room service, and many are within walking distance. The five family units have kitchenettes.

248 Bourbong St., Bundaberg, QLD 4670. © **1800/351 735** in Australia, or 07/4152 3411. Fax 07/4152 2387. acabund@fc-hotels.com.au. 26 units (all with shower only). A$72 (US$47) double. Additional person A$11 (US$7.15) adults, A$6 (US$3.90) children under 12. A$5 (US$3.25) crib. AE, DC, MC, V. Covered parking. **Amenities:** Outdoor saltwater pool; nearby golf course; access to nearby health club; bike rental; tour desk; limited room service; in-room massage; coin-op laundry; same-day dry cleaning; nonsmoking rooms. *In room:* A/C, TV/VCR w/pay movies, dataport, minibar, coffeemaker, hair dryer, iron.

LADY ELLIOT ISLAND ⑨
80km (50 miles) NE of Bundaberg

The southernmost Great Barrier Reef island, Lady Elliot is a 42-hectare (104-acre) coral cay ringed by a wide shallow lagoon filled with dazzling coral life. Reef walking, snorkeling, and diving are the main reasons people come to this coral cay that's so small you can walk across it in 15 minutes. You may snorkel and reef walk during only the 2 to 3 hours before and after high tide, so plan your schedule accordingly. You will see dazzling corals and brilliantly colored fish, clams, sponges, urchins, and anemones. Divers will see a good range of marine life, including green and loggerhead turtles (which nest on the beach Nov–Mar). Whales pass by June through September.

Lady Elliot is a sparse, grassy island rookery, not a lush tropical paradise, so don't expect white sand and palm trees. Some people will find it too spartan; others will relish chilling out in a beautiful, peaceful location with reef all around. Just be prepared for the smell and constant noise of those birds.

GETTING THERE   You reach the island by a 30-minute flight from Bundaberg or Hervey Bay. Book your air travel along with your accommodations. Round-trip fares are A$175 (US$114) for adults and A$88 (US$57) for children 3 to 12. There is a 10-kilogram (22-lb.) luggage limit. **Seair Pacific** (© **07/ 5599 4509;** www.seairpacific.com.au) operates day tours from Brisbane and the Gold Coast, which include flights, snorkel gear, glass-bottom-boat ride, lunch, and guided activities.

WHERE TO STAY
Lady Elliot Island Resort ⑨   Accommodations here are fairly basic, but visitors come for the reef, not the room. Top of the range are the Island Suites, which have one or two separate bedrooms, and great sea views from the deck. Most Reef rooms have a double bed and two bunks, and a deck with views through the trees to the sea. Shearwater bunk rooms sleep up to six, and all room types have modern private bathrooms. The cool, spacious tent cabins have

---

Tips **Look Out Below!**

When you land on the grass airstrip at Lady Elliot Island, you'll think you're on the set of Hitchcock's *The Birds*. The air is thick with tens of thousands of swirling noddy terns and bridled terns that nest in every available branch and leave their mark on every available surface—including you— so bring a big, cheap straw hat for "protection."

---

four bunks, electric lighting, and timber floors, but share the public toilets and showers used by day guests. All accommodations have fans. The limited facilities include a boutique, a dive shop, and an education center. There is no air-conditioning, no keys (secure storage is at front desk), no TVs, no radio, and one public telephone. The food is basic. A low-key program of mostly free activities is run, including glass-bottom boat rides, badminton, guided walks, and beach volleyball, and because of the relatively low number of guests, you pretty much get the reef to yourself.

Great Barrier Reef via Bundaberg. (P.O. Box 206, Torquay, QLD 4655). ℂ 1800/072 200 in Australia, or 07/5536 3644. Fax 07/5536 7285. www.ladyelliot.com.au. 40 units, 20 with bathroom (shower only). A$290 (US$189) double for tent cabins; A$330 (US$215) double for Shearwater bunk rooms; A$390 (US$254) double for Reef units; A$450 (US$293) double for 1 bedroom or A$480 (US$312) double for 2-bedroom Island Suites. A$75 (US$49) extra child 3–12. Minimum 3-night stay Dec 24–Jan 5. Ask about 2-, 4-, 5-, and 7-night packages, and dive packages. Rates include breakfast and dinner. AE, DC, MC, V. **Amenities:** Cafe/bistro and dining room; saltwater pool; children's program for children 5–12 (on Queensland school holidays only). *In room:* Ceiling or wall fans, no phone.

7 Fraser Island: Ecoadventures & Four-Wheel-Drive Fun

1,547km (959 miles) S of Cairns; 260km (161 miles) N of Brisbane; 15km (9½ miles) E of Hervey Bay

The biggest sand island in the world, this 162,000-hectare (400,140-acre) World Heritage–listed island off the central Queensland coast attracts a mix of ecotourists and Aussie fishermen. Fraser is a pristine vista of eucalyptus woodlands, dunes, clear creeks, ancient rainforest, blue lakes, ocher-colored sand cliffs, and a stunning 121km (75 mile) long beach. For four-wheel-drive fans though, Fraser's true beauty lies in its complete absence of paved roads. On weekends when the fish are running, it's nothing to see 100 four-wheel-drives lining 75-Mile Beach, which is an authorized road. Pedestrians should beware!

You'll need more than a day here to see everything and to truly appreciate how stunning this place is. Allow at least 3 days to soak it all up, and to allow for the slow pace dictated by the sandy trails that call themselves roads.

ESSENTIALS

GETTING THERE   Hervey (pronounced *har*-vey) Bay is the main gateway to the island. Take the Bruce Highway to Maryborough, then the 34km (21-mile) road to Hervey Bay. If approaching from the north, turn off the highway at Torbanlea, north of Maryborough, and cut across to Hervey Bay. Allow 3 hours from the Sunshine Coast, a good 5 hours from Brisbane.

Guests at Kingfisher Bay Resort (p. 340) can get to the resort aboard the Kingfisher Bay Fastcat, which departs Urangan Boat Harbour at Hervey Bay four times a day between 8:30am and 6:30pm (7pm Fri–Sat). Round-trip fare for the 40-minute crossing is A$35 (US$23) adults and A$17 (US$11.05) kids 4 to 14. The resort runs a courtesy shuttle from Hervey Bay's airport and coach

---

Tips Four-Wheel-Drive Fundamentals

Driving a four-wheel-drive vehicle is great fun and not hard for a beginner to learn, but if you've never driven one before, get a good briefing from your rental company before you head out. Fraser's loose sand tracks can be tricky, and getting bogged is common. The beach can be dangerous for the novice—if you travel too high up on the beach, you can get trapped in soft sand; if you travel too low, a surprise wave can bog your vehicle in treacherously soft sand under the water (and rust your car). Car-rental companies don't like that, and they can smell salt on an axle a mile away! Stick to the firmest tracks, know the tides, and don't be afraid to ask for advice. You'll have to drive a lot slower on a four-wheel-drive trail than you would on a conventional road; take that into account when you plan your day. For example, it takes a full day to get to Indian Head and back, and then only when the tide is favorable. Look out for light planes landing on the beach (which is a runway as well as a road).

---

terminal to the harbor. You can park free in the open at the Fastcat terminal; Parking Great Sandy Straits (© **07/4128 9999**) has secure, uncovered car parking on the left as you enter the Urangan Boat Harbour parking lot. Drive to the terminal first to unload your luggage at the Kingfisher Bay reception desk, then return to the parking lot and walk back (only 100m/328 ft.). **Fraser Coast Secure Vehicle Storage,** at 629 The Esplanade (© **07/4125 2783**), a 5-minute walk from the terminal, has covered parking for A$7.70 to A$9.90 (US$5–US$6.45) per 24 hours.

Both **Greyhound Pioneer** and **McCafferty's** coaches stop several times a day in Hervey Bay on their Brisbane-Cairns-Brisbane routes. The 6-hour trip from Brisbane costs A$43 (US$28). From Cairns, the fare is A$177 (US$115) for a 23-hour trip.

The nearest train station is in **Maryborough West,** 34km (20 miles) from Hervey Bay. Passengers on the high-speed **Tilt Train** (Sun–Fri) can book a connecting bus service to Pialba via **Queensland Rail** (© **13 22 32** in Queensland, or 07/3235 1122). The fare from Brisbane for the 3½-hour Tilt Train trip is A$52 (US$34) economy class and A$78 (US$51) business class, plus nominal bus connection fare. Fares are A$175 (US$113) in a seat and A$334 (US$217) in a first-class sleeper from Cairns (trip time: just under 27 hr.). Train passengers from the north must take a courtesy shuttle to Maryborough Central, then take the next available local bus to Pialba.

GETTING THERE & AROUND BY FOUR-WHEEL-DRIVE 🚙 Four-wheel-drives are the only permissible mode of vehicle transportation on the island. Many four-wheel-drive-rental outfits are based in Hervey Bay. You must be 21 or over to rent a 4WD. You'll pay about A$100 and A$195 (US$65–US$126) a day, plus around A$20 to A$35 (US$13–US$23) per day to reduce the deductible, which is usually A$4,000 (US$2,600), plus a bond (typically A$500/US$325). You must also buy a government Vehicle Access Permit, which costs A$30 (US$20) from your rental-car company, Urangan Boat Harbour, or the River Heads boat ramp; or A$40 (US$26) from a Queensland Parks and Wildlife Service office on the island. Both **Bay 4WD Centre** (© **07/4128 2981;** www.bay4wd.com.au) and **Ausbay 4WD Rentals** (© **07/4124 6177)**

rent four-wheel-drives, offer camping and accommodated four-wheel-drive packages; rent camping gear; organize Vehicle Access Permits, barge bookings, camping permits, and secure storage for your car; and pick you up free from the airport, coach terminal, or your hotel.

Four-wheel-drives transfer by **Fraser Venture** barge (© **07/4125 4444**), which runs three times a day from River Heads, 17km (11 miles) south of Urangan Boat Harbour. The round-trip fare for vehicle and driver is A$82 (US$53), plus A$5.50 (US$3.60) per extra passenger. It is a good idea to book a place for the 45-minute crossing.

Kingfisher Bay 4WD Hire (© **07/4120 3366**) within Kingfisher Bay Resort (see below) rents four-wheel-drives for A$195 (US$127) a day, plus a A$30 (US$20) Fraser Island driving permit and a A$2,000 (US$1,300) security deposit (by credit card) held until return of the vehicle in the same condition as hired. They allow 1-day rentals. Book well in advance. **Fraser Island Taxi Service** (© **07/4127 9188**) is another option for getting around, and they use four-wheel-drives, of course. It's based at Eurong on the island's eastern side. A typical fare, from Kingfisher Bay Resort across the island to go fishing on 75-Mile Beach, for example, is A$65 (US$42). The taxi seats five.

VISITOR INFORMATION   Contact the **Hervey Bay Tourism Bureau,** Urraween Road at Maryborough-Hervey Bay road, Pialba (P.O. Box 8, Hervey Bay, QLD 4655; © **1800/811 728** in Australia, or 07/4124 2912; www.hervey baytourism.com.au). A better source for Web-connected travelers is www. hervey.com.au. The **Marina Kiosk** (© **07/4128 9800**) at Urangan Boat Harbour is a one-stop booking and information agency for all Fraser-related travel. Several Queensland Parks and Wildlife Service information offices are on the island.

There are no towns and very few facilities, food stores, or services on the island, so if you're camping, take all supplies with you.

ECOEXPLORING THE ISLAND

Fraser's turquoise lakes and tea-colored "perched" lakes in the dunes are among the island's biggest attractions. The brilliant blue **Lake McKenzie** is absolutely beautiful; a swim here may be the highlight of your visit. Lake Birrabeen is another popular swimming spot. Don't miss a refreshing swim in the fast-flowing clear shallows of **Eli Creek.** Wade up the creek for a mile or two and let the current carry you back down. You should also take the boardwalk through a verdant forest of palms and ferns along the banks of Wanggoolba Creek.

Don't swim at **75-Mile Beach,** which hugs the eastern edge of the island— there are dangerously strong currents and a healthy shark population to contend with. Instead, swim in the **Champagne Pools** (also called the Aquarium)— pockets of soft sand protected from the worst of the waves by rocks. The bubbling seawater turns the pools into miniature spas. The pools are just north

---

(Tips Please Don't Feed the Dingoes

The dingoes that roam the island are emboldened by visitors who have— sometimes deliberately and sometimes unwittingly—fed them over the years. These dangerous wild animals have been responsible for one death and several serious attacks in recent years. Do not feed them, and keep your distance. There are fines of up to A$3,000 (US$1,950) for feeding dingoes on Fraser Island.

of **Indian Head,** a 60m (197-ft.) rocky outcrop at the northern end of the beach.

View the island's famous colored sand in its natural setting—the 70m (230-ft.) cliffs called **the Cathedrals,** which stretch for miles north of the settlement of Happy Valley on the eastern side of the Island.

Some of Queensland's best fishing is on Fraser Island. Anglers can throw a line in the surf gutters off the beach. (Freshwater fishing is not allowed.) Bream, whiting, flathead, and swallowtail are the beach catches. Indian Head is good for rock species and tailor; and the waters east off **Waddy Point** yield northern and southern reef fish. **Kingfisher Bay Resort** (see below) offers free fish clinics, rents tackle, and organizes half-day fishing jaunts.

August through October, tour boats crowd the straits to see humpback whales returning to Antarctica with calves in tow. Kingfisher Bay Resort runs a whale-watching cruise from Urangan Harbour.

WHERE TO STAY

Fraser Island Retreat ⊁ *Finds*   This is the wild side of Fraser Island, just minutes from 75-Mile Beach. Don't come expecting a luxury resort, but one that has comfortable timber cottages and all the amenities you need. There's a small swimming pool, surrounded by a deck and deck chairs, and each cottage has a small veranda. The rooms all have fans, limited cooking facilities, and a VCR. (You can rent videos.) The bar/bistro is open for all meals, but be warned that day-tour buses stop here for lunch so it can be crowded at that time. If you want to cook for yourself, there's a general store selling food and liquor. The store also has fuel, ice, and gas for campers. You can also hire a four-wheel-drive from the resort. There's a public phone to use. The only access is by plane (**Air Fraser Island,** 🕾 **07/4125 3600**) or bus. **Fraser Island Tours** (🕾 **1800/446 655** in Australia, or 07/4125 3933) will transfer guests to the resort from Hervey Bay and also runs day tours of the island for A$99 (US$64) adults and A$55 (US$36) children 4 to 14.

Happy Valley, Fraser Island, QLD 4650. 🕾 **1800/446 655** in Australia, or 07/4127 9144. Fax 07/4127 9131. www.fraserislandco.com.au. 9 units (all with shower only). A$110 (US$72) 1-bedroom lodge (sleeps 3); A$150 (US$98) family lodge (sleeps 5). Ask about package deals. AE, MC, V. **Amenities:** Restaurant; bar; outdoor pool; tour desk; car-rental desk; babysitting; coin-op laundry. *In room:* TV/VCR, kitchenette, small fridge, no phone.

Kingfisher Bay Resort ⊁⊁ *Kids*   This sleek, environment-friendly ecoresort lies low along Fraser's west coast. Hotel guest rooms are smart and contemporary, with a Japanese-style screen opening onto a balcony looking into the bush, but my pick is the two- and three-bedroom villas just a short walk from the main resort area and pools. The hillside villas, which have Jacuzzis on their balconies, are fairly luxurious, but there's that long haul up the hill to contend with. An impressive lineup of ecoeducational activities includes daily four-wheel-drive tours with a ranger to points of interest around the island, free guided walks daily, and an excellent free Junior Eco-Ranger program on weekends and school vacations. You can also join bird-watching tours, guided canoe trips, sunset champagne sails, and dolphin and dugong (manatee) spotting cruises. Wildlife videos play continuously in the lobby, and the on-site ranger office lists the animals and plants you are most likely to spot.

Fraser Island (PMB 1, Urangan, QLD 4655). 🕾 **1800/072 555** in Australia, or 07/4120 3333. Fax 07/4120 3326. www.kingfisherbay.com. 262 units. A$270 (US$176) double for hotel rooms; A$825 (US$536) 3 nights in 2-bedroom villa (sleeps 5); A$1,260 (US$819) 3 nights in 3-bedroom villa (sleeps 6); minimum 3-night stay in villas. Additional person A$22 (US$14). Free crib. Ask about package deals. AE, DC, MC, V. **Amenities:**

Another Great Walk

The stunning Fraser Island World Heritage Area is the location for the second of Queensland's six Great Walks (p. 323). To open in June 2004, the **Fraser Island Great Walk** (℃ 07/5459 6114; www.env.qld.gov.au) will provide a continuous winding track from Dilli Village to Lake Garawongera. The main trail will be 85km (53-mile) long and take 6 to 8 days to complete, but there are off-shoots which provide short, full day, overnight, and 2- to 3-day walks. The walk will take you to many of the island's popular landmarks such as Lake McKenzie, Central Station, Wangoolba Creek, Valley of the Giants, and Lake Wabby.

3 restaurants; 4 bars; 4 outdoor saltwater pools (heated main pool has water slide for the kids); day/night tennis courts; Jacuzzi; watersports equipment and fishing tackle for hire; kids' club; game room; tour desk, babysitting. *In room:* A/C (hotel rooms only), TV, kitchen (villas only), fridge, coffeemaker, hair dryer, iron, washing machine and dryer (villas only).

8 The Sunshine Coast

Warm weather, miles of pleasant beaches, trendy restaurants, and a relaxed lifestyle attract Aussies to the Sunshine Coast in droves. Despite some rather unsightly commercial development in recent years, the Sunshine Coast is still a great spot if you like lazing on sandy beaches and enjoying a good meal.

The Sunshine Coast starts at **Caloundra,** 83km (51 miles) north of Brisbane and runs all the way to **Rainbow Beach,** 40km (25 miles) north of **Noosa Heads** 🐾, where the fashionable crowd goes. There's a wide range of accommodations, from inexpensive motels and holiday apartments to AAA-rated five-star hotels and resorts.

Most of the Noosa's sunbathing, dining, shopping, and socializing takes place on trendy Hastings Street, Noosa Heads, and on the adjacent Main Beach. The commercial strip of Noosa Junction is a 1-minute drive away; a 3-minute drive west along the river takes you to the low-key town of Noosaville, where Australian families rent holiday apartments. Giving Noosa a run for its money in recent years is the newly spruced up Mooloolaba, about 30km (19 miles) south, which has a better beach and about 90 great restaurants.

A short drive away, in the hinterland, mountain towns like **Maleny, Montville,** and **Mapleton** lead to the stunning beauty of the **Glass House Mountains,** a dramatic series of 13 volcanic plugs.

SUNSHINE COAST ESSENTIALS

GETTING THERE   If you're driving from Brisbane, take the Bruce Highway north to Aussie World theme park at Palmview, then exit onto the Sunshine Motorway to Mooloolaba, Maroochydore, or Noosa Heads. The trip takes about 2 hours.

Sunstate Airlines (book through Qantas) has two or three flights daily (trip time: 30 min.) from Brisbane to the Sunshine Coast Airport in Maroochydore, 42km (26 miles) south of Noosa Heads. **Qantas** flies direct from Melbourne. **Henry's Airport Bus Service** (℃ 07/5474 0199) meets all flights; door-to-door transfers to Noosa Heads are A$15 (US$9.75) for adults and A$8 (US$5.20) for kids 4 to 14, one-way. Bookings are not necessary for arrival pickups but should be made for transfers back to the airport about 24 hours ahead.

The nearest train station to Noosa Heads is in **Cooroy,** 25km (16 miles) away, to which **Queensland Rail** (© **13 22 32** in Queensland, or 07/3235 1122) operates two daily services from Brisbane on its **CityTrain** (© **07/3235 5555**) network. The trip takes about 2½ hours and the fare is A$18 (US$9.75) including bus connection to Noosa Heads. Queensland Rail's long-distance trains departing Brisbane pick up but do not drop off passengers in Cooroy, with the exception of the high-speed **Tilt Train** (which runs Sun–Fri). The fare is A$28 (US$18). *The Sunlander* makes several trips from Cairns each week; the fare is A$183 (US$119) for a seat, A$345 (US$224) for a first-class sleeper. Local bus company **Sunbus** (© **13 12 30** or 07/5450 7888) meets most trains at Cooroy station and travels to Noosa Heads; take bus no. 12.

Several coach companies have service to Noosa Heads from Brisbane, including **Sun-air** (© **1800/804 340** in Australia, or 07/5478 2811) and **Suncoast Pacific** (© **07/5443 1011** on the Sunshine Coast, or 07/3236 1901 in Brisbane). **McCafferty's** and **Greyhound Pioneer** have many daily services from all major towns along the Bruce Highway between Brisbane and Cairns. Trip time to Noosa Heads is 2 hours and 20 minutes from Brisbane, and just under 26 hours from Cairns. The single fare is A$21 (US$14) from Brisbane and A$186 (US$121) from Cairns.

VISITOR INFORMATION   Write to **Tourism Sunshine Coast Ltd,** P.O. Box 264, Mooloolaba, QLD 4557 (© **07/5477 7311;** fax 07/5477 7322; www. sunshinecoast.org) for information. In Noosa, drop into the **Noosa Tourist Information Centre** (© **07/5447 4988;** fax 07/5474 9494) at the eastern roundabout on Hastings Street where it intersects Noosa Drive. It's open daily from 9am to 5pm. Other tourist information centers are: **Nambour Tourist Information Centre,** 5 Coronation Ave., Nambour (© **07/5476 1933**); **Maroochy Tourism,** Sixth Avenue and Aerodrome Rd., Maroochydore, (© **07/5479 1566**); and **Caloundra City Information Centre,** 7 Caloundra Rd., Caloundra (© **07/5491 0202**).

GETTING AROUND   Major car-rental companies on the Sunshine Coast are **Avis** (© **07/5443 5055** Sunshine Coast Airport, or 07/5447 4933 Noosa Heads), **Budget** (© **07/5448 7455** airport, or 07/5447 4588 Noosa Heads), **Hertz** (© **07/5448 9731** airport or 07/5447 2253 Noosa Heads), and **Thrifty** (© **07/5443 1733** airport, or 07/5447 2299 Noosa Heads). Many local companies rent cars and four-wheel-drives, including **Trusty** (© **07/5491 2444**).

The local bus company is **Sunbus** (© **07/5492 8700,** or 13 12 30 in Australia).

EXPLORING THE AREA

HITTING THE BEACH & OTHER OUTDOOR FUN   Main Beach, Noosa Heads, is the place to swim, surf, and sunbathe. If the bikini-clad supermodel look-alikes are too much for you, head to Sunshine Beach, just behind Noosa Junction off the David Low Way, about 2km (1¼ miles) from Noosa Heads. It's just as beautiful. Both beaches are patrolled 365 days a year.

Learn to surf with two-time Australian and World Pro-Am champion **Merrick Davis** (© **0418/787 577** mobile phone; www.learntosurf.com.au), who's lived in Noosa for 10 years. Merrick and his team run 2-hour lessons on Main Beach daily for A$35 (US$23), 3-day certificate courses for A$95 (US$62), and 5-day courses for A$125 (US$82). They will pick you up and drop you off at your accommodations, and also rent surfboards, body boards, and sea kayaks.

If you want to rent a Windsurfer, canoe, kayak, surf ski, catamaran, jet ski, or fishing boat that you can play with on the Noosa River, or take upriver into

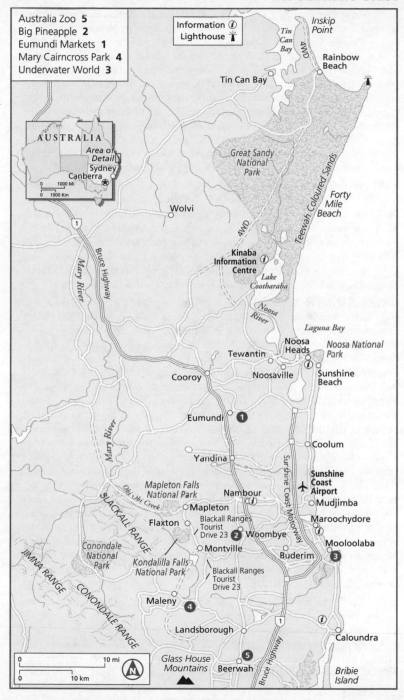

The Sunshine Coast

Australia Zoo **5**
Big Pineapple **2**
Eumundi Markets **1**
Mary Cairncross Park **4**
Underwater World **3**

Information ⓘ
Lighthouse ⍊

Inskip Point

Tin Can Bay

Rainbow Beach

Tin Can Bay

4WD

AUSTRALIA

Area of Detail

Sydney
Canberra ⊛

1000 Mi
0
0   1000 Km

Great Sandy National Park

Wolvi

Teewah Coloured Sands

Forty Mile Beach

1

Bruce Highway

Mary River

4WD

Kinaba Information Centre ⓘ

Lake Cootharaba

Noosa River

Laguna Bay

Tewantin

Noosa Heads

Noosa National Park

ⓘ Sunshine Beach

Cooroy

Noosaville

Mary River

Eumundi ❶

Coolum

Yandina

Sunshine Coast Airport ✈

Mapleton Falls National Park

Nambour ⓘ

Mudjimba

Maroochydore

BLACKALL RANGE

Obi Obi Creek

Mapleton

Blackall Ranges Tourist Drive 23 ❷ Woombye

ⓘ

Conondale National Park

Flaxton

Mooloolaba ❸

JIMNA RANGE

Kondalilla Falls National Park

Montville

Buderim

Blackall Ranges Tourist Drive 23

CONONDALE RANGE

Maleny ❹

Landsborough

1

ⓘ

Caloundra

0   10 mi
0   10 km

N

Glass House Mountains

❺
Beerwah

Bruce Highway

Bribie Island

343

Great Sandy National Park (see below), check out the dozens of outfits along Gympie Terrace between James Street and Robert Street in Noosaville.

The **Aussie Sea Kayak Company** (© 07/5477 5335; www.ausseakayak. com.au), at The Wharf, Mooloolaba, runs a 2-hour sunset paddle on the Maroochy River every day for A$40 (US$26)—including a glass of champagne on your return as reward for all the hard work! Owner/operators Natalie Stephenson and Rod Withyman are qualified kayak guides and instructors who worked in the U.S., Canada, and Mexico before returning to Australia to set up their tours. Half-day tours run every day for 3 to 4 hours at Mooloolaba (A$60/US$39), day tours for 6 hours, Tuesday, Wednesday, Friday, and Saturday at Noosa (A$110/US$68). The company also runs overnight adventures to Moreton and North Stradbroke Islands, and to Fraser Island, Great Keppel, and the Whitsundays for up to 6 days.

EXPLORING NOOSA NATIONAL PARK   A 10-minute stroll northeast from Hastings Street brings you to the 432-hectare (1,067-acre) **Noosa National Park.** Anywhere you see a crowd looking upwards, you're sure to spot a koala. They're often seen in the unlikely setting of the parking lot at the entrance to the park. A network of well-signposted walking trails leads through the bush. The most scenic is the 2.7km (1.5-mile) coastal trail. The shortest trail is the 1km (just over .5-mile) Palm Grove circuit; the longest is the 4.8km (3-mile) Tanglewood trail inland to Hell's Gates—definitely worth the effort.

GREAT SANDY NATIONAL PARK   Stretching north of Noosa along the coast is the 56,000-hectare (138,320-acre) Great Sandy National Park (often called Cooloola National Park), home to forests, beach, and freshwater lakes, including the state's largest, Lake Cootharaba. A popular thing to do is cruise the Everglades formed by the Noosa River and tributary creeks. The park's information office, the **Sir Thomas Hiley Information Centre** (© 07/5449 7364; daily 9am–3pm), is on the western shore of Lake Cootharaba, about 30km (19 miles) from Noosaville. It has a display on the area's geography and a mangrove boardwalk to explore; it's accessible only by boat, which you can easily rent from the numerous boat-rental outfits in Noosaville. There are several half-day cruises into the Everglades, and guided kayak tours explore the park's lower reaches.

The other option is to take a four-wheel-drive along 40-Mile Beach, a designated highway with traffic laws, for a close-up view of the Teewah colored sand cliffs. This is a great place to get away from the crowds and enjoy nature's wonders. Lifeguards do not patrol the beach, so do not swim alone, and take care. Tours are available, or you can rent a four-wheel-drive and explore on your own. To reach the beach, cross Noosa River on the ferry at Tewantin, then take Maximilian Drive for 4km (2½ miles) to the beach. Stock up on water, food, and gas in Tewantin. The ferry (© 07/5449 8013) costs A$8 (US$5.20) per vehicle round-trip; it operates from 6am to 10pm Sunday through Thursday, and 6am to midnight Friday and Saturday.

WILDLIFE PARKS & THEME PARKS   Small theme parks seem to thrive on the Sunshine Coast. Don't expect thrill rides, but you might find some of them a pleasant way to spend a few hours.

A transparent tunnel with an 80m (262-ft.) moving walkway that takes you through a tank filled with sharks, stingrays, groupers, eels, and coral is the highlight at **Underwater World** (© 07/5444 8488), at The Wharf, Mooloolaba. Kids can pick up starfish and sea cucumbers in the touch pool, and there are static displays on whales and sharks, shark breeding, and freshwater crocodile talks, an otter enclosure, and a 30-minute seal show. You can also swim with the seals (A$75/US$49), or dive with the sharks (A$95/US$62 for certified divers, including gear, or A$125/US$81 for nondivers). It's open daily from 9am to 6pm (last entry at 5pm). Closed Christmas. Admission is A$23 (US$15) for adults, A$15 (US$9.75) for seniors, A$16 (US$10) for students, A$13 (US$8.45) for children 3 to 15, and A$59 (US$38) for a family of five. Allow 2 hours to see everything, more if you want to attend all the talks.

At the **Big Pineapple** (© 07/5442 1333; www.bigpineapple.com.au), 6km (3¾ miles) south of Nambour on the Nambour Connection Road in Woombye—don't worry, you can't miss the 16m (52-ft.) tall monument—you can take a train ride through a working pineapple plantation, ride through a rainforest and a macadamia farm in a macadamia-shaped carriage, and take a boat ride through a hydroponics greenhouse. The park also has a baby animal farm, kangaroos, koalas, a rainforest walk, a small but excellent nocturnal house called "Creatures of the Night," and a gift shop. It's open 365 days a year from 9am to 5pm (opens later on Christmas and Anzac Day; call for exact time). Entry is free; each tour is priced separately so you can do all or just one, but the best option is to buy a family pass to all tours, which costs A$69 (US$45) for two adults and up to four children. Allow half a day if you do everything.

Farther south on Glass House Mountains Tourist Drive 24 at Beerwah, off the Bruce Highway, is crocodile hunter Steve Irwin's **Australia Zoo** ☆ (© 07/ 5494 1134; www.crocodilehunter.com). Steve and his wife, Terri, stars of the *Crocodile Hunter* television shows, are renowned for handling dangerous saltwater crocs and are often around to say hello. The zoo is in the process of a A$40 million (US$26 million) upgrade, which will expand it from 8.8 hectares (22 acres) to 100 hectares (251 acres) in the next 5 years. Watch out for new themed sections displaying animals from around the world including Madagascar, South East Asia, Africa, the Americas, and Asia. Demonstrations and feedings are held regularly throughout the day, but the highlight is the saltwater croc show at 1:30pm. You can also hand-feed 'roos, pat a koala, check out foxes and camels, and watch (even hold!) venomous snakes and pythons. Admission is A$23 (US$15) for adults, A$19 (US$12) for seniors and students, A$14 (US$9.10) for kids 3 to 14, and A$65 (US$42) for a family of five. The park is open daily from 8:30am to 4pm. Closed Christmas. Courtesy buses will pick you up and return you to Beerwah and Landsborough railway stations or from Noosa, Maroochydore, Alexandra Headlands, Mooloolaba, and Caloundra.

A SCENIC MOUNTAINTOP DRIVE THROUGH THE SUNSHINE COAST HINTERLAND

A leisurely drive along the lush green ridge-top of the **Blackall Ranges** ☆ behind Noosa is a popular half- or full-day excursion. Mountain villages, full of crafts shops and cafes, and terrific views of the coast are the main attractions. Macadamia nuts, peaches, and other homegrown produce are often for sale by the road at dirt-cheap prices.

On Saturdays, start at the colorful outdoor **Eumundi Markets** ☆☆ in the historical village of Eumundi, 13km (8 miles) west of Noosa along the Eumundi Road. Locals and visitors wander under the huge shady trees among dozens of stalls selling locally grown organic lemonade, fruit, groovy hats, teddy bears, antique linen, homemade soaps, handcrafted hardwood furniture—even live emu chicks! Get your face painted, your palm read, or your feet massaged. Listen to some didgeridoo music or bush poetry. When shopping's done, everyone pops into the cafes on Eumundi's main street. The market runs from 6:30am to 2pm.

From Eumundi, take the Bruce Highway to Nambour and turn right onto the **Nambour-Mapleton Road.** (The turnoff is just before you enter Nambour, so if you hit the town, you've gone too far.) A winding 12km (7½-mile) climb up the range between rolling farmland and forest brings you to Mapleton. Stop at the pub for some spectacular views from the veranda. From here, detour almost 4km (2½ miles) to see the 120m (394-ft.) Mapleton Falls. A 200m (656-ft.) bushwalk departs from the picnic grounds and ends with great views over the Obi Obi Valley. There is also a 1.3km (¾ mile) circuit.

Back on the main **Mapleton-Maleny Road,** head south 3.5km (2 miles) through lush forest and farms to Flaxton Gardens. Perched on the cliff with breathtaking coast views is a wine cellar offering tastings and sales, plus a pottery, cafe, and gift shop. A bit farther south you can detour right and walk the 4.6km (2¾-mile) round-trip trail to the base of 80m (262-ft.) Kondalilla Falls. You can swim here, too. It's a slippery downhill walk, and the climb back up can be tough.

Take the main road south for 5.5km (3½ miles) to **Montville.** This English-style village has become such a tourist stop that it has lost some of its character and lots of people decry its touristy facade. But everyone still ends up strolling the tree-lined streets and browsing the gift shops and galleries.

About 13km (8 miles) down the road is **Maleny,** more modern and less com-mercialized than Montville. Be sure to follow the signs around to **Mary Cairn-cross Park** for spectacular views of the **Glass House Mountains** ⟨⟨, 11 volcanic plugs protruding out of the plains. The park has a food kiosk, a playground, free wood barbecues, and a rainforest information center; a 1.7km (1-mile) walking trail loops through the rainforest past some giant strangler figs.

You can either return to Noosa the way you came or, if you're in a hurry, drive down to Landsborough and rejoin the Bruce Highway.

WHERE TO STAY

The **Sunshine Coast Booking Centre** (© **1300/553 800** in Australia; www.scbc.biz) offers competitive up-to-the-minute accommodations deals at a range of self-contained apartment resorts in Mooloolaba, Alexandra Headland, and Noosa.

EXPENSIVE

Hyatt Regency Coolum ⟨⟨   A couple of hours under the expert care of the therapists at the Sun Spa and you'll feel years younger! This is one of the reasons the well heeled flock to this sprawling bushland resort. The other is its 18-hole Robert Trent Jones Jr.–designed golf course. The Sun Spa (there are entrance fees of around A$13/US$8.45 a day as well as the cost of treatments) does everything from aromatherapy baths to triglyceride checks (130 treatments in all) and has massage rooms, aqua-aerobics, yoga, a 25m (82-ft.) lap pool, and much more. An almost-6-hour body detox costs A$400 (US$260), but you can get a minifacial or a half-hour massage for A$60 (US$39). *Australian Golf Digest* rated the golf course as one of Australia's top five resort courses in 2000. Golf widows and widowers can play tennis; do decoupage in the Creative Arts Center; take the twice-daily free shuttle into Noosa to shop; and surf at the resort's private beach. A nightly shut-tle runs to Noosa Heads restaurants for A$15 (US$9.75) per person, round-trip.

So spread out are the low-rise accommodations that guests rent a bike to get around, wait 15 minutes for the two free resort shuttles (frustrating sometimes!), or get into the healthy swing of things and walk. Accommodations all sport con-temporary decor and come as "suites" (a single room divided into living and sleeping quarters); two-bedroom President's Villas with a kitchenette; villas within the Ambassador Club, which has its own concierge, pool, tennis court, and lounge; and two-story, three-bedroom Ambassador Club residences boasting rooftop terraces with a Jacuzzi.

The Village Square is just that: an attractive cluster of shops, restaurants, bars, and takeout joints that provides the heart of the resort.

Warran Rd., off David Low Way (approx. 2km/1¼ miles south of town), Coolum Beach, QLD 4573. © **13 12 34** in Australia, 800/633-7313 in the U.S. and Canada, 0845/758 1666 in the U.K. or 020/8335 1220 in London, 0800/44 1234 in New Zealand, or 07/5446 1234. Fax 07/5446 2957. www.coolum.hyatt.com. 323 units (some with Jacuzzis). A$220–A$395 (US$143–US$256) double; A$320–A$1,400 (US$208–US$910) villa; A$1,030–A$2,200 (US$670–US$1,430) Ambassadors' residences. Rates include continental breakfast. Extra person A$45 (US$29). Children under 13 stay free in parent's room with existing bedding. Ask about golf, spa, and other packages. AE, MC, V. Valet parking A$18 (US$12) or self-parking. Resort shuttle meets all flights at Sunshine Coast Airport for A$18 (US$12) per person, one-way. Town car transfers from Brisbane Airport A$79 (US$51) per person, one-way (shared service with other guests); limousine transfers available. **Amenities:** 4 restaurants; 3 bars; 9 outdoor pools (main pool and lap pool heated); golf course; 9 night/day tennis courts; health club and spa; watersports equipment rental; bike rental; children's programs daily for kids ages 6 weeks to 12 years (for a fee); concierge; tour desk; car-rental desk; business center; shopping arcade; limited room service; massage; babysitting; same-day dry cleaning; nonsmoking rooms; executive rooms. *In room:* A/C, TV w/pay movies, fax, dataport, kitchenette, minibar, coffeemaker, hair dryer, iron, safe.

Sheraton Noosa Resort & Spa 🌟🌟🌟

Another great place to enjoy a day spa by the sea is at Noosa's first AAA-rated five-star resort. Right in the heart of Hastings Street, the Sheraton has a prime spot among the chic boutiques and restaurants. There are several different styles of rooms, but the best in my book are those with views away from the beach but looking right down the Noosa River to the mountains. Sit on the balcony at sunset and drink it in. All the rooms are extra-large, and all have Jacuzzis. You'll pay more for the two-level poolside villas, which have private access to the pool area, but there's no view. Some rooms have ocean (but not beach) views. The Aqua Day Spa has a Roman-bathhouse feel to it and offers a wide range of treatments in its seven treatment rooms. The hotel restaurant, **Cato's**—named for Australian novelist Nancy Cato, who lived in Noosa until her death a few years ago—fronts onto Hastings Street and is a great place to watch the world go by.

Hastings St., Noosa Heads, QLD 4567. © **1800/073 535** in Australia, 888/625-5144 in the U.S., or 07/5449 4888. Fax 07/5449 2230. www.sheraton.com. 169 units. A$280–A$530 (US$182–US$345) double low season; A$535–A$650 (US$348–US$423) double high season (Dec 25–Jan 4). Secure covered parking and valet parking. **Amenities:** Restaurant; 2 bars; outdoor heated pool; health club and sauna; spa; Jacuzzi; daily child care center for ages 6 weeks to 10 years; kids' club programs on weekends and during school vacations for ages 9–15 (for a fee); game room; concierge; tour desk; limited room service; massage (poolside and in-room); babysitting; laundry/dry cleaning service or use of free guest laundry. *In room:* A/C, TV w/free and pay-per-view movies, kitchenette with microwave, minibar, fridge, coffeemaker, hair dryer, iron, safe.

MODERATE

Noosa Village Motel 𝘝𝘢𝘭𝘶𝘦

All the letters from satisfied guests pinned up on the wall here are a testament to owners John and Mary Skelton's hard work in continually sprucing up this clean, bright little motel in the heart of Hastings Street. The pleasant rooms are spacious and freshly painted, with a cheerful atmosphere. There's no air-conditioning, but the rooms all have ceiling fans. And at these rates, it's one of Hastings Street's best values.

10 Hastings St., Noosa Heads, QLD 4567. © **07/5447 5800.** Fax 07/5474 9282. www.noosavillage.com.au. 11 units (9 with shower only). High season (Dec 24–Jan 14) A$175 (US$114) double, A$230 (US$150) family room; low season A$100–A$110 (US$65–US$72) double, A$155 (US$101) family room. Additional person A$11–A$15 (US$7.15–US$9.75). Discounts for longer stays. Ask about May/June specials. MC, V. Free parking. **Amenities:** Bike rental; tour desk; car-rental desk; room-service breakfast; babysitting; coin-op laundry; nonsmoking rooms. *In room:* TV, kitchenette, fridge, hair dryer.

Tips **The Seasons of the Sunshine Coast**

Room rates on the Sunshine Coast are mostly moderate, but they jump sharply in the Christmas period from December 26 to January 26, during school holidays, and in the week following Easter. Book well ahead at these times. Weekends are often busy, too.

IN THE HINTERLAND

Avocado Grove Bed & Breakfast   Joy and Brian Baxter's modern, red cedar Queenslander home is in a peaceful rural setting in the middle of an avocado grove just off the ridge-top road. The cozy, comfortable rooms have country-style furniture, full-length windows opening onto private verandas, and oil heaters for cool mountain nights. The big suite downstairs has a TV and kitchen facilities. Colorful parrots and other birds are a common sight. Guests are welcome to picnic on the peaceful sloping lawns that have wonderful views west to Obi Obi Gorge in the Connondale Ranges.

10 Carramar Ct., Flaxton via Montville, QLD 4560. ℭ and fax **07/5445 7585.** www.avocadogrove.com.au. 4 units, 3 with bathroom (shower only), 1 with private adjacent bathroom. A$130 (US$85) double; A$150 (US$98) suite. Rates include full breakfast. Ask about weekend and midweek packages. MC, V. Turn right off ridge-top road onto Ensbey Rd.; Carramar Ct. is the first left. **Amenities:** Tour desk; in-room massage; non-smoking rooms. *In room:* Ceiling fan, coffeemaker, hair dryer.

WHERE TO DINE

Noosa's Hastings Street comes alive at night with vacationers wining and dining at restaurants as sophisticated as those in Sydney and Melbourne. Just stroll along and see what appeals to you—but be prepared to need a booking at high seasons. For a great breakfast try **Café Le Monde** at the southern end of Hastings Street (opposite the back of the Surf Club), or **Bistro C,** one of the few restaurants offering beachfront dining. Noosa Junction is a less attractive place to eat, but the prices are cheaper. There are about 90 restaurants at Mooloolaba from which to choose.

Ricky Ricardo's 𝒢 MODERN AUSTRALIAN   Owners Leonie Palmer and Steven "Stef" Fisher, stalwarts of the Noosa restaurant scene, named their latest one not for a Latin TV idol, but for Stef's great-uncle Ricky, a "gentleman scallywag" whose zest for life is reflected here. I'd choose it for lunch over dinner simply because of the fantastic setting; the food is sensational at any time. You can sit over a long lunch drinking in the view across the Noosa River while nibbling from an innovative tapas menu or something more substantial. The menu is Mediterranean style, with fresh seafood and regional produce used throughout, and changes seasonally.

2/2 Quamby Place (inside the shopping center), Noosa Sound, QLD 4567. ℭ **07/5447 2455.** Reservations recommended. Main courses A$17–A$33 (US$11–US$21). AE, DC, MC, V. Daily noon–midnight.

Season 𝒢 MODERN AUSTRALIAN   With one of the few beachfront restaurant locations, this is one of Noosa's most popular restaurants. Former Sydney chef Gary Skelton has maintained his following, with vacationers from southern states rediscovering Season, and even if the locals balk at the A$10 (US$6.50) corkage for BYO wine there's no question the food remains superb. Breakfast dishes start from A$4 (US$2.60) for muffins or you can indulge yourself with buttermilk and banana pancakes (with palm sugar butter and maple syrup) for A$12 (US$7.80). For dinner? How about the pan-fried reef fish filet with crushed pinkeye potatoes, leek, and tomato, or even simpler, the barbecued seafood antipasto. Smoking is not permitted.

25 Hastings St., Noosa Heads, QLD 4567. (𝐶) 07/5447 3747. Reservations accepted on the day you dine only. Main courses A$21–A$26 (US$14–US$17). AE, DC, MC, V. Daily 8am–10pm.

9 The Gold Coast

Love it or hate it, the Gold Coast is one of Australia's icons. Bronzed lifeguards, bikini-clad meter maids, tanned tourists draped with gold jewelry, high-rise apartment towers that cast long shadows over some parts of the beach . . . but the glitz, the glitter, and the overdevelopment pales as soon as you hit the beach. The white sands stretch uninterrupted for 70km (43 miles), making up for the long strips of neon-lit motels and cheap souvenir shops. Since the '50s, Australians have been flocking to this strip of coastline, and that hasn't changed. Today, they're lining up with tourists from all around the world to get in to the theme parks, but everyone can still find a quiet spot on the beach and the sun shines on.

The Gold Coast's theme parks are not as large or as sophisticated as Disneyland, but they're exciting enough. Apart from the three major parks—Dreamworld, Warner Bros. Movie World, and Sea World—there are of plenty of smaller-scale ones. If theme parks aren't your thing, there are also 40 golf courses, dinner cruises, and loads of adrenaline-based outdoor activities, from bungee jumping to jet-skiing. The best activity on the Gold Coast, though, is the natural kind, and it doesn't cost a cent—hitting the surf and lazing on the beach.

GOLD COAST ESSENTIALS

GETTING THERE   By Car   Access to the Gold Coast Highway, which runs the length of the Coast, is off the Pacific Highway from Sydney or Brisbane. The drive takes about 80 minutes from Brisbane. From Sydney it's an 11-hour trip, sometimes longer, on the crowded, rundown Pacific Highway.

By Plane   Domestic flights land at Gold Coast Airport, Coolangatta, 25km (16 miles) south of Surfers Paradise. **Qantas** ((𝐶) **13 13 13**) operates plenty of direct flights from Sydney, Melbourne, and Brisbane. **Virgin Blue** ((𝐶) **13 67 89**) flies direct from Sydney, Melbourne and Adelaide. The **Gold Coast Tourist Shuttle** ((𝐶) **13 12 30**) meets every flight and will transfer you to your accommodations; the fare is A$14 (US$9.10) one-way and A$24 (US$16) round-trip. A taxi from the airport to Surfers Paradise is about A$30 (US$20), depending on the traffic, which can be heavy.

The nearest international gateway is **Brisbane International Airport** (see chapter 5). The Coachtrans Airporter bus meets most flights and makes about 20 trips a day from the domestic and international terminals at Brisbane Airport to Gold Coast accommodations for A$35 (US$23) adults, A$18 (US$12) children 4 to 14. The trip takes about 90 minutes to Surfers Paradise. You do not need to book in advance unless you are on an evening flight.

AirtrainConnect services link Brisbane Airport and the Gold Coast by train and bus for A$25 (US$16) adults, A$15 (US$9.75) children 5 to 14, or A$80 (US$52) for a group of four. Take Airtrain to the Gold Coast, then an air-conditioned coach shuttle will take you to any accommodations house between Southport Spit at the northern end of the Gold Coast and Burleigh Heads to the south. Airtrain's SmartPass, for which you pay A$89 (US$58) per adult, A$43 (US$28) per child, or A$215 (US$140) for a family of four for 3 days, covers AirtrainConnect transfers, as well as unlimited door-to-door theme park transfers on the Gold Coast Tourist Shuttle and use of the local Surfside bus network, 24 hours a day. Passes are also available for 5, 7, 10, and 14 days.

By Bus   Coachtrans (© 13 12 30 in Queensland, or 07/5506 9777) also offers a transfer service between Brisbane and Gold Coast hotels. The fare is A$30 (US$20) adults one-way, half price for kids.

McCafferty's (© 13 14 99) and **Greyhound Pioneer** (© 13 20 30) make daily stops at Surfers Paradise from Sydney and Brisbane. The trip from Sydney takes 15 to 16 hours, and the fare is A$93 (US$60). Trip time from Brisbane is 90 minutes, and the fare is $17 (US$11).

By Train   Suburban trains (call **Queensland Rail Citytrain;** © 07/3235 5555) depart Brisbane Central and Roma Street stations every 30 minutes for the 72-minute trip to the Gold Coast suburb of Robina. The fare is A$9.30 (US$6.05) adults, A$4.70 (US$3.05) children ages 5 to 14. Numerous local buses meet the trains to take passengers to Surfers Paradise.

If you come by train to Surfers Paradise from Sydney or other southern cities (call **Countrylink** at © 13 22 32 in Australia; www.countrylink.nsw.gov.au), you will need to transfer to a connecting coach in Casino or Murwillumbah, which are just south of the Queensland border. The trip from Sydney takes 14 to 15 hours and the fare is A$105 (US$68) for a sitting berth, and A$218 (US$142) for a sleeper.

VISITOR INFORMATION   The **Gold Coast Tourism Bureau** (www.gold coasttourism.com.au) has an information kiosk on Cavill Avenue in Surfers Paradise (© 07/5538 4419). It is stacked with brochures on things to see and do, and they will book tours and arrange accommodations for you. The kiosk is open Monday through Friday from 8:30am to 5:30pm, Saturdays and public holidays from 9am to 5:30pm, and Sundays from 9am to 3:30pm. A second information booth is at the corner of Griffith and Warner streets in Coolangatta (© 07/5536 7765). It is open from 8am to 4pm weekdays, from 8am to 3pm Saturdays, from 8am to 1pm public holidays, and closed Sundays.

To obtain material in advance, e-mail info@gctb.com.au or write to the bureau at P.O. Box 7091, Gold Coast Mail Centre, QLD 9726.

ORIENTATION   The heart of the Gold Coast is **Surfers Paradise**—"Surfers" to the locals—a high-rise forest of apartment towers, shops, cheap eateries, taverns, and amusement parlors. The pedestrians-only Cavill Mall in the center of town connects the Gold Coast Highway to The Esplanade, which runs along the beach.

The Gold Coast Highway is the main artery that connects the endless beach-side suburbs lining the coast. Just north of Surfers is **Main Beach** 𝕬, where Tedder Avenue is lined with shops, restaurants, and cafes. Heading south from Surfers, the main beach centers are Broadbeach, where retail complexes and restaurants are mushrooming; family-oriented Burleigh Heads; and the twin towns of Coolangatta in Queensland and Tweed Heads just over the border

---

⸛ *Tips* The Secret of the Gold Coast Seasons

School holidays, especially the Christmas vacation from mid-December to the end of January, are peak season on the Gold Coast. Accommodations are booked months in advance at these times. The rest of the year, occupancy levels plummet and so do rates! Packages and deals abound in the off season, so make sure you ask.

The Gold Coast

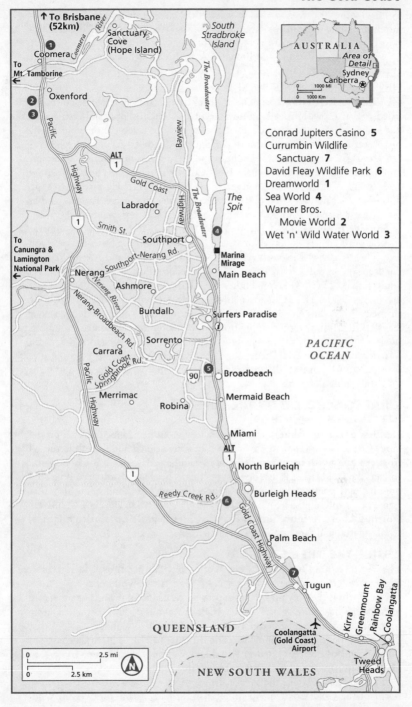

To Brisbane (52km)

Coomera

To Mt. Tamborine

Oxenford

Sanctuary Cove (Hope Island)

South Stradbroke Island

Coomera River

The Broadwater

AUSTRALIA
Area of Detail
Sydney
Canberra

Conrad Jupiters Casino **5**
Currumbin Wildlife Sanctuary **7**
David Fleay Wildlife Park **6**
Dreamworld **1**
Sea World **4**
Warner Bros. Movie World **2**
Wet 'n' Wild Water World **3**

ALT 1

Gold Coast Highway

Bayview

Labrador

The Spit

The Broadwater

Smith St.

Southport

Marina Mirage

Main Beach

To Canungra & Lamington National Park

Southport-Nerang Rd.

Nerang

Ashmore

Nerang River

Bundall

Surfers Paradise

Nerang-Broadbeach Rd.

Carrara

Sorrento

Gold Coast Springbrook Rd.

Pacific Highway

90

Broadbeach

Merrimac

Mermaid Beach

Robina

Miami

ALT 1

North Burleigh

Reedy Creek Rd.

Burleigh Heads

Gold Coast Highway

Palm Beach

Tugun

QUEENSLAND

Kirra

Greenmount

Rainbow Bay

Coolangatta

Coolangatta (Gold Coast) Airport

Tweed Heads

NEW SOUTH WALES

PACIFIC OCEAN

0   2.5 mi
0   2.5 km

in New South Wales. Coolangatta still has the sleepy small-town feel ideal for families, despite some major development in the past few years. Gold Coast Airport is on the other side of the highway from Coolangatta township.

West of Surfers Paradise and Broadbeach are the affluent suburbs of Ashmore and Nerang, where luxury residential estates and many of the region's championship golf courses have sprung up.

GETTING AROUND   It's not necessary to have a car to get around. The hotels listed below are within walking distance of the beach, shops, and restaurants, and many tour companies pick up at hotels. You can reach the theme parks by bus. A car is handy for a day trip to the hinterland, and to get around to restaurants and golf courses. Parking is cheap and plentiful in numerous parking lots and on the side streets between the Gold Coast Highway and The Esplanade.

Avis (© 07/5539 9388), **Budget** (© 07/5538 1344), **Hertz** (© 07/5538 5366), and **Thrifty** (© 07/5570 9999) have outlets in Surfers Paradise and at Gold Coast Airport. Endless local outfits rent cars at cheap rates.

Surfside Buslines (© 13 12 30 or 07/5574 5111) is the local bus company. Its best deals are passes that allow you to hop on and off the buses anytime you like. The 1-day Ezy Pass costs A$10 (US$6.50) for adults and A$5 (US$3.25) children and is valid for 24 hours. The **Freedom Pass** costs A$45 (US$29) adults and A$22 (US$14) for children for 3 days; 5-, 7-, 10-, and 14-day passes are also available. This is a particularly good deal if you're planning to visit the theme parks, as the company's Gold Coast Tourist Shuttle operates door-to-door transfers four times every morning from anywhere on the coastal strip. You must book for this, but if you are staying in Surfers Paradise or Broadbeach you can just hop on the Surfside Theme Park Express, which leaves every 15 minutes from 8:30 to 11am from Pacific Fair shopping center at Broadbeach and picks up at bus stops along the way.

WHAT TO SEE & DO ON THE COAST
HITTING THE BEACHES
Needless to say, the white sandy beaches are the number one attraction on the Gold Coast. No fewer than 35 patrolled beaches stretch almost uninterrupted from the Spit north of Surfers Paradise to Rainbow Bay, south of Coolangatta. In fact, the Gold Coast is just one long fabulous beach—all you need do is step onto it at any point, and you will spot the nearest set of red and yellow flags that signal safe swimming. The most popular beaches are **Main Beach** , **Surfers North, Elkhorn Avenue, Surfers Paradise, Mermaid Beach, Burleigh Heads, Coolangatta,** and **Greenmount.** All are patrolled 365 days a year.

DOING THE THEME PARKS
The big three are Dreamworld, Sea World, and Warner Bros. Movie World. Right next door to Movie World is Wet 'n' Wild Water World.

Sea World is the only major theme park in the center of town. The others are in northern bushland on the Pacific Highway, about 15 to 20 minutes away from Surfers Paradise. You can ride to the theme parks on the Gold Coast Tourist Shuttle (see above) or on **Surfside Buslines** (© **13 12 30** in Queensland) buses. Take Bus no. 1A to Movie World and Wet 'n' Wild; Bus no. 1A or X to Dreamworld; and Bus no. 2 or 9 to Sea World.

If you are driving, take the M1 Pacific Motorway for about 15 to 20 minutes north of the Gold Coast or 40 minutes south of Brisbane for Wet 'n' Wild, Warner Bros Movie World, and Dreamworld. Exits are all well signposted. All the theme parks have huge free car parks.

Tips A Money-Saving Theme Park Pass

Sea World, Warner Bros. Movie World, and Wet 'n' Wild sell a **3 Park Super Pass** that gets you a full-day's entry to each park plus a free return visit to the one you like best. It costs A$150 (US$98) for adults and A$94 (US$61) for kids 4 to 13. You can buy it at any of the parks, online, from a travel agency, or at most Gold Coast hotels, apartments, and tour desks. **Dreamworld** has a second-day return pass for an extra A$10 (US$6.50), but you must buy it before leaving on your first day.

Trains (© **13 12 30**) run to Coomera and Helensvale on the Brisbane–Gold Coast line. Queensland Rail Citytrain sells "Fun Tickets" to the theme parks, which include return rail travel to the nearest station, coach transfer and entry tickets. There's no real savings, just the convenience of not having to stand in line to get in.

Coachtrans (© **13 12 30** or 07/5506 9777) does daily door-to-door transfers to the big three parks, as well as Wet 'n' Wild and Currumbin Sanctuary. Round-trip fare is A$15 (US$9.75) for adults, A$9 (US$5.85) for kids, or A$38 (US$25) for a family of four. Book a day ahead if you can, especially in peak season.

Dreamworld ☆ *(Kids)* Adrenaline-crazed thrill-seekers will love the action rides here, such as the aptly named Giant Drop, in which you free-fall 39 stories in 5 seconds, or the Tower of Terror, which propels you forward and upward at 4.5Gs before falling backwards 38 stories in 7 seconds. They'll also get a kick out of the hair-raising Cyclone roller coaster, with its 360-degree loop and the Wipe-out, which spins, twists, and tumbles you upside down in a random sequence (but only exerts a sissy 2.5Gs units of pressure). These high-octane offerings make the park's other offerings look tame. Dreamworld is a family fun park, Disney-style—except that here giant koalas called Kenny and Belinda roam the streets instead of Mickey Mouse. Kids will love Nick Central, the only Nick-elodeon cartoon attraction outside the U.S. Other activities include an IMAX theater, a native wildlife park where you can cuddle a koala and hand-feed kangaroos, river cruises livened up by a bushranger shoot-out, and a carousel and other rides for young kids. A big highlight is to watch trainers swim, wrestle, and play with Bengal tigers on Tiger Island. Souvenir stores, restaurants, cafes, and ice-cream shops abound, and there's a water-slide park, so bring your swimsuit.

Pacific Hwy. (25km/16 miles north of Surfers Paradise), Coomera. © **1800/073 300** in Australia, 07/5588 1111, or 07/5588 1122 (24-hr. info line). www.dreamworld.com.au. Admission (all-inclusive except skill games, souvenir photos, and helicopter rides) A$56 (US$36) adults, A$36 (US$23) children 4–13. Daily 10am–5pm; Main St., Plaza Restaurant, and Koala Country open at 9am. Closed Christmas and until 1:30pm Anzac Day. Extended hours during Easter and Dec–Jan. Free parking for 1,600 cars.

Sea World ☆☆ *(Kids)* Four polar bears—two adults called Ping Ping and Kanook, and two cubs, Lia and Lutik—are the star attractions at this marine park, and crowds flock to see them frolic, dive, and hunt for fish in a large pool. The cubs are usually out in the mornings, and the big bears on show in the after-noons, but as you'll probably make a day of it, you'll get to see them all. You can also do a "behind-the-scenes" tour of their habitat for A$40 (US$26) adults, A$20 (US$13) children 4 and over. Sea World may not be as sophisticated as similar parks in the United States, but it's got its own charm and has all the things you'd expect to see—performing dolphins and sea lions, ski shows, an aquarium, shark feeding, and an array of rides. A monorail gets you around the grounds, and there's a free water-slide playground. Water-sports are available for an extra fee. Adults (14 and over) can snorkel with seals or dolphins for A$80 or A$115 (US$52–US$75), including a souvenir photo. An hour-long Dolphin Dive Encounter uses "ocean-walker" technology to allow guests without dive qualifications to have a divelike encounter with dolphins. It costs A$165 (US$107) per person (you must be 14 or older). Younger kids can attend a 30-minute dolphin talk, pat one, and have their photo taken with it for A$50 (US$33).

Sea World Dr. (3km/1¾ miles north of Surfers Paradise), The Spit, Main Beach. © **07/5588 2222**, or 07/5588 2205 (24-hr. info line). Fax: 07/5591 1056. www.seaworld.com.au. Admission (all-inclusive except dolphin experiences, helicopter rides, and powered watersports) A$56 (US$36) adults, A$36 (US$23) children 4–13. AE, DC, MC, V. Daily 10am–5pm; Anzac Day (Apr 25) 1:30–6:30pm. Closed Christmas. Free parking.

Warner Bros. Movie World 🔆 *Kids*   Australia's answer to Universal Studios just about matches its U.S. counterpart for thrills and spills. The park is based around working studios where *Scooby Doo* starring Sarah Michelle Gellar and Freddie Prinze Jr.; *The Phantom,* starring Billy Zane; *20,000 Leagues Under the Sea,* with Michael Caine; and *Streetfighter,* with Jean-Claude Van Damme, were filmed. If you already know how Superman flies across skyscrapers and you've heard a Foley sound studio in action before, the train ride around the sets might not interest you, but it's a great introduction to cinema tricks for first-timers. The latest hair-raising tummy-turning ride is the A$13 million indoor Scooby-Doo Spooky Coaster roller coaster, which joins the Lethal Weapon roller coaster and the simulated high-speed chase of Batman—The Ride in keeping thrill-seekers happy. Don't miss the hilarious Police Academy Stunt Show. Young kids can take rides and see stage shows by Yosemite Sam and Porky Pig in the Looney Tunes Village, and there's a Looney Tunes Parade through the streets each day. Most parades and shows take place between 11am and 4pm.

Pacific Hwy. (21km/13 miles north of Surfers Paradise), Oxenford. © **07/5573 3999**, or 07/5573 8485 for recorded information. www.movieworld.com.au. Admission (all-inclusive) A$56 (US$36) adults, A$36 (US$23) children 4–13. AE, DC, MC, V. Daily 9:30am–5:30pm; rides and attractions operate 10am–5pm. Closed Christmas and until 1:30pm Apr 25. Free parking.

Wet 'n' Wild Water World *Kids*   Hurtling down a seven-story piece of fiberglass at 70kmph (43 mph) is just one of many water-slide options at this aquatic fun park. The rides have names like Double Screamer, Mammoth Falls, The Twister, Terror Canyon, and White Water Mountain. That just about says it all. Scaredy-cats can stick to the four regular white-water flumes, float gently past palm-studded "islands" at Calypso Beach, swim in the artificial breakers in the Wave Pool or in the regular pool, or soak in a spa at Whirlpool Springs. There's also a water playground for young kids. Every night in January, and Saturday night September through April, is Dive-In Movie night, during which film fans can recline on a rubber tube in the pool while watching the flick on a giant screen. *Warning:* It is very popular and very crowded, and to get a tube or a seat you have to get there early. A stunt show plays at 2:30pm (5pm on movie nights). The water is heated to 79°F (26°C) April to September, there are lifeguards on duty, you can rent towels and lockers, and you can use the hot showers.

Pacific Hwy. (next to Warner Bros. Movie World), Oxenford. © **07/5556 1610** (administration), or 07/5573 2255 for 24-hr. recorded information. www.wetnwild.com.au. Admission A$35 (US$23) adults, A$22 (US$14) children 4–13. AE, DC, MC, V. Daily Jan 10am–9pm; Feb 10am–5pm; Mar–Apr 10am–4:30pm; May–Aug 10am–4pm; Sept–Oct 10am–4:30pm; Nov–Dec 10am–5pm. Open to 9pm on Dive-In Movie nights. Closed Christmas and open from 1:30pm Anzac Day (Apr 25).

EXPLORING THE WILDLIFE PARKS

Currumbin Wildlife Sanctuary *(Kids*   Currumbin began life as a bird sanctuary, and is almost synonymous with the wild rainbow lorikeets which flock here in the hundreds twice a day for feeding. It's quite an experience, as flocks of chattering birds descend onto visitors holding trays of food for them. Photographers go crazy and the tourists love it. These amazingly beautiful birds have a vivid green back, blue head, and red and yellow chest. Lorikeet feeding is at 8am and 4pm. Don't miss it. You can also have your photo taken cuddling a koala, hand-feed kangaroos, stroll, or take a free miniature steam-train ride through the park, and attend animal talks and feeding demonstrations. An Aboriginal song and dance show takes place daily. The park's 27 hectares (67 acres) are home to 1,400 native birds and animals, including two enormous saltwater crocodiles, and lots of native birds are also drawn to the wetlands within the grounds. It also offers behind-the-scenes tours that take in the animal hospital and endangered-species-breeding area, a birds-of-prey display, and nighttime tours. Allow several hours to see everything.

28 Tomewin St., Currumbin (18km/11 miles south of Surfers Paradise). © 07/5534 1266. www.currumbin-sanctuary.org.au. Admission A$22 (US$14) adults, A$14 (US$9.10) children 4–13. AE, DC, MC, V. Daily 8am–5pm. Closed Christmas and until 1pm Anzac Day (Apr 25). Ample free off-street parking. Bus stop 15m (49 ft.) from entrance.

David Fleay Wildlife Park *(Value*   Established in 1952 by Australian naturalist David Fleay, this is one of Australia's premier wildlife parks. You'll see a platypus, saltwater and freshwater crocodiles, wallabies, kangaroos, glider possums, dingoes, wombats, the rare Lumholtz's tree kangaroo, and a big range of Australian birds, including emus, cassowaries, wedge-tailed eagles, black swans, and lorikeets. You walk on a series of raised boardwalks through picturesque mangrove, rainforest, and eucalyptus habitats, where most of the animals roam free. The nocturnal house is open from 11am to 5pm daily, and this is where you'll see many of the most elusive animals including Australia's answer to the Easter bunny, the bilby. Talks and feeding demonstrations throughout the day include a reptile show and saltwater croc feeding—usually only October through April, when the crocs are hungry. Aboriginal rangers give talks about weaponry, bush medicine, and their links with this region. Volunteers also give free guided tours throughout the day. The Queensland National Parks and Wildlife Service (QNPWS) has run the park since 1983, but David Fleay continued to live here until his death in 1993. Because the QNPWS frowns on handling animals, you can't cuddle a koala or hand-feed kangaroos here. There's a cafe, gift shop, and picnic tables.

West Burleigh Rd. (17km/11 miles south of Surfers Paradise), West Burleigh. © 07/5576 2411. Admission A$13 (US$8.45) adults, A$8.50 (US$5.50) seniors and students, A$6.50 (US$4.20) children 4–17, A$33 (US$21) family of 6. MC, V. Daily 9am–5pm. Closed Christmas. Ample free parking.

WHERE TO STAY
VERY EXPENSIVE

Palazzo Versace   You almost have to see this to believe it. In the unlikely location of the Australian Gold Coast, fashion designer Donatella Versace has created a tribute to her late brother Gianni in the form of an extravagantly opulent resort, furnished exclusively with Versace gear. You'll either love it or hate it . . . there's no in-between. Everything has been imported from Italy, from the river stones that pave the porte-cochere to the massive antique chandelier that dominates the vast, marbled lobby. Vaulted ceilings are hand-detailed in gold and huge marble columns dominate. The rooms are decorated in four colors, red, blue, gold, and orange, but are less confronting than the public areas of the hotel. Everything in them—furniture, cutlery, crockery, toiletries, the lot—is Versace (either from the home wares collection or specially created for the hotel). Many of the rooms overlook the huge swimming pool, the Broadwater, and marina. As you'd expect, everything is beautifully appointed, and you'll enjoy strolling the corridors that are lined with Gianni's artwork and designs. There's an extensive spa and health club in the basement. You can choose from eight room types (Donatella stays in the A$3,000-a-night/US$1,950 Imperial Suite when she comes) or from a pool of two- or three-bedroom condominiums. And of course, should you get the urge to shop, there's a Versace boutique.

94 Sea World Dr., Main Beach, QLD 4217. ⓒ 1800/098 000 in Australia, or 07/5509 8000. Fax 07/5509 8888. www.palazzoversace.com. 205 units and 72 condominiums. A$695 (US$452) double superior room; A$745 (US$484) double superior suite; A$765 (US$497) double superior lagoon view room; A$895 (US$582) deluxe suite; A$1,045 (US$679) Broadwater suite; condominiums A$1,080–A$1,380 (US$702–US$897) per night. AE, DC, MC, V. **Amenities:** 3 restaurants; 2 bars; saltwater heated lagoon pool and 27 other pools (some of them exclusive to condos); health club and spa; wet and dry sauna; concierge; tour desk; business center and secretarial services; salon; 24-hr. room service; massage; laundry service; dry cleaning; half the rooms are nonsmoking. *In room:* A/C, TV w/pay movies, dataport, PlayStation, kitchen (condos only), minibar, fridge, coffeemaker, hair dryer, iron, safe, Jacuzzi (all rooms and suites).

MODERATE

Mercure Resort Surfers Paradise 🛋 *Kids*   If you're a parent and your idea of a holiday is to not even see your kids for most of the day, this place is for you. The resort has a licensed child-care center for little ones as young as 6 weeks and up to 5 years old. For 5- to 12-year-olds, there's the Gecko Club, complete with pedal minicars, the Leonardo painting room, and an underwater themed pirate adventure world. You can laze around the leafy pool area and watch the kids play on the water slide. The child-care center charges moderate fees, but the Gecko Club is free; both operate daily year-round. The low-rise building is comfortable and rooms have views of the pool or the gardens. All rooms were refurbished in November 2000. Family quarters sleep up to five in two separate rooms, and some have kitchenettes. The resort rents a wide range of kiddy stuff such as prams (strollers), bottle warmers, car seats, and PlayStations, and there is a mini supermarket and take-out meal service. The big range of activities makes this a great value place for families, and the center of Surfers Paradise and the patrolled beach are a few blocks across the highway. Some rooms are near the highway, so ask for a quiet spot.

122 Ferny Ave., Surfers Paradise, QLD 4217. ⓒ 1800/074 111 in Australia, 800/221-4542 in the U.S. and Canada, 0181/283 4500 in the U.K., 0800/44 4422 in New Zealand, or 07/5579 4444. Fax 07/5579 4496. www.mercuresurfers.com.au. 405 units. A$205 (US$133) resort room (sleeps 4); A$235 (US$153) deluxe room (sleeps 4); A$265 (US$172) resort family room (sleeps 5); A$300 (US$195) family studio (sleeps 5). Ask about special packages. AE, DC, MC, V. Free covered security parking. Local bus stop outside the resort. **Amenities:** 2 restaurants; cafe/sandwich bar; bar; 4 outdoor pools; 2 tennis courts; exercise room; Jacuzzi; sauna; child-care center and kids' club; games room/video arcade; concierge; tour desk; shuttle bus; business center; babysitting; coin-op laundry; dry cleaning. *In room:* A/C, TV/VCR w/free and pay-per-view movies, kitchenette (family studios only), fridge, coffeemaker, hair dryer, iron, safe (some rooms only).

GOOD-VALUE VACATION APARTMENTS

Apartments make good sense for families and for any traveler who wants to self-cater to save money. Because the Gold Coast has a dramatic oversupply of apartments that stand empty outside school vacations, you can get a spacious modern unit with ocean views for the cost of a low-priced midrange hotel. Apartment block developers got in quick to snag the best beachfront spots when the Gold Coast boomed in the 1970s, so it's apartment buildings, not hotels, that have the best ocean views. The **Gold Coast Booking Centre** is a centralized booking

---

Tips **Book Ahead for Indy & Easter Madness!**

Most accommodations will require a 1-week minimum stay during school holiday periods, and a 4-day minimum stay at Easter. When the Gold Coast Indy car race takes over the town for 4 days in October, hotel rates skyrocket and most hostelries demand a minimum stay of 3 or 4 nights. Don't leave accommodations bookings to the last minute! Contact the **Gold Coast Tourism Bureau** (© **07/5538 4419**; fax 07/5570 3259) to find out the exact dates.

---

service that offers great deals at more than 1,200 apartments in Surfers Paradise and Broadbeach. Book via www.gcbc.com.au or © **1300/553 800.**

Enderley Gardens   Just a block from the beach, and centered around a large lagoon-style pool, this older-style apartment block is a short walk from the Cavill Mall. Units are spacious, and all have balconies. They are simply but neatly furnished with a large kitchen and laundry facilities. Like many apartments on the Gold Coast, these are not air-conditioned, but the sea breeze is a good substitute. There are two barbecue areas, and the low-rise (four-story) block makes this a good choice for families or older people.

38 Enderley Ave., Surfers Paradise, QLD 4217. © 07/5570 1511. Fax 07/5592 3878. www.enderleygardens. com.au. 86 units. High season A$149 (US$97) double 1-bedroom apt, A$198 (US$129) double 2-bedroom apt. Low season A$109 (US$71) 1-bedroom apt, A$138 (US$90) 2-bedroom apt. Extra person A$20 (US$13). Weekly rates and discounts on stays of 3 nights or more available. AE, DC, MC, V. **Amenities:** Large outdoor pool (heated in winter); half-court tennis; Jacuzzi; sauna; children's playground and wading pool; tour desk; babysitting; secure covered parking. *In room:* TV, kitchen, iron.

Equinox Resort *(Value (Kids*   This clean, well-maintained older-style apartment block is just across the road from the beach and a short walk from Cavill Mall. You can choose between a studio with a balcony and basic tea-and-coffeemaking facilities, or forego the balcony for a full kitchen in a suite. Or you can join a studio and suite together for a two-bedroom apartment that has it all. Some of the studios have air-conditioning, and they are ideal for up to three people. It's good value for location, price, and comfort.

3458 Main Beach Parade, Surfers Paradise, QLD 4217. © 07/5538 3288. Fax 07/5538 6862. www. equinoxresort.com.au. 90 units. High season A$148 (US$96) studio, A$169 (US$110) suite, A$249 (US$162) 2-bedroom apt. Low season A$109 (US$71) studio or suite, A$138 (US$90) 2-bedroom apt. Extra person A$20 (US$13). Minimum 4-night stay during Indy, 5 nights at Christmas. MC, V. Free underground security parking. **Amenities:** Outdoor pool (heated in winter); 2 tennis half-courts; squash court; gymnasium; Jacuzzi; sauna; children's playground; games room; tour desk; babysitting. *In room:* TV, kitchen, fridge, hair dryer, iron.

WHERE TO DINE

The Gold Coast is full to the rafters with good restaurants. Many stylish new restaurants and cafes, most reasonably priced, are springing up around **Surf Parade** and **Victoria Avenue** at Broadbeach, as well as in the nearby **Oasis shopping mall.** Another of the trendy spots to be seen dining is in the stylish **Marina Mirage** shopping center opposite the Sheraton on Sea World Drive at Main Beach, or at one of the hip **Tedder Avenue** cafes in Main Beach.

THE GOLD COAST AFTER DARK

There's a genuine Rolls Royce parked in the corner at **Rolls** nightclub at the Sheraton Mirage, Sea World Drive, Main Beach (© **07/5591 1488**)—you can reserve it as your booth for the night. A mixed-age crowd of sophisticated locals rubs shoulders with hotel guests. There is a A$5 (US$3.25) cover; the club opens Friday and Saturday night. At 10:30pm they push back the tables at **Saks,** Marina Mirage, Sea World Drive, Main Beach (*C* **07/5591 2755**) and this elegant cafe/wine bar turns into a dance floor for fashionable 20- and 30-somethings. Friday, Saturday, and Sunday are the coolest nights to turn up, and there's a live band Sundays; no cover.

It's not as big as some Vegas casinos, but **Conrad Jupiters Casino,** Gold Coast Highway, Broadbeach (*C* **07/5592 8282**), has plenty to keep the gambler amused—70 gaming tables and 1,200-plus slot machines with roulette, blackjack, Caribbean stud poker, baccarat and minibaccarat, craps, Pai Gow, and Sic Bo. Downstairs the 1,100-seat Jupiter's Theatre stages floor shows and concerts; and there are three bars, including an English-style pub. Of the five restaurants, the good-value **Food Fantasy** buffet is outrageously popular, so be prepared to wait. The casino is open 24 hours. You must be 18 to enter, and smart, casual dress is required.

10 The Gold Coast Hinterland: Back to Nature

The cool, green Gold Coast hinterland is only a half-hour drive from the Coast, but it is a world away from the neon lights, theme parks, and crowds. Up here, at an altitude of 500m to 1,000m (about 1,640 ft.–3,280 ft.), the tree ferns drip moisture, the air is crisp, and the pace is slow.

Mt. Tamborine shelters several villages known for their crafts shops, galleries, cafes, and B&Bs. Easy walking trails wander from the streets through rainforest and eucalyptus woodland, and as you drive you will discover magnificent views.

The impressive 20,200-hectare (49,895-acre) **Lamington National Park** lies to the south of Mt. Tamborine. The park, at around 1,000m (3,328 ft.) above sea level, is a eucalyptus and rainforest wilderness crisscrossed with walking trails. It's famous for its colorful bird life, wallabies, possums, and other wildlife. The road to the park is full of twists and tight turns, and as you wind higher and higher, tangled vines and dense eucalyptus and ferns make a canopy across the road, so dark you need headlights. The park is about 90 minutes from the coast—but once you're ensconced in your mountain retreat, the world will seem remote.

The hinterland is close enough to the Gold Coast and Brisbane to make a pleasant day trip, but you will almost certainly want to stay overnight, or longer, once you breathe that restorative mountain air.

MT. TAMBORINE
40km (25 miles) NW of Surfers Paradise; 70km (43 miles) S of Brisbane

Crafts shops, teahouses, and idyllic vistas are Mt. Tamborine's attractions. The mountaintop is more a plateau than a peak, and it's home to a string of villages, all a mile or two apart—Eagle Heights, North Tamborine, and Mt. Tamborine proper. Many shops and cafes are only open Thursday, Friday, and weekends.

ESSENTIALS
GETTING THERE & GETTING AROUND   From the Gold Coast, head to Nerang and follow signs to Beaudesert. The Mt. Tamborine turnoff is off this road. Alternatively, take the Pacific Highway north to Oxenford and take the Mt. Tamborine turnoff, the first exit after Warner Bros. Movie World. Many tour operators run minibus and four-wheel-drive day trips from the Gold Coast, and

some run tours from Brisbane. Another option is to pay A$15 (US$9.75) for the day to ride the **Tamborine Trolley Co.** buses (℃ **07/5545 2782**), modeled on early-20th-century trams, which run on a 25km (16-mile) circuit linking four wineries, a distillery, pub, cafes, restaurants, antiques shops, markets, galleries, hang-gliding lookouts, and rainforest walks. The circuit takes an hour and you can hop on and off as you like. Owner/operator Sue Netherway will organize transport to Mt. Tamborine on request. She also runs a food and wine tour, with pick-ups at the Gold Coast, every Thursday and an antiques tour on Fridays.

VISITOR INFORMATION   Head to the **Gold Coast Tourism Bureau** (see "Visitor Information" in the "The Gold Coast" section, earlier in this chapter) to stock up on information and tourist maps before you head out. Brisbane Marketing (See "Visitor Information" in chapter 5) also has information. Once you arrive, the **Tamborine Mountain Information Centre** is in Doughety Park, where Geissmann Drive becomes Main Western Road in North Tamborine (℃ **07/5545 3200**). It's open daily from 10:30am to 3:30pm.

EXPLORING THE MOUNTAIN
With a map at hand, you are well equipped to drive around Mt. Tamborine's roads to admire the wonderful views over the valleys and to poke around the shops. New Age candles, homemade soaps, maple-pecan fudge, framed tropical watercolors, German cuckoo clocks, and Aussie antiques are some of the things you can buy in the many stores. The best place to shop is the quaint strip of galleries, cafes, and shops known as Gallery Walk on Long Road, between North Tamborine and Eagle Heights. Eagle Heights has few shops but great views back toward the coast. North Tamborine is mainly a commercial center where you still find the odd nice gallery or two. Mt. Tamborine itself is mainly residential.

Allow time to walk some of the trails that wind through forest throughout the villages. Most are reasonably short and easy. The Mt. Tamborine Information Centre has maps marking them.

WHERE TO STAY
Tamborine Mountain Bed & Breakfast ℛ   Tony and Pam Lambert's restful timber home has stunning 180-degree views to the ocean from the breakfast balcony. Laze by the open fire in the timber-lined living room, or out on the lovely veranda where rainbow lorikeets, kookaburras, and crimson rosellas flit about over the bird feeders. The ferny gardens have four purpose-built rustic timber rooms, each individually decorated in cottage style and linked to the house by covered walkways. The rooms are heated in winter. No smoking indoors.

19–23 Witherby Crescent, Eagle Heights, QLD 4721. ℃ **07/5545 3595.** Fax 07/5545 3322. www.tmbb.com. au. 4 units (all with shower only). A$127 (US$83) double mid-week; A$149 (US$97) double at weekends. Rates include continental breakfast Mon–Fri and full breakfast at weekends. MC, V. Free parking. No children under 12. *In room:* A/C, TV/VCR, small fridge, coffeemaker, iron.

LAMINGTON NATIONAL PARK ℛℛ
70km (43 miles) W of Gold Coast; 115km (71 miles) S of Brisbane

Subtropical rainforest, 2,000-year-old, moss-covered Antarctic beech trees, giant strangler figs, and misty mountain air characterize Lamington's high narrow ridges and plunging valleys. Its great stretches of dense rainforest make it one of the most important subtropical parks in southeast Queensland, and one of the loveliest. The park has 160km (99 miles) of walking trails that track through thick forest, past ferny waterfalls, and along mountain ridges with soaring views across green valleys. The trails vary in difficulty and length, from 1km (.5-mile) strolls up to 23km (14-mile) treks. The park is a haven for bird lovers who come to see and photograph the rosellas, bowerbirds, rare lyrebirds, and other species that live here, but that's not the only wildlife you will see. Groups of small wallabies, called pademelons, graze outside your room. In summer you may see giant carpet pythons curled up in a tree or large goannas sunning themselves on rock ledges. Near streams you may be stopped by a hissing Lamington spiny crayfish, an aggressive little monster 6 inches long, patterned in royal blue and white. The park comes alive with owls, possums, and sugar-gliders at night.

Most visitors are fascinated by the park's Antarctic beech trees, which begin to appear above the 1,000m (3,280-ft.) line. Like something from a medieval fairy tale, these mossy monarchs of the forest stand 20m (66 ft.) tall and measure up to 8m (26 ft.) in girth. They are survivors of a time when Australia and Antarctica belonged to the supercontinent, Gondwana, when it was covered by wet, tropical rainforest. The species survived the last Ice Age, and the trees at Lamington are about 2,000 years old, suckered off root systems about 8,000 years old. The trees are a 2½-hour walk from O'Reilly's Rainforest Guesthouse (see below).

EXPLORING LAMINGTON NATIONAL PARK

The easiest way to explore the park is to base yourself at **O'Reilly's Rainforest Guesthouse** in the Green Mountains section of the park, or at **Binna Burra Mountain Lodge** in the Binna Burra section (see "Where to Stay & Dine," below). Most of the trails lead from one or the other of these resorts, and a 23km (14-mile) **Border Trail** connects them; it follows the New South Wales–Queensland border for much of the way, and can be walked by most reasonably fit folk in a day. Guided walks and activities at both resorts are for houseguests only; however, both properties welcome day visitors who just want to walk the trails for free. Both have inexpensive cafes for day-trippers.

It is a good idea to bring a torch (flashlight) and maybe binoculars for wildlife spotting. The temperature is often 10°F to 20°F (4°C–5°C) cooler than on the Gold Coast, so bring a sweater in summer and bundle up in winter when nights get close to freezing. September through October is orchid season, and the frogs come out in noisy abundance in February and March.

GETTING THERE   By Car   O'Reilly's is 37km (23 miles) from the town of Canungra. The road is twisty and winding, so take it slowly, allow yourself an hour from Canungra to reach O'Reilly's, and plan to arrive before dark. Binna Burra is 35km (22 miles) from Nerang via Beechmont, or 26km (16 miles) from Canungra, on a winding mountain road. From the Gold Coast go west to Nerang, where you can turn off to Binna Burra via Beechmont, or go on to Canungra where you will see the O'Reilly's and Binna Burra turnoffs. From Brisbane, follow the Pacific Highway south and take the Beenleigh/Mt. Tamborine exit to Mt. Tamborine. From there follow the signs to Canungra. Allow a good 2½ hours to get to either resort from Brisbane, and 90 minutes from the Gold Coast. Binna Burra sells unleaded fuel; O'Reilly's has emergency supplies only.

By Coach   The **Mountain Coach Company** (© **07/5524 4249**) does daily transfers to O'Reilly's and Binna Burra from the Gold Coast, leaving the airport at 8am, picking up at hotels along the way, and arriving at O'Reilly's at 12:30pm. The return trip leaves O'Reilly's at 2:30pm, arriving at the airport by 5:30pm. **Allstate Scenic Tours** (© **07/3003 0700**) makes a coach run from outside the Roma Street Transit Centre in Brisbane every day except Saturday at 9:30am, arriving at O'Reilly's at 12:30pm.

The Binna Burra resort runs a shuttle from Gold Coast Airport at 1:30pm daily and from Nerang railway station at 2pm, both arriving at Binna Burra at 3pm. Reserve a spot when making accommodations bookings.

VISITOR INFORMATION   The best sources of information on hiking are O'Reilly's Rainforest Guesthouse and Binna Burra Mountain Lodge (see "Where to Stay & Dine" below for both); ask them to send you copies of their walking maps. There is a national parks information office at both properties. For detailed information on hiking and camping in the park, contact the ranger at Lamington National Park, Green Mountains section (which is at O'Reilly's), via Canungra, QLD 4211 (© **07/5544 0634**).

WHERE TO STAY & DINE

Both of these mountain-top retreats have long and interesting histories. Both offer walking trails of a similar type and distance; guided walks, including nighttime wildlife-spotting trips; hearty food; and a restful, enjoyable experience. Look into the special-interest workshops both properties run throughout the year, which can be anything from gourmet weekends to mountain-jogging programs.

Binna Burra Mountain Lodge 👁👁 (Kids)   Binna Burra is a postcard-perfect mountain lodge. The original cabins, built in 1935, are still in use today; they've been outfitted with modern comforts, but not 20th-century "inconveniences," such as telephones, televisions, radios, or clocks. All the accommodations have pine-paneled walls, floral bedcovers, heaters, and electric blankets. The most attractive and spacious are the mud-brick and weatherboard Acacia cabins, which have private bathrooms and the best views over the Numinbah Valley. There are two kinds of less-expensive Casuarina cabins—the nicest are the small and very cozy huts with a pitched ceiling, a washbasin, and a nice aspect into the forest and over the valley. Less atmospheric are the bunk room style rooms that sleep four to six people—good for families and groups of friends. Guests in Casuarina cabins share bathroom facilities, which include a Jacuzzi. Meals are served in the lovely stone-and-timber dining room. Seating is communal, so you get to meet other travelers. Free tea and coffee is on the boil all day. There is also a crafts shop, a natural history library, and conference rooms.

Beechmont via Canungra, QLD 4211. © **1800/074 260** in Australia, or 07/5533 3622. Fax 07/5533 3747. www.BinnaBurralodge.com.au. 41 cabins, 22 with bathroom (shower only). A$230–A$292 (US$150–US$190) double for bed and breakfast only; A$334–A$396 (US$217–US$257) double for all-inclusive meals and activities. Single supplement A$11 (US$7.15) per night; A$32 (US$21) B&B or A$58 (US$38) all-inclusive for children 5–16. Ask about packages. Minimum 2-night stay weekends, 3-night stay public holiday weekends, 4-nights Easter, and 5 nights at Christmas. AE, DC, MC, V. **Amenities:** Restaurant; bar; free kids' club Sat and school vacations for children 5–14; babysitting; coin-op laundry. *In room:* Minibar, fridge, coffeemaker, no phone.

O'Reilly's Rainforest Guesthouse 👁👁 (Kids)   Highlights of your stay will be the chance to hand-feed brilliantly colored rainforest birds every morning and the fact that the staff will remember you by name for your entire stay. Nestled high on a cleared plateau, the buildings are closed in on three sides by dense tangled rainforest and open to picturesque mountain views to the west. The timber-resort complex is inviting rather than grand, but up-market new suites and the refurbishment of older rooms have added a touch of luxury in the past year. The comfortable guest lounge has an open fire and is scattered with old-fashioned sofas, chairs, and an upright piano. The six rooms in the Tooloona block, which dates from the 1930s, have communal bathrooms and basic furniture. The recently refurbished motel-style Elabana rooms have en-suite bathrooms and handcrafted maple furniture and some have small balconies. The 37 Bithonga-bel rooms have the best views and also have en-suite bathrooms. Seven are single rooms; the six family rooms in this block have bunks for kids, and two rooms have wheelchair access. The newest, and most expensive, rooms are the three Canopy Suites, which are twice as large as any other rooms and have a king-size four-poster bed, fireplace, Jacuzzi, library, audio system, and bar. At meal times, the maitre d' assigns you to a table in the dining room, so you get to meet other guests. If you do not buy a meal package, buffet breakfast costs A$22 (US$14), lunch costs A$26 (US$17), and a three-course dinner is A$37 (US$24). Before dinner, guests head to the hexagonal timber bar, perched up high for great sunset views and half-price cocktails (5–6:30pm). Among other facilities are a cafe and gift shop, a basketball court, and free tea, coffee, and cookies all day.

Via Canungra, Lamington National Park Rd., Lamington National Park, QLD 4275. © **1800/688 722** in Australia, or 07/5544 0644. Fax 07/5544 0638. www.oreillys.com.au. 70 units. A$194–A$448 (US$126–US$291) double; A$578 (US$375) canopy suites. Additional person A$25 or A$40 (US$16 or US$26) in Canopy Suites; children under 18 stay free in parent's room with existing bedding. Free crib. Rates include all meals and activities. Rates decrease with every night you stay. Minimum 2-night stay weekends, 3-night stay long weekends, 4-night stay Easter and Christmas. Ask about packages for stays of 2 nights or more. Meal plans A$69 (US$45) adults, A$34 (US$22) children 10–17, A$17 (US$11) children 4–9 for 3 meals per day; 2-meal packages available. AE, DC, MC, V. **Amenities:** Restaurant; bar; heated outdoor plunge pool; day/night tennis court; Jacuzzi; sauna; kids' club for over-5s on weekends and school vacations; game room; massage; babysitting; coin-op laundry. *In room:* Fridge, coffeemaker. In canopy suites only: Minibar, Jacuzzi, stereo/CD player.

7

The Red Centre

by Marc Llewellyn

The Red Centre is the landscape many of us conjure up when we think of the Outback—vast horizons, red sand as far as the eye can see, mysterious monoliths, cloudless blue sky, harsh sunlight, and the rhythmic twang of the didgeridoo. It's home to sprawling cattle ranches; ancient mountain ranges; "living fossil" palm trees that survived the Ice Age; cockatoos and kangaroos; red gorges; pretty water holes; and, Ayers Rock, now officially called by its Aboriginal name, Uluru. Aboriginal people have lived here for thousands of years, long before the Pyramids were a twinkle in a Pharaoh's eye, but the Centre is still largely unexplored by non-Aboriginal Australians. One highway cuts from Adelaide in the south to Darwin in the north, and a few roads and four-wheel-drive tracks make a lonely spider web across it; there are many areas where non Aborigines have never set foot.

Alice Springs is the only big town in central Australia. So let's get one thing straight—Alice Springs and Uluru are *not* side by side. Uluru is 462km (286 miles) away. You can see it in a day from Alice, but it's an effort. The Red Centre is more than just the Rock. Give yourself a few days to experience all there is—visiting the impressive Olgas (or Kata Tjuta by its Aboriginal name) near Ayers Rock/Uluru, walking the rim of Kings Canyon, riding a camel down a dry riverbed, poking around Aboriginal rock carvings, swimming in water holes, or staying at an Outback homestead. A stay in Alice Springs also gives you a better flavor for the Outback than Uluru. If you base yourself in Alice, it's easy to radiate out to less crowded but still beautiful attractions like Palm Valley, Ormiston Gorge, and Trephina Gorge Nature Park, each easily handled as a day trip. Too many visitors jet in, snap a photo of the Rock, and head home, only to miss the essence of the desert.

1 Exploring the Red Centre

VISITOR INFORMATION The **Central Australian Tourism Industry Association** (see "Visitor Information" under "Alice Springs," below) can send you a brochure pack. It is your best one-stop source of information.

Most of the Red Centre lies within the Northern Territory. The **Northern Territory Tourist Commission (NTTC),** Tourism House, 43 Mitchell St., Darwin, NT 0800 (© **13 61 10** in Australia, or 08/8999 3900; **www.ntholidays. com**), maintains a site for adventurous independent travelers at **www.ozoutback. com**. The commission publishes a helpful annual guide to central Australia that details many hotels, tour operators, car-rental companies, and attractions, and operates a division that offers package deals on complete trips.

WHEN TO GO   April/May and September/October have sunny days (coolish in May, hot in Oct). Winter (that's June–Aug) means mild temperatures with cold nights. Summer (Nov–Mar) is ferociously hot and best avoided. In summer, limit exertions to early morning and late afternoon, and choose air-conditioned accommodations. Rain is rare but can come at any time of year.

DRIVING TIPS   The **Automobile Association of the Northern Territory (AANT),** 79–81 Smith St., Darwin, NT 0800 (© **08/8981 3837**), offers emergency breakdown service to members of affiliated overseas automobile associations and dispenses maps and advice. It has no office in the Red Centre. For **road conditions,** call © **1800/246 199** in Australia for a recorded report.

Only a handful of highways and arterial roads are sealed (paved) roads in the Northern Territory. A conventional two-wheel-drive car will get you to 95% of all you want to see, but consider renting a four-wheel-drive for complete freedom. All the big car-rental chains rent them. Some attractions are on unpaved roads good enough for a two-wheel-drive car, but your car-rental company will not insure a two-wheel-drive for driving on them.

Outside settled areas, the Territory has no speed limit, but before you hit the gas, consider the risk of hitting wild camels, kangaroos, and protected native wildlife. Locals stick to a comfortable 120kmph (75 mph) or less. Avoid driving at night, early morning, and late afternoon when 'roos feed; beware of cattle lying down on the warm bitumen at night. A white road sign bearing a black circle outline crossed by a diagonal black line indicates the point when speed restrictions no longer apply. Make sure you have a full tank of gas before setting out.

Road trains (trucks hauling more than one container) and fatigue caused by driving long distances are two other major threats. For details on safe driving, review the tips in the "By Car" section of "Getting Around Australia," in chapter 2.

If you plan to "go bush" in remote regions not covered by this guide, you may need a permit to cross Aboriginal land from the relevant Aboriginal lands council. This can be a drawn-out bureaucratic affair taking weeks, so plan ahead. The Northern Territory Tourist Commission (see "Visitor Information," above) can put you in touch with the appropriate council. All good road maps mark Aboriginal lands clearly.

OTHER TRAVEL TIPS   **Always carry drinking water.** When hiking, carry 4 liters (about a gallon) per person per day in winter, and a liter (¼ gal.) per person per hour in summer. Wear a broad-brimmed hat, high-factor sunscreen lotion, and insect repellent.

Bring warm clothing for chilly evenings in winter.

TOUR OPERATORS   Numerous coach, minicoach, and four-wheel-drive tour operators run tours taking in Alice Springs, Kings Canyon, and Uluru. They depart either Alice Springs or Uluru, offering accommodations ranging

---

Tips **Buzz Off!**

Uluru is notorious for plagues of flies in summer. Don't be embarrassed to cover your head with the fly nets sold in souvenir stores—you'll look like the Dreamtime Beekeeper from Outer Space, but there will be "no flies on you, mate," an Aussie way of saying you are doing the right thing.

The Red Centre

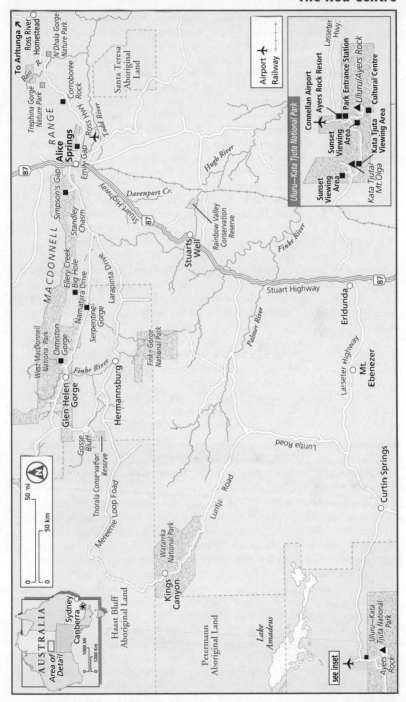

Uluru—Kata Tjuta National Park

Airport ✈
Railway ┼┼┼┼

Connellan Airport
Ayers Rock Resort
Park Entrance Station
Uluru/Ayers Rock
Cultural Centre
Lasseter Hwy.
Sunset Viewing Area
Kata Tjuta Viewing Area
Sunset Viewing Area
Kata Tjuta/Mt. Olga

To Artunga ↗
Ross River Homestead
N'Dhala Gorge Nature Park
Trephina Gorge Nature Park
Corroboree Rock
Santa Teresa Aboriginal Land
Ross Hwy. Rock
Todd River
RANGE
Alice Springs
Emily Gap
Ross Hwy.
Hugh River
87
Stuart Highway
Davenport Cr.
Simpson's Gap
Standley Chasm
Rainbow Valley Conservation Reserve
Stuarts Well
Finke River
Ellery Creek Big Hole
Namatjira Drive
Serpentine Gorge
Larapinta Drive
Finke Gorge National Park
Palmer River
Stuart Highway
87
Erldunda
MACDONNELL
Ormiston Gorge
West MacDonnell National Park
Finke River
Glen Helen Gorge
Hermannsburg
Lasseter Highway
Mt. Ebenezer
Gosse Bluff
Tnorala Conservation Reserve
Lurltja Road
50 mi
50 km
0
0
Mereenie Loop Road
Luritje Road
Curtin Springs
Watarrka National Park
Kings Canyon
Petermann Aboriginal Land
Lake Amadeus
Uluru—Kata Tjuta National Park
see inset ✈
Ayers Rock
Haast Bluff Aboriginal Land
AUSTRALIA
Area of Detail
Sydney
Canberra ✷
1000 Mi
0
1000 Km

from spiffy resorts, comfortable motels, and basic cabins to shared bunkhouses, tents, or swags (sleeping bags) under the stars. Most pack the highlights into a 2- or 3-day trip, though leisurely trips of 6 days or more are available. Many offer one-way itineraries between Alice and the Rock (via Kings Canyon if you like), or vice versa, which will allow you to avoid backtracking.

Among the reputable companies are **AAT Kings** (© **1800/334 009** in Australia, or 03/9274 7422 for the Melbourne central reservations office; www.aat kings.com), which specializes in coach tours but also has four-wheel-drive camping itineraries; **Alice Springs Holidays** (© **08/8953 1411;** www.alicesprings holidays.com.au), which does upscale soft-adventure tours for groups; **Sahara Outback Tours** (© **08/8953 0881;** www.saharatours.com.au), which conducts camping safaris in small groups for all ages; and **Discovery Ecotours** (formerly Uluru Experience and Alice Experience) (© **1800/803 174** in Australia, or 08/8956 2563; www.ecotours.com.au), which specializes in ecotours for groups. Coach operator **Greyhound Pioneer** (© **13 20 30** in Australia; www.greyhound. com.au) provides good-value, large bus tours. One of these is a 3-day tour from Alice Springs to Uluru, Kings Canyon and the Olgas costing A$279 (US$181). A 2-day tour including Uluru and the Olgas costs A$250 (US$162).

Tailormade Tours (© **08/8952 1731**) and **VIP Travel Australia** (© **1800/ 806 412** in Australia, or 08/8956 2388; www.vipaustralia.com.au) customizes luxury tours in limos, minicoaches, and four-wheel-drives, and offers treats like desert barbecues and champagne tailgate dinners overlooking the Rock or the Olgas.

You can book Sahara Outback Tours and Tailormade Tours via **Alice Springs Tour Professionals** (© **08/8953 0666;** www.alicetourprofessionals.com.au), a one-stop shop that represents a number of Alice Springs–based tour and sightseeing companies.

Aboriginal Desert Discovery Tours (© **08/8952 3408;** www.aboriginalart. com.au), owned by Alice Springs Aboriginal people, teams up its Aboriginal guides with Alice-based tour companies to offer tours with an Aboriginal slant.

2 Alice Springs

462km (286 miles) NE of Ayers Rock; 1,491km (924 miles) S of Darwin; 1,544km (957 miles) N of Adelaide; 2,954km (1,831 miles) NW of Sydney

"The Alice," as Australians fondly dub it, is the unofficial capital of Outback Australia. In the early 1870s, a handful of telegraph-station workers struggled nearly 1,600km (992 miles) north from Adelaide through the desert to settle by a small spring in what must have seemed like the end of the earth. Alice Springs, as the place was called, was just a few huts around a repeater station on the ambitious telegraph line that was to link Adelaide with Darwin and the rest of the world.

Today Alice is a city of 27,000 people, with supermarkets, banks, and the odd nightclub. It's a friendly, rambling, unsophisticated kind of place. No matter what direction you come from, you will soar for hours over a vast, flat landscape to get here. That's why folks are so surprised when they reach Alice Springs and see low but dramatic mountain ranges, rippling red in the sunshine. Many people excitedly mistake them for Uluru, but that baby is about 462km (286 miles) down the road. The hills that jut their craggy faces up close by are the **Mac-Donnell Ranges.**

Many tourists visit Alice only to get to Uluru, but Alice has charms all its own, albeit mostly of a small-town kind. The red folds of the MacDonnell Ranges hide

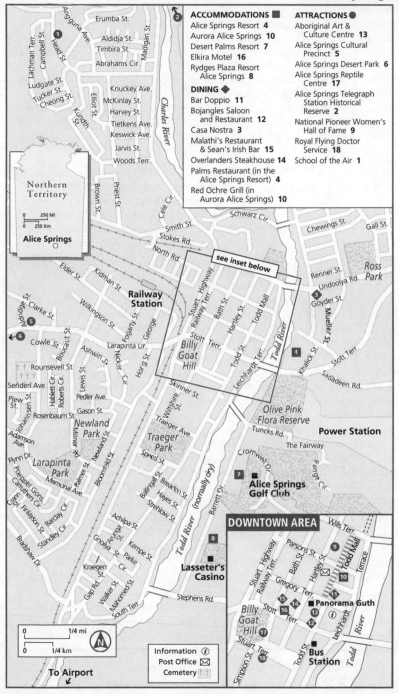

Alice Springs

ACCOMMODATIONS ■
Alice Springs Resort **4**
Aurora Alice Springs **10**
Desert Palms Resort **7**
Elkira Motel **16**
Rydges Plaza Resort
 Alice Springs **8**

DINING ◆
Bar Doppio **11**
Bojangles Saloon
 and Restaurant **12**
Casa Nostra **3**
Malathi's Restaurant
 & Sean's Irish Bar **15**
Overlanders Steakhouse **14**
Palms Restaurant (in the
 Alice Springs Resort) **4**
Red Ochre Grill (in
 Aurora Alice Springs) **10**

ATTRACTIONS ●
Aboriginal Art &
 Culture Centre **13**
Alice Springs Cultural
 Precinct **5**
Alice Springs Desert Park **6**
Alice Springs Reptile
 Centre **17**
Alice Springs Telegraph
 Station Historical
 Reserve **2**
National Pioneer Women's
 Hall of Fame **9**
Royal Flying Doctor
 Service **18**
School of the Air **1**

Northern Territory

0   250 Mi
0   250 Km

Alice Springs ○

Information ⓘ
Post Office ✉
Cemetery

0   1/4 mi
0   1/4 km

To Airport

DOWNTOWN AREA

lovely gorges with shady picnic grounds. A planned 250km (155-mile) hiking trail is partly ready for your boots now. There is an old gold-rush town to poke around in, quirky little museums, wildlife parks, a couple of cattle stations (ranches) that welcome visitors, a couple of nice day trips out of town, and one of the world's top-10 desert golf courses. You could easily fill 2 or 3 days in the area.

This is the heart of the Aboriginal Arrernte people's country, and Alice is a rich source of tours, shops, and galleries for those interested in Aboriginal culture, art, or souvenirs. There is a sad side to this story. Not every Aborigine succeeds in splicing his or her ancient civilization with the 21st century, and the result is dislocated communities living in the riverbed with only alcohol for company.

ESSENTIALS

GETTING THERE   By Plane   Qantas (© 13 13 13 in Australia) flies direct from Sydney, Adelaide, Darwin, Cairns, Broome, and Ayers Rock. Flights from most other cities connect via Sydney or Adelaide. **Virgin Blue** (© 13 67 80 in Australia; www.virginblue.com.au) flies to Alice Springs direct from Sydney, with connections from Adelaide, Brisbane, the Gold Coast, and Melbourne. The company offers heavily discounted prices if you book on the net and well in advance. Prices start from around A$199 (US$165) one-way. **Airnorth** (© 1800/ 627 474 in Australia, or 08/8945 2866) does a "Centre Run" from Darwin via Katherine and Tennant Creek daily except Sunday.

The **Alice Springs Airport Shuttle** (© 1800/621 188 in the Northern Territory, or 08/8953 0310) meets all major flights (but not always those from small towns like Tennant Creek) and transfers you to your Alice hotel door for A$10 (US$6.50) one-way or A$18 (US$12) round-trip, per person. A taxi from the airport to town, a distance of 15km (9⅓ miles), is around A$25 (US$16).

By Train   The *Ghan* train, named after Afghani camel-train drivers who carried supplies in the Red Centre during the last century, makes a 2-day trip from Sydney or Melbourne via Adelaide to Alice every week. The twice-weekly Adelaide-Alice stretch takes roughly 24 hours. It is treeless and empty, if fascinatingly so, so don't be concerned you'll miss it by overnighting on the train. The train has sleeper berths. For fares and schedules, call **Great Southern Railway** (© 13 21 47 in Australia, or 08/8213 4592; www.gsr.com.au) or see "Getting Around Australia," in chapter 2, for its booking agencies abroad. The Ghan will extend its run to Darwin in 2004, with the completion of a new 1,410km (874-mile) rail link.

By Bus   Greyhound Pioneer (© 13 20 30 in Australia) runs from Adelaide and Darwin. It's about a 19½-hour trip from Adelaide, and the fare is around A$168 (US$109). The 21-hour trip from Darwin costs about A$180 (US$117). Greyhound does a daily 5¾-hour run from Ayers Rock; the fare is around A$71 (US$46). It also does a daily trip from Kings Canyon for $54 (US$35).

By Car   Alice Springs is on the Stuart Highway linking Adelaide and Darwin. Allow a very long 2 days or a more comfortable 3 days to drive from Adelaide, the same from Darwin. From Sydney, connect to the Stuart Highway via Broken Hill and Port Augusta north of Adelaide; from Cairns head south to Townsville,

---

Tips **Safety in the Centre**

Alice is a safe place, but steer clear of dark streets and the riverbed at night, as some teenagers can make a nuisance of themselves.

then west via the town of Mt. Isa to join the Stuart Highway at Tennant Creek. Both routes are long and dull. From Perth it is an even longer, duller drive across the Nullarbor Plain to connect with the Stuart Highway at Port Augusta.

VISITOR INFORMATION   The **Central Australian Tourism Industry Association (CATIA) Visitor Information Centre,** 60 Gregory Terrace, Alice Springs, NT 0870 (© **08/8952 5800;** www.centralaustraliantourism.com), is the official one-stop shop for bookings and touring information for the Red Centre, including Alice Springs, Kings Canyon, and Uluru-Kata Tjuta National Park (Ayers Rock). It also acts as the visitor center for the Parks & Wildlife Commission of the Northern Territory. It's open Monday through Friday from 8:30am to 5:30pm and from 9am to 4pm weekends and public holidays. It also has a desk at the airport.

SPECIAL EVENTS   The town hosts a couple of bizarre events. The **Camel Cup** camel race takes place on the second Saturday in July. In late September, folks from hundreds of miles come out to cheer the **Henley-on-Todd Regatta,** during which gaudily decorated, homemade bottomless "boats" are raced down the dry Todd River bed. Well, what else do you do on a river that flows only 3 days a year? See "Australia Calendar of Events" in chapter 2 for more details on this event.

GETTING AROUND   Virtually all tours pick you up at your hotel.

If your itinerary traverses unpaved roads, as it may do in outlying areas from Alice, you will need to rent a four-wheel-drive vehicle, as regular cars will not be insured on an unpaved road surface. However, a regular car will get you to most attractions. **Avis** (© 08/8953 5533), **Budget** (© 08/8952 8899), **Europ-Car** (© 08/8955 5994), **Hertz** (© 08/8952 2644), local company **Outback Auto Rentals** (© 1800/652 133 in Australia, or 08/8953 5333), and **Thrifty** (© 08/8952 9999) all rent conventional and four-wheel-drive vehicles. You may get a better deal on car rental by going through the booking agent **The Outback Travel Shop** (© 08/8955 5288; www.outbacktravelshop.com.au) in Alice Springs, as it negotiates bulk rates with most Alice car-rental companies.

Hertz, Thrifty Car Rental, and Outback Auto Rentals rent **camping kits** holding everything you need, including a tent, sleeping bags, and a gas stove. A kit will cost around A$15 (US$9.75) per person per day. Book them in advance. Camping gear usually only fits into four-wheel-drive vehicles, not sedans.

Many rental outfits for motor homes (camper vans) have Alice offices, including **Britz Campervan Rentals** (© 08/8952 8814), **Hertz Campervans** (© 08/8953 5333), **Kea Camper (Australia)** (© 1800/252 555), and **Maui Rentals** (© 08/8952 8049). As an example of price, another outfitter, **Apollo Campers** (© 1800/777 779 in Australia; www.apollocamper.com), rents two- to three-berth vans for around $100 (US$65) a day, with pickup and drop-off at several major centers. A four-wheel drive version costs between A$165 and A$220 (US$107 and US$143) a day. This can work out significantly cheaper than staying in hotels and going on tours.

The best way to get around town without your own transport is aboard the **Alice Wanderer** bus (see "Organized Tours," below). Taxi fares are exorbitant, presumably because there's only one main outfit in town, **Alice Springs Taxis** (© **13 10 08**).

CITY LAYOUT   **Todd Mall** is the heart of town. Most shops, businesses, and restaurants are here or within a few blocks' walk. Most hotels, the casino, the golf course, and many of the town's attractions are located a few kilometers outside of town. The dry Todd River "flows" through the city east of Todd Mall.

SEEING THE SIGHTS IN ALICE

Aboriginal Art & Culture Centre   Set up by the Southern Arrernte Aboriginal people, this center houses a small, intriguing museum with exhibits on Aboriginal life. It displays a timeline of the Aboriginal view of history since "contact" (the arrival of Europeans). It's worth a visit if you're interested in indigenous cultures. It sells artifacts and art. Allow from 15 minutes to 1 hour.

86 Todd St. ℂ 08/8952 3408. Free admission. Daily 8am–5pm.

Alice Springs Cultural Precinct   At least one or two of the attractions here will probably pique your interest. All of them are within walking distance of each another. The **Museum of Central Australia** mostly shows local fossils, natural history, and meteorites. Some impressive Aboriginal and contemporary Aussie art is shown at the **Araluen Centre,** the town's performing arts center; check out the "Honey Ant Dreaming" stained-glass window in its foyer. Aviation nuts may want to browse the old radios, aircraft, and wreckage in the **Aviation Museum,** which preserves the Territory's aerial history. You can buy stylish crafts, and sometimes catch artists at work, in the Territory Craft gallery. You may want to amble among the outdoor sculptures, including the 15m (49 ft.) *Yeperenye Dreamtime Caterpillar;* or among the gravestones in the cemetery, where "Afghani" (Pakistani) camel herders are buried facing Mecca. There is a picnic area, but save your picnic for the Alice Springs Telegraph Station Historical Reserve (below).

Larapinta Dr. at Memorial Ave., 2km (1¼ miles) south of town. ℂ 08/8951 1120. Incorporating the Museum of Central Australia, Araluen Centre (ℂ 08/8951 1122 box office), Central Australian Aviation Museum, Territory Craft, and Memorial Cemetery. Admission (includes all attractions) A$8 (US$5.20) adults; A$5 (US$3.25) children 5–16, seniors, and students; A$20 (US$13) families. Daily 10am–5pm. Closed Christmas and Good Friday. Take a cab, Alice Wanderer bus, or Desert Park Transfers (see "Organized Tours," below).

 Earning a Degree from Didgeridoo University

Fancy yourself a Wynton Marsalis of the desert? Then Didgeridoo University, at the Aboriginal Art & Culture Centre is the place for you.

Local Aboriginal Paul Ah Chee-Ngala set up his "campus" to satisfy an ever-growing demand from world travelers to master the didgeridoo's evocative rhythms. In truth, the university is an alcove in the culture center, and the degree takes just 1 hour. Classes begin every day at 1pm and cost A$12 (US$7.50) adults, A$5.50 (US$3.25) kids (or are free as part of the Centre's half-day tour described in "Organized Tours," below). Paul guarantees you will make kangaroo hopping sounds on the darn thing within the hour. The trick is to breathe in and out at the same time, a technique known as "circular breathing."

When buying a didgeridoo, keep in mind there is no such thing as a "good" or a "bad" one. The diameter, the wood used, and the unique surface of the instrument's insides are what makes each one unique. The pitch of the instrument can vary from a high wail on G to a deep and somber A; the shorter the instrument, the higher the pitch.

If you can't take a "degree" in Alice, learn to play the thing in your own living room via an audio lesson on the center's website, www. aboriginalart.com.au. The site sells didgeridoos, too.

Alice Springs Desert Park ⋆ⓡ By means of an easy 1.6km (1-mile) trail through three reconstructed natural habitats, this impressive wildlife and flora park shows you 120 or so of the animal species that live in the desert around Alice, but that you won't spot too easily in the wild (including kangaroos you can walk among). Most of the creatures are small mammals (like the big-eared bilby), reptiles (cute thorny devil lizards), and birds. Don't miss the excellent **Birds of Prey** ⓡⓡ show at 10am and 3:30pm. There's a cafe here, too. Allow 2 to 3 hours.

Larapinta Dr., 6km (3¾ miles) west of town. ⓒ **08/8951 8788**. Admission A$18 (US$12) adults, A$9 (US$5.85) students and children 5–16, A$40 (US$26) families. Daily 7:30am–6pm (last suggested entry 4pm; 'roo and emu exhibit closes 4:30pm). Closed Christmas. **Desert Park Transfers** ((ⓒ **08/8952 4667**) provides round-trip transfers from anywhere in Alice for A$30 (US$20) adults, A$25 (US$17) students and seniors, A$20 (US$13) kids 5–16, A$77 (US$50) families; includes park admission.

Alice Springs Reptile Centre ⓡⓘⓓⓢ Kids can walk around with pythons or bearded dragons (lizards) on their shoulders, all day if they want, at this Aussie reptile park. The easy-going proprietor lifts up the cages' glass fronts for better photos, and lets kids hand-feed bugs to the animals at feeding time. Some 30 species are on display, including the world's deadliest snake—Australia's inland taipan—and big goannas. Allow an hour.

9 Stuart Terrace (opposite the Royal Flying Doctor Service). ⓒ **08/8952 8900**. Admission A$7 (US$4.55) adults, A$4 (US$2.60) children under 17, A$20 (US$13) families. Daily 9am–5pm. Closed Christmas and New Year's Day.

Alice Springs Telegraph Station Historical Reserve ⋆ⓡ ⓕⓘⓝⓓⓢ Alice Springs began life as this charming telegraph repeater station in 1871, set by a pretty water hole amid red bouldery hills, sprawling gums full of parrots, and mercifully green lawns. An oasis in the harsh Alice landscape, it's a place tourists often overlook. Arm yourself with the free map, or join a free 45-minute tour, and wander around the old station master's residence; the telegraph office, with its Morse code machine tap-tapping away; the shoeing yard packed with blacksmith's equipment; and the stables, housing vintage buggies and saddlery. By the time you arrive, you may be able to "telegraph" e-mails to your friends from the on-site computer. May through October, "kitchen maids" in period dress serve scones (biscuits) and damper from the original wood-fired ovens. The park has pet camels, and sometimes orphaned kangaroo joeys. Allow a good hour, more to walk one of the several hiking trails leading from the extensive grounds. This is a lovely picnic spot. There is a gift shop and coffee and snacks for sale, too.

On the Stuart Hwy. 4km (2½ miles) north of town (beyond the School of the Air turnoff). ⓒ **08/8952 3993**. Free admission to picnic grounds and trails; station A$6.60 (US$4.30) adults, A$4.95 (US$3.10) seniors and students, A$3.30 (US$2.15) children 5–15. Daily 8am–5pm (picnic grounds, trails open until 9pm). Station closed Christmas; picnic grounds open 365 days a year. Take a cab or Alice Wanderer bus (see "Organized Tours," below) or the 4km (2½-mile) riverside pedestrian/bike track that starts near the corner of Wills Terrace and Undoolya Rd.

National Pioneer Women's Hall of Fame With a collection of photographs, domestic items, and other memorabilia, this engrossing museum tells the stories of more than 100 Aussie women who were pioneers in their fields, be they Olympic gold medalists, priests, or pilots.

The Old Courthouse, 27 Hartley St. ⓒ **08/8952 9406**. www.pioneerwomen.com.au. Admission A$3 (US$1.95) adults, free for children under 15. Daily 10am–5pm. Closed mid-Dec to Feb 1.

Royal Flying Doctor Service Alice is a major base for this airborne medical service that treats people living and traveling in the vast Outback. An interesting 20-minute tour runs every half-hour, featuring a video and a talk in the communications room; allow another 30 minutes or so to browse the small museum. Some of the recorded conversations between doctors and patients are intriguing. There is a nice garden cafe and a gift shop.

8–10 Stuart Terrace (at end of Hartley St.). ℂ 08/8952 1129. www.flyingdoctor.net. Admission A$6 (US$3.90) adults, A$2.50 (US$1.60) children 6–15. Mon–Sat 9am–5pm (last tour departs 4pm); Sun and public holidays 1–5pm. Closed Christmas and New Year's Day.

School of the Air   Sitting in on school lessons may not be your idea of a vacation, but this school is different—it broadcasts by radio to a 1,300,000-sq.-km (507,000-sq.-mile) "schoolroom" of 140 children on Outback stations. That's as big as Germany, Great Britain, Ireland, New Zealand, and Japan combined—or twice the size of Texas. The attraction is to watch and listen in when classes are in session, but outside class hours you may hear taped classes, and browse the kids' artwork, photos, video, and many other displays in the well-organized visitor gallery. Free 30-minute tours run throughout the day.

80 Head St. (2.5km/1½ miles from town). ℂ 08/8951 6834. Admission A$3.50 (US$2.30) adults, A$2 (US$1.30) seniors and children 5–16, A$12 (US$7.80) families. Mon–Sat and public holidays 8:30am–4:30pm; Sun 1:30–4:30pm. Closed Christmas, Boxing Day (Dec 26), and New Year's Day. Bus: 3, or take the Alice Wanderer (see "Organized Tours," below).

ORGANIZED TOURS

AROUND TOWN & OUT IN THE DESERT   The **Alice Wanderer** bus (ℂ **1800/722 111** in Australia, or 08/8952 2111) does a running loop of town attractions every 70 minutes from 9am, with the last departure at 4pm. Hop on and off as you please, and enjoy the commentary from the driver. The bus departs daily from the south end of Todd Mall. Tickets are sold on board and cost A$30 (US$20) for adults, A$25 (US$16) for seniors and students, and A$15 (US$9.75) for kids 4 to 14. Call for a free pickup from your hotel.

The bus calls at most of the attractions above, plus the **National Road Transport Hall** of Fame; the **Ghan Preservation Society** (formally the Old Ghan Museum), housing the original Ghan train that plied the Adelaide–Alice Springs line from 1929 to 1980; and **Panorama Guth,** an art gallery housing a 360-degree painting by artist Henk Guth of central Australian landscapes.

The company can also tack on a Desert Park tour for an extra A$25 (US$16), and also offers a tour to the rocky West MacDonnell Ranges.

Many Alice-based companies offer minicoach or four-wheel-drive day trips and extended tours not only of Alice, but also of outlying areas including the East or West Macs, Hermannsburg, and Finke Gorge National Park. Among the well-regarded ones are: **Discovery Ecotours** (ℂ **08/8956 2563;** www.ecotours.com. au); **Alice Springs Holidays** (ℂ **1800/801 401** in Australia, or 08/8953 1411; www.alicespringsholidays.com.au); and **Alice Springs Tour Professionals** (ℂ **1800/673 391** in Australia, or 08/8953 0666; www.alicetourprofessionals. com.au), a one-stop shopping place for a number of reliable tour operators and adventure outfitters. See also "Exploring the Red Centre," at the beginning of this chapter, for companies running tours throughout the area.

Several companies run tours by motorcycle or four-wheel-drive ATV (all-terrain vehicle). One option is **Central Oz Tours** (ℂ **08/8953 4755;** http://centraloz. biz).

ABORIGINAL TOURS   I recommend those offered by the **Aboriginal Art & Culture Centre** (see "Seeing the Sights in Alice," above). All their tours have Aboriginal guides. Their **half-day tour** 𝓯 features an explanation of the

---

(Fun Fact Billy Tea & Damper

Any tours in the Outback aren't complete without the traditional bush-man's meal of billy tea and damper. Billy tea is made from tea leaves, and sometimes eucalyptus leaves, put into water (traditionally from a water hole or river) and boiled in an open-topped canister on an open fire. You don't have to stir it; the trick is to pick up the canister by the wire handle and swing the whole thing around, sometimes over your head—gravity keeps the liquid in (don't try this at home though). Damper is simply flour, water, and salt mixed up into a dough and thrown in the ashes of the fire to cook into bread. Yummy.

Dreamtime creation era; a gentle bush tucker walk; a chance to throw a boomerang and spear; talks about tools and weapons over billy tea and damper; and a dance performance at which you can have a go yourself, and have your photo taken with the dancers. You may have seen these dancers performing in the opening ceremony of the Sydney 2000 Olympic Games. Threaded through all this is an ongoing discussion of Aboriginal culture, beliefs, family relationships, and a view of history both ancient and modern through Aboriginal eyes. You have a chance to buy art during the morning. The experience wraps up with a didgeridoo lesson at 1pm. The tour departs daily at 8am and costs A$83 (US$54) adults and A$44 (US$29) children under 12 (including hotel pickup).

CAMEL SAFARIS   You might not associate camels with Australia, but the camel's ability to get by without water was key to opening up the arid inland parts of the country to European settlement in the 1800s. With the advent of cars, they were released into the wild, and today there are more than 200,000 roaming central Australia. Australia even exports them to the Middle East! **Frontier Camel Tours** (© **1800/806 499** in Australia, or 08/8953 0444; www.camel tours.com.au) runs a 1-hour **Camel Ramble** down the dry Todd River bed. This is followed by a tasty three-course meal of kangaroo sausages, smoked camel (we hope not the one you rode on), wattle-seed beer bread, and seasonal "bush tucker" samples like peppercress or native mistletoe, barramundi, or steak; and dessert, plus wine and beer. Dinner is served at the company's camel farm, where you can browse its camel museum and shop. With hotel transfers and dinner, it costs A$100 (US$65) for adults and A$75 (US$49) for kids 5 to 12. It departs daily at 4pm April through October, and at 5pm November through March, and gets back around 5½ hours later. Kids under 6 can join the ride if the cameleer on duty agrees. A breakfast ride costs A$75 (US$49) for adults and A$45 (US$92) for children, leaving at 6:30am and returning at 9:30am.

HOT-AIR BALLOON FLIGHTS   Dawn balloon flights above the desert are popular in central Australia. You have to get up 90 minutes before dawn, though. Several companies offer flights. **Outback Ballooning** (© **1800/809 790** in Australia, or 08/8952 8723; www.outbackballooning.com.au) is one of the most upscale. A 1-hour flight followed by champagne breakfast in the bush costs A$290 (US$188), with a 20% discount for kids under 17. A 30-minute breakfast flight costs A$190 (US$123). Kids under 6 are discouraged from participating because they cannot see over the basket. Don't make any other morning plans, as you probably won't get back to your hotel until close to noon.

ACTIVE PURSUITS

BIKING　A gently undulating 17km (11-mile) **bike trail** weaves from John Flynn's Grave on Larapinta Drive, 7km (4⅓ miles) west of town, through the bushland and desert foothills of the MacDonnell Ranges to Simpson's Gap (p. 379). **Centre Cycles** (© 08/8953 2966) on Lindsay Avenue at Undoolya Road rents bikes for around A$10 (US$6.50) for 4 hours (plus a A$50/US$33 refundable deposit). *Note:* Carry water, because the two taps en route are a long way apart. Bike in cooler months only.

BUSHWALKING　The 250km (155-mile) **Larapinta Trail** winds west from Alice through the sparse red ranges, picturesque semidesert scenery, and rich bird life of the West MacDonnell National Park (p. 379). Sections range from easy to hard. The shortest is 8km (5 miles), ranging up to several 23km to 29km (14- to 18-mile) stretches. Trail maps and information are dispensed by the **Parks & Wildlife Commission of the Northern Territory** office in Alice Springs (© 08/8951 8211), or the **CATIA Visitor Centre** (see "Visitor Information," earlier in this chapter). Camp facilities are simple at best on popular routes, non-existent on less traveled sections. *Warning:* Always carry drinking water. The trail may close in extremely hot summer periods.

　　Alice Wanderer Centre Sightseeing Tours (© 1800/66 9111 in Australia, or 08/8952 2111) runs transfers to road access points along the trail, where you can mostly pick up a choice of 1-, 2-, or 3-day hikes. Several outfitters run guided, supported hikes along trail sections.

GOLF　The **Alice Springs Golf Club** ✿, 1km (just over ½ mile) from town on Cromwell Drive (© 08/8952 5440), boasts a Thomson-Wolveridge course rated among the world's top desert courses by touring pros. The course opens from sunup to sundown. For nine holes you will pay A$17 (US$11), for 18 holes, A$22 (US$14). Then there's A$22 (US$14) for clubs, and A$30 (US$20) for a cart, which many locals don't bother with. It's best to book a tee time.

SHOPPING AT THE SOURCE FOR ABORIGINAL ART

Alice Springs is the best place in Australia to buy **Aboriginal art and crafts** ✿. You will find no shortage of stuff: linen and canvas paintings, didgeridoos, spears, clapping sticks, *coolamons* (a dish used by women to carry anything from water to babies), animal carvings, baskets, and jewelry, as well as books, CDs, and all kinds of non-Aboriginal merchandise printed with Aboriginal designs. Prices can soar into the thousands for large canvases by world-renowned painters, but you will find plenty of small works for under A$250 (US$163). Major artworks sell unmounted for ease of shipment, which most galleries arrange on your behalf. Store hours can vary with the seasons and the crowds, so it pays to check ahead.

　　See artists at work when you drop by **Jukurrpa Artists,** on Stott Terrace between Gap Road and Leichhardt Terrace (© 08/8953 1052). This Aboriginal women's cooperative studio/gallery sells the "pattern and dot" paintings of the Western Desert style, plus crafts such as carvings and jewelry, weapons and tools.

　　Aboriginal-owned **Warumpi Arts,** 105 Gregory Terrace (© 08/8952 9066), sells wooden artifacts, seed necklaces, and canvas and linen paintings in the earth-hued designs of the Papunya people, who live 250km (155 miles) west of Alice. Another Aboriginal-owned gallery, **Papunya Tula Artists,** 78 Todd St. (© 08/8952 4731), sells paintings on canvas and linen from Papunya and other artists living in the desert as far as 700km (434 miles) west of Alice Springs.

Several stores on Todd Mall sell affordable Aboriginal art and souvenirs. The biggest, the **Original Dreamtime Gallery,** 63 Todd Mall (℃ **08/8952 8861**), stocks a huge selection, and packs, mails, and insures your purchases free of charge anywhere in the world. It also shows visiting exhibitions of Aboriginal art.

Arunta Art Gallery & Bookshop, 70 Todd St. (℃ **08/8952 1544**), stocks a great range of books on Aboriginal art, language, and archaeology, as well as Australian history, geology, wildlife, and biographies.

If you're interested in investing in serious artwork, speak to Roslyn Premont, proprietor of **Gallery Gondwana,** 43 Todd Mall (℃ **08/8953 1577**). She has written a book on desert art, and her gallery sells only top-notch works.

A big range of art, didgeridoos, artifacts, music, and books is sold by the **Aboriginal Art & Culture Centre** (see "Seeing the Sights in Alice," above) via its website at **www.aboriginalart.com.au.**

Today's Aboriginal bands mix ancient and hip new rhythms to create some wonderful sounds. For the country's biggest range of indigenous music, head to the **CAAMA (Central Australian Aboriginal Media Association)** ☆ store at 101 Todd St. (℃ **08/8952 9207**). It also stocks books on Aboriginal art and issues; videos in PAL and NTSC format (on everything from how to fix your broken-down Ford the bushman's way, to Aboriginal people's memories of their first contact with "white man"); children's books with Aboriginal story lines; a line of Aboriginal-print fabrics, clothes, diaries, stationery, and greeting cards; Aboriginal artifacts and jewelry; and cute Yamba the Honey Ant dolls, modeled after a kids' character on the local Aboriginal television station, Imparja.

WHERE TO STAY

Alice's hotel stock is not grand. Many properties have dated rooms and modest facilities, no match for the gleaming standard of **Ayers Rock Resort** (described later in this chapter). You may pay lower rates than those listed in the summer off season (Dec–Mar), and even as late as June. Peak season typically runs July through October or November. As well as the more upmarket properties below, there are several backpacker resorts offering dorm rooms and doubles.

EXPENSIVE

Alice Springs Resort ☆ This friendly, well-run, low-rise property is a 3-minute walk from town over the Todd River. Ask for one of the standard rooms renovated in 2002 (the unrenovated ones are airy and comfortable, but those bright green carpets and dated peach floral curtains are hard on the eye!), or go for the big deluxe rooms built in 1999. In summer, it's nice to repair to the pool under a couple of desert palms after a hot day's sightseeing. A fire glows in the Gumtree Lounge bar on winter evenings.

34 Stott Terrace, Alice Springs, NT 0870. ℃ **1300/8139 889** in Australia, or 08/8951 4545. Fax 08/8953 0995. www.alicespringsresort.com.au. 144 units (108 shower only). A$200–A$234 (US$130–US$152) double. Extra person A$25 (US$16). Children under 12 stay free in parent's room with existing bedding. Ask about packages with Ayers Rock Resort and/or Kings Canyon Resort. AE, DC, MC, V. Free parking. Airport shuttle. **Amenities:** Restaurant; 2 bars; solar-heated outdoor swimming pool; bike rental; concierge; tour desk; secretarial services; limited room service; in-room massage; babysitting; same-day laundry/dry-cleaning service. *In room:* A/C, TV w/pay movies, minibar, hair dryer, iron.

Bond Springs Outback Retreat ☆ *(Finds* This working 1,515-sq.-km (585-sq.-mile) cattle ranch is a great place to get a taste of Outback life with a real Aussie family. A reader said it reminded her of the kind of place you'd see in *The Thornbirds.* Janice Heaslip welcomes guests to her homestead, inviting them to join country dinners with the family and accommodating them in simple but appealing rooms or self-contained cottages. A TV is located in the guest lounge. The Heaslips run a good range of day trips, overnight bush camps, and tours throughout the Red Centre, making this a good base for a Red Centre stay. Ask about 3- and 5-day packages, some combining tours, and accommodations at Kings Canyon Resort and Ayers Rock Resort also. No smoking indoors.

25km (16 miles) north of Alice Springs (P.O. Box 4, Alice Springs, NT 0870). © 08/8952 9888. Fax 08/8953 0963. www.outbackretreat.com.au. 5 units, 3 with bathroom, 2 sharing a private bathroom. A$231–A$277 (US$150–US$180) double. Rates include full breakfast. Extra adult A$58 (US$38), extra child 6–15 A$47 (US$31). Dinner A$55 (US$36) per person extra. MC, V. Closed Christmas–Jan. Transfers from Alice Springs A$40 (US$26) from town, A$80 (US$52) from airport, one-way, per vehicle. **Note:** All but the last 6km (3¾ miles) of the road is paved; while car-rental companies do not allow driving on unpaved roads, they may permit it here. Check with your company. **Amenities:** Unheated outdoor pool; outdoor tennis court; laundry service. *In room:* A/C, fridge, coffeemaker (in cottages), hair dryer, no phone.

MODERATE

Aurora Alice Springs This pleasant hotel (formally The Territory Inn) is smack in the center of town. Rooms in the newer wing are your standard quality motel-style variety, all clean, large, and decorated nicely. Those in the original wing are small and a little dark; they have a pretty heritage theme with floral bedcovers and lace curtains. The courtyard has a barbecue and the front desk loans hair dryers. The tiny pool and Jacuzzi are tucked away in a utilitarian corner, so this is not the place for chilling out poolside; stay here to be within walking distance of shops and restaurants. Room service is from the **Red Ochre Grill** (p. 378).

Leichhardt Terrace (backing on to Todd Mall), Alice Springs, NT 0870. © 1800/089 644 in Australia, or 08/8950 6666. Fax 08/8952 7829. www.aurora-resorts.com.au. 108 units (all with shower only, 1 suite w/Jacuzzi). A$150–A$170 (US$98–US$110) double. Extra person A$20 (US$13). Children under 14 stay free in parent's room with existing bedding. AE, DC, MC, V. Free parking. Hotel provides transfers from airport A$10 (US$6.50) per person, round-trip. Airport shuttle. **Amenities:** Restaurant; small heated outdoor pool; Jacuzzi; tour desk; limited room service; babysitting; same-day laundry/dry-cleaning service; barbecue area. *In room:* A/C, TV w/pay movies, fridge, minibar, iron, hair dryer (available on request).

Rydges Plaza Resort Alice Springs *Value* Next to the golf club and near Lasseter's Casino, this is one of Alice's fanciest resorts. Three stories of rooms wrap around the pool and an ample sun deck. All rooms are spacious and around half were refurbished in 2001. Each has a balcony—some looking onto the pool, some back toward town—while others look over the red ranges. Barbecues take place every lunch and dinner around the pool September through March.

Barrett Dr. (1.5km/1 mile from town center), Alice Springs, NT 0870. © 1800/226 466 in Australia, 0800/446 187 in New Zealand, or resort direct 1800/675 212 in Australia, or 08/8950 8000. Fax 08/8953 0475. www.rydges.com. 235 units. A$160–A$215 (US$104–US$139) double; A$350–A$500 (US$228–US$325) suite. Extra person A$25 (US$16). Children under 13 stay free in parent's room with existing bedding. Free crib. Ask about packages. AE, DC, MC, V. Free parking. Airport shuttle. **Amenities:** Restaurant; bar; heated outdoor pool; 2 lit tennis courts; exercise room with plunge pool; Jacuzzi; sauna; bike rental; tour desk; secretarial service; 24-hr. room service; babysitting; laundry service; same-day laundry/dry-cleaning service. *In room:* A/C, TV w/pay movies, dataport, minibar, hair dryer, iron.

INEXPENSIVE

Desert Palms Resort *Value* Next to Lasseter's Casino (where the food can be awful) and the Alice Springs Golf Club (to which guests enjoy honorary membership), these cheery cabins set behind manicured palms and pink bougainvillea are one of the nicest places to stay in Alice. Don't be deterred by their poky prefab appearance; inside they are surprisingly large, well kept, and inviting, with a pine-pitched ceiling, a minikitchen, a sliver of bathroom sporting white tiles and fittings, and a pert furnished front deck. Four rooms are suitable for travelers with disabilities. A sun deck and pool with its own little island is out front. The pleasant staff at the front desk loans hair dryers, processes your film, does laundry service, sells basic grocery and liquor supplies, and books your tours.

74 Barrett Dr. (1km/½ mile from town), Alice Springs, NT 0870. (C) **1800/678 037** in Australia, or 08/8952 5977. Fax 08/8953 4176. www.desertpalms.com.au. 80 units (all with shower only), with parking in front of units. A$99 (US$64) double. Extra person A$10 (US$6.50). AE, DC, MC, V. Airport shuttle. Free coach station/train station/airport shuttle twice daily; free resort-to-town shuttle 4 times daily. **Amenities:** Large unheated outdoor pool; golf course nearby; half-size tennis court; access to nearby health club; tour desk; car-rental desk; massage available by appointment; laundry service; same-day laundry/dry-cleaning service; nonsmoking rooms. *In room:* A/C, TV, kitchenette, dataport, fridge, coffeemaker.

Elkira Motel   The cheapest rooms in the heart of town—that are still decent, that is—are at this unpretentious, clean Best Western motel. Standard rooms are dated, with lots of wood and tile floors, and a fridge and shower. Two standard family rooms come with a double bed and three singles. The 42 deluxe rooms have a little more space, and nine have microwaves and some have queen-size beds. Nine family rooms are nicer still, and come with a kitchenette—and as they cost the same as normal deluxe room are well worth asking for even if you're traveling as a couple. All deluxe family rooms and a few deluxe doubles have bathrooms. Ask for a room away from the road, as the traffic is noisy during the day. The seven budget rooms are also a little dated, but though small, are comfortable and quiet. They come with a double bed, a TV, shower, fridge, and hair dryer. Look out for the friendly Doberman called Charlie.

65 Bath St. (opposite Kmart), Alice Springs, NT 0870. (C) **1800/809 252** in Australia, or 08/8952 1222. Fax 08/8953 1370. www.elkira.com.au. 58 units (some with shower only, 2 with Jacuzzi). A$100–A$120 (US$65–US$78) all rooms. Extra person A$15 (US$9.75); extra child under 3 A$5 (US$3.25). AE, DC, MC, V. Free parking. Airport shuttle. **Amenities:** 2 restaurants; unheated outdoor pool; nearby golf course; Jacuzzi; tour desk; car-rental desk; limited room service; same-day laundry/dry-cleaning service; nonsmoking rooms. *In room:* A/C, TV, fax, dataport, fridge, coffeemaker, hair dryer, iron, safe.

WHERE TO DINE
EXPENSIVE
Overlanders Steakhouse 𝕮 STEAK/AUSSIE TUCKER   This landmark on the Alice dining scene is famous for its "Drover's Blowout" menu, which assaults the megahungry with soup and damper, then a platter of crocodile vol-au-vents, camel and kangaroo filet, and emu medallions—these are just the *appetizers*—followed by Scotch filet or barramundi, and dessert. There's a regular menu with a 700 gram (1-lb., 10-oz.) steak, plus lots of lighter fare like oysters or spinach crepes. The barnlike interior is Outback all through, from the rustic bar to the saddlebags hanging from the roof beams. An "Overlanders' Table" seats solo diners together.

72 Hartley St. (C) **08/8952 2159.** Reservations required in peak season. Main courses A$19–A$26 (US$12–US$17); Drover's Blowout A$44 (US$29). AE, DC, DISC, MC, V. Daily 6–10pm.

Palms Restaurant 𝕮𝕮 MODERN AUSTRALIAN   Ask the locals for the best chow in town, and this is where they'll send you. It serves sophisticated fare, like catch of the day done in a carrot and blood orange *beurre blanc*. Bush tucker creeps onto the menu, in dishes such as the peppered kangaroo filet with sweet potato mash. A lighter menu is served at lunch. The wine list is split between easy-drinkers at reasonable prices and a "Premium" list carrying some wonderful Australian labels, even Henschke's Hill of Grace, which some say is Australia's best red. Live piano music plays nightly. No smoking inside until 9pm.

At the Alice Springs Resort, 34 Stott Terrace. (C) **08/8951 4545.** Reservations recommended at dinner. Main courses A$25–A$28 (US$16–US$18). AE, DC, MC, V. Daily 6am–9:30pm.

MODERATE

Malathi's Restaurant & Sean's Irish Bar ASIAN/WESTERN   Located in an unprepossessing building a couple of blocks from Todd Mall, Malathi's serves up an eclectic assortment of Asian dishes plus a few Aussie choices, such as grain-fed steak. The Asian food is outstanding. I can recommend the lamb korma, a kind of mild curry. You might want to try the Lakshmi king prawns cooked in Indian flavors, or the Thai coconut curry. Vegetarians have some good choices. They do takeout, too. The bar serves cheap Irish stews, live bands play (sometimes), and there always Guinness available. The restaurant has a wine list, but permits BYO wine at A$5 (US$3.25) corkage per bottle.

51 Bath St. (opposite Kmart). ⓒ **08/8952 1858.** Reservations recommended. Main courses A$15–A$28 (US$9.75–US$18); many dishes under A$21 (US$14). AE, DC, MC, V. Restaurant Mon–Sat 5:30–10pm or later; bar daily 3:30–9:30pm.

Red Ochre Grill ⋒ GOURMET BUSH TUCKER   If you've never tried wallaby mignons on a bed of native pasta and polenta cake with a native berry and red-wine cream sauce, or barramundi baked in paperbark with wild lime and coriander butter, here's your chance. The chef at this upscale chain fuses native Aussie ingredients with dishes from around the world. Although it might seem a touristy formula, the food is mouthwatering. Dine in the contemporary interior fronting Todd Mall, or outside in the attractive courtyard.

Under the Territory Inn on Todd Mall. ⓒ **08/8952 9614.** Reservations recommended at dinner. Main courses A$9–A$21 (US$5.80–US$14) lunch; A$15–A$23 (US$9.75–US$15) dinner; A$13–A$16 (US$8.10–US$10) buffet breakfast. AE, DC, MC, V. Daily 6:30am–10pm.

INEXPENSIVE

Bar Doppio ⋒ EAST/WEST CAFE FARE   If you're in need of a dose of cool—style, that is, as well as air-conditioning—this arcade cafe is the place to chill over good coffee and feast on cheap, wholesome food. Sacks of coffee beans are stacked all over, gypsy music plays, no tables and chairs match, and the staff doesn't care if you sit here all day. It's largely vegetarian, but fish and meat figure on the blackboard menu. Try lamb chermoula cutlets on Gabriella potatoes with rocket, red onion and tomato salad; chickpea curry; warm Turkish flat bread with dips; or spuds with hot toppings. Hot and cold breakfast choices stay on the menu until 11am. They do takeout. BYO.

2 and 3 Fan Arcade (off the southern end of Todd Mall). ⓒ **08/8952 6525.** Reservations accepted at dinner only. Main courses A$7–A$16 (US$4.55–US$10); sandwiches average A$6 (US$3.90). No credit cards. Mon–Fri 7:30am–5:30pm; Sat 7:30am–4:30pm; Sun 10am–4:30pm; dinner Fri–Sat only 6–9pm. Closed holidays and Christmas–New Year.

Bojangles Saloon and Restaurant ⋒ TEX-MEX/MIXED   Swing open the saloon doors and enter a world of cowhide seats, thick wooden tables, assorted Western-style knickknacks, original American Civil War guns, and so on. The front bar is friendly and serves up good beers by the bottle or schooner, and food such as burgers, nachos, salads, and fish and chips. The restaurant out back has more gourmet offerings, but either way it's a great atmosphere. Aussie-style country and folk singers strum away in the evenings, and the bar staff is terrific.

80 Todd St. ⓒ **08/8952 2873.** Reservations not needed. Main courses A$7–A$18 (US$4.55–US$12) front bar, A$12–A$25 (US$7.80–US$16) restaurant. AE, DC, MC, V. Lunch noon–3pm daily; dinner 6–10pm daily.

Casa Nostra ⋒⋒ ⟨Value⟩ ITALIAN   The only difference between this cheery homespun family eatery and every other Italian restaurant in the world is that this one has autographed photos of Tom Selleck pinned to the wall. Judging by his scrawled praise, Tom loved eating here (when on location in Alice filming *Quigley Down Under*) as much as the locals do. You've seen the red-checked table-cloths and the basket-clad Chianti bottles before, but the food is surprisingly good. A long list of pastas (like the masterful carbonara), pizzas, and chicken and veal dishes are the main offerings. All meals can come as takeout. BYO.

Corner of Undoolya Rd. and Sturt Terrace. ☎ **08/8952 0549.** Reservations strongly recommended. Main courses A$11–A$18 (US$7.15–US$12). MC, V. Mon–Sat 5–10pm. Closed Christmas to end of Jan.

3 Road Trips from Alice Springs

The key attraction of a day trip into the MacDonnell Ranges is unspoiled natural scenery and few crowds. Many companies run coach or four-wheel-drive tours of a half day or a day, sometimes overnight, to the West and East Macs. Some of these appear in "Organized Tours," earlier in the "Alice Springs" section. Expect to pay about A$100 (US$65) for a full-day trip.

THE WEST MACDONNELL RANGES ✦

WEST MACDONNELL NATIONAL PARK The 300km (186-mile) round-trip drive west from Alice Springs into West MacDonnell National Park is a stark but picturesque trip to a series of red gorges, semidesert country, and the occasional peaceful swimming hole.

From Alice, take Larapinta Drive west for 18km (11 miles) to the 8km (5-mile) turnoff to **Simpson's Gap,** a water hole lined with ghost gums. Black-footed rock wallabies hop out on the cliffs in the late afternoon (so you may want to time a visit here on your way back to Alice). There are a couple of short trails, including a ½km (⅓-mile) Ghost Gum circuit, and a 17km (11-mile) round-trip trail to Bond Gap. Swimming is not permitted. The place has an information center/ranger station and free barbecues.

Twenty-three kilometers (14 miles) farther down Larapinta Road, 9km (5½ miles) down a turnoff, is **Standley Chasm** (☎ **08/8956 7440**). This rock cleft is only a few meters wide but 80m (262 ft.) high, reached by a 10-minute creek-side trail. Aim to be here at midday, when the walls glow orange in the overhead sun. A kiosk sells snacks and drinks. Admission is A$6 (US$3.90) for adults and A$4.50 (US$2.90) for seniors and children 5 to 14. The Chasm is open from 8am to 6pm daily, with last entry at 5pm (closed Christmas).

Six kilometers (3¾ miles) past Standley Chasm, you can branch right onto Namatjira Drive, or carry on to Hermannsburg Historical Precinct (see below). Assuming you take Namatjira Drive, you'll head 42km (26 miles) on to **picturesque Ellery Creek Big Hole.** The spring-fed water is so nippy that the tourism authority warns swimmers to take a flotation device in case of cramping. A 3km (2-mile) walking trail explains the area's geological history.

Eleven kilometers (7 miles) farther along Namatjira Drive is **Serpentine Gorge,** where a trail leads up to a lookout for a lovely view of the ranges through the gorge walls. Another 12km (7½ miles) on are **ocher pits,** which Aboriginal people quarried for body paint and for decorating objects used in ceremonial performances. Twenty-six kilometers (16 miles) farther west, 8km (5 miles) from the main road, is **Ormiston Gorge and Pound** (☎ **08/8956 7799** for the ranger station/visitor center). This is a good spot to picnic, swim in the wide deep pool below red cliffs, and walk a choice of trails, such as the 30-minute Ghost Gum Lookout trail or the easy 7km (4-mile) scenic loop (allow 3–4 hr.). The water is warm enough to swim in the summer. You can camp here for A$6.60 (US$4.30)

Road-Trip Tips for the East & West Macs

Facilities are scarce outside Alice, so bring food (a picnic perhaps, or meat to barbecue), drinking water, and a full gas tank. Leaded, unleaded, and diesel fuel is sold at Glen Helen Resort, Hermannsburg, and Ross River Resort. Wear walking shoes.

Many of the water holes dry up too much to be good for swimming—those at Ellery Creek, Ormiston Gorge, and Glen Helen are the most permanent. Being spring-fed, they can be intensely cold, so take only short dips to avoid cramping and hypothermia, don't swim alone, and be careful of underwater snags. Don't wear sunscreen because it pollutes drinking water for native animals.

Two-wheel-drive rental cars will not be insured on unsealed (unpaved) roads—that means the last few miles into Trephina Gorge Nature Park, and the 11km (7-mile) road into N'Dhala Gorge Nature Park, both in the East Macs. If you are prepared to risk it, you will probably get into Trephina in a two-wheel-drive car, but you will need a four-wheel-drive for N'Dhala and Arltunga. The West MacDonnell road is paved to Glen Helen Gorge; a few points of interest may require driving for short lengths on unpaved road. Before setting off, drop into the CATIA Visitor Information Centre (see "Visitor Information," earlier in this chapter) for tips on road conditions, and for details on the free ranger talks, walks, and slide shows that take place in the West and East Macs April through October. Entry to all sights, parks, and reserves (except for Standley Chasm) is free.

per adult, and A$3.30 (US$1.90) per child 5 to 15. The campground has no powered sites but does have hot showers, toilets, and free barbecues.

A bit farther on is **Glen Helen Gorge,** where the Finke River cuts through the ranges, with more gorge swimming, a walking trail, guided hikes, and helicopter flights. Modest **Glen Helen Resort** (⊘ **1800/896 110** in Australia, or 08/8956 7489; www.melanka.com.au/melanka_glenghelen/gh_index.html) has 25 motel rooms (A$143/US$93) double; bunkhouses for four (A$19/US$12 per person) and campgrounds (A$9/US$5.85 per person for a tent site, and A$22/US$14 double for a powered campsite); a restaurant serving three meals a day; a bar; and barbecues for which they sell meat packs.

HERMANNSBURG HISTORICAL PRECINCT   An alternative to visiting the West Mac gorges is to stay on Larapinta Drive all 128km (79 miles) from Alice Springs to the old **Lutheran Mission** at the **Hermannsburg Historical Precinct** (⊘ **08/8956 7402**). Some maps will show this route as an unpaved road, but it is now paved. Settled by German missionaries in the 1870s, this is a cluster of restored farmhouse-style mission buildings. There are a museum, a gallery housing landscapes by Aussie artist Albert Namatjira, and tearooms serving an apple strudel from an old German recipe. The Mission is open daily from 9am to 4pm (from 10am Nov–Mar). Admission to the precinct with tea or coffee is A$4.50 (US$2.90) for adults, A$3 (US$1.95) for school-age kids, or A$12 (US$7.80) for a family, plus A$3.50 (US$2.30) per adult or A$2.50 (US$1.60) per child for a guided gallery tour, which departs every hour. The precinct is closed from December 24 to January 2 or 3, and on Good Friday.

FINKE GORGE NATIONAL PARK   Just west of Hermannsburg is the turnoff to the 46,000-hectare (113,620-acre) **Finke Gorge National Park,** 16km (10 miles) to the south on an unpaved road. The park is most famous for **Palm Valley,** where groves of rare *Livistona mariae* cabbage palms have survived since central Australia was a jungle millions of years ago. You will need a four-wheel-drive to explore this park. Four walking trails between 1.5km (1 mile) and 5km (3 miles) take you among the palms or up to a lookout over cliffs; one is a signposted trail exploring Aboriginal culture. There is a campsite about 4km (2½ miles) from the palms; it has showers, toilets, and free barbecues. Collect your firewood outside the park. Camping is A$6.60 (US$4.30) for adults, A$3.30 (US$2.10) for kids 5 to 15. For information, call the CATIA Visitor Information Centre in Alice Springs before you leave, because there is no visitor center in the park. The ranger station (© **08/8956 7401**) is for emergencies only.

THE EAST MACDONNELL RANGES

Not as many tourists tread the path on the Ross Highway into the East Macs, but if you do, you'll be rewarded with lush walking trails, fewer crowds, and traces of Aboriginal history. I even spotted wild camels on my visit. At the end of the drive, 86km (53 miles) from Alice, is the *dinky-di* (that's Australian for "authentic"—as is "fair dinkum") **Ross River Resort** (see "Where to Stay," below), where day-trippers are welcome. The homestead stages a boomerang-throwing and whip-cracking experience over billy tea and damper from 10am to noon daily for A$5.50 (US$3.60) per person, so consider heading there first, then dropping in on the attractions below as you return.

The first points of interest are **Emily Gap,** 10km (6 miles) from Alice, and Jessie Gap, an additional 7km (4 ½ miles), a pretty picnic spot. You can cool off in the Emily Gap swimming hole if there is any water. Don't miss the "Caterpillar Dreaming" Aboriginal art on the wall, on your right as you walk through.

At **Corroboree Rock,** 37km (23 miles) farther, you can make a short climb up this outcrop that was important to local Aborigines. The polished rock "seat" at the hole high up in it means Aboriginal people must have used this rock for eons.

Twenty-two kilometers (13¾ miles) farther is the turnoff to **Trephina Gorge Nature Park,** an 18-sq.-km (7-sq.-mile) beauty spot with peaceful walking trails ranging from 45 minutes to 4½ hours. The last 5km (3 miles) of the 9km (5½-mile) road into the park are unpaved, but you can make it in a two-wheel-drive car.

N'Dhala Gorge Nature Park, 10km (6 miles) past Trephina Gorge Nature Park, just before you reach Ross River Resort, houses an "open-air art gallery" of rock carvings, or petroglyphs, left by the Eastern Arrernte Aboriginal people. An interesting 1.5km (1-mile) signposted trail explains the Dreamtime meanings of a few of the 6,000 rock carvings, hundreds or thousands of years old, that are thought to be in this eerily quiet gorge. A four-wheel-drive vehicle is a must to traverse the 11km (7-mile) access road.

The Ross Highway is paved all the way to Ross River Resort.

WHERE TO STAY

Ross River Resort   This fair dinkum, 100-year-old station offers both day visitors and overnight guests a condensed taste of Outback life. Overnight accommodations are rustic, roomy log cabins; there are also basic quad-share bunkhouses, with shared bathrooms, and shady campgrounds with a general store.

The whitewashed original homestead has been converted to a restaurant with Edwardian furniture, open for breakfast, lunch, and dinner at moderate prices. Entry to the homestead, its rustic restaurant and bar, the barbecue, four bush-walking trails, and kangaroo enclosure is free (get feed for them from the stables); so are the pool and Jacuzzi if you patronize the bar or restaurant. The resort ended up being closed for most of 2003—it was rented out to a private guest—but it should reopen sometime in 2004.

Ross Hwy., 86km (53 miles) east of Alice Springs (P.O. Box 3271), Alice Springs, NT 0871. © 1800/241 711 in Australia, or 08/8956 9711. Fax 08/8956 9823. www.rossriverresort.com.au. 48 units, 30 with bathroom (shower only). A$125 (US$81) double; family of 4 A$150 (US$98); bunkhouse quad-share adults A$33 (US$21), with linen, without linen adults A$22 (US$14). Extra person A$30 (US$20). Unpowered campsite A$10 (US$6.50) per adult; powered campsite A$15 (US$9.75) per adult. Lower rates for kids in bunkhouses and campgrounds. AE, DC, MC, V. Coach transfers from Alice Springs A$110 (US$72) per person, round-trip. Pets are not accepted except in campground if they are kept on a leash at all times. **Amenities:** Restaurant; bar; small unheated outdoor pool; Jacuzzi. *In room:* A/C, fridge, tea and coffeemaker, no phone.

4 Kings Canyon ⦿

Anyone who saw the movie *The Adventures of Priscilla, Queen of the Desert* will remember the stony plateau the transvestites climb to gaze over the plain below. You can stand on that same spot (wearing sequined underpants is optional) at **Kings Canyon** ⦿ in **Watarrka National Park** (© **08/8956 7460** for park headquarters). As the crow flies, it is 320km (198 miles) southwest of Alice Springs. The sandstone walls of the canyon drop about 100m (330 ft.) to rock pools and centuries-old gum trees. There is little to do except walk the dramatic canyon rim for a sense of the peaceful emptiness of the Australian Outback.

GETTING THERE No regular flights operate, but **Ayers Rock Scenic Flights** (© **08/8956 2345**) does an aerial day trip from Ayers Rock Resort that incorporates a guided canyon walk at A$425 (US$276) per adult, A$390 (US$254) per child 3 to 12.

Greyhound Pioneer (© **13 20 30** in Australia) and coach tour company **AAT Kings** (© **08/8952 1700** in Alice Springs, or 08/8956 2171 in Ayers Rock) make daily transfers from Ayers Rock; Greyhound's fare is about A$54 (US$35) one-way.

Numerous **coach** and **four-wheel-drive** tour outfits call at Kings Canyon from Alice Springs or Ayers Rock, with time allowed for the rim walk. See "Exploring the Red Centre," at the beginning of this chapter, for recommended companies.

With a four-wheel-drive, you can get to Kings Canyon from Alice Springs on the unpaved Mereenie Loop Road.

The regular route is the 480km (349-mile) trip from Alice Springs south via the Stuart Highway, then west onto the Lasseter Highway, then north and west on the Luritja Road. All three roads are paved. Ayers Rock/Uluru is 306km (190 miles) to the south on a paved road; from Yulara, take the Lasseter Highway east for 125km (78 miles), then turn left onto Luritja Road for 168km (104 miles) to Kings Canyon Resort. The resort sells leaded and unleaded petrol and diesel.

Uluru Motorcycle Tours (© **08/8956 2019;** www.ozemail.com.au/~uluru harleys) will take you there on a 1-day tour via Harley Davidson from Ayers Rock Resort, with you as a passenger or driving.

GETTING AROUND   AAT Kings provides a guided rim or creek-bed walk from Kings Canyon Resort, 7km (4 ⅓ miles) away, for A$40 (US$26) for adults, A$20 (US$13) for kids under 15, round-trip. It departs daily at 6:15am October through March, and at 7am April through September. You can book this through AAT Kings or the resort.

EXPLORING THE PARK

The way to explore the canyon is on the 6km (3¾-mile) **walk** up the side (short but steep!) and around the rim. Even if you're in good shape, it's a strenuous 3- to 4-hour hike. It leads through a maze of rounded sandstone formations called the Lost City, across a bridge to a fern-fringed pocket of water holes called the Garden of Eden, and back along the other side through more sandstone rocks. There are lookout points en route. If you visit after the odd rainfall, the walls teem with waterfalls. In winter, don't set off too early, because sunlight doesn't light up the canyon walls to good effect until midmorning.

If you're not up to making the rim walk, take the shady 2.6km (1½-mile) round-trip trail along the mostly dry **Kings Creek bed** on the canyon floor. It takes about an hour. Wear sturdy boots, because the ground can be rocky. This walk is all right for young kids and travelers in wheelchairs for the first 1km (just over ½ mile).

Both walks are signposted. Avoid the rim walk in the middle of the day between September and May, when it's too hot.

You can also explore the park from an Aboriginal viewpoint with **Lilla Aboriginal Tours** (book through Kings Canyon Resort). Aboriginal guides take you on an easy 1km (just over a ½-mile) walk to sacred caves and rock-painting sites. You learn about the artworks, hear the Dreamtime events that created the land around you, discover plant medicines and food, and have a go at throwing a spear and a boomerang. The tour lasts 1½ to 2 hours and departs at 9am and 4pm daily (closed mid-Dec to mid-Jan) from the Lilla community, 14km (8¾ miles) from Kings Canyon Resort. The resort does transfers for A$20 (US$13) per person, round-trip, or A$30 (US$20) for two of you. The tour costs A$39 (US$25) for adults, A$33 (US$21) for seniors and students, and A$27 (US$18) for kids 5 to 16.

Professional Helicopter Services (© **08/8956 7873;** www.phs.com.au) makes 15-minute flights over the canyon for A$90 (US$59) per person.

WHERE TO STAY & DINE

Apart from campgrounds, the only place to stay in Watarrka National Park is at Kings Canyon Resort.

Kings Canyon Resort 🏕   This attractive, low-slung complex 7km (4⅓ miles) from Kings Canyon blends into its surroundings. All but four of the larger deluxe rooms were built in 1999 and have desert views from glass-enclosed Jacuzzis. The remaining rooms are typical hotel rooms, comfortable enough, with restful range views from the balcony; they were refurbished in 2001. The double/twin, quad, and family lodge rooms are adequate low-budget choices, with a communal kitchen and bathroom facilities. The resort has a well-stocked minimart where you can buy meat for the barbecues. Live entertainment plays some nights, and a ranger gives a slide show several nights a week. Internet access is available.

Luritja Rd., Watarrka National Park, NT 0872. © **1800/817 622** in Australia, or 08/8956 7442. Fax 08/8956 7426. www.voyages.com.au. 164 units, 128 with bathroom, of which 32 have Jacuzzis; 72 powered campsites and tent sites. High season (July–Nov) A$330–A$397 (US$215–US$258) hotel room double; low season

(Dec–June) A$277–A$343 (US$180–US$223) hotel room double. Extra adult A$27 (US$18). Children under 16 stay free in parent's room with existing bedding. High season A$100 (US$65) lodge room double; A$168 (US$109) quad-share; A$185 (US$120) family (to sleep 5). Low season A$98 (US$64) lodge room double; A$163 (US$106) quad-share; A$178 (US$116) family. No children in lodge rooms unless you book entire room. Tent sites A$28 (US$18) double; powered sites A$32 (US$21) double. Extra person A$11 (US$7.15) adults, A$5 (US$3.25) children 6–15 in powered campsite. Children under 16 dine free at breakfast and dinner buffets at Carmichael's with an adult. Ask about packages in conjunction with Ayers Rock Resort and Alice Springs Resort. AE, DC, MC, V. **Amenities:** Restaurant; cafe; 2 bars; 2 outdoor unheated pools; outdoor lit tennis court; volleyball court; bike rental (from nearby gas station); tour desk; limited room service; coin-op laundry. *In room:* A/C, TV, fridge. Hotel only: TV w/pay movies, minibar, hair dryer, iron.

5 Uluru-Kata Tjuta National Park (Ayers Rock/The Olgas) ⋆

462km (286 miles) SW of Alice Springs; 1,934km (1,199 miles) S of Darwin; 1,571km (974 miles) N of Adelaide; 2,841km (1,761 miles) NW of Sydney

Ayers Rock/Uluru is the Australia tourism industry's pinup icon, a glamorous red stone that has probably been splashed on more posters than Cindy Crawford has been on magazine covers. Just why people trek from all over the world to gawk at it is a bit of a mystery. For its size? Hardly, nearby Mt. Conner is three times as big. For its shape? Probably not, when most folks agree the neighboring Kata Tjuta/Olgas are more picturesque. You can put its popularity down to the faint shiver up the spine and the indescribable sense of place it evokes in anyone who looks at it. Even Aussie bushmen reckon it's "got somethin' spiritual about it."

In 1985 the **Uluru-Kata Tjuta National Park** ⋆ was returned to its Aboriginal owners, the Pitjantjatjara and Yankunytjatjara people, known as the Anangu, who manage the property jointly with the Australian government. People used to speculate that the Rock was a meteorite, but we now know it was formed by sediments laid down 600 million to 700 million years ago in an inland sea and thrust up above ground 348m (1,141 ft.) by geological forces. With a circumference of 9.4km (6 miles), the Rock is no pebble, especially because two-thirds of it is thought to be underground. On photos it looks like a big smooth blob. In the flesh, it's more interesting—dappled with holes and overhangs, and its sides draped with curtains of stone, creating little coves hiding water holes and Aboriginal rock art. It also changes color from pink to a deep wine red depending on the slant of the sun.

Don't think a visit to Uluru is just about snapping a few photos and going home. You can walk around the Rock, climb it (although the local Aborigines prefer you don't), fly over it, ride a camel to it, motorcycle around it on a Harley-Davidson, trek through the Olgas, eat in an outdoor restaurant, tour the night sky, and join Aboriginal people on guided walks.

Give yourself at least a day in the Uluru area; you could easily stay two or three.

Isolation (and a lack of competition) makes things like accommodations, meals and transfers expensive at Ayers Rock. A coach tour or four-wheel-drive camping safari is often the cheapest way to see the place. See "Exploring the Red Centre," at the beginning of this chapter, for recommended tour companies.

ESSENTIALS
GETTING THERE   By Plane   Qantas (© 13 13 13 in Australia) flies to Ayers Rock (Connellan) Airport direct from Sydney, Alice Springs, Perth, and Cairns. Flights from other ports go via Alice Springs. The airport is 6km (3¾ miles) from Ayers Rock Resort. Expect to pay around A$115 (US$75) one-way. A free shuttle ferries all resort guests, including campers, to their door.

Tips **The Rock in a Day?**

It's a loooong day to visit Uluru in a day from Alice by road. Many organized coach tours pack a lot—perhaps a Rock base walk or climb, Kata Tjuta/the Olgas, the Uluru-Kata Tjuta Cultural Centre, and a champagne sunset at the Rock—into a busy trip that leaves Alice around 5:30 or 6am and gets you back late at night. **Murray Cosson's Australian Outback Flights** (© 08/8952 4625; www.australianoutbackflights.com.au) does an aerial day trip from Alice Springs that includes flights over Kings Canyon, Gosse Bluff meteorite crater, and Lake Amadeus; a rental car at Ayers Rock; National Park entry fee; and lunch. It costs A$512 (US$332) per person (based on a minimum two passengers).

You should consider a day trip only between May and September. Other times, it's too hot to do much from early morning to late afternoon.

By Bus   **Greyhound Pioneer** (© 13 20 30 in Australia) makes a daily trip from Alice Springs (trip time: 5½ hr.), dropping you to your hotel door at Ayers Rock Resort. The fare is around A$71 (US$46).

By Car   Take the Stuart Highway south from Alice Springs 199km (123 miles), and turn right onto the Lasseter Highway for 244km (151 miles) to Ayers Rock Resort. The Rock itself is 18km (11 miles) farther on. (Everyone mistakes the flat-topped mesa they see en route for Ayers Rock; it's Mt. Conner.)

If you want to rent a car in Alice Springs and drop it at Ayers Rock, brace yourself for a one-way penalty. Only Avis, Hertz, and Thrifty have Uluru depots: Thrifty charges a one-way fee of around A$110 (US$72) for bookings under 3 days; Hertz charges A$137 (US$89) for bookings under 7 days; and Avis charges A$137 (US$89) for bookings of 2 days or less.

VISITOR INFORMATION   For information before you leave, contact the **Central Australian Tourism Industry Association (CATIA),** 60 Gregory Terrace, Alice Springs (© **08/8952 5800;** www.centralaustraliantourism.com), or drop in to its **Visitor Information Centre** if you visit Alice Springs. One of the best online sources is Ayers Rock Resort's site (**www.voyages.com.au**).

The **Ayers Rock Resort Visitor Centre,** next to the Desert Gardens Hotel (© **08/8957 7377**), has displays on the area's geology, wildlife, and Aboriginal heritage, plus a souvenir store. It's open daily from 8:30am to 7:30pm. You can book tours at the **tour desk** in every hotel at Ayers Rock Resort, or visit the **Ayers Rock Resort Tour & Information Centre** (© **08/8957 7324**) at the shopping center in the resort complex. It dispenses information on and books tours as far afield as Kings Canyon and Alice Springs. It's open daily from 7:30am to 8:30pm.

One kilometer (just over ½ mile) from the base of the Rock is the **Uluru-Kata Tjuta Cultural Centre** ℛ (© **08/8956 3138**), owned and run by the Anangu, the Aboriginal owners of Uluru. It uses eye-catching wall displays, frescoes, interactive recordings, and videos to tell about Aboriginal Dreamtime myths and laws. It's worth spending some time here to understand a little about Aboriginal culture. A National Park desk has information on ranger-guided activities and animal, plant, and bird-watching checklists. The Centre also has a cafe, a souvenir shop, and two Aboriginal arts and crafts galleries. It opens daily from early in the morning to after sundown; exact hours vary from month to month.

PARK ENTRANCE FEES   Entry to the Uluru-Kata Tjuta National Park is A$16 (US$11) per adult, free for children under 16, valid for 3 days. The cost of the pass is included in many organized tours.

ETIQUETTE   The Anangu ask you not to photograph sacred sites or Aboriginal people without permission, and to approach quietly and respectfully.

GETTING AROUND

Getting around the park is expensive. Ayers Rock Resort runs a **free shuttle** every 15 minutes or so around the resort complex from 10:30am to after midnight, but to get to the Rock or Kata Tjuta/the Olgas, you will need to take transfers, join a tour, or have your own wheels.

BY SHUTTLE   Uluru Express (© 08/8956 2152) provides a minibus shuttle from Ayers Rock Resort to and from the Rock about every 50 minutes from before sunrise to sundown, and several times a day to the Olgas. The basic shuttle costs A$35 (US$3) for adults and A$20 (US$13) for kids, while a sunrise trip costs A$40 (US$26) for adults and A$20 (US$13) for kids. To the Olgas it costs A$50 (US$33) for adults and A$25 (US$16) for children. A 3-day pass covering as many trips as you like to both sites costs A$130 (US$85) for adults and A$60 (US$39) for kids, while a combined Uluru and Olgas trip costs A$55 (US$36) for adults and A$30 (US$20) for kids. All fares are round-trip.

BY CAR   If there are two of you, the easiest and cheapest way to get around is likely to be renting a car. All roads in the area are paved, so a four-wheel-drive is unnecessary. Expect to pay around A$70 to A$95 (US$46–US$62) per day for a medium-size car. Rates drop a little in low season. Most car-rental companies give you the first 100km (63 miles) free, and then charge A30¢ (US20¢) per kilometer after that. Take this into account, because the round-trip from the resort to the Olgas is just over 100km (63 miles), and that's without driving about 20km (12½ miles) to the Rock and back. **Avis** (© 08/8956 2266), **Hertz** (© 08/8956 2244), and **Thrifty** (© 08/8956 2030) book four-wheel-drives through their Darwin offices. All rent regular cars and four-wheel-drives.

  Booking agent **The Outback Travel Shop** ⚘ (© 08/8955 5288; www.outback travelshop.com.au) in Alice Springs often has better deals on car-rental rates than you'll get by booking direct.

BY ORGANIZED TOUR   Several tour companies run a big range of daily sunrise and sunset viewings, circumnavigations of the Rock by coach or on foot, guided walks at the Rock or the Olgas, camel rides, observatory evenings, visits to the Uluru-Kata Tjuta Cultural Centre, and innumerable permutations and combinations of all these. Some offer "passes" containing the most popular activities. Virtually every company picks you up at your hotel. Among the most reputable are **Discovery Ecotours** (formerly Uluru Experience and Alice Experience), AAT Kings, Tailormade Tours, and **VIP Travel Australia** (see "Exploring the Red Centre" at the start of this chapter for details).

ABORIGINAL TOURS   Because **Anangu Tours** ⚘ (© 08/8956 2123; www. anangutours.com.au) is owned and run by the Rock's Aboriginal owners, its tours give you firsthand insight into Aboriginal culture. Tours are in the Anangu language and translated by an interpreter. They are not cheap, but if you are going to spend money on just one tour, this group is a good choice.

  The company does a **Kuniya** walk, where you visit the Kata Tjuta Cultural Centre and the Mutitjulu water hole at the base of the Rock, learn about bush foods, and see rock paintings, before watching the sunset. It departs daily at

---

Tips Water, Water . . .

Water taps are scarce and kiosks nonexistent in Uluru-Kata Tjuta National Park. Always carry your own drinking water when sightseeing.

2:30pm March through October, 3:30pm November through February. With hotel pickup, the tour costs A$84 (US$55) for adults and A$58 (US$38) for children. Self-drive and it costs A$52 (US$34) for adults and A$27 (US$18) for kids.

For an Aboriginal insight into the Rock without paying for a tour, join the free **Mala Walk** _(see "Walking, Driving, or Busing Around It," below); it discusses Aboriginal culture and is often led by an Aboriginal park ranger.

DISCOVERING AYERS ROCK/ULURU

AT SUNRISE & SUNSET   Sunset is the peak time to catch the Rock's beauty, when oranges, peaches, pinks, reds, and then indigo and deep violet creep across its face as if it were a giant opal. Some days it's fiery, other days the colors are muted. A sunset-viewing car park is located on the Rock's western side. Plenty of sunset and sunrise tours operate from the resort. A typical sunset tour is that offered by **AAT Kings** (© **08/8956 2171**), which departs 90 minutes before sunset, includes a free glass of wine with which to watch the "show," and returns 20 minutes after sundown; the cost is A$29 (US$19) for adults, A$15 (US$9.75) for children 4 to 14.

At sunrise the colors are less dramatic, but many folks enjoy the spectacle of the Rock unveiled by the dawn to bird song. You'll need an early start—most tours leave about 75 minutes before sunup.

CLIMBING IT   Aborigines refer to tourists as _minga_—little ants—because that's what we look like crawling up Uluru. Climbing this thing is no picnic—there's sometimes a ferociously strong wind that can blow you right off, the walls are almost vertical in places so you have to hold onto a chain, and it can be freezing cold or insanely hot. Quite a few people have died climbing the rock from heart attacks, heat stress, or simply falling off, so if you're not in good shape; have breathing difficulties, heart trouble, or high or low blood pressure; or are just plain scared of heights, don't do it. The Rock is closed to climbers during bad weather; when temperatures exceed 97°F (36°C) (which they often do from Nov–Mar); and when wind speed exceeds 25 knots, so climb in the stillness of early morning. _Warning:_ Wherever you go at Uluru and Kata Tjuta/the Olgas, bring lots of drinking water with you from the resort.

If that doesn't put you off, you'll be rewarded with views of the plain, Kata Tjuta/the Olgas, and Mt. Conner. The surface is rutted with ravines about 2.5m (8¼ ft.) deep, which demand scrambling. The climb takes at least 1 hour up for the fit, and 1 hour down. The less sure-footed should allow 3 to 4 hours all told.

Note: The Anangu do not like people climbing Uluru, because the climb follows the trail their ancestral Dreamtime Mala men took when they first came to Uluru. They allow people to climb but strongly prefer that they don't.

WALKING, DRIVING, OR BUSING AROUND IT   The easy 9.4km (6-mile) **Base Walk** circumnavigating Uluru takes about 2 hours, but allow time to linger around the water holes, caves, folds, and overhangs that make up its walls. A shorter walk is the easy 1km (just over ½ mile) round-trip trail from the **Mutitjulu** parking lot to the pretty water hole near the Rock's base, where there

Dinner in the Desert

Why sit in a restaurant when you can eat outside in the dust? Because you came to the Outback to be outside, that's why. Ayers Rock Resort's **Sounds of Silence dinner** ✦ makes outside eating a fascinating event. In an outdoor clearing, you sip champagne and nibble canapés as the sun sets over the Rock to the strains of a didgeridoo—played by a white man (the excuse is that didgeridoos don't come from this part of the world, but from Arnhem Land)—though there seem to be plenty of local Aboriginals who play. We hope you've zeroed in on people you want to sit with by now, because you head to communal white-clothed, candlelit tables and a serve-yourself a meal of kangaroo and barramundi (a large fresh-water fish). Last time I was here they served pretty poor pumpkin soup to begin, the main courses varied from bland to nice, and the Aussie wines were bad examples. However, after dinner, the lanterns fade, and you are left with stillness (apart from an occasional dingo looking for scraps). It is the first time some city folk have ever heard silence. Next, an astronomer points out the constellations of the Southern Hemisphere, and you have a chance to see the stars through telescopes. Sounds of Silence is held nightly, weather permitting, and costs A$120 (US$78) for adults and A$60 (US$39) for children under 15, including transfers from Ayers Rock Resort. It's mighty popular, so book 3 months ahead in peak season. Book through the Ayers Rock Resort office in Sydney (✆ **1300/139 889** or 02/9339 1040).

is some rock art. The **Liru Track** is another easy trail; it runs 2km (1¼ miles) from the Cultural Centre to Uluru, where it links with the Base Walk.

Make time for the free daily 2km (1¼-mile) **Mala Walk** ✦, where the ranger, who is often an Aborigine, explains the Dreamtime myths behind Uluru, talks about Aboriginal lifestyles and hunting techniques in days past, and explains the significance of the rock art and other sites you see along the way. The 90-minute trip leaves the Mala Walk sign at the base of the Uluru climb at 10am May through September, and at a cooler 8am October through April.

Before setting off on any walk, it's a good idea to arm yourself with the self-guided walking notes available for A$1.10 (US70¢) from the Cultural Centre (see "Visitor Information," above).

A paved road runs around the Rock.

Most companies offer base tours. As an example, **Discovery Ecotours** (formerly Uluru Experience) (✆ **1800/803 174;** www.discoveryecotours.com.au) conducts two guided base tours that give you an insight into natural history, rock art, and Dreamtime beliefs. Both arrive in time for sunrise: one is a 5-hour walk, the other is a 4-hour tour in a four-wheel-drive vehicle that incorporates short walks to the Rock base and a stop at the Uluru-Kata Tjuta Cultural Centre. Both include the park entry fee and breakfast, and cost A$105 (US$68) for adults and A$70 (US$46) for children 6 to 15. Admission is free for kids under 6 but their meals are not included. The 5-hour walk is not suited for kids under 10.

FLYING OVER IT   Several companies do scenic flights by light aircraft or helicopter over Uluru and/or Kata Tjuta/the Olgas, nearby Mt. Conner, the vast white salt pan of Lake Amadeus, and as far as Kings Canyon. Helicopters don't land on top of the Rock, however. As a guide to the flights available, **Professional Helicopter Services** (② **08/8956 2003;** www.phs.com.au) does a 12- to 15-minute flight over Uluru for A$95 (US$62) per adult, and a 25- to 30-minute flight for A$190 (US$124). Kids under 13 usually pay half-price (that depends more on their weight than on their age). You can drive to the helicopter site on a Harley-Davidson for A$50 (US$33) one-way and A$75 (US$49) round-trip.

MOTORCYCLING AROUND IT   Harley-Davidson tours are available as sunrise or sunset rides, laps of the Rock, and various other Rock and/or Kata Tjuta/Olgas tours with time for the Olgas walks. A blast out to the Rock at sunset with **Uluru Motorcycle Tours** (② **08/8956 2019**) will set you back A$135 (US$88) with a glass of champagne. They drive the bike, you sit behind and hang on. Self-ride tours are available, too, at a hefty price.

VIEWING IT ON CAMEL BACK   They say a soul travels at the same pace as a camel; it's certainly a peaceful way to see the Rock. **Frontier Camel Tours** (② **1800/806 499** in Australia, or 08/8956 2444) makes daily forays aboard "ships of the desert" to view Uluru. Amble through red sand dunes with great views of the Rock, dismount to watch the sun rise or sink over it, and ride back to the depot for billy tea and beer bread in the morning, or champagne in the evening. The 1-hour rides depart Ayers Rock Resort 1 hour before sunrise, or 1½ hours before sunset, and cost A$90 (US$59) per person, including transfers from your hotel. Each day between 10:30am and midday, you can visit the camels free of charge and take a short ride for A$10 (US$6.50) for adults, A$5 (US$3.25) for kids 6 to 12, or A$25 (US$16) for a family.

EXPLORING THE OLGAS

Although not everyone has heard of massive **Mt. Olga** ⭐ (or "the Olgas"), a sister monolith an easy 50km (31-mile) drive west of Uluru, many folks who have say it's lovelier and more mysterious, and I agree. Known to the Aborigines as Kata Tjuta or "many heads," the Olgas's 36 momentous red domes bulge out of the earth like turned clay on a potter's wheel. The tallest dome is actually 200m (656 ft.) higher than Ayers Rock. The Olgas are more important in Aboriginal Dreamtime legend than Uluru.

Two walking trails take you in among the domes: the 7.4km (4½-mile) **Valley of the Winds** ⭐ walk, which is fairly challenging and takes 3 to 5 hours, and the 2.6km (1½-mile) **Gorge walk,** which is easy and takes about an hour. The Valley of the Winds trail is the more rewarding in terms of scenery. Both have lookout points and shady stretches. The Valley of the Winds trail is closed when temperatures rise above 97°F (36°C).

WHERE TO STAY & DINE

Ayers Rock Resort not only is in the township of Yulara—it is the township. Located about 30km (19 miles) from the Rock, outside the national park

---

Tips Travel Tip

Most tourists visit Uluru in the mornings and Kata Tjuta/the Olgas in the afternoon. Reverse the order (do the Valley of the Winds walk in the morning and Uluru in the afternoon) and you'll find both spots a little more silent and spiritual.

boundary, it is the only place to stay. It is an impressive, contemporary complex, built to a high standard, very efficiently run, and attractive—all things you can end up paying an arm and a leg for. Because everyone either is a tourist or lives and works here, it has a village atmosphere—with a supermarket; a bank; a post office; a news agency; babysitting services; a medical center; a beauty salon; several gift, clothing, and souvenir shops; a place to buy beer; and a gas station. You have a choice of seven places to stay within the complex, from hotel rooms and apartments to luxury and basic campsites. In keeping with this village feel, no matter where you stay, even in the campground, you are free to use all the pools, restaurants, and other facilities of every hostelry, except the rather glamorous Sails in the Desert pool, which is reserved for Sails guests.

Ayers Rock Resort, Alice Springs Resort, and Kings Canyon Resort are managed by **Voyages Hotels & Resorts.** You can book accommodations for all three properties through the central reservations office in Sydney (© **1300/139 889** in Australia, or 02/9339 1040; fax 02/9332 4555; www.voyages.com.au). Ask about packages for stays at one, two, or all three resorts. *Warning:* Shop around for prices on the Internet and with travel agencies. My experience is that people staying here have paid a whole range of prices.

High season is from July 1 to November 30. Book well ahead.

A tour desk, same-day dry-cleaning and laundry service, and babysitting are all available at each hostelry and campground.

As well as the dining options below, the resort's small shopping center has the pleasant **Gecko's Café,** which offers wood-fired pizzas, pastas and sandwiches; a bakery; an ice-creamery; and takeout. Sails in the Desert, Desert Gardens, and the Outback Pioneer Hotel & Lodge can provide picnic hampers and breakfast backpacks. Kids under 15 dine free at any of the hotels' buffets in the company of an adult. It's a good idea to bring some wine with you because the place has really got things sewn up, including prices.

VERY EXPENSIVE

Longitude 131 👟👟👟 You can find this African-style luxury safari camp, with perfect views of Uluru, in the sand dunes a mile or two from the main complex. The camp, which was finished in June 2002, offers 15 top-class air-conditioned tents, each with a private bathroom and a balcony overlooking the rock. The resort is promoting them as "six star." (How long until we have a seven star, and an eight star rather than the usual five?) Whatever, A$9 million (US$5.85 million) on 15 tents makes them pretty expensive. A central facility, Dune House, houses a restaurant, bar, library, and shop.

Yulara Dr., Yulara, NT 0872. © **08/8957 7888.** Fax 08/8957 7474. 15 units. A$1,495 (US$941) per night, minimum 2-night stay. Tours, meals, and selected drinks included. AE, DC, MC, V. **Amenities:** Restaurant; bar; unheated outdoor pool. *In room:* No phone.

Sails in the Desert 👟👟 This top-of-the-range hotel choice offers expensive, contemporary-style rooms, many overlooking the pool and some with Jacuzzis (though watch your head on the glass doors leading onto the private balcony if you have one—I had a bruise for days). You can't see the Rock from your room, but most guests are too busy sipping cocktails by the pool to care. The pool area is shaded by white "sails" and surrounded by sun lounges. The lobby art gallery has artists-in-residence. The **Kuniya** restaurant serves elegant a la carte fine-dining fare with bush tucker ingredients; **Winkiku** is a smart a la carte and buffet venue; and the lively **Rockpool** (open seasonally) serves alfresco Thai fare poolside.

Yulara Dr., Yulara, NT 0872. ℂ 08/8957 7888. Fax 08/8957 7474. 232 units (6 with Jacuzzis). High season A$507–A$595 (US$329–US$387) double; A$894 (US$581) suite. Low season A$466–A$544 (US$303–US$254) double; A$830 (US$540) suite. Extra person A$36 (US$23). AE, DC, MC, V. Free airport shuttle. **Amenities:** 3 restaurants; bar; large unheated outdoor pool; 2 outdoor lit tennis courts; limited room service. *In room:* A/C, TV w/pay movies, dataport, minibar, hair dryer, iron.

EXPENSIVE

Desert Gardens Hotel ℛ   This is the only hotel with views of the Rock (rather distant ones), from some of the 84 deluxe rooms. The accommodations are not as lavish as Sails in the Desert, but they're as comfortable, and done up with elegant furnishings. In 2002, 34 new rooms were built, and in 2001 the existing 100 standard rooms were refurbished with new bathrooms, bedding, and carpets. The refurbished **White Gums** restaurant serves a la carte flame grill and buffet meals.

Yulara Drive, Yulara, NT 0872. ℂ 08/8957 7888. Fax 08/8957 7716. 218 units (100 with shower only). High season A$426–A$494 (US$277–US$321) double. Low season A$395–A$460 (US$257–US$299) double. Extra person A$27 (US$18). AE, DC, MC, V. Free airport shuttle. **Amenities:** 2 restaurants; bar; unheated outdoor pool; limited room service. *In room:* A/C, TV w/pay movies, minibar, hair dryer, iron.

Emu Walk Apartments ℛ   These bright, contemporary apartments have full kitchens, separate bedrooms, and roomy living areas, and are serviced daily. There's no restaurant or pool; but Gecko's Café and the market are close, and you can cool off in the Desert Gardens Hotel pool next door.

Yulara Dr., Yulara, NT 0872. ℂ 08/8957 7888. Fax 08/8957 7742. 59 apts. (all with shower only). High season A$426 (US$277) 1-bedroom apt; A$512 (US$333) 2-bedroom apt for 4. Low season A$395 (US$257) 1-bedroom apt; A$472 (US$307) 2-bedroom apt. Extra person A$36 (US$23). AE, DC, MC, V. Free airport shuttle. **Amenities:** Limited room service. *In room:* A/C, TV w/pay movies, kitchen, minibar, hair dryer, iron.

The Lost Camel ℛ   This AAA rated 3½ star hotel opened its doors in late 2002 on the site of the resort's demolished Spinifex Lodge, which once offered the best budget deals outside the campgrounds. It's aimed at young urbanites and is as bright, crisp, and modern as something you might find in Sydney's Darlinghurst. (Don't you just love that urban feel in the red dirt? You could forget you are in the Outback altogether.) The Red Camel offers lush courtyards and a generous swimming pool. Bang goes that budget though.

Yulara Dr., Yulara, NT 0872. ℂ 08/8957 7888. Fax 08/8957 7474. 99 units. High season A$385 (US$250) double; low season A$350 (US$228) double. AE, DC, MC, V. Free airport shuttle. **Amenities:** Bar; unheated outdoor pool. *In room:* A/C, minibar, hair dryer, iron, safe.

Outback Pioneer Hotel and Lodge   A happy, all-ages crowd congregates at this midrange collection of hotel rooms, budget rooms, bunkrooms, and dorms. Thirty new rooms were added in 2002, offering clean, simple accommodations with private bathrooms; these are cheaper than the hotel rooms but more expensive than the existing budget rooms. The budget rooms have double beds and bunks, and shared bathroom and kitchen facilities. By the pool, are plenty of lounge chairs, and there's also an Internet lounge. The **Bough House Restaurant** does buffets, and there is a dirt-cheap kiosk selling burger-style fare; but what seems like the entire resort gathers nightly at the great-value **Outback Pioneer Barbeque** ℛℛ. This barn with big tables, lots of beer, and live music is the place to join the throngs throwing a kangaroo steak or emu sausage on the communal cook-it-yourself barbie.

Yulara Dr., Yulara, NT 0872. ℂ 08/8957 7888. Fax 08/8957 7615. 125 units, all with private bathroom; 12 budget rooms without bathrooms; 30 budget rooms with bathrooms; 32 quad-share bunkrooms and 2, 40-bed single-sex dorms, none with bathroom. High season A$383 (US$249) double; A$184 (US$119) budget

> ### *Moments* When You See the Southern Cross for the First Time . . .
>
> Light pollution is extremely low out in the Red Centre, so the night sky is a dazzler. At the Ayers Rock Observatory, you can check out your zodiac constellation and take a 1-hour tour of the Southern Hemisphere heavens. (They're different from the Northern Hemisphere stars.)
>
> To visit the observatory, you must join a tour with **Discovery Ecotours** (formerly Uluru Experience) (© **1800/803 174** in Australia, or 08/8956 2563), which provides hotel pickup and a tour. Tours depart twice a night; times vary. It costs A$30 (US$20) for adults, A$22 (US$14) for children 6 to 15, and A$63 (US$41) for a family.

room with bathroom; A$162 (US$105) budget room without bathroom. Low season A$350 (US$227) double; A$172 (US$112) budget room with bathroom; A$152 (US$99) budget room without bathroom. Bunkroom bed A$40 (US$26), dorm bed A$32 (US$21) year-round. No children under 16 in bunkhouses unless you book entire room. AE, DC, MC, V. Free airport shuttle. **Amenities:** 2 restaurants; bar; unheated outdoor swimming pool. *In room:* A/C. Hotel and some budget rooms only: TV (w/pay movies in hotel), fridge. Hotel only: Minibar, hair dryer, iron. Phones in hotel rooms only.

INEXPENSIVE

Moderately priced cabins and inexpensive bunkhouse and dorm beds are available at the Outback Pioneer Hotel and Lodge, above.

Ayers Rock Campground   Instead of red dust you get green lawns at this campground, which has barbecues, a playground, Internet access, and clean communal bathrooms and kitchen. If you don't want to camp but want to travel cheap, consider the cabins. They're clean, modern, and a great value; each has a kitchenette, dining furniture, a double bed, and four bunks. **Thrifty** (© **08/8956 2030**) at Uluru rents a complete camping kit with sleeping bags, tents, cooking equipment, and so on, to its customers for A$36 (US$23) per day for two people; book it ahead. **Hertz** (© **08/8956 2244**) rents camping gear if you rent a large four-wheel-drive for a week or more.

Yulara Dr., Yulara, NT 0872. © **08/8956 2055.** Fax 08/8956 2260. 220 tent sites, 198 powered sites, 14 cabins, none with bathroom. A$148 (US$96) cabin for up to 6 people; A$24 (US$16) double tent site. Powered sites for motor homes A$15 (US$9.75) for the first 2 people, A$12 (US$7.50) for each additional adult, A$5.80 (US$3.80) for each additional child 6-15. Unpowered sites A$12 (US$8.20) for the first 2 people, A$11 (US$7.15) for each additional adult, A$5.80 (US$3.80) for each additional child. Family rate A$36 (US$23). AE, DC, MC, V. Free airport shuttle. **Amenities:** Unheated outdoor pool; coin-op laundry; small general store. *In room:* Cabins only: A/C, TV, fridge, no phone.

The Top End

by Lee Mylne

The "Top End" is a last frontier, a vast sweep of barely inhabited country from Broome on the west coast to Arnhemland in the Northern Territory and eastern Queensland. Most of it is in the Northern Territory, and the term is also used to differentiate the northern part of the Territory from the "Red Centre." It is a place of wild, rugged beauty and, sometimes, hardship.

The Northern Territory's capital, Darwin, is a small city, rich, modern, and tropical. Katherine is famous for its river gorge. Visit an Aboriginal community, canoe along lonely rivers,

and soak in thermal pools. To the east of Darwin is Kakadu National Park, home to wetlands teeming with crocs and birds; one-third of the country's bird species are here. Farther east is Arnhemland, a stretch of rocky escarpments and rivers owned by Aborigines and seen by few others.

Life in the Top End is different than elsewhere in Australia. Its slightly lawless image is one the locals enjoy. Isolation, the summer wet season, monsoons, predatory crocodiles, and other dangers make 'em tough up here.

1 Exploring the Top End

Read "Exploring the Red Centre," at the start of chapter 7; it contains information on traveling the entire Northern Territory.

VISITOR INFORMATION The **Northern Territory Tourist Commission (NTTC),** Tourism House, 43 Mitchell St., Darwin, NT 0800 (© **13 30 68** for trip-planning inquiries in Australia, or 08/8999 3900 for administration; www.nt holidays.com), can supply you with information on Darwin, Litchfield National Park, Kakadu National Park, Katherine, and other destinations in the Territory. The commission has a website tailored for international travelers at **www.australiasoutback.com**, and another at **www.ntexplore.com** for the self-drive market. It also publishes a helpful annual guide to the Top End that details many hotels, tour operators, rental-car companies, and attractions, and a separate fishing guide. The Commission's Territory Discoveries division offers package deals.

The **Tourism Top End** information center in Darwin and **Katherine Region Tourist Association** (listed in the "Darwin" and "Katherine" sections of this chapter) can supply information about the Top End in addition to their local regions.

WHEN TO GO Most folks visit the Top End in the winter **dry season** ("the Dry"). Not a cloud will grace the sky more than likely, and temperatures will be comfortable, even hot in the middle of the day. The Dry runs from **late April to late October/early November.** It is high season, so book every hotel or tour in advance.

The **wet season** ("the Wet") runs **November (sometimes as early as Oct) through March or April,** sometimes a few weeks longer in the Kimberley. While it does not rain 24 hours a day, it still comes down in buckets for an hour or two each day, mainly in the late afternoon or during the night. The land floods as far as the eye can see, the humidity is murderous, and the temperatures hit nearly 104°F (40°C). The floods cut off many attractions, sometimes suddenly, and some tour companies shut up shop for the season. Cyclones may hit the coast during the Wet, with the same savagery and frequency as hurricanes hit Florida. Many people find the "buildup" to the Wet in October and November, when clouds gather but do not break, to be the toughest time.

Despite that, many people love traveling in the Wet. Waterfalls become massive torrents, fork lightning storms crackle across the afternoon sky, the land turns green, cloud cover keeps the worst of the sun off you, crowds vanish, and there is an eerie beauty to it all. Keep your plans flexible to account for floods, take it slowly in the heat, and carry lots of drinking water. Even if you normally camp, sleep in air-conditioned accommodations now. Book tours ahead, because most will operate on a reduced schedule. See the tips about traveling in the Wet, below.

GETTING AROUND   The **Automobile Association of the Northern Territory (AANT),** 79–81 Smith St., Darwin, NT 0800 (© **08/8981 3837;** www. aaa.asn.au), is a good source of maps and road advice. See also the Northern Territory Tourist Commission's site at www.ntexplore.com, which is designed specifically for those setting out on a driving holiday.

The Northern Territory has no open road speed limit, but drivers should be careful to keep to a reasonable speed and leave enough distance to stop safely.

Most Aboriginal land is open to visitors, but in some cases you must obtain a permit first. If you are taking a tour, this will be taken care of, but independent travelers should apply to the relevant Aboriginal Land Council for permission.

Always carry 4 liters (1 gal.) of **drinking water** per person a day when walking (increase to 1 liter/¼ gal. per person per hr. in summer). Wear a broad-brimmed hat, high-factor sunscreen lotion, and insect repellent containing DEET (Aerogard and RID brands both contain it) to protect against the dangerous Ross River Fever virus carried by mosquitoes in these parts.

Deadly **marine stingers** (see "Bugs, Bites & Other Wildlife Concerns," in chapter 2) put a stop to ocean swimming in the Top End from roughly October to April or May.

TRAVELING IN THE WET   Some roads will be underwater throughout the Wet, while others can flood unexpectedly, leaving you cut off for hours, days, or even months. Flash floods pose dangers to unwary motorists. Don't cross a flooded road unless you know the water is shallow, the current gentle, and the road intact. Never wade into the water, because crocodiles may be present. If you're cut off, the only thing to do is wait, so it's smart to travel with food and drinking water in remote parts. Check road conditions every day by calling the **Northern Territory Department of Transport & Works's 24-hour recorded report on road conditions** (© **1800/246 199** in Australia); dropping into or

---

Tips   **Croc Alert!**

Saltwater crocodiles are a threat in the sea, estuaries, lakes, wetlands, pools, and rivers of the Top End—even well inland. They may be called "saltwater" crocs, but they live in fresh water, too. Never jump in the water or stand on the bank unless you want to be lunch.

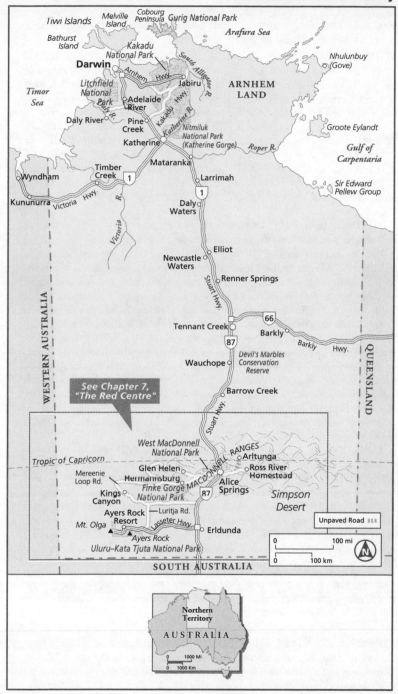

The Northern Territory

Tiwi Islands

Melville Island

Cobourg Peninsula

Gurig National Park

Arafura Sea

Bathurst Island

Kakadu National Park

Darwin

Litchfield National Park

Adelaide River

Daly River

Pine Creek

Katherine

South Alligator R.

Arnhem Hwy.

Jabiru

Kakadu Hwy.

Katherine R.

Nitmiluk National Park (Katherine Gorge)

ARNHEM LAND

Nhulunbuy (Gove)

Timor Sea

Roper R.

Groote Eylandt

Gulf of Carpentaria

Matarenka

Timber Creek

Wyndham

Kununurra

Victoria Hwy.

Victoria R.

1

Larrimah

1

Daly Waters

Sir Edward Pellew Group

WESTERN AUSTRALIA

Newcastle Waters

Elliot

Renner Springs

Stuart Hwy.

66

Tennant Creek

87

Barkly

Barkly Hwy.

QUEENSLAND

Wauchope

Devil's Marbles Conservation Reserve

See Chapter 7, "The Red Centre"

Barrow Creek

Tropic of Capricorn

West MacDonnell National Park

Glen Helen

Mereenie Loop Rd.

Hermannsburg

Finke Gorge National Park

MACDONNELL RANGES

Arltunga

Ross River Homestead

Alice Springs

Simpson Desert

Kings Canyon

87

Ayers Rock Resort

—Luritja Rd.

Lasseter Hwy.

Mt. Olga

Ayers Rock

Uluru–Kata Tjuta National Park

Erldunda

Unpaved Road

0   100 mi

0   100 km

N

SOUTH AUSTRALIA

Northern Territory

AUSTRALIA

0   1000 Mi

0   1000 Km

calling the AANT (above) in Darwin during office hours; or tuning in to the local radio stations as you drive. Local tour companies, tourist bureaus, and police stations should also be able to help.

TOUR OPERATORS Organized tours can bust the hassles posed by distance, isolation, and Wet floods in the Top End, and the guides will show and tell you things you almost certainly would not discover on your own. A loop through Darwin, Litchfield National Park, Kakadu National Park, and Katherine is a popular triangle that shows you a lot in a short time.

Reputable companies include **AAT Kings** (✆ **1300/556 100** in Australia, or 08/8941 3844; www.aatkings.com); **Odyssey Safaris** (✆ **1800/891 190** or 08/8948 0091; www.odysaf.com.au); **Sahara Outback Tours** (✆ **1800/806 240** in Australia, or 08/8953 0881; www.saharatours.com.au); **Adventure Tours** (✆ **1300/654 604** in Australia, or 08/8309 2277; www.adventuretours.com. au); and **Billy Can Tours** (✆ **1800/813 484** in Australia, or 08/8981 9813; www. billycan.com.au).

VIP Travel Australia (✆ **1800/806 412** in Australia, or 08/8956 2388; www. vipaustralia.com.au) does luxury organized and tailor-made tours.

Far Out Adventures ☆ (✆ **02/6557 6076** or 0427/152288; www.farout.com. au) does tailor-made four-wheel-drive safaris into Kakadu, Darwin, Arnhemland, Litchfield National Park, Katherine, the Kimberley, and more Top End regions. Proprietor/guide Mike Keighley will create a private adventure to suit your interests, budget, and time restrictions. Accommodations can range from luxury hotels to "under the stars" in Aussie bush swags. Touring with Mike can involve hiking, fishing, meeting or camping with his Aboriginal mates, canoeing, exploring seldom-seen Aboriginal rock art, taking extras like scenic flights, and swimming under (croc-free) waterfalls. Mike is one of a select group of operators with Australia's Advanced Eco Tour Accreditation and Savannah Guide status, and has a tremendous knowledge of the Top End's geography, Aboriginal culture, and ecology. Fun and personal, his trips are accompanied by good wine (sometimes in locations like a bird-filled lagoon at sunset) and "bush gourmet" meals.

Lord's Kakadu & Arnhemland Safaris (✆ **08/8979 2970;** www.lords-safaris.com) is based in Jabiru and operates charter tours throughout Kakadu and Arnhemland. Owner Sab Lord was born on a buffalo station in Kakadu before it was a National Park, and has a strong rapport with local Aborigines. His small-group 4WD tours, which can be tailor-made, visit the Injalak Hill rock-art sites in Arnhemland and the arts center at Oenpelli and have exclusive access to the Minkinj Valley. Day tours to Arnhemland cost A$165 (US$107) adults and A$130 (US$85) children under 14 and operate May to November. They also run tours to Jim Jim and Twin Falls.

2 Darwin

1,489km (923 miles) N of Alice Springs

Australia's proximity to Asia is never more apparent than when you are in Darwin. The northernmost capital, named after Charles Darwin, is an exotic blend of frontier town, Asian village, and modern life. With a population of about 90,000, Darwin has had a turbulent history—and it shows. This city has battled just about everything that man and nature could throw at it. Most of its buildings date from the mid-1970s, after Cyclone Tracy wiped out the city on Christmas Eve 1974. Don't bother bringing a jacket and tie here. Shorts and sandals will get you most

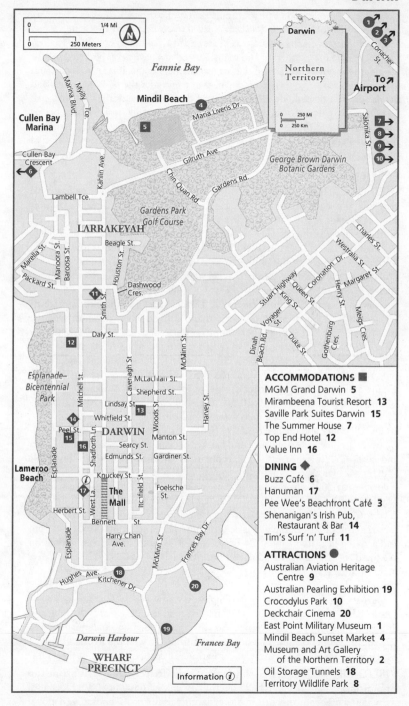

Darwin

Fannie Bay

Mindil Beach 4

Maria Liveris Dr.

Cullen Bay Marina

Cullen Bay Crescent 6

Lambell Tce.

Myilly Tce.

Marina Blvd

Kahlin Ave.

Gilruth Ave.

Chin Quan Rd.

Gardens Rd.

Gardens Park Golf Course

LARRAKEYAH

Beagle St.

Marella St.
Manoora St.
Baroosa St.

Packard St.

Houston St.

Dashwood Cres.

Smith St. 11

Daly St.

12

McLachlan St.

McMinn St.

Esplanade–Bicentennial Park

Mitchell St.

Cavenagh St.

Shepherd St.

Lindsay St. 13

Whitfield St.

14

Peel St.

15

16

DARWIN

Shadforth Ln.

Searcy St.

Edmunds St.

Woods St.

Manton St.

Gardiner St.

Harvey St.

Lameroo Beach

Esplanade

Knuckey St.

17

West La.

The Mall

Foelsche St.

Herbert St.

Bennett St.

Esplanade

Harry Chan Ave.

McMinn St.

Litchfield St.

Frances Bay Dr.

Hughes Ave.

18

Kitchener Dr.

20

19

Darwin Harbour

Frances Bay

WHARF PRECINCT

Information ⓘ

Darwin (inset map)

Northern Territory

0   250 Mi
0   250 Km

1
2
3

Conacher St.

To Airport

Salonika St.

7
8
9
10

George Brown Darwin Botanic Gardens

Charles St.

Westralia St.

Margaret St.

Stuart Highway

Queen St.

Coronation Dr.

Henry St.

Meigs Cres.

King St.

Voyager St.

Duke St.

Gothenburg Cres.

Dinah Beach Rd.

0   1/4 Mi
0   250 Meters

N

ACCOMMODATIONS ■
MGM Grand Darwin **5**
Mirambeena Tourist Resort **13**
Saville Park Suites Darwin **15**
The Summer House **7**
Top End Hotel **12**
Value Inn **16**

DINING ◆
Buzz Café **6**
Hanuman **17**
Pee Wee's Beachfront Café **3**
Shenanigan's Irish Pub, Restaurant & Bar **14**
Tim's Surf 'n' Turf **11**

ATTRACTIONS ●
Australian Aviation Heritage Centre **9**
Australian Pearling Exhibition **19**
Crocodylus Park **10**
Deckchair Cinema **20**
East Point Military Museum **1**
Mindil Beach Sunset Market **4**
Museum and Art Gallery of the Northern Territory **2**
Oil Storage Tunnels **18**
Territory Wildlife Park **8**

places—even the swankiest official state invitations stipulate dress as "Territory Rig," meaning long pants and a short-sleeved open-neck shirt for men.

Darwin is most commonly used as a gateway to Kakadu National Park, Katherine Gorge, and the Kimberley, and many Australians have never bothered to visit it—or at least not for long. And that's a real shame, because it is an attractive and interesting place. Give yourself a day or two to wander the pleasant streets and parklands, visit the wildlife attractions, and discover some of the city's rich history. Then take time for some wetlands fishing in outlying regions, or shop for Aboriginal art and the Top End's South Sea pearls. An easy day trip is **Litchfield National Park** 🐾🐾, one of the Territory's best-kept secrets, boasting the kind of beautiful waterfalls to swim under that you only see on holiday brochures.

ESSENTIALS

GETTING THERE   Qantas (℃ 13 13 13 in Australia; www.qantas.com) serves Darwin daily from most state capitals; flights either are direct or connect in Alice Springs. Qantas also flies direct from Cairns. **Virgin Blue** (℃ 13 67 89 in Australia; www.virginblue.com) flies to Darwin from Brisbane, with connections from Townsville, Sydney, and Melbourne. **Airnorth** (℃ 1800/627 474 in Australia, or 08/8920 4001) flies from Alice Springs via Tennant Creek and Katherine, as well as from Broome in Western Australia and Cairns in Queensland. There are also direct flights to Darwin from Asia.

Darwin Airport Shuttle Services (℃ 1800/358 945 in the Northern Territory, or 08/8981 5066) meets every flight and delivers to any hotel between the airport and city (including The Summer House and the MGM Grand) for A$7.50 (US$4.90) one-way or A$13 (US$8.45) round-trip. Children 6 to 13 pay A$4.50 (US$2.90), or A$8 (US$5.20) round-trip. Bookings aren't essential. A cab to the city is around A$25 (US$16). **Avis, Budget, Hertz,** and **Thrifty** have airport desks (see "Getting Around," below, for telephone numbers).

Greyhound Pioneer (℃ 13 20 30 in Australia) and **McCafferty's** (℃ 13 14 99 in Australia) both make a daily coach run from Alice Springs. The trip takes around 20 hours, and the fare is A$194 (US$126). Greyhound also has daily service from Broome via Kununurra and Katherine; this trip takes around 24 hours and costs A$226 (US$147). Both companies run from Cairns via Townsville and Tennant Creek, a 40-hour trip costing A$265 (US$172).

From early 2004, the opening of the long-awaited Alice Springs–Darwin railway line will give the Top End its first rail link. Great Southern Railway's *The Ghan* (℃13 21 47 in Australia; www.trainways.com.au) will run one weekly return journey between the two cities, leaving Alice Springs on Mondays at 4pm and arriving in Darwin about 24 hours later. The return trip leaves Darwin on Wednesdays at 10am. The adult one-way fare is A$480 (US$312) for a "day-nighter" seat, A$1,390 (US$904) for a sleeper, or A$1,760 (US$1,144) for a first-class sleeper.

Darwin is at the end of the Stuart Highway. Allow at least 2 long days, 3 to be comfortable, to drive from Alice. The nearest road from the east is the long and dull Barkly Highway, which connects with the Stuart Highway at Tennant Creek, 922km (572 miles) south. The nearest road from the west is Victoria Highway, which joins the Stuart Highway at Katherine, 314km (195 miles) to the south.

VISITOR INFORMATION   The official visitor center is run by **Tourism Top End,** Knuckey Street at Mitchell Street, Darwin, NT 0800 (℃ 08/8936 2488; www.tourismtopend.com.au). It is the place to go for maps, bookings, national park notes, and information on Darwin and other regions throughout the

Northern Territory, including Arnhemland, Katherine, and Kakadu and Litchfield National Parks. It's open Monday to Friday from 8:30am to 5:45pm, Saturday from 9am to 2:45pm, and Sunday and public holidays from 10am to 1:45pm.

CITY LAYOUT   The city heart is the **Smith Street pedestrian mall.** One street over is the **Mitchell Street Tourist Precinct** with backpacker lodges, cheap eateries, and souvenir stores. Two streets away is the harbor-front **Esplanade.** In the **Old Wharf precinct,** a walk from town, are a couple of tourist attractions, a jetty popular with fishermen and a working dock. **Cullen Bay Marina** is a hub for restaurants, cafes, and expensive boats; it's about a 25-minute walk northwest of town. Northwest of town is **Fannie Bay,** where you'll find the Botanic Gardens, sailing club, golf course, museum and art gallery, and casino.

GETTING AROUND   For car and four-wheel-drive rentals, call **Avis** (© 08/8981 9922), **Budget** (© 08/8981 9800), **EuropCar** (© 08/8941 0300), **Hertz** (© 08/8941 0944), or **Thrifty** (© 08/8924 0000).

Darwinbus (© 08/8924 7666) is the local bus company. Its 1-day Tourcard allows unlimited travel on the network until midnight for A$5 (US$3.25) adults, A$2.50 (US$1.60) kids 5 to 14. The city terminus is on Harry Chan Avenue (behind the Commonwealth Bank and Qantas buildings). Get timetables there, or from the Tourism Top End visitor center (see "Visitor Information," above).

The **Tour Tub bus** (© 08/8985 6322) does a loop of most city attractions and major hotels between 9am and 4pm daily. Hop on and off as you like all day for A$25 (US$16) for adults, A$15 (US$9.75) for children 4 to 12. It departs the Knuckey Street end of Smith Street Mall, opposite Woolworths. The **Territory Shuttle** (© 08/8928 1155) is a minibus service that picks you up and drops you off anywhere in the Darwin area—hotels, attractions, shops, the wharf precincts, the burbs, and so on. It will come by as promptly as it can when you call, or you can prebook it. It runs daily, usually 24 hours Wednesday through Saturday. The fares are low; a trip within the downtown area or out as far as the MGM Grand Casino and Mindil Beach Sunset Markets will set you back just A$2.50 (US$1.60) per person.

Darwin Day Tours (©1800/811 633 or 08/8924 1111) has a range of sightseeing tours.

Darwin Radio Taxis (© 131 008) is the main cab company. The starting rate is A$3.10 (US$2), or A$3.70 (US$2.40) on weekends and holidays. Taxi stands are at the Knuckey Street and Bennett Street ends of Smith Street Mall.

EXPLORING DARWIN

Darwin's parks, harbor, and tropical clime make it lovely for strolling in during the Dry. It's worth picking up the free map from the tourist office of a Historical Stroll of 17 points of interest around town. The **Esplanade** makes a pleasantly short and shady saunter, and the 42-hectare (104-acre) **George Brown Darwin Botanic Gardens** (© 08/8981 1958), on Gardens Road 2km (1¼ mile) from town, has paths through palms, orchids, every species of baobab in the world, and mangroves. Entry is free. Take bus no. 4 or 6; the buses drop you at the Gardens Road entrance, but you might want to walk straight to the visitor center (open 8.30am–4pm daily) near the Geranium Street entrance (open 24 hr.) to pick up self-guiding maps to the Aboriginal plant-use trails.

The pleasant 5km (3-mile) trail along **Fannie Bay** from the MGM Grand to the East Point Military Museum is also worth doing. Keep a lookout for some of the 2,000 wild wallabies on the east side of the road near the museum.

Darwin has two wildlife parks worth visiting. At the **Territory Wildlife Park** (℡ **08/8988 7200**), 61km (38 miles) south of Darwin at Berry Springs, you can take a free shuttle or walk 6km (3¾ miles) of bush trails to see native Northern Territory wildlife in wonderfully re-created natural habitats including monsoon rainforest boardwalks, lagoons with hides (shelters for watching birds), a walk-through aviary, a walk-through aquarium housing sting rays and sawfish, and a nocturnal house with marsupials such as the bilby. Bats, birds, spiders, crocs, frill-neck lizards, kangaroos, and other creatures also make their home here (but not koalas, because they don't live in the Territory). A program of animal talks runs throughout the day. The best is the birds of prey show, at 10am and 3pm. Go first thing to see the animals at their liveliest, and allow 4 hours to see everything, plus 45 minutes traveling time. Open daily from 8:30am to 6pm (last entry at 4pm), and closed Christmas. Admission is A$18 (US$12) for adults, A$9 (US$5.85) for students and children 5 to 16, and A$40 (US$26) for a family. Take the Stuart Highway for 50km (31 miles) and turn right onto the Cox Peninsula Road for another 11km (7 miles). If you don't have your own wheels, the cheapest way to get there is aboard the **Rainbow Down the Track and Back** (℡ **08/8948 4248**) bus service that runs direct to the park for A$25 (US$16) per person, round-trip, half price for kids under 5. It departs from the McCafferty's/Greyhound Pioneer coach terminal at 67–69 Mitchell St. (behind the Darwin YHA hostel). Call for schedule details.

In addition to housing a small crocodile museum, **Crocodylus Park** (℡ **08/ 8922 4500**), a 15-minute drive from town at 815 McMillan's Rd., Berrimah (opposite the police station), holds croc-feeding sessions and free, guided tours at 10am, noon, 2 and 3:30pm. It also doubles as Darwin's zoo, with exotic species including lions, Bengal tigers, and monkeys on display. It's open daily from 9am to 5pm (closed Christmas). Admission is A$22 (US$14) for adults, A$18 (US$12) for seniors, A$11 (US$7.15) for children 4 to 15, and A$57 (US$37) for a family of four. Take bus no. 5 (Mon–Fri only) or the park shuttle bus (℡ **08/8928 1100**) that costs A$35 (US$23) adults or A$90 (US$59) family for return transport from the city and park entrance.

The **Museum and Art Gallery of the Northern Territory,** Conacher Street, Bullocky Point (℡ **08/8999 8201**), also holds an attraction for crocodile fans— the preserved body of **Sweetheart,** a 5m (16-ft.) man-eating saltwater croc captured in Kakadu National Park. The museum and gallery is a great place to learn about Darwin's place in Australia's modern history. It has sections on Aboriginal, Southeast Asian, and Pacific art and culture, and a maritime gallery with a pearling lugger and other boats that have sailed into Darwin from Indonesia and other northern parts. A highlight is the Cyclone Tracey gallery, where you can stand in a small, dark room as the sound of the cyclone rages around you. Gallery and museum are open from 9am to 5pm Monday through Friday, and 10am to 5pm weekends and public holidays; closed Christmas, Boxing Day (Dec 26), New Year's Day, and Good Friday. The cafe has lovely bay views. Admission is free to the permanent exhibits. Take bus no. 4 or 6.

Darwin was bombed 64 times during World War II, and 12 ships were sunk in the harbor. It was an Allied supply base, and many American airmen were based here. The **East Point Military Museum,** East Point Road, East Point (℡ **08/ 8981 9702;** www.epmm.com.au), housed in a World War II gun command post, plays a video of the 1942 to 1943 Japanese bombings and has small but fine displays of photos, memorabilia, artillery, armored vehicles, weaponry old and new, and gun emplacements outside. Open daily from 9:30am to 5pm (closed Christmas and Good Friday). Admission is A$10 (US$6.50) adults, A$9 (US$5.85) seniors, A$5 (US$3.25) children, and A$28 (US$18) family.

Even if you are not a military or aircraft buff you may still enjoy the excellent **Australian Aviation Heritage Centre** ⚓, 557 Stuart Hwy., Winnellie (℃ **08/ 8947 2145**). A B-52 bomber on loan from the United States is the prized exhibit, but the center also boasts a B-25 Mitchell bomber, Mirage and Sabre jet fighters, rare Japanese Zero fighter wreckage, and funny, sad, and heart-warming (and heart-wrenching) displays on World War II and Vietnam. Hours are daily from 9am to 5pm (closed Christmas and Good Friday). Admission is A$11 (US$7.15) for adults, A$8 (US$5.20) for seniors and students, A$6 (US$3.90) for children 6 to 12, and A$28 (US$18) for a family. Guided tours are at 10am, 2pm and 4pm. The Centre is 10 minutes from town; take the no. 5 or 8 bus.

Empty **World War II oil storage tunnels** (℃ **08/8985 6333**) on Kitchener Drive in the Wharf precinct, house a collection of black-and-white photographs of the war in Darwin, each lit up in the dark. It's a simple but haunting attraction worth a visit. Admission is A$4.50 (US$2.90) per person. The tunnels are closed December 10 to 27. They open from 9am to 5pm daily May through September; October through April, hours are Tuesday through Friday from 10am to 2pm, weekends and holidays from 10am to 4pm.

On the Esplanade stands a monument to the destroyer **USS *Robert E. Peary*,** which went down in Darwin Harbour, with a loss of 88 lives.

Despite all this destruction, some of Darwin's historic buildings—or at least parts of them—have survived, and you can see them around the city center.

For an insight into Darwin's pearling industry, visit the **Australian Pearling Exhibition** (℃ **08/8999 6573**) on Kitchener Drive near the Wharf Precinct. It has displays following the industry from the days of the lugger and hard-hat diving to modern farming and culture techniques. It's open from 10am to 5pm daily, except Good Friday, Christmas, Boxing Day (Dec 26) and New Year's Day. Tickets cost A$6.60 (US$4.30) adults, A$3.30 (US$2.15) children, and A$17 (US$11) family of five. And if you've got an evening free, get out on the harbor with **Darwin Pearl Lugger Cruises** (℃ **08/8942 3131**). For A$46 (US$30) adults (kids half price), you can spent about 3 hours aboard the lugger *Kim,* built in 1953 and now restored to take up to 30 guests on sunset cruises, which leave Cullen Bay Marina daily at 5:15pm. They even throw in a free glass of bubbly and some nibbles, and you can buy more drinks.

The Top End's wetlands and warm oceans are **fishing heaven** ⚓. The big prey is barramundi. Loads of charter boats conduct jaunts of up to 10 days in the river and wetland systems around Darwin, Kakadu National Park, and into remote Arnhemland. The same company that runs Darwin's Tour Tub bus also runs the **Northern Territory Fishing Office** (℃ **08/8985 6333;** www.ntfishing office.com.au), a booking agent for a number of fishing charter boats offering barramundi day trips and extended wetland safaris, reef fishing, light tackle sportfishing, fly fishing, and estuary fishing. A day's barra fishing on wetlands near Darwin will cost you around A$250 (US$163) per person; for an extended barra safari, budget about A$420 (US$273) per person per day. If you simply want to cast a line in Darwin Harbour for trevally, queenfish, and barra, they will take you out for A$75 (US$49) per person for a half day, or A$135 (US$88) per person for a full day. They also rent skipper-yourself fishing boats and tackle. Check out **www.fishingtheterritory.com** for detailed information on fishing tours, guides and everything you need to know to make your arms ache from reeling 'em in!

THE DARWIN SHOPPING SCENE

Darwin's best buys are Aboriginal art and crafts, pearls, opals, and diamonds. For a good range of authentic Aboriginal artworks and artifacts at reasonable prices, check out **Raintree Aboriginal Fine Arts,** 20 Knuckey St. (© **08/8941 9933).** For a heavyweight investment in works by internationally sought-after artists, visit the Aboriginal-owned **Aboriginal Fine Arts Gallery,** on the second floor on the corner of Knuckey and Mitchell streets (© **08/8981 1315**). Its website at **www.aaia.com.au** is a useful guide to art and artists.

The world's best South Sea pearls are farmed in the Top End seas. Buy, or just drool in the window, at **Paspaley Pearls,** off Smith Street Mall on Bennett Street (© **08/8982 5515**). **The World of Opal,** 44 Smith St. Mall (© **08/8981 8981**), has a re-creation of an opal mine in their showroom. If you fancy a pink diamond (the world's rarest) from the Argyle Diamond Mine in Kununurra (see "Kununurra," in chapter 9), you can get them at **Creative Jewellers,** 27 Smith St. Mall (© **08/8941 1233**), an Argyle-appointed supplier that buys direct from the mine. They also stock the champagne diamonds for which Argyle is renowned and other Argyle diamond colors, as well as South Sea pearls and opals. They try to fashion pieces for overseas visitors in a short time frame to match your traveling schedule.

Jokes about "snapping handbags" abound in croc country, but for your own croc-skin fashion statement, head to **di Croco,** in the Paspaley Pearls building in Smith Street Mall (©**08/8941 4106**). You'll find bags, purses, wallets, card holders, belts, pens and other accessories, all made from saltwater croc skins farmed locally.

WHERE TO STAY

April through October is the peak dry season; hotels usually drop their rates November through March, which is the wet season.

VERY EXPENSIVE

MGM Grand Darwin ⍟ *Value*   Attached to Darwin's casino on Fannie Bay, this grand hotel is well priced for such an upscale place. The complex resembles a tropical palace with its white blocky architecture and 7 hectares (18 acres) of gardens on Mindil Beach, next to the Botanic Gardens. The rooms are a cocktail of European-style/contemporary Spanish furniture, and the tropical elegance of timber louvers and potted palms. All rooms have king-size beds and balconies. It's worth paying a little extra for an ocean-facing room in the dry season so you can watch Darwin's great sunsets. A longish beachside stroll brings you to the Museum and Art Gallery, and the Mindil Beach Sunset Markets take place right outside on Thursday and Sunday nights. A free shuttle runs four times a day to the city.

Gilruth Ave., Mindil Beach, Darwin, NT 0800. © 1800/89 1118 in Australia, or 08/8943 8888. Fax 08/8943 8999. www.mgmgrand.com.au. 97 units, all with bathroom. A$216 (US$140) double; A$324–A$700 (US$211–US$455) suite. Extra person A$44 (US$29). Children under 14 stay free in parent's room with existing bedding. AE, DC, MC, V. Free valet and self-parking. Bus: 4 or 6. **Amenities:** 3 restaurants; 3 bars; nightclub; outdoor pool; children's pool; access to nearby 9-hole golf course and 20 tennis courts; exercise room; Jacuzzi; sauna; concierge; tour desk; car-rental desk; business center; 24-hr. room service; massage; babysitting; free guest laundry; same-day dry-cleaning/laundry service; VIP suites. *In room:* A/C, TV/VCR w/pay movies, dataport, minibar, coffeemaker, hair dryer, iron, safe (suites only).

EXPENSIVE

Saville Park Suites Darwin ⍟⍟   Built in 1998 and renovated in 2001, this eight-floor hotel and apartment complex, a block from Smith Street Mall and overlooking the Esplanade, is one of Darwin's most comfortable, elegant lodgings.

> **Tips** **Where Can I Swim?**
>
> Crocodiles and stingers render Darwin's lovely beaches a no-swim zone year-round. Locals sunbathe on Casuarina Beach, and swim within view of the sea in **Lake Alexander** in East Point Reserve. About an hour's drive from the city, on the way to the Territory Wildlife Park, **Berry Springs Nature Park** has swimming holes along Berry Creek, with steps for easy access, and small waterfalls which create a natural Jacuzzi. They may be closed in the wet season.

Royal blue and turquoise lobby armchairs shout up-to-the-minute style, carried over in a more muted way in the rooms, which are mostly contemporary-style spacious studio, one-, two- or three-bedroom apartments. Those on the higher floors have sea views. A pantry-stocking service does your grocery shopping. "Premium" apartments have CD players and dataports, and you can request a video gaming station. There are also hotel rooms, lacking a balcony but still a good size.

88 The Esplanade at Peel St., Darwin, NT 0800. © **1800/681 686** in Australia, or 08/8943 4333. Fax 08/8943 4388. www.savillesuites.com.au. 204 units. A$180 (US$117) double; A$180 (US$117) studio apt; A$207 (US$135) 1-bedroom apt; A$317 (US$206) 2-bedroom apt; A$355 (US$231) 3-bedroom apt. Additional person A$28 (US$18). Children 14 and under stay free in parent's room w/existing bedding. AE, DC, MC, V. Free parking. **Amenities:** Restaurant; bar; outdoor pool; access to nearby golf course and health club; Jacuzzi; bike rental; concierge; tour desk; car-rental desk; business center; salon; limited room service; massage; babysitting; same-day dry-cleaning/laundry service (except Sun); nonsmoking rooms; executive level rooms. *In room:* A/C, TV w/pay movies, kitchen and laundry facilities in apts, minibar, coffeemaker, hair dryer, iron.

MODERATE

Mirambeena Tourist Resort   You're just a stone's throw from the city center at this modern hotel complex, where the tempting swimming pools, the Jacuzzis, and the treetop restaurant, all shaded by the leaves of a sprawling strangler fig, have a castaway island feel. Each room is a decent size and has some kind of garden or pool view. Town houses with kitchenettes are good for families, if you can handle sharing the compact bathroom with your kids.

64 Cavenagh St., Darwin, NT 0800. © **1800/891 100** in Australia, or 08/8946 0111. Fax 08/8981 5116. www.mirambeena.com.au. 225 units (all with shower only). High season (Apr–Oct) A$152–A$195 (US$99–US$127) double; A$230 (US$150) town house (sleeps 4). Low season (Nov–Mar) A$117–A$148 (US$76–US$96) double; A$180 (US$117) town house. Extra person A$25 (US$16). Children under 3 stay free. AE, DC, MC, V. Free parking for limited cars, plus on-street parking. Bus: 4, 5, 6, 8, or 10. **Amenities:** Restaurant; poolside cafe; 2 bars; 2 outdoor pools (in a single complex); children's pool; exercise room; 2 Jacuzzis; bike rental; game room; minigolf; tour desk; secretarial services; limited room service; babysitting; coin-op laundry; same-day dry cleaning/laundry service. *In room:* A/C, TV w/free movies, minibar (on request), fridge, hair dryer, iron, safe.

The Summer House ★★ *Finds*   A groovy, stylish tropical hideaway is a rare thing in the rough-and-ready Territory, but that's what Jill Farrand has created in her home in this converted apartment block. The place is in a leafy suburb 3km (2 miles) from town, on the local bus route, or a A$2 (US$1.30) shuttle ride away. Two roomy suites sport white walls, trendy polished concrete floors, and wrought-iron furniture (one has giant Balinese armchairs and 3m/10-ft.-high exotic flower arrangements), while a third has a retro look. All have louvered windows to encourage a breeze, hip mosaic bathrooms, and one or two bedrooms, a living area, and a kitchenette. Jill delivers a nice continental breakfast.

A Jacuzzi in the jungly garden is great for cooling off on hot nights. Gay and lesbian guests and children are welcome. No smoking indoors.

3 Quarry Crescent, Stuart Park (P.O. Box 104, Parap, NT 0820). © 08/8981 9992. www.interbed.com. au/summerhouse.htm. 3 units (all shower only). A$120 (US$78) double; A$160 (US$104) 2-bedroom apt (sleeps 4). Rates include continental breakfast. AE, MC, V. Free parking. Bus: 5, 6, 8, or 10. From the airport, take the Stuart Hwy. 5km (3 miles) to Stuart Park; turn left onto Woolner Rd., right onto Iliffe St., right onto Armidale St., and left onto Quarry Crescent. **Amenities:** Jacuzzi; coin-op laundry; dry cleaning by arrangement. *In room:* A/C,TV (apt only) kitchenette, hair dryer, iron, no phone.

INEXPENSIVE

Top End Hotel This two-story hotel has a quiet ambience, despite the trendy complex of bars, restaurant, sports-betting outlets, and a liquor store on one side. Most of the rooms face a rectangular saltwater swimming pool surrounded by an inviting lawn, sun lounges, and tall palms rather than the bar complex. The front desk sells breakfast and dinner meat packs for you to cook up on the barbie. Rooms were renovated in 2000, and each is a good size, with quality fittings and a furnished patio or balcony. You're just across the road from the Esplanade (where fish come in to shore at high tide to be hand-fed by visitors), close to restaurants, and a 1km (½-mile) stroll from Smith Street Mall.

Mitchell St. at Daly St., Darwin, NT 0801. © 1800/626 151 in Australia, or 08/8981 6511. Fax 08/8941 1253. www.bestwestern.com.au/topend. 40 units (all with shower only). Dry season A$132 (US$86) double. Wet season A$115 (US$75) double. AE, DC, MC, V. Free parking. Bus: 4, 5, 6, 8, or 10. **Amenities:** Restaurant; 3 bars; outdoor saltwater pool; tour desk; room service; babysitting; coin-laundry; same-day dry cleaning/ laundry service. *In room:* A/C, TV w/free movies, fridge, coffeemaker.

Value Inn *(Value* The cheerful rooms at this neat little hotel in the Mitchell Street Tourist Precinct are extremely compact but tidy, and have colorful modern fittings. Each room is just big enough to hold both a queen-size and a single bed, and a small writing table. The views aren't much, but you'll probably spend your time in the cafes along the street. Smith Street Mall and the Esplanade walking path are 2 blocks away. There is a public pay phone, cold drink and coffee vending machines, and an iron on each floor, and a very small garden swimming pool off the parking lot.

50 Mitchell St., Darwin, NT 0800. © 08/8981 4733. Fax 08/8981 4730. www.valueinn.com.au. 93 units (all with shower only). Dry season A$75–A$89 (US$49–US$58) double. Wet season A$65–A$69 (US$42–US$45) double. No charge for extra person. AE, MC, V. Limited free parking. **Amenities:** Outdoor pool; tour desk; dry cleaning; coin-op laundry. *In room:* A/C, TV, fridge, no phone.

WHERE TO DINE

Cullen Bay Marina, a 25-minute walk from town or a short cab ride, is packed with trendy restaurants and cafes. If it's Thursday, don't even think about eating anywhere other than the **Mindil Beach Sunset Market** . And on Saturdays head to the suburban Parap markets for Asian goodies (see the box, "Cheap Eats & More!" below). The cool crowd hangs at **Roma Bar,** 30 Cavenagh St. (© 08/ 8981 6729), for good coffee and cheap nosh; it's open from 7am to 5pm Monday through Friday, from 8am to 2pm Saturday and Sunday.

EXPENSIVE

Buzz Café MODERN AUSTRALIAN This smart, busy waterfront cafe is as well known for its loo-with-a-view as it is for its terrific food and relaxed atmosphere. The men's bathroom just nudges out the women's for interest value—ladies, get a man to take you in there to see what I mean—everybody does! The food is flavorsome East-meets-West fare like jungle curry of chicken with snake beans and green peppercorns, or pan-fried barramundi on potato mash in a lemon butter sauce; the lamb shanks are so huge almost no one can finish them. Wash it down with a cocktail.

The Slipway, Cullen Bay Marina. (© **08/8941 1141**. Reservations recommended in the Dry. Main courses A$17–A$30 (US$11–US$20). AE, DC, MC, V. Mon–Fri noon–2am; Sat–Sun 10:30am–2am (including brunch). Bus: 4 or 6.

Hanuman ✿ CONTEMPORARY THAI/NONYA/TANDOORI Elegant black walls and a moody Eastern atmosphere make this city restaurant popular as a business-lunch venue by day and as a rendezvous for couples, families, and more business folk by night. You can rely on it to serve up interesting dishes such as roasted duck in a red curry of coconut, fresh pineapple, kaffir lime, and sweet basil, or fish baked whole in banana leaves, Melaccan-style, with ground galangai, hot chile, lemon grass, and kaffir lime leaves. There is also a separate tandoori menu. Service is prompt and friendly.

28 Mitchell St. (© **08/8941 3500**. Reservations recommended. Main courses A$17–A$24 (US$11–US$16). AE, DC, MC, V. Mon–Fri noon–2:30pm; daily 6:30–11pm.

Pee Wee's Beachfront Café ✿✿ MODERN AUSTRALIAN Surrounded on three sides by forest, this modern steel-and-glass venue affords views of Fannie Bay from just about every table, inside, out on the deck, or down on the lawn. New owners—two chefs and a sommelier—have introduced a full a la carte service, and an extensive wine list that includes some older and hard-to-find Australian wines. The food has an emphasis on fresh local produce, and

---

Value **Cheap Eats & More!**

If it's Thursday, join the entire city at the **Mindil Beach Sunset Market** ✿✿ to feast at the 60 terrific (and cheap—most dishes are A$4–A$6/US$2.60–US$3.90 a serving!) Asian, Greek, Italian, and Aussie food stalls; listen to live music; wander among almost 200 arts-and-crafts stalls; and mix and mingle with the masseurs, tarot card readers, and street performers as the sun sets into the sea. The action runs from 5 to 10pm in the Dry (approximately May–Oct). A smaller market of about 50 stalls runs Sunday between about mid-May and late September from 4 to 9pm. The markets' season changes from year to year, so if you're visiting Darwin on the seasonal cusp in April or September, check whether they have started or ended by calling the organizers ((© **08/8981 3454**). The beach is about a A$7.50 (US$4.85) cab ride from town, or take bus no. 4, or call the **Territory Shuttle** ((© **08/8928 1155**), which charges A$2.50 (US$1.60) per person from downtown. The Tour Tub's last run of the day at 4pm (see "Getting Around," earlier in the chapter) goes by the markets.

On Saturday mornings, head to suburban **Parap Markets** ✿, which transform a small street into a corner of Asia as stall holders ply their wares. The focus is on food, with a sprinkling of arts and crafts, and it's a favorite place for locals to have breakfast or brunch, choosing from the southeast Asian soups, noodle dishes, and satays, washed down with fresh-squeezed tropical fruit drinks. The markets are only about a block long, on Parap Road in Parap ((© **08/8948 2373**).

some interesting tastes such as corned buffalo silverside. Some of the dishes have an Asian twist, and local fare includes kangaroo filet, Humpty Doo barramundi, or local shell scallops—try them sizzled in lime zest chile butter, with a marinated green papaw salad. Get there in time to watch the sun set.

Alec Fong Lim Dr., East Point Reserve (4km/2½ miles from town). ℂ 08/8981 6868. Reservations recommended. Main courses A$20–A$32 (US$13–US$21). AE, DC, MC, V. Daily 5pm–late and for lunch May–Oct only. Free parking. A cab fare from the city is about A$15 (US$9.75) or you can catch the 24-hr. shuttle bus.

MODERATE

Shenanigan's Irish Pub, Restaurant & Bar ⍟ IRISH PUB FARE   Hearty Irish stews and braised beef and Guinness pies (plus the odd pint of Guinness itself) gets everyone in the mood for eating, talking, and dancing at this convivial bar/restaurant. A friendly mix of solo travelers, families, seniors, and backpackers eat and drink in atmospheric wooden booths, standing up at bar tables, or by the fire. As well as hearty meat dishes, there is lighter stuff like salmon salad or vegetarian brochettes, and nightly specials, such as chicken and chile pasta or poached barramundi in white-wine sauce with fries and salad. Live bands on Wednesday, Friday, Saturday, and Sunday nights.

69 Mitchell St. at Peel St. ℂ 08/8981 2100. Reservations recommended. Daily specials A$9.50–A$14 (US$6.15–US$9.10). Main courses A$12–A$24 (US$7.80–US$16). AE, DC, MC, V. Weekdays 10am–2am; from 11am weekends.

INEXPENSIVE

Tim's Surf 'n' Turf ⍟ ⟨Value⟩ ⟨Kids⟩ STEAK/SEAFOOD   Locals fairly bash down the door to get into this unpretentious restaurant under a cheap motel on the city fringe. The surroundings are not the attraction, so what is? Hearty, no-nonsense food cooked well, and served in portions big enough to feed an army. No namby-pamby steaks here—Tim's are monsters up to 700 grams (25½ oz.), over an inch thick, and grain-fed (a boon in Australia, where the beef is mostly grass-fed and a little chewy). Garlic prawns, crocodile schnitzel, lasagna, oysters, quiche, and roast of the day are typical menu items. There are meals for kids, who eat free before 6:30pm (one kid for every adult in the party). You'll get a complimentary port after dinner and free ice cream for dessert.

In the Asti Motel, Smith St. at Packard Place. ℂ 08/8981 9979. Main courses A$7–A$21 (US$4.55–US$14) (many dishes around A$12/US$7.80); seafood platter for 2 A$35 (US$23); crocodile from A$13 (US$8.40). AE, DC, MC, V. Daily 7–9am, noon–2pm, and 5:30–9:30pm. Bus: 4 or 6; bus stop within 100m (328 ft.).

DARWIN AFTER DARK

Lie back in a deck chair at the **Deckchair Cinema** (ℂ 08/8981 0700; www. deckchaircinema.com) to watch Aussie hits, foreign films, and cult classics

---

⟨Moments⟩ Lizards & Sunsets

A good spot to catch Darwin's Technicolor sunsets is the supercasual **Darwin Sailing Club**, Atkins Drive on Fannie Bay (ℂ 08/8981 1700). Ask the manager to sign you in. Dine on affordable meals outdoors while a family of goannas (monitor lizards) swirls around your feet looking for meaty scraps. The bar is open from 10am until midnight, and until 2am Friday and Saturday. The cafes and restaurants of **Cullen Bay Marina** are a good place to be day or night, but especially for dry season sunsets. If it's Thursday, you are mad to be anywhere except the **Mindil Beach Sunset Markets** ⍟⍟ (see "Cheap Eats & More!" above).

---

under the stars. Movies are screened at 7:30pm Wednesday through Sunday in the Dry (Apr or May–Oct or Nov) with late sessions Friday and Saturday nights. It is on the beachfront opposite Parliament House on the Esplanade. Tickets are A$12 (US$7.80) adults, A$6 (US$3.90) children, and A$30 (US$20) family, and there's a bar.

The gaming tables at the **MGM Grand Casino,** Gilruth Avenue, Mindil Beach (© **08/8943 8888**), are in play from noon until 4am Sunday to Thursday, 6am Friday and Saturday. Slot machines are in play 24 hours. The dress regulation allows neat jeans, shorts, and sneakers, but men's shirts must have a collar.

A SIDE TRIP TO LITCHFIELD NATIONAL PARK 🦘🦘
120km (74 miles) S of Darwin

An easy 90-minute drive south of Darwin is a miniature Garden of Eden full of forests, waterfalls, rocky sandstone escarpments, glorious swimming holes, and prehistoric cycads that look like they belong on the set of *Jurassic Park*. Litchfield National Park is much smaller (a mere 146,000 hectares/360,620 acres) and much less famous than its big sister, Kakadu, but it is no less stunning.

The park's main attractions are the spring-fed swimming holes, like the magical plunge pool at **Florence Falls** 🦘🦘🦘, 29km (18 miles) from the forest. It's a 15-minute hike down stairs to the water, so the easily accessible pool at **Wangi Falls** 🦘, 49km (30 miles) from the eastern entrance, gets more crowds. (It's a beautiful spot, surrounded by cliffs and forests with a lookout from the top.) More idyllic grottos are 4km (2½ miles) from Florence Falls at **Buley Rockhole,** a series of tiered rock pools and waterfalls. You can't swim at Tolmer Falls, but during the Wet when they're flowing, take the boardwalk about 400m (1,312 ft.) to the lookout and see the cascade against a backdrop of red cliffs.

There are a number of short walking trails through the park, too, such as the half-hour Shady Creek Circuit from Florence Falls up to the parking lot.

Parts of the park are also home to thousands of 2m (6½-ft.) high **"magnetic" termite mounds,** so called because they run north-south to escape the fierce midday heat. There is a display hut and a viewing point 17km (10½ miles) from the park's eastern entrance.

Most of the park's swimming holes are regarded as crocodile-free; the same is *not* true of the Finniss and Reynolds rivers in the park, so no leaping into those!

To get there from Darwin, head south for 86km (53 miles) on the Stuart Highway and follow the park turnoff on the right through the town of Batchelor for 34km (21 miles). A number of minicoach and four-wheel-drive day trips run from Darwin. Katherine-based tour operator **Travel North** (© **1800/089 103** in Australia, or 08/8971 9999) runs a day tour to Litchfield that starts in Darwin and ends in Katherine, a convenient way to combine sightseeing and transport if you plan to visit both. It costs A$139 (US$90) adults and A$114 (US$74) children. Crowds of locals can shatter the peace in Litchfield on weekends, especially in the dry season, but the park is worth visiting, crowds or no crowds.

The **Parks & Wildlife Commission** office in Batchelor, on the corner of Nurdina Street and Pinaroo Crescent (© **08/8976 0282**), has maps and information; most locations of interest have signboards. Entry to the park is free.

Roads to most swimming holes are paved, although a few are accessible only by four-wheel-drive. In the wet season (approx. Nov–Apr), some roads may be closed, usually the four-wheel-drive ones, and the Wangi water hole may be off-limits due to turbulence and strong currents. Check with the Parks & Wildlife Commission before you leave Darwin during this time.

There are basic campsites at a number of locations throughout the park. The camping fee is A$6.60 (US$4.30) for adults, A$3.30 (US$2.15) for kids under 16, or A$15 (US$9.75) for a family of two adults and four kids, per night. A kiosk at Wangi Falls sells some supplies, but stock up on fuel and alcohol in Batchelor.

3 Kakadu National Park 🌟

257km (159 miles) E of Darwin

Kakadu National Park 🌟, a World Heritage area, is Australia's largest national park, covering a massive 1,755,200 hectares (4,335,344 acres).

Cruising the lily-clad wetlands to spot crocodiles, plunging into exquisite natural swimming holes, hiking through spear grass and cycads, fishing for prized barramundi, soaring in a light aircraft over torrential waterfalls during the wet season, photographing thousands of birds flying over the eerie red sandstone escarpment that juts 200m (650 ft.) above the floodplain, and admiring some of Australia's most superb Aboriginal rock-art sites—these are the activities that draw people to Kakadu. Some 275 species of birds and 75 species of reptiles inhabit the park, making it one of the richest wildlife habitats in the country. Kakadu is an ecological jewel. But be aware that the vast distances between points of interest in the park, and that sameness that infects so much Australian landscape, can detract from Kakadu's appeal for some people. Wildlife here is not the breathtaking equivalent of an African game park, where herds roam the plains, which is why even Australians get so excited when they spot a kangaroo in the wild. It is best in the late Dry around September and October, when crocs and birds gather around shrinking water holes. Wildlife viewing is not particularly good in the wet season, when birds disperse widely and you may not see a single croc.

The name "Kakadu" comes from "Gagudju," the group of languages spoken by Aborigines in the northern part of the park, where they and their ancestors are believed to have lived for 50,000 years. Today, Aborigines manage the park as its owners with the Australian government. This is one of the few places in Australia where some Aborigines stick to a traditional lifestyle of hunting and living off the land. You won't see them, because they keep away from prying eyes, but their culture is on display at a cultural center and at rock-art sites. Kakadu and the vast wilds of Arnhemland to the east are the birthplace of the "X-ray" style of art for which Aboriginal artists are famous.

JUST THE FACTS

VISITOR INFORMATION   Both the park entrances—the northern station on the Arnhem Highway used by visitors from Darwin and the southern station on the Kakadu Highway for visitors from Katherine—hand out free visitor guides with maps, and in the Dry they also issue a timetable of free ranger-guided bushwalks, art-site talks, and slide shows taking place that week.

Park headquarters is at the **Bowali Visitor Centre** (✆ **08/8938 1120**) on the Kakadu Highway, 5km (3 miles) from Jabiru, 100km (62 miles) from the northern entry station, and 131km (81 miles) from the southern entry station. This attractive, environmentally friendly Outback-style center shows a program of 1-hour videos on the park's natural history and Aboriginal culture, stocks maps and park notes, has a library and displays, has information officers on hand to help you plan your visit (they provide tour times, costs, and telephone numbers, but do not make bookings), and has a gift shop and a cafe. You may want to spend a good hour or so here, more to see a video. It is open daily from 8am to 5pm.

You can also book tours and get information at the **Jabiru Travel Centre,** Shop 6, Tasman Plaza, Jabiru, NT 0886 (℃ **08/8979 2548).**

Before you arrive, you can find information on Kakadu, and book tours to it, at the Tourism Top End visitor information center in Darwin. You can also contact the rangers at **Kakadu National Park** (℃ **08/8938 1120;** www.ea.gov.au/parks/kakadu).

WHEN TO GO   Kakadu has two distinct seasons: wet and dry. The Dry (May–Oct) is overwhelmingly the best time to go, with temperatures around 86°F (30°C) and sunny days. Many tours, hotels, and even campsites are booked a year in advance, so make sure you have reservations.

In the wet season, November through April, floodwaters cover much of the park, some attractions are cut off, and the heat and humidity are extreme. Some tour companies do not run during the Wet, and ranger talks, walks, and slide shows are not offered. The upside is that the crowds vanish, the brownish vegetation bursts into green, waterfalls swell from a trickle to a roar, and lightning storms are spectacular, especially in the hot "buildup" to the season in October and November. The landscape can change dramatically from one day to the next as floodwaters rise and fall, so be prepared for surprises, both nice ones (like giant flocks of geese) and unwelcome ones (like blocked roads). Although it can pour down all day, it's more common for the rain to fall in late-afternoon storms and at night. Take it easy in the humidity and don't even think about camping in this heat—stay in air-conditioned accommodations.

GETTING THERE   Follow the Stuart Highway 34km (21 miles) south of Darwin, and turn left onto the Arnhem Highway to the park's northern entrance station. The trip takes 2½ to 3 hours. If you're coming from the south, turn off the Stuart Highway at Pine Creek onto the Kakadu Highway, and follow the Kakadu Highway for 79km (49 miles) to the park's southern entrance. **Greyhound Pioneer** (℃ **13 20 30** in Australia) travels daily from Darwin stopping at Jabiru and Cooinda for A$84 (US$55) round-trip.

A big range of coach, minibus, and four-wheel-drive tours and camping safaris usually taking 1, 2 or 3 days depart from Darwin daily. These are a good idea, because many of Kakadu's geological, ecological, and Aboriginal attractions come to life only with a guide, and the best water holes, lookouts, and wildlife-viewing spots change dramatically from month to month, even from day to day.

FEES & REGULATIONS   The park entry fee of A$16 (US$10) per adult is valid for 14 days. Children 15 and under enter free.

LOGISTICAL TIPS   Kakadu is a big place—about 200km (124 miles) long by 100km (62 miles) wide—so spend at least a night. Day trips are available from Darwin, but it's too far and too big to see much in a day.

Most major attractions are accessible in a two-wheel-drive vehicle on sealed (paved) roads, but a four-wheel-drive vehicle allows you to get to more falls, water holes, and campsites. Car-rental companies will not permit you to take two-wheel-drive vehicles on unpaved roads. **Thrifty** (℃ **08/8979 2552**) rents cars at the Mobil service station, Lakeside Drive, Jabiru; otherwise, rent a car in Darwin. If you four-wheel-drive it in the wet season (Nov–Apr), always check floodwater levels on all roads at the **Bowali Visitor Centre** (℃ **08/8938 1120**). The Bowali Visitor Centre, many attractions such as Nourlangie and Yellow Water Billabong, and the towns of Jabiru and Cooinda usually stay above the floodwaters year-round.

Tips **Never Smile at a You-Know-What**

The Aboriginal Gagudju people of the Top End have long worshipped a giant crocodile called Ginga, but the way white Australians go on about these reptilian relics of a primeval age, you'd think they worshipped them too. There is scarcely a soul in the Northern Territory who will not regale you with his or her personal croc story, and each one will be more outrageous than the last.

Aussies may be good at pulling your leg with tall tales, but when they warn you not to swim in crocodile country, they're deadly serious. After all, crocodiles are good at pulling your leg, too—literally. Here are some tips:

1. There are two kinds of crocodile in Australia, the highly dangerous and enormously powerful saltwater or "estuarine" croc, and the "harmless" freshwater croc, which will attack only if threatened or accidentally stood on. Saltwater crocs can and do swim in the ocean, but live in fresh water.

2. Don't swim in *any* waterway, swimming hole, or waterfall unless you have been specifically told it is safe. Take advice only from someone like a recognized tour operator or a park ranger. You can never be sure where crocodiles lurk from year to year, because every wet season crocs head upriver to breed and spread out over a wide flooded area. As the floodwaters subside, they are trapped in whatever water they happen to be in at the time—so what was a safe swimming hole last dry season might not be croc-free this year.

3. Never stand on or walk along a riverbank, and stand well back when fishing. A 6m (20-ft.) croc can be 1 inch beneath the surface of that muddy water yet remain invisible. It moves fast, so you won't see it until you're in its jaws.

4. Plant your campsite and clean your fish at least 25m (82 ft.) back from the bank.

And if you do come face to face with a crocodile? There is little you can do. Just don't get into this situation in the first place!

Facilities are limited. The only town of any size is **Jabiru** (pop. 1,455), a mining community where you can find banking facilities and a few shops. The only other real settlements are the park's four accommodations houses.

SEEING THE HIGHLIGHTS
EN ROUTE TO KAKADU

En route to the park, stop in at the **Fogg Dam Conservation Reserve** (© 08/ 8988 8009 is the ranger station), 25km (16 miles) down the Arnhem Highway plus 7km (4⅓ miles) off the highway. You'll get a close-up look at geese, finches, ibis, brolgas, and other wetland birds from lookouts looking over ponds of giant lilies, or leading through monsoon forests to viewing blinds. There are two lookouts on the road and three walks, two at 2.2km (1½ miles) round-trip and one at 3.6km (2¼ miles) round-trip. Entry is free every day of the year. (Crocs live here, so don't swim, and keep well away from the water's edge.) Or take a ranger-guided walk, which you must book by calling ✆ **08/8988 8188.**

Four kilometers (2½ miles) down the Arnhem Highway at Beatrice Hill, you may want to stop at the **Window on the Wetlands Visitor Centre** (✆ **08/8988 8188**), a hilltop center with views across the Adelaide River floodplain and displays and touch-screen information on the wetlands' ecology. It's free and open daily from 7:30am to 7:30pm.

Just past Beatrice Hill on the highway at the Adelaide River Bridge (look out for the statue of a grinning croc), you can join the **Original Jumping Crocodiles cruise** (✆ **1800/888 542** in Australia, or 08/8988 8144) aboard the *Adelaide River Queen* to watch wild crocodiles leap out of the water for hunks of meat dangled over the edge by the boat crew. It's an unabashed tourist trap, and not to my taste, but because crocs typically only move fast when they attack, it may be your only chance to witness their immense power and speed. The 90-minute cruise departs at 9 and 11am, and 1 and 3pm May through August, and 9 and 11am, and 2:30pm September through April (closed Dec 24–25). A free shuttle runs from Darwin twice a day. It costs A$36 (US$23) for adults, A$29 (US$19) for seniors, and A$20 (US$13) for children 5 to 15. The souvenir shop sells all things croc, including crocodile toilet seat covers!

TOP PARK ATTRACTIONS

WETLANDS CRUISES   One of the biggest attractions in the park is **Yellow Water Billabong,** a lake 50km (31 miles) south of the Bowali Visitor Centre at Cooinda (pop. about 20). It's rich with freshwater mangroves, paperbarks, pandanus palms, water lilies, and masses of birds gathering here to drink—sea eagles, honking magpie geese, kites, china blue kingfishers, and jacanas, called "Jesus birds" because they seem to walk on water as they step across the lily pads. This is also one of the best places in the park to spot saltwater crocs. Cruises in canopied boats with a running commentary depart near Gagudju Lodge Cooinda six times a day from 6:45am in the Dry (Apr–Nov) and four times a day from 8:30am in the Wet (Dec–Mar). A 90-minute cruise costs A$36 (US$23) for adults and A$15 (US$9.75) for children 2 to 14. A 2-hour cruise (available in the Dry only) costs A$41 (US$27) for adults and A$17 (US$11) for children. Book through **Gagudju Lodge Cooinda** (p. 414).

In the Wet, when the Billabong floods to join up with Jim Jim Creek and the South Alligator River, the bird life spreads far and wide over the park and the crocs head upriver to breed, so don't expect wildlife viewing to be spectacular.

Another good cruise is the **Guluyambi East Alligator River Cruise** (✆ **1800/089 113** in Australia, or 08/8979 2411). The East Alligator River forms the border between Kakadu and isolated Arnhemland, and unlike the Yellow Water cruise, which focuses on crocs, birds, and plants, on this you will learn about Aboriginal myths, bush tucker, and hunting techniques. The cruise lasts 1 hour, starting at 9 and 11am, and 1 and 3pm daily May through October. A free shuttle will take you from the Border Store to the boat ramp. It costs A$30 (US$20) for adults and A$15 (US$9.75) for children 4 to 14.

ABORIGINAL ART & CULTURE   There are as many as 5,000 art sites throughout the park, though for cultural reasons the Aboriginal owners make only a few accessible to visitors. Dating the rock art is controversial, but it is thought some paintings may be 50,000 years old. The best are **Nourlangie Rock** and **Ubirr Rock.** Nourlangie, 31km (19 miles) southeast of the Bowali Visitor Centre, features "X-ray"-style paintings of animals and a vivid, energetic striped Dreamtime figure of **Namarrgon** ⚐, the "Lightning Man," and modern depictions of a white man in boots, a rifle, and a sailing ship. You'll also find rock paintings at **Nanguluwur**, on the other side of Nourlangie Rock, and a variety of excellent sites at Ubirr Rock, which is worth the 250m (820-ft.) steep climb for the additional art sites higher up the cliff, and for the views of the floodplain.

Ubirr Rock can be cut off in the Wet, but the views of afternoon lightning storms from the top at that time are breathtaking.

Unlike most sites in Kakadu, Ubirr is not open 24 hours—it opens at 8:30am April through November and at 2pm December through March, and closes at sunset. There is a 1.5km (1-mile) signposted trail past Nourlangie's paintings (short trails into the art sites shoot off it), an easy 1.7km (1-mile) trail from the car park into Nanguluwur, and a 1km (½-mile) circuit at Ubirr. Access to the sites is free.

Displays and videos of the bush tucker, Dreamtime creation myths, and lifestyles of the local Bininj Aborigines are on show at the **Warradjan Aboriginal Cultural Centre** ⚐ (© 08/8979 0051) at Cooinda. This building was built in the shape of a pig-nose turtle at the direction of the Aboriginal owners. There is also a quality gift shop selling items like didgeridoos, bark paintings by local artists, and baskets woven from pandanus fronds. The center is open daily from 9am to 5pm, and admission is free. It is connected to Gagudju Lodge Cooinda and the Yellow Water Billabong by a 1km (½-mile) long trail.

A SIDE TRIP TO THE TIWI ISLANDS

Separated from the northern mainland by a narrow strait are the Tiwi Islands, Bathurst and Melville. The Tiwi people have a separate culture from that of the Aborigines, and one of the main reasons for visiting is to see firsthand their distinctive art style. **Tiwi Tours** (© 08/8924 1111) take small groups on 1- and 2-day tours to Bathurst Island which include visits to two art centers where you can watch artists at work and buy their paintings, carvings, silk-screen printing, and basketwork at "island prices"—usually up to a third cheaper than buying the same thing in Darwin. You will learn the history of the islands, have morning tea with some Tiwi women and see them making baskets, and visit a mock burial site. The 2-day tour includes overnight camping. There is no commercial accommodations on the island, and the 1-day tour probably satisfies most people's curiosity. The 1-day tour costs A$298 (US$194) per person and the 2-day tour is A$564 (US$367). Both include round-trip light plane airfares from Darwin (it's about a 30-min. flight) and meals.

SCENIC FLIGHTS Scenic flights over the floodplains and the surprising rainforest-filled ravines of the escarpment are worth taking if the strain is not too great on your wallet. They're much more interesting in the Wet than in the Dry, when the floodplains spread and Jim Jim Falls and Twin Falls swell from their dry season trickle to a roaring flood. From the air is also the best way to appreciate the clever crocodile shape of the Gagudju Crocodile Holiday Inn. **North Australian Helicopters** (© 1800/898 977 in Australia, or 08/8972 2444) operates flights from Jabiru from A$80 (US$52), but to see Jim Jim and Twin Falls, you must take the flight costing A$420 (US$273) per person. **Kakadu Air** (© 1800/089 113 in Australia, or 08/8979 2411) runs fixed-wing flights from Jabiru and Cooinda for A$80 (US$52) per person for 30 minutes.

SWIMMING, FISHING & BUSHWALKING IN THE PARK

In the eastern section of the park rises a massive red sandstone escarpment that sets the stage for two waterfalls, **Jim Jim Falls** and **Twin Falls**. In the Dry, the volume of water may not be all that impressive, but their settings are magical. Both are accessible by four-wheel-drive only, and neither is open in the Wet.

WHERE CAN I SWIM?

Many people swim at spots that are generally regarded as croc-free, such as Jim Jim, Twin Falls, and water holes such as Gubara (it's a long walk to it, but it can be lovely in the Wet), Maguk, and Koolpin Gorge. However, you do so at your own risk. Although rangers survey the swimming holes at the start of the season, and crocodiles are territorial creatures that stick to one spot, there can never be an ironclad guarantee that a saltwater crocodile has not moved into a swimming hole. A good indication that the hole is croc-free is the presence of many other people already swimming in the water hole. Crocs tend to eat whatever's moving pretty much immediately, so if there are people swimming happily, the pool is almost certainly croc-free! Macabre it may be, but it's a tool many people use to gauge a pool's safety. Ask at the Bowali Visitor Centre which pools are croc-free that year (it can change from year to year) before setting off into the park. If you are unsure about a water hole's safety, the only place rangers recommend you swim is your hotel pool. Water hole depths change dramatically with the season. Check with the Bowali Visitor Centre for the swimming spots that are best at the time you visit.

A 1km (½-mile) walk over rocks and through rainforest leads to a **deep green plunge pool** ⋒ at Jim Jim Falls, 103km (64 miles) from the Bowali Visitor Centre. An almost perfectly circular 150m (492-ft.) cliff surrounds the water. Allow 2 hours to drive the final 60 unpaved kilometers (37 miles) off the highway. Due to floodwaters, Jim Jim Falls may not open until as late as June. **Swimming** ⋒ at nearby Twin Falls is great, too. The falls descend into a natural pool edged by a sandy beach, surrounded by bush and high cliffs.

Kakadu Gorge and Waterfall Tours ⋒ (book through Gagudju Lodge Cooinda; © **08/8979 0145**) run an excellent small-group day trip for active people. You bushwalk into Jim Jim Falls for a swim and morning tea, four-wheel-drive through the bush, and then paddle in a canoe past a "friendly" freshwater crocodile (the kind that does not typically attack humans) to Twin Falls for swimming and lunch. Tours depart daily from Jabiru and Cooinda May through November and cost A$135 (US$88) for adults, A$115 (US$75) for kids 4 to 14 (no kids under 4 allowed). Book in advance for July, the busiest month.

Kakadu's wetlands are brimful of barramundi, and there is nothing Territorians like more than to hop in a tin dinghy barely big enough to resist a croc attack and go looking for them. **Kakadu Fishing Tours** (book through **Gagudju Lodge Cooinda;** © **08/8979 0145**) takes you fishing in a 5m (16½-ft.) sportfishing boat. Tours depart from Jabiru, 5km (3 miles) east of the Bowali Visitor Centre, and cost A$120 (US$78) per person for a half day (A$190/US$124 if there is only one of you) and A$240 (US$156) per person for a full day. They will pick you up from your Kakadu accommodations.

Wide-ranging **bush and wetlands walking trails** lead throughout the park, including many short strolls and six half- to full-day treks. Typical trails include a ¾km (less than ½-mile) amble through the Manngarre Monsoon Forest near Ubirr Rock, an easy 3.8km (2½-mile) circular walk at the Iligadjar Wetlands near the Bowali Visitor Centre, or a tough 12km (7½-mile) round-trip trek through rugged sandstone country at Nourlangie Rock.

One of the best wetlands walks is at **Mamukala wetlands,** 29km (18 miles) from Jabiru. Thousands of magpie geese feed here, especially in the late dry season

---

Moments **A Swim in the Falls**

Remember the idyllic pool that Paul Hogan and Linda Koslowski plunged into in *Crocodile Dundee*? That was **Gunlom Falls,** 170km (105 miles) south of the Bowali Visitor Centre. A climb to the top rewards you with great views of southern Kakadu. It is generally regarded as croc-free and safe for swimming. Access is by four-wheel-drive; it is cut off in the Wet.

---

around October. An observation platform gives you a good view, and a sign explains the dramatic seasonal changes the wetlands undergo. Choose from a 1km (½-mile) or 3km (1¾-mile) round-trip meander. The Bowali Visitor Centre sells hiking-trail maps. There are also some challenging unmarked trails along creeks and gorges, for which you will need good navigational skills.

WHERE TO STAY & DINE

High season is usually from April 1 to late October/early November.

Gagudju Crocodile Holiday Inn 🛪 Some people think this hotel is grossly kitsch; others declare it an architectural masterpiece. I liked it. It was built to the specifications of its owners, the Gagudju Aborigines, in the form of their spirit ancestor, a giant crocodile called "Ginga." The building's entrance is the "jaws," the two floors of rooms are in the "belly," the circular parking lot clusters are "eggs," and so on. From the ground, it's hard to work out, but from the air the shape is quite distinct. Love it or hate it, it is the most luxurious place to stay in Kakadu; a stylish modern hotel with basic but comfortable rooms. Guests can access the town's nine-hole golf course, tennis courts, and Olympic-size swimming pool a few blocks away. The lobby doubles as an art gallery selling the works of local Aborigines, and a trail leads to the Bowali Visitor Centre.

1 Flinders St. (5km/3 miles by road east of Bowali Visitor Centre), Jabiru, NT 0886. © **1300/666 747** in Australia, 800/465-4329 in the U.S. and Canada, 0800/405060 in the U.K., 1800/553 155 in Ireland, 0800/322 222 in New Zealand, or 08/8979 2800. Fax 08/8979 2707. www.gagudju-crocodile.holiday-inn.com. 110 units. A$340 (US$221) double. Rates often reduced in the Wet. Extra adult A$33 (US$21). Children and teenagers under 20 stay free in parent's room with existing bedding. Free crib. AE, DC, MC, V. **Amenities:** Restaurant; 2 bars; small outdoor pool; tour desk; car-rental desk; secretarial services; limited room service; concierge; babysitting; coin-op laundry; laundry service. *In room:* A/C, TV w/free movies, minibar, coffeemaker, hair dryer, iron.

Gagudju Lodge Cooinda This modest but pleasant lodge set among tropical gardens is at the departure point for Yellow Water Billabong cruises. Simply furnished tile-floor bungalows are big and comfortable, and there are also "budget rooms"—just bunk beds (four have double beds) in an air-conditioned corrugated iron demountable (portable cabin) with shared bathrooms. They rent on a "per bed" basis, so you may share with a stranger.

The lodge is something of a town center, so there is a general store, gift shop, currency exchange, post office, fuel, and other useful facilities. Cook up a 'roo steak in the nightly do-it-yourself barbecue in the rustic and ultracasual Barra Bar & Bistro, or go for the bush tucker a la carte meals at lunch or dinner in **Mimi's** 🛪, which has a nice "bush-sophisticated" ambience. The **Barra Bistro** does full buffet breakfast and an all-day snack menu, with live entertainment in the dry season. Scenic flights take off from the lodge's airstrip, and the Warradjan Aboriginal Cultural Centre is a 15-minute walk away.

Kakadu Hwy. (50km/31 miles south of Bowali Visitor Centre), Jim Jim, NT 0886. Ⓒ **1800/500 401** in Australia, 800/835-7742 in the U.S. and Canada, 0800/897 121 in the U.K., 1800/553 155 in Ireland, 0800/801 111 in New Zealand, or 08/8979 0145. Fax 08/8979 0148. www.sphc.com.au. 48 lodge units (all with shower only), 24 budget rooms (none with bathroom), 80 powered and 300 unpowered campsites. Lodge room A$198 (US$129) double. Extra person A$28 (US$18); children under 14 stay free. Budget room A$31 (US$20) per bed. A$13 (US$8.45) per adult, powered campsite; A$10 (US$6.50) per adult, unpowered campsite. Children under 14 stay free in campsite. Rates in bungalows and budget rooms are often reduced in the wet season. AE, DC, MC, V. **Amenities:** Small outdoor pool; tour desk; babysitting; coin-op laundry. *In room* (lodge rooms only): A/C and ceiling fans, TV, fridge, coffeemaker, hair dryers (on request), iron, free cots and rollaway beds.

4 Katherine

314km (195 miles) S of Darwin; 512km (317 miles) E of Kununurra; 1,177km (730 miles) N of Alice Springs

The key draw to the farming town of Katherine (pop. 11,000) is Katherine (Nitmiluk) Gorge. It's small by the standards of, say, the Grand Canyon, but its dramatic sheer orange walls dropping to a blue-green river make it an unexpected delight in the middle of the dry Arnhemland plateau that stretches to the horizon.

The gorge and its surrounding river ecosystem are located in the 292,008-hectare (721,260-acre) **Nitmiluk National Park.** In the Dry, the gorge is a haven not just for cruisers but for canoeists, who must dodge the odd "friendly" freshwater crocodile as they paddle between its walls. In the Wet, the gorge can become a torrent at times, and jet boating is sometimes the only way to tackle it. Hikers will find trails any time of year throughout the park. Farther afield are hot springs, water holes, uncrowded rivers to canoe, and Aboriginal communities where visitors can make dot paintings and find bush tucker.

ESSENTIALS
GETTING THERE   Airnorth (Ⓒ **1800/627 474** in Australia, or 08/8920 4000) flies from Darwin, and from Alice Springs via Tennant Creek.

McCafferty's (Ⓒ **13 14 99** in Australia) and **Greyhound Pioneer** (Ⓒ **13 20 30** in Australia) stop in Katherine on their Darwin–Alice Springs routes, which both companies run twice a day. It's about a 4½-hour trip from Darwin, costing A$52 (US$34); from Alice it's about a 15-hour journey for which the fare is A$179 (US$116). Greyhound also calls daily from Broome via Kununurra; a journey of about 19 hours costs A$226 (US$147).

Beginning in early 2004, visitors to Katherine can hop aboard *The Ghan* (see "Getting Around" in chapter 2) in Adelaide or Alice Springs and hop off in Katherine. The train leaves Adelaide on Sundays at 5:15pm and Alice Springs on Mondays at 4pm. The trip from Alice takes about 16 hours and costs A$480 (US$312) for a "day-nighter" seat or A$1,760 to A$2,200 (US$1,144–US$1,430) for a sleeper. Contact **Great Southern Railways** (Ⓒ **13 21 47** in Australia; www.trainways.com.au) for details on connections from Sydney and Melbourne.

Katherine is on the Stuart Highway, which links Darwin and Alice Springs. From Alice Springs, allow a good 2 days to make the drive. The Victoria Highway links Katherine with Kununurra to the west. There is no direct route from the east; from, say, Cairns, you need to go via Townsville, Mt. Isa, and Tennant Creek, a long and dull journey.

VISITOR INFORMATION   The **Katherine Visitor Information Centre,** Lindsay Street at Katherine Terrace, Katherine, NT 0850 (Ⓒ **1800/653 142** or 08/8972 2650; www.krta.com.au), has information on things to see—not only all around Katherine, but as far afield as Kakadu National Park and the Kimberley. It's open Monday through Friday from 8:30am to 6pm and weekends from 10am to 3pm in the Dry season; in the Wet it's open Monday through Friday from 9am to 5pm.

The **Nitmiluk Visitor Centre** (© 08/8972 1886) on the Gorge Road, 32km (20 miles) from town, dispenses information on the Nitmiluk National Park and sells tickets for gorge cruises, which depart outside. The Centre has maps; displays on the park's plant life, birds, geology, and Aboriginal history; a gift shop; and a cafe. It's open daily from 7am to 7pm, sometimes closing a little earlier in the Wet. Entry to the park is free.

GETTING AROUND Budget (© 08/8971 1333), Hertz (© 08/8971 1111), Europcar (© 08/8971 2777), and Thrifty (© 08/8972 3183) have outlets in Katherine.

Travel North (© 1800/089 103 in Australia, or 08/8971 9999) makes transfers from Katherine hotels to the cruise, canoe, and helicopter departure points at the Nitmiluk Visitor Centre four times a day. Round-trip fares are A$20 (US$13) per adult or A$10 (US$6.50) for children. Most Katherine activities and attractions can be booked through Travel North. The company runs many local tours and activities such as horseback cattle musters, visits to an old homestead, half-day trips to Mataranka Thermal Pools (see below), and tour packages of up to 5 days taking in Katherine, Darwin, Litchfield and Kakadu National Parks, and outlying Aboriginal communities.

For personalized tours both off the beaten path and around town, contact **Far Out Adventures** ☆ (© 0427 152288), described below.

EXPLORING KATHERINE GORGE (NITMILUK NATIONAL PARK)

Cruising the gorge in an **open-sided boat** is the most popular way to appreciate its beauty. Katherine Gorge is actually a series of 13 gorges, but most cruises ply only the first two, because the second gorge is the most photogenic.

Travel North (above) operates all cruises. Most people take the 2-hour cruise, which departs four times a day and costs A$40 (US$26) for adults and A$15 (US$9.75) for children 5 to 15. There is also a 4-hour cruise at least once daily, although you will probably be satisfied with 2 hours, and an 8-hour cruise/hike safari to the fifth gorge (available from about May–Oct only). Wear sturdy shoes; because each gorge is cut off from the next by rapids, all the cruises involve some walking along the bank to transfer to a boat in the next gorge.

In the height of the wet season, the cruises may not operate when the floodwaters really start to swirl. Instead, Travel North runs a **jet boat** as far as the third gorge. This 45-minute adventure costs A$47 (US$31) for adults and A$34 (US$22) for kids 5 to 15. Departure times vary with the floodwater conditions.

Cruising is nice, but in a **canoe** ☆ you can discover sandy banks and waterfalls, and get up close to the gorge walls, the birds, and those crocs. (Don't worry, they're the freshwater kind that are not typically regarded as dangerous to humans.) The gorges are separated by rocks, so be prepared to carry your canoe quite often. You may even want to camp out on the banks overnight. A half-day canoe rental from Travel North is A$31 (US$20) for a single canoe and A$47 (US$31) for a double, with a A$20 (US$13) cash deposit. Canoeing the gorge is popular, so book canoes ahead, especially in the dry season.

Guided paddles are a good idea as you will learn and see more. The most knowledgeable company is **Gecko Canoeing** ☆ (© 1800/634 319 in Australia, or 08/8972 2224; www.geckocanoeing.com.au), whose tours are known for their ecotourism content. Gecko's founder, Martin "Snowy" Wohling, and three other Gecko guides have Australia's elite "Savannah Guide" ecotour guide status. They do 3- to 5-day canoeing/camping safaris on the Katherine River, but also run a 1-day canoe safari at a cost of A$178 (US$116) per person. The company also runs canoeing and camping safaris (with any other activities you like thrown in such as mountain biking, rock climbing, wildlife photography, hiking, or fishing) of up to 18 days in little-explored wildernesses and river systems across the Top End. Tours only run between April and November, with departures on request, and can be tailored to your needs.

Some 100km (62 miles) of **hiking trails** crisscross Nitmiluk National Park, ranging in duration from 1 hour to the lookout to 5 days to Edith Falls (see below). Trails—through rocky terrain and forests, past water holes and along the gorge—depart the Nitmiluk National Park ranger station, located in the Nitmiluk Visitor Centre, where you can pick up trail maps. Overnight walks require a deposit of between A$20 and $50 (US$13 and US$33) per person, and a A$3.30 (US$2.15) per-person camping permit, payable at the Nitmiluk Visitor Centre.

One of the nicest spots in the Park is actually 42km (26 miles) north of Katherine, 20km (12½ miles) off the Stuart Highway. **Edith Falls** ⚓ is a real Eden of natural (croc-free) swimming holes bordered by red cliffs, monsoonal forest, and pandanus palms. Among the couple of bushwalks leading from the Falls is a 2.6km (1½-mile) round-trip trail, which takes about 2 hours, and incorporates a dip at the upper pool en route.

More than the gorge itself, the aerial views of the ravine-ridden Arnhem Plateau, which stretches uninhabited to the horizon, are arresting. **North Australian Helicopters** (ⓒ **1800/089 103** in Australia, or 08/8972 1253) does daily flights of 3, 8, and all 13 gorges for between A$60 and A$150 (US$39 and US$98) per person, adult or child. Take at least an eight-gorge flight to get a sense of Australia's wild vastness. In the Wet it also makes flights from Katherine to see Jim Jim Falls in Kakadu National Park.

ABORIGINAL CULTURE TOURS, HOT SPRINGS & MORE

On a 1-day visit to the **Manyallaluk Aboriginal community** ⚓, a 90-minute drive southeast from Katherine, you chat with Aborigines about how they balance traditional ways with modern living; take a short bushwalk to look for native medicines and bush tucker like green ants (they're refreshing!); try lighting a fire with two sticks, weaving baskets, throwing spears, painting on bark, and playing a didgeridoo; take a dip in a natural water hole; and buy locally made Aboriginal art and artifacts at better prices than you may find elsewhere. Lunch is a barbecue featuring stuff like high-grade kangaroo filet, kangaroo tail, Scotch filet steak, or barramundi cooked on hot coals. Some visitors rush into these tours and expect the community to be a kind of Aboriginal Disney World theme park with a new attraction every 10 minutes, but that's not how it is. It's an unstructured experience (this is the community's home), so it's up to you to take part. A 1-day tour from Katherine costs A$143 (US$93) for adults and A$79 (US$51) for children 5 to 15, or A$110 (US$72) adults and A$67 (US$44) for kids if you drive yourself. There are basic camping facilities including tent sites and powered and unpowered sites. The last 35km (22 miles) of road is unsealed (unpaved), for which rental cars will be insured only if they are four-wheel-drive. The tour runs Monday through Friday in July and August, and Monday, Wednesday, and Friday from October to mid-December, but hours may be reduced, or the place may close, in the Wet. Call ahead before setting off no matter what the time of year, as sometimes the place closes for cultural reasons. Call Manyallaluk—The Dreaming Place (© **08/8975 4727**), or book through Travel North, above.

About 110km (68 miles) south of Katherine, you can soak your aches away at the **Mataranka Thermal Pools.** This man-made pool is fed by 93°F (34°C) spring water, which bubbles up from the earth naturally at a rate of 16,495 liters (4,124 gal.) per minute! It's a little paradise, surrounded by palms, pandanus, and a colony of flying foxes. The pools are open 24 hours and admission is free. They are 7km (4⅓ miles) along Homestead Road, which is off the Stuart Highway 1½km (1 mile) south of Mataranka township. They make a welcome stop on the very long drive from Alice Springs.

If you can't be bothered driving to Mataranka, you can soak in the pleasantly warm **Katherine Hot Springs,** under shady trees 3km (2 miles) from town on Riverbank Drive. Entry is free. At the **School of the Air,** Giles Street (© **08/ 8972 1833**), you can sit in on an 800,000-sq.-km (312,000-sq.-mile) "classroom" as children from the Outback do their lessons by radio. Forty-five-minute tours begin on the hour from 9am up to and including 2pm (there's no tour at noon). Tours also run during school holidays and public holidays minus the on-air classes. The school is open Monday through Friday from 9am to 3pm from April until December. Admission is A$5 (US$3.25) for adults and A$2 (US$1.30) for school-age kids.

Mike Keighley of **Far Out Adventures** (© **0427/152288**) runs upmarket tailor-made tours which include areas around Katherine such as the 5,000-sq.-km. (1,930-sq.-mile or 1.2 million acres) Elsey Cattle Station, 140km (87 miles) southeast of Katherine, made famous as the setting of the Aussie book and film *We of the Never Never.* Meet children of the Mangarrayi Aborigines, sample bush tucker, learn a little bush medicine, and swim in a vine-clad natural "spa-pool" in the Roper River. Mike has been accepted as an honorary family member of the Mangarrayi people and is a mine of information about Aboriginal culture and the bush.

WHERE TO STAY

The Nitmiluk National Park ranger station in the Nitmiluk Visitor Centre has maps of available "bush campsites" throughout the park. These are very basic sites—no showers, no soaps or shampoos allowed because they pollute the river system, and simple pit toilets or none at all. Most are beside natural swimming holes. You must stop for a camping permit from the ranger station beforehand; the camping fee is A$3.30 (US$2.15) per person per night.

Travel North runs the **Nitmiluk Gorge Caravan Park** (© **1800/089 103** in Australia, or 08/8972 1253; fax 08/8972 3989) next to the Nitmiluk Visitor Centre, where wallabies often hop into the grounds. Fees are A$8.50 (US$5.50) per adult, A$5 (US$3.25) per child for a tent site, and A$21 (US$14) double for a powered site.

Knotts Crossing Resort   At this low-key resort, you have a choice of huge, well-furnished motel rooms, some with kitchenettes, minibars, and in-room dataports and fax machines; cabins with a kitchenette inside and their own private bathrooms just outside the door; or campgrounds, all located among the tropical landscaping. The "village" rooms are a good penny-wise choice, built in 1998 and smartly furnished with a double bed and bunks, a kitchenette, and joint veranda facing a small private pool with a barbecue. Locals meet at the casual bar beside the pool, and Katie's Bistro is one of the smartest places to eat in town.

Corner Giles and Cameron sts., Katherine, NT 0850. © **1800/222 511** in Australia, or 08/8972 2511. Fax 08/ 8972 2628. www.knottscrossing.com.au. 123 units (some with shower only; cabins have adjacent private bathroom), 75 powered and unpowered campsites. A$75 (US$49) double cabin; A$85 (US$55) double "village" room; A$120–A$145 (US$78–US$94) double motel room; A$135 (US$88) family of 4, motel family room. Extra person A$10 (US$6.50) adult and A$5 (US$3.25) child under 13, cabin or village room; A$10 (US$6.50) per extra adult, motel room. Unpowered site A$10 (US$6.50) per person per night. Powered site A$22 (US$14) per night single or double; A$5 (US$3.50) extra child, $10 (US$6.50) extra adult. AE, DC, MC, V. Complimentary transfers from airport or bus stop. **Amenities:** Restaurant; bar; free barbecues; 2 outdoor pools (1 large and attractive, 1 small); Jacuzzi; tour desk; car-rental desk; limited room service; coin-op laundry; same-day dry cleaning/laundry service. *In room:* A/C, TV w/pay movies, fridge, no phone in cabins.

9

Perth & Western Australia

by Lee Mylne

Many international visitors—and for that matter, many east-coast Australians—never make the trek to Western Australia. It's too far away, too expensive to fly to, and too big when you get there, they say. That's all true, especially about it being big (2.5 million sq. km/975,000 sq. miles), but don't dismiss a trip out of hand. Flights need not be expensive (if you're an international traveler you can use air coupons—see chapter 2), and some of Australia's best snorkeling and diving, most historic towns, splendid natural scenery, and fantastic wine regions are here. Every spring (that's Sept–Nov Down Under), a good deal of the state is carpeted with wildflowers. The capital, **Perth** ✿, has great food, a fabulous outdoor life of biking and beaches, plenty of smallish museums that are well worth a look, and a beautiful historic port called Fremantle.

The **Southwest** ✿✿ "hook" of the state, below Perth, is the prettiest part of Western Australia, and also the easiest region to visit outside of Perth. Massive stands of karri and jarrah trees stretch to the sky, the surf is world-class, and the coastline is wave-smashed and rugged. The Southwest's Margaret River region turns out some of Australia's most acclaimed wines. En route to the Southwest is a special phenomenon—a visit by **wild dolphins** ✿✿ to the town of Bunbury. You can swim with them, if they are in the mood for socializing.

Head east 644km (400 miles) inland from Perth and you strike what, in the 1890s, was the richest square mile of gold-bearing earth the world has ever seen. The mining town of **Kalgoorlie** ✿, still Australia's biggest gold producer (nearly 2,000 oz. a day), is a place of ornate 19th-century architecture. If Australia has an answer to the Wild West, then Kalgoorlie is it.

Head north of Perth and you're in the Outback. Red sands, scrubby trees, and spinifex grass are all you see for hundreds of miles. About 850km (527 miles) north of Perth, **wild dolphins** ✿ make daily visits to the shores of Monkey Mia. Another 872km (541 miles) on is one of Australia's best-kept secrets, a 260km (161-mile) coral reef called **Ningaloo** ✿✿, along the isolated Outback shore. It's a second Great Barrier Reef, undiscovered by world travelers or Aussies themselves.

The rugged northwest portion of Western Australia is known as the Kimberley, where cattle farming, pearl farming, and tourism thrive in a rocky moonscape of red cliffs, waterfalls, rivers, sparse gums, and wetland lagoons. Here you can visit a million-acre cattle station rich in Aboriginal rock-art sites, tour the world's largest diamond mine, cruise the lush Ord River to see hundreds of native birds, ride a camel on the beach, and shop for the world's biggest South Sea pearls.

Western Australia

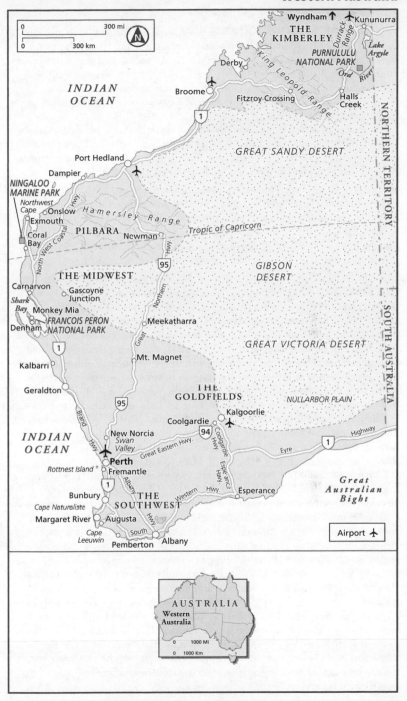

EXPLORING THE STATE

VISITOR INFORMATION   The **Western Australian Tourism Commission** (**WATC**) is the official source of information on the state. Its website (www. westernaustralia.net) provides a good overview, and you may find the **Australian Tourist Commission's** website (www.australia.com), or the Web pages of local tourism boards (found under "Visitor Information" in each regional section of this chapter) useful. Private company **Visit WA** (www.visitwa.com.au) offers an online tour-planning service.

Also contact the Western Australia **Visitor Centre** in Perth, which dispenses information about the state, and makes bookings. See section 1 of this chapter for information. The Department of Conservation and Land Management (CALM) has information on national and marine parks at www.calm.wa.gov.au.

WHEN TO GO   Perth is blessed with long, dry summers and mild, wet winters. You'll want warm gear in the Southwest winters, but temperatures rarely hit the freezing point. Much north of Perth, summer is hell, when temperatures soar to between 104°F and 120°F (40°C–49°C). Avoid these parts from December to March; February is worst. Winter (June–Aug) in the mid-, northern, and inland reaches of the state is pleasantly cool—warm enough for ocean swimming—and sometimes even hot.

GETTING AROUND   Before you plan a driving tour of this state, consider the distances (it's three times as big as Texas) and the mostly flat, monotonous countryside. The Southwest forests make pretty driving; elsewhere, you should fly, unless you want to count sheep in all those paddocks you will be driving past.

If you do hit the road, remember that Western Australia is largely devoid of people, gas stations (keep the gas tank full), and emergency help. Road trains and wildlife pose a road threat more so here than in any other state. Avoid driving at night, dusk, and dawn—all prime animal feeding times. Read "Road Conditions & Safety," in "Getting Around Australia" in chapter 2, before setting off.

The **Royal Automobile Club of Western Australia (RACWA),** 228 Adelaide Terrace, Perth, WA 6000 (② **13 17 03;** www.aaa.asn.au), is a good source of maps and motoring advice. For a recorded road-condition report, call **Main Roads Western Australia** (② **1800/013 314** in Australia).

Skywest (② **1300/66 00 88 in Australia;** www.skywest.com.au) is the state's major regional airline, with **Qantas** (② **13 13 13** in Australia; www.qantas.com. au) also providing services to smaller centers.

Greyhound Pioneer (② **13 20 30** in Australia) is the only interstate coach company serving Western Australia. It travels the highway from Adelaide over to Perth, then up the coast to Broome and across to Darwin; it also travels the remote inland Newman Highway calling at Outback mining towns.

The only train to Western Australia from outside the state is the *Indian Pacific* ℛ, from Sydney via Adelaide and Kalgoorlie to Perth (see "Getting Around Australia," in chapter 2). Inside the state, long-distance trains run only in the southern third. They are operated by **WAGR** (② **13 10 53** in Western Australia, or 08/9326 2000; www.wagr.wa.gov.au) from Perth to Bunbury 2¼ hours south of Perth, Northam an hour or so eastward in the Avon Valley, and Kalgoorlie. WAGR also runs coach services to the Southwest and the southern coast.

All major car- and motor-home-rental companies have offices in Perth.

TOUR OPERATORS   Between them, Western Australia's two biggest coach tour companies, **Australian Pinnacle Tours** (② **1800/999 069** in Australia, or

Moments Tiptoeing Through the Wildflowers

Every year from August to mid-November, the southern half of Western Australia is blessed with a carpet of 12,000 species of white, yellow, mauve, pink, red, and blue **wildflowers** ᐊᐊ.

Wildflower shows and festivals in country towns throughout the state accompany this annual blossoming, and coach- and rail-tour companies ferry enthusiasts from all around Australia and the globe on wildflower tours. You can check out the wildflowers on day trips from Perth, or on longer jaunts of up to 5 days or so. September and October are the peak months.

If time is short, you can go to Perth's Kings Park & Botanic Garden, which conducts free guided walks through its 2,000 species during its 10-day Wildflower Festival every September.

Because Australian flora is adapted to desert conditions, it tends to sprout on dry, sunny days following a rain shower. The Western Australian Tourism Commission's Perth Visitor Centre (see "Visitor Information," above) can keep you up to speed on whatever spot is blooming brightest that week, and they can book you on one of the coach and rail wildflower tours. The Commission produces a 32-page **Wildflower Holiday Guide** brochure that describes self-drive wildflower routes, accommodations houses and events en route, and wildflower tour operators. It is downloadable from the Commission's website (www.westernaustralia.net).

Interstate buses, trains, and hotels fill up fast in wildflower season, so book ahead.

08/9417 5555; www.pinnacletours.com.au) and **Feature Tours** (© **1800/999 819** in Australia, or 08/9475 2900; www.ft.com.au) visit Perth, the Southwest, Monkey Mia, the Northwest Cape, and attractions about a day's drive away, such as Wave Rock (a large wave-shaped rock; see the box "Catching a Silent Wave") and the Pinnacles (weird limestone formations in the desert). Australian Pinnacle Tours also does four-wheel-drive tours. **Overland 4WD Safaris** (© **08/ 9524 7122**) runs four-wheel-drive safaris from Perth throughout the state with an off-the-beaten-track bent.

Aerial tours make sense in Western Australia. Look into the personalized or preset tours offered by **Complete Aviation Services** (© **1800/632 221** in Australia, or 08/9478 2749; www.casair.com.au) or **Kookaburra Air** (© **08/9354 1158;** www.kookaburra.iinet.net.au). Their tours from Perth can take you throughout Western Australia, including the Kimberley, the Top End, and the Red Centre.

Landscope Expeditions ᐊᐊ is an excellent tour program run by the state Conservation and Land Management Department, or **CALM.** The University of Western Australia handles books (© **08/9380 2433;** fax 08/9380 1066 for a free schedule; www.calm.wa.gov.au). You'll be helping CALM scientists on research projects, such as monitoring endangered loggerhead turtles on Dirk Hartog Island, traveling through the evocative landscapes of the Gascoyne Region's rugged hinterland with an artist and a botanist, or sailing the remote islands of the Pilbara coast.

Moments Catching a Silent Wave

The incredible Wave Rock, a 4-hour drive east of Perth, attracts thousands of visitors each year. Standing 15m (45-ft.) tall and running for 110m (330 ft.), this multi-colored "wave" of granite has been shaped by wind and water over an estimated 2,700 million years. Stand at its base, and it feels as if a huge, silent surf wave will break right on top of you!

Wave Rock is about 340km (210 miles) east of Perth, near the wheat-belt town of Hyden. See "Tour Operators" for details on two companies that stop here.

1 Perth *

4,405km (2,731 miles) W of Sydney; 2,389km (1,481 miles) S of Broome

If you like Sydney, you'll like Perth. It has the same silver skyscrapers glinting under a blue sky, the same youthful, energetic outdoorsy vibrancy, and, like Sydney, the sparkling ocean and glorious white beaches are just a bus ride from downtown. Perth likes to boast it gets more sunshine than any other city in Australia, some 300 days a year. Wander through the impressively restored historic warehouses, museums, and working docks of bustling **Fremantle;** stock up at the plentiful Aboriginal art and souvenir stores; visit some great art galleries and museums; eat at some of the country's best restaurants; go snorkeling and sea kayaking with wild sea lions; bushwalk through a 400-hectare (1,000-acre) park in the middle of the city; and pedal your bike to a great snorkeling spot on **Rottnest Island** *, a miniature reef resort 19km (12 miles) offshore.

More than most other Aussie capitals, Perth gives you several good choices of side trips: Drop in on the Benedictine monks in the Spanish Renaissance monastery town of **New Norcia** *, nip out to the Swan Valley vineyards, or spend a few days in **Margaret River** * country, one of Australia's top wine regions. The long, dry summer is the best time to visit; winter is rainy.

ORIENTATION

ARRIVING   By Plane   Qantas (© **13 13 13** in Australia; www.qantas. au) flies at least once a day, if not more often, from all mainland state capitals, either direct or with mostly only one stop. **Airlink** (book through Qantas) flies direct from Alice Springs, and from Cairns via Ayers Rock. Airlink also flies from Broome and Darwin, and operates flights from many small towns within Western Australia. **Virgin Blue** (© **13 67 89** in Australia; www.virginblue.com) flies direct from Sydney, Melbourne, Brisbane, and Adelaide, with connections from other cities.

Perth Airport is 12km (7½ miles) northeast of the city. Allow a 15- to 20-minute transfer time between the international and domestic terminals. Both have ATMs, showers, baby-change rooms, lockers, a post box (newsdealers sell stamps), and a limited range of tourist information. Internet kiosks and currency-exchange bureaus are in the international and Qantas domestic terminals. The international terminal has cellphones for rent.

Avis (© 08/9277 1177 domestic terminal, 08/9477 1302 international terminal), **Budget** (© 08/9277 9277), **EuropCar** (© 08/9237 4320), **Hertz** (© 08/9479 4788), and **Thrifty** (© 08/9464 7333) have desks at both terminals.

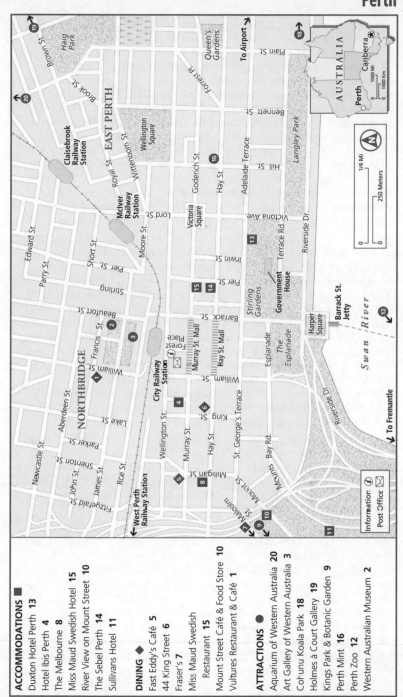

ACCOMMODATIONS
Duxton Hotel Perth **13**
Hotel Ibis Perth **4**
The Melbourne **8**
Miss Maud Swedish Hotel **15**
River View on Mount Street **10**
The Sebel Perth **14**
Sullivans Hotel **11**

DINING
Fast Eddy's Café **5**
44 King Street **6**
Fraser's **7**
Miss Maud Swedish
  Restaurant **15**
Mount Street Café & Food Store **10**
Vultures Restaurant & Café **1**

ATTRACTIONS
Aquarium of Western Australia **20**
Art Gallery of Western Australia **3**
Cohunu Koala Park **18**
Holmes à Court Gallery **19**
Kings Park & Botanic Garden **9**
Perth Mint **16**
Perth Zoo **12**
Western Australian Museum **2**

Feature Tours runs the **airport-city shuttle** (© **1800/999 819** in Australia, or 08/9479 4131), which meets all international and interstate flights. It does not specifically meet intrastate flights. There is no need to book. City transfers from the international terminal cost A$11 (US$7.15) adults one-way; domestic terminal-city transfers are A$9 (US$5.85) one-way. Transfers between the domestic and international terminals are A$5.50 (US$3.55) for adults. The **Fremantle Airport Shuttle** (© **1300/668 687** in Australia, or 08/9335 1614) operates regular services each day from the airport to hotels, or anywhere else in Fremantle you want to go; you must book in advance. The fare is A$20 (US$13) per person, but gets cheaper the bigger your group is—down to A$10 (US$6.50) per person for five or more people traveling together.

Public bus nos. 37 and 39 run to the city from the domestic terminal. No buses run from the international terminal. A taxi to the city is about A$28 (US$18) from the international terminal and A$21 (US$14) from the domestic terminal, including a A$1 (US65¢) fee for picking up a taxi at the airport.

By Train   The 3-day journey to Perth from Sydney via Broken Hill, Adelaide, and Kalgoorlie aboard the *Indian Pacific* 🦘, operated by Great Southern Railway (© **13 21 47** in Australia; www.trainways.com.au), is an experience itself. The train runs twice a week each direction. The one-way fare ranges from A$1,506 (US$979) in first class with meals and en-suite bathroom, to A$1,250 (US$813) in comfy second class (meals cost extra, and bathrooms are shared), down to A$513 (US$333) for the sit-up-all-the-way coach class (not a good idea). Connections are available from Melbourne on the *Overland* train. See "Getting Around Australia," in chapter 2, for contact details in Australia and abroad. The **Prospector** train makes the 7¾-hour trip from Kalgoorlie daily; call **WAGR** (© **13 10 53** in Western Australia, or 08/9326 2000).

All long-distance trains pull into the East Perth Terminal, Summers Street off Lord Street, East Perth. A taxi to the city center costs about A$10 (US$6.50).

By Bus   **Greyhound Pioneer** (© **13 20 30** in Australia) runs daily from Sydney (58 hr.) to Adelaide and once a week from Adelaide to Perth, trip time about 34 hours. It also has service daily from Darwin via Kununurra and Broome (trip time: about 59 hr.). Traveling from Alice Springs requires a connection in Adelaide and takes about 53 hours. The Sydney-Perth fare is A$397 (US$258), Adelaide-Perth is A$264 (US$172), Darwin-Perth is A$550 (US$358), and Alice Springs–Perth is A$441 (US$287).

By Car   There are only two road routes from interstate—the 2,389km (1,481-mile) route from Broome in the north, and the 2,708km (1,679-mile) odyssey from Adelaide, which includes hundreds of miles along some of the world's straightest roads on the treeless Nullarbor Plain. Arm yourself with an up-to-date road map before setting off. It's not a bad idea to contact the South Australian or Western Australian state auto clubs (listed under "Getting Around Australia," in chapter 2) for advice on crossing the lonely Nullarbor. Both routes cross mostly featureless and semidesert, sheep ranches or wheat fields most of the way, with very few towns en route. For that reason, I don't recommend either!

VISITOR INFORMATION   The **Western Australian Visitor Centre,** Albert Facey House, 469 Wellington St. on the corner of Forrest Place, Perth (© **1300/361 351** in Australia, or 08/9483 1111; www.westernaustralia.net), is the official visitor information source for Perth and the state. It's open Monday through Thursday from 8:30am to 6pm (5:30pm in winter May–July), Friday from 8:30am to 7pm (6pm in winter), Saturday from 8:30am to 12:30pm year-round, and closed Sundays. Another source of information and maps (plus a free booking service) is **Perth Tourist Lounge,** Level 2, Carillon Arcade off 207 Murray Street Mall (© **08/9481 4400**), open Monday through Thursday from 9am to 5:30pm, Friday 9am to 9pm, Saturday 9am to 5pm and Sunday from noon to 5pm.

For an untouristy lowdown on the city's restaurants, cultural life, shops, bars, nightlife, concerts, and the like, buy the excellent local glossy quarterly magazine *Scoop* (A$8.90/US$5.80; www.scoop.com.au), available in bigger newsstands.

CITY LAYOUT   The city center is 19km (12 miles) upriver from the Indian Ocean, on the north bank of a broad reach of the Swan River. **Hay Street** and **Murray Street** are the two major thoroughfares, 1 block apart; both are bisected by pedestrian malls between William and Barrack streets. It helps to know that Adelaide Terrace and St. Georges Terrace appear to be one and the same street. The name change occurs at Victoria Avenue.

MAPS   Of the many free pocket guides to Perth available at tour desks and in hotel lobbies, *Your Guide to Perth & Fremantle* (Countrywide Publications) has the **best street map,** because it shows one-way streets, public toilets and telephones, taxi stands, post offices, police stations, and street numbers, as well as most attractions and hotels. The **Royal Automobile Club of Western Australia** (see "Exploring the State," at the start of this chapter) is a good source of maps to the state, as is **Map World,** 900 Hay St. (© **08/9322 5733**). You will find tourist maps at the Perth Visitor Centre and the Perth Tourist Lounge (see "Visitor Information," above).

NEIGHBORHOODS IN BRIEF

City Center The central business district (called the CBD in Australia) is home to shops and department stores. A good introduction to Perth's charms is to take in the views from the pedestrian/bike path that skirts the river along Riverside Drive. Within walking distance is Kings Park & Botanic Garden.

Northbridge Just about all of Perth's nightclubs, and a good many of its cool restaurants, bars, and cafes, are in this 5-block precinct north of the railway line, within easy walking distance of the city center, or take the free Blue CAT buses. It's roughly bounded by James, Beaufort, Aberdeen, and Lake streets. What locals call the Cultural Centre—which means the Western Australian Museum, the Art Gallery of Western Australia, the State Library, and the Perth Institute of Contemporary Arts—is here, too.

Subiaco This well-heeled suburb is on the other side of Kings Park. Saturday morning just wouldn't be the same for Perth's see-and-be-seen crowd without a stroll through "Subi's" villagelike concoction of cafes, markets, boutiques, antiques shops, and art galleries. Most of the action is near the intersection of Hay Street and Rokeby (pronounced *Rock*-er-bee) Road. Take the train to Subiaco station.

Fremantle Not only is "Freo" a working port, it's also Perth's second city heart, and a favorite weekend spot to eat, shop, and sail. A 1980s restoration of Victorian warehouses turned Freo into a marvelous example of a 19th-century seaport—like San Francisco's Fisherman's Wharf without the commercial taint. Fremantle is 19km (12 miles) downriver on the mouth of the Swan.

Scarborough Beach This is one of Perth's prize beaches, 12km

(7½ miles) north of the city center. The district is a little tatty with an oversupply of cheap takeout food outlets, but if you like sun, sand, and surf, this is the place to be. You will find bars, restaurants, and surf-gear rental stores here. Allow 15 to 20 minutes to get there by car, 35 minutes on the bus.

GETTING AROUND

BY PUBLIC TRANSPORTATION   **Transperth** (www.transperth.wa.gov.au) runs Perth's buses, trains, and ferries. For route, bus stop, and timetable information, call © **13 62 13** in Western Australia, or drop into the Transperth Info-Centres at the Plaza Arcade off Hay Street Mall, the Perth Railway Station, the Wellington Street bus station, or the City Bus Port on Mounts Bay Road. You can transfer from bus to ferry to train on one ticket within its expiration time of 2 or 3 hours. Travel costs A$1.90 (US$1.20) in one zone (to Subiaco, for instance), and A$2.90 (US$1.90) in two, which gets you most places, including Fremantle. Non–West Australian seniors and students don't qualify for discounted fares; kids ages 5 to 14 do.

By Bus   The Wellington Street Bus Station, located next to Perth Railway Station at Forrest Place, and the City Bus Port on Mounts Bay Road, are the two main depots. The vast majority of buses travel along St. Georges Terrace. Drivers do not always stop unless you hail. Buy tickets from the driver. Buses run from about 5:30am until about 10:30 or 11:30pm, depending on the route.

Tips   **Take a Free Ride**

A welcome freebie in Perth is the **Free Transit Zone (FTZ)**. You can travel free on trains and buses within this zone any hour, day or night. It is bounded by Kings Park Road, Fraser Avenue, Thomas Street, and Loftus Street in the west; Newcastle Street in the north; and the river in the south and east. Basically, this means you can travel to Kings Park, Northbridge, east to major sporting grounds, and anywhere in the city center free. Signs mark the FTZ boundaries; just ask the driver if you're unsure. FTZ boundaries for trains are City West station on the Fremantle line and Claisebrook on the Midland and Armadale lines.

MultiRider passes give you 10 trips at a savings of 15%; they come in a range of prices good for various numbers of zones. A **DayRider** pass allows 1 day's unlimited travel after 9am on weekdays and all day on weekends and public holidays, and costs A$7.30 (US$4.75). A FamilyRider pass is valid for unlimited all-day travel to any destination and back, for a group of seven people with a maximum of two adults. FamilyRiders are aimed at Perth families and so are valid only weekends, public holidays, after 9am weekdays, and during Western Australian school holidays, after 6pm year-round Monday through Thursday, and after 3pm Friday. They cost A$7.30 (US$4.75). Passes, collectively known as FastCards, are sold at newsagents and at Transperth InfoCentres. To use the passes, validate them in the machines located on board in the case of buses, and on the platform or wharf in the case of trains and ferries.

The best way to get around town is on the free **CAT** (Central Area Transit) buses that run a continual loop of the city and Northbridge. The Red CAT runs east-west every 5 minutes, Monday through Friday from 6:50am to 6:20pm, and once every 35 minutes from 10am to 6:15pm weekends. The Blue CAT runs north-south as far north as Northbridge and south to Barrack Street Jetty every 7 minutes from 6:50am. The last Blue CAT service is at 6:20pm Monday through Thursday, and on Friday it continues every 15 minutes from 6:20pm until 1am Saturday morning. Saturdays it runs from 8:30am to 1am (Sun morning) every 15 minutes, and Sundays every 15 minutes from 10am to 6:15pm. The Yellow CAT runs between East Perth and the city center every 10 minutes from 6:50am to 6:20pm weekdays and every 15 minutes 10am to 6:15pm weekends. There are no CAT services on public holidays. Look for the silver CAT bus stops. Transperth InfoCentres (see above) dispense free route maps.

The Perth Tram Co. tours (see "Whale-Watching Cruises, Tram Trips & Other Tours," later in this chapter) are a good way to get around, too.

By Train Trains are fast, clean, and safe. They start from about 5:30am and run every 15 minutes or even more often during the day, and every half-hour at night until midnight. NightRider trains depart Perth at 1 and 2am Friday and Saturday night (meaning Sat–Sun morning) December through March, stopping at all stations on all lines. All trains leave from Perth Railway Station opposite Forrest Place on Wellington Street. Buy your ticket before you board, at the vending machines on the platform.

By Ferry You will probably use ferries only to visit Perth Zoo. They run every half-hour or so, more often in peak hours, every day from 6:50am weekdays and 7:50am weekends and public holidays, until 7:15pm (or until 9:15pm on Fri–Sat nights in summer between Sept and Apr) from the Barrack Street Jetty to Mends Street in South Perth. Buy tickets before you board from the vending machine on the wharf. The trip takes 7 minutes.

By Taxi Perth's two biggest taxi companies are **Swan Taxis** (✆ **13 13 30**) and **Black & White Taxis** (✆ **13 10 08**). Ranks are located at Perth Railway Station, and at both ends of Hay Street Mall.

By Car Perth's signposting is notorious for telling you where you have been, not where you are going — for example, some interstate highways are announced with insignificant signs more suited to a side street.

The major car-rental companies are **Avis** (✆ 08/9325 7677), **Budget** (✆ 08/9480 3111), **EuropCar** (✆ 08/9226 0026), **Hertz** (✆ 08/9321 7777), and **Thrifty** (✆ 08/9464 7444). All except Hertz also have outlets in Fremantle. **ATC Rent-A-Car** (✆ 1800/999 888 in Australia, or 08/9325 1833) is a locally owned outfit with offices in Monkey Mia and Broome; it also rents camping kits.

 FAST FACTS: **Perth**

American Express The bureau at 645 Hay Street Mall (✆ **08/9221 0777**) is open Monday through Friday from 9am to 5pm and Saturday from 9am to noon.

Business Hours Banks are open Monday through Thursday from 9:30am to 4pm and until 5pm Friday. Shopping hours are usually from 9am to

5:30pm Monday through Friday (until 9pm on Thurs in the suburbs and Fremantle, and until 9pm Fri in the city), and from 9am to 5pm on Saturday. On Sunday most major stores (but not all) open from noon to 4pm or later in the city, and from noon to 6pm in Fremantle.

Currency Exchange Go to the American Express office (see above) or **Interforex,** Shop 24, London Court off Hay Street Mall (✆ **08/9325 7418**), open daily from 9am to 6pm, and until 9pm Friday. Interforex has a Fremantle bureau at the corner of William and Adelaide streets (✆ **08/9431 7022**), open daily from 8am to 8pm.

Dentist **LifeCare Dental** (✆ **08/9221 2777**) is on the Upper Walkway Level, Forrest Chase shopping complex, 425 Wellington St. opposite Perth Railway Station. Open daily from 8am to 8pm, it can be reached after hours at ✆ **08/9383 1620**.

Doctor **Central City Medical Centre** is on the Perth Railway Station concourse, 420 Wellington St. (✆ **08/9221 4747**). Open daily 8am to 7pm.

Embassies/Consulates The **United States Consulate-General** is at 16 St. Georges Terrace (✆ **08/9202 1224**). The **Canadian Consulate** is at 267 St. Georges Terrace (✆ **08/9322 7930**). The **British Consulate-General** is at 77 St. Georges Terrace (✆ **08/9224 4700**). The Irish **Consulate-General** is at 10 Lilika Rd., City Beach (✆ **08/9385 8247**).

Emergencies Dial ✆ **000** for fire, ambulance, or police in an emergency. This is a free call; no coins are needed from a public phone.

Hospitals **Royal Perth Hospital** in the city center has a public emergency/casualty ward (✆ **08/9224 2244**). Enter from Victoria Square, which is accessed from Murray Street.

Luggage Storage/Lockers The **Perth Tourist Lounge** (see "Visitor Information," earlier in this chapter) stores luggage, and there are baggage lockers at the international and domestic terminals at the airport.

Pharmacies **Forrest Chase Pharmacy** (✆ **08/9221 1691**), on the upper level of the Forrest Chase shopping center, 425 Wellington St. (near the dentist's office listed above), is open Monday through Thursday from 8am to 7pm (and until 9pm Fri), Saturday from 8:30am to 6pm, and Sunday from 10am to 6pm. **Shenton Pharmacy,** 214 Nicholson Rd., Subiaco (✆ **08/9381 1358** business and after hours), will deliver across Perth.

Police Dial ✆ **000** in an emergency. **Central Police Station,** 1 Hay St., East Perth (✆ **08/9263 2300**) and **Fremantle Police Station,** 45 Henderson St. (✆ **08/9430 1222**), are open 24 hours. To be connected to the nearest station, dial ✆ **13 14 44**.

Safety Perth is safe, but steer clear of the back streets of Northbridge—where groups of teenagers sometimes congregate at night—even if you are not alone.

Time Zone Western Australian time (WST) is Greenwich Mean Time plus 8 hours and has no daylight saving. This means it is normally 2 hours behind Sydney, except October through March when New South Wales goes to daylight saving. Call ✆ **1194** for the exact local time.

Weather Call ✆ **1196** for a recorded local weather forecast.

WHERE TO STAY

Perth has loads of hotels in the city center. That means competition can be high, especially Friday through Sunday when the business travelers go home, so ask about lower rates on weekends. You may strike a deal on a weeknight if business is slow. Many hotels throw a free breakfast or some other added value into mid-week packages. Most hotels have rooms for travelers with disabilities.

IN THE CITY CENTER
Very Expensive
Duxton Hotel Perth *ʀʀ*   The best uninterrupted views of the Swan River from a hotel room are found from the south-side rooms at this chic 21st century–meets–Art Deco hotel, located downtown. Only a few years old as a hotel, the place was created out of old tax office chambers. A sandstone portico fronts the bronze-paneled lobby with its Siena marble floor, and the rooms— given a soft refurbishment in 2003—sport blond oak furniture with 1930s curves, elegant marquetry, and ample bathrooms. Superior rooms have extra-large bathrooms (some with Jacuzzis); executive-level rooms have TVs in the bathroom, CD players, and a fax and printer; and suites have separate living rooms. Make time to see and be seen lazing around that petite swimming pool colonnaded like a Roman bath.

1 St. Georges Terrace (at Victoria Ave. next to Perth Concert Hall), Perth, WA 6000. Ⓒ 1800/681 118 in Australia, or 08/9261 8000. Fax 08/9261 8020. www.duxton.com. 306 units (several with shower only). A$360–A$440 (US$234–US$286) double; A$470(US$306) suite. Extra person A$28 (US$18). Children under 16 stay free in parent's room with existing bedding. Ask about packages and upgrades. AE, DC, MC, V. Valet parking A$15 (US$9.75); no self-parking. Bus: Red CAT Stop 11 "Victoria Ave." Airport shuttle. **Amenities:** Restaurant; bar; small heated pool; Jacuzzi; fitness center; concierge; business center; 24-hr. room service; in-room massage; babysitting; coin-op laundry; same-day dry cleaning/laundry service; executive-level rooms. In room: A/C, TV w/pay movies, dataport, minibar, hair dryer, iron.

Expensive
The Sebel Perth *ʀ*   In the middle of town, the Sebel has the biggest standard hotel rooms in Perth, and a friendly ambience that's a welcome contrast to the frosty hauteur of many AAA-rated five-star properties. Nice touches are every-where—like a free gift with every stay (such as locally made soap), free tea and coffee in the lobby every morning, and a weekly General Manager's cocktail party. All 99 standard rooms were refurbished in 2000. All have big desks, walk-in closets, bathrobes, armchairs or sofas, and windows that open for fresh air. Suites have a separate sitting room. Every Monday, Wednesday, and Friday at 6:15am, you, three other guests, and a senior member of management can jump into the hotel's "Cottesloe Express" Rolls-Royce and motor in style to **Cottesloe Beach** *ʀ* (20 min. away) for a swim, a walk, or a jog. They get you back to the hotel by 7:40am or so. Some packages are often less than half the "rack" rates.

37 Pier St., Perth, WA 6000. Ⓒ 1800/999 004 Mirvac in Australia, or 08/9325 7655. Fax 08/9325 7383. www.mirvac.com.au. 119 units. A$260 (US$169) double; A$300 (US$195) suite. Extra person A$25 (US$16). Children under 12 stay free in parent's room with existing bedding. Ask about weekend, overnight, honeymoon, and suite packages. AE, DC, MC, V. Free valet and self-parking. Train: Perth. Bus: Red CAT Stop 12 "Town Hall East"; Blue CAT Stop 4 "Town Hall" or Stop 5 "Murray St. Mall East." Airport shuttle. **Amenities:** Restaurant; poolside bar/cafe; heated outdoor pool; access to nearby health club; free bike rental; concierge; tour desk; secretarial services; 24-hr. room service; babysitting; coin-op laundry; laundry service; dry cleaning. In room: A/C, TV w/pay movies, dataport, minibar, coffeemaker, hair dryer, iron.

Moderate
The Melbourne *ʀ* *(Value)*   This 1897 hotel in Perth's downtown West End, restored to its ornate gold rush–era originality in 1997, is a great value, because

its facilities and rooms match most AAA-rated five-star hotels. The public areas and restaurant have a New Orleans theme, aided by original trappings like decorative pressed metal ceilings and floral carpets, and have been refurbished in 2003, along with almost half the guest rooms. Rooms favor modern convenience but retain a hint of the South with wooden blinds, summery friezes, and brass-trimmed fans. Suites are a single room with a sitting area. Go for the outside rooms (those on the second floor open onto the wide veranda), as inside rooms lack views. The recently renovated atmospheric street-front **Bar @ The Melbourne** has live jazz on Friday nights.

Corner of Hay and Milligan sts., Perth, WA 6000. ℃ 1800/68 5671 in Australia, or 08/9320 3333. Fax 08/9320 3344. www.melbournehotel.com.au. 36 units (all with shower only). A$165 (US$107) double; A$185 (US$120) suite. Extra person A$20 (US$13). Up to 2 children under 12 stay free in parent's room. Ask about overnight packages. AE, DC, MC, V. Valet parking A$14 (US$9.10); no self-parking. Bus: Red CAT Stop 18 "QVI." Airport shuttle. Train: Perth Central. **Amenities:** Restaurant; cafe; bar; access to a nearby health club, golf course, and tennis courts; concierge; tour desk; car-rental desk; secretarial in-room services; 24-hr room service; babysitting; same-day dry cleaning/laundry service (except Sun). *In room:* A/C, TV w/free movies, fax and dataport, minibar, coffeemaker, hair dryer, iron.

Miss Maud Swedish Hotel ✿ About half the rooms in this homey hotel in the heart of town have been gutted and totally rebuilt in the past year. New furnishings include the Scandinavian colors of yellow and blue, while others have a crisp Nordic look of cream and pale blue. A private sun deck is tucked away as a surprise up among the rooftops. The real Miss Maud, Maud Edmiston, wants guests to feel they are in a European family hotel like those in her Swedish homeland, and she succeeds—in part due to the staff, which is more polite and on the ball than in most AAA-rated five-star hotels. A fabulous buffet breakfast is included at **Miss Maud Swedish Restaurant** downstairs (p. 435).

97 Murray St. (at Pier St.), Perth, WA 6000. ℃ 1800/998 022 in Australia, or 08/9325 3900. Fax 08/9221 3225. www.missmaud.com.au. 52 units (40 with shower only). A$112–A$150 (US$73–US$98) double. Extra person A$15 (US$9.75). Rates include smorgasbord breakfast. AE, DC, MC, V. Discounted parking A$7 (US$4.55) at the Kings Hotel car park 1 block away. Bus: Red CAT Stop 1 "Pier St."; Blue CAT Stop 5 "Murray St. Mall East." Airport shuttle. **Amenities:** Restaurant/bar; takeout pastry shop; tour desk; limited room service; coin-op laundry; laundry/dry cleaning service. *In room:* A/C, TV, minibar, coffeemaker, hair dryer.

Sullivans Hotel This family-owned hotel about 1.5km (1 mile) from town is popular with Europeans for its small-scale ambience. Despite being on the main road into the city, none of the rooms seem to be noisy. They're simply furnished with laminate fittings, not glamorous but clean and roomy. Larger deluxe rooms come with desks, safes, and balconies with views over parkland and the freeway to the river. There are also two-bedroom apartments with kitchenettes. Out back is a pleasant little swimming pool with a sun deck and barbecue. Bikes are free, the restaurant is affordable, and the front desk has free 24-hour Internet access for guests. Some rooms have dataports. The Swan River is a stroll away, the city is a 10-minute walk, and Kings Park is a short, steep climb up the hill.

166 Mounts Bay Rd., Perth, WA 6000. ℃ 1800/99 9294 in Australia, or 08/9321 8022. Fax 08/9481 6762. www.sullivans.com.au. 68 units (66 with shower only). A$110–A$130 (US$72–US$85) up to 4 people in room; A$190 (US$124) 2-bedroom apt. Ask about packages. Weekly rates available. AE, DC, MC, V. Free parking. Bus: 71, 72, or 78 (the hotel is within the Free Transit Zone). Airport shuttle. **Amenities:** Restaurant/bar; small outside pool; free bikes; tour desk; limited room service for meals and drinks; babysitting; coin-op laundry; same-day laundry/dry cleaning service; Internet access. *In room:* A/C, TV w/free movies, dataport (some rooms), coffeemaker, hair dryer.

Inexpensive

Hotel Ibis Perth ✿ *Value* Ibis is one of those reputable chain brands of the "four-star facilities at a three-star price" variety. Shops, cinemas, and Hay Street

Mall are a block or two away from this hotel. The neat, no-frills rooms were thoroughly renovated with funky colors and high-quality beds in 2001, and the lobby, restaurant and bar were refurbished in 2003. The rooms are small, but a nice room in this location for this price can't be beaten.

334 Murray St. (between William and King sts.), Perth, WA 6000. © 08/9322 2844; Accor, 1300/88 4400 in Australia, 800/221-4542 in the U.S. and Canada, 020/8283 4500 in the U.K., or 0800/44 4422 in New Zealand. Fax 08/9321 6314. www.accorhotels.com.au. 192 units (all with shower only). A$95 (US$62) double. Extra person A$27 (US$18). Children under 13 stay free in parent's room with existing bedding. AE, DC, MC, V. Discounted self-parking A$9.90 (US$6.45) at the nearby Queen St. car park. Bus: Red CAT Stop 15 "Murray St. Mall West"; Blue CAT Stop 17 "Hay St. Mall West." Airport shuttle. **Amenities:** Restaurant; 2 bars; tour desk; car-rental desk; business center; babysitting; coin-op laundry; same-day dry cleaning. *In room:* A/C, TV w/pay movies, fridge, coffeemaker, hair dryer, iron.

River View on Mount Street 🐾 *Value*   On a quiet leafy street a short walk from the city and Kings Park, these roomy studio apartments in a 1960s block were refurbished in 1999 with new kitchens and bathrooms, fresh carpets and curtains, and smart-looking fittings. The result is great style at a great price. Some have distant views of the river a few blocks away. Maid service is weekly. The helpful on-site managers loan hair dryers and irons. You can breakfast at the **Mount Street Café** downstairs (p. 435), which also sells prepared curries and deli items. No smoking.

42 Mount St., Perth, WA 6000. © 08/9321 8963. Fax 08/9322 5956. www.riverview.au.com (not "riverview.com.au"). 50 units (all with shower only). A$85–A$95 (US$55–US$62) apt (some sleep up to 3). Weekly rates available. AE, MC, V. Limited free parking. Bus: Red CAT Stop 18 "QVI" (over the fwy. footbridge accessed from the corner of St. Georges Terrace and Milligan St.). Airport shuttle. **Amenities:** Cafe; access to nearby golf course and health club; tour desk; car-rental desk; coin-op laundry; laundry/same-day dry cleaning service; nonsmoking rooms. *In room:* A/C, TV, dataport, kitchenette, fridge, coffeemaker, hair dryer, iron.

ON THE BEACH
Hotel Rendezvous Observation City Perth 🐾   One of the few beachside places to stay in Perth is this 17-story complex right on the never-ending sands of Scarborough Beach. Its no-fuss ambience makes it popular with vacationing Aussies. Most of the rooms, which will be refurbished from mid-2003, have private balconies with ocean views. Some rooms have dataports, and most suites have separate sleeping quarters. Among the entertainment venues is a British-style pub popular with locals, a live music lounge, and a dance club.

The Esplanade, Scarborough Beach, WA 6019. © 1800/067 680 in Australia, or 08/9245 1000. Fax 08/9245 1345. www.rendezvoushotels.com. 333 units (150 with shower only). A$230–A$350 (US$150–US$228) double; A$550 (US$358) and up, suite. Extra person A$50 (US$33). Children under 18 stay free in parent's room with existing bedding. Ask about packages. AE, DC, MC, V. Valet parking A$20 (US$13); self-parking A$7 (US$4.55). A daily courtesy shuttle operates between the hotel, Perth city, Burswood Casino, Fremantle, and a local mall. Bus: 400. **Amenities:** 3 restaurants; 4 bars; heated outdoor pool; children's wading pool; 2 outdoor day/night tennis courts; health club; Jacuzzi; sauna; limited watersports-equipment rentals; bike rental; children's recreation room; concierge; tour desk; business center (Mon–Fri); shopping arcade; salon; 24-hr. room service; in-room massage; babysitting; coin-op laundry; same-day laundry/dry cleaning; executive-level rooms. *In room:* A/C, TV w/pay movies, kitchenette, minibar, coffeemaker, hair dryer, iron.

IN FREMANTLE
There's a perpetual holiday atmosphere in this picturesque port city. Although you're 19km (12 miles) from Perth's city center, public transport is good, so you can happily explore all of Perth from here—and most of the top attractions are in Freo anyhow. There are good restaurants and a happening nightlife, too.

Danum House 🐾🐾   Hostess Christine Sherwin has created a welcoming haven in her beautiful Federation (ca. 1909) home, a short walk from town. One room, decked out in heritage reds and greens, opens onto a cottage garden.

The other very large room has an ornate mantle, floral wallpaper, long drapes, and that most colonial of furnishings, a daybed, as well as a real bed for sleeping. Both sport antiques, ornate ceiling roses and cornices, fireplaces, high ceilings and fans, and have a private entrance. Even the bathrooms (one en suite, one with private access) share the colonial decor. Christine serves a hearty breakfast, and you can relax in the comfy lounge over books, CDs, free coffee, and complimentary port and chocolates. Hair dryers and irons are available. No smoking.

6 Fothergill St. (at Bellevue Terrace), Fremantle, WA 6160. © 08/9336 3735. Fax 08/9335 3414. www. staywa.net.au/ads/danum. 2 units (both with shower only). A$90–A$110 (US$59–US$72) double. Minimum 2-night stay. Rates include full breakfast. MC, V. Ample on-street parking. Bus: 105 from Perth. Train: Fremantle. Fremantle airport shuttle (see "Arriving: By Plane," earlier in this chapter). Children not permitted. *In room:* TV.

Esplanade Hotel Fremantle ⓕ   Freo's best hotel is this low-rise 1897 colonial building wrapped by two verandas, centered around a buzzing four-story atrium lobby. A A$15 million (US$9.7 million) expansion in 2003 added 41 rooms to the hotel as well as a 1,000-seat convention center. The nicely maintained rooms have views of the street, the pool, or the distant harbor across a park. The attractive larger pool in the courtyard is a good place to chill out without getting buffeted by the pesky local sea breeze, the "Fremantle Doctor." It's a minute's walk to Freo's cafes, shops, and attractions.

Marine Terrace at Essex St., Fremantle, WA 6160. © 1800/998 201 in Australia, or 08/9432 4000. Fax 08/ 9430 4539. www.esplanadehotelfremantle.com.au. 300 units (some with shower only). A$270–A$599 (US$176–US$389) double. Extra person A$38 (US$25). Children under 13 stay free in parent's room with existing bedding; cribs free. Ask about packages. AE, DC, MC, V. Valet parking A$15 (US$9.75); fee-paying street parking available and a 450-space parking lot is nearby on Collie St. Train: Fremantle. Fremantle Airport Shuttle (see "Arriving: By Plane," earlier in this chapter). **Amenities:** 2 restaurants; cafe; bar; 2 heated outdoor pools; gymnasium; 3 outdoor Jacuzzis; sauna; bike rental; concierge; tour desk; business center; 24-hr. room service; in-room massage; babysitting; coin-op laundry; same-day laundry/dry cleaning service. *In room:* A/C, TV w/pay movies, dataport, minibar, coffeemaker, hair dryer, iron.

WHERE TO DINE

An array of upscale choices, plus terrific, cheap ethnic spots makes Perth's restaurant scene as sophisticated as Sydney's and Melbourne's—which is to say, great. You'll find many good choices in "restaurant city," Northbridge.

For inexpensive pasta, a Turkish bread sandwich, or excellent coffee and cake, you can't beat Perth's homegrown **DOME** chain of cafes. You will spot their dark green logo at Trinity Arcade between Hay Street Mall and St. Georges Terrace (© **08/9226 0210**); 149 James St., Northbridge (© **08/9328 8094**); 13 South Terrace, Fremantle (© **08/9336 3040**); 19 Napoleon St., Cottesloe (© **08/ 9383 1071**); 26 Rokeby Rd., Subiaco (© **08/9381 5664**); and at Henderson Street on Rottnest Island (© **08/9292 5026**)—to name just a few.

Western Australian law bans smoking in enclosed public spaces, including restaurants.

IN THE CITY CENTER
Expensive
Fraser's ⓕⓕⓕ *(Moments)* MODERN AUSTRALIAN/SEAFOOD   What a sensational view from this hilltop restaurant! The city skyscrapers and Swan River look so close you could almost reach out and touch them—and even better, the victuals match the vista. Executive chef Chris Taylor's sure hand with seafood, which composes about 70% of the long menu, has made the place a finalist in national "restaurant of the year" awards more than once. Seared Atlantic salmon

with snow peas, abalone mushrooms, and mandarin soy is typical. The duck is legendary. To maximize the view, ask for a seat on the terrace.

Fraser Ave. (near the Information Kiosk), Kings Park. ℂ **08/9481 7100.** Reservations required. Main courses A$22–A$45 (US$14–US$29); average A$26 (US$17). AE, DC, MC, V. Daily 7:30am–late. Closed Good Friday. Ample free parking. Bus: 33 stops outside the Information Kiosk. Red CAT Stop 25 "Havelock St." is 1 block to the north of the gates.

Moderate

44 King Street ★★ MODERN AUSTRALIAN   Socialites and hip corporate types adorn this sophisticated hangout, whose interior is a mix of industrial design and European cafe with dark timber tables, exposed air ducts, and windows onto the street. The open kitchen produces a daily changing menu of weird and wonderful choices with exotic ingredients—such as lamb shank stifhadtho with broad bean skordalia, or black risotto with squid and scallops and salsa verde. Not only does the menu helpfully list wine suggestions for each dish, but it also does taster-size glasses from around A$3 (US$1.95) to A$8.50 (US$5.50) from a 200-strong wine list. Lots of folks drop in just for coffee, roasted on-site, and the famous cakes. All meals are available as takeout.

44 King St. ℂ **08/9321 4476.** Reservations not accepted. Tasting menu A$3.50–A$13 (US$2.30–US$8.45) breakfast, A$19–A$27 (US$12–US$18) lunch and dinner. AE, DC, MC, V. Daily 7am–midnight. Bus: Red CAT Stop 28 "King St."; Blue CAT Stop 1 "Cloisters."

Miss Maud Swedish Restaurant *Value* INTERNATIONAL   "Good food and plenty of it" is the motto at Miss Maud's homey establishment, and the crowds packing the place prove it works. Most diners skip the long a la carte menu and go straight for the smorgasbord. At breakfast, that means 50 dishes including pancakes cooked before your eyes. At lunch and dinner you can tuck into soup, 10 salads, a big range of seafood (including oysters at dinner), cold meats, roasts, hot vegetables, pasta, cheeses, European-style breads, half a dozen tortes, fruit, and ice cream—65 dishes in all. Service is fast and polite.

97 Murray St. at Pier St. (below Miss Maud Swedish Hotel). ℂ **08/9325 3900.** Reservations recommended. Smorgasbord breakfast A$17 (US$11) Mon–Sat, A$18 (US$12) Sun and public holidays; lunch A$25 (US$16) Mon–Sat, A$26 (US$17) Sun and public holidays; dinner A$31 (US$20) Sun–Fri, A$35 (US$23) Sat and public holidays. Cheaper smorgasbord prices for children 4–13. A la carte main courses, sandwiches, and light meals A$5.75–A$20 (US$3.75–US$13). Dine and leave by 7:15pm Mon–Sat for a A$5 (US$3.25) discount. AE, DC, MC, V. Open all day for coffee and cake. Meals daily 6:45–10am, noon–2:30pm, 5:30–7pm, and 7:15–10pm (until about 11:30pm weekends). Bus: Red CAT Stop 1 "Pier St."; Blue CAT Stop 5 "Murray St. Mall East."

Mount Street Café and Food Store ★★ MODERN AUSTRALIAN   Chef Toby Uhlrich turns out yummy dine-in and takeout fare from this charming alfresco cafe on the edge of the central business district. Come for lunches like risotto with asparagus, chicken, roasted almonds, and Parmesan, or your choice of light snacks from the deli cabinet. Breakfasts are equally fresh and delicious. Dine inside at a few tables, or out on the shaded stone terrace. Drop by anytime for cakes and good coffee, but be prepared to fight the regulars for a table. BYO (corkage A$2.50/US$1.60).

Under the "River View on Mount Street" apts, 42 Mount St. ℂ **08/9485 1411.** Reservations recommended on weekends. Breakfast A$5.80–A$17 (US$3.75–US$11); main courses A$14–A$21 (US$9.10–US$14). AE, MC, V. Daily 7:30am–5pm. Bus: Red CAT Stop 18 "QVI" (over the fwy. footbridge accessed from corner of St. Georges Terrace and Milligan St.).

Inexpensive

Fast Eddy's Café FAST FOOD   A hefty menu of steaks, burgers, sandwiches, soups, pancakes, sundaes, shakes, and full fry-up brekkies (breakfasts) are served all hours at this popular chain. The interior is decked out with 1930s soap-pow-der posters and Coca-Cola advertisements. One side is table service; the same food minus the side orders will cost you about half the already low prices at the Victorian-era-meets-1950s counter service diner and takeout section on the other side.

454 Murray St. (at Milligan St.). © 08/9321 2552. Main courses A$5–A$15 (US$3.25–US$9.75). MC, V. Daily 24 hr. Red CAT Stop 27 "Milligan St."

IN NORTHBRIDGE
Vulture's Restaurant & Café *ECLECTIC/MODERN AUSTRALIAN* This roomy, relaxed, and groovy "coffee lounge–cum–restaurant" has a knack of suiting all occasions and all folk, from couples doing a romantic dinner in the street-side courtyard to teenage nightclubbers hanging out after a big night. The place is scattered with funky bric-a-brac from Indian eagle totems to Balinese four-poster wedding beds—you can even sit inside them on cushions and eat at a low coffee table, instead of at the regular tables. The main courses are surpris-ingly sophisticated and skillfully cooked for such a casual joint—crispy skinned Exmouth Pink snapper, served with seafood, leek, and mushroom risotto, and finished with lemon hollandaise, or lamb loin stuffed with an apricot and sage farce, for example. There is also plenty of light stuff such as roast-chicken nachos or pastas. Fancy cocktails are a specialty, and there's a grazing menu after 10pm.

Francis St. at William St., Northbridge. © 08/9227 9087. Reservations recommended for dinner Fri–Sat. Main courses A$15–A$25 (US$9.75–US$16); dine-in or takeout sandwiches at lunch A$6.60–A$8.30 (US$4.30–US$5.40). Kids' menu A$7 (US$4.55). AE, DC, MC, V. Sun–Thurs 11am–1am; Fri–Sat 11am–2am or later. Bus: Blue CAT Stop 9 "TAFE."

ON THE BEACH
The Blue Duck *Kids* INTERNATIONAL/PIZZAS For ocean views and a lively atmosphere, it's hard to beat this casual restaurant perched right over the sand. Although the interior lacks the balcony's panoramic position, it has an upbeat seaside ambience and is just as packed as the porch. The all-day menu (from noon) has lots of light choices like chargrilled chicken salad, as well as steaks, grilled fish, gourmet burgers, and wood-fired pizzas with creative top-pings. The store is licensed to sell alcohol, but you can also BYO (bottled wine).

151 Marine Parade, North Cottesloe. © 08/9385 2499. Reservations recommended. Main courses A$4–A$14 (US$2.60–US$9.10), breakfast A$11–A$27 (US$7.15–US$18), all-day menu (many meals under A$20/US$13). Buffet breakfast Sat–Sun and holidays A$15–A$25 (US$9.75–US$16). Kids' menu A$7–A$9 (US$4.55–US$5.85). AE, DC, MC, V. Open Mon–Fri 6am–late (from 6:30am in winter); weekends and public holidays 7am–late. Bus: 71, 72, 73, or 883.

Indiana Tea House *MODERN AUSTRALIAN* The colonial Asian trap-pings (bamboo birdcages, plaster lions, and palms) at this bathhouse-turned-restaurant on Cottesloe Beach make me want to head for the tropical timber bar and order a Singapore Sling. Actually, the tasteful stucco building with bay win-dows and wooden floors is new—it just looks old. The menu mostly sticks to basics like rack of lamb or seafood dishes, with a couple of tasty vegetarian dishes thrown in. This place is just as popular with business folk cutting deals as it is with arty types browsing the papers over their cafe latte. Go in the daytime to make the most of those ocean views, or at sunset.

99 Marine Parade (on Cottesloe Beach opposite Forrest St.), Cottesloe. © 08/9385 5005. Reservations recommended. Main courses A$22–A$48 (US$14–US$24). AE, DC, MC, V. Daily noon–4pm and 6pm–late. Bus: 71, 72, 73, or 883.

> **Tips Java Joints**
>
> Don't leave Freo without a "short black" (that's an espresso) or a "flat white" (coffee with milk) at the port's "cappuccino strip" on South Terrace. On weekends this street bursts at the seams with locals flocking to alfresco Italian-style cafes serving good java and excellent focaccia, pasta, and pizza. **DOME, Old Papa's,** and **Gino's** are three to look for.

IN FREMANTLE

There's a Fremantle branch of **Fast Eddy's Café** (p. 435) at 13 Essex St. (© **08/ 9336 1671**) and another **Miss Maud Swedish Restaurant** (p. 435) at 33 South Terrace (© **08/9336 1599**), though this branch serves only the breakfast buffet on weekends.

La Pizzeria WOOD-FIRED PIZZA/SEAFOOD   Freo has loads of restaurants, but this joint has an upbeat, easy ambience with its terrazzo tables, concrete and timber floor, and stainless-steel bar. Wood-fired pizzas come straight from the funky oven at the rear, bearing toppings like grilled eggplant, roast capsicum, and mushrooms. Traditional pastas and seafood main courses get served up, too. Licensed to serve alcohol but you can also BYO beer and wine.

95 Market St. © **08/9430 6126.** Pizzas A$13–A$18 (US$8.45–US$12); main courses A$16–A$22 (US$10–US$14). AE, DC, MC, V. Mon–Thurs noon–10pm; Fri–Sun noon–10.30pm. Train: Fremantle.

WHAT TO SEE & DO IN PERTH

AQWA (Aquarium of Western Australia) *Kids*   You won't catch performing dolphins a la Sea World, but there's plenty to see here, including a moving walkway through an underwater tunnel of sharks, rays, turtles, and fish; a touch pool that even has a (small!) shark; and lots of aquariums that showcase the marine life of the Western Australian coast, including pretty leafy sea dragons, coral reefs, jellyfish, cuttlefish, sea snakes, crocodiles, and deadly stonefish that look remarkably like stones. Keepers feed the sharks and the touch-pool creatures daily, and a program of talks and movies on marine creatures is scheduled throughout the day. For A$90 (US$59) plus A$30 (US$20) for dive gear, qualified divers can dive with sharks. You may need to book this experience weeks in advance. Allow half a day here.

Sorrento Quay at Hillarys Boat Harbour, 91 Southside Dr., Hillarys. © **08/9447 7500.** Admission A$20 (US$13) adults, A$17 (US$11) seniors and students, A$13 (US$8.45) children 4–14, free for children under 4; A$58 (US$38) for a family of 4. Daily 10am–5pm; until 9pm Wed (Dec–Apr). Closed Christmas. Train and bus: Take Joondalup train line to Warwick, transfer to bus 423. By car, take Mitchell Fwy. 23km (14 miles) north, turn left into Hepburn Ave. and carry on to roundabout at entrance to Hillarys Boat Harbour; AQWA is at the western end of the harbor. Free parking.

Art Gallery of Western Australia   Most outstanding among this state gallery's international and Australian works is the Aboriginal art collection, regarded as the finest in Australia. Free 1-hour tours of a particular collection run once or twice a day, Tuesday through Friday and Sunday; call for times.

Roe St. and Beaufort St. (enter near the walkway opposite Perth Railway Station), Northbridge. © **08/9492 6600** administration, or 08/9492 6622 recorded information line. Free admission. Entry fee may apply to special exhibitions. Daily 10am–5pm; from 1pm Anzac Day. Closed Christmas and Good Friday. Train: Perth. Bus: Blue CAT Stop 7 "Museum."

Cohunu Koala Park   Not all states in Australia permit **koala cuddling,** but Western Australia does, and this large park set in bushland is a good place to try it. You can also feed 100 kangaroos, wallabies, and emus wandering in natural enclosures, see wombats and dingoes, walk through an aviary housing Aussie native birds, and see wild water birds on the ponds. The Caversham Wildlife Park in the Swan Valley (see "Side Trips from Perth," later in the chapter) has a bigger and more intriguing range of native species, but it does not allow koala cuddling.

Off Mills Rd. E., Gosnells (in the suburb of Martin on some maps). ℂ 08/9390 6090. Admission A$18 (US$12) adults, A$16 (US$10) seniors and students, A$9 (US$5.85) children 5–14. Koala-cuddling photos A$15–A$25 (US$9.75–US$16), or A$12 (US$7.80) if you take the photo yourself. Daily 10am–5pm; koala photo sessions 10am–4pm. Closed Christmas. Train: Gosnells on Armadale line then a cab (about A$15/US$9.75). Bus: 219. By car: Take Riverside Dr. across Swan River onto Albany Hwy., follow for approximately 25km (16 miles) to Gosnells, turn left onto Tonkin Hwy. and right (onto Mills Rd. E.; approx. 35-min. drive from city). A cab from the city is approx. A$40 (US$26).

Holmes à Court Gallery   This glamorous riverside gallery offers rotating exhibitions from one of the country's most outstanding private art collections, that of Janet Holmes à Court, Australia's richest woman. Many of the works are Aboriginal or by well-known Australian artists such as Sidney Nolan. The shop sells some impressive crafts pieces.

11 Brown St., East Perth. ℂ 08/9218 4540. Free admission. Thurs–Sun noon to 5pm. Closed public holidays. Train: Claisebrook.

Kings Park & Botanic Garden   Smack against the city center and Swan River is this 400-hectare (988-acre) hilltop park of botanic gardens and bushland. You can inspect weird and wonderful Western Australian flora, get to know the solitude of the bush, and bike, hike, or drive an extensive network of roads and trails. Visiting the spring **wildflower displays** (which peak in Sept–Oct) is a highlight for many. On weekends close to special occasions such as Easter, St. Patrick's Day, or Anzac Day (Apr 25) the lemon-scented gums lining Fraser Avenue are illuminated. There are barbecue and picnic facilities, several extensive playgrounds, bikes for rent (behind the Visitor Information Centre), tearooms, and the incomparable **Fraser's** restaurant (p. 434).

Pick up self-guiding maps from the Visitor Information Centre, or join one of the daily free, guided walks leaving from opposite the flower clock on Fraser Avenue. Walks depart 10am and 2pm and take 1½ hours, or 2 or 3 hours on bushwalks (May–Oct only). The **Perth Tram Co.** (ℂ **08/9322 2006**) runs 1-hour tours of the park and neighboring University of Western Australia in replica 1899 wooden trams. Tours depart daily from outside the Information Kiosk on Fraser Avenue at 11am, 12:15, 1:15 and 2:15pm. Tickets cost A$12 (US$7.80) for adults, A$10 (US$6.50) for seniors, A$6 (US$3.90) for children under 15, and A$30 (US$20) for families. Buy tickets on board. You can stop en route and rejoin a later tram if you like.

Fraser Ave. off Kings Park Rd. ℂ 08/9480 3659 information kiosk, or 08/9480 3600 administration. Free admission. Daily 24 hr. The Information Kiosk on Fraser Ave. inside the park is open daily from approximately 9:30am–4:30pm (closed Christmas). Hours can vary. Bus: 33 stops outside the Information Kiosk and extends into the park on Sat afternoon, and much of the day Sun and public holidays. Red CAT Stop 25 "Havelock St." is 1 block north of the gates.

Moments **Picture Perfect**

For the only photo of Perth you'll need, snap the view over the city and river from the War Memorial in Kings Park—it's superb day or night.

Perth Mint ⨁   This lovely historic building—built in the 1890s to mint currency from the Kalgoorlie gold rush—produced the victors' gold medals in the Sydney 2000 Olympic Games. Bullion is still traded here. The key event is a gold pour demonstration (on the hour from 10am weekdays, and from 10am–noon inclusive on weekends). You can also see samples of the 2000 Olympics medals, engrave a medallion with your own message, handle a 400-ounce gold bar, see gold coins being minted, and ogle the country's biggest collection of nuggets. A 30-minute free guided tour departs half an hour before every pour. A shop sells gold coins and nugget jewelry.

310 Hay St. at Hill St., East Perth. ✆ **08/9421 7277**. Admission A$6.50 (US$4.20) adults, A$5.50 (US$3.60) seniors and students, A$3.30 (US$2.15) school-age children; shop admission free. Mon–Fri 9am–4pm; Sat–Sun and holidays 9am–1pm. Closed Christmas, New Year's Day, Anzac Day (Apr 25), and Good Friday. Red CAT Stop 10 "Perth Mint."

Perth Zoo *Kids*   This is a good place to see kangaroos, koalas, numbats, wombats, quokkas, emus, echidnas (the Aussie answer to the porcupine), dingoes, snakes, frogs, and just about every other kind of Aussie wildlife, mostly housed in natural habitats, or in a walk-through aviary. There are plenty of exotic animals, too, including orangutans, Rothschild's giraffes, zebras, lions, rhinos, and elephants. Feeding demonstrations and talks run throughout the day. Koala cuddling is not permitted; for that, head to Cohunu Koala Park (see above).

20 Labouchere Rd., South Perth. ✆ **08/9474 3551** for recorded information, or 08/9474 0444 administration. Admission A$14 (US$9.10) adults, A$7 (US$4.55) children 4–15, A$38 (US$25) family of 4. Daily 9am–5pm. Ferry: Barrack St. Jetty to Mends St. Jetty, South Perth. Bus: 35. Ample free parking.

Western Australian Museum *Kids*   Kids will like the dinosaur gallery, the drawers full of insects, the blue-whale skeleton on the well-stocked aquatic zoology floor, the "megamouth" shark preserved in a tank set in the ground in the courtyard, and assorted other examples of Australia's weird natural creatures. The main attraction for grown-ups is one of the best collections of Aboriginal artifacts and rare photographs in the country. Allow 90 minutes to see most highlights.

Francis St. at Beaufort St. (or enter off James St. Mall), Northbridge. ✆ **08/9427 2700**. Free admission (donation requested); fee may apply to temporary exhibitions. Daily 9:30am–5pm; Anzac Day (Apr 25) and Boxing Day (Dec 26) 1–5pm. Closed Christmas and Good Friday. Train: Perth. Bus: Blue CAT Stop 8 "Museum."

HITTING THE BEACHES
Perth shares Sydney's good luck in having beaches in the metropolitan area—19 of them, in fact, laid end to end along the 35km (21-mile) Sunset Coast from Cottesloe in the south to Quinns Rocks in the north. Mornings are best, because a strong afternoon wind, known as the "Fremantle Doctor," can be unpleasant, especially in summer. Always swim between the red and yellow flags, which denote a "safe swimming" zone.

On weekends and public holidays from the last Saturday in September to the last Sunday in April, bus no. 458 stops hourly during the day at most beaches from Fremantle to Hillarys. It operates in both directions. You can take a surfboard under 2m (6½ ft.) on the bus.

The three most popular beaches are Cottesloe, Scarborough, and Trigg.

COTTESLOE   This pretty crescent, graced by the Edwardian-style Indiana Tea House (see above), is Perth's most fashionable beach. It has safe swimming and a small surf break. A couple of good cafes are nearby. Train: Cottesloe, then a walk of several hundred meters. Bus: 71, 72, 73, or 883.

SCARBOROUGH   Scarborough's white sands stretch for miles from the base of the Hotel Rendezvous Observation City, Perth. Swimming is generally safe, and surfers are always guaranteed a wave, although inexperienced swimmers should take a rain check when the surf is rough. The busy shopping precinct across the road means there's always somewhere to buy lunch and drinks. Bus: 400.

TRIGG   Surfers like Trigg best for its consistent swells. Bus: 400 to Scarborough, then a 10-minute walk north.

A DAY OUT IN FREMANTLE 𝕽𝕽

The heritage port precinct of **Fremantle,** 19km (12 miles) from downtown Perth on the mouth of the Swan River, is probably best known outside Australia as the site of the 1987 America's Cup challenge. Before that event, the city embarked on a major restoration of its gracious but derelict warehouses and Victorian buildings. Today "Freo" is a bustling district of 150 National Trust buildings, alfresco cafes, museums, galleries, pubs, markets, and shops in a masterfully preserved historical atmosphere. It's still a working port so you will see fishing boats unloading and yachts gliding in and out of the harbor. The ambience is so authentic that locals make a beeline for the place every weekend, resulting in a wonderful hubbub of buzzing shoppers, market-stall holders, java drinkers, yachties, tourists, and fishermen. Allow a full day to take in even half the sights—and don't forget to knock back an ale or two on the veranda of one of the gorgeous old pubs.

ESSENTIALS

GETTING THERE   Parking is plentiful, but driving is frustrating in the maze of one-way traffic. Most attractions are within walking distance (or hop on the free CAT bus, below), so take the train to Fremantle and explore on foot.

A nice way to get to Freo and see Perth's river suburbs is on the cruises that run once or twice a day from Barrack Street Jetty. See "Whale-Watching Cruises, Tram Trips & Other Tours," later in this chapter, for cruise operators.

GETTING AROUND   The silver Fremantle CAT bus makes a running loop of local attractions every 10 minutes Monday through Friday from 7:30am to 6pm, and on weekends and holidays from 10am to 6pm, except Christmas, Boxing Day (Dec 26), and Good Friday. It is free and departs from the train station.

VISITOR INFORMATION   The **Fremantle Tourist Bureau** is located in Town Hall, Kings Square at High Street, Fremantle, WA 6160 (© **08/9431 7878**). It's open Monday through Saturday from 9am to 5pm (until 4pm Sat in winter) and Sunday noon to 4:30pm. The best website is that of the Fremantle Council, www.fremantle.wa.gov.au.

SEEING THE SIGHTS IN FREMANTLE

You'll want to explore some of Freo's excellent museums and other attractions, but take time to stroll the streets and admire the 19th-century offices and warehouses, many painted in rich, historically accurate colors. When you arrive, wander down to the docks—either Victoria Quay, where sailing craft come and go, or Fishing Boat Harbour off Mews Road, where the boats bring in their catches—to get a breath of salt air.

Freo's best **shopping** is arts and crafts, from hand-blown glass to Aboriginal art to alpaca-wool clothing. Worth a look are the assorted art, crafts, and souvenir stores on High Street west of the mall; those in the **E Shed markets** on Victoria Quay (open Fri–Sun only, and public holidays that fall on a Mon,

9am–6pm); and **Bannister Street CraftWorks,** 8–12 Bannister St. (© **08/9336 2035**), an arts cooperative where you often spy the artists at work (open 11am–5:30pm; closed Mon). The 150 stalls at the **Fremantle Markets,** 74 South Terrace at Henderson Street (© **08/9335 2515**), mostly sell cheap imported handcrafts, jewelry, housewares, and clothing, as well as inexpensive food. They're open Friday from 9am to 9pm, Saturday from 9am to 5pm, and Sunday and any public holidays that fall on a Monday from 10am to 5pm.

The most popular watering holes are the **Sail & Anchor,** 64 S. Terrace (© **08/9335 8433**), which brews its own Brass Monkey Stout; the **Norfolk,** 47 South Terrace at Norfolk Street (© **08/9335 5405**); and the beautifully restored front bar and garden courtyard at **Phillimore's Café & Bar** at His Majesty's Hotel, on Phillimore Street at Mouat Street (© **08/9335 9596**). The happening "cappuccino strip" on South Terrace is good for people-watching.

Fremantle Arts Centre   Housed in a striking neo-Gothic 1860s building built by convicts, this center contains one of Western Australia's best contemporary arts-and-crafts galleries with a constantly changing array of works. A shop sells crafts from Western Australia, a bookstore stocks Australian art books and literature, and the courtyard cafe is the perfect place to hang out. Free concerts play on the lawn every Sunday and public holiday between October and April from 2 to 4pm.

1 Finnerty St. © 08/9432 9555. Free admission. Daily 10am–5pm. Closed Christmas, Boxing Day (Dec 26), Good Friday, and New Year's Day.

Fremantle History Museum *♠*   Housed in a convict-built former lunatic asylum next to the Fremantle Arts Centre, this small but densely packed museum uses lots of old photographs and personal possessions to paint a realistic picture of what life was like for Fremantle's first settlers, the Aborigines they displaced, and later generations up to the present day.

1 Finnerty St. at Ord St. (part of the Fremantle Arts Centre, see above). © 08/9430 7966. Free admission (donation requested). Sun–Fri 10:30am–4:30pm; Sat 1–5pm. Closed Christmas and Good Friday.

Fremantle Prison *♠*   Even jails sported attractive architecture back in the 1850s. This limestone jail, built to house 1,000 inmates by convicts who no doubt ended up inside it, was a maximum-security prison until 1991. Take the 75-minute tour, or guide yourself with an audio headset to see cells re-created in the style of past periods of the jail's history, bushranger (highwayman) Joe Moondyne's "escape-proof" cell, the gallows, the workshops, the chapel, the hospital, the jailers' houses, and cell walls featuring some wonderful artwork by the former inmates. An additional 45-minute tour visits the women's prison every hour, after the main tour and is included in the ticket price. You must book for the Wednesday- and Friday-night **candlelight tours** *♠*, which take 90 minutes.

1 The Terrace. © 08/9336 9200. Free admission to prison precinct and visitor center. Tours A$14 (US$9.10) adults, A$11 (US$7.15) seniors and students, A$7.15 (US$4.65) children 4–15, A$39 (US$25) families of 5; candlelight tours Wed and Fri A$18 (US$12) adults, A$13 (US$8.45) seniors and students, A$8.80 (US$5.70) children, A$47 (US$31) families. Daily 10am–6pm. Main tours run every 30 min. from 10am; last tour 5pm. Women's prison tours run every hour from 11:30am; last tour 4:30pm. Candlelight tours Wed and Fri 7pm (winter) or 7:30pm (summer). Closed Christmas and Good Friday.

The Roundhouse   This 12-sided jail is the oldest public building in the state (built around 1830). There are no displays or memorabilia, but it's worth a visit for history's sake, and for the sea views on the other side. The time cannon just to its west, a replica of a gun salvaged from an 1878 wreck, is fired and a **time**

ball dropped at 1pm daily, just as it was in the 1800s, from a deck overlooking the ocean. You might be that day's honorary gunner chosen from the crowd! The Roundhouse is a short walk from the Fremantle train station.

10 Arthur Head (enter over the railway line from High St.). © **08/9336 6897.** Admission by gold coin donation, A$1 or A$2 (US65¢ or US$1.30). Daily 10:30am–3:30pm. Closed Good Friday and Christmas.

Shipwrecks Museum   You will love the tales of old wrecks and displays of pieces of eight, glassware, cannon, and other deep-sea treasure recovered off the Western Australian coast. The museum is renowned for its work in maritime archaeology. Displays date from the 1600s, when Dutch explorers became the first Europeans to encounter Australia. One of the best displays is the appalling tale of the *Batavia,* wrecked north of Perth in 1629, where most of the survivors were massacred by a handful of mutineers.

Cliff Street. © **08/9431 8444.** Free admission. Daily 9:30am–5pm; from 1pm on Anzac Day (Apr 25) and Boxing Day (Dec 26). Closed Good Friday and Christmas.

Western Australian Maritime Museum 𝕽𝕽   This fascinating museum moved into a new home at the western end of Victoria Quay in December 2002. The museum looks at Fremantle's history and present-day operations as a port, signaling and piloting, navigation ancient and modern, current sailing technology, naval defense, sea trade, and Aboriginal maritime heritage. It also features historic or rare boats, including *Australia II* (the Aussie yacht that won the America's Cup), and you can also tour the HMAS *Ovens,* an Oberon-class submarine, every half-hour from 10am daily. You can buy either a joint ticket for the museum and sub, or just for the sub. Museum staffer Elaine Berry leads a 90-minute **Maritime Precinct Walk** for A$10 (US$6.50) for adults, A$7.50 (US$4.90) for seniors and groups of 4 or more, and A$3 (US$1.95) for school-age kids; book by calling the museum © **08/9431 8455,** or Elaine at home (© **08/9336 1906**) on weekends. Tours can be scheduled for a day and time to suit you.

Victoria Quay, Fremantle. © **08/9335 8921.** Admission A$10 (US$6.50) adults, A$3 (US$2) children 5–15, A$5 (US$3.25) concessions, A$22 (US$14) for family of 6. Entry to submarine only A$8 (US$5.20) adults, A$3 (US$2) children 5–15. Daily 9:30am–5pm, and from 1–5pm on Anzac Day (Apr 25) and Boxing Day (Dec 26). Closed Good Friday and Christmas.

WHALE-WATCHING CRUISES, TRAM TRIPS & OTHER TOURS

Boat Torque Cruises (© **08/9430 5844**), **Golden Sun Cruises** (© **08/9325 9916**), and **Oceanic Cruises** (© **08/9325 1191**) run an assortment of morning, afternoon, sunset, luncheon, dinner, half-, and full-day cruises on the Swan River, some as far as Fremantle, and to historic homes and vineyards in the Swan Valley. Oceanic Cruises does a lunch cruise to see wild sea lions at Carnac Island just off Fremantle. The cruise costs A$79 (US$51) adults, A$69 (US$45) ages 13 to 17, and A$39 (US$25) kids 4 to 12 from Perth, less from Fremantle. **Captain Cook Cruises** (© **08/9325 3341**) also runs cruises on the Perth-Fremantle route, and does an Aboriginal cultural cruise that includes a guided bushland walk and costs A$35 (US$23) adults, A$30 (US$20) seniors and students, and A$20 (US$13) kids 4 to 14. Cruise with lunch is slightly more.

September through November, Perth's waters are alive with southern right and humpback **whales** returning from the north with their calves. To join a 2- or 3-hour jaunt to watch them, contact Boat Torque Cruises, Oceanic Cruises, or the **Rottnest Express ferry** (© **08/9335 6406**), which does whale-watch trips between ferry runs. Departure days and times vary from year to year with every cruise operator, so check ahead. Prices range from A$25 (US$16) on the Rottnest Express up to around A$40 (US$26) for the other companies, and about half price for kids. Most depart Fremantle; Boat Torque also does them from Hillarys Boat Harbour (near the AQWA aquarium; see "What to See & Do in Perth," earlier in this chapter). The company provides coach connections to Hillarys from Perth.

The **Aquarium of Western Australia (AQWA;** © **08/9447 7500)** runs whale-watching tours on Wednesdays, weekends, and public holidays during the season (Sept to early Dec) at 9am and 11:30am. Tours, limited to 12 people, are on board an ocean rafter that gives "eye level" encounters with these magnificent mammals. The cost is A$90 (US$59) per person and includes admission to AQWA. Bookings are essential.

The Perth Tram Co. (© **08/9322 2006**) makes a daily loop of the city, the casino, and Kings Park in replica 1899 wooden trams; hop on and off as often as you wish. Tickets, which you buy on board, cost A$15 (US$9.75) for adults, A$13 (US$8.45) for seniors, A$7 (US$4.55) for children under 15, and A$37 (US$24) for families. City-casino, city–Kings Park, and casino–Kings Park single legs are also available. Join anywhere; the tram starts at 565 Hay St. at 9:40am and makes six 90-minute loops a day, with a commentary.

Feature Tours (© **1800/999 819** in Australia, or 08/9475 2900; www.ft. com.au) runs half- and full-day coach tours to attractions in and around Perth.

ACTIVE PURSUITS

BIKING   Perth's superb bike-track network stretches for miles along the Swan River, through Kings Park, around Fremantle, and all the way down the beaches. There is a great 9.5km (6-mile) track around Perth Water, the broad expanse of river in front of the central business district, that starts at the Swan River on Riverside Drive and goes over the Causeway bridge, back along the other bank and over the bridge at the Narrows back to the city. The state Department of Transport's cycling division, Bikewest, publishes a range of useful bike-route maps to the city. They are available in bike shops, most newsagents, and at **Map World,** 900 Hay St. (© **08/9322 5733**).

Rental from **Koala Bike Hire,** located in the car park behind Fraser's restaurant in Kings Park (© **08/9321 3061**), is A$5 (US$3.25) for an hour, or A$16 (US$10) for the day, which includes a helmet (required by law in Australia), lock, and maps of Kings Park.

GOLF   Most convenient to the city is Burswood Park Golf Course, part of the **Burswood International Resort Casino,** across the river on the Great Eastern Highway, Burswood (© **08/9362 7576** for the pro shop). A nine-hole round is just A$14 (US$9.10) weekdays and A$17 (US$11) weekends. A cart for nine holes is A$22 (US$14) and club rental is A$17 (US$11).

Even more scenic are the 27 championship fairways designed by Robert Trent Jones Jr. at **Joondalup Resort,** Country Club Boulevard, Connolly, a 25km (15½-mile) drive north of Perth (© **08/9400 8811** pro shop); and **The Vines** in the Swan Valley (© **08/9297 3000** for the resort, or 08/9297 0777 for the pro shop), which has two 18-hole bushland courses. Joondalup was ranked the No. 1 Resort Golf Course in Australia by *Golf Australia* magazine in 2003. Kangaroos often come onto both courses. Expect to pay between A$35 and A$55 (US$23–US$36) for nine holes at either resort, and A$90 (US$59) at Joondalup on weekends.

SAILING   The tallest Tall Ship in Australia, the lovely three-masted barquen-tine **STS *Leeuwin II*** (© 08/9430 4105; www.leeuwin.com), sails from B Shed at Victoria Quay, Fremantle, when it is not out on voyages around Australia. You may be one of up to 40 passengers, but you still get the chance to try your hand at sailing the way it used to be done. Day trips—usually on weekends—are from 10am to 3pm and cost A$99 (US$64) for adults and A$55 (US$36) for chil-dren under 12. The ship sometimes does 3- or 4-hour sails in the mornings, afternoons, and at sunset.

Experienced sailors can sail on Wednesday afternoons in summer from about 3 to 5pm with members of the **Royal Perth Yacht Club,** Australia II Drive, Crawley (© 08/9389 1555; ask for the sailing administrator), if there is a place available. It's not spinnaker sailing on Wednesdays, so the action is at an easy pace. All-white dress standards apply.

SCUBA DIVING & SNORKELING   Just 19km (12 miles) off Perth, Rot-tnest Island's corals, reef fish, wrecks, and limestone caverns, in 18m to 35m (59- to 115-ft.) visibility, are a gift from heaven to Perth divers and snorkelers. Contact **Rottnest Malibu Diving** (© 08/9292 5111) on Rottnest Island (see "Side Trips from Perth," below) to rent gear or join a dive trip. **Diving Ventures,** at 384 S. Terrace, Fremantle (© 1800/655 330 in Australia, or 08/9430 5130; www.dventures.com.au/dv.shtml), also conducts dive day trips from Perth to Rottnest Island, and also to the wreck of the HMAS *Swan,* located off Duns-borough in the state's Southwest, a 113m (246-ft.) long destroyer which was scuttled for divers' pleasure a couple of years ago. This trip costs A$160 (US$104) with two dives, including all gear. The company also does 3-day live-aboard trips to Ningaloo Reef, and "introductory" dives for any adventurer without dive qualifications who wants to try the sport in the company of an instructor. The company also rents scuba gear and conducts dive courses. It has a city outlet at 222 William St., Northbridge, in Perth (© 08/9228 2630).

SURFING   You will find good surfing at many city beaches, Scarborough and Trigg in particular. See the "Hitting the Beaches" section, earlier in this chapter. Rottnest Island (see "Side Trips from Perth," below) also has good breaks. **Mur-ray Smith Surf Centre,** Shop 14, Luna Maxi Mart, Scarborough (© 08/9245 2988), rents long boards for A$20 (US$13) for half a day or A$30 (US$20) for the day, plus a A$100 (US$65) refundable deposit. They also rent body boards. **Surfing WA** (© 08/9448 0004) runs 2-hour surfing classes for A$110 (US$72) per person on Saturday and Sunday mornings. Boards, wet suits, and sunscreen are provided.

THE SHOPPING SCENE

Most shops are located downtown on the parallel **Hay Street** and **Murray Street malls,** located 1 block apart, and in the network of arcades running off them such as the Plaza, City, Carillon, and the Tudor-style **London Court** arcades. Off Murray Street Mall on Forrest Place is the **Forrest Chase shopping com-plex,** housing the Myer department store and boutiques on two levels. Add to your collection of international designer brands on posh **King Street.**

If you want to avoid the chains, spend half a day in **Subiaco** ⚘ or "Subi," where Hay Street and Rokeby Road are lined with smart boutiques, art galleries, cafes, antiques shops, and markets. The Colonnade shopping center at 388 Hay St. showcases groovy young Aussie fashion designers in its Studio 388 section.

Fremantle's shopping is mostly limited to a good selection of crafts, markets, and Aboriginal souvenirs.

> ## *Finds* Desert Designs
>
> Aboriginal artist **Jimmy Pike** grew up in Western Australia's Sandy Desert and was one of the first to start transferring his Dreamtime art and designs to fabrics, in 1981. He died in late 2002, but his commercial work lives on in clothing and accessories—including cute children's gear—bearing his designs at the **Desert Designs** boutique at 114 High Street Mall, Fremantle (© **08/9430 4101**). For paintings and limited-edition prints by Jimmy Pike and many other Aboriginal artists, visit the **Japingka Gallery**, 47 High St., Fremantle (© **08/9335 8265**), which also stocks didgeridoos, artifacts, and stunning high-quality hand-tufted woolen floor rugs.

Shops are open until 9pm on Friday in the city, and until 9pm on Thursday in Subiaco and Fremantle.

ABORIGINAL ARTS & CRAFTS   Creative Native, 32 King St. (© **08/9322 3398**), stocks Perth's widest range of Aboriginal arts and crafts. Upstairs is a gallery selling original works by some renowned Aboriginal artists. There's another branch at 65 High St., Fremantle (© **08/9335 6995**).

Indigenart, 115 Hay St., Subiaco (© **08/9388 2899**), and 82 High St., Fremantle (© **08/9335 2911**), stocks works on canvas, paper, and bark, as well as artifacts, textiles, pottery, didgeridoos, boomerangs, and sculpture, by world-famous and lesser-known Aboriginal artists from all over Australia.

JEWELRY   Western Australia is renowned for farming the world's best **South Sea pearls** off Broome, for Argyle **diamonds** mined in the Kimberley, and for being one of the world's biggest **gold** producers.

Artisans of the Sea, corner of Marine Terrace and Collie Street, Fremantle (© **08/9336 3633**), sells elegant South Sea pearl and gold jewelry.

Some of Perth's other leading jewelers, where you can buy opals, Argyle diamonds, and Broome pearls, are family-owned sister stores, **Costello's,** Shop 5–6, London Court (© **08/9325 8588**), and **Swan Diamonds,** Shop 4, London Court (© **08/9325 8166**), and also **Linneys,** 37 Rokeby Rd., Subiaco (© **08/9382 4077**).

For opals to suit all budgets, head to the Perth outlet of opal retailer, **Quilpie Opals,** Shop 6, Piccadilly Arcade off Hay Street Mall (© **08/9321 8687**).

PERTH AFTER DARK

Scoop (see "Visitor Information," earlier in this chapter) is a good source of information on festivals and concerts, performing arts, classical music, exhibitions, and the like. Your best guide to dance clubs, rock concerts, gig listings, art-house cinemas, theater and art galleries is the free weekly *X-press* magazine available at pubs, cafes, and music venues every Thursday. The *West Australian* and *Sunday Times* newspapers publish a limited amount of entertainment information, including cinema guides.

Two booking agents handle bookings to most of the city's major performing arts, entertainment, and sporting events: the performing arts–oriented **BOCS** (© **1800/193 300** in Australia, or 08/9484 1133; www.bocsticketing.com.au) and the sports- and family entertainment–oriented **Ticketmaster 7** (© **136 109**; www.ticketmaster7.com). Book opera, ballet, the orchestra, and the Black Swan Theatre Company (see below) through BOCS.

THE PERFORMING ARTS   The **West Australian Opera** (© **08/9321 5869** administration or 08/9265-0950 bookings) and **West Australian Ballet** (© **08/9481 0707** administration) usually perform at **His Majesty's Theatre,** 825 Hay St., a restored "grande dame" venue from the early 1900s. Perth's leading theatrical company, the **Black Swan Theatre Company** (© **08/9388 9388** administration), plays at theaters around town. The **West Australian Symphony Orchestra** (© **08/9326 0000**) usually performs at the **Perth Concert Hall,** 5 St. Georges Terrace next to the Duxton Hotel. This hall has the best acoustics of any such venue in Australia; such acts as the London Philharmonic, comedian Billy Connolly, and legendary blues guitarist B. B. King have performed here.

Perth is an outdoors kinda place. In summer, look for outdoor concerts or jazz at **Perth Zoo** (© **08/9474 3551** for recorded information, or 08/9474 0449 administration); movies at Perth's several outdoor cinemas; and open-air concerts, plays, and movies in **Kings Park** (© **08/9480 3600**).

PUBS, BARS & NIGHTCLUBS   Northbridge houses most of city's lively pubs and dance clubs. Don't forget Freo has good pubs, too (see "A Day Out in Fremantle," earlier in this chapter).

For a trendy take on the traditional pub, head to **The Brass Monkey,** 209 William St. at James Street, Northbridge (© **08/9227 9596**). Downstairs are several bars including a wine bar serving gourmet pizzas, and a beer garden. Wednesday to Saturday head upstairs to the Glasshouse for live entertainment, including the Laugh Resort comedy club from 8pm Wednesdays for a A$10 (US$6.50) cover.

In Subiaco, suits flock to the "Subi," also known as the **Subiaco Hotel,** 465 Hay St. at Rokeby Road, Subiaco (© **08/9381 3069**), a popular historic pub with a stylish cafe, great cocktails, and live jazz on Wednesday and Saturday nights.

Metropolis Concert Club, 146 Roe St., Northbridge (© **08/9228 0500**), is a huge complex of dance floors and bars over several levels. It's open Friday from 9pm and Saturday from 8pm, until very late. If your "dancing till 6am" days are over but you still know how to hit the dance floor, check out **Margeaux's,** a nightclub popular with the over-30s crowd, located in the Parmelia Hilton, 14 Mill St. (© **08/9215 2000**). It's open Wednesdays, Fridays, and Saturdays from 9pm until 3:30am.

BURSWOOD CASINO   A 2,300-seat theater that hosts some major international stars is located in the **Burswood International Resort Casino,** on the Great Eastern Highway just over the river (© **08/9362 7646** for information, or call BOCS for bookings—see above). Live bands, disco, cabaret performers, or karaoke play nightly in the free Cabaret Nightclub, and there are nine restaurants and six bars within the complex. On the main gaming floor are 88 tables and 1,300 computerized gaming machines. Some of the Casino's most popular games include roulette, blackjack, and two-up. There's also a VIP players' room and a Keno Lounge. Except for Christmas Day, Good Friday, and Anzac Day, the casino is open 24 hours. Dress code is "neat and tidy" with smarter standards required after 7pm. The Casino is open to everyone over the age of 18. It's about a A$13 (US$8.45) cab ride from the city, or take a train to Burswood station.

2 Side Trips from Perth

ROTTNEST ISLAND: GETTING FACE TO FACE WITH THE FISHES *☆☆*

19km (12 miles) W of Perth

The delightful wildlife reserve of Rottnest Island off the Perth coast is like the city's own Great Barrier Reef in miniature. Its jewel-bright waters, warm currents, rocky coves, and many sheltered beaches harbor **coral reefs** and 360 kinds of fish that make for fabulous snorkeling. You may spot humpback whales September through December, and dolphins surfing the waves anytime. The island is also home to 10,000 **quokkas,** cute otterlike marsupials that reach up to your knees. A wonderful thing about Rottnest is that there are no cars. Everyone gets around by bike (or bus, if you tire of pedaling over the mostly moderate-grade hills). The island is 11km (7 miles) long and 4.5km (3 miles) across at its widest point.

ESSENTIALS

GETTING THERE   Boat Torque Cruises (© 08/9221 5888) and **Oceanic Cruises** (© 08/9325 1191) operate services at least three times a day from Perth (trip time: about 1 hr. 45 min.), and four to seven times a day from Fremantle (trip time: about 25 min.). The **Rottnest Express ferry** (© 08/9335 6406) runs four or five times a day from Fremantle only. Round-trip fares from Perth average about A$60 (US$39), or about A$40 (US$26) from Fremantle. Boat Torque and Oceanic pick you up free from most Perth and Fremantle hotels. You pay about A$5 (US$3.25) more if you return on a later day. Most boat operators offer day-trip and accommodations packages, as well as straight transfers.

   Kookaburra Air (© 08/9354 1158; www.kookaburra.iinet.net.au) and **Rottnest Air Taxi** (© 1800/500 006 in Western Australia, or 08/9292 5027; www.rottnest.de) provide aerial transfers. A round-trip in a four-seater (including the pilot) aircraft with Rottnest Air Taxi is A$180 (US$117) for the plane.

VISITOR INFORMATION   Information is dispensed by the **Rottnest Island Visitor & Information Centre** (© 08/9372 9752), which is right at the end of the jetty on the island. The center is run by the **Rottnest Island Authority** (© 08/9432 9300; www.rottnest.wa.gov.au). The Perth Visitor Centre (see "Visitor Information," in the Perth section, earlier in this chapter) also has information.

GETTING AROUND   Ferries pull into the jetty in the main town, called "Settlement" at Thomson Bay. **Rottnest Bike Hire** (© 08/9292 5105), next to the Rottnest Hotel near the jetty, rents 2,300 bikes in every size, speed, and type, as well as holders for everything from surfboards to babies. An 18-speed bike is A$20 (US$13) for a 24-hour day (plus a A$25/US$16 refundable deposit), including a helmet (compulsory in Australia) and lock. There is no need to book a bike.

   The yellow **Bayseeker** bus does half-hourly circumnavigations calling at 16 stops including all the best bays. An all-day ticket costs A$7 (US$4.55) for adults, A$3.50 (US$2.25) for children 4 to 12, and A$17 (US$11) for families of 4 (extra child A$1.65/US$1.05). Buy tickets on board.

   A free bus runs regularly between the airport and four of the five small communities around the island—Thomson Bay Settlement, Geordie, Fay's and Longreach Bays. It does not run to the Basin, which is a 15-minute walk from the Settlement.

ISLAND ORIENTATION TOURS

Many first-time visitors take the **2-hour Island Bus Tour** because it is a good introduction to the bays and the island's cultural and natural history—and because it includes a stop to see the quokkas. It costs A$22 (US$14) for adults, A$11 (US$7.15) for kids 4 to 12, and A$50 (US$33) for families of four (extra child A$5/US$3.25). Departure times vary, but you can expect them to run twice a day, usually around 10:30am and 1:30pm. Buy tickets from the Visitor Centre.

SNORKELING, DIVING, SURFING & FISHING

Most people come to Rottnest to snorkel, swim, surf, dive, or fish. As soon as you arrive, rent a bike and your preferred aquatic gear, and pedal around the coast until you come to a beach that suits you. (Don't forget to carry drinking water and food, because the only shops are at Settlement.) The Basin, Little Parakeet Bay, Little Salmon Bay, and Parker Point are good snorkel spots. The Visitor Centre sells maps to suggested **snorkel trails.** Surfers should try Cathedral Rocks or Strickland Bay. Fishermen will catch squid, salmon, and tailor, as well as all kinds of reef fish. The island's dive shop, **Rottnest Malibu Diving** (© **08/9292 5111**), near the jetty, rents snorkel gear, dive gear, wet suits, surfboards, body boards, aqua-bikes, and fishing tackle. The company conducts two daily trips to some of the 100-plus dive sites around Rottnest. Some feature limestone caverns and some of the island's 14 shipwrecks. A shore or boat dive with all gear included is A$60 (US$39). If you have never dived before but want to try, a 1- to 2-hour theory lesson followed by a boat dive is A$200 (US$130) including return transport from Perth.

FOR HISTORY BUFFS

Rottnest has quite a bit to offer history buffs, who may want to walk (45-min. trip), cycle, or take the train to the Oliver Hill 1930s gun emplacements, which has intact 9.2-inch guns and battery tunnels housing an engine room, a plotting room, and observation posts. You can explore the 1.5km (1-mile) heritage trail on your own (maps are at the Visitor Centre), or take a guided 1-hour tour on the hour between 11am and 2pm inclusive. The train fare, which includes the tour except for the last trip of the day, costs A$15 (US$9.75) for adults, A$7.70 (US$5) for children 4 to 12, and A$39 (US$25) for families of four (extra child A$3.85/US$2.50). It departs from the station near the Visitor Centre hourly from 10:30am to 2:30pm inclusive.

Volunteer guides run several free 1-hour walking tours. One is a historical tour of architectural points of interest around Thomson Bay, many of which were built in the 19th century, such as the Governor's residence, the chapel, the octagonal prison, the small **museum** (© **08/9372 9753;** open daily 11am–4pm), and the former Boys' Reformatory. Another heritage trail takes you to the memorial marking de Vlamingh, the Dutch explorer who named the island Rott Enest (Rat Nest) in 1696 when he mistook quokkas for rats. There are also quokka walks, an Aboriginal historical walk, and a walk to Bathurst lighthouse.

WHERE TO STAY & DINE

Call the **Rottnest Island Authority's accommodations booking service** (© **08/9432 9111**) to book one of the island's 250-plus holiday homes, apartments, cabins, historic cottages, or the campground. Don't expect anything new or upscale. Water and electricity restrictions mean no accommodations are air-conditioned. Book well in advance all through summer; accommodations during the peak Western Australian school vacation times are allotted on a ballot system, for which you must submit an application form.

Apart from the very nice restaurants at the hotels listed below, the casual tearooms, and a couple of lackluster takeout joints, your only other dining option is the excellent DOME cafe at the jetty.

Shoulder season is usually April through May, and again September through November or December. Winter is June through August.

Rottnest Hotel   This 1864 building near the jetty, once the state governor's summer residence, is now the local pub where day-trippers gather in the sports bar or the large open-air beer garden to admire the ocean views over an ale or two. The building contains pleasant, modern motel-style rooms, some with a small patio and sea views. Apart from the Lakeside units at Rottnest Lodge, below, these are the best hotel rooms on the island. No smoking indoors.

Bedford Ave, Rottnest Island, WA 6161. © 08/9292 5011. Fax 08/9292 5188. rottnesthotel@axis mgt.com.au. 18 units (all with shower only). Peak (Dec 21–Jan 31) A$180–A$199 (US$117–US$129) double; summer (Feb to mid-Apr, Sept–Dec) A$140–A$160 (US$91–US$104) double; winter (June–Aug) A$115–A$135 (US$75–US$88) double. Extra person A$30 (US$20). Rates include continental breakfast. Ask about midweek packages in winter. AE, DC, MC, V. **Amenities:** Restaurant; cook-your-own barbecue; 2 bars; beer garden. *In room:* TV, fridge, no phone.

Rottnest Lodge   The Lakeside Rooms at this former colonial barracks and prison are Rottnest's most luxurious accommodations, built in 1989 with flagstone floors, cream painted brick walls, contemporary furnishings, and a living area with a wood fireplace. Some have salt-lake views, not always pretty when the water dries up. The remaining Deluxe, Standard, "Quod," and Family rooms, which sleep from 2 to 10, are in the historic quarters and are mostly dark, viewless, and small. The two-bedroom family rooms have the advantage of a kitchen and laundry. You are just a few minutes' stroll from the jetty and Visitor Centre here.

Kitson St., Rottnest Island, WA 6161. © 08/9292 5161. Fax 08/9292 5158. www.rottnestlodge.com.au. 80 units (all with shower only). High season (mid-Dec to late Jan) A$175–A$265 (US$114–US$172) double. Shoulder (Feb–Apr, Sept to mid-Dec) A$165–A$240 (US$107–US$156) double. Winter (May to early Sept) A$130–A$185 (US$85–US$120) double. Additional person A$60 (US$39) extra. Quod rooms (sleep 4) A$180–A$235 (US$117–US$153). Family apts A$375–A$450 (US$244–US$293). Ask about packages. AE, DC, MC, V. **Amenities:** Restaurant; 2 bars; small lagoon-style swimming pool. *In room:* TV, fridge, coffeemaker; hair dryer, iron in Lakeside rooms only.

IN PURSUIT OF THE GRAPE IN THE SWAN VALLEY ✿
20km (13 miles) NE of Perth

Twenty minutes from the city center is the Swan Valley, home to two of Australia's biggest wine labels. There are 30 or so wineries, along with a wildlife park, antiques shops, a few galleries, several good restaurants, and Australia's best golf resort. Some restaurants and wineries close Monday and Tuesday.

Lord Street from the Perth city center becomes Guildford Road and takes you to the historic Art-Deco town of Guildford at the start of the Swan Valley. The **Swan Valley and Eastern Region Visitors Centre** is at the corner of Meadow and Swan streets, Guildford (© **08/9379 9400;** www.swanvalley.com.au). It's open daily from 9am to 4pm. Several companies (see "Whale-Watching Cruises, Tram Trips & Other Tours," above) run day tours or day cruises from Perth, and local companies run tours by black cab or Rolls Royce. The winery at **Sandalford Caversham Estate** (© **08/9374 0000**) runs its own upscale cruise from Perth daily that includes a 2-hour winery tour, three-course lunch matched to wines, wine tasting en route and at the winery, souvenir wine glass, and a wine-education kit. It costs A$129 (US$84) per person and includes coach return to Perth.

TOURING THE WINERIES & OTHER THINGS TO DO

Most Swan wineries are small family-run affairs, but an exception is **Houghton Wines,** Dale Road, Middle Swan (© **08/9274 9540**), Western Australia's oldest, biggest, and most venerable winery. The big-beamed timber cellar has old wine-making machinery on show, and there are beautiful picnic grounds (especially nice in Nov when mauve jacaranda trees blossom gloriously), a cafe, and an art gallery selling works by local artists. Open 10am to 5pm daily except Good Friday and Christmas. The other big-name winery is **Sandalford Caversham Estate,** 3210 West Swan Rd., Caversham (© **08/9374 9300**). You may want to take its 90-minute winery tour, which takes you along walkways over the hi-tech production areas. The A$15 (US$9.75) fee includes a tasting of premium wine and a wine-education kit. It runs three times daily. The winery also has a good gift shop, a pretty vine-covered casual dining area, and a pleasant restaurant. Both wineries' cellar doors are open daily for free tastings from 10am to 5pm.

The popular **Margaret River Chocolate Company** has an outlet at 5123 W. Swan Rd. (near the Reid Hwy.), West Swan (© **08/9250 1588**), open daily from 10am to 5pm. It does sales and tasting, and you can see the chocolate being made through the viewing window.

After a move in 2003 to a new site in Whiteman Park, West Swan, the **Caversham Wildlife Park & Zoo** (© **08/9274 2202**) has smart new homes for its collection of 200 species of mostly Western Australian wildlife. You can stroke koalas (but not hold them), cuddle wombats and joeys sometimes, feed kangaroos, pet farm animals, and take a camel ride. It's open daily from 9am to 5pm, closed Christmas. Admission is A$12 (US$7.80) for adults, A$9 (US$5.85) for seniors and students, and A$5 (US$3.25) for children 2 to 14.

Lovers of old stuff should browse the **junk-shop strip** on James Street, in Guildford (most shops are open daily), or visit **Woodbridge House,** a beautifully restored 1883 manor at Ford Street, in West Midland (© **08/9274 2432**). The house is open daily (closed Wed) from 1 to 4pm; closed all July for maintenance, and Christmas, Boxing Day (Dec 26) and Good Friday. Admission is A$3.85 (US$2.50) for adults, A$1.65 (US$1.10) for seniors and school-age children, and A$8.80 (US$5.70) for a family. Its river-view tearooms open for lunch.

One of Perth's best boutiques, the **Swan Valley Boutique** (© **08/9377 2070**) is in the unlikely location of 4 Johnson St., Guildford; it serves coffee while you try on clothes by big-name Aussie fashion designers.

WHERE TO STAY

Hansons Swan Valley ⨀⨀   "At last!" some of you will cry as you step into the sleek entry hall—it's a B&B that's not hokey or drowning in chintz. Instead, these rooms have stark white walls and groovy furniture a la Philippe Starck. Most rooms have king-size beds; all have bathrobes and minibars stocked with cheeses, chocolates, and other goodies. Hair dryers and irons are available. Former advertising executives Jon and Selina Hanson built this house to create a slick B&B of the kind they would like to stay in themselves. It is set on a 10-hectare (25-acre) farm. It also has great breakfasts and dinners. No smoking indoors.

60 Forest Rd., Henley Brook, WA 6055. © **08/9296 3366.** Fax 08/9296 3332. www.hansons.com.au. 10 units (6 with Jacuzzis and shower, 4 with shower only). A$195–A$290 (US$127–US$189) double. Rates include full

breakfast. Ask about packages. AE, DC, MC, V. Take West Swan Rd. to Henley Brook and turn right at Little River Winery into Forest Rd. Hansons is on the left at the end of the road. No children under 15. **Amenities:** Restaurant; small outdoor pool; limited room service; in-room massage (with 2 hr. notice); laundry/dry cleaning service; nonsmoking rooms. *In room:* A/C, TV/VCR, minibar.

Novotel Vines Resort 🏆 This rural retreat is one of the best resort golf courses in Australia, and is the most upscale place in the Swan Valley. Most rooms or apartments in the low-rise accommodations have balconies looking onto one of two 18-hole courses where kangaroos often join the players, or over the pool or vineyard. The rooms are of a high standard, if a bit stiff and citified. A suite consists of a room with a living area and a Jacuzzi.

Verdelho Dr., Belhus near Upper Swan, WA 6069. © Accor, **1300/65 6565** in Australia, 800/221 4542 in the U.S. and Canada, 020/8283 4500 in the U.K., 0800/44 4422 in New Zealand, or 08/9297 3000. Fax 08/9297 3333. www.novotelvines.com.au. 147 units. A$220–A$415 (US$143–US$270) double; A$265–A$444 (US$172–US$289) suite; A$300 (US$195) 2-bedroom apt; A$375 (US$244) 3-bedroom apt. Extra person A$33 (US$21). Children under 16 stay free in parent's room with existing bedding. Ask about packages. AE, DC, MC, V. Take West Swan Rd. to the Upper Swan and turn left on to Millhouse Rd. The resort entrance is about 1.5km (1 mile) on the right. **Amenities:** 2 restaurants (1 open Fri–Sat night only); large outdoor lap pool; w/adjacent children's pool; 4 all-weather tennis courts (2 floodlit); 2 squash courts; exercise room; Jacuzzi; concierge; tour desk; salon; limited room service; same-day laundry/dry cleaning service. *In room:* A/C, TV w/pay movies, dataport, minibar, hair dryer, iron.

WHERE TO DINE

Hansons 🏆 MODERN AUSTRALIAN This new restaurant attached to Hansons Swan Valley (see "Where to Stay," above) seats 80 inside and 120 outside. You can choose from a prix-fixe blackboard menu (with a glass of wine) (noon–2pm, or 6:30–8:30pm) or the a la carte menu, which includes hearty fare such as venison bourguignon or grilled milk-fed pork sausages with caramel onion soubise and royal blue potato mash. For something lighter, there's warm poached ocean trout with potato cakes and herbed salad. Desserts include a wickedly "adults only" hot fudge sundae.

60 Forest Rd., Henley Brook, WA 6055. © **08/9296 3366.** Reservations recommended. www.hansons. com.au. Breakfast A$16–A$35 (US$10–US$23). Main courses A$15–A$25 (US$9.75–US$16) dinner. AE, DC, MC, V. Daily from noon for lunch, and from 6:30pm for dinner. Take West Swan Rd. to Henley Brook and turn right at Little River Winery into Forest Rd. Hansons is on the left at the end of the road.

Lamont's Winery, Restaurant & Gallery 🏆🏆 MODERN AUSTRALIAN This highly regarded restaurant is housed in a rustic timber building at Lamont Winery. Full-flavored main courses such as chargrilled beef with field mushrooms, beet and walnut tapenade, and delicious desserts such as white chocolate parfait with poached stone fruit and almond biscotti, ensure lots of regulars make the drive from Perth. Marron, a local crustacean, is a specialty. An alfresco menu serves up casual fare like pizza or antipasto to eat outside at the farm tables on weekends. A gallery on the grounds shows Western Australian art and crafts.

85 Bisdee Rd. (off Moore Rd.), Millendon near Upper Swan. © **08/9296 4485.** Reservations recommended, especially for dinner. Main courses A$29–A$32 (US$18–US$21). Alfresco menu A$8.80–A$18 (US$5.70–US$12). AE, DC, MC, V. Wed–Sun 10am–5pm; open for dinner 1st Sat of month 6:30pm–late. Closed Christmas to New Year's Day. Take the Great Northern Hwy. to Baskerville near Upper Swan, take a right onto Haddrill Rd. for 1.6km (1 mile), right onto Moore Rd. for 1km (just over ½ mile), and right onto Bisdee Rd.

NEW NORCIA: A TOUCH OF EUROPE IN AUSTRALIA 🏆
132km (82 miles) N of Perth

It's the last thing you expect to see in the Australian bush—a Benedictine monastery town with elegant European architecture, a fine museum, and a collection of Renaissance art—but New Norcia is no mirage. Boasting a population of 70 (when everyone's at home), this pretty town and the surrounding 8,000-hectare (19,760-acre) farm were established in 1846 by Spanish Benedictine missionaries. Visitors can tour beautifully frescoed chapels, marvel at one of the finest religious art collections in Australia, stock up on famous New Norcia nut cake straight from the monastery's 120-year-old wood-fired ovens, and attend prayers with the 18 monks who live here.

New Norcia is an easy 2-hour drive from Perth. From downtown, take Lord Street, which becomes Guildford Road, to Midland; here join the Great Northern Highway to New Norcia. Government rail organization **WAGR** (© **13 10 53** in Western Australia, or 08/9326 2000) runs a coach service (there is no rail line) Sunday, Tuesday, Thursday, and Friday from Perth for A$14 (US$9.10) one-way. **Greyhound Pioneer** (© **13 20 30** in Australia) coaches run from Perth on Fridays only for A$40 (US$26). Coach schedules will probably require you to stay at least overnight, if not longer, in order to have time to see anything. Check ahead if you plan to travel on a public holiday or during Western Australian school vacations, because schedules sometimes change then. Day tours from Perth are available.

Conference groups can book the town solid, so reserve accommodations and tours in advance, especially in wildflower season August through October.

You can get information at the **New Norcia Tourist Information Centre,** New Norcia, WA 6509 (© **08/9654 8056;** www.newnorcia.wa.edu.au), in the Museum and Art Gallery, off the highway behind St. Joseph's, beside the Trading Post and Roadhouse. Its hours are those of the museum and gallery (see below).

EXPLORING THE TOWN & MONASTERY

The New Norcia Tourist Information Centre's intriguing 2-hour walking tours are a must. Tickets cost A$12 (US$7.80) for adults and A$5.50 (US$3.60) for children 12 to 17, free for younger children. Tours depart daily except Christmas at 11am and 1:30pm, and they allow time for you to attend prayers with the monks if you wish. The guide strolls you around some of the town's 27 National Trust–classified buildings and gives an insight into the monks' lifestyle. You will also see the frescoes in the old monastery chapel and in St. Ildephonsus's and St. Gertrude's colleges. Much of the monastery is closed to visitors, but the tour does show you the fruit gardens and a glimpse of the men-only courtyard. Heritage walking-trail maps sold for A$3.30 (US$2.15) at the Tourist Information Centre include more buildings not visited on the tour, such as the octagonal apiary.

The **museum and art gallery** ℛ is full of relics from the monks' past—old mechanical and musical instruments, artifacts from the days when New Norcia was an Aboriginal mission, gifts to the monks from the Queen of Spain, and an astounding collection of paintings by Spanish and Italian artists, dating back to the 1400s. Give yourself at least an hour here. The museum and gallery are open daily from 9:30am to 5pm August through October, and from 10am to 4:30pm November through July (closed Christmas). Admission is A$4.50 (US$2.90) for adults, A$3.50 (US$2.30) for seniors and students, and A$1 (US65¢) for children 6 to 12.

Apart from joining the monks for 15-minute prayers in the monastery chapel five times a day (noon and 2:30pm are the most convenient for day visitors), you can join them for Mass in the Holy Trinity Abbey Church Monday through Saturday at 7:30am and on Sunday at 9am, or at 5:30pm for vespers.

WHERE TO STAY & DINE

New Norcia Hotel   When they thought a Spanish royal visit to New Norcia was imminent in 1926, the monks built this grandiose white hotel fit for, well, a king. Sadly, the royals never materialized, and the building was used as a hostel for parents of the children boarding at the town's colleges. In 1955, it became a hotel. Only the grand central staircase, soaring pressed-metal ceilings, and imposing Iberian facade hint at the splendor that was. About 4 years ago, new carpets, curtains, and beds were put in, but be prepared for rather grim rooms. Only one has an en suite bathroom, air-conditioning, and a TV. Still, it's rather nice to eat a meal at the dated bar or the charmingly faded dining room, and to sit on the football field–size front veranda upstairs. The bar gets jumping on Friday and Saturday nights when local farmers come to town. This is the only place to stay in town. No smoking.

Great Northern Hwy., New Norcia, WA 6509. © **08/9654 8034.** Fax 08/9654 8011. hotel_nn@hotmail.com. 17 units, 1 only with bathroom. A$77 (US$50) double without bathroom, A$90 (US$59) double with bathroom. Extra person A$15 (US$9.75). Breakfast A$11 (US$7.15) continental or A$18 (US$12) cooked; kids eat for half price. AE, MC, V. **Amenities:** Restaurant; bar; nonsmoking rooms. *In room:* Fridge, coffeemaker, iron, no phone.

3 Margaret River & the Southwest: Wine Tasting in the Forests ★★

Margaret River: 290km (180 miles) S of Perth

Say "Margaret River" to Australians and their eyes light up as they reply "great wine!" The area's 42 wineries nestle among statuesque forests of karri, the world's third-tallest tree. The wineries contribute only around 1% of Australia's wine output, yet they turn out some 10% of the country's top-notch "premium" wines. Not even most Aussies know about the Southwest's other drawing cards—like the spectacular surf breaks on the 130km (81-mile) coast from Cape Naturaliste in the north to Cape Leeuwin on the southwest tip of Australia; the coastal cliffs, perfect for abseiling (rappelling) and rock climbing; and the honeycomb of limestone caves filled with stalagmites and stalactites. Whales pass by June through December, wildflowers line the roads August through October, and wild birds, kangaroos, and shingle-backed lizards are everywhere. If you like hiking, pack your boots, because there are plenty of trails, from a 15-minute stroll around Margaret River township, to a 6-day **Cape-to-Cape trek** ★ along the sea cliffs. The Southwest is one of Australia's last great wildernesses.

Like wine regions the world over, the Southwest has more than its fair share of cozy B&Bs, galleries, and some super restaurants. Plan to stay at least 2 days.

ESSENTIALS

GETTING THERE   It's a 3½-hour drive to Margaret River from Perth; take the inland South Western Highway (the quickest route) or the more scenic Old Coast Road to Bunbury, and pick up the Bussell Highway to Margaret River.

Air Australia (© **9332 5011;** www.airaustralia.net) operates charter flights from Perth's Jandakot airport and a Busselton-Margaret River air taxi service twice a day on weekdays for A$140 (US$91) per person one-way. **Leeuwin Estate** winery does charter flights from Perth. Contact the Fremantle office (© **08/9430 4099;** www.leeuwinestate.com.au) for details.

Southwest Coachlines (© **1800/800 530** in Australia, or 08/9324 2333) runs a daily service, and two on weekends and public and Western Australian school holidays, to Margaret River from Perth for about A$25 (US$16). There is no train, but government rail organization **WAGR** (© **13 10 53** in Western

Australia, or 08/9326 2000) runs a coach service from Perth, twice daily every day except Saturday. It takes over 5 hours, and on some services you transfer by local bus (which does not run Sun or public holidays) to a different coach in Bunbury. You could also connect to this coach service in Bunbury by taking WAGR's twice-daily *Australind* train from Perth to Bunbury—it shaves travel time down to a bit over 4½ hours. Fares are A$28 (US$18) with either mode. WAGR schedules can differ on a public holiday or during Western Australian school vacations.

VISITOR INFORMATION   You will pass many wineries before you get to Margaret River township, but it's worth heading first to the **Margaret River Visitor Centre** to pick up a winery guide. It's at 100 Bussell Hwy. (at Tunbridge St.), Margaret River, WA 6285 (℘ **08/9757 2911;** www.margaretriverwa.com). It is open daily from 9am to 5pm; closed Christmas.

GETTING AROUND   Nine kilometers (5½ miles) past Busselton, which marks the start of the Southwest, the Bussell Highway makes a sharp left and

---

 Taking a Dip with Flipper

The wild dolphins that come to Monkey Mia's shore (see "The Midwest & the Northwest: Where the Outback Meets the Sea," later in this chapter) are justly famous. But just 2½ hours' drive south of Perth, en route to Margaret River, is a place where you can *swim* 🐬🐬 with these creatures. And the tourist hordes that invade Monkey Mia are largely absent!

At the **Dolphin Discovery Centre** in the town of Bunbury, bottlenose dolphins come into shore in Koombana Bay. You can "float" with them free in the "interaction zone" on the beach in front of the Centre, under the watchful eye of volunteer guides. The water is only waist-deep so you can stand if you like. You must not actively swim, chase, or touch them, but they are free to touch you. Bookings are not necessary.

From December to April the Centre runs **2-hour boat tours** to swim with some of the bay's 100-plus dolphins in deeper water for A$99 (US$64); you must be over 8. **Naturaliste Charters** (℘ **1300/361 351** in Australia, or 08/9755 2276) runs excellent 90-minute **dolphin watch cruises** twice daily (except Christmas or in bad weather) from the Centre at 11am and 2pm; they cost A$27 (US$18) adults and A$20 (US$13) kids 4 to 12. The Centre has showers, a cafe, and a good little ecodisplay on the dolphin life cycle; admission to that is A$2 (US$1.30) adults; A$1 (US65¢) seniors, students, and children; A$5 (US$3.25) family. The Centre is open from 8am to 5pm (Oct–May) and from 10am to 3pm (June–Sept). The Centre is located on Koombana Drive, Bunbury (℘ **08/9791 3088;** www.dolphindiscovery.com.au).

Monkey Mia's fame as a dolphin spot means it draws crowds, so rangers control interaction with the dolphins. You are unlikely to get to touch or swim with dolphins there. So why go all the way to Monkey Mia? Because sightings are almost guaranteed every day. At Bunbury, dolphins don't show up about a third of the time (the best chance of seeing them is 8am–noon). *Note:* You can hand-feed wild dolphins at **Tangalooma Wild Dolphin Resort** near Brisbane (see chapter 5).

Moments   **Under the Stars with the Stars**

Every February or March, **Leeuwin Estate Winery** (© **08/9430 4099;** www. leeuwinestate.com.au) stages an **outdoor concert** starring some leading showbiz light (in 2003 it was k.d. lang; past performers include Shirley Bassey, Julio Iglesias, and Diana Ross) and usually a major orchestra, attended by 6,000 picnicking guests. Tickets are A\$105 (US\$68). This is a big local event, so book months ahead.

heads south among the wineries through Vasse, then 25km (16 miles) on through the tiny village of Cowaramup, 11km (7 miles) farther through Margaret River proper, and 43km (27 miles) on to windswept Cape Leeuwin and the tiny fishing port of Augusta on Australia's south coast.

A car is close to essential. **Avis** (© **1800/679 880** in Australia for reservations in the Southwest, or 08/9757 3686) and **Hertz** (© **13 30 39** in Australia ,or 08/9758 8331) have offices in Margaret River.

Several companies run sightseeing and winery tours from Margaret River or Perth.

TOURING THE WINERIES

Fans of premium wines will have a field day. Cabernet sauvignon and merlot are the star red varieties, while chardonnay, semillon, and sauvignon blanc are the pick of the bunch of whites. Most wineries offer free tastings from 10am to 4:30pm daily. Most cluster north of Margaret River, around Cowaramup.

The region's top winery is **Leeuwin Estate** , Stevens Road, Margaret River (© **08/9759 0000**). It has a towering reputation, especially for chardonnay; its Art Series label is among the country's best. Winery tours are scheduled three times a day. A relative newcomer, **Voyager Estate,** Stevens Road, Margaret River (© **08/9757 6354**), has exquisite rose gardens and a South African Cape Dutch–style cellar. These wines are gaining a good reputation. Other labels to look for are Arlewood Estate, Cape Mentelle, Cullen Wines, Devil's Lair, Evans & Tate, Lenton Brae, Pierro (at least one wine writer claims it makes Australia's best chardonnay), and Sandalford Wines. Vasse Felix winery makes two highly drinkable "quaffers"—Aussie slang for easy-drinking, inexpensive wines—called Theatre Red and Theatre White. They are served in the London West End theaters owned by the winery's proprietor, Janet Holmes à Court, Australia's wealthiest woman.

BEYOND THE WINERIES: CAVES, BUSH TUCKER & MORE

Six of the Southwest's 350 or so limestone caves are open to the public, some with elaborate stalactite formations. Before or after you visit, call at **CaveWorks** ecointerpretive center at Lake Cave, Caves Road, 15km (9 miles) south of Margaret River's Wallcliffe Road (© **08/9757 7411**), open daily except Christmas from 9am to 5pm. Entry is free if you tour Lake, Jewel, or Mammoth caves, or else A\$3 (US\$1.95) for adults, A\$2 (US\$1.30) for children 4 to 15.

Lake Cave, right outside CaveWorks and 300 steps down an ancient sinkhole, contains a tranquil pond in which exquisite stalactites are reflected. Four kilometers (2½ miles) north along Caves Road is **Mammoth Cave,** where you can see the fossilized jaw of a baby zygotaurus trilobus, an extinct giant wombat. **Jewel Cave,** 8km (5 miles) north of Augusta on Caves Road, is the prettiest. Tours of Lake and Jewel and self-guided tours (using a CD audio system) of Mammoth cost A\$14 (US\$9.10) for adults, A\$5.50 (US\$3.60) for children 4 to 15. A 7-day Grand Pass to all three plus CaveWorks saves you money. Mammoth is open from 9am to 5pm (last tour at 4pm); tours of Lake and Jewel run hourly from 9:30am to the last tour at 3:30pm. Sometimes extra tours are scheduled during school vacations. The caves are open every day except Christmas. Book tours through CaveWorks.

Calgardup and **Giants** caves, run by the Department of Conservation and Land Management (CALM), are a more challenging experience. The caves are not electrically lit and there are no guides. Visitors are equipped with helmets, lamps, and information, and allowed to spend as long as they like exploring. Calgardup goes to a depth of 27m (81ft.) and has boardwalks to help negotiate it. Calgardup Cave is on Caves Road, about 12 minutes' drive south of Margaret River and 3 minutes north of Conto's Road turnoff. It is open from 9am to 4:15pm daily. Giants Cave, 20 minutes South of Margaret River on Caves Road, is one of the largest and deepest caves on the Leeuwin-Naturaliste Ridge. It is 575m (1,725 ft.) long and about 86m (258 ft.) deep. Entry is from 9:30am to 3:30pm school and public holidays, and some other times. Entry to Calgardup and Giants each costs A$10 (US$6.50) adult, A$5 (US$3.25) child, or A$30 (US$20) a family of six (includes helmets and lamps). Buy your tickets at the **National Park Information Centre** (© 08/9757 7422) at Calgardup Cave. The center also has walking maps and information on camping sites and other activities in the Leeuwin-Naturaliste National Park.

Another "adventure cave" where you get down and dirty crawling on your hands and knees, in the protective clothing supplied, is offered at **Ngilgi Cave,** Caves Road, Yallingup (© 08/9755 2152), for A$40 (US$26) for anyone over 15. It departs daily at 9:30am and takes about 3 hours. Book 24 hours ahead. Ngilgi's main chamber has translucent stalactite "shawls," which anyone can explore on a semiguided tour. This costs A$14 (US$9.10) for adults and A$8 (US$5.20) for children 5 to 17, or A$38 (US$25) for a family, and runs half-hourly from 9:30am, with the last tour at 3:30pm (4pm during school vacations, 5pm during Christmas school vacations). Flashlight tours cost A$14 (US$9.10) adults and A$9 (US$5.85) children (minimum A$80/US$52 group). The cave opens every day except Christmas.

Food-based attractions are opening up in the area all the time. You can pick your own kiwi, raspberries, and other fruit at **The Berry Farm,** 222 Bessell Rd. outside Margaret River (© 08/9757 5054), or buy them ready-made as attractively packaged sparkling, dessert, and port wines; jams; and vinegars. At the **Margaret River Chocolate Company,** Harman's Mill Rd. (at Harman's Rd S.), Willyabrup (© 08/9755 6555), you can do free tastings, watch the candy making through a window, and, of course, buy the stuff. Open daily 9am to 5pm.

Tips A Wine-Buying Tip

The place to buy wine if you want to take it out of Australia is the **Margaret River Regional Wine Centre**, 9 Bussell Hwy., Cowaramup (© 08/9755-5501), because most wineries don't deliver internationally. It stocks about every local wine, does daily tastings of select vintages, sells maps, visitor guides, and winery guides, and has an expert staff to help you purchase, and even tailor your day's foray. It is open Monday through Saturday from 10am to 7pm, and Sunday from noon to 6pm (closed Christmas, Good Friday, and sometimes New Year's Day). Order off its website at www.mrwines.com.

Moments Scenic Drives

Boranup Drive is a magical detour off Caves Road through towering karris (though keep in mind that your rental car is not insured on its unpaved surface). It departs Caves Road 6km (3¾ miles) south of Mammoth Cave and rejoins it after a 14km (8¾-mile) meander. **Caves Road** is a 106km (66-mile) north-south drive through forest and farms, from Busselton to Augusta on Cape Leeuwin in the south.

Allow time to browse the area's arts-and-crafts galleries, too. One of the most upscale is **Gunyulgup Galleries,** Gunyulgup Valley Drive (off Caves Rd.) near Yallingup (© **08/9755 2177**), which has elegant jewelry, glass, ceramics, and artworks by 120 artists. It is open daily from 10am to 5pm.

Plenty of **hiking trails** are available in this area, whether you want an easy stroll to a whale-watch lookout, an afternoon's ramble through the forest, or an overnight trek. The tourist information center in Margaret River (see "Visitor Information," above) sells trail maps, including maps to all the open sections of the Cape-to-Cape cliff-edge walk from Cape Naturaliste to Cape Leeuwin.

Try to make time for a tour offered by **"Bushtucker Woman" Helen Lee** (© **08/9757 1084** or 0419/91 1971; www.bushtuckertours.com). On one tour, she has you canoeing up the river, exploring a cave, and eating smoked emu, grub paté, and other Aboriginal delicacies on a river island. It runs from 10am to 2pm (no tour Tues and Thurs in winter), and costs A$40 (US$26) for adults and A$20 (US$13) for kids under 16. Her winery tour has an alternative bent incorporating short karri-forest walks, insights into organic winemaking, tastings of up to 40 wines at five wineries, a visit to Leeuwin Estate's herb garden, and a picnic lunch of bush tucker and local cheeses, hams, and dips. She'll teach you things like how vaporized peppermint oil from the native trees condenses on the grapes to create the distinctive flavor of Margaret River whites. The 5-hour tour departs daily at noon and costs A$55 (US$36) per person.

Surfing lessons from four-time Western Australian professional surfing champion **Josh Palmateer** (© **08/9757 3850** or 0418/958 264) are a must! Two-hour lessons in the gentle waist-deep surf at Prevelly Park Beach, 9km (5½ miles) west of Margaret River, run daily and cost A$80 (US$52) per person, or A$40 (US$26) per person for two or more. Lessons run September through June. If you are already a Master of the Surf Universe, try legendary Smiths Beach or the Three Bears (Mama, Papa, and Baby) break at Yallingup, the double-barreled North Point at Gracetown, or the plentiful breaks at Prevelly Park. **Beach Life,** 117 Bussell Hwy., Margaret River (© **08/9757 2888**), rents boards for A$40 (US$26) for 24 hours.

June through December **whales** play just offshore all along the coast. There is a whale lookout near the Cape Naturaliste lighthouse. Daily 3-hour whale-watching cruises with **Naturaliste Charters** (© **08/9755 2276**) depart June through September from Augusta (where you'll also see fur seals and often dolphins). September through December, cruise departures switch to Dunsborough, where whales rest their calves. The boat is fitted with an underwater camera connected to a TV and a hydrophone, so you can see and hear the creatures. Cruises cost A$45 (US$29) for adults, A$42 (US$27) for seniors and students, and A$25 (US$16) for children 4 to 12; free for children under 4.

WHERE TO STAY

It's not the prettiest village in the Southwest, but **Margaret River** has the advantage of banks, a supermarket, and a few restaurants and shops. The blink-and-you'll-miss-it hamlet of **Cowaramup,** 11km (6¾ miles) north of Margaret River township, is closer to more wineries and has a general store, a cafe, and one or two interesting crafts shops. **Vasse** is a tiny settlement at the northern edge of the Southwest, 36km (22½ miles) north of Margaret River. Some places may demand a minimum 2-night stay on weekends.

IN MARGARET RIVER

Basildene Manor ⚑   This lovely National Trust–classified farmhouse was built by the local lighthouse keeper in 1912 out of local stone. Following a supremely tasteful refurbishment in 1997 by the friendly proprietors, Garry Nielsen and Julie Whittingham, it's now a gentrified B&B with attractive bedrooms. Some lead off an impressive jarrah gallery overlooking the cozy "Main Hall" with its open fire. Suites are large rooms with their own sitting areas, and eight of them added in 1999 have Jacuzzi bathrooms. A stylish, cooked breakfast is served in the pretty conservatory overlooking the 5.5-hectare (14-acre) grounds, and your hosts point you along a walking trail to spy on a mob of kangaroos. No smoking indoors.

Lot 100 Wallcliffe Rd. (2km/1¼ miles west of town), Margaret River, WA 6285. (℃ **08/9757 3140.** Fax 08/9757 3383. www.basildene.com.au. 17 units (all with shower only, 8 with Jacuzzis). A$229–A$334 (US$149–US$217) double. 2-night stay required on weekends. Rates include full breakfast. AE, DC, MC, V. Children under 15 not permitted. **Amenities:** Same-day laundry/dry cleaning service; nonsmoking rooms. *In room:* A/C, TV/VCR, nonalcoholic minibar, coffeemaker, hair dryer, iron.

Heritage Trail Lodge ⚑   Although they're on the highway and "in" Margaret River (within walking distance of restaurants), this cute row of salmon-pink cabin-style rooms, built in 1997, are huddled in a serene karri forest, out of sight of town. Inside, each spacious unit has king double or king twin beds and a fabulous double Jacuzzi (even the room for people with disabilities), from which you can see the forest. The rooms back onto a 35-minute bushwalk trail. Welcoming proprietors Hugh and Maxine Beckingham serve up a delicious gourmet breakfast of local produce including cereals, yogurt, and local jams, cheeses, and breads in the sunny pine dining room. 'Roos even hop into the car park sometimes. No smoking indoors.

31 Bussell Hwy. (almost .5km/¼ mile north of town), Margaret River, WA 6285. (℃ **08/9757 9595.** Fax 08/9757 9596. www.heritage-trail-lodge.com.au. 10 units (all with shower and Jacuzzi). A$210–A$259 (US$137–US$168) double. Extra person A$35 (US$23). Rates include gourmet continental breakfast. Ask about midweek packages. AE, DC, MC, V. Children under 16 not permitted. **Amenities:** Nonsmoking rooms. *In room:* A/C, TV, minibar, coffeemaker, hair dryer, iron.

IN COWARAMUP

The Noble Grape   English cottage gardens surround this B&B, recently built in a colonial style. Each well-maintained room is motel-like, but homey and welcoming with a modern bathroom, heating, ceiling fans, a comfy sitting area, and a small rear patio opening onto bird-filled trees. One caters to travelers with disabilities, and a family room sleeps five. Although you're on the highway here, the rooms are quiet. Hair dryers are at reception. No smoking indoors.

Lot 18, Bussell Hwy., Cowaramup, WA 6284. (℃/fax **08/9755 5538.** www.babs.com.au/noblegrape. 6 units (all with shower only). A$99 (US$64) double. Additional person A$22 (US$14). Rates include continental breakfast. Ask about packages. AE, DC, MC, V. **Amenities:** Coin-op laundry; nonsmoking rooms. *In room:* TV, fridge, coffeemaker, no phone.

IN VASSE

Newtown House   Set in lavender and rose gardens nice for lazing in after a hard day's wine tasting, this National Trust–listed 1851 homestead has four pretty rooms with "contemporary country" decor, furnished with wrought-iron table and chairs, pine furniture, and cute touches like potpourri "dream sacks" on your pillow. All have ceiling fans. The fixings for a gourmet continental breakfast are sent up to your room the night before. Don't miss the excellent restaurant (see "Where to Dine," below). No smoking indoors.

Bussell Hwy. (9km/5½ miles past Busselton), Vasse, WA 6280. © and fax **08/9755 4485**. 4 units (all with shower only). A$138 (US$90) double. Rates include continental breakfast. AE, DC, MC, V. The property is on the right just after the Bussell Hwy. turns left (south). Children not permitted. **Amenities:** Restaurant; nonsmoking rooms. *In room:* TV, minibar, coffeemaker, no phone.

WHERE TO DINE

Good restaurants are attached to a number of wineries, including Vasse Felix, Driftwood Estate, and Brookland Valley Vineyard. Most outstanding is **Leeuwin Estate's restaurant** 𝄐𝄐, Stevens Road, Margaret River (© **08/9759 0000**); it has terrific food, it's cozy in winter, and in summer its wide deck overlooking lawns is just the place to be for lunch.

You can stock up for a picnic at the supermarket in Margaret River. Cape Mentelle and Vasse Felix both have shady picnic areas beside a brook.

Newtown House 𝄐𝄐 MODERN FRENCH/AUSTRALIAN   The Southwest boasts some of the best restaurants in Australia, and this is one of 'em. Folks come from far and wide to savor chef Stephen Reagan's skill in preparing such dishes as rare local venison with roast pears, beets, and red-wine glaze. Desserts are no let-down, either—caramel soufflé with lavender ice cream and hot caramel sauce is typical. Located in a historic homestead, the restaurant consists of two simple, intimate rooms with sisal matting and contemporary, boldly colored walls. Even better, it's BYO. Drop by for morning or afternoon tea, if you like.

737 Bussell Hwy. (9km/5½ miles past Busselton), Vasse. © **08/9755 4485**. Reservations recommended, especially at dinner. Main courses A$20–A$25 (US$13–US$16) lunch, A$27–A$32 (US$18–US$21) dinner. AE, DC, MC, V. Tues–Sat 10am–10:30pm or later.

The Valley Café 𝄐 MODERN AUSTRALIAN   Voted most popular Southwest cafe in 1998, 1999, and 2000, this pleasant place serves up stylish fare with views over the countryside. Lunch might be risotto with Augusta smoked chicken, sun-dried capsicum (bell pepper), and shaved Parmesan. Dinner might be cured Atlantic salmon with polenta, asparagus, and caramelized balsamic vinegar. Courses are "Medium" and "Large," so you can eat light if you wish, or just come for coffee and cake. BYO.

Carters Rd. (near Caves Rd.), Margaret River. © **08/9757 3225**. Reservations recommended. Main courses A$18–A$30 (US$12–US$20), average A$24 (US$16). AE, MC, V. Wed–Sun 10am–4pm; Fri–Sat (and Sun on 3-day weekends) 6–10pm.

4 The Goldfields 𝄐

595km (369 miles) E of Perth

After Paddy Hannan struck gold in 1893, the wheat-belt town of Kalgoorlie found itself sitting on the "Golden Mile," the richest square mile of gold-bearing earth in the world. Today **Kalgoorlie** 𝄐 (pop. 32,000) is still an Outback gold-rush boomtown, a mixture of yesteryear charm and 21st-century corporate gold fever. The town is perched on the edge of the Super Pit, the world's biggest open-cut gold mine, 4.5km (2¾ miles) long, 1.5km (1 mile) wide, and 290m (951 ft.) deep. It yields up to 850,000 ounces of the yellow stuff every year—over 2,000 ounces a day. An estimated 13 million ounces is still in the ground.

Walking down the wide streets fronted with wrought-iron lace verandas is like stumbling onto a Western movie set. Countless bars still do the roaring trade they notched up in the 1890s—only now they serve suited-up gold-mining executives from Adelaide and Perth.

Life on the Golden Mile is not so lively for everyone, however. Just down the road 39km (24 miles) is **Coolgardie** (pop. 1,100), another 1890s boomtown where the gold ran out in 1963. The town's semiabandoned air is a sad foil to Kalgoorlie's energy; but much of the lovely architecture remains, so you can wander the gracious streets and a few museums for a pleasant nostalgia buzz.

ESSENTIALS

GETTING THERE **Airlink** (book through Qantas ⓒ **13 13 13** in Australia) flies to Kalgoorlie from Perth daily. Skywest (ⓒ **1300/660 088** in Australia; www.skywest.com.au) flies daily from Perth, except Saturdays.

Greyhound Pioneer (ⓒ **13 20 30** in Australia) makes the 8-hour trip once a week from Perth for A$118 (US$77). Greyhound's service from Adelaide also runs once a week, takes around 27 hours, and costs A$264 (US$172). **Goldrush Tours** (ⓒ **1800/62 0440** in Australia, or 08/9021 2954) runs a 6¾-hour express coach service from Perth every day for A$88 (US$57).

Kalgoorlie is a stop on the 3-day *Indian Pacific* train service, which runs between Sydney and Perth through Adelaide twice a week in both directions. See section 12, "Getting Around Australia," in chapter 2, for contact details. The *Prospector* train makes 10 trips a week from Perth to Kalgoorlie for A$55 (US$36). Call the government rail organization **WAGR** (ⓒ **13 10 53** in Western Australia, or 08/9326 2000).

From Perth, take the Great Eastern Highway. If you want to make the extremely dull 2,182km (1,353-mile) journey on the Eyre Highway from Adelaide, which features the longest straight stretch of highway in the world on the empty Nullarbor Plain, contact the South Australian or Western Australian state auto clubs listed under "Getting Around Australia," in chapter 2, for advice. There are only a handful of small towns and gas stops en route.

VISITOR INFORMATION The **Kalgoorlie-Boulder Tourist Centre,** 250 Hannan St., Kalgoorlie, WA 6430 (ⓒ **1800/00 1880** in Australia, or 08/9021 1966; www.kalgoorlieandwagoldfields.com.au), dispenses information on Kalgoorlie, Coolgardie, and outlying ghost towns and regions. Boulder is a suburb of Kalgoorlie. The center's walking trail map to the town's architecture, which sells for a few dollars, is worth buying. The center is open Monday through Friday from 8:30am to 5pm, and Saturday, Sunday, and public holidays from 9am to

---

⟨*Fun Fact* **Streets Paved with Gold . . .**

In Kalgoorlie's young days, its streets were paved with a blackish spoil from the mining process called "tellurides." When someone realized tellurides contain up to 40% gold and 10% silver, those streets were ripped up in one big hurry. The city fathers had paved the streets with gold and didn't even know it!

5pm. The **Coolgardie Tourist Bureau,** 68 Bayley St., Coolgardie, WA 6429 (℗ 08/9026 6090), is open daily from 9am to 5pm.

GETTING AROUND   Avis (℗ 08/9021 1722), **Budget** (℗ 08/9093 2300), **Hertz** (℗ 08/9093 2211), and **Thrifty** (℗ 08/9021 4722) have offices in Kalgoorlie.

Local tour operators will take you prospecting in outlying regions, as well as offering coach, four-wheel-drive, and four-wheel-drive bush tours of Kalgoorlie, Coolgardie, and outlying ghost towns. Tours range from half a day to several days.

WHAT TO SEE & DO

As you might guess, gold is a common thread running through many of the town's attractions. One of the best is the **Mining Hall of Fame** (℗ 08/9026 2700; www.mininghall.com), Broad Arrow Road, 6km (3¾ miles) north of the Tourist Centre on the Goldfields Highway. Opened in late 2001, it has five interactive galleries focusing on mining's modern high-tech face. Find out how prospecting is done, how the business of mining is conducted, go underground in an old mine, pan for gold, watch a gold pour, see a video in a re-created miner's tent, and pore over an extensive collection of mining memorabilia, machinery, and huts in a miners' village. It's open daily from 9am to 4:30pm, except Christmas, Boxing Day (Dec 26) and New Year's Day. Admission A$12 (US$7.80) adults, A$10 (US$6.50) seniors and students, A$6 (US$3.90) children, and A$35 (US$23) families for aboveground activities only; if you want to join the underground tour too, the prices are A$20 (US$13) adults, A$15 (US$9.75) seniors and students, A$10 (US$6.50) children, and A$50 (US$33) families. Underground tours and gold panning are run four times a day, more often in WA school holidays. Allow half a day to see everything. The complex is still a work-in-progress with new attractions, including a Chinese garden and more galleries to open during 2003.

The **WA Museum Kalgoorlie-Boulder,** 17 Hannan St. (℗ 08/9021 8533), is worth a look for the first 400-ounce gold bar minted in town, nuggets and jewelry, and historical displays. It is open daily from 10am to 4:30pm, closed Christmas and Good Friday. Admission is free (donation requested). Tours are at 11am and 2:30pm. Allow an hour.

Don't leave town without ogling the **Super Pit** open-cut mine—it makes giant dump trucks look like ants. The lookout is at Outram Street in Boulder, off the Goldfields Highway. It's open daily from about 6am to about 7pm. A blast takes place daily; check the time with the visitor center. Entry is free.

Another reminder of the days when miners spent their spare time trying for riches of another kind by indulging in two-up (a simple game involving betting on a penny landing heads or tails) can be found about 12km (7½ miles) north of Boulder on the Goldfields Highway. The original shanty that housed the **Bush Two-Up School** still stands, but if you want to try your hand, the only place to do it is at Sheffields restaurant in the **Recreation Hotel,** 140 Burt St., Boulder (℗ 08/9093 3467), which runs two-up games on Wednesday and Sunday at 3pm. You must be 18 or over to play.

The **Royal Flying Doctor Service** (℗ 08/9093 7500) base at Kalgoorlie-Boulder Airport is open for visitors to browse memorabilia, see a video, and look over an aircraft if one is in. It is open Monday through Friday from 11am to 3pm. Admission is A$2 (US$1.30) adults, free for children under 6. Allow 45 minutes.

Full-blood Aboriginal Geoffrey Stokes of **Yamatji Bitja Aboriginal Bush Tours** ☆ (℗ 08/9093 3745 or 0407/378 602) grew up the Aboriginal way in the bush. On his full-day four-wheel-drive tours, you'll forage for bush tucker, learn bushcraft, and do things like eat witchetty grubs, cook kangaroo over a fire, or track emus. Tours cost A$80 (US$52), half price for kids 4 to 12. Geoff also does twilight campfire evenings, and overnight or longer tours in the bush.

Candidate for "Kalgoorlie's Most Unusual Attraction" award goes to **Langtrees 181,** 181 Hay St. (© **08/9026 2181**), a working brothel styled into a sex industry museum in the heart of Kalgoorlie's (in)famous red-light district. For the most part housed in red and pink corrugated iron sheds festooned with colored lights, this neck of town is a popular drive-by spot among the blue-rinse bus-tour set, who get a kick out of returning the cheery waves of the workers standing in their doorways. Ninety-minute tours, fun rather than sleazy, of some of the 12 themed rooms cost A$25 (US$16). Tours depart 1, 3, and 7pm daily.

Wandering **Coolgardie's** quiet streets, which are graced with historic facades, is a stroll back in time. More than 100 signboards erected around the place, many with photos, detail what each site was like at the turn of the 20th century. The **Goldfields Exhibition,** 62 Bayley St. (© **08/9026 6090**), tells the town's story in a lovely 1898 building once used as the mining warden's court-house. (The Tourist Bureau is also here.) Admission is A$3.30 (US$2.15) for adults, A$2.75 (US$1.80) for seniors, A$1.10 (US70¢) for children under 16, or A$7.70 (US$5) for a family. It's open daily except Christmas from 9am to 5pm. Coolgardie also has a couple of small museums, including a neat little pharmaceutical museum, a railway museum, and a National Trust–owned 1895 house open for tours, now restored with period interiors.

The **Coolgardie Camel Farm,** 4km (2½ miles) west of Coolgardie on the Great Eastern Highway (© **08/9026 6159**), leads rides through the bush on the mode of transport they used in the goldfields in the old days—camels.

WHERE TO STAY

Mercure Hotel Plaza Kalgoorlie   Corporate travelers like the practical comforts, upscale restaurant, and walking distance to the heart of Kalgoorlie's nightlife and main street at this AAA-rated four-star property. Many appreciate the extra touches such as bathrobes, toiletries, magazines, herbal tea, and real coffee. The rooms are spacious, well appointed, and have balcony views over the city and Golden Mile. The restaurant has an extensive wine list, and the cocktail bar buzzes in the evenings.

45 Egan St., Kalgoorlie, WA 6430. (© **1300/656 565** in Australia, 800/221-4542 in the U.S. and Canada, 020/8283 4500 in the U.K., 0800/44 4422 in New Zealand, or 08/9021 4544. Fax 08/9091 2195. www.accor hotels.com.au. 100 units (all with shower only). A$183–A$199 (US$119–US$129) double; A$276 (US$179) suite. Extra person A$30 (US$20). Ask about weekend packages. AE, DC, MC, V. **Amenities:** Restaurant; bar; outdoor pool; tour desk; secretarial services; limited room service; coin-op laundry; same-day laundry/dry cleaning service. *In room:* A/C, TV w/pay movies, minibar, coffeemaker, hair dryer, iron.

WHERE TO DINE

Akudjura 🔎 MODERN AUSTRALIAN   The Italianate outdoor terrace under sailcloth and the timber floors, curved silver bar, and blond-wood furniture make this Kalgoorlie's first groovy restaurant. Bright young waitstaff provide snappy service from a long and stylish menu featuring items like chicken Caesar salad, smoked salmon fettuccine, kangaroo steak, and seafood dishes (yep, even in the desert) like Tasmanian salmon in a citrus and cilantro dressing. Lighter fare is available outside meal hours.

418 Hannan St. (next to Hannan's View Motel). (© **08/9091 3311.** Reservations recommended. Main courses A$13–A$32 (US$8.45–US$21); lunch averages A$13 (US$8.45). AE, DC, MC, V. Daily 7am to approximately 10pm.

5 The Midwest & the Northwest: Where the Outback Meets the Sea ⟨*⟩

The Midwest and Northwest coasts of Western Australia are treeless, riverless semi-desert, occupied by vast sheep stations and a handful of people. Temperatures soar to over 115°F (46°C) in summer, and the Outback sand burns orange in the blazing sun. But it's not the land you come here for—it's what's in the sea. Since the 1960s, a pod of **bottlenose dolphins** has been coming into shallow water at **Monkey Mia** ⟨*⟩, the World Heritage–listed Shark Bay Marine Park, to greet shore-bound humans. Their magical presence has generated worldwide publicity and drawn people from every corner of the globe.

Another 87km (54 miles) by road north on the Northwest Cape, adventure seekers from around the world come to **snorkel with awesome whale sharks** ⟨*⟩—measuring up to 18m (59 ft.) long—every fall (Mar to early June). The Cape's parched shore and green waters hide an even more dazzling secret though—a second barrier reef 260km (161 miles) long and 2km (1¼ miles) wide called **Ningaloo Marine Park** ⟨**⟩. It protects 250 species of coral and 450 kinds of fish, dolphins, mantas, whales, turtles, and dugongs (manatees) in its 5,000 sq. km (1,950 sq. miles). Some people say Ningaloo is as good, if not better, than the Great Barrier Reef. Even the Great Barrier Reef can't beat Ningaloo Reef's proximity to shore—just a step or two off the beach delivers you into a magical underwater garden. What is so amazing about the reef is not that it is here, but that so few people know about it—a mere 8,000 tourists a year. That means beaches pretty much to yourself, seas teeming with life because humans haven't scared it away, unspoiled scenery, and a genuine sense of the frontier.

The Midwest and Northwest are lonely, remote, and really too hot to visit between November and March. The best time to visit is April through October, when it is still warm enough to swim, though snorkelers might want a wet suit June through August. Both regions are too far south to get the Top End's sticky Wet Season, and humidity is always low. Facilities, gas, and freshwater are scarce, and distances immense in this neck of the woods, so be prepared.

SHARK BAY (MONKEY MIA) ⟨*⟩
853km (529 miles) N of Perth; 1,867km (1,157 miles) S of Broome

Monkey Mia's celebrity dolphins may not show on time—or at all—but they rarely pass up a visit. Apart from these delightful sea mammals, Shark Bay's waters heave with fish, dolphins, turtles, the world's biggest population of dugongs (10,000 at last count), manta rays, sea snakes, and, June through October, humpback whales. On the tip of the Peron Peninsula, which juts out into the Shark Bay Marine Park, is **Francois Peron National Park.** The park is home to many endangered species, white beaches composed entirely of shells, and "living fossils"— rocklike structures on the shore (called stromatolites) that are Earth's first life. The bay's only town is the one-time pearling town of **Denham** (pop. 500), 129km (80 miles) from the main coastal highway, which has a hotel or two, a bakery, a news agency, and a few fishing-charter and tour operators. There is no settlement, only the pleasant but basic Monkey Mia Dolphin Resort (p. 466).

ESSENTIALS
GETTING THERE   Skywest (© **1300/660 088** in Australia; www.skywest. com.au) flies four times a week from Perth to Shark Bay Airport (also called Monkey Mia Airport), 18km (11 miles) from Monkey Mia Dolphin Resort. The fare

is A$362 (US$235), cheaper for advance purchase tickets. The **Shark Bay Airport Bus** (✆ **08/9948 1358**) meets every flight and transfers you to Monkey Mia Dolphin Resort for A$7.70 (US$5) per person one-way.

There is no train to Shark Bay. **Greyhound Pioneer** (✆ **13 20 30** in Australia) travels daily from Perth and Broome. These services connect three times a week at the Overlander Roadhouse at the Shark Bay turnoff on the North West Coastal Highway. The trip from Perth costs A$136 (US$88) and takes about 15 hours. From Broome it costs A$293 (US$190) and takes about 24 hours through featureless landscape—not recommended.

Beware of wildlife on the lonely, uninteresting 9- to 10-hour drive from Perth, and keep the gas tank full. From Perth take the Brand Highway 424km (263 miles) north to Geraldton, then the North West Coastal Highway for 280km (174 miles) to the Overlander Roadhouse. Turn left onto the Denham-Hamelin Road and follow it for 152km (94 miles) to Monkey Mia, which is 27km (17 miles) past Denham. If you want to break the journey, the **Mercure Inn Geraldton,** Brand Highway, Geraldton, WA 6530 (✆ **08/9921 2455**), has smart, clean motel rooms. Rates are A$131 (US$85) double; specials are available most nights.

Numerous coach, four-wheel-drive, and aerial tours run from Perth. **World Heritage Tours & Travel** (✆ **08/9581 5666;** book via www.visitwa.com.au) offers a wide range.

VISITOR INFORMATION   Wide-ranging ecological information on Shark Bay Marine Park, Francois Peron National Park, and Hamelin Pool Marine Nature Reserve, as well as details on local tours, is available at the **Monkey Mia Visitor Centre** (✆ **08/9948 1366**) within Monkey Mia Dolphin Resort (see "Where to Stay & Dine," below). Videos run throughout the day, and researchers (who are mostly from American universities) give free talks and slide shows most nights. The state Department of Conservation and Land Management runs the center (www.calm.wa.gov.au). The official information outlet is the **Shark Bay Tourist Bureau** at 71 Knight Terrace, Denham, WA 6537 (✆ **08/9948 1253;** www.sharkbay.asn.au), open daily from 8am to 5pm (until 6pm in winter), though you will probably find the Monkey Mia Visitor Centre just as helpful.

GETTING AROUND   **Shark Bay Car Hire** (✆ **08/9948 1247**) delivers cars and four-wheel-drives to the airport and the resort from its Denham office. Several companies run tours to all the main attractions.

FAST FACTS   Admission to the Monkey Mia Reserve, in which Monkey Mia Dolphin Resort is located, is A$6 (US$3.90) per adult, A$2 (US$1.30) per child 7 to 16, and A$12 (US$7.80) per family. If you stay longer than 2 days and a night, you need a 4-week pass costing A$9 (US$5.85) for adults, A$4 (US$2.60) for kids, and A$22 (US$14.30) for a family.

There's an ATM at **The Heritage Resort,** 73 Knight Terrace (at Durlacher St.), Denham (✆ **08/9948 1133**), but banks are nonexistent. A banking agency is located within the post office in Denham.

MEETING THE DOLPHINS

At 7am guests at Monkey Mia Dolphin Resort are already gathering on the beach in quiet anticipation of the dolphins' arrival. By 8am three or more dolphins usually show, and they come and go until the early afternoon. Because of the crowds the dolphins attract (about 40 people a session in low season, coach loads in high season), a park ranger instructs everyone to line up knee-deep in the water as the playful swimsters cruise by your legs. You may not approach

---

Tips **Where Can I See the Dolphins?**

The main advantage to making the trek to **Monkey Mia** to see dolphins is that sightings are virtually guaranteed every day. But it's crowded, and rangers strictly monitor behavior with the dolphins—not the interactive frolic you might have imagined. At **Bunbury** 🐬🐬, a 2½-hour drive south of Perth, you can *swim* with wild dolphins (see "Taking a Dip with Flipper," earlier in this chapter). Here the critters show up near shore only about two-thirds of the time. But the daily dolphin-watch cruise into deeper water has an almost 100% sighting success rate.

---

them or reach out to pat them, but they come up to touch people of their own accord sometimes. Feeding times are different each day so the dolphins won't become dependent on the food. Once the crowd disperses, savvy swimmers dive into the water just up the beach outside the no-swimmers-allowed Dolphin Interaction Area, because the dolphins may head there after the "show." Apart from the Monkey Mia Reserve entry fee, there is no charge to see the creatures.

A GREAT SEA-LIFE CRUISE, LIVING "FOSSILS" & MORE

Don't do what so many visitors do—see the dolphins, then shoot back to Perth. Stay to see Shark Bay's incredible marine life on the sailing catamaran ***Shotover*** 🐬 (© **1800/24 1481** in Australia, or 08/9948 1481). During a 2½-hour dugong (manatee) cruise, you will see a huge range of creatures, possibly hammerhead sharks, a baby great white, sea snakes, turtles, dolphins, and, of course, dugongs. Every passenger is given polarized sunglasses, which help you spot underwater animals. Sometimes you see dozens of dugongs (though they leave the area from mid-May to Aug). The cruise departs 1pm daily from Monkey Mia Dolphin Resort and costs A$54 (US$35). The *Shotover* also does a fascinating 2-hour dolphin cruise every morning—worth doing even if you already saw the dolphins on the shore. It costs A$49 (US$32). Children 7 to 16 pay half price.

On your way in or out of Monkey Mia, stop by **the Hamelin Pool Historic Telegraph Station** (© **08/9942 5905**), 41km (25½ miles) from the highway turnoff. A small museum houses old equipment, farming tools, and historical odds and sods from the 19th-century days when Monkey Mia was a repeater station on a telegraph line. The A$5.50 (US$3.60) admission fee to the museum includes an explanation of the **stromatolites,** rocky formations about a foot high that were created by the planet's first oxygen-breathing cells—in other words, Earth's first life. You might want to skip the museum, but wander down to **Shell Beach** and have a look. The "sand" on the beach consists of millions of tiny white shells, which were quarried as bricks to build some of the local buildings. There is a cafe and gift store here, too.

You can explore the saltpans, dunes, coastal cliffs, short walking trails, and old homestead in the nearby 52,500-hectare (129,675-acre) **Francois Peron National Park,** either alone (you will need a four-wheel-drive) or on a half- or full-day tour—although not everyone will appreciate the park's harsh scenery. You should spot wallabies, birds, and emus, and you may see turtles, dolphins, rays, dugongs, and, in season, whales from the cliffs. Other activities include half- and full-day game and deep-sea-fishing trips from Denham, scuba diving, excursions to the deserted beaches and 180m (590-ft.) cliffs of nearby Dirk Hartog Island, and a couple of pearl-farm tours.

WHERE TO STAY & DINE

Monkey Mia Dolphin Resort   Set right on the beach the dolphins visit, this oasis of green lawns and palms doubles as a town settlement. Most comfortable are the spacious air-conditioned motel rooms; safari tent "canvas condos" with carpeted floors, bathrooms, electricity, a fridge, and a separate kitchen/dining area from the bedroom (but no air-conditioning); and air-conditioned demountable "park homes" with cooking facilities. The pleasant open-sided all-day restaurant overlooks the sea. Most tours in the area depart from the resort. A 1.5km (1-mile) nature trail leads from the resort.

Monkey Mia Rd., Shark Bay (P.O. Box 119, Denham, WA 6537). © 1800/653 611 in Australia, or 08/9948 1320. Fax 08/9948 1034. www.monkeymia.com.au. Tent sites: 58 powered sites; 10 on-site trailers; 6 "canvas condo" permanent tents to sleep 6; 13 park homes to sleep 6, none with bathroom; 72 motel rooms. A$40–A$55 (US$26–US$36) for 2–4 people sharing a trailer rented from resort; A$82 (US$53) up to 4 people in canvas condo; A$92 (US$60) up to 4 people in park home; A$163–A$186 (US$106–US$121) double or triple motel room. Extra person A$8.80–A$11 (US$5.70–US$7.15). Linen A$11 (US$7.15) per person in park homes, canvas condos, and trailers for duration of stay. Lower rates Feb 1–Mar 31 (excluding Easter) and May 1–June 30 except in on-site vans. Weekly rates available. AE, DC, MC, V. **Amenities:** Restaurant/bar; takeout cafe; outdoor pool; 2 outdoor tennis courts; Jacuzzi (fed by naturally warm underground water); volleyball court; snorkel gear; tour desk; minimarket; coin-op laundry. *In room:* Fridge, hair dryer (in motel rooms only).

THE NORTHWEST CAPE

1,272km (789 miles) N of Perth; 1,567km (972 miles) S of Broome

Driving along the only road on the Northwest Cape is like driving on the moon. Hundreds of red anthills taller than you march away to the horizon, sheep and 'roos threaten to get under the wheels, and the sun beats down from a harsh blue sky. On the Cape's western shore is coral-filled **Coral Bay** (pop. 120), a tiny cluster of dive shops, backpacker lodges, a low-key resort, and charter boats nestled on sand so white, water so blue, and ochre dust so orange you think the townsfolk computer-enhanced the colors. North of town are deserted sandy beaches edged by coral. On the Cape's east coast is **Exmouth** (pop. 3,500), born in 1967 as a support town to the Harold E. Holt Naval Communications Station, a joint Australian–United States center. Apart from whale-shark diving, the reason you come here is to scuba dive and snorkel in Ningaloo Marine Park. You can also take four-wheel-drive trips over the Cape Range National Park, which covers much of the cape, and surrounding sheep stations. Ningaloo Marine Park stretches from Bundegi Beach on the Cape's east coast around its northern tip and down its western side.

Exmouth and Coral Bay are 150km (93 miles) apart. Coral Bay is several degrees cooler than Exmouth and has divine diving, swimming, and snorkeling; a restaurant, some takeout, and a bar or two; a small supermarket; and little else. It has no ATMs. Exmouth is hot and charmless, but it has more facilities, including a supermarket, an ATM, an outdoor cinema, rental cars, a swimming beach 1km (just over ½ mile) away, and one or two smarter accommodations and dining options. Most tours not having to do with the reef, such as four-wheel-drive safaris, leave from Exmouth. Both towns have plenty of dive, snorkel, fishing, and whale-watch companies. Wherever you stay, it's best to book ahead in whale-shark season (from Mar to early June). Carry drinking water everywhere you go.

ESSENTIALS

GETTING THERE   Skywest (© **1300/660 088** in Australia; www.skywest. com.au) flies daily from Perth, and **Northwest Regional Airlines** (© **1300/136 629** in Australia, or 08/9192 1369; www.northwestregional.com.au) flies from

Broome. A shuttle bus meets every flight and takes you to your Exmouth hotel for A$18 (US$12) one-way. It does not take bookings. (Have the cash on you; there's no ATM at the airport.) **Coral Bay Adventures** (© **08/9942 5955**) makes transfers, on demand, from the airport to Coral Bay, approximately 120km (74 miles) away, for A$85 (US$55) adults, A$41 (US$27) children under 13, one-way.

Greyhound Pioneer (© **13 20 30**) operates three services a week from Perth (trip time: 18–20 hr.). The fare is A$177 (US$115) to both Coral Bay and Exmouth. Another option, which takes about the same time, is Greyhound's daily Perth-Broome service, which connects with a local service to Exmouth at the turnoff on the highway at Giralia in the wee hours of the morning. The Perth-Exmouth fare in that case is A$184 (US$120).

There is no train.

The 14-hour drive from Perth (plus rest stops) is through lonely country on a two-lane highway. Check that your contract allows you to drive your rental car this far north, and has unlimited mileage. Wildlife will be thick on the ground, and gas stations thin. From Perth, take the Brand Highway north to Geraldton, 424km (263 miles), then the North West Coastal Highway for 623km (386 miles) to Minilya gas station; the Exmouth turnoff is 7km (4⅓ miles) north of Minilya. Exmouth is a further 225km (140 miles) along the cape from the turnoff. Overnight at the **Mercure Inn Geraldton,** Brand Highway, Geraldton, WA 6530 (© **08/9921 2455;** A$131/US$85 double), or in Carnarvon, the only town between Geraldton and Exmouth. Everything else that looks like a town on your map is just a gas station. But keep in mind that even the gas stations can be 200km (130 miles) apart. The longer, lonelier drive from Broome is even less recommended.

VISITOR INFORMATION The **Exmouth Visitor Centre,** Murat Road, Exmouth, WA 6707 (© **1800/287 328** within Western Australia, or 08/9949 1176; www.exmouth-australia.com), is open daily from 8:30am to 5pm, or from 10am to 3pm on weekends November through March. The **Milyering Visitors Centre,** 52km (32 miles) northwest of Exmouth, is the Cape Range National Park's information center, run by the Department of Conservation and Land Management (CALM). It is open daily from 10am to 4pm but closes for lunch from 12:30pm to 1:15pm. You can pick up a hiking-trail map of the park from CALM's office in Nimitz Street, Exmouth. **Coral Bay Adventures** runs a tour information and booking center on Robinson Street, Coral Bay, WA 6701 (© **08/9942 5955;** www.users.bigpond.com/coralbay).

The entry fee to the Cape Range National Park, payable at the Milyering Visitor Centre, is A$9 (US$5.85) per vehicle.

There is only one ATM cash machine on the Cape, in Exmouth.

GETTING AROUND Tours and dive operators pick up from either Exmouth or Coral Bay accommodations, but not usually both. The roads to Exmouth and Coral Bay are paved, and so is the only road around the Cape's coast. **Avis** (© **08/9949 2942**), **Budget** (© **08/9949 1534**), **Hertz** (© **08/9949 2792**), and local operator **Allens Car Hire** (© **08/9949 2403**) have offices in Exmouth; there is no car rental in Coral Bay.

Ningaloo Reef Bus (© **08/9949 1776**) runs from Exmouth hotels to various beaches around the cape, calling at the Milyering Visitors Centre en route. It runs every day except Thursday April through September, and Tuesday, Wednesday, Friday, and Sunday October through March. The round-trip fare to the snorkel beauty spot of Turquoise Bay is A$22 (US$14), including the park entry fee.

DIVING WITH WHALE SHARKS 𝒜𝒜

Diving is not the correct term for this activity, because it's by snorkeling that you get close to these leviathans of the deep. Whale sharks are sharks, not whales, and are the world's biggest fish, reaching an alarming 12m to 18m (39 ft.–58 ft.) in length. Terrified? Don't be. Their gigantic size belies a gentle nature and swimming speed; despite having a mouth big enough to swallow a boatload of snorkelers, they eat plankton. Several boat operators take people out to swim alongside the fish when they appear from late March to mid-June. A day trip with one of the longest established whale-shark companies, **Exmouth Diving Centre** (② 1800/ 655 156 in Australia, or 08/9949 1201; www.exmouthdiving.com.au) or its Coral Bay sister company, **Ningaloo Reef Diving Centre** (② 08/9942 5824; www. users.bigpond.com/ningaloo), costs A$320 (US$208) for snorkeling or A$360 (US$234) including a scuba dive, with all gear included.

DIVING, SNORKELING, FISHING & 4WD TOURS

Scuba dive 𝒜 the Cape's unspoiled waters, and you will see marvelous reef formations, grouper, manta rays, octopus, morays, potato cod (which you can hand-feed), and other marvels at a dozen or more sites. Divers often spot humpback and false killer whales and large sharks, while snorkelers may see dolphins, dugongs, and turtles. Loads of dive companies in Exmouth and Coral Bay rent gear and run daily dive trips and learn-to-dive courses, including the two listed in "Diving with Whale Sharks," above. A two-dive day trip costs between A$125 (US$81) and A$160 (US$104) with all gear supplied.

Three great snorkeling spots are: right off the shore at Coral Bay; Bundegi Beach, 14km (nearly 9 miles) north of Exmouth; and at **Turquoise Bay** 𝒜, a 60km (37-mile) drive from Exmouth. In deeper waters off Coral Bay, you can snorkel with **manta rays** 𝒜 with a "wingspan" up to 7m (23 ft.). Companies in either town run manta and reef-snorkel trips, and rent snorkel gear. The Cape has loads of swimming beaches; for safety's sake, never swim alone.

Reef fish, tuna, and Spanish mackerel are common catches in these waters, and black, blue, and striped marlin run outside the reef September through January. Up to a dozen boats operate reef and **game-fishing day trips** 𝒜 out of Exmouth and Coral Bay, and tackle and tin fishing dinghies are easily rented in either town.

Green and loggerhead **turtles** 𝒜 lay eggs at night November through February or March on the Cape's beaches. Take a flashlight and go looking for them, or join one of several turtle-watch tours from either town. August through October, boats run cruises from either town to spot **humpback whales.**

Because the Cape has few roads, and even fewer sights along the way, take an off-road 240km (149-mile) four-wheel-drive escapade with **Neil McLeod's Ningaloo Safari Tours** 𝒜 (② 08/9949 1550; www.ningaloosafari.com). You will explore the arid limestone ridges of 50,581-hectare (124,935-acre) Cape Range National Park, snorkel Turquoise Bay, climb up a lighthouse, and cruise orange-walled Yardie Creek Gorge to spot rock wallabies—snacking on Neil's mum's fruitcake along the way. This full-day trip departs your Exmouth hotel at 7:30am and returns at 6pm. It costs A$145 (US$94) for adults and A$105 (US$68) for children under 13.

WHERE TO STAY & DINE
IN EXMOUTH

Potshot Hotel Resort   The grounds are hot and dusty, but the building is in a modern complex. The cocktail bar around the pool is the only shady place in town to enjoy a drink, which explains its popularity with locals. The restaurant is scant on atmosphere but has a long menu, good food, and a nice wine list. There's a seafood buffet on Friday and Saturday nights. The brick motel rooms are cool and spacious; the homestead rooms are smaller, older, and more basic. There are two-bedroom apartments, and across the road are newer three-bedroom apartments, some with Jacuzzis.

Murat Rd., Exmouth, WA 6707. © 08/9949 1200. Fax 08/9949 1486. www.potshotresort.com. 97 units (all with shower only). A$85 (US$55) double homestead room; A$118–A$129 (US$77–US$84) resort studio room (sleeps 4); A$139–A$175 (US$90–US$114) 2-bedroom apt; A$195–A$205 (US$127–US$133) 3-bedroom apt. Maid service in apts A$22–A$33 (US$14–US$21) per day. AE, DC, MC, V. **Amenities:** 2 restaurants; 4 bars; 3 small outdoor pools; coin-op laundry; hair dryers; irons. *In room:* A/C, TV, fridge, coffeemaker; no phone in Homestead rooms only.

IN CORAL BAY

Ningaloo Reef Resort   This low-rise complex of motel rooms, studios, and apartments stands out as the best place to stay among Coral Bay's profusion of backpacker hostels. Located on a blissfully green lawn with a swimming pool overlooking the bay, the rooms are nothing fancy or new, but they're clean, with views toward the bay and the pool. The place has a nice communal air, thanks to the bar doubling as the local pub.

At the end of Robinson St., Coral Bay, WA 6701. © 08/9942 5934. Fax 08/9942 5953. www.coralbay.org/resort.htm. 34 units, all with bathroom (shower only). A$138–A$143 (US$90–US$93) double; A$175–A$285 (US$114–US$185) apt. Extra person A$11 (US$7.15) adults, A$5.50–A$11 (US$3.60–US$7.15) children. Weekly rates available. MC, V. **Amenities:** Restaurant; bar; outdoor pool; coin-op laundry; hair dryers; irons. *In room:* A/C, TV, no phone.

6 The Kimberley: A Far-Flung Wilderness ⊀

Most Aussies would be hard put to name a single settlement, river, or mountain within the Kimberley, so rarely visited and sparsely inhabited is this wilderness. This is an ancient land of red, rocky plateaus stretching for thousands of miles, jungly ravines, endless bush, crocodile-infested wetlands, surreal-looking boab trees with trunks shaped like bottles, lily-filled rock pools, lonely island-strewn coastline, droughts in winter, and floods in summer. The dry, spreading scenery might call to mind Africa or India. In the dry season (the Dry), the area's biggest river, the Fitzroy, is empty, but in the wet season (the Wet), its swollen banks are second only to the Amazon in the volume of water that surges to the sea. Aqua and scarlet are two colors that will hit you in the eye in the Kimberley—a luminous aqua for the sea and the fiery scarlet of the fine soil hereabouts called "pindan." The area is famous for Wandjina-style Aboriginal rock art depicting people with circular hairdos that look more than a little like beings from outer space. It is also known for another kind of rock art known as "Bradshaw figures," sticklike representations of human forms, which may be the oldest art on earth. A mere 25,000 people live in the Kimberley's 420,000 sq. km (1,638,000 sq. miles). That's three times the size of England.

The unofficial capital of the East Kimberley is **Kununurra.** It's a small agricultural town that serves as the gateway to wildlife river cruises; the **Bungle Bungles**⊀, a massive labyrinth of beehive-shaped rock formations; and **El Questro**⊀⊀, a million-acre cattle ranch where you can hike, fish, and cruise palm-filled gorges by day and sleep in comfy permanent safari tents or glamorous homestead rooms by night (it's open from Apr to early Nov). The main town in the West Kimberley is the Outback port of **Broome**⊀ whose waters give up the world's biggest and best South Sea pearls. Linking Kununurra and Derby, near

Broome, is the Gibb River Road, an isolated four-wheel-drive track through cattle-station country that is becoming popular with adventure travelers.

Off the West Kimberley coast lies a jigsaw puzzle of 10,000 or more barely inhabited islands, the **Bonaparte** ⚓ and **Buccaneer Archipelagos** ⚓, the last named in honor of the pirate's pirate, William Dampier, who sailed here in 1688. In fact, much of the appeal of this coastline lies in the knowledge that few Westerners have laid eyes on it since the first explorers of the 17th century.

ESSENTIALS

VISITOR INFORMATION   The **Kimberley Tourism Association,** P.O. Box 554, Broome, WA 6725 (© **08/9193 6660;** www.kimberleytourism.com), supplies information on the entire region. The **Kununurra Visitor Centre** and the **Broome Visitor Centre** (which appear later in this chapter) also handle inquiries on things to see and do across the entire Kimberley, and you can drop into their information offices once you arrive.

Best of the Kimberley (© **1800/450 850** in Australia, or 08/9192 6070; www.kimberleytravel.net) is a Broome-based agency marketing a large range of tours and experiences, including four-wheel-drive safaris, aerial tours, bushwalking and horseback riding, and cruising. It sells accommodations and tour packages, and a huge range of day trips, tours, and activities, and specializes in personalized vacations. Visits to the remote Dampier Peninsula to fish and go mud-crabbing with an Aboriginal family, or to self-fly packages around this vast region for private pilots (aircraft hire included) are among their more unusual offerings.

GETTING AROUND   Enormous distances, high gasoline costs (often A$1 per liter or more, equivalent to US$2 per U.S. gal.), wet season floods, and very limited roads and facilities can make traveling the Kimberley expensive and time-consuming. The place has lots of attractions so remote they can only be reached by aerial tours or charter boats. Many more are accessible only on unpaved roads, for which your two-wheel-drive rental car is not insured and which it probably can't handle, so if you don't want to rely on tours, rent a four-wheel-drive (available in Broome and Kununurra). Allow for an average speed of 60kmph (37 mph) on the area's rough unsealed roads, and never exceed 80kmph (50 mph), because unexpected dips and smooth patches can take you by surprise. Most outfits will allow one-way rentals between Broome and Kununurra, or vice versa, at a ballpark surcharge of A$350 to A$550 (US$228–US$358). Review "Road Conditions & Safety," "What If Your Vehicle Breaks Down?," and "Tips for Four-Wheel Drivers," in the "Getting Around Australia" section of chapter 2, before setting off.

Kimberley Camping & Outback Supplies, 65 Frederick St., Broome (© **08/ 9193 5909**), sells and rents every piece of camping equipment you need, from tents and "mozzie" (mosquito) nets to cooking utensils, plus outdoor clothing.

Taking a guided four-wheel-drive camping or accommodated safari is a neat way to sidestep the challenges of Kimberley travel. Safaris depart Broome, Kununurra, or Darwin, and last between 2 days and 2 weeks. A popular route is the cross-Kimberley journey between Broome and Kununurra. If you opt for this route, look for tours that traverse the Gibb River Road, rather than the scenically dull highway via Halls Creek and Fitzroy Crossing. The Gibb River Road is an adventurous unpaved "back road" between Kununurra and Broome that offers gorges, low red ranges, swimming holes (ask directions to croc-free ones), walking trails, barramundi fishing, and campsites or basic homestead accommodations on vast cattle stations (ranches). Most safaris run only in the dry season, April/May

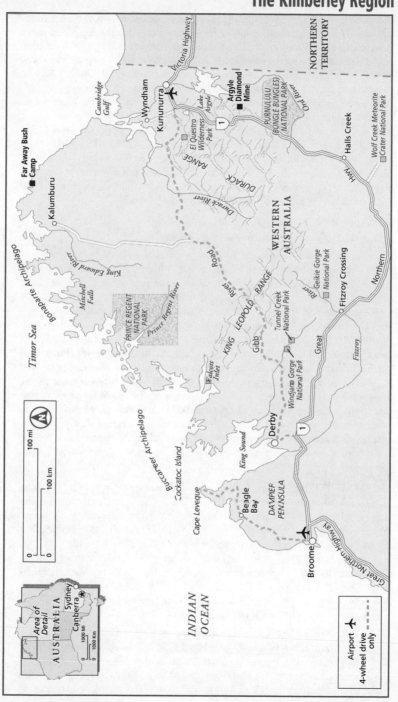

The Kimberley Region

NORTHERN TERRITORY

WESTERN AUSTRALIA

Victoria Highway

Cambridge Gulf

Wyndham

Kununurra

Lake Argyle

Argyle Diamond Mine

PURNULULU (BUNGLE BUNGLES) NATIONAL PARK

Ord River

El Questro Wilderness Park

DURACK RANGE

Halls Creek

Wolf Creek Meteorite Crater National Park

Hwy.

Far Away Bush Camp

Kalumburu

Durack River

Bonaparte Archipelago

King Edward River

Mitchell Falls

Timor Sea

PRINCE REGENT NATIONAL PARK

Prince Regent River

Gibb River Road

LEOPOLD RANGE

KING

Geikie Gorge National Park

Fitzroy Crossing

Northern

Tunnel Creek National Park

River

Great

Fitzroy

Buccaneer Archipelago

Cockatoc Island

Walcott Inlet

Windjana Gorge National Park

Derby

King Sound

Cape Leveque

Beagle Bay

DAMPIER PENINSULA

Great Northern Highway

Broome

INDIAN OCEAN

100 mi

100 km

Area of Detail

AUSTRALIA

Sydney

Canberra

1000 Mi

1000 Km

Airport ✈
4-wheel drive only

through October/November. Respected operators include **East Kimberley Tours** (© **08/9168 2213;** www.eastkimberleytours.com.au); **Kimberley Wilderness Adventures** (© **1800/804 005** in Australia, or 08/9192 5741; www.kimberley wilderness.com.au); **Adventure Tours** (© **1300/654 604** in Australia; www. adventuretours.com.au); and **Australian Pinnacle Tours** (© **1800/999 069** in Australia, or 08/9417 5555; www.pinnacletours.com.au).

Broome Aviation (© **1300/13 66 29** in Australia, or 08/9192 1369; www. broomeaviation.com) and **King Leopold Air** (© **08/9193 7155;** www.king leopoldair.com.au), based in Broome, and **Alligator Airways** (© **08/9168 1333;** www.alligatorairways.com.au) and **Slingair Heliwork** (© **1800/095 500** in Australia, or 08/9169 1300; www.slingair.com.au), based in Kununurra, run a range of flight-seeing tours all over the Kimberley, lasting from a couple of hours to several days. Some involve sightseeing on the ground, hiking, four-wheel-drive trips, overnights at fishing camps, or calls into cattle stations.

KUNUNURRA
827km (513 miles) SW of Darwin; 1,032km (640 miles) E of Broome

Given the arid conditions in the Kimberley, it's quite a surprise to swoop over a field of sugar cane as you come in to land at Kununurra. This rather ramshackle little town (pop. 5,000) is an agricultural center created by the damming of the mighty Ord River to form **Lake Argyle.**

Kununurra itself (the name is Aboriginal for "Meeting of Big Waters") has little to spark your interest, but it is the gateway to several outstanding attractions. A cruise or canoe trip down the **Ord River** to see wild birds, dramatic cliffs, and crocs is a must. So is a flight over, or a hike into, the **Bungle Bungles (Purnululu National Park)** *⭑*, monumental orange domes of rock that look like giant beehives. The world's biggest diamond mine is not in South Africa but out in the rugged Kimberley wilds near Kununurra, and it can be visited by air every day. The town is also a gateway to **El Questro Wilderness Park** *⭑⭑*, a million-acre cattle station (ranch) where you can hike magnificent gorges, fish, cruise rivers, ride horses, and see some of Australia's most breathtaking Aboriginal art. It is open from April to early November, closed over summer due to the wet season.

ESSENTIALS
GETTING THERE   There is no train to Kununurra. **Greyhound Pioneer** (© **13 20 30** in Australia) serves the town daily from Perth via Broome and daily from Darwin via Katherine. From Perth the trip takes about 34 hours, from Broome about 15 hours. The one-way fare from Perth is A$468 (US$304). From Darwin, the trip time is around 9 hours, and the fare is A$129 (US$84).

Kununurra is 512km (323 miles) west of Katherine on the Victoria Highway. The Great Northern Highway from Broome connects with the Victoria Highway 45km (28 miles) west of Kununurra. The Gibb River Road is an alternative four-wheel-drive scenic route from Derby near Broome; it connects with the Great Northern Highway 53km (33 miles) west of town.

VISITOR INFORMATION   The **Kununurra Visitor Centre** is at Coolibah Drive, Kununurra, WA 6743 (© **08/9168 1177;** kununurratb@bigpond.com). The hours change with the season, but it's usually open from 9am to 5pm every day from April to September, and from 9am to 5pm weekdays and 9am to noon Saturdays between October and March (closed Sun and public holidays during this time).

GETTING AROUND   Avis (℡ 08/9169 1258), **Budget** (℡ 08/9168 2033), **Hertz** (℡ 08/9169 1424), and **Thrifty** (℡ 08/9169 1911) all rent four-wheel-drive vehicles. Hertz rents camping gear also.

WHAT TO SEE & DO

ON THE ORD RIVER   Several cruise outfits will offer you the option of cruising the Ord River or Lake Argyle, a massive man-made blue inland sea ringed by red cliffs and bigger than 19 Sydney Harbours, but go for the Ord. The Ord River is one of the most picturesque waterways in Australia, lined by red cliffs in parts, and teeming with all kinds of wetland birds and freshwater crocodiles. Jeff Haley of **Triple J. Tours** (℡ 08/9168 2682; www.triplejtours.net.au) runs excellent cruises. There are several itineraries, and they vary from dry season to wet, but the most popular starts with a 70km (43-mile) coach ride and commentary to Lake Argyle, a wander through a historic homestead, then the 55km (34-mile) cruise down the Ord back to Kununurra. The boat travels fast and is a bit noisy, but Jeff pulls in at numerous tranquil spots. This costs A$140 (US$91) for adults and A$70 (US$46) for children 4 to 15, including pickup from your hotel. It takes most of the day.

Big Waters Kimberley Canoe Safaris (℡ 1800/641 998 in Australia, or 08/9169 1998; www.adventure.kimberley.net.au) offers a popular 3-day self-guided canoeing/camping safari down the Class I (that means "gentle") Ord River in two-person Canadian canoes. It costs A$145 (US$94) per person. During the Wet you can do a 1-day tour for A$45 (US$29) per person.

A day on the river to fish for barramundi with Greg Harman's **Ultimate Adventures** (℡ 08/9168 2310; www.wn.com.au/ultimateadvent) costs around A$230 (US$150) per person, more if there is only one of you. Greg also does trips of up to 10 days to remote fishing camps.

DIAMONDS IN THE ROUGH   Turning out an impressive 38 million carats a year—that's more than 8 tons of pure diamond—is the world's biggest diamond mine, the **Argyle Diamond Mine,** 176km (109 miles) from Kununurra. It is the only mine in the world to produce the pink diamond in commercial quantities, as well as champagne, cognac, yellow, green, and white rocks. During a 3½- to 4-hour visit, you will see rough and polished gems in the viewing room, see gems get extracted from the open-cut mine (as long as safety conditions permit), and, if you like, buy diamonds. For security reasons, you must join an aerial tour with **Belray Diamond Tours** (℡ 08/9168 1014), which you can also book through **Alligator Airways** (℡ 08/9168 1333; www.alligatorairways.com.au). Opt for a flight that covers the nearby Purnululu National Park (Bungle Bungles) and Lake Argyle as well, an option costing A$325 (US$211). Belray Diamond Tours does a coach trip Thursdays only June through September, which costs A$180 (US$117) per person, but it's a 2½-hour drive each way. Kids under 12 are not permitted on mine tours.

SPENDING THE DAY AT EL QUESTRO WILDERNESS PARK   You do not have to stay at El Questro (see "Where to Stay," below) to enjoy the wonderful facilities. After aristocratic Englishman Will Burrell bought this million-acre cattle ranch in 1991, he turned it into a kind of Outback holiday camp where anyone from international celebrities to humble four-wheel-drive enthusiasts could revel in its rugged beauty. Although it's a working farm, guests don't get involved in that side of things. Instead, they go barramundi fishing and heli-fishing in croc-infested wetlands and rivers, soak under palm trees in the thermal waters of Zebedee Springs (closed from noon daily), hike gorges, some of which hide pockets of rainforest, take half-day four-wheel-drive fishing safaris, cruise tranquil Chamberlain Gorge, horseback ride across stony plains, photograph red rocky ranges, join rangers on bird-watching or "bush-tucker" tours, or explore a rich lode of Aboriginal rock paintings. It's an unspoiled, primeval place.

El Questro is open from April 1 to early November (it closes in the Wet, Nov–Mar). It is 100km (62 miles) west of Kununurra by road (58km/36 miles on the sealed Great Northern Highway towards Wyndham, with the remainder on the graded gravel Gibb River Rd.). Visitors must purchase a 7-day Wilderness Park Permit to enter, which costs A$13 (US$8.45) per person; children under 12 enter free. Buy permits from El Questro's office in Kununurra, on Banksia Street, where the staff will give you a map and point out all there is to see and do, or at the Station Township. The Township acts as a kind of headquarters—most tours and activities depart here, and it's where you can buy road and other supplies and fuel, and rent four-wheel-drives and camping gear. Consider renting a four-wheel-drive in Kununurra or at the Station Township. Transfers from the Homestead and Emma Gorge cost A$60 (US$39) per person to join tours and activities departing the Station Township, so while it is not crucial to have your own four-wheel-drive, it is less costly. Having your own vehicle also means you can explore independently. The Station Township rents them for A$130 to A$176 (US$85–US$114) per day, plus A30¢ (US20¢) per kilometer after the first 100km (62 miles) (best to book them ahead as the fleet size is limited).

If you're short on time, the station's 12-hour ranger-guided day trips from Kununurra are a good idea. They include the highlights of a Chamberlain Gorge cruise to see Aboriginal Wandjina rock art and a soak in Zebedee Springs, plus a gorge walk, lunch at the Station Township restaurant, and four-wheel-drive transfers, for A$145 (US$94) per person. Ask staff to identify which swimming spots are croc-free, and don't swim anywhere else!

You pay for most activities—between A$60 (US$39) for a 2-hour horse ride to A$565 (US$367) for a half-day's saltwater heli-fishing. Typical prices are A$42 (US$27) for a gorge cruise, A$75 (US$49) for a 4-hour four-wheel-drive trip to watch the sun set over the Cockburn Range, or A$175 (US$114) for a half-day four-wheel-drive barramundi-fishing trip. The rangers are friendly and knowledgeable. The tour desk also arranges such off-station activities as day trips on the Ord River or around Kununurra, trips to the Argyle diamond mine and the Bungle Bungles, and extended tours throughout the Kimberley as far afield as Mitchell Falls.

GETTING THERE   4WD transfers for guests operate from Kununurra and are driven by a ranger who gives a commentary en route. The cost is A$144 (US$94) per adult round-trip to Emma Gorge only, or A$180 (US$117) to the Station Township; children under 12 are half price. If you are driving yourself, take the Great Northern Highway 58km (36 miles) from Kununurra toward Wyndham, then the (unsealed) Gibb River Road 25km (15½ miles) to Emma Gorge Resort (which is 2km/1¼ miles along an access road), or a further 27km (17 miles) to the station store.

WHERE TO STAY
At El Questro
All of the accommodations accept American Express, Diners Club, MasterCard, and Visa. All have public pay phones only, not in-room phones (or TVs).

El Questro Homestead 🏵🏵🏵 Perched over the Chamberlain River on the edge of a gorge, this homestead is one of the world's most luxurious yet simple getaways. Visitors (make that *wealthy* visitors) come for the sense of seclusion and the wilderness experience. You stay in airy rooms furnished in a blend of Aussie country style and Indonesian antiques, with a view of the gardens and the river from your veranda. The premier suite even has a bathtub on the veranda! Guests relax outside or in the inviting TV lounge. Everyone dines at one big communal table at breakfast and lunch. At dinner you dine at tables for two set up wherever you like—halfway down the gorge cliff face overhanging the river, out by the pool, and so on. The Station Township is 9km (5½ miles) away.

Gibb River Rd., approximately 100km (62 miles) southwest of Kununurra (P.O. Box 909, Kununurra, WA 6743). Accor, 📞 **1300/65 65 65** in Australia, 800/221-4542 in the U.S. and Canada, 020/8283 4500 in the U.K., 0800/44 4422 in New Zealand, or 08/9169 1777. Fax 08/9169 1383. www.elquestro.com.au. 6 units (shower only; 1 with veranda tub). A$750–A$850 (US$488–US$553) per person per night double or twin (including all meals, open bar, laundry service, and all activities except helicopter flights). Minimum 2-night stay. The homestead is 119km (74 miles) from Kununurra (about 1¾ hr.). Round-trip 4-wheel-drive transfers from Kununurra A$75 (US$49) per person (scheduled) or A$150 (US$98) per person (private). Air transfers from Kununurra, Broome, Darwin, Alice Springs, and Ayers Rock available on request—baggage limit can be as little as 5kg (11 lb.) on flights from Kununurra or Darwin. Children under 16 not permitted. **Amenities:** Home-style kitchen "restaurant"; free alcoholic beverages; small outdoor pool; tennis court; Jacuzzi; tour bookings; laundry service. *In room:* A/C, hair dryer.

Emma Gorge Resort 🏵🏵 This neatly kept oasis of cute permanent tents mounted on lush lawns under pandanus palms at the foot of the soaring red Cockburn Range is a great way to "camp" in the wilderness without sacrificing comfort. Although they are "only" tents, accommodations are comfortable, with wooden floors, electric lights, fans, insect screens, nice firm beds with quilts, and flashlights for getting around at night. Those without bathrooms share clean and modern facilities. The reception desk stocks stuff like sunscreen and souvenirs, and lends hair dryers. The rustic restaurant serves up gourmet bush-tucker meals that would put many big-city restaurants to shame, and has a retractable roof for stargazing. Free to guests is access to a 1.6km (1-mile) trail along lush Emma Gorge to the natural swimming hole and trickling waterfall enclosed by 46m (150-ft.) cliffs. The Station Township is 27km (17 miles) away.

See contact details for El Questro Homestead, above. 45 tent cabins, 27 with bathroom (shower only). A$133–A$182 (US$86–US$118) double; A$198 (US$129) deluxe tent (sleeps 4). Emma Gorge is 85km (53 miles), an hour's drive, from Kununurra. Transfers are A$48 (US$31) per person each way (children under 12 half price). **Amenities:** Restaurant; bar; outdoor pool; tour desk; coin-op laundry; hair dryer (at front desk). *In room:* No phone.

Station Township Bungalows These basic but comfortable cabin-style rooms located by the store at the heart of Station Township are good for anyone without their own transportation, as tours depart from right outside. The nicest are the eight newish ones with balconies overlooking the Pentecost River. Two of the four original stone bungalows sleep six but are the same price. **The Steakhouse** restaurant and bar serves three meals a day of the steak and barramundi kind, and there is often live music around the campfire. A swimming hole is nearby.

See contact details for El Questro Homestead, above. 12 bungalows (with shower only). A$198 (US$129) per bungalow (sleeps 4). The Bungalows are 110km (68 miles), about 90 min., from Kununurra. **Amenities:** Restaurant; bar; tour desk; 4-wheel-drive rental desk; coin-op laundry; hair dryer (at front desk). *In room:* A/C, fridge, coffeemaker.

Station Township Riverside Camping In addition to the other El Questro options, there are two camping areas. **Black Cockatoo Riverside Camping** has

45 campsites near the station store, and there are another 28 more secluded riverside campsites within a 6km (3¾-mile) drive. All campsites are the same price, A$13 (US$8.45) per person per night; free for children under 12. Campers share shower facilities and a laundry, and use the bungalows' restaurant. No bookings are taken for campsites. *Note:* The Wilderness Park Permit fee is not included in the campground fee. For contact details see above.

In Kununurra
Country Club Hotel   Just down the road from the tourist bureau, this low-rise hotel is your best bet among Kununurra's modest choice of accommodations. Set in tropical gardens, it has a lovely shaded pool with sun lounges and a bar, and a couple of simple dining and bar venues. The rooms are nothing flashy, but they're neat and clean, with plenty of space.

47 Coolibah Dr., Kununurra, WA 6743. ℂ 1800/808 999 in Australia, or 08/9168 1024. Fax 08/9168 1189. www. countryclubhotel.com.au. 88 units, all with bathroom (8 with tub). Dry season (Apr–Oct) A$168 (US$109) double; A$222 (US$144) 2-bedroom apt. Wet season (Nov–Mar) A$148 (US$97) double; A$191 (US$124) 2-bedroom apt. Extra person A$24 (US$16). AE, DC, MC, V. **Amenities:** 2 restaurants, 3 bars; outdoor pool; tour desk; coin-op laundry; hair dryer (at front desk). *In room:* A/C, TV, fridge.

PURNULULU (BUNGLE BUNGLES) NATIONAL PARK ✦
250km (156 miles) S of Kununurra

Rising out of the landscape 250km (155 miles) south of Kununurra are thousands of enormous sandstone domes 200m to 300m (656 ft.–984 ft.) high called the Bungle Bungles. They are thought to have been named after either "bundle bundle" grass or the bungle beetle. The Bungle Bungles get their distinctive orange-and-gray stripes from algae found in the permeable layers and mineral graining in nonpermeable layers. The formations are 360 million years old.

The domes look spectacular from the air—that's the way most people see them, and it's the only way to see them in the Wet, because the park is closed to ground traffic from January 1 to March 31, sometimes later. As the waters subside, the soaring gorges and forested creeks at the base of the Bungle Bungles are accessible to hikers. Highlights are the beehive-shaped walls of Cathedral Gorge, the rock pool at Frog Hole Gorge, and palm-filled Echidna Chasm. Keep an eye peeled for rainbow bee-eaters, flocks of budgerigars, rare nail-tailed wallabies, and euros, a kind of kangaroo. It's a lonely, quiet, contemplative, and dramatic place.

VISITOR INFORMATION   For information call the **Department of Conservation and Land Management (CALM)** (ℂ 08/9168 4200) in Kununurra. There's also a **visitor center/ranger station** (ℂ 08/9168 7300) in the park.

GETTING THERE & GETTING AROUND   Most folks take a scenic flight over the park in a light aircraft from Kununurra offered by **Slingair Heliwork** (ℂ **1800/095 500** in Australia, or 08/9169 1300) or **Alligator Airways** (ℂ **1800/632 533** in Australia, or 08/9168 1333). The flight takes about 2 hours, incorporates a flight over Lake Argyle and the impressive Argyle Diamond Mine, and costs A$190 (US$124) per adult and A$110 (US$72) per child 3 to 12 years. Both companies also do combined air/hiking day trips, though they're pricey, starting at A$445 (US$289) per person. **East Kimberley Tours** (see "Getting Around," earlier in the Kimberley section) runs an array of four-wheel-drive and fly/four-wheel-drive camping and hiking safaris into the park, including some 1-day "express" versions.

BROOME ℛ

2,389km (1,481 miles) N of Perth; 1,859km (1,152 miles) SW of Darwin

Part rough Outback town, part glam seaside resort, the pearling port of **Broome** ℛ (pop. 11,000) is a hybrid of Australia and Asia you won't see anywhere else. Chinese and Japanese pearl divers used to work the pearling luggers in this isolated little town in the old days, and as the Chinese settled here, they affixed their distinctive architecture to typical Australian buildings. The result is a main street so cute it could be a movie set, with neat rows of Australian corrugated iron stores wrapped by verandas and trimmed with Chinese peaked roofs.

The people are unique, too, because Anglo-Saxon/Irish Aussies and Chinese, Filipino, and Malayan pearl workers often married Aboriginal women. The Japanese tended to return home, but not all of them made it as cyclones, the "bends," sharks, and crocodiles all took their toll. The Japanese legacy in the town is a divers' cemetery with Asian inscriptions on 900 rough-hewn headstones.

For such a small and remote place, Broome is surprisingly sophisticated. Walk the streets of Chinatown and you'll rub shoulders with Aussie tourists, itinerant workers, Asian food-store proprietors, tough-as-nails cattle hands, and well-heeled visitors from Europe and America downing good coffee at a couple of trendy cafes. Broome's South Sea pearls are still its bread and butter, but the old-timber pearling luggers have been replaced with gleaming high-tech vessels equipped with helipads and stainless-steel security doors.

To be honest, it's kind of hard to explain Broome's appeal. There is not much to do, but it's a nice place to be. You can shop for pearls, and it's a good base for exploring the Kimberley. But most people simply come to laze by the jade-green Indian Ocean on Cable Beach, ride camels along the sand as the sun plops into the sea, fish the unplundered seas, mosey around the art galleries and jewelry stores, and soak up the gorgeous reds, blues, and greens of the Kimberley coast.

ESSENTIALS

GETTING THERE   Airlink (book through **Qantas** ℂ **13 13 13** in Australia) flies direct from Perth, Ayers Rock, and Alice Springs. Virgin Blue (ℂ **13 67 89** in Australia) flies direct to Broome from Adelaide once a week on Saturdays. The trip to Broome from Sydney and other capitals is a lengthy affair via Perth or Alice Springs.

Greyhound Pioneer (ℂ **13 20 30** in Australia) has a daily service from Perth that takes around 30 hours. The fare is A$295 (US$192). Greyhound's daily service from Darwin via Katherine and Kununurra takes around 24 hours; the one-way fare is A$255 (US$166).

There is no train service to Broome.

Broome is 34km (21 miles) off the Great Northern Highway, which leads from Perth in the south, Kununurra to the east. Many companies (including those listed under Kimberley's "Essentials," earlier in this chapter) run four-wheel-drive camping safaris to Broome on the Gibb River Road, an unpaved Outback scenic route from Kununurra.

VISITOR INFORMATION   The **Broome Visitor Centre** is on the Great Northern Highway (locals call it the Broome Hwy.) at Bagot Street, Broome, WA 6725 (ℂ **08/9192 2222;** www.kimberleytourism.com). It's open Monday through Friday from 8am to 5pm. On Saturday, Sunday, and public holidays, it's open from 9am to 4pm in the Dry (Apr–Sept), and from 9am to 1pm in the Wet (Oct–Mar).

Book hotels and tours well in advance of the peak June-through-August season.

GETTING AROUND Avis (℅ 08/9193 5980), **Broome Broome Car Rentals** (℅ 1800/676 725 in Western Australia, or 08/9192 2210), **Budget** (℅ 08/9193 5355), **Europcar** (℅ 08/9193 7788), and **Hertz** (℅ 08/9192 1428) all rent conventional cars and four-wheel-drives. Hertz also rents camping-gear kits and car-top tents that affix to the larger four-wheel-drives. Among the motor-home companies are **Apollo Motorhome Holidays** (℅ 08/9192 3087) and **Britz** (℅ 08/9192 2647).

The **Town Bus Service** (℅ **08/9193 6585**) does an hourly loop of most attractions starting at 7:10am and finishing at 6:35pm daily. Tours depart every half-hour from June to mid-September. A single fare is A$2.70 (US$1.75), and a day pass is A$8.50 (US$5.50).

Broome Taxis (℅ **08/9192 1133**) operates the airport shuttle; book ahead if you want a transfer to your hotel door. For a cab call **Roebuck Taxis** (℅ **1800/ 880 330**).

Several coach or four-wheel-drive companies run a variety of day tours of the town, plus trips of a day or several days to natural attractions farther afield like Windjana and Geikie Gorges, Tunnel Creek, and the Dampier Peninsula (described in "Beyond Broome," below).

WHAT TO SEE & DO

Head to **Chinatown,** in the town center on Carnarvon Street and Dampier Terrace, when you arrive to get a feel for the town. It's not all that Chinese anymore, but most shops, cafes, and galleries are here.

Probably the most popular dry season pastime is lazing on the 22km (14 miles) of glorious, white sandy **Cable Beach** 🏖. The beach is 6km (3¾ miles) out of town; the bus runs there regularly. A beach hut near Cable Beach Club Resort Broome (see "Where to Stay & Dine," below) rents beach and water-sports equipment in the Dry. In the Wet, about November through April, the water is off-limits due to marine stingers—it's incredibly frustrating! Crocodiles, on the other hand, do not like surf, so you should be safe swimming here. Go to the beach for at least one of the magnificent sunsets in the Dry, when the sun sinks into the sea behind the romantic outlines of pearling luggers.

A novel way to experience the beach is on a camel ride. Several outfits operate; the most popular time is at sunset as the sun drops over the ocean. A 1-hour sunset ride with **Red Sun Camel Safaris** (℅ **08/9193 7423**) costs A$33 (US$21) adults, A$22 (US$14) kids 11 to 16, and A$11 (US$7.15) kids 6 to 10. Kids under 6 pay A$10 (US$6.50), but they must ride with an adult.

Four-time state surf champ **Josh Palmateer** 🏄 (℅ **0418/958 264**) gives 2-hour surf lessons on the beach through July and August for A$80 (US$52) per person, or A$40 (US$26) per person for two. He supplies the boards and the wet suits, and the lessons are great fun.

Don't miss the **Pearl Luggers** 🏄🏄, 31 Dampier Terrace (℅ **08/9192 2059**). A 75-minute session includes a look over two restored Broome pearling luggers, a browse through a small pearling museum, and a riveting and hilarious talk about pearl diving by former pearl divers, including Richard "Salty" Baillieu. Salty is so entertaining it's worth timing your visit for the days he's on duty. Admission is A$17 (US$11) adults, A$15 (US$9.75) seniors and students, A$9 (US$5.85) kids 8 to 17. The attraction is open from 9am to 5pm May through October, and from

10am to 3:30pm November through April. Tours depart at 9am, 11am, and 2pm in the Dry, and 11am and 2pm in the Wet. Closed Christmas.

A **dinosaur footprint** 120 million years old is on show at very low tide on the cliff at Gantheaume Point, 6km (3¾ miles) from town. The town authorities have set a plaster cast of it higher up on the rocks, so you can see it anytime. Bring your camera to snap the point's breathtaking palette of glowing scarlet cliffs, white beach, and jade-turquoise water.

You should also take a peek at the haunting **Japanese pearl divers' cemetery** on Port Drive. Entry is free.

During a tour of the **Willie Creek Pearl Farm** (© **08/9192 6000**), 38km (24 miles) north of town, you will see the delicate process of an oyster getting "seeded" with a nucleus to form a pearl, learn about pearl farming, and learn what to look for when buying a pearl. You can also buy them in the showroom. The tour costs A$25 (US$16) adults, A$12 (US$7.80) children, and A$65 (US$42) for a family of four. The road to the farm is four-wheel-drive-only, and tides can cut it off; it is wise to take a coach tour, which will cost you A$59 (US$38) adults, A$30 (US$20) children or A$160 (US$104) for a family of four. Tours run daily April to September and every day except Tuesday and Saturday from October to March. You must book for the tour whether you self-drive or not.

If you have not seen any crocs in the wild during your travels, you can see them on a 1-hour tour at the **Broome Crocodile Park,** next to Cable Beach Club Resort Broome, Cable Beach Road (© **08/9192 1489**). Admission is A$15 (US$9.75) for adults, A$12 (US$7.80) for seniors and students, A$8 (US$5.20) for kids 5 to 15, and A$38 (US$25) for a family. Tours run once or twice daily, but hours vary with the seasons, so call ahead.

Several art galleries sell vivid oil and watercolor Kimberley landscapes and a small range of Aboriginal art. A historic pearling master's house, **Matso's,** 60 Hamersley St. (© **08/9193 5811**), stocks the biggest range of European and Aboriginal paintings, sculpture, pottery, carvings, and books in its Monsoon Gallery. It has a lovely veranda cafe and boutique brewery turning out unusual recipes like alcoholic ginger beer. The gallery is open daily from 10am to 5pm; the cafe is open daily from 8am until late.

On Saturday from 8am to 1pm, browse the **markets** in the gardens of the colonial Courthouse at the corner of Frederick and Hamersley streets. It used to be the official station for the cable from Broome to Java. Don't bet the ranch on this tale being gospel, but locals like to tell you that when the British authorities

---

Moments Staircase to the Moon

You've heard of a stairway to heaven? Well, Broome has a **staircase to the moon** 🕭. On the happy coincidence of a full moon and a 10m (33-ft.) tide (which happens about 3 consecutive nights a month Mar–Oct), nature treats the town to a special show, as the light of the rising moon falls on the rippled sand and mudflats in Roebuck Bay, looking for all the world like a "staircase to the moon." The best place to see it is from the cliff-top restaurant at the **Mangrove Hotel** (see "Where to Stay & Dine," below), or from the food and crafts markets held at Town Beach. Live music plays at the Mangrove most staircase nights, including a didgeridoo player to accompany the rising moon.

packed up the building materials for the courthouse in Britain and addressed it to "The Kimberley," they meant them to end up in the Kimberley, South Africa. Instead, the stuff arrived in the Kimberley, Australia. The town kept the building and so can proudly lay claim to having Australia's only Zulu-proof courthouse.

A number of boats run sunset cruises on Roebuck Bay or off Cable Beach.

Fishing ⚲ for trevally, barracuda, barramundi, queenfish, tuna, shark, sailfish, marlin, salmon (in the May–Aug run), and reef fish is excellent around Broome; fly- and sportfishing are also worth a try. Rent tackle and try your luck from the deep-water jetty near Town Beach 2km (1¼ miles) south of town, or join one of several charter boats, such as **FAD Game Fishing Charters** (© **08/9192 3998;** www.fadcharters.com.au), for a day trip. **Pearl Sea Coastal Cruises** (see "Boating the Kimberley Coast," below) runs live-aboard fishing trips up the coast. Cyclones, rain, high winds, and strong tides can restrict fishing December through March.

More than one-third of Australia's bird species live in the Kimberley. The blue, green, yellow, and violet Gouldian finch, Nankeen night heron, tawny frogmouth, and hundreds more species get "twitchers" excited. **The Broome Bird Observatory** research station (© **08/9193 5600**), 25km (16 miles) out of town on Roebuck Bay, monitors the thousands of migratory wetlands birds that gather here from Siberia. It offers 2½-hour tours from Broome, and has basic accommodations and camping facilities for real enthusiasts.

Australia's "first family" of pearling, the Paspaleys, sell their wonderfully elegant jewelry at **Paspaley Pearls,** Carnarvon Street at Short Street (© **08/9192 2203**). **Linneys** (© **08/9192 2430**) is another reputable jeweler nearby.

Don't leave without taking in a recent-release movie at the wonderful **Sun Pictures** outdoor cinema, Carnarvon Street near Short Street (© **08/9192 1077**). Built in 1916, these are the oldest "picture gardens" in the world, where the audience sits in (saggy) canvas deck chairs. Films are even screened through the rain in the Wet. Tickets are A$12 (US$7.80). Open nightly except Christmas.

WHERE TO STAY & DINE

Cable Beach Club Resort Broome ⚲⚲⚲   For some Aussies, a visit to Broome is just an excuse to stay at this chic Asia-meets-Outback resort, which blends Australian frontier architecture and decor—corrugated iron walls inside as well as out, verandas, Aboriginal art—with Chinese elements like red and green latticework, pagoda roofs, silky red bathrobes, and Asian cotton bedcovers. The huge standard rooms are gorgeous and have a decent-size living area and balcony. Bungalows (which sleep five or six) were renovated in 2000; they have central bedrooms wrapped on three sides by a veranda, and kitchens. For glamour, it's tough to match the colonial-pearling-master suites, lavishly decked out with eye-popping Asiatic antiques and valuable Australian art. These are truly to die for, so ask about suite packages, which offer remarkably good value. A dune blocks true sea views, because the authorities won't allow buildings visible from the sand. Unlike many resorts, this one has a choice of dining venues worth eating in. It is a 5-minute drive or a 6km (3¾-mile) bus ride into town.

Cable Beach Rd., Broome, WA 6725. © **1800/099 199** in Australia, or 08/9192 0400. Fax 08/9192 2249. www.cablebeachclub.com. 263 units (some with shower only). High season (July–Sept) A$345–A$445 (US$224–US$289) double; A$299–A$575 (US$194–US$374) bungalow. Slight discounts in Apr–June; significantly lower rates Oct–Mar. Lower rates for a 3-night stay. Ask about packages. Extra person A$38 (US$25). Children under 20 stay free in parent's room with existing bedding. AE, DC, MC, V. Airport shuttle A$6 (US$3.90) per person return. Town bus. **Amenities:** 5 restaurants (2 close in the Wet); cafe; bar; outdoor pool and an adults-only saltwater pool chilled in humid wet season; 8 floodlit tennis courts (4 indoor); health club; massages, yoga, float tank, personal trainers; Jacuzzi; kids' club for kids 3–12; guest-activities program;

concierge; tour desk; business center; limited room service; in-room massage; babysitting; same-day dry cleaning/laundry service; art gallery/pearl boutique. *In room:* A/C, TV w/pay movies, fridge, hair dryer, iron.

Mangrove Hotel 𝄢   The best views in Broome are across Roebuck Bay from this modest but appealing cliff-top hotel, a 5 minutes' walk from town. There's no faulting the clean, well-kept, roomy deluxe rooms with sea views. Sixteen extra-large Executive Suite rooms were added in 2002; there are also three suites with kitchenettes, separate bedrooms, and Jacuzzis; and two two-bedroom apartments. The swimming pools and Jacuzzis are set in the lawns overlooking the bay. It's worth hightailing it back from sightseeing just to watch dusk fall over the bay from **The Tides** 𝄢, a lovely outdoor restaurant serving fresh, affordable food. The restaurant's tables and chairs are set out on the lawns under the palms and along the cliff edge. Inside, **Charters** restaurant is one of Broome's best. The town bus stops across the road.

120 Carnarvon St., Broome, WA 6725. ℂ **1800/094 818** in Australia, or 08/9192 1303. Fax 08/9193 5169. www.mangrovehotel.com.au. 70 units, all with bathroom (65 with shower only, 3 with Jacuzzi). High season (Apr–Sept) A$165–A$198 (US$107–US$129) double; A$253–A$275 (US$164–US$179) suite; A$264 (US$172) 2-bedroom apt. Low season (Oct–Mar) A$143 (US$93) double; A$176–A$253 (US$114–US$164) suite; A$242 (US$157) 2-bedroom apt. Extra person A$33 (US$21). Children under 3 stay free. Ask about packages in the wet season. AE, DC, MC, V. Courtesy car from airport. **Amenities:** 2 restaurants; 2 bars; 2 outdoor pools; 2 Jacuzzis; tour desk; secretarial services; limited room service; coin-op laundry; same-day dry cleaning/laundry service. *In room:* A/C, TV w/movies, dataport (Executive Suites only), fridge, hair dryer, iron.

BEYOND BROOME

North of Broome, the Kimberley gets wild. It's a place with almost no human settlement, best suited to those who love nature at its most raw and isolated. Swimming in the ocean and rivers is off-limits, except in croc-free rock-pools.

Stretching 220km (136 miles) north of Broome, the **Dampier Peninsula** is home to several Aboriginal communities that sell artworks, and a wonderful pearl-shell church built by missionaries.

The 350-million-year-old walls of **Windjana Gorge,** 240km (149 miles) east of Broome reveal fossilized marine creatures laid down in the Devonian period. A trail leads you past the walls, which rise up to 100m (328 ft.) above the desert floor. The 30m (98-ft.) high walls of **Geikie Gorge** (pronounced *geek*-ee), 418km (259 miles) east of Broome, are part of the same ancient coral-reef system as Windjana, which you explore by walk trails or a short cruise run by rangers. Either gorge can be explored on a long day trip from Broome.

The 10,000 or more islands of the **Buccaneer and Bonaparte Archipelagos** 𝄢 are mostly uninhabited except for **Cockatoo Island Resort** (ℂ **08/9191 7477;** fax 08/9191 7484; www.cockatooisland.com), several hundred kilometers north of Broome, a glamorously simple hideaway that puts guests in salmon-pink former miners' huts perched high on a rock wall over the sea. Fishing, taking nature walks, and lazing by the cliff-top pool are the main activities. The sight of the archipelago's red rocky islands and the clouds reflecting in the jade-green sea is wonderful from the air.

Much farther north are the tidal whirlpools, gorges, and rainforested waterfalls of **Walcott Inlet;** the utter isolation of the gorges, rock plateaus, and river of the 600,000-hectare (1,482,000-acre) **Prince Regent Nature Reserve;** and the four tiers of the picturesque **Mitchell Falls.**

There are no roads to most of these places (except for four-wheel-drive tracks to the Dampier Peninsula and Mitchell Falls), so you need to explore by scenic flight from Broome or Kununurra or by boat. July through September or later, plane and boat passengers often spot humpback whales along this coast.

BOATING THE KIMBERLEY COAST

Boating this vast, unspoiled Kimberley coastline is a true adventure. Here you can fish in rivers without names, hike through spectacular gorges, laze on isolated beaches, gaze at Aboriginal rock art, eat oysters fresh off the rocks, spot giant marine turtles, shower under waterfalls, swim in the odd croc-free rainforest pool, and feel the wilderness is yours. But extremely strong tidal currents of up to 11m (36 ft.), high cliffs, sharks, and saltwater crocodiles all pose dangers, so you should be reasonably fit and independent to travel by boat. This is a big region, so you will need to take an extended charter trip lasting anywhere from 5 to 14 days.

Half a dozen or so boat operators run fishing and adventure trips from Broome or Derby 221km (137 miles) north, or from Darwin. Some incorporate short inland expeditions on foot, or by light aircraft or four-wheel-drive. North Star Charters, below, even travels with its own helicopter for flight-seeing and heli-fishing. Some boats take scuba divers to Rowley Shoals, a marvelous outcrop of coral reef and giant clams 260km (161 miles) west off Broome. Find a vessel that suits you—some offer comfortable private cabins, while others are camp-on-the-beach jobs. Some of the most established are **North Star Cruises** (© **08/9192 1829;** www.northstarcruises.com.au) and **Pearl Sea Coastal Cruises** (© **08/9193 6131;** www.pearlseacruises.com), both operating from Broome, and **Buccaneer Sea Safaris** (© **08/9191 1991;** www.westnet.com.au/buccaneer) operating out of Derby. Contact the Broome Tourist Bureau for an up-to-date list of the boats plying the coast, because some boats come and go from year to year.

The *Coral Princess* makes 10-day Broome-Darwin or reverse voyages April through September. It's a 35m (115-ft.) motorized catamaran carrying no more than 48 passengers in standard and deluxe staterooms or in budget cabins (all with bathrooms en suite). Facilities include a Jacuzzi, sun deck, cocktail bar, and dining room. The voyages depart about 10 times a year and give you the opportunity to go ashore at least once a day to swim (in croc-free pools only), fish, hike in spectacular scenery, croc-spot on river cruises, have a barbecue on an island beach, take optional scenic helicopter flights over the Mitchell Falls, or see Aboriginal art. Fares for 2004 range from A$5,660 to A$6,990 (US$3,679–US$4,544) per person, twin-share. Contact **Coral Princess Cruises,** © **07/4040 9999;** www.coral princesscruises.com; in the U.S., contact S. H. Enterprises, 245-M, Mt. Hermon Rd. #B, Scotts Valley, CA 05066 (© **800/441-6880** or 831/335-4954; Coralpss@ aol.com).

Adelaide & South Australia

by Marc Llewellyn

Adelaide (pop. 1 million) has a major advantage over the other state capitals in that it has Outback, vineyards, wetlands, animal sanctuaries, a major river, and mountain ranges virtually on its doorstep. Meals and lodgings are cheaper in Adelaide than in Sydney or Melbourne. If you plan to travel outside the city, then a trip to one of the wine-growing areas has to be on your itinerary. Of all the wine areas, the **Barossa Valley** ✿ is the most interesting. Centered on Tanunda, the Barossa is known for its German architecture as well as its dozens of pretty hamlets, fine restaurants, and vineyards offering cellar-door tastings.

If you want to see animals instead of, or in addition to, grapes, you're in luck. You're likely to come across the odd kangaroo or wallaby near the main settlements, especially at dusk, or you could visit one of the area's wildlife reserves. Otherwise head out into the Outback or over to **Kangaroo Island,** without a doubt the best place in Australia to see concentrated numbers of native animals in the wild.

Another place well worth visiting is the craggy **Flinders Ranges,** some 460km (285 miles) north of Adelaide. Though the scenery along the way is mostly unattractive grazing properties devoid of trees, the Flinders Ranges offer an incredible landscape of multi-colored rocks, rough-and-ready characters, and even camel treks in the semidesert. On the other side of the mountains, the real Outback starts.

The **South Australian Outback** is serenely beautiful, with giant skies, red earth, little water, and wildflowers after the rains. Out here you'll find bizarre opal-mining towns, such as **Coober Pedy,** where summer temperatures can reach 122°F (50°C) and where most people live underground to escape the heat.

If you prefer your landscape with more moisture, head to the **Coorong,** a water-bird sanctuary rivaled only by Kakadu National Park in the Northern Territory (see chapter 8).

EXPLORING THE STATE

VISITOR INFORMATION The **South Australian Visitor & Travel Centre,** 18 King William St. (© **1300/655 276** in Australia; fax 08/8303 2249; southaustralia.com), is the best place to find information on Adelaide and South Australia. It's open weekdays from 8:30am to 5pm and weekends from 9am to 2pm. Also try www.southaustralia.com.

For general information about South Australia's national parks contact the **Department of Environment and Natural Resources Information Centre,** Australis House, 77 Grenfell St., Adelaide 5000 (© **08/8204 1910**). It's open Monday through Friday from 9am to 5pm.

GETTING AROUND South Australia, at four times the size of the United Kingdom, has a lot of empty space between places of interest. The best way to see it is by car, though a limited rail service connects Adelaide with some areas. The Stuart Highway bisects the state from south to north; it runs from Adelaide through the industrial center of Port Augusta (gateway to the Flinders Ranges), and through Coober Pedy to Alice Springs in the Red Centre. The Eyre Highway travels westward along the coastline and into Western Australia, while the Barrier Highway enters New South Wales just before the mining city of Broken Hill (see chapter 4). The Princes Highway takes you east to Melbourne. You should seek travel advice from the **Royal Automobile Association of South Australia (RAA),** 41 Hindmarsh Square, Adelaide, SA 5000 (© **13 11 11** in South Australia only, or 08/8202 4500; www.raa.net), if you are planning to drive into the Outback regions. The RAA provides route maps and emergency breakdown service.

Both **Greyhound Pioneer** (© **13 20 30** in Australia) and **McCafferty's** (© **13 14 99** in Australia) operate bus service within South Australia. Within the state the largest operator is **Stateliner** (© **08/8415 5555**).

1 Adelaide

Adelaide has a reputation as a quieter place than some of the other state capitals and relishes in the peace of its parklands and surrounding vineyards. In many ways it's something of a throwback to the comfortable lifestyle of 1950s Australia—a lifestyle that the more progressive state capitals have left behind.

Numerous parks and gardens, wide tree-lined streets, the River Torrens running through its center, sidewalk cafes, colonial architecture, and, of course, the churches help make it a pleasant, open city, perfect for strolling or bicycling.

Though the immigrant population has added a cosmopolitan flair to the restaurant scene, Adelaide still has a feeling of old England about it. That's not surprising when you learn that Adelaide was the only capital settled by English free settlers rather than convicts, and that it attracted more after World War II, when Brits flocked here to work in the city's car and appliance factories.

But it was earlier immigrants, from Germany, who gave Adelaide and the surrounding area a romantic twist. Arriving as refugees from their religious-torn country in the 1830s, German immigrants brought with them their winemaking skills and established wineries. Today, more than one-third of all Australian wine—including some of the world's best—comes from areas mostly within an hour's drive from Adelaide. As a result, Adelaidians of all socioeconomic groups are more versed in wine than even the French and regularly compare vintages, wine-growing regions, and winemaking trends.

Any time of the year is a good time to visit Adelaide, though May through August can be chilly and January and February hot.

ESSENTIALS

GETTING THERE   By Plane   Qantas (© **13 13 13** in Australia) flies to Adelaide from the other major state capitals. **Virgin Blue** (© **13 67 89** in Australia) flies direct from Melbourne with connections from other state capitals and some major towns. Check their Internet site for cheap deals. Adelaide International Airport is 5km (3 miles) west of the city center. Major car-rental companies (Avis, Budget, Hertz, and Thrifty) have desks in both the international and domestic terminals.

The **Skylink** (© **08/8332 0528;** www.coachaust.com.au) links the airport with major hotels and the rail and bus stations. On weekdays, buses leave the terminals at 30-minute intervals from 5:30am to 9:30pm, and on weekends and

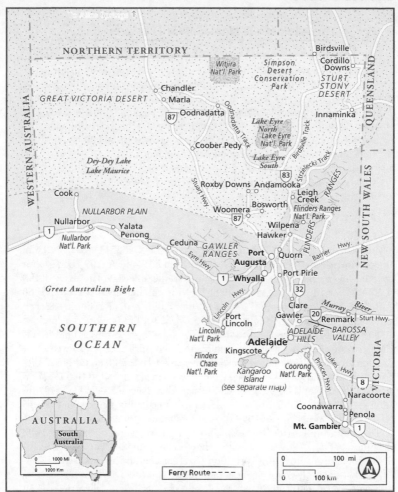

public holidays hourly (on the half-hour). Adult tickets are A$7 (US$4.55) one-way, A$12 (US$7.80) round-trip. Children's tickets cost A$2.50 (US$1.60) each way.

By Taxi　A taxi to the city will cost around A$17 (US$11).

By Train　The **Keswick Interstate Rail Passenger Terminal,** located 2km (1¼ miles) west of the city center, is Adelaide's main railway station. The terminal has a small snack bar and a cafe.

Call **Great Southern Railways** (© **13 21 47** in Australia, or 08/8213 4530) for information and bookings for all trains described below, or check out the timetables and fares on their website (www.gsr.com.au).

One of the great trains of Australia, The *Indian Pacific* transports passengers from Sydney to Adelaide (trip time: 28 hr.) and from Perth to Adelaide (trip time: 36 hr.) twice a week on Monday and Thursday. One-way tickets from Sydney to Adelaide are A$570 (US$370) for adults and A$445 (US$289) for children

The Adelaide & Womadelaide Festivals

Adelaide is home to Australia's largest performing arts festival, the **Adelaide Festival,** which takes place over 3 weeks in March during even-numbered years. The festival includes literary and visual arts as well as dance, opera, classical music, jazz, cabaret, and comedy. The festival encompasses Writers' Week and the **Adelaide Fringe Festival.**

In February and March of odd-numbered years the 3-day **Womadelaide Festival** of world music takes place. Crowds of 60,000 or more turn up to watch Australian and international artists.

For more information on the Adelaide Festival check out the website at www.adelaidefestival.org.au, and for the Adelaide Fringe Festival visit www.adelaidefringe.com.au.

in first class; A$450 (US$292) for adults and A$325 (US$211) for children in an economy sleeper; and A$227 (US$148) for adults and A$109 (US$71) for children in coach. From Perth to Adelaide the one-way fare is A$1,190 (US$773) for adults and A$809 (US$526) for children in first class; A$960 (US$624) for adults and A$576 (US$375) for children in an economy sleeper; and A$309 (US$200) for adults and A$155 (US$100) for children in coach.

The other legendary Australian train is *The Ghan,* which runs from Adelaide and up to Alice Springs weekly November through April and twice a week May through October. Trip time from Alice Springs to Adelaide is 20 hours. From Alice Springs to Adelaide and vice versa, the one-way fare costs A$850 (US$552) for adults and A$578 (US$375) for children in first class; A$680 (US$442) for adults and A$408 (US$265) for children in an economy sleeper; and A$215 (US$140) for adults and A$105 (US$68) for children for an economy seat.

The round-trip fare for the *Indian Pacific* and *Ghan* works out to either twice the one-way fare, or just a few dollars cheaper. Full-time students with a recognized student card from any institution travel for child prices on all trains.

Another train, *Overland,* operates four weekly services: a daylight service from Adelaide to Melbourne and a return overnight service from Melbourne to Adelaide (trip time: 12 hr.). From Melbourne to Adelaide, one-way ticket prices are A$175 (US$114) for adults and A$139 (US$90) for children in first class, and A$59 (US$38) for adults and A$42 (US$27) for children in an economy seat. It's a little cheaper from Adelaide to Melbourne, and there are good discounts for return fares.

By Bus   Intercity coaches terminate at the central bus station, 101 Franklin St. (© **08/8415 5533**), near Morphett Street in the city center.

Adventurous types should consider traveling to Adelaide from Melbourne (or vice versa) on the **Wayward Bus,** operated by the Wayward Bus Touring Company, P.O. Box 7076, Adelaide, SA 5000 (© **1800/882 823** in Australia, or 08/8232 6646; www.waywardbus.com.au). These 21-seat buses make the trip in 3½ days via the Great Ocean Road; the fare is A$310 (US$201) with backpacker's accommodations and around A$440 (US$286) with motel accommodations. You spend around 3 hours a day on the bus, and the driver acts as your guide. A picnic or cafe lunch each day and entry to national parks are included. You can leave the trip and rejoin another later. Reservations are essential. Wayward

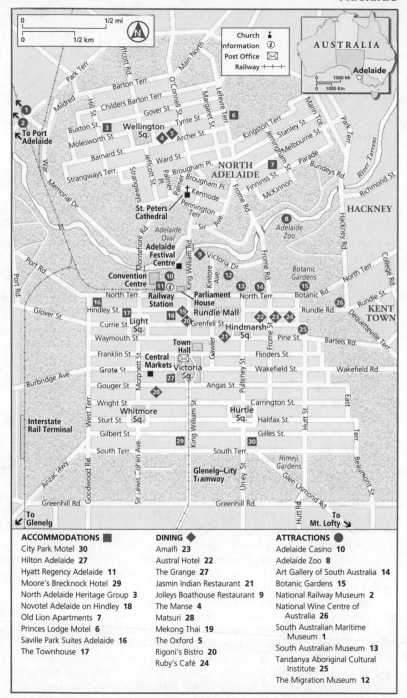

Adelaide

Church ⛪
Information ℹ
Post Office ✉
Railway +++

AUSTRALIA

Adelaide

ACCOMMODATIONS
City Park Motel **30**
Hilton Adelaide **27**
Hyatt Regency Adelaide **11**
Moore's Brecknock Hotel **29**
North Adelaide Heritage Group **3**
Novotel Adelaide on Hindley **18**
Old Lion Apartments **7**
Princes Lodge Motel **6**
Saville Park Suites Adelaide **16**
The Townhouse **17**

DINING
Amalfi **23**
Austral Hotel **22**
The Grange **27**
Jasmin Indian Restaurant **21**
Jolleys Boathouse Restaurant **9**
The Manse **4**
Matsuri **28**
Mekong Thai **19**
The Oxford **5**
Rigoni's Bistro **20**
Ruby's Café **24**

ATTRACTIONS
Adelaide Casino **10**
Adelaide Zoo **8**
Art Gallery of South Australia **14**
Botanic Gardens **15**
National Railway Museum **2**
National Wine Centre of Australia **26**
South Australian Maritime Museum **1**
South Australian Museum **13**
Tandanya Aboriginal Cultural Institute **25**
The Migration Museum **12**

487

Bus also runs a 4-day trip from Alice Springs to Adelaide, via Coober Pedy and the Flinders National Park (and vice versa) leaving twice weekly. This includes 2 nights camping and 2 nights in a bunkhouse. The trip costs A$395 (US$257) from Adelaide to Coober Pedy, and A$770 (US$500) from Adelaide to Alice Springs.

Another bus company the **Nullabor Traveller** (P.O. Box 72, Glensside, SA 5065; © **08/8364 0407;** www.the-traveller.com.au) takes adventurous travelers from Adelaide to Perth in 9 days across the Nullabor Plain. The tour includes a mixture of camping and pub accommodations and most meals. It costs A$945 (US$614) in summer, and A$72 (US$47) more in winter (with more accommodations instead of camping). The company offers a range of other tours, including a 6-day trip to Coober Pedy, Lake Eyre, and the Flinders Ranges for A$550 (US$357); a 2-day tour to Kangaroo Island for A$310 (US$201) in dorm rooms and A$365 (US$237) in a double; a full-day tour of the Barossa Valley for A$49 (US$32); and a 3½-day trip along the Great Ocean Road for A$310 (US$201) in a dorm and A$440 (US$286) in a double.

By Car   To drive from Sydney to Adelaide takes roughly 20 hours via the Hume and Sturt highways; from Melbourne it takes around 10 hours via the Great Ocean Road and Princess Highway; from Perth it takes 32 hours via the Great Eastern and Princess highways; and from Alice Springs it takes 15 hours of remote driving on the Stuart Highway. For more information on driving distances consult www.auinfo.com/distancecalc_process.asp.

VISITOR INFORMATION   Go to the **South Australia Visitor & Travel Centre,** 18 King William St. (© **1300/655 276** in Australia, or 08/8303 2033; fax 08/8303 2249), for maps, travel advice, and hotel and tour bookings. It's open weekdays from 8:30am to 5pm, weekends from 9am to 2pm. There's an info booth on Rundle Mall (© **08/8203 7611**), open daily from 10am to 5pm.

CITY LAYOUT   Adelaide is easy to navigate because of its gridlike pattern, planned down to each wide street and airy square by Colonel William Light in 1836. The city's official center is **Victoria Square,** where you'll find the Town Hall. Bisecting the city from south to north is the city's main thoroughfare, **King William Street.** Streets running perpendicular to King William Street change their names on either side, so that Franklin Street, for example, changes into Flinders Street. Of these cross streets, the most interesting are the restaurant strips of **Gouger Street** and **Rundle Street,** the latter running into the pedestrian-only shopping precinct of Rundle Mall. Another is **Hindley Street,** with its inexpensive restaurants and nightlife. On the banks of the River Torrens just north of the city center, you'll find the Riverbank Precinct, the home of the Festival Centre, the Convention Centre, and the Skycity Adelaide Casino. Bordering the city center on the north and south are **North Terrace,** which is lined with galleries and museums and leads to the Botanic Gardens, and **South Terrace.**

Follow King William Street south and you'll be chasing the tram to the beachside suburb of **Glenelg;** follow it north, and it crosses the River Torrens and flows into sophisticated **North Adelaide,** an area crammed with Victorian and Edwardian architecture. The main avenues in North Adelaide, **O'Connell and Melbourne streets,** are lined with restaurants, cafes, and bistros that offer the tastes of a multicultural city.

To the northwest of the city center is **Port Adelaide,** a seaport and the historic maritime heart of South Australia—home to some of the finest colonial buildings in the state, as well as good pubs and restaurants.

GETTING AROUND   By Bus   Adelaide's public bus network is divided into three zones, and fares are calculated according to the number of zones traveled. The city center is classed as Zone 1. The fare in Zone 1 is A$1.80 (US$1.20) from 9am to 3pm on weekdays and A$3 (US$1.95) most other times. You can buy tickets on board or at kiosks around the city. You can pick up free metro information and get timetable and destination information over the phone, or at the **Passenger Transport Board Information Centre** (© 08/ 8210 1000), on the corner of Currie and King William streets. It's open Monday through Saturday from 8am to 6pm and Sunday from 10:30am to 5.30pm.

The **CityLoop bus** (no. 99C) operates free bus service every 15 minutes (Mon–Thurs 8:30am–6pm; Fri to 9pm and Sat to 5pm) around the city center, along North Terrace, East Terrace, Grenfell Street, Pulteney Street, Wakefield Street, Grote Street, Morphett Street, Light Square, Hindley Street, and West Terrace. Another free bus, **the Bee Line** (no. 99B), runs along North Terrace, down King William Street to Victoria Street. Routes are well signposted. All city free buses are wheelchair-accessible.

Bus nos. 181 and 182 run from the city to North Adelaide.

The **Adelaide Explorer bus** (© 08/8231 7172; www.adelaideexplorer.com. au) stops at 26 sights around town, including Glenelg, and costs A$30 (US$20) for adults, A$19 (US$12) for children, and A$70 (US$46) for families of four. The loop takes a leisurely 3 hours, with commentary, and you can get on and off when you want. The first bus departs from 38 King William St., on the corner of Rundle Mall (next to Haigh's Chocolates) at 9am. The company will pick you up from your hotel between 8 and 8:30am if you call ahead, and will drop you off at the airport (with your luggage) as part of the fare. Call or e-mail ahead. Buy tickets on the bus.

By Tram   The **Glenelg Tram** runs between Victoria Square and the beachside suburb of Glenelg. Tickets are valid for 2 hours and cost A$1.80 (US$1.15) for adults and A90¢ (US60¢) for children 5 to 14 from 9am to 3pm, and A$3 (US$1.95) for adults and A$1.30 (US85¢) for children at other times. The journey takes 29 minutes.

By Taxi & Car   The major cab companies are **Yellow Cabs** (© 13 22 27 in South Australia only), **Suburban** (© 08/8211 8888), and **Amalgamated** (© 08/ 8223 3333). **Access Cabs** (© 1300/360 940 in South Australia only) offers wheelchair taxis.

Major car-rental companies are **Avis**, 136 North Terrace (© 08/8410 5727); **Budget**, 274 North Terrace (© 08/8223 1400); **Hertz**, 233 Morphett St. (© 08/ 8231 2856); and **Thrifty**, 296 Hindley St. (© 08/8211 8788).

Value **A Money-Saving Transit Pass**

If you plan to get around the city via public transportation, it's a good idea to purchase a **Daytrip ticket**, which covers unlimited travel on buses, trams, and city trains within the metropolitan area for 1 day. The pass costs A$5.70 (US$3.65) for adults and A$2.90 (US$1.90) for children 5 to 15 and is available at most train stations, newsstands, and the **Passenger Transport Board Information Centre** (© 08/8210 1000).

The **Royal Automobile Association of South Australia (RAA),** 41 Hindmarsh Sq. (© **13 11 11** in South Australia, or 08/8202 4500; www.raa.net), has route maps and provides emergency breakdown services.

 FAST FACTS: **Adelaide**

American Express The Amex office, at 13 Grenfell St. (© **08/8202 1400**), is open during normal business hours.

Business Hours Generally, banks are open Monday through Thursday from 9:30am to 4pm and Friday from 9:30am to 5pm. Stores are generally open Monday through Thursday from 9am to 5:30pm, Friday from 9am to 9pm, Saturday from 9am to 5pm, and Sunday from 11am to 5pm.

Currency Exchange Banks and hotels, the casino, and the Myer department store in Rundle Mall all cash traveler's checks. The **Thomas Cook** office is at 45 Grenfell St. (© **08/8212 3354**).

Dentist Contact the **Australian Dental Association Emergency Information Service** (© **08/8272 8111**), open weeknights from 5 to 9pm, and Saturday and Sunday from 9am to 9pm. It will put you in touch with a dentist. You can also contact the office of **Dr. Brook,** 231 North Terrace (© **08/8223 6988**), available during normal business hours.

Doctor Contact the **Royal Adelaide Hospital,** on North Terrace (© **08/8222 4000**). **The Travellers' Medical & Vaccination Centre,** 29 Gilbert Place (© **08/8212 7522**), offers vaccinations and travel-related medicines.

Emergencies Dial © **000** to call an ambulance, the fire department, or the police in a emergency.

Hospitals The **Royal Adelaide Hospital,** North Terrace (© **08/8222 4000**), is located in the city center.

Hot Lines Call the **Crisis Care Centre** at © **13 16 11** (in Australia), the **Royal Automobile Association of South Australia (RAA)** at © **08/8202 4500,** and the **Disability Information and Resource Centre** at © **08/8223 7522.**

Internet Access The **Ngapartji Multimedia Centre,** 211 Rundle St. (© **08/8232 0839**), offers e-mail and Internet access Monday through Thursday from 8:30am to 9pm, Friday and Saturday from 9am to 10pm, and Sunday from noon to 7pm. Other access points are on Hindley Street: **Talking Cents,** 53 Hindley St., (© **08/8212 1266**), and **Café Boulevard,** 13 Hindley St. (© **08/8231 5734**).

Lost Property If you've lost something on the street, contact the nearest police station. For items left on public transport contact the **Lost Property Office,** on the main concourse of the Adelaide Railway Station on North Terrace (© **08/8218 2552**); it's open Monday through Friday from 9am to 5pm.

Luggage Storage/Lockers There are luggage lockers at Adelaide Airport in the domestic terminal. At the **Central Bus Station** on Franklin Street (© **08/8415 5533**), luggage lockers cost A$2 (US$1.30) for 24 hours.

Pharmacies Called "chemist shops" in Australia. **Burden Chemists,** Shop 11, Southern Cross Arcade, King William St. (© **08/8231 4701**), is open Monday through Thursday from 8am to 6pm, Friday from 8am to 8pm, and Saturday from 9am to 1pm.

Post Office The **General Post Office (GPO)**, 141 King William St., Adelaide, SA 5000 (℡ **08/8216 2222**), is open Monday through Friday from 8am to 6pm and Saturday from 8:30am to noon. General delivery mail (poste restante) can be collected Monday through Friday from 8am to 5pm and Saturday 8:30 to noon.

Restrooms Public restrooms can be found at the Central Market Arcade, between Grote and Gouger streets, in both Hindmarsh and Victoria squares, and at James Place (off Rundle Mall).

Safety Adelaide is a safe city, though it's wise to avoid walking along the River Torrens and through side streets near Hindley Street after dark.

WHERE TO STAY

The **South Australia Visitor & Travel Centre** (see "Visitor Information," above) can supply information on B&Bs and homestays around the state. Satellite or cable TV is rare in South Australian hotels, though some provide pay-per-view movies.

IN THE CITY CENTER
Very Expensive

Hilton Adelaide ⭐⭐ The Hilton is a luxurious establishment on Victoria Square just around the corner from a host of restaurants on Gouger Street. The lobby is polished marble with a cascading fountain and piano music tinkling throughout. Guest rooms are pleasant with all you might expect from a classy establishment. There are 11 rooms equipped for travelers with disabilities. The Hilton has fabulous deals—A$210 (US$137) for standard and $235 (US$143) for executive rooms—"subject to availability" (which means when it's not full). Five floors of mostly executive rooms were refurbished in early 2001. I was surprised to find **Charlie's Bar**—full of photos of famous Charlies—virtually empty even on a Saturday night. In a pinch I'd probably choose the Hyatt (see below) for the extensive views, but there's not much difference between them.

233 Victoria Sq., Adelaide, SA 5000. (℡ **1800/222 255** in Australia, or 08/8217 2000. Fax 08/8217 2001. www.hilton.com. 380 units. A$325–A$335 (US$211–US$218) double; A$440 (US$286) executive floor; A$650 (US$423) suite. Extra person A$45 (US$29). Children under 12 stay free In parent's room. AE, DC, MC, V. Parking A$16 (US$10). The tram stops in front of the hotel; a bus stop is adjacent. **Amenities:** 2 restaurants; bar; heated outdoor pool; tennis court; health club; Jacuzzi; sauna; concierge; salon; 24-hr. room service; massage; babysitting; laundry service; dry cleaning; nonsmoking rooms. *In room:* A/C, TV w/pay movies, modem port and fax (in business rooms), dataport, minibar, coffeemaker, hair dryer, iron, safe.

Hyatt Regency Adelaide ⭐⭐ The 20-story Hyatt Regency is in the heart of the city and part of the complex that includes the Adelaide Festival Centre, the Casino, the Exhibition Hall, and the Convention Centre. The property overlooks the River Torrens and nearby parklands, and there are some wonderful views from the higher floors. The Hyatt doesn't scrimp, which shows in the attention to detail in the rooms. Guests staying in the club-level Regency rooms get a good complimentary breakfast and free evening drinks and canapés. **Waves**, a cabaret/nightclub, offers a lively combination of video, disco, and live music; it's free for guests, though it can be dull and the drinks are expensive. Afternoon tea is served in the Atrium Lounge, which gets surprisingly full as the night wears on.

North Terrace, Adelaide, SA 5000. (℡ **13 12 34** in Australia, 800/233-1234 in the U.S. and Canada, or 08/8231 1234. Fax 08/8231 1120. www.hyatt.com. 367 units. A$250–A$300 (US$162–US$195) double (depending on

---

> ### ⌒Tips Plan Ahead
>
> If you plan to be in town during the Adelaide Festival, make sure you book accommodations well in advance. The town can be packed during Christmas and New Year's, so it's wise to book well in advance then, too.

---

season, availability); A$300–A$340 (US$195–US$221) Regency Club City View (including breakfast); A$320–A$360 (US$221–US$234) Club River Park View (including breakfast); A$390 (US$254) executive suite; A$840 (US$546) deluxe suite. Extra person A$50 (US$33). Children under 13 stay free in parent's room. Ask about packages and lower weekend rates. AE, DC, MC, V. Parking A$18 (US$12). **Amenities:** 3 restaurants; lounge; bar; nightclub; heated outdoor swimming pool; health club and Jacuzzi; concierge; business center; 24-hr. room service; massage; babysitting; laundry service; dry cleaning. *In room:* A/C, TV w/pay movies, high-speed Internet access, minibar, hair dryer, iron.

Expensive

Novotel Adelaide on Hindley   Only a short stroll from the center of town, the Novotel is a good value, especially if you happen to be staying on the weekend when the rates go down. Otherwise, it's not as classy as either the Hyatt or the Hilton. What you get for your money is a good, recently renovated, bright room. Ask at the reception desk for a robe, as they aren't included in the standard rooms.

65 Hindley St., Adelaide, SA 5000. ℂ **08/8231 5552.** Fax 08/8237 3800. www.accorhotel.com. 217 units. Midweek A$202 (US$131) double; A$245 (US$156) suite. Weekend A$150 (US$98) double; A$193 (US$125) suite. Children under 15 stay free in parent's room. Ask about package deals. AE, DC, MC, V. Parking A$17 (US$11). **Amenities:** Brasserie; bar; heated outdoor pool; health club; concierge; business center; 24-hr. room service. *In room:* A/C, TV w/pay movies, modem and fax, minibar, hair dryer, iron.

Moderate

The Townhouse *(Value*   Totally refurbished in 2001, The Townhouse is Adelaide's newest boutique hotel. It's a 10- to 15-minute walk from the center of town, 5 minutes from the casino, and near the nightclub and red-light district. Rooms are spacious, comfortable, modern, and clean. The major refurbishment did not result in a massive hike in prices, which leaves this place a good value option.

164 Hindley St., Adelaide, SA 5000. ℂ **1800/888 241** in Australia, 800/624-3524 in the U.S. and Canada, 0800/892 407 in the U.K., 0800/803 524 in New Zealand, or 08/8211 8255. Fax 08/8231 1179. www.barron townhouse.com.au. 68 units. A$135 (US$88) single or twin share; A$172 (US$112) business double; and A$182 (US$118) executive double. Children under 12 stay free in parent's room. Lower rates in off-season and weekends. Check for Internet specials. Ask about package deals. AE, DC, MC, V. Free parking. **Amenities:** Restaurant; bar; heated outdoor pool; golf course nearby; access to nearby health club; sauna; concierge; limited room service; laundry service; dry cleaning; nonsmoking rooms. *In room:* A/C, TV, DVD w/free movies, dataport, minibar, hair dryer, iron.

Inexpensive

City Park Motel   The rooms in this motel just outside the city center have modern furnishings and nice bathrooms with showers. Some rooms have private balconies. Also on the premises is a separate bathroom with a tub. The best room is no. 45. Downstairs there's a cocktail bar, nightclub, and bistro.

471 Pulteney St., Adelaide, SA 5000. ℂ **08/8223 1444.** Fax 08/8223 1133. 18 units, 14 with bathroom (shower only). A$55 (US$36) double without bathroom; A$75 (US$49) double with bathroom; A$110 (US$72) deluxe double with balcony. Extra person A$10 (US$6.50). AE, DC, MC, V. Limited parking by arrangement. The tram to Glenelg stops around the corner; 3 streets up is a bus stop for the free City Loop bus. **Amenities:** Restaurant; bar; nightclub; tour desk; car-rental desk; limited room service; dry cleaning service; nonsmoking rooms. *In room:* A/C, TV, fridge, coffeemaker, iron.

Moore's Brecknock Hotel   Adelaide's original Irish pub, built in 1851, still attracts a lot of Irish who come here for the great selection of beer and reasonably priced home-style cooking—it reputedly serves Adelaide's best hamburgers. It's also very popular with American guests who use the hotel accommodations upstairs as a base from which to discover Kangaroo Island and other parts of the state. The Brecknock is about 4 blocks from Victoria Square and is run by Kerry Moore and his Canadian wife Tricia. There are live bands downstairs on Friday, Saturday, and Sunday evenings, but the music finishes at 1am on Friday and Saturday, and 10pm on Sunday, so you shouldn't have too much trouble sleeping. Rooms are large and pleasantly done out in old-world style. Each has a double and a single bed, and a sink, with the bathrooms down the hall.

Next door to Moore's is **Nomads Backpackers** (© **08/8211 8985;** www. nomads-backpackers.com), which is associated with the hotel.

401 King William St., Adelaide, SA 5000. © **08/8231 5467.** Fax 08/8410 1968. www.breconinn.com.au. 10 units, none with bathroom. A$65 (US$42) double; A$85 (US$55) triple. Rates include continental breakfast. AE, DC, MC, V. Free parking. The Glenelg tram stops in front of the hotel. **Amenities:** Restaurant; 3 bars; bike rental; tour desk; car-rental desk; coin-op laundry; dry cleaning; nonsmoking rooms. *In room:* A/C, fax, fridge, coffeemaker, iron, safe.

Saville Park Suites Adelaide ℛ   You can't miss this conglomerate of russet-red bricks just on the outskirts of the city center (about a 10-min. walk). Rooms are nice and spacious, if a bit formal, which is not surprising because the place is popular with business travelers. On the premises is the **Zipp Restaurant and Wine Bar,** where Tommy Chang serves up an innovative menu.

255 Hindley St., Adelaide, SA 5000. © **1800/882 601** in Australia, or 08/8217 2500. Fax 08/8217 2519. www.savillesuites.com. 142 units. A$146 (US$95) studio; A$167 (US$109) 2-bedroom suite. Up to 2 people in studio and 4 in other units. Facilities for travelers with disabilities in some rooms. AE, DC, MC, V. Parking A$5 (US$3.25) per day. **Amenities:** Restaurant; free access to nearby City Gym; outdoor Jacuzzi; concierge; tour desk; car-rental desk; limited room service; babysitting; coin-op laundry; dry cleaning; nonsmoking rooms; safe. *In room:* A/C, TV w/pay movies, VCR (on request), dataport, kitchen, minibar, fridge, tea/coffeemaker, hair dryer, iron.

IN NORTH ADELAIDE

This suburb across the river is an interesting place with nice architecture and good restaurants. It's about a 10-minute bus ride from the city center.

Expensive

North Adelaide Heritage Group ℛℛℛ *(Finds* It's worth coming all the way to Adelaide just for the experience of staying in one of these out-of-this-world apartments, cottages, or suites. Each of the 21 properties in North Adelaide and Eastwood are fabulous. I recommend particularly the former Friendly Meeting Chapel Hall, which was once the headquarters of the mouthwatering "Albert Lodge No. 6 of the Independent Order of Oddfellows, Manchester Unity Friendly Society, and the Court Huntsman's Pride No. 2478 of the Ancient Order of Foresters Friendly Society." The structure is a small, simple gabled hall of bluestone rubble trimmed with brick and resembles a small church. Built in 1878, it's stocked with period pieces and antiques and rounded off with a modern, fully stocked kitchen; a huge Jacuzzi; a queen-size bed; and a CD player and TV.

Another standout place is the George Lowe Esquire unit. This huge 19th-century apartment is also stocked with antiques, has a huge four-poster bed, a separate bathroom, a lounge, and a full kitchen. Guests also have use of nice gardens. Owners Rodney and Regina Twiss have added all those little touches that make you feel like home, from magazines liberally piled up everywhere to bacon and eggs in the fridge. The company also offers three apartments in the old North Adelaide Fire Station, where the ground-floor apartment even comes with a full-size, bright red, and very old, fire engine. All properties are within easy walking distance of the main attractions in the area, as well as tennis courts (around A$20/US$13 an hour) and Adelaide Golf Links (© **08/8267 2171;** A$18/US$12 weekdays, A$21/US$14 weekends).

Office: 109 Glen Osmond Rd., Eastwood, SA 5063. © **08/8272 1355,** or 0418/289 494 (mobile phone). Fax 08/8272 1355. www.adelaideheritage.com. 21 units. A$145–A$330 (US$94–US$215) double, depending on accommodations. Extra person A$60–A$85 (US$39–US$55). Children under 12 A$30 (US$20). AE, DC, MC, V. Free parking. **Amenities:** Golf/tennis courts nearby; Jacuzzi; concierge; car-rental desk; free bus to city center; limited room service; massage; dry cleaning service. *In room:* A/C, TV, kitchenette, fridge, coffeemaker, hair dryer, iron.

Old Lion Apartments ⚸

These pleasant apartments are located inside a renovated brewery. The complex is about a 15-minute walk from the city center and is on a direct bus route. Rooms are spacious, with high ceilings, and come with a kitchenette, a living room, French doors separating bedrooms from living quarters, a shower and bathtub, and a good-size balcony. All apartments also have use of a washing machine and dryer. VCRs and videos are available for rent at the front desk. Continental breakfast costs A$8.50 (US$5.50) extra.

9 Jerningham St., North Adelaide, SA 5006. © **08/8223 0500.** Fax 08/8223 0588. www.majapts.com.au. 57 units. A$182 (US$118) studio apt; A$193 (US$125) 1-bedroom apt; A$221 (US$144) 2-bedroom apt; A$262 (US$170) 3-bedroom apt. Extra adult A$17 (US$11), extra child 3–12 A$5.50 (US$3.60). AE, DC, MC, V. Free parking. Bus: 184, 224, 226, 228, or 229. **Amenities:** Concierge; tour desk; car-rental desk; limited room service; dry cleaning. *In room:* A/C, TV (VCRs and videos by request), kitchenette, fridge, coffeemaker, hair dryer, iron.

Princes Lodge Motel

One of the best motels in Adelaide, the Princes Lodge looks more like a large private home than your simple brick roadside structure. Rooms are nicely decorated and generally come with a double and a single bed. There are three family rooms available, one of which has a double and three singles, while another has six beds in one room. The motel is within walking distance of the restaurant strip on O'Connell Street, and a A$6 (US$3.90) taxi ride from the city center.

73 Lefevre Terrace, North Adelaide, 5006. © **08/8267 5566.** Fax 08/8239 0787. princeslodge@senet. com.au. 21 units. A$60 (US$39) double with separate private bathroom; A$70 (US$46) double with attached bathroom. Rates include continental breakfast. AE, DC, MC, V. Bus: 222 from Victoria Sq. (with pickups along King William St.). **Amenities:** Golf course nearby; tour desk; car-rental desk; coin-op laundry. *In room:* A/C, TV, dataport, fridge, coffeemaker, hair dryer, iron.

IN GLENELG

I'd recommend anyone, without hesitation, to stay in Glenelg rather than in the city center. The journey to the city center by car or tram takes less than 30 minutes, and the airport is less than 10 minutes away. Add to this the sea, the lovely beach, the fun fair, the great shops, the good pub, and the nice accommodations, and you have a perfect place to relax on your holiday.

Atlantic Tower Motor Inn

If you're looking for relatively inexpensive accommodations near the beach, this is your place. You can't miss this tubular building not far from the sea, with its slowly revolving restaurant on the 12th floor. Rooms are simple, but bright, and have nice park views through large windows. Each room has a double and a single bed. The Deluxe rooms are a bit nicer and come with bathrooms rather than just showers. Suites have two rooms and excellent views; the most expensive have Jacuzzis. The gently turning **Rock Lobster Cafe** upstairs is open for lunch on Thursday, Friday, and Sunday (no lunch on Sat) and dinner every evening.

760 Anzac Hwy., Glenelg, SA 5045. © **08/8294 1011.** Fax 08/8376 0964. www.atlantictower.citysearch. com.au. 27 units (20 with shower only). A$90 (US$59) double; A$110 (US$72) deluxe double; A$155

(US$101) suite. Extra person A$12 (US$7.80). Children under 15 stay free in parent's room. AE, DC, MC, V. Free parking. Hotel is 1 block from tram stop 20. **Amenities:** Restaurant; tour desk; car-rental desk; room service; laundry service; same-day dry cleaning; nonsmoking rooms. *In room:* A/C, TV, fax, minibar, hair dryer, iron.

Stamford Grand Adelaide 🎔🎔 A classic Adelaide photo is of the trams awaiting passengers in front of the facade of the Stamford Grand. Located right on the beach, this classy hotel offers nice rooms with modern furnishings; many overlook the beach, the ocean, and the pier. **The Pier and Pines** is a popular bar bursting with youngish crowds most nights; for a mellower scene, there's **Horizons** piano bar, which offers quality live music particularly on weekends.

Moseley Sq. (P.O. Box 600), Glenelg, SA 5045. ✆ **1800/882 777** in Australia, or 08/8376 1222. Fax 08/8376 1111. 240 units. A$322 (US$209) double; A$349–A$546 (US$227–US$355) suite. Children under 12 stay free in parent's room. AE, DC, MC, V. Parking A$10 (US$6.50). The tram from Adelaide stops in front of the hotel. **Amenities:** 2 restaurants; 2 bars; indoor pool; health club and Jacuzzi; concierge; business center; 24-hr. room service. *In room:* A/C, TV w/pay movies, minibar, hair dryer, iron.

WHERE TO DINE

With more than 600 restaurants, pubs, and cafes, Adelaide boasts more dining spots per capita than anywhere else in Australia. Many are clustered in areas such as Rundle Street in the city and Gouger Street and North Adelaide—where you'll find almost every style of cuisine you can imagine. For cheap noodles, laksas, sushi, and cakes head to Adelaide's popular Central Markets (✆ **08/8203 7494**), behind the Adelaide Hilton Hotel between Gouger and Grote streets.

Because of South Australia's healthy wine industry, you'll find that many of the more expensive restaurants have extensive wine lists—though with spicier foods, it's probably wiser to stick with beer or a fruity white in a pinch. Many Adelaide restaurants allow diners to bring their own wine (BYO), but most charge a steep corkage fee to open your bottle—A$6 (US$3.90) or so is not uncommon.

IN THE CITY CENTRE
Very Expensive

The Grange 🎔🎔 MODERN AUSTRALIAN The Grange is an open-plan restaurant specializing in contemporary food by Adelaide's most influential chef, Cheong Liew. Liew offers an innovative fusion of Western and Asian ingredients, rounded off with an extensive wine list. The menu begins with a choice of two starters, among them Liew's signature dish "The four dances of the sea" —an antipasto of fish, octopus in a garlic sauce, prawn sushi, raw cuttlefish, and black noodles. For the next course you could choose baby abalone, or lobster baked with bourbon and lime, or Japanese quail with chestnuts and Chinese mushrooms.

In the Hilton Adelaide, 233 Victoria Sq. ✆ **08/8217 2000.** Reservations required. 3-course dinner A$81 (US$53); 4 courses A$97 (US$63). AE, DC, MC, V. Tues–Sat 7–10:30pm.

Finds **Something Different—Dining Tours**

If you like good food and wine, but can't decide on just one restaurant, try one of **Graeme Andrews' tours** (✆ **08/8336 8333**, or 0412/842 242 mobile; fax/message 08/8336 4075; www.food-fun-wine.com.au). He offers eight food and food-and-wine tours showcasing the Central Market, Chinatown, and Gouger Street restaurant precincts. Prices start from A$28 (US$18). Private tours are also available on request.

Moderate

Amalfi ITALIAN   Come here for good Italian cooking at reasonable prices in a lively atmosphere. The pizzas are the best in Adelaide—though a little expensive—and good veal and pasta dishes are always on the menu. Be sure to check out the daily specials, where you can pick out a very good fish dish or two.

29 Frome St. (just of Rundle St.). © 08/8223 1948. Reservations recommended. Main courses A$14–A$17 (US$8.80–US$11). AE, DC, MC, V. Mon–Thurs 11:30am–3pm and 5:30–11pm (until midnight Fri); Sat 5:30pm–midnight.

Austral Hotel *Value* MODERN AUSTRALIAN   This large pub, with its dark timber and forest-colored wallpaper, is a pleasant place for a good-value pub meal. You can either eat at the bar, outside on the street, or in the dining room. The bistro serves burgers, fish and chips, pastas, laksas, and Thai curries. The restaurant is a bit more upscale and offers risotto, handmade crab ravioli, beef filets, chicken dishes, venison, paella, and baby octopus.

205 Rundle St. © 08/8223 4660. www.theaustral.com. Reservations recommended. Main courses A$6.50–A$14 (US$4.20–US$8.80) in bistro and A$15–A$22 (US$9.70–US$14) in restaurant. AE, MC, V. Mon–Sun 11pm–late. Metro station nearby.

Jasmin Indian Restaurant NORTH INDIAN   Prices have crept up as this place has gotten more popular, but this family-run Adelaide institution a block south of Rundle Mall is still a good value—and it won the Restaurant Association's award for best Indian restaurant in 2000. Indian artifacts and signed cricket bats from visiting Indian teams decorate the walls. The atmosphere is comfortable yet busy, and the service is professional. The house special is the very hot beef vindaloo, but all the old favorites, such as tandoori chicken, butter chicken (a big seller here), lamb korma, and malabari beef with coconut cream, ginger and garlic, are here, too. Mop it all up with naan bread, and cool your palate with a side dish of raita. The *suji halwa* (a semolina pudding with nuts) is the best I've tasted. Smoking is not permitted.

31 Hindmarsh Sq. © 08/8223 7837. Reservations recommended. Main courses A$19–A$20 (US$12–US$13). Lunch banquet A$27 (US$18); dinner banquet A$35 (US$23). AE, DC, MC, V. Tues–Fri noon–2.30pm; Tues–Sat 5:30–10.30pm.

Jolleys Boathouse Restaurant *Ʀ* MODERN AUSTRALIAN   Jolleys is on the banks of the River Torrens, with views of boats, ducks, and black swans. Business people and ladies-who-lunch rush for the three outside tables, but if you miss out, the bright and airy interior, with its cream-colored tablecloths and directors' chairs, isn't too much of a letdown. You might start with the goat's curd ravioli with red pesto and chives. Moving on, you could tuck into the roasted duck with hazelnut risotto. (Close your eyes to the peaceful quacking out on the river if you can.) The banana and cardamom soufflé for dessert is wicked.

Jolleys Lane. © 08/8223 2891. Reservations recommended. Main courses A$21–A$27 (US$14–US$18). AE, DC, MC, V. Daily noon–2:30pm; Mon–Sat 6:30–9.30pm.

Matsuri *Ʀ* JAPANESE   I like the atmosphere in this very good Japanese restaurant on the popular Gouger Street restaurant strip. Takaomi Kitamura, world-famous ice sculptor and sushi master, prepares the sushi and sashimi dishes, some of the best in Australia. Monday night is "sushi festival night," when sushi is half price. During happy hour Wednesday through Sunday, sushi is 30% off if you place your order before 7pm. (You can preorder over the phone and eat later.) Promised too is a 10% discount if you show this Frommer's guide. Other popular dishes include vegetarian and seafood tempura, *yose nobe* (a hot pot of vegetables, seafood, and chicken), and *chawan mushi* (a steamed custard dish). The service is friendly and considerate. Corkage fee is a steep A$4.50 (US$2.90) a bottle.

167 Gouger St. © **08/8231 3494**. Reservations recommended. Main courses A$8.60–A$28 (US$5.60–US$18). AE, DC, MC, V. Lunch Fri noon–2pm; dinner Wed–Mon 5:30–10pm.

Mekong Thai THAI/MALAYSIAN/HALAL *Value*   Though this place is not much to look at—with simple tables and chairs, some outside in a portico—it has a fiery reputation for good food among in-the-know locals. The food is spicy and authentic, and the portions are filling. It's also a vegetarian's paradise, with at least 16 meat-free mains on the ethnically varied menu. It's Adelaide's only fully halal (suitable for Muslims) restaurant.

68 Hindley St. © **08/8231 2914**. Main courses A$11–A$13 (US$7–US$8.40). AE, DC, MC, V. Daily 5:15pm–late.

Rigoni's Bistro ITALIAN   Located on a narrow lane west of King William Street, this traditional Italian trattoria is often packed at lunch, though less frantic in the evening. It's big and bright with high ceilings and russet quarry tiles. A long bar runs through the middle of the dining room; brass plates mark the stools of regular diners. The food is very traditional and quite good. The chalkboard menu often changes, but you are quite likely to find lasagna, veal in white wine, marinated fish, and various pasta dishes. There's also an extensive salad bar with a variety of antipasto and an outside dining area.

27 Leigh St. © **08/8231 5160**. Reservations recommended. Main courses A$15–A$22 (US$9.50–US$14); antipasto bar (lunch only) A$12–A$14 (US$7.50–US$8.90). AE, DC, MC, V. Mon–Fri noon–2:30pm and 6:30–10pm; Sat 6.30–10pm.

Ruby's Café *&* MODERN AUSTRALIAN   Situated in suitably unpretentious surroundings for a former market cafe catering to the local workers, Ruby's is an Adelaide institution. It still has its laminated tables and the "no spitting, no coarse language" sign behind the bar, despite being far more upmarket than that. Basically, you get a very good restaurant meal in an old-cafe atmosphere at very good prices. Served up are filling curries and pasta dishes, hearty meals such as lamb shanks, and quite a few vegetarian options. For dessert I recommend the toffee pudding with toffee sauce. The menu changes every 6 weeks.

255b Rundle St. © **08/8224 0365**. Main courses A$11–A$20 (US$7.15–US$13). AE, MC, V. Sun 9am–5pm and 6:30–11.30pm; daily 6:30–11.30pm.

IN NORTH ADELAIDE

The Manse *&&* SEAFOOD   Swiss chef Bernhard Oehrli has a fine touch when it comes to seafood, and I recommend this place wholeheartedly. This cozy restaurant spreads out into several rooms, with log fires to keep you warm in winter and room to dine outside on sunnier days. As for the food, the scallops are almost fresh enough to waddle off the warmed cucumber base and head for sea, while the rare tuna in Japanese-style tempura is so delicate it literally melts in your mouth. If you want something other than seafood, then you can't go wrong with a signature dish of venison with black pepper and a spiced beet glaze. For dessert try the warm chocolate gâteau or the rhubarb gratin with ice cream.

142 Tynte St., North Adelaide. © **08/8267 4636**. Reservations recommended. A$30 (US$20) for 2 courses. AE, DC, MC, V. Fri noon–3pm (set menu); Mon–Sat 6:30–10pm. Bus: 182, 224, 226, 228, or 229.

The Oxford *&* MODERN AUSTRALIAN   This restaurant has won nearly twice as many gold medals for cooking as Mark Spitz won for swimming (seven golds in 1972 Olympic Games, by the way). The Oxford is praised for its creative, contemporary food in a range of mixed-up styles—sometimes too mixed in my opinion. It's big and busy and housed in a character-filled 1870s building. Inside you'll find crisp white tablecloths, a single-page menu, and a stainless steel kitchen whipping up steam. The signature dishes are the red-roasted spatchcock (a small chicken) with water chestnut, chicken-and-cashew spring roll, black-bean mayonnaise, and coconut broth; and the wonderful Caesar salad. Other favorites include jellyfish with Moroccan-spiced salsa; and poached prawns with natural oysters, served with wasabi, nori rolls, and soy dressing. The wine list is extensive.

101 O'Connell St., North Adelaide. ℂ 08/8267 2652. theoxfordhotel@ozemail.com.au. Reservations recommended, especially for lunch and dinner Fri and dinner Sat. Main courses A$15–A$21 (US$9.40–US$13). AE, DC, MC, V. Sun–Thurs 9am–2am; Fri–Sat 9am–3am. Bus: 182, 22, 224, 226, 228, or 229.

SEEING THE SIGHTS

Adelaide is a very laid-back city. It's not jam-packed with tourist-oriented attractions like some of the larger state capitals, though the Migration Museum (see below) is easily one of the best museums in Australia. The best way to enjoy this pleasant city is to take things nice and easy. Take a walk beside the River Torrens, take the tram to the beachside suburb of Glenelg, and spend the evenings sipping wine and sampling some of the country's best alfresco dining.

THE TOP ATTRACTIONS

Art Gallery of South Australia ℛ   Adelaide's premier public art gallery has a good range of local and overseas works and a fine Asian ceramics collection. Of particular interest are Charles Hall's *Proclamation of South Australia 1836,* Nicholas Chevalier's painting of the departure of explorers Burke and Wills from Melbourne; several examples of works by Australian painters Sidney Nolan, Albert Tucker, and Arthur Boyd; and some excellent contemporary art. The bookshop has an extensive collection of art publications. Allow 1 to 2 hours.

North Terrace. ℂ 08/8207 7000. Free admission. Daily 10am–5pm. Guided tours Mon–Fri 11am and 2pm; Sat–Sun 11am and 3pm. Closed Christmas Day. Bus: City Loop.

The Migration Museum ℛ *Finds*   This tiny museum, dedicated to immigration and multiculturalism, is one of the most important and fascinating in Australia. With touching, personal displays, it tells the story of the waves of immigrants who have helped shape this multicultural society, from the boatloads of convicts who came here in 1788 to the ethnic groups who have been trickling in over the past 2 centuries. Allow 1 hour.

82 Kintore Ave. ℂ 08/8207 7580. Admission by donation. Mon–Fri 10am–5pm; Sat–Sun and public holidays 1–5pm. Closed Good Friday and Christmas. Bus: Any to North Terrace.

The National Wine Centre of Australia ℛ   This architectural masterpiece concentrates on Australia's 53 wine regions. Interactive exhibits and displays allow you to blend your own virtual wine. The Tasting Gallery displays an extensive range of Australian wines, and the wine tasting packages allow you to taste some of the rarest vintages. A restaurant and bar overlook the Centre, which has its own vineyard. You can fit the Wine Centre in with a visit to the nearby Botanic Gardens.

Hackney Rd. (eastern end of Northern Terrace). ℂ 08/8222 9288. wineaustralia.com.au. Admission A$11 (US$7.15) adults, A$6 (US$3.90) children under 18 (must be accompanied by an adult), A$29 (US$19) families. Wine-tasting packages from A$5–A$20 (US$3.25–US$13). Mon–Fri 9am–5.30pm. Closed Good Friday and Christmas Day. Limited parking on-site. Bus: Adelaide free bus, stop at Botanic Gardens

South Australian Maritime Museum   Over 150 years of maritime history are commemorated in this Port Adelaide museum. Most of the exhibits can be found in the 1850s Bond Store, but the museum also incorporates an 1863 lighthouse and three vessels moored alongside Wharf No. 1, just a short walk away. The fully rigged replica of the 16m (54-ft.) ketch *Active II* is very impressive. Allow 1½ hours. Port Adelaide is approximately 30 minutes from the city center by bus.

126 Lipson St., Port Adelaide. © 08/8207 6255. Admission A$8.50 (US$5.50) adults, A$3.50 (US$2.30) children, A$22 (US$14) families. Daily 10am–5pm. Closed Christmas. Bus: 151 or 153 from North Terrace in the city (opposite Parliament House) to Stop 40 (Port Adelaide). Train: Port Adelaide.

South Australian Museum   The star attraction of this interesting museum is the new Australian Aboriginal Cultures Gallery which opened in March 2000. On display is an extensive collection of utensils, spears, tools, bush medicine, food samples, photographs, and the like. Also within the museum is a sorry-looking collection of stuffed native animals (sadly also including a few extinct marsupials, including the Tasmanian Tiger); a good collection of Papua New Guinea artifacts; and excellent mineral and butterfly collections.

If you're interested in learning even more about the exhibits, take one of the Behind-the-Scenes Tours. The tours are conducted after museum hours and cost A$12 (US$7.80) for adults. Allow 2 hours.

On North Terrace between the State Library and the Art Gallery. © 08/8207 7500. Free admission. Daily 10am–5pm. Closed Good Friday and Christmas.

Tandanya Aboriginal Cultural Institute   This place offers a great opportunity to experience Aboriginal life through Aboriginal eyes. Exhibits change regularly, but all give insight into Aboriginal art and cultural activities. At noon every day there's a didgeridoo performance. A shop sells Aboriginal art and books on Aboriginal culture, while a cafe on the premises serves up several bush tucker (native food) items. Allow 1 hour.

253 Grenfell St. © 08/8224 3200. Admission A$4 (US$2.60) adults, A$3 (US$1.95) children 13 and under, A$10 (US$6.50) families. Daily 10am–5pm. Bus: City Loop.

THE FLORA & THE FAUNA

Adelaide Zoo *Kids*   To be honest, if you've experienced the wonderful Melbourne Zoo, or even Taronga Zoo in Sydney, it's probably not worth your while coming here. But if this is going to be your only chance to see a kangaroo in captivity, then plan a visit. Of course, other Australian animals live at the zoo, too, and the nicely landscaped gardens and lack of crowds make it a pleasant place for an entertaining stroll. The zoo houses the only pygmy blue-tongue lizard in captivity in Australia, a species thought to be extinct since the 1940s, until a specimen was discovered inside the belly of a dead snake. Allow 1 hour.

Frome Rd. © 08/8267 3255. Admission A$15 (US$9.75) adults, A$8 (US$5.20) children. Daily 9:30am–5pm. Bus: 272 or 273 from Currie St. to bus stop 2 (5 min.).

Botanic Gardens   You'll feel like you're at the heart of the city when you stroll through the huddles of office workers having picnic lunches on the lawns. Highlights include a broad avenue of Moreton Bay figs, duck ponds, giant water lilies, an Italianate garden, a palm house, and the Bicentennial Conservatory—a glass dome full of rainforest species. You might want to have lunch in the **Botanic Gardens Restaurant** (© 08/8223 3526) surrounded by bird song and lush vegetation, in the center of the park; it's open daily from 10am to 5pm.

North Terrace. © 08/8222 9311. Free admission. Mon–Fri 8am–sundown; Sat–Sun 9am–sundown.

FOR TRAIN BUFFS

National Railway Museum   This former Port Adelaide railway yard houses Australia's largest and finest collection of locomotive engines and rolling stock—with around 104 items on display including some 30 engines. Among the most impressive trains on show are the gigantic "Mountain" class engines, and so-called "Tea and Sugar" trains that once ran between railway camps in remote parts of the desert. Entrance includes a train ride. Allow 1½ hours.

Lipton St., North Adelaide. ℭ 08/8341 1690. Admission A$9 (US$5.85) adults, A$3.50 (US$2.30) children, and A$20 (US$13) families. Daily 10am–5pm. Bus: 151 or 153 from North terrace, opposite Parliament House, to stop number 40 (approx. 30-min. journey).

ORGANIZED TOURS

Grayline Day Tours (ℭ 1300/858 687 in Australia; www.grayline.com) operates a city sightseeing tour for A$39 (US$25) for adults and A$20 (US$13) for children. It operates from 9:30am to noon every day except Sunday. The bus can pick you up at your hotel. Grayline also does other tours taking in central Adelaide with either Hahndorf or Cleland Wildlife Park included, as well as tours to the Flinders ranges and Kangaroo Island.

ENJOYING THE GREAT OUTDOORS

BIKING   Adelaide's parks and riverbanks are very popular with cyclists. Rent your bicycle from **Linear Park Hire** (ℭ 018/844 588 mobile phone). The going rate is A$15 to A$20 (US$9.75–US$13) for 24 hours, including helmet, lock, and baby seat (if needed). **Recreation SA** (ℭ 08/8226 7301) publishes a brochure showing Adelaide's bike routes. Pick one up at the **South Australian Visitor & Travel Centre** (see "Visitor Information," earlier in chapter). **The Map Shop,** 6 Peel St. (ℭ 08/8231 2033), is also a good source for maps.

HIKING & JOGGING   The banks of the River Torrens are a good place for a jog. The truly fit and/or adventurous, might want to tackle the **Heysen Trail,** a spectacular 1,600km (992-mile) walk through bush, farmland, and rugged hill country that starts 80km (50 miles) south of Adelaide and goes to the Flinders Ranges by way of the Adelaide Hills and the Barossa Valley. For more information on the trail, visit the **South Australian Visitor & Travel Centre** (see "Visitor Information," earlier in this chapter).

GOLF   The **City of Adelaide Golf Course** (ℭ 08/8267 2171) is quite close to town and has two short 18-hole courses and a full-size championship course. Greens fees are A$14 to A$17 (US$9.10–US$11) weekdays and A$17 to A$19 (US$11–US$12) weekends, depending on the course. Club rental is available. Ask about cheaper prices after 4pm.

TAKING IN AN AUSSIE RULES GAME & OTHER SPECTATOR SPORTS

CRICKET   The **Adelaide Oval** (ℭ 08/8300 3800), on the corner of War Memorial Drive and King William Street, is the venue for international matches during the summer season. The Institute Building, part of the State Library of S.A., displays the **Don Bradman Collection** ℭ 08/8207 7595. The cricket legend died in Adelaide in 2001.

FOOTBALL   Unlike New South Wales, where Rugby League is the most popular winter sport, in Adelaide you'll find plenty of Australian Rules fanatics. Games are usually played on a Saturday at the **Adelaide Oval** (see above) or **Football Park** (ℭ 08/8268 2088), on Turner Drive, West Lakes. The home teams are the Adelaide Crows and the Port Adelaide Power. Games are played

February through October, with the finals held in September and October. Tickets must be purchased well in advance from **BASS** (© **13 12 46** in South Australia, or 08/8400 2205).

THE SHOPPING SCENE

Rundle Mall (between King Williams and Pulteney sts.) is Adelaide's main shopping street. This pedestrian-only thoroughfare is home to the big names in fashion.

Adelaide's Central Markets (© **08/8203 7494**), behind the Adelaide Hilton Hotel between Gouger and Grote streets, make up the largest produce market in the Southern Hemisphere. They're a good place to shop for vegetables, fruit, meat, fish, and the like, although the markets are worth popping into even if you're not looking for picnic fixings. The markets, held in a warehouselike structure, are open Tuesday from 7am to 5:30pm, Thursday from 9am to 5:30pm, Friday from 7am to 9pm, and Saturday from 7am to 3pm. **Market Adventures** (© **08/8336 8333,** or mobile 0412/842 242; fax/message 08/8336 4075) runs behind-the-scenes tours of the markets every Tuesday and Thursday at 10:30am and 1:30pm, Friday at 10am and 2pm, and Saturday at 8:30am. Tours cost A$35 (US$23) for adults and A$18 (US$12) for children 3 to 11. Phone for directions.

The six-story **Myer Centre,** next door to the Myer department store, 22–38 Rundle Mall, has a Body Shop (on the ground floor), for beauty products; an Australian Geographic shop (on level 3), for top-quality Australiana; and Exotica (level 2), where you can find unusual futuristic gifts.

Just off Rundle Mall, at Shop no. 6 in the City Cross Arcade, is **L'Unique** (© **08/8231 0030**), a good crafts shop selling South Australian pottery, jewelry, woodcraft, hand-blown glass, and original paintings.

Elsewhere, the renowned **Jam Factory Craft and Design Centre,** in the Lions Art Centre, 19 Morphett St. (© **08/8410 0727**), sells an excellent range of locally made ceramics, glass, furniture, and metal items. You can also watch the craftspeople at work here.

For the best boots in Australia, head to the **R.M. Williams** shop on Gawler Place (© **08/8232 3611**) for the best simple boots you're likely to find, as well as other Aussie fashion icons, including Akubra hats, moleskin pants, and Drizabone coats.

ADELAIDE AFTER DARK

The *Adelaide Advertiser* lists all performances and exhibitions in its entertainment pages. The free tourist guide *Today in Adelaide,* available in most hotels, also has information. Tickets for theater and other entertainment events in Adelaide can be purchased from **BASS ticket outlets** at the following locations: Festival Theatre, Adelaide Festival Centre, King William Road; Centre Pharmacy, 19 Central Market Arcade; Verandah Music, 182 Rundle St.; and on the

---

Finds Shopping for Opals

South Australia is home to the world's largest sources of white opals. (The more expensive black opals generally come from Lightning Ridge in New South Wales.) There are plenty of places to buy around town, but **Opal Field Gems,** 33 King William St. (© **08/8212 5300**), is one of the best. As a rule, you're not going to find any bargains, so just buy what you like (and can afford—good opals cost many thousands of dollars).

5th floor of the Myer department store, Rundle Mall. Call BASS at 🕾 **13 12 46** in South Australia, or 08/8400 2205.

THE PERFORMING ARTS

The major concert hall in town is the **Adelaide Festival Centre,** King William Road (🕾 **08/8216 8600** for general inquiries, 08/8400 2205 for box office). The Festival Centre encompasses three auditoriums: the 1,978-seat Festival Theatre, the 612-seat Playhouse, and the 350-seat Space Centre. This is the place in Adelaide to see opera, ballet, drama, orchestral concerts, the Adelaide Symphony Orchestra, plays, and experimental drama.

The complex also includes an outdoor amphitheater used for jazz, rock 'n' roll, and country music concerts; an art gallery; a bistro; a piano bar; and the Silver Jubilee Organ, the world's largest transportable concert-hall organ (built in Austria to commemorate Queen Elizabeth II's Silver Jubilee).

The Adelaide Repertory Festival presents a season of five productions a year, ranging from drama to comedy, at the **Arts Theatre,** 53 Angus St. (🕾 **08/8221 5644**). Playwrights Alan Ayckbourne and Terrence Rattigan are among the many who have had plays performed here. The theater, which is a short walk away from many hotels and restaurants, is also the home of the Metropolitan Musical Theatre Company, which presents two musical comedy productions a year. Tickets cost around A$16 (US$10) for adults and A$11 (US$7.15) for children.

Her Majesty's Theatre, 58 Grote St. (🕾 **08/8216 8600**), is a 1,000-seat venue opposite Central Markets that presents drama, comedy, musicals, dance, opera, and recitals. Tickets are generally A$30 to A$55 (US$20–US$36).

THE BAR & CLUB SCENE

Adelaide's nightlife ranges from twiddling your thumbs to nude lap dancers. For adult entertainment (clubs with the word *strip* in the name) head to **Hindley Street**—there are a few pubs there, but I wouldn't recommend them. For information on gay and lesbian options, pick up the *Adelaide Gay Times.*

Popular **Universal Wine Bar** at 285 Rundle St. (🕾 **08/8232 5000**) is the perfect place to start an evening, with great atmosphere and good wines by the glass.

As for all-age pubs, the locals will point you toward **The Austral,** 205 Rundle St. (🕾 **08/8223 4660**); **The Exeter,** 246 Rundle St. (🕾 **08/8223 2623**); **The Lion,** at the corner of Melbourne and Jerningham sts. (🕾 **08/8367 0222**); and the **British Hotel,** 58 Finniss St. (🕾 **08/8267 2188**), in North Adelaide, where you can cook your own steak on the courtyard barbecue. Also popular with both visitors and locals alike is the **Earl of Aberdeen,** 316 Pulteney St., at Carrington Street (🕾 **08/8223 6433**), a colonial-style pub popular for after-work drinks. **The Port Dock,** 10 Todd St., Port Adelaide (🕾 **08/8240 0187**), was licensed as a pub in 1864 and has kept up with tradition ever since; it even brews four of its own beers and pumps them directly to its three bars with old English beer engines. Most pubs are open from 11am to midnight.

TRYING YOUR LUCK AT THE CASINO

Right next to the Adelaide Hyatt, and dwarfed by the old railway station containing it, is the **Adelaide Casino** (now officially called "SkyCity" to make it sound trendier), North Terrace (🕾 **1800/888 711** in Australia, or 08/8212 2811). The casino has two floors of gaming tables and slot machines, as well as four bars and several dining options, including a fast-food station and the excellent Pullman buffet restaurant. The casino is open Sunday through Thursday from 10am to 4am and Friday and Saturday from 10am to 6am.

2 Side Trips from Adelaide

THE BAROSSA: ON THE TRAIL OF THE GRAPE ௸

More than a quarter of Australia's wines, and a disproportionate number of top labels, originate in the Barossa and Eden valleys—collectively known as the **Barossa.** Beginning just 45km (28 miles) northeast of Adelaide and easily accessible, the area has had an enormous influence on the city's culture. In fact, Adelaidians of all socioeconomic levels partake in more wine talk than the French. German settlers from Silesia, who came to escape religious persecution, first settled the area. They brought with them their culture, their food, and their vines. They built the Lutheran churches that dominate the Barossa's skyline. With the help of English aristocrats, the wine industry went from strength to strength. Today, there are over 50 wineries in an area that retains its German flavor.

The focal points of the area are **Angaston,** farthest away from Adelaide; **Nuriootpa,** the center of the rural services industry; and **Tanunda,** the nearest town to the city. Each has interesting architecture, crafts and antiques shops, and specialty food outlets. If you are adventurous, you might want to hire a bike in Adelaide and take it on the train to **Gawler,** and cycle through the Barossa. Other options are exploring the area by hot-air balloon, motorcycle, or limousine.

ESSENTIALS

WHEN TO GO   The best times to visit the Barossa and other South Australian wine regions are in the spring (Sept–Oct), when it's not too hot and there are plenty of flowering trees and shrubs, and in the fall (Apr–May), when the leaves turn red. The main wine harvest is late summer/early autumn (Feb–Apr). The least crowded time is winter (June–Aug). Hotel prices can be more expensive on the weekend.

GETTING THERE   If you have a car (by far the most flexible way to visit the Barossa), I recommend taking the scenic route from Adelaide. (The route doesn't have a specific name, but it's obvious on a map.) It takes about half an hour longer than the Main North Road through Gawler, but the trip is well worth it. Follow the signs to Birdwood, Springton, Mount Pleasant, and Angaston.

So Much Wine, So Little Time

If you have the choice of exploring the Barossa or the Hunter Valley in New South Wales (see chapter 4), I recommend the **Barossa,** which despite being a little more touristy, has more to offer in history and architecture.

Another famous wine-producing region is the **Coonawarra,** 381km (236 miles) southeast of Adelaide and near the border with Victoria; it's particularly convenient if you're driving from Melbourne. The area is just 12km (7½ miles) long and 2km (just over 1 mile) wide, but the scenic countryside is crammed with historical villages and 16 wineries. The **Clare Valley,** 135km (84 miles) north of Adelaide, is another pretty area; it produces some outstanding examples of cool-climate wine. Finally, the **McLaren Vale,** south of Adelaide, offers some 42 vineries producing some of Australia's best aromatic white wines as well as shiraz.

Public buses run infrequently to the major centers from Adelaide. There are no buses between wineries.

ORGANIZED TOURS FROM ADELAIDE Various companies run limited sightseeing tours. One of the best, **Grayline Day Tours** (© **1300/858 687;** www.grayline.com), offers a day trip visiting three wineries and other attractions every day. It costs A$75 (US$49) for adults and A$37 (US$24) for children, including a restaurant lunch. It also offers a daylong Grand Barossa Tour stopping off at two wineries, the Adelaide Hills and Hahndorf. This costs A$85 (US$55) for adults and A$50 (US$33) for children, and heads out Monday through Wednesday and Friday in summer (Wed and Fri in winter). Both tours depart at 9am from the bus terminal at 101 Franklin St., Adelaide. Another option is the **Barossa Wine Train** (© **08/8212 7888**), which departs from Adelaide Railway Station on Thursday, Saturday and Sunday. There are a variety of day tour and overnight packages available. Another option is to do it in style in a vintage car with the **Mirror Image Vintage Touring Co** (© **08/8621 1400;** www.mirror-image.com.au). Chevrolets, stretch limos, or Caravelles can be hired from 1 hour to 2 days with a chauffeur/guide.

VISITOR INFORMATION The **Barossa Wine and Visitor Information Centre,** 66–68 Murray St., Tanunda, SA 5352 (© **08/8563 0600;** www.barossa-region.org), is open Monday through Friday from 9am to 5pm, and Saturday and Sunday from 10am to 4pm. It's worth popping into the center's small audio-visual display for an introduction to the world of wine; entry is A$2.75 (US$1.80) for adults, free for children. You'll need an hour or so to look around.

Wines are often cheaper at the **Tanunda Cellars** bottleshop, or retail outlet, at 14 Murray St., Tanunda (© **08/8563 3544;** tanundacellars@dove.com.au) than at the winery door. This historic 1858 stone shop also houses one of Australia's finest collections of vintage wines, so pop in if you appreciate wines.

TOURING THE WINERIES

With some 50 wineries offering free cellar-door tastings and/or daily tours charting the winemaking process, you won't be stuck for places to visit. All wineries are well signposted. Below are just a few of my favorite places, but don't be shy about just stopping whenever you come across a winery that takes your fancy. *A tip:* Try a sparkling red. It may turn up noses elsewhere, and it takes some getting used to, but bearing in mind that the world's wine industry now hangs on Australia's every wine offering, it may well be the great tipple of the future.

Orlando and Jacobs Creek Visitor Centre This large winery was established in 1847 and is the home of many award-winning brands. Its big seller is the Jacobs Creek brand, now sold worldwide. Premium wines include the Lawson Shiraz and the Jacaranda Ridge Cabernet, and new vintages of either will set you back at least A$45 (US$29) a bottle. There's a cafe and a picnic area with barbecues. The new Visitor Centre opened in May 2002.

Barossa Hwy., Rowland Flat. © 08/8521 3000. Daily 10am–5pm.

Penfolds Australia's biggest wine producer churns out some 22.5 million liters (5.8 million gal.) from this one winery every year. Penfolds also owns other wineries all over the country. It all started when Dr. Christopher Rawson planted a few vines in 1844 to make wine for his patients. The winery now houses the largest oak barrel maturation cellars in the Southern Hemisphere.

Nuriootpa. © 08/8568 9408. Mon–Fri 10am–5pm; weekends 11am–5pm.

The Barossa

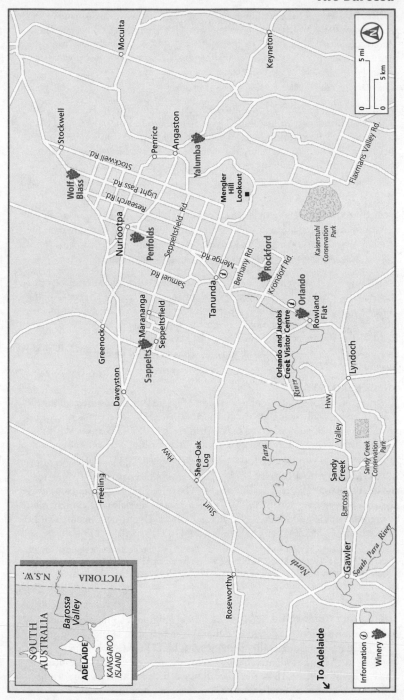

Rockford   Most of the buildings here were constructed in 1984 out of recycled local materials, but you'd never know it. The wine is pressed between mid-March and the end of April, in the traditional way with machinery from the turn of the 20th century. It's a fascinating sight. Demand for Rockford wines, especially the Basket Pressed Shiraz, far exceeds supply.

Krondorf Rd., Tanunda. © 08/8568 9408. Mon–Sat 11am–5pm.

Seppelts   This National Trust–listed property was founded in 1857 by Joseph Seppelt, an immigrant from Silesia. The wine tour around the gardens and bluestone buildings is considered one of the best in the world. On a nearby slope, check out the family's Romanesque mausoleum, skirted by planted roadside palms, built during the 1930s recession to keep winery workers employed.

Seppeltsfield. © 08/8568 6200. Adults A$7 (US$4.55), children 5–16 A$2 (US$1.30). Mon–Fri 10am–5pm; Sat–Sun 11am–5pm. Tours hourly Mon–Fri 11am–3pm; Sat–Sun 11:30am, and 1:30 and 2:30pm.

Wolf Blass   This winery's Germanic-style black-label vintages have an excellent international reputation, while its cheaper yellow-label vintages are the toast of many a Sydney dinner party. The Wolf Blass museum is worth a peek.

Sturt Hwy., Nuriootpa. © 08/8568 7300. Mon–Fri 9am–5pm; Sat–Sun 10am–5pm.

Yalumba   This winery was built in 1849, making it the oldest family-owned winemaking business in Australia. It's also huge. Look out for the sad-looking Himalayan bear in the corner of the large tasting room; following a run-in with a hunting rifle, it's been Yalumba's advertising gimmick. The winery's Signature Red Cabernet-Shiraz is among the best you'll ever taste.

Eden Valley Rd., Angaston. © 08/8561 3200. www.yalumba.com.au. Mon–Fri 8:30am–5pm; Sat 10am–5pm; Sun noon–5pm.

WHERE TO STAY

There are plenty of standard motels and lots of interesting B&Bs throughout the Barossa, some with rooms for as little as A$60 (US$39). Weekends often find rooms are booked out and prices higher than weekdays. The **Barossa Wine and Visitor Information Centre** (see "Visitor Information," above) can provide information on additional accommodations choices and off-season deals.

Barossa Valley (SA) Tourist Park   This peaceful place is back from the road and abuts a nature lake and wildlife reserve. The cabins are simple but come with just about everything you'll need for a pleasant stay. Cabins have a combination of doubles, singles, and bunk beds. If you don't have your own linen you'll be charged A$5 (US$3.25) per single bed and A$10 (US$6.50) per double.

Penrice Rd., Nuriootpa 5355. © 08/8562 1404. Fax 08/85622 615. www.barossa-tourist-park.com.au. 27 cabins, 19 with bathroom. A$36 (US$23) double without bathroom; A$45–A$60 (US$30–US$39) double with bathroom. Family unit A$65 (US$42). Extra adult A$5 (US$3.25), extra child 3–15 A$3 (US$1.95). AE, DC, MC, V. **Amenities:** Outdoor pool (nearby); 2 tennis courts; coin-op laundry. *In room:* A/C, TV, kitchenette, coffeemaker, iron.

Collingrove Homestead ✩✩✩ *Finds*   In my opinion, Collingrove is not just the best country-house experience in the Barossa but, dare I say it, in Australia. Built in 1856, it was originally the home of John Howard Angas, one of those involved in the initial settlement of South Australia. Additions were made as Angas's sheep business prospered. The hallway is festooned with spears, artillery shells, rifles, oil-painted portraits, and the mounted heads of various stags and tigers. English oak paneling and creaky floorboards add a certain nuance, and the cedar kitchen, library, glorious dining room, and various other places are all bursting with antiques and knickknacks. What the quaint, individually decorated guest rooms lack in modern amenities—no phones or TVs—they make up for in charm. The modern communal Jacuzzi is set in the old stables, with its flagstone floors and old horse harnesses; there's also a flagstone-floored tennis court. Even if you don't stay here, you can indulge in Devonshire tea on the terrace daily for A$5 (US$3.25) and can tour the property Monday through Friday from 1 to 4:30pm and Saturday and Sunday from 11am to 4:30pm. The tour costs A$4 (US$2.60) for adults and A$1.50 (US$1) for children. Sunday brunch is also popular. Dinner by prior arrangement for guests costs A$95 (US$62) per person.

Eden Valley Rd., Angaston, SA 5353. © 08/8564 2061. Fax 08/8564 3600. www.collinggrovehomestead. com.au. 6 units, 4 with bathroom. A$210 (US$136) luxury double; A$250 (US$162) deluxe double. Rates include full breakfast. AE, DC, MC, V. **Amenities:** Restaurant; tennis court; Jacuzzi; in-room massage; babysitting; nonsmoking rooms. *In room:* TV w/pay movies (room 5 only), minibar (room 5 only), hair dryer.

The Hermitage of Marananga ⭐ This is far and away the best of the area's motels. The rooms are awkwardly shaped but have been recently renovated. Each has a small balcony. The main building is old-fashioned and bursting with character. It's also cool in the heat of summer. Outside there are fantastic views over the valley and to the ranges beyond. Good walks lead around the property, and at dusk you'll see plenty of kangaroos in the surrounding fields. The new apartment has a private balcony overlooking the vineyards, a separate bedroom, and a double sleeper sofa in the living room.

Corner of Seppltsfield and Stonewell rds., Marananga, SA 5351. © 08/8562 2722. Fax 08/8562 3133. www. hermitageofmarananga.com.au. 11 units, including 1 apt. A$230 (US$150) double; A$330 (US$214) Jacuzzi room; $330 (US$214) apt. Rates include breakfast and cost A$100 (US$65) more on Sat. AE, DC, MC, V. Free parking. **Amenities:** Restaurant; heated outdoor pool; tour desk; massage; dry cleaning. *In room:* A/C, TV/DVD, minibar, coffeemaker, hair dryer, iron.

Marble Lodge ⭐⭐ Wake up and smell the roses—there are plenty in the beautiful gardens surrounding this romantic historic property (as well as a tennis court, and several deer and kangaroos). Away from the main house is a lodge made of local marble that's divided into two suites. The larger suite has two rooms and an open fireplace. The second is a large bed/sitting room, with an open fireplace. Both have access to the shared Jacuzzi and are tastefully furnished in antiques. There's always fresh fruit, homemade biscuits, and chocolates in the room, and it's a 5-minute walk to three local restaurants. A double room, with shared bathroom, is sometimes available in the homestead itself.

21 Dean St., Angaston, SA 5351. © 08/8564 2478. Fax 08/8564 2941. www.marblelodge.com.au. 2 units. A$170 (US$111) double. Rate includes breakfast, bottle of champagne, and minibar drinks. MC, V. **Amenities:** Tennis court; Jacuzzi; room service until 8pm; laundry/dry cleaning service available nearby; nonsmoking rooms; e-mail and fax facilities. *In room:* A/C, TV w/pay movies, fax, minibar, fridge, coffeemaker, hair dryer, iron.

WHERE TO DINE

The Barossa prides itself on its cuisine as well as its wine, so you'll find plenty of places of note to eat, many of them serving up traditional German foods in line with the area's heritage. A hot spot, for lunch or dinner, is **Vintner's Bar & Grill,** Nuriootpa Road, Angaston (© **08/8564 2488**); the wine list here is six pages long! Try the bay leaf risotto with prawns or the roast veal rack with crisp polenta. Main courses cost A$22 to A$27 (US$14–US$18). It's open for lunch daily and closed on Sunday for dinner. Another choice is **Salters,** Satram Winery, Nuriootpa Road, Angaston (© **08/8564 3344**); local produce is the specialty here, with main courses such as slow-roasted baby pork, milk-fed lamb, and crisp-based pizzas. Main courses are between A$20 and A$26 (US$13–US$17). It's open daily for lunch and from 6pm Wednesdays to Saturdays for dinner. You'll find perhaps the valley's best German-style bakery in Lyndoch, the **Lyndoch Bakery,** on the Barossa Highway (© **08/8524 4422**). In Angaston you must stop off at **The Seasons of the Valley,** 6 Washington St. (© **08/8564 3688**). This restored 1840 homestead houses has cottage gardens and a sunny verandah as well as delicious meals from A$15 to A$18 (US$9.50–US$11). It's open daily 10am to 5pm.

THE ADELAIDE HILLS

A 25-minute drive from Adelaide and visible even from the main shopping street, you'll find the tree-lined slopes and pretty valleys, orchards, vineyards, winding roads, and historic townships of the **Adelaide Hills.** You might want to walk part of the Heysen Trail (see "Enjoying the Great Outdoors" in the Adelaide section, earlier in this chapter), browse through the shops in Hahndorf, stop in Melba's Chocolate Factory in Woodside, or visit Cleland Wildlife Park or Warrawong Sanctuary. Otherwise, it's a nice outing just to hit the road and drive. Should you decide to stay overnight, the area offers lots of cozy B&Bs.

ESSENTIALS

GETTING THERE The Adelaide Hills are 25 minutes from Adelaide by car via Greenhill and Glen Osmond roads. **Adelaide Sightseeing** (© **08/8231 4144;** www.adelaidesightseeing.com.au) runs outings to the gorgeous town of Hahndorf (see below) as well as to Cleland Wildlife Park. An afternoon excursion to Hahndorf costs A$43 (US$28) for adults and A$23 (US$15) for children; the tour to Cleland costs A$38 (US$25) for adults and A$23 (US$15) for children, including park entry. Check their Web site to compare trips to the Barossa valley, Flinders Ranges, Great Ocean Road, and Kangaroo Island.

VISITOR INFORMATION Visitor information and bookings are available through the **Adelaide Hills Tourist Information Centre,** 41 Main St., Hahndorf (© **08/8388 1185**). It's open Monday through Friday from 9am to 4pm. Otherwise, maps are available at the **South Australia Travel Centre** in Adelaide.

WOODSIDE: CHOCOLATE LOVERS UNITE!

Visitors come here for **Melba's Chocolate Factory,** Henry Street (© **08/8389 7868**), where chocoholics will find a huge range of handmade chocolates. Melba's is part of Heritage Park, a complex that includes a wood turner, a cheese maker, a ceramics studio, a leather maker, and a crafts shop. It's open Monday through Friday from 10am to 4pm, and Saturday, Sunday, and holidays from noon to 5pm.

MYLOR: GETTING BACK TO NATURE

Mylor is located 25km (16 miles) southeast of Adelaide, and 10km (6 miles) south of Mt. Lofty via the town of Crafters. Here you'll find the **Warrawong Sanctuary,** Stock Road, Mylor (P.O. Box 1135), Stirling, SA 5152 (© **08/8370 9197;** fax 08/8370 8332; www.efl.com.au). Unlike many other wildlife parks, the animals here are not kept in enclosed runs. Instead, park founder Dr. John Wamsley took a 14-hectare (35-acre) tract of farmland, replanted it with natural bush, fenced it off, and went around shooting the introduced rabbits, cats, dogs, and foxes that plague much of Australia. Then the good doctor took to reintroducing animals native to the site—such as kangaroos, various types of wallabies, bandicoots, beetongs, platypuses, possums, frogs, birds, and reptiles.

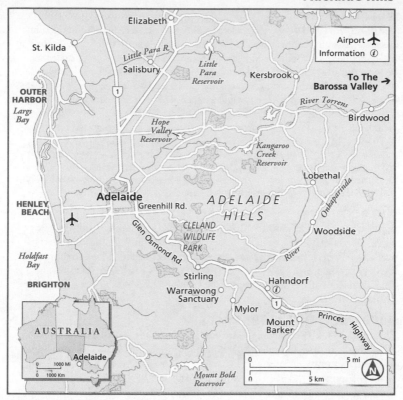

They are all thriving, not only because he eliminated their unnatural predators, but also because he re-created waterways, rainforests, and blackwater ponds. The animals roam free while you're guided through on 1½-hour dawn or sunset walks (A$18/US$12 adults, A$12/US$7.80 children). There's a restaurant on the premises, and you can even stay overnight in large cabins with bathrooms, wall-to-wall carpeting, and air-conditioning. The cabins cost A$125 (US$81) per person with both dawn and dusk tours, a two-course dinner, and breakfast.

Compared to **Cleland Wildlife Park** (see below), there is less variety of animals here (you won't find any koalas, for example), but it's more educational and you get the feeling that you're in the wild rather than in a zoo.

HAHNDORF: GERMAN HERITAGE, CRAFTS & MORE ⊛

This historic German-style village is one of South Australia's most popular tourist destinations. Lutherans fleeing religious persecution in eastern Prussia founded the town, which is 29km (18 miles) southeast of Adelaide, in 1839. They brought with them their winemaking skills, foods, and architectural inheritance, and put it all together here. Hahndorf still resembles a small German town in appearance and atmosphere, and is included on the World Heritage List as a Historical German Settlement. Walking around you'll **see St. Paul's Lutheran Church,** erected in 1890. **The Wool Factory, L'Unique Fine Arts & Craft,** and **Bamfurlong Fine Crafts** are worth checking out and are within walking distance of Main Street.

WHERE TO STAY

The Hahndorf Resort 🅰️   This large resort has a variety of accommodations available, as well as approximately 80 trailer and tent sites. Here, too, are fully self-contained, air-conditioned cabins, and motel-style rooms with queen-size beds (some have an extra single) and a shower. The chalets look like they're straight out of Bavaria; each can accommodate from two to five people in either one or two bedrooms. Each has a full kitchen and an attached bathroom with shower. Some of them overlook a small lake. The larger spa chalets come with Jacuzzis. An on-site animal sanctuary has a few emus, kangaroos, and horses.

145A Main St., Hahndorf, SA 5245. © 08/8388 7921. Fax 08/8388 7282. www.hahndorfresort.com.au. 60 units. A$61 (US$40) cabin; A$87 (US$57) motel room; $A98–A$165 (US$64–US$107) chalet. A$11 (US$7.15) extra adult, A$5.50 (US$3.60) extra child. AE, DC, MC, V. **Amenities:** Restaurant; heated outdoor pool; 2 putting greens; half-size tennis court; small gym; bike rental; limited room service; coin-op laundry. *In room:* A/C, TV, kitchenette, minibar, coffeemaker, iron.

WHERE TO DINE

If you want a treat head to the **Bridgewater Mill,** Mt Barker Road, Bridgewater (© **08/8339 3422**). Set in an impressive 1860s stone building with a terrace near a waterwheel, this places serves some of the best-regarded food in the country. Try the duck with braised cherries. Main courses cost A$31 (US$20) and a three-course menu serviced Sunday only is A$68 (US$44). It's open for lunch Thursday to Monday.

OAKBANK: A DAY AT THE RACES

The **Easter Oakbank Racing Carnival** is part of the Australia-wide "picnic races" that take place in small towns throughout the nation. The Oakbank horse races attract crowds in excess of 110,000 a day over the long Easter weekend. General admission is A$10 (US$6.50), plus another A$5 (US$3.25) for admission to the grandstand. The **Oakbank Racing Club** (© **08/8212 6279**) is just off the main road; you can't miss it.

WHERE TO STAY

Adelaide Hills Country Cottages 🅰️🅰️   These three cottages have won several tourism awards, including the 1998 Australian Tourist Commission award for hosted accommodations in Australia—which is quite a big deal. They are 1km (½ mile) apart and surrounded by 60 hectares (150 acres) of scenic countryside. The Apple Tree cottage, from around 1860, sleeps up to five, has a Jacuzzi and antiques, and overlooks an orchard and a lake; the Gum Tree Cottage sleeps four and has wonderful country views; and the Lavender Fields Cottage sleeps up to four and overlooks a lily-fringed duck pond. All of the cottages have open fireplaces and full kitchens. This is a great place to relax and a good base for exploring the area. You'll get a couple of free drinks and a fruit basket upon arrival.

P.O. Box 100, Oakbank, SA 5243. © 08/8388 4193. Fax 08/8388 4733. www.ahcc.com.au. 5 cottages. A$205–A$260 (US$133–US$169). Extra person A$70 (US$46). Rates include provisions for breakfast. A 1-night rate will include a surcharge of A$30 (US$20). Ask about lower weekly rates. AE, DC, MC, V. Oakbank is 30 min. from Adelaide, 7 min. from Hahndorf, and less than 1 hr. from the Barossa Valley. **Amenities:** Jacuzzi; tour desk; coin-op laundry; nonsmoking rooms. *In room:* A/C, TV/VCR, kitchen, coffeemaker, hair dryer, iron.

MT. LOFTY: VIEWS & 'ROOS

Visitors make the pilgrimage to the top of the 690m (2,263-ft.) **Mt. Lofty,** 16km (10 miles) southeast of Adelaide, for the panoramic views over Adelaide, the Adelaide plains, and the Mt. Lofty Ranges. There are several nice bushwalks from the top.

Almost at the top of Mt. Lofty, off Summit Road, is the **Cleland Wildlife Park** (© **08/8339 2444**). Here you'll find all the usual Australian animals on view—including the largest male red kangaroo I've ever seen. Though the park is not as good as similar wildlife parks in Australia, it does have a very good wetlands aviary. One of the drawbacks of Cleland is that it's got some unimaginative enclosures, notably the one for the Tasmanian devils. The park is open daily from 9:30am to 4:30pm. Visitors can meet at the Tasmanian devil enclosure at 2pm and join the animal feed run by following a tractor around the park as it drops off food.

Admission to Cleland is A$12 (US$7.80) for adults, A$8 (US$5.20) for children 3 to 14, and A$31 (US$20) for families. Koala holding is allowed during the photo sessions held daily from 2 to 4pm daily (but not on very hot summer days); on Sunday and public holidays there's an additional session from 10am to noon. The privilege will cost you A$12 (US$7.80) per photo. A kiosk and restaurant are on the premises.

It's a bit of a hassle getting to either place by public transport. To get to the Mt. Lofty Lookout take bus no. 163 Monday through Friday, and no. 165 Saturday and Sunday from Currie Street in the city. Ask the driver to drop you off at "Crafters." The trip takes 30 minutes. From there you'll need to take a short taxi ride to the top, so prearrange pick up with **Tony's Taxi's** at © **08/8388 5988.**

To get to Cleland take bus no. 822 from Currie Street and get off at bus stop 19b. There are only two services daily, at 10am and noon, Monday through Friday. Take the 10am bus and ask the bus driver for the exact return time. The trip to Cleland takes 40 minutes.

WHERE TO DINE

While you're atop Mt. Lofty, have lunch at **The Summit** restaurant (© **08/8339 2600**). Look out for the kangaroo fillet with chile, lemon grass, and coconut sauce, and venison on rosemary polenta. Mains cost from A$22 to A$26 (US$14–US$17). It's open for lunch Monday and Tuesday, and for dinner Wednesday to Sunday. The **Summit Café** here also sells good sandwiches and cakes, and Devonshire tea for A$8 (US$5.20).

3 Kangaroo Island ⟨★⟨★⟨★

110km (68 miles) S of Adelaide

There is nowhere better than Kangaroo Island to see Australian marsupials in the wild. Spend a few days here with the right guide and you can walk along a beach past a colony of sea lions; spot hundreds of New Zealand fur seals playing; creep through the bush on the trail of wallabies or kangaroos; spot sea eagles, black swans, sacred ibis, pelicans, little penguins, the rare glossy black cockatoo and other birds; come across goannas; pick out bunches of koalas hanging sleepily in the trees above your head; and, if you're lucky, see platypus, echidna, bandicoots, reclusive pygmy possums—the list goes on.

The secrets to Kangaroo Island's success are its perfect conditions, the most important of which is the fact that there are no introduced foxes or rabbits to take their toll on the native inhabitants or their environment. The island was also never colonized by the dingo—Australia's "native" dog—which was believed to have been introduced from Asia some 4,000 years ago. About one-third of the island is unspoiled national park, and there are plenty of wildlife corridors to give the animals a chance to move about the island, lessening the problems of inbreeding.

While the animals are what most people come to see, no one goes away without also being impressed by the scenery. Kangaroo Island has low mallee

Kangaroo Island

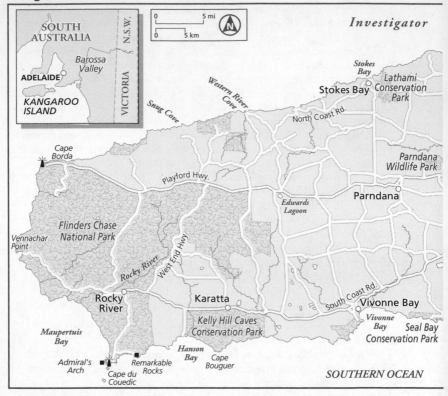

scrubland, dense eucalyptus forests, rugged coastal scenery, gorgeous beaches, caves, lagoons, and blackwater swamps. The effect of 150 years of European colonization has taken its toll, though. In South Australia as a whole, some 27 mammal, 5 bird, 1 reptile, and 30 plant species have become extinct since the state was discovered by the English seafarer Matthew Flinders in 1802.

The island's history is a harsh one. Aborigines inhabited the island as early as 10,000 years ago but abandoned it for unexplained reasons. In the 19th century it was settled by pirates, mutineers, deserters from English, French, and American ships, and escaped convicts from the eastern colonies. Sealers also arrived and took a heavy toll on the seal and sea lion population—in just 1 year, 1803 to 1804, they managed to kill more than 20,000 of these animals. Between 1802 and 1836, Aboriginal women from both the mainland and Tasmania were kidnapped, brought to Kangaroo Island, and forced to work catching and skinning seals, kangaroos, and wallabies, and lugging salt from the salt mines.

In 1836, Kangaroo Island became the first place in South Australia to be officially settled. The state's capital was Kingscote, until it was abandoned a couple of years later in favor of Adelaide. In spite of its early settlement, Kangaroo Island had very few residents until after World War II, when returned soldiers set up farms here. Today, more than a million sheep are raised on the island. The island also acts as an official bee sanctuary to protect the genetic purity of the Ligurian bee, introduced in 1881, and it is believed to be the only place in the world where this strain of bee survives.

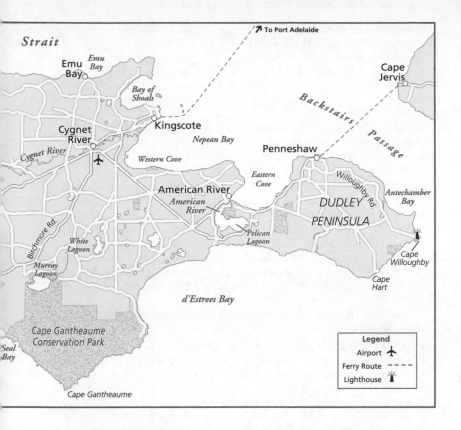

ISLAND ESSENTIALS

WHEN TO GO   The best time to visit Kangaroo Island is between November and March (though you'll have difficulty finding accommodations over the Christmas school holiday period). July and August tend to be rainy, and winter can be cold (though often milder than on the mainland around Adelaide). Many companies offer 1-day trips to Kangaroo Island from Adelaide, but I would advise you to tailor your holiday to spend at least 2 days here, though 3 or even 5 days would be better. There really is a lot to see, and you won't regret spending the extra time.

GETTING THERE   Emu Airways (© **08/8234 3711**) is the only airline servicing Kangaroo Island. Up to six daily departures ensure a frequent service to the Island. **Regional Express** (© **13 17 13** in Australia; www.regionalexpress. com.au) also flies from Adelaide (check their website for offers). Flights leave from the General Aviation Terminal, Kel Barclay Avenue, Adelaide. The General Aviation Terminal is about a 20-minute walk (or shorter taxi ride!) from the main airport terminal. The flight from Adelaide to Kangaroo Island usually takes about 25 minutes.

If you prefer to go by sea, **Kangaroo Island SeaLink** (© **13 13 01** in Australia, or 08/8202 8688; www.sealink.com.au) operates two oceangoing vehicle and passenger ferries four times daily (up to 10 times in peak periods) from Cape Jervis on the tip of the Fleurieu Peninsula on the mainland to Penneshaw on

Kangaroo Island. The trip takes 40 minutes and costs A$64 (US$42) round-trip for adults, A$32 (US$21) for children 3 to 14, and A$138 (US$90) for cars. Connecting bus service from Adelaide to Cape Jervis is provided at an extra A$36 (US$23) for adults, and A$18 (US$12) for children round-trip. There are some cheaper off-peak prices, but check when booking. Count on 3 hours for the whole trip from Adelaide if you take the connecting bus. Bookings are essential.

SeaLink also runs a range of island tours, including the 2-day/1-night "K.I. coast to coast," which costs from A$289 (US$188) per person twin share. SeaLink also offers a wide range of accommodations, day tours, and adventure activities and offers Adelaide hotel pickups for selected tours.

VISITOR INFORMATION   Tourism Kangaroo Island, The Gateway Information Centre, Howard Drive, Penneshaw (P.O. Box 336, Penneshaw, Kangaroo Island, SA 5222; © 08/8553 1185; fax 08/8553 1255; www.tourkangarooisland. com.au), has plenty of maps and information and can assist visitors with accommodations and island tours information. For more information on the island's national parks, contact the National Parks and Wildlife South Australia (NP & W SA) office, 39 Dauncey St. (P.O. Box 39), Kingscote, SA 5223 (© 08/8553 2381; fax 08/8553 2531), open Monday through Friday from 9am to 5pm.

In addition, hotel and motel staff generally carry a stack of tourist brochures and can point you in the right direction as far as where to go and what to see.

ISLAND LAYOUT   Kangaroo Island is Australia's third largest island, at 156km (97 miles) long and 57km (35 miles) wide at its widest point. The distance across the narrowest point is only 2km (1¼ miles). Approximately 3,900 people live on the island. More than half live on the northeast coast in one of the three main towns: Kingscote (pop. 1,800), Penneshaw (pop. 250), and American River (pop. 200). The island's major attractions are located farther from the mainland: Flinders Chase National Park is in the far west, Lathami Conservation Park is on the north coast, and Seal Bay and Kelly's Caves are on the south coast.

GETTING AROUND   Apart from a twice daily SeaLink bus service which connects Kingscote, Penneshaw, and American River, there is no public transport on the island. An Airport Shuttle Service (© 1800/750 850) meets all flights to Kangaroo Island and will take passengers to Kingscote, Emu Bay, and American River. Return transfers from your accommodations to the airport need to booked in advance. Kingscote shuttle costs A$10 (US$6.50) for adults and A$5 (US$3.25) for children one-way. Emu Bay shuttle costs A$17 (US$11) for adults and A$8 (US$5.20) for children one-way. American River shuttle costs A$33 (US$21) for adults and A$15 (US$9.75) for children one way. The shuttle drops off to Kingscote first (approx. 15 min. from airport), then Emu Bay, then American River.

Major roads between Penneshaw, American River, Kingscote, and Parndana are paved, as is the road to Seal Bay and all major roads within Flinders Chase National Park. Most other roads are made of ironstone gravel, and can be very slippery if corners are approached too quickly. All roads are accessible by two-wheel-drive vehicles, but if you're bringing over a rental car from the mainland make sure your policy allows you to drive on Kangaroo Island's roads. Avoid driving at night—animals rarely fare best in a car collision.

Car-rental agencies on the island include Budget (© 08/8553 3133 or 08/ 8553 1034; fax 08/8553 2888), Hertz & Kangaroo Island Rental Cars

> *Tips* **An Island Bargain**
>
> I'd advise buying an **NP&WSA Island Pass** if you'll be exploring the island on your own for 3 days or more and visiting the National Park and attractions more than once. It costs A$32 (US$21) for adults, A$23 (US$15) for children, and A$84 (US$55) for families, and includes guided tours of Seal Bay, Kelly Hill Caves, Cape Borda, and Cape Willoughby. The pass also includes access to Flinders Chase National Park. The pass doesn't cover penguin tours or camping fees.

(© **1800/088 296** in Australia, or 08/8553 2390; fax 08/8553 2878), and **Wheels over Kangaroo Island** (©1800/750 850 in Australia, or 08/8553 3030; woki@ozemail.com.au). You can pick up cars at the airport or ferry terminals.

ORGANIZED TOURS If you want to keep expenses down, you can't go wrong with one of the tours organized by **Penneshaw Youth Hostel,** 43 North Terrace, Penneshaw, Kangaroo Island, SA 5222 (© **08/8553 1284;** fax 08/8553 1295; www.ki-ferryconnections.com/yha_hostel/yha_hostel.). The most popular includes an afternoon pickup from the main bus station in Adelaide, coach and ferry to the island, a penguin tour that evening, and dorm accommodations (you can pay a little extra to upgrade to a double room, but book ahead). The next day involves 10 hours of touring, taking in most of the main attractions. That evening you return to Adelaide. The tour costs A$220 (US$143).

More expensive options include a tour by **Kangaroo Island Wilderness Tours** (© **08/8559 5033;** www.wildernesstours.com.au), which operates from the island with several small four-wheel-drive vehicles (maximum six people). Three different one-day trips cost between A$270 and A$290 (US$176–US$189) per person, including transfers, an excellent lunch with wine, and park entry fees. Two-, 3-, and 4-day trips, with all meals and accommodations included, cost A$710 (US$461), A$1,150 (US$745), and A$1,590 (US$1,033) per person, respectively.

Another excellent operator based on the island is **Adventure Charters of Kangaroo Island,** Playford Highway, Cygnet River, SA 5223 (© **08/8553 9119;** www.adventurecharters.com.au), with the knowledgeable and gregarious Craig Wickham at the helm. Day trips cost A$272 (US$177) a day with a big lunch, or A$501 (US$325) for a 1-day safari including flights from and to Adelaide.

Another option is with **Wayward Bus** (© **08/8410 8833;** www.wayward bus.com.au) from Adelaide. Two-day trips depart Monday, Wednesday, and Saturday and cost A$365 (US$237) in hostel accommodations (you can pay extra for an upgrade).

EXPLORING THE ISLAND

The island is bigger than you might think, and you can spend a fair bit of time getting from one place of interest to the next. Of the many places to see on the island, **Flinders Chase National Park** *ℛ* is one of the most important. First port of call should be the Flinders Chase Visitors Centre where you can purchase park entry, view the interpretive display, dine at the licensed cafe, purchase souvenirs, and obtain Parks information. It took 30 years of lobbying until reluctant politicians finally agreed to preserve this western region of the island in 1919. Today, it makes up around 17% of the island and is home to true wilderness, some beautiful coastal scenery, two old lighthouses, and plenty of animals. Bird-watchers have recorded at least 243 species of birds here. Koalas are so common that they're almost falling out of the trees. Platypus have been seen, but you'll probably need to make a special effort and sit next to a stream in the dark for a few hours for any chance of spotting one. The new Platypus Waterholes walk is a 2-hour return walk, great for all ages. The walk begins at the Flinders Chase Visitors Centre and has a shorter walk suitable for wheelchairs. This walk offers the best opportunity to see the elusive platypus. Kangaroos, wallabies, and brush-tailed possums, on the other hand, are so tame and numerous that the authorities were forced to erect a barrier around the Rocky River Campground to stop them from carrying away picnickers' sandwiches!

The most impressive coastal scenery can be found at **Cape du Couedic** at the southern tip of the park, where millions of years of crashing ocean have created curious structures—like the hollowed-out limestone promontory called Admiral's Arch and the aptly named Remarkable Rocks, where you'll see huge boulders balancing on top of a massive granite dome. At Admiral's Arch there is a colony of some 4,000 New Zealand fur seals that are easily spotted playing in the rock pools and resting on the rocks. During rough weather this place can be spectacular. Recently, the road from Rocky River Park Headquarters to Admiral's Arch and Remarkable Rocks was paved. A new parking lot and loop trail also has been developed at Remarkable Rocks. There's also a new road, parking lot, and trail system around the Cape du Couedic heritage lighthouse district.

You also shouldn't miss out on the unforgettable experience of walking through a colony of Australian sea lions at Seal Bay. The **Seal Bay Conservation Park** (© **08/8559 4207**) was created in 1972, and some 100,000 people visit it each year. Boardwalks have been built through the dunes to the beach to reduce the impact of so many feet. The colony consists of about 500 animals, but at any one time you might see up to 100 basking with their pups here. The rangers who supervise the area lead guided trips throughout the day, every 15 to 30 minutes from 9am to 4:15pm. If you come here without a coach group, you must join a tour. Tours cost A$11 (US$6.80) for adults and A$7.50 (US$4.90) for children.

Lathami Conservation Park, just to the east of Stokes Bay, is a wonderful place to see wallabies in the wild. Just dip in under the low canopy of casuarina pines and walk silently, keeping your eyes peeled, and you're almost certain to spot them. If you're fortunate you may even come across a very rare glossy cockatoo—it's big and black and feeds mainly on casuarina nuts.

Another interesting spot, especially for bird-watchers, is **Murray Lagoon,** on the northern edge of Cape Gantheaume Conservation Park. It's the largest lagoon on the island and a habitat for thousands of water birds. Contact the NP & W SA (see "Visitor Information," above) for information on a ranger-guided Wetland Wade.

If you want to see little **penguins**—tiny animals that stand just 33 centimeters (13 in.) tall—forget the touristy show at Phillip Island near Melbourne. On Kangaroo Island you get to see them in a natural environment at both Kingscote

---

Tips **Don't Feed the Animals, Please**

Don't feed *any* native animals. Kangaroos and wallabies might beg, but they are lactose-intolerant and can go blind or catch disease from being fed human food.

Culling Koalas—A National Dilemma

Koalas are cute. They're fluffy, they're sleepy, and they're awesomely cuddly. The problem is they eat an awful lot. In the early 1920s, 18 koalas were introduced to Kangaroo Island. Over the years, without predators and disease, and with an abundant supply of eucalyptus trees, they have prospered. By 1996, there were an estimated 4,000 koalas, and their favorite trees were looking ragged. Some of the koalas were already suffering; some people even claimed the animals were starving to death.

The South Australian Government decided the only option was to shoot Australia's ambassador to the world. The public outcry was enormous; Japan even threatened to advise their citizens to boycott Down Under. But what could be done? Some scientists maintained that the koalas could not be relocated to the mainland because there were few places left to put them. Conservationists blamed Kangaroo Island's farmers for depleting the island of more than 50% of its vegetation. The koala is endangered; the smaller northern variety is threatened with extinction in New South Wales and the larger subspecies in Victoria, which includes the Kangaroo Island koalas, are also under threat. A compromise was reached; the koalas are to be trapped and neutered, a few thousand per year, until their numbers stabilize. A few conscientious farmers will plant more trees. Other farmers will, no doubt, continue to see the koalas as pests.

and Penneshaw. Tours are conducted nightly in Kingscote by the NP & W SA and cost A$7.50 (US$4.90) for adults and A$6 (US$3.90) for children. Times of tours change seasonally, so call **NP & W SA** at © **08/8553 2381** to confirm. Kingscote Tours depart from the reception desk at the Ozone Seafront Hotel. The Penneshaw Penguin Centre has the largest penguin colony on the Island. Tours depart from the Interpretive Centre (adjacent to the beach and Lloyd Collins Reserve) twice per evening. Call the NP & W SA for times, as they can change. Tours cost A$6 (US$3.90) for adults, and A$4.50 (US$2.90) for kids, though children under 12 go free.

For a fabulous, though pricey, day **boat fishing** for everything from King George Whiting, trevally, and snapper to mullet and mackerel, contact **Kangaroo Island Fishing Charters** (© **08/8553 1328;** www.kifishchart.com.au). A day out costs from A$125 (US$82), including lunch; a half-day trip costs A$90 (US$59) and you keep what you catch! American River Fishing Charters (© **0417/869 346** mobile) also runs trips.

Finally, Kangaroo Island is renowned for its fresh food, and across the island you'll see signs beckoning to you to come and have a taste of cheese, honey, wine, or the like. One place worth stopping off at is **Clifford's Honey Farm** (© **08/8553 8295**), which is open daily from 9am to 5pm. The farm is the home of the protected Ligurian honeybee, found nowhere else on earth but on the island. **Island Pure Sheep Dairy** (© **08/8553 9110**) is another worthwhile stop. Tours and tastings are conducted at milking time (1–5pm). It's a great chance to sample delicious sheep's milk, yogurts, and mouthwatering haloumi cheese.

WHERE TO STAY

There are a wide variety of places to choose from, from B&Bs to campgrounds. If you feel like sleeping in one of 40 self-contained cottages or coastal lodgings, then contact **Kangaroo Island Remote and Coastal Farm Accommodation** (© **08/8553 1233;** fax 08/8553 1190; www.ki-ferryconnections.com). Standards vary and prices range from A$65 to A$100 (US$42–US$65) for each. The staff can also arrange lodgings in local farms, homes, and B&Bs for A$60 to A$110 (US$39–US$72) for a double with breakfast.

The NP & W SA (see "Visitor Information," above) also offers basic but comfortable lodgings for rent, including relatively isolated **lighthouse cottages** ★★ at Cape Willoughby, Cape Borda, and Cape du Couedic, from A$21 to A$37 (US$14–US$24) per adult per night—though the minimum charge per stay is between A$49 and A$110 (US$32–US$72) a cottage.

If you're on a super-tight budget, head to the **Penneshaw Youth Hostel,** 43 North Terrace, Penneshaw, Kangaroo Island, SA 5222 (© **08/8553 1284;** fax 08/8553 1295), with dorm beds for A$22 (US$14) and doubles for A$72 (US$47). It costs a few dollars less for YHA members.

Camping is allowed at designated sites around the Island and in National Parks for a minimal fee. There are many beach, river, and bush camping spots to choose from including the Rocky River site within the Flinders Chase National Park.

IN & NEAR KINGSCOTE

Ozone Seafront Hotel   The best known of Kangaroo Island's lodging alternatives, the Ozone gets its name from the aroma from the sea—which virtually laps at its door. It's a nice, centrally located choice offering comfortable rooms with plenty of space; the majority of the more expensive ones have water views of Nepean Bay. Family rooms have a double bed and two single beds.

The Foreshore (P.O. Box 145), Kingscote, SA 5223. © **08/8553 2011.** Fax 08/8553 2249. www.ozonehotel. com. 37 units. A$220–A$286 (US$143–US$186) double; A$242–A$308 (US$157–US$200) Victorian double; A$297–A$374 (US$193–US$243) suite. More expensive prices are for Sat night. Extra person A$13 (US$8.45). AE, DC, MC, V. **Amenities:** 2 restaurants; 3 bars; heated outdoor pool; golf course nearby; Jacuzzi; sauna; tour desk; limited room service; babysitting; laundry service. *In room:* A/C, TV, fridge, coffeemaker, hair dryer, iron.

Wisteria Lodge ★   All rooms at the modern and definitely unglamorous-looking Wisteria Lodge are standard motel-type, with exposed brick walls and gray carpets, boosted by ocean views over Nepean Bay. Deluxe rooms offer a Jacuzzi and queen-size beds. Reservations are essential for the restaurant.

7 Cygnet Rd., Kingscote, SA 5223. © **08/8553 2707.** Fax 08/8553 2200. www.users.on.net/wisteria. Reservations can be made through Flag Inns (© **800/624-3524** in the U.S. and Canada, 0800/892 407 in the U.K., 0800/803 524 in New Zealand, or 13 24 00 in Australia). 20 units. A$140 (US$91) double; A$160 (US$104) triple; A$178 (US$116) double Jacuzzi room; A$200 (US$130) triple Jacuzzi room. Extra adult A$20–A$22 (US$13–US$14), extra child 3–12 A$15–A$19 (US$9.75–US$12). Ask about money-saving packages (with transport to the island, transfers, meals, and day tours). AE, DC, MC, V. **Amenities:** Restaurant; heated outdoor pool; half tennis court; Jacuzzi; children's center; tour desk; car-rental desk; limited business center; limited room service; laundry service; dry cleaning; nonsmoking rooms. *In room:* A/C, TV, minibar, fridge coffeemaker, hair dryer.

IN AMERICAN RIVER

Popular with fishermen and located 37km (23 miles) from Kingscote, American River lacks a beach but offers black swans on Pelican Lagoon. Wild wallabies abound, and egrets, magpies, and cockatoos offer early morning wake-up calls.

Casuarina Holiday Units These simple, country-style units are not flashy, but they offer a clean and cozy budget option. Each comes with a double bed, two singles, and an attached shower.

9 Ryberg Rd., American River, SA 5221. © and fax **08/8553 7020.** 6 units. A$60 (US$39) double; A$50 (US$33) double for more than 1 night. MC, V. **Amenities:** Children's playground; coin-op laundry; barbecue; fish-cleaning facilities. *In room:* TV.

Kangaroo Island Lodge ⟨★⟩ Though Kangaroo Island Lodge was built in 1801, renovations in late 1999 so overhauled the place that you would be hard pressed to find anything rustic remaining. What you have is a very nicely appointed property with pleasant, quiet motel-style rooms, a good swimming pool, Jacuzzi and sauna, and a restaurant and bar (entrees average A$20/US$13). The lodge looks over Pelican Lagoon (famous for its, well, pelicans), but it's a little too far away from it to make the waterview double rooms really worth the extra cost.

Scenic Rd., American River, SA 5221. © **08/8553 7053.** Fax 08/8553 7030. www.kilodge.com.au. 38 units. A$165 (US$107) waterview double; A$135 (US$88) poolside double. A$24 (US$16) extra person. AE, DC, MC, V. **Amenities:** Restaurant; heated outdoor pool; unlit tennis court; game room; tour desk; car-rental desk; limited room service; coin-op laundry; nonsmoking rooms. *In room:* A/C, TV, kitchen (some rooms), fridge, hair dryer, iron.

Wanderers Rest This pleasant guesthouse is set on a hillside with panoramic views across the sea to the mainland. It has large, comfortably furnished rooms with balconies. All rooms come with king-size beds that convert to twins. You get a shower, but no tub. Breakfasts are hearty, packed lunches are available, and dinnertime can be a hoot, with guests sipping beers and wine around the dining-room table and tucking into King George whiting caught that day. There are other meals available, such as steak, lamb chops, local oysters, and a vegetarian stir-fry.

Bayview Rd. (P.O. Box 34), American River, SA 5221. © **08/8553 7140.** Fax 08/8553 7282. www.wanderers rest.com.au. 9 units. A$189 (US$123) double; A$244 (US$158) triple. Rates include full breakfast. Ask about packages and ferry transport deals. AE, DC, MC, V. Limited parking. Children under 12 not accepted. **Amenities:** Restaurant; heated outdoor pool; game room; tour desk; car-rental desk. *In room:* A/C, TV, mini-bar, coffeemaker, hair dryer.

IN PARNDANA

Developed by soldier-settlers after World War II, Parndana today is a rural service center situated a 25-minute drive from Seal Bay and Stokes Bay, and just around the corner from Parndana Wildlife Park, which has more than 50 aviaries with collections of native and other birds, some of them rare and protected.

The Open House ⟨★⟩ The best thing about the Open House is mealtimes, when the guests get together and sit around a communal table and dive into delicious home-cooked meals. The rooms—two with queen-size beds, one with two singles, and a family room sleeping up to four—are comfortable and homey and come with a private bathroom with shower. The owners are friendly and can offer good advice on what to do around the island.

70 Smith St., Parndana, SA 5221. © **08/8559 6113.** Fax 08/8559 6088. www.theopenhouse.com.au. 4 units. A$136 (US$88) per person with dinner and breakfast included; A$104 (US$68) per person with just breakfast included; A$85 (US$55) per child under 14 with dinner and breakfast included; A$104 (US$52) per child with just breakfast included. MC, V. **Amenities:** Restaurant; nonsmoking rooms. *In room:* Ceiling fans, hair dryer.

ON THE SOUTHWEST COAST

Hanson Bay Cabins ⟨★⟩ *(Finds* Located on the southwest coast of the island on the South Coast Road, Hanson Bay Cabins are a row of four comfortable log cabins perched above a fabulous beach. Each cabin has a large picture window facing the southern ocean, and comes with a full kitchen, a bathroom, two bedrooms (including a double bed and three singles in all), and a wood stove. Bring your own food and supplies from Kingscote, American River, or Penneshaw. The ocean can get really wild and dramatic around here with strong offshore winds whipping up the sand and spray. The cottages are near to most of the major attractions, so they make a good base. Salmon are often caught off the beach.

Hanson Bay Company, P.O. Box 614, Kingscote, SA 5225. (℃ **08/8853 2603.** Fax 08/8853 2673. hansbay@ kin.net.au. 6 units. A$132 (US$86) cabin for 2. A$18 (US$12) extra adult, A$12 (US$7.80) extra child. There's an A$18 (US$12) surcharge for staying only 1 night. AE, DC, MC, V. **Amenities:** Bike rental; free coin-op laundry; nonsmoking rooms. *In room:* Kitchen, fridge, coffeemaker, hair dryer, iron (on request).

WHERE TO DINE

You'll find that most accommodations on Kangaroo Island provide meals for guests (at an additional cost, usually). In addition, most day tours around the island include lunch. You'll find a few cheap takeout booths scattered around the island at the most popular tourist spots. For lunch you could get sandwiches at Roger's Deli on Dauncey Street, behind the Ozone Hotel, in Kingscote.

IN PENNESHAW

Dolphin Rock Café FAST FOOD   Plastic tables and chairs and budget meals are what's offered here. The budget meals including individual pizzas, and french fries and gravy, are popular with backpackers. Also on offer are fish and chips, hamburgers, and chicken. Across the road, the fairy penguins come in at dusk.

43 North Terrace (next to the YHA). (℃ **08/8553 1284.** Main courses A$4–A$12 (US$2.60–US$7.80). AE, MC, V. Winter Wed–Mon 7:30am–7:30pm; summer daily 7am–8:30pm.

ELSEWHERE

Cape Willoughby Café ☆☆ LOCAL PRODUCE   This fabulous restaurant is perched on a cliff top on the far eastern tip of the island, right next to Cape Willoughby Lighthouse (an attraction in itself), and about 30km (19 miles) from Penneshaw. One wall is all glass, and there's a veranda outside with terrific ocean views. King George Whiting is a specialty, as are the desserts (the sticky date pudding is mouthwatering). Forty-five-minute tours of the lighthouse leave from the lighthouse office at 10 and 11am, and 12:30 and 2pm daily. They cost A$6 (US$3.90) for adults, A$4.50 (US$2.90) for children, and A$17 (US$11) for a family.

Cape Willoughby. (℃ **08/8553 1333.** Reservations necessary. Main courses A$20–A$27 (US$13–US$18). MC, V. Open 10am–4pm for coffee and cakes; 12.30–2.30pm for lunch.

4 Outback South Australia

South Australia is the driest state in Australia. This is well borne out once you leave behind the parklands of Adelaide and head into the interior. The Outback is as harsh as it is beautiful. Much of it is made up of stony desert, saltpans, and sand hills, roamed by kangaroos and wild goats. After spring rains, though, the area can burst alive with wildflowers.

It was always difficult to travel through these parts, and even today there are only four main routes that traverse it. One of them, the **Birdsville Track,** is famed in Outback history as the trail along which stockmen once drove their herds of cattle south from Queensland. Another, the **Strzelecki Track,** runs through remote sand dune country to Innamincka and on to Coopers Creek.

⟨ Tips **An Outback Travel Warning**

If you intend to drive through the Outback, take care. Distances between points of interest can be vast; water, gas, food, and accommodations are far apart. Always travel with a good map and plenty of advice. If you plan to travel off-road, a four-wheel-drive vehicle is a must.

Both of these tracks cut through the "dog fence"—a 5,600km (3,472-mile) long barrier designed to keep dingoes out of the pastoral lands to the south.

If you follow the **Stuart Highway,** or the **Oodnadatta Track,** you'll pass the mining towns of Coober Pedy, Andamooka, and Mintabie, where people from all over the world have been turned loose in the maddening search for opal. Out here, too, are national parks, such as the daunting Simpson Desert Conservation Park, with its seemingly endless blood-red sand dunes and spinifex plains; and Lake Eyre National Park, with its dried-up salt pan that, during the rare event of a flood, is a temporary home to thousands of water birds.

THE FLINDERS RANGES NATIONAL PARK ⟨⟨
460km (285 miles) N of Adelaide

The dramatic craggy peaks and ridges that make up the Flinders Ranges rise out of the South Australian desert. The colors of the rock vary from deep red to orange, with sedimentary lines visible as they run down the sides of cliffs. Much of the greenery around here is stunted arid land vegetation. Ever since the introduction of a devastating rabbit virus in 1996, and with the continued culling of hundreds of thousands of wild goats, growing shoots and saplings, which for decades were nibbled away before they grew up, have started to turn what was once bare land back into bush. The most remarkable attraction is **Wilpena Pound,** a natural circle of cliff faces that form a gigantic depression on top of a mountainous ledge. The wind whipping over the cliff edges can produce some exhilarating white-knuckle turbulence if you fly over it in a light aircraft. Kangaroos and emus can sometimes be seen wandering around the park, but outside the park kangaroos are heavily culled.

ESSENTIALS
GETTING THERE   By car, you can take Highway 1 out of Adelaide to Port Augusta (3½ hr.), then head east on Route 47 via Quorn and Hawker (another 45 min.). It's another hour to Wilpena Pound. Alternatively, take the scenic route (it doesn't have a specific name) through the Clare Valley (around 5 hr.): From Adelaide head to Gawler and then through the Clare Valley; follow signs to Gladstone, Melrose, Wilmington, and Quorn.

Premier Stateliner (© 08/8415 5555; www.premierstateliner.com.au) runs five buses every day from Adelaide to Port Augusta for A$35 (US$23) one-way. The company also runs buses to Wilpena Pound via Hawker and Quorn, leaving Adelaide at 8:30am on Wednesday and 11am on Friday. Fares each way are A$44 (US$29) to Quorn, A$58 (US$38) to Hawker, and A$63 (US$41) to Wilpena Pound. Buses return to Adelaide from Wilpena Pound at 11am on Thursday, 7:15pm on Friday (arriving in Adelaide at 5am), and 3:05pm on Sunday.

Heading Bush Adventures (www.headingbush.com) has great trips, including a 10-day tour to the Flinders Ranges, the Oodnatta Track, Coober Pedy, the Simpson Desert, Ayres Rock, the Olgas, Kings Canyon, and Aboriginal communities. This remarkable trip, which focuses on Aboriginal culture, costs A$1,200 (US$780) (or A$995/US$647 with a YHA card), and includes meals and bush camping.

Another good operator is **Banksia Adventures** (© **08/8236 9141;** www. banksia-adventures.com.au), which has 1-, 2-, or 4-day trips to the Flinders, either in hotels or camping. The 1-day trip, including a hotel, costs A$225 (US$146), the 2-day trip A$585 (US$380), and the 3-day trip A$925 (US$601). Camping is about 25% cheaper. This company also offers camping trips to salty Lake Eyre when it floods (it flooded in 2000 and was due to flood again at the time of writing), as well as the Great Aussie Pub Crawl. On this trip you fly by light plane from Adelaide and visit remote Outback pubs. You stay overnight at good hotels including The Prairie Hotel in the Flinders and underground at Coober Pedy. The trip costs A$3,795 (US$2,466) and is all inclusive (with as much beer as you can drink).

Covering a huge slice of the Outback from Adelaide is another great operator, **South Australian Scenic Tours** (© **08/8289 3970;** www.oztourism.com.au/ sascenictours), which hits the dirt roads and heads off on 10-day trips up the Birdsville Track to remote townships and historic sites. You continue along the Strezelecki Track to Innamincka (where the explorers Burke and Wills came to a tragic end), cruise on Cooper Creek, and also take in the Sturt Stony Desert and the Flinders Ranges. Expect to see plenty of wildlife, including kangaroos, emus, and possibly even the very rare yellow-footed rock wallaby. The trip costs A$2,167 (US$1,408). A 3-day Flinders Ranges trip with this company costs A$682 (US$443), and a 4-day Kangaroo Island tour is A$946 (US$615).

Most operators will also make up personalized tours on request.

VISITOR INFORMATION   Before setting off, contact the **Flinders Ranges and Outback of South Australia Regional Tourism Association (FROSATA),** at P.O. Box 2083, Port Augusta (© **1800/633 060** in Australia), for advice on roads and conditions. I strongly recommend a visit to the **Wadlata Outback Centre** at 41 Flinders Terrace, Port Augusta (© **08/8642 4511**), an award-winning interactive museum and information center. The museum costs A$7 (US$4.55) for adults and A$4.50 (US$2.90) for children and is open Monday through Friday from 9am to 5:30pm, Saturday and Sunday from 10am to 4pm.

In Hawker, both the Mobil service station and the post office also act as information outlets.

GETTING AROUND   By Car   If you decide to explore on your own using a rental car, I recommend renting one in Adelaide before setting out.

By Camel   Kev's Kamel Kapers (© **08/8648 4299,** or 0419/839 288 mobile phone onboard camel) offers remarkable 2-hour sunset camel safaris for A$25 (US$16); half-day excursions for A$50 (US$33); and full-day safaris including a champagne lunch for A$80 (US$52) for adults and A$60 (US$39) for children under 16. Overnight camel treks are available, and on weekends and public holidays 15-minute rides cost just A$5 (US$3.25). The tours only run from March to the end of October and leave from Hawker (call beforehand for exact pickup spot). Kev is often unreachable, so check with the tourist association for his whereabouts.

WHERE TO STAY

Andu Lodge ⋆   This fabulous backpackers' lodge is one of the best in Australia. Situated in Quorn, in the central Flinders Ranges (42km/26 miles from Port Augusta), this upscale former hotel is air-conditioned in summer, heated in winter, and has nice clean rooms (dorms sleep six). There's also a nice TV room, a laundry, a computer for e-mailing, and a kitchen area. The hostel offers transfers from Port Augusta for A$10 (US$6.50) each way and runs a range of trips with an emphasis on Aboriginal culture and ecotourism. Guests can also rent mountain bikes. Quorn (pop. 1,300) was where the old Ghan railway used to start and finish from, and where part of the movie *Gallipoli* was filmed. The town has four friendly pubs, all serving meals from A$6.50 to A$7.50 (US$4.20–US$4.90). The lodge also offers 1-, 2-, and 3-day tours of the Ranges.

12 First St., Quorn, SA 5043. © 1800/639 933 in Australia, or 08/8648 6655. Fax 08/8648 6898. www. headingbush.com. 64 units. A$50 (US$33) double; A$82 (US$53) family room (sleeps 4); A$24 (US$16) dorm bed; A$29 (US$19) twin. Discounts for YHA members. MC, V. Free parking. Bus: 3 per week, pickup from Port Augusta for A$6 (US$3.90). **Amenities:** Shared lounge with VCR; push-bike rental; tour desk; coin-op laundry; nonsmoking rooms. *In room:* No phone.

Prairie Hotel 🌟🌟 *Finds* If you are going to stay anywhere near the Flinders Ranges, stay here. This tiny, tin-roofed, stonewalled pub offers a memorable experience and is well worth the dusty 89km (55-mile) drive north alongside the Ranges from Hawker on the A83. A new addition to the pub contains nice rooms, each with a queen-size bed and a shower. The older-style rooms are smaller and quaint. Three units have Jacuzzis. The bar out front is a great place to meet the locals and other travelers (who all shake their heads in wonder that this magnificent place is still so undiscovered). Meals here, prepared by "Flinders Feral Food," are top-notch—very nearly the best I've had in Australia. Among their specialties are kangaroo tail soup to start and a mixed grill of emu sausages, camel steak, and kangaroo as a main course. The owner's brother runs remarkable scenic flights over Wilpena Pound and out to the salt lakes. From here you could head to the township of William Creek for a side trip to see the giant salt lake, Lake Eyre, and then onwards west to Coober Pedy.

Corner of High St. and West Terrace, Parachilna, SA 5730. © 08/8648 4844. Fax 08/8648 4606. www.prairie hotel.com.au. 12 units. A$125–A$170 (US$81–US$111) double; A$225 (US$146) double with Jacuzzi. Extra person A$35–A$45 (US$23–US$29). Rates include light breakfast. AE, DC, MC, V. **Amenities:** Restaurant; bar. *In room:* A/C, minibar, coffeemaker.

Wilpena Pound Resort The nearest place to the Wilpena Pound itself, this partly refurbished resort almost monopolizes the overnight tourist market around here. Standard rooms are adequate and offer respite from the summer heat. The self-contained units come with a stove top, a microwave, a basin, and cooking utensils. The resort also operates a campground. Campsites cost A$22 (US$14) per night for two people with power and A$18 (US$12) without power, and A$4 (US$2.60) for each extra person. There are some good walks around the area. Also on offer are half-hour scenic flights over the Ranges for A$95 (US$62) per person for two people, or A$80 (US$52) per person for 20 minutes. They also operate four-wheel-drive tours of the area.

Wilpena Pound, SA 5434. © 1800/805 802 in Australia, or 08/8648 0004. Fax 08/8648 0028. www.wilpena pound.com.au. 60 units. A$115–A$145 (US$75–US$94) motel double; A$160–A$170 (US$104–US$111) self-contained units. Extra adult A$22 (US$6.50), extra child 2–14 A$6.50 (US$4.25). AE, DC, MC, V. **Amenities:** Restaurant; bar; bistro; general store; pool; game room; tour desk; laundry service; 4-wheel-drive tours; scenic flights; nonsmoking rooms. *In room:* A/C, TV, kitchenette (some rooms), fridge, coffeemaker, hair dryer (available at reception), iron (some rooms).

WHERE TO DINE

The **Old Ghan Restaurant** on Leigh Creek Road, Hawker (© **08/8648 4176**), is open for lunch and dinner Wednesday through Sunday; the restaurant used to be a railway station on the Ghan railway line to Alice Springs before the line was shifted sideways due to flooding. The food here is unexciting, but the home-made pies have a following. If you find yourself in Port Augusta, the area's main town, head to the **Standpipe Motor Inn** (© **08/8642 4033**) for excellent Indian food. The rooms here are nice enough, and quiet, and cost A$80 (US$52) for a double.

COOBER PEDY ✦
854km (529 miles) NW of Adelaide; 689km (427 miles) S of Alice Springs

Tourists come to this Outback opal-mining town for one thing: the people. More than 3,500 people, from 44 nations, work mainly underground here—the majority suffering from opal fever, which keeps you digging on the trail of the elusive shimmering rocks. Though some residents are secretive and keep to themselves, many others are colorful characters ready to stop for a chat and spin a few yarns.

Historically, Coober Pedy was a rough place, and it still has a certain Wild West air about it. The first opal was found here in 1915, but it wasn't until 1917 when the Trans Continental Railway was completed, that people began seriously digging for opals. Since then, they have mainly lived underground—not surprising when you encounter the heat, the dust, and the flies for yourself.

The town got its name from the Aboriginal words *kupa piti,* commonly thought to mean "white man's burrow." Remnants of the holes left by early miners are everywhere, mostly in the form of bleached-white hills of waste called "mullock heaps." It's rather discouraged for tourists to wander around the tailing sites because locals get fed up when tourists fall down the mine shafts.

As for the town, there isn't much to look at, except a couple of underground churches, some casual restaurants, a handful of opal stores, and the necessary service-type businesses. In the center of town you'll find lots of outdoor buildings; the hotels and youth hostel have aboveground entrances but rooms below ground. These are all within stumbling distance of each other on the main street.

ESSENTIALS
GETTING THERE   **Regional Express** (© **13 17 13** in Australia; www.regionalexpress.com.au) flies to Coober Pedy from Adelaide. It's a new airline and fares are fluctuating as we update this guide. Check the website for discounted fares and specials. **Greyhound Pioneer** (© **13 20 30** in Australia) runs buses from Adelaide to Coober Pedy for A$76 (US$50) for adults and A$61 (US$40) for children one-way. The trip takes about 12 hours. The bus from Alice Springs to Coober Pedy costs A$75 (US$49) for adults and A$60 (US$39) for children. Passengers bound for Ayres Rock transfer at Erldunda.

If you drive from Adelaide it will take you about 9 hours to reach Coober Pedy along the Stuart Highway. It will take you another 7 hours to drive the 700km (434 miles) to Alice Springs.

VISITOR INFORMATION   The **Coober Pedy Tourist Information Centre,** Hutchison Street, Coober Pedy (© **1800/637 076** in Australia, or 08/8672 5298), is open Monday through Friday from 8:30am to 5pm (closed holidays). A good website, www.opalcapitaloftheworld.com.au, gives a rundown of other adventure operators in the area.

SEEING THE TOWN
Radeka's Downunder Motel (see "Where to Stay," below) runs half-day tours of the opal fields, including a visit to an underground mine. It costs A$30 (US$20) for adults and A$15 (US$9.75) for kids.

If you want to see parts of Australia that most Australians never see, join an honest-to-goodness **Mail Run** for a 12-hour journey out into the bush. Tours leave every Monday and Thursday from **Underground Books** (© **08/8672 5558**) in Coober Pedy (yep, it's a bookshop underground) and travel along 600km (372 miles) of dirt roads to Oodnatta and William Creek cattle station, stopping off at five different stations along the route. It can get pretty hot and dusty outside (think endless horizons of flat lands), but it's relatively comfortable inside the air-conditioned four-wheel-drive, and you'll have the chance to see such wildlife as eagles, emus, and the ever-present kangaroos. Bring your own lunch or buy it along the way. Tours cost around A$120 (US$78) for adults and A$75 (US$49) for children under 12, though kids might find the long trip difficult. This could easily be one of the most memorable experiences you have in Australia, for its up-close-and-personal look at life in the bush.

WHERE TO STAY

The Backpacker's Inn at Radeka's Downunder Motel   Whereas all other "underground" rooms in Coober Pedy are actually built into the side of a hill, the centrally located hostel here is actually underground—some 6.5m (21 ft.) directly below the topside building, that is. This makes for nice all-year-round temperatures. Odd-looking dorms have no doors and are scooped out of the rock. They contain just four beds, though there are two large dorms sleeping up to 20 people. The twin rooms are simply furnished but pleasant. The motel rooms are quite comfortable and come with attached bathrooms with a shower. Some have a kitchenette. Room no. 9 is huge with a double and two sets of bunk beds. All motel rooms are dug out of the side of a hill. Radeka's also runs a good opal tour.

1 Oliver St., Coober Pedy, SA 5723. © 08/8672 5223. Fax 08/86725821. 150 units, 10 motel rooms. Dorm beds A$22 (US$14); A$52 (US$34) double. In motel: A$90 (US$59) double; A$110 (US$72) family suite. A$15 (US$9.75) extra person. AE, MC, V. Free parking. **Amenities:** Bar; kitchen/dining room; tour desk; coin-operated laundry service; TV and video room; pool table. *In room:* Motel only: TV, coffeemaker.

Moments A Fabulous Four-Wheel-Drive Adventure

With a hired vehicle from Adelaide, it's a day's drive north through the Clare Valley wine region to the **Prairie Hotel** (p. 523). Stop off along the way for a traditional Aussie lunch at **Bluey Blundstone's Café** in Melrose (© **08/8666 2173**). The next day it's a 3- to 4-hour drive to William Creek, an Outback town with a takeout restaurant, pub/hotel, satellite phone box, campground, and general store. **Explore the Outback Camel Safaris** (© **08/8672 3968**; www.austcamel.com.au/explore) offers 4-day camel safaris across the desert from here (check alternate ways to get to William Creek from their website). Just 20km (12 miles) before you reach town is a turnoff to **Lake Eyre,** a giant salt lake which flooded in 2000, and again in 2001, and should hold water for a couple of years. **Wrightsair** offers 1-hour flights over Lake Eyre for A$110 (US$72) per person; call © **0418 336 748** (mobile). Camping beside the lake is a magical experience. The next day it's a 166km (103-mile) drive to Coober Pedy, and then a 9-hour drive back to Adelaide.

The Desert Cave Hotel   Though not the only underground hotel in the world (there's another wonderful one in White Cliffs in New South Wales), this is the only one with a pool and Jacuzzi. Personally, I find the place to be a little soul-less. The bar's "pokie" machines are noisy, and you can hear your neighbors in the next room. (Heaven help you if the TV is turned up loud enough for you to hear.) The hotel can arrange transfers from the airport (A$6.50/US$4.25).

Hutchison St., Coober Pedy (P.O. Box 223, Coober Pedy, SA 5723). © 1800/088 521 in Australia, or 08/8672 5688. Fax 08/8672 5198. www.desertcave.com.au. 50 units (19 underground). A$175 (US$114) double; A$195 (US$127) family room sleeping 5. Extra person A$20 (US$13). Ask about packages. AE, DC, MC, V. Free parking. **Amenities:** Restaurant; bar; outdoor pool; golf nearby; health club w/Jacuzzi; sauna; tour desk; car-rental desk (Thrifty only); limited room service; laundry service; dry cleaning; nonsmoking rooms. *In room:* TV, minibar, coffeemaker, hair dryer, iron.

WHERE TO DINE

The **Opal Inn** (© 08/8672 5054) offers good-value counter meals of the typical pub-grub variety. Head to **Traces** (© 08/8672 5147), the township's favorite Greek restaurant, for something a bit different.

5 The Coorong

Few places in the world attract as much wildfowl as the **Coorong,** one of Australia's most precious sanctuaries. The Coorong is made up of an area that includes the mouth of the Murray River, the huge Lake Alexandrina, the smaller Lake Albert, and a long, thin sand spit called the Younghusband Peninsula. A small, but by far the most scenic, part of this area is encompassed in the **Coorong National Park.** The area is under environmental threat due to pollutants coming south via the Murray River from farmlands to the north. It still manages to play host to large colonies of native and visiting birds, such as the Australian pelican, black swans, royal spoonbills, greenshanks, and the extremely rare hooded plover.

If it were possible to count all the birds here you'd probably run out of steam after some 45,000 ducks, 5,000 black swans, 2,000 Cape Barren geese, and 122,000 waders. This last figure is even more significant when you consider it corresponds to a total South Australian population of waders standing at 200,000, and an overall Australian population of some 403,000.

Add to these figures the thousands of pelicans—with around 3,000 birds nesting here it's the largest permanent breeding colony in Australia—and gulls, terns, and cormorants, and you'll realize why the Coorong and Lower Murray Lakes form one of the most important waterbird habitats in Australia.

The national park, which stands out starkly against the degraded farmland surrounding it, is also home to several species of marsupials, including wombats.

The best time to visit the Coorong is in December and January, when the lakes are full of migratory birds from overseas. However, plenty of birds can be spotted year-round. *Note:* Binoculars and patience are highly recommended.

ESSENTIALS

GETTING THERE   The best way to visit the Coorong is by car, though a guided tour of the area is highly recommended once you arrive at either the main settlement of Goolwa on the western fringe of the waterways, or at Meningie, on the eastern boundary. From Adelaide follow the Princes Highway along the coast.

VISITOR INFORMATION   The **Goolwa Tourist Information Centre,** BF Lawrie Lane, Goolwa (© 08/8555 1144; www.alexandrina.sa.gov), has information on the area and can book accommodations. It's open from 9am to 5pm daily.

GETTING AROUND   The best operator in the area is **Coorong Nature Tours** (© **08/8574 0037,** or 0428/714 793 mobile phone; www.lm.net. au/~coorongnat), based in Narrung. The tours are run by David Dadd, a delightful, unassuming Cockney, who fell in love with the Coorong when he arrived at the age of 11. He offers memorable 1-, 2-, and 3-day tours of the area, with pickup either in Meningie or Adelaide. Full-day tours cost A$132 (US$86) per person from Meningie or A$185 (US$120) per person from Adelaide. Reservations are essential.

WHERE TO STAY

There are plenty of hotels, B&Bs, campgrounds, and trailer parks in Goolwa and along the main road that runs parallel to the national park. One of the ones I prefer is the **Goolwa Camping and Tourist Park,** 40 Castle Rd., Goolwa, SA 5214 (© **08/8555 2144**). It has 70 trailer sites and a large area for tents. A two-berth van costs A$25 (US$16) a night, and a six-berth A$35 (US$23) for the first two people and A$5 (US$3.25) for an extra adult or A$3 (US$1.95) for an extra child. Bring your own bedding.

Grahams Castle Resort   This former conference center is classified as a three-star backpacker's accommodations. Rooms are very basic with two single beds, heating, and a shower shared between two rooms. It's very popular with budget groups, so it could get noisy.

Corner of Castle and Bradford sts., Goolwa, SA 5214. © 1800/243 303 in Australia, or 08/8555 3300. Fax 08/8555 3828. 22 units. A$15 (US$9.75) per person. AE, DC, MC, V. **Amenities:** Restaurant; bar; heated outdoor pool; tennis court; tour desk. *In room:* No phone.

Poltalloch ★★   Located smack in the middle of nowhere on the eastern edge of the Coorong, Poltalloch is a working farm property—with plenty of cows, ducks, chickens, and dogs wandering about—that seems more like a village. The whole place is classified by the National Trust of South Australia, and history is evident everywhere, from the cottages once used by farmhands to the giant wooden shearing shed and other outbuildings crammed with relics from the past.

You can stay in a choice of five cottages on the property. The Shearer's Hut is a stone cottage that sleeps up to nine people; the Overseers stone cottage sleeps up to eight people; the Boundary Rider's Cottage is built of timber, iron, and stone, and sleeps five; and the Station Hand's Cottage sleeps four. The Shearer's Quarters is mainly for large groups and sleeps 12. All of the units are modern and comfortable inside and have their own kitchen facilities and barbecues. I stayed in the Station Hand's Cottage, once the home of Aboriginal workers. I loved the mix of rural feeling and modern conveniences.

There's a private beach if you want to swim in the lake, and guests have the use of a dinghy, a canoe, and a Ping-Pong table. Historical tours of the property cost A$9 (US$5.85) for adults, and A$4.50 (US$2.90) for children with a minimum charge of A$27 (US$18). Bookings are essential. Breakfast provisions are available for A$13 (US$8.45) per person. Coorong Nature Tours will pick you up from here for no extra charge. There's plenty of bird life all around.

Poltalloch. P.M.B. 3, Narrung via Tailem Bend, SA 5260. © 08/8574 0088. Fax 08/8574 0065. www. poltalloch.com.au. 3 units. A$105–A$175 (US$68–US$114) per cottage. Extra person A$25 (US$16). MC, V. **Amenities:** Tennis court; use of watersports equipment; nonsmoking rooms. *In room:* A/C, TV, kitchen, fridge, coffeemaker, iron.

11

Melbourne

by Marc Llewellyn

Melbourne (pronounced *Mel*-bun), the capital of Victoria and Australia's second-largest city, with a population well over three million, is a cultural melting pot. For a start, more people of Greek descent live here than in any other city except Athens. Chinese, Italian, Vietnamese, and Lebanese immigrants have all left their mark. In fact, almost one-third of Melburnians were born overseas or have parents who were born overseas. With such a diverse population, and with trams rattling through the streets and a host of stately European architecture surrounding you, you could easily forget you're in Australia.

Melbourne has a reputation of being at the head of the pack when it comes to shopping, restaurants, fashion, music, nightlife, and cafe culture. It frequently beats out other state capitals in bids for major international concerts, plays, exhibitions, and sporting events, such as the Formula One Grand Prix.

The city also revels in a healthy rivalry with its northern neighbor, Sydney, but it's interesting to note that almost every Melbournian adores their city—often described as the "most livable" in the world—whereas Sydneysiders are mostly half-hearted in their praise for their own abode.

Melbourne's roots go back to the 1850s, when gold was found in the surrounding hills. British settlers took up residence and have since prided themselves on coming freely to their city, rather than having been forced here in convict chains. The city grew wealthy and remained largely a conservative bastion until World War II, when another wave of immigration, this time mainly from southern Europe, made it a more relaxed place.

1 Orientation

ARRIVING

BY PLANE Melbourne's main international and domestic airport is **Tullamarine Airport,** located 22km (14 miles) northwest of the city center. If you're traveling from Sydney, the flight will take you around 1 hour, 20 minutes. It's a 5-minute walk between the international and domestic terminals. Travelers' information desks are open on both levels of the international terminal building from 6am until the last flight. There are snack bars, a restaurant, currency-exchange facilities, and duty-free shops in the international terminal. There's also a post office, open daily from 9am to 5pm, but stamps are available from vending machines after hours, as well as mail boxes. ATMs are available at both terminals. Showers are on the first floor of the international area. Baggage trolleys are free in the international baggage claim hall but cost A$2 (US$1.30) if hired in the parking lot, departure lounge, or the domestic terminal. Baggage lockers cost A$4 to A$8 (US$2.60–US$5.60) per day, depending on size. The **Hilton Melbourne Airport** is walking distance from the terminals (© **03/9338 2322**).

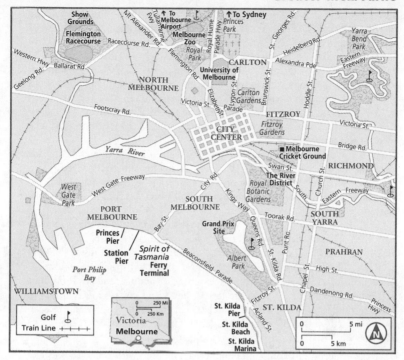

Thrifty (© **1800/652 008** in Australia, or 03/9330 1522), **Budget** (© **13 27 27** in Australia), **Avis** (© **1800/225 533** in Australia, or 03/9338 1800), and **Hertz** (© **13 30 39** in Australia, or 03/9379 9955), **Delta Europcar** (© **1300/ 131390** in Australia, or 03/9417 2311) have airport rental desks. The Tullamarine freeway to and from the airport joins with the Citylink, an electronic tollway system. Drivers need a CityLink pass. A 24-Hour pass costs $9.10 (US$5.90). Check with your car-rental company.

Skybus (© **03/9335 2811;** www.skybus.com.au) picks up passengers in front of the baggage claim area every 15 minutes from 6am to 12pm, and hourly from 12pm to 6:am. The trip into the center takes around 35 minutes and costs A$13 (US$7.80) one-way for adults and A$5 (US$3.25) for children under 15. The service travels direct to Spencer Street Railway Station, where free shuttle buses transfer you to city hotels. When you want to return to the airport, book the Skybus service a few hours in advance and allow at least 40 minutes for traveling time. Buy tickets on board, or from Skybus desks outside the baggage claim areas.

A taxi to the city center takes about 30 minutes and costs around A$45 to A$50 (US$29–US$35).

An alternative is the **Super Shuttle,** a multihire limousine service that departs approximately every 20 minutes from in front of the arrival terminal. Airport to city hotels costs $16 (US$10). Bookings are not necessary from the airport, but from the city call © **03/9338 4401.**

BY TRAIN   Interstate trains arrive at **Spencer Street Railway Station,** at Spencer and Little Collins streets (5 blocks from Swanston St. in the city center). Taxis and buses connect with the city. The **Sydney-Melbourne XPT** travels between Australia's two largest cities daily; trip time is 10½ hours. The full fare for economy class is A$110 (US$72) on the day of travel; A$66 (US$43) 1 week in advance; and A$55 (US$36) 2 weeks in advance. The first-class fare is A$154 (US$100) on day of travel, A$92 (US$60) 1 week in advance, and A$77 (US$50) 2 weeks in advance. A first-class sleeper costs $231 (US$150) on day of travel, A$169 (US$110) 1 week in advance, and A$154 (US$100) 2 weeks in advance. Students presenting an ISIC international student card travel at "2 week in advance price" in all categories, even if booked on the day of travel. For more information, contact **Countrylink** (© **13 22 32** in Australia; www.countrylink.info).

The *Overland* provides daily service to and from Melbourne and Adelaide (trip time: 12 hr.). Fares are A$57 (US$37) in economy and A$105 (US$68) for a first-class sleeper. You can transport your car on the *Overland* for A$168. For more information, contact **Great Southern Railways** (© **13 21 47** in Australia; www.gsr.com.au).

Daylink services also connect Melbourne with Adelaide. This trip is by train from Melbourne to Bendigo, and by bus from Bendigo to Adelaide. Total trip time is 11 hours, and the fare is A$60 (US$39) economy and A$69 (US$45) first-class. The **Canberra Link** connects Melbourne with the nation's capital, and consists of a train journey from Melbourne to Wadonga, and bus from there to Canberra. The journey takes around 11 hours and costs A$45 (US$30) in economy, and A$64 (US$42) in first-class. For train information and reservations for the daylink services to Adelaide and Canberra, contact **V/Line** (© **13 61 96** in Australia; www.vlinepassenger.com.au).

BY BUS   Several bus companies connect Melbourne with other capitals and regional areas of Victoria. Among the biggest are **Greyhound Pioneer** and **McCafferty's** (© **13 20 30** in Australia, or 03/9670 2533; www.greyhound.com.au). Greyhound Pioneer buses and McCafferty's coaches depart and arrive at Melbourne's Transit Centre, at 58 Franklin St., 2 blocks north of the Spencer Street Railway Station. New arrivals can take a tram or taxi from the station to their hotel. **V/Line buses** (© **13 61 96** in Australia), which travel all over Victoria, depart from the Spencer Street Bus Terminal.

BY CAR   You can drive from Sydney to Melbourne along the Hume Highway (a straight trip of about 9½ hr.), although a much nicer route is via the coastal Princes Highway, for which you will need a minimum of 2 days, with stops. For information on all aspects of road travel in Victoria, contact the **Royal Automotive Club of Victoria** (© **03/9607 2222;** www.racv.com.au).

VISITOR INFORMATION

The first stop on any visitor's itinerary should be the **Melbourne Visitor Centre,** Federation Square, Swanston Street and Flinders Street (© **03/9658 9658**). The center, which opened in 2002, serves as a one-stop-shop for tourism information, accommodations and tour bookings, event ticketing, public transport information, and ticket sales. Also here are an ATM, self-help Internet terminals, and interactive multimedia providing information on Melbourne and Victoria. The center is open 7 days from 9am to 6pm. The Melbourne Greeter Service also operates from the Melbourne Visitor Centre. This service is available in 20 different languages and connects visitors to enthusiastic local volunteers who offer free one-on-one orientation tours of the city. Book at least 3 days in advance (© **03/9658 9658;** greeter@melbourne.vic.gov.au).

You'll find some information services at **Information Victoria,** 356 Collins St. (© **1300/366 356** in Australia). Staffed information booths for Melbourne Visitors Centre are also found in Bourke Street Mall. In the central city area, also look for **Melbourne's City Ambassadors** for tourist information and directions.

Good websites on the city include CitySearch Melbourne, http://melbourne. citysearch.com.au; www.melbourne.vic.gov.au; and www.visitmelbourne.com.

CITY LAYOUT

Melbourne is situated on the Yarra River and stretches inland from Port Philip Bay, which lies to its south. Look at a map, and you'll see a distinct central oblong area surrounded by Flinders Street to the south, Latrobe Street to the north, Spring Street to the east, and Spencer Street to the west. Cutting north-to-south through its center are the two main shopping thoroughfares, Swanston Street and Elizabeth Street. A series of cross streets, including Bourke Street Mall (a pedestrians-only shopping promenade), runs between these major thorough-fares. If you continue south along Swanston Street, and over the river, it turns into St. Kilda Road, which runs to the coast. The central area is surrounded by Melbourne's various urban "villages," including South Yarra, Richmond, Carl-ton, and Fitzroy. The seaside suburb of St. Kilda known for its diverse selection of restaurants is also positioned very near to the beach. If you've visited Sydney, you'll find Melbourne's city center to be smaller and far less congested with peo-ple and cars.

NEIGHBORHOODS IN BRIEF

Melbourne is huge. At more than 6,110 sq. km (7,383 sq. miles), it's one of the biggest cities in the world. Below are the areas of most interest to visitors.

City Center Made up of a grid of streets north of the Yarra River, the city center is bordered to the south by Flinders Street and to the north by Latrobe Street. The eastern and western borders are Spring Street and Spencer Street, respectively. There's some good shopping and charming cafes, and in recent years an active nightlife has sprung up with the opening of a swath of funky bars and restaurants playing live and recorded music to suit all ages. The gateway to the city is Flinders Street Station, with its dome and clock tower, flanked by the stunning new Federation Square precinct.

Chinatown This colorful section of the city is centered on Little Bourke Street between Swanston and Exhi-bition streets. The area marks Aus-tralia's oldest permanent Chinese settlement, dating from the 1850s, when a few boardinghouses catered to Chinese prospectors lured by gold

rushes. Plenty of cheap restaurants crowd its alleyways. Tram: Any to the city.

Carlton North of the city center, Carlton is a rambling inner-city suburb famous for the Italian restaurants along Lygon Street with outdoor seating—though the qual-ity of the food served is variable. It's the home of the University of Mel-bourne, so there's a healthy student scene. From Bourke Street Mall count on a 15-minute walk to reach the restaurant strip. Tram: 1 or 22 from Swanston Street.

Fitzroy A ruggedly Bohemian place, 2km (1¼ miles) north of the city center, Fitzroy is raw and funky, filled with students and artists and popular for people-watching. Fitzroy revolves around Brunswick Street, with its cheap restaurant scene, busy cafes, late-night book-shops, art galleries, and pubs. Around the corner, on Johnston

Street, is a growing Spanish quarter with tapas bars, Flamenco restaurants, and Spanish clubs. Tram: 11 from Collins Street.

Richmond One of Melbourne's earliest settlements is a multicultural quarter based around historic streets and back lanes. Victoria Street is reminiscent of Ho Chi Minh City, with Vietnamese sights, sounds, aromas, and restaurants everywhere. Bridge Road is a bustling cut-price fashion precinct. Tram: 48 or 75 from Flinders Street to Bridge Road; 70 from Batmans Avenue at Princes Bridge to Swan Street; 109 from Bourke Street to Victoria Street.

Southgate & Southbank This flashy entertainment district on the banks of the Yarra River opposite Flinders Street Station (linked by a pedestrian bridge) is home to the Crown Casino—Australia's largest gaming venue. Southbank has a myriad of themed restaurants, bars, cafes, nightclubs, cinemas, and designer shops. On the city side of the river is the new Melbourne Aquarium. All are a 10-minute stroll from Flinders Street Station. Tram: 8 from Swanston Street.

Docklands Near the city center, at the rear of the Spencer Street station, this old industrial docking area has become the biggest development in Melbourne. NewQuay on the waterfront has a diverse range of restaurants, shops, and cinemas. To celebrate the dominance of the Australian Rules Football, Melbournians recently constructed a purpose-built 52,000 seat stadium, the Telstra Dome, to house their favorite game. Docklands is accessible by the free city circle tram.

St. Kilda Hip and Bohemian in a shabby-chic sort of way, this bayside suburb (6km/3¾ miles south of the city center) has Melbourne's highest concentration of restaurants,

ranging from glitzy to cheap, as well as some superb cake shops and delis. Historically it was Melbourne red-light district. The Esplanade hugs a pleasant "beach" (with brown waters) and is the scene of a lively arts and crafts market on Sundays. Acland Street houses many restaurants. Check out Luna Park, one of the world's oldest fun parks, built in 1912, and take a ride on the historic wooden roller coaster. Tram: 10 or 12 from Collins Street; 15 or 16 from Swanston Street; 96 from Bourke Street.

South Yarra/Prahan This posh part of town is crammed with chic boutiques, cinemas, nightclubs, and galleries. Chapel Street is famous for its well-heeled eateries and designer fashion houses, while Commercial Road is popular with the gay and lesbian community. Just off Chapel Street in Prahan is Greville Street, a Bohemian enclave featuring retro boutiques and music outlets. Every Sunday the Greville Street Market offers arts, crafts, old clothes, and jewelry from noon to 5pm. Tram: 8 or 72 from Swanston Street.

South Melbourne One of the city's oldest working-class districts, South Melbourne is known for its historic buildings, old-fashioned pubs and hotels, and markets. Tram: 12 from Collins Street; 1 from Swanston Street.

The River District The muddy-looking Yarra River runs southeast past the fabulous Botanic Gardens and nearby to other attractions such as the Victorian Arts Centre, the National Gallery of Victoria, the Sidney Myer Music Bowl, and the Melbourne Cricket Ground (MCG), all described later in this chapter. Birrarung Marr is the first new major parkland in Melbourne in over a 100 years.

Williamstown A lack of extensive development has left this outer waterfront suburb with a rich architectural heritage centered on Ferguson Street and Nelson Place—both reminiscent of old England. On the Strand overlooking the sea are a line of bistros and restaurants, and a World War II warship museum. Ferry: from Southgate, the World Trade Center, or St. Kilda Pier.

2 Getting Around

BY PUBLIC TRANSPORTATION

Trams, trains, and buses are operated by several private companies including the National Bus Company, Yarra Trams, and Connex to name a few. Generally, both tourists and locals travel around the city and inner suburbs by tram.

BY TRAM Melbourne has the oldest tram network in the world. Trams are still an essential part of the city, and a major cultural icon. There are several hundred trams running over 325km (202 miles) of track. Instead of phasing this non-smoggy method of transport out, Melbourne is busily expanding the network.

Tram travel within the city and to all suburbs mentioned in this chapter costs A$1.80 (US$1.20) for adults, A90¢ (US52¢) for children for a single journey. Or you can buy a **2-Hour Metcard** good for unlimited transport on buses or trains for up to 2 hours. The 2-Hour Metcards cost A$2.70 (US$1.75) for adults and A$1.50 (US$1) for children. If you plan to pack in the sightseeing, try the **Zone 1 Metcard Daily ticket,** which allows travel on all transport (trams and trains) within the city and close surrounding suburbs mentioned in this chapter from 5:30am to midnight (when transportation stops). It costs A$5.20 for adults and A$2.70 (US$1.75) for children. **Metcard Weekly tickets** cost A$23 (US$15) for adults and A$11 (US$7.40) for children.

Buy single-trip and 2-hour tram tickets at ticket machines on trams, special ticket offices (such as at the tram terminal on Elizabeth St., near the corner of Flinders St.), at most newsdealers, and at Metcard vending machines at many railway stations. A Metcard needs to be validated by the Metcard Validator machine on the tram, station platforms, or on board buses before each journey; the only exception to this is the 2-hour Metcard ticket purchased from a vending machine on a tram, which is automatically validated starting from that journey only. Vending machines on trams only accept coins—but give change—whereas larger vending machines at train stations give change up to A$10 (US$6.50).

You can pick up a free route map from the Melbourne Visitors Centre, at Federation Square, or at the **Met Information Centre,** 103 Elizabeth St., at the corner of Collins Street (© **13 16 38** in Australia; www.victrip.com.au), which is open Monday through Friday from 8:30am to 4:30pm, and Saturday from 9am to 1pm.

The **City Circle Tram** is the best way to get around the center of Melbourne—and it's free. These burgundy-and-cream trams travel a circular route between all

ⓥ*Value* Money-Saving Transit Pass

The **Getabout Travelcard,** which can be used by two adults and up to four children, is good 1 day of travel on Saturdays, Sundays, and public holidays only. The card costs A$11 (US$7). Buy it at newsdealers.

the major central attractions, and past shopping malls and arcades. The trams run, in both directions, every 10 minutes between 10am and 6pm, except Good Friday and Christmas Day. City Circle Tram stops are marked with a burgundy sign.

Trams can be hailed at numbered green-and-gold tram-stop signs. To get off the tram, press the red button near handrails or pull the cord above your head.

BY EXPLORER BUS

Melbourne Explorer Gray Line (✆ **1300/858 687** in Australia) operates buses that pick up and drop off at 21 stops around the city, including the Melbourne Aquarium, Crown Casino, Queen Victoria Markets, Captain Cook's Cottage, Chinatown, Melbourne Zoo, and the Botanic Gardens, among others. There's full commentary on board. You can hop on and off during the day. A bus returns to each stop half-hourly. The first bus leaves Town Hall on Swanston Street at 9:30am and the last at 2:30pm. Tickets cost A$32 (US$21) for adults, A$16 (US$10) for children under 14. Buy from the driver or at the little tour booth outside Melbourne Town Hall.

BY TAXI

Cabs are plentiful in the city, but it may be difficult to hail one in the city center late Friday and Saturday nights. Taxi companies include **Silver Top** (✆ **13 10 08** in Australia, or 03/9345 3455), **Embassy** (✆ **13 17 55** in Australia, or 03/9277 3444), and **Black Cabs Combined** (✆ **13 22 27** in Australia). A large, illuminated rooftop light indicates that a cab is free.

BY CAR

Driving in Melbourne is not always fun. Roads can be confusing, there are trams and aggressive drivers everywhere, and there is a strange rule about turning right from the left lane at major intersections in the downtown center (which leaves the left-hand lane free for oncoming trams and through traffic). Here, you must wait for the lights to turn amber before turning. Also, you must always stop behind a tram if it stops, as passengers usually step directly into the road. Add to this the general lack of parking spaces and expensive hotel valet-parking charges, and you'll know why it's better to get on a tram instead. For road rules pick up a copy of the Victorian Road Traffic handbook from bookshops or from a **Vic Roads** office (✆ **131171** in Australia for the nearest office).

Major car-rental companies, all with offices at Tullamarine Airport, include **Avis,** 400 Elizabeth St. (✆ **03/9663 6366**); **Budget,** 398 Elizabeth St. (✆ **03/9203 4844**); **Hertz,** 97 Franklin St. (✆ **03/9698 2555**); **Thrifty,** 390 Elizabeth St. (✆ **03/9663 5200**); and **National,** 110 A'beckett St. (✆ **13 10 45** in Australia). Expect to pay from A$40 (US$26) a day for a small car.

 FAST FACTS: **Melbourne**

American Express The main Amex office is at 235 Collins St. (✆ **03/9633 6333**). It's open Monday through Friday from 9am to 5:30pm, and Saturday from 9am to noon.

Business Hours In general, stores are open Monday through Wednesday from 9am to 5:30pm, Friday from 9am to 9pm, Saturday from 9am to 5:30pm, and Sunday from 10am to 5pm. The larger department stores stay open on Thursday till 6pm and Friday until 9pm. Banks are open Monday through Thursday from 9:30am to 4pm, and Friday from 9:30am to 5pm.

Camera Repair **Vintech Camera Repairs,** 5th Floor, 358 Lonsdale St. (✆ 03/ **9602 1820,** or 0418-515 662 mobile), is well regarded.

Consulates The following English-speaking countries have consulates in Melbourne: United States, Level 6, 553 St. Kilda Rd. (✆ **03/9526 5900**); United Kingdom, Level 17, 90 Collins St. (✆ **03/9650 4155**); and Canada, 1st Floor, 123 Camberwell Rd., Hawthorn (✆ **03/9811 9999**).

Dentist Call the **Dental Emergency Service** (✆ **03/9341 0222**) for emergency referral to a local dentist.

Doctor The "casualty" department at the **Royal Melbourne Hospital,** Grattan Street, Parkville (✆ **03/9342 7000**) responds to emergencies. The **Traveller's Medical & Vaccination Centre,** 2nd Floor, 393 Little Bourke St. (✆ **03/9602 5788**), offers full vaccination and travel medical services.

Emergencies In an emergency, call ✆ **000** for police, ambulance, or the fire department.

Internet Access There are numerous Internet cafes along Elizabeth Street, between Flinders and La Trobe streets, and also around Flinders Lane, and Little Bourke Street in the Chinatown area. Most are open from early until well into the night.

Lost Property Contact your nearest police station, or call in at the Melbourne Town Hall, Swanston Street (✆ **03/9658 9774**).

Pharmacies The **McGibbony & Beaumont Pharmacy** is in the Grand Hyatt hotel complex, 123 Collins St. (✆ **03/9650 1823**). It's open Monday through Thursday from 8am to 6:30pm, Friday from 8am to 7pm, Saturday from 9:30am to 2:30pm, and Sunday from 9:30am to noon.

Post Office The well-known **General Post Office (G.P.O.)** at the corner of Bourke Street Mall and Elizabeth Street has closed and will be made into a new hotel. Postal services are now available at two nearby locations: De Bono Centre, 257 Collins St., or corner of Elizabeth and Little Bourke streets. Both are open Monday through Friday 8:30am to 5:00pm. Poste Restante hours are the same.

Safety St. Kilda might be coming up in the world, but walking there alone at night still isn't wise. Parks and gardens can also be risky at night, as can the area around the King Street nightclubs.

Taxes Sales tax, where it exists, is included in the price, as is the 10% Goods and Services Tax (GST). There is no hotel tax as yet in Melbourne.

Telephones For Directory Assistance call ✆ **1223**; for International Directory Assistance call ✆ **1225**.

Weather Call ✆ **1196** for recorded weather information.

3 Where to Stay

Getting a room is generally easy enough on weekends, when business travelers are back home. You need to book well in advance, however, during the city's hallmark events (say, the weekend before the Melbourne Cup, and during the

Grand Prix and the Ford Australia Open). Hostels in the St. Kilda area tend to fill up quickly in December and January.

Once considered dead after offices closed for the day, the city center has been rejuvenated in recent years, and you'll feel right in the heart of the action if you stay here. Otherwise, the suburbs are all exciting satellites, with good street life, restaurants, and pubs—just a quick tram ride from the city center. (Transportation from the airport to the suburbs is a little more expensive and complicated than to the city center, however.)

If you arrive without booked accommodations, contact either of the **travelers' information desks** (© 03/9297 1814), located on both floors of the international terminal and open daily from 6am to the last flight. Or try the **Best of Victoria Booking Service,** at new Melbourne Visitor Centre at Federation Square (© 03/9650 3663), open weekdays from 9am to 6pm and weekends from 9am to 5pm.

IN THE CITY CENTER
VERY EXPENSIVE

Crown Towers 🏨🏨   One of Melbourne's finest hotels, Crown Towers is part of the Crown Casino complex, on the banks of the Yarra River. The hotel itself is grand and impressive. People often gasp as they enter the glittering lobby paved in black marble. This leads on to an enormous collection of gambling machines (called "pokies" in Australia), as well as gaming tables. Upstairs in the hotel, standard guest rooms are cozy. Superior guest rooms occupy floors 5 to 15— those above the 10th floor have spectacular city views. Deluxe rooms, which run up to the 28th floor, are similar, but all have great views. The hotel is a 10-minute walk from the main shopping streets, although trams stop right outside.

Crown Casino offers 24-hour gambling. The 900-seat Showroom features live entertainment nightly, and a 14-screen cinema complex and three cabaret theaters provide additional activities. There are plenty of eateries and designer shops around here, too.

8 Whiteman St., Southbank, Melbourne 3006. © **1800/811653** in Australia, or 03/9292 6868. Fax 03/9292 6600. www.crownltd.com.au. 500 units. A$720 (US$468) double; A$1150–A$1,250 (US$747–US$812) suite. Extra person A$55 (US$36). Children under 12 stay free in parent's room. AE, DC, MC, V. Parking A$25 (US$16). **Amenities:** 3 restaurants; Olympic-size indoor pool; health club; concierge; tour desk; car-rental desk; business center; 24-hr. room service; massage; babysitting; laundry service; same-day dry cleaning; non-smoking rooms; executive rooms. *In room:* A/C, TV w/pay movies, dataport, minibar, coffeemaker, hair dryer, iron.

Grand Hyatt Melbourne 🏨🏨   The Grand Hyatt is a glitzy, glamorous affair, situated in the best part of town, just a short walk from Swanston Street, Elizabeth Street, Chinatown, and public transport. Rooms are large and luxurious, and come with a nice-size marble bathroom and all those details you'd expect from a five-star establishment. Prices vary with the view over the city, which can be almost Hong Kong–like from the top floors. Regency Club guests get free sushi and drinks in the evening, snacks all day, and a complimentary breakfast. Monsoon's is a popular late-night disco in the hotel.

123 Collins St., Melbourne, VIC 3000. © **13 12 34** in Australia, 800/233-1234 in the U.S. and Canada, or 03/8843 1300. Fax 03/9650 3491. www.melbourne.grand.hyatt.com. 547 units. A$450 (US$292) Hyatt Guest double; A$570 (US$370) deluxe double; A$600 (US$390) Regency Club double; A$840–A$3,300 (US$546–US$2,145) suite. Extra person A$55 (US$33). Children under 18 stay free in parent's room. Ask about weekend rates and packages. AE, DC, MC, V. Parking A$4 (US$2.60). **Amenities:** 2 restaurants; large indoor pool; 2 outdoor lighted tennis courts; health club; concierge; tour desk; car-rental desk; business center; 24-hr. room service; in-room massage; babysitting; laundry service; same-day dry cleaning; nonsmoking rooms; executive-level rooms. *In room:* A/C, TV w/pay movies, dataport, minibar, coffeemaker, hair dryer.

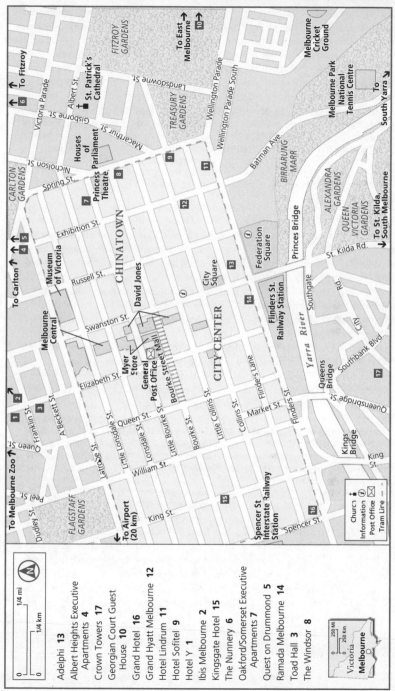

Melbourne Accommodations

Adelphi **13**
Albert Heights Executive Apartments **4**
Crown Towers **17**
Georgian Court Guest House **10**
Grand Hotel **16**
Grand Hyatt Melbourne **12**
Hotel Lindrum **11**
Hotel Sofitel **9**
Hotel Y **1**
Ibis Melbourne **2**
Kingsgate Hotel **15**
The Nunnery **6**
Oakford/Somerset Executive Apartments **7**
Quest on Drummond **5**
Ramada Melbourne **14**
Toad Hall **3**
The Windsor **8**

Hotel Sofitel 🦘🦘 I guarantee you'll like this beautiful luxury hotel, located in the best area of Collins Street, just a short walk from the major shopping and business area. The hotel features a glass-topped atrium that allows natural light to flood in. Rooms are large and very pleasant, with high-quality furniture, two TVs, and a large bathroom with a tub/shower combination. More expensive rooms have two walls of tall windows and magnificent views over the city. The service is very impressive.

25 Collins St., Melbourne, VIC 3000. ℂ 1300/65 65 65 in Australia, 800/221-4542 in the U.S. and Canada, 0800/44 4422 in New Zealand, or 03/9653 0000. Fax 03/9650 4261. www.sofitel.com. 363 units. A$274 double (US$178); A$374–A$1,700 (US$243–US$1,105) suite. Extra person A$44 (US$29). 1 child under 12 stays free in parent's room. Ask about weekend rates and packages. AE, DC, MC, V. Parking A$26 (US$17). **Amenities:** 2 restaurants; bar; exercise room; Jacuzzi; concierge; tour desk; car-rental desk; business center; shopping arcade; 24-hr. room service; babysitting; laundry service; same-day dry cleaning; nonsmoking rooms. *In room:* A/C, TV/VCR, dataport, minibar, coffeemaker, hair dryer, iron.

The Windsor 🦘🦘 The Windsor is Australia's only surviving authentic "grand" hotel. It opened in 1883, literally as "The Grand," and was restored to its original condition by Oberoi Hotels International. This charmingly upper-crust establishment oozes sophistication and has hosted such notable guests as Lauren Bacall, Muhammad Ali, and Omar Sharif. The lobby is luxuriously carpeted, and the staff friendly and efficient. Standard rooms are comfortable, with high ceilings and tasteful furnishings. Each has a good-size bathroom. Deluxe rooms are twice as big, and many have striking views of Parliament House and the Melbourne Cathedral across the way. Suites are huge and furnished with antiques. Guests can choose from among 10 types of pillows, including an aromatherapy version filled with rose petals and herbs. The Windsor is a member of both Leading Hotels of the World and Small Luxury Hotels of the World.

The **Grand Ballroom,** with ornate ceilings, leather furniture, gorgeous carpets, and plenty of gold leaf, is a most impressive place to eat; it's open to nonguests for a buffet lunch Fridays at noon.

103 Spring St., Melbourne, VIC 3000. ℂ 1800/033 100 in Australia, or 03/9633 6000. Fax 03/9633 6001. www.thewindsor.com.au. 180 units. A$500 (US$325) superior double; A$580 (US$377) deluxe double; A$650–A$2400 (US$393–US$1,560) suite. AE, DC, MC, V. Parking A$20 (US$13). **Amenities:** Restaurant; 2 bars; health club; concierge; business center; 24-hr. room service; babysitting; laundry service; dry cleaning service. *In room:* A/C, TV w/pay movies, minibar, coffeemaker, hair dryer, iron.

EXPENSIVE

Adelphi 🦘 It may be worth staying in this designer boutique hotel, a minute's walk from the city center, just for the experience of taking a dip in its top-floor 25m (82-ft.) lap pool, which juts out from the end of the building and hangs over the city streets below. The pool has a glass bottom, so you can watch pedestrians below as you float upside down. The rooms are similarly modernist, with colorful leather seating and lots of burnished metal. Within the hotel is Ezard, a particularly well-regarded restaurant offering Modern Australian fare at its best. You might find some of the staff to be quite self-important, though, so just smile and humor them.

187 Flinders Lane, Melbourne, VIC 3000. ℂ 03/9650 7555, or 1800/800 177 in Australia. Fax 03/9650 2710. www.adelphi.com.au. 34 units (most with shower only). A$305 (US$198) standard double; A$340 (US$221) deluxe double; A$570 (US$370) executive suite. Rates include breakfast. Extra person A$65 (US$42). AE, DC, MC, V. Parking A$14 (US$9.10). **Amenities:** Restaurant; cafe/bar; heated outdoor pool; exercise room; sauna; bike rental; concierge; tour desk; business center; babysitting; same-day dry cleaning; nonsmoking rooms; executive rooms. *In room:* A/C, TV, dataport, DVD/CD, minibar, coffeemaker, hair dryer, iron.

Grand Hotel ⭐⭐ This majestic former railway department headquarters is striking for its remarkable scale and imposing Italianate facade. Building started on the six-story site in 1887, and additions were still being made in 1958. It finally became a hotel in late 1997, and is now managed by Sofitel. Suites have plush red Pullman carpets, a full kitchen with a dishwasher, a CD player, a second TV in the bedroom, and great views over the railway tracks and onto the new Docklands area beyond—though rooms are whisper quiet. All rooms are similar but vary in size, though some have balconies. Many of the suites are split level, with bedrooms on the second floor.

33 Spencer St., Melbourne, VIC 3000. ⓒ **1300/361 455** in Australia, or 03/9611 4567. Fax 03/9611 4655. www.accorhotel.com. 118 units. A$209–A$435 (US$135–US$283) studio suite; A$229–A$475 (US$149–US$309) 1-bedroom suite; A$364–A$590 (US$236–US$384) 2-bedroom suite; A$800 (US$520) 3-bedroom suite. Extra person A$44 (US$29). Children under 14 stay free in parent's room. Ask about weekend and seasonal packages. AE, DC, MC, V. Parking A$13 (US$8.45). Tram: 48 or 75 from Flinders St. **Amenities:** Restaurant; bar; golf course nearby; exercise room; Jacuzzi; sauna; concierge; tour desk; car-rental desk; 24-hr. room service; in-room massage; babysitting; laundry service; same-day dry cleaning; nonsmoking rooms. *In room:* A/C, TV w/pay movies, dataport, kitchen, minibar, fridge, coffeemaker, hair dryer, iron.

MODERATE

Hotel Lindrum ⭐⭐ *Finds* If you like your hotels stylish and contemporary then the Hotel Lindrum is for you. It's quite typical of the new wave of modern hotels that puts great emphasis on trendy interior design. Standard rooms, if you can call them that, have lots of hardwood, soft lighting, and forest greens—and even a CD player. Superior rooms have king-size beds and lovely polished wood floorboards, while deluxe rooms have wonderful views across to the Botanic Gardens through large bay windows. The hotel boasts a smart restaurant and a cigar bar with open fire.

26 Flinders St., Melbourne, Vic 3000. ⓒ **03/9668 1111.** www.hotellindrum.com.au. 59 units. A$215–A$300 (US$140–US$266) double; A$260–A$410 (US$169–US$266) junior suite. AE, DC, MC, V. Parking A$11 (US$5.20) off-site. **Amenities:** Restaurant; cigar bar; billiard room; fully equipped board room; same-day laundry service; valet; nonsmoking rooms; rooms for guests with disabilities. *In room:* A/C, TV w/free movies, coffeemaker, dataport, iron.

Ibis Melbourne ⭐ *Value* The good-value Ibis is right next door to the bus station and a short walk from the central shopping areas. The four-star rooms are spacious, immaculate, and bright, and have attached showers. Apartments come with kitchenettes and tubs. All guests have free use of the swimming pool, sauna, and Jacuzzi just up the road at the historic Melbourne City Baths.

15–21 Therry St., Melbourne, VIC 3000. ⓒ **1300/65 65 65** in Australia, 03/9639 2399, 800/221-4542 in the U.S. and Canada, 0800/44 44 22 in New Zealand. Fax 03/9662 9263. www.ibishotel.com. 250 units (some with shower only). A$109–A$119 (US$71–US$77) double (depending on high/low season); A$149–A$149 (US$97–US$97) 1-bedroom apt. Additional person A$30 (US$20). Children under 12 stay free in parent's room. Ask about package deals. AE, DC, MC, V. Parking A$11 (US7). **Amenities:** Free use of nearby swimming pool, sauna, and Jacuzzi. *In room:* A/C, TV, kitchens (in apts), minibar, coffeemaker, iron.

Oakford/Somerset Executive Apartments ⭐⭐ These serviced apartments, located inside an 1884 National Trust–listed building, are some of the best I've seen, and are a good alternative for travelers who like to cook their own food. The spacious apartments come with full kitchens, including a dishwasher. Those in the south block are older in style but still have contemporary furnishings. Those in the north block are new and a little more upscale; they're set farther back from the road, too. More than half the units have a tub, but specify when booking to make sure.

Another option to consider is the well-placed **Oakford on Lygon** ★★, on Lygon Street (© **03/8341 4777**), about a 10-minute walk from the city center. The rooms here have no kitchen but offer great value and I highly recommend them.

24 Little Bourke St., Melbourne, VIC 3000. © **1800/818 237** in Australia, or 03/9663 2888. Fax 03/9639 1537. www.oakford.com. 82 apts. A$105–A$115 studio (US$68–US$75); A$125 (US$81) 1-bedroom apt; A$211–A$145 (US$137–US$155) 2-bedroom apt; A$226–A$325 (US$147–US$211) split-level 3-bedroom apt. Extra person A$22 (US$14). Ask about weekend packages, corporate rates, and long-term stays. AE, DC, MC, V. Parking A$10–A$20 (US$6.50–US$13). **Amenities:** Restaurant; small heated outdoor pool; exercise room; Jacuzzi; sauna; business center; limited room service; dry-cleaning; nonsmoking rooms. *In room:* A/C, TV w/pay movies, dataport, kitchen, minibar, fridge, coffeemaker, hair dryer, iron.

Ramada Melbourne ★ *(Finds* Opened in 2003, this compact four-star hotel opposite Flinders Street Railway Station offers light and comfortable rooms at a good price. It's quiet and pleasantly welcoming and is a short walk to the main shopping streets. It's also a stroll away from the new Federation Square, the Crown Casino Entertainment Complex, and the Southbank district. You can get some wonderful packages here, including a weekend special for A$145 (US$94) per night with breakfast.

270 Flinders St., Melbourne, VIC 3000. © **1300/726 232** in Australia, or 03/9654 6888. Fax 03/9654 0368. www.ramadamelbourne.com.au. 179 units. A$340 (US$221) standard room; A$350 (US$227) with water views. Additional person A$45 (US$29). Ask about packages. AE, DC, MC, V. Parking A$20 (US$13). **Amenities:** Restaurant; bar; business center; 24-hour room service; nonsmoking rooms. *In room:* A/C, TV w/pay movies, high-speed Internet, safe, minibar, coffeemaker, hair dryer, iron.

INEXPENSIVE

Hotel Y All rooms at the Y are sparsely furnished and not overly large, and as such do not represent such great value. The most expensive doubles and triples have been refurbished recently and have a TV, a refrigerator, and air-conditioning. The one-bedroom apartment has a queen-size bed with en-suite bathroom, and the lounge has a double pullout bed and a small kitchenette. A cafe on the premises serves breakfast, lunch, and light snacks. The Y welcomes both women and men. The hotel is situated right near the Queen Victoria Market and is a short tram ride down Elizabeth Street or a 10-minute walk from the city center.

YWCA Melbourne, 489 Elizabeth St., Melbourne, VIC 3000. © **03/9329 5188.** Fax 03/9329 1469. www. ywca.net. 60 units. A$98–A$120 (US$64–US$78) double; A$109–A$131 (US$71–US$85) triple; A$185 (US$120) apt (for 2 people). Additional person A$17 (US$11). AE, DC, MC, V. No parking. **Amenities:** Cafe; access to health club; tour desk; car-rental desk; coin-op laundry; kitchen; TV room. *In room:* A/C (more expensive rooms only), phone, TV (more expensive rooms only), fridge, coffeemakers.

Kingsgate Hotel Only a 10-minute walk from the city, this hotel, an interesting place, feels like a basic B&B, though a total refurbishment—"to attract airline staff"—gave it a better look. From the outside, it resembles a terrace building, but inside it's a maze of corridors and rooms. The staff is very friendly. The least-expensive "economy" rooms are for backpackers only. They're dark and have two single beds and a hand basin; there's barely enough room to swing a backpack. Pricier "executive" rooms, however, are light, spacious, and have double beds (or two twins) as well as en-suite bathrooms. A cooked breakfast costs A$7 (US$4.50) extra. The 15 or so deluxe quad rooms have double beds and two singles.

131 King St., Melbourne, VIC 3000. © **1300/73 41 71** in Australia, or 03/9629 417. Fax 03/9629 7110. www. kingsgatehotel.com.au. 225 units, 104 with bathroom. A$69–A$99 (US$23–US$64) double; A$89–A$119 (US$58–US$77) triple; A$139 (US$90) deluxe quad. AE, DC, MC, V. Parking A$7 (US$4.55) a day at Crown Casino, a 5-min. walk away. **Amenities:** Tour desk; executive-level rooms. *In room:* TV.

Toad Hall ⚡ *Value*   "It's one of the best in Australia" is what one well-traveled guest said of Toad Hall. I have to agree; this 1858 mansion offers excellent value. It's just down the road from Queen Victoria Market, Melbourne Central train/tram station, and only a few minutes' walk to the main shopping areas. Dorms are segregated by sex, with four to six bunk beds in each. Doubles and twins are small, but like the dorms, are clean and quite comfortable, with springy beds. I really liked the large communal kitchen, dining room, and outdoor courtyard.

441 Elizabeth St., Melbourne, VIC 3000. ✆ 03/9600 9010. Fax 03/9600 9013. www.Toadhall-hotel.com.au. 85 dorm beds in 16 rooms; 8 doubles, 4 with bathroom; 12 twin rooms, 2 with bathroom. A$60 (US$39) double/twin without bathroom; A$90 (US$58) double/twin with bathroom; A$25 (US$16) dorm bed. MC, V. Parking A$6 (US$3.90). **Amenities:** Tour desk; coin-op laundry; nonsmoking rooms; roof garden; 3 TV lounges. *In room:* Fridge, coffeemaker.

IN CARLTON

Albert Heights Executive Apartments ⚡   For good, moderately priced accommodations with cooking facilities so you can cut down on meal costs, you can't go wrong with the Albert Heights, a favorite of American travelers. It's in a nice area of Melbourne, a few minutes' walk from the city center. There are parks at each end of the street. Each self-contained unit in this brick building is large and attractive. If you want your own space, or are traveling with your family, you can use the sofa bed in the living room. Each unit comes with a full kitchen with a microwave (no conventional oven), dining area, and large bathroom.

83 Albert St., East Melbourne, VIC 3002. ✆ 1800/800 117 in Australia, or 03/9419 0955. Fax 03/9419 9517. www.albertheights.com.au. 34 units. A$130 (US$85) double. Additional adult A$20 (US$13), additional child A$15 (US$9.75). Ask about special deals. AE, DC, MC, V. Free parking. Tram: 42 or 109; or a 10-min. walk to city. **Amenities:** Jacuzzi; tour desk; car-rental desk; babysitting; dry cleaning; laundry service; nonsmoking rooms. *In room:* A/C, TV, dataport, kitchen, fridge, coffeemaker, hair dryer, iron, safe.

Georgian Court Guest House   The comfortable Georgian Court's appearance hasn't changed much since it was built in 1910—and it still fits like a favorite shirt. The sitting and dining rooms both have high ceilings, and offer old-world atmosphere. The bedrooms, furnished with little more than plain pine furniture and a double bed, still have charm.

21 George St., East Melbourne, VIC 3002. ✆ 03/9419 6353. Fax 03/9416 0895. www.georgiancourt.aunz. com 31 units, 21 with bathroom. A$99 (US$64) double without bathroom; A$119 (US$76) double with bathroom. A$10–A$20 (US$6.50–US$13) surcharge during busy periods, such as the Melbourne Grand Prix and other major sporting events. Additional adult A$20 (US$13), additional child under 15 A$13 (US$8.45) Rates include buffet breakfast. AE, DC, MC, V. Free parking. Tram: 75 from Flinders St., or 48 from Spencer St. Georgian Court is behind the Hilton, a 15-min. walk from the city center. **Amenities:** Access to nearby health club; tour desk; car-rental desk; coin-op laundry; same-day dry cleaning; nonsmoking rooms. *In room:* A/C, TV, fridge, coffeemaker, hair dryer, iron, safe.

Quest on Drummond   Very nice and functional three-star self-catering apartments at a decent price are what you'll find at this good, semibudget option. All apartments are modern and clean, and come with a full kitchen. One-bedroom apartments also have a sofa bed. Breakfast items are available on request, but no reception is on the premises (though the management is only a phone call and a 2-min. walk away). It's within walking distance of the city center.

371 Drummond St., Carlton, VIC 3053. ✆ 03/9486 1777. Fax 03/9482 2649. www.questapartments.com.au. 10 units. A$121 (US$79) studio apt; A$132 (US$86) 1-bedroom apt. AE, DC, MC, V. Off-street parking. Tram: 1 or 22 from Swanston St. **Amenities:** Access to nearby health club; babysitting; coin-op laundry; nonsmoking rooms. *In room:* TV, kitchen, fridge, coffeemaker, iron.

IN FITZROY

The Nunnery Guesthouse *(★) (Value)* This former convent offers pleasant accommodations, just a short tram ride to the city center. Set in a terrace on the city's edge, the Nunnery is perfectly situated near the restaurant and nightlife scenes on Brunswick and Lygon streets, in nearby Carlton. This informal, friendly place is well suited to couples and families. Rooms have wooden floors, rugs, and leafy views. All rooms share good bathrooms, one with a tub. Attached is a backpackers' place with simple rooms and shared bathrooms. There's a spacious communal lounge with wicker furniture, self-catering kitchen, and a cobbled courtyard with lots of greenery.

116 Nicholson St., Fitzroy, Melbourne, VIC 3065. © **1800/032 635** in Australia, or 03/9419 8637. Fax 03/9417 7736. www.bakpak.com/nunnery. 30 units, none with bathroom. A$90–$100 (US$59–$65) double (more expensive price for larger rooms); A$115 (US$75) triple; A$130 (US$85) quad. In backpackers' section: A$23–$27 (US$15–$18) bunk rooms; A$55 (US$36) single; A$70 (US$46) double. Guesthouse rates include breakfast. MC, V. Free parking available (but book in advance). Tram: 96 to East Brunswick (stop 13). **Amenities:** Tour desk; car-rental desk; kitchen; lounge; coin-op laundry; all nonsmoking rooms. *In room:* TV.

IN ST. KILDA

Hotel Tolarno *(★)* The quirky Hotel Tolarno is right in the middle of St. Kilda's cafe and restaurant strip, and a long stone's throw away from the beach. Rich red carpets bedeck the corridors throughout this 1950s and 1960s retro-style building. Rooms vary, but all are modern and nice. The most popular rooms are in the front of the building and have balconies overlooking the main street. The more expensive of those come with a separate kitchen and lounge. Suites vary from one and two bedrooms and don't have balconies, though some have Jacuzzis.

42 Fitzroy St., St. Kilda, Melbourne, VIC 3182. © **1800/620 363** in Australia, or 03/9537 0200. Fax 03/9534 7800. www.hoteltolarno.com.au. 31 units. A$115–A$125 (US$75–US$81) standard double; A$145–A$165 (US$94–US$107) deluxe double; A$145–A$165 (US$94–US$107) balcony double; A$180–A$275 (US$117–US$179) suite (sleeps up to 4). Additional person A$20 (US$13). AE, DC, MC, V. On-street parking. Tram: 16 from Swanston St.; 96 from Flinders St. **Amenities:** Restaurant; bar; 4 lit tennis courts; bike rental; concierge; tour desk; car-rental desk; room service; massage; babysitting; laundry/dry cleaning service opposite hotel; nonsmoking rooms. *In room:* A/C, TV, dataport, kitchenette, fridge, coffeemaker, hair dryer, iron.

Olembia Private Hotel This sprawling Edwardian house, built in 1922, is set back from a busy St. Kilda Street behind a leafy courtyard. It's popular with tourists, business travelers, and young families; and everyone gets together for the frequent video nights, wine and cheese parties, and barbecues. The clean bedrooms are simply furnished, with little more than a double bed, or two singles, a desk, a hand basin, and a wardrobe. Guests share six bathrooms. There's a very comfortable sitting room, and a courtyard area with barbecues. The Olembia is near St. Kilda beach and the host of restaurants lining Acland Street.

96 Barkly St., St. Kilda, Melbourne, VIC 3182. © **03/9537 1412.** Fax 03/9537 1600. www.olembia.com.au. 23 units, none with bathroom. A$74 (US$48) double; A$24 (US$16) dorm rooms. AE, MC, V. Free parking. Tram: 96 from Bourke St. to stop 138. **Amenities:** Bike rental; coin-op laundry; nonsmoking rooms. *In room:* No phone.

Robinson's by the Sea *(★★) (Finds)* For something special, Robinson's by the Sea fits the bill. Both the management and pet dog are incredibly friendly at this 1870s heritage B&B just across from the beach. They encourage an evening social scene, and downstairs you'll find a comfortable, antiques-filled living room, and a dining room. Four of the five bedrooms are upstairs. Each is unique. The Eastern Room has a four-poster queen-size bed and Indian and Chinese furniture, whereas the Rose Room is decorated with patterned flowers and pastel colors. The units all share three communal bathrooms, one with a tub and shower, a second with a shower, and the third with a Jacuzzi tub and shower. There are wood floorboards and fireplaces throughout.

335 Beaconsfield Parade, St. Kilda, Melbourne, VIC 3182. ℂ 03/9534 2683. Fax 03/9534 2683. www. robinsonsbythesea.com.au. 5 units, none with bathroom, 2 self-contained studios. A$155–A$195 (US$100–US$127) double; A$95 (US$62) studio. Rates include cooked breakfast. AE, DC, MC, V. Free parking. Tram: 112 to Cowderoy St., St. Kilda. **Amenities:** Health club nearby; bike rental; babysitting; laundry service; nonsmoking rooms. *In room:* TV, coffeemaker, hair dryer.

IN SOUTH YARRA

Hotel Claremont   The high ceilings and the mosaic tiles in the lobby welcome visitors into the interior of this old-world hotel. It's an attractive place, though sparsely furnished. The AAA-rated two-star rooms are comfortable enough, and each comes with either a double or a single bed. There is no elevator in this three-story building with 72 stairs, so it could be a bad choice for travelers with disabilities. Internet access is available.

189 Toorak Rd., South Yarra, VIC 3141. ℂ **1300/301 630** in Australia, or 03/9826 8000. Fax 03/9827 8652. www.hotelclaremont.com. 80 units, none with bathroom. A$68 (US$44) double. Additional person A$10 (US$6.50). Children stay free in parent's room. Rates include continental breakfast. AE, DC, MC, V. On-street parking. **Amenities:** Coin-op laundry; nonsmoking rooms. *In room:* TV.

The Hotel Como ★★★   Winner of many tourism awards, the Hotel Como deservedly basks in its reputation for excellent service and terrific accommodations, which include studio rooms (some with shower only), one-room suites (some with kitchen or kitchenette), one- or two-bedroom suites (all with kitchen, some with an office), and luxurious (and pricey) penthouse and executive suites. Some units have a private Japanese garden. The hotel is especially adept at accommodating business travelers: all rooms have video-conferencing capability and three complimentary limousines carry guests to the city center each weekday morning. Weekend packages are very good value.

630 Chapel St., South Yarra, Melbourne, VIC 3141. ℂ **1800/033 400** in Australia, 800/552-6844 in the U.S. and Canada, 0800/389 7791 in the U.K., 0800/446 110 in New Zealand, or 03/9825 2222. Fax 03/9824 1263. www.mirvachotels.com.au. 107 units. A$600 (US$390) studio; A$680 (US$442) 1-bedroom suite; A$800 (US$520) 2-bedroom suite; A$930 (US$604) penthouse; A$1,300 (US$845) Como/Executive Suite. Ask about weekend package deals. AE, DC, MC, V. Parking $15 (US$9.75). **Amenities:** 2 restaurants; bar; indoor pool; health club; Jacuzzi; sauna; bike rental; game room; concierge; tour desk; car-rental desk; business center; salon; 24-hr. room service; massage; babysitting; laundry service; dry cleaning; nonsmoking rooms; currency exchange. *In room:* A/C, TV w/pay movies, CD stereos, dataport, kitchen, minibar, coffeemaker, hair dryer, iron, safe.

4 Where to Dine

Melbourne's ethnically diverse population ensures a healthy selection of international cooking styles. Chinatown, in the city center, is a fabulous hunting ground for Chinese, Malaysian, Thai, Indonesian, Japanese, and Vietnamese fare, often at bargain prices. Carlton has plenty of Italian cuisine, but the outdoor restaurants on Lygon Street are aimed at unsuspecting tourists, and can be overpriced and disappointing, so avoid them; Richmond is crammed with Greek and Vietnamese restaurants; and Fitzroy has cheap Asian, Turkish, Mediterranean, and vegetarian food. To see and be seen, head to Chapel Street or Toorak Road in South Yarra, or to St. Kilda and join the throng of Melbournians dining out along Fitzroy and Acland streets. Most of the cheaper places in Melbourne are strictly BYO (bring your own wine or beer). Smoking is no longer possible in cafes and restaurants, so please think twice before offending both staff and fellow patrons.

IN THE CITY CENTER
EXPENSIVE

Flower Drum ☆☆☆ CANTONESE   Praise pours in from all quarters for this upscale restaurant situated just off Little Bourke Street, Chinatown's main drag. Take a slow elevator up to the restaurant, which has widely spaced tables (perfect for politicians and businesspeople to clinch their deals). Take note of the specials—the chefs are extremely creative and utilize the best ingredients they find in the markets each day. The signature dish here is the Peking duck, although the buttered garfish is my favorite. The king crab dumplings in soup is a great starter. One or 2 days in advance, you can order a banquet for two or more diners during which you'll be served more unusual dishes such as abalone.

17 Market Lane. ℂ **03/9662 3655.** Reservations required. Main courses A$30–A$45 (US$20–US$29). AE, DC, MC, V. Mon–Sat noon–2:30pm and 6–10pm; Sun 6–10:30pm.

Koko ☆☆ JAPANESE   Though you'll find plenty of Japanese sushi and noodle bars around Chinatown, there's nothing quite like raw fish eaten with a bit of panache. A visit to Crown Casino Entertainment Complex can be a memorable experience in itself, but stop off here and you'll wish you could remember these tastes forever. The restaurant has a mixed contemporary/traditional decor, with a goldfish pond in the center of the main dining room and wonderful views over the city. There are separate teppanyaki grills and screened tatami rooms where you sit on the matted floor. If you can manage the boiled eel with rice then go for it. Otherwise the yaki udon, or the cooked "sushi" of roast chicken, duck, prawns, and rare beef is popular. A selection of 10 different sakes helps digestion.

Level 3, Crown Towers, Southbank. ℂ **03/9292 6886.** Reservations required. Main courses A$27–A$32 (US$18–US$21). AE, DC, MC, V. Daily noon–2:30pm and 6–10:30pm.

Le Restaurant ☆☆☆ MODERN AUSTRALIAN   You might not want to leave the hotel once you've experienced the Sofitel's dining options. If having the wonderful **Café La** on the premises wasn't enough, it is blessed with Le Restaurant, one of Melbourne's premier fine-dining choices. The service is exquisite, the cuisine inventive, and the views fixating. The dishes here are well crafted and combine wonderful flavors and colors. The menu changes regularly, but you might find the King Island crayfish in a crust of kaffir lime leaf and morel dust served up with scallop ravioli, shiitake mushroom, and tarragon essence. The enormous wine list is mostly populated with expensive vintages.

In the Sofitel Melbourne, 35th floor, 25 Collins St. ℂ **03/9653 7744.** Fax 03/9657 7753. restaurant-res@ sofitelmelbourne.com.au. Reservations recommended. Main courses A$35–A$45 (US$23–US$29). AE, DC, MC, V. Tues–Sat 6.30–10:30pm.

MODERATE

ah mu MALAYSIAN   Voted best Malaysian in 2002 and 2003 by Melbourne's *The Age Good Food Guide*, this restaurant continues to inspire. The cool and contemporary interiors enhance the menu of chef Allen Woo whose characteristic modern Asian cooking can lead to marinated fish grilled in banana leaf with citric sambal belachan or lightly floured king prawns seared in ginger flower syrup.

51 Bourke St. ℂ **03/9654 6800.** www.ahmu.com. Reservations recommended Fri–Sat nights. Main courses $18–A$29 (US$12–US$19). AE, DC, MC, V. Mon–Fri noon–10:30pm; daily 6–10:30pm.

Bamboo House ☆ NORTHERN REGIONAL CHINESE/CANTONESE   If Flower Drum (see above) is full (or breaks your budget), try this place, which is esteemed by both the Chinese community and local business big shots. The service here is a pleasure, and the food (especially the chicken with shallot sauce)

Melbourne Dining

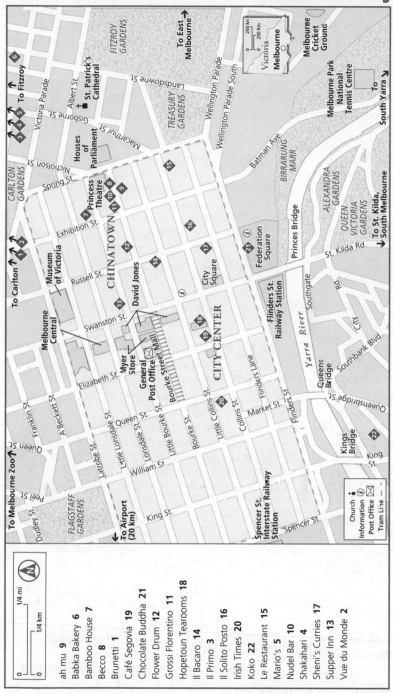

ah mu **9**
Babka Bakery **6**
Bamboo House **7**
Becco **8**
Brunetti **1**
Café Segovia **19**
Chocolate Buddha **21**
Flower Drum **12**
Grossi Florentino **11**
Hopetoun Tearooms **18**
Il Bacaro **14**
Il Primo **3**
Il Solito Posto **16**
Irish Times **20**
Koko **22**
Le Restaurant **15**
Mario's **5**
Nudel Bar **10**
Shakahari **4**
Sheni's Curries **17**
Supper Inn **13**
Vue du Monde **2**

is worth writing home about. The waiters are all eager to help you construct a feast from the myriad Cantonese and northern Chinese dishes. (Don't leave without a taste of the duck in plum sauce!) Other popular dishes include pan-fried dumplings, spring onion pancakes, and the signature dish, Szechuan smoked duck.

47 Little Bourke St. ℂ 03/9662 1565. Reservations recommended. Main courses A$20–A$28 (US$13–US$18). AE, DC, MC, V. Mon–Fri noon–3pm; Mon–Sat 5:30–11pm; Sun 5:30–10pm.

Becco ⊕ MODERN ITALIAN   Tucked away in a lane, this favorite of Melbournians has not disappointed in 6 years of winning awards and accolades. Here you find stylish service—and stylish clients all without pretension. The cuisine mixes Italian favors with Australian flair in such offerings as crumbed prawns with radicchio and chile aioli, or the delicate panettone pudding with cinnamon. On the upstairs level is the ultracool late-night bar, **Bella Vista Social Club** (p. 562).

11–25 Crossley St., near Bourke St., City. ℂ 03/9663 3000. Main courses A$22–A$31 (US$7.15–US$20). AE, DC, MC, V. Mon–Sat noon–3pm and 6–11pm; Sun 5:30–10pm.

Grossi Florentino ⊕ ITALIAN   Under the management of the Grossi family, this restaurant is probably the best Italian restaurant in Melbourne. It's split into separate sections, with a casual bistro downstairs, next to the **Cellar bar** (where you can pick up a bowl of pasta for around A$13/US$8.50), while upstairs you can find the fine dining restaurant with its chandeliers and murals reflecting the Florentine way of life. The food is traditional Italian, including the signature wet-roasted suckling lamb and the suckling pig. On the menu, too, are risotto, seafood, and steak dishes. The chocolate soufflé is very special.

80 Bourke St. ℂ 03/9662 1811. Fax 03/9662 2518. www.grossiflorentino.com. Reservations recommended. Main courses A$38–A$42 (US$25–US$27). AE, DC, MC, V. Mon–Fri noon–3pm; Mon–Sat 6–11pm.

Il Bacaro ⊕ ITALIAN   Walk into Il Bacaro and you'll feel you've been transported to Venice. Dominated by a horseshoe-shaped bar, it's jam-packed with small tables and weaving waiters carrying dishes like carpaccio of tuna or semolina gnocchetti with duck ragout. The pasta dishes and the risotto of the day always go down well, as do the salad side dishes. It's often crowded at lunch with local businesspeople digging deep into the excellent wine list.

168–170 Little Collins St. ℂ 03/9654 6778. Reservations recommended. Main courses A$20–A$32 (US$13–US$20). AE, DC, MC, V. Mon–Fri noon–4pm; Mon–Sat 6pm–midnight.

Il Solito Posto NORTHERN ITALIAN   This below-ground restaurant is split into two parts. The casual bistro has a blackboard menu offering good pastas, soups, and salads. Then there's the sharper and more upmarket trattoria, with its a la carte menu offering the likes of steak, fish, and veal dishes. The coffee is excellent, too.

Basement of 113 Collins St. (enter via George Parade). ℂ 03/9654 4466. Reservations recommended. Main courses A$15–A$17 (US$9.75–US$11) in bistro, A$25–A$33 (US$16–US$21) in trattoria. AE, DC, MC, V. Mon–Fri 7:30am–1am; Sat 9am–1am. Closed late Dec to early Jan.

Irish Times IRISH/MODERN AUSTRALIAN   An Irish bar more authentic than most, the character-filled Irish Times serves up generous portions and Guinness on tap. Popular dishes include the warm chicken salad, mussels in a creamy broth, Caesar salad, and Irish dishes such as "boxty"—patties of mashed potato, leek, and onion with an accompanying tomato relish. There's a live band on Thursday and Friday evenings from 9:30pm and on Saturday from 10:30pm.

427 Little Collins St. ℂ 03/9642 1699. Reservations recommended. Main courses A$10–A$25 (US$6.50–US$16). AE, DC, MC, V. Mon–Fri 5pm–midnight; Sat 5pm–3am.

Nudel Bar NOODLES   A favorite with city slickers, the Nudel Bar serves up a variety of noodle dishes to the crowded tables and bar. Examples of what you might find here are cold spicy green tea noodles and *mee goring* (a noodle dish with peanuts and, here, often chicken). Sticky rice pudding is a favorite for dessert.

76 Bourke St. ℂ 03/9662 9100. Reservations recommended Fri–Sat night. Main courses A$13–A$18 (US$8.40–US$12). AE, DC, MC, V. Mon–Fri 11am–10:30pm; Sat 11am–11pm; Sun 4–10:30pm.

INEXPENSIVE

Café Segovia ⭐⭐ *Finds* CAFE   Café Segovia is one of the most atmospheric cafes in Australia, with a smoky, sensual interior reminiscent of Spain. Seating is also available outside in the arcade, but you'll have to come early at lunchtime to nab a chair. Typical cafe food is on offer, such as focaccias, cakes, and light meals. Live music Thursdays and Fridays.

33 Block Arcade. ℂ 03/9650 2373. Main courses A$8–A$13 (US$5.20–US$8.50). AE, DC, MC, V. Mon–Fri 7:30am–11pm; Sat 8am–6pm; Sun 9am–5pm.

Chocolate Buddha NOODLES   Located within the precinct of Federation Square, this place offers mostly organic produce, including some organic wines. Based mostly on Japanese inspired noodle, ramen, and soba dishes to which meat, chicken, or seafood is added, it's casual yet particularly satisfying dining. Food is creative and the view across the square to the Yarra River and Southbank is a delight at dusk.

Federation Square, corner of Flinders and Swanson sts. ℂ 03/9654 5688. Main courses A$13–A$17 (US$8.45–US$11). AE, MC, V. Daily noon–10:30pm.

Hopetoun Tearooms ⭐ CAFE   The first cup of coffee served in this Melbourne institution left the pot in 1892. It's very civilized, with green-and-white Regency wallpaper and marble tables. The cakes are very good; the sandwiches go for A$4.50 to A$6.50 (US$2.90–US$4.25) and the focaccias for A$7 to A$8.50 (US$4.50–US$5.50). Scones, croissants, and grilled food are also available.

Shops 1 and 2, Block Arcade, 280–282 Collins St. ℂ and fax 03/9650 2777. Main courses A$4.50–A$8.50 (US$2.90–US$5.55) (minimum charge A$5/US$3.25 per person noon–2pm). AE, DC, MC, V. Mon–Thurs 8:30am–5pm; Fri 8:30am–6pm; Sat 10am–3:30pm. Closed Sun.

Sheni's Curries SRI LANKAN   This tiny, basic but very busy place (it seats 30) offers a range of excellent-value, authentic Sri Lankan curries. You can either dine here or take your lunch special to go. Choose between three vegetable dishes and a choice of meat and seafood dishes. All meals come with rice, three types of chutney, and a papadam. You can also buy extra items such as samosas and roti.

Shop 16, 161 Collins St. (on the corner of Flinders Lane and Russell St., opposite the entrance to the Grand Hyatt). ℂ 03/9654 3535. Lunch specials A$5.50–A$12 (US$3.60–US$7.80). No credit cards. Mon–Fri 11am–4pm.

Supper Inn CANTONESE   Head here if you get the Chinese-food munchies late at night. It's a friendly place with a mixed crowd of locals and tourists chowing down on such dishes as steaming bowls of *congee* (a rice-based porridge), barbecued suckling pig, mud crab, or stuffed scallops. Everything here is the "real thing!"

15 Celestial Ave. ℂ and fax 03/9663 4759. Reservations recommended. Main courses A$10–A$15 (US$6.50–US$9.75). AE, DC, MC, V. Daily 5:30pm–2:30am.

CARLTON

Brunetti ☏ TRATTORIA/PASTICCERIA   For a real Italian experience, come here for excellent cakes, gelato, and coffee while gazing at the trompe l'oeil paintings and frescoes on the walls. Their very authentic range of lunch dishes are also worth sampling. The best thing this side of Rome.

198–204 Faraday St., Carlton. ℂ 03/9347 2801. Main courses A$12–A$25 (US$7.80–US$16). Cafe dishes A$3–A$8 (US$2–US$5.20). AE, DC, MC, V. Mon–Fri 7:am–10.30pm; Sat 8am–10.30pm. Tram: All trams traveling north on Swanston St.

Il Primo ☏ SOUTHERN EUROPEAN   This restaurant is tucked away in a pair of historic houses in the Italian sector of Carlton. There are three, cozy dining areas in all, with antique bricks, wood-beamed ceilings, and tiled floors. It feels like you're dining in a wine cellar, and indeed, there's a great wine list, including a range of unlabeled local wines at rock-bottom prices. The menu changes regularly, but you'll often see the likes of veal parmigiana, warm kangaroo salad, fish, garlic prawns, risotto, and several pasta dishes. Live jazz brings in the customers every night from 10 or 11pm to closing time.

242 Lygon St., Carlton. ℂ 03/9663 6100. Reservations recommended. Main courses A$17–A$28 (US$11–US$18). AE, DC, MC, V. Sun–Tues 6:30am–1am; Wed–Sat 6:30am–3am. Tram: 1, 15, 21, or 22 traveling north on Swanston St. (Stop 12).

Shakahari VEGETARIAN   Good vegetarian food isn't just a meal without meat; it's a creation in its own right. At Shakahari you are assured of a creative meal that's not at all bland. The large restaurant is quite low-key, but the service can be a bit inconsistent. The Sate Samsara (skewered, lightly fried vegetables and tofu pieces with a peanut dip) is a winner, as is the couscous, served in a vast earthenware pot. Also served up are curries, croquets, tempura avocado, and veggie burgers (on a plate with salad, not in a bun).

201–203 Faraday St., Carlton. ℂ 03/9347 3848. Main courses A$15 (US$9.40). AE, DC, MC, V. Mon–Sat noon–3:30pm; Sun–Thurs 6–9:30pm; Fri–Sat 6–10:30pm. Tram: Any tram going north along Swanston St. toward Melbourne University.

Vue du Monde MODERN FRENCH   Striving for a refined experience similar to that of a European Michelin-starred restaurant, this small but oh-so-stylish establishment produces mostly exceptional food. If pig's trotter stuffed with caramelized sweetbreads or assiette of mushrooms and truffle are what you desire, then you will not be disappointed. An excellent wine list.

295 Drummond St., Carlton. ℂ 03/9347 0199. Main courses A$36 (US$23), 2-course dinner A$50 (US$33). AE, DC, MC, V. Tues–Fri noon–2:30pm; Tues–Sat 6:30–11pm. Tram: All trams traveling north on Swanston St.

FITZROY

Mario's ITALIAN   This place has ambience, groovy '60s decor, great coffee, and impeccable professional service. Offerings include a varied range of pastas and cakes. Breakfast is served all day. The art on the wall, all by local artists, is always interesting and for sale, too.

303 Brunswick St., Fitzroy. ℂ 03/9417 3343. Main courses A$12–A$18 (US$7.80–US$12). AE, DC, MC, V. Mon–Fri 7:am–10.30pm; Sat 8am–10.30pm.

SEASIDE DINING IN ST. KILDA

Chinta Blues MALAYSIAN   Head to this very popular eatery if you're looking for simple, satisfying food with a healthy touch of spice. The big sellers are the laksa, the mei goreng, the chicken curry, the sambal spinach, and a chicken dish called ayam blues. Lots of noodles, too. It's very busy, especially at lunch.

> **Tips The Staff of Life**
>
> The enticing aroma of fresh bread is what attracts you to **Babka Bakery,**
> a Russian-style cafe-bakery run by a delightful gaggle of girls. Come for
> breakfast or a light lunch of eggs on fresh sourdough, quiches, tarts, and
> brioches. Or perhaps try the homemade borscht? It's at 358 Brunswick St.
> in Fitzroy (© **03/9416 0091).**

6 Acland St., St. Kilda. © **03/9534 9233.** Reservations recommended. Main courses A$10–A$19 (US$6.50–
US$12). AE, MC, V. Mon–Wed noon–2:30pm and 6–10pm; Thurs–Sat noon–2:30pm and 6–10:45pm;
Sun noon–9:45pm. Tram: 16 from Swanston St. or 96 from Bourke St.

Donovans &&& MODERN MEDITERRANEAN   Donovans is so near the
sea you expect the fish to jump through the door and onto the plate—and
indeed, you do get extremely fresh seafood. The restaurant is all higgledy-piggledy
and charming, with lots of cushions, a log fire, and the sound of jazz and breakers on the beach. The menu includes a mind-boggling array of dishes, many big
enough for two. Chef Robert Castellani's trademarks include steamed mussels,
linguini with seafood, and stuffed squid. The bar is perfect for watching the sun
go down.

40 Jacka Blvd., St. Kilda. © **03/9534 8221.** Reservations recommended. Main courses A$23–A$36
(US$15–US$23). AE, DC, MC, V. Daily noon–10:30pm. Tram: 12 from Collins St., 16 from Swanston St., 94 or
96 from Bourke St.

La Porchetta Pizza Restaurant *Value* PIZZA   This busy, large, very noisy
pizza joint is a good value. There are some 22 different pizzas to choose from,
with the largest ranging in price from A$6 to A$7.80 (US$4.20–US$4.50)
being just large enough to fill two. A range of pasta dishes costs from A$6 to
A$9 (US$4.20–US$6.30). Chicken, seafood, veal, and steaks are also on the
menu. The heart-pounding pace here means it's not for the faint-hearted.

80 Acland St., St. Kilda. © **03/9534 1888.** Main courses A$5–A$14 (US$3.20–US$9.10). No credit cards.
Sun–Thurs 11am–midnight; Fri–Sat 11am–2am. Tram: 16 from Swanston St. or 96 from Bourke St.

MORE ETHNIC EATS IN SOUTH YARRA

Kanpai JAPANESE   You have to book early in the day to get a seat at this popular restaurant on the Chapel Street restaurant strip. The sushi and sashimi
dishes are very fresh, and the miso soup is well worth plundering with your
chopsticks. There's also a good vegetarian selection as well.

569 Chapel St., South Yarra. © **03/9827 4379.** Reservations recommended. Main courses A$12–A$34
(US$7.80–US$22). AE, DC, MC, V. Daily noon–11pm. Tram: 6, 8, or 72 from Swanston St.

Tandoor Indian Restaurant & INDIAN   This basic Indian restaurant was
far less crowded than many of the others on the Chapel Street strip when I last
visited—all I can say is that the "in" crowd didn't know what they were missing.
The curries here are rich and spicy, with the vegetarian paneer–butter masala
and the cheese kofta being some of the best I've tasted in Australia. Some dishes,
such as the crab masala curry, are truly inspirational. The main courses are quite
large, so you'll probably not need a first course, but I highly recommend side
dishes of naan bread (one per person) and a cucumber raita to cool the palate.

517 Chapel St., South Yarra. © **03/9827 8247.** Reservations recommended Fri–Sat night. Main courses
A$11–A$22 (US$7.15–US$14). AE, DC, MC, V. Tues–Fri and Sun noon–2:30pm; daily 6–11pm. Tram: 6, 8, or
72 from Swanston St.

Yeah Maan ⚘ CARIBBEAN   Is this the coolest restaurant in Australia or what? Calypso music wafts amid the homemade triangle-backed chairs, diners wait in the lounge or at the new bar for a table to become free, palm trees sway—and the food! Wow! The whole place is rockin', with seats almost continually occupied. The authentic Trinidadian goat curry is a must, as is the Barbados burrito. The Jamaican KFC (chicken marinated for 2 days in approximately 30 spices and then smoked), and the Jumbo-Jumbie cassava shoestring fries (cassava is similar to a potato) are very, very popular. An upstairs dining room has recently opened. The staff is ultrafriendly. Licensed and BYO.

340 Punt Rd. (at Fawkner St.), South Yarra. ℂ **03/9820 2707**. Main courses A$13–A$19 (US$8.45–US$12). MC, V. Tues–Sat 6–11:30pm. Tram: 6, 8, or 72 from Swanston St.

5 Seeing the Sights

Melbourne's attractions may not have quite the fame as some of Sydney's, but visitors come here to experience the contrasts of old-world architecture and the exciting feel of a truly multicultural city.

If you'd like to see the city aboard a leisurely cruise, call **Melbourne River Cruises** (ℂ **03/9614 1215** Mon–Fri, or 03/9650 2055 Sat–Sun). This company offers a 2½-hour round-trip cruise on the Yarra River costing A$17 (US$11) for adults, A$8.80 (US$5.70) for children 3 to 12, A$13 (US$8.45) for students, and A$42 (US$27) for a family.

THE TOP ATTRACTIONS

Federation Square   Touted as "Melbourne's civic and cultural hub for the 21st century," Federation Square is a conglomerate of attractions centered around wacky architecture and a large open piazza-type area cobbled with misshapen paving. Here you'll find the National Gallery of Victoria: the Ian Potter Centre—Australian Art (p. 553), the new Australian Centre for the Moving Image (ACMI), and the new one-stop Visitor Centre (see "Visitor Information," earlier in this chapter). The three-level Nation Gallery of Victoria building is huge and hosts the largest collection of Australian art in the country, including many works by Sidney Nolan, Russell Drysdale, and Tom Roberts, as well as Aboriginal and Torres Strait Islanders. The Gallery is already a major focus for art festivals and special events. Numerous cafes and coffee shops operate throughout the precinct. The ACMI center includes two state-of-the-art cinemas and large areas where visitors can access movies, videos, and digital media. It's worth visiting the square though just to see the extraordinary architecture, made up of strangely reflective geometrical designs, and the impressive glassed Atrium. Lots of events are planned for the square's 450-seat amphitheater, including theatrical performances and free concerts. Other events will take place on the plaza and along areas of the banks of the Yarra River.

Runs north-south from Flinders St. to the Yarra River (near Flinders St. Railway Station, to the left as you look at it). www.federationsquare.com.au. Outdoor spaces open 24 hr. Free entry (though charges for some special events and exhibitions). Tram: City Circle.

Gold Treasury Museum   Designed by the architect J. J. Clarke (when he was only 19) and built in 1857, the Old Treasury Building is an imposing neoclassical sandstone building, which once housed precious metal from the Ballarat and Bendigo gold rushes. The gold was stored in eight thick-walled vaults underground and protected by iron bars. The "Built on Gold" Exhibition within the vaults is a high-tech multimedia show featuring videos and displays showing how the gold was dug up, sold, transported, and housed. In the basement are

Melbourne Attractions

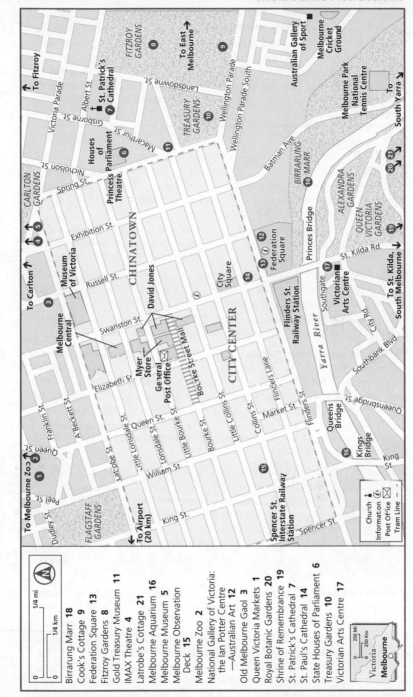

Birrarung Marr **18**
Cook's Cottage **9**
Federation Square **13**
Fitzroy Gardens **8**
Gold Treasury Museum **11**
IMAX Theatre **4**
Latrobe's Cottage **21**
Melbourne Aquarium **16**
Melbourne Museum **5**
Melbourne Observation Deck **15**
Melbourne Zoo **2**
National Gallery of Victoria: the Ian Potter Centre—Australian Art **12**
Old Melbourne Gaol **3**
Queen Victoria Markets **1**
Royal Botanic Gardens **20**
Shrine of Remembrance **19**
St. Patrick's Cathedral **7**
St. Paul's Cathedral **14**
State Houses of Parliament **6**
Treasury Gardens **10**
Victorian Arts Centre **17**

Tips **A Few Sightseeing Suggestions**

Much of Melbourne's appeal comes from soaking up the atmosphere on a walk around the city. But if you have time to see only one major attraction, by all means make it the **Melbourne Zoo.** Other top-of-the-list sights include **Federation Square,** the **National Gallery of Victoria,** and the **Botanic Gardens.** If you have time, head to **Phillip Island** to see the fairy penguins.

---

the restored quarters of a caretaker who lived there from 1916 to 1928. The ground floor is taken up by the "Melbourne: A City Built On Gold" display which shows how Melbourne was built using the profits from the gold rushes. A temporary exhibition gallery on the premises can feature anything from prints to gold-thread embroidery. Allow about 1 hour.

Old Treasury Building. Spring St. (top of Collins St.). © **03/9651 2233.** A$7 (US$4.55) adults, A$3.50 (US$2.30) children, A$18 (US$12) families. Mon–Fri 9am–5pm; weekends and public holidays 10am–4pm. Bus: City Explorer.

IMAX Theatre *(Kids* This eight-story movie screen rivals the world's largest screen at Sydney's Darling Harbour. Recent subjects have been outer space, the African Serengeti, and the deep oceans.

Melbourne Museum Complex, Rathdowne St., Carlton. © **03/9663 5454.** Admission from A$14 (US$9) adults, A$9.95 (US$6.50) children. Daily 10am–10pm. Tram: 1 or 22 from Swanston St.

Melbourne Aquarium *(Overrated* Opened in early 2000, the Melbourne Aquarium stretches over three levels and features a Barrier Reef–type exhibit, some interesting jellyfish displays, and an enormous walk-through tank with larger fish, sharks, and rays. However, it's pretty disappointing compared to the ones in Sydney and doesn't live up to the hype. Allow 30 minutes.

Corner Queens Wharf Rd and Kings sts., opposite Crown Casino. © **03/9620 0999.** www.melbourne aquarium.com.au. Admission A$21 (US$13) adults, A$11 (US$7) children under 16, A$49 (US$32) families. Daily 9:30am–6pm. Tram: City Circle.

Melbourne Museum *(Kids* This newly constructed museum is Australia's largest, and is located opposite the 19th-century Royal Exhibition Buildings. It houses interactive exhibits and science displays; Bunjikata, the award winning Aboriginal and Torres Strait Islander Centre; and bits and pieces of social history among other exhibits. Check out the brightly colored Children's Museum, which will bring hours of enjoyment to the little ones.

Melbourne Museum Complex, Rathdowne St., Carlton. © **13 11 02** in Australia. Admission A$15 (US$9.75) adults, A$8 (US$5.20) children, A$35 (US$22.75) families. Daily 10am–6pm. Tram: 1 or 22 from Swanston St.

Melbourne Observation Desk From the observation deck on the 55th floor, near the top of the tallest building in the Southern Hemisphere, you get 360-degree views of the whole of Melbourne and beyond. See if you can spot the Melbourne Cricket Ground (MCG) and the Crown Casino. A 20-minute film costing A$2 (US$1.30) shows you what you're looking at, but you might as well just take a map up with you and figure it out for yourself. Of interest are the displays telling about life in Melbourne, past and present. There's a cafe here, too. Allow 1 hour.

Rialto Building, 55th Floor, Collins St. (between William and King sts.). © **03/9629 8222.** Admission A$12 (US$7.70) adults, A$6.50 (US$4.20) children, A$34 (US$22) families. Daily 10am–11pm. Parking underneath. Tram: Any tram on Collins St.

Melbourne Zoo *(Kids)*   This place is a must-see. Built in 1862, it's the oldest zoo in the world, and among the best. There are some 3,000 animals here, including the ever-popular kangaroos, wallabies, echidnas, koalas, wombats, and platypuses. Rather than being locked up in cages, most animals are set in almost natural surroundings or well-tended gardens. Don't miss the butterfly house, with its thousands of colorful butterflies flying around; the free-flight aviary; the lowland gorilla exhibit; and the tree-top monkey displays. Allow at least 1 hour if you just want to see the Australian natives and around 2½ hours for the whole zoo.

Elliott Ave., Parkville. ℂ 03/9285 9300. www.zoo.org.au. Admission A$16 (US$10) adults, A$8.10 (US$5.25) children under 14, A$44 (US$29) families. Daily 9am–5pm. Free guided tours daily; go to the Friends of the Zoo Office to arrange tours. Free parking. Tram: 55 going north on William St. to stop 25; 19 from Elizabeth St. to Stop 16 (then it's a short walk to your left following signposts). Train: Royal Park Station.

National Gallery of Australia: the Ian Potter Centre—Australian Art   This fascinating gallery, featuring 20 rooms dedicated to Australian art, opened in 2002 in the heart of Federation Square. Some 20,000 objects are stored here but only about 800 are on display at any one time. Aboriginal art and colonial art collections are the centerpieces of the gallery, but you will find modern paintings here, too. Temporary exhibitions include anything from ceramics to shoes. There are also a couple of cafes here.

Federation Square (runs north-south from Flinders St. to the Yarra River). ℂ 03/8662 1555. Free admission. Mon–Thurs 10am–5pm; Fri 10am–9pm; Sat–Sun 10am–6pm. Bus: City Explorer.

Old Melbourne Gaol *(Finds)*   I love this cramped former prison with its tiny cells and spooky collection of death masks and artifacts of 19th-century prison life. Some 135 hangings took place here, including that of notorious bandit (and Australian hero) Ned Kelly, in 1880. The scaffold where he was hung is still in place, and his gun, as well as a suit of armor used by a member of his gang, is on display. The jail closed in 1929. Profiles of former prisoners give a fabulous perspective of what it was like to be locked up here. Chilling night tours run every Sunday and Wednesday (call ahead and check the schedule); they cost A$18 (US$12) for adults and A$10 (US$6.50) for children (though the tour is not recommended for children under 12). Allow 1 hour or more.

Russell St. ℂ 03/9663 7228. Admission A$10 (US$6.50) adults, A$6.60 (US$4.30) children, A$45 (US$29) families. Daily 9:30am–4:30pm. Tram: City Circle tram to corner of Russell and Latrobe sts.

Queen Victoria Markets   The Queen Victoria Market is a Melbourne institution covering several blocks. There are hundreds of indoor and outdoor stalls, where you can find anything from live rabbits to bargain-basement clothes. The markets can get cramped, and there's a lot of junk to sort through, but you'll get a real taste of Melbourne and its ethnic mix. Look out for the interesting delicatessen section and cheap eateries. Allow at least an hour.

Two 2-hour tours of the market take in its food and heritage. The **Foodies Dream Tour** departs every Tuesday, Thursday, Friday, and Saturday at 10am and costs A$22 (US$14) for adults and A$15 (US$9.75) for children under 15, including sampling. Well-known chefs give cooking classes, costing $65 (US$42) per session. Call ℂ 03/9320 5835 for reservations.

Between Peel, Victoria, Elizabeth, and Therry sts. on the northern edge of the city center. ℂ 03/9269 5835. www.qvm.com.au. Tues–Thurs 6am–2pm; Fri 6am–6pm; Sat 6am–3pm; Sun 9am–4pm. Tram: Any tram traveling north along William St. or Elizabeth St.

Rippon Lea House Museum & Historic Garden   This grand Victorian house, 8km (5 miles) from the city center, is worth a visit to get a feel for old-money Melbourne. With dozens of rooms, Rippon Lea House was built by socialite Sir Frederick Thomas Sargood between 1868 and 1903; a pool and ballroom were added in the 1930s. Though the Romanesque architecture is interesting (note the stained glass and polychrome brickwork), the real attraction is the surrounding 5.3 hectares (13 acres) of landscaped gardens, which include a conservatory, a lake, a lookout tower, an orchard, and extensive flower beds and shrubbery. If you're here on a weekend, a public holiday, or during school vacations, you might like to drop into the tearoom, which is open from 11am to 4pm. Allow 2 hours.

192 Hotham St., Elsternwick. ℭ 03/9523 6095. Admission A$9 (US$5.85) adults, A$5 (US$3.25) children 5–16, A$20 (US$13) families. Daily 10am–5pm (house closes at 4:45pm). Daily guided tours of house every half-hour 10:30am–4pm and tour of estate at 2pm. Closed Good Friday and Christmas Day. Tram: 67 to Stop 40, then walk up Hotham St. Bus: 216/219 from Bourke and Queen sts. in the city to Stop 4. Train: Sandringham Line from Flinders St. Station to Rippon Lea Station.

St. Patrick's Cathedral   Though lacking the intricacy of design of St. Paul's, the Roman Catholic St. Patrick's is another interesting Gothic Revival construction with exceptional stained-glass windows. Built between 1858 and 1940 (consecrated in 1897), St. Patrick's was closely associated with immigrants from Ireland escaping the mid-19th-century potato famine. In the courtyard out front is a statue of the Irish patriot Daniel O'Connell. Allow 15 minutes.

Cathedral Place. ℭ **03/9662 2233.** Mon–Fri 6:30am–6pm; Sat–Sun 7:15am–7:30pm.

St. Paul's Cathedral   Built from 1880 to 1892 from the designs of William Butterfield, a famous English Gothic revival architect, the Anglican St. Paul's Cathedral is noteworthy for its highly-decorative interior and the English organ built by T. S Lewis. Step inside to see gold mosaics on walls, Victorian tessellated tiles on the floors, intricate woodcarvings, and stained-glass windows. The cathedral sports the second highest spire (at 98m/321 ft.) in the Anglican Communion. A boy's choir sings at 5:10pm Monday through Friday during school times, and twice on Sunday at 10:30am and 6pm. Outside is a statue of Matthew Flinders, the first sailor to navigate the Australian mainland between 1801 and 1803. Allow 15 minutes.

Flinders and Swanston sts. ℭ **03/9650 3791.** Daily 7:30am–6pm. Services: Sun 8, 9, and 10.30am; Eucharist 6pm. Choral evensong Mon–Fri 7:45am, and 12:15 and 5:10pm. Cathedral shop open 10am–4pm daily.

State Houses of Parliament   Now the home of the Victorian Parliament, this imposing monument to Victorian (as in Queen Victoria) architecture at the top of a run of sandstone steps was built in 1856. Between the time of the Australian Federation (1900–27), it was used as the National Parliament. When the State Government is in session—generally on Tuesday afternoon and all day Wednesday and Thursday between March and July, and again between August and November—you can view the proceedings from the public gallery. However, you should ring ahead and check as sitting times do vary. During non-sitting times both the extremely opulent Upper House and the less ornate Lower House chambers are open to the public. Allow 30 minutes.

Spring St. ℭ **03/9651 8568** or 03/9651 8569. www.parliament.vic.gov.au. Mon–Fri 9am–5pm. Free guided tours 10 and 11am, noon, and 2, 3, and 3:45pm on weekdays when parliament is not in session. Reservations recommended.

PARKS & GARDENS

Birrarung Marr, along the Yarra River and east of Federation Square on Batman Avenue (ℭ **03/9658 9658;** www.melbourne.vic.gov.au/parks), is Melbourne's first new major parkland in more than 100 years. Birrarung means "river of mists" in the Woiwurrung language of the Wurundjeri people who originally inhabited the area, while "Marr" equates with the side of the river. Wide, open spaces and large, sculptured terraces have been specially designed to host some of Melbourne's best events and festivals throughout the year, and the terraces give way to spectacular views of the City, Southbank, King's Domain, and the Yarra River.

The **Royal Botanic Gardens** ✿✿, 2km (1¼ miles) south of the city on Birdwood Avenue, off St. Kilda Road (✆ **03/9252 2300**), are the best gardens in Australia and well worth a few hours wander. More than 40 hectares (99 acres) are lush and blooming with more than 12,000 plant species from all over the world. Don't miss a visit to the oldest part of the garden, the Tennyson Lawn, with its 120-year-old English elm trees. Other special corners include a fern gully, camellia gardens, an herb garden, rainforests packed with fruit bats, and ponds full of ducks and black swans. You can either discover the gardens by wandering at your own pace, or you can take one of the free guided walks that leave the National Herbarium Building, F Gate, Sunday through Friday at 11am and noon. Bring snacks and your picnic blanket to Shakespeare in the Park, a popular summer event. Performances are in January and February, and tickets cost around A$30 (US$20). Call ✆ **03/9252 2300** for details. The gardens are open from November through March from 7:30am to 8:30pm, April and September through October from 7:30am to 6pm, and May through August from 7:30am to 5:30pm. Admission is free. To get there, catch the tram on Route 8, traveling south, and get off at Stop 21. Allow 2 to 4 hours.

Nearby, in King's Domain, take a look at Victoria's first Government House, **Latrobe's Cottage** (✆ **03/9654 5528**). It was built in England and transported to Australia brick by brick in 1836. Admission is A$2 (US$1.30) per person. The cottage is open from 11am to 4pm every Monday, Wednesday, Saturday, and Sunday. On the other side of Birdwood Avenue is the **Shrine of Remembrance,** a memorial to the servicemen lost in Australia's wars. It's designed so that at 11am on Remembrance Day (Nov 11), a beam of sunlight hits the Stone of Remembrance in the Inner Shrine. Note the eternal flame in the forecourt. King's Domain is Stop 12 on the Route 15 tram traveling south along St. Kilda Road.

In Fitzroy Gardens, off Wellington Parade, is **Cooks' Cottage** (✆ **03/9419 4677**), which was moved to Melbourne from Great Ayton, in Yorkshire, England, in 1934 to mark Victoria's centenary. The cottage was built by the parents of Captain Cook, and today provides the opportunity to learn about his voyages of discovery around the world. Inside, it's spartan and cramped, not unlike a ship's cabin. Admission is A$3.70 (US$2.40) for adults, A$1.80 (US$1.15) for children 5 to 15, and A$8.80 (US$5.70) for a family. It's open daily from 9am to 5pm (until 5:30pm during summer). Also east of the central business district are the **Treasury Gardens.** Look for the memorial to John F. Kennedy near the lake. Treasury Gardens and Fitzroy Gardens can be reached by tram no. 75 traveling east along Flinders Street. Get off at Stop 14 for Treasury Gardens and Stop 14A for Fitzroy Gardens.

6 Enjoying the Great Outdoors or Catching an Aussie Rules Football Match

OUTDOOR ACTIVITIES

BALLOONING   Melbourne by Balloon, Balloon Sunrise Office, 41 Dover St., Richmond (✆ **03/9427 7596;** fax 03/9427 7597), offers flights over the city plus a champagne breakfast once you've hit the ground again. Dawn flights cost A$265 (US$146) for adults, and A$175 (US$101) for children under 12 (but if they're under 1.2m (4 ft.) tall they won't be able to see over the basket). Reservations are essential.

BIKING Extensive bicycle paths wind through the city and suburbs. For details on the 20 most popular routes, pick up a copy of *Melbourne Bike Tours,* published by **Bicycle Victoria** (© **03/9328 3000;** fax 03/9328 2288; www.bv.com. au), available at most bookshops. Bicycle Victoria also runs several major cycling tours throughout the state every year.

Bike Now, 320 Toorak Rd., South Yarra (© **03/9826 6870**), rents bicycles for A$15 (US$9.75) for 2 hours, A$20 (US$13) for 4 hours, A$30 (US$20) for a full day, and A$70 (US$46) for a week. The shop is open Monday through Friday from 9am to 7pm, Saturday from 9am to 5pm, and Sunday from 11am to 5pm. Take tram no. 8 to Toorak Road.

You can also rent a bike from **Hire a Bike** at St. Kilda Pier (© **03/9531 7403**); non-Australians must show their passports.

GOLF One of the best public golf courses in Australia is **Yarra Bend,** Yarra Bend Road, Fairfield (© **03/9481 3729**). Greens fees are about A$15 (US$9.75), and club rental is an extra A$10 (US$6.50) for a half set and A$25 (US$16) for a full set.

The exclusive **Royal Melbourne Golf Club,** in the suburb of Black Rock, 24km (15 miles) from the city center, is rated as one of the world's 10 best golf courses. It's open to members only, but if you belong to a top-notch golf club at home, you might be able to wheedle your way in.

For more information on golf in Victoria, contact the **Victorian Golf Association,** 15 Bardolph St., Burwood (© **03/9889 6731**).

IN-LINE SKATING The promenade in St. Kilda is the most popular place to strap on a pair of skates. You can rent all you need at **Rock'n 'n' Roll'n,** 11a Fitzroy St., St. Kilda (© **03/9525 3434**). The first hour costs A$8 (US$5.20). Successive hours are less expensive.

TENNIS The venue for the Australian Open, the **Melbourne Park National Tennis Centre,** on Batman Avenue (© **03/9286 1244**), is a great place to play tennis. When tournaments are not scheduled, its 22 outdoor courts and four indoor courts are open to the public. You can rent courts Monday through Friday from 7am to 11pm, and Saturday and Sunday from 9am to 6pm. Charges range from A$14 to A$30 (US$9.10–US$20) per hour, depending on the court and time of day (outdoor courts are cheapest). Show courts 1, 2, and 3 are also for rent at the same prices. Racquets are also available for A$3 (US$1.95).

SPECTATOR SPORTS

CAR RACING The annual **Australian Formula One Grand Prix** takes place in early March. Call Ticketmaster (© **13 61 22** in Australia), or the Grand Prix Hotline (© **13 16 41** in Australia, or 03/9258 7100) for information on tickets, accommodations, and airfares. Also check out the Grand Prix's website at www.grandprix.com.au.

CRICKET From October through March, cricket's the name of the game in Melbourne. The **Melbourne Cricket Ground (MCG),** Brunton Avenue, Yarra Park, Jolimont (© **03/9657 8879**), once the main stadium for the 1956 Melbourne Olympic Games, is perhaps Australia's most hallowed cricket field. The stadium can accommodate 97,500 people. For the uninitiated, "one-day" games are the ones to look out for; "Test" games take several days to complete. Buy tickets at the gate or in advance from **Ticketmaster** (✆ **13 61 00** in Australia; www.ticketmaster7.com).

Tours of the MCG and its museum leave every half-hour daily from 10am to 3pm. The Australian Gallery of Sport and the Olympic Museum are also at the MCG. The Olympic Museum traces the development of the modern Olympics with individual display sections for each city.

FOOTBALL   Melbourne's number-one sport is **Australian Rules Football**— or simply, "the footy"—a skillful, often violent, ball game the likes of which you've never seen (unless you have ESPN). Melbourne sports 10 of the 16 Australian Football League (AFL) teams, with the others coming from Adelaide, Perth, Sydney, and Brisbane. The season starts on the third weekend in March and ends with the Grand Final on the last Saturday in September. The most accessible grounds are at The Melbourne Cricket Ground (MCG)—take tram no. 75 along Wellington Parade—and the Optus Oval at Carlton—take tram no. 19 from Elizabeth Street. Entrance tickets cost around A$16 (US$10.40) per person, or A$30 (US$20) for a family. For game information, call **AFL Headquarters** at ✆ **03/9643 1999.** Buy tickets at **Ticketmaster** (✆ **13 61 00** in Australia; www.ticketmaster7.com).

HORSE RACING   The **Melbourne Cup,** on the first Tuesday in November, has been fought for by the best of Australia's thoroughbreds (and a few from overseas) since 1861. Melbourne society puts on a show when they dress up for the occasion, and the entire nation stops in its tracks to at least tune in on TV.

The city has four race tracks: **Flemington** (which holds the Melbourne Cup), on Epson Road in Flemington (✆ **03/9371 7171**); **Moonee Valley,** on McPherson Street in Mooney Ponds (✆ **03/9373 2222**); **Caulfield,** on Station Street in Caulfield (✆ **03/9257 7200**); and **Sandown,** on Racecourse Drive in Springvale (✆ **03/9518 1300**). If you're staying in the city center, Flemington and Moonee Valley tracks are the easiest to get to. Take tram no. 57 from Flinders Street to reach the Flemington racetrack, and catch tram no. 59 from Elizabeth Street to travel to Moonee Valley.

TENNIS   The **Australian Open,** one of the world's four Grand Slam events, is played during the last 2 weeks of January every year at the Melbourne Park National Tennis Center, on Batman Avenue (✆ **03/9286 1244**). Tickets for the Australian Open go on sale in mid-October and are available through **Ticketek** (✆ **03/9299 9079**) and also on the Open's website, www.ausopen.org. Guided tours of the center are offered from April through October, Wednesday through Friday, when events aren't scheduled. Tours cost A$5 (US$3.25) for adults and A$2.50 (US$1.60) for children. To get there, take a train from the Flinders Street Station to Richmond Station and catch the special Tennis Center tram from there.

7 Shopping

Ask almost any Melbournian to help you plan your time in the city, and they'll advise you to shop till you drop. All Australia regards Melbourne as a shopping capital—it's got everything, from fashion houses to major department stores and unusual souvenir shops. If you're coming from Sydney, I say save your money until you get to Melbourne, and then indulge!

Start at the magnificent city arcades, such as the **Block Arcade** (running between Collins and Little Collins sts.), which has more than 30 shops, including the historic Hopetoun Tearooms (p. 547), and the Royal Arcade (stretching from Little Collins St. to the Bourke St. Mall). Then hit the courts and lanes around **Swanston Street** and the huge **Melbourne Central shopping complex** between Latrobe and Lonsdale streets.

Next, take your wallet as you fan out across the city, taking in **Chapel Street** in South Yarra, for its Australian fashions; and **The Jam Factory,** 500 Chapel St., South Yarra (© **03/9826 0537**), which is a series of buildings with a range of shops and food outlets, including a branch of the U.S.-based Borders, as well as 16 cinema screens. Get there on tram no. 8 or no. 72 from Swanston Street.

There's also **Toorak Road** in Toorak, for Gucci and other high-priced, high-fashion names; **Bridge Road** in Richmond for budget fashions; **Lygon Street** in Carlton for Italian fashion, footwear, and accessories; and **Brunswick Street** in Fitzroy for a more alternative scene.

Serious shoppers might like to contact **Shopping Spree Tours** (© **03/9596 6600**), a company that takes you to all those exclusive and alternative shopping venues, manufacturers, and importers you wouldn't be likely to find by yourself. Tours depart Monday through Saturday at 8:30am and cost A$60 (US$39) per person including lunch and a visit to the Melbourne Observation Deck.

MELBOURNE SHOPPING FROM A TO Z
ABORIGINAL CRAFTS
The Aboriginal Gallery of the Dreaming   This place stocks an extensive range of acrylic dot paintings and represents more than 120 artists. Boomerangs, didgeridoos, pottery, jewelry, bark paintings, prints, books, and music are also available. 73–77 Bourke St., Mall, City. © **03/9650 3277.**

Original & Authentic Aboriginal Art   Stop here for original artworks, traditional bark paintings, and informative aboriginal art presentations. 90 Bourke St. © **03/9663 5133.** www.authaboriginalart.com.au

CRAFTS
An interesting arts-and-crafts market is held on The Esplanade in St. Kilda on Sunday from 9am to 4pm. Take tram no. 16 from Swanston Street or no. 96 from Bourke Street.

The Australian Geographic Shop   Head here for high-quality Australiana, including crafts, books, and various gadgets. Shop 130, Melbourne Central, 300 Londsdale St. © **03/9639 2478** and Galleria Shopping Plaza, Little Collins St. © **03/9670 5813.**

DEPARTMENT STORES
David Jones   Like Myer, its direct competition, David Jones (or DJ's as it's affectionately known) spans 2 blocks (separated into men's and women's stores) and offers similar goods. The men's fashions, in particular, leave a lot to be desired. 310 Bourke St. Mall, City. © **03/9643 2222.**

Myer   The grand dame of Melbourne's department stores has 12 floors of household goods, perfume, jewelry, and fashions stretching over 2 blocks. It's one of the largest stores in the world. There's a good food section on the ground floor offering, among other things, good sushi. The clothes are better here than at David Jones and it has a good shoe shop next door. 314 Bourke St. Mall, City. © **03/9661 1111.**

FASHION
High-fashion boutiques also line the eastern stretch of Collins Street between the Grand Hyatt and the Hotel Sofitel, and Chapel Street in South Yarra. In addition, many thousands of retail shops and factory outlets are dotted around

the city, many of them concentrated on Bridge Road near Punt Road and Swan Street near Church Street in Richmond. You'll be able to find designer clothes, many just last season's fashions, at a fraction of the original price.

Collins Street features most international labels and also shoe heaven **Miss Louise** (123 Collins St.; © **03/9654 7730**). Nearby Flinders Lane has earned style status with the likes of **Alice Euphemia** (241 Flinders Lane; © **03/9650 4300**) that stocks upcoming Australian and New Zealand designers. Stop at **Aesop** (238 Flinders Lane; © **03/9654 1331**) for its aromatherapy creams and lotions; while down the stairs is **Christine** (181 Flinders Lane; © **03/9654 2011**), where women have been known to faint over the accessories. Little Collins Street is another fashion rat run. At 150 Little Collins St. look for local fashion labels **Bettina Liano** (© **03/9654 1912**), **Scanlan & Theodore** (© **03/ 9650 6195**), and **Verve** (© **03/9639 5886**).

Country Road   Country Road is one of Australia's best-known names for men's and women's fashion. The cool, classic looks don't come cheap, but the quality is worth it. County Road also sells designer cooking equipment and housewares. 252 Toorak Rd., and other sites, including Chapel St., South Yarra. © **1800/801 911** in Australia, or **03/9824 0133**.

R. M. Williams   Head here for genuine Australian gear: boots, Driza-bone coats, and Akubra hats. In the Melbourne Central complex. © **03/9663 7126**.

Saba   Australian designer Joseph Saba has several very vogue, very expensive boutiques for men and women in Melbourne, including one for each sex on Chapel Street (nos. 538 and 548) in South Yarra. This store caters to both men and women. 264 Collins St., City. © **03/9654 3524**.

Sam Bear   Sam Bear is another good bet for Outback-style fashions: Driza-bone coats, Akubra bush hats, R. M. Williams boots and clothing, and Blundstone boots (my favorite). They also sell a solid range of camping equipment. 225 Russell St., City. © **03/9663 2191**.

Surf, Dive 'N Ski Australia   As well as surfboards, boogie boards, and sunglasses, this store stocks a wide range of hip and happening beachwear, all at reasonable prices. All the big names in Australian surf wear can be found here, including Ripcurl, Quicksilver, and Billabong. The Jam Factory, Chapel St., South Yarra. © **03/9826 4071**.

Vegan Wares   Instead of leather, Vegan Wares uses microfiber to create tough, stylish shoes, bags, and belts. It's not just for vegetarians; carnivores enjoy it, too! 78 Smith St., Collingwood. © **03/9417 0230**.

FOODSTUFFS

Haigh's Chocolates   Indulge in some 50 types of Australia's best chocolate, from milk to dark to fruit flavored. I recommend the Sparkling Shiraz truffle if you need a serious treat. Two locations: 26 Collins St. © **03/9650 2114**; and Shop 27, the Block Arcade, 282 Collins St. © **03/9654 7673**.

Melbourne Candy Kitchen   If you have a sweet tooth, you're likely to spend a fortune at this traditional little candy shop that makes its goodies before your eyes. Rock candy is a specialty, and you can get your name (or the name of someone back home) spelled out in its center. Shop 20, Royal Arcade, City. © **03/9663 5654**.

JEWELRY

Altman & Cherny   Even if you're not in the market to buy, it's worth coming here to check out "Olympic Australia," the largest precious-gem opal in the

Death by Chocolate

If you love chocolate, sign up now for the **Chocolate Indulgence Walk** and the **Chocolates & Other Desserts Walk** (© 03/9815 1228 or 04/1215 8017). The former takes you on a tasting tour of Cadbury's, Myer, New Zealand Natural Ice Creamery, Chocolate Box, and Darrell Lea, and finishes off over chocolate cake at a cafe. This 2-hour tour leaves every Saturday at 12:30pm and costs A$25 (US$16) for adults (children under 6 go free). The latter tour includes tasting plenty of ice creams and chocolates around town as you tour kitchens and talk to chefs. The tour finishes with afternoon tea at the Grand Hyatt. This tour leaves every Saturday at 2:30pm and also costs A$25 (US$16). A third tour has been recently added, the **Chocolate Brunch Walk,** during which you try coffee and pastries at some of Melbourne's grooviest cafes. This tour costs A$22 (US$14). Reservations are essential.

world. It was found in Coober Pedy in South Australia in 1956 and is valued at A$2.5 million (US$1.6 million). The store offers tax-free shopping for tourists armed with both a passport and an international airline ticket. 128 Exhibition St., near Little Collins St. © 03/9650 9685.

Dinosaur Designs Dinosaur Designs is taking the jewelry design world by storm with its range of very artistic jewelry made out of resin. The shop has modern housewares as well. None of it's cheap, but the odd item won't break the bank. 562 Chapel St., South Yarra. © 03/9827 2600.

e.g.etal Shop here for fresh innovative jewelry by 50 or so of Australia's leading and emerging designers. 185 Little Collins St. © 03/9663 4334.

8 Melbourne After Dark

Melbourne can be an exciting place once the sun has set. The pubs and bars are far better than those in Sydney. Friday and Saturday nights will see most pubs (of both the trendy and the down-to-earth variety) packed to the rafters, and at lunchtimes those that serve food are popular, too. To find out what's happening, check the entertainment guide in the *Age,* Melbourne's daily broadsheet, each Friday.

THE PERFORMING ARTS

Melbourne is the most dynamic performing arts city in Australia. Its theaters offer the whole gamut from offbeat independent productions to large-scale musicals the like you'd find on Broadway. The city is also the home of the most prestigious festivals, with the annual **Melbourne Fringe Festival** (the first 3 weeks in Oct) and the annual **Melbourne International Comedy Festival** (from the end of Mar to roughly the end of Apr), attracting the best of Australian and international talent.

The Melbourne International Comedy Festival sees venues all over the city putting on performances, while the Fringe Festival sees the streets, pubs, theaters, and restaurants playing host to everyone from jugglers and fire-eaters to musicians and independent productions covering all art forms. Try to get tickets if you're in town during either festival, but keep in mind that hotels fill up fast at these times. For more information about these festivals consult their websites, www.melbournefringe.org.au or www.comedyfestival.com.au.

Another good time to plan your visit is during the annual **Melbourne International Film Festival** (from mid-July to the end of the first week in Aug), when new releases, shorts, and avant-garde movies are shown at varying venues around the city. For details or to check schedules check the festival's website, www.melbournefilmfestival.com.au.

For information on upcoming theater productions and reviews check out www.stageleft.com.au, or the official government entertainment information site, www.melbourne.vic.gov.au/events, which shows "What's On" in the theater world for up to 2 months in advance, as well as what's happening in dance, film, comedy, music, exhibitions, sports, and tours.

The best place to buy tickets for everything from theater to major sporting events, and to obtain details on schedules, is **Ticketmaster** (② **1800/062 849** in Australia, 13 28 849, or 03/9299 9079; www.ticketmaster7.com).

THE HEART OF MELBOURNE'S CULTURAL LIFE

Victorian Arts Centre ⟨⟨⟨   The spire atop the Theatre Building of the Victorian Arts Center, on the banks of the Yarra River, crowns the city's leading performing-arts complex. Beneath it, the State Theatre, the Playhouse, and the Fairfax present performances that are the focal point of Melbourne's cultural life.

The **State Theatre,** seating 2,079 on three levels, can accommodate elaborate stagings of opera, ballet, musicals, and more. The **Playhouse** is a smaller venue that often hosts the Melbourne Theatre Company. The **Fairfax** is more intimate still, and is often used for experimental theater or cabaret.

Adjacent to the Theatres Building is the **Melbourne Concert Hall,** home of the Melbourne Symphony Orchestra and the State Orchestra of Victoria, and often host to visiting orchestras. Many international stars have graced this stage, which is known for its excellent acoustics.

One-hour guided tours of the Concert Hall and theaters run Monday through Saturday at noon and 2:30pm (Saturday also at 10:30am). They cost A$10 (US$6.50) for adults, A$7.50 (US$4.90) for children, and A$23 (US$15) for families. Backstage tours on Sunday at 12:15pm cost A$14 (US$8.80). Children under 11 are not permitted. Call ② **03/9281 8000** between 9:30am and 5pm for information.

100 St Kilda Rd. ② **1300/136 166** for ticket purchase, or 03/9281 8000. Fax 03/9281 8282. www.viccarts centre.com.au. Tickets priced from A$20–A$140 (US$13–US$91).

ADDITIONAL VENUES & THEATERS

Check the *Age* to see what productions are scheduled during your visit. Odds are that the leading shows will be produced in one of the following venues:

The Comedy Club   The Comedy Club is a Melbourne institution. Come here to see local and international comedy acts, musicals, and special shows. Dinner and show Friday through Saturday A$40 to A$45 (US$26–US$29) depending on performer; show only Thursday through Saturday approximately A$20 (US$13). Level 1, 380 Lygon St., Carlton. ② **03/9348 1622.**

Comedy Theatre   The Comedy Theatre, with its ornate Spanish Rococo interior, manages to feel intimate even though it seats more than 1,000 people. Plays and musicals usually fill the bill, but dance companies and comedians also appear. 240 Exhibition St., City. ② **03/9299 9886** (or tickets can be purchased from Ticketek at ② 13 28 49).

(Value Half-Price Tickets

Buy your tickets for entertainment events, including opera, dance, and drama, on the day of the performance from the Half-Tix Desk in the Melbourne Town Hall on Swanston Street (✆ **03/9650 9420**). The booth is open Monday from 10am to 2pm, Tuesday through Thursday from 11am to 6pm, Friday from 11am to 6:30pm, and Saturday from 10am to 2pm. Tickets must be purchased in cash. Available shows are displayed on the booth door; note that you can't get show information over the phone.

The Forum Theatre   The Forum hosts well-known bands and international comedians. Tables and chairs are set up in cabaret-style booths, from which you can order drinks and meals. 154 Flinders St., City. ✆ **03/9299 9886.**

Her Majesty's Theatre   A fire destroyed the original theater here, but the current structure still retains the original facade and the Art-Deco interior added during a 1936 renovation. Musicals, such as the Australian premier of *Chicago,* frequent the boards. 219 Exhibition St., City. ✆ **03/9663 3211.**

The Princess Theatre   This huge facility hosts extravaganza productions. The theater opened its doors in 1886, and it still retains a dramatic marble staircase and ornate plaster ceilings. 163 Spring St., City. ✆ **03/9 663 3300.**

The Regent Theatre   Built in 1929, the Regent fell into disrepair and its stage was dark for 25 years. Now, after a recent A\$35 million (US\$23 million) renovation, it's been restored to its former glory. Tickets are available in the U.S. through ATS Tours at ✆ **800/423-2880.** The theater offers a range of dining packages. 191 Collins St., City. ✆ **03/9299 9800.**

Sidney Myer Music Bowl   This huge outdoor entertainment center is run under the auspices of the Victorian Arts Center Trust, and hosts opera, jazz, and ballet in the warmer months (and ice skating in the winter). It underwent extensive renovations in 2000. King's Domain, Alexandra Ave., City. ✆ **03/9281 8360.**

CINEMAS

Most of the city cinemas are situated within 2 blocks of the intersection of Bourke and Russell streets. Tickets cost between A\$9 and A\$14 (US\$5.90– US\$9.10). Among the independent cinemas, the one that stands out is the **Astor,** 3 Chapel St., East St. Kilda, at the corner of Chapel and Dandenong roads (✆ **03 9510 1414**). Housed in a superb Art Nouveau building, the Astor shows well-chosen classic movies.

THE CLUB & MUSIC SCENE

Melbourne's nightclub scene used to be centered along King Street, and while this area is still popular with large disco-style venues, the city is now awash with unique, hidden bars and clubs. It's best just to follow the crowds—or in some cases that couple slipping down a side lane and disappearing into a dimly lit entrance. Otherwise, the following options are more enduring in their appeal.

Bella Vista Social Club   Owned by the team at Becco, BVSC is upstairs above this perennially favorite restaurant. Ultra modern in a microsuede kind of way, this place jumps with a late-night crowd of many splendid hues—arty young things mingling with the suits, and all watching the goings on in the laneway below via a large screen hookup. 11–25 Crossley St. ✆ **03/9663 3000.**

Bennetts Lane Jazz Club   Often exceptional and always varied, this venue is simply the best in Melbourne for jazz. The back-lane location may be a little hard to find, but inside it's everything you've always imagined a jazz club to be. The best international players seek it out. 25 Bennetts Lane. ℭ 03/9663 2856. www.bennettslane.com. Cover A$10 (US$6.50).

Cicciolina Back Bar   This softly lit, alluring hideaway offers plush leather booths and a fine range of cocktails. Add in a particularly attentive staff, and you've got one of the best little bars in the greater St Kilda region. 130 Acland St. (enter from arcade), St Kilda. ℭ 03/9525 3333.

Double Happiness   This tiny but hugely atmospheric bar is detail at its best. The retro-oriental theme would make Chairman Mao proud. Mix with the hip crowd from the CBD (Central Business District), and try the "Gang of Four" cocktail (mango, vodka, Cointreau, and lemon). 21 Liverpool St (off Bourke St). ℭ 03/9650 4488. www.double-happiness.org.

Hi-Fi Bar & Ballroom   Featuring lots of live music mostly of the hard rock and contemporary persuasion and patronized by the younger set, this cavernous, underground venue features many visiting acts. 125 Swanson St., City. ℭ 03/9654 7617. www.thehifi.com.au. Cover Sat A$20 (US$13).

Honky Tonks   Head down a dark lane into a nondescript warehouse and up a flight of wooden stairs to discover this bar's happy revelers enjoying live but laid-back jazz or a DJ weaving his magic on the turntables. The cocktail bar is buzzing and the view from the deep lounges across the Yarra River to the botanical gardens is surreal. Duckboard Place. ℭ 03/9662 4555.

KingPin   Why not combine your two favorite pastimes? Ten-pin bowling and drinking! Experience the newly refurbished lanes and the new purple lounge, which really mixes it up with cool live DJs and great cocktails. Situated in the Crown Casino complex, this venue is open 24/7, so happy days really are here again. 8 Whiteman St., Southbank. ℭ 03/9292 7009. Cover varies. Bowling around A$20 (US$13).

Melbourne Supper Club   Upstairs above the ever-popular "European" cafe/restaurant, the Melbourne Supper Club is a perfect posttheater venue. Deep, leather lounges and a giant circular window that looks directly onto the beautifully lit Parliament House buildings make this bar a place to idle, smoke a cigar, or dwell over a bottle of your favorite wine. 161 Spring St. ℭ 03/9654 6300.

Misty   Funk meets Barbarella in this ultrahip and arty venue, one of the quintessential Melbourne bars, down a cobbled lane. Here smooth cocktails mix with live combos or soulful DJs. 3–5 Hosier Lane. ℭ 03/9663 9202.

Revolver   This venue usually pumps with techno music, although bands play on weekends with dancing later. 229 Chapel St., Prahan. ℭ 03/9521 5985. Cover $10 (US$6.50) on weekends.

Tony Starrs Kitten Club   Don't be put off by the name because this is one great place. A restaurant/bar on the lower level serves an array of excellent tapas and more exotic fare. But the action is at the upstairs Galaxy Lounge, where most nights you'll find entertainment—ranging from the peculiar to the animated to just plain bizarre. Don't forget to visit the Love Lounge, with its floor-to-ceiling red fabric, heart-shaped lounges, and secluded booths. The club is open for lunch and dinner until 1am. 267 Little Collins St. ℭ 03/9650 2448. Cover Sat A$5 (US$3.25).

WHERE TO SHARE A PINT

Something fun to do if you want to have a few drinks and meet a few people is to take one of the **City Pub Walks** (© **03/9384 0655** or 04/1208 5661). The 2½- to 3-hour walks stop off at a variety of interesting pubs and bars where you can sample the local brews (at your own expense). Tours leave from "under the clocks" at Flinders Street Station at 6:30pm Tuesday and Thursday.

Pubs have varying hours of operation, but generally stay open from mid-morning until at least midnight most nights. Many remain open until 2am or 3am on Friday and Saturday nights, and you can always find a few open 24 hours.

Bridie O'Reillys   Bridie O'Reillys is one of Melbourne's best Irish pubs, complete with traditional dark-wood decor and good beer. The two-level pub has 19 different beers on tap (7 of them Irish). There is live Irish music every night from around 9pm. The place gets quite crowded on weekends. 62 Little Collins St. (just off Exhibition St.), City. © **03/9650 0840.**

Belgian Beer Café Bluestone   Belgian beer culture in all its forms. Pretend that you're in Brussels in this extremely atmospheric cafe. Full-bodied Belgian brews dominate. While downing your pint, try the traditional streamed mussels. In warmer weather sitting in the parklike garden outside is a delight. 557 St Kilda Rd. © **03/9529 2899.**

The Cricketers Club Bar   Locals come to this popular English-style pub to lift a glass surrounded by the relics of Australia's summer passion. Glass cases are packed full of cricket bats, pads, and stumps, whereas the plush green carpets and solid mahogany woodwork give the place a touch of class. In the Windsor Hotel, 103 Spring St., City. © **03/9653 0653.**

Jimmy Watson's Wine Bar   While probably not the best spot for a pint, Jimmy's is somewhat of an institution and is one of Melbourne's oldest wine bars. The bar itself is a cozy affair where all types of people chat while sampling a vast range of wines. In the attached dining area, excellent food is expertly teamed with the perfect wine. Come to talk or simply read the paper. 333 Lygon St., Carlton. © **03/9347 3985.**

The Prince St. Kilda   This pub is a legend among the locals. Though recently refurbished, it retains its original rough-at-the-edges appearance. Bands, some of them big names, play most nights. 2 Acland St., St Kilda. © **03/9536 1100.**

Windsor Castle   Up Chapel Street and through Prahran is Windsor and its best-kept secret, the Windsor Castle Hotel, home of the local stylemeisters. This is a perfect weekend meeting place for good pub food, which can be enjoyed in the sunny courtyard or in the plush interior. You'll find DJs and barbecue on weekends. Look for the giant pink elephants outside. At the corner of Albert and Upton sts., Windsor. © **03/9525 0239.**

The Young and Jacksons Hotel   After a major renovation, Melbourne's oldest (and arguably most famous) pub is a newfound pleasure whether for a drink or a full dining experience in the stylish upstairs restaurant or bistro areas. Head upstairs to see the naked *Chloe,* a famous painting brought to Melbourne for the Great Exhibition in 1880. The pub, which was built in 1853 and started selling beer in 1861, has a few years on *Chloe,* which was painted in Paris in 1875. The painting has a special place in the hearts of customers. At the corner of Flinders and Swanston sts. © **03/9650 3884.**

THE CASINO

Crown Casino Australia's largest casino is a plush affair open 24 hours. You'll find all the usual roulette and blackjack tables and so on, as well as an array of gaming machines. Believe me, you can lose big here. There are some 25 restaurants and 40 bars on the premises. Clarendon St., Southbank. ℭ 03/9292 6868.

While you're here, have lunch at the **Red Emperor.** Its Cantonese yum cha is superb as is the service. There's a great view of the Yarra River. 3 Southgate Ave., upper level Southgate. ℭ 03/9699 4170. Yum cha items from A$3.85–A$8.80 (US$2.50–US$5.70). AE, DC, MC. V. Mon–Sat noon–3pm; Sun 11am–4pm.

9 Side Trips from Melbourne

DANDENONG RANGES

40km (25 miles) E of Melbourne

Melbournian traditionally do a "day in the Dandenongs" from time to time, topping off their getaway with Devonshire tea with scones and jam at one of the many cafes en route. Up in the cool, high country you'll find native bush, famous gardens, the Dandenong Ranges National Park, historic attractions such as the Puffing Billy—a vintage steam train—and plenty of restaurants and cozy B&Bs. The Dandenong Ranges National Park is one of the state's oldest, set aside in 1882 to protect its Mountain Ash forests and lush tree-fern gullies.

Auswalk, P.O. Box 516, Jindabyne, NSW 2627 (ℭ 02/6457 2220; fax 02/6457 2206; info@auswalk.com.au), offers 4-day/3-night, self-guided tours of the Dandenongs for two or more people, including accommodations, most meals, a ride on the Puffing Billy steam train (p. 566), national park entrance fees, vehicle transfers, and an itinerary and maps. The tour costs around A$590 (US$384) per person but could be a little cheaper depending on the season.

Parkwood Personalised Tours (ℭ 03/5334 2428; www.oztour.com; info@oztour.com) runs personalized day and multiday tours of the Yarra Valley as well as other places in Victoria, and the Great Ocean Road, staying at quaint B&B guesthouses or boutique hotels, from $60 (US$39) per hour.

GETTING THERE To get to the area, take the Burwood Highway from Melbourne, then the Mt. Dandenong Tourist Road, which starts at Upper Ferntree Gully and then winds its way through the villages of Sassafras, Olinda, Mount Dandenong, and Kalorama to Montrose. If you take a turnoff to Sherbrook, or extend your journey into a loop taking in Seville, Woori Yallock, Emerald, and Belgrave you'll see a fair slice of the local scenery.

VISITOR INFORMATION The **Dandenong Ranges & Knox Visitor Information Centre,** 1211 Burwood Hwy., Upper Ferntree Gully, VIC 3156 (ℭ 1800/645 505 in Australia, or 03/9758 7522; fax 03/9758 7533), is open daily from 9am to 5pm.

NATURE WALKS

Most people come here to get out of the city for a pleasant bushwalk, so in that way it's the equivalent of Sydney's Blue Mountains. Some of the better walks include the easy 2.5km (1.5-mile) stroll from the **Sherbrook Picnic Ground** through the forest, and the **Thousand Steps** and the **Kokoda Track Memorial Walk,** a challenging rainforest track from the Fern Tree Gully Picnic Ground up to One Tree Hill. Along the way are plaques commemorating Australian troops who fought and died in Papua New Guinea in World War II.

FOR GARDENING BUFFS

Bonsai Farm   If you don't like to crane your neck when it comes to looking at trees, then visit this large display of petite bonsais. Some of them are many decades old and cost a pretty penny.

Mt. Dandenong Tourist Rd., Mt. Dandenong. ☎ 03/9751 1150. Free admission. Wed–Sun 11am–5pm. Transportation: See William Ricketts Sanctuary below.

National Rhododendron Gardens   From September through November, thousands of rhododendrons and azaleas burst into bloom in these magnificent gardens. There are 42 lovely hectares (104 acres) in all, with a 3km (1.75-mile) walking path leading past flowering exotics and native trees as well as great vistas over the Yarra Valley. A tearoom is open every day during spring and on weekends at other times. Visitors flock here in summer for the glorious walks, and again in autumn when the leaves are turning.

The Georgian Rd., Olinda. ☎ 03/9751 1980. Admission: Sept 1–Nov 30 A$6.70 (US$4.35) adults, A$2.20 (US$1.40) children 10–16, A$14 (US$8.80) families; Dec 1–Aug 31 A$5.60 (US$3.60) adults, A$2.20 (US$1.40) children, A$13.50 (US$8.80) families. Daily 10am–4:30pm. Closed Christmas Day. Train to Croydon and then bus no. 688 to the gardens, or train to Belgrave and bus no. 694.

Tesselaar's Bulbs and Flowers   There are literally tens of thousands of flowers on display here, putting on a flamboyantly colorful show in the spring (Sept–Oct). Expect to see a dazzling variety of tulips, daffodils, rhododendrons, azaleas, fuchsias, and ranunculi. Bulbs are on sale at discount prices at other times.

357 Monbulk Rd., Silvan. ☎ 03/9737 9811. Admission during tulip festival, A$12 (US$7.80) adults, children under 16 admitted free if accompanied by an adult; free for everyone rest of the year. During tulip festival (approx. Sept 12–Oct 11) daily 10am–5pm; rest of year Mon–Fri 8am–4:30pm, Sat–Sun 1–5pm. Take the train to Lilydale and then bus no. 679.

William Ricketts Sanctuary   This wonderful garden, set in a forest of mountain ash, features clay figures representing the Aboriginal Dreamtime. The sculptures were created over the lifetime of sculptor William Ricketts, who died in 1993 at the age of 94. The garden encompasses fern gullies and waterfalls spread out over 13 hectares (32 acres), with the sculptures occupying .8 hectares (2 acres).

Mt. Dandenong Tourist Rd., Mt. Dandenong. ☎ 03/9751 1300. www.parkweb.vic.gov.au. Admission A$5.20 (US$3.40) adults, A$2 (US$1.30) children 10–16, A$13 (US$8.15) families. A$4.20 (US$2.75) concessions. Daily 10am–4:30pm. Closed Christmas and days of total fire ban. Train to Croydon then bus no. 688 to the sanctuary.

FOR TRAIN BUFFS

Puffing Billy Railway *Kids*   For almost a century, Puffing Billy steam railway has been chugging over a 13km (8-mile) track from Belgrave to Emerald Lake. Passengers take trips on open carriages and are treated to lovely views as the train passes through forests and fern gullies and over a National Trust–classified wooden trestle bridge. Trips take around an hour each way. Trains leave at 10:30 and 11:15am, noon, and 2:30pm on weekdays; and at 10:30 and 11:45am, and 1:30 and 3:15pm on Saturday and Sunday. A further stretch of track to Gembrook was opened in 1998. Daily trips to Gembrook take an extra 45 minutes and cost A$25 (US$16) for adults, A$14 ($9.10) for children, and A$72 (US$47) for families. Night trains also run on occasional Saturday nights.

Belgrave Station, Belgrave. ☎ 03/9754 6800 for 24-hr. recorded information. www.puffingbilly.com.au. Admission A$18 (US$12) adults, A$10 (US$6.50) children 4–16, A$51 (US$33) families. Operates daily except Christmas. Train from Flinders Street Station in Melbourne to Belgrave; the Puffing Billy station is a short walk away.

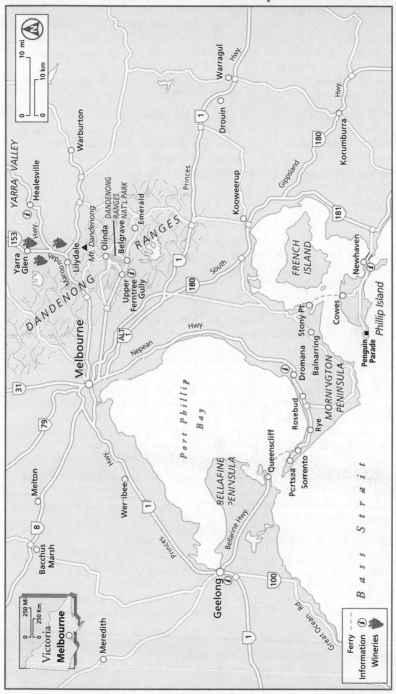

WHERE TO DINE

Churinga Café CAFE   This is a nice place for a quick lunch or morning or afternoon tea. It has nice gardens and is just across from the William Ricketts Sanctuary. You can get everything here from curries to traditional British fare. Devonshire tea costs A$6 (US$3.90).

1381 Mt. Dandenong Tourist Rd., Mt. Dandenong. ℂ 03/9751 1242. Main courses A$13–A$14 (US$8.45–US$9.10). AE, DC, MC, V. Sat–Wed 10:30am–4:30pm.

Wild Oak Café MODERN AUSTRALIAN   For good home cooking you can't beat this cozy cafe. The food includes the likes of chargrilled steak, smoked Atlantic salmon risotto, linguini with prawns, and Cajun chicken. The restaurant has a few vegetarian selections and a roaring log fire in winter.

232 Ridge Rd., Mt. Dandenong. ℂ 03/9751 2033. Main courses A$16–A$19 (US$10–US$12). DC, MC, V. Daily 10am–10pm.

YARRA VALLEY ℱ
61km (40 miles) E of Melbourne

The Yarra Valley is a wine-growing region east of Melbourne. It's dotted with villages, historic houses, gardens, crafts shops, antiques centers, and restaurants, as well as dozens of wineries. There are some good bushwalks around here and the Healesville Sanctuary is one of the best places in Australia to see native animals.

ESSENTIALS

GETTING THERE   McKenzie's Bus Lines (ℂ 03/9853 6264) operates a bus service from Lilydale Railway Station to Healesville. (Catch a train from Melbourne's Spencer Street Station to Lilydale; the trip takes about an hour.) Buses connect with trains roughly 12 times a day; call for exact connection times.

If you're driving, pick up a map of the area from the Royal Automotive Club of Victoria (ℂ 03/9790 3333) in Melbourne. Maps here are free if you're a member of an auto club in your home country, but remember to bring along your membership card. Alternatively, you can pick up a map at the tourist office. Take the Maroondah Highway from Melbourne to Lilydale and on to Healesville. The trip takes around 1 hour and 15 minutes.

VISITOR INFORMATION   Pick up details on attractions and lodging at the **Yarra Valley Visitor Information Centre,** Old Court House, Harker Street, Healesville (ℂ 03/5962 2600; fax 03/5962 2040). It's open daily from 9am to 5pm.

EXPLORING THE VALLEY

There are three principal roads in the valley: Melba Highway, Maroondah Highway, and Myers Creek Road, which together form a triangle. Within the triangle are three smaller roads, Healesville–Yarra Glen Road, Old Healesville Road, and Chum Creek Road, which all access wineries. Most people start their tour of the Yarra Valley from Lilydale and take in several cellar-door tastings at vineyards along the route.

Balloon Aloft (ℂ 1800/028 568 in Australia) offers dawn balloon rides over the wineries for A$195 (US$127) for adults and A$130 (US$85) for children over 8. The flight includes a champagne breakfast. **Peregrin Adventures** (ℂ 03/9662 2800; www.peregrine.net.au) also has balloon flights over the valley, with free pickup from Adelaide for A$195 (US$127) on weekends and A$175 (US$114) on weekdays. Peregrine can also arrange accommodations.

Healesville Sanctuary *(Finds)* Forget about seeing animals in cages—this preserve is a great place to spot native animals in almost natural surroundings. You can see wedge-tailed eagles, dingos, koalas, wombats, reptiles, and more, all while strolling through the peppermint-scented gum forest, which rings with the chiming of bell birds. Sir Colin McKenzie started the sanctuary in 1921 as a center to preserve endangered species and educate the public. There's a gift shop, a cafe serving light meals, and picnic grounds.

Badger Creek Rd., Healesville. © 03/5957 2800. Fax 03/5957 2870. www.zoo.org.au. Admission A$16 (US$10) adults, A$8.10 (US$5.25) children, A$44 (US$29) families; A$12 (US$7.80) concession. Daily 9am–5pm. Train from Flinders Street Station to Lilydale, then bus no. 685 to the sanctuary.

WHERE TO STAY & DINE

Melba Lodge *∕ℛ* These stylish, modern accommodations opened in Yarra Glen, in the heart of the Yarra Valley wine region, in early 1999. Of the six luxurious bedrooms, four have queen-size beds and two have king-size beds and a Jacuzzi; all have private bathrooms. There's a comfortable lounge with an open fire, and a billiard room. The lodge is only a few minutes' walk from historic Yarra Glen, which has antiques shops and a crafts market. There are plenty of restaurants and wineries around, too. It's a short drive to the Healesville Sanctuary.

939 Melba Hwy., Yarra Glen, VIC 3775. © 03/9730 1511. Fax 03/9730 1566. www.melbalodge.com.au. 8 units. A$130 (US$98) queen room; A$190 (US$117) king room. Rates include cooked breakfast. AE, DC, MC, V. **Amenities:** Bar; Jacuzzi; business center; massage; billiard room; nonsmoking rooms. *In room:* A/C, TV.

Sanctuary House Motel Healesville This place is very handy for visiting the sanctuary and even better if you want to relax and sample some good Yarra Valley wine. Just 400m (1,312 ft.) from the Healesville Sanctuary, Sanctuary House is set in some 4 hectares (10 acres) of beautiful bushland. The rooms are motel-style, and were completely refurbished in 2001 and awarded a government three-and-one-half star rating. There is also a five-bedroom farmhouse nearby on 8 hectares (20 acres) featuring a pool and log fireplace that can be hired through the motel.

Badger Creek Rd. (P.O. Box 162 Healesville, VIC 3777). © 03/5962 5148. Fax 03/5962 5392. www. sanctuaryhouse.com.au. 12 units (all with shower). A$80–A$88 (US$52–US$57) double. There are also 2 self-contained units available at a higher rate with amenities to assist travelers with disabilities. MC, V. Transportation: See the Healesville Sanctuary above. **Amenities:** Restaurant; small outdoor heated pool; Jacuzzi; sauna; games room; children's play area; massage; babysitting; laundry service; nonsmoking rooms. *In room:* A/C, TV, shower, fridge, hair dryer, iron.

PHILLIP ISLAND: PENGUINS ON PARADE *∕ℛ*
139km (86 miles) S of Melbourne

Phillip Island's **penguin parade,** which happens every evening at dusk, is one of Australia's most popular animal attractions. There are other (less crowded) places in Australia where watching homecoming penguins feels less staged—Kangaroo Island in South Australia comes to mind—but at least the little ones and their nesting holes are protected from the throngs by guides and boardwalks. Nevertheless, the commercialism of the Penguin Parade puts a lot of people off—busloads of tourists squashed into a sort of amphitheater is hardly being one with nature. Phillip Island also offers nice beaches, good bushwalking, fishing, and Seal Rocks. If you have the time, you could spend at least 2 days here.

ESSENTIALS
GETTING THERE Most visitors come to Phillip Island on a day trip from Melbourne and arrive in time for the Penguin Parade and dinner. Several tour

companies run day trips. Among them are **Gray Line** (© **03/9663 4455**), which operates penguin trips daily departing Melbourne at 1:30pm and returning at around 11:30pm. Tours cost A$80 (US$52) for adults and A$40 (US$26) for children. Gray Line also offers full-day trips including the Dandenong Ranges and a ride on the Puffing Billy Steam Train.

Down Under Day Tours (© **03/9650 2600**) offers a similar half-day tour for A$80 (US$52) for adults and A$40 (US$26) for children; tours depart Melbourne at 1:30pm and return at 11:30pm. It also offers a daylong trip that combines a Melbourne sightseeing tour with the penguin tour for A$106 (US$69) for adults, and A$53 (US$34) for children, and a half-day combined Dandenong Ranges/Phillip Island tour costing A$96 (US$63) for adults and A$48 (US$31) for children.

An excellent budget option is a half-day trip with **Melbourne Sightseeing** (© **03/9663 3388**). Tours depart Melbourne daily at 1:30pm and include visits to a cattle farm where you can hand-feed kangaroos, the Koala Conservation Centre, a seal colony, as well as the Penguin Parade. The coach returns to Melbourne at 10:30pm. The trip costs A$75 (US$49) for adults (A$49/US$32 with a YHA card) and A$38 (US$25) for children. For the same price, an express bus leaves Melbourne at 5:30pm (returning at 11pm) and travels directly to the Penguin Parade.

Auswalk, P.O. Box 516, Jindabyne, NSW 2627 (© **02/6457 2220;** fax 02/ 6457 2206; monica@auswalk.com.au), offers a 4-night self-guided tour of Phillip Island for two or more people for A$760 (US$494) per person. The price includes accommodations, most meals, park and entrance fees to the main places of interest, some vehicle transfers, an itinerary, and maps.

If you're driving on your own, it's an easy 2-hour trip from Melbourne along the South Gippsland Highway and then the Bass Highway. A bridge connects the highway to the mainland.

V/Line trains (© **13 22 32** in Australia, or 03/9619 5000) run in summer from Flinders Street Station to Phillip Island via Dandenong. The trip takes 2¼ hours and costs A$13 (US$8.70).

VISITOR INFORMATION   The **Phillip Island Information Centre,** Phillip Island Tourist Road, Newhaven (© **1300/366 422** in Australia, or 03/5956 7447; www.phillipisland.net.au), is an attraction in itself, with interactive computer displays, relevant information, dioramas giving visitors a glimpse into the penguin's world, and a small theater. It's open daily from 9am to 5pm (to 6pm in summer).

EXPLORING THE AREA
Visitors approach the island from the east, passing through the town of **Newhaven.** Just a little past Newhaven is the Phillip Island Information Centre.

The main town on the island, **Cowes** (pop. 2,400), is on the far north coast. It's worth taking a stroll along its Esplanade. The Penguin Parade is on the far southwest coast.

The trip to the west coast of the Summerland Peninsula ends in an interesting rock formation called **The Nobbies.** This strange-looking outcropping can be reached at low tide by a basalt causeway. You'll get some spectacular views of the coastline and two offshore islands from here. On the farthest of these islands is a population of up to **12,000 Australian fur seals,** the largest colony in Australia. (Bring your binoculars.) This area is also home to thousands of nesting silver gulls.

On the north coast you can explore **Rhyll Inlet,** an intertidal mangrove wetland, where you can see wading birds such as spoonbills, oystercatchers, herons, egrets, cormorants, and the rare bar-tailed godwit and the whimbrel.

Bird-watchers will also love **Swan Lake,** another breeding habitat for wetland birds.

Elsewhere, walking trails lead through heath and pink granite to **Cape Woolamai,** the island's highest point, where there are fabulous coastal views. September through April the cape is home to thousands of short-tailed shearwaters, or muttonbirds as they are sometimes called.

If you really want to see a bit of the island (instead of just seeing the parade and dashing off), consider taking one of the 15 different tours offered by **Mike Cleeland** and his **Island Nature Tours,** RMB 6080, Cowes, Phillip Island, VIC 3922 (© **03/5956 7883**).

A pedestrian bridge is the only connection to **Churchill Island,** an islet where you can visit beautiful gardens and a villa situated 1km (½ mile) from Newhaven, open every day (except Christmas Day). Admission is A$7.70 (US$5) adults, A$3.70 (US$2.40) children.

Koala Conservation Centre ⚞

Koalas were introduced to Phillip Island in the 1880s and at first they thrived in the predator-free environment. However, overpopulation, the introduction of foxes and dogs, and the clearing of land for farmland and roads, have all taken their toll. Though today you can still see a few koalas in the wild, the best place to find them is at this sanctuary, set up for research and breeding purposes. Visitors can get quite close to them, especially on the elevated boardwalk, which lets you peek into their treetop homes. For the best viewing come around 4pm, when the ordinarily sleepy koalas are on the move.

At Fiveways, Phillip Island Tourist Road, Cowes © **03/5952 1307.** A$5.60 (US$3.65) adults, A$2.60 (US$1.70) children under 16, A$14 (US$9) families. Daily 10am–5pm.

Phillip Island Penguin Reserve ⚞ *Kids*

The Penguin Parade takes place every night of the year at dusk, when hundreds of little penguins appear at the water's edge, gather together in the shallows, and waddle up the beach toward their burrows in the dunes. They're the smallest of the world's 17 species of penguins, standing just 33 centimeters (13 in.) high, and they're the only penguins that breed on the Australian mainland. Fences and viewing stands were erected in the 1960s to protect the nesting areas. Flash photography is banned because it scares the little guys. Wear a sweater or jacket, since it gets chilly after the sun goes down. A kiosk selling food opens an hour before the penguins turn up. Reservations for the Penguin Parade are essential on weekends and public holidays and in summer—all times when tickets can be difficult to get.

If you get to Phillip Island on your own and don't have a car, the **Penguin Parade Bus** (© **03/5952 1042** or 04/1736 0370) will pick you up from your hotel. The round-trip price is A$19 (US$12) for adults and A$11 (US$7.15) for children and includes a prebooked ticket for the Penguin Parade.

Summerland Beach, Phillip Island Tourist Rd., Cowes. © **03/5951 2800.** www.penguins.org.au. Admission A$14 (US$9.10) adults, A$7 (US$4.55) children 4–13, A$35 (US$23) families. Visitor center opens 10am; penguins arrive at sunset.

WHERE TO STAY

Penguin Hill Country House B&B   This private home with views over sheep paddocks to Bass Strait is within walking distance of the Penguin Parade. Each room has good views and is stocked with antiques (as is much of the house) and queen-size beds. Two have an attached bathroom with shower, and the third has a private bathroom across the hall. There's a TV and a phone in the cozy lounge. The hosts can pick you up from Cowes.

At Backbeach and Ventnor roads. (RMB 1093, Cowes, Phillip Island, VIC 3922). ℂ and fax **03/5956 8777.** 3 units. A$130 (US$85) double. Rates include cooked breakfast. AE, MC, V. Not suitable for children. **Amenities:** TV lounge; tour desk; business center; limited room service; coin-op laundry; nonsmoking rooms. *In room:* TV, fax, hair dryer, iron.

Rothsaye on Lovers Walk 🕊🕊   The penguins are just down the road and the beach is right on the doorstep—who could ask for anything more? The two suites here are adjacent to the owner's home, and the one-bedroom cottage is set slightly apart. All rooms come with antiques and king-size beds. You also get a fruit basket, free fishing gear, beach chairs and umbrellas, magazines, and fresh flowers. Lovers Walk, a romantic floodlit path, leads from the doorstep to the center of Cowes. The owners also have a new beachside property nearby called Abaleigh on Lovers Walk. The two gorgeous apartments here come with kitchens, barbecues, and good water views. They cost A$215 (US$140) a night.

2 Roy Ct., Cowes 3922. ℂ and fax **03/5952 2691.** www.rothsaye.com. 4 suites, 1 cottage. A$140–A$190 (US$91–US$124) suite; A$130–A$170 (US$85–US$111) cottage. Rates include breakfast. MC, V. Children not permitted. **Amenities:** Golf course nearby; tour desk; laundry; nonsmoking rooms. *In room:* A/C (portable), TV/VCR, kitchen, coffeemaker, hair dryer, iron.

AROUND PORT PHILLIP BAY

West of Melbourne, the Princes Freeway (or M1) heads toward Geelong via a bypass at Werribee. To the east of Melbourne, the Nepean Highway travels along the coast to the Mornington Peninsula as far as Portsea. If you have time to stay the night, you can combine the two options, heading first down to the Mornington Peninsula (see below) and then taking the car and passenger ferry from Sorrento to Queenscliff (see below).

WERRIBEE

This small country town is 32km (20 miles) southwest of Melbourne, a 30-minute drive along the Princes Freeway. Trains run from Melbourne to Werribee station; a taxi from the station to the zoo will cost around A$5 (US$3.25).

The Mansion at Werribee Park   Known as "the palace in the paddock," this 60-room Italianate mansion was built in 1877. It was quite the extravagant project in its day. In addition to touring the house, you may stroll around the grounds and have a picnic; it's surrounded by 132 hectares (326 acres) of bushland fronting the Werribee River. You can also prearrange to take one of the popular carriage rides that make their way through the property. Allow 1 to 2 hours. Great afternoon tea.

K Rd., Werribee. ℂ **13 19 63** in Australia, or 03/9741 2444. www.visitvictoria.com/mansions. Free admission park and picnic grounds; admission to mansion A$11 (US$6.50) adults, A$5.40 (US$3.40) children 5–15, A$28 (US$18) families. Nov–Mar daily 10am–5pm; Apr–Oct daily 10am–4pm. Closed Christmas.

Victoria's Open Range Zoo at Werribee   From inside your zebra-striped safari bus you can almost touch the mainly African animals that wander almost freely over the plains—no depressing cages here. This high-caliber open-air zoo is closely associated with the Melbourne Zoo. There is also a walk-through section featuring African cats, including cheetahs, and monkeys. The safari-bus tour takes 50 minutes.

K Rd., Werribee. (C) **03/9731 9600**. www.zoo.org.au. Admission A$16 (US$10) adults, A$7.80 (US$5.05) children, A$43 (US$28) families. Daily 9am–5pm (the entrance gate closes at 3:30pm). Safari tours hourly 10am–3pm.

THE MORNINGTON PENINSULA

The Mornington Peninsula, a scenic 40km (25 miles) stretch of windswept coastline and hinterland 80km (50 miles) south of Melbourne, is one of Melbourne's favorite day-trip and weekend-getaway destinations. The coast is lined with good beaches and thick bush consisting almost entirely of tea trees. (Early colonists used it as a tea substitute.) The **Cape Shanck Coastal Park** stretches along the peninsula's Bass Strait foreshore from Portsea to Cape Shanck. It's home to gray kangaroos, southern brown bandicoots, echidnas, native rats, mice, reptiles, bats, and many forest and ocean birds. The park has many interconnecting walking tracks providing access to some remote beaches.

The Mornington Peninsula has become a very popular wine-producing region. The Peninsula's fertile soil, temperate climate, and rolling hills produce excellent wine, particularly pinot noir, shiraz, and chardonnay. Many wineries offer cellar door tastings, others have excellent restaurants located among the wineries.

Along the route to the south you could stop off at the **Morning Peninsula Regional Gallery,** 4 Vancouver St., Mornington (© **03/5975 4395**), to check out the work of famous Australian artists (open Tues–Sun 10am–5pm), or visit Arthurs Seat State Park to take a short hike or ride a chair lift to a 300m (984-ft.) summit offering glorious views over the surrounding bush. At Sorrento, take time out to spot pelicans on the jetty, or visit the town's many galleries.

Also on the Mornington Peninsula is Australia's oldest and most famous maze, **Ashcombe Maze & Water Gardens,** Red Hill Road, Shoreham (© **03/5989 8387**), which also has extensive water and woodland gardens. There is even a rose maze made out of 1,300 rose bushes, which is spectacular when in full bloom over the spring and summer months. There's also a pleasant cafe with indoor and outdoor dining. The park is open daily from 10am to 5pm; admission is A$7 (US$4.35) for adults, and A$4 (US$2.50) for children.

GETTING THERE   From Melbourne, take the Mornington Peninsula Freeway to Rosebud, and then the Point Nepean Road. If you want to cross Port Phillip Bay from Sorrento to Queenscliff, take the **Queenscliff Sea Road Ferry** (© **03/5258 3255;** fax 03/5258 1877), which operates daily departing every hour on the hour between 8am and 6pm (there's an 8pm ferry Fri–Sat from mid-Sept to mid-Dec and daily from mid-Dec until Easter Thurs). Ferries from Queenscliff operate from 7am to 5pm (plus a 7pm ferry on days listed above). The fare is A$32 to A$34 (US$21–US$22) for cars depending on season, plus A$3 (US$1.95) for adults, A$2 (US$1.30) for children 5 to 15, and A$1 (US65¢) for children 4 and under. Passenger-only fares are A$7 (US$4.50) for adults, A$5 (US$3.25) for children 5 to 15, and A$1 (US65¢) for children under 4. The crossing takes 35 to 40 minutes.

VISITOR INFORMATION   The **Peninsula Visitor Information Centre,** Point Nepean Road, Dromana (© **1800/804 009** in Australia, or 03/5987 3078), has plenty of maps and information on the area and can also help book accommodations. It's open daily from 9am to 5pm. You can get more information on this and all the other Victorian National Parks by calling © **13 19 63,** or via the Internet on www.parks.vic.gov.au.

Where to Stay & Dine

The Portsea Hotel   The rooms in this typical Australian motel situated on the seafront are done up in country-style furnishings. The standard twin rooms are basic; all share bathrooms. En-suite doubles have double beds and attached bathrooms with showers. The outdoor beer garden is pleasant on a sunny day.

3746 Point Nepean Rd., Portsea, Vic 3944. ✆ **03/5984 2213.** Fax 03/5984 4066. www.portseahotel.com.au. 25 units, 6 with bathroom. A$116 (US$75) double without bathroom; A$143 (US$93) double with bathroom; A$176 (US$114) bay-view suite. Rates are around 20% cheaper in winter. AE, DC, MC. V. **Amenities:** Restaurant; 3 bars; golf course nearby; tour desk; laundry service. *In room:* A/C, TV (in 6 rooms with bathroom only), fridge (in rooms with bathroom), coffeemaker.

12

Victoria

by Marc Llewellyn

Australia's southernmost mainland state is astoundingly diverse. Within its boundaries are 35 national parks, encompassing every possible terrain, from rainforest and mountain ranges to sun-baked Outback desert and a coast where waves crash dramatically onto rugged sandstone outcroppings.

Melbourne (see chapter 11) may be this rugged state's heart, but the mighty Murray River, which separates Victoria from New South Wales, is its lifeblood, providing irrigation for vast tracks of semidesert land.

Most visitors to Victoria start out exploring Melbourne's cosmopolitan streets, and then visit a few local wineries, before heading for the gold fields around the historic city of Ballarat. Lots of them only experience a fraction of Victoria, but this wonderful and not overly touristed region is worth a closer look.

Visitors with more time might head inland to the mountains (perhaps for skiing or bushwalking at Mt. Hotham or Falls Creek), or seek out the wilderness of Snowy River National Park. Others head to the outback, to the Grampians National Park, and Mildura through open deserts and past pink lakes and red sand dunes.

Lots of options await, and because many of them are rural, you'll find prices for accommodations very affordable. Whatever itinerary you choose, you're sure to find adventure and dramatic scenery.

See "Side Trips from Melbourne," in chapter 11, for information on the Dandenong Ranges, Yarra Valley, Phillip Island, and the Mornington Peninsula.

EXPLORING THE STATE

VISITOR INFORMATION Pick up brochures and maps at the Victoria Visitor Information Centre (see chapter 11, "Melbourne"), or call the **Victoria Tourism Information Service** (© **13 28 42**) from anywhere in Australia to talk to a consultant about your plans. The service, open daily from 8am to 6pm, will also send out brochures. If you need information along the way, look for blue road signs with a white or yellow information symbol.

GETTING THERE V/Line (© **13 61 96** in Victoria, or 13 22 32 in New South Wales) runs a limited network of trains to various places in Victoria, continuing trips to most major centers with connecting buses. Several bus companies connect Melbourne with regional areas of Victoria; the biggest operator is **McCafferty's** (© **13 20 30** in Australia, or 03/9670 2533).

1 Ballarat: Gold-Rush City ⋆⋆

113km (70 miles) W of Melbourne

Ballarat, Victoria's largest inland city (pop. 90,000), is all about gold. In 1851, two prospectors found gold nuggets scattered on the ground at a place known as, ironically, Poverty Point. Within a year, 20,000 people had drifted into the area, and Australia's El Dorado gold rush had begun.

In 1858, the second-largest chunk of gold discovered in Australia (the Welcome Nugget) was found, but by the early 1860s, most of the easily obtainable yellow metal was gone. Larger operators continued digging until 1918, and by then Ballarat had developed enough industry to survive without mining. Today, you can still see the gold rush's effects in the impressive buildings, built from the miners' fortunes, lining Ballarat's streets.

ESSENTIALS

GETTING THERE   From Melbourne, Ballarat is a 1½-hour drive via the Great Western Highway. **V/Line** (© **13 61 96** in Victoria or 13 22 32 in New South Wales) runs trains between the cities every day, and the trip takes less than 2 hours. The one-way fare is approximately A$17 (US$11) for adults and A$9 (US$5.85) for children. Ask about family-saver fares. A public bus connects the Ballarat train station with the town center.

Several companies offer day trips from Melbourne. **Melbourne Sightseeing** (© **03/9663 3388**) offers one of the most affordable choices, a full-day tour that costs A$98 (US$64) for adults and A$49 (US$32) for children.

VISITOR INFORMATION   The **Ballarat Visitor Information Centre** at 39 Sturt St. (at the corner of Albert St.), Ballarat, VIC 3350 (© **1800/648 450** in Australia, or 03/5320 5741; www.ballarat.com), is open daily from 9am to 5pm.

SEEING THE SIGHTS

Ballarat contains many reminders of the gold-rush era, but it all really comes to life in the colonial-era re-creation on Sovereign Hill.

Ballarat Fine Art Gallery   After you've learned the story of the Eureka Uprising (see the next listing), you may find it moving to come here and see the original Eureka flag. This provincial gallery also houses a collection of Australian art, including works by Sydney Nolan, Fred Williams, and Russell Drysdale. Look out for Tom Roberts' *Charcoal Burners* and Phillip Fox's *Love Story.*

40 Lydiard St. N., Ballarat. © 03/5320 5858. Admission A$4 (US$2.60) adults, A$2 (US$1.30) students, free for children under 16. Daily 9am–5pm. Closed Good Friday and Christmas.

Blood on the Southern Cross ⭑   This 80-minute show re-creates the Eureka Uprising, one of the most important events in Australia's history, in a breathtaking light-and-sound show that covers Sovereign Hill's 25 hectares (62 acres). Bring something warm to wear, because it can get chilly at night.

After gold was discovered, the government devised a system of gold licenses, charging miners a monthly fee, even if they came up empty-handed. The miners had to buy a new license every month, and corrupt gold field police (many of whom were former convicts) instituted a vicious campaign to extract the money.

When license checks intensified in 1854, even though most of the surface gold was gone, resentment flared, and prospectors began demanding political reforms, such as the right to vote, parliamentary elections, and secret ballots.

The situation exploded when the Eureka Hotel's owner murdered a miner but was set free by the government. The hotel was burned down in revenge, and more than 20,000 prospectors joined together, burned their licenses in a huge bonfire, and built a stockade over which they raised a flag.

Troops arrived at the "Eureka Stockade" the following month, but by then only 150 miners remained behind its walls. The stockade was attacked at dawn,

Victoria

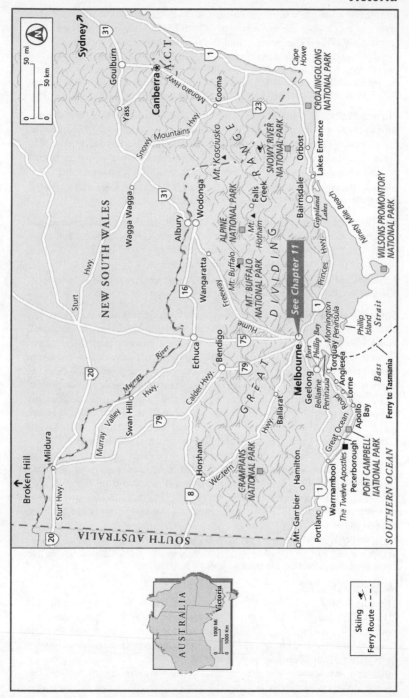

and in the 15-minute skirmish, 24 miners were killed and 30 wounded. The civil uprising forced the government to act: The licenses were replaced with "miners rights" and cheaper fees, and the vote was introduced to Victoria.

At Sovereign Hill, Bradshaw St. ☏ 03/5333 5777. www.sovereignhill.com.au. Reservations required. Admission A$30 (US$20) adults, A$16 (US$10) children 5–15, A$84 (US$55) families. Other packages include daytime entry to Sovereign Hill: A$51 (US$33) adults, A$26 (US$17) children, A$140 (US$91) families. Call ahead for information about other packages. 2 shows nightly Mon–Sat (times vary seasonally). Closed early Aug.

Eureka Stockade Centre   You can't miss this building with its huge sail, signifying the flag of the Southern Cross, which was raised above the original miners' stockade. Relive the action of the battle through multimedia displays. The Contemplation Room, where you are asked to think about Australian history while listening to a trickling water soundscape, is a bit too hokey for me.

Eureka St. ☏ 03/5333 1854. Admission A$8 (US$5.20) adults, A$4 (US$2.60) children, A$22 (US$14) families. Daily 9am–5pm. Closed Christmas and Mon except public holidays.

The Gold Museum   This interesting museum houses a large collection of gold nuggets found at Ballarat, as well as alluvial deposits, gold ornaments, and coins. There are also gallery displays relating to the history of gold mining in the area. One hour should be enough to take in the museum.

Bradshaw St. (opposite Sovereign Hill), Ballarat. ☏ 03/5337 1107. Admission included with Sovereign Hill ticket; otherwise, A$6.30 (US$4) adults, A$3.10 (US$1.95) children. Daily 10am–5:30pm.

Sovereign Hill 𝄆𝄆 𝘒𝘪𝘥𝘴   Australia's best outdoor museum transports you back to the 1850s and the heady days of the gold rush. More than 40 stone-and-wood reproduction buildings, including shops and businesses on Main Street, sit on this 25-hectare (62-acre) former gold-mining site. There are also tent camps around the diggings on the lowest part of the site, which would have been the outskirts of town. There is lots to see and do, so expect to spend at least 4 hours.

The Township bustles with actors in period costumes going about their daily business. In addition to seeing how miners and their families lived, visitors can pan for real gold, watch lessons in Victorian classrooms, ride in horse-drawn carriages, and watch potters, blacksmiths, and tanners make their wares.

On top of Sovereign Hill are the mineshafts and their pithead equipment. The fascinating tour of a typical underground gold mine takes around 45 minutes.

The Voyage to Discovery museum has various artifacts from the gold rush, dioramas of mining scenes, and interactive computer displays.

A restaurant and several cafes, coffee shops, and souvenir stores can be found around the site.

Bradshaw St. ☏ 03/5331 1944. www.sovereignhill.com.au. Admission (including mine tour and admission to Gold Museum) A$27 (US$18) adults, A$13 (US$8.45) children 5–15, A$70 (US$46) families. Daily 10am–5pm. Closed Christmas. Bus: From Ballarat catch the Buninyong bus.

WHERE TO STAY

The Ansonia 𝘢   This boutique hotel in a restored Victorian building sports a glass atrium that runs the length of the property and is filled with plants and wicker chairs. Studio rooms are simply but comfortably furnished, and have nice polished floorboards. The executive doubles are larger and a little plusher. The two family rooms can sleep four people in two bedrooms. There is a comfortable library and sitting room with an open fire and tea- and coffeemaking facilities, and plenty of flowers and art everywhere. Smoking is not allowed on the property.

32 Lydiard St. S., Ballarat 3350. ☏ 03/5332 4678. Fax 03/5332 4698. www.ballarat.com/ansonia.htm. 20 units. A$135 (US$88) double; A$150 (US$98) executive double; A$175 (US$114) suite; A$215 (US$140)

family room; A$210 (US$137) apt. AE, DC, MC, V. Free parking. **Amenities:** Restaurant; tour desk; baby-sitting; laundry service; same-day dry cleaning; nonsmoking rooms. *In room:* TV, dataport, hair dryer, iron.

Ballarat Heritage Homestay ✸ *(Finds* If you'd enjoy staying in a historic cottage, you might want to try Ballarat Heritage Homestay. Some of these Victorian and Edwardian cottages date from the gold rush days. All of them are very different, but all have a historic feel. Three cottages have claw-foot tubs, and one has a Jacuzzi. Generally there's a queen and a double, and sometimes two singles in each cottage. All the cottages have three bedrooms, open fires, and gas heating. The B&B room has a queen-size bed and sole use of a lounge.

185 Victoria St. (P.O. Box 1360, Ballarat Mail Centre, VIC 3354). ℂ **1800/813 369** in Australia, or 03/5332 8296. Fax 03/5331 3358. www.heritagehomestay.com. 5 cottages, 1 B&B unit. A$175 (US$114) for 2 people for 1-night weekend stay (available for some cottages only); A$275–A$350 (US$179–US$228) 2-night weekend stay; A$145–A$160 (US$94–US$104) 1-night weekday stay. Rates include breakfast. Extra adult A$30 (US$20), extra child under 18 A$15 (US$9.65). AE, DC, MC, V. **Amenities:** TV lounge. *In room:* Kitchen, hair dryer, iron.

The Sovereign Hill Lodge The colonial-style wooden buildings adjacent to the Sovereign Hill were built to resemble an 1850s Government Camp that was used to control (and tax) the mine fields. The residence building has rooms with queen-size beds and a set of single bunks, and the Offices building has heritage rooms with four-poster beds and Baltic pine furnishings, some with Jacuzzis. There are eight double rooms in the Superintendent's house, while the Barracks houses dorm rooms sleep up to eight people (A$55/US$36 double; A$32/US$21 single). There's a bar, 24-hour reception, and a game room. Guests get a 10% discount off entry to Sovereign Hill.

Magpie St., Ballarat, VIC 3350. ℂ **03/5333 3409.** Fax 03/5333 5861. www.sovereignhill.com.au. 37 units. A$126 (US$82) double; A$138 (US$90) heritage room. Extra person A$14 (US$9.10). Ask about packages. AE, DC, MC, V. Free parking. **Amenities:** Restaurant; bar; Jacuzzi (in heritage room); babysitting; laundry service; nonsmoking rooms. *In room:* A/C, TV, iron.

WHERE TO DINE

Lake Pavilion Restaurant Café INTERNATIONAL I like this restaurant across from the Botanical Gardens and on the shores of Lake Wendouree. The Lake Pavilion was constructed in 1890 and still has that old-world atmosphere, with polished floorboards and high ceilings. You can eat either indoors or outside, but either way you have some good views across the gardens and the lake. The menu includes pizzas, focaccia sandwiches, various pasta dishes, salads, steaks, and seafood. It's licensed but you can also bring your own wine. A kiosk adjacent to the restaurant sells cheap snacks.

Wendouree Parade (across from the Botanical Gardens). ℂ **03/5334 1811.** Main courses around A$11 (US$7.15). AE, MC, V. Daily 9am–6pm. Bus: 15 Mon–Sat.

Robin Hood Family Bistro BISTRO The Robin Hood is located in a big old pub—not exactly a place where you'd expect to find a bistro catering to healthy eating. The bistro, though, is a past winner of the Real Meal Award, handed out by the Australian Hoteliers Association and aimed at promoting healthier pub food. Everything here is made with low-fat/low-cholesterol ingredients. On the menu you'll find steak-and-kidney pie, beef curry, and several types of steak. Not healthy so far, perhaps, but there's an extensive salad bar, and all main courses come with a healthy dollop of vegetables.

33 Peel St. N. ℂ **03/5331 3348.** Reservations recommended Fri–Sat. Main courses A$8–A$20 (US$5.20–US$13). AE, DC, MC, V. Daily 11:30am–2pm and 5:30–8pm.

2 The Great Ocean Road: One of the World's Most Scenic Drives ⋆⋆

Geelong: 75km (47 miles) SW of Melbourne; Torquay: 94km (58 miles) SW of Melbourne; Port Campbell National Park: 285km (177 miles) SW of Melbourne; Peterborough: 200km (124 miles) SW of Melbourne

The Great Ocean Road—which hugs the coast from Torquay, and onwards through Anglesea, Lorne, Apollo Bay, and Port Campbell, until it ends at Peterborough—is one of Australia's most spectacular drives. The scenery along the 106km (66-mile) route includes huge cliffs, ocean vistas, beaches, rainforests, and some incredible rock formations. The settlements along the highway are small, but they offer a number of accommodations choices.

The best way to travel along the Great Ocean Road is to drive yourself at a leisurely pace, stopping off wherever your fancy takes you. The main attractions are in the coastal Port Campbell National Park, so don't be surprised if you're not overly impressed until you get there. If you are traveling on to Adelaide, you could stop off for 1 night along the Great Ocean Road, and spend another night in the Coorong in South Australia (see section 5, "The Coorong," in chapter 10).

ESSENTIALS

ORGANIZED TOURS   **Melbourne Sightseeing** (✆ 03/9663 3388) offers a bus trip featuring the highlights of the Great Ocean Road. Buses leave from Melbourne daily at 8:15am and return at 8:30pm—a journey I wouldn't like to attempt in a day. Tours cost A$97 (US$63) for adults—A$54 (US$35) if you have a YHA card—and A$49 (US$32) for children. The trip can be stretched out over 2 days with overnight accommodations; the price for the overnight trip ranges between A$136 and A$170 (US$88–US$111) depending on where you stay. **Grayline Sightseeing Tours** (✆ 03/9663 4455) also has daily trips that cost A$102 (US$66) for adults and A$51 (US$33) for children.

Another option worth considering is a 2-day excursion with **Let's Go Bush Tours** (✆ 03/9662 3969), which departs Melbourne every Wednesday and Saturday. The trip is less rushed than others, and you get to stay in the company's own house situated on the highest point of the Great Ocean Road. The trip costs A$99 (US$64), including dinner, breakfast, and accommodations.

Wild-Life Tours (✆ 1300/650 288 or 03/9747 1882; www.wildlifetours.com. au) offers a 3-day Great Ocean Road tour from Melbourne, including a visit to The Grampians, for A$135 (US$88). The company also offers a 2-day trip from Melbourne to Adelaide along the Great Ocean Road for A$129 (US$84) one-way. Prices do not include accommodations or food. Inquire about discounts.

V/Line (✆ 13 61 96 in Victoria, or 03/9619 5000) runs a combined train/coach Coast Link service to Warrnambool, via Geelong, Lorne, Apollo Bay, and Port Campbell. The train leaves Melbourne daily at 8:50am, and 12:40 and 6:08pm—but check before turning up—and then you transfer onto a bus at Geelong. The bus tours the Great Ocean Road, stopping off at lookout points (and for lunch) and then carries on to Warrnambool. The round-trip cost is A$80 (US$52) for adults and A$39 (US$23) for children. Ask about family-saver fares.

VISITOR INFORMATION   Most places along the route have their own information centers. If you're coming from Melbourne, stop at the Geelong & Great Ocean Road Visitors Centre, Stead Park, Princess Highway, Geelong, VIC 3220 (✆ and fax 03/5275 5797; www.greatoceanrd.org.au). You can book accommodations here, which you should do in advance, especially in summer.

There's also a visitor center at the National Wool Museum, 26 Moorabool St., Geelong (© **1800/620 888** in Australia, or 03/5222 2900).

Along the route, the **Port Campbell Visitor Information Centre,** at Port Campbell National Park, Morris Street, Port Campbell (© **03/5598 6382**), is also a good place to pick up brochures. It has some interesting displays and an audiovisual show of the area, and also acts as a hotel-booking service for the area. It's open from 9am to 5pm daily.

If you're approaching from the north, visit the **Camperdown Visitor Information Centre,** "Court House," Manifold Street, Princes Highway, Camperdown (© **03/5593 3390**). It's open Monday through Friday from 9:30am to 5pm, Saturday from 9:30am to 4pm, and Sunday from 11am to 4pm.

EXPLORING THE COASTAL ROAD

Along the route you might want to stop off at **Torquay,** a township dedicated to surfing. The main surf beach here is much nicer than the one farther down the coast in Lorne. While in Torquay, check out **Surfworld Museum,** Surfcity Plaza, Beach Road, West Torquay (© **03/5261 4606**), which has interactive exhibits dealing with surfboard design and surfing history, and video of the world's best surfers. Admission is A$6.50 (US$4.20) for adults, A$4.50 (US$2.90) for children, and A$18 (US$11) for families. **Bells Beach,** just down the road, is world-famous in surfing circles for its perfect waves.

Lorne has some nice boutiques and is a good place to stop off for lunch or stay the night. The stretch from Lorne to Apollo Bay is one of the most spectacular sections of the route, as the road narrows and twists and turns along a cliff edge with the ocean on the other side. **Apollo Bay** is a pleasant town that was once a whaling station. It has good sandy beaches and is more low-key than Lorne.

Next, you come to the **Angahook-Lorne State Park,** which protects most of the coastal section of the Otway Ranges from Aireys Inlet, south of Anglesea, to Kennett River. It has plenty of well-marked rainforest walks and picnic areas at Shelly Beach, Elliot River, and Blanket Bay. There's plenty of wildlife around.

About 13km (8 miles) past Apollo Bay, just off the main road, you can take a stroll through the rainforest on the **Maits Rest Rainforest Boardwalk.** A little farther along the main road, an unpaved road leads north past Hopetoun Falls and Beauchamp Falls to the settlement of **Beech Forest.** Seven kilometers (4⅓ miles) farther along the main road another unpaved road heads off south for 15km (9⅓ miles) to a windswept headland and the **Cape Otway Lighthouse.** Built by convicts in 1848, the 100m (328-ft.) tall lighthouse is open to tourists. Admission is A$6.50 (US$4.20) for adults and A$3.50 (US$2.30) for children. It's open daily from 9am to 5pm. Ask about guided tours.

Back on the main road again, your route heads inland through an area known as **Horden Vale,** before running to the sea at Glenaire—there's good surfing and camping at Johanna, 6km (3¾ miles) north of here. Then the Great Ocean Road heads north again to **Lavers Hill,** a former timber town. Five kilometers (3 miles) southwest of Lavers Hill is the small **Melba Gully State Park,** where you can spot glowworms at night and walk along routes of rainforest ferns. Keep an eye out for one of the last giant gum trees that escaped the loggers—it's some 27m (88 ft.) in circumference and is estimated to be more than 300 years old.

The next place of note is Moonlight Head, which marks the start of the **"Shipwreck Coast"**—a 120km (74-mile) stretch of coastline running to Port Fairy that claimed more than 80 ships in only 40 years at the end of the 19th century and the beginning of the 20th.

Just past Princetown starts the biggest attraction of the trip, **Port Campbell National Park** 🐸🐸. With its sheer cliffs and coastal rock sculptures, it's one of the most immediately recognizable images of natural Australia. You can't miss the **Twelve Apostles,** a series of rock pillars standing in the foam just offshore. Other attractions are the **Blowhole,** which throws up huge sprays of water; the **Grotto,** a rock formation intricately carved by the waves; **London Bridge,** which looked quite like the real thing until the center crashed into the sea in 1990 (leaving a bunch of tourists stranded on the wrong end); and the **Loch Ard Gorge. Port Fairy,** a lovely fishing town once known as Belfast by Irish immigrants who settled here to escape the potato famine, is also on the Shipwreck Coast.

Not far past the town of Peterborough, the Great Ocean Road heads inland to Warrnambool to eventually join the Princes Highway heading toward Adelaide.

WHERE TO STAY ALONG THE WAY

The **Great Ocean Road Accommodation Centre,** 136 Mountjoy Parade, Lorne, VIC 3232 (© **03/5289 1800**), rents out cottages and units along the route.

IN LORNE

Lorne is a good option for a night's rest. Though the beach is nothing special it's a great place to learn to surf. There are plenty of restaurants, and lots of boutiques.

Cumberland Lorne Conference & Leisure Resort 🐸 *Value*   This sporty resort, totally renovated in 2003, stands out like a sore thumb from its location between the sea and the foothills of the Otway Ranges. Still, I highly recommend it, as it's good value and quite luxurious. Every apartment has a queen-size bed and a foldout sofa bed, a kitchen, a laundry, a Jacuzzi, a balcony, and free in-house movies. All units have large bathrooms with shower/tub combinations. More than half of the rooms have panoramic ocean views; the rest look out onto gardens. Two-bedroom apartments have two extra single beds, and split-level penthouses have two Jacuzzis and two balconies.

150–178 Mountjoy Parade, Lorne, VIC 3232. © **1800/037 010** in Australia, or 03/5289 2400. Fax 03/5289 2256. www.cumberland.com.au. 99 units. Summer A$285–A$325 (US$185–US$211) 1-bedroom apt; A$345–A$385 (US$224–US$250) 2-bedroom apt; A$385–A$425 (US$250–US$276) penthouse. Off-season A$230–A$270 (US$150–US$176) 1-bedroom apt; A$290–A$330 (US$189–US$212) 2-bedroom apt; A$330–A$370 (US$215–US$241) penthouse. Ask about packages. AE, DC, MC, V. **Amenities:** Restaurant; small indoor pool; 2 lit tennis courts; exercise room; Jacuzzi; sauna; watersports rental; children's center; concierge; tour desk; business center; 24-hr. room service; in-room massage; babysitting; same-day dry cleaning; nonsmoking rooms. *In room:* A/C, TV w/pay movies, kitchenette, fridge, coffeemaker, hair dryer, iron.

Great Ocean Road Cottages *Kids*   This complex has it all, although with so many people around (and quite a few children), it can be a little noisy in summer. There's a set of self-contained cottages, set away from each other in a quiet patch of bushland, about a 5-minute walk from the town center. Each cottage is a two-story wooden hut with a double bed, two twin beds, and a pullout mattress. There's also a bathroom and a full kitchen. Just down the road is Waverley House, a historic mansion that has been divided into seven apartments. All of them are nice, but they vary enormously in size and furnishing.

Also on the property is **Great Ocean Road Backpackers,** which offers dorm-style accommodations for A$18 (US$12) for YHA members and A$21 (US$13) for non-members. They also have a few family rooms. (Discounts apply to all backpacker beds for YHA members.)

10 Erskine Ave. (P.O. Box 60), Lorne, VIC 3232. © **03/5289 1070.** Fax 03/5289 2508. greatoceanrdcotts@ iprimus.com.au. 10 cottages, 7 apts, dorms sleeping 40. A$130 (US$85) double off-season midweek; A$220 (US$143) double peak season; apts A$145–A$220 (US$94–US$143). AE, DC, MC, V. **Amenities:** Jacuzzi; free

bike rental; free laundry; nonsmoking rooms. *In room:* A/C (cottages only), TV/VCR, kitchenette, fridge, coffeemaker, hair dryer.

IN APOLLO BAY

Bayside Gardens Opposite the beach, with good ocean views from the front rooms, Bayside Gardens is a pleasant place to stay—and you can save money on meals by cooking in your own kitchen. Each unit has a separate bedroom with a double bed, a lounge area, kitchen, and attached bathroom with shower. Rooms at the front can be noisy if you're not used to living beside an ocean. There are wood fires in some of the units, and all rooms have central heating. Fry your fish on barbecues scattered around the grounds. It's a 10-minute walk to town.

219 Great Ocean Rd., Apollo Bay, VIC 3233. C and fax **03/5237 6248.** baysidegardens@iprimus.com.au. 10 units. A$70–A$110 (US$46–US$72) 1- and 2-bedroom apts. Higher rates apply Christmas, Jan, Easter, and public holidays. Minimum 1-week stay in Jan, $980 (US$637) per week. MC, V. **Amenities:** Coin-op laundry; nonsmoking rooms. *In room:* TV, kitchen, fridge.

IN PORT CAMPBELL

Macka's Farm *(Finds (Kids* This working farm is inland from the Twelve Apostles. (Continue on from the Twelve Apostles for 2km/1¼ miles and turn off at the sign for Macka's farm—it's another 4km/2½ miles inland from there.) The units all have kitchens, so you can cook your own feast. Otherwise, you can order meals by prior arrangement outside peak season, or visit one of the nearby restaurants. Rooms sleep between six and eight in a mixture of singles and doubles. There's no TV—but who needs it when there are lots of pigs, cows, ducks, and chickens running around? Overall, it's a great farm experience.

RSD 2305 Princetown Rd., Princetown, VIC 3269. C **03/5598 8261.** Fax 03/5598 8201. www.mackasfarm. com.au. 3 units. A$94–A$110 (US$61–US$72) double, depending on season. Extra person A$28 (US$18). MC, V. *In room:* Kitchen, fridge, hair dryer.

WHERE TO DINE IN LORNE

Arab Restaurant *(R* INTERNATIONAL This popular bistro serves some of the best food along this part of the coast. The house specialty is chicken Kiev, but you can also tuck into dishes such as the fish of the day or chicken schnitzel. The apple crumble is delicious.

Mount Joy Parade. C **03/5289 1435.** Reservations recommended. Main courses A$11–A$19 (US$6.80–US$12). AE, DC, MC, V. Mon–Fri 9am–9pm; Sat 8am–11pm; Sun 7:30am–10pm. Closed Christmas.

Marks *(R* INTERNATIONAL Lorne's best restaurant is a classy joint with simple wooden chairs and tables set in an elegant fashion in a cool, yellow-walled interior. Dishes include fried calamari salad, spicy octopus, risotto, and the oven-baked vine-wrapped goat cheese and macadamia nut parcel on eggplant paté with red capsicum purée. The bar is open for coffee and drinks all day.

Mount Joy Parade. C **03/5289 2787.** Main courses A$12–A$23 (US$7.80–US$15). AE, MC, V. Daily noon–2:30pm (only Sat–Sun in winter) and 6–9pm. Closed in May.

Ozone Milk Bar *(Value* AUSTRALIAN MILK BAR An Ozzie icon, a milk bar is a kind of downmarket cafe that sells everything from shakes and pies to newspapers. This one sells good pies and quiche, a veggie burger I wouldn't recommend, chicken-filet burgers, cookies, ice cream, and small homemade cakes. The milk shakes are particularly good. You can sit inside or around three tables outside. There's a Thai place next door, but it's very unwelcoming.

Mount Joy Parade. C **03/5289 1780.** Menu items A$1.80–A$4 (US$1.20–US$2.60). No credit cards. Daily 7am–6pm (to 11pm Christmas to the end of Jan).

3 The Murray River ★

Mildura: 544km (337 miles) NW of Melbourne; Albury-Wadonga: 305km (189 miles) N of Melbourne; Echuca: 210km (130 miles) N of Melbourne

The Murray is Australia's version of the Mississippi River. Though it's a rushing torrent of white water at its source in the Snowy Mountains, it becomes slow moving and muddy brown by the time it becomes the meandering border between Victoria and New South Wales. The Darling River, which starts off in Queensland, feeds the Murray; together they make Australia's longest river.

Aborigines once used the Murray as a source of food and transportation, and later the water was plied by paddle steamers, laden with wool and crops from the land it helped irrigate. In 1842, the Murray was "discovered" by explorers Hamilton Hume and William Howell on the first overland trek from Sydney to Port Phillip, near Melbourne. As Hume later wrote, on their trek the explorers "suddenly arrived at the bank of a very fine river—at least 60m wide, apparently deep, the bank being 2.4m or 2.7m above the level, which is overflowed at the time of flood . . . In the solid wood of a healthy tree I carved my name." You can still see the carved initials on a tree standing by the riverbank in Albury, on the border between the two states.

ESSENTIALS

GETTING THERE   Most visitors cross the river during an overland drive between cities. There are two routes to get to the Murray from Melbourne: Either take the Calder Highway to Mildura, which is a 6-hour drive, or take the 2½-hour route down the Midland Highway to Echuca. Traveling from Melbourne to Mildura is only practical if you're continuing on to Broken Hill, which is 297km (184 miles) north of Mildura. Those in a hurry to get to and from Sydney can travel via the river-straddling twin towns of Albury-Wodonga on the Hume Highway (about a 12-hr. trip with short stops).

V/Line (© **13 61 96** in Victoria, or 03/9619 5000) runs regular train services to Mildura, Echuca, and Albury-Wodonga.

VISITOR INFORMATION   The **Echuca and Moama and District Visitor Information Centre,** 2 Heygarth St., Echuca, VIC 3564 (© **1800/804 446** or 03/5480 7555; fax 03/5482 6413; www.echucamoama.com), has plenty of maps and information about accommodations and river cruises. It's open daily from 9am to 5pm. The **Mildura Visitor Information & Booking Centre,** 180–190 Deakin Ave., Mildura, VIC 3502 (© **1800/039 043** or 03/5021 4424; fax 03/5021 1836; www.milduratourism.com), offers similar services. It's open Monday through Friday from 9am to 5:30pm and weekends from 9am to 5pm. If you're passing through Albury, contact the **Gateway Visitors Information Centre,** Gateway Village, Lincoln Causeway, Wadonga, VIC 3690 (© **1800/800 743** or 02/6041 3875; fax 02/6021 0322), open daily from 9am to 5pm.

RIVER CRUISES & OTHER FUN STUFF

IN MILDURA   Mildura is one of Australia's most important fruit-growing areas. There was a time, however, when this was just semiarid, red dust country. The area bloomed due to a little ingenuity and, of course, the Murray. The original irrigation system consisted of two English water pumps and the manual labor of hundreds of immigrants, who were put to work clearing the scrub and digging channels through the new fields. Today, the hungry land soaks up the water.

Several paddle steamers leave from Mildura wharf. One of the nicest boats is the **PS *Melbourne*** (© **03/5023 2200;** fax 03/5021 3017), which was built in

1912 and is still powered by steam. It offers 2-hour trips leaving at 10:50am and 1:50pm. The fare is A$19 (US$12) for adults and A$7.50 (US$4.90) for children (free for children under 5).

The PS *Melbourne*'s sister ship, the **Rothbury**, was built in 1881, but its steam-driven engine has been replaced by a conventional engine. It churns out a winery cruise every Thursday from 10:30am to 3:30pm, stopping off at a winery for tastings and a barbecue lunch. The trip costs A$42 (US$27) for adults and A$20 (US$13) for children. The *Rothbury* has evening dinner cruises every Thursday from 7 to 10pm for A$40 (US$26) for adults and A$18 (US$12) for children. You can also take the paddleboat to the Golden River Zoo (see below) during school holiday periods leaving Mildura Wharf at 9:50am on Wednesday morning (returning at 3pm). The trip costs A$32 (US$21) for adults and A$16 (US$10) for children 5 to 14, including zoo entry.

On dry land, the **Golden River Zoo**, Flora Avenue, Mildura (© **03/5023 5540;** www.goldenriverzoo.com.au), is a pleasant place to see native animals. The zoo fronts onto the river 4km (2½ miles) from the city center down 11th Street. The animals here virtually follow you around (on the lookout for food) as you walk through their large enclosures. Admission is A$12 (US$7.80) for adults and A$6 (US$3.90) for children, including a free barbecue lunch at noon and a free tractor-train ride down to the river at 1:30pm and an animal show. The zoo is open daily, except Christmas Day, from 10am to 5pm.

IN ECHUCA   In Echuca, another paddle steamer is the **Emmylou** (© **03/5480 2237;** fax 03/5480 2927; www.emmylou.com.au). A 2-day/2-night cruise leaves the Port of Echuca Wednesday at 6pm and returns at noon on Friday (check sailings beforehand). The cruise includes a visit to the Barmah, an area famous for its wetlands and the largest red gum trees in the world, or depending on river levels, a stop at Perricoota Station. The trip costs A$415 to A$435 (US$270–US$283) per person, depending on cabin. Children 4 to 14 receive a 25% discount. An overnight trip leaves on Saturday at 6pm and returns at 10am on Sunday. It costs A$195 to A$210 (US$127–US$137) per person including breakfast; dinner is extra. The *Emmylou* also offers day trips costing A$15 (US$9.75) for adults and A$7.50 (US$4.90) for kids for 1 hour, and A$18 (US$12) for adults and A$9 (US$5.90) for kids for 1½ hours.

The **Port of Echuca** (© **03/5482 4248;** www.portofechuca.org.au) is definitely worth a look. The three-level red gum wharf was built in 1865 and is still used by paddle steamers. The Port owns the PS *Adelaide,* the oldest operating wooden-hulled paddle steamer in the world (1866), the PS *Pevensey* (1911), and the PS *Alexander Arbuthnot* (1923). One-hour cruises on the latter two are offered daily at 10:15 and 11:30am, and 1, 2:15, and 3:30pm for A$15 (US$9.90) for adults and A$6.50 (US$4.20) for children. You can take a look around the wharf on a guided tour, priced at A$10 (US$6.50) for adults and A$6.50 (US$4.20) for children. Ask about combined and family prices. Outside the Port, in the Echuca Port Precinct, there are various things to do, including carriage rides and old penny arcade machines in Sharpes Magic Movies, in an old riverboat warehouse.

TRIPS INTO THE OUTBACK   If you want to get out into the Outback, then trips from Mildura with **Mallee Outback Experiences,** P.O. Box 82, Nichols Point, VIC 3501 (© and fax **03/5021 1621,** or mobile 0418/521 0030), are worth the effort. The company offers two trips. The first goes to **Mungo National Park** ⍟, which is famous for its red sand dunes and shifting sands, and which I highly recommend you go and see. The second is to **Hattah**

National Park, which has some gorgeous river plains, Murray River lakes, pine forests, and more mallee scrub. The Mungo trip leaves every Wednesday and Saturday, and the Hattah National Park trip every Friday. All trips cost A$55 (US$36) for adults, A$33 (US$21) for children, and A$132 (US$86) for a family of five.

You can get to these two national parks on your own, but it's best to have a four-wheel-drive vehicle—even better if you go with an experienced guide. Mungo National Park is a unique, arid region 110km (68 miles) northeast of Mildura, off the Sturt Highway. People come here to see the Walls of China, a moonscape of intricately weathered red sand. The walls edge onto Lake Mungo, once a huge freshwater lake during the last Ice Age, now dry. A 60km (37-mile) driving tour starting at the visitor center at the park's entrance takes you across the lake bed to the Walls of China. There are several short walks leading off from the campsites at the park entrance. Call the **National Parks & Wildlife Service NSW** (© **1300/361 967** in Australia) for more information on Mungo. Just outside the park, the **Mungo Lodge** (© **03/5029 7297;** www.mungolodge.com. au) offers affordable motel accommodations and a casual restaurant.

WHERE TO STAY
IN MILDURA

Mildura Grand Hotel 𝒦𝒦𝒦   This huge 19th-century hotel is right in the center of Mildura, overlooking the Murray River. Double rooms are comfortable, and many have been recently refurbished. Suites are bigger, and some have balconies and garden views. State suites are plush and come with a king-size bed. The Presidential suite (the most expensive) is Art Deco inspired, with a large marble bathroom and Jacuzzi. This place is now very famous for **Stefano's,** the restaurant of celeb chef Stefano di Pietri. Voted best restaurant in 2002, the place offers a set menu of five to six courses for $66 (US$43), featuring the best local produce.

Seventh St., Mildura, VIC 3500. © **1800/034 228** in Australia, or 03/5023 0511. Fax 03/5022 1801. www. milduragrand.com. 102 units. A$110–A$143 (US$72–US$93) grand room double; A$176–A$462 (US$114–US$300) suite. Rates include breakfast. Additional person A$22 (US$14). Ask about packages. AE, DC, MC, V. **Amenities:** 3 restaurants; 4 bars; large heated outdoor pool; golf course nearby; access to nearby health club, Jacuzzi, sauna; 24-hr. concierge; shopping arcade; 24-hr. room service; in-room massage; laundry service; dry cleaning; nonsmoking rooms; executive rooms. In room: A/C, TV w/pay movies, minibar, coffeemaker, hair dryer, iron.

IN ECHUCA

Echuca Gardens B&B and YHA   There are evening gatherings around the piano at this popular two-story log cabin B&B, as well as a pretty neat Jacuzzi in the front yard surrounded by murals and landscaped water gardens. Rooms are decorated in native flower themes, and all have balconies. Two rooms have showers in the bathroom, and another has a shower on the second floor. It's a short stroll from the B&B to either the river or a state forest. The YHA has a basic twin room inside and three tentlike cabins outside, one with a double bed and the other with two singles. There are also three basic dorm rooms with beds going for A$18 (US$12) for YHA members and A$22 (US$14) for nonmembers.

103 Mitchell St., Echuca, VIC 3564. © **03/5480 6522,** or 0419 881 054 mobile. Fax 03/5482 6951. www. echucagardens.com. 6 units (3 in B&B and 3 in hostel). B&B room A$150 (US$98) weekends, A$120 (US$78) weekdays. Rates include breakfast. MC, V. **Amenities:** Jacuzzi; sauna; bike rental; tour desk; massage; coin-operated laundry services; nonsmoking rooms. In room: A/C, TV, hair dryer.

IN ALBURY

Hume Country Golf Club Motor Inn   This is a good place to stop if you're making the trip north to Sydney. Just on the New South Wales side of the border, this motor inn has typical motel rooms and two large family rooms, one sleeping five the other seven. Suites are also large and come with a Jacuzzi. All rooms overlook the 27-hole golf course, where a round of golf costs A$20 (US$13).

736 Logan Rd., Albury, NSW 2640. (© 02/6025 8233. Fax 02/6040 4999. humegolfmotel@primus.com.au. 25 units. A$82 (US$53) double; A$90 (US$59) family room; A$115 (US$75) suite. Extra person A$10 (US$6.50). AE, DC, MC, V. **Amenities:** Heated outdoor pool; golf course on the premises; babysitting; coin-op laundry; dry cleaning; nonsmoking rooms. *In room:* A/C, TV, kitchen, minibar, coffeemaker, hair dryer, iron.

4 The Southeast Coast

The Princes Highway wanders down the coast from Sydney just past Eden, and then darts across into Victoria, passing through the logging town of Orbost, and then dipping down toward Lakes Entrance. The highway continues to the southwest, swooping in an arch to Melbourne.

This region's most interesting sights are Wilsons Promontory National Park, and—to a lesser extent—the Snowy River National Park.

WILSONS PROMONTORY NATIONAL PARK 🐾
200km (124 miles) SE of Melbourne

"The Prom," as it's called, is Victoria's best-loved national park. Dipping down into Bass Strait, the park—named after a prominent London businessman—marks the southernmost point on Australia's mainland. It's thought to once have been joined to Tasmania by a land bridge. The best time to visit the park is from late September to early December, when all the bush flowers are in bloom.

Visitors come here for the spectacular granite mountains, the thick forests and vast plains, and some of the country's best beaches. Wildlife abounds in the park, including plenty of koalas, kangaroos, wallabies, possums, echidnas, wombats, and emus. You can hand-feed crimson rosellas at the capital of the Prom, Tidal River, but you'll find little more here than the national park's **Tourist Information Centre** (© **1800/350 552** in Australia, or 03/5680 9555) and camping and motor-home grounds. There are plenty of trails leading off into the mountains: Following the longer trails can turn into a 2- or 3-day excursion, though shorter day hikes are possible. One of the best trails is the 1-hour Mt. Oberon walk, which starts from the Mt. Oberon parking lot and offers superb views. Visitors also rave about the Squeaky Beach Nature Walk, a 1½-hour walk from Tidal River to the next bay and back.

There are some 30 beaches, some of which are easily accessible. Norman's Beach in Tidal River is the most popular, and it's the only one recommended for swimming. No snorkeling or lifeguards are at these beaches, but they're gorgeous.

ENTRY FEES   Park entry costs A$9 (US$5.90) for cars, which you pay at the park entrance gate, 30km (19 miles) north of Tidal River. The gate is open 24 hours, but if you arrive late and the collection station is closed, pay the following morning at Tidal River.

GETTING THERE   From Melbourne, take the South Gippsland Highway (B440), turning south at Meeniyan and again at Fish Creek or Foster. The route is well signposted. Tidal River is 30km (19 miles) inside the park boundary.

There's no public transportation to the park. You can, however, take the V/Line bus from Melbourne to Foster (fare: A$21/US$14), which is 60km (37 miles) north of the park. In Foster, you can stay at the **Foster Backpackers Hostel,** 17 Pioneer St., Foster, VIC 3960 (© **03/5682 2614**). It's basically a private home with a few spare rooms; the two doubles cost A$44 (US$29), and dorm beds go for A$19 (US$12). There are also two fully self-contained apartments for $55 (US$36). The owner offers daily transport to Tidal River for A$22 (US$14) each way; the trip takes around 45 minutes.

WHERE TO STAY

The national park's Tourist Information Centre operates 17 self-contained cabins costing A$119 to A$130 (US$77–US$84) a night for two, depending on the season. They can accommodate up to six people; each extra adult costs A$17 (US$11) and each child A$11 (US$7.15). In addition, five "Lorikeet" units cost A$58 to A$93 (US$38–US$60) a night for two and A$94 to A$134 (US$61–US$87) for three or four (higher prices in summer). For bookings call ✆ **03/5680 9500** or fax 03/568 09516.

Waratah Park Country House   If you don't feel like roughing it, this is the only place within the park that will do. Rooms, with king-size beds and double Jacuzzis, offer stunning views over Wilsons Promontory and a dozen or so islands. The food here is excellent, too. The hotel is also next to the new Cape Liptrap Coastal Park, home to some 120 species of birds.

It's a friendly place, and the hosts will sit down with you and go through the things you want to do in the area. A V/Line coach operates from Melbourne to Fish Creek (about 10 min. away), and the owner will pick you up at the station.

Thomson Rd., Waratah Bay, VIC 3959. ✆ 03/5683 2575. Fax 03/5683 2275. www.wpe.com.au. 6 units. A$78 (US$51) including breakfast; A$115 (US$75) Sun–Thurs (including 4-course dinner and breakfast); A$280 (US$182) for weekend package including 2 nights' lodgings, 2 breakfasts, and 2 4-course dinners. All rates are per person. AE, MC, V. **Amenities:** Restaurant; babysitting (for dinnertime only); nonsmoking rooms. *In room:* TV, fridge, coffeemaker, hair dryer, iron.

5 The High Country

Victoria's High Country is made up of the hills and mountains of the Great Dividing Range, which runs from Queensland, through New South Wales, to just before Ballarat, where it drops away and reappears in the mountains of the Grampians, in the western part of Victoria. The range separates inland Australia from the greener coastal belt. The highest mountain in the Victorian segment of the range is Mt. Bogong, which at just 1,988m (6,521 ft.) is minuscule by world mountain standards.

The main attractions of the High Country are its natural features, which include moorland and typical mountainous alpine scenery. It's also popular for its outdoor activities, including hiking, canoeing, white-water rafting, mountain bike riding and rock climbing. The High Country is also the home of the Victorian ski fields, based around Mt. Buller, Mt. Stirling, Falls Creek, Mt. Buffalo, and Mt. Hotham. If you plan to go walking here make sure you have plenty of water and sunscreen, as well as a tent and a good-quality sleeping bag. As in any alpine region temperatures can plummet dramatically. In summer, days can be very hot, and nights very cold.

SNOWY RIVER NATIONAL PARK ✿
390km (242 miles) NE of Melbourne

The Snowy River National Park, with its lovely river scenery and magnificent gorges, protects Victoria's largest forest wilderness areas. The Snowy River was once a torrent worthy of Banjo Paterson's famous poem, but since Snowy Mountain Hydro-Electric came along and erected a series of dams, it's become a mere trickle of its former self.

GETTING THERE & GETTING AROUND There are two main access roads to the park, the Gelantipy Road from Buchan and the Bonang Freeway from the logging township of Orbost. MacKillop's Road (also known as Deddick River Rd.) runs across the park's northern border from Bonang to a little south of Wulgulmerang. Around MacKillop's Bridge, along MacKillop's Road, is some spectacular scenery, and the park's best campgrounds, set beside some nice swimming holes and sandy river beaches. The Barry Way leads through the main township of Buchan, where you'll find some of Australia's best caves.

VISITOR INFORMATION The main place to get information on Snowy River National Park and Alpine National Park is the **Buchan Caves Information Centre,** in the Buchan Caves complex. It's open daily from 9am to 4pm (closed Christmas). Or call **Parks Victoria** (© **13 19 63** in Victoria, or 03/5155 9264).

EXPLORING THE BUCHAN CAVES

The **Buchan Caves** ⚲ (© **03/5155 9264**) are set in a scenic valley that is particularly beautiful in autumn, when all the European trees are losing their leaves. Tourists can visit the Royal and Fairy caves (which are quite similar), with their fabulous stalactites and stalagmites. There are several tours daily: April to September at 11am, and 1 and 3pm; October to March at 10 and 11:15am, and 1, 2:15, and 3:30pm. Entry to one cave costs A$10 (US$6.50) for adults, A$5 (US$3.25) for children 5 to 16, and A$25 (US$16) for families of five.

To reach the caves from the Princes Highway, turn off at Nowa Nowa (it's well signposted), or if you're coming south from Jindabyne in New South Wales (see chapter 4) follow the Barry Way, which runs alongside the Snowy River.

Want to feel like the man from Snowy River? **Snowy Mountain Rider Tours,** Karoonda Park, Gelantipy (© **03/5155 0220;** fax 03/5155 0308), offers half-day horseback rides in the Snowy River National Park for A$60 (US$39), and full-day tours for A$120 (US$78) including lunch. Four-day trips including camping and all meals cost A$520 (US$338). The company also arranges rafting on Snowy River for A$120 (US$78) a day including lunch.

ALPINE NATIONAL PARK ⚲⚲
333km (206 miles) NE of Melbourne, 670km (415 miles) SW of Sydney

Victoria's largest national park at 646,000 hectares (1,595,620 acres), the Alpine National Park connects the High Country areas of New South Wales and the Australian Capital Territory (ACT). The park's scenery is spectacular, encompassing most of the state's highest mountains, wild rivers, impressive escarpments, forests, and high plains. Much of the park was devastated by horrific bushfires in December 2002, but at the time of writing it was recovering quickly. The flora is diverse; in all, some 1,100 plant species have been recorded within the park's boundaries, including 12 not found anywhere else. Walking here is particularly good in spring and summer, when the Bogong High Plains are covered in a carpet of wildflowers. Other impressive walking trails include the 5.7km (3.5-mile) route through Bryce Gorge to The Bluff, a 200m (356-ft.) high rocky escarpment with panoramic views. Of the numerous other walking trails in the park, the most well known is the Alpine Walking Track, which bisects the park for 400km (248 miles) from Walhalla to the township of Tom Groggin, on the New South Wales border. There are plenty of access roads into the park, though some close in winter.

If you are a keen walker, you could strap on your boots and see the area by foot. **Ecotrek** (✆ **08/8383 7198;** ecotrek@ozemail.com.au) offers an 8-day Bogong Alpine Traverse trek, including 4 nights camping and 3 nights in ski lodges. You carry your own pack, but the pain is worth it for the incredible panoramic views of peaks, plains, and forested valleys. The trek costs A$1,150 (US$748), including round-trip transport to Melbourne. The company also offers a 5-day trek that involves camping and day walks through extremely rugged country. It costs A$630 (US$410), including round-trip transport to Melbourne.

Horseback-riding treks are another option for seeing the area. One of the best operators is **Stoney's Bluff & Beyond Rides** (✆ **03/5775 2212;** www.stoneys.com.au).

GETTING THERE The Alpine National Park can be accessed by several routes from Melbourne, including the Great Alpine Road (B500), the Kiewa Valley Highway (C531), and the Lincoln Road from Heyfield. Get to The Bluff from Mansfield along the Maroodah Highway.

HITTING THE SLOPES: THE HIGH COUNTRY SKI RESORTS

Most of **Victoria's ski areas** 𝕽 are in, or on the edge of, the Alpine National Park (see above). The ski season in the Victorian High Country lasts June through October, with July and August being the most popular months.

MT. HOTHAM
373km (231 miles) NE of Melbourne

Mt. Hotham (1,750m/5,740 ft.) is an intimate ski resort significantly smaller than those at Falls Creek (see below). There are eight lifts offering runs from beginners to advanced. It also offers some good off-piste (off-trail) cross-country skiing, including a route across the Bogong High Plains to Falls Creek. Some of the lifts are quite far apart, although there's a free "zoo cart" and bus transport system in winter along the main road. Resort entry costs A$20 (US$13) per car for a day, payable at the resort entry gates, or at the Mount Hotham Resort Management office (see "Visitor Information," below). Ski tickets are available from Mount Hotham Skiing Company (✆ **03/5759 4444**). Full-day lift tickets cost between A$59 and A$72 (US$38–US$47) for adults and A$33 and A$39 (US$21–US$25) for children, depending on time of season.

GETTING THERE From Melbourne, take the Hume Highway via Harrietville, or the Princes Highway via Omeo. The trip takes around 5½ hours (the trip is slightly quicker on the Hume Hwy.). Fly to Mt. Hotham Airport from Melbourne and Sydney with **Qantas** (✆ **13 13 13** in Australia).

Trekset Mount Hotham Snow Service (✆ **03/9370 9055**) runs buses to Mt. Hotham daily during the ski season departing Melbourne's Spencer Street Coach Terminal at 9am. The trip takes 6 hours and costs A$70 (US$46) one-way or A$105 (US$68) round-trip. You need to book in advance.

VISITOR INFORMATION **Mount Hotham Resort Management,** Great Alpine Road, Mt. Hotham (✆ **03/5759 3550**), is as close as you'll come to an information office. It has plenty of brochures. It's open daily from 8am to 5pm during ski season, and Monday through Friday from 9am to 5pm at other times. The general Mt. Hotham Web page is **www.mthotham.com.au**.

WHERE TO STAY The **Mt. Hotham Accommodation Service** (✆ **1800/ 032 061;** www.mthothamaccommodation.com.au) can book rooms and advise you on special deals during both off-peak and peak periods, including flights.

Another option is **Falls Creek Reservations Centre** (© **1800/453 525** in Australia). During the ski season, most places will want you to book for an entire week. Prices are significantly lower in the non-ski season.

FALLS CREEK ⊛
375km (233 miles) NE of Melbourne

One of Victoria's best ski resorts, and my favorite, Falls Creek is situated on the edge of the Bogong High Plains overlooking the Kiewa Valley. This compact alpine village is the only one in Australia where you can ski from your lodge to the lifts and back again from the ski slopes. The nightlife is also very good in the ski season, with plenty of party options as well as a range of walk-in lodge restaurants.

The ski fields are split into two parts, the Village Bowl and Sun Valley, with 17 lifts covering more than 90 trails. There are plenty of intermediate and advanced runs, as well as a sprinkling for beginners. You'll also find some of Australia's best cross-country skiing here; Australia's major cross-country skiing event, the Kangaroo Hoppet, is held here on the last Saturday in August every year. Entry to the resort costs A$6 (US$3.90). Full-day lift tickets cost from A$59 to A$75 (US$38–US$49) for adults and A$33 to A$39 (US$21–US$25) for children, depending on the time you ski (July 31–Aug 31 is the most expensive time, and June and after mid-Sept is the cheapest). Combined lift and ski lesson tickets are also available. Call the **Falls Creek Ski Lifts** (© **03/5758 3280**) for details. The ski lifts can also organize accommodations options.

Falls Creek is also a pleasant place to visit in summer, when you can go bushwalking, horseback riding, and trout fishing. **Angling Expeditions** (© and fax **03/5754 1466**) is the best option for fly-fishing for trout in the alpine area during spring, summer, and fall. Trips last from 3 hours to all day and are suitable for everyone from beginners to experts. Overnight trips are also available. Horseback riding operators include **Falls Creek Trail Rides** (© **03/5758 3655**) and **Bogong Horseback Adventures** (© **03/5754 4849**).

GETTING THERE   **Pyles Coaches** (© **03/5754 4024**) runs buses to the ski resort from Melbourne every day during the ski season (from the end of June to the end of Sept), departing Melbourne at 9am and Falls Creek at 5pm. The round-trip fare is A$100 (US$65) for adults and A$75 (US$49) for children and includes the resort entrance fee. The company also runs shuttle buses to and from Albury just over the border in New South Wales (accessible by train from Sydney), and between Mt. Beauty and Falls Creek. Bookings are essential.

If you're driving from Melbourne take the Hume Highway to Wangaratta, and then through Myrtleford and Mt. Beauty to Falls Creek. The trip takes around 4½ hours. From Sydney take the Hume Highway to Albury-Wodonga and follow the signs to Mt. Beauty and the snowfields. If you arrive in the ski season, a resort worker will direct you to a car park, and bring you back to the resort entrance, from where you can take a caterpillar-tracked "troop-carrier" to your hotel, or attempt the short but (probably) slippery, walk yourself.

VISITOR INFORMATION   The **Falls Creek Information Centre,** 1 Bogong High Plains Rd., Falls Creek (© **03/5758 3490**), is open daily from 8am to 5pm. Buy lift tickets in the booth next door, between mid-June and October.

Where to Stay & Dine
Falls Creek is a year-round resort, with a good range of accommodations available, though it tends to fill up fast during the ski season. As you might expect

room rates are much higher during the ski season. The **Falls Creek Reservation Centre** (© **1800/453 525** in Australia, or 03/5758 3100; fax 03/5758 3337; www.fallscreek.net) can tell you what deals are on offer and can book rooms for you. The cheapest winter option is the very basic **Frying Pan Inn,** P.O. Box 55, Falls Creek, VIC 3699 (© **03/5758 3390;** fax 03/5758 3416), right in the village next to the ski lifts. Bunks in four- or six-bed rooms cost A$58 (US$38) per night Sunday through Thursday, and A$68 (US$44) Friday through Saturday, in the ski season. Packages are available.

If you fancy a self-contained apartment or freestanding chalet, try the **Frueauf Village** complex (© **03/9593 6125;** www.fvfalls.com.au). These 28 properties were built in 2001 and 2002. In peak season they work out at about A$100 (US$65) per person per night for two or more.

Feathertop Alpine Lodge ⋇ *Finds*   I really like this pleasant old-fashioned ski lodge nestled among the gum trees. Hosts Pip and Mark Whittaker have made it into one of the friendliest getaways in the mountains, and its relatively small size makes it easy to get to know a few of the other guests. Rooms are functional yet cozy, and sleep two to four people. All have showers attached. The lounge room is large and comfortable with good views, a well-stocked bar, and a library.

Parallel St. (P.O. Box 259), Falls Creek, VIC 3699. © **03/5758 3232.** Fax 03/5758 3514. www.ski.com.au/ feathertop. 10 units. Winter A$95–A$185 (US$62–US$120); summer A$70 (US$46). Rates are per person and include dinner and breakfast. AE, MC, V. **Amenities:** Restaurant; golf course nearby; 4 tennis courts (summer); health club nearby; children's center; tour/activities counter; business center on request; babysitting; coin-op laundry; nonsmoking rooms.

Summit Ridge Alpine Lodge ⋇   Summit Ridge is a AAA-rated 4½-star property made from local rock and timber. It caters to discerning guests. All rooms are quite nice, if a little stark. The mezzanine suites are split-level with the bedroom upstairs; they have king-size beds and an attached bathroom with tub. There's a lounge and dining room on the ground floor and a library on the second. If the mist holds off there are some fine valley views. The hosts pay a lot of attention to detail, and the homemade bread is worth an early rise. The restaurant excels in fine dining. The owner can take you on early-morning ski runs.

Schuss St., Falls Creek, VIC 3699. © **03/5758 3800.** Fax 03/5758 3833. sunridge@fallscreek.albury.net.au. Winter A$140–A$230 (US$88–US$150) queen room per person. Summer A$110 (US$72) queen room per person. AE, DC, MC, V. Children 5–14 25% off adult rate. Rates include breakfast and dinner. Children under 5 not permitted. **Amenities:** Restaurant; bar; exercise room; sauna; Jacuzzi; in-room massage; babysitting; coin-op laundry. *In room:* TV, minibar, coffeemaker, hair dryer.

MT. BUFFALO NATIONAL PARK ⋇⋇
350km (217 miles) NE of Melbourne

Based around Mt. Buffalo, this is the oldest national park in the Victorian High Country, declared in 1898. The scenery is spectacular, with huge granite outcrops and plenty of waterfalls. As you ascend the mountain you pass through dramatic vegetation changes, from tall snow gum forests to subalpine grasslands. In summer, carpets of silver snow daisies, royal bluebells, and yellow Billy Button flowers bloom on the plateau. Animals and birds here include wallabies and wombats, cockatoos, lyrebirds, and mobs of crimson rosellas, which congregate around the campsite at Lake Catani (popular for swimming and canoeing). Other popular sports around and about include advanced hang gliding and some very serious rock climbing. There are also more than 90km (56 miles) of walking trails. The area is regenerating after bushfires in late 2002.

Mt. Buffalo is also home to Victoria's smallest ski resort, with just five lifts, and a vertical drop of 157m (515 ft.). There are also 11km (6¾ miles) of marked cross-country ski trails.

ENTRY FEES & LIFT TICKETS   Entry to Mt. Buffalo ski resort is A$20 (US$13) per car. Full-day lift tickets cost around A$39 (US$25) for adults, A$25 (US$16) for children under 15, and A$15 (US$9.75) for children under 8. Combination lift and ski lesson packages are available. Buy lift tickets at the park offices (© **13 19 63** in Victoria, or 03/5756 2328) from 9am to 3pm.

GETTING THERE   From Melbourne take the Hume Freeway (M31) to Wangaratta, then follow the Great Alpine Road to Porepunkah. From there follow the Mount Buffalo Tourist Road.

VISITOR INFORMATION   The nearest visitor information center is in the town of Bright. Find the **Bright Visitor Information Centre** at 1A Delaney Ave., Bright (© **03/5755 2275**).

WHERE TO STAY

Mt. Buffalo Chalet *★/★ (Finds*   This rambling mountain guesthouse was built in 1910 and retains a wonderful old-world feel. Standard rooms are small with a comfortable bed and share a bathroom with others. Classic rooms are small but have their own bathroom. Heritage rooms are larger, have a nice old-time feel about them, and some have good views (ask for the View Heritage rooms). Tower rooms have excellent National Park views and are popular with honeymooners. Treetops rooms, which also have great views, are set apart from the main building. These also have a kitchenette and separate lounge, which makes them good for small families. There's a large lounge room and a billiards room, both with open fireplaces. Meals are available for both guests and visitors.

Mt. Buffalo National Park, VIC 3740. © 1800/037 038 in Australia, or 03/5755 1500. Fax 03/5755 1892. www.mtbuffalochalet.com.au. 97 units, 72 with bathroom (some with shower only). A$100–A$150 (US$65–US$98) standard room without bathroom; A$140–A$200 (US$91–US$130) classic room with bathroom; A$190–A$300 (US$156–US$195) Heritage view room with bathroom; A$210–A$320 (US$137–US$208) Tower; A$240–A$350 (US$156–US$195) Treetops with balcony. Rates include park entry. Highest rates Christmas to mid-Jan and Easter weekend; lower rates in summer. Children rates 50% less. AE, DC, MC, V. **Amenities:** Restaurant; bar; 2 grass tennis courts; exercise room; Jacuzzi; sauna; canoe rental; bike rental; kids' club on weekends and school holidays; activities desk; massage; babysitting; coin-op laundry; nonsmoking rooms. *In room:* Fridge, coffeemaker.

13

Canberra

by Marc Llewellyn

If you mention you're heading to Canberra (pronounced *Can*-bra, with very open vowels), most Australians will raise an eyebrow and say, "Why bother?" Even many Canberrans will admit that it's a great place to live but they wouldn't want to visit.

So what is it about Canberra that draws so much lackluster comment? Simply put, Australians aren't used to having things so nice and ordered. In many ways, Canberra is like Washington, D.C., or any town that was a planned community from the start. Some see its virtues as bland: The roads are wide and in good order, the buildings are modern, and the suburbs are pleasant and leafy. Canberra is also the seat of government and the home of thousands of civil servants—enough to make almost any freethinking, individualist Aussie shudder.

But to me, Canberra's differences are the very things that make it special. The streets aren't clogged with traffic, and there are plenty of opportunities for safe biking—try that in almost any other city center and you'll be dusting the sides of cars and pushed onto the sidewalks in no time. There are plenty of open spaces, parklands, and monuments, and there is an awful lot to see and do—from museum and gallery hopping to ballooning with a champagne glass in your hand or boating on Lake Burley Griffin. You can pack a lot into a few days' visit.

Canberra was born after the Commonwealth of Australia was created in 1901. Melbourne and Sydney, even then jockeying for preeminence, each put in their bid to become the federal capital. In the end, Australian leaders decided to follow the example of their U.S. counterparts by creating a federal district; in 1908 they chose an undeveloped area between the two cities.

Designing the new capital fell to Chicago landscape architect Walter Burley Griffin, a contemporary of Frank Lloyd Wright. The city he mapped out was christened Canberra (a local Aboriginal word meaning "meeting place"), and by 1927, the first meeting of parliament took place. The business of government was underway.

Originally the land that became Canberra was predominantly grass plains. Over the years millions of trees have been planted in and around the city—earning it the nickname "the bush capital." Unfortunately, massive bushfires in January 2003 destroyed much of the surrounding forest and more than 500 homes in the suburbs.

1 Orientation

ARRIVING

BY PLANE   **Qantas** (© 13 13 13 in Australia) runs frequent daily services to Canberra. **Virgin Blue** (© 13 67 89; www.virginblue.com.au) also connects Canberra to Sydney, and offers discount Web fares.

Canberra

Black Mountain ▲ ❶
AUSTRALIAN NATIONAL BOTANIC GARDENS ❷

BRADDON

General Post Office ✉

Mount Ainslie →

Bunda St.

Black Mountain Dr.

ACTON

Childers St.
Alinga St.

Australian National University ❺

Vernon Circle

Northbourne Avenue

Ballumbir Ave.
Ainslie Ave.

❻ Caffe Della Piazza
❼
❽
❾
❿
⓫ Binara St.
⓬

Petrie St.
Akuna St.
Coranderrk St.
Euree St.

REID

⓭

Limestone Ave.

London Circuit

Constitution Ave.

RUSSELL

Anzac Parade

COMMONWEALTH PARK
⓮

Lake Burley Griffin

❹

Commonwealth Ave. Bridge

National Library of Australia ■

Commonwealth Avenue

KINGS PARK

STIRLING PARK

⓯

⓰

PARKES

King George Terrace

⓱
⓲
⓳

GREVILLEA PARK

United States Embassy

⓴ Old Parliament House

Kings Avenue

Kings Ave. Bridge

YARRALUMLA

CAPITAL HILL

㉑

Capital Circle
State Circle

Brisbane Ave.

Adelaide Ave.

Melbourne Ave.

National Circuit
Dominion Circuit

㉘

㉒

TELOPEA PARK

㉓

Wentworth

㉔

Giles St.

㉕

KINGSTON

㉖ Canberra Railway Station

FORREST

Empire Circuit

COLLINS PARK

㉗

MANUKA PARK

GRIFFITH

Canberra Ave.

0   1/4 mi
0   1/4 km

N

ACCOMMODATIONS ■
The Brassey of Canberra **22**
City Walk Hotel **8**
Crowne Plaza Canberra **11**
Forest Inn and Apartments **28**
Hyatt Hotel Canberra **15**
Kingston Court Apartments **23**
University House **5**
Victor Lodge **25**

DINING ◆
The Boat House by the Lake **24**
Caffe Della Piazza **6**
Chairman and Yip **10**
Juniperberry **19**
Little Saigon **7**
The Palette Cafe **29**
Portia's Place **26**
Tosolini's **9**
The Tryst **27**

ATTRACTIONS ●
Australian Institute of Sport **3**
Australian National Botanic Gardens **2**
Australian War Museum **13**
Casino Canberra **12**
High Court of Australia **17**
National Capital Exhibition **14**
National Gallery of Australia **18**
National Museum of Australia **4**
Old Parliment House **20**
Parliament House **21**
Questacon–The National Science and Technology Centre **16**
Telstra Tower **1**

AUSTRALIA

Sydney
Canberra

1000 Mi
1000 Km

Information ⓘ
Post Office ✉
Mountain ▲

The Canberra Airport is about 10 minutes from the city center. Car-rental desks can be found there, as well as a currency exchange, a bar, and a bistro. Stamps are sold at the newsdealer and a mailbox is provided for cards and letters. The airport lacks lockers, showers, and a post office.

The **Airliner Bus** (© 02/6299 3722) operates a 20-minute shuttle between the CBD and the airport Monday to Friday, leaving hourly. They charge A$5 (US$3.25) per person one-way.

BY TRAIN A nice way to see the countryside while you're in Australia is to take the train. **Countrylink** (© 13 22 32 in Australia; www.countrylink.nsw. gov.au) runs three Canberra Xplorer trains daily between Sydney and Canberra. The 4-hour trip costs around A$70 (US$46) in first class and A$50 (US$33) in economy; children are charged half price, and a return trip costs double. Many people make use of Countrylink transport/hotel packages (call **Countrylink Holidays** at © 13 28 29), which can save you quite a bit. You can choose between a range of accommodations in Canberra from A$90 to A$190 (US$59–US$124) a night for a couple, and if you book in advance (they recommend 2 weeks), you can save up to 40% on the fare (through a Rail Escape package). Find the Countrylink office at Wynyard CityRail station in Sydney.

From Melbourne, the **Canberra Link,** run by **V/Line** (© 13 61 96 in Australia), involves a 5-hour bus trip and a 3½-hour train trip. It costs A$55 (US$36) for adults and A$34 (US$22) for children and students.

Canberra Railway Station (© 02/6239 6707) is on Wentworth Avenue, Kingston, about 5km (3 miles) southeast of the city center. Coaches connect the railway station to the center.

BY BUS **Greyhound Pioneer** (© 13 20 30 in Australia; www.greyhound. com.au) does six runs a day from Sydney to Canberra. Tickets cost A$35 (US$23) for adults, A$32 (US$21) for students with ISAC (International Student Activity Card), and A$28 (US$18) for children 3 to 14; the trip takes 4 to 4½ hours.

From Melbourne, tickets to Canberra cost A$56 (US$36) for adults, A$50 (US$33) for students, and A$45 (US$29) for children. (Advanced purchase fares can save you up to 35%.)

Murrays Australia (© 13 22 51 in Australia) runs three services a day from Sydney to Canberra for A$35 (US$23) for adults and A$19 (US$12) for children. Ask for YHA member discounts. Several sightseeing companies in Sydney, including **AAT King's, Murrays,** and **Australia Pacific Tours,** offer day trips to Canberra as well.

Interstate buses arrive at **Jolimont Tourist Centre,** at the corner of Northbourne Avenue and Alinga Street, in Canberra City.

BY CAR The ACT (Australian Capital Territory) is surrounded by New South Wales. Sydney is 306km (190 miles) northeast, and Melbourne is 651km (404 miles) southwest of Canberra. In late 2001 the traveling time to Canberra was cut significantly following the opening of an extension to the M5 motorway that linked with the Eastern Distributor near Sydney Airport. (Turn right before you reach the airport and follow the signs to Wollongong, then the M5.) Now the drive takes between 3 and 3½ hours. From Melbourne, take the Hume Highway to Yass, switch to the Barton Highway; the trip will take about 8 hours.

VISITOR INFORMATION

The **Canberra Visitors' Centre,** 330 Northbourne Ave., Dickson (© **1300/554 114** in Australia, or 02/6205 0044), dispenses information and books accommodations. The office is open Monday through Friday from 9am to 5:30pm, and Saturday and Sunday from 9am to 4pm. The official government website (www.visitcanberra.com.au) is worth checking out.

SPECIAL EVENTS   A host of free events—from concerts to competitions— is part of the annual **Canberra National Multicultural Festival** held in the first 3 weeks of March. The fun includes Canberra Day (a local public holiday— always the 3rd Mon in Mar), a hot-air balloon fiesta, fireworks displays, food and wine promotions, plenty of music, and a large range of activities organized by Australia's ethnic mix. Visitors could find it a little more difficult to book accommodations during this time, but you should always be able to find something. There are many other major events including the flower show Floriade, the Subaru Rally of Canberra, the Canberra 400 V8 Supercars meeting, and the National Folk Festival. Check dates at www.visitcanberra.com.au.

CITY LAYOUT

The first thing that strikes a visitor to Canberra is its parklike feel (amazing, because there was barely a tree on the original site). Half a dozen avenues radiate from **Capital Hill,** where the Parliament House stands. Each of these broad, tree-shaded streets leads to a traffic circle, from which yet more streets emanate. Around each hub, the streets form a pattern of concentric circles—not the easiest layout for visitors trying to find their way.

Another of Canberra's most notable features is **Lake Burley Griffin,** a manmade lake created by damming the Molonglo River. The centerpiece of the lake is the **Captain Cook Memorial Jet,** a spire of water that reaches 147m (482 ft.) into the air. Wedged between Commonwealth Avenue and Kings Avenue is the suburb of **Parkes,** also known as the National Triangle. Here you'll find many of the city's most impressive attractions, such as the National Gallery of Australia, the High Court of Australia, and Questacon—the National Science and Technology Center. (All sites here can be accessed via www.nationaltriangle.com.au/tri.)

Canberra's main shopping district is on the other side of the lake, centered around Northbourne Avenue, one of the city's main thoroughfares. Officially labeled Canberra City, this area is more commonly known as **"Civic."** Northeast of Civic is **Mount Ainslie,** with the Australian War Memorial at its foot; from its summit there are spectacular views of the city and beyond. Another good lookout point is from the top of the **Telstra Tower** on Black Mountain, reached by Black Mountain Drive. Many of the embassies and consulates are concentrated in the suburb of **Yarralumla,** east of Capital Hill, while most of the other suburbs are filled with pleasant homes and small retail areas.

2 Getting Around

BY CAR   **Advantage Car Rentals,** 74 Northbourne Ave. (corner of Barry Dr.; © 1800/504 460 in Australia, or 02/6257 6888), has cars from A$35 (US$23) per day, including 200km (124 miles) per day. **Budget** (© 02/6257 1305), **Hertz** (© 02/6249 6211), **Thrifty** (© 1300/367 227), **Avis** (© 02/6249 6088), and **Delta Europcar** (© 13 13 90) have desks at the airport.

If you rent your own wheels, you might follow one or more of the six tourist drives marked with signs; pick up details from the Canberra Visitors' Centre.

BY TAXI   Canberra's only taxi company is **Canberra Cabs** (© 13 22 27 in Australia).

BY BUS   Canberra's bus system is coordinated by **ACTION** (© 02/6207 7611; www.action.act.gov.au). The central bus terminal is on Alinga Street, in Civic.

Single tickets cost A$2.40 (US$1.55) for adults and A$1.30 (US85¢) for children 5 to 15. Weekly tickets cost A$24 (US$15) and 10-ride tickets cost A$21 (US$14). Children travel for around half price. Purchase all tickets on the bus or from most newsdealers and ACTION interchanges.

For timetable information, call ACTION Monday through Saturday from 7am to 9pm, and Sunday from 8am to 6pm. Pick up bus route maps at bus interchanges, newsagents, and the Canberra Visitors' Centre.

Canberra City Sightseeing Tours (℘ 02/6257 3423) has double-decker buses, which pull in at 11 attractions around the city. Visitors can get off and on when they like. An all-day ticket costs A$25 (US$16) for adults and A$13 (US$8) for children.

BY BICYCLE   Canberra is unique in Australia for its extensive system of cycle tracks—some 120km (74 miles) of them—which makes sightseeing on two wheels a very pleasurable experience. See "Outdoor Pursuits," later in this chapter, for details on bike rental.

 FAST FACTS: Canberra

American Express   The office at **Centerpoint,** Shop 1, 185 City Walk (at the corner of Petrie Plaza), Civic (℘ **02/6247 2333**), is open Monday through Friday from 9am to 5pm, and Saturday from 9am to noon.

Business Hours   Banks are generally open Monday through Thursday from 9:30am to 4pm and Friday from 9:30am to 5pm. Stores and offices are open Monday through Friday from 9am to 5:30pm. Many shops, particularly in the large malls, stay open weekends and until 9pm Fridays.

Climate   The best time to visit Canberra is in spring (Sept–Nov) or autumn (Mar–May). Summers are hot and winters are cool and crisp.

Currency Exchange   Cash traveler's checks at banks, at **American Express** (above), or at **Thomas Cook,** at the Petrie Plaza entrance of the Canberra Centre (℘ **02/6257 2222**), open Monday through Friday from 9am to 5pm and Saturday from 9:30am to 12:30pm.

Dentist   Canberra lacks a dental emergency referral service. A reputable dentist in town is **Lachland B. Lewis,** Level 3, 40 Allara St., Civic (℘ **02/6257 2777,** or for emergency calls only 02/6295 9495 on weekends).

Doctor   The **Capital Medical Centre,** 2 Mort St., Civic (℘ **02/6257 3766**), is open Monday through Friday from 8:30am to 4:30pm. A standard consultation costs A$30 (US$20). The **Travellers' Medical & Vaccination Centre,** Level 5, 8–10 Hobart Place, Civic (℘ **02/6257 7154**), offers vaccinations and travel medicines. Standard consultations cost from A$40 (US$26).

E-mail   The **National Library,** Parkes Place, Parkes (℘ **02/6262 1111**), has e-mail facilities available during opening hours: Monday through Thursday 9am to 5pm. Internet access is readily available around town at other libraries and in Internet cafes. The Canberra Visitors' Centre can provide you with a full list of places.

Embassies/Consulates   The **British High Commission** (consular section) is on the 10th floor of SAP Building, corner of Bunda and Akuna Streets, Canberra City. (℘ **02/6270 6666**). The **Canadian High Commission** is at

Commonwealth Avenue, Yarralumla (© **02/6270 4000**); the **U.S. Embassy** is found at Moonah Place, Yarralumla (© **02/6214 5600**); and the **New Zealand High Commission** is at Commonwealth Avenue, Yarralumla (© **02/6270 4211**).

Emergencies Call © **000** for an ambulance, the police, or the fire department.

Eyeglasses For repairs, glasses, and contact lenses try **OPSM Express,** shop 5, Lower Ground Floor, The Canberra Centre, Civic (© **02/6249 7344**). It's open 9am to 5:30pm weekdays (to 9pm on Fri) and 9am to 4pm on Saturday.

Hospitals For medical attention, go to the **Canberra Hospital,** Yamba Drive, Garran (© **02/6244 2222**), or call the **Accident & Emergency Department** at © **02/6244 2324** (24 hr.).

Hot Lines In Canberra you have access to the **Rape Crisis Centre** (© 02/ 6247 2525); **Drug/Alcohol Crisis Line** (© 02/6205 4545, 24 hr.); **Lifeline Crisis Councelling** (© 13 11 14); **Salvation Army Councelling Service** (© 02/ 9331 6000); **Poison Information Centre** (© 02/6285 2852); and **National Roads & Motorists Association (NRMA)** (© 13 21 32).

Pharmacies **The Canberra Centre Pharmacy,** Civic (© **02/6249 8074**), is open during general shopping hours. A number of after-hours pharmacies are listed in the Canberra Yellow Pages.

Photographic Needs **Fletchers Fotographics,** Shop 2, 38 Akuna St., Civic (© **02/6247 8460**), is the best place to buy camera gear and films. They also repair cameras and sell secondhand equipment.

Post Office The **Canberra GPO,** 53–73 Alinga St., Civic (© **02/6209 1680**), is open Monday through Friday from 8:30am to 5:30pm. The Poste Restante address is c/o Canberra GPO, ACT 2601.

Restrooms Found near the city bus exchange, City Hall, and London Circuit.

3 Where to Stay

Canberra has a good scattering of places to stay, and generally accommodations are much cheaper than in most other state capitals. Many people travel to Canberra during the week, so many hotels offer cheaper weekend rates to put heads on beds. You should always ask about special deals. The rates given below are rack rates, or what the hotels hope they'll get on a good day—you can often get a room for less. The Canberra Visitors' Centre (© **1300/554 114**) can also provide you information about accommodations options.

VERY EXPENSIVE

Hyatt Hotel Canberra ✶✶ Visiting heads of state and pop stars make this their residence of choice in Canberra, and it's not hard to see why. It has a great location, only a 2-minute drive from the city center, in the shadow of Parliament House, and between Lake Burley Griffin and the Parliamentary Triangle. Originally the Hotel Canberra, it was opened in 1924 and was based on the low-slung "prairie" design of the now-destroyed Imperial Hotel in Tokyo. For many years the Hyatt was an important part of Canberra's social and political life, with key decisions affecting all Australians being consistently made over drinks in the bar. All staff members wear 1920s costumes to add to the atmosphere. Some 39 rooms are in the original two-story section. The rooms have more historic appeal, but they are darker than their modern counterparts, which were added in the 1980s. Standard rooms have a king-size bed and marble bathrooms. They all come with all the little luxuries you'd expect from a hotel of this class.

Commonwealth Ave., Yarralumla, ACT 2600. ℂ 13 12 34 in Australia, or 02/6270 1234, 800/233-1234 in the U.S. and Canada, 0181/335 1220 in London or 0845/758 1666 elsewhere in the U.K., 0800/441 234 in New Zealand, or 02/6270 1234. Fax 02/6281 5998. www.hyatt.com.au. 249 units. A$380 (US$247) standard double; A$605 (US$436) executive suite; A$1,200 (US$780) diplomatic suite. Extra person A$28 (US$18). Children under 18 stay free in parent's room. Ask about weekend packages and special rates. AE, DC, MC, V. Free parking. Amenities: Restaurant; cafe; indoor pool; lighted tennis court; extensive health club and spa; bike rental; concierge; business center; 24-hr. room service; laundry service. In room: A/C, TV w/pay movies, minibar, hair dryer, iron, safe.

EXPENSIVE

Crowne Plaza Canberra 🏵🏵

This centrally located hotel, formerly the Parkroyal Canberra (it changed owners in mid-2001), is next door to the National Convention Centre and Casino Canberra. Its car-oriented approach makes it a little inconvenient for pedestrians, but the gardens (Glebe Park) at the back are good for early morning strolls. Rooms face onto internal balconies that look down to the restaurants below. Standard rooms are user-friendly and comfortable; most come with one queen-size bed or two doubles. Park-view doubles look over the gardens. Weekend rates drop dramatically here. For example the standard rooms drop from A$300 (US$195) to A$190 (US$124), with breakfast thrown in, too.

1 Binara St., Canberra, ACT 2601. ℂ 1300/363 300 in Australia. Fax 02/6257 4903. www.crowneplaza.com. 295 units. A$300 (US$195) standard double; A$315 (US$205) park-view double; A$425–A$500 (US$276–US$325) suite. Extra person A$35 (US$23). Lower weekend rates. Children under 15 stay free in parent's room. AE, DC, MC, V. Free parking. Amenities: Restaurant; bar; medium-size indoor pool; health club; concierge; business center; 24-hr. room service; laundry service. In room: A/C, TV, minibar, hair dryer, iron, safe.

MODERATE

The Brassey of Canberra 🏵

Rooms in this 1927 heritage-listed building, formerly a boardinghouse for visiting government officials, are large, quiet, and somewhat plush. The garden bar and piano lounge are popular. Other good points include its proximity to Parliament House and other major attractions, and the hearty breakfasts. The hotel underwent extensive renovations in early 2000, which included the remodeling of many of the doubles into larger heritage rooms.

Belmore Gardens, Barton, ACT 2600. ℂ 1800/659 191 in Australia, or 02/6273 3766. Fax 02/6273 2791. www.brassey.net.au. 81 units. A$132 (US$86) double; A$165 (US$107) double family room; A$141 (US$92) heritage double; A$187 (US$122) heritage family room. Rates include full breakfast. Check for specials. AE, DC, MC, V. Free parking. Bus: 36 (get off outside the National Press Club). Amenities: Restaurant; bar; coin-op laundry; dry cleaning. In room: A/C, TV, dataport, minibar, coffeemaker, hair dryer, iron.

Forrest Inn and Apartments

The Forrest Inn is far from fancy, but it's close to the Manuka shops and restaurants and Parliament House. The outside of this 1960s property looks tacky, but the interior has been recently refurbished. The motel-style rooms are small and colorless, but clean; the apartments are nicer and have full-size kitchens, so for the same price I'd go for one of these. Two-bedroom apartments are perfect for families, and even the one-bedroom apartments have a single bed in the living room.

30 National Circuit, Forrest, ACT 2603. © 1800/676 372 in Australia, or 02/6295 3433. Fax 02/6295 2119. www.forrestinn.com.au. 102 units. A$110 (US$72) motel room; A$150 (US$98) 1-bedroom apt; A$175 (US$114) 2-bedroom apt. AE, DC, MC, V. Free parking. Bus: 39 (get off at the Rydges Hotel). **Amenities:** Restaurant; limited room service (motel only); coin-op laundry. *In room:* A/C, TV, minibar, hair dryer, iron.

Kingston Court Apartments ⋒ Situated about 1km (½ mile) from the Parliamentary Triangle and 6km (3¾ miles) from Civic, this apartment complex is a good option if you're looking for the comforts of home. The apartments are modern and spacious and come with a full kitchen, washer and dryer, a balcony, and a courtyard. The rooms underwent a full renovation in 2000.

4 Tench St., Kingston, ACT 2604. © 1800/655 754 in Australia, or 02/6295 2244. Fax 02/6295 5300. www. kingstonterrace.com.au. 36 units. A$160 (US$104) apt for 2. Extra adult A$20 (US$13), extra child A$10 (US$3.50). AE, DC, MC, V. Free parking. Bus: 38. **Amenities:** Small outdoor heated pool; half-size tennis court. *In room:* A/C, TV/VCR, dataport, kitchen, minibar, fridge, hair dryer, iron, washing machine, dryer.

University House ⋒ University House, situated less than 2km (1¼ miles) from the city center, offers a pleasant alternative to run-of-the-mill hotels in a similar price bracket. Large twin rooms come with two single beds; suites have a sitting room and a queen-size bed; the one-bedroom apartments have a bedroom with a queen-size bed, a sitting room, and a kitchenette; and the two-bedroom apartments are huge, with two large bedrooms, a dining room, a lounge room, and a full kitchen. All units have bathrooms with showers and tubs.

The hotel at the Australian National University, Balmain Crescent, Acton (G.P.O. Box 1535, Canberra, ACT 2601). © 1800/814 864 in Australia, or 02/6249 5211. Fax 02/6249 5252. www.anu.edu.au/unihouse. 104 units. A$124 (US$81) twin; A$126–A$149 (US$82–US$97) suite; A$136 (US$88) 1-bedroom apt; A$190 (US$124) 2-bedroom apt. Ask about packages, especially during low season. AE, DC, MC, V. Free secured parking. Bus: 34. **Amenities:** Restaurant; cafe; tennis court; access to nearby health club; bike rentals; car-rental desk; babysitting; coin-op laundry; laundry service/dry cleaning; nonsmoking rooms. *In room:* TV, fridge, hair dryer.

INEXPENSIVE

City Walk Hotel You can hardly get closer to the city center than at this former YWCA-turned-budget-travel hotel. Being right near the Jolimont Tourist Centre bus interchange, it picks up a lot of business from backpackers and budget travelers arriving by bus. The rooms are pretty basic, but clean. The hostel was completely refurbished in 2003. There are five double rooms with shared bathrooms, and three of these also have two extra single beds. One room (no. 204) has air-conditioning. Family rooms sleep up to 10 people, all in one room. The hotel has a bunch of communal facilities for the weary traveler, including a kitchen, telephone, tea- and coffeemakers, and a lounge area with TV and VCR.

2 Mort St., Civic, ACT 2601. © 1800/600 124 in Australia, or 02/6257 0124. Fax 02/6257 0116. www.city walkhotel.com.au. 55 units, 18 with bathroom (shower only). A$60 (US$39) double without bathroom; A$70 (US$46) double with bathroom; A$95–A$125 (US$62–US$81) family room; A$22–A$24 (US$14–US$16) dorm bed. Extra adult A$12 (US$7.80), extra child stays free. MC, V. **Amenities:** Coin-op laundry; Internet cafe. *In room:* TV, fridge, coffeemaker, no phone.

Victor Lodge (*Value* Backpackers, parliamentary staff, and budget travelers frequent this friendly place, situated right next to Kingston shops and about a 15-minute drive from the city center. Rooms vary from dorms with three, four, or five beds, to modern, simple doubles. There are communal showers and toilets and a courtyard. The staff picks up guests from the train and bus stations daily and drops off guests in town every morning. It's a nice place overall, but you'll have to decide whether or not you want to put up with the short trek into the city.

The owners also own the reasonable **Best Western** motel next door, which has standby rates of A$89 (US$58) for a double. Apparently, long-suffering parents often dump their teenage kids at the lodge and live it up at the motel.

29 Dawes St., Kingston, ACT 2604. ℂ **02/6295 7777.** Fax 02/6295 2466. www.victorlodge.com.au. 29 units, none with bathroom. A$59 (US$38) double; A$23 (US$15) dorm bed. Rates include continental breakfast. MC, V. Free parking. Bus: 38, 39, or 50. **Amenities:** Bike rental; tour desk; coin-op laundry; nonsmoking rooms; Internet facilities; TV room. *In room:* A/C, TV, iron, washbasin.

4 Where to Dine

EXPENSIVE

The Boat House by the Lake ⨂⨂ MODERN AUSTRALIAN   Set on the shores of Lake Burley Griffin, the Boat House is a very pleasant dining retreat enjoying uninterrupted water views. The large dining room offers floor to ceiling windows to capture the view, and the outside terrace is nice for a pre- or postdinner retreat. To start with try the Coffin Bay oysters, either natural with lemon, or topped with lychee avocado and chile salsa. Then go for the Japanese peppered beef filet on garlic mash potatoes with braised mushrooms, asparagus tempura, and wasabi hollandaise sauce. The wine list features locally produced wines. The Boat House was named the best restaurant in the ACT in 2001, and was a finalist in the American Express Best Restaurant awards the same year.

Grevillea Park, Menindee Drive, Barton, ACT. ℂ **02/6273 5500.** Reservations required. Main courses A$16–A$22 (US$10–US$14). AE, DC, MC, V. Mon–Fri noon–3pm; Mon–Sat 6–10:30pm.

Chairman and Yip ⨂⨂ ASIAN AUSTRALIAN   This is, without doubt, one of Canberra's best restaurants. Upbeat and popular with political bigwigs, it really is the place to see and be seen. The fish specials are good and spicy, with combinations of chile, cilantro, lemon grass, and galangal perking up your taste buds. I always go for the prawns with homemade chile jam, served on vermicelli noodles with mango salsa. Abalone and lobster also find their way onto the menu. The panna cotta is the signature dessert.

108 Bunda St., Civic. ℂ **02/6248 7109.** Reservations required. Main courses A$16–A$22 (US$10–US$14). AE, DC, MC, V. Sun–Fri noon–3pm; daily 6–11pm.

Juniperberry ⨂⨂ MODERN AUSTRALIAN   It sits on a lake edged with rushes and sculptures, full of goldfish. Add smoke machines (they call it a fog sculpture) on the far bank to send mysterious white eddies across the lake's surface toward your lakeside table, and you have a charming fantasy world in which to dine. The menu is small, with only a choice of six dishes each for first course, mains, and desserts. Main courses may include duck legs on figs, Atlantic salmon on polenta, a vegetarian option, and chicken and veal sausages.

Juniperberry Restaurant in the Sculpture Garden of the National Gallery of Australia, Parkes. ℂ **02/6240 6665.** Reservations recommended. Main courses A$25 (US$16). AE, DC, MC, V. Daily noon–2:30pm; check for dinner opening times in summer.

MODERATE

The Palette Café ⨂ CAFE/MODERN AUSTRALIAN   This is a great choice for lunch, especially because it's in the same building as Canberra's largest private art gallery. You can either eat inside, surrounded by artwork, or claim a table outside in the sunny courtyard. Standout dishes include grilled asparagus spears with Japanese scallops and almond hollandaise, and the chile-salted baby octopus. The Caesar salads are particularly good, as are the mushrooms with a sauce of soy, Japanese rice wine, honey, and coriander. The etchings, paintings, and sculptures on display are of high quality and are well priced.

Beaver Gallery, 81 Denison St., Deakin. © 02/6282 8416. Main courses A$12–A$18 (US$7.80–US$12). AE, MC, V. Daily 10am–5pm.

Tosolini's ⓚ CAFE/MODERN AUSTRALIAN   Because it's situated right next to the busy central bus terminal and close to the major shopping areas, Tosolini's really pulls in the passing crowd. You can sit out on the sidewalk terrace and watch the world go by. The eggs Benedict (A$7.50/US$4.90) served here at breakfast could be the best you've ever eaten. Lunchtime fare is almost as good. Both the battered flathead and the pan-fried broad bill (both are local fish) are tasty, but Tosolini's really made its name with its pastas and focaccias.

Corner of London Circuit at East Row, Civic. © 02/6247 4317. Main courses A$15–A$18 (US$9.75–US$12). AE, DC, MC, V. Daily 7:30am–5pm (Tues–Sat until 10:30pm).

The Tryst ⓚⓚ *Finds* MODERN AUSTRALIAN   The personal touches and service shine through at The Tryst, and the food is consistently delicious. The restaurant is tastefully decorated in an upscale cafe style, with the kitchen staff on show as they rustle up some of the capital's best tucker. It's relaxed, feeling more communal than intimate on busy nights. My favorite dish is the Atlantic salmon served with beurre blanc sauce and potatoes, but other popular dishes include the eye filet steak and the pumpkin risotto. If you have room left for dessert, don't miss out on the sticky date pudding served with hot butterscotch sauce, pralines, and ice cream—it's as good as it sounds. Otherwise, the long list of daily specials that complement the extensive menu could keep you busy for weeks.

Bougainville St., Manuka. © 02/6239 4422. Reservations recommended. Main courses A$15–A$23 (US$9.75–US$15). AE, DC, MC, V. Daily noon–2:30pm; Mon–Sat 6–10pm.

INEXPENSIVE

Caffe Della Piazza ⓚ ITALIAN/CAFE   Good eating isn't hard to find in Canberra, but this place is up there with the best. It won several awards for its Italian-inspired cooking, including the catering industries award for the best restaurant in the state. The restaurant offers both indoor and outdoor dining in pleasant surrounds, and is a good place to pop in for a light meal and a coffee, or something more substantial. Pastas here cost around A$11 (US$7.15), and the best seller is chicken breast strips in a machiato sauce. You need to book early for Friday or Saturday evenings.

19 Garema Place, Civic © 02/6248 9711. Reservations recommended. Main courses A$6.50–A$18 (US$4.20–US$12). AE, DC, MC, V. Daily 10:30am–midnight.

Little Saigon *Value* VIETNAMESE   This spacious restaurant has minimalist decor and floor-to-ceiling windows offering views of the city center. Tables are set up on either side of an indoor pond, and there's a bar in the back of the restaurant. The menu is vast, with lots of noodle dishes as well as spicy seafood, duck, chicken, pork, beef, and lamb. The top seller is the lemon grass and chile chicken.

Alinga St. and Northbourne Ave., Civic. © 02/6230 5003. Main courses A$12–A$15 (US$7.80–US$9.75). AE, DC, MC, V. Daily 10am–3pm and 5–10:30pm.

Portia's Place CANTONESE/MALAYSIAN/PEKING   A small restaurant serving up excellent traditional cookery, Portia's Place often fills up early and does a roaring lunchtime trade. The best things on the menu are the lamb ribs in shang tung sauce, the King Island filet steak in pepper sauce, the flaming pork (brought to your table wrapped in foil and bursting with flames), and the Queensland trout stir-fried with snow peas.

11 Kennedy St., Kingston. © **02/6239 7970.** Main courses A$9.80–A$19 (US$6.40–US$12). AE, DC, MC, V. Daily noon–2:30pm; Sun–Wed 5–10pm; Thurs–Sat 5–10:30pm.

5 Seeing the Sights

Australian Institute of Sport   This institution provides first-class training and facilities for Australia's elite athletes. Tours, led by one of the institute's athletes, include visits to the gymnasium, basketball courts, and Olympic swimming pool to see training in progress. There is also a fascinating interactive sports display where visitors can test their sporting skills.

Leverrier Crescent, Bruce. © **02/6214 1444.** Admission A$12 (US$7.80) adults, A$6 (US$3.90) children, A$33 (US$21) families. Tours leave the AIS shop Mon–Fri at 11:30am and 2:30pm; Sat–Sun at 10, 10:20, and 11:30am, and 1 and 2:30pm. Bus: 80 from City Center.

Australian War Memorial 🟌🟌   This monument to Australian troops who gave their lives for their country is truly moving and well worth a visit. Artifacts and displays tell the story of Australia's conflicts abroad. You won't soon forget the exhibition on Gallipoli, the bloody World War I battle in which so many Anzac (Australian and New Zealand Army Corps) servicemen were slaughtered. The Hall of Memory is the focus of the memorial, where the body of the Unknown Soldier lies entombed. (His remains were brought back from a World War I battlefield in 1993.) The Memorial also holds one of the largest collections of Australian art in the world, including works by Tom Roberts, Arthur Streeton, and Grace Cossington-Smith. Recently added exhibits include a film showing the surrender of Singapore, projected onto the actual table on which the surrender was signed, and a simulated ride aboard an original Lancaster bomber. ANZAC Hall and Bradbury Aircraft Hall are recent additions to the Memorial, housing significant aircraft and large pieces of war memorabilia.

At the head of Anzac Parade on Limestone Ave. © **02/6243 4211.** Free admission. Daily 10am–5pm (when the Last Post is played). Closed Christmas. Guided tours at 10, 10:30, and 11am, and 1:30 and 2pm. Bus: 33 or 40.

Canberra Deep Space Communication Complex 🟌   This information center, which stands beside huge tracking dishes, is a must for anyone interested in space. There are plenty of models, audiovisual recordings, and displays,

---

⟨Finds⟩ Up, Up & Away

Balloon Aloft (© **02/4938 1955;** www.balloonaloft.com.au) offers fabulous 45-minute sunrise flights over Canberra Monday through Friday for A$210 (US$137) for adults and A$120 (US$78) for children 6 to 12, including a champagne breakfast on touchdown. On weekends a 1-hour trip costs A$250 (US$163) for adults and A$150 (US$98) for children; breakfast costs A$25 (US$16) for adults and A$10 (US$6.50) for kids.

   Dawn Drifters (© **02/6285 4450;** fax 02/6281 5315; www.dawn drifters.com.au) will also send you soaring. One-hour champagne flights are A$185 (US$120) for adults Monday through Friday; A$215 (US$140) on weekends and holidays. Children go for 40% of the adult price. Breakfast is A$20 (US$13) extra.

including a space suit, space food, and archive film footage of the Apollo moon landings. The complex is still active, tracking and recording results from the Mars Pathfinder, *Voyager 1* and *2*, and the Cassini, Soho, Galileo, and Ulysses space exploration projects, as well as providing a link with NASA spacecraft. This is a great stop-off on the way back from the Tidbinbilla Nature Reserve (p. 607).

Tidbinbilla, 39km (24 miles) southwest of Civic. Ⓒ **02/6201 7880.** www.cdscc.nasa.gov. Free admission. Summer daily 9am–8pm; rest of year daily 9am–5pm. No public bus service, but several tour companies offer programs that include the complex.

High Court of Australia   The High Court, an impressive concrete-and-glass building that overlooks Lake Burley Griffin and stands next to the National Gallery of Australia, was opened by Elizabeth II in 1980. It is home to the highest court in Australia's judicial system and contains three courtrooms, a video display, and a huge seven-story-high public hall. When the court is in session, visitors can observe the proceedings from the public gallery. Call or e-mail for session details.

Overlooking Lake Burley Griffin, Parkes Place. Ⓒ **02/6270 6346.** www.hcourt.gov.au. Free admission. Mon–Fri 9:45am–4:30pm. Closed public holidays. Bus: 34.

National Capital Exhibition   If you want to find out more about Canberra's beginnings—and get a memorable view of Lake Burley Griffin, the Captain Cook Memorial Water Jet, and the Carillon in the bargain—then head here. The displays are well done, and there's a film that provides an overview of the city's design.

On the lake shore at Regatta Point in Commonwealth Park. Ⓒ **02/6257 1068.** Free admission. Daily 9am–6pm (5pm in winter).

National Gallery of Australia   Linked to the High Court by a pedestrian bridge, the National Gallery showcases both Australian and international art. The permanent collection and traveling exhibitions are displayed in 11 separate galleries. You'll find paintings by big names such as Claude Monet and Jackson Pollock, and Australian painters Arthur Boyd, Sidney Nolan, Arthur Streeton, Charles Condor, Tom Roberts, and Albert Tucker. The exhibition of Tiwi islander burial poles in the foyer is also interesting (the Tiwi Islands include Melville and Bathurst islands off Darwin), and there's a large collection of Aboriginal bark paintings from central Australia. A sculpture garden surrounding the gallery has 24 sculptures and is always open to the public.

Parkes Place. Ⓒ **02/6240 6502.** www.nga.gov.au. Free admission (except for major touring exhibitions). Daily 10am–5pm, closed Christmas. Guided tours daily at 11am and 2pm; Thurs and Sun at 11am there's a free tour focusing on Aboriginal art. Bus: 36 or 39 from Old Parliament House, or 34 from Parkes Place in front of the High Court.

National Museum of Australia   This, the first official all-encompassing museum dedicated to the nation of Australia, opened in 2001 to rave reviews. Using state-of-the-art technology and hands-on exhibits, the museum is based on three main themes: Australian society and its history since 1788; the interaction of people with the Australian environment; and Aboriginal and Torres Strait Islander cultures and histories. In reality it doesn't so much rely on actual historic objects to tell the stories of Australia but on images and sound. Allow a couple of hours if it grabs you, and 30 minutes to rush around baffled if it doesn't.

Acton Peninsula (about 5km/3 miles from the city center). Ⓒ **1800/026 132** or 02/6208 5000. www.nma. gov.au. Free admission (fees for special exhibitions). Daily 9am–5pm.

Old Parliament House The seat of government from 1927 to 1988, the Old Parliament House is now home to exhibitions from the National Museum and the Australian Archives. The National Portrait Gallery is also here, and outside on the lawn is the Aboriginal Tent Embassy, which was set up in 1972 in a bid to persuade the authorities to recognize the land ownership claims of Aboriginal and Torres Strait Islander people. The red, black, and yellow Aboriginal flag first came to prominence here. Interestingly, the Australian Heritage Commission now recognizes the campsite as a place of special cultural significance. On King George Terrace, midway between the new Parliament House (see below) and the lake. ℂ 02/6270 8222. www.oldparliamenthouse.gov.au. Admission A$2 (US$1.30) adults, A$1 (US65¢) children, A$5 (US$3.25) families. Daily 9am–5pm. Bus: 39.

Parliament House Conceived by American architect Walter Burley Griffin in 1912, but only built in 1988, Canberra's focal point was designed to blend organically into its setting at the top of Capital Hill; only a national flag supported by a giant four-footed flagpole rises above the peak of the hill. In good weather, picnickers crowd the grass that covers the roof, where the view is spectacular. Inside are more than 3,000 works of Australian arts and crafts, and extensive areas of the building are open to the general public. Look for a mosaic by Michael Tjakamarra Nelson entitled *Meeting Place,* which represents a gathering of Aboriginal tribes, and can be found just inside the main entrance. There's also a 20m (66-ft.) long tapestry by Arthur Boyd in the Great Hall on the first floor and one of the four known versions of the Magna Carta in the Great Hall beneath the flagpole. Free 50-minute guided tours are offered throughout the day.

Parliament is usually in session Monday through Thursday between mid-February and late June, and mid-August to mid-December. Both the Lower House—the House of Representatives (where the prime minister sits)—and the Upper House—the Senate—have public viewing galleries. The best time to see the action is during Question Time, which starts at 2pm in the Lower House. If you turn up early, you might get a seat; otherwise, make reservations for gallery tickets via the **sergeant-at-arms** (ℂ 02/6277 4889), at least a day in advance. Free tours of the building go for 45 minutes and start at 9am (then follow every 30 min.).

Capital Hill. ℂ 02/6277 5399. Free admission. Daily 9am–5pm. Closed Christmas. Bus: 39.

Questacon—The National Science and Technology Centre (*Kids*) Questacon offers some 200 hands-on exhibits that can keep you and your inner child occupied for hours. Exhibits are clustered into six galleries, each representing a different aspect of science. The artificial earthquake is a big attraction. The center is great for kids, but give it a miss if you've already visited the Powerhouse Museum (p. 149) in Sydney.

King Edward Terrace, Parkes. ℂ 02/6270 2800. Admission A$10 (US$6.50) adults, A$5 (US$3.25) children, A$6.50 (US$4.20) students, A$28 (US$18) families. Daily 10am–5pm. Closed Christmas. Bus: 34.

Telstra Tower The tower, which rises 195m (640 ft.) above the summit of Black Mountain, has both open-air and enclosed viewing galleries that provide magnificent 360-degree views over Canberra and the surrounding countryside. Those who dine in the pricey, revolving **Tower Restaurant** (ℂ 02/6248 7096) are thoughtfully entitled to a refund of their admission charge.

Black Mountain Dr. ℂ 02/6248 1911. Admission A$3.30 (US$2.15) adults, A$1.10 (US70¢) children. Daily 9am–10pm. No bus service.

Tidbinbilla Nature Reserve *(Moments* This is a great place to see native animals such as kangaroos, wallabies, koalas, platypuses, and birds in their natural environment. Unlike other wildlife parks around the country, this one has plenty of space, so sometimes you'll have to look hard to spot the animals. (On a recent quick visit, I saw a few birds and not much else, but on previous visits I've been almost stomped on by kangaroos.) A guide is available from the visitor center. **Go Bush Tours** (✆ **02/6231 3023;** www.gobushtours.com.au) runs tours to the reserve as well as the neighboring Canberra Deep Space Communication Complex for A$66 (US$43). This includes morning tea and lunch.

Tidbinbilla. Paddys River Rd., RMB 141 via Tharwa, ACT 2620. ✆ 02/6205 1233. Fax 02/6205 1232. www.environment.act.gov.au. Admission A$9 (US$5.85) per vehicle day. Daily 9am–6pm (8pm in summer). Visitor center Mon–Fri 9am–4:30pm; Sat–Sun 9am–5:30pm. No public bus service, but several tour companies offer programs that include the reserve

BOTANIC GARDENS & A NEARBY NATIONAL PARK

The **Australian National Botanic Gardens** *(*, Clunies Ross Street, Black Mountain, Acton (✆ **02/6250 9540**), are home to the best collection of Australian native plants anywhere. The gardens are situated on 51 hectares (126 acres) on the lower slopes of Black Mountain and feature a Eucalyptus Lawn containing more than 600 species of eucalyptus, a rainforest area, a Tasmanian alpine garden, and self-guided walking trails. Free, guided tours depart from the visitor center at 11am on weekdays and 11am and 2pm on weekends. The gardens are open daily from 9am to 5pm (to 8pm in summer). The visitor center is open daily from 9:30am to 4:30pm. There's no bus service to the gardens.

The **Namadgi National Park** *(* covers almost half of the Australian Capital Territory. Parts of the park, which has rolling plateaus, good trout-fishing streams, and dense forest, are just 30km (19 miles) from Canberra. Marked hiking trails can be found throughout the park. Spring is the best time to visit for the prolific display of bush flowers. In the past, sections of the park were cleared for sheep grazing, but these days the pastures are popular with hundreds of gray kangaroos. (They're easiest to spot in the early morning and late afternoon.) At Yankee Hat, off the Nass/Boboyan Road, is an Aboriginal rock-art site. The **Namadgi Visitors Centre** (✆ **02/6207 2900**), on the Nass/Boboyan Road, 3km (1¾ miles) south of the township of Tharwa, has maps and information on walking trails.

6 Outdoor Pursuits

BIKING   With 120km (74 miles) of bike paths, Canberra is made for exploring on two wheels. Rent a bike from **Mr. Spoke's Bike Hire** on Barrine Drive near the ferry terminal in Acton (✆ **02/6257 1188**). Bikes for adults cost A$10 (US$6.50) for the first hour and A$9 (US$5.85) for each hour afterward; rates are A$9 (US$5.85) for kids, going down to A$8 (US$5.20) for each subsequent hour.

BOATING   **Burley Griffin Boat Hire,** on Barrine Drive near the ferry terminal in Acton (✆ **02/6249 6861**), rents paddle boats for A$20 (US$13) per hour and canoes for A$14 (US$9.10) per hour. **Row 'n' Ride,** near the MacDermott Place Boat Ramp, Belconnen (✆ **02/6254 7838**), is open on weekends and school and public holidays and offers canoes from A$9 (US$5.85) per hour, kayaks for A$10 (US$6.50) per hour, and mountain bikes for A$9 (US$5.85) per hour.

GLIDING   The **Canberra Gliding Club** (© **02/6257 1494** or 02/6452 3994) offers joy flights and trial instructional flights on weekends and public holidays from the Bunyan Airfield. Flights cost A$60 (US$39).

SWIMMING   The indoor heated pool at the **Australian Institute of Sport** (© **02/6214 1281**), on Leverrier Crescent in Bruce, a short drive northwest of Civic, is open to the public at certain times during the day (call ahead to check schedules). Adults pay A$4 (US$2.60) to swim, and children pay A$2 (US$1.30). It's compulsory to wear swimming caps, which can be bought there for A$2.50 (US$1.60). It costs A$6 (US$3.90) to use the pool, Jacuzzi, and sauna.

TENNIS   The **National Tennis and Squash Centre,** Federal Highway, Lyneham (© **02/6247 0929**), has squash courts available for A$12 to A$16 (US$7.80–US$10) per hour, depending on when you want to play. Tennis courts can be booked for A$9.50 to A$15 (US$6.20–US$9.75). The Australian Institute of Sport (p. 604) also rents courts.

7 Canberra After Dark

The **"Times Out"** section in Thursday's the *Canberra Times* has listings on what's on offer around town.

Of the pubs in town, the best in the city center are the British-style **Wig & Pen,** on the corner of Limestone and Alinga Street (© **02/6248 0171**); the popular **Moosehead's Pub,** at 105 London Circuit in the south of the city (© **02/6257 6496**); the **Phoenix,** at 21 East Row (© **02/6247 1606**), which has live music upstairs for a cover charge; and **P. J. O'Reileys** (© **02/6230 4752**), on the corner of West Row and Alinga Street, an authentic-style Irish pub. **King O'Malleys** (© **02/6257 0111**), on Mort Street, is another popular Irish pub in the city.

A good nightclub for the young at heart is the American-style **Bobby McGee's Entertainment Lounge** in the Rydges Canberra Hotel on London Circuit (© **02/6257 7999**). It's open Monday, Thursday, Friday and Saturday nights. Entry varies from A$3 to A$7 (US$1.95–US$4.55).

If you're looking to roll some dice, the **Casino Canberra,** in Glebe Park, 21 Binara St., Civic (© **1800/806 833** in Australia, or 02/6257 7074), is a small, older-style casino offering all the usual casino games from noon to 6am. Dress regulations prohibit leisure wear, running shoes, and denim, but overall it's a casual place to lose some money.

14

Tasmania

by Marc Llewellyn

The name "Tasmania" suggests an unspoiled place, with vast stretches of wilderness roamed by strange creatures like the Tasmanian devil. Many mainland residents still half-jokingly refer to their "country cousins" on this island as rednecks. In truth, most Tasmanians are hospitable and friendly people, lacking the harsh edge that big cities can foster. Most also care passionately for the environment, decrying the belief that anything that moves deserves a bullet and anything that stands still needs chopping down.

Visitors to Tasmania are surprised by its size, though compared to the rest of Australia the distances are certainly more manageable. Dense rainforests, mountain peaks, alpine meadows, great lakes, eucalyptus stands, and fertile stretches of farmland are all easily accessible, but you should be prepared for several hours of concentrated driving to get you between the main attractions. Among Tasmania's chief attractions is its natural environment. More than 20% of the island has been declared a World Heritage area, and nearly a third of the island is protected within its 14 national parks.

Tasmania's other main draw is its history. Remains of the Aborigine people that lived here for tens of thousands of years are evident in isolated rock paintings, engraving, stories, and the aura of spirituality that still holds tight in places where modern civilization has not yet reached.

Europeans discovered Tasmania (or Van Diemen's Land, as it was once known) in 1642, when the seafarer Abel Tasman set anchor off its southwest coast, although it wasn't identified as an island until 1798. Tasmania made its mark as a dumping ground for convicts, who were more often than not transported for petty crimes in their homeland. The brutal system of control, still evident in the ruins at Port Arthur and elsewhere, spilled over into persecution of the native population. The last full-blooded Tasmanian Aborigine died in 1876, 15 years after the last convict transportation. Most had already died of disease and maltreatment at the hands of the settlers.

1 Exploring Tasmania

VISITOR INFORMATION   The **Tasmanian Travel and Information Centre** (© **1300/655 145** in Australia; www.discovertasmania.com.au) operates visitor centers located in more than 30 towns throughout the state. It can arrange travel passes, ferry and bus tickets, car rental, cruises, and accommodations.

Pick up a copy of *Travelways,* Tourism Tasmania's tourist tabloid, for details on transportation, accommodations, restaurants, and attractions around Tasmania.

WHEN TO GO   The best time to visit Tasmania is between October and April, when the weather is at its best. By May nights are getting cold, the days are getting shorter, and the deciduous trees are starting to turn golden. Winters

(June–Aug), especially in the high country, can be quite harsh—though that's the best time to curl up in front of a blazing fire. The east coast is generally milder than the west coast, which is buffeted by the "Roaring 40s"—the winds that blow across the ocean and the 40° meridian, from as far away as Argentina.

The busy season for tourism here runs December through February, as well as during public holiday and school holiday periods. Unlike the rest of Australia, Tasmanian schools have three terms. Term dates are from the second week in February to the last week in May; the third week in June to the first week in September; and the fourth week in September to the first week in December.

GETTING THERE   The quickest way to get to Tasmania is by air. **Qantas** (© **13 13 13** in Australia; www.qantas.com) flies from the mainland to Hobart and Launceston. **Virgin Blue** (© **13 67 89** in Australia; www.virginblue.com.au) offers discounted trips from Melbourne, with connections from other capitals, if you book early from their website. **Regional Express** (© **03/13 17 13** in Australia; www.regionalexpress.com.au) flies from Melbourne to Devonport and Burnie in the State's north.

In 2002, two new high-speed ferry services replaced the DevilCat and the old *Spirit of Tasmania* ferry that plied the waters between Melbourne and Tasmania for years. The new car ferries—the *Spirit of Tasmania I* and *II*—are each capable of carrying 1,400 passengers as well as cars. They make the crossing from Melbourne's Station Pier to Tasmania's Devonport (on the north coast) in around 10 hours. The ferries leave both Melbourne and Devonport at 9pm and arrive at around 7am. From roughly December 20 to April 27, there's also day service on weekends, leaving both ports at 9am and arriving at 7pm. Prices are based on "shoulder" and "peak" times: The shoulder seasons run from roughly August 31 to December 6, and from January 27 to April 27. A one-way seat costs between A$99 and A$135 (US$65–US$88) for adults, and A$75 and A$99 (US$49–US$65) for children. Three- to four-berth cabins cost from A$187 to A$234 (US$121–US$152) for adults and A$91 to A$105 (US$59–US$68) for kids depending on the season and if you have a porthole. Twin cabins cost from A$200 to A$261 (US$130–US$169) for adults and A$101 to A$132 (US$66–US$86) for children. Deluxe cabins cost A$283 to A$369 (US$184–US$240) for adults and children alike. Standard-size cars cost $55 (US$36) from December 6 to January 25 but are free to transport the rest of the year.

In early 2004, the *Spirit of Tasmania III* will commence sailing between Sydney and Devonport. The ferry will depart Sydney at 3pm on Tuesday, Friday, and Sunday, and Devonport at 3pm on Monday, Thursday, and Saturday. The trip will take 20 hours and cost from A$230 to A$371 (US$150–US$242), depending on accommodations. Prices are one-way and cars travel free.

Make reservations for any of the ferries through **TT-Line** (© **03/9206 6211;** www.spiritoftasmania.com.au). Special offers are regularly available. **Tasmanian**

⌒Tips   Tasmania's Tricky Roads

Driving in Tasmania can be dangerous; there are more accidents involving tourists on Tasmania's roads than anywhere else in Australia. Many roads are narrow and bends can be tight, especially in the mountainous inland regions—where you may also come across black ice early in the morning or at anytime in winter. Marsupials are also common around dusk, and swerving to avoid them has caused countless crashes.

Tasmania

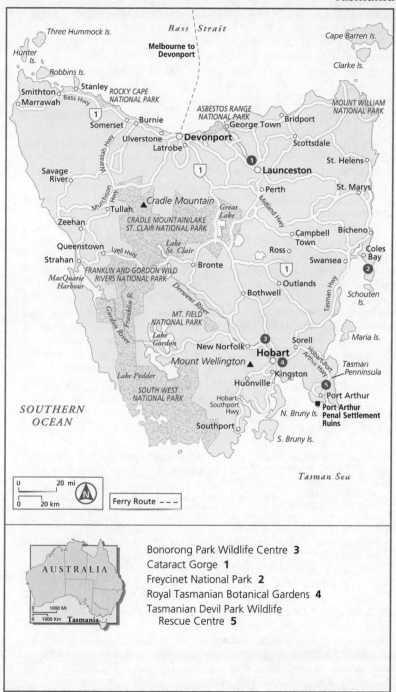

Bass Strait

Three Hummock Is.

Cape Barren Is.

Hunter Is.

Clarke Is.

Robbins Is.

Melbourne to Devonport

Stanley

Smithton   ROCKY CAPE NATIONAL PARK

Marrawah   Bass Hwy

MOUNT WILLIAM NATIONAL PARK

Somerset   Burnie

ASBESTOS RANGE NATIONAL PARK

Bridport

Ulverstone   George Town

Devonport

Scottsdale

Latrobe

St. Helens

Savage River

Launceston

Perth

St. Marys

Cradle Mountain

Great Lake

Tullah

CRADLE MOUNTAIN/LAKE ST. CLAIR NATIONAL PARK

Midland Hwy

Zeehan

Campbell Town

Bicheno

Queenstown   Lyell Hwy

Lake St. Clair

Ross

Coles Bay

Strahan

FRANKLIN AND GORDON WILD RIVERS NATIONAL PARK

Bronte

Swansea

MacQuarie Harbour

Outlands

Schouten Is.

Gordon River

Franklin R.

Derwent River

Bothwell

Tasman Hwy

MT. FIELD NATIONAL PARK

Lake Gordon

New Norfolk

Sorell

Maria Is.

Mount Wellington

Hobart

Kingston

Tasman Penninsula

Lake Pedder

SOUTH WEST NATIONAL PARK

Huonville

Port Arthur

SOUTHERN OCEAN

Hobart-Southport Hwy

Port Arthur Penal Settlement Ruins

N. Bruny Is.

Southport

S. Bruny Is.

Tasman Sea

20 mi

0   20 km

Ferry Route – – –

AUSTRALIA

1000 Mi

1000 Km   **Tasmania**

Bonorong Park Wildlife Centre **3**
Cataract Gorge **1**
Freycinet National Park **2**
Royal Tasmanian Botanical Gardens **4**
Tasmanian Devil Park Wildlife
    Rescue Centre **5**

611

Redline Coaches (℡ 03/6336 1446) connect with each ferry and transfer passengers to Launceston, and on to Hobart.

McCafferty's (℡ 13 14 99 in Australia) can organize coach travel from the eastern mainland states, with transfers to Tasmania by ferry.

GETTING AROUND   The regional airline **Tasair** (℡ 03/6248 5088; www. tasair.com.au) flies to some settlements in Tasmania. **Par Avion** (℡ 03/6248 5390; www.paravion.com.au) concentrates on the southwest World Heritage areas of the state and also operates wonderful sightseeing tours. A 2½-hour southwest wilderness flight, for example, costs A$176 (US$114).

Statewide coach services are provided by **Tasmanian Redline Coaches** (℡ 03/ 6336 1446; www.redlinecoaches.com.au) and **Tassielink** (℡ 1300/300 520 in Australia, or 03/6272 6611; www.tigerline.com.au). Associated with Tassielink are **Tigerline Coaches** (contactable by same phone and website), which offers a series of coach tours to major places of interest. **Hobart Coaches** (℡ 1800/030 620 in Australia, or 03/6234 4077) runs trips around the Hobart area.

The cheapest way to get around by coach is to buy a travel pass. The **Tassie Link Explorer Pass,** which can be used on all Tassielink routes, comes in four categories: A 7-day pass good for travel within 15 days is A$160 (US$104); a 10-day pass good for travel in 15 days is A$190 (US$124); a 14-day pass good for travel within 20 days is A$220 (US$143); a 21-day pass valid for travel in 30 days is A$265 (US$172).

Driving a car from Devonport on the north coast to Hobart on the south coast takes less than 4 hours. From Hobart to Strahan on the west coast also takes around 4 hours, while the journey from Launceston to Hobart takes about 2 hours. The **Royal Automobile Club of Tasmania (RACT),** at Murray and Patrick streets in Hobart (℡ 13 27 22 in Australia), can supply you with touring maps.

TOUR OPERATORS   Dozens of operators run organized hiking, horse trekking, sailing, caving, fishing, bushwalking, diving, cycling, rafting, climbing, kayaking, or canoeing trips in Tasmania. For a full listing, see the "Outdoor Adventure" section of *Travelways,* the Tasmanian tourist board's publication (see "Visitor Information," above).

One of the best operators is **Tasmania Adventure Tours** (℡ 1300/654 604 in Australia, or 038/8309 2277; www.adventuretours.com.au). They offer a 3-day East Coast Explorer tour from Devonport, taking in Launceston, Freycinet National Park, and Port Arthur, before finishing in Hobart. The tour costs A$375 to $495 (US$144–US$322) depending on accommodations. Their 6-day Taste of Tasmania Tour starts off in Devonport, takes in all the attractions in their other two tours, and ends up in Hobart. This tour costs A$720 to $950 (US$468–US$617). Call for departure days.

Peregrine Adventures (℡ 03/9662 2800; www.peregrine.net.au) runs rafting tours of the Franklin River, which carves its way through some of the most beautiful, rugged, and inaccessible wilderness in the world. Another good operator is the **Roaring 40°s Ocean Kayaking Company** (℡ 1800/653 712 in Australia; www.roaring40skayaking.com.au); both companies offer paddling expeditions lasting from 1 to 11 days. **Tasmanian Expeditions,** based in Launceston (℡ 1800/030 230 in Australia, or 03/6267 5000; www.tasmanianexpeditions. com.|au), runs a whole range of cycling, trekking, and rafting trips around the country, some starting or finishing in Hobart.

SUGGESTED ITINERARIES   Planning my first trip to Tasmania, I'd pack my walking boots, raincoat, and shorts, and head off first to either **Launceston** or

> ## ⌒Tips National Park Entry Fees
>
> A **Tassie Holiday Pass** costs A$33 (US$21) and allows entry for a car and passengers to Tasmania's national parks for 2 months. Pedestrians, cyclists, motorcyclists, and coach passengers pay A$14 (US$8.80) for 2 months. Occasional users can buy a 24-hour pass for A$10 (US$6.50) per car, while walkers, cyclists, motorcyclists, and coach passengers pay $3.50 (US$2.30) per day. Passes are available at all major parks and Tasmanian Visitor Information Centres. For more information, contact the **Parks and Wildlife Service** at ✆ **03/6233 8203.** Look up the Tasmanian Parks and Wildlife Service's website (www.parks.tas.gov.au) for information on Tasmania's national parks.

Hobart, the island's two main cities. I'd take in **Freycinet National Park** for its wonderful scenery and abundant wildlife, stop in at **Port Arthur** for its beautiful setting and disturbing convict past, and head to the central highlands for a stomp around **Cradle Mountain.**

2 Hobart

198km (123 miles) S of Launceston

Tasmania's capital (pop. 126,000), second in age only to Sydney, is an appealing place worth visiting for a couple of days. Hobart's main features are its wonderful harbor and the colonial cottages that line the narrow lanes of Battery Point. As with Sydney, Hobart's harbor is the city's focal point, attracting yachts from all over the world. Down by the waterfront, picturesque Salamanca Place bursts with galleries, pubs, cafes, and an excellent market on Saturdays. Europeans settled in Hobart in 1804, a year after Tasmania's first colony was set up at Risdon (10km/6¼ miles up the Derwent River). Hobart, the most southerly Australian state capital, is closer to the Antarctic coast than it is to Perth in Western Australia, and has long been regarded by navigators, whalers, and explorers as the gateway to the south.

ESSENTIALS

GETTING THERE   Qantas (✆ **13 13 13** in Australia) and **Virgin Blue** (✆ **13 67 89** in Australia) carry passengers from the mainland. The trip from the airport to the city center takes about 20 minutes and costs about A$25 (US$16) by taxi. The **Airporter Bus** (✆ **0419/382 240**) meets planes and delivers passengers to hotels in the city and farther afield.

Car- and camper-rental offices at the airport include **Hertz** (✆ 03/6237 1155), **Advance** (✆ 1800/030 118 in Australia; www.advancecars.com.au), **Avis** (✆ 03/6248 5424), **Budget** (✆ 1300/362 848 in Australia, or 03/6248 5333), and **Thrifty** (✆ 1800/030 730 in Australia, or 03/6234 1341). Cars cost around A$55 (US$36) for 1 day, A$50 (US$32) per day for 2 days, A$45 (US$29) per day for 4 days, and A$40 (US$26) per day for a week or more. You might find even better bargains in town with lower-priced rental companies such as **Lo-Cost Auto Rent** (✆ 1800/030 023 in Australia, or 03/6231 0550) and **Range Rent-a-Bug** (✆ 03/6231 0300).

VISITOR INFORMATION   Information is available from the **Tasmanian Travel and Information Centre,** at Davey and Elizabeth streets (✆ **03/6230 8233**). It's open Monday through Friday from 8:30am to 5:15pm, Saturday and public holidays from 9am to 4pm, and Sunday from 9am to 1pm (9am–4pm

Dec–Apr). You can pick up information on the State's National Parks at the **Lands Information Bureau,** 134 Macquarie St. (© **03/6233 8011**).

CITY LAYOUT Hobart straddles the Derwent River on the south coast of the Tasmania. **Salamanca Place** and nearby **Battery Point** abut Sullivan's Cove, home to hundreds of yachts. The row of sandstone warehouses that dominate Salamanca Place date back to the city's importance as a whaling base in the 1830s. Behind Princes Wharf, Battery Point is the city's historic district, which in colonial times was the home of sailors, fishermen, whalers, coopers, merchants, shipwrights, and master mariners. The open ocean is about 50km (31 miles) farther down the river, though the Derwent empties out into Storm Bay, just 20km (12 miles) downstream. The central business district is on the west side of the water, with the main thoroughfares—**Campbell, Argyle, Elizabeth, Murray, and Harrington streets**—sloping down to the busy harbor. The Tasman Bridge and regular passenger ferries reach across the Derwent River. Set back from the city, but overlooking it, is the 1,270m (4,166-ft.) tall **Mount Wellington.**

GETTING AROUND Central Hobart is very small, and most of the attractions are in easy walking distance. **Metro Tasmania** (© **03/6233 4232** or 13 22 01; www.metrotas.com.au) operates a system of public metro buses throughout the city and suburban areas. Single tickets cost from A$1.40 to A$3.20 (US91¢–US$2.10) depending on how far you're going. Day Tripper tickets can be used between 9am and 4:30pm and after 6pm during the week and all day on weekends; they cost A$3.60 (US$2.35). Purchase tickets from bus drivers. If you plan on busing about, stop off at the Metro Shop situated in the General Post Office building on the corner of Elizabeth and Macquarie streets and pick up a timetable, brochures, and sightseeing information.

The **Roche-O'May ferry company** (© **03/6223 1914;** www.ontas.com.au/cartela) operates morning and afternoon tea cruises, and lunch and dinner cruises on the *Cartela,* a wooden-hulled, former steam-powered ferry built in Hobart in 1912. One-hour afternoon coffee cruises cost A$12 (US$7.80), 2-hour afternoon cruises cost A$16 (US$10), and lunch and dinner cruises are A$24 (US$16). Call for departure times. The company also runs a ferry service on the *Wanderer,* with coffee, tea, and full commentary. It stops at the Wrest Point Casino, the Royal Tasmanian Botanical Gardens, Sullivan's Cove, and the old suburb of Belle Reeve. These ferries leave Brooke Street Pier on Franklin Wharf at 10:30am, noon, and 1:30 and 3pm. The 1½-hour cruise costs A$10 (US$6.50) for adults, A$5 (US$3.25) for children, and A$25 (US$16) for a family.

Tasmanian Tours & Travel Tigerline (© **1300/653 633** in Australia, or 03/6272 6611) offer a range of sightseeing tours of Hobart and its surroundings.

SPECIAL EVENTS The **Sydney-to-Hobart Yacht Race,** starting in Sydney on December 26, fills the Constitution Dock Marina and harbor area close to overflowing with spectators and partygoers when the ships turn up in Tasmania. The race takes anywhere from 2 to 4 days, and the sailors and fans stay on to celebrate

---

Tips **Staying Connected**

It's relatively hard to find public access to the Internet in Hobart, but you can try **Drifters Internet Café,** Shop 9/33 Salamanca Place, Hobart (in Salamanca Galleria) (© **03/6224 3244**). The cafe charges A$5 (US$3.25) per half-hour.

Hobart

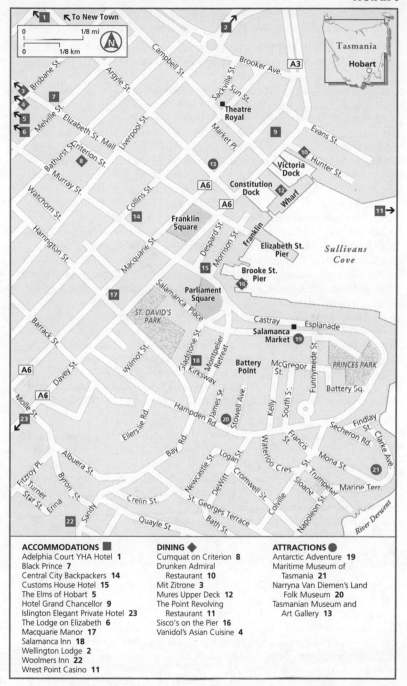

To New Town

0   1/8 mi
0   1/8 km

Tasmania

Hobart

Campbell St.
Brisbane St.
Argyle St.
Brooker Ave.
A3
Sackville St.
Sun St.
Theatre Royal
Evans St.
Melville St.
Elizabeth St. Mall
Liverpool St.
Market Pl.
Hunter St.
Victoria Dock
Bathurst St.
Criterion St.
Murray St.
Collins St.
A6
Constitution Dock
Wharf
Watchorn St.
Harrington St.
Macquarie St.
Franklin Square
Despard St.
Morrison St.
Franklin
Elizabeth St. Pier
Sullivans Cove
Brooke St. Pier
Barrack St.
Salamanca Place
Parliament Square
ST. DAVID'S PARK
Castray
Esplanade
Salamanca Market
Davey St.
A6
A6
Wilmot St.
Gladstone St.
Kirksway
Montpelier Retreat
Battery Point
McGregor St.
PRINCES PARK
Battery Sq.
Molle St.
Hampden Rd.
Runnymede St.
Findlay St.
Clarke Ave.
Ellerslie Rd.
Bay Rd.
Stowell Ave.
Kelly
South S.
Secheron Rd.
Mona St.
Albuera St.
Newcastle St.
Logan St.
DeWitt
Cromwell St.
Waterloo Cres.
Francis St.
Sloane
Trumpeter
Marine Terr.
Fitzroy Pl.
Turner St.
Star St.
Erina
Byron St.
Sandy
Crelin St.
St. Georges Terrace
Quayle St.
Bath St.
Colville
Napoleon St.
River Derwent

ACCOMMODATIONS ■
Adelphia Court YHA Hotel **1**
Black Prince **7**
Central City Backpackers **14**
Customs House Hotel **15**
The Elms of Hobart **5**
Hotel Grand Chancellor **9**
Islington Elegant Private Hotel **23**
The Lodge on Elizabeth **6**
Macquarie Manor **17**
Salamanca Inn **18**
Wellington Lodge **2**
Woolmers Inn **22**
Wrest Point Casino **11**

DINING ◆
Cumquat on Criterion **8**
Drunken Admiral
   Restaurant **10**
Mit Zitrone **3**
Mures Upper Deck **12**
The Point Revolving
   Restaurant **11**
Sisco's on the Pier **16**
Vanidol's Asian Cuisine **4**

ATTRACTIONS ●
Antarctic Adventure **19**
Maritime Museum of
   Tasmania **21**
Narryna Van Diemen's Land
   Folk Museum **20**
Tasmanian Museum and
   Art Gallery **13**

New Year's Eve. Food and wine lovers indulge themselves after the race during the 2-month-long **Hobart Summer Festival,** which starts on December 28.

EXPLORING THE CITY & ENVIRONS

Simply strolling around the harbor and popping into the shops at Salamanca Place can keep you nicely occupied.

Also take a look around Battery Point, an area chock-full of colonial stone cottages. The area gets its name from a battery of guns set up on the promontory in 1818 to defend the town against potential invaders (particularly the French). Today, there are plenty of tearooms, antiques shops, cozy restaurants, and atmospheric pubs interspersed between grand dwellings. One of the houses worth looking into is **Narryna Van Diemen's Land Folk Museum,** 103 Hampden Rd. (© **03/6234 2791**), which depicts the life of upper-class pioneers. It's open Tuesday through Friday from 10:30am to 5pm and Saturday and Sunday from 2 to 5pm (closed July). Admission is A$5 (US$3.25) for adults and A$2 (US$1.30) for children. Also in this area is the **Maritime Museum of Tasmania,** 16 Argyle St. (© **03/6234 1427**), one of the best museums of its type in Australia. It's open daily from 10am to 5pm, and admission is A$7 (US$4.55) for adults, A$4 (US$2.60) for children 4 to 16, and A$16 (US$10) for a family.

The National Trust (© **03/6223 7570**) offers a 3-hour **Battery Point Heritage Walk** leaving at 9:30am every Saturday from the wishing well in Franklin Square. It costs A$11 (US$7.15) for adults and A$3 (US$1.95) for children 6 to 16 and includes morning tea.

For magnificent views over Hobart and across a fair-size chunk of Tasmania, drive to **The Pinnacle** on top of Mount Wellington, about 40 minutes from the city center. Take a warm coat though; the wind in this alpine area can bite. An extensive network of walking trails offers good hiking. Pick up a copy of *Mt. Wellington Day Walk Map and Notes* from the **Department of Environment Tasmap Centre,** at the Lands Building, 134 Macquarie St. (© **03/6233 3382**).

THE TOP ATTRACTIONS

Antarctic Adventure & *Kids*   Hobart is the last port of call for expeditions to Antarctica. You can experience the cold continent yourself at this highly recommended attraction. It doesn't look like much at first, but I promise you'll be sucked in. You can experience an Antarctic blizzard, climb all over heavy machinery, experience a downhill ski simulator (I'm not sure how that fits in), and get computer access to Antarctic weather conditions and communications. The photos and other displays are also interesting. The irresistible stuffed huskies in the souvenir shop will take a hefty bite out of your wallet. Allow 1 to 2 hours.

Salamanca Sq. © 03/6220 8220. Admission A$16 (US$10) adults, A$13 (US$8.45) students, A$8 (US$5.20) children 4–13, A$40 (US$26) families. Daily 10am–5pm. Closed Christmas.

Bonorong Park Wildlife Centre *Kids*   I don't think I've ever seen so many wallabies in one place as I saw here—they were hopping all over the place. There are lots of other native animals around, too, including snakes, koalas, Tasmanian devils, and wombats. The Bush Tucker shed serves lunch, billy teas (basically tea brewed up in a metal pot with a gum leaf thrown in), and damper (Australian-style campfire bread). Koala cuddling isn't allowed in Tasmania, but if you're around at feeding times it's possible to stroke one—they're not as shy as you might think. Feeding times are 12:30 and 3pm daily. The park is on the side of a steep hill, so travelers in wheelchairs are likely to fare badly. Allow 1 hour.

Briggs Rd., Brighton. © 03/6268 1184. Admission A$11 (US$7.15) adults, A$6 (US$3.90) children under 15. Daily 9am–5pm. Closed Christmas Day. Bus to Glenorchy from the central bus terminal in Hobart (about 10 min.), then take bus 125 or 126 to the park. Drive north on rte. 1 to Brighton; it's about 25 min. north of Hobart and is well signposted.

Cadbury Chocolate Factory   Eat chocolates until they make you sick on this Willy Wonka–type trip. Book well ahead, because chocolate tours are very popular. Keep in mind you'll need to climb lots of stairs inside the factory. You can visit the factory on a ferry tour (details below), or go through Tasmanian Tours & Travel Tigerline (© **1300/653 633** or 03/6272 6611), which runs half-day coach tours out of Hobart Monday through Friday from 9:30am. These cost A$35 (US$23) for adults, A$12 (US$7.80) for children, and A$99 (US$65) for a family.

Claremont, 16km (10 miles) north of Hobart. © 1800/627 367 in Australia, or 03/6249 0333. Tours A$13 (US$8) adults, A$6.50 (US$4.20) children, A$32 (US$21) families. Tours Mon–Fri 9, 9:30, 10, and 10:30am, 11am, noon, and 1 and 1.30pm.

Cascade Brewery Tours   Cascade Premium is one of the best beers in the country, in my opinion. To see how this heady amber nectar is produced, head to Australia's oldest brewery and tag along on a fascinating 2-hour tour, which includes a stroll through the grand old Woodstock Gardens behind the factory. There's lots of stairs involved.

Cascade Rd., South Hobart. © **03/6221 8300.** Tours A$11 (US$7.15) adults, A$4.50 (US$2.90) children 5–12. Mon–Fri 9:30am and 1pm. Closed public holidays. Reservations required. Bus: 44, 46, or 49; get off at stop 18.

Female Factory Historic Site and Island Produce Fudge Factory ⊛ *Finds*
This is an interesting stopover if you're visiting the Cascade Brewery or Mount Wellington. Not only do you get a trip around a successful fudge-making factory, but a guided tour around the remains of the women's prison next door. The tales told here will make the hairs on your neck stand on end—like the fact that 17 out of every 20 children born within the walls of the institution died soon after birth, and that women who died were tossed into an unmarked mass grave. All the proceeds of the tour go into preserving the prison. Allow 1½ hours.

Female Factory Historic Site and Island Produce Fudge Factory, 16 Degraves St., South Hobart. © **03/6223 1559.** Fax 03/6223 1556. www.femalefactory.com.au. Tours A$9 (US$5.90) adults, A$7 (US$4.50) students, A$4.50 (US$3) children, A$25 (US$16) family. M/C, V. Tours Easter Tues to Dec 24, Mon–Fri 9.30am (closed weekends and public holidays); Dec 26 to Easter Mon, Mon–Fri 9.30am and 2pm, and weekends and public holidays 9.30am. Bus 43, 44, 46, or 49 from GPO to South Hobart and Cascade Rd. Get off at stop 14.

Royal Tasmanian Botanical Gardens ⊛   Established in 1818, these gardens are known for English-style plant and tree layouts—including a great conifer collection—a superb Japanese garden (better than some I've seen in Kyoto, Japan), and colorful seasonal blooming plants. The peaceful atmosphere is disturbed somewhat by a nearby busy road. A restaurant provides lunch and teas. To walk here from the city center, partly along a pleasant country lane known as Soldier's Walk, takes around 40 minutes—but it's badly signposted. (When you come to a shelter and plaque with a missing YOU-ARE-HERE marker turn right—the gardens are walled and there's an obvious entrance gate.)

On the Queens Domain near Government House. © 03/6234 6299. Admission free to Botanical Shop and Botanical Discovery Center; conservatory A$2 (US$1.30) donation. Daily 8am–6:30pm (until 5pm in winter). Bus: 17.

Tasmanian Museum and Art Gallery ⊛   Come here to find out more about Tasmania's Aboriginal heritage, its history since settlement, and the island's wildlife. Traveling art exhibitions are mounted from time to time, but always on display are the paintings of the colonial era. The art gallery has a particularly impressive collection of paintings by Tom Roberts and by several convict artists. The pride of the entire collection, though, is *The Conciliation by Benjamin Duttereau,* the second-most painting of historical significance in Australia, after Tom Roberts' *Shearing of the Rams,* which you can see in the National Gallery of Victoria in Melbourne. Allow 1 to 2 hours.

40 Macquarie St. ℭ **03/6211 4177.** Free admission. Daily 10am–5pm.

ORGANIZED TOURS

You'll get a good introduction to the city on the daily **Hobart Historic Walk** (ℭ **03/6225 4806**), a 2-hour leisurely stroll through historic Sullivan's Cove and Battery Point. Tours start at 10am daily from September through May and on request from June through August and cost A$17 (US$11) for adults, free for children under 12. The tour requires a minimum of six people for a walk to go ahead; group discounts are provided.

Several companies run boat tours of the harbor. **Captain Fells Ferries** (ℭ **03/ 6223 5893**) offers a range of morning tea, lunch, afternoon, and dinner cruises. The company also runs Cadbury Factory Tours, which include coach transfers, a tour of the factory, a harbor cruise, and two-course lunch for A$32 (US$21) for adults and A$18 (US$12) for children; these leave at 9:45am Monday through Thursday. Cruises depart from Franklin Wharf behind the wooden cruise-sales booths beside Elizabeth Street Wharf at the bottom of Elizabeth Street.

The Cruise Company (ℭ **03/6234 9294**) operates river trips along the Derwent to the Cadbury Chocolate Factory. Cruises depart at 10am Monday through Friday, returning at 2:30pm, and cost A$33 (US$21) for adults, A$16 (US$10) for children 5 to 15, and A$93 (US$60) for a family, including entry and a guided tour of the factory; free for children under 5. The boat leaves from Brooke Street Pier. Also of interest is the company's 2-hour Ironpot Cruise (to the lighthouse of that name at the mouth of the Derwent). The scenic tour of the river leaves Brooke Street Pier at 2pm every Saturday and costs A$20 (US$13) for adults; free for children under 15.

THE SHOPPING SCENE

If you are in Hobart on a Saturday don't miss the **Salamanca Market** ⟨★★⟩, in Salamanca Place—it's one of the best markets in Australia. Some 200 stalls offer everything from fruit and vegetables to crafts made from pottery, glass, and native woods. The market is open from 8:30am to 3pm.

Salamanca Place itself has plenty of crafts and souvenir shops that are worth exploring, though you pay for the privilege of buying in such a fashionable area. The best bookshop in town is a beauty and sells a large range of new and secondhand books, many relating to Tasmania. Find the **Hobart Bookshop** at 22 Salamanca Sq. (ℭ **03/6223 1803**). For great chocolate and the best licorice, head to **Darrell Lea,** shop 36 in the Cat & Fiddle Arcade between Collins and Liverpool streets. There are plenty of other interesting shops here, too.

Store hours are Monday through Thursday from 9am to 6pm, Friday from 9am to 9pm, and Saturday from 9am to noon (though some open all day).

WHERE TO STAY

Hobart has some of the best hotels, guesthouses, and B&Bs in Australia. For something different, you can stay with a Tasmanian family either in town or at a farm in the country or arrange accommodations in one of the many boutique B&Bs found throughout Tasmania. Contact **Heritage Tasmania Pty Ltd.,** P.O. Box 780, Sandy Bay, TAS 7005 (✆ **03/6233 5511;** fax 03/6233 5510). Nightly B&B rates range from about A$60 (US$39) to around A$160 (US$104) for a double. There are 20 **YHA youth hostels** in Tasmania, including ones in Devonport (✆ **03/6424 5696**), Bicheno (✆ **03/6375 1293**), Coles Bay (✆ **03/6257 0115**), Mt. Field National Park (✆ **03/6288 1369**), Stanley (✆ **03/6458 1266**), and Strahan (✆ **03/6471 7255**). Most have dorms as well as inexpensive double rooms. The state YHA office is located at 28 Critereon St., Hobart (✆ **03/6234 9617**).

VERY EXPENSIVE

Hotel Grand Chancellor ✺   If you prefer standard hotel accommodations to a stately old homestead, then you should book a room at this imposing property overlooking the yachts and fishing boats parked in Victoria Dock. Standard rooms are large and comfortable, with large polished granite bathrooms. More than 50% of the rooms have water views. Eight rooms are equipped for travelers with disabilities. The lobby is an impressive marble-and-granite construction complete with a large curved window to catch the action on the docks. There's also a first-class restaurant specializing in innovative Tasmanian cuisine.

1 Davey St., Hobart, TAS 7000. ✆ **03/6235 4535.** Fax 03/6223 8175. www.hgchobart.com.au. 234 units. A$260 (US$169) double; A$365 (US$237) executive suite. Extra person A$30 (US$20). Children under 15 stay free in parent's room. AE, DC, MC, V. Free parking. **Amenities:** Restaurant; lounge with good views; heated indoor pool; health club; concierge; business center; salon; 24-hr. room service; massage; babysitting; laundry service. *In room:* A/C, TV w/pay movies, dataport, minibar, hair dryer, iron.

Wrest Point Casino ✺✺   A pricey face-lift in 1998 transformed this Hobart icon, built in 1973, giving birth to Australia's annual A$2 billion (US$1.3 billion) casino industry. Beside the Derwent River, 3km (almost 2 miles) from the city center, the complex looks out across the harbor and the city and up to Mount Wellington. All rooms feature Tasmanian oak furniture and plush carpets, and the more expensive rooms have exceptional views. While it may not be as convenient to the city center as the Hotel Grand Chancellor (though it's certainly walkable), the views make it a class above. Adjacent to the casino is the 61-room **Wrest Point Motor Inn,** which has nice rooms costing between A$120 and A$131 (US$78–US$85). Taxis from Wrest Point to the city cost around A$7 (US$4.55), and the bus operates to and from the city every 15 minutes.

410 Sandy Bay Rd., Sandy Bay, TAS 7005. ✆ **03/6225 0112.** Fax 03/6225 3744. www.wrestpoint.com.au. 197 units. A$242–A$264 (US$157–US$172) double; A$330 (US$215) suite with Jacuzzi. Extra adult A$33 (US$21). AE, DC, MC, V. Free parking. **Amenities:** 3 restaurants; 3 bars; nightclub; large indoor pool; 9-hole putting course; 2 lighted tennis courts; health club; children's playground; concierge; business center; 24-hr. room service; massage; babysitting; laundry service; harbor boardwalk with indoor and outdoor entertainment; boutique casino. *In room:* A/C, TV w/pay movies, dataport, minibar, hair dryer, iron, safe.

Value Booking Accommodations Online

Asia Travel (http://asiatravel.com/australia.html) offers substantial savings on some of the properties recommended in this chapter if you book online. At the time of writing, these included the Hotel Grand Chancellor in Hobart, the Colonial Motor Inn in Launceston, Freycinet Lodge, and Cradle Mountain Lodge.

EXPENSIVE

The Elms of Hobart   This lovely National Trust–classified mansion is too far from the city to walk to, and I think both the Islington and Macquarie Manor are nicer. However, it's just .5km (⅓ mile) from a wide range of restaurants along the popular North Hobart food strip. Each room has heritage appeal and is furnished with antiques. There is a "grog" room where guests can help themselves to beers and wines on an honor system and a quaint front living room. Two outstanding features are the Tasmanian Oak staircase and paneling. Bedrooms at the front face onto the road and can be noisy. Smoking is not permitted.

452 Elizabeth St., North Hobart, TAS 7000. ℂ **03/6231 3277.** Fax 03/6231 3276. www.theelmsofhobart. com. 6 units. A$150–A$220 (US$98–US$143) double. Rates include full breakfast. AE, DC, MC, V. Free off-street parking. The hotel is 2km (1¼ miles) from the city center. Bus: Any up Elizabeth St. from the city. Children over 10 accepted. **Amenities:** Lounge; tour desk; nonsmoking rooms. *In room:* TV, dataport, coffeemaker, hair dryer.

Islington Elegant Private Hotel   This 1845 private home is popular with American travelers. Rooms are large and simple, each with a queen-size bed and TV. The Grand rooms are slightly roomier. Antiques, cedar woodwork, and elegant furnishings contribute to an air of gentility. French doors open onto a garden and a pool. The breakfast room is small and sunny, and the chessboard, piano, and open fire add charm to the front parlor. The last time I visited, the guests had found the place so relaxing they'd all retired for their afternoon snooze. Smoking is not permitted.

321 Davey St., Hobart, TAS 7004. ℂ **03/6223 3900.** Fax 03/6224 3167. www.historichouses.com.au. 8 units. A$170 (US$110) standard double; A$180 (US$117) grand double. Rates include continental breakfast. AE, DC, MC, V. Free parking. The Islington is 1.5km (1 mile) from the city on the way to Mt. Wellington. Take the A6 Hwy. from the airport to Davey St.; stay in the right lane and go straight ahead when the road turns left. Bus: 44, 46, 48, or 49 from the city. Free secure parking. Children not accepted. **Amenities:** Heated outdoor pool. *In room:* TV, coffeemaker.

The Lodge on Elizabeth   The Lodge on Elizabeth is located in the second-oldest building in Tasmania, with some parts of it dating back to 1810. Originally a gentleman's residence, it later became the first private boy's school in Tasmania. It's well situated just a 12-minute walk from Salamanca Place and is surrounded by restaurants. All rooms are decorated with antiques, and many are quite romantic, with four-poster beds. Standard rooms have just a shower, whereas the deluxe rooms come with more antiques and a large granite bathroom with a tub. Complimentary drinks are served in the communal living room in the evenings, and a good continental breakfast buffet goes for A$12 (US$7.80).

249 Elizabeth St., Hobart, TAS 7000. ℂ **03/6231 3830.** Fax 03/6234 2566. www.thelodge.com.au. 13 units. A$135 (US$88) standard double; A$149 (US$97) deluxe double (with Jacuzzi). AE, DC, MC, V. **Amenities:** Tour desk; car-rental desk; coin-op laundry; dry cleaning, nonsmoking rooms. *In room:* TV, dataport, fridge, coffeemaker, hair dryer, iron.

Macquarie Manor   As soon as you walk into this classic colonial-style manor you'll know you want to stay. Macquarie Manor was built in 1875 as a doctor's surgery and residence. Extra rooms were added in 1950. Thick carpets and double-glazed windows keep the place very quiet, even though the Manor is on the main road. Rooms, which vary enormously, are comfortable and elegantly furnished. One room is suitable for people with disabilities. The staff is very friendly and will be happy to escort you around the premises in search of your favorite room. Check out the delightful dining room, and the drawing room complete with old couches and a grand piano. Parking is just to the left down the side of the main building. Smoking is not permitted.

172 Macquarie St., Hobart, TAS 7000. (©) **1800/243 044** in Australia, or 03/6224 4999. Fax 03/6224 4333. www.macmanor.com.au. 18 units (most with shower only). A$160 (US$104) Heritage double; A$190 (US$124) Heritage suite; A$210 (US$137) Macquarie suite. Extra adult A$33 (US$21), extra child A$17 (US$11). Rates include full breakfast. AE, DC, MC, V. Free parking. 2 blocks from central bus terminal. **Amenities:** Tour desk; dry cleaning service. *In room:* TV, minibar, coffeemaker, hair dryer, iron.

Salamanca Inn   Conveniently located on the edge of the central business district and toward the waterfront near Battery Point, Salamanca Inn features modern and pleasant apartments. The whole place was refurbished in 2000 and features queen-size beds, leather couches, Tasmanian oak furniture, galley-style kitchens, and spacious living areas. The more expensive suites are a bit plusher.

10 Gladstone St., Hobart, TAS 7000. (©) **1800/030 944** in Australia, or 03/6223 3300. Fax 03/6223 7167. www.salamancainn.com.au. 68 units. A$198 (US$129) 1-bedroom apt; A$220 (US$143) 2-bedroom suite; A$260 (US$169) 2-bedroom deluxe suite. Extra adult A$25 (US$16), extra child 3–14 A$15 (US$9.75). Ask about weekend and long-stay packages. AE, DC, MC, V. Free parking. Bus: Sandy Bay Rd. **Amenities:** Restaurant; bar; indoor pool; Jacuzzi; tour desk; business center; room service; babysitting; laundry/dry cleaning service. *In room:* TV, free in-house movies, dataport, kitchenette, minibar, fridge, coffeemaker, hair dryer, iron.

MODERATE

Black Prince   If you're looking for someplace centrally located, clean, and unfussy, then try the Black Prince, an American-influenced pub with a 1950s bent. All rooms come with a shower and a bathtub. Room no. 8 is the landlord's favorite here, because "it's nearer to the stairs so you don't have to walk too far" (presumably beneficial when you've had a few beers). Downstairs, the American-style bar called Joe's Garage is popular, especially on weekends. The American-influenced restaurant serves up budget-priced steaks and chicken dishes. Lunch is offered Monday through Friday, and dinner Monday through Saturday.

145 Elizabeth St., Hobart, TAS 7000. (©) **03/6234 3501.** Fax 03/6234 3502. 10 units. A$70 (US$46) double, including breakfast. AE, DC, MC, V. **Amenities:** Restaurant; bar. *In room:* TV, coffeemaker.

Wellington Lodge (⋆)   This charming Victorian-style town house (ca. 1885) is just a 10-minute walk (through Hobart's Rose Garden) from the main shopping area and Salamanca Place. Expect wooden floorboards, a country feel, and period antiques. Complimentary port is served every evening in the guest lounge. Smoking is not permitted.

7 Scott St., Hobart, TAS 7000. (©) **03/6231 0614.** Fax 03/6234 1551. www.wwt.com.au/wellingtonlodge. 4 units. A$100–A$120 (US$65–US$78) double. Extra person A$30 (US$20). Rates include full breakfast. MC, V. Free off-street parking. The airport bus will drop you off here, as will any bus to the Aquatic Center. Children under 11 not accepted. *In room:* TV, fridge, hair dryer.

Woolmers Inn   Situated 2km (1¼ miles) south of the city, Woolmers Inn offers cozy one- or two-bedroom units with fully equipped kitchens. One unit is suitable for travelers with disabilities. Sandy Bay is Hobart's main suburb; it's halfway between the casino and the city (within walking distance of Salamanca Place) and features a "golden mile" of boutique shopping. The inn was upgraded throughout in 1999.

123–127 Sandy Bay Rd., Hobart, TAS 7000. (©) **1800/030 780** in Australia, or 03/6223 7355. Fax 03/6223 1981. woolmersinn@bigpond.com.au. 36 units. A$121 (US$79) 1-bedroom apt; A$149 (US$97) 2-bedroom apt. Rates 10% higher from mid-Dec to end of Jan, and cheaper in winter. AE, DC, MC, V. Free parking. Bus: Catch the Sandy Bay (no number) bus from Elizabeth St. Mall on Elizabeth St. **Amenities:** Tour desk; babysitting; coin-op laundry; dry cleaning. *In room:* TV/VCR, telephone, kitchen, fridge, coffeemaker, hair dryer, iron.

INEXPENSIVE

Adelphi Court YHA Hostel   The Adelphi is a typical clean and friendly Australian youth hostel. All dorm rooms sleep four people. There is a communal kitchen, a dining room serving breakfast, and a barbecue area. It's situated 3km (less than 2 miles) from the city center.

17 Stoke St., New Town (YHA Tasmania, G.P.O. Box 174, Hobart, TAS 7001). © **03/6228 4829**. Fax 03/6278 2047. www.yha.com.au. 9 dorms, 16 doubles, 2 with bathroom. A$56 (US$36) per person twin/double without bathroom; A$65 (US$42) double with bathroom; A$20 (US$13) dorm bed. Non-YHA members pay A$3.50 (US$2.30) per person extra. MC, V. Free parking. Bus: 15 or 16 from Argyle St. to stop no. 8A, or any bus from Stop E at Elizabeth St. Mall to bus stop no. 13. **Amenities:** Game and TV room; tour-booking desk; coin-op laundry; nonsmoking rooms; barbecue area; kitchen.

Central City Backpackers   This place is typical of backpacker-type accommodations—cheap and cheerful, a little frayed around the edges, but right in the heart of things. The central shopping district is right outside the door, and it's only a short walk to the harbor.

138 Collins St., Hobart, TAS 7000. © **1800/811 507** in Australia, or 03/6224 2404. Fax 03/6224 2316. www.centralbackpackers.com.au. 80 units. A$22 (US$14) twin per person; A$44 (US$29) double; A$18 (US$12) dorm bed. Cash or traveler's checks only. 2-min. walk from central bus terminal. **Amenities:** Bar (open in summer); tour desk; coin-op laundry; Internet access; pool table; kitchen; dining room. *In room:* No phone.

Customs House Hotel   You won't find a better value than the rooms above this historic sandstone pub overlooking the waterfront. Built in 1846, the property offers simple, colonial-style rooms, without luxuries such as a TV and telephone. Four have water views overlooking the old sailing ship the *May Queen,* which used to carry wood up the Derwent River. Other rooms look across Parliament House. Guests make the best of a shared TV room. Downstairs, a friendly public bar overlooks the water, and at the back of the building is a popular seafood restaurant known for its scallops.

1 Murray St., Hobart, TAS 7000. © **03/6234 6645**. Fax 03/6223 8750. www.customshousehotel.com. 13 units, 2 with bathroom. A$75 (US$49) double without bathroom; A$80 (US$52) double with bathroom. Rates include continental breakfast. AE, DC, MC, V. **Amenities:** Restaurant; 2 bars; dry cleaning; kitchenette with fridge. *In room:* No phone.

WHERE TO DINE

Tasmania is known for its fresh seafood, including oysters, crab, crayfish, salmon, and trout. Once cheap, in recent years prices have crept up to match or even surpass those on the mainland. Generally though, the food is of a good quality.

EXPENSIVE

Mures Upper Deck   SEAFOOD   This large and bustling waterfront restaurant offers great views of bobbing yachts as well as very fine seafood caught on the owner's very own fishing boats. I recommend starting with a bowl of potato soup, or the signature Mures Oysters topped with smoked salmon, sour cream, and salmon caviar. The most popular main courses are the blue-eye filet Martinique—a Creole-inspired sweet fish curry with coconut cream and banana sauce—or the giant seafood platter for two. The best summer dessert on the menu is the restaurant's famous summer pudding, which almost bursts with berries. In winter, come here if only for the Granny Leatherwood Pudding—made of apples and Australian leatherwood honey and served with cinnamon ice cream. The complex also includes **Lower Deck,** a very popular self-service family restaurant where you can dine very well for under A$15 (US$9.75).

Between Victoria and Constitution Docks, Hobart. © 03/6231 2121. Reservations recommended. Main courses A$20–A$25 (US$13–US$16). AE, DC, MC, V. Daily noon–10pm.

The Point Revolving Restaurant TASMANIAN/AUSTRALIAN This revolving restaurant on the 17th floor of the Wrest Point Hotel Casino is known for its spectacular harbor and mountain views. Criticism of its consistency has led to a complete review of its cuisine over the last couple of years, but fortunately its specialties—prawns flambé in a curry sauce and the Caesar salad—have remained through regular menu upgrades. The crêpes suzette dessert is also wonderful. The service is friendly and relaxed. This place is packed on weekends.

In the Wrest Point Hotel Casino, 410 Sandy Bay Rd. ℂ **03/6225 0112**. Reservations recommended. Main courses from A$12 (US$7.50) at lunch, from A$17 (US$11) at dinner. Fixed-price 3-course lunch menu A$26 (US$17); fixed-price 3-course dinner menu A$43 (US$28) Fri–Sat, A$34 (US$22) Sun–Thurs. AE, DC, MC, V. Daily noon–2pm and 6:30–9:30pm.

MODERATE

Drunken Admiral Restaurant ⍟ SEAFOOD The Drunken Admiral, opposite the Hotel Grand Chancellor on the waterfront, is an extremely popular spot with tourists, and can get raucous on busy evenings. The main attraction is its famous seafood chowder, swimming with anything that was on sale at the docks that morning. The large Yachties seafood grill is a full plate of squid, scallops, fish, mussels, and prawns, but there are plenty of simpler fish dishes on the menu, too. Otherwise splash out on Sperm Whale Sally's Shellfish Platter or perhaps Captain Nimrod's Depth Charge Platter. The salad bar is spread in a sailing dingy and can be raided as often as you want, but it's rather uninteresting, so you'll probably be content with just one dip.

17–19 Hunter St. ℂ **03/6234 1903**. Reservations required. Main courses A$14–A$23 (US$8.80–US$15). AE, DC, MC, V. Daily 6–10:30pm.

Mit Zitrone ⍟⍟ MODERN AUSTRALIAN Chef and owner Chris Jackman has earned quite a reputation in Tasmania. His twice-cooked eggs with chile-palm sugar are a huge seller, while the hot smoked blue-eye cod with ginger and wok-fried greens, and the chicken and mushroom sausages with wide noodles, spinach, and anchovy sauce are sensational. The informal restaurant, which is basically an old shop, has bright yellow citrus walls and wooden floors and furniture. You can also drop in for coffee and cake.

333 Elizabeth St., North Hobart. ℂ **03/6234 8113**. Reservations recommended. Main courses A$17 (US$11). AE, DC, MC, V. Mon–Sat 10am–2pm; Tues–Sat 6–10pm.

Sisco's on the Pier SPANISH/MEDITERRANEAN/INTERNATIONAL Sisco's has undergone a transformation from a typical Spanish eatery with roving guitar players to a more upmarket international affair in recent years. Today it's known for its paella, Morton Bay bugs (a kind of small crayfish) with chocolate, garlic prawns with squid-ink spaghetti, and chargrilled octopus. The restaurant is light and bright with a large outdoor balcony.

Upper Level, Murray St. Pier. ℂ **03/6223 2059**. Reservations recommended. Main courses A$17–A$18 (US$11–US$12). AE, DC, MC V. Mon–Fri noon–3pm; Mon–Sat 6pm–12am.

Vanidol's Asian Cuisine ASIAN Another restaurant very popular with both locals and tourists, Vanidol's serves up a variety of Thai, Indonesian, and Indian dishes. The beef salad with basil, chile, and mint is very good, as are the barbecue prawns served with a sweet tamarind sauce. The fish cooked in a light red curry sauce is another specialty. Smoking is not permitted between 6 and 9pm.

353 Elizabeth St., North Hobart. ℂ **03/6234 9307**. Reservations recommended. Main courses A$13–A$18 (US$8.45–US$12). AE, MC, V. Tues–Sun 6 to around 11pm.

INEXPENSIVE

Cumquat on Criterion 𝔾 *Value* MIXED ASIAN/AUSTRALIAN   This cafe is an excellent breakfast venue, offering everything from egg on toast to traditional porridge with brown sugar. On the menu for lunch and dinner you could find Thai beef curry, laksa, a daily risotto, and chermoula-marinated fish. The desserts can be great. Vegetarians and vegans, and those on a gluten-free diet, are very well catered for, as are your average carnivores.

10 Criterion St. ℂ **03/6234 5858.** Reservations recommended. Main courses A$7.50–A$15 (US$4.90–US$9.75). No credit cards. Mon–Fri 8am–6pm.

HOBART AFTER DARK

Built in 1837, the 747-seat **Theatre Royal,** 29 Campbell St. (ℂ **03/6233 2299),** is the oldest remaining live theater in the country. It's known for its excellent acoustics and its classical Victorian decor. Ticket prices vary depending on the performance, but A$25 (US$16) is average.

If theater's not your thing, you may be interested in the **Hobart Historic Pub Tour** (ℂ **03/6225 4806),** which traces the city's development through hotel drinking holes—an important part of life in Hobart early last century. The 2-hour tour takes in four pubs; visitors enjoy a drink in each as guides give an account of the building's place in Hobart's drinking history. Tours depart Sunday through Thursday at 5pm, and cost A$35 (US$23), including a drink at each pub.

Opened in 1829 as a tavern and a brothel frequented by whalers, **Knopwood's Retreat,** 39 Salamanca Place (ℂ **03/6223 5808),** is still a raucous place to be on Friday and Saturday evenings, when crowds cram the historic interior and spill out onto the streets. Light lunches are popular throughout the week, and occasionally you'll find jazz or blues on the menu.

My favorite drinking hole in Hobart is **Irish Murphy's,** 21 Salamanca Place (ℂ **03/6223 1119),** an atmospheric pub with stone walls and lots of dark wood. Local bands play Friday and Saturday evenings.

If you want to tempt Lady Luck, head to the **Wrest Point Casino,** in the Wrest Point Hotel, 410 Sandy Bay Rd. (ℂ **03/6225 0112),** Australia's first legal gambling club. Smart, casual attire required (collared shirts for men).

3 Port Arthur: Discovering Tasmania's Convict Heritage ⊛

102km (63 miles) SE of Hobart

Port Arthur, on the Tasman Peninsula, is one of Australia's prettiest harbors and houses the extensive remains of Tasmania's largest penal colony—essentially Australia's version of Devil's Island. It's the state's number-one tourist destination, and you really should plan to spend at least a whole day in this incredibly picturesque, yet haunting, place.

From 1830 to 1877, Port Arthur was one of the harshest institutions of its type anywhere in the world. It was built to house the settlement's most notorious prisoners, often prisoners who had escaped into the bush from lesser institutions. Nearly 13,000 convicts found their way here, and nearly 2,000 died while incarcerated. Port Arthur was, and still is, connected to the rest of Tasmania by a strip of land called Eaglehawk Neck. Guards and dogs kept watch over this narrow path, while the authorities circulated rumors that the waters around the peninsula were shark-infested. Only a few convicts ever managed to escape, and most of those either perished in the bush or were tracked down and hanged. Look out for the blowhole and other coastal formations, including Tasman's

Arch, Devil's Kitchen, and the Tessellated Pavement, as you pass through Eagle-hawk Neck.

ESSENTIALS

GETTING THERE   Port Arthur is a 1½-hour drive from Hobart via the Lyell and Arthur highways. **Tasmanian Tours & Travel Tigerline** (© **1300/653 633** in Australia, or 03/6272 6611; www.tigerline.com.au) runs trips from Hobart to the former penal settlement on Tuesdays, Wednesdays (in summer only), Thursdays, Fridays, and Sundays. Tours cost A$60 (US$39) for adults and A$38 (US$25) for children 4 to 16. Another option also takes in Bushmills Pioneer Settlement, a sawmill with old buildings, which features a narrow-gauge steam railway. It's near Port Arthur. This tour costs A$70 (US$46) for adults and A$60 (US$39) for children 4 to 16. Tours depart from 199 Collins St. at 9am and return around 5:30pm. Both trips include a guided tour of the Port Arthur site.

EXPLORING THE SITE

The **Port Arthur Historic Site** ✦✦ (© **03/6251 2310;** www.portarthur.org.au) is large and scattered, with some 30, 19th-century buildings. (Most of the main ones were damaged during bushfires in 1877, shortly after the property ceased to be a penal institution.) You can tour the remains of the church, guard tower, model prison, and several other buildings. It's best to tour the area with a guide, who can describe what the buildings were originally used for. Don't miss the fascinating museum in the old lunatic asylum, which has a scale model of the prison complex, as well as leg irons and chains.

The site is open daily from 9am to 5pm; admission is A$22 (US$14) for adults, A$10 (US$6.50) for children 4 to 12, and A$48 (US$31) for a family. The admission price is good for 2 consecutive days and includes a walking tour and a boat cruise around the harbor, which leaves eight times daily in summer. There is also a separate cruise to the **Isle of the Dead** off the coast of Port Arthur twice a day; some 1,769 convicts and 180 free settlers were buried here, mostly in mass graves with no headstones. The cruise costs an extra A$5 (US$3.25) per person.

A new visitor center opened in January 1999. The main feature is a fabulous **Interpretive Gallery,** which takes visitors through the process of sentencing in England to transportation to Van Dieman's Land. The gallery contains a court-room, a section of a transport ship's hull, a blacksmith's shop, a lunatic asylum, and more. Allow between 3 and 4 hours to explore the site and the gallery.

EN ROUTE TO PORT ARTHUR

On the way to Port Arthur you might want to stop off at the historic village of Richmond and at the Tasmanian Devil Park Wildlife Rescue Centre.

Richmond is just 26km (16 miles) northeast of Hobart and is the site of the country's oldest bridge (1823), the best-preserved convict jail in Australia (1825), and several old churches, including St. John's Church (1836)—the oldest Catholic church in the country. Richmond also has plenty of tearooms, crafts shops, galleries, and antiques stores.

Eighty kilometers (50 miles) from Hobart is the **Tasmanian Devil Park Wildlife Rescue Centre,** Port Arthur Highway, Taranna (© **03/6250 3230;** fax 03/6230 3406), which houses orphaned or injured native animals, including Tasmanian devils, quolls, kangaroos, eagles, and owls. The park is open daily from 9am to 5pm. Admission is A$12 (US$7.80) for adults, A$6 (US$3.90) for children, and A$30 (US$20) for a family. Tasmanian devils are fed daily at 10

Finds **Something Spooky**

The **Ghost Tours of Port Arthur** ⭐ leave nightly by lantern at 6:30, 8:30, and 9:30pm (only 8:30pm during winter months) and cost A$14 (US$9) for adults and A$8.60 (US$5.60) for children. You can purchase a Family ticket, costing A$36 (US$24), which includes two adults and up to six children. Reservations are essential; call ℂ **1800/659 101** in Australia.

---

and 11am, and 5pm. The adjoining World Tiger Snake Centre, a unique medical research project, contains some 1,500 highly venomous snakes.

WHERE TO STAY & DINE

Port Arthur Motor Inn   If you decide to stop over rather than drive all the way back to Hobart (remember marsupials get killed all the time on the roads at night—and they can do a lot of damage to a rental car), then this AAA-rated 3½-star motor inn is a good choice. The rooms are attractive and overlook the historic site. A range of packages are available, including a room with dinner, breakfast and the ghost tour for A$99 (US$65) per person, or a room, 2-day's entrance to the Port Arthur site, the ghost tour, and breakfast for A$103 (US$67) per person.

Port Arthur Historic Site, Arthur Hwy., Port Arthur, TAS 7182. ℂ **1800/030 747** in Australia, or 03/6250 2101. Fax 03/6250 2417. www.portarthur-inn.com.au. 35 units. A$99 (US$72) double. Extra person A$15 (US$9.75). Children 11 and under stay free in parent's room. AE, DC, MC, V. Free parking. Bus: Hobart Coaches run from Hobart on weekdays. **Amenities:** Restaurant; kids' playground; coin-op laundry. *In room:* TV, coffeemaker, iron.

4 Freycinet National Park ⭐⭐

206km (128miles) NE of Hobart; 214km (133 miles) SW of Launceston

If you only have time to visit one place in Tasmania, make sure it's **Freycinet National Park.** The Freycinet Peninsula hangs down off the eastern coast of Tasmania. It's a place of craggy pink granite peaks, spectacular white beaches, wetlands, heathlands, coastal dunes, and dry eucalyptus forests. This is the place to come to spot sea eagles, wallabies, seals, pods of dolphins, and humpback and southern right whales during their migration to and from the warmer waters of northern New South Wales from May through August. The township of **Coles Bay** is the main staging post, and there are many **bushwalks** in the area. The **Moulting Lagoon Game Reserve**—an important breeding ground for black swans and wild ducks—is signposted along the highway into Coles Bay from Bicheno. Some 10,000 black swans inhabit the lake, so it's very rare not to see them. Six kilometers (3¾ miles) outside town and inside the national park is the **Cape Tourville Lighthouse,** from where there are extensive views north and south along the coast and across several of the small islands in the Tasman Ocean.

The spectacular **Wineglass Bay** ⭐⭐, named as one of the world's top 10 beaches by *Outside* magazine, is a lovely spot for a walk.

ESSENTIALS

GETTING THERE   Tasmanian Redline Coaches (ℂ **03/6336 1446**) runs between Launceston (112 George St.) at 2pm Monday through Thursday, and at 3:45pm on Friday, and take less than 3 hours. From Bicheno catch a local bus run by **Bicheno Coach Services** (ℂ **03/6257 0293,** or mobile 0419 570 293).

Buses leave at 9am and 3pm every day (except Sat, when there's no 3pm service). Buses also meet every coach from Launceston, but you need to book in advance. There are no direct buses from Hobart. **Tassielink** (℃ **1300/300 520** in Australia, or 03/6272 6611; www.tigerline.com.au) runs buses from Launceston to Bicheno on Monday, Wednesday, Friday, and Sunday leaving at 8:30am. **Tasmanian Tours & Travel Tigerline** (℃ **1300/653 633** in Australia, or 03/6272 6611; www. tigerline.com.au) offers a day trip to Freycinet with an optional walking trip to Wineglass Bay (see below) from Hobart on Friday and Sunday in summer only. It costs A$59 (US$38) for adults and A$40 (US$26) for children. Car entry to the park costs A$10 (US$6.50) per day.

From Hobart it's about a 3-hour drive to the park.

VISITOR INFORMATION   The **Visitor Information Centre** (℃ **03/6375 1333;** fax 03/6375 1533) on the Tasman Highway at Bicheno can arrange tour bookings. Otherwise, the **Tasmanian Travel and Information Centre** in Hobart (℃ **03/6230 8383**) can supply you with maps and details. Daily entry to the park costs A$9 (US$5.85) per vehicle.

EXPLORING THE PARK

If you only have time to do one walk, then head out from Freycinet Lodge on the 30-minute uphill hike past spectacularly beautiful pink granite outcrops to **Wineglass Bay Lookout** for breathtaking views. You can then head down to Wineglass Bay itself and back up again. The walk takes around 2½ hours. A longer walk takes you along the length of **Hazards Beach,** where you'll find plenty of shell middens—seashell refuge heaps—left behind by the Aborigines who once lived here. This walk takes 6 hours.

Tasmanian Expeditions (℃ **1800/030 230** in Australia, or 03/6334 3477; fax 03/6334 3463; www.tas-ex.com) offers a 3-day trip from Launceston and back that includes 2 nights in cabins at Coles Bay. The trip includes guided walks to Wineglass Bay and Mt. Amor. It costs A$540 (US$351) and departs year-round on Wednesday. The company also offers 6- and 12-night walking, rafting, and cycling trips.

Not to be missed is a trip aboard Freycinet Sea Charter's vessel *Kahala* (℃ **03/ 6257 0355;** fax 03/6375 1461), which offers whale-watching between June and September, bay and game fishing, dolphin watching, diving, scenic and marine wildlife cruises, and sunset cruises. Half-day cruises cost A$60 (US$39) per person with a minimum of four adults onboard. Full day cruises cost A$100 (US$65) per person.

WHERE TO STAY & DINE

Camping is available in the park itself for A$10 (US$6.50) a tent, though water is scarce. For inquiries, call the **Parks and Wildlife Service** (℃ **03/6257 0107**).

Freycinet Lodge ✿✿   I can't praise this ecofriendly lodge enough. Comfortable one- and two-room cabins are spread unobtrusively through the bush and connected by raised walking tracks. Each has a balcony, and the more expensive ones have a huge Jacuzzi. (The deluxe cabins are newly furnished, and some have water views.) Twenty cabins have their own kitchens. The main part of the lodge houses a lounge room and a truly excellent restaurant that sweeps out onto a veranda overlooking the limpid green waters of Great Oyster Bay. The lodge is right next to the white sands of Hazards Beach, and from here it's an easy stroll to the start of the Wineglass Bay walk.

Freycinet National Park, Coles Bay 7215. 📞 **03/6257 0101.** Fax 03/6257 0278. www.freycinetlodge.com.au. 60 units. A$190 (US$124) standard cabin; A$225 (US$146) cabin with Jacuzzi; $255 (US$166) deluxe cabin with Jacuzzi. AE, DC, MC, V. **Amenities:** 2 restaurants; bar; golf course nearby; outdoor tennis court; bike rental; activities desk; coin-op laundry; Internet kiosk; nonsmoking rooms. *In room:* Fridge, coffeemaker, hair dryer.

HOBART TO LAUNCESTON: THE "HERITAGE HIGHWAY"

By the 1820s several garrison towns had been built between Launceston and Hobart, and by the middle of the 19th century convict labor had produced what was considered to be the finest highway of its time in Australia. Today, many of the towns along the route harbor magnificent examples of Georgian and Victorian architecture. It takes about 2 hours to drive between Launceston and Hobart on the "Heritage Highway" (officially known as the A1, or the Midland Highway), but you really need 2 days to fully explore.

ROSS 𝒢
121km (75 miles) N of Hobart; 78km (48 miles) S of Launceston

One of Tasmania's best preserved historic villages, picturesque Ross was established as a garrison town in 1812 on a strategically important crossing point on the Macquarie River. **Ross Bridge,** the third oldest in Australia, was built in 1836 to replace an earlier one made of logs. The bridge is decorated with Celtic symbols, animals, and faces of notable people of the time. It is lit up at night, and there are good views of it from a dirt track that runs along the river's north bank.

The town's **main crossroads** is edged by four historic buildings, humorously known as "temptation" (represented by the Man-o'-Ross Hotel), "salvation" (the Catholic church), "recreation" (the town hall), and "damnation" (the old jail). The **Ross Female Factory,** built in the early 1840s, consists of ruins, a few interpretive signs, and a model of the original site and buildings inside the original Overseer's Cottage. Entry is free. Women convicts were imprisoned here from 1847 to 1854.

At the **Tasmanian Wool Centre** and tourist information center on Church Street (📞 **03/6381 5466**), there is an exhibition detailing the growth of the region and the wool industry since settlement. It's open daily from 9am to 5pm (until 6pm Jan–Mar), and entry costs A$4 (US$2.60) for adults, A$2 (US$1.30) for children, and A$10 (US$6.50) for a family.

Where to Stay & Dine

Colonial Cottages of Ross 𝒢   To feel the part, why not stay in one of these delightful historic cottages. Apple Dumpling Cottage (from around 1880) is a two-bedroom wooden cottage, sleeping four, with impressive sandstone fireplaces set on the edge of the village in a rural setting. The spacious Church Mouse Cottage (around 1840), set in an old Sunday School, sleeps just two. Captain Samuel's Cottage (around 1830), accommodates six people in three bedrooms, with two double and two single beds. Finally, Hudson Cottage (around 1850) sleeps four. All cottages have modern bathrooms and kitchen facilities.

12 Church St., Ross, Tasmania 7209. 📞 03/6381 5354. Fax 03/6381 5408. mjohnson@southcom.com.au. 4 units. A$138–A$156 (US$90–US$101) for 2 (depending on cottage and season). A$25–A$33 (US$13–US$21) extra person. MC, V. *In room:* TV, kitchen.

The Ross Village Bakery and Inn   This coaching inn, built in 1832, offers four homey rooms done in old English style. One room has a double bed, another a double and two singles. The third is a double, which opens up onto a fourth room that has two singles (suitable as a family room). A separate lounge has a TV and free tea, coffee, sherry, and cakes. The bakery on the premises is an excellent place for lunch, serving things like filled baked potatoes and some of the best pies in Australia, baked in a wood-fired oven dating from 1860.

15 Church St., Ross, Tasmania 7209. © **03/6381 5246.** Fax 03/6381 5360. 4 units. www.rossbakery.com.au. A$110 (US$72) all rooms. AE, MC, V. **Amenities:** Bakery; TV lounge. *In room:* Hair dryer.

5 Launceston ⟨★

198km (123 miles) N of Hobart

Tasmania's second largest city is Australia's third oldest after Sydney and Hobart. Situated at the head of the Tamar River, 50km (31 miles) inland from the state's north coast, and surrounded by delightful undulating farmland, **Launceston** is a pleasant city crammed with elegant Victorian and Georgian architecture and plenty of remnants from convict days. Unfortunately, shortsighted local and state governments are gradually overseeing the chipping away of its great architectural heritage in favor of the usual parking garages and ugly concrete monoliths. However, Launceston (pop. 104,000) is still one of Australia's most beautiful cities and has plenty of delightful parks and churches. It's also well placed as the gateway to the wineries of the Tamar Valley, the highlands and alpine lakes of the north, and the stunning beaches to the east.

ESSENTIALS

GETTING THERE **Qantas** (© **13 13 13** in Australia; www.qantas.com) flies to Launceston from Melbourne and Sydney. The **Airport Shuttle** (© **0500/512 009** in Australia) provides transportation between city hotels and the airport from 8.45am to 5pm daily at a cost of A$10 (US$6.50) each way.

Tasmanian Redline Coaches depart Hobart for Launceston several times daily (trip time: around 2 hr., 40 min.). The one-way fare is A$25 (US$16). Launceston is 1½ hours from Devonport if you plan to take a ferry from Melbourne across Bass Strait to Devonport. The bus ride from Devonport to Launceston costs around A$17 (US$11).

The drive from Hobart to Launceston takes just over 2 hours on Highway 1.

VISITOR INFORMATION The **Gateway Tasmania Travel Centre** on the corner of St. John and Paterson streets (© **03/6336 3133;** fax 03/6336 3118; gateway.tas@microtech.com.au) is open Monday through Friday from 9am to 5pm, Saturday from 9am to 3pm, and Sunday and holidays from 9am to noon.

CITY LAYOUT The main pedestrian shopping mall, Brisbane Street, along with St. John and Charles streets on either side, forms the heart of the central area. The Victorian-Italianate Town Hall is 2 blocks north on Civic Square, and opposite the red brick Post Office building dating from 1889. The Tamar River slips quietly past the city's northern edge and is crossed at two points by Charles Bridge and Tamar Street. City Park, to the northeast of the central business district, is a nice place for a stroll.

EXPLORING THE CITY & ENVIRONS

Launceston is easily explored by foot. A must for any visitor is a stroll with **Launceston Historic Walks** ⟨★ (© **03/6331 3679;** harris.m@bigpond.com), which leave from the Gateway Tasmania Travel Centre Monday through Friday at 9:45am. (Weekend walks can also be arranged.) The 1-hour walk gives a fascinating insight into Launceston's history and costs A$10 (US$6.50). **City Sights**

(© **03/6336 3122**), on the corner of St. John and Paterson streets, runs city tours daily by replica tram. Tours cost A$23 (US$15) for adults and A$16 (US$10) for children under 16. Otherwise, **Tasmanian Tours & Travel Tigerline** (© **1300/ 653 633** or 03/6272 6611) operates a half-day coach tour of the city, plus a boat cruise, on Mondays, Wednesdays, and Fridays from 9:30am. It costs A$39 (US$25) for adults and A$23 (US$15) for children.

A must see is **Cataract Gorge** ✿, the result of violent earthquakes that rattled Tasmania some 40 million years ago. It's a wonderfully scenic area just 10 minutes from Launceston. The South Esk River flows through the gorge and collects in a small lake traversed by a striking yellow suspension bridge and the longest single span chair lift in the world. The chair lift (© **03/6331 5915**) is open daily from 9am to 4:30pm (except June 23–Aug 11, when it operates on Sat–Sun only), and costs A$5 (US$3.25) for adults and A$3 (US$1.95) for children under 16. Outdoor concerts are sometimes held on the lake bank. The hike to the Duck Reach Power Station takes about 45 minutes. Take good footwear and a raincoat. Other walks in the area are shorter and easier. The **Gorge Restaurant** (© **03/6331 3330**) and the kiosk next door serve meals with glorious views from the outdoor tables.

Tamar River Cruises (© **03/6334 9900**) offers lunch, afternoon, and evening buffet dinner cruises up the Tamar River from Home Point Wharf in Launceston.

Mountain biking is popular in this area. Contact **Tasmanian Expeditions** (© **1800/030 230** in Australia, or 03/6334 3477) for information on its 4- to 7-day trips along the east coast in summer. You can rent bicycles from the youth hostel at 36 Thistle St. (© **03/6344 9779**) for A$11 (US$7.15) per day for a touring bike or A$18 (US$12) per day for a mountain bike. (You can also rent bushwalking equipment, including boots, tents, sleeping bags, and stoves.)

The **Trevallyn State Recreation Area,** on the outskirts of Launceston off Reatta Road, is a man-made lake surrounded by a beautiful wildlife reserve with several walking tracks. There are barbecue facilities, picnic areas, and a beach.

OTHER ATTRACTIONS

Aquarius Roman Baths   Adorned with gold, Italian marble, and works of art, this remarkable Romanesque structure is worth visiting just for the architectural experience. Indulge in warm-, hot-, and cold-water baths; visit the steam room; or get a massage or a beauty makeover.

127 George St. © 03/6331 2255. Admission to baths and hot rooms A$20 (US$13) for 1, A$33 (US$21) for 2. Treatments extra. Mon–Fri 8:30am–9pm; Sat–Sun 9am–6pm.

The Old Umbrella Shop   Built in the 1860s, this unique shop is the last genuine period store in Tasmania and has been operated by the same family since the turn of the 20th century. Umbrellas spanning the last 100 years are on display, while modern "brollies" and souvenirs are for sale. Allow 15 minutes.

60 George St. © 03/6331 9248. Free admission. Mon–Fri 9am–5pm; Sat 9am–noon.

The Penny Royal World & Gunpowder Mill   This amusement park, with its sailboat, barges and trams, and historic gunpowder mills, is large enough to occupy an entire day. Admission also includes a tram ride and a trip up Cataract Gorge and the Tamar River on the paddle steamer MV *Lady Stelfox.*

Off Bridge Rd. © 03/6331 6699. Admission A$18 (US$12) adults, A$7.50 (US$4.90) children, A$45 (US$30) family of 2 adults and up to 6 children. Daily 9am–4:30pm. Closed Christmas.

The Queen Victoria Museum & Art Gallery Opened in honor of Queen Victoria's Golden Jubilee in 1891, this museum houses a large collection of stuffed wildlife, including the extinct Tasmanian tiger, or thylacine. There are also temporary exhibits and historical items on display. Allow 1 hour.

2 Wellington St. © **03/6323 3777.** Free admission for those under 18 and Launceston residents; otherwise, A$10 (US$6.50). Daily 10am–5pm, except Christmas.

Waverley Woollen Mills Established in 1874 on a site 5km (3 miles) northeast of town, this business still uses a waterwheel to turn the looms that help make woolen blankets and rugs. Tours show how the process works. Everything from woolen hats to ties is sold on the premises. Allow 1 hour.

Waverley Rd. © **03/6339 1106.** Tours A$4 (US$2.60) adults, A$2 (US$1.30) children, A$12 (US$7.80) families. Tours daily 9am–4pm (there's usually a 20-min. wait).

WHERE TO STAY
EXPENSIVE
Alice's Cottages & Spa Hideaways ✸✸✸ I highly recommend these two delightful cottages. **Alice's Place,** which sleeps two, was made entirely from bits and pieces of razed historic buildings. **Ivy Cottage,** on the other hand, is a restored Georgian house (ca. 1831). Both places are furnished with antiques and fascinating period bric-a-brac. Kitchens are fully equipped, and both units have large Jacuzzis. Guests come and go as they please and stay here on their own. (Check in at the reception at 129 Balfour St.) Both cottages share the same garden. Also available for rent are five other cottages in a colonial Australian theme (some sleeping four), called **Alice's Hideaways;** and four cute cottages collectively known as **The Shambles.** A recent addition is **Aphrodites Delux Spa,** a very large and regal setup with a formal dining room.

129 Balfour St., TAS 7250. © **03/6334 2231.** Fax 03/6334 2696. www.alicescottages.com.au. 11 units. Alice's Place A$197 (US$125) cottage for 2 people; Ivy Cottage A$197 (US$125) cottage for 2 people. Shambles cottages A$160 (US$102); Aphrodites A$230 (US$143) (2-night minimum stay). Alice's Hideaways: Bonnie Doon, Captain Stirlings, Camelot, and French Boudoir A$197 (US$128). A$55 (US$36) extra person. Rates include breakfast ingredients left in your fridge. AE, DC, MC, V. Free parking. *In room:* A/C, TV, kitchen, washing machine and dryer (in cottages).

Launceston International ✸✸ This former Novotel hotel underwent major refurbishment in late 2002. In its previous guise it had some of the most comfortable and homey rooms of any major hotel in Australia, and that hasn't changed. Standard rooms have two double beds or a king-size bed and all new furnishings. There's a new fine-dining restaurant, a piano bar, and a brasserie, too. Smoking is not permitted.

29 Cameron St., Launceston, TAS 7250. © **1800/555 811** in Australia, or 03/6334 3434. Fax 03/6331 7347. www.launceston@dohertyhotels.com. 162 units. A$220 (US$143) double; A$245 (US$159) room with Jacuzzi; A$290–A$500 (US$189–UA$325) suite. Children stay free in parent's room. Ask about packages. AE, DC, MC, V. Free parking. **Amenities:** Restaurant; bar; concierge; car-rental desk; business center; 24-hr. room service; massage by arrangement; babysitting; coin-op laundry; laundry service; nonsmoking rooms. *In room:* A/C, TV, dataport, minibar, coffeemaker, hair dryer, iron.

York Mansions ✸✸✸ If you feel that where you stay is as important to your visit as what you see, then you must stay here. Within the walls of the National Trust–classified York Mansions, built in 1840, are five very spacious apartments, each with a distinctly individual character. The Duke of York apartment is fashioned after a gentleman's drawing room, complete with rich leather sofa, antiques, and an extensive collection of historic books. The two-bedroom, light and airy Duchess of York unit has hand-painted silk panels and a Jacuzzi. Each apartment is self-contained and has its own separate kitchen, dining room, living room, bedrooms, bathroom, and laundry. A CD player and large-screen TV add modern touches. The ingredients for a hearty breakfast can be found in the refrigerator. There's also a delightful cottage garden.

9–11 York St., Launceston, TAS 7250. © 03/6334 2933. Fax 03/6334 2870. www.yorkmansions.com.au. 5 units. A$198–A$224 (US$129–US$146) depending on apt. A$55 (US$36) extra person. Rates include breakfast provisions supplied to your kitchen. AE, DC, MC, V. Free parking. **Amenities:** Tour desk; laundry service; nonsmoking rooms. In room: TV/VCR, dataport, kitchen, minibar, coffeemaker, hair dryer, iron.

MODERATE

Innkeepers Colonial Motor Inn   Those who desire tried-and-true motel lodging will feel at home at the Colonial, a place that combines old-world ambience with modern facilities. The rooms are large and have attractive furnishings. The Old Grammar School next door has been incorporated into the complex, with the **Quill and Cane Restaurant** operating in what once was a schoolroom, and **Three Steps On George,** Launceston's liveliest nightspot, making use of the former boys' gym. Rooms are fairly standard and attract a large corporate clientele.

31 Elizabeth St., Launceston, TAS 7250. © 03/6331 6588. Fax 03/6334 2765. www.colonialinn.com.au. 63 units. A$145 (US$78) double; A$195 (US$127) suite. Extra person A$15 (US$9.75). Lower weekend rates. Children under 3 stay free in parent's room. AE, DC, MC, V. Free parking. **Amenities:** Restaurant; lounge; tour desk; limited room service; laundry service. In room: A/C, TV, minibar, coffeemaker, hair dryer, iron.

Waratah on York ★★   The Waratah on York is a carefully renovated Victorian mansion, built in 1862 for Alexander Webster, an ironmonger by trade and mayor of Launceston in the 1860s and 1870s. The current owners have spent considerable time and energy restoring the property to its former glory. Some of the original features—pressed brass ceiling roses and a staircase with a cast-iron balustrade—remain, while others have been faithfully re-created. Of the nine rooms, six come with a Jacuzzi, one with a balcony, and another with a sunroom. All have high ceilings and ornate (but nonfunctional) fireplaces. The executive rooms have four-poster beds and sweeping views down upon the Tamar River.

12 York St., Launceston, TAS 7250. © 03/6331 2081. Fax 03/6331 9200. www.waratahonyork.com.au. 9 units. A$156 (US$96) standard double; A$176 (US$109) double with Jacuzzi; A$208 (US$130) executive suite with Jacuzzi. Rates include continental breakfast. AE, DC, MC, V. Free off-street parking. **Amenities:** Bar; lounge with fireplace; tour desk; business facilities; massage; laundry service; same day dry cleaning; nonsmoking rooms. In room: TV, minibar, coffeemaker, hair dryer, iron.

INEXPENSIVE

Hillview House   The rooms at this restored farmhouse are nothing fancy, but are quite comfortable. They come with a double bed and a shower. The family room has an extra single bed; it's the nicest room and has the best views. The hotel overlooks the city, and the large veranda and colonial dining room both have extensive views over the city and the Tamar River.

193 George St., Launceston, TAS 7250. © 03/6331 7388. Fax 03/6331 7388. 9 units. A$90 (US$59) double; A$105 (US$68) family room for 3. Rates include full breakfast. MC, V. **Amenities:** Laundry service. In room: TV.

Hotel Tasmania   Situated in the heart of town, this budget hotel offers simple rooms with modern furnishings and attached showers. All the rooms were renovated in 1998, which helped win the hotel the Australian Hoteliers Association's award for the best budget pub-style accommodations in Tasmania. Downstairs there's a saloon-style bar with a cowboy theme which hosts live music Wednesday, Friday and Saturday. The popular UNI nightclub also kicks off late on Wednesdays, and it's free for students before 11pm.

191 Charles St., Launceston, TAS 7250. 𝒞 **03/6331 7355.** Fax 03/6331 2414. www.saloon.com.au. 25 units. A$64 (US$42) double. Extra person A$19 (US$12). Rates include continental breakfast. AF, MC, V. Free on-street parking. **Amenities:** Restaurant; bar. *In room:* TV, fridge, coffeemaker.

Lloyd's Hotel   This older-style centrally located property offers comfortable lodging at a modest budget. It underwent a change of hands in 2002, and by some reports has lost some of its friendly feel. It was getting a bit grubby, so the refurbishment in 2001 was welcome. Best to spend a little more on the Hotel Tasmania above in my opinion.

23 George St., Launceston, TAS 7250. 𝒞 **03/6331 4966.** Fax 03/6331 5589. 18 units (some with shower only). A$54 (US$35) double. Extra person A$20 (US$13). Rates include full breakfast. MC, V. Free parking. **Amenities:** Coin-op laundry; nonsmoking rooms. *In room:* TV, fridge, coffeemaker.

WHERE TO DINE

You'll find most places to eat in Launceston don't have a fixed closing time; rather, they close up shop when the last customer has been served and has eaten.

EXPENSIVE

Fee & Me Restaurant 𝕘𝕘 MODERN AUSTRALIAN   What is perhaps Launceston's best restaurant is found in a grand old mansion. The menu is structured so that diners choose a selection from five categories, each one moving from light to rich. An extensive wine list has been designed to complement selections for each course. A five-course meal could go something like this: Tasmanian smoked salmon with salad, capers, and a soft poached egg; followed by chile oysters with a coconut sauce and vermicelli noodles; then ricotta and goat cheese gnocchi with creamed tomato and red capsicum; followed by Asian-style duck on bok choy with a citrus sauce; topped off with a coffee and chicory soufflé. The dishes change frequently, so you never know what you might find.

Corner of Charles and Frederick sts. 𝒞 **03/6331 3195.** Reservations recommended. A$42 (US$27) for 3 courses, A$48 (US$31) for 4 courses, A$50 (US$33) for 5 courses. AE, DC, MC, V. Mon–Sat 7–10:30pm.

MODERATE

O'Keefe's Hotel ASIAN/TASMANIAN   This pub-based eatery earns high praise for its variety of well-prepared dishes. You can choose between such delicacies as Thai curry and laksa, seafood dishes such as scallops, prawns, and sushi, and plenty of pastas and grills. There's also a range of good salads.

124 George St. 𝒞 **03/6331 4015.** Reservations recommended. Main courses A$11–A$25 (US$7–US$16). AE, MC, V. Daily 11am–2am.

Shrimps 𝕘 SEAFOOD   Come here for the best selection of seafood in Launceston. Built in 1824 by convict labor, it has a classic Georgian exterior. Tables are small and well spaced, and the best meals are off the blackboard menu, which generally includes at least eight fish dishes. Usually available are wonderful Tasmanian mussels, whitebait, Thai-style fish cakes, and freshly split oysters. Everything is very fresh and seasonal.

72 George St. (at the corner of Paterson St.). 𝒞 **03/6334 0584.** Reservations recommended. Main courses A$14–A$19 (US$9.10–US$12). AE, DC, MC, V. Mon–Sat noon–2pm and 6:30–10pm.

Star Bar Cafe 𝕘 MEDITERRANEAN   Many consider this Tasmania's best bistro. It offers a range of dishes, such as mee goreng, beets, and quail risotto; grilled octopus, steaks, and chicken livers; and pizzas and breads cooked in the wood-fired oven. In winter, guests congregate around a large open fire.

113 Charles St. 𝒞 **03/6331 9659.** Reservations recommended. Main courses A$12–A$20 (US$6.80–US$11). AE, MC, V. Mon–Wed 11am–11pm; Thurs–Sat 11am–midnight; Sun noon–10pm.

INEXPENSIVE

Konditorei Cafe Manfred PATISSERIE   This German patisserie has recently moved to larger premises to keep up with demand for its sensational cakes and breads. It's also added an a la carte restaurant serving up the likes of pastas and steaks. Light meals include croissants, salads, and cakes. You can eat inside or outside.

106 George St. ℂ **03/6334 2490.** Light meals A$4–A$5 (US$2.60–US$3.25); main courses A$9–A$18 (US$5.85–US$12). AE, DC, MC, V. Mon–Fri 9am–5:30pm; Sat 8.30am–4pm.

A CAFE

Croplines Coffee Bar ⓡ *(Finds)* CAFE   If you crave good coffee, bypass every other place in Launceston and head here. It's a bit hard to find, and you may have to ask for directions, but basically it's behind the old Brisbane Arcade. The owners are dedicated to coffee, grinding their beans on the premises daily. If coffee's not your cup of tea, then try the hot chocolate—it's the best I've tasted.

Brisbane Court, off Brisbane St. ℂ **03/6331 4023.** Coffees and teas A$1.60–A$2.40 (US$1–US$1.60). Cakes under A$2 (US$1.30). AE, MC, V. Daily 8am–5:30pm.

---

6 Cradle Mountain & Lake St. Clair National Park ⓡⓡ

85km (53 miles) S of Devonport; 175km (109 miles) NW of Hobart

The national park and World Heritage area that encompasses both Cradle Mountain and Lake St. Clair is one of the most spectacular regions in Australia and, after Hobart and Port Arthur, the most visited place in Tasmania. The 1,545m (5,068-ft.) mountain dominates the north part of the island, and the long, deep lake is to its south. Between them lie more steep slopes, button grass plains, majestic alpine forests, dozens of lakes filled with trout, and several rivers. **Mount Ossa,** in the center of the park, is Tasmania's highest point at 1,617m (5,304 ft.). The **Overland Track** (see "Hiking the Overland Track," below), links Cradle Mountain with Lake St. Clair and is the best known of Australia's walking trails. Another option in the area is a visit to the **Walls of Jerusalem National Park,** a high alpine area with spectacular granite walls, small lakes, and old-growth forest.

ESSENTIALS

GETTING THERE   Tassielink (ℂ **1300/300 520** in Australia, or 03/6272 6611; www.tigerline.com.au) runs buses to Cradle Mountain from Hobart, Launceston, Devonport, and Strahan. A special summer Overland Track service (provided by Tassielink) drops off passengers at the beginning of the walk (Lake St. Clair) and picks them up at Cradle Mountain. From Launceston this service costs A$99 (US$65) one-way for adults and A$89 (US$58) for students. From Hobart it costs A$90 (US$59) one-way for adults and A$81 (US$53) for students. Another option is to be picked up in Launceston and dropped off in Lake St. Clair, and then picked up in Cradle Mountain and driven to Hobart, for A$70 (US$46) for adults and A$63 (US$41) for students. Check the website for departure times as they do change. The company also runs a day tour from Launceston, including short walks, for A$89 (US$58) for adults and A$55 (US$36) for children.

    Maxwells Cradle Mountain–Lake St. Clair Charter Bus and Taxi Service (ℂ and fax **03/6492 1431**) runs buses from Devonport and Launceston to Cradle Mountain from A$35 (US$23), depending on how many people are onboard. The buses also travel to other areas nearby, such as the Walls of Jerusalem, as well as Lake St. Clair. Buses also run from the Cradle Mountain campground to the start of the Overland Track.

Motorists enter the park via the Lyall Highway from Hobart, via Deloraine or Poatina from Launceston, and via Sheffield or Wilmot from Devonport. Both Cradle Mountain and Lake St. Clair are well signposted.

VISITOR INFORMATION   The park headquarters, **Cradle Mountain Visitor Centre** (© 03/6492 1133; fax 03/6492 1120; www.parks.tas.gov.au), on the northern edge of the park outside Cradle Mountain Lodge, offers the best information on walks and treks. It's open 8am to 5pm (6pm in summer) daily.

EXPLORING THE PARK

Cradle Mountain Lodge (see "Where to Stay & Dine," below) runs a daily program of guided walks, abseiling (rappelling), rock-climbing, and trout-fishing excursions for lodge guests. There are also plenty of trails that can be attempted by people equipped with directions from the staff at the park headquarters (see "Visitor Information," above). Be warned, though, that the weather changes quickly in the high country; so go prepared with wet-weather gear and always tell someone where you are headed. Of the shorter walks, the stroll to Pencil Pines and the 5km (3-mile) walk to Dove Lake are the most pleasant. Between June and October it's sometimes possible to cross-country ski in the park.

WHERE TO STAY & DINE

Cradle Mountain Lodge 🐾🐾   If you like luxury with your rainforests, then this award-winning lodge is the place for you. Cradle Mountain Lodge is marvelous. Just minutes from your bed are the giant buttresses of 1,500-year-old trees, moss forests, mountain ridges, limpid pools and lakes, and hoards of scampering marsupials. The cabins are comfortable, the food excellent, the staff friendly, and the open fireplaces well worth cuddling up in front of for a couple of days. Each modern wood cabin has a pot-bellied stove as well as an electric heater for chilly evenings, a shower, and a small kitchen. There are no telephones or TV in the rooms—but who needs them? Spa cabins come with carpets, a Jacuzzi, and a balcony offering a variety of views. Some have a separate bedroom. Two cabins have limited facilities for travelers with disabilities. Guests have the use of the casual, comfortable main lodge where almost every room has a log fire.

G.P.O. Box 478, Sydney, NSW 2001. © 13 24 69 in Australia, 800/225-9849 in the U.S., 0171/805-3875 in the U.K., or 03/6492 1303. Fax 02/9299 2477. www.poresorts.com.au. 96 units. A$230 (US$150) Pencil Pine cabin; A$290 (US$188) spa cabin; A$360 (US$234) spa suite. Extra person A$58 (US$38). Children under 3 stay free in parent's room. Ask about special winter packages. AE, DC, MC, V. Free parking. **Amenities:** Cafe; 2 bars; laundry service. *In room:* Kitchenette, no phone.

Waldheim Cabins   If you want a real wilderness experience then head for these cabins run by the Parks and Wildlife Service and located 5km (3 miles) from Cradle Mountain Lodge. Nestled between button grass plains and temperate rainforest, they are simple and affordable and offer good access to plenty of walking tracks. Each cabin is equipped with heating, single bunk beds, basic cooking utensils, crockery, cutlery, and a gas stove. They are serviced by two composting toilets and showers. Generated power is provided for lighting between 6 and 11pm only. Stores and fuel can be bought at Cradle Mountain Lodge. Bring your own bed linen and toiletries.

Cradle Mountain Visitor Centre, P.O. Box 20, Sheffield, TAS 7306. © 03/6492 1110. Fax 03/6492 1120. Cradle @dpiwe.tas.gov.au. Minimum cabin charge A$70 (US$46) for 2 adults, A$25 (US$16) for each additional adult, A$9.90 (US$6.45) for each additional child 6–16, children under 6 stay free. Linen is provided for A$5.50 (US$3.60) per person. MC, V. Collect cabin keys from the National Park Visitor Centre, just inside the boundary of the national park, daily 8am–5:30pm. *In room:* No phone.

Finds Hiking the Overland Track

The most well-known hiking trail in Australia is the **Overland Track** 🌟🌟, an 85km (53-mile) route between Cradle Mountain and Lake St. Clair. The trek takes from 5 to 10 days and goes through high alpine plateaus, button grass plains, heathland, and rainforests, and passes glacial lakes, ice-carved crags, and waterfalls. The trek gives you a good look at the beauty of Tasmania's pristine wilderness, and although the first day is quite tough, you soon get into the rhythm. After climbing to Pelion Gap, the track gradually descends southwards toward the towering myrtle forests on the shores of Lake St. Clair. There are many rewarding side trips, including the 1-day ascent of Mt. Ossa (1,617m/5,304 ft.), Tasmania's highest peak.

Several companies offer guided walks of the Overland Track from October through April, although simple public huts, on a first-come, first-served basis, and camping areas are available for those who wish to do it solo. Every summer up to 200 people a day start the trek. Most trekking companies employ at least two guides who carry tents and cooking gear, while you carry your sleeping bag, lunch, and personal belongings. Wet-weather gear is essential as heavy downpours can be frequent, and make sure your boots are well worn in to avoid blisters.

Tasmanian Expeditions (🕿 **1800/030 230** in Australia, or 03/6334 3477; www.tas.ex.com) offers 3-day walking tours around Cradle Mountain, staying at Waldheim Cabins. The tours depart from Launceston and cost A$595 (US$387), all-inclusive. Trips leave every Sunday and Wednesday between November and April, with extra trips from Christmas to the end of January. The company also offers a full 8-day trek on the Overland Track for A$1,395 (US$906), all-inclusive, from Launceston (wet-weather gear costs A$55/US$36 extra to rent). These trips depart every Saturday between November and April, with extra trips from late December to the end of January. Another trip, a 6-day Cradle Mountain and Walls of Jerusalem National Park trip, includes 3 nights of wilderness camping and 3 nights in a cabin. It costs A$1,170 (US$760) and leaves every Sunday between October and April. Many people have reported this trek to be the highlight of their trip to Australia.

Craclair Tours (🕿 and fax **03/6424 7833**; www.craclairtours.com.au) also offers a quality 8-day Overland Track tour, including 5 nights of camping, between October and mid-April (leaving every Sun and Wed) for A$1,440 (US$705).

For an organized trek in this area, I recommend **Cradle Mountain Huts**, P.O. Box 1879, Launceston, TAS 7250 (🕿 **03/6331 2006;** fax 03/6331 5525; cradle@tassie.net.au). Six-day walks cost A$1,895 (US$1,231); rates are all-inclusive and include transfers to and from Launceston. Children under 12 are not permitted. The huts are fully equipped, heated, and quite comfortable, with showers, a main living area, and a full kitchen. You get a good three-course meal every night. The treks leave every day between Christmas Day and early February, and around five times a week between November and April.

Moments A Lakeside Fishing Lodge

Tasmania's extensive hydroelectric schemes have created many new lakes, all seeded with some of the biggest wild brown and rainbow trout in the world. At **London Lakes Lodge** *★★★*, it's all about low-key, high-action trout fishing; guides—one to every two people—take guests out on area lakes, rivers, and streams, offering personal tips and lessons. The lodge caters to just 10 guests in 5 simple twin-bedded rooms, each with an en-suite bathroom; the chef here produces marvelous food. Such personalized attention doesn't come cheap; prices start at A$693 (US$451) with guide, A$495 (US$322) without guide, including meals, tackle, rods, clothing, and transportation. Prebooking is mandatory; contact Post Office, Bronte Park, TAS 7140 (*©* **03/6289 1159;** fax 03/6289 1122; www.londonlakes.com.au). *Note:* The lodge is so exclusive that the owners won't even post a road sign to tell you where it is; it's off the first dirt track after the Bronte Park turnoff on the road from Strahan to Hobart. The lodge is closed May through July.

LAKE ST. CLAIR *★*

Australia's deepest natural freshwater lake is a narrow, 15km (9⅓-mile) long water-way, enclosed within the Cradle Mountain—Lake St. Clair National Park. On the lake's southern edge is **Cynthia Bay,** site of an informative ranger station where you must register if you're attempting the Overland Track from this end, as well as a restaurant, cabin accommodations, and a backpackers' hostel (the latter operated by **Lakeside St. Clair** at *©* **03/6289 1137**). National park rangers run several tours between Boxing Day and the end of February, including spotlighting tours and guided walks around the area. Call for details at *©* **03/6289 1172.**

Appendix:
Australia in Depth

by Marc Llewellyn

The land Down Under is a modern nation coming to terms with its identity. The umbilical cord with Mother England has been cut, and the nation is still trying to find its position within Asia.

One thing Australia realized early on was the importance of tourism to its economy. Millions flock here every year. You'll find Australians to be helpful and friendly, and services, tours, and food and drink to rival any in the world. Factor in the landscape, the native Australian culture, the sunshine, the animals, and some of the world's best cities, and you've got a fascinating, accessible destination full of amazing diversity and variety.

1 Australia's Natural World

THE LAND OF THE NEVER-NEVER

People who have never visited Australia wonder why such a huge country has a population of just 19 million people. The truth is, Australia can barely support that many. About 90% of those 19 million people live on only 2.6% of the continent. Climatic and physical land conditions ensure that the only relatively decent rainfall occurs along a thin strip of land around Australia's coast. The vast majority of Australia is harsh Outback, characterized by saltbush plains, arid brown crags, shifting sand deserts, and salt lake country. People survive where they can in this great arid land because of one thing—the Great Artesian Basin. This saucer-shaped geological formation comprises about one-fifth of Australia's landmass, stretching over much of inland New South Wales, Queensland, South Australia, and the Northern Territory. Beneath it are massive underground water supplies stored during Jurassic and Cretaceous times (some 66 million–208 million years ago), when the area was much like the Amazon basin is today. Bore holes bring water to the surface and allow sheep, cattle, and humans a respite from the dryness.

The Queensland coast is blessed with one of the greatest natural attractions in the world. The **Great Barrier Reef** stretches some 2,000km (1,240 miles) from off Gladstone in Queensland, to the Gulf of Papua, near New Guinea. It's relatively new, not more than 8,000 years old, although many fear that rising seawater, caused by global warming, will cause its demise. As it is, the non-native Crown of Thorns starfish and a bleaching process believed to be the result of excessive nutrients flowing into the sea from Australia's farming land, is already causing significant damage. The Reef is covered in chapter 6.

AUSTRALIA'S FAUNA

NATIVE ANIMALS Australia's isolation from the rest of the world over millions of years has led to the evolution of forms of life found nowhere else. Probably the strangest of all is the **platypus.** This monotreme, or egg-laying marsupial, has webbed feet, a ducklike bill, and a tail like a beaver's. It lays eggs, and the young suckle from their mother. When a specimen was first brought back to Europe, skeptical scientists insisted it was a fake—a concoction of several different animals sewn together. You will probably never see this shy, nocturnal creature in the wild, although there are a few at Sydney's Taronga Zoo.

Another strange one is the **koala.** This fluffy marsupial eats virtually indigestible gum leaves and sleeps about 20 hours a day. There's just one koala species, although those found in Victoria are substantially larger than their brethren in more northern climes. Australia is also famous for **kangaroos.** There are 45 different kinds of kangaroos and wallabies, ranging in scale from small rat-size kangaroos to the man-size red kangaroos.

The animal you're most likely to come across in your trip is the **possum,** named by Capt. James Cook after the North American "opossum," which he thought they resembled. (In fact they are from an entirely different family of the animal kingdom.) The brush-tailed possum is commonly found in suburban gardens, including those in Sydney. Then there's the **wombat.** There are four species of this bulky burrower in Australia, but the common wombat is most frequently found. You might come across the smaller hairy-nosed wombat in South Australia and Western Australia.

The **dingo,** thought by many to be a native of Australia, was in fact introduced—probably by Aborigines. They vary in color from yellow to a russet red, and are heavily persecuted by farmers. Commonly seen **birds** include the fairy penguin along the coast, black swans, parrots and cockatoos, and honeyeaters. **Tasmanian devils** can be found in (you guessed it) the island/state of Tasmania.

DANGEROUS NATIVES   Snakes are common throughout Australia, but you will rarely see one. The most dangerous land snake is the taipan, which hides in the grasslands in northern Australia—one bite contains enough venom to kill up to 200 sheep. If by the remotest chance you are bitten, you must immediately demobilize the limb, wrapping it quite tightly (but not tight enough to restrict the blood flow) with a cloth or bandage, and head to the nearest hospital where antivenin should be available.

There are two types of **crocodile** in Australia: the harmless freshwater croc, which grows to 3m (10 ft.); and the dangerous estuarine (or saltwater) crocodile, which reaches 5m to 7m (16 ft.–23 ft.). Freshwater crocs eat fish; estuarine crocs aren't so picky. *Never* swim in, or stand on the bank of, any river, swamp, or pool in northern Australia unless you know *for certain* it's croc-free.

Spiders are common all over Australia, with the funnel web spider and the red-back spider being the most aggressive. Funnel webs live in holes in the ground (they spin their webs around a hole's entrance) and stand on their back legs when they're about to attack. Red-backs have a habit of resting under toilet seats and in car trunks, generally outside the main cities. Caution is a good policy.

If you go bushwalking, check your body carefully. **Ticks** are common, especially in eastern Australia, and can cause severe itching and fever. If you find one on you, dab it with methylated spirits or another noxious chemical. Wait a while and pull it out gently with tweezers, taking care not to leave the head behind.

Fish to avoid are stingrays, porcupine fish, stonefish, lionfish, and puffer fish. Never touch an **octopus** if it has blue rings on it, or a cone shell, and be wary of the painful and sometimes deadly tentacles of the box **jellyfish** along the northern Queensland coast in summer. If you happen to brush past one of these creatures, pour vinegar over the affected site immediately—local authorities leave bottles of vinegar on the beach for this purpose. Vinegar deactivates the stinging cells that haven't already affected you, but doesn't affect the ones that already have.

In Sydney, you might come across "stingers" or "blue bottles" as they are also called. These long-tentacled blue jellyfish can inflict a very nasty stinging burn that can last for hours. Sometimes you'll see warning signs on patrolled beaches. The best remedy if you are severely stung is to wash the affected water with fresh water and have a very hot bath or shower.

2 The People Down Under

It's generally considered that more races of people live in Australia at the present time than anywhere else in the world, including North America. Heavy immigration has led to people from some 165 nations making the country their home. In general, relations between the different ethnic groups have been peaceful. Today Australia is an example of a multicultural society, despite an increasingly vocal minority that believes that Australia has come too far in welcoming people from races other than their own.

THE ABORIGINES   When Capt. James Cook landed at Botany Bay in 1770 determined to claim the land for the British Empire, at least 300,000 Aborigines were already on the continent. Whether you believe a version of history that suggests the Aboriginal people were descendants of migrants from Indonesia to the north, or the Aboriginal belief that they have occupied Australia since the beginning of time, there is scientific evidence that people were walking the continent at least 120,000 years ago.

At the time of the white "invasion" of their lands, there were at least 600 different, largely nomadic tribal communities, each linked to their ancestral land by **"sacred sites"** (certain features of the land, such as hills or rock formations). They were hunter-gatherers, spending about 20 hours a week harvesting the resources of the land, rivers, and the ocean. The rest of the time was taken up by a complex social and belief system, as well as by life's practicalities, such as making utensils, weapons, and musical instruments such as didgeridoos and clapsticks.

The basis of Aboriginal spirituality rests in the **Dreamtime** stories, in which spirits created everything—land, stars, mountains, the moon, the sun, the oceans, water holes, animals, and humans. Much Aboriginal art is related to their land and the sacred sites that are home to the Dreamtime spirits. Some Aboriginal groups believe these spirits came in giant human form, while others believed they were animals or huge snakes. According to Aboriginal custom, individuals can draw on the power of the Dreamtime spirits by reenacting various stories and practicing certain ceremonies.

Aboriginal groups had encountered people from other lands before the British arrived. Dutch records from 1451 show that the Macassans, from islands now belonging to Indonesia, had a long relationship trading Dutch glass, smoking pipes, and alcohol for edible sea slugs, from Australia's northern coastal waters, which they sold to the Chinese in the Canton markets. Dutch, Portuguese, French, and Chinese vessels also encountered Australia—in fact, the Dutch fashion for pointy beards caught on through northern Australia long before the 1770 invasion.

When the British came, bringing their **diseases** with them, coastal communities were virtually wiped out by smallpox. Even as late as the 1950s, large numbers of Aborigines in remote regions of South Australia and the Northern Territory succumbed to deadly outbreaks of influenza and measles.

Although relationships between the settlers and local Aborigines were initially peaceful, conflicts over land and food soon led to skirmishes in which Aborigines were massacred and settlers and convicts attacked—Governor Phillip was speared in the back by an Aborigine in 1790.

Within a few years, some 10,000 Aborigines and 1,000 Europeans had been killed in Queensland alone, while in Tasmania, a campaign to rid the island entirely of local Aborigines was ultimately successful, with the last full-blooded Tasmanian Aborigine dying in 1876. By the start of the 20th century, the Aboriginal people were considered a dying race. Most of those who remained lived in government-owned reserves or Church-controlled missions.

Massacres of Aborigines continued to go largely or wholly unpunished into the 1920s, by which time it became official government policy to remove light-skinned Aboriginal children from their families and to sterilize young, Aboriginal women. Many children of the "stolen generation" were brought up in white foster homes or church refuges and never reunited with their biological families— many children with living parents were told that their parents were dead.

Today, there are some 283,000 Aborigines living in Australia, and in general a great divide still exists between them and the rest of the population. Aboriginal life expectancy is 20 years lower than that of other Australians, with overall death rates between two and four times higher. Aborigines make up the highest percentage of the country's prison population, and many Aborigines die while incarcerated.

A landmark in Aboriginal affairs occurred in 1992 when the High Court determined that Australia was not an empty land *(terra nullius)* as it had been seen officially since the British invasion. The **"Mabo" decision** resulted in the **1993 Native Title Act,** which allowed Aboriginal groups, and the ethnically distinct people living in the Torres Strait islands off northern Queensland, to claim government-owned land if they could prove continual association with it since 1788. The later **"Wik" decision** determined that Aborigines could make claims on government land leased to agriculturists. The federal government, led by the right-leaning Prime Minister John Howard, curtailed these rights following pressure from farming and mining interests.

Issues currently facing the Aboriginal population include harsh mandatory sentencing laws (enacted in Western Australia and the Northern Territory state governments in 1996 and 1997, respectively), which came to international attention in 2000. The Aboriginal community believes such laws specifically target them. When a 15-year-old Aboriginal boy allegedly committed suicide less than a week before he was due to be released from a Northern Territory prison in early 2000, and a 21-year-old Aboriginal youth was imprisoned for a year for stealing A$23 (US$15) worth of fruit cordial and cookies, Aboriginal people protested, activists of all colors demonstrated, and even the United Nations weighed in with criticism.

Added to this was the simmering issue of the federal government's decision not to apologize to the Aboriginal people for the "stolen generation." In March 2000, a government-sponsored report stated there was never a "stolen generation," while independent researchers believed the report underestimated how many people were personally affected.

Before the Sydney 2000 Olympic Games, a popular movement involving people of all colors and classes called for reconciliation and an apology to the Aboriginal people. In Sydney, an estimated 250,000 people marched across the Sydney Harbour Bridge. The Liberal (read "conservative") Government refused to bow to public pressure. Despite threats of boycotts and rallies during the Olympics, the Games passed without major disturbance, and a worldwide audience watched as Aboriginal runner Cathy Freeman lit the Olympic cauldron.

THE REST OF AUSTRALIA   "White" Australia was always used to distinguish the Anglo-Saxon population from that of the Aboriginal population. These days, though, a walk through any of the major cities would show that things have changed dramatically. About 100,000 people emigrate to Australia each year. Of these, approximately 12% were born in the U.K. or Ireland and 11% in New Zealand. More than 21% hail from China, Hong Kong, Vietnam, or the Philippines. Waves of immigration have brought in millions of people since the end of World War II. At the last census in 1996, more than a quarter of a million Australian residents were born in Italy, for example, some 186,000 in the former Yugoslavia, 144,000 in Greece, 118,000 in Germany, and 103,000 in China. So what's the typical Australian like? Well, he's hardly Crocodile Dundee.

3 Australian History 101

IN THE BEGINNING In the beginning there was the **Dreamtime**—at least according to the Aborigines of Australia. Between then and now, perhaps, the supercontinent referred to as **Pangaea** split into two huge continents called **Laurasia** and **Gondwanaland.** Over millions of years, continental drift carried the landmasses apart. Laurasia broke up and formed North America, Europe, and most of Asia. Meanwhile, Gondwanaland divided into South America, Africa, India, Australia and New Guinea, and Antarctica. **Giant marsupials** evolved to roam the continent of Australia: Among them were a plant-eating animal that looked like a wombat the size of a rhinoceros; a giant squashed-face kangaroo standing 3m (10 ft.) high; and a flightless bird the same size as an emu, but four times heavier. The last of these giant marsupials are believed to have died out some 40,000 years ago, possibly helped towards extinction by Aborigines.

EARLY EXPLORERS The existence of Australia had been in the minds of Europeans since the Greek astronomer Ptolemy drew a map of the world in about A.D. 150 showing a large land mass in the south, which he believed had to be there to balance out the land in the northern hemisphere. He called it *Terra Australia Incognita*—the unknown southland.

Evidence suggests Portuguese ships reached Australia as early as 1536 and

Dateline

- **120,000 B.C.** Evidence suggests Aborigines living in Australia.
- **60,000 B.C.** Aborigines living in Arnham Land in the far north fashion stone tools.
- **24,500 B.C.** The world's oldest known ritual cremation takes place at Lake Mungo.
- **1606 A.D.** Dutch explorer Willem Jansz lands on far north coast of Van Diemen's Land (Tasmania).
- **1622** First English ship to reach Australia wrecks on the west coast.
- **1642** Abel Tasman charts the Tasmanian coast.
- **1770** Capt. James Cook lands at Botany Bay.
- **1787** Capt. Arthur Phillip's First Fleet leaves England with convicts aboard.
- **1788** Captain Phillip raises British flag at Port Jackson (Sydney Harbour).
- **1788–1868** Convicts are transported from England to the colony of Australia.
- **1793** The first free settlers arrive.
- **1830** Governor Arthur lines up 5,000 settlers across Van Diemen's Land to walk the length of the island to capture and rid it of all Aborigines.
- **1850** Gold discovered in Bathurst, New South Wales.
- **1852** Gold rush begins in Ballarat, Victoria.
- **1853** The last convict arrives in Van Diemen's Land and to celebrate, the colony is renamed Tasmania after Abel Tasman.
- **1860** The white population of Australia reaches more than one million.

even charted part of its coastline. In 1606 William Jansz was sent by the Dutch East India Company to open up a new route to the Spice Islands, and to find New Guinea, which was supposed to be rich in gold. He landed on the north coast of Queensland and fought with local Aborigines. Between 1616 and 1640, many more Dutch ships made contact with Australia as they hugged the west coast of what they called "New Holland," after sailing with the *westerlies* (west winds) from the Cape of Good Hope.

In 1642, the Dutch East India Company, through the Governor General of the Indies, Anthony Van Diemen, sent Abel Tasman to search out and map the great south land. During two voyages, he charted the northern Australian coastline and discovered Tasmania, which he named Van Diemen's Land.

THE ARRIVAL OF THE BRITISH

In 1697, English pirate William Dampier published a book about his adventures. The text mentions Shark Beach on the northwest coast of Australia as the place his pirate ship made its repairs after robbing ships on the Pacific Ocean. Sent to further explore by England's King William III, Dampier returned and found little to recommend.

Capt. James Cook turned up in 1770 and charted the east coast in his ship HMS *Endeavor*. He claimed the land for Britain and named it New South Wales, probably as a favor to Thomas Pennant, a Welsh patriot and botanist who was a friend of the *Endeavour's* botanist, Joseph Banks. On April 29, Cook landed at Botany Bay, which he named after the discovery of scores of plants hitherto unknown to science. Turning northwards, Cook passed an entrance to a possible harbor, which appeared to offer safe anchorage, and named it Port Jackson after the

- **1875** Silver found at Broken Hill, New South Wales.
- **1889** Australian troops fight in the Boer War in South Africa.
- **1895** Banjo Paterson's "The Man from Snowy River" published.
- **1901** The six states join together to become the Commonwealth of Australia.
- **1902** Women gain the right to vote.
- **1911** Australian (non-Aboriginal) population reaches 4,455,005.
- **1915** Australian and New Zealand troops massacred at Gallipoli.
- **1927** The federal capital is moved from Melbourne to Canberra.
- **1931** The first airmail letters are delivered to England by Charles Kingsford Smith and Charles Ulm.
- **1931** The Arnham Land Aboriginal Reserve is proclaimed.
- **1932** Sydney Harbour Bridge opens.
- **1942** Darwin bombed; Japanese mini-submarines found in Sydney Harbour.
- **1953** British nuclear tests at Emu in South Australia lead to a radioactive cloud that kills and injures many Aborigines.
- **1956** Olympics held in Melbourne.
- **1957** British atomic tests conducted at Maralinga, South Australia. Aborigines again affected by radiation.
- **1962** Commonwealth government gives Aborigines the right to vote.
- **1967** Aborigines granted Australian citizenship and are counted in census.
- **1968** Australia's population passes 12 million following heavy immigration.
- **1971** The black, red, and yellow Aboriginal flag flown for the first time.
- **1973** Sydney Opera House completed.
- **1976** The Aboriginal Land Rights (Northern Territory) Act gives some land back to native people.
- **1983** Ayers Rock given back to local Aborigines, who rename it Uluru.
- **1983** Australia wins the Americas Cup, ending 112 years of American domination of the event.
- **1986** Queen Elizabeth II severs the Australian Constitution from Great Britain's.

continues

Secretary to the Admiralty, George Jackson. Back in Britain, King George III viewed Australia as a potential colony and repository of Britain's overflowing prison population, which could no longer be transported to the United States of America following the War of Independence.

The First Fleet left England in May 1787, made up of 11 store and transport ships (none of them was bigger than the passenger ferries that ply modern-day Sydney Harbour from Circular Quay to Manly) led by Arthur Phillip. Aboard were 1,480 people, including 759 convicts. Phillip's flagship, *The Supply,* reached Botany Bay in January 1788, but Phillip decided the soil was poor and the surroundings too swampy. On January 26, now celebrated as Australia Day, he settled for Port Jackson (Sydney Harbour) instead.

SETTLING DOWN The convicts were immediately put to work clearing land, planting crops, and constructing buildings. The early food harvests were failures, and by early 1790, the fledgling colony was facing starvation.

Phillip decided to give some convicts pardons for good behavior and service, and even grant small land parcels to those who were really industrious. In 1795, coal was discovered; in 1810 Governor Macquarie began

- **1988** Aborigines demonstrate as Australia celebrates its Bicentennial with a reenactment of the First Fleet's entry into Sydney Harbour.
- **1991** Australia's population reaches 17 million.
- **1993** Sydney chosen as the site of 2000 Olympics.
- **1994** High Court "Mabo" decision overturns the principle of *terra nullius,* which suggested Australia was unoccupied at time of white settlement.
- **1995** Australians protest as France explodes nuclear weapons in the South Pacific.
- **1996** High Court hands down *Wik* decision, which allows Aborigines the right to claim some Commonwealth land.
- **1998** The right-wing One Nation Party holds the balance of power in Queensland elections on an anti-immigration and anti-Aboriginal platform.
- **2000** A 10% Goods and Services tax becomes part of everyday life in Australia.
- **2000** Sydney Olympics held.
- **2001–2002** Massive bushfires start on Christmas Day in NSW and rage through much of January. Massive areas of bushland and national parks destroyed.
- **2003** Bushfires again ravage much of NSW and Victoria. Hundreds of homes are burned to the ground in the capital city, Canberra. The country faces a severe drought.

extensive city building projects; and in 1813 the explorers Blaxland, Wentworth, and Lawson forged a passage over the Blue Mountains to the fertile plains beyond.

When gold was discovered in Victoria in 1852, and in Western Australia 12 years later, hundreds of thousands of immigrants from Europe, America, and China flooded into the country in search of their fortunes. By 1860, more than a million non-Aboriginal people were living in Australia.

The last 10,000 convicts were transported to Western Australia between 1850 and 1868, bringing the total shipped to Australia to 168,000.

FEDERATION & THE GREAT WARS On January 1, 1901, the six states that made up Australia proclaimed themselves to be part of one nation, and the Commonwealth of Australia was formed. In the same ceremony, the first Governor General was sworn in as the representative of the Queen, who remained head of state. In 1914, Australia joined the Mother Country in war. In April the following year, the Australian and New Zealand Army Corps (ANZAC) formed a beachhead on the peninsula of Gallipoli in Turkey. The Turkish troops had been warned, and 8 months of fighting ended with 8,587 Australian dead and more than 19,000 wounded.

Australians fought in World War II in North Africa, Greece, and the Middle East. In March 1942, Japanese aircraft bombed Broome in Western Australia and Darwin in the Northern Territory. In May 1942, Japanese midget submarines entered Sydney Harbour and torpedoed a ferry before being destroyed. Later that year, Australian volunteers fought an incredibly brave retreat through the jungles of Papua New Guinea on the Kokoda Trail against superior Japanese forces. Australian troops fought alongside Americans in subsequent wars in Korea and Vietnam and sent military support to the Persian Gulf conflicts.

RECENT TIMES Following World War II, mass immigration to Australia, primarily from Europe, boosted the population. In 1974 the left-of-center Whitlam government put an end to the White Australia policy that had largely restricted black and Asian immigration since 1901. In 1986 the official umbilical cord to Britain was cut when the Australian Constitution was separated from that of its motherland. Australia had begun the march to complete independence.

In 1992 the High Court handed down the "Mabo" decision that ruled that Aborigines had a right to claim government-owned land if they could prove a continued connection with it. The following year, huge crowds filled Sydney's Circular Quay to hear that the city had won the 2000 Olympic Games.

New venues were built for the Olympics; some of these were temporary, while others are now used as arenas for professional and amateur sports. A new expressway and train link were built to connect the spruced-up airport to the city center, and Sydney welcomed thousands of international visitors to the 2-week extravaganza starting in September 2000. The Games put medal-winning Australian athletes Cathy Freeman and swimmer Ian Thorpe in the spotlight, and spurred a new wave of interest and tourism in the land Down Under.

4 Aussie Eats & Drinks

THE EATS

It took a long time for the average Australian to realize that there is more to food than English-style sausage and mashed potatoes, "meat and three veg," and a Sunday roast. It wasn't long ago that spaghetti was something foreigners ate, and zucchini and eggplant were considered exotic. Then came mass immigration and all sorts of foods that people had only read about in *National Geographic*.

The first big wave of Italian immigrants in the 1950s caused a national scandal. The great Aussie dream was to have a ¼-acre block of land with a Hills Hoist (a circular revolving clothesline) in the backyard. When Italians started hanging their freshly made pasta out to dry on this Aussie icon, it caused an uproar, and some clamored for the new arrivals to be shipped back. As Australia matured, southern European cuisine became increasingly popular until olive oil was sizzling in frying pans the way only lard had previously done.

In the 1980s, waves of Asian immigrants hit Australia's shores. Suddenly, everyone was cooking with woks. These days, this fusion of flavors and styles has melded into what's now commonly referred to as "Modern Australian"—a distinctive cuisine blending the spices of the east with the flavors of the west.

Note: Tipping is not widely expected in Australia, but it is usual to tip around 5% to 10% or round up to the nearest A$10 (US$6.50) for a substantial meal in a good restaurant.

THE DRINKS

THE AMBER NECTAR   The great Aussie drink is a "tinnie" (a can) of beer. Barbecues would not be the same without a case of tinnies, or "stubbies" (small bottles). In the hotter climes, you may be offered a polystyrene container or "stubby holder" in which to place your beer to keep it cool.

Australian beers vary considerably in quality, but, of course, there's no accounting for tastes. Among the most popular are Victoria Bitter (known as "VB"), XXXX (pronounced "four ex"), Fosters, and various brews produced by the Tooheys company. All are popular in cans, bottles, or on tap (draft). My favorite beer is Cascade, a German-style beer that you'll usually find only in a bottle. It's light in color, strong in taste, and made from Tasmanian water straight off a mountain. If you want to get plastered, try Coopers—it's rather cloudy in looks, very strong, and usually ends up causing a terrific hangover. Most Australian beers range from 4.8% to 5.2% alcohol.

In New South Wales, bars serve beer by the glass in a "schooner" or a smaller "midi"—though in a few places it's also served in British measurements, by pints and half pints. In Victoria you should ask for a "pot," or the less copious "glass." In South Australia a schooner is the size of a NSW midi, and in Western Australia a midi is the same size as a New South Wales midi, but a glass about half its size is called a "pony." Confused? My advice is to gesture with your hands like a local to show whether you want a small glass or a larger one.

By the way, you have to be 18 to buy alcohol.

THE VINO   Australian winemaking has come a long way since the first grape vines were brought to Australia on the First Fleet in 1788. These days, more than 550 major companies and small winemakers produce wine commercially in Australia. Vintages from Down Under consistently beat competitors from other wine-producing nations in major international shows. The demand for Australian wine overseas has increased so dramatically in the past few years that domestic prices have risen, and new vineyards are being planted at a frantic pace.

Australian wines are generally named after the grape varieties from which they are made. Of the white wines, big favorites include the fruity chardonnay and riesling varieties, the "herbaceous" or "grassy" sauvignon blanc, and the dry semillon. Of the reds, the dry cabernet sauvignon, the fruity merlot, the burgundy-type pinot noir, and the big and bold shiraz come out tops.

The best recent vintages are 1988 and 2002. The 2003 vintage also promises to be a cracker, with low rainfall meaning smaller, and more intensely flavored grapes.

Index

Great Trips Like Great Days Begin with a Plan

FranklinCovey and Frommer's Bring You *Frommer's Favorite Places* Planner

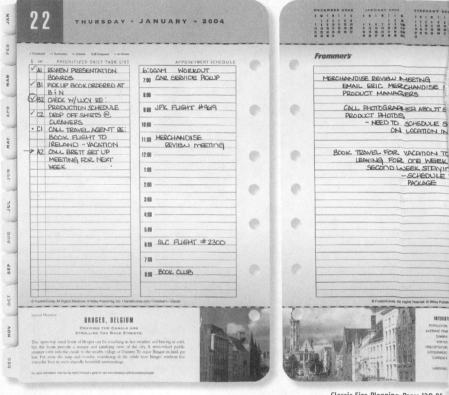

Classic Size Planning Pages $39.95

The planning experts at FranklinCovey have teamed up with the travel experts at Frommer's. The result is a full-year travel-themed planner filled with rich images and travel tips covering fifty-two of Frommer's Favorite Places.

- Each week will make you an expert about an intriguing corner of the world
- New facts and tips every day
- Beautiful, full-color photos of some of the most beautiful places on earth
- Proven planning tools from FranklinCovey for keeping track of tasks, appointments, notes, address/phone numbers, and more

Save 15%

when you purchase Frommer's Favorite Places travel-themed planner and a binder.

Order today before your next big trip.

www.franklincovey.com/frommers
Enter promo code 12252 at checkout for discount. Offer expires June 1, 2005.

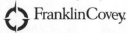

Frommer's is a trademark of Arthur Frommer.